Key Readings in Criminology

University of Liverpool

Key Readings in Criminology

Edited by Tim Newburn

WILLAN
PUBLISHING

Published by

Willan Publishing
Culmcott House
Mill Street, Uffculme
Cullompton, Devon
EX15 3AT, UK
Tel: +44(0)1884 840337
Fax: +44(0)1884 840251
e-mail: info@willanpublishing.co.uk
Website: www.willanpublishing.co.uk

Published simultaneously in the USA and Canada by

Willan Publishing
c/o ISBS, 920 NE 58th Ave, Suite 300,
Portland, Oregon 97213-3786, USA
Tel: +001(0)503 287 3093
Fax: +001(0)503 280 8832
e-mail: info@isbs.com
Website: www.isbs.com

First published 2009

ISBN 978-1-84392-402-9 paperback
        978-1-84392-403-6 hardback

British Library Cataloguing-in-Publication Data

A catalogue record for this book is available from the British Library

Project managed by Deer Park Productions
Typeset by Pantek Arts Ltd, Maidstone, Kent
Printed and bound by Ashford Colour Press, Gosport, Hants

PEFC™
PEFC/16-33-366

Contents

List of abbreviations   xvi

Acknowledgements   xviii

General Introduction   xix

1 Understanding crime and criminology   1

   Introduction, key concepts and questions for discussion   2

   1.1 What is crime?   4
        Paul W. Tappan

   1.2 Conceptions of deviance, official data and deviants   7
        Steven Box

   1.3 The construction and deconstruction of crime   11
        John Muncie

   1.4 A suitable amount of crime   17
        Nils Christie

2 Crime and punishment in history   19

   Introduction, key concepts and questions for discussion   20

   2.1 Execution and the English people   22
        Vic Gatrell

   2.2 Eighteenth-century punishment   24
        Michael Ignatieff

   2.3 Prosecutors and the courts   27
        Clive Emsley

   2.4 Police and people: the birth of Mr Peel's blue locusts   31
        Michael Ignatieff

   2.5 The London garotting panic of 1862: a moral panic and the creation   34
        of a criminal class in mid-Victorian England
        Jennifer Davis

3 Crime data and crime trends   41

   Introduction, key concepts and questions for discussion   42

   3.1 The social construction of official statistics on criminal deviance   44
        Steven Box

   3.2 A note on the use of official statistics   48
        John I. Kitsuse and Aaron V. Cicourel

3.3   The origins of the British Crime Survey   54
      Mike Hough, Mike Maxfield, Bob Morris and Jon Simmons

3.4   Unravelling recent crime patterns and trends   59
      Robert Reiner

4   Crime and the media   65

Introduction, key concepts and questions for discussion   66

4.1   What makes crime 'news'?   68
      Jack Katz

4.2   The media politics of crime and criminal justice   71
      Philip Schlesinger, Howard Tumber and Graham Murdock

4.3   On the continuing problem of media effects   75
      Sonia Livingstone

4.4   The sociology of moral panics   79
      Stanley Cohen

5   Classicism and positivism   85

Introduction, key concepts and questions for discussion   86

5.1   On crimes and punishments   88
      Cesare Beccaria

5.2   The female born criminal   93
      Cesare Lombroso and Guglielmo Ferrero

5.3   The positive school of criminology   99
      Enrico Ferri

6   Biological positivism   105

Introduction, key concepts and questions for discussion   106

6.1   Criminal anthropology in the United States   108
      Nicole Hahn Rafter

6.2   The increasing appropriation of genetic explanations   113
      Troy Duster

6.3   Biosocial studies of antisocial and violent behaviour in children and adults   119
      Adrian Raine

6.4   Evolutionary psychology and crime   127
      Satoshi Kanazawa

7   Psychological positivism   137

Introduction, key concepts and questions for discussion   138

7.1   Differential association   140
      Edwin H. Sutherland and Donald R. Cressey

7.2 Social structure and social learning   142
Ronald L. Akers

7.3 Crime as choice   149
James Q. Wilson and Richard J. Herrnstein

7.4 The link between cognitive ability and criminal behavior   154
Richard J. Herrnstein and Charles Murray

8 Durkheim, anomie and strain   159

Introduction, key concepts and questions for discussion   160

8.1 The normal and the pathological   162
Emile Durkheim

8.2 Social structure and anomie   165
Robert K. Merton

8.3 Why do individuals engage in crime?   169
Robert Agnew

8.4 Crime and the American Dream: an institutional analysis   174
Richard Rosenfeld and Steven F. Messner

8.5 The vertigo of late modernity   181
Jock Young

9 The Chicago School, culture and subcultures   187

Introduction, key concepts and questions for discussion   188

9.1 Juvenile delinquency and urban areas   190
Clifford R. Shaw and Henry D. McKay

9.2 Delinquent boys: the culture of the gang   194
Albert K. Cohen

9.3 Subcultural conflict and working-class community   198
Phil Cohen

9.4 Subcultures, cultures and class   201
John Clarke, Stuart Hall, Tony Jefferson and Brian Roberts

9.5 Cultural criminology   203
Jeff Ferrell

10 Interactionism and labelling theory   209

Introduction, key concepts and questions for discussion   210

10.1 Primary and secondary deviation   212
Edwin M. Lemert

10.2 Notes on the sociology of deviance   214
Kai T. Erikson

10.3 Outsiders   216
Howard S. Becker

10.4 Misunderstanding labelling perspectives   220
Ken Plummer

10.5 The social reaction against drugtaking   224
Jock Young

11 Control theories   231

Introduction, key concepts and questions for discussion   232

11.1 Techniques of neutralization: a theory of delinquency   234
Gresham M. Sykes and David Matza

11.2 A control theory of delinquency   236
Travis Hirschi

11.3 A general theory of crime   241
Michael R. Gottfredson and Travis Hirschi

11.4 Charles Tittle's control balance and criminological theory   246
John Braithwaite

12 Radical and critical criminology   255

Introduction, key concepts and questions for discussion   256

12.1 Toward a political economy of crime   258
William J. Chambliss

12.2 The theoretical and political priorities of critical criminology 261
Phil Scraton and Kathryn Chadwick

12.3 Radical criminology in Britain   267
Jock Young

12.4 Abolitionism and crime control   271
Willem de Haan

13 Left and right realism   275

Introduction, key concepts and questions for discussion   276

13.1 Reflections on realism   278
Roger Matthews and Jock Young

13.2 The failure of criminology: the need for a radical realism   282
Jock Young

13.3 The emerging underclass   288
Charles Murray

13.4 Broken windows   295
James Q. Wilson and George L. Kelling

14 Contemporary classicism   301

Introduction, key concepts and questions for discussion   302

14.1 The new criminologies of everyday life   304
David Garland

14.2 'Situational' crime prevention: theory and practice   307
Ronald V. Clarke

14.3 Opportunity makes the thief: practical theory for crime prevention 312
Marcus Felson and Ronald V. Clarke

14.4 Social change and crime rate trends: a routine activity approach   318
Lawrence E. Cohen and Marcus Felson

15 Feminist criminology   325

Introduction, key concepts and questions for discussion   326

15.1 The etiology of female crime   328
Dorie Klein

15.2 Girls, crime and woman's place: toward a feminist model of female 335
delinquency
Meda Chesney-Lind

15.3 Feminism and criminology   340
Kathleen Daly and Meda Chesney-Lind

15.4 Feminist approaches to criminology or postmodern woman meets   347
atavistic man
Carol Smart

16 Late modernity, governmentality and risk   357

Introduction, key concepts and questions for discussion   358

16.1 The new penology: notes on the emerging strategy for corrections   360
Malcolm M. Feeley and Jonathan Simon

16.2 Actuarialism and the risk society   367
Jock Young

16.3 Risk, power and crime prevention   373
Pat O'Malley

16.4 Say 'Cheese!' The Disney order that is not so Mickey Mouse   379
Clifford D. Shearing and Philip C. Stenning

17 Victims, victimization and victimology   385

Introduction, key concepts and questions for discussion   386

17.1 On becoming a victim   388
Paul Rock

17.2   Fiefs and peasants: accomplishing change for victims in the criminal   397
       justice system
       Joanna Shapland

17.3   Violence against women and children: the contradictions of crime   402
       control under patriarchy
       Jill Radford and Elizabeth A. Stanko

17.4   Multiple victimisation: its extent and significance   409
       Graham Farrell

18   White-collar and corporate crime   417

Introduction, key concepts and questions for discussion   418

18.1   The problem of white-collar crime   420
       Edwin H. Sutherland

18.2   Who is the criminal?   423
       Paul W. Tappan

18.3   Defining white-collar crime   425
       David O. Friedrichs

18.4   Iraq and Halliburton   430
       Dawn Rothe

19   Organised crime   437

Introduction, key concepts and questions for discussion   438

19.1   Organised crime: the structural skeleton   440
       Donald R. Cressey

19.2   Fishy business: the mafia and the Fulton Fish Market   444
       James B. Jacobs

19.3   The crime network   449
       William J. Chambliss

19.4   The profession of violence: the Krays   453
       John Pearson

19.5   Perspectives on 'organised crime'   454
       Michael Levi

20   Violent and property crime   461

Introduction, key concepts and questions for discussion   462

20.1   The social organization of burglary   464
       Neal Shover

20.2   American lethal violence   470
       Franklin E. Zimring and Gordon Hawkins

20.3 Modernization, self-control and lethal violence   476
     Manuel Eisner

20.4 Racial harassment and the process of victimization   481
     Benjamin Bowling

21 Drugs and alcohol   487

Introduction, key concepts and questions for discussion   488

21.1 Booze, the urban night and the human ecology of violence   490
      Dick Hobbs, Phil Hadfield, Stuart Lister and Simon Winlow

21.2 Heroin use and street crime   496
      James A. Inciardi

21.3 Drug prohibition in the United States: costs, consequences and   499
      alternatives
      Ethan A. Nadelmann

21.4 The war on drugs and the African American community   506
      Marc Mauer

22 Penology and punishment   511

Introduction, key concepts and questions for discussion   512

22.1 The body of the condemned   514
      Michel Foucault

22.2 What works? Questions and answers about prison reform   517
      Robert Martinson

22.3 Censure and proportionality   520
      Andrew von Hirsch

22.4 The largest penal experiment in American history   524
      Franklin E. Zimring, Gordon Hawkins and Sam Kamin

23 Understanding criminal justice   529

Introduction, key concepts and questions for discussion   530

23.1 Two models of the criminal process   532
      Herbert L. Packer

23.2 Models of justice: Portia or Persephone? Some thoughts on equality,   536
      fairness and gender in the field of criminal justice
      Frances Heidensohn

23.3 The antecedents of compliant behavior   542
      Tom R. Tyler

23.4 Defiance, deterrence and irrelevance: a theory of the criminal sanction   545
      Lawrence W. Sherman

24 Crime prevention and community safety — 551

Introduction, key concepts and questions for discussion — 552

24.1 A conceptual model of crime prevention — 554
Paul J. Brantingham and Frederic L. Faust

24.2 The British gas suicide story and its criminological implications — 559
Ronald V. Clarke and Pat Mayhew

24.3 Neighborhoods and violent crime: a multilevel study of collective efficacy — 563
Robert J. Sampson, Stephen W. Raudenbusch and Felton Earls

24.4 The uses of sidewalks: safety — 568
Jane Jacobs

25 The police and policing — 571

Introduction, key concepts and questions for discussion — 572

25.1 What do the police do? — 574
David H. Bayley

25.2 A sketch of the policeman's 'working personality' — 580
Jerome H. Skolnick

25.3 The rhetoric of community policing — 585
Carl B. Klockars

25.4 The future of policing — 592
David H. Bayley and Clifford D. Shearing

26 Criminal courts and the court process — 601

Introduction, key concepts and questions for discussion — 602

26.1 Conditions of successful degradation ceremonies — 604
Harold Garfinkel

26.2 Materials of control — 608
Pat Carlen

26.3 The adversarial system — 613
Paul Rock

26.4 Understanding law enforcement — 619
Doreen McBarnet

27 Sentencing and non-custodial penalties — 625

Introduction, key concepts and questions for discussion — 626

27.1 Crime, inequality and sentencing — 628
Pat Carlen

27.2 The punitive city: notes on the dispersal of social control — 633
Stanley Cohen

27.3 The dispersal of discipline thesis 640
Anthony Bottoms

27.4 Understanding the growth in the prison population in England and Wales 644
Andrew Millie, Jessica Jacobson and Mike Hough

28 Prisons and imprisonment 649

Introduction, key concepts and questions for discussion 650

28.1 The 'disciplinary' origins of the prison 652
David Garland

28.2 Prisons and the contested nature of punishment 657
Richard Sparks

28.3 The inmate world 664
Erving Goffman

28.4 Women in prison: the facts 669
Pat Carlen and Anne Worrall

29 Youth crime and youth justice 677

Introduction, key concepts and questions for discussion 678

29.1 Present tense: moderates and hooligans 680
Geoffrey Pearson

29.2 The coming of the super-predators 684
John J. Dilulio

29.3 Penal custody: intolerance, irrationality and indifference 689
Barry Goldson

29.4 Comparative youth justice 698
Michael Cavadino and James Dignan

30 Restorative justice 709

Introduction, key concepts and questions for discussion 710

30.1 Conflicts as property 712
Nils Christie

30.2 Restorative justice: an overview 719
Tony Marshall

30.3 Responsibilities, rights and restorative justice 726
Andrew Ashworth

30.4 Critiquing the critics: a brief response to critics of restorative justice 732
Allison Morris

31   Race, crime and justice   739

Introduction, key concepts and questions for discussion   740

31.1 The racism of criminalization: police and the reproduction of the   742
      criminal other
      Tony Jefferson

31.2 From Scarman to Stephen Lawrence   747
      Stuart Hall

31.3 In proportion: race, and police stop and search   754
      P.A.J. Waddington, Kevin Stenson and David Don

31.4 Deadly symbiosis: when ghetto and prison meet and mesh   759
      Loïc Wacquant

32   Gender, crime and justice   767

Introduction, key concepts and questions for discussion   768

32.1 Women and criminal justice: saying it again, again and again   770
      Loraine Gelsthorpe

32.2 The woman of legal discourse   772
      Carol Smart

32.3 Women and social control   779
      Frances Heidensohn

32.4 Common sense, routine precaution and normal violence   786
      Elizabeth A. Stanko

32.5 Hegemonic and subordinated masculinities   791
      James W. Messerschmidt

33   Criminal and forensic psychology   797

Introduction, key concepts and questions for discussion   798

33.1 Individual factors in offending   800
      David P. Farrington and Brandon C. Welsh

33.2 Adolescent-limited and life-course-persistent antisocial behavior: 807
      a developmental taxonomy
      Terrie E. Moffitt

33.3 A sociogenic developmental theory of offending   818
      Robert J. Sampson and John H. Laub

34   Globalisation, terrorism and human rights   823

Introduction, key concepts and questions for discussion   824

34.1 Crime control as industry   826
      Nils Christie

34.2 Human rights and crimes of the state: the culture of denial 827
Stanley Cohen

34.3 The new regulatory state and the transformation of criminology 837
John Braithwaite

34.4 Criminal justice and political cultures 844
Tim Newburn and Richard Sparks

35 Doing criminological research 851

Introduction, key concepts and questions for discussion 852

35.1 The relationship between theory and empirical observations in 854
criminology
Anthony Bottoms

35.2 The fieldwork approach 860
Howard Parker

35.3 A snowball's chance in hell: doing fieldwork with active residential 865
burglars
Richard Wright, Scott H. Decker, Allison K. Redfern and Dietrich L. Smith

35.4 Doing research in prison: breaking the silence? 870
Alison Liebling

35.5 Feminist methodologies in criminology: a new approach or old 875
wine in new bottles?
Loraine Gelsthorpe

35.6 Writing: the problem of getting started 882
Howard S. Becker

Publisher's Acknowledgements 886
Index 893

List of abbreviations

ACLU	American Civil Liberties Union
ACPS	Advisory Council on the Penal System
ASBO	anti-social behaviour order
BCS	British Crime Survey
BKA	Bundeskriminalamt
CASI	computer-assisted self-interviewing
CIA	Central Intelligence Agency
CJA	Criminal Justice Act
CO	Carbon Monoxide
CPA	Coalition Provisional Authority
CPPU	Crime Policy Planning Unit
CPS	Crown Prosecution Service
CYPA	Children and Young Persons' Act
DNA	deoxyribonucleic acid
DFI	Development Fund for Iraq
EEG	electroencephalogram
Eses	street corner youths
EU	European Union
EWO	Education Welfare Officer
FAR	Federal Acquisitions Regulations
FBI	Federal Bureau of Investigation
GHS	General Household Survey
GST	General Strain Theory
HIV	Human immunodeficiency virus
HORU	Home Office Research Unit
IMF	International Monetary Fund
IQ	Intelligence Quotient
JCAR	Joint Committee Against Racialism
KBR	Kellogg, Brown and Root
LOGCAP	Logistics Civil Augmentation Program
MPA	Minor Physical Anomaly
NATO	North Atlantic Treaty Organization
NAVSS	National Association of Victim Support Schemes
NCIS	National Criminal Intelligence Service
NCS	National Crime Squad
NCS	US National Crime Survey
Ncs	Neighborhood Clusters
NCVS	National Crime Victimization Survey

NEO-PI	Neuroticism-Extraversion-Openness Personality Inventory
NF	National Front
NGO	non-governmental organisations
NIDA	National Institute on Drug Abuse
NLSY	National Longitudinal Survey of Youth
NOMS	National Offender Management Service
NOVA	National Organization for Victim Assistance
NYPD	New York Police Department
OPCS	Office of Population, Census and Surveys
PACE	Police and Criminal Evidence Act 1984
PHDCN	Project on Human Development in Chicago Neighborhoods
Quango	Quasi-autonomous nongovernmental organisations
RPU	(Home Office) Research and Planning Unit
RSOI	Reception, Staging, Onward Movement and Integration
SAMHSA	Substance Abuse and Mental Health Services Administration
SCPR	Social and Community Planning Research
SEC	US Securities and Exchange Commission
SES	socioeconomic status
Socs	socialites
SOMA	State Oil Marketing Organization
SS&A	Social Structure and Anomie
SSSL	Social Structure and Social Learning theory of crime
SWAT	special weapons and tactics team
VAT	Value Added Tax
VORP	Victim-Offender Reconciliation Projects
VSS	Victim Support Scheme
WANO	World Association of Nuclear Operators
YOI	Young Offender Institution

Acknowledgements

Completing a sizeable undertaking such as this means that a lot of debts are incurred. Once again Brian Willan has brought all his skills to bear on the project (from planning and design, through careful handling of the whole production, all the way to proof-reading). I owe him, and Jim, Julia, Simone, Lucinda, Jake and everyone associated with Willan Publishing a considerable debt. My thanks to Julia Willan for all the hard work in chasing the permissions for the selections in the volume, and to Bill and Michelle Antrobus at Deer Park Productions, together with Emma Gubb and Becky Little, who had the unenviable task of checking and double-checking the text/proofs. My gratitude to Kevin Ancient for the work on the cover and to all those – family, friends, colleagues – who helped in the process of getting the right pictures in the right order. As ever, I'd like to thank my family for being, well, my family.

Tim Newburn

General Introduction

Welcome to Key *Readings in Criminology*. In 2007 I published a large introductory textbook simply entitled *Criminology*. This volume is intended as a companion to that book and my hope is that the two books will complement each other. That said, *Key Readings* has been developed as a stand-alone text and the intention is that it can be used in that way or with any of the main criminology textbooks that are available.

As its title suggests, this volume consists primarily of a selection of excerpts from original criminological texts. They are organised to correspond to the running order of the chapters in *Criminology* (with the exception of the final chapter in *Key Readings* which covers elements of the two final chapters in the textbook). Given the size of this enterprise I have limited the number of readings to approximately four in each chapter. You will anticipate straight away, therefore, that there is no suggestion that the readings in any one chapter cover *all* of the main issues connected with the subject of that chapter. Rather, the intention is to give a flavour of some of the more important and interesting questions that are raised in that particular topic, and to do so in a way that will hopefully stimulate debate and discussion.

Wherever possible I have attempted to make selections that are worth reading. By this I mean a number of things. First, in all cases I hope the selection has been of writing that makes some important contribution to the subject concerned, either by introducing new ideas, by offering interesting or provocative ideas, or in the way they bring together or summarise particular arguments.

Second, taking the volume as a whole, I have attempted to include as much 'classic' criminology as I can. I have resisted the temptation to stick to materials that were published in the last few years. One of the unfortunate characteristics of criminology is what my colleague Paul Rock has called 'chronocentrism': a preoccupation with the new and a tendency to 'forget' about materials published more than a few years ago even though they may be among the most important in the subject.

The aim here, therefore, has been to offer a broad range of criminological materials – in terms of when they were written, who they were written by and what they cover. In addition, wherever possible, I have also tried to find materials that are well written. There is nothing worse than having to slog through badly written journal articles and books. It is a dispiriting experience and, crucially, is precisely what is likely to drain away any enthusiasm a student may have. I don't suppose that I have succeeded in absolutely every case but, honestly, I did try.

The task of making a selection for a volume such as this necessarily means leaving out an awful lot even when it contains almost 150 selections. I will be intrigued to see what students make of the selection and how useful they find it. I will also be fascinated to discover what my colleagues – those running criminology courses in universities – will make of the selection. Are there particular things that it astonishes them that are missing? If so I should like to know and I hope they will tell me (politely)!

What I have attempted to do, in sum, is to produce a volume for students that:

- Provides you with access to a broad range of materials with which to follow up your reading of other textbooks;

- Incorporates readings that include both more recent summaries of particularly important criminological issues as well as excerpts from criminological *classics*; and

- Introduces you not only to criminological argument and debate but also offers you the opportunity to read primary as well as secondary or summary sources.

The overall objective is that this volume could be used in a number of ways in support of university teaching:

- As a source of both 'key' and 'supplementary' reading for lectures
- As the basis for organised reading in advance of seminars and tutorials
- As the basis for classroom discussion and analysis
- As a broad source of reading for exam revision

In almost every case, each reading is simply an excerpt from a longer work – sometimes a journal article, sometimes a book. In almost every case I have had to edit the text quite substantially. Had I not it would have been physically impossible to glue the pages of this book together such would have been its size. One consequence of this is that you are getting the kernel of people's arguments; not necessarily all the supporting detail. I hope that reading excerpts in this volume will stimulate to visit the originals and to read the works in their original form. This volume is not a substitute for the original texts – it is simply a way of getting you to a lot of material quickly and easily. Nor is it a substitute for going to the library and browsing. Naturally, the bulk of material in any topic does not appear in this book. The more you can read around your subject – following the suggestions that your teachers make, but also following your own nose – the more you will get from your studies.

Features of this book

Each chapter in *Key Readings in Criminology* opens with a short essay introducing the particular readings and explaining aspects of their content and their relevance. At the start of this introduction there is also a list of *key concepts*, and also a series of *questions for discussion*. Both of these features pick up key, salient points in the readings.

The *key concepts* are included to alert you to elements you may wish to look out for as you read.

The *questions for discussion* are there to provide a focus for classroom discussion or for further reading. They are deliberately located at the beginning rather than at the end of each chapter. It is often quite helpful, in my view, to have some sense of what you might want to look for before you set out on the task of reading something. The questions only pick up on some of the key issues – there will be other aspects of the readings which you or others may want to raise for discussion. The questions, together with the key concepts, will at least give you a start, suggesting to you in advance certain avenues of inquiry and possible controversy. From there on it is up to you, but it should be an exciting journey. I wish you luck with your reading.

Tim Newburn
London
t.newburn@lse.ac.uk

1

Understanding crime and criminology

1.1 What is crime?
Paul W. Tappan
4

1.2 Conceptions of deviance, official data and deviants
Steven Box
7

1.3 The construction and deconstruction of crime
John Muncie
11

1.4 A suitable amount of crime
Nils Christie
17

Introduction

KEY CONCEPTS black letter law; censure; crime; criminalization; deviance; enforcement; morality; norms; (official) deviants; social construction; social harm; social order

There are four readings in this chapter and each offers a slightly different view of the subject-matter of criminology. If you have done any initial reading (perhaps read the opening chapter in the textbook *Criminology*) then you will have learned that criminology is multi-disciplinary in nature, drawing on a broad range of academic subjects and methodologies. It is, as David Downes once described it, a 'rendezvous subject'. It is a place where people from a variety of disciplinary origins come together to study three core issues, identified by Edwin Sutherland in the 1930s as: the making of laws, the breaking of laws and society's reaction to the breaking of laws. Actually, there is rather more to it than that, of course, but Sutherland captures a goodly chunk of what we would still recognize today as criminology. One way or another, pretty much irrespective of one's approach to criminology, the core of the subject-matter boils down to those things that we refer to as 'crime'. Like so much of the social world, the term 'crime' seems initially and superficially straightforward but gets increasingly complex the more one attempts to define and analyse it. The readings selected for this chapter are designed to offer some reflections on this apparently simple, but actually deeply problematic term. Given how central the term is to the rest of what you will study in criminology this is consequently an important starting point.

In 'What is crime?' **(Reading 1.1)** Paul Tappan challenges those who argue that *crime* is not a particularly meaningful category, and suggests that the most straightforward and reliable way of understanding what we mean by the term is to limit it to infractions of the criminal law. Although we cannot possibly know of every occasion when a law is broken (just think of how often people speed in their cars or shoplift without ever being caught) it remains the case, he argues, that those who are arrested and processed by the criminal justice system are a good enough approximation of those that break the law to be a reasonable focus for criminological study.

By contrast, Steven Box **(Reading 1.2)** focuses on something rather broader than crime – namely, *deviance* or *rule-violating behaviour*. He describes how early writers in this field were especially concerned to try to identify the individual differences between those engaged in deviant behaviour and others, but that this later gave way to a search for causes in the social environment rather than within the individual. One problem with work in both these traditions, he argues, is that they have tended to confine themselves to the study of those 'officially defined' as deviant. In contrast to Tappan, however, Box takes the view that such a group is in fact a 'highly selected population' and therefore unlikely to give rise to accurate generalizations.

The excerpt from John Muncie **(Reading 1.3)** provides an overview of differing approaches to understanding crime, beginning with Tappan's narrow definition and moving through a series of alternative, often radical analyses. The latter vary from Marxist approaches which emphasize the ways in which the criminal law protects and reinforces the privileged position of the powerful, to those scholars who question the whole idea of criminology as a project – or at least one that tries to focus on crime – and which proposes 'social harms' as a better alternative. The final reading by Nils Christie **(Reading 1.4)** shares a similar outlook to these latter critics. In it, he suggests that crime is an 'unlimited natural resource'. It is, from this point of view, not something that we should think of as being limited in quantity – a certain number of burglaries, or thefts or violent attacks – but, rather, as being the product of social processes, decisions and institutional reactions to respond to particular behaviours in particular ways. In short, Christie wants us to ask questions of crime that we tend often to ignore, most notably the issue of *when is enough, enough?* He wants us to dilute our preoccupation with attempting to measure how much crime there is in our society and, instead, use the data we have in a critical manner to tell us something about what we treat as criminal, what we decide to process and prosecute and so on, and what these decisions tell us about the nature of our social world.

Questions for discussion

1. Can you identify any problems in Tappan's observation that 'adjudicated offenders represent the closest possible approximation of those who have in fact violated the law'?

2. In what ways might concentrating only on those who break the law be too narrow a focus for criminology?

3. According to Box what, historically, have been the two main approaches to understanding deviance within criminology?

4. In what ways might it be significant to distinguish between *actors* and *acts* in criminology?

5. What do we mean when we suggest that crime is a 'social construct'?

6. Give some examples of the way in which definitions of crime change historically.

7. What might be the advantages of a focus on *social harm* compared with one on *crime*?

8. What does Christie mean when he says crime is an 'unlimited natural resource'?

1.1 What is crime?
Paul W. Tappan

Another increasingly widespread and seductive movement to revolutionize the concepts of crime and criminal has developed around the currently fashionable dogma of 'white collar crime.' This is actually a particular school among those who contend that the criminologist should study antisocial behavior rather than law violation. The dominant contention of the group appears to be that the convict classes are merely our 'petty' criminals, the few whose depredations against society have been on a small scale, who have blundered into difficulties with the police and courts through their ignorance and stupidity. The important criminals, those who do irreparable damage with impunity, deftly evade the machinery of justice, either by remaining 'technically' within the law or by exercising their intelligence, financial prowess, or political connections in its violation. We seek a definition of the white collar criminal and find an amazing diversity, even among those flowing from the same pen, and observe that characteristically they are loose, doctrinaire, and invective. When Professor Sutherland launched the term, it was applied to those individuals of upper socioeconomic class who violate the criminal law, usually by breach of trust, in the ordinary course of their business activities.[1] This original usage accords with legal ideas of crime and points moreover to the significant and difficult problems of enforcement in the areas of business crimes, particularly where those violations are made criminal by recent statutory enactment. From this fruitful beginning the term has spread into vacuity, wide and handsome. We learn that the white collar criminal may be the suave and deceptive merchant prince or 'robber baron,' that the existence of such crime may be determined readily 'in casual conversation with a representative of an occupation by asking him, "What crooked practices are found in your occupation?"'[2]

Confusion grows as we learn from another proponent of this concept that, 'There are various phases of white-collar criminality that touch the lives of the common man almost daily. The large majority of them are operating within the letter and spirit of the law ....' and that 'In short, greed, not need, lies at the basis of white-collar crime.'[3]

Apparently the criminal may be law obedient but greedy; the specific quality of his crimes is far from clear.

Another avenue is taken in Professor Sutherland's more recent definition of crime as a 'legal description of an act as socially injurious and legal provision of penalty for the act.'[4] Here he has deemed the connotation of his term too narrow if confined to violations of the criminal code; he includes by a slight modification conduct violative of any law, civil or criminal, when it is 'socially injurious.'

In light of these definitions, the normative issue is pointed. Who should be considered the white collar criminal? Is it the merchant who, out of greed, business acumen, or competitive motivations, breaches a trust with his consumer by 'puffing his wares' beyond their merits, by pricing them beyond their value, or by ordinary advertising? Is it he who breaks trust with his employees in order to keep wages down, refusing to permit labor organization or to bargain collectively, and who is found guilty by a labor relations board of an unfair labor practice? May it be the white collar worker who breaches trust with his employers by inefficient performance at work, by sympathetic strike or secondary boycott? Or is it the merchandiser who violates ethics by under-cutting the prices of his fellow merchants? In general these acts do not violate the criminal law. All in some manner breach a trust for motives which a criminologist may (or may not) disapprove for one reason or another. All are within the framework of the norms of ordinary business practice. One seeks in vain for criteria to determine this white collar criminality. It is the conduct of one who wears a white collar and who indulges in occupational behavior to which some particular criminologist takes exception. It may easily be a term of propaganda. For purposes of empirical research or objective description, what is it?

Whether criminology aspires one day to become a science or a repository of reasonably accurate descriptive information, it cannot tolerate a nomenclature of such loose and variable usage. A special hazard exists in the employment of the term, 'white collar criminal,' in that it invites individual systems of private values to run riot in an area (economic ethics) where gross variation exists among criminologists as well as others. The rebel may enjoy a veritable orgy of delight in damning as criminal most anyone he pleases; one imagines that some experts would thus consign to the criminal classes any successful capitalistic business man; the reactionary or conservative, complacently viewing the occupational practices of the business world, might find all in perfect order in this best of all possible worlds. The result may be fine indoctrination or catharsis achieved through blustering broadsides against the 'existing system.' It is not criminology. It is not social science. The terms 'unfair,' 'infringement,' 'discrimination,' 'injury to society,' and so on, employed by the white collar criminologists cannot, taken alone, differentiate criminal and non-criminal. Until refined to mean certain specific actions, they are merely epithets.

Vague, omnibus concepts defining crime are a blight upon either a legal system or a system of sociology that strives to be objective. They allow judge, administrator, or conceivably sociologist, in an undirected, freely operating discretion, to attribute the status 'criminal' to any individual or class which he conceives nefarious. This can accomplish no desirable objective, either politically or sociologically.[5]

Worse than futile, it is courting disaster, political, economic, and social, to promulgate a system of justice in which the individual may be held criminal without having committed a crime, defined with some precision by statute and case law. To describe crime the sociologist, like the lawyer legislator, must do more than condemn conduct deviation in the abstract. He must avoid definitions predicated simply upon state of mind or social injury and determine what particular types of deviation, in what directions, and to what degree, shall be considered criminal. This is exactly what the criminal code today attempts to do, though imperfectly of course. More slowly and conservatively than many of us would wish: that is in the nature of legal institutions, as it is in other social institutions as well. But law has defined with greater clarity and precision the conduct which is criminal than our anti-legalistic criminologists promise to do; it has moreover promoted a stability, a security and dependability of justice through its exactness, its so-called technicalities, and its moderation in inspecting proposals for change.

Having considered the conceptions of an innovating sociology in ascribing the terms 'crime' and 'criminal,' let us state here the juristic view: Only those are criminals who have been adjudicated as such by the courts. Crime is an intentional act in violation of the criminal law (statutory and case law), committed without defense or excuse, and penalized by the state as a felony or misdemeanor. In studying the offender there can be no presumption that arrested, arraigned, indicted, or prosecuted persons are criminals unless they also be held guilty beyond a reasonable doubt of a particular offense.'[6]

Even less than the unconvicted suspect can those individuals be considered criminal who have violated no law. Only those are criminals who have been selected by a clear substantive and a careful adjective law, such as obtains in our courts. The unconvicted offenders of whom the criminologist may wish to take cognizance are an important but unselected group; it has no specific membership presently ascertainable. Sociologists may strive, as does the legal profession, to perfect measures for more complete and accurate ascertainment of offenders, but it is futile simply to rail against a machinery of justice which is, and to a large extent must inevitably remain, something less than entirely accurate or efficient. [...]

We reiterate and defend the contention that crime, as legally defined, is a sociologically significant province of study. The view that it is not appears to be based upon either of two premises: 1. that offenders convicted under the criminal law are not representative of all criminals and 2. that criminal law violation (and, therefore, the criminal himself) is not significant to the sociologist because it is composed of a set of legal, non-sociological categories irrelevant to the understanding of group behavior and/or social control. Through these contentions to invalidate the traditional and legal frame of reference adopted by the criminologist, several considerations, briefly enumerated below, must be met.

1 Convicted criminals as a sample of law
   violators:

   a Adjudicated offenders represent the closest
      possible approximation to those who have in
      fact violated the law, carefully selected by the
      sieving of the due process of law; no other
      province of social control attempts to
      ascertain the breach of norms with such rigor
      and precision.

b It is as futile to contend that this group should not be studied on the grounds that it is incomplete or non-representative as it would be to maintain that psychology should terminate its description, analysis, diagnosis, and treatment of deviants who cannot be completely representative as selected. Convicted persons are nearly all criminals. They offer large and varied samples of all types; their origins, traits, dynamics of development, and treatment influences can be studied profitably for purposes of description, understanding, and control. To be sure, they are not necessarily representative of all offenders; if characteristics observed among them are imputed to law violators generally, it must be with the qualification implied by the selective processes of discovery and adjudication.

c Convicted criminals are important as a sociological category, furthermore, in that they have been exposed and respond to the influences of court contact, official punitive treatment, and public stigma as convicts.

2 The relevance of violation of the criminal law:

a The criminal law establishes substantive norms of behavior, standards more clear cut, specific, and detailed than the norms in any other category of social controls.

b The behavior prohibited has been considered significantly in derogation of group welfare by deliberative and representative assembly, formally constituted for the purpose of establishing such norms; nowhere else in the field of social control is there directed comparable rational effort to elaborate standards conforming to the predominant needs, desires, and interests of the community.

c There are legislative and juridical lags which reduce the social value of the legal norms; as an important characteristic of law, such lag does not reduce the relevance of law as a province of sociological inquiry. From a detached sociological view, the significant thing is not the absolute goodness or badness of the norms but the fact that these norms do control behavior. The sociologist is interested in the results of such control, the correlates of violation, and in the lags themselves.

d Upon breach of these legal (and social) norms, the refractory are treated officially in punitive and/or rehabilitative ways, not for being generally anti-social, immoral, unconventional, or bad, but for violation of the specific legal norms of control.

e Law becomes the peculiarly important and ultimate pressure toward conformity to minimum standards of conduct deemed essential to group welfare as other systems of norms and mechanics of control deteriorate.

f Criminals, therefore, are a sociologically distinct group of violators of specific legal norms, subjected to official state treatment. They and the non-criminals respond, though differentially of course, to the standards, threats, and correctional devices established in this system of social control.

g The norms, their violation, the mechanics of dealing with breach constitute major provinces of legal sociology. They are basic to the theoretical framework of sociological criminology.[7]

> From P.W. Tappan (1947) 'Who is the criminal?', American Sociological Review, *12(1): 96–102.*

Notes

1 E.H. Sutherland, 'Crime and Business,' 217 *The Annals of the American Academy of Political and Social Science* 112, (1941).
2 Sutherland, 'White-Collar Criminality,' 5 *American Sociological Review* 1, (1940).
3 Harry Elmer Barnes and Negley K. Teeters, *New Horizons in Criminology*, pp. 42–43, (1943).
4 Sutherland, 'Is 'White-Collar Crime' Crime?' 10 *American Sociological Review* 132, (1945).
5 In the province of juvenile delinquency we may observe already the evil that flows from this sort of loose definition in applied sociology. In many jurisdictions, under broad statutory definition of delinquency, it has become common practice to adjudicate as delinquent any child deemed to be anti-social or a behavior problem. Instead of requiring sound systematic proof of specific reprehensible conduct, the courts can attach to children the odious label of delinquent through the evaluations and recommendations of over-worked, undertrained case investigators who convey to the judge their hearsay testimony of neighborhood gossip and personal predilection. Thus these vaunted 'socialized tribunals' sometimes become themselves a source of delinquent and criminal careers as they adjudge individuals who are innocent of proven wrong to a depraved offender's status through an administrative determination of something they know vaguely as

anti-social conduct. See Introduction by Roscoe Pound of Pauline V. Young, *Social Treatment in Probation and Delinquency*, (1937). See also Paul W. Tappan, *Delinquent Girls in Court*, (1947) and 'Treatment Without Trial,' 24 *Social Forces*, 306, (1946).

6   The unconvicted suspect cannot be known as a violator of the law: to assume him so would be in derogation of our most basic political and ethical philosophies. In empirical research it would be quite inaccurate, obviously, to study all suspects of defendants as criminals.

7   For other expositions of this view, see articles by Jerome Hall: 'Prolegomena to a Science of Criminal Law,' 89 *University of Pennsylvania Law Review* 570, (1941); 'Criminology and a Modern Penal Code,' 57 *Journal of Criminal Law and Criminology* 4, (May–June, 1936); 'Criminology,' *Twentieth Century Sociology*, pp. 342–65, (1945).

1.2 Conceptions of deviance, official data and deviants
Steven Box

To begin at the beginning is to be confronted by the most perplexing question of all 'What are we studying?' Although the subject-matter of deviance has teased and tantalized the minds of thinkers for centuries, they seem to have been taught on carousel, going up and down, and round and round, but not progressing noticeably beyond the starting points of concern and curiosity. There is a reason for this lack of development: most people who have attempted to study deviance have been confused about *what* they were studying, and consequently mistaken in *how* they should study it.

For most of the nineteenth century and even well into the twentieth, writers and researchers on deviance were sustained in their activities by a kind of alchemical belief that their pursuits would lead them to discover one of nature's dark secrets – *what* caused a human being to be an inhuman deviant. Since it was widely believed that deviants are particular types of people, distinctly different from ordinary law-abiding citizens, this pursuit of the cause of deviance must have seemed – at least in the abstract – to be one without obstacles. Indeed, it was perceived in exactly these terms: simply discover the difference between deviants and conformists, and there revealed for all, would be the cause, or at least the clue to the cause.

According to this perspective there was no worthwhile distinction between *deviance*, i.e. rule-violating behavior, and *deviants*, i.e. people who assume a deviate identity. The two were perceived as being intricately part of the same phenomenon They were *causally* linked because deviants commit deviance, and they were *conceptually* linked because it was widely inferred that people who commit deviate behavior could, because of that behavior, be classified as deviant, in other words, a person's behavior reveals *who* s/he is essentially, and that essential self is the ultimate cause of the behavior. Given this presumed fusion of self and deviance, the only remaining intellectual problem for traditional criminology was 'Why are a minority of persons essentially deviant?'

At an abstract level, there was consensus amongst most early theorists concerned to answer this question, 'Why are *they* like they are?' There was a commonly shared belief that people who break the rules of society were defective, and that the root of this defect lay within them; beyond this commonly shared belief, there existed little agreement. When it came down to detailed analysis of the difference between deviants and conformists, there was only the comedy of the academic game, the bewildering myriad of claims and counterclaims, results and insults, assertions and desertions, eurekas and raspberries. The deviant was defective, that was agreed, but the nature of this defect remained a contentious issue. Indeed, as recent textbooks verify (Davis, 1975; Gibbons, 1979; Gibbons and Jones, 1975; Nettler, 1974, 1978; Reid, 1976; Schafer, 1969; Suchar, 1978; Thio, 1978), the everyday theoretical and conceptual squabbles still persist with as much vigour and rancour as ever.

For some thinkers, particular those versed in the mystic arts, demonology and in some cases theology, deviants were perceived as persons possessed by evil forces, or bewitched by black magic, or seduced by sorcery, or demented by demons, or earmarked by God. For example, Erikson (1966) suggests that

> according to the Puritan reading of the Bible . . . there were only two important classes of people on earth – those who had been elected to ever-lasting life and those who had been consigned forever to hell . . . persons who had reasons to fear the worst would drift sullenly into the lower echelons of society, highly susceptible to deviant forms of behavior. (p. 189)

Preordained, or held firmly in the grip of some less magisterial but none the less suprahuman power, individuals were viewed as helpless; they lived out their fated lives, the mark of Cain allowed them no other alternative.

Other writers, convinced of a more positive and empiric route to knowledge, considered that deviant behavior could be explained by linking it to a *physiological* defect. For most of these thinkers the actual defect remained a mystery, although in some quarters it was thought to be that quality which divided primitive man from civilized people. Baffled by the defect's exact nature, researchers concentrated on discovering *indicators* of it. Since the most obvious candidate for such an indicator was the human anatomy, this became the object fit for scrutiny. In no time, deviants were characterized as having deviations in their head shapes, peculiarities in their eyes, receding foreheads, weak chins, compressed faces, flared nostrils, long ape-like arms and agile and muscular bodies. We have progressed (sic) considerably since these Lombrosian mistaken preoccupations. Now 'experts' (Jeffery, 1979; Rosenthal, 1973; Shah and Roth, 1974) reassure us that the root cause of crime and delinquency lies within the human body. Thus our attention is drawn to the deviant's minimal brain damage (Cantwell, 1977), nutritional deficiency (Hippchen, 1977), abnormal chromosomes (West, 1969) and the hereditary transmission of low intelligence (Austin, 1978; Hirschi and Hindelang, 1977).

Adherents to another viewpoint were more inclined to favour the idea that deviants suffered from a *psychological* defect, although again there were differences of opinion on the nature of this flaw. To behavioral psychologists, deviants were individuals whose personalities were not amenable to the 'normal' processes of social learning (Eysenck, 1964, 1977; Trasler, 1962); to numerous thinkers with a psychoanalytic leaning, the deviant was perceived as a person whose weak super-ego had abdicated control to a riotous id (Alexander and Ross, 1952); to the vocal middle class intelligentsia, caught on the rising fashion of psychiatry, all deviants were insane (Menninger, 1969; Prins, 1980).

The tapestry of assertions could be extended, almost infinitely, but this would serve only to distract attention away from the point on which all these theorists agreed. It did not matter much whether they subscribed to a demonological, physiological, psychological or psychiatric explanation of deviant behavior, the belief that the deviant was a defective was a belief committing the theorist to a five fold fracture in the unity between a person and (i) the *meaning* of his/her behavior, (ii) the *perception* of his/her own predicament, (iii) the *reaction* of the person to the reaction of others, (iv) the *reaction* to the reactions of state officials, and (v) the State as the creator of rules whose violation constitutes the grounds for deviance attribution. Furthermore, given the strict paring away from the person of any meaningful connection with the social world, the deviant, in the view of these theoreticians, was someone who needed to be *corrected*. Whether the theorist took a tough-minded view and called penal sanctions punishment – a view now unfashionable, at least to admit to – or took a tenderminded view and called them treatment – currently much more acceptable as a motive for depriving others of their liberty – the fate for the deviant that lay implicit in these theoretical perspectives was always the same. The deviant was a defective person, and since that defect was *internal*, and hence inseparable, it was the deviant who had to be subjected to various correctional technologies. Until these were successfully applied, it remained unsafe to allow a 'defective' – dangerous – deviant either to stay in or return to the community.

However, before different correctional technologies could be put into practice, each theorist, or his disciples, had to convert those who administered the judicial and penal institutions. The issue was, how could they *demonstrate* their beliefs to be worth accepting? Fortunately for them, but unfortunately for the growth of our knowledge of deviance, this appeared to be an issue not worthy of much thought; the answer seemed quite obvious. Simply take a sample of *official deviants*, that is, men in prison or other penal institutions; conclude what is peculiar about this population – besides their being institutionalized – and declare this peculiarity to be the cause, or connected with the cause, of their deviant behavior.

At first only institutionalized populations were studied; however, it became apparent that what was peculiar about this population might also be a peculiarity of a 'normal' population. Consequently, to be more rigorous and strengthen their arguments, and at the same time to imitate the method of natural science, some researchers took the step, although not always very carefully, of comparing official deviants with a control group of conformists.

The holy trinity of the subject-matter of deviance was thus forged: study *official deviants*, for these are the equivalents of *deviants*, who are the people who engage in *deviance*. Armed with these theoretical correspondences, the positivist non-sociological students of deviance visited penal institutions and, in the honourable name of scientific research, proceeded to harass the inmates with a battery of pseudo-scientific gadgetry and mindless questions, such as 'How often do you get this problem?' (e.g. feeling sexually frustrated, being bored, feeling your life is wasted, missing social life, and missing little luxuries) (Richards, 1978; Sapsford, 1978). Depending on the fashion of the day or the fad of the researcher, prisoners had their heads measured for irregularities, their bodies somatotyped, their unconsciouses probed and analysed, their intelligence rated, their personalities typed, their brains scanned, and their gene structure investigated.

Millions, perhaps billions, of pounds and man-hours were, and still are being, expended in this manner. The result, however, hardly bears the fruit of these efforts; no consistent and valid differences between official deviants and a control group of conformists have been revealed. Some researchers have indeed discovered clear differences between the two groups, but other researchers, replicating or re-examining these studies, have consistently been unable to substantiate the original claim.

The sociological establishment was, at first, pleased to explain this failure – these researchers were simply looking in the wrong place. The reason for people's behavior, deviant or otherwise, did not lie within them, but in their social and cultural surroundings. No wonder those with physiological or psychological presuppositions had come up with so little: they had been guilty of a misconception. Deviant behavior was not to be perceived as the *manifestation* of a defective human being, but as the *indicator* of a defective social environment. No longer were deviants to be viewed as innately deviant; instead their deviant character was to be explained primarily as a result of the unfavourable and pathological circumstances of their environment.

Carried along by this new presupposition, sociologists then proceeded to reveal the nature of this *external* cause of deviant behavior. A list of these revelations would include nearly every institution and association that has ever been subsumed under the canopy 'society'. However, those aetiological accounts which have most preoccupied sociologists, at least until recently, have been family breakdown, corrupting friends, socially disorganized neighborhoods and anomie-inducing culture.

Unfortunately, like their non-sociological counterparts, sociological accounts of deviance have been dazzling in their rich variety, but disappointing in their substantiveness. They do represent a significant shift of emphasis from a defective individual to defective social circumstances, but their adherents hardly broke with the traditional assumption that, in order to test hypotheses on deviants and deviance, it was adequate to study official deviants and compare them with samples of conformists. In other words, the holy trinity which had sustained writers with a physiological or psychological leaning had also sustained generations of sociologists. When it came to the question of what they were studying, sociologists failed to make distinct a significant difference between *actors* and *acts*, and they refused to accept what they at least implied they knew, namely that *official deviants* are a highly selected population of deviants and, as such, an entirely inappropriate basis from which to make generalizations on deviants and deviant behavior. This is why, for so long, sociological explanations remained unsubstantiated.

To escape this carousel, it became increasingly clear that the subject-matter of the sociology of deviance needed to be opened up from the concertina'd position in which it had originally been cast. During the last two decades, this has been attempted and, as a result, the sociology of deviance has been completely remoulded. It seems clear now that there are *at least* three distinct questions to be answered:

1 Why do people engage in deviant behavior? This is the question of deviance.

2 Why do people with certain attributes, both social and psychological, appear more

frequently in the official data on deviants? This is the question of official deviants.

3 Why do some people assume a deviant identity? This is the question of deviants.

From S. Box (1981) 'Changing conceptions of deviance, official data and deviants', Deviance, Reality and Society *(London: Holt, Rinehart and Winston), pp. 1–5.*

References

Alexander, F: & Ross, H. (Ed.) (1952) *Dynamic Psychiatry*. Chicago: Chicago University Press.

Austin, R.L. (1978) Intelligence and adolescent theft. *Criminal Justice and Behavior*, 5, 212–225.

Cantwell, D. (1977) The hyperkinetic syndrome. In *Child Psychiatry* (Ed.) Rutter, M. & Hersov, L. pp. 524–555. London: Blackwell.

Davis, N.J. (1975) *Sociological Constructions of Deviance*. Dubuque, Ia: Wm C. Brown.

Erikson, K.T. (1966) *Wayward Puritans*. New York: Wiley.

Eysenck, H.J. (1964) *Crime and Personality*. London: Routledge and Kegan Paul.

Gibbons, D.C. (1979) *The Criminological Enterprise: Theorists and Perspectives*. New Jersey: Prentice-Hall.

Gibbons, D.C. & Jones, J.F. (1975) *The Study of Deviance*. New Jersey: Prentice-Hall.

Hippchen, L.J. (1977) Biochemical research: its contribution to criminological theory. In *Theory in Criminology: Contemporary Views* (Ed.) Meier, R.F. pp. 57–68. London: Sage.

Hirschi, T. & Hindelang, M.J. (1977) Intelligence and crime. *American Sociological Review*, 42, 571–586.

Jeffery, C.R. (Ed.) (1979) *Biology and Crime*. Beverley Hills: Sage.

Menninger, K. (1969) *The Crime of Punishment*. New York: Viking.

Nettler, G. (1974) *Explaining Crime*. New York: McGraw-Hill.

Nettler, G. (1978) *Explaining Crime* (2nd ed.) New York: McGraw-Hill.

Prins, H. (1980) *Offenders, Deviants or Patients*? London: Tavistock.

Reid, T. (1976) *Crime and Criminology*. Hinsdale, Ill: Dryden Press.

Richards, B. (1978) The experience of long-term imprisonment. *British Journal of Criminology*, 18, 162–169.

Rosenthal, D. (1973) Heredity in criminality, *Criminal Justice and Behavior*, 2, 3–21.

Sapsford, R.J. (1978) Life-sentence prisoners: psychological changes during sentence. *British Journal of Criminology*, 18, 128–145.

Schafer, S. (1969) *Theories in Criminology*. New York: Random House.

Shah, S.A. & Roth, L.H. (1974) Biological and psychological factors in criminality. In *Handbook of Criminology* (Ed.) Glaser, D. pp. 101–173. New York: Rand McNally.

Suchar, C.S. (1978) *Social Deviance: Perspectives and Prospectives*. New York: Holt, Rinehart and Winston.

Thio, A. (1978) *Deviant Behavior*. Boston: Houghton Mifflin.

Trasler, G. (1962) *Explanation of Criminality*. London: Routledge and Kegan Paul.

West, D.J. (Ed.) (1969) *Criminological Implications of Chromosome Abnormalities*. Cambridge: Institute of Criminology.

1.3 The construction and deconstruction of crime
John Muncie

Defining crime

What is crime? The *Oxford English Dictionary* states that crime is:

> An act punishable by law, as being forbidden by statute or injurious to the public welfare. ... An evil or injurious act; an offence, a sin; esp. of a grave character.

At first sight, such a definition appears straightforward and uncontroversial: a crime is an illegal act. However, on closer examination things are not so simple. [...]

To appreciate fully the complexities of the question 'what is crime', we need to broaden our enquiry to include some understanding of criminal law, social mores and social order.

Crime as criminal law violation

The most common and frequently applied definition of crime is that which links it to substantive criminal law. In other words, an act is only a crime when it violates the prevailing legal code of the jurisdiction in which it occurs. Michael and Adler are thus able to argue that the most precise and least ambiguous definition of crime is 'behavior which is prohibited by the criminal code' (Michael and Adler, 1933, p.5) **(DEFINITION 1)**. [...]

This logic was taken to its extreme by Tappan's argument that: 'Only those are criminals who have been adjudicated as such by the courts. Crime is an intentional act in violation of the criminal law (statutory and case law), committed without defense or excuse and penalized by the state as a felony or misdemeanor' (Tappan, 1947, p.100) **(DEFINITION 2)**. This black letter law approach – that the application of a legal sanction through court processes and practices must be pursued before a crime can be formally established to have occurred – maintains that no act can be considered criminal before and unless a court has meted out some penalty.

Again, this may appear clear-cut and uncontroversial, but two important consequences flow from such formulations. First, there would be no crime without criminal law. No behavior can be considered criminal unless a formal sanction exists to prohibit it. Michael and Adler (1933, p.5) contend that: 'if crime is merely an instance of conduct which is proscribed by the criminal code, it follows that the criminal law is the formal cause of crime'. Second, there would be no crime until an offender is caught, tried, convicted and punished. No behavior or individual can be considered criminal until formally decided upon by the criminal justice system.

By drawing these lines of argument together, Sutherland and Cressey proposed a definition of crime which (at least up to the 1960s) was adopted by most social scientists and legal scholars:

> Criminal behavior is behavior in violation of the criminal law ... it is not a crime unless it is prohibited by the criminal law. The criminal law, in turn, is defined conventionally as a body of specific rules regarding human conduct which have been promulgated by political authority, which apply uniformly to all members of the classes to which the rules refer and which are enforced by punishment administered by the state.
> (Sutherland and Cressey, 1924/1970, p.4)
> **(DEFINITION 3)**

In a similar vein, a number of conditions must be met before an act can be legally defined as a crime:

- The act must be legally prohibited at the time it is committed.
- The perpetrator must have criminal intent (mens rea).
- The perpetrator must have acted voluntarily (actus rea).
- There must be some legally prescribed punishment for committal of the act.

What this means is that we can only understand crime by identifying the distinctive procedural rules of evidence, burdens and standards of proof and particular forms of trial established within criminal law. It also assumes that people act with free will and should be made responsible for their actions. Yet the argument is circular: criminal law and court procedures claim to respond to crime, yet crime can only be defined by looking to the criminal law itself. Lacey *et al.* suggest that, in order to break out of this impasse and move towards a more adequate answer to the apparently straightforward question, 'what is crime?', 'we must enter upon some broader reflection about how our society comes to define "deviance"; how it comes to be decided which deviance calls for a legal response; and what determines that legal response as a criminal as opposed to, or as well as, a civil response' (Lacey *et al.*, 1990, pp. 2–3). [...]

We can identify a number of other issues and consequences that flow from legally based definitions:

- An act can only be considered a 'crime' once it is identified as such by law – thus criminals can only be identified once processed and convicted by the courts. But not all of those who break criminal laws are caught and prosecuted. The study of criminal behavior is thus severely hampered, and may be particularly one-dimensional if restricted only to those persons who are convicted of offences.

- The approach neglects the basic issues of why and how some acts are legislated as criminal, while others may remain subject only to informal control or rebuke.

- A black letter law approach tends to refer only to the formal constitution and enactment of law and underplays the different ways in which it is enforced. It divorces the criminal process from its social context, masking the ways in which the law is not simply applied by the courts, but is actively made and interpreted by key court personnel (for example, in plea bargaining, the quality of legal representation, and judicial discretion). In turn, this may have important consequences for what kinds of behavior should be regarded as truly criminal. Are theft and violence more serious than violations of health and safety codes in the work place? Both may be dealt with by the criminal law, but the tendency to view the former as 'real crime' and the latter as 'regulatory offences' may only lead us (unjustifiably?) to exclude these latter behaviors from our legitimate subject matter.

Crime as violation of moral codes

Sellin (1938) argued that the concept of crime should be extended beyond legal violations of *moral* and *social* codes. He contended that every society has its own standards of behavior or 'con-duct norms', but that not all these standards are necessarily reflected in law. In this context, terms such as 'deviance', 'non-conformity' and 'anti-social conduct' are preferred to that of 'crime', because the latter is incapable of encompassing all acts of wrong-doing. [...]

Although clearly a social, rather than a legal, category, [the term deviance] suffers from an extreme cultural relativism and is inextricably related to difficulties in establishing what is 'nor-mal'. As Simmons (1969, p.3) found in public responses to the question, 'who's deviant?', the concept can be as readily applied to Christians, pacifists, divorcees, 'know-it-all' professors and the president of the United States as it can to criminals and law-breakers. [...]

Sutherland's (1949) research into unethical practices among corporate managers in the USA found that, despite their serious and injurious nature, such practices were often considered non-criminal: as violations of civil, rather than criminal, law. As a result, he argued that crime should be defined not on the basis of criminal law, but on the more abstract notions of 'social injury' and 'social harm'. Thus:

> The essential characteristic of crime is that it is behavior which is prohibited by the state as an *injury* to the state ... The two abstract criteria ... as necessary elements in a definition of crime are legal descriptions of an act as *socially harmful* and legal provision of a penalty for the act.
>
> (Sutherland, 1949, p.31, emphasis added)
>
> **(DEFINITION 4)**

Sutherland implied that some moral criteria of social injury must be applied before any compre-hensive definition of crime can be formulated. However, whether morality has any more an objec-tive status than law also remains disputed.

Subsequent moral 'readings' of crime have been most forcibly put by those on the right of the political spectrum but not confined to them. The American neo-conservative social policy analyst Charles Murray, for example, has maintained that increases in crime are directly the result of a break-down in family relationships and a growth in illegitimacy (Murray, 1990). [...]

Behaviors such as taking the life of another, sexual violence and stealing for personal gain may be considered to be particularly heinous and abhor-rent. Each though has at some time also been considered quite legitimate. Criminal laws are never static or permanent features of any society. [...]

As Wilkins (1964, p.46) warns: 'there are no absolute standards. At some time or another, some form of society or another has defined almost all forms of behavior that we now call "criminal" as desirable for the functioning of that form of society'. The temporal and cultural relativity of 'crime' ensures that 'there is no one behavioral entity which we can call crime, there is no behavior which is always and everywhere criminal' (Phillipson, 1971, p.5). Similarly, if there are no clear and unambiguous rules to decide which actions should be subject to moral and legal sanction, can it be argued that any consensus exists in society? Can the law or moral codes be relied upon to reveal any such consensus?

Crime as social construct

A vast array of behaviors have been (or can be) deemed 'deviant' or 'criminal' because they violate legal or normative prescriptions. But there is no common behavioral denominator that ties all of these acts together. Propositions, such as society is based upon a moral consensus or that the criminal law is merely a reflection of that consensus, also remain contentious. The interactionist school of sociology, for example, argues that there is no underlying or enduring consensus in society. [...] Rather, crime is viewed as a consequence of social interaction: that is, as a result of a *negotiated process* that involves the rule-violator, the police, the courts, lawyers and the law-makers who define a person's behavior as criminal.

Behavior may be *labelled* criminal, but it is not this behavior in itself that constitutes crime. Rather, behavior is *criminalized* by a process of social perception and reaction as applied and interpreted by agents of the law. Crime exists only when the label and the law are successfully applied to an individual's behavior. It is not what people do, but how they are perceived and evaluated by others, that constitutes crime. Whereas law-violation approaches argue that the existence of 'crime' depends on the prior existence of criminal law, interactionism logically contends that, without the *enforcement and enactment* of criminal law (or social reaction to certain behaviors), there would be no crime. [...]

Social groups create deviance by making the rules whose infraction constitutes deviance, and by applying those rules to particular people and labelling them as outsiders. From this point of view deviance is not a quality of the act a person commits, but rather a consequence of the application by others of rules and sanctions to an 'offender'. The deviant is one to whom that label has been successfully applied; deviant behavior is behavior that people so label. (Becker, 1963, p.9) **(DEFINITION 5)**

Thus 'crime' has no universal or objective existence, but is relative to the subjective contingencies of social and historical circumstance. This in turn opens up and expands the range of criminological inquiry away from behavioral questions – Why did they do it? – towards *definitional issues* – Why is that rule there? Who created it? In whose interests? How is it enforced? What are the consequences of this enforcement? (Cohen, 1973a, p.623). It implies that we will only come to understand why an action is regarded as criminal by examining both the processes of rule creation and law enforcement. [...]

The interactionist approach refutes the notion that criminality is driven by some peculiar motivation or that criminals are a species apart. Rather, it contends that criminality *is ordinary, natural* and *widespread* and as a result requires no more explanation than that which might be attached to any 'ordinary' activity. However, what does require explanation is the complex process by which agencies of social control are able to construct a public identification of *certain* people as criminal, and how social reaction and labelling are able to produce and reproduce a recognizable criminal population. [...]

Crime as ideological censure

Conflict-based analyses of the social order have expanded on the basic premise of interactionism – that crime only exists through the labelling of certain behaviors as such – by arguing that it is essential to ground such generalities in specific relations of power and domination. It is not a simple question of interest groups acting in competition with each other (as the interactionists would argue), but of the systematic and consistent empowerment of some groups to the detriment of others. [...]

In developing a Marxist theory of crime and criminal law, Chambliss (1975, p.152) argues that acts are defined as criminal only when it is in the interest of the ruling class to define them so. Crime is a reality which exists only as it is created by those in society whose interests are served by its presence. In capitalist societies, 'crime' performs the vital function of diverting the lower classes' attention away from the conditions and source of their exploitation, and enables the bourgeoisie to expand penal law in their efforts to coerce the proletariat into submission. Behaviors are criminalized in order to maintain political control and to counter any perceived threat to the legitimacy of the ruling class (the clearest examples of such a process being the creation of public order offences to curtail political demonstration and trade union legislation to prevent 'wildcat' strikes):

> Criminality is simply *not* something that people have or don't have; crime is not something some people do and others don't. Crime is a matter of who can pin the label on whom, and underlying this socio-political process is the structure of social relations determined by the political economy.
>
> (Chambliss, 1975, p.165) **(DEFINITION 6)**

Sumner (1990) presents a development of this line of argument which continues to recognize how criminal law (and thus crime) can be a crucial instrument of class power, but also argues that it cannot be simply reduced to class relations and class conflict. He prefers to treat crime and deviance as matters of moral and political judgement – as social censures rooted in particular ideologies. The concept of crime, then, is neither a behavioral nor a legal category, but an expression of particular cultural and political conditions. Neither is 'crime' simply a label, but a generic term to describe a series of 'negative ideological categories with specific historical applications ... categories of denunciation or abuse lodged within very complex, historically loaded practical conflicts and moral debates ... these negative categories of moral ideology are social censures' (Sumner, 1990, pp.26, 28) **(DEFINITION 7)**.

Crime as historical invention

Troublesome behaviors have been called 'crimes' (whether or not recognized in law) for so long that the term is habitually used to condemn 'unwanted' or 'undesirable' acts or people. If 'crime' is intrinsically tied to 'criminal law', as various definitions assume, then we only discover the origins of crime in the development of criminal law in the eighteenth century. Up till then, the newly emergent nation states in Europe lacked the resources to

invest in the wholesale formulation and enforcement of state law. At the time, many behaviors that are today deemed criminal were governed by civil law and religion. In other words, there was less 'crime' and more 'sin', 'civil wrongs' and 'private disputes'. The terms in which crime might be construed as a problem had not yet been formed. [...]

Many explanations of the origins of criminal law have pointed to the symbiotic relationship that existed between economic power and the forging of new legislation tailored to protect the unique interests of dominant groups. Chambliss (1964) demonstrates how vagrancy laws find their origins in economic circumstance and class power: originating in 1349, these laws made it a crime to give alms to unemployed people. The law was passed following a chronic labour shortage experienced by landowners as a consequence of the Black Death of 1348. The traditional custom of migratory and free labour was criminalized in order to ensure an abundant supply of local, cheap labour. Agricultural labourers could no longer move from county to county to seek higher wages. Once the labour market was full, the laws fell into disuse, but were revived in 1530 to protect the interests of the new mercantile class. The emphasis shifted to controlling the movement of 'rogues' and 'vagabonds' in order to reduce the risk of robberies of commercial goods while in transit. By 1743, a person could be liable for prosecution if unable to give a 'good account of themselves'. The legislation was designed to serve the interests of powerful interest groups who needed a stable and static workforce to fill the fields and the emergent factories. [...]

From such analyses, 'crime' has been defined as 'human conduct that is created by authorised agents in a politically organised society' and used to describe 'behaviors that conflict with the interests of the segments of the society that have the power to shape public policy' (Quinney, 1970, pp.15–16) **(DEFINITION 8)**. This definition suggests that the identification and delineation of 'crime' is an inherently political process. The law (and thus crime) is created and applied by those who have the power to translate their private interests into public policy. Criminal law is coercive and partial, its political neutrality a myth. Developing this line of argument, De Haan claims that 'crime' is an ideological concept which 'serves to maintain political power relations; justifies inequality and serves to distract public attention from more serious problems and injustices' (De Haan, 1991, p.207) **(DEFINITION 9)**. In a similar vein, the historian, E.P. Thompson (1975, p.194), has asserted that 'crime' is a disabling and moralistic category. To restrict the analysis of crime to those definitions constructed by property owners and the state can only hinder accurate historical research and produce pre-given moral interpretations.

Crime as social harm

In the section 'Crime as violation of moral codes' we noted that Sutherland's (1949) pathbreaking study of corporate malpractices led to a recognition among criminologists of the need to move beyond legally defined conceptions of crime if the existence of other more damaging forms of 'injury' or 'social harm' are to be recognized and incorporated into the criminological agenda. By the 1970s, the critical criminologists, the Schwendingers, for example, expanded the list of potentially injurious practices to include the systematic violation of basic human rights. Working within a theoretical tradition which maintains that capitalist and imperialist social orders (and their state practices) contain their own criminogenic tendencies, they promoted a definition of crime based on a conception of the denial of basic fundamental human rights:

> The abrogation of these rights certainly limits the individual's chance to fulfil himself in many spheres of life. It can be stated that individuals who deny these rights to others are criminal. Likewise social relationships and social systems which regularly cause the abrogation of these rights are also criminal. If the terms imperialism, racism, sexism and poverty are abbreviated signs for theories of social relationships or social systems which cause the systematic abrogation of basic rights, then imperialism, racism, sexism and poverty can be called crimes.
> (Schwendinger and Schwendinger, 1970, p.148) **(DEFINITION 10)**

And in the 1990s, a whole range of 'injurious practices' or 'non-crimes' such as the failure to enforce health and safety standards at work, the deliberate marketing of known faulty products, the 'culpable negligence' of tobacco and food companies knowingly promoting unsafe and life-threatening substances, the international dumping of toxic waste, the abuse involved in the transportation of live animals, the extent of violence in the home or the systematic flouting of export controls to certain countries by arms manufacturers not only

came to enter public idiom as 'crime', but also began to be taken seriously by academic criminologists. What all such cases reveal is that a legal concept of 'crime' is not only partial but that many of the most harmful acts are actually supported by the law (Tifft, 1994/5). They also suggest that victimization is far more prevalent and widespread than official definitions would have us believe.

To tackle such partiality, some authors have begun to place 'crime' within a broader context of social harm in which the visible and the obscured, the legally recognized and the legally sanctioned can be included in a comprehensive, continuous and integrated vision of criminal and harmful acts. Henry and Milovanovic (1996, p.1–16), for example, work within a broad conception of 'crime' as the 'power to deny others': 'crime is the expression of some agency's energy to make a difference on others and it is the exclusion of those others who in the instant are rendered powerless to maintain and express their humanity' **(DEFINITION 11)**. For others, given the vast diversity of behaviors or acts that have been (or can be) considered 'criminal', there remains no sense in retaining the concept of 'crime' at all. Hulsman (1986, p.71), for example, has argued that 'crime has no ontological reality. Crime is not the *object* but the *product* of criminal policy.' He prefers to work with the less emotionally charged concepts of 'trouble', 'problematic situation' and 'undesirable occurrence'. In a similar vein, De Haan (1991, p.208) contends that 'what we need is not a better theory of crime, but a more powerful critique of crime.' Again, this requires an alternative series of conceptualizations: 'unfortunate events'; 'more or less serious troubles'; 'conflicts which can result in suffering, harm or damage'. The key point is that 'crime' can never be defined in any consistent or conclusive manner. 'What is crime?' will always remain 'essentially contested'. [...]

Definitions of crime are neither objectively right nor wrong: they do, however, point out the elusive and the contested nature of our subject matter. [...] The strength of explanations based on crime of law prescription is that they provide an objective criteria by which 'crime' can be reliably identified: 'crime' is whatever the law deems to be illegal at particular times and in particular jurisdictions. Such a definition does, nevertheless, bind us to state-generated notions of lawbreaking. It narrows our attention to formulations enshrined in legal statutes, and, while it may assume a greater objectivity, it overlooks the fact that 'the law' itself is deeply problematic, as a site of struggle, dispute, construction and contestation. In addition, a legal-based definition systematically excludes notions of harm, deviance, anti-social conduct, injustices and rule-breaking. We lose sight of how and why it is only *certain* behaviors that come to be considered deviant and how and why it is only *some* harmful practices that are ultimately subject to criminal sanction. In short, we lose sight of 'crime' as a for-ever shifting concept, as a morally and politically loaded term.

Importantly, the various conceptions of crime appear to be generated from competing accounts of the social order. If that order is considered consensual (as we discussed earlier), 'crime' can be defined as the infraction of legal, moral or conduct norms. When the social order is considered pluralist or conflict based (as we showed in 'Crime as social construct' and 'Crime as ideologi-cal censure' above), 'crime' refers not to particular behaviors, but to the social and political processes whereby those actions are subjected to criminaliza-tion. Accordingly, it can be argued that any definition of crime rests on prior assumptions about the nature of social order and how that order is conceived and maintained. Indeed, this has led some to argue that crime only comes to be a problem when order is a problem. Our key prob-lematic then may not be 'crime', but the 'struggle around order and the products it produces among which are crime and criminal justice' (Shearing, 1989, p. 178).

> *From J. Muncie, 'The construction and deconstruction of crime', in J. Muncie and E. McLaughlin (eds)* The Problem of Crime *(London: Sage), 2001, pp. 9–23.*

References

Becker, H. (1963) *Outsiders: Studies in the Sociology of Deviance*, New York, Free Press. (Extract reprinted as 'Outsiders' in Muncie *et al.*, 1996.)

Chambliss, W.J. (1964) 'A sociological analysis of the law of vagrancy', *Social Problems*, no. 12, pp.67–77.

Chambliss, W.J. (1975) 'Toward a political economy of crime', *Theory and Society*, vol. 2, pp.149–70. (Extract reprinted in Muncie *et al.*, 1996.)

Cohen, S. (1973a) 'The failures of criminology', *The Listener*, 8 November.

De Haan, W. (1991) 'Abolitionism and crime control: a contradiction in terms', in Stenson and Cowell (1991). (Extract reprinted as 'Abolitionism and crime control' in Muncie *et al.*, 1996.)

Henry, S. and Milovanovic, D. (1996) *Constitutive Criminology*, London, Sage.

Hulsman, L (1986) 'Critical criminology and the con-cept of crime', *Contemporary Crises*, vol.10, no.1, pp.63–80. (Extract reprinted in Muncie *et al.*, 1996.)

Lacey, N., Wells, C. and Meure, D. (1990) *Reconstructing Criminal Law*, London, Weidenfeld and Nicolson.

Michael, J. and Adler, M. (1933) *Crime, Law and Social Science*, New York, Harcourt, Brace Jovanovich.

Murray, C. (1990) *The Emerging British Underclass*, London, Institute of Economic Affairs. (Extract reprinted as 'The Underclass' in Muncie *et al.*, 1996.)

Phillipson, M. (1971) *Sociological Aspects of Crime and Delinquency*, London, Routledge and Kegan Paul.

Quinney, R. (1970) *The Social Reality of Crime*, Boston, MA, Little Brown.

Schwendinger, H. and Schwendinger, J. (1970) 'Defenders of order or guardians of human rights?', *Issues in Criminology*, vol.5, no.2, pp.123–57.

Sellin, T. (1938) *Culture, Conflict and Crime*, New York, Social Science Research Council.

Shearing, C. (1989) 'Decriminalising criminology', *Canadian Journal of Criminology*, vol.31, no.2, pp.169–78.

Simmons, J.L. (1969) *Deviants*, Berkeley, CA, Glendessary Press.

Sumner, C. (ed.) (1990) *Censure, Politics and Criminal Justice*, Buckingham, Open University Press.

Sutherland, E. (1949) *White Collar Crime*, New York, Dryden Press.

Sutherland, E. and Cressey, D. (1924/1970) *Criminology*, 8th edn, Philadelphia, PA, Lippincott.

Tappan, P.W. (1947) 'Who is the criminal?', *American Sociological Review*, vol.12, pp.96–102.

Thompson, E.P. (1975) *Whigs and Hunters*, London, Allen Lane.

Tifft, L. (1994/5) 'Social harm definitions of crime', *The Critical Criminologist*, vol.6, no.3, pp.9–13.

Wilkins, L. (1964) *Social Deviance*, London, Tavistock.

1.4 A suitable amount of crime
Nils Christie

Crime is in endless supply. Acts with the potentiality of being seen as crimes are like an unlimited natural resource. We can take out a little in the form of crime – or a lot. Acts are not, they become; their meanings are created as they occur. To classify and to evaluate are core activities for human beings. The world comes to us as we constitute it. Crime is thus a product of cultural, social and mental processes. For all acts, including those seen as unwanted, there are dozens of possible alternatives to their understanding: bad, mad, evil, misplaced honour, youth bravado, political heroism – or crime. The 'same' acts can thus be met within several parallel systems as judicial, psychiatric, pedagogical, theological

But let it be quite clear: I do not say, here or later, that unacceptable acts, completely unacceptable also to me do not exist. I do not deny that some people get bullets into their bodies due to other people's guns. Nor do I deny that some are killed due to other people's cars, that money is taken away from people's drawers or bank accounts without their consent. And I do not deny that I have strong moral objections to most of these acts, try to stop them, and try to prevent them. Nor do I deny that it might be useful to see some of these acts as crime.

I am interested in how meanings are born and are shaped. But that is no immoral position. My world is filled with values, many of which command me to act and re-act. But that does not hinder a keen interest in how acts get their meaning.

With this general perspective, there are some traditional questions in criminology I will *not* ask. Particularly, I will not find it useful asking what is the development in the crime situation. This does not mean that crime statistics are without interest. Such statistics inform on phenomena seen and registered by a particular society as crime and also what happens to those seen as major actors. But crime statistics are themselves social phenomena. They tell what the system sees as crime and bothers to cope with, or has capacity to cope with. Crime statistics are a social fact in dire need for interpretation. This view on crime statistics has consequences. It means that it is not useful to ask if crime is on the increase, stable, or on the decrease. Crime does not exist as a given entity. To measure the variations in the occurrence of a phenomenon that changes its content over time is not among the most tempting of tasks.

I am on this point probably in some disagreement with David Garland (2001) in his book on *The Culture of Control*. I say 'probably' in disagreement. That is because Garland in his interesting book to me is unclear on this point. I am of the impression that he says that crime exists as a phenomenon we can describe as an entity that varies over time and that we can say it is on the increase or decrease. I am also of the impression that he is of the opinion that crime has increased, and that this belief is an important element in his analysis. But he is guarded on this point. I hope his basic position is that we have moved into a social situation where an impression is created of a situation of increased crime, and that this *impression* has all sorts of social consequences.

This general perspective on crime makes it possible to raise two interrelated central questions: First, what is behind increases or decreases in acts generally perceived as unwanted or unacceptable? And how is it eventually possible to influence the occurrence of these unwanted acts?

Second, what is it that makes a shifting quota of these unwanted acts to appear as crimes and the actors as criminals? Particularly, under what material, social, cultural and political conditions will crime and criminals appear as the dominant metaphors, the dominant way of seeing the unwanted acts and actors?

This is a liberating perspective. It opens for the general theme of this book: When is enough, enough? Or, as in the title, what is a suitable amount of crime? This question leads naturally into the next: What is a suitable amount of punishment?

From N. Christie, A Suitable Amount of Crime *(London: Routledge), 2004, pp. 10–12.*

2

Crime and punishment in history

2.1 Execution and the English people
Vic Gatrell   22

2.2 Eighteenth-century punishment
Michael Ignatieff   24

2.3 Prosecutors and the courts
Clive Emsley   27

2.4 Police and people: the birth of Mr Peel's blue locusts
Michael Ignatieff   31

2.5 The London garotting panic of 1862: a moral panic and the creation of a criminal class in mid-Victorian England
Jennifer Davis   34

Introduction

Without some sense of the history of our systems of policing and punishment it is very hard to grasp fully the nature and significance of the way we do things now. It is all too easy when thinking about pretty much any aspect of our contemporary world to assume that things have generally always been thus. Thus, in relation to crime and justice one could be forgiven for assuming, say, that we have always had something that looks like a police force for maintaining order or that when people commit serious crimes we have tended to respond by sending them to prison. History shows us something different – namely that both police forces and prisons, at least in roughly the forms we understand and have them today, are the product of the modern world. Before the industrial revolution, approximately speaking, we did things differently. The five readings in this chapter give some sense of this changing history.

In the excerpt from his wonderful book, *The Hanging Tree*, Vic Gatrell **(Reading 2.1)** discusses the use of the death penalty in the decades between the 1770s and the 1830s. This was a time when there was a very substantial range of offences potentially punishable by death – often what appear relatively minor offences from today's vantage point. Moreover, not only were people hanged in relatively large numbers, but the death penalty was carried out in public. Then, all of a sudden, there was a substantial drop in the use of capital punishment and alternatives were preferred. One of these was imprisonment and the second reading **(Reading 2.2)**, from Michael Ignatieff's *A Just Measure of Pain*, links the emergence of the modern prison, and the growing use of transportation with changing views of, and practices in relation to, the death penalty.

During this time there was also a series of far-reaching changes taking place in relation to prosecutors and the courts. In the third reading **(Reading 2.3)**, Clive Emsley examines these and more particularly notes the gradual shift away from private prosecutions brought by individual citizens (usually the victim of the crime) toward more formalized systems of magistrates, courts etc. Nevertheless, for much of the eighteenth and nineteenth centuries a wide variety of alternatives to prosecution were utilized by victims and their communities – sometimes this might involve the payment of some restitution; other times it might involve a rougher form of community response. Emsley also illustrates how communities often took a dim view of prosecutors, especially when they felt that charges were too severe or were unreasonable in some other way. He also notes the widespread use of rewards offered for recovery of goods and sometimes paid to thief-takers – one of the early precursors of formal police forces.

In the fourth of the readings **(Reading 2.4)** Michael Ignatieff turns his attention to the beginnings of modern police forces and, more particularly, the Metropolitan Police in London established by Robert Peel in 1829. Although some histories present the introduction of formal policing systems as a logical and functional response to the demands of rapidly industrializing society, as Ignatieff shows there was, in practice, much hostility and many sources of resistance. The new police were by no means universally welcome. The idea of the state encroaching on territory that had traditionally been the preserve of local communities and citizens caused much concern. Nor did such concern and resistance quickly disappear – indeed, one might ask whether it ever disappeared?

The final reading **(Reading 2.5)** by Jennifer Davis concerns crime rather than criminal justice institutions or punishment. Her focus is upon what she refers to as the 'London garotting panic' of 1862 – in effect something close to what in more modern parlance might be thought of as 'mugging' or street robbery. In fact, what she describes is something that we often think of as a very modern phenomenon: rising concern about particular types of crime in which the media play an important role in stirring up public fears and which, in turn, seems to result in an apparent 'crime wave'. In this article, Davis uses a variety of criminological ideas – most notably 'folk devils', 'moral panics' and 'deviancy amplification' – which we will meet in later chapters (especially chapter 4). As with all good historical writing, in doing so she makes us think both about the differences between the 1860s and the times we live in now, as well as some of the continuities.

Questions for discussion

1. Why do you think that in the eighteenth and much of the nineteenth century the death penalty and other punishments were carried out in public?

2. What was the Bloody Code? Why might it not have been quite as severe as it sounded?

3. What was the purpose of the Black Act and what might such legislation tell you about the functions of the criminal law?

4. What evidence is there that in the eighteenth century there was growing unease at the use of the death penalty for relatively minor offences?

5. Why do you think that local communities in the eighteenth and nineteenth centuries sometimes attacked prosecutors?

6. What were the sources of hostility to the introduction of the 'new police' in the 1820s and beyond?

7. According to Ignatieff, what techniques were used by the police in the nineteenth century to increase co-operation and trust among those communities that were most reluctant to accept them?

8. Describe the ways in which it might be argued that the police 'created' the garotting crime panic in the 1860s.

2.1 Execution and the English people
Vic Gatrell

Late eighteenth- and early nineteenth-century English people were very familiar with the grimy business of hanging. This is so large a social fact separating that era from our own that although it is not the most obvious way of defining modern times, it must be one of them. Admittedly the English noose and axe had been at their most active long before then: 75,000 people are thought to have been executed in the century 1530–1630, and nothing like this was seen again.[1] Execution rates declined in the second third of the seventeenth century as transportation to the American colonies absorbed many who would once have hanged; and political stability kept hanging rates stable across the next half-century. But then, dramatically, in the later eighteenth century it looked as if the bad old killing days were returning. There had been a mere 281 London hangings between 1701 and 1750; there were nearly *five* times as many between 1751 and 1800. The slaughter rate thereafter stayed high. As many were hanged in London in the 1820s as in the 1790s, and twice as many hanged in London in the thirty years 1801–30 as hanged in the fifty years 1701–50. How easily this extraordinary fact has been forgotten – that the noose was at its most active on the very eve of capital law repeals!

I estimate that some 35,000 people were condemned to death in England and Wales between 1770 and 1830. Most were reprieved by the king's prerogative of mercy and sent to prison hulks or transported to Australia. But about 7,000 were less lucky. Eight times a year at Tyburn or Newgate, once or twice a year in most counties, terrified men and women were hanged before large and excited crowds. Audiences of up to 100,000 were occasionally claimed in London, and of 30,000 or 40,000 quite often. Crowds of 3,000–7,000 were standard. When famous felons hanged, polite people watched as well as vulgar.

What they watched was horrific. There was no nice calculation of body weights and lengths of drop in those days; few died cleanly. Kicking their bound legs, many choked over minutes. Until 1790 women hanged for coining or murdering their husbands had their corpses publicly burnt after hanging. As late as 1820 male traitors had their heads hacked off and held up to the crowd. Even though, notoriously, there were over two hundred capital crimes on the statute-books, most of the hanged were strangled straightforwardly for standard crimes which (except for forgery) had been capital for centuries. In the 1820s a fifth were hanged for murder, a twentieth for attempted murder, another twentieth or so for rape, and somewhat fewer for sodomy. Two-thirds were hanged for property crimes: over a fifth of these for burglary and housebreaking, a sixth for robbery, a tenth for stealing horses, sheep, or cattle and a twelfth for forgery and uttering false coins. Forgery convictions killed off one in five of those hanged between 1805 and 1818.

Who were these people? Fewer women were hanged than men. Of the 1,242 London people condemned in 1703–72, only 92 were women; and of the 59 people executed in London in 1827–30, only 4 were women, all murderesses. Many men imprisoned in Newgate were listed as 'labourers'. But most claimed craft and trade status: leather-dressers, weavers, wiredrawers, brush-makers, printers, servants, porters, clerks, tailors, errand-boys, smiths, painters, sawyers, brass-founders, upholsterers, grooms, chair-carvers, drapers, whip-makers, steel-polishers, plasterers, glass-cutters, etc.[2] None the less, apart from the execution of a few wealthy forgers or murderers, most of the hanged were poor and marginalized people – 'the very lowest and worst of the people... the scum both of the city and the country', as Elizabeth Fry amiably described her Newgate charges in 1818. The more rootless the felon, the more likely the execution. Some 90 per cent of men hanged in London in the 1780s were aged under 21. A high proportion were recent immigrants to the city.[3]

The frequency of English executions was widely noted by foreign observers. It was in vain that English commentators replied that this was the price the English cheerfully paid for liberty and prosperity, that a few hangings were better than the ubiquitous police controls of a despotic state, and that most of the condemned were reprieved anyway. Foreign (and Scottish) eyebrows continued to be raised, for despite population differences, comparisons were startling. Scotland effectively excludes itself from this book if only because a meagre four or so a year hanged there in the 1780s; this rose to 5.4 a year in 1805–14, as against the English average of 67. Scotland's (and Ireland's) relative innocence of the noose continued into the mid-nineteenth century.[4] Other countries could crow too. The Prussian code had restricted capital punishment as early as 1743, and after 1794 only murderers were executed. Catherine's reforms to similar effect followed in Russia in 1767 and Joseph II's in Austria in 1787. Philadelphia Quakers dispensed with capital punishment after the American Revolution. In Amsterdam in the 1780s less than 1 a year were killed; barely 15 were executed annually in Prussia in the 1770s, and a little over 10 in Sweden in the 1780s. Towards 1770 about 300 people a year were condemned in the whole of France; over twice that number were condemned annually between 1781 and 1785 in London alone. Before the guillotine's invention French punishments were crueller than English. Stretchings, flayings, burnings, and breakings on wheels were common; hands were cut off before execution and hanged bodies routinely burnt. Even so, only 32 people were executed in Paris in 1774–7, against 139 in London, and when London hangings rose from annual averages of 48 in the 1770s to 70 in 1783–7, men and women dangled outside Newgate prison up to 20 at a time, a sight unknown elsewhere. There were on average 23 metropolitan hangings a year throughout the 1820s (more if Surrey hangings south of the Thames are included). Berliners would be unlucky to see a couple in the whole decade. While only 9 were executed in Prussia in 1818, 5 in 1822, and 9 in 1831, in no year of the 1820s did English executions fall below the 50 of 1825, and there were 107 in 1820, 114 in 1821, 74 in 1829. In the 1820s, 672 were executed in England and Wales, more (again) than had been hanged in the whole of either the first or the second quarter of the eighteenth century.[5]

Then suddenly – and I mean suddenly – this ancient killing system collapsed. After nearly forty years' exclusion from office, the whigs came to power with large reformist ambitions. The 1832 Reform Act also opened parliament to some hundred independent MPs, largely middle-class advocates of progress and critics of the *ancien régime*, fervently advocating the bloody code's repeal. Hangings shrank to a tenth of their score a decade before. When most capital statutes were at last repealed in 1837, only eight people were killed that year in the whole country, and six in the year following, all murderers, while the numbers sentenced to death dropped from 438 in 1837 to 56 in

1839. Penitentiaries and prisons acquired new importance in penal practice. Prison inspectors announced confidently that 'the law intends that the suffering of the offender shall be proportioned to the enormity of his offence'.[6] Uniformity was more striven for than achieved, just as the reformative idea was more alive in theory than in practice (in transportation it was not alive at all), and it addressed lesser offenders chiefly.[7] None the less it was as if England had become another and gentler country – or a little more like other countries. In most northern states of America executions had been confined to murder since the 1780s, and by the end of the 1830s most north-eastern states had already transferred executions from public spaces to the interiors of prisons.[8] England was only catching up. But at least ideas of just and proportionate punishment were tacitly acknowledged. At least, too, only murderers hanged in England and Wales, even if they continued to hang in large numbers compared to other countries (347 between 1837 and 1868 inclusive), and still in public.[9] Finally, public hanging was itself abolished in 1868. Thereafter until 1964 the state's killing business was done discreetly inside prisons, where nobody could see. The civilized public in whose interest punishments were inflicted could keep its emotional and physical distance from them, as it still does.

There has been no greater nor more sudden revolution in English penal history than this retreat from hanging in the 1830s. It was far more dramatic than the invention of the prison, for example even though the two processes were inextricably linked.

> *From V.A.C Gatrell*, The Hanging Tree *(Oxford: OUP), 1996, pp. 6–10.*

Notes

1 P. Jenkins 'From gallows to prison? The execution rate in early modern England', *Criminal Justice History* (1986), 52.

2 P. Linbaugh, *The London hanged: Crime and civil society in the eighteenth century* (1991), 91–2, 143; PP 180–1, xii. 463–91. Of the 416 prisoners locked up (for all reasons) in Newgate in Oct. 1828, 29 were women: Newgate Prison Register, 1829 (London Corporation RO: PD.28.15).

3 E. Fry to J.J. Gurney, 14 Nov. 1818 (Gurney papers, i. 203: Library of the Society of Friends, Temp. MS; Radzinowicz, i. 14; Linebaugh, *The London hanged*, ch. 3; A. R. Ekirch, *Bound for America: The transporta-*

tion of British convicts to the colonies, 1718–1775 (Oxford, 1987), 47–8.

4 Scottish executions dropped to little over 1 a year by 1836–42, eight to ten times less than the English rate; 5 murderers hanged in Scotland in 1857–63, as against 96 in England and Wales. In Ireland 81 were hanged in 1813-14, as against 19 in Scotland; but only 15 murderers hanged in Ireland in 1857–63, compared with the English 96 (PP 1812, x. 217ff; 1814–15. ix. 293ff.; 1844, xxix. 367–73; 1865. xlix).

5 French executions caught up with English in the 1820s. The Napoleonic code allowed for 36 capital offences (22 in 1832). In 1826–30 French courts delivered fewer death sentences than English (111 a year on average), but they pardoned fewer too; on average 72 a year were guillotined, 32 after 1832: G. Wright, *Between the guillotine and liberty: Two centuries of the crime problem in France* (Oxford, 1983), 39, 168–70. See also G. A. Kelly, *Mortal politics in eighteenth-century France* (Waterloo, Ontario, 1986), 187; J. R. Ruff, *Crime, justice and public order in old régime France* (1984), 60–2; Radzinowicz, i 288, 290, 295–7; I. Gilmore, *Riot, risings and revolution: Governance and*

violence in 18th century England (1992), 180; R. J. Evans, 'Offentlichkeit und Autoritat: Zur Geschichte der Hinrichtungcn in Deutschland vom Allgemeinen Landrecht bis zurm Dritten Reich', in H. Reif (ed.), *Räuber, Volk und Obrigkeit* (Frankfurt, 1984),208–28.

6 *Prison inspectors' third report (Home district)*, PP 1837–8, xxx, 8.

7 Over a quarter of felons convicted at English and Welsh assizes and quarter sessions were transported in the 1830s with no pretence at their reformation: a fifth died on the journey anyway. About 43,500 men and 7,700 women were transported in the 1830s, as against about 9,300 and 2,500 in 1787–1810, 15,400 and 2,000 in 1811–20, and 28,700 and 4,100 in 1821–30. Some third were Irish. The total from England and Wales was about 41,000 in 1787–1830: A. G. L. Shaw, *Convicts and the colonies: A study of penal transportation* (1966), 147–50.

8 L. P. Masur, *Rites of execution: Capital punishment and the transformation of American culture, 1776–1865* (Oxford, 1989), 4–5.

9 Before 1841, this included 3 who had attempted murder.

2.2 Eighteenth-century punishment
Michael Ignatieff

Before 1775, imprisonment was rarely used as a punishment for felony. At the Old Bailey, the major criminal court for London and Middlesex, imprisonments accounted for no more than 2.3 percent of the judges' sentences in the years between 1770 and 1774.[1] These terms of imprisonment were short – never longer than three years and usually a year or less – and they were inflicted on a narrow range of offenders – those convicted of manslaughter, commercial frauds, perjury, combining against employers, or rioting. The Wilkes and Liberty rioters and the London tailors, coal-heavers, hatters, and sailors who demonstrated for higher wages during the 1760s were all punished with prison terms.[2] Only minor offenders of this sort received imprisonment. Those convicted for their part in the violent frame-cutting war in the Spitalfields silk trade in 1769 and 1770 were either executed or transported to America.

The rationale behind the judges' use of imprisonment in these cases is far from clear. In cases arising from conflicts between masters and workers, however, some of their criteria are revealed in the correspondence between the Lord Chief Justice and the Secretary of State in 1773 about the fate of seven journeymen weavers in Paisley convicted of rioting and combining against their employers.[3] The judge sensed that the execution of these men might so inflame the weavers that they would riot again or else emigrate to America en masse. The situation in the town was, as he put it, 'very delicate.' Deciding that a show of mercy was more likely to succeed in restoring order than a display of force, he ordered their punishments mitigated to imprisonment.[4] In Paisley, therefore, imprisonment figured in the tactics of concession as an 'intermediate' and therefore 'merciful' compromise between transportation and hanging. Apart from such special occasions, however, judges rarely used the prison as a place of punishment for major felonies.

For these crimes – the most frequent being highway robbery, housebreaking, beast stealing of various kinds, grand larceny, murder, and arson – the nominal penalty was death. The number of crimes bearing the punishment for death increased from about 50 in 1688 to about 160 by 1765 and reached something like 225 (no one was quite sure of the new number) by the end of the Napoleonic Wars.[5] Some of these new statutes, the Riot Act for example, made offenses capital that had long been subject to lesser penalties. Others like the Black Act penalized activities that had not been criminal before, such as stealing hedges, underwood, fruit from trees, and timber; damaging orchards, hop-bines, or woodland; and taking fish from ponds or breaking the ponds to let fish escape.[6] The Black Act was enacted to make possible the conviction of the small farmers and tenants who were waging a guerrilla-style resistance to the encroachment upon their customary forest rights by *nouveaux riches* estate holders and royal foresters in the woodlands of Hampshire and Berkshire. While passed as an emergency measure, the Black Act became a permanent addition to the armory of the game laws.[7]

Since other new statutes of the time have not yet received historical attention, it is not clear why this gradual and inchoate extension of the definition of crime took place over the course of the century. In very general terms it appears that the new acts reflected the commercialization of eighteenth century agriculture and the desire of landlords to make profit from woodlands, ponds, and wastes on their estates, which they had previously ignored or allowed the poor to use without hindrance. The new criminal penalties were required as a legitimizing sanction for this assertion of property right because laborers, cottagers, and small farmers had customary use rights over game, wood, deadfall, peat, and other bounty of nature, rights which the gentry had formerly accepted as part of the binding order of custom in the countryside. Thus the extension of the definition of crime, brought about in the Black Act and in other new capital penalties, appears to represent the aggrandizement of the property rights of the gentry at the expense of common right and custom.[8]

In other cases, the criminalization of popular activity served the needs of commerce, the best example being the proliferation of new forgery and counterfeiting statutes in the first forty years of the century. The judge and jurist William Blackstone explained the growth of law in this field as an attempt by banking and commercial interests to secure protection for the new systems of paper credit and exchange created in response to the rise of a national market.[9] These interests apparently succeeded in convincing both the Crown and the judiciary that a rigorous enforcement of these new laws was of critical importance to commerce. Throughout the century, two-thirds of those convicted of forgery were actually executed.[10] With the exception of murder, no offense was more relentlessly punished.

In theory, the Bloody Code, as the criminal law was popularly known, appeared rigid and inflexible, prescribing death alike for murder and for the forgery of a petty deed of sale. In practice, the application of penalties was flexible indeed, allowing a large measure of play for judicial discretion, executive clemency in response to appeals for mercy, or exemplary displays of terror. The Paisley example already cited illustrates how judges could use their powers to temper the code in the direction of mercy. The same power, of course, could be used in the opposite direction. In 1775, two Halifax justices secured the approval of the Secretary of State to hang the body of Matthew Normanton, convicted for the murder of the supervisor of excise in Halifax, in chains on the top of Beacon Hill. It was unusual to hang a man in chains, the justices admitted, but they had been urged to do so by 'very many respectable Gentlemen and Merchants in and about Halifax and Rochdale,' who felt that 'such a notorious and public example' would deter others from making counterfeit coin, the crime that Normanton had been engaged in when discovered by the luckless exciseman.[11] A legal system that allowed the judges to heighten the symbolic impact of the hanging ritual in response to the pressures of 'respectable' citizens (or to forego it entirely in response to rebellious weavers) was obviously more flexible than its unvarying bloody penalties gave it the appearance of being.

There were of course more merciful uses of judicial and executive discretion. Judges in the Home Circuit during the 1750s, for example, pardoned a third of the offenders they had sentenced to death and sent them to transportation instead.[12] Their pardon power enabled them to mitigate capital penalties in 'special' or 'deserving' cases, to save 'respectable' offenders who could enlist a patron to plead for their lives, and in general to temper the severest criminal code in Europe with an elastic measure of mercy.

The code was also modified in practice by the traditional privilege of benefit of clergy. At first a privilege enjoyed by clerics who came before the royal courts of the Middle Ages, a privilege that was then extended gradually to other groups until 1705 when it was made available to men and women universally, benefit of clergy was a plea that offenders convicted of a range of minor capital crimes could enter to save themselves from the gallows [...].

The judicial habit of pardoning capital offenders, especially those convicted for newly criminalized activities, contributed to the rapid growth of transportation as a punishment. So did the act passed in 1717 changing the punishment for petty larceny from whipping to transportation. Other acts likewise substituted transportation for whipping as a penalty for robbery, minor kinds of coining, and the receipt of stolen goods.[13] While the substitution of transportation for whipping and branding might be interpreted, like the expansion of the Bloody Code itself, as an attempt by Parliament to increase the rigors of traditional punishment, the rising rate of pardons in capital cases after 1750 appears to indicate the opposite tendency among judges – a growing doubt about the fairness of visiting minor infractions with the punishment of death.[14]

Likewise, certain practices of juries suggest their unease about sending petty offenders to the gallows. Juries, like judges, were allowed a measure of discretion in arriving at verdicts. It was common for them to commit the 'pious perjury' of convicting those charged with grand larceny (a capital offense) with petty larceny (punishable by transportation) by valuing the goods stolen at less than a shilling regardless of their real value.[15] Comments by legal authorities like Blackstone suggest that 'pious perjury' became more common after 1750, indicating growing public dissatisfaction with the Bloody Code.[16] [...]

Like hanging, whipping was a public ritual inflicted by a parish officer or court official for the edification of the populace. Hence it was considered important to stage the ritual at a time and a place sure of attracting attention. The Surrey justices seem keenly aware of this in a sentence recorded in their order books in 1775:

> Robert Snowdon ... convicted of felony is committed to your custody for the space of three months and on Saturday the 15th instant between the hours of 12 and 2 of that day to be stripped from the middle upwards and tied to a cart's tail and publicly whipped from the stockhouse round thro' the Market Place at Kingston upon Thames and back again 'til his back is bloody and at the end of the said three months to be discharged without fees.[17]

Like their colleagues in Halifax who orchestrated the hanging of the coiner in chains, the Surrey justices displayed that shrewd sense of theater and

timing on which the deterrent effect of ritual punishment relied.

Another punishment of public shame was the pillory. Offenders who aroused a high degree of public indignation, such as shopkeepers found using false weights, persons convicted of hoarding or speculating in the grain trade, or persons convicted of homosexual assault, were locked in head stocks in a marketplace or in front of a jail and sentenced to endure an hour of the crowd's abuse.[18] Such a punishment relied for its enforcement on the feeling of the populace. It could be a horror if the crowd pelted them with stones and offal, but if it sympathized with them there was little the magistrate could do to prevent the hour in the pillory from becoming a public triumph. Such was the case when Daniel Isaac Eaton, the aged and distinguished radical printer, was sentenced to an hour's pillory in Newgate in 1813. Much to the government' chagrin, Eaton's head was garlanded with flowers and he was brought refreshment during his ordeal, while the police and magistrates in attendance were reviled and abused.[19]

All such ritual punishments depended for their effectiveness as ceremonial of deterrence on the crowd's tacit support of the authorities' sentence.[20]

> *From M. Ignatieff, 'Eighteenth century punishment', (1978)* A Just Measure of Pain *(Basingstoke: MacMillan), 1978, pp. 15–21.*

Notes

1 *Proceedings*, Old Bailey, 1770–1774 (Harvard Law School Collection); see also J. M. Beattie, 'Punishment in England, 1660–1800,' an unpublished paper, 1972, on sentencing patterns in Surrey assize and sessions.

2 *Proceedings*, 1763, session 3; 1764, session 4; 1767, session 6; 1771, session 1; see also George Rudé, *Wilkes and Liberty*, 1962, pp. 65–103.

3 Calendar of Home Office Papers, Geo. III, October 25, 1773.

4 Douglas Hay, 'Property, Authority and the Criminal Law,' in Hay *et al.*, *Albion's Fatal Tree*, 1975, pp. 17–64.

5 Leon Radzinowicz, *A History of English Criminal Law, 1947–1956*, 1, p. 4.

6 E. P. Thompson, *Whigs and Hunters*, 1975, passim.

7 William Blackstone, *Commentaries on the Laws of England*, 1769, IV, pp. 233–37.

8 Thompson, *Whigs and Hunters*, p. 22.

9 Blackstone, *Commentaries*, IV, p. 246; also Peter

Linebaugh in Society for the Study of Labour History, *Bulletin*, no. 25, 1972.

10 Radzinowicz, *History of Criminal Law*, I, p. 156.

11 PRO/SP/44/92, Criminal Letter Book, April 8, 1775.

12 John Howard, *An Account of the Principal Lazarettos of Europe*, 1789, table 1, Appendix; on the operation and ideological function of pardons see Hay, 'Property, Authority and Criminal Law.'

13 Blackstone, *Commentaries*, IV, pp. 132, 241.

14 Radzinowicz, *History of Criminal Law*, I, p. 150.

15 Blackstone, *Commentaries*, IV, p. 390; Samuel Romilly, *Observations on a Late Publication ...*, 1786, p. 42.

16 Blackstone, *Commentaries*, IV, pp. 277–78; Richard Burn, *The Justice of the Peace and Parish Officer*, 1st ed., 1755, II, 'Summary Justice.'

17 Surrey R.O., QS/2/1/24, 1775.

18 E. P. Thomson, 'The Moral Economy of the Eighteenth Century Crowd,' *Past and Present* 50, 1971, pp. 76–136.

19 Place Mss. B. M. Add. Mss. 27826/178.

20 Peter Linebaugh, 'The Tyburn Riot Against the Surgeons,' in Hay *et al.*, *Albion's Fatal Tree*, pp. 65–118.

2.3 Prosecutors and the courts
Clive Emsley

There were significant changes in prosecution and court practice during the period 1750 to 1900. There were also significant changes in the kind of court environments in which criminal cases were heard. On occasions it was an act of parliament which heralded a change; sometimes, however, legislation simply formalised and sanctioned what had come to be existing practice; and many changes were gradual, almost imperceptible except over a long period.

The English legal system provides for any private citizen to initiate a prosecution. During the eighteenth century a few prosecutions were directed by the Treasury Solicitor, notably in coining offences. Some were conducted by the Attorney General, principally cases of treason or sedition; but again the numbers remained small and during the 1790s, the period of the English 'reign of terror', the Crown Law Officers regularly refused to finance prosecutions for sedition and urged magistrates – not always successfully – to organise these locally. The overwhelming majority of criminal prosecutions, more than eighty per cent, were conducted by the victims of crimes or, rather less frequently, by private individuals acting on the victim's behalf, and, reflecting the dominance of the male in eighteenth- and nineteenth-century society, most prosecutors were men.[1]

Victims of a criminal offence had a variety of choices. They could, for example, let the matter drop regarding it as too insignificant or unimportant for a criminal prosecution. Sometimes, and especially in the earlier part of the period under consideration, an offender was dealt with by community action rather than by recourse to the law: a Jewish hawker, caught attempting to steal a ring from a young woman at Huntingdon races in 1753, was seized by a crowd and ducked in a horse pond.[2] However crowds, and individuals, could not be relied upon always to help a victim. Stories were reported in the courts of victims, in hot pursuit of thieves, being deliberately impeded either by individuals or by crowds.[3] Probably what happened in these instances was that the activist individuals or crowds took the part of the person who appeared to be the underdog. Arthur Harding recalled crowds taking the part of children at the end of the nineteenth century who, well aware of what they were doing and certain of getting popular support because of their tender years, openly stole from traders' carts and barrows or from shops and stalls.[4]

The occasional attack on, or 'rough musicing' of, a prosecutor is suggestive of communities which felt that certain offenders should not have been prosecuted, or at least should have been proceeded against on a lesser charge. In the summer of 1763 Mrs White, a Spitalfield victualler, prosecuted her servant, Cornelius Saunders, for theft after he had stumbled across her savings in her basement and decked himself out in new clothes. Saunders was found guilty and executed. Many inhabitants of Spitalfields were incensed; Saunders was well-known in the neighbourhood primarily, perhaps, because he had been blind from birth. Mrs White's house was attacked by large crowds; her furniture and possessions were thrown out into the street and burned.[5] [...]

Violent hostility towards prosecutors and their witnesses in unpopular cases was not confined to the Georgian period. In Blackburn in November 1862, after the prosecution of four men for night poaching on the land of J. Butler Bowden, crowds turned on the gamekeepers who had given evidence as they left the town hall escorted by eight men from the Lancashire Constabulary. An estimated 400 people then marched on Bowden's house, Pleasington Hall, which they proceeded to stone until driven off by Bowden and his servants firing two or three shots over their heads. A troop of the 16th Lancers and squads of the county constabulary were rushed into Blackburn to maintain order.[6] Traditional rough musicing, with all of its folkloric paraphernalia, tended to fade away during the nineteenth century, though its Welsh variant, *ceffyl pren*, has been noted as being deployed against unpopular offenders and prosecutors in the Victorian period, and manifestations were not unknown in the great cities of mid nineteenth-century England.[7]

If the offender was known to, or instantly apprehended by, the victim, some personal retribution or private settlement could be sought, or offered, to avoid recourse to the law. Though it must be noted that this was not always the case, no matter how close the bonds between individuals. There are, for example, court records of children stealing from their parents, and being prosecuted for it. There are also examples of parents urging the prosecution of their offspring by those who had been their victims; thus the law could be brought into play as a means of discipline within the family.[8] [...]

Other alternatives to prosecution continued to be exploited throughout the nineteenth century. Employers could, and often did simply dismiss pilfering workmen; this, together with the threat that the offender would never be employed again was a tougher sanction than many courts could impose. Many victims were often satisfied with the return of their stolen property and/or with the scare which they gave the accused by the very fact of involving the police; once property had been restored and the offender had been warned by police involvement, some victims declined to press ahead with prosecutions, or else simply did not turn up for the trials.[9]

Legally assaults were different from thefts in that they were not necessarily felonious. During the eighteenth century many cases of assault were settled with a financial payment being made by the assailant to the victim. Magistrates could be involved in such settlements at petty sessions. At quarter sessions, if it was noted that agreement had been reached between the parties, the punishment imposed by the court could be nominal. In January 1766, for example, William Wesson prosecuted Thomas Turner, a grocer of Derby at the Nottinghamshire Sessions for assault; 'it appearing to the court that [the] prosecutor was satisfied', Turner was fined one penny and discharged.[10] But alleged agreements to make amends with a money payment could be as fraught with difficulties in assault cases as in larceny cases. At the Easter Sessions for Bedfordshire in 1833 Emily Crossley prosecuted Robert Wells for an assault after which she had suffered a miscarriage. Wells complained that 'the woman offered to make it up and did for 5/–'.[11] Again alternative settlements to prosecution continued to be sought and found in cases of assault throughout the nineteenth century. Moreover it would seem that many working-class prosecutions for assault were part of continuing feuds between families or groups, with the law being employed as one way of the complainant achieving a measure of what he or she considered to be justice, but certainly not bringing the affair to an end.[12]

Some victims of theft who reported their loss to constables or thief-takers, were prepared to pay a reward for the return of their property and to ignore the prosecution of the offender; corrupt and unscrupulous constables and thief-takers, working in league with thieves, were happy to fall in with these wishes splitting the rewards with the offender.[13] Newspaper advertisements or handbills describing the stolen property and offering a reward were regularly employed by victims and not without success in both the recovery of goods, the identification of the offender and thus in his or her prosecution and conviction; the circulation of information about offences became central to the Fieldings' proposals for improving the system of policing.[14] Some victims went to considerable personal lengths to pursue offenders and regain their property. In the summer of 1769 Richard Wallis, a baker, and William Thornton, a tallow chandler, spent several days chasing the men who had stolen their horses around the southern environs of London. After the theft of ten ferrets, a box, a spud, a dog and a gun John Jeffries and Thomas Asplen of Thurleigh pursued Samuel Colgrave for two days through the villages surrounding Bedford; subsequently they continued their pursuit into Huntingdonshire and Cambridgeshire, eventually running their quarry to earth in a Cambridge pub.[15] It was also possible for the victim to apply to a magistrate for a warrant to search a suspect's house or lodgings.[16] When an individual had gone to the effort and, like as not, the expense of an advertisement, of finding a constable or thief-taker, or of a personal pursuit, he or she was less likely to balk at the effort and expense of a prosecution. Once judicial agents, particularly magistrates, were involved there was less likelihood of crime not being heard in court; and a warrant for an arrest, generally entrusted to a constable meant, at least, a hearing before a magistrate once the suspect was apprehended.[17]

The number of offences which could be heard and resolved summarily before a single magistrate sitting informally in his parlour or in a local tavern, or before one or two magistrates sitting with rather more formality in petty sessions, increased during the eighteenth century as legislation altered penalties and consolidated existing laws. Summary offences included specific minor thefts such as embezzlement by textile workers, stealing wood or vegetables, as well as, most notoriously, certain poaching offences and, by the Combination Acts, trade union activity. The prosecutor had the opportunity to decide whether he wished to have the accused tried summarily or before higher court; summary justice was prompt, but the penalties were less severe involving only a fine or a short period of imprisonment. If the prosecutor was determined to make an example he probably would opt for a higher court and it was also possible for magistrates to advise victims to prosecute in a higher court so as to make an example. [...]

But even if there did seem a felony case to answer, magistrates often encouraged reconciliation and interpreted some theft accusations as disputes over ownership. During the 1740s William Hunt studiously avoided the word 'theft' when noting certain cases in his justice book.[18] Samuel Whitbread's notebooks, kept seventy years later, reveal him occasionally seeking to settle matters by correspondence, threats, and bringing parties together, rather than simply committing an offender to trial.[19] In those instances where magistrates persuaded the accuser to drop a charge they were not, at least in their own eyes, compounding the offence, rather they were effectively establishing that there had not been a criminal offence in the first place. Some cases, especially assault cases, might be settled with a monetary payment from the accused to the victim; in poaching cases the accused could have proceedings against him dropped if he entered into a bond not to poach on the victim's land again; in other instances an apology inserted in a newspaper might suffice.[20] In wartime the accused could be recruited into the army or navy without the case going beyond the magistrate; this saved the accused from a possibly lengthy pre-trial imprisonment, and it saved the accuser the expense of a prosecution. In eighteenth-century Essex, at least, such a policy was also pursued in peacetime with the accused being encouraged to enlist in the East India Company's service.[21] Finally it is apparent that magistrates used their wide powers over vagrants, servants, or those who could be described as 'idle and disorderly' to imprison, or otherwise punish offenders guilty of petty crimes, particularly petty theft.

If it was resolved to take the accused to a higher court the magistrate committed him, or her for trial; bail was very rarely given in larceny cases and committal generally meant the accused being put in gaol, often for several months before appearing in court – after all, with the exception of London and its environs, there were only four quarter sessions and only two assizes each year for the eighteenth and much of the nineteenth centuries. The magistrate also bound over the prosecutor and any witnesses to attend at the higher court. Still the prosecutor's discretion was not at an end. An indictment had to be prepared for the court; this was then submitted to the grand jury, together with any depositions, for a decision on whether or not there was sufficient cause for the case to proceed to a hearing before magistrates and a petty jury at quarter sessions, or judge and jury at assizes. The bill of indictment was generally prepared by the clerk of the peace, for quarter sessions, or the clerk of assizes. These clerks were solicitors, but very often in cases of theft their task was no more than taking a printed bill and filling in the names of the accused, the victim, and the details of the offence; these details sometimes simply involved writing the word 'larceny' or 'felony'. A particularly determined, or particularly wealthy prosecutor, might employ his own, independent solicitor to prepare the bill of indictment in which case the bill could incorporate several separate counts to ensure that, if the accused escaped on one charge, he could be caught by another. Following an attempted robbery of his Soho Works in 1800 Matthew Boulton was determined to have the four accused executed on a charge of burglary. Boulton's son was most impressed with the eight-count indictment prepared by his father's solicitors: 'it appears to be formed like a swivel gun and may be directed to all points as circumstances require'.[22] Yet, during the eighteenth and early nineteenth centuries, prosecutorial discretion in the bill of indictment could also lead to an offence being downgraded so as to ensure that the accused did not face the most serious, generally capital, charge available. Joseph Stenson, a hatter, was prosecuted for theft at the Borough Sessions in Leeds in January 1801: he was accused of taking one canvas bag value two pence, 500 shilling pieces value three pence, 500 sixpenny pieces value two pence and one gold half guinea value one penny.[23] The total value of the money which Stenson was accused of stealing was £38.0.6d. but by downgrading its value to a mere six pence he could be tried before the borough magistrates on a non-capital charge.

From C. Emsley, 'Prosecutors and the courts', Crime and Society in England 1750–1900, (Harlow: Longman), 1987, pp. 178–185.

Notes

1 Douglas Hay, 'Controlling the English Prosecutor' *Osgoode Hall Law Journal*, 21 (1983), pp.165–86 (at p.167); Clive Emsley, 'An aspect of Pitt's 'Terror': Prosecutions for sedition during the 1790s', *Social History*, 6, (1981), pp.155–84; idem, 'Repression, 'terror' and the rule of law in England during the decade of the English Revolution', *E.H.R.C.* 1985), pp.801–25.

2 *Northampton Mercury*, 6 and 13 August 1753.

3 George Rudé, *Criminal and Victim: Crime and society in early nineteenth-century England*, Clarendon Press: Oxford, 1985, pp.59–60. Rudé cites four examples; the first three were instances of the victim being impeded in his pursuit of the offender; in the fourth instance the victim was helped. Rudé asks: 'does this denote a change in popular attitudes towards criminal and victim?' Obviously it will take far more than four examples to prove anything like this, and it should also be remembered that the hue and cry had a long pedigree.

4 Raphael Samuel (ed.) *East End Underworld: Chapters in the life of Arthur Harding*, RKP, London, 1981, pp.43–5.

5 Peter Linebaugh, 'The Tyburn riot against the surgeons', in Douglas Hay, Peter Linebaugh *et al.*, *Albion's Fatal Tree: Crime and Society in Eighteenth Century England*, Allen Lane, 1975, pp.107–8.

6 H.O. 45.7323. My thanks to Professor John Bohstedt for this reference.

7 David Jones, 'The Welsh and crime, 1801–91', in Clive Emsley and James Walvin (eds), *Artisans, Peasants and Proletarians 1760–1860*, Croom Helm, London, 1985, pp. 89–91; for an example of charivari or rough music in mid nineteenth-century Liverpool see *Liverpool Mercury*, 12 November 1855, though the cause appears to have been sexual transgression rather than crime.

8 In June 1847, for example, Ann Wood, a widow of Edingley, Nottinghamshire, left her house in the care of one of her daughters. In the mother's absence a second daughter stole several articles of clothing together with some money and then ran off. She was eventually arrested in Derbyshire by a police constable. Notts. R.O. QSD/1847. See also Jennifer Davis, 'Prosecutions and their context. The use of the criminal law in late nineteenth-century London'. in Douglas Hay and Francis Snyder (eds), *Policing and Prosecution in Britain 1750–1850*, Oxford U.P., 1989, pp. 415–16.This issue has been rarely noted with reference to England; recent research in France has shown that the law, the police and the infamous *lettre de cachet* were regularly used to discipline unruly children. See, inter alia, Claude Quetel, *De Par Le Roy: Essai sur les lettres de cachet*, Privat, Toulouse, 1981, pp. 137–40 and 146–8; Arlette Farge and Michel Foucault, *Le Desordre des Familles: Lettres de cachet des archives de la Bastille*, Gallimard Julliard, Paris, 1982, chap. 3.

9 Jennifer Davis, 'Law breaking and law enforcement: The creation of a criminal class in mid-Victorian London', unpublished Ph.D. Boston College, 1984, chap. 5 especially.

10 Notts. R.O. QSM 1761–67; Nottingham 13 January 1766.

11 Beds. R.O. PM 2629, Notebook of Pym.

12 Davis, 'Law breaking and law enforcement', pp. 307–10. 18.

13 See below pp. 175 and 177.

14 John Styles, 'Sir John Fielding and the problem of criminal investigation in eighteenth-century England', *TR.H.S.* 5th series, 33 (1983), pp. 127–50; idem, 'Crime in the eighteenth-century provincial newspaper', unpublished paper, has estimated from depositions from the Northern Assize Circuit that certainly twenty-five per cent of arrests for horse stealing and perhaps as many as forty-three per cent were, at least partially, the result of advertisements in newspapers. In 1827 John Pilstow, a shopkeeper of Northampton stopped at a Woburn Inn on his way to London. During the night he was robbed. He promptly had some handbills printed offering a £1 reward for the arrest of a suspect; the handbills led directly to an arrest two days after the robbery, in Leicester. Beds. R.O. 1827/295.

15 Elizabeth Silverthorne (ed.), *Deposition Book of Richard Wyatt J.P.* 1767–76, Surrey Records Society, vol. xxx (1978), nos 64–7; Beds. R.O. QSR 1830/495.

16 Wilts. R.O. Stourhead Archive, 383/955 Justice Book of R. C. Hoare 1785–1815 has several examples of warrants issued on suspicion, for example: '21 Feby

[1795] Granted a Warrant on Information of Giles Jupe of Mere to search the houses of Edmund Williams, Thomas Herridge, Hugh Deverill, Edward Mills, John Miles and Edward Avery, for wood stolen from the coppice of Deverill Longwood.' Wood was found in the possession of Herridge and Mills, and acting summarily Hoare fined them both 10s. For an example leading to a more serious charge see *O.B.S.P.* 1800–01, no. 99 for a warrant issued to Richard Jones, a soap and perfume manufacturer of Shoreditch, to search the lodgings of his former foreman whom he rightly suspected of pilfering large quantities of goods to set up in the trade on his own account.

17 Beds. R.O. 25/1822/610 contains a letter from a magistrate, the Rev Orlebar Smith suggested that a certain Sinfield be indicted for felony. Sinfield had gone to Smith for a warrant accusing William Pilgrim of stealing his watch. He had then used the warrant to frighten Pilgrim into returning the watch and to paying Sinfield 30s. in compensation; the business completed to his satisfaction, Sinfield had then, illegally, destroyed the warrant.

18 Elizabeth Crittal (ed.), *The Justicing Notebook of William Hunt 1744–49*, Wiltshire Record Society, xxxvii (1982), pp. 13–14.

19 Alan F. Cirket (ed.), *Samuel Whitbread's Notebooks*, 1810–11, 1813–14, Bedfordshire Historical Records Society, vol. 50 (1971), nos 210, 215, 224.

20 P. B. Munsche, *Gentlemen and Poachers: The English Game Laws* 1671–1831, Cambridge U.P., 1981, p. 92. The apology inserted in the newspaper could be used in assault cases (e.g. Beds. R.O. QSR 16/1789/284), in seditious libel cases during the 1790s (Emsley, 'An aspect of Pitt's "Terror" ', pp. 159–60) and even in poaching cases (e.g. *Sussex Weekly Advertiser*, 11 June 1796).

21 P. J. R. King, 'Crime, law and society in Essex 1740–1820', unpublished Ph.D. Cambridge University, 1984, p. 258.

22 Hay, 'Controlling the English prosecutor', p. 168; idem, 'Manufacturers and the criminal law in the later eighteenth century: Crime and 'police' in South Staffordshire', *Past and Present Society Colloquium: Police and policing*, 1983, pp. 39–41.

23 Leeds City Archives, LC/QS 1/12, f. 132; and for similar examples see ibid. f 126 (William Hartley), £175 (Thomas Brumfutt), and f 176 (Jesse Holmes).

2.4 Police and people: the birth of Mr Peel's blue locusts
Michael Ignatieff

Thinking about the history of the police requires a certain mental struggle against one's sense of their social necessity. Over the past 150 years, the London police have inserted themselves into our social subconscious as facts of life. Whether we trust them or not, we cannot imagine the city doing without them. It takes a small but appreciable stretch of the historical imagination to put oneself back into the time when there were no professional police on the streets, and when the idea of such a force seemed pregnant with danger for the 'liberties of Englishmen'.

The first patrols of the Metropolitan police set out on their beats on 29 September 1829, dressed in top hats, blue swallowtail coats, heavy serge trousers and boots, and equipped with a wooden rattle and a truncheon. To us, their coming has the weight of historical inevitability, but this was not so for the Londoners of 1829. So pervasive was the resistance to their arrival that we need to ask ourselves, as we approach their 150th anniversary, how such a decisive enlargement of the powers of the state became possible at all.

The crowds who surged across Blackfriars Bridge on a November night in 1830, after listening to orator Hunt at the Rotunda, chanted, 'Reform! No Wellington! No Peel! No New Police!' Next day, when the King stepped from his carriage in St James Palace Yard after opening parliament, the crowds surged against the line of blue serge protecting him and called out, 'Down with the Raw Lobsters! No Martial Law! No Standing Armies!' At nightfall, abusive crowds eddied accusingly around constables who were patrolling in the West End.

The agitation against the new police was stubborn and protracted, continuing in the pages of the radical press and in meetings of parish vestries, and then bursting out into the streets again in 1833 when police used the flats of their sabres to disperse a radical meeting in Coldbath Fields. A coroner's jury, outraged by the brutality of the force, handed in a verdict of justifiable manslaughter on the body of a policeman killed in the affray. The jurymen were heroes of British fair play. Pewter mugs with their portraits were on the mantelpiece of many a radical parlour.

In London, opposition to the police passed out of the vocabulary of radical politics sometime after 1848, but a brooding residue of collective hostility remained among the London poor. This was especially so among costermongers who, as Mayhew reported in 1851, continued to regard 'serving out a copper' as a matter of honour, well worth the inevitable prison sentence. Outside London, the introduction of the 'blue locusts' brought angry crowds into the streets of many northern industrial towns during the 1840s.

There was something weightier than prejudice in the momentum of this resistance. In the cry, 'No Standing Armies,' there resonated an echo of the 18th century commonwealth and country party comparison between 'continental despotism' (meaning standing armies, police spies, *lettres de cachet* and Bastilles) and 'English liberty' (meaning rule of law, balanced constitution, unpaid constables and local justices of the peace). It was this robust constitutionalism which damned Pitt's Police Bill of 1785 as 'a new engine of power and authority, so enormous and extensive as to threaten a species of despotism'. These arguments held the field until 1829.

The idea of a bureaucratic central force also offended against a tradition which held that social control should be a private, local and voluntary matter, best left to the master of the household, the parish beadle, and the JP. A 'paid police', no longer responsible to the community, would set servant spying on master and master denouncing servant. In this rhetoric, there is resistance to something we now take for granted – the right of the state to intervene in the disputes of the household.

From our vantage point today, this localism may seem an obvious anachronism in the London of the 1820s. But it was not so for many Londoners, for whom the parish still seemed a genuine boundary of administration and community. While discernibly swollen by new population, the London of the 1820s had not been ravaged by industrialism. The myth of the 'dangerous classes' was not yet a waking nightmare of the propertied. The social chasm between East End and West End had still to be dug. The geographic separation of classes in the city had not yet replaced the 18th century jumble. A Londoner like the Bow Street Runner, Townshend, could still discern the lineaments of the London of his youth in the city of his old age. He could plausibly assert that the London of the Gordon riots, the criminal 'Alsatias' and the twisting corpses atop Temple Bar, was at least as turbulent and unruly as the London of the 1820s.

Certainly there were many philanthropists, police magistrates and MPs who had concluded by 1820 that the growth of the city made policing inevitable. Yet their views did not command the consensus of the powerful and the propertied. Looking back ourselves, we tend to view the London of the 1820s through the bifocals of alarmists (from Fielding through Colquhoun to Chadwick). We fail to notice that they were contending unequally against a deeply entrenched constitutionalist libertarianism as well as a more subconscious and reflexive sense of social continuity. As late as 1822, the alarmists were having the worst of the argument. The county gentlemen and urban professional men on the 1822 police committee concluded that a professional police could not be reconciled with the liberties of Englishmen.

To interpret the coming of the new police, therefore, as a 'response' to crime and disorder, 'caused' by urban growth – to see the force as the work of a bourgeois consensus brought together by social fear – is to rewrite history in the language of a retrospective fatalism.

The most that can be said is that Wellington convinced Peel he should set up a civilian force specialising in crowd control after witnessing the embarrassingly inept performance of the soldiery called out to control rioting after Queen Caroline's trial. This may have been the motivation of the Police Bill of 1829; but it doesn't explain how, within three generations, the force had managed to insert itself into popular awareness as a legitimate fact of London life.

The social history of the police's insertion into the warrens, courts and alleyways of St Giles, Spitalfields and Bethnal Green is usually told as a straightforward Whiggish progress from suspicion to cooperation. Yet how rapidly or easily was this progress to legitimacy achieved? Obviously, some of the skilled or regularly employed working class benefited immediately from the new police. To the extent that the washing on their lines or the tools in their boxes were now marginally more secure from theft, and they could use the police courts to secure a stay of eviction or to recover a small debt, they had some reason to believe the rhetoric proclaiming the police as 'servants' of the community.

The submerged tenth

But among the 'submerged tenth' who struggled to survive in the catch-as-catch-can labour market of the docks and the sweated trades, the rhetoric encountered rougher sailing. To the casual poor, the coming of the new police only meant a greater chance of being arrested for 'drunkenness', 'loitering', 'common assault', 'vagrancy' or whatever else the duty sergeant decided to write in his big book. The hackney coachmen and the street sellers, for their part, knew the police as their licensers, as the ones with whom they waged a bickering, bantering struggle for control of a 'pitch' or a profitable position on the street. For the destitute, the police were the prying inspectors of common lodging houses, the inquisitors at the entrance to the workhouse and the cloaked figures who trained the sharp light of the bulls-eye lantern on your face as you lay awake at night in the 'coffins' of the night refuge.

In all these guises, the poor of London experienced the coming of the new police as a massive intensification of outside supervision over their ways of living and surviving – an intrusion which broke the casual, callous contract of disregard between rich and poor in the 18th century. A new contract between rich and poor, between police and people, had to be made.

The Police Commissioners' speeches about the necessity of securing the 'cooperation' of the public were more than hollow pieties. Without poor people willing to come forward as witnesses and as prosecutors, or simply to point a breathless constable in the direction of the running figure who had just vanished down an alley, the police would have been powerless over all but the most transparent street illegal behaviour.

The history of the emerging inter-dependence between police and people has not yet been written, but we know what questions to ask. When would a fight in the street or a stairway be handled by bystanders or neighbours, and when would a child be sent running for 'the constable'? When a publican or shopkeeper found his till empty, when would he go to the police, and when would he pay a visit himself to the shopboy's mother, or to a fence?

For the working poor; it must be remembered, going to the police was usually the last in a range of responses to crisis – a range which included dealing directly with the families of suspected persons, or engaging the services of the underworld network of fences, informers, enforcers, loan-sharks and debt collectors. The success of the police in securing the cooperation of the public depended less on keeping a rosy image of impartiality than on securing a near-monopoly over the market in violence and redress.

We still do not understand which range of 'official' crimes were also accepted as 'crimes' within different working class communities, and which were not. There were at least two, often three or four, overlapping definitions of crime competing for the allegiances of the community. The success of the police, both ideologically and practically, depended on convincing people to accept the official code of illegal behaviour, and turn to 'official' channels for redress.

To win this cooperation, the police manipulated their powers of discretion. They often chose not to take their authority to the letter of the law, preferring not to 'press their luck' in return for tacit compliance from the community. In each neighbourhood, and sometimes street by street, the police negotiated a complex, shifting, largely unspoken 'contract'. They defined the activities they would turn a blind eye to, and those which they would suppress, harass or control. This 'tacit contract' between normal neighbourhood activities and police objectives was sometimes oiled by corruption, but more often sealed by favours and friendships. This was the microscopic basis of police legitimacy, and it was a fragile basis at best. A violent or unfair eviction by the police, for example, could bring a whole watching street together in a hostility to be visited on the policeman afterwards, in the frozen silence which would descend when he stepped into the 'local'.

The bargain might also be overturned by events outside the community. The memory of the Trafalgar Square police charges in 1886 must have cast a pall over policemen's beats in Poplar, Stepney and Bethnal Green.

Fair play?

In this social history, there is no clear passage in popular behaviour from suspicion to cooperation. Support for the police, then as now, was inherently unstable. This was because of the inevitable conflict between their image as impartial embodiments of British fair play, and their social role as defenders of property against the propertied.

Given this conflict, such acceptance as they could secure depended less on rhetoric and myth, than on imperceptibly slipping into the realm of necessary and inevitable facts of British life. To argue that their legitimacy rested on a massive popular consensus in the 19th century is to ignore the depth of the opposition to their coming, the highly sectorial character of their appeal, and the fragility of the contract they negotiated with the urban neighbourhood.

It is worth emphasising the fragile character of public support for the police in the last century, because our deepening economic and social crisis is fostering a plaintive nostalgia for a simpler, happier past. It is widely believed that there used to be a time, 'before this crisis', 'when Macmillan was Prime Minister', 'before the war', when policemen were 'respected', and police work could count on unstinting popular support. For those of us whose memories were formed by television, this undertow of feeling carries us back to the mythic figure of Dixon of Dock Green, on smiling patrol down a leafy, eternally sunlit suburban lane.

This longing to return to a past when 'authority' was 'respected' only takes us one small step closer to the 'law and order' state. Against this use of the past, the historically minded can plausibly object.

From M. Ignatieff, 'Police and people: the birth of Mr. Peel's blue locusts', New Society, 1979, Vol. 49, pp. 443–5.

2.5 The London garotting panic of 1862: a moral panic and the creation of a criminal class in mid-Victorian England Jennifer Davis

On 17 July 1862 Hugh Pilkington, M.P., was accosted by two men as he walked along Pall Mall on his way from the House of Commons to the Reform Club. He was struck on the head and choked by one malefactor, while another relieved him of his watch. In common parlance, he had been 'garotted'. Press reaction was immediate and intense. The *Sun*'s comment was characteristic: 'the case of Mr. Pilkington is not, in itself, an exceptional case' since 'the statistics of garotting in recent years would present a very frightful catalogue of outrages'.[1] The sense of alarm over the safety of the metropolis expressed in the press throughout July and the following month was shared by much of London and, indeed, England. This period of intense public concern is now known as the garotting panic of 1862.

Where the garotting panic is mentioned by historians of nineteenth century crime, it is largely dismissed as a quite comprehensible reaction to a rash of violent street robberies which presaged a general increase in most categories of violent crime over the next few years.[2] [...]

However, a closer study of the Metropolitan Police returns reveals that [...] the start of the panic preceded any 'crime wave', and that the subsequent bulge in the number of recorded street robberies is attributable more to the panic itself than to an actual increase in robberies with violence. In fact, it was the actions and reactions of the press, public and various government agencies involved in control which created the 1862 'crime wave' rather than any significant increase in criminal activity in the streets. Thus, the garotting panic was clearly a 'moral panic'. [...]

The garotting panic occurred during a period of intense public debate over the treatment of England's law-breakers. During the 1850s and 1860s the reformative principles on which England's prison system was based came in for increasing criticism from those who favoured more punitive treatment and stricter control of convicts. It is in the context of this debate that the panic's origins and significance must be located. [...]

The threat felt by the English ruling classes in the 1850s and 60s was that posed by the release of several thousand convicts who had previously been transported. The 'folk devils' identified during the panic as personifying this threat were the convicts released on tickets of leave, of whom the garotters were perceived as a small but particularly dangerous subgroup. Press and public opinion focused not only on the ticket-of-leave men/garotters, but also on the 'philanthropists' and 'reformers' behind the prison system which had produced this threatening criminal class. [...]

How did the garotting panic unfold? What did the press, as the instigator and mouthpiece of public opinion, reveal of popular feelings about crime and the penal system in mid-Victorian England? What was the course of events of the panic, and how did it serve to create deviance? On 17 July there were two garottings. Immediately, the press expressed its relief that these crimes would finally draw attention to the fact that:

Highway robbery is becoming an institution in London, and roads like the Bayswater Road are as unsafe as Naples. Case after case has been reported this week, without the slightest improvement, till some ruffian with less brains than his fellows, attacked an M.P.[3]

At first the police came in for a certain amount of criticism especially because the garottings had occurred in areas of London which were supposedly well policed and not known for their criminal element. But, in general, before long the police were absolved of any major blame for the panic. As the *Observer* concluded,

Even if our police force were doubled it would be doubtful whether they could put a stop to the wholesale highway robberies that are daily committed.[4]

As *The Times* observed, these were 'fresh and bold geniuses' unawed by the police. Indeed, on the whole, *The Times* felt that 'Crime is evidently making a fresh start, it is becoming young again, there is a spring and saliency of a new morning life about its ways and habits.'[5]

The *Observer* echoed a general feeling that England was facing a qualitatively different threat from its law-breakers. In the past robbery had been 'a sort of forced taxation' when

the traveller. . . cashed up, and gave the tax and gathered the (highwayman's) hearty blessing – as soon as his back was turned – and there was no very great harm done after all. But how changed is all this now! The 'gentlemanly' highwayman and the simply surly footpad have degenerated into a coarse, brutal ruffian who disdains the outskirts of towns.[6]

And it was quite obvious to the *Manchester Guardian* on whose shoulders blame for this threat should be placed:

Under the influence of our humanity mongers, we have nursed and fostered a race of hardened villains, who are perfectly well acquainted with the comforts of all the gaols in the kingdom, who have fully learned the liberality with which the penalties appointed by law and awarded by the judges are mitigated in practice and who, for all we know, look upon their brief intervals in confinement as seasonable opportunities for renovating their health and strength.

Well the public is now learning, in rather a startling fashion, what is the natural result of making pets of thieves and garrotters.[7]

The Times saw only one solution to the state of affairs:

The Garotters and their species have displayed themselves in the true colours of their class as the profound enemies of the human race, and their outrages must be suppressed before society can take time to consider how far any imperfect social condition is responsible for their perversity.[8] [...]

In their creation of 'folk devils' on which to project public anxieties, the press must set them off as a clearly distinguishable group. Convicts fulfilled this role well. As *The Times* put it in an editorial:

Though a large portion of the population is plunged in distress, that distress is patiently endured and munificently relieved. It is with slighter elements of danger that we have to deal, but they are proving too strong for us. Whether the irredeemably criminal class be a large class or a small one seems to be doubted, but, whether small or large, it defies our treatment, and comes off winner in the contest between crime and law.[9] [...]

Once an irredeemable criminal class had been identified there were apparently few holds barred as to what might be done with it: 'The first object of punishment, whatever may be said, is not to reform the criminal, but to deter others from crime.'[10] Certainly, it was unnecessary to treat convicts kindly in prison. [...]

Even if prisons were made notoriously deterrent, there still came a point at which the convict must be released. Generally there was a call to bring back transportation. [...]

Supposing transportation were impossible, then the length of sentences might be increased. But even longer sentences were only a temporary solution, of course, since eventually the prisoner had to be let out. [...] The general consensus was that tickets of leave were, indeed, a necessary evil, but that they should be distributed and their terms enforced in the strictest manner possible. It was clear that the ticket-of-leave man was after all 'liberated merely on sufferance', so that 'if his conduct is not satisfactory to the authorities, he may at once be sent to prison'. [...]

[The Home Secretary] claimed that the ability to determine whether a ticket-of-leave man was living honestly, according to the terms of his licence, necessitated a degree of police surveillance not only 'continental' in its implications of espionage, but also inimical to the convict's chances of finding employment. Fortuitously, once it was concluded that the convicts formed a dangerous and irredeemable class, these concerns might be safely overridden. [...] To the upper classes and the press the convicts were a special and threatening group who were proving, by their responsibility for the present 'crime wave', that they merited harsher treatment in prison and stricter control without.

It is necessary to offer a tentative explanation why the 'crime wave' apparently began after the panic itself. The amplification of the perceived threat from the criminal class resulted from the way the police, the courts, and the public reacted to the press's presentation of the initial threat posed by the garottings in July. The manner in which the press, in turn, represented the results of the actions of these three groups perpetuated the panic and persuaded society that its fears were justified.

First of all, let us look at the police's role in creating the panic. The Metropolitan Police returns of 1862 show that there were 779 more arrests of suspicious characters and reputed thieves than in 1861, and 256 more arrests for persons loitering with intent. Do these figures then represent a real increase in criminal activity which would go some way to justify the panic? A closer look at the figures reveals that in both categories of crime, like that of robberies with violence, the increase in arrests coincided with the panic itself, and can almost certainly be explained by increased police activity.[11] [...]

A clear illustration of how police activity 'created' crime is revealed by the fate of two men, both ex-ticket-of-leave holders, arrested for the Pilkington garotting. Because the police magistrate found no actual proof that they committed the crime part from information the police claimed to have received, he sentenced them only to three months as suspicious characters. The press none the less presented their arrests as the first concrete proof that the crime wave was attributable to licence holders.[12] The police not only reacted to public concern during the panic but probably also used it for their own purposes. In one case, the police described in court what was clearly a public-house quarrel among acquaintances as a garotting because they were interested in taking the 'thieves and suspected thieves' involved off the streets. This

probability appears even stronger if it is remembered that, ideally, Mayne [Metropolitan Police Commissioner] would have liked to exercise strict police surveillance over ticket holders. Certainly, the existence of a crime wave would be (and was) a decisive reason for altering policy in his favour.[13]

The second contribution to the creation of a crime wave came from magistrates and judges, in the police courts and quarter sessions. There is ample evidence that police magistrates and judges tended to define criminal actions of alleged offenders more seriously during the panic. An illegal action that might have been a simple theft before July might be treated by a magistrate, after July, as a robbery with violence. [...]

The garotting panic peaked in November 1862. In September there were only two alleged robberies with violence reported to the police, and very little press comment. But in October there were 12 alleged cases of robbery with violence, and in November there was a spate of garottings given much play in the newspapers, which finally amounted to an extraordinary 32 alleged crimes.[14] The contribution that the general public made to the inflation of the garotting statistics may be inferred from the case of a woman who, caught in the act of attempting suicide 'by tying a handkerchief around her neck', claimed in court that, in fact, she had been garotted. Whereupon the chief clerk was moved to remark that, it was another of those extraordinary stories that were now a float, as to people being stopped in the street and garotted. It was a pity that the public should be so needlessly alarmed for half the cases that were reported to the police were not true ...'. None the less, whether true or not, a great many of these alleged robberies were duly reported in the press, increasing the seriousness with which the public perceived the criminal threat.[15] [...]

It is simpler to explain why a panic begins than why it ends. The number of garottings began to tail off. There were 14 garottings in December, but only two in January, 1863. There is evidence that by December the police and the courts were taking steps to dampen public anxieties. The head of the City Department, William Hamilton, appeared at the Guildhall on 9 December, one day after a press report that 'three individuals have died from the effects of being garotted', to state that 'he had caused inquiries to be made into several of the most serious cases and found that they were wholly untrue...'. They included the three allegedly fatal garottings, and he promised that the author of the spurious 'garotting deaths' article would be prosecuted. He assured the public that 'the insecurity of the metropolis was not so great as those frequently concocted garotte cases' would lead then to suppose. Alderman Besley agreed that 'the public mind had been unnecessarily excited'.[16]

Despite the efforts of such as Hamilton and Besley, public and press concern with crime and convicts continued into the early months of 1863 although the crime wave was over. [...]

The end of the panic, at least as it manifested itself in the press, almost exactly coincided with the second reading of Adderley's Bill [which imposed a sentence of whipping along with imprisonment for robberies with violence] on 23 March, 1863. It is as if the legalized violence against convicts permitted by the Act provided the necessary catharsis for public fears aroused ten months earlier. [...]

The question remains as to how much the changes in penal policy were part of a wider ruling-class strategy of control aimed at the working-class population, which as recently as the 1840s had appeared to constitute a clear threat to the social order.

One striking feature of the popular discontent over penal policy during the 1860s is that not once was the existence of the penitentiary itself challenged. Ignatieff has noted that by the 1860s the penitentiary had 'slowly inserted itself into the realm of the taken for granted' as one of a whole series of Victorian disciplinary institutions, including 'asylums, workhouses, monitorial schools, night refuges, and reformatories'. [...] It still needs to be explained why penitentiaries continued to be accepted in the 1860s alongside a widespread conviction that prisons were, in fact, producing a more ruthless and persistent criminal class than had hitherto existed.

Michel Foucault, in his seminal work on the birth of the prison, argues that the creation of such a class through the penal system was not the system's greatest failure, but its greatest success.[17] According to Foucault, during the eighteenth century, popular illegalities, such as petty theft, were widely practised by the lower classes, and were, for the most part, tolerated by the government. Criminals were often popular heroes, and the frequently spectacular and exemplary punishment meted out to them offered potential rallying points for lower-class opposition to authority. The coming of industrialism brought a need to stamp out popular law-breaking, to discipline the working class to the constraints of factory production, and, because

of the political uncertainties of the early nineteenth century, to sever the connection between crime and popular rebellion. Although the first prisons were actually planned as weapons in the war against criminality,

> from 1820 it was realized that prisons, far from transforming criminals into honest people, serve only to manufacture new criminals and to drive existing criminals still deeper into criminality. It was then there took place, as always in the mechanics of power, a strategic utilization of what had been experienced as a drawback. The prison manufactured delinquents but delinquents turned out to be useful.[18]

According to Foucault, the new criminal class had a multiplicity of functions. For one thing, the professional criminals could develop and maintain illegal economies which were tolerated because useful to the ruling class. An example would be 'the great prostitution business' which thrived in the Victorian cities. Furthermore, the creation through the penal system of a specific 'delinquent' group also 'effected the separation between the criminal and the popular classes'. While the criminal class remained the repository of most illegal activity, the rest of the working class was bombarded with moral propaganda; it was both exhorted and threatened into repudiating the illegalities of the past. The menacing and persuasive presence of the penitentiary and the police served as a grim warning to those of the working class tempted to cross the border between honesty and crime: that once crossed it might be closed for ever. The criminal domain now belonged not to the popular hero, but to the criminal mastermind or the anti-social delinquent.[19] [...]

To Foucault, the crucial function of the criminal class was to legitimate the sweeping extension in the power of the nineteenth-century state represented by the creation of a vigorous police force and its deployment in working-class areas.

In many respects, the events of the garotting panic buttress Foucault's claims. There is no doubt that widespread fear and anxiety about crime, during this period, allowed for a considerable extension of police powers, and, indeed, effectively silenced any lingering opposition within the middle class to the whole idea of an English police force. And it is clear that the police welcomed the opportunity the panic offered them to reinforce their position in the state's control apparatus. Furthermore, the panic does appear to mark a key point at which the idea of a separate, irredeemable criminal class was firmly embedded in popular consciousness. Changes in the laws regarding ex-convicts which made it more difficult for them to find employment on release confirm that the authorities believed they were dealing with a separate class of criminals, and that they were willing to employ strategies of control which they admitted, at the time, would inevitably perpetuate this class. One might go further and agree with Foucault that the usefulness of a distinct separation between this dangerous criminal class and its poor but honest brothers and sisters was not lost on the upper classes; hence the press's concern to point out that the garotters and ticket-of-leave men were inhuman (or sub-human) 'folk devils' who bore only a coincidental resemblance, if any, to those starving but tenaciously law-abiding Lancashire cotton weavers.

So Foucault argues that the nineteenth-century penal system was a successful failure. While it failed in its apparent function of eradicating criminals and crime, it succeeded in its implicit function of rescuing crime from the working class and confining it to a small group of well-controlled, prison-created delinquents, to whom the rest of the working class saw itself opposed. While Foucault's description of the implicit function of the penal system is convincing, especially given the evidence of the garotting panic, his assumption that the state, through the penal system, succeeded in limiting most law-breaking activity to a separate criminal class seems much less justified. Ironically, by confining himself to largely literary proof for the existence of such a class, Foucault accepts the same questionable evidence as the mid-Victorians, who were convinced they were threatened by a small group of irredeemable convicts. We have seen, through a study of the panic, just how unreliable such literary evidence can be. Not only is it open to question whether the crime wave in the 1860s was the responsibility of this new group of delinquents but it is unclear whether there was a crime wave at all. Might not the presumed existence of a delinquent class with a virtual monopoly on crime be equally open to challenge?

It seems clear that in order to discover whether or not popular lawbreaking was indeed curtailed in nineteenth-century England, literary evidence must be rejected in favour of that presented by the lives of those actually caught up in the judicial and penal systems, and investiga-tion into the material conditions in which these law-breakers lived.

It may well be, and preliminary research into existing conviction records tends to support this supposition, that law-breaking activity remained a common feature of London working-class life throughout the nineteenth century. Given the exigencies of survival in the seasonal, underpaid, and overstocked London labour market, it is hardly surprising if attempts by the state to limit most law-breaking to a small group of professional criminals and known delinquents made little headway. Indeed, the compulsion to engage in those illegalities which require little skill, and for which there was so much opportunity in London, such as shoplifting, robbery, and petty theft from docks, workshops, buildings, or even one's neighbours, must have been overwhelming to a population of both skilled workers and casual labourers whose margin for survival was so slim. Indeed, one vital question to be asked about all those individuals who were involved in the criminal justice system is not how often they had been arrested, but rather, how much of their time was spent not in crime, but as participants in the legal economy. Given the poverty of the majority of the working class, it seems unlikely that any but a tiny number of convicted individuals could have supported themselves totally through the proceeds of crime. The rest may have differed from their apparently more law-abiding fellows only in that they were caught breaking the law.[20]

Until such questions as these are answered, it would be wrong to assume with Foucault that the penal system and its adjuncts, the police and the courts, succeeded in dividing the working class into opposing camps of law-breaking and law-abiding citizens. Because he has largely ignored the empirical evidence of the material conditions in which the London poor laboured, Foucault has credited the Victorian state with a hegemony over working-class behaviour it almost surely did not possess. While it may be an exaggeration to suggest that London's casual labour market only survived through its recourse to crime, further research may well show that lawbreaking activity provided an important source of outdoor relief in an age when legal charity was so difficult to come by. Under such circumstances it seems doubtful that any clear division existed either in reality or in the minds of the working class between the poor but honest and the merely poor.

From J. Davis, 'The London Garotting Panic of 1862: A Moral Panic and the Creation of a Criminal Class in mid-Victorian England', in V. Gatrell, B. Lenman and G. Parker (eds) Crime and the Law *(London: Europa Publications), 1980, pp. 190–213.*

Notes

1 *Sun*, 18 July 1862; see also, *Observer*, 21 July 1862.
2 See for example T. R. Gurr *et al., The Politics of Crime and Conflict: a Comparative History of Four Cities* (London, 1977); pp. 66–7.
3 *Spectator*, no. 1777, 19 July 1862; see also *Observer*, 21 July 1862.
4 *Observer*, 21 July 1862; for early articles critical of police, see *Examiner*, 19 July 1862, *Sun*, 18 July 1862, *Spectator* no 1777, 19 July 1862.
5 *The Times*, 14 Aug. 1862.
6 *Observer*, 23 Nov. 1862; see also, *The Times*, 26 Nov. 1862 and 30 Dec. 1862, *Sun*, 26 Nov. 1862.
7 *Manchester Guardian*, 2 Dec. 1862.
8 *The Times*, 30 Dec. 1862.
9 *The Times*, 2 Jan. 1863 (reprinted in the *Sun*).
10 *Spectator*, no. 1796, 29 Nov. 1862; see also, *The Times*, 5 Nov. 1862.
11 *R.C. on Penal Servitude* (P. P. 1863, XXI) appendix C.
12 *R.C. on Penal Servitude* (P. P. 1863, XXI), qq. 1548–1552. For examples of how police orders created crime see, *Morning Herald* police reports, 'Precautions against garotters', 10 Nov. 1862, and 'Capture of a burglar and garotter', 29 Nov. 1862.
13 'Garotte robber', *Morning Herald* police report, 3 Dec. 1862.
14 *R.C. on Penal Servitude* (P. P. 1863, XXI) appendix B.
15 'Singular attempted suicide – extraordinary story as to being garotted', *Morning Herald* police report, 11 Dec. 1862; see also, 'Increase of garotte robberies', 20 Nov. 1862 and speech of the Recorder of the central criminal court, reported in *Morning Herald*, 24 Nov. 1862. See 'Daring garotte robbery in Sloane Square', 25 Nov. 1862, as an example of the ambiguities involved in the public's crime reporting.
16 Quoted in *Morning Herald* police report, 'A policeman's opinion on garotting', 9 Dec. 1862. Report on the alleged murders in the *Morning Herald*, 8 Dec 1862; Kellow Chesney, in *The Victorian Underworld*, is the latest to fall victim to spurious report, p.163.
17 Michel Foucault, *Discipline and Punish: the Birth of the Prison* (Harmondsworth, 1979).
18 Quoted in 'Prison talk: an interview with Michel Foucault by J. J. Brochier', *Radical Philosophy*, 16 (Spring, 1977), p. 10.
19 Ibid., p. 10.
20 Compare the analogous discussion by Dr. Gatrell, [1980, *Crime and the Law*] pp. 265–6.

3

Crime data and crime trends

3.1 The social construction of official statistics on criminal deviance
Steven Box   44

3.2 A note on the use of official statistics
John I. Kitsuse and Aaron V. Cicourel   48

3.3 The origins of the British Crime Survey
Mike Hough, Mike Maxfield, Bob Morris
and Jon Simmons   54

3.4 Unravelling recent crime patterns and trends
Robert Reiner   59

Introduction

KEY CONCEPTS

attrition; British Crime Survey; counting rules; discretion; official statistics; rates of crime; risk; social construction; victimization survey

How much crime is there in our society (bearing in mind the lessons from chapter 1 about what *crime* actually means) and how do we know? Although there are numerous sources of data on crime, we tend to rely on two main types of data for much of what we say about levels and trends in crime. These are, first of all, police-recorded crime statistics (sometimes referred to as 'official statistics') and, second, information from victimization surveys. The four readings in this chapter illustrate a number of aspects of these two main sources of data – both positive and negative – and also tell us a little about what has apparently been happening in recent years to trends in crime in the UK.

In the first reading **(Reading 3.1)** Steven Box looks at the key criminological problem of the social construction of official statistics on crime. At heart this issue concerns the layers and layers of processes and decisions that lie between the commission of a crime and its appearance in the statistics: Will the victim report it? Will the police record it? Is there sufficient evidence and will to prosecute? What happens in court? And so on. All this serves to limit the usefulness of this particular source of data. As he shows, this is not some technical or neutral question either. The use of discretion in the criminal justice system – whether or not to arrest, prosecute etc – is argued by some to be applied unequally. For a variety of reasons it is the poor and disadvantaged who are most likely to be processed by the criminal justice system. Nevertheless, there are a number of limits to the application of discretion and Box's excerpt ends with a review of the limits that are placed on the decisions of police officers.

The second reading **(Reading 3.2)** – a classic from John Kitsuse and Aaron Cicourel – picks up critical arguments about official statistics and argues that there is much to be gained from the use of such data, so long as one is asking the appropriate questions of them. That is to say, rather than treating the data as self-evidently meaningful (or not), it is important to see within them the possibility of analysing what such information tells us about the workings of official bodies (the police, the courts etc) and about the application of deviant labels in our society (how some behaviours – and, see the Nils Christie reading in chapter 1 – indeed, certain amounts of certain behaviours, become defined as deviant).

Largely as a result of the limitations of official statistics, governments have sought other means of assessing levels and trends in crime. Foremost amongst these is the victimization survey – generally a household survey asking individual citizens about their experiences of criminal victimization and other aspects of criminal justice. The excerpt from Mike Hough and Mike Maxfield **(Reading 3.3)** recounts the origins of the British Crime Survey (the BCS) and explains what potential advantages it was thought to offer over other sources of data. Established in the early 1980s, the BCS has become a key tool for government and for criminologists and, arguably, has had a major impact on our knowledge of crime levels and trends and, as Hough and Maxfield in particular argue, on such matters as fear of crime, attitudes toward the police and other criminal justice agencies, risks of victimization, and on drug use.

In the final excerpt **(Reading 3.4)** Robert Reiner draws on a range of data sources to unpick patterns and trends in crime since the 1950s. The pattern he illustrates is one of steadily rising crime, with a particularly steep increase in the 1980s, followed by what appears to be generally falling crime rates since the mid-1990s. The word *appears* here is important, however, for the messages from the data are by no means unambiguous, and this lack of clarity serves to remind us that all sources of data are necessarily limited in what they are able to tell us. Crucially, as Reiner notes, 'because there are now two alternative measures of trends and patterns for offences covered by the [BCS], there can be greater confidence when they point in the same direction'. The difficulty, as you will discover, occurs when the different data sources appear to point in differing directions.

Questions for discussion

1. Why might it be that the poor and disadvantaged are most likely to find themselves being processed in the criminal justice system?

2. What are the main shortcomings of 'official statistics' on crime?

3. To what uses can 'official statistics' be put?

4. In what ways is police discretion circumscribed?

5. What are the main advantages of victimization surveys argued to be?

6. What have been the main contributions of the British Crime Survey since its inception?

7. What have been the main trends in crime since the 1950s and how do we know?

8. What are the main sources of controversy over crime trends since the mid-1990s?

3.1 The social construction of official statistics on criminal deviance Steven Box

As dreamers, we imagine ideals which because of their very nature (and ours!) are difficult to realize; but, not wanting to confront our shortcomings directly, we frequently bridge the gap between ideal and reality by constructing a comforting myth that the hiatus does not exist. Such a human ideal is justice, and the accompanying myth is that this ideal is realized in the everyday practices and routine procedures of those bureaucracies which comprise the legal system. Unfortunately, despite the fact that we are generally able to mystify ourselves in this matter, there are too many discrepant facts for this particular myth to be universally accepted. In the administration of justice, 'inconsistencies' in police decisions to make arrests and prosecute are too systematically biased, court decisions of guilt and innocence are too skewed, and penal sanctions against the guilty are often too inconsistent among similar offenders and too incommensurate with the offence. The result is that in more than a few people's minds there is a persistent and discomforting nag that the ideal is one thing, but the practice is 'something else again'.

In traditional Western philosophy the pivotal interpretation of justice has been equal treatment for equals. But the criteria by which people are to be equated are, and always have been, problematical. The organizing principle, 'equal in regard to relevant criteria', has an instant common-sense appeal, but deceives few into thinking the matter is closed; for when day-to-day decisions have to be made, the relevance of various criteria is contentious. Consequently, decisions taken in the face of genuine differences of opinion concerning relevance lead to antagonisms: what is justice to one person is rampant injustice to another.

This issue of justice is one that confronts us directly when we continue to develop our account of the process of an individual becoming deviant and the official construction of crime rates. After a person has committed an illegal act (or one whose meaning is ambiguous in relation to criminal codes), and thereby rendered him/herself vulnerable to penal sanction, it is far from automatic that anything detrimental will happen to him/her. In a phrase, law-violators often 'get away with it', and the more powerful they are the more likely they

are to make crime pay. From illegal act to legal punishment there are numerous escape routes. It is as though the offender has to pass through a corridor of connected rooms. In each, there is only one door which leads on to the garden of official registration and criminalization, whilst all the others offer a retreat into safety from the 'long arm of the law'. Naturally, given the deeply ingrained inequalities in our society, some persons have more keys to escape-doors than others, and indeed some, often the same persons, have escape-doors held wide open for them by the very officials paid to protect us from criminals! Our justice system is, in other words, a selective process in which the powerful are unlikely to be criminalized, whilst the powerless are more likely to end up behind the walls of crumbling, overcrowded, Victorian prisons, even though in aggregate the 'crimes' of the former cause more damage or loss to life, limbs and property (Reiman, 1979).

For the purpose of illustrating this selective process, we will concentrate on a few of the more important stages. The victim, if one exists, has to decide to report the incident to the police. The offence has to be officially recorded, because the police either take a complaint seriously from a victim of a crime, or directly observe illegal behaviour and do not turn a blind eye to it. If there is a victim, in addition to his/her being willing to report the incident, a conviction will be forthcoming only if s/he is prepared to offer the police information necessary for detection, and to be a witness at any criminal trial. Although many victims are willing to report incidents, many of them refuse to go further because a criminal trial involves more effort and results in more punishment of the offender than they consider appropriate. But even when the victim displays the necessary degree of cooperation, the police still need to find the offender and establish, and be willing to establish, a reasonable legal case against him/her. Finally, s/he has to be persuaded to plead guilty, or be found guilty in a court of law, and then sentenced.

Only at this final stage is the offender incorporated into public official records: simultaneously s/he becomes someone fit for official punishment and ripe for transformation into a deviant person.

Until this point, s/he has been a normal person dabbling in dicey and dubious behaviour – just like most other normal people! But being officially sentenced constitutes one of the crucial forking paths on the route towards a deviant career; for having been officially cast as deviant forces anyone to consider, if only momentarily, what kind of person s/he really is. The experiences during and subsequent to punishment, particularly imprisonment and its stigmatizing consequences, may help an individual to resolve this matter of identity uncertainty, not necessarily in a way that serves him/herself. S/he may actually become deviant and hence make him/herself available for inclusion time and time again in the officially recognized 'dangerous criminal classes'.

Organizing principles in the administration of justice

To understand the dynamics of the selective process in the administration of justice, we must first grasp the organizing principles which govern that process. Probably one of the briefest and most instructive assessments of these principles has been provided by Chambliss (1969). He suggested that

> Those persons are arrested, tried and sentenced who can offer the fewest rewards for non-enforcement of the laws and who can be processed without creating any undue strain for the organizations which comprise the legal system. (pp. 84–85)

One implication to which this statement draws our attention is that full law enforcement does not exist. Obviously such an accomplishment would be impossible: the police cannot be everywhere all the time; they cannot rely upon being given consistent and complete information on criminal incidents, even from a law-conscious community; they cannot muster the necessary technical know-how, human resources and ingenuity to solve every case which comes to theft attention. But these are not the reasons that lie implicit in Chambliss's statement. He is suggesting that, surrounding the decisions to proceed with the administration of justice, such as patrolling, taking complaints seriously, detection work, arresting, prosecuting, reaching verdicts and sentencing, there are community and personal pressures which not only have the effect of constraining state officials from enforcing the law as fully as they reasonably could, but also, and more importantly, influence officials

to enforce the law in such a way that bias is shown against some sections of the community and favours are given to others. In a hierarchical society such as ours, those persons 'who can be processed without creating any undue strain' are more likely to be drawn from the disorganized and economically marginalized sections of the working class, the ethnically oppressed, and other social groups without resources or power to protect themselves from criminalization.

To put this matter in the blunt language of *conflict theorists*:

> In general, the greater the power difference in favour of the authorities, the greater the probability of criminalisation of the opposition. (Turk, 1966; p. 349)

> The lower-class person is (1) more likely to be scrutinized and therefore to be observed in any violation of the law, (2) more likely to be arrested if discovered under suspicious circumstances, (3) more likely to spend the time between arrest and trial in jail, (4) more likely to come to trial, (5) more likely to be found guilty, and (6) if found guilty, more likely to receive harsh punishment than this middle- or upper-class counterpart. (Chambliss, 1969; p. 86)

> Where laws are so stated that people of all classes are equally likely to violate them, the lower the social position of the offender, the greater is the likelihood that sanctions will be imposed on him. [And) when sanctions are imposed, the most severe sanctions will be imposed on persons in the lowest social class. (Chambliss and Seidman, 1971; p. 475)

> Obviously judicial decisions are not made uniformly. Decisions are made according to a host of *extra-legal* factors, including the age of the offender, his race and social class. Perhaps the most obvious example of judicial discretion occurs in the handling of cases of persons from minority groups. Negroes in comparison to whites, are convicted with lesser evidence and sentenced to more severe punishments. (Quinney, 1970; p. 142)

To understand how judicial bias could and does occur, it is only necessary to realize that in the process of registering criminals, or transforming normals into (official) deviants, state agents have considerable discretion. In the initial and, therefore, the most critical stages of the registration process, the police are particularly influential. As Turk (1969) suggests:

> The norms of the police have a critical impact upon criminality rates, because police have a wide range of alternatives to strict and dedicated enforcement, some of them legal, some not, and many in a gray area not explicitly covered by manuals and laws. Police may go all out to detect and apprehend offenders, or they may act only when evidence is thrust upon them. They may ignore an illegality unless it is found in combination with other factors, as when police officers ignore weekly suburban poker parties but stay on the lookout for cards and craps in Negro slums. They may administer justice on or off the records, and may warn or arrest. In short, the police have available to them all the possibilities from enthusiasm to goldbricking, from fanaticism to a fine discrimination among legally similar situations, and from legal to illegal behaviour. But policemen too are not entirely free to do so as they please. (p. 65)

The police then have considerable discretion, but they feel constrained to employ this discretion in a routine manner. These constraints can be identified briefly, and an analysis of their influence held over until a detailed examination of police decisions is made.

In the first place, the police are technically prohibited from resorting to certain methods of gaining information to solve crimes. These technical constraints exist because whilst the community desires law-enforcement it does not want it at all costs. Other societal values, such as individual liberty under the law and freedom from administrative tyranny, have to be delicately balanced against the needs of the police to have sufficient latitude to capture and control offenders. A critically important constraint in this respect is the *institution of privacy*. In practice this means that persons who are afforded more protection under this institution, or whom the police consider are more able to claim such protection, will be comparatively immune from routine police scrutiny and harassment. As far as the police are concerned, an infringement on their part against the institution of privacy represents a cost. For such an infringement often leads to public disapproval, and this has to be set against the rewards of probable crime solution. Such disapproval is more likely when it is middle- and upper-class persons and

organizations whose privacy has been violated by the police. As a consequence, other things being equal, the police are more likely to violate the institution of privacy when it affords 'protection' to the lower strata. It is quite clear, for example, that the way in which police interpret the British 'sus' laws and immigration control laws is such that ethnic minorities are constantly at risk of their privacy rights being totally ignored.

Secondly, the police experience societal pressure not to enforce certain laws, so that enforcement carries with it the potential cost of adversely affecting police–public relations. This occurs, for instance, when there develops a discontinuity between current moral standards and existing legal codes which were established during a previous and different moral climate. Although the police do episodically enforce antiquated moral laws, they certainly refrain from anything more than minimal enforcement, and when they do evoke these laws, it is frequently for reasons other than that the suspect has offended against them. For the most part, the police discreetly fail to enforce laws when the middle and upper class no longer regard them as moral. Naturally, when the middle class itself takes divergent views on the morality of certain laws such as laws against pornography, the decision of the police to enforce or not is made more complicated, for no matter what action is taken one important section of the community will not be satisfied.

Thirdly police bureaucracies are embedded in a network of relations with other bureaucracies, and out of these there develop *reciprocal obligations* which, in part, have the effect of constraining the police from full law-enforcement. The sometime symbiotic relationship between police departments and organized crime in America (Chambliss, 1978; Pearce, 1976; pp. 113–160) and in England (Coxetal, 1977) provides a dramatic example of this reciprocity, but at the same time it makes opaque the more mundane inter-organizational ties which have a binding effect on police activity. For example, universities, schools, commercial firms, and professional organizations are frequently allowed by the police to administer their own justice to members who have violated a state legal code. Thus, a university may send down a student for possessing marijuana, a school may expel a boy for stealing from a class-mate, a commercial firm may sack an employee for physically assaulting another employee, and a profession can dismiss a member for disgraceful conduct which also happens to be criminal. In such instances the police remain in the wings, only becoming involved if their assistance is requested. This non-intervention is doubly rewarding: first, it keeps down the amount of work for the police to handle, and second, it fosters a sense of mutual respect between the police and high-ranking officials in other bureaucracies for the latter like being permitted to keep their own houses in order.

Fourthly, the police are constrained by *interpretational* issues. Behaviour is behaviour is behaviour; it only becomes meaningful when influential human beings have decided what meaning to attribute to it. This universal ambiguity of meaning makes the policeman's task difficult. Not only does he have to impute meaning to behaviour, but he also has to decide whether, with regard to ambiguously worded statutes, it constitutes a breach of the law. In this negotiation process over 'What really happened?' and 'Was it illegal?' the interactants, including the suspect, may be differentially endowed with dramaturgical skills. In the social construction of reality the suspect may sometimes be better able to manipulate the symbolic meaning of behaviour and the situational context so as to persuade the police that nothing really wrong occurred, or, even if it did, that it was accidental and reflected little about his character. Furthermore, if the suspect is able only to maintain the ambiguity of the situation, the police may refrain from proceeding because the chances of getting a good clean pinch may appear comparatively poor.

Fifthly, the police are constrained in their work by *ideological* and *theoretical* considerations. To the layperson all policemen may look alike; but it is naïve to deceive ourselves into thinking that in every policeman there is a human being struggling to get out. The fact is, the human being does get out whenever the policeman exercises his considerable discretionary powers to evoke the law. What he decides is frequently coloured by his ideological values, his moral standards, his beliefs about the causes of criminal behaviour and his stereotypical conceptions of criminals. To the extent that police are conservative, puritanical, and believe that crime and criminals are associated with poverty and similar social conditions, then it is the least privileged sections of the community against whom police decisions are biased. This is probably the most crucial factor. For to understand police behaviour, we need to understand police-men, not in the obvious psychological sense of 'Are they authoritarian?' but in the sociological sense of 'How do they view their role in society?' and 'How do they recognize criminal types?'

Finally, all policemen, like other employees, have *occupational* and *career worries*. Physical threats or the fear of physical threats may occasionally persuade a policeman that retreat from the scene is the better course of action. But more influential in persuading the police not to enforce the law is the symbolic threat posed by the suspect. If he is a person of privilege, influence or power, the policeman may be swayed by the possibility that ordinary law-enforcement might be defined by his superiors as over enforcement, with consequent detriment to his career advancement. Thus, Bayley and Mendelsohn (1969) suggest that 'class status very clearly carries with it, in the minds of policemen, an implied threat. Police officers know that the higher the class of the complainant, the greater the likelihood that he will appeal over the officer's head' (p. 102). And in reply to the question about which social locations pose the greatest threat of an appeal to a superior officer, patrolmen replied, 'the wealthy section . . . associated in the public mind with a relatively high concentration of ... professional people'.

The organizing principle governing the performance of bureaucracies responsible for the administration of justice is to maintain a precarious balance between reward and costs: that is, to secure sufficient convictions of the right kind to allay community fears that crime is getting out of hand, and refrain from over-enforcement, particularly of some offences, so as to avoid giving the impression, at least to the influential sections of the community, that the police are getting out of hand. In calculating rewards and costs, police administrators and policemen take into account the institution of privacy, legal constraints, middle-class shifting moral standards, reciprocal obligations with other bureaucracies, the danger of misinterpreting behaviour and thus not securing convictions, the values of the middle establishment, and the occupational and career risks accompanying law-enforcement. It is out of the matrix of considerations given to each of these issues that the police take decisions calculated to maximize rewards and minimize costs. Since, with few exceptions, 'the rewards which can be offered for non-enforcement of the law and the amount of trouble a suspected offender can create for the legal system are closely linked to the individual's social class position' (Chambliss, 1969; p. 86), it is not to be wondered at that the official profile of criminals suggests that they derive from the lower strata.

From S. Box, *'The social construction of official statistics on criminal deviance'*, Deviance, Reality and Society *(London: Holt, Rinehart & Winston), 1981, pp. 157–163.*

References

Bayley, D.H. & Mendelsohn, H. (1969) *Minorities and the Police.* New York: Free Press.

Chambliss, W.J. (1969) *Crime and the Legal Process.* New York: McGraw-Hill.

Chambliss, W.J. (1978) *On The Take.* Bloomington: Indiana University Press.

Chambliss, W.J. & Seidman, R.B. (1971) *Law, Order and Power.* Massachusetts: Addison Wesley.

Quinney, R. (1970) *The Social Reality of Crime.* Boston: Little Brown.

Reiman, J.H. (1979) *The Rich get Richer and the Poor get Prison.* New York: Wiley.

Turk, A.T. (1966) Conflict and criminality. *American Sociological Review,* 31, 338–352.

Turk, A. (1969) *Criminality and Legal Order.* Chicago: Rand-McNally.

3.2 **A note on the use of official statistics**
John I. Kitsuse and Aaron V. Cicourel

Current theoretical and research formulations in the sociology of deviance are cast within the general framework of social and cultural differentiation, deviance, and social control. [...] These forms of deviation are conceived as social products of the organization of groups, social structures, and institutions.

Three major lines of inquiry have developed within this general framework. One development has been the problem of explaining the rates of various forms of deviation among various segments of the population. The research devoted to this problem has produced a large body of literature in which individual, group, and areal (e.g., census tracts, regions, states, etc.) characteristics are correlated with rates of deviation. Durkheim's pioneer study of suicide is a classic example of this sociological interest. Merton's more general theory of social structure and anomie[1] may be cited as the most widely circulated statement of this problem.

The second line of investigation has been directed to the question of how individuals come to engage in various types of deviant behavior. From the theoretical standpoint, this question has been posed by the fact that although an aggregate of individuals may be exposed to the 'same' sociogenic factors associated with deviant behavior, some individuals become deviant while others do not. [...]

A third line of inquiry has been concerned with the developmental processes of 'behavior systems.' Theory and research on this aspect of deviant behavior focuses on the relation between the social differentiation of the deviant, the organization of deviant activity, and the individual's conception of himself as deviant. Studies of the professional thief, convicts, prostitutes, alcoholics, hoboes, drug addicts, carnival men, and others describe and analyze the deviant sub-culture and its patterning effects on the interaction between deviant and others. [...]

Although the three lines of investigation share a common interest in the organizational 'sources' of deviant behavior, a theoretical integration between them has not been achieved. This is particularly apparent in the theoretical and methodological difficulties posed by the problem of relating the rates of deviant behavior to the distribution of 'sociogenic' factors within the social structure. These difficulties may be stated in the form of two questions: (1) How is 'deviant behavior' to be defined sociologically, and (2) what are the relevant rates of deviant behavior which constitute the 'facts to be explained'? We shall propose that these difficulties arise as a consequence of the failure to distinguish between the social conduct which produces a unit of behavior (the behavior-producing processes) and organizational activity which produces a unit in the rate of deviant behavior (the rate-producing processes). The failure to make this distinction has led sociologists to direct their theoretical and empirical investigations to the behavior-producing processes on the implicit assumption that the rates of deviant behavior may be explained by them. We shall discuss some of the consequences of this distinction for theory and research in the sociology of deviance by examining the problems of the 'appropriateness' and 'reliability' of official statistics.

I

The following statement by Merton is a pertinent and instructive point of departure for a discussion of the questions raised above:

> Our primary aim is to discover how some *social structures exert a definite pressure upon certain persons in the society to engage in non-conforming rather than conforming conduct.* If we can locate groups peculiarly subject to such pressures, we would expect to find fairly high rates of deviant behavior in those groups, not because the human beings comprising them are compounded of distinctive biological tendencies but because they are responding normally to the social situation in which they find themselves. Our perspective is sociological. We look at variations in the rates of deviant behavior, not at its incidence.[2]

The central hypothesis that Merton derives from his theory is that 'aberrant behavior may be regarded as a symptom of dissociation between culturally prescribed aspirations[3] and socially structured avenues for realizing these aspirations.' The test of this general hypothesis, he suggests, would be to compare the variations in the rates of aberrant behavior among populations occupying different positions within the social structure. The question arises: What are the units of behavior which are to be tabulated to compile these rates of aberrant behavior?

Merton answers this question by discussing the kinds of rates which are 'inappropriate,' but he

is less explicit about what may be considered 'appropriate' data for sociological research. Discussing the relevance of his theory for research on juvenile delinquency, Merton presents two arguments against the use of 'official' rates of deviant behavior. He asks:

> ... to what extent and for which purposes is it feasible to make use of existing data in the study of deviant behavior? By existing data I mean the data which the machinery of society makes available – census data, delinquency rates as recorded in official or unofficial sources, data on the income distribution of an area, on the state of housing in an area, and the like.
>
> There is little in the history of how statistical series on the incidence of juvenile delinquency came to be collected that shows them to be the result of efforts to identify either the sources or the contexts of juvenile delinquency. These are social bookkeeping data. And it would be a happy coincidence if some of them turned out to be in a form relevant for research.
>
> From the sociological standpoint, 'juvenile delinquency' and what it encompasses is a form of deviant behavior for which the epidemiological data, as it were, may not be at hand. You may have to go out and collect your own appropriately organized data rather than to take those which are ready-made by governmental agencies.[4]

Our interpretation of this statement is that for the purposes of sociological research, official statistics may use categories which are unsuitable for the classification of deviant behavior. At best such statistics classify the 'same' forms of deviant behavior in different categories and 'different' forms in the same categories. Thus, the 'sources or the contexts' of the behavior are obscured.

Merton also argues against the use of official statistics on quite different grounds. He states that such data are 'unreliable' because 'successive layers of error intervene between the actual event and the recorded event, between the actual rates of deviant behavior and the records of deviant behavior.'[5] In this statement, the argument is that the statistics are unreliable because some individuals who manifest deviant behavior are apprehended, classified and duly recorded while others are not. It is assumed that if the acts of all such individuals were called to the attention of the official agencies they would be defined as deviant and so classified and recorded. In referring to the 'unreliability' of the statistics in this sense, however, Merton appears to suspend his 'sociologically relevant' definition of deviant behavior and implicitly invokes the definitions applied by the agencies which have compiled the statistics. That is, the 'unreliability' is viewed as a technical and organizational problem, not a matter of differences concerning the definition of deviant behavior.

Thus, Merton argues against the use of official statistics on two separate grounds. On the one hand, official statistics are not appropriately organized for sociological research because they are not collected by the application of a 'sociologically relevant' definition of deviant behavior. On the other hand, he implies that official statistics *could* be used if 'successive layers of error' did not make them 'unreliable.' But if the statistics are inappropriate for sociological research on the first ground, would they not be inappropriate regardless of their 'unreliability'?

It is evident, however, that 'inappropriate' or not, sociologists, including Merton himself,[6] do make use of the official statistics after a few conventional words of caution concerning the 'unreliability' of such statistics. The 'social bookkeeping data' are, after all, considered to bear some, if unknown, relation to the 'actual' rates of deviant behavior that interest sociologists. But granted that there are practical reasons for the use of official statistics, are there any theoretical grounds which justify their use, or is this large body of data useless for research in the sociology of deviance? This question directs us to examine more closely the theoretical and methodological bases of the two arguments against their use.

II

The objection to the official statistics because they are 'inappropriate' is, as indicated above, on definitional grounds. The argument is that insofar as the definitions of deviant behavior incorporated in the official statistics are not 'sociologically relevant,' such statistics are *in principle* 'inappropriate' for sociological research. What then is a sociologically relevant definition of deviant behavior and what are to be considered 'appropriately organized data' for sociological research?

We suggest that the question of the theoretical significance of the official statistics can be rephrased by shifting the focus of investigation from the processes by which *certain forms of behavior* are socially and culturally generated to the processes by which *rates of deviant behavior* are produced. Merton states that his primary aim is to explain the former processes, and he proposes to look at variations in the rates of deviant behavior as indices of the processes. Implicit in this proposal is the assumption that an explanation of the behavior-producing processes is also an explanation of the rate-producing processes. This assumption leads Merton to consider the correspondence between the forms of behavior which his theory is designed to explain and their distribution in the social structure as reflected in some set of statistics, including those commonly used official statistics 'which are ready-made by governmental agencies.'

Let us propose, however, the following: Our primary aim is to explain the *rates of deviant behavior*. So stated, the question which orients the investigation is not how individuals are motivated to engage in behavior defined by the sociologist as 'deviant.' Rather, the definition and content of deviant behavior are viewed as problematic, and the focus of inquiry shifts from the forms of behavior (modes of individual adaptation in Merton's terminology) to the 'societal reactions' which define various forms of behavior as deviant.[7] In contrast to Merton's formulation which focuses on forms of behavior as dependent variables (with structural pressures conceived to be the independent variables), we propose here to view the rates of deviant behavior as dependent variables. Thus, the explanation of rates of deviant behavior would be concerned specifically with the processes of rate construction.

The problem of the definition of 'deviant behavior' is directly related to the shift in focus proposed here. The theoretical conception which guides us is that the *rates of deviant behavior* are produced by the *actions taken by persons in the social system* which define, classify and record certain behaviors as deviant.[8] If a given form of behavior is not interpreted as deviant by such persons it would not appear as a unit in whatever set of rates we may attempt to explain (e.g., the statistics of local social welfare agencies, 'crimes known to the police,' Uniform Crime Reports, court records, etc.). The persons who define and activate the rate-producing processes may range from the neighborhood 'busybody' to officials of law enforcement agencies.[9] From this point of view, *deviant behavior* is behavior which is organizationally defined, processed, and treated as 'strange,' 'abnormal,' 'theft,' 'delinquent,' etc., by the personnel in the social system which has produced the rate. By these definitions, a sociological theory of deviance would focus on three interrelated problems of explanation: (1) How different forms of behavior come to be defined as deviant by various groups or organizations in the society, (2) how individuals manifesting such behaviors are organizationally processed to produce rates of deviant behavior among various segments of the population, and (3) how acts which are officially or unofficially defined as deviant are generated by such conditions as family organization, role inconsistencies or situational 'pressures.'

What are the consequences of these definitions for the question regarding the relevance of official statistics for sociological research? First, the focus on the processes by which rates are produced allows us to consider any set of statistics, 'official' as well as 'unofficial,' to be relevant. The question of whether or not the statistics are 'appropriately organized' is not one which is determined by reference to the correspondence between the sociologist's definition of deviant behavior and the organizational criteria used to compile the statistics. Rather the categories which organize a given set of statistics are taken as given – the 'cultural definitions,' to use Merton's term, of deviant behavior are *par excellence* the relevant definitions for research. The specification of the definitions explicitly or implicitly stated in the statistical categories is viewed as an empirical problem. Thus, the question to he asked is not about the 'appropriateness' of the statistics, but about the definitions incorporated in the categories applied by the personnel of the rate-producing social system to identify, classify, and record behavior as deviant.

Second, a unit in a given rate of deviant behavior is not defined in terms of a given form of behavior or a 'syndrome' of behavior. The behaviors which result in the classification of individuals in a given deviant category are *not necessarily* similar, i.e., the 'objective' manifestation of the 'same' forms of behavior may result in the classification of some individuals as deviant but not others. For example, with reference to the rates of delinquency reported by the police department, we would ask: What are the criteria that the police personnel use to identify and process a youth as 'incorrigible,' 'sex offender,' 'vandal,' etc.? The criteria of such categories are vague enough to include a wide range of behaviors which in turn may be produced by various 'sources and contexts' within the social structure.[10]

Third, the definition of deviant behavior as behavior which is organizationally processed as deviant provides a different perspective on the problem of the 'unreliability' of the official statistics. Insofar as we are primarily concerned with explaining rates rather than the forms of deviant behavior, such statistics may be accepted as a record of the number of those who have been differentiated as variously deviant at different levels of social control and treatment. The 'successive layers of error' which may result from the failure of control agencies to record all instances of certain forms of behavior, or from the exclusion of cases from one set of statistics that are included in another, do not render such statistics 'unreliable,' unless they are assigned self-evident status. By the definition of deviance proposed here, such cases are not among those processed as deviant by the organizations which have produced the statistics and thus are not officially deviant. To reject these statistics as 'unreliable' because they fail to record the 'actual' rate of deviant behavior assumes that certain behavior is always deviant independent of social actions which define it as deviant.

Fourth, the conception of rates of deviant behavior as the product of the socially organized activities of social structures provides a method of specifying the 'relevant structure' to be investigated. The rates are constructed from the statistics compiled by specifiable organizations, and those rates must be explained in terms of the deviant processing activities of those organizations. Thus, rates can be viewed as indices of organizational processes rather than as indices of the incidence of certain forms of behavior. For example, variations in the rates of deviant behavior among a given group (e.g., Negroes) as reflected in the statistics of different organizations may be a product of the differing definitions of deviant behavior used by those organizations, differences in the processing of deviant behavior, differences in the ideological, political, and other organizational conditions which affect the rate-making processes.

III

We wish now to discuss briefly some recent work[11] concerning adult and juvenile criminal acts which lends support to the thesis presented above. Let us assume that an ideal system of law-enforcement would lead to the apprehension of all persons who have committed criminal acts as defined by the statutes, and adjudicated in the manner prescribed by those statutes. In the ideal case, there would be little room for administrative interpretation and discretion. The adjudication process would proceed on the basis of evidence deemed legally admissible and the use of the adversary system to convict those who are guilty and exonerate those against whom there is insufficient evidence.[12] Criminologists have long recognized that the practiced and enforced system of criminal law, at all levels of the process, does not fulfill this ideal conception of criminal justice strictly governed by the definitions and prescriptions of statutes. Therefore, criminal statistics clearly cannot be assumed to reflect a system of criminal justice functioning as ideally conceived, and 'labels assigned convicted defendants' are not to be viewed as 'the statutory equivalents of their actual conduct.'[13]

What such statistics do reflect, however, are the specifically organizational contingencies which condition the application of specific statutes to actual conduct through the interpretations, decisions and actions of law enforcement personnel. The decisions and discretionary actions of persons who administer criminal justice have been documented by the American Bar Foundation study cited above. That study and other research[14] indicates the following:

1   There is considerable ambiguity in defining the nature of criminal conduct within the limits defined by the statutes. Categories of criminal conduct are the product of actual practices within these limits, and the decisions which must be made to provide the basis for choosing the laws which will receive the greatest attention.

2   The discretion allowed within the administration of criminal justice means that admissible evidence may give way to the prosecutor's power to determine whether or not to proceed, even in cases where there is adequate evidence to prosecute. The judge, as well as the police or the victim, also has discretion (e.g., sentencing), and some discretion is also extended to correctional institutions.

3   Most persons charged with criminal conduct plead guilty (from 80 to 90 per cent, according to the references cited by Newman) and jury trials are rare. Thus, the adversary aspect of the law is not always practiced because many of the lower income offenders cannot afford lawyers and often distrust public defenders. Criminal justice depends upon a large number of guilty pleas. Many of these cases would be acquitted if there were more trials.

4   Statistics are affected by such accommodations in the conviction process. Some offenders are excluded because they are not processed even though known to be guilty (e.g., drug addicts, prostitutes and gamblers are often hired by the police or coerced by them to help apprehend other offenders), and the practice of re-labeling offenses and reducing sentences because of insufficient evidence, 'deals,' and tricks (e.g., telling the defendant or his lawyer that because the offender 'seems like a decent person' the charge will be reduced from a felony to a misdemeanor, when in fact the prosecution finds there is insufficient evidence for either charge). These accommodations may occur at the time of arrest, or during prior or subsequent investigation of crimes, filing of complaints, adjudication, sentencing and post-sentencing relations with authorities, and so on.

The significance of the American Bar Foundation study goes beyond the documentation of the usual complaints about inadequate recording, inflated recording, and the like. More importantly, it underlines the way criminal statistics fail to reflect the decisions made and discretion used by law-enforcement personnel and administrators, and the general accommodations that can and do occur. An offender's record, then, may never reflect the ambiguous decisions, administrative discretions, or accommodations of law enforcement personnel; a statistical account may thus seriously distort an offender's past activities. [...]

We wish to state explicitly that the interpretation of official statistics proposed here does *not* imply that the forms of behavior which the sociologist might define and categorize as deviant (e.g., Merton's modes of adaptation) have no factual basis or theoretical importance. Nor do we wish to imply that the question of how behaviors so defined are produced by the social structure is not a sociologically relevant question. The implication of our interpretation is rather that *with respect to the problem of rates of deviant behavior* the theoretical question is: what forms of behavior are organizationally defined as deviant, and how are they classified, recorded and treated by persons in the society?

In our discussion, we have taken the view that official statistics, reflecting as they do the variety of organizational contingencies in the process by which deviants are differentiated from non-deviants, are sociologically relevant data. An individual who is processed as 'convicted,' for example, is sociologically differentiable from one who is 'known to the police' as criminal – the former may legally be incarcerated, incapacitated and socially ostracized, while the latter remains 'free.' The fact that both may have 'objectively' committed the same crime is of theoretical and empirical significance, but it does not alter the sociological difference between them. The *pattern* of such 'errors' is among the facts that a sociological theory of deviance must explain, for they are indications of the organizationally defined processes by which individuals are differentiated as deviant.

Indeed, in modern societies where bureaucratically organized agencies are increasingly invested with social control functions, the activities of such agencies are centrally important 'sources and contexts' which generate as well as maintain definitions of deviance and produce populations of deviants. Thus, rates of deviance constructed by the use of statistics routinely issued by these agencies are social facts *par excellence*. A further implication of this view is that if the sociologist is interested in how forms of *deviant* behavior are produced by social structures, the forms that must be explained are those which not only are defined as deviant by members of such structures but those which also activate the unofficial and/or 'official' processes of social control. By directing attention to such processes, the behavior-producing and rate-producing processes may be investigated and compared within a single framework.

> *From J.I. Kitsuse and A.V. Cicourel, 'A note on the use of official statistics'*, Social Problems, 1963, *11:131–139*

Notes

1 Robert K. Merton, *Social Theory and Social Structure*, revised, Glencoe: The Free Press, 1957, Chapter 4.

2 Robert K. Merton, *op. cit.*, p. 147. Merton's comments on the theory of social structure and anomie may be found in Chapter 5 of that volume, and in 'Social Conformity, Deviation, and Opportunity Structures: A Comment on the Contributions of Dubin and Cloward,' *American Sociological Review*, 24 (April, 1959), pp. 177–189; See also his remarks in *New Perspectives for Research on Juvenile Delinquency*, H. Witmer and R. Kotinsky, editors, U. S. Government Printing Office, 1956.

3 *Social Theory and Social Structure, op, cit.*, p. 134.

4 *New Perspectives for Research on Juvenile Delinquency, op. cit.*, p. 32.

5 *Ibid.*, p. 31.

6 For example, '…crude (and not necessarily reliable) crime statistics suggest…' etc., *Social Theory and Social Structure, op. cit.*, p. 147.

7 For a discussion of the concept of 'societal reaction' see Edwin M. Lemert, *op. cit.*, Chapter 4.

8 For a preliminary research application of this formulation, see John I. Kitsuse, 'Societal Reaction to Deviant Behavior: Problems of Theory and Method,' *Social Problems*, 9 (Winter, 1962), pp. 247–56.

9 We recognize, of course, that many individuals, may be labeled 'strange,' 'crooks,' 'crazy,' etc., and ostracized by members of a community, yet be unknown to the police or any other official agency. Insofar as such individuals are labeled and treated as deviants, they constitute a population which must be explained in any theory of deviance. In this paper, however, we are primarily concerned with the theoretical relevance of official statistics for the study of deviance.

10 In any empirical investigation of such criteria, it is necessary to distinguish between the formal (official) interpretive rules (as defined by a manual of procedures, constitution, and the like) which are to be employed by the personnel of the organizations in question, and the unofficial rules used by the personnel in their deviant-processing activities, e.g., differential treatment on the basis of social class, race, ethnicity, or varying conceptions of 'deviant' behavior.

11 The material in this section is taken from an unpublished paper by Cicourel entitled 'Social Class, Family Structure and the Administration of Juvenile Justice,' and is based on a study of the social organization of juvenile justice in two Southern California communities with populations of approximately 100,000 each.

12 See Donald J. Newman, 'The Effects of Accommodations in Justice Administration on Criminal Statistics,' *Sociology and Social Research*, 46 (Jan., 1962), pp. 144155; *Administration of Criminal Justice*, Chicago: American Bar Foundation, 1955, unpublished.

13 Newman, 'The Effects of Accommodations…,' *op. cit.*, pp. 145–146,

14 See *ibid.*, pp. 146–151, and the references cited.

3.3　The origins of the British Crime Survey
Mike Hough, Mike Maxfield, Bob Morris and Jon Simmons

Origins of the BCS

This section describes how the decision to initiate crime surveys was reached within the policy-making structures of the Home Office of the day. The viewpoints expressed are those of the two coauthors of this chapter who were involved in the process. One of us (Bob Morris) was a 'generalist' Home Office official, and was at the time director of the Home Office's Crime Policy Planning Unit (CPPU).[1] The other (Mike Hough) was one of the initial BCS research team in the Home Office Research Unit (HORU).[2] The core BCS team was small, the other members being Pat Mayhew and Ron Clarke, who at the time was Deputy Director of the Unit. The Director, John Croft, also played an important role in supporting the concept of a national survey, and – crucially – in being able to commit the necessary finance to the project.

The context

HORU had commissioned the first crime survey of any significance in Britain in the early 1970s, published as *Surveying Victims* (Sparks, Genn and Dodd, 1977).[3] This study was conducted in London on a scale that was very modest by current standards, but it addressed all of the key conceptual and methodological issues relating to crime surveys, and the British Crime Survey (BCS) certainly owes a debt to this work. [...]

Crime surveys came tentatively back on to the Home Office policy agenda in the late 1970s. By this time, HORU and CPPU had discussed the possibility of mounting a national survey, both recognising the possibilities that this represented. Early discussion took account of the United States experience, the HORU sponsorship of the Sparks *et al.* survey, the outcome of the few questions inserted twice in the General Household Survey (GHS), and some early forays into local crime surveys.[4] A CPPU review in 1978 had touched without enthusiasm on crime surveys in the context of a more general review. It was not until later in 1979 that the CPPU began to look at the prospect in more depth, when the 1979 general election resulted in a change of government.

The new government was committed to a strong law and order agenda. Not only was there the penology of the 'short, sharp shock,' but immediate payment of the second instalment of the Edmund Davies pay award to the police as part of a commitment to fight crime. In another part of the new woods, a 'Quango cull'[5] swept away the Advisory Council on the Penal System (ACPS), the standing, independent body that had brought together academics and criminal justice practitioners and acted as a continuing source of policy advice. On the face of it, this might not have seemed like a government that would welcome novel depictions of crime levels (for example, calibrating the 'dark figure') that might be thought to call the success of their policies into question or to make them more difficult to achieve.

Making the case for a national crime survey

Throughout 1979, HORU and CPPU had been collaborating in working up a case for a crime survey. The CPPU was ready to make its case to the Crime Policy Planning Committee in February 1980.[6] The case that was made placed less importance on the 'dark' figure of unreported crime than on obtaining more intelligence in respect of crime prevention, fear of crime, and for informing enforcement responses. Because nothing was to be gained from offering an unbalanced account, the CPPU paper was also frank about the drawbacks of expense and uncertainty of impact. Discussion revealed the battle lines to be as indicated above. In addition, SD [Statistical Department] was concerned about the proposed methodology and, assuming that the Office of Population, Census and Surveys (OPCS) would be the right body to undertake any survey, pointed out that recent Rayner manpower cuts had reduced its capacity for doing so. After a further airing of the issues at a New Options seminar initiated by the Permanent Under Secretary in June 1980, the CPPC agreed – not unanimously – in October that there should be a spring workshop in 1981 to ventilate the issues as thoroughly as possible.[7]

Chaired by the head of the Criminal Department, this was a crucial initiative, co-organised by CPPU and HORU and funded by the latter. It involved a much wider group than hitherto, together with strong academic and official representation, including in the former case from North America[8] and Europe. Also present were researchers who had much practical experience of surveys on the scale being contemplated. [...]

The seminar allayed some opposition but did not end it. [...] The chairperson thereupon put the proposal to ministers. [...] Much beleaguered at the time, the Home Secretary could have easily postponed or simply rejected a proposal that was likely to complicate rather than directly assist his tasks. He did not, however, take the easy route:

The Home Secretary said that he was inclined to think the project should go ahead, despite the reservations that had been expressed (some of which he shared) since it would be desirable for the Home Office to show its willingness to contribute to the public debate about crime, which would inevitably follow the recent urban disorders.[9]

And that was that – except that the RPU then, of course, had to shoulder the considerable amount of work involved in establishing the new venture. The RPU awarded a contract to Social and Community Planning Research (now the National Centre for Social Research). A crime survey team was set up under the direction of Ron Clarke and work began on the survey immediately. The sampling strategy and the questionnaire were devised by Douglas Wood of SCPR, Pat Mayhew, and Mike Hough, with the academic advice of Hazel Genn, David Farrington, and Wes Skogan. The first survey went into the field in January 1982. This could genuinely claim to be a *British* crime survey, in that the Scottish Office decided to conduct a parallel survey using a near-identical questionnaire.[10]

The first BCS report (Hough and Mayhew, 1983) was published a year later. Although it may not appear unusual now, it was in many ways a groundbreaking piece of work. It was produced very rapidly by the standards of the time, at low cost. It was written in a style that was less formal and more accessible than conventional Home Office research reports. We were also careful to ensure that the results could withstand methodological criticism – partly by ensuring that it was technically competent, and partly by being as open as possible about the limitations of the survey method. The research

team were also heavily involved in the preparation of press notices, and more broadly in the development of media handling strategies. This contrasts with what subsequently became the norm, with increasingly less involvement by research professionals with media contact. The first survey was largely well received. Whilst its findings attracted a great deal of attention, press coverage largely avoided the sort of sensationalism that had always been recognised as a risk inherent in revealing a 'dark figure' of crime.

The second BCS was mounted in 1984, followed by sweeps in 1988, 1992, and biennially thereafter until 2001, when it was changed into a continuous survey.

The BCS: key contributions since 1982

[...] The idea for the BCS originated in the United States in the form of the National Crime Victimization Survey (NCVS), which predates the British version and provided the main model for the BCS to adapt to its own local purpose. Serving as an alternate count for police statistics has always been the most important goal of the American NCVS. This was among the objectives of the BCS – although reports always took care to present the survey as a complementary measure of crime, rather than as a substitute. The BCS always had a broader range of objectives to the NCVS, benefiting from the lessons that could be drawn from this earlier exercise.

Rather than looking only at today's issues, the BCS has been adept at looking forward at tomorrow's concerns, providing a bedrock of knowledge on some of the key issues that only subsequently became a matter of widespread political or public concern.

Serial surveys are well suited for such purposes. As knowledge is acquired and funnelled into policy development, new topics can be added to the next sweep. From its outset, the BCS combined a set of core items to monitor levels of victimisation, reporting to police, and concern about crime. Periodic supplements gathered information on special topics of particular interest to public officials and researchers. Results were presented in Home Office reports and academic publications. The scope of basic and applied research produced with BCS data is much broader than that from any other single source of data on crime, its correlates and impact. This influence is a product of the survey's design.

Design elements

Several design elements have contributed to the survey's utility as a research and policy instrument, which in combination give the BCS its distinctive shape.

Research platform

As a product of an agency engaged in research (the Home Office Research and Planning Unit, later to be absorbed into the Research and Statistics Directorate), the BCS was designed to accommodate varying clusters of questions that would supplement its core crime-counting function. This made it possible to add questions as needed to meet emerging interests, while maintaining a standard series to monitor victimisation consistently over time. It is especially important that the BCS was designed to incorporate standard, rotating, and purpose-built questionnaire modules.

Independent and dependent variables

As a research platform, each sweep of the BCS included bundles of items that are antecedents or consequences of victimisation. These have largely been developed from criminological theories, and their inclusion has supported basic research. Measures based on opportunity-related ideas have been prominent. The first sweep asked about routine behaviour thought to be linked with victimisation risk. Among these were items on self-reported offending. Later sweeps expanded on the latter, as research documented how the same factors were associated with higher victimisation and offending, within different population groups, and more importantly how victimisation was linked to offending at the individual level.

Policy development

The BCS has also supported applied research to develop and clarify justice policies. Various sweeps of the BCS have centred on special topics such as contacts with police, domestic violence, drug misuse, fraud and technology offences, and attitudes toward criminal justice agencies. Selected survey results have been presented in special publications that target the criminal justice community. Reducing repeat victimisation is one especially well-known example of a policy initiative rooted in findings from the BCS. Just as locally targeted surveys are tools for local police forces, national surveys are well suited to exploring general features of social problems that can subsequently inform broader policy initiatives.

Contextual analysis

In collaboration with the research firm CAC, neighbourhood-level data from the decennial census were appended to each BCS interview record from the 1984 sweep onward. This innovation played an important role in supporting multilevel contextual analysis of crime and disorder problems. The specific area identifiers have been changed, and the BCS is now stratified by police force area.

Sampling

Until the 2000 revisions, the BCS was based on a core sample of moderately large size, supplemented by booster samples that targeted groups and areas of particular interest. This approach yielded sufficient numbers of cases for analysis of most crimes and topics, while avoiding the expense of interviewing very large numbers of people as is done in the US. Booster samples yield victims in higher-risk areas, or they are used to oversample groups of particular interest, as in boosters for ethnic minority respondents or young people. This was innovative, offering a good example of adaptive sampling. In its current configuration, the BCS has moved toward the US model, with concomitant increases in cost. This is appropriate for developing more precise estimates of infrequent crimes and for obtaining representative samples within police force areas. Yet, larger sample sizes are not necessary for the broader uses supported by former sampling practices. The final chapter returns to this point.

Asking sensitive questions

Asking respondents about their experiences of victimisation is at the core of crime survey methodology. Yet some types of victimisation seemed to demand a more anonymous approach than direct questions put by interviewers. This led to the adoption in the BCS in 1994 of computer-assisted self-interviewing (CASI) – where the respondent inputs responses to the interviewer's laptop computer themselves – to look at family violence and sexual victimisation, Moreover, although self-reported offending questions have been included in the BCS since its first sweep, there was also a shift to the use of CASI to try and elicit more honest responses – for instance, in relation to drug-taking, stalking, being offered and buying goods known to be stolen, fraud, and technology crimes.

Influence on criminological research and justice policy

Tracing the influence of a survey such as the BCS is inevitably a subjective process. Here we offer simply one version of the impact that it has had on criminal policy and on criminological thinking.

Various lists of publications using BCS data have been produced over the last 20 years or so. One included in a guide to BCS analysis (Budd and Mattinson, 2001) lists more than 20 topics covered by hundreds of publications. With the combination of RDS published overviews of annual findings, RDS publications on particular topics rotated through different sweeps, and publications in academic journals, results from the BCS have been widely disseminated. A Google search of Web references located around 300,000 references to the phrase 'British Crime Survey.' The survey's influence has been particularly important in certain areas, most of which are represented by other chapters in this volume.

Multiple victimisation

This is arguably the body of research that can be linked most closely and most exclusively to the BCS. It is especially interesting because BCS data have been used to identify multiple victimisation as a problem, while serial victimisation has not received much attention in US crime surveys. Victimisation data also prompted researchers to begin to seek out measures of repeat crimes in police data. This revealed links between area-level measures of crime concentration (hot spots) and repeat victimisation. Repeat victimisation is perhaps the best available illustration of the progression from exploratory research findings through further research, crafting interventions, and ultimately the measurement of the impact of crime reduction policies.

Experience and attitudes to police

Although victim surveys emerged to measure the crimes not reported to police, they are also well suited to measuring respondent experiences with police. Like unreported crime, such experiences may not be included in police records. The specific police-contact modules added to follow-up forms are good examples of how the survey has been supplemented to assess emerging issues in crime and justice. Special attention was first devoted to police contacts in the 1984 survey. Special Home Office research studies on police contacts were published in 1984, 1990, and 1995. With police force areas as primary sampling units, the BCS is currently able to monitor police/public contacts routinely in geographic context. As with data on repeat victimisation, BCS data were first used to understand better police/public contacts, which have now become a central focus of the survey. Perhaps reflecting its centrality as a specific policy issue, BCS-based research on policing has been published infrequently in journals. On the other hand, the BCS interest in this topic spread to the US, where a supplement to the NCVS now gathers information on police/ public contacts.

Crime and communities

This stems from the multilevel analysis supported by area identifiers in the BCS. Research published in the US is widely recognised for demonstrating how community-level measures of social disorganisation are related to crime and its perceptions. Further studies by UK researchers have expanded our knowledge of the role macro-level community characteristics play in criminal victimisation.

Fear of crime

'Fear of crime' is what psychometricians call an indirect observable. One may want to argue whether 'fear' is the right term for the phenomenon, but it is clear that worries or anxieties about crime are, in principle, well suited for measurement by surveys. Parts of the BCS have tackled this topic since the first wave for two related reasons. First, despite its attitudinal content, fear has been difficult to measure in ways that researchers and policy makers can agree on. Second is the persisting gap between subjective measures such as fear and more objective measures of crime risks. Research has established, after a fashion, that fear is a complex, multidimensional construct – and one that would be better labelled as anxiety. The topic has attracted quite a lot of interest from researchers and public officials. Officials view fear as a policy problem at least partly independent of crime and linked to confidence in the criminal justice system. Researchers have long been engaged in attempts to better measure fear and model it with resulting data. Though not alone in covering fear, the BCS has offered much more detailed measures of the concept than surveys in the U.S. and most other nations. As a result, more has been learned about fear from analysis of BCS data than from any other national crime survey.

Attitudes toward justice issues

This is another topic that has been viewed as an important policy issue. Again, surveys are best at measuring attitudes, since they are subjective concepts elicited through questioning. The BCS has covered attitudes almost as a social indicator, seeking public views of punishment as a rough gauge for lawmaking. Because attitudes to punishment and other criminal justice processes do not travel well internationally, most BCS research on this topic has appeared in the UK. To the extent that democratic nations should benchmark policy against the preferences of citizens, however, the BCS serves as something of a model for periodically assessing public views, and several other countries have adopted or adapted the approach taken from the 1996 ECS onwards.

Risks of crime

The body of BCS-based research on risks of crime encompasses policy relevance and criminological theory. Two influential publications in the late 1970s laid out lifestyle and routine activity theories of crime and victimisation (Cohen and Felson, 1979; Hindelang, Gottfredson, and Garofalo, 1978). Lifestyle theories of crime had a significant impact especially on early sweeps of the survey.[11] The first sweep included a variety of items to measure directly certain dimensions of behaviour that had only been inferred from previous crime surveys. Research on this topic has continued with subsequent sweeps, published in highly regarded journals in the US and Europe. Research on crime risks has also contributed to crime prevention initiatives. As with data on fear, the BCS has been the single most fruitful source of data on crime risks.

Drug use

From the 1992 sweep, the BCS incorporated detailed self-report drug use items collected through computer-assisted interviewing. Results from that and subsequent sweeps have been reported in the continuing series of *Drug misuse declared* Home Office publications (most recently, Roe and Man, 2006). This segment of the BCS is important for four related reasons. First, as a national crime survey it provides regular data for monitoring the scope of drug use among the general population. Second, occasional booster samples make it possible to assess drug use among targeted populations. Third, drug use can be examined against the variety of other variables measuring behaviour and experiences. Finally, the use of CASI (computer-assisted self-interviewing) produces better estimates than those obtained through other means – although no one would claim that the survey provides reliable information on dependent or problematic use of drugs such as crack or heroin.

> From M. Hough and M. Maxfield, (Eds) Surveying Crime in the 21st Century *(Monsey, NY: Criminal Justice Press), 2007, pp. 9–22.*

Notes

1 This was a small, freestanding outfit in the Criminal Department headed by an Assistant Secretary assisted by a Principal and, crucially, also by a Principal Research Officer. Its work has been described in Train (1977) and Morris (1980a). It involved wholly intra-Home Office coordination. 'Tripartism' – coordination between the Home Office, the then Lord Chancellor's Department and the Law Officers' Department – emerged in rather different circumstances later.

2 HORU was reorganised and re-badged as the Home Office Research and Planning Unit in 1981, and much later incorporated into a larger Research Statistics and Development department.

3 From 1972 the General Household Survey had included a question on burglary, which suggested that much of the increase in this offence over the course of the 1970s was due to increased recording by the police rather than any increase in public propensity to report or any real increase in offences. This was reported in a Home Office Statistical Bulletin around the time the BCS was launched (see Home Office, 1982, for details).

4 Two local surveys predated the first BCS: in Sheffield (Bottoms, Mawby & Walker, 1987), and a Home Office survey in Mosside comparing black and white residents (Tuck & Southgate, 1981).

5 Quangos were 'Quasi-autonomous nongovernmental organisations' – essentially, governmental organisations set up at arm's length from government departments. Their proliferation was a source of political concern at the time.

6 RES 80 0508/001/12/078, CPP(80)3 'Public Surveys of Crime' and CPP(M)58.

7 Meeting of 13 October 1980, CPP(M)61.

8 It was significant that Al Biderman, Al Reiss, and Wes Skogan all attended the workshop.

9 *Ibid*. Note of meeting on 22 July 1981.

10 There have been six published sweeps of the Scottish Crime Survey, with varying degrees of comparability to the BCS. The 2005 sweep involved an unhappy experience with telephone interviews.

11 With a degree of obsession that now seems mis-placed, we designed the first questionnaire to grill respondents not only on the mode of transport they used when going out in the evening, but also about their mode of return. The small subsample who used different modes of transport to go out and to return never led to any significant criminological breakthrough!

References

Budd, T., & Mattinson, J. (2001). *British Crime Survey training notes* (Unpublished Technical Report). London: Home Office, Crime Surveys Section, Crime and Criminal Justice Unit, Research, Development and Statistics Directorate. Available at http://www.ndad.nationalarchives.gov.uk/CRDA/2/DD/detail.html

Cohen, L.E., & Felson, M. (1979). Social change and crime rate trends: A routine activity approach. *American Sociological Review*, 44, 588–608.

Hindelang, M.J., Gottfredson, M.R., Cohen, L.E., &

Garofalo, J. (1978) *Victims of personal crime: An empirical foundation for a theory of personal victimization.* Cambridge, MA: Ballinger.

Hough, M., & Mayhew, P. (1983). *The British Crime Survey: First report.* Home Office Research Study No. 76. London: Her Majesty's Stationery Office.

Roe, S., & Man, L. (2006). *Drug misuse declared: Findings from the 2005/06 British crime survey, England and Wales. Statistic Bulletin 15/06.* London: Home Office.

Sparks, R., Genn, H., & Dodd, D. (1977). *Surveying victims.* London: Wiley.

3.4 Unravelling recent crime patterns and trends
Robert Reiner

The official police recorded crime statistics have severe limitations as an index of trends or patterns in crime. The advent of the BCS twenty-five years ago has shed much light on reporting and recording practices, allowing the statistics to he interpreted more confidently. Above all, because there are now two alternative measures of trends and patterns for offences covered by the survey, there can be greater confidence when they point in the same direction, as they did for most of the history of the BCS. However, in recent years the trends indicated by the police statistics and the BCS have begun to diverge, producing a politicization of the debate about their interpretation and the relative merits of different measuring instruments.

Patterns of crime

An important point to bear in mind is that recorded crime consists overwhelmingly of property crime, above all the so-called 'volume' crimes of burglary, other theft and handling, and thefts of and from cars. Nearly three-quarters (73 per cent) of crimes recorded by the police in 2005–6 were property crimes.[1] Violent crimes accounted for 22 per cent, and drugs and other offences 4 per cent. This is very similar to the picture given by the BCS, which estimated that 77 per cent were property crimes, and 23 per cent violent offences (as indicated earlier, the BCS does not include drug and other offences without specific individual victims). The pattern of an overwhelming preponderance of property offences has been true throughout the history of crime statistics, although there has been some growth of violent relative to property offences in the last thirty years, and particularly in the last decade (largely because of shifts in the recording rules). In 1976, for example, the proportion of recorded property offences was 94 per cent, and violent and sexual crimes were just 5 per cent.[2] This had changed only slightly by 1997: 91 per cent of recorded crimes were property offences, and 8 per cent were violent.[3] Thus trends in overall crime primarily track fluctuations in the level of property offences.

| **Figure 3.4.1** | Crimes recorded by the police, 1857–1997 |

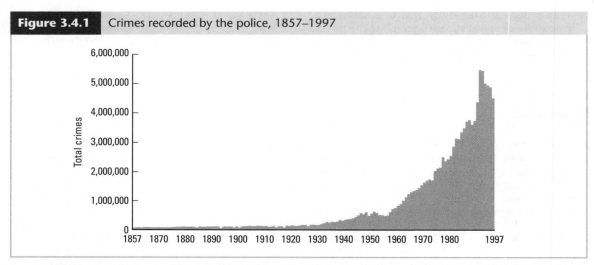

Source: G. Barclay and C. Tavares, Digest 4: *Information on the Criminal Justice System in England and Wales* (London: Home Office, 1999).

Trends in crime

Putting together the different sorts of data available, what can be said about the trends in the last half century? The most apparent trend is the spectacular rise in recorded crime since the late 1950s. Figure 3.4.1 sets this in a longer term historical context. It underlines the dramatic extent of the rise in recorded crime since the mid-1950s. Between the 1850s and the 1920s recorded crime remained on a plateau.[4] During the 1930s there was a period of substantial and sustained increase, continuing through the early years of the Second World War. In the decade following the war there were several short cycles of rising and falling rates, but no clear trend. But from 1955 recorded crime began a massive and sustained long-term growth.

In the early 1950s the police recorded fewer than half a million offences per annum. By the mid-1960s this had increased to around 1 million, and by the mid-1970s 2 million. The 1980s showed even more staggering rises, with recorded crime peaking in 1992 at over 5.5 million – a tenfold increase in less than four decades. By 1997 recorded crime had fallen back to 4.5 million. The counting rule changes introduced in 1998 and 2002 make comparison of the subsequent figures especially fraught, but on the new rules (which undoubtedly exaggerate the increase) just under 6 million offences were recorded by the police for 2003–4 – the highest on record – but this had fallen back to just over 5.6 million in 2005–6.[5]

The big question is to what extent the huge increase in recorded crime is a product of varia-tions in reporting and recording, and how much of it is a genuine increase in offending. For all the reasons discussed earlier, it is impossible to be certain about either the level or trends in crime. Nonetheless, with the advent of regular alternative measures, and much more knowledge of reporting and recording processes, it is possible to interpret the trends with some confidence. Three sub-periods can be distinguished, corresponding not only to the relationship between the recorded crime figures and alternative statistical series, notably the BCS, but also to major changes in political economy, culture and society. The three distinct periods are from the late 1950s to 1980; the 1980s and early 1990s; the 1990s and the early years of the twenty-first century.

Period 1, late 1950s–1980: rapid recorded crime rise

Until the 1970s there were no alternative measures of crime apart from the police statistics. Criminologists were wont to give cautionary warnings about whether crime really was increasing as the figures indicated, but it was impossible to know how much of any change was due to new patterns of reporting and/or recording crime.

However, during the 1970s the General Household Survey began to ask respondents about their experience of burglary. For the first time this allowed some insight into the extent to which reporting or recording changes contributed to rising crime rates. Burglary was not only a common offence, accounting for something like a fifth of recorded crime, but was of crucial importance for public anxieties about crime and the emerging politics of law and order. The GHS showed that during the 1970s the substantial rise in recorded burglaries was mainly accounted for by an increase in victims' propensity to report burglary to the police, not an increase in victimization. Between 1972 and 1983 recorded burglaries doubled, but victimization increased by only 20 per cent according to the surveys.[6] There was a considerable increase in the proportion of victims reporting burglaries to the police, and the reason is plain from the GHS. In 1972 the property stolen was insured in only 19 per cent of burglary incidents, but by 1980 this had increased to 42 per cent.[7] Thus the first set of victimization statistics, from the GHS in the 1970s, reinforced criminological scepticism about how much of the huge increase in recorded crime statistics was really due to increased offending.

It is impossible to be sure about whether the rise in the recorded rates for other offences was due to increased reporting on the same scale as burglary, and indeed how much of the increase in recorded burglary before the 1970s was a reporting phenomenon. But it is plausible that at least a substantial part of the rise in recorded crime was due to more being reported by victims. It was not only that a higher proportion of goods enjoyed insurance cover, but also that this reflected the spread of ownership of expensive consumer durables that were more likely to be reported if stolen. Thus a substantial part of the increase in crime rates from the late 1950s to the late 1970s was probably due to greater reporting rather than to increased offending. Nonetheless the public and political panic that (apparently) rising crime fuelled was a

major factor in the 1970s politicization of law and order, and the Conservative election victory of 1979 with all the epochal changes it precipitated.

Period 2, 1980s–1992: crime explosion

However, as the BCS came to be repeated in several sweeps during the 1980s and early 1990s the discrepancy in the trends recorded by the surveys and by the police figures began to lessen. Although there was still some increase in reporting and recording, most of the huge rise in recorded crime in the 1980s and early 1990s corresponded to an increase in victimization. Between 1981 and 1993, the number of crimes recorded by the police increased 111 per cent, while BCS offences rose by 77 per cent. The proportion of offences reported to the police by victims increased from 31 per cent in 1981 to 41 per cent in 1993 according to the BCS.[8] In the most common types of property crime, such as car thefts and burglary with loss, reporting and recording rates had reached almost 100 per cent. When there is almost complete recording of victimization by the police the trends in the BCS and police figures will of course be almost identical. This is shown by figures 3.4.2 and 3.4.3 which chart the trends in BCS crime and police recorded crime since 1981.

Figure 3.4.3 shows that between 1981 and 1993 recorded crime roughly doubled. The reality of most of this increase is confirmed by the correspondingly huge increase in overall crime recorded by the BCS, which also went up by nearly 80 per cent, as shown by figure 3.4.2 The BCS also shows that there was an increase in the reporting of crime by victims, which accounts for the discrepancy in the trends. Nonetheless the overwhelming bulk of

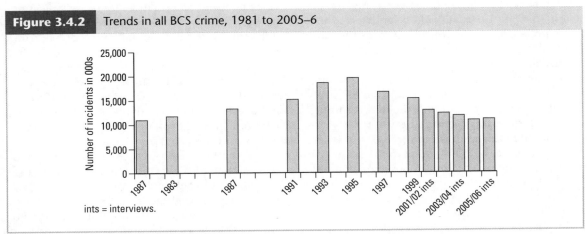

Figure 3.4.2   Trends in all BCS crime, 1981 to 2005–6

Source: A. Walker, C. Kershaw and S. Nicholas, *Crime in England and Wales 2005/06* (London: Home Office, 2006).

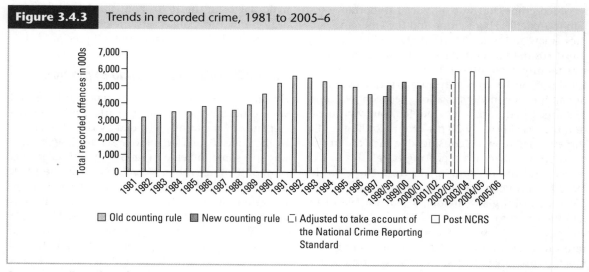

Figure 3.4.3   Trends in recorded crime, 1981 to 2005–6

Legend: ☐ Old counting rule ■ New counting rule ☐ Adjusted to take account of the National Crime Reporting Standard ☐ Post NCRS

Source: A. Walker, C. Kershaw and S. Nicholas, *Crime in England and Wales 2005/06* (London: Home Office, 2006).

the vast increase in recorded crime during the 1980s and early 1990s seems to have been a genuine increase in offending and victimization. The 1980s were a decade of explosive crime increase.

Period 3, 1992 onwards: ambiguously falling crime, rising fear

In the first decade of its existence the BCS seemed largely to confirm the patterns and trends shown by the police recorded crime statistics. While charting a somewhat slower rise in crime than the police statistics (because there was some increase in reporting by victims), for the most part the trends were similar. As the main volume crimes had reached rates of reporting that were nearly 100 per cent by the late 1980s, it could be anticipated that this parallelism would continue. From the early 1990s, however, the two sets of statistics begin to diverge, in complicated ways.

Between 1992 and 1995 the police statistics began to decline from their record height of nearly 6 million recorded crimes. But the BCS continued to register increasing victimization in these years. The 'missing crimes' in the police statistics were due to a reversal of the trend towards saturation reporting of the most common property offences.[9] Paradoxically, the very high levels of crime set in train processes leading victims to report less, and the police to record fewer of the crimes reported to them. Victims in higher risk categories faced more onerous conditions for insurance, reducing the

incentive to report crimes (as making claims could trigger increased premiums, or other burdens such as expensive and stringent domestic security arrangements). The 'deductibles' (the proportion of claims victims themselves had to pay) were increasing for most insurance policies, creating further disincentives to reporting.

At the same time, the police were coming under a tighter performance measurement regime that began to bite hard in the early 1990s.[10] There were stronger pressures to record fewer crimes if at all possible, especially for key target offences. It was not only that overall crime levels, and rates for crucial categories like burglary, were in themselves performance indicators. Minimizing the recording of hard-to-investigate offences like burglary also helped boost detection rates, another key measure. The significance of declining recording by the police for explaining the fall in recorded crime from 1992 to 1995, at a time of increasing victimization according to the BCS, is shown in figure 3.4.4, which charts the shifting balance between recorded, reported and BCS crime since 1981. As can be seen, recording by the police fell from 1991 to 1995, while reporting by victims measured by the BCS continued to rise.

After 1997 the divergence between the police and BCS statistics continues, but in the reverse direction, The BCS figures, however, show continuing declines in total victimization from 1995 to 2005–6. The trend is substantial and sustained, with the risks of victimization by crime measured by the BCS now below the level of the first survey

Figure 3.4.4   Indexed trends in the reporting of crime and all BCS crime, 1981 to 2005–6 (1981 = 100)

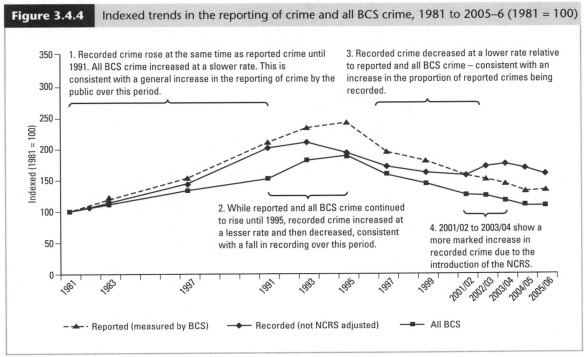

Source: A. Walker, C. Kershaw and S. Nicholas, *Crime in England and Wales 2005/06* (London: Home Office, 2006).

in 1981. This is the basis of the claims by Labour to have brought crime down substantially. By contrast, the police figures record increases from 1997 to 2004–5, if no allowance is made for the two major shifts in counting rules and procedures in 1998 and 2002 that were discussed earlier. However, if the impact of the new counting rules and the National Crime Recording Standard is estimated, there is only a very small increase in recorded crime from 1997 to 2004, and decline since then. The rise in recorded crime after 1997, at a time of sharp decline in BCS-measured victimization, is thus largely accounted for by the two changes in counting rules over this period.

> From R. Reiner, 'What happened? Unravelling crime patterns and trends', Law and Order (Cambridge: Polity Press), 2007, pp. 61–70.

Notes

1 Walker, Kershaw and Nicholas, *Crime in England and Wales* 2005/06, p. 17.
2 Home Office, *Criminal Statistics* (1976), p. 22.

3 Barclay and Tavares, *Digest 4*, p. 4.
4 Although there are no figures for crimes that were not prosecuted prior to 1856, on the basis of the judicial statistics historians generally believe that the mid-Victorian levels represent a decline from much higher levels in the early nineteenth century (Gatrell, 'The decline of theft'; Emsley, 'The history of crime', pp. 204–7). There is some debate about whether the flat trend indicated in figure 3.4.1 is attributable to supply-side rationing of the figures driven both by fiscal parsimony and the wish to present an appearance of success for the new police forces and other nineteenth-century criminal justice reforms (H. Taylor, 'Rising crime: the political economy of criminal statistics' and 'Rising crime: a crisis of 'modernisation'; R. Morris, ''Lies, damned lies and criminal statistics''; Emsley, 'The history of crime').
5 Walker, Kershaw and Nicholas. *Crime in England and Wales 2005/06*, p. 14.
6 Hough and Mayhew, *Taking Account of Crime*, p. 16.
7 Mayhew, Elliott and Dowds, *The 1988 British Crime Survey*, pp. 19–22.
8 Barclay, Tavares and Prout, *Digest 3*, p. 7.
9 Reiner, 'The case of the missing crimes'.
10 Weatheritt, 'Measuring police performance'; McLaughlin and Murji, 'Lost connections and new directions'; Long, 'Leadership and performance management'.

4

Crime and the media

4.1 What makes crime 'news'?
Jack Katz   68

**4.2 The media politics of crime
and criminal justice**
Philip Schlesinger, Howard Tumber
and Graham Murdock   71

**4.3 On the continuing problem of
media effects**
Sonia Livingstone   75

4.4 The sociology of moral panics
Stanley Cohen   79

Introduction

Much of what we know, or we think we know, about crime is drawn from the mass media: television, newspapers, radio, cinema and, increasingly, the internet. Take a look at today's television schedules. Have a quick scan of the titles of the films that are on the cinema this week. Pick up today's newspaper and see what the main news stories are. I'm sure you will quickly come across a whole range of crime-related material. Given the centrality of the mass media it is important that we think about the impact it has on crime. Is what we see and read an accurate representation of what is actually happening in our society and, if not, why not? How are the media used by criminal justice institutions such as the police? Does the emergence of new media, such as the internet, lead to new criminal opportunities? These are just a few of the questions that concern criminologists.

One apparently simple question is what makes crime 'news'? As Jack Katz **(Reading 4.1)** shows, however, this is another example which appears straightforward but is actually deceptively complex. Katz illustrates a number of ways in which the reporting of crime in the news departs in important ways from what we know about the frequency of crime in reality. However, he argues that the appearance of particular types of crime story illustrates the capacity of such stories to illuminate and help us deal with particular problems, dilemmas and moral problems that are the stuff of everyday life. Consuming crime news, he argues, is part of our 'daily moral routine'.

The excerpt from Philip Schlesinger and colleagues **(Reading 4.2)** also explores media content, and looks in some detail at what television and print media publish by way of crime-related information and stories. They illustrate the relative preoccupation with violence against the person in the national press and the television news, and the variation that exists amongst newspapers – according to the nature of their intended audience – of their crime coverage. What is the relevance of this? Well, first, it helps us in our attempts to interpret how the media work and, second, it potentially enables us to become more sophisticated readers and consumers of what such outlets produce.

One very long-standing segment of media research has been that on so-called 'media effects': focusing primarily on the impact of television on its audience. Sonia Livingstone **(Reading 4.3)** reviews this research and shows how difficult it is to draw hard and fast conclusions. She examines research which suggests that there may be some beneficial effects as well as that work which points in more negative directions. As you will see her overall conclusion, echoing that of Schramm *et al.* (1964), is studiously limited in the claims it makes.

Stan Cohen **(Reading 4.4)** looks at the role of the mass media in selecting targets for news production and, more particularly, how such choices can serve to trigger a variety of public responses. His focus is on a series of disturbances between two youth subcultural groups – the mods and the rockers – in the early 1960s, and how the disorder that was involved was exaggerated and distorted. Cohen suggests that the social scientific preoccupation with direct 'media effects' on individuals, particularly those who break rules and laws, has been at the expense of attempting to understand the effects of the media on the control agents themselves and, indirectly, through processes such as 'amplification' on deviancy itself. Cohen introduces the important term *moral panics* and illustrates how the process of deviancy amplification works – in effect a cycle in which initial problems provoke social reactions, leading to a response by control organizations, the creation of new deviancy and, as a consequence, the confirmation of the initial stereotype.

Questions for discussion

1. In what ways might representations of crime in the media be inaccurate (and why)?

2. What does Katz mean when he suggests that the preponderance of serious crimes in the news is evidence of interest that is 'less morbid than inspirational'?

3. What are the main differences between national newspapers in their crime coverage?

4. What are the main difficulties encountered when trying to assess the nature and degree of 'media effects'?

5. What are the main ways in which the mass media might influence human behaviour?

6. How would you summarize the overall conclusion of media effects research?

7. What is meant by the terms 'folk devil' and 'moral panic'?

8. How does 'deviancy amplification' work?

4.1 What makes crime 'news'?
Jack Katz

Crime news, crime statistics and reader interest

As an initial point, it is clear that the meaning of crime news, whatever it may be, is important to news readers. Crime news has been continually present in the metropolitan daily for about 150 years. It might be argued that if this long record ever did indicate a strong interest among readers, it no longer does. Perhaps today's more educated (and presumably more sophisticated) readers ignore crime news or read with only superficial interest, failing to absorb content. The evidence is otherwise. Graber (1980: 50–1) asked a panel of Chicago-area news readers to recite details of news stories on a variety of topics. She found their recall of stories on crime exceeded their recall of stories on many other matters, including education, congressional activities, conflicts in the Middle East, and state government. Recall of news about crime was at about the same, relatively high, level as recall of news about accidents and political gossip. On an average day, stories on crime and justice comprise about 15 percent of the topics actually read.[1]

The fact that readers find crime news spontaneously involving does not mean that news organizations are not biasing the public appearance of crime in the news. Indeed there are systematic biases in the reporting of crime news, at least in the respect that crime as presented in the daily news differs consistently from crime as described in official police statistics. In order to home in on what it is that readers find so interesting in crime news, we should clarify the nature of this 'bias.'

Comparisons of crime news and crime statistics have produced consistent findings. In study after study, the content of crime news has been found to diverge widely from the patterns available in official statistics. The relationship does not appear to be random or incoherent: in many respects, the picture one obtains about crime from reading the newspapers inverts the picture about crime one gets from reading police statistics. In a recent study of thirty years of front-page crime news in each of nine cities, Jacob (1980) found that violent crime made up about 70 percent of crime news and about 20 percent of the official crime rate. Sherizen (1978: 215) computed the percentages of crimes known to the police (FBI Schedule 1 types) that were reported in four Chicago newspapers in 1975: 70 percent of homicide cases were reported, five percent of the rapes, one percent of larceny/thefts. He concluded: 'the more prevalent the crime, the less…reported'. This systematic 'over-representation' of violent crime in the news is also characteristic of black community newspapers (Ammons et al., 1982). And in a study of British newspapers, Roshier (1973) similarly found that crimes against the person were consistently over-represented in contrast to official criminal statistics. (See also Jones, 1976, on St. Louis; and the review in Garofalo, 1981: 323).

News reporting of white-collar and common crimes has also been found to reverse the relationship found in official statistics. In our set of federal crime news stories published in New York between 1974 and 1978, about 66 percent concerned white-collar crimes and 21 percent, common crimes. In a separate study, we counted the types of cases which, according to federal court records, were actually prosecuted during these years in the local jurisdictions. Court records showed the inverse of news reports: about 22 percent of filed criminal cases charged white-collar crimes, 70 percent, common crimes. This over-representation of white-collar crime has been documented in studies of newspaper coverage of all crimes, state and federal. Roshier (1973: 34), on British papers, and Graber (1980: 38, 40) on Chicago papers, also found an over-representation of higher social class offenders: the *Chicago Tribune* identified about 70 percent of the criminals as white and about 75 percent as from middle or upper socioeconomic statuses.[2]

Daily crime news reading as a ritual moral exercise

Although the frequency of news stories on homicides, violent robberies and rapes might seem evidence of a 'lowbrow' insensitivity in the modern public, an opposite interpretation is more revealing and more consistent with the overall patterns in crime news. The interest is less morbid than inspirational. If portrayals of violent crime show in the extreme the lack of sensibility with which members of our society may treat each other, readers' appetites for such stories suggest that they are not so coarse as to take for granted a destructive personal insensitivity. The fact that assaults on property are far less newsworthy than assaults on the person indicates that readers' fundamental concerns are more humanistic than material. Or rather, by picking up the paper to read about yet another brutal crime, readers can attempt to sustain their conviction that their own moral sensibility has not yet been brutalized into a jaded indifference. The predominance of stories on violent crime in contemporary newspapers can be understood as serving readers' interests in re-creating daily their moral sensibilities through shock and impulses of outrage.

Instead of the empirically ambiguous idea that crime becomes interesting to the extent that it is 'unexpected', and in place of a simple invocation of Durkheim's ideas, I would argue that crime news is taken as interesting in a process through which adults in contemporary society work out individual perspectives on moral questions of a quite general yet eminently personal relevance.

Each of the categories of crime news relates to a type of non-criminal, moral question that adults confront daily. First, crime stories with implications about personal competence and sensibility are taken as interesting because readers sense that they must deal with analogous questions in everyday life. In routine interactions with others, we must make assumptions about their essential qualities, assumptions about the age competencies of the young or old, about qualities related to gender, or about qualities like intelligence (which today are less politically controversial but no more visible than the competencies supposedly associated with age and sex). If children can hold up banks, should we take as serious the statement by our 7-year-old that he would like to kill his younger brother? If there is a 'Grandma Mafia', should we be concerned that the elderly woman behind us in the supermarket line may have a lethal intent as she rams her cart into our rear?

We must also make assumptions constantly about our own essential competencies and sensibilities. The question of audacity is faced not only by criminals. How daring, how ingenious, can I be? Would it be admirably daring; just reasonably cautious; or really, recklessly foolish to submit a paper for publication in its current draft? Crime news is of widespread interest because it speaks dramatically to issues that are of direct relevance to readers' existential challenges, whether or not readers are preoccupied with the possible personal misfortune of becoming victims to crime.

Similarly, the second group of crime news stories, those that depict threats to sacred centres of society, are deemed interesting because readers understand that they themselves must work day after day, to define moral perspectives on questions about elusive collective entities. The interest in such stories comes not just from the practical necessity of evaluating the physical safety of different places, but from inescapable encounters with enigmas of collective identity. In contemporary bourgeois life, questions of physical safety are of minor relevance compared to questions about collective moral character – mundane, recurrent questions such as, What's a 'nice' (morally clean) place to take the family to dinner? [...]

As to the third category of crime news, stories reflecting preexisting tensions among groups, people in persistent political conflict often hunger for moral charges to use against the character of their opponents. They find satisfying morsels in crime news.

Finally, what process of daily stimulation might be behind the widespread taste for news of white-collar crime? I would suggest that the newsworthiness of white-collar crime is constructed in a dialectical relationship to the moral routines of everyday life. The crimes of people in high white-collar occupations are especially newsworthy, not because they are shocking or surprising – not because such people are presumed to be more conforming, decent, respectable or trustworthy than blue-collar workers or the unemployed; but because they *have to be treated as if they are.*

It is certainly inadequate to attribute the newsworthiness of white-collar crime to shocked expressions of honour. News readers maintain appetites for stories of white-collar crime, day after day – another congressman caught taking bribes!; another multinational corporation caught corrupting foreign governments! – while common crimes committed by poor, young, minority males continue in their redundant, typically non-newsworthy procession, because every day, in infinite ways, news readers only feel forced to enact trust in and deference towards the former. However cynical a person's view of the morality of business, political, and civic institutional leaders, he or she lives surrounded by symbols of their superior status: their towering offices, their advertised qualities on subway or bus placards or on TV commercials, their names on hospitals. Readers of a news story about white-collar crime recall that they have made many payments to that firm; that they were moved around by that airplane or bus company; that they have had their neighbourhood or recreational environment defined by the politicians or lay leaders; that each day at work they must defer to person in that type of superior status. The newsworthiness of white-collar crime owes much to the routine moral character of the division of labour. (On the 'moral division of labour', see Hughes, 1971).

I have argued that crime news takes its interest from routinely encountered dilemmas, not from concerns focused on crime. The reading of crime news is not a process of idle moral reflection on past life; it is an eminently practical, future-oriented activity. In reading crime news, people recognize and use the moral tale within the slot to orient themselves towards existential dilemmas they cannot help but confront. [...]

The experience of reading crime news induces the reader into a perspective useful for taking a stand on existential moral dilemmas. The dilemmas of imputing personal competence and sustaining one's own moral sensibility, of honouring sacred centres of collective being, of morally crediting and discrediting political opponents, and of deferring to the moral superiority of elites, cannot be resolved by deduction from rational discourse. In these moral areas, a measure of faith – of understanding a position of making a commitment that underlies the reasons that can be given for one's beliefs – is an essential part of everyday social life. Crime news accordingly moves the reader through emotions rather than discursive logic, triggering anger and fear rather than argumentation.

Like vitamins useful in the body only for a day, like physical exercise whose value comes from its recurrent practice, crime news is experienced as interesting by readers because of its place in a daily moral routine.

> *From J. Katz, 'What makes crime 'news'?',* Media, Culture and Society, *1987, 9: 47–75.*

Notes

1   Other studies are supportive (Dominick, 1978: 110). Schramm (1949: 264) found no patterned difference in the reading of 'intermediate reward news', a category which included the comics, crime news, sports and society news, although economic status was significantly (and directly) related to reading of public affairs news.

2   Dominick (1978) studied crimes reported on the front pages of the *New York Times* and the *Los Angeles Times* in 1950, 1960 and 1969. Although he found that violent crime was covered at three times the rate of white-collar crime, these figures, when compared to statistics on prosecution, still indicate an over-representation of white-collar crime. State district attorneys file more than ten times as many cases as do federal district attorneys, and white-collar criminal cases are so rare as to be virtually invisible in state court statistics. See the literature review in Davis (1982: 32). Gans (1980: 141), examining the news on TV and in weekly magazines, found about equal coverage of 'knowns' and 'unknowns' in trouble with the law, a pattern of equality which again, when compared to statistics on official action, shows a strong bias towards the coverage of people of higher social status.

References

Ammons, L., Dimmick, J. and Pilotta, J. (1982) 'Crime News Reporting in a Black Weekly', *Journalism Quarterly*, 59: 310–13.

Davis, J.R. (1982) *The Sentencing Dispositions of New York City Lower Court Criminal Judges*. Washington, DC: University Press of America.

Dominick, J.R. (1978) 'Crime and Law Enforcement in the Mass Media', pp. 105–28 in C. Winick (ed.), *Deviance and Mass Media*. Beverly Hills: Sage.

Gans, H. (1980) *Deciding What's News*. New York: Vintage Books.

Garofalo, J. (1981) 'Crime and the Mass Media: A Selective Review of Research', *Journal of Research in Crime and Delinquency*, 18: 319–49.

Graber, D. (1980) *Crime News and the Public*. New York: Praeger.

Hughes, E.C. (1971) 'The Study of Occupations', pp. 283–97 in E.C. Hughes, *The Sociological Eye*, Vol. 1. Chicago: Aldine-Atherton.

Jamb, H. (1980) 'Police and Newspaper Presentations of Crime: An Examination of Nine Cities, 1948–78'. Unpublished manuscript, Department of Political

Science, Northwestern University, Evanston, Illinois.

Jones, E.T. (1976) 'The Press as Metropolitan Monitor', *Public Opinion Quarterly*, 40: 239–44.

Roshier, B. (1973) 'The Selection of Crime News by the Press', pp. 28–39 in S. Cohen and J. Young (eds), *The Manufacture of News*. Beverly Hills: Sage.

Schramm, W. (1949) 'The Nature of News', *Journalism Quarterly*. 26: 259–69.

Sherizen, S. (1978) 'Social Creation of Crime News', pp. 203–24 in C. Winick (ed.), *Deviance and Mass Media*. Beverly Hills: Sage.

4.2 The media politics of crime and criminal justice
Philip Schlesinger, Howard Tumber and Graham Murdock

Much recent media research has been based upon a 'dominant ideology thesis'.[1] Using either a neo-Gramscian theory of hegemony[2] or a 'propaganda model',[3] it has been argued that the power of politically and economically dominant groups in the society defines the parameters of debate, ensures the privileged reproduction of their discourse, and by extension, largely determines the contours of the dominant ideology of what is socially thinkable.

Whether culturalist or political-economic in emphasis, such work has paid inadequate attention to the communication process as a whole. Specifically, it has neglected the conflictual processes that lie behind the moment of definition both inside central social institutions and within the media themselves. Furthermore, such work has been characterised by a tendency to treat media as homogeneous, as the media. This largely ignores the distinctiveness of particular media (say, the press or television) and the ways in which such media are internally differentiated (e.g. the 'popular' vs the 'quality' press). [...]

Some features of media content

Media representations are a key moment in the process whereby public discourses concerning crime and justice are made available for general consumption. They are the end result of the strategies and practices deployed by sources and media personnel outlined earlier and one of the means whereby audiences make sense of this domain. Consequently, we have aimed to provide an account of patterns of coverage in the two major mass media, the national press and television. We were particularly interested in charting the similarities and divergencies in coverage within and between these two media. Did tabloid, mid-market and quality newspapers differ significantly in their patterns of attention and exclusion and in the ways in which they presented material? Did broadcast television 'hold the middle ground'? [...]

Tables 4.2.1 and 4.2.2 show between 18 and 29 percent of all crime-related items recorded for the national daily press and national television news mentioned offences against property, and more detailed analysis revealed that most of these were related to City scandals rather than to more routine property offences such as burglary and theft.

Recent American studies of prime-time fiction and entertainment programming also show a strong bias towards the misdeeds of the powerful with the majority of offenders being white males aged between 20 and 50 in white collar jobs. Conversely, blacks, young people and members of the working class are under-represented.[4] We need to be cautious in applying this argument directly to British television, however, since it takes no account of the mediating effects of genre.[5]

Also noteworthy is the distribution of attention to different kinds of discourse in the print media. This is somewhat crudely indicated by variations in the space allocated to the views of different groups and individuals. As Table 4.2.3 shows, there are important differences between the top and bottom ends of the newspaper market, particularly amongst daily titles. Whilst the quality dailies are focused upon Parliament and government, and offer space to the views of experts, elites and pressure groups, tabloid newspapers give far greater play to the opinions and perspectives offered by the victims of crime and their relatives and by those suspected or convicted of crimes. They are more oriented, that is, to 'common sense' thinking and discourse, and less to professionalised debate and the evaluation of policy. These variations throw light upon the complexity of the process of 'secondary definition' through

Table 4.2.1: Percentages of crime-related items in national daily newspapers mentioning various types of offence

Type of offence	Type of newspaper		
	Quality	Mid-market	Tabloid
Non-sexual violence against the person	24.7%	38.8%	45.9%
Sexual offences	7.2%	9.3%	11.3%
Non-violent offences against the person	3.7%	5.1%	4.4%
Drug offences	3.1%	5.4%	6.4%
Offences against animals	0.4%	0.2%	0.3%
Property offences	25.7%	23.2%	18.8%
Corporate offences	5.3%	5.9%	4.1%
Offences against the justice system	1.9%	2.4%	2.3%
Offences against the state	5.0%	4.6%	2.8%
Number of items	835	410	388

Notes: (1) More than one type of offence could be recorded for each item.
(2) Only items dealing with the UK are represented in these figures.

the media, as they suggest that the distribution and hierarchy of discourses between different types of daily newspaper may vary significantly in relation to different readerships.

The second major set of differences concerns variations in the general pattern of attention to crime within the national press. As Table 4.2.1 shows, the overall distribution confirms the commonsense distinctions made between quality, mid-market and tabloid newspapers. Whereas almost half (46 per cent) of crime-related items in the daily tabloids mention violent crimes against

Table 4.2.2: Percentages of crime-related television news items mentioning various types of offence

Type of offence	News items on		National news bulletins on		
	National bulletins	Local bulletins	ITV	BBC1	Channel 4
Non-sexual violence against the person	40.0%	63.2%	43.5%	42.3%	18.2%
Sexual offences	5.5%	8.8%	8.7%	–	9.1%
Non-violent offences against the person	8.3%	8.8%	10.0%	5.8%	9.1%
Drug offences	4.8%	1.8%	5.8%	3.8%	4.5%
Offences against animals	0.7%	5.3%	–	1.9%	–
Property offences	23.4%	12.3%	20.3%	26.9%	27.3%
Corporate offences	2.1%	1.8%	2.9%	1.9%	–
Public order offences	18.6%	5.3%	14.5%	23.1%	18.2%
Offences against the justice system	7.6%	7.0%	10.1%	7.7%	–
Offences against the state	6.2%	–	4.3%	9.6%	4.5%
Number of items	145	57	69	52	22

Notes: (1) More than one type of offence could be recorded for each item.
(2) Only items dealing with the UK are represented in these figures.
(3) This table refers solely to news bulletins and excludes daily current affairs programmes. Consequently, BBC2, which does not carry a nightly bulletin, has not been included in the channel columns. However, two news flashes on BBC are included in the item total for all national bulletins.

Table 4.2.3: Percentages of crime-related items in national daily newspapers containing the views or comments of selected groups

Group	Type of newspaper		
	Quality	Mid-market	Tabloid
Members of the Government and Conservative MPs	15.7%	8.0%	5.7%
MPs from opposition parties	11.9%	8.0%	3.6%
Local goverment officials and local politicians	3.8%	3.4%	1.0%
Judges, lawyers and court officials	19.9%	17.6%	18.8%
Police and law enforcement sources	12.2.%	15.1%	16.2%
Probation and prison workers	1.3%	1.0%	1.8%
Experts/elites/members of lobby and pressure group	21.7%	17.3%	11.3%
Victims, suspects' relatives and criminals	13.4%	22.9%	24.2%
Vox pops, members of general public	3.0%	4.4%	7.0%
Number of items	835	410	388

Notes: (1) More than one type of offence could be recorded for each item.
　　　 (2) Only items dealing with the UK are represented in these figures.

the person, the corresponding figure for the quality dailies is only 25 per cent, with mid-market papers falling almost exactly in between. A similar, though far less dramatic, pattern emerges in the coverage of sexual offences and offences involving drugs.

As Table 4.2.4 shows, these differences are also evident in variations in the prominence given to stories featuring different kinds of crime. Although their smaller page size results in mid-market and tabloid dailies carrying far fewer crime-related items on their front pages than the quality titles, those that do appear are twice as likely to feature violent crimes against the person (45 per cent as against 22 per cent). Tabloids and mid-market papers are also far more likely to feature sexual offences on the front page than are quality papers. In other words, the world of front-page crime in the 'popular' press (both tabloid and mid-market)

Table 4.2.4: Percentages of crime-related items on the front pages of national daily newspapers mentioning various types of offence

Type of offence	Type of newspaper		
	Quality	Mid-market	Tabloid
Non-sexual violence against the person	22.0%	45.0%	45.5%
Sexual offences	2.8%	20.0%	22.7%
Non-violent offences against the person	5.5%	10.0%	22.7%
Drug offences	–	5.0%	4.5%
Property offences	35.8%	40.0%	27.3%
Corporate offences	6.4%	–	–
Public order offences	6.4%	5.0%	–
Offences against the justice system	0.9%	–	13.6%
Offences against the state	8.3%	10.0%	–
Number of items	109	20	22

Notes: (1) More than one type of offence could be recorded for each item.
　　　 (2) Only items dealing with the UK are represented in these figures.

is primarily oriented towards personalised crime affecting identifiable individuals, with a strong emphasis on interpersonal violence.

Turning now to some of the findings for television news (shown in Table 4.2.2), several points are worth noting. First, the overall pattern of attention to different kinds of violent crimes against the person, drug offences, and property offences in national television news approximates to the pattern established for the mid-market dailies, lending weight to the argument that in certain key areas television news seeks the 'middle ground'. However, as Table 4.2.2 also shows, this pattern is by no means consistent across all categories of offence. Compared to all types of national daily paper, television news pays rather more attention to offences relating to public order, to the justice system and to the state.

Second, compared to the national bulletins, local news gives markedly more attention to violent crimes against the person, which perhaps suggests a heavy reliance on the police and courts (and the local press) as sources of news items. Third, there are some important differences between channels, with violent crimes against the person attracting many more mentions on the two 'popular' channels, BBCI and ITV, than on the more 'upmarket' Channel 4. Indeed, the pattern for ITV more closely approximates to the pattern displayed by the tabloid dailies – particularly in the areas of interpersonal violence, sexual crimes, and drug offences.

These different patterns of emphasis in coverage have important implications for our understanding of audience perceptions, since they suggest that differences in newspaper readership and television viewing may regulate access to significant variations in discourses about crime.

From P. Schlesinger, H. Tumbler and G. Murdock, 'The media politics of crime and criminal justice', British Journal of Sociology, *1991, 42: 397–420.*

Notes

1 N. Abercrombie, S. Hill, and B. S. Turner, *The Dominant Ideology Thesis*, London: George Allen and Unwin, 1980, and *ibid.*, *Sovereign Individuals of Capitalism*, London, Allen and Unwin, 1986.
2 S. Hall, C. Critcher, T. Jefferson, J. Clarke, and B. Roberts, *Policing the Critic: Mugging, the State and Law and Order*, London, MacMillan, 1978.
3 E.H. Herman and N. Chomsky, *Manufacturing Consent: The Political Economy of the Mass Media*, New York, Pantheon Books, 1988.
4 L.S. Lichter and S.R. Lichter, *Prime Time Crime: Criminals and Law Enforcers in TV Entertainment*, Washington DC, The Media Institute, 1983.
5 Crime is shown in a greater variety of contexts on this side of the Atlantic because the system supports a wider range of programme formats – from the street-level inner city policing of *The Bill*, through the complexly contextualised offences in *EastEnders*, to the boardroom struggles of *Howard's Way*. Different formats organise discourse and imagery diversely though their patterns of exclusion and emphasis and their construction of varying points of view of the actions presented. In soap operas such as *Brookside or EastEnders*, routine crimes emerge out of well-established situations and milieux and are committed by characters the audience knows well. In contrast, the action in *The Bill* (which shares many of the basic features of a soap opera) is viewed through the eyes of the police. We see only the incident or its aftermath. It is something to be dealt with. The motivations involved often remain obscure. These variations suggest a possible link between differences in patterns of media consumption and differences in public perceptions and attitudes.

4.3 On the continuing problem of media effects
Sonia Livingstone

The scope and context of media effects research

The effects tradition

The 'effects tradition' focuses predominantly but not exclusively on the effects of television rather than other media, on the effects on the child audience especially, on the effects of violent or stereotyped programmes, on effects on individuals rather than on groups, cultures or institutions.

Media effects: a matter of change or reinforcement?

If by media effects we mean that exposure to the media changes people's behaviour or beliefs, then the first task is to see whether significant correlations exist between levels of exposure and variations in behaviour or beliefs. 'Change' theories – on which this chapter will focus – generally presume that the more we watch the greater the effect. Most research does show such a correlation (Signorelli and Morgan, 1990), albeit a small and not always consistent one. The next question concerns the direction of causality. For example, having shown that those who watch more violent television tend to be more aggressive (Huesmann, 1982), researchers must ask whether more aggressive people choose to watch violent programmes (i.e. selective exposure), whether violent programmes make viewers aggressive (i.e. media effects), or whether certain social circumstances both make people more aggressive and lead them to watch more violent television (i.e. a common third cause). To resolve this issue, the effects tradition has generally adopted an experimental approach, arguing that only in controlled experiments can people be randomly assigned to experimental and control conditions, thereby controlling for any other variables in the situation. Only then can causal inferences be drawn concerning any observed correlation between the experimental manipulation (generally media exposure) and resultant behaviour.

In research on media violence, some researchers offer a bidirectional argument, concluding that there is evidence for both selective viewing and media effects (Huesmann et al., 1984). Undoubtedly, many viewers choose selectively to watch violent or stereotyped programmes (after all there has always been a market for violent images). However, it does not necessarily follow that there are no effects of viewing such programmes or that motivated viewers can successfully undermine any possible effects. Many remain concerned especially for the effects of violent programmes on children and so-called vulnerable individuals, irrespective of whether they chose to watch them.

However, if by media effects we mean that the media do not generate specific changes but rather reinforce the status quo, then empirical demonstration of media effects becomes near impossible.

The contested findings of experimental effects research

The classic experiment

Let us first consider the prototypical effects study. As part of a series of experiments during the 1960s, Bandura and colleagues (Bandura et al., 1961, 1963) investigated the notion that children imitate the behaviours they see on television, particularly when enacted by admired role models or when the behaviours viewed are rewarded. Four- to five-year-old children were shown a five-minute film in the researcher's office and then taken to a toy room and observed for twenty minutes through a one-way mirror. Children had been randomly assigned to watch one of three films, each involving a boy picking a fight with another boy and attacking some toys. In the first, the attacker won the fight and was rewarded by getting all the toys to play with; in the second the attacker is beaten by his opponent and is punished; in the third, the two children play together with no aggression. In addition, a fourth group of children was observed with no prior exposure to a film. The results showed that those children, especially the boys, who had seen the rewarded aggressive model spontaneously performed twice as much imitative aggression as all other groups (including kicking a large 'Bobo' doll), but no more non-imitative aggression. When interviewed afterwards, these children were found to disapprove of the model's behaviour and yet they were influenced to imitate him because his aggression led to success.

Turner *et al.* (1986) argue that there are significant parallels between the situation in Bandura's experiment and that of the domestic viewing situation; children may and often do identify with characters who are rewarded for their aggression in television programmes. More aggressive children are more likely to watch violent television (Huesmann and Eron, 1986), thus enhancing the likelihood of an effect. Being arbitrarily provoked before viewing also enhances the effect. Borden (1975) argues that such findings are an artefact of the demand characteristics of the experiment (that children sense what is expected of them and try to please), for children are more likely to imitate the aggressive behaviour if an adult in the test situation is seen to approve. Yet arguably, in the context of the playground, and sometimes in the home, aggressive behaviour is indeed approved by others, especially by and for boys. Does it make sense to suggest that the 'real' child has been taken over by one influenced by social desirability if such influences also occur elsewhere?

What kinds of violence portrayals are effective?

As, increasingly, real television programmes, rather than artificial extracts, are shown to viewers, questions about types of portrayal can be addressed. The greatest antisocial effects are found to be associated with the news, particularly the portrayal of justified and realistic violence with no negative consequences (such as when police control a riot). Cartoons, containing no justified violence and the negative consequences of aggression, are much less effective (Hearold, 1986). Whether or not the consequences of violence are shown – even if children can connect a portrayed action to its consequences (Collins, 1983) – seems less important than whether the programme provides a justification for the violence and whether the portrayal is realistic (Dorr, 1983; Hodge and Tripp, 1986). As there is some suggestion that these conclusions are reversed for very young children, the need to differentiate children of different ages is critical.

What about positive effects of television?

The bulk of effects research is concentrated on harmful media effects, with some exceptions (Davies, 1989). There are far fewer studies of the prosocial effects (such as helping, kindness, cooperation) which might result from viewing positive images of social relations. Interestingly, the results

for such studies are far less controversial, although the same methodological problems apply. Generally researchers conclude that while, unfortunately, few prosocial television programmes exist, they have broadly beneficial effects and these effects are more substantial than for harmful effects. Comparing across many experiments, Hearold (1986) found that the overall effect size is around an extra 20 per cent of antisocial responses following violent or stereotyped content compared with an extra 50 per cent of prosocial responses following prosocial content, after a single viewing session.

How big are the effects of television?

Hearold (1986) conducted a meta-analysis of 1043 media effects reported in 230 studies with over 100,000 subjects over the past 60 years. In general, the correlations between viewing and effect vary between 0.1 and 0.3. These are small effects, and findings which meet the criteria for statistical significance are not necessarily socially significant. It is a matter of judgement whether effects which account for some 5 per cent of the variation in the behaviour concerned are important or not and whether they are more or less important than other factors. A satisfactory explanation of social phenomena, such as violence, stereotypes, consumerism or prejudice, will involve understanding the combined and interactive effects of multiple factors, of which television may be one such factor, although probably not a major one.

How long do the effects last?

Few experiments follow up media effects over time. Those which do tend to show a drop in effect size of about one quarter over the two weeks following exposure, but the effects are still present (Hearold, 1986). Hicks (1965) showed that a Bandura-type experiment resulted in aggressive behaviours being well remembered, although little performed, six months after viewing. However, given the daily nature of television exposure, one might argue that persistent effects are less important than immediate and cumulative effects.

One advantage of correlational studies is that, although they cannot easily discriminate either causal direction or the operation of underlying causes, they can follow up their respondents over several years. Eron *et al.* (1972), Huesmann *et al.* (1984) and others generally show a positive correlation between viewing at one time and aggression some years later, even when parental, family, and socio-economic variables are taken into account.

Common criticisms of experimental research

The artificiality of effects experiments has been heavily criticized (Cumberbatch, 1989b; Freedman, 1984; Noble, 1975) – for example, for their use of artificial stimuli rather than real programmes (which was especially true of earlier but not of more recent studies), and for their measurement of short-term effects, with few follow-up studies.

Can we draw any conclusions?

Most reviews of the literature agree that viewers learn both prosocial and antisocial attitudes and behaviour from television portrayals (Comstock and Paik, 1991; Liehert *et al.*, 1982; Roberts and Bachen, 1981; Rubinstein, 1983). Children can learn new prosocial or aggressive behaviours from a single exposure; violence portrayed as punished is less likely to be imitated; violent images in the news affect older children more, while younger children are more affected by cartoons; boys, younger children and more aggressive children are more influenced by antisocial content; and so forth. Most would also agree that, having learned these behaviours, viewers can be shown to reenact these or related behaviours under experimental conditions.

However, none of this need imply, and it certainly does not show, that beliefs or behaviours learned under experimental conditions can be generalized to viewers' everyday lives, whether routinely or on occasion. Indeed, results which are relatively consistent in the experimental literature have generally been poorly replicated under naturalistic conditions, although relatively few studies have attempted this. [...] This leads us then to field experiments, which study the possible changes in children's ordinary behaviour as a result of an experimental intervention into an everyday setting, and to naturalistic experiments, where real life, on occasion, provides the conditions for an experimental test with no intervention required.

Different research designs, different results

A central problem for effects research is the lack, at least in contemporary western society, of a group of people who have not been exposed to the media in their lives but who in all other respects are similar to those who have been exposed to the media.

With whom can we compare television viewers: the problem of control groups

Interestingly, naturalistic experiments – studies with 'real' control groups which were either conducted during the 1950s or on data from the 1950s – tend to show rather minor effects, although of course, labelling effects as 'minor' especially when they are cumulative, is a matter of judgement about what is socially important. Two kinds of study will be illustrated below: the first involved analyses of social statistics from the 1950s; the second compared those with and without television and was conducted during the 1950s. Hennigan *et al.* (1982) reasoned that, if television violence was making its audience more aggressive and violent, then this should be reflected in the crime statistics. Fortunately for them, the introduction of television across America during the 1950s was interrupted by the Federal Communications Commission between 1949 and 1952, so that there existed cities equivalent in other respects which gained television at different points in time. Analysis of the crime statistics for both categories of city before and after the freeze on introduction of television, showed no impact whatsoever on the incidence of violent crimes. However, they found that:

> in 1951, larceny increased in a sample of 34 cities where television had just been introduced, relative to a sample of 34 cities where the FCC freeze prevented access to television broadcasts. In 1955, larceny theft increased in the 34 cities that had just gained access to television, relative to the 34 cities that had been receiving broadcasts for several years. (p. 473)

The observed increase was of the order of 5 per cent. They suggest that explanations other than that of a media effect are hard to support. For example, it may be that television content makes the police and public more crime-conscious and so increases reported statistics, but why would this occur just for property crime? Hennigan *et al.* (1982) explain their findings by noting that the overwhelming majority of television programmes portray middle-class characters enjoying comfortable material lifestyles while poorer characters receive more negative portrayals. Combined with the exposure to television advertising, they suggest an effect of increasingly materialistic values, frustration at inequalities, and, for some, the resort to crime.

This explanation fits the findings of Himmelweit *et al.* (1958) from their comparison of children with and without television, matched for age, sex, social class and intelligence, during the 1950s. They also compared the responses of a smaller sample in Norwich both before and one year after the city received television transmission, again pairing those with and without television. As a multi-method, naturalistic experiment conducted with nearly 2000 children, this study has been given considerable weight in the literature. Yet the study did not find large effects. Of a range of findings, some key points can he summarized. While they reported similar thoughts about jobs, values and success before television entered their homes, after a year of having television children reported more ambitions, more 'middle-class' job values, and more concern with self-confidence and success than did the control sample, although their actual job expectations were unchanged. The lower ability 13-14-year olds, irrespective of social class, were most affected in these values.

Laboratory and field studies compared

[...] We are faced with a less than ideal situation, as four incompatible conclusions could be drawn: that the laboratory experiment demonstrates the existence of causal effects while the null effect of field experiments reflects their poor design and conduct; that the laboratory experiment is too artificial to be generalized to everyday life while the absence of effects under naturalistic conditions justifies this 'no effects' conclusion; that research findings depend on the method used, so no general conclusions are justified and researchers set out to show what they want to show; or that we can only draw conclusions from studies designed to examine causal processes under naturalistic conditions and so more and better field studies, with high internal and external validity, must be conducted.

Aren't all the findings contradictory?

Broad generalizations about the overall balance of evidence tend to be bland and cautious. For example, as a broad generality, it is still true, over thirty years later, that the fairest conclusion from research is that:

> for some children, under some conditions, some television is harmful. For some children under the same conditions, or for the same children under other conditions, it may be beneficial. For most children, under most conditions, most television is probably neither particularly harmful nor particularly beneficial. (Schramm *et al.* 1961: 11)

> *From S. Livingstone, 'On the continuing problem of media effects', in J. Curran and Gurevitch (eds)* Mass Media and Society, *2nd edn (London: Arnold), 1996, pp. 305–324.*

References

Bandura, A., Ross, D. and Ross, S.A. 1961: 'Transmission of aggression through imitation of aggressive models.' *Journal of Abnormal and Social Psychology* 63(3), 575–82.

— 1963: Vicarious reinforcement and imitative learning. *Journal of Abnormal and Social Psychology*, 67(6), 601–607.

Borden, R. J. 1975: 'Witnesses aggression: Influence of an observer's sex and values on aggressive responding.' *Journal of Personality and Social Psychology*, 31, 567–73.

Collins, W.A. 1983: 'Interpretation and inference in children's television viewing.' In J. Bryant and D.A. Anderson (eds), *Children's understanding of television*. New York: Academic Press.

Comstock, G. (1975) *Television and human behaviour: the key studies*. Santa Monica: The Rand Corporation.

Cumberbatch, G. 1989a: 'Overview of the effects of the mass media.' In G. Cumberbatch and D. Howitt (eds), *A measure of uncertainty: the effects of the mass media*. London: John Libbey and Company Ltd.

— 1989b: 'Violence and the mass media: the research evidence.' In G. Cumberbatch and D. Howitt (eds), *A measure of uncertainty: the effects of the mass media*. London: John Libbey & Company Ltd.

Davies. M.M. 1989: *Television is good for your kids*. London: Hilary Shipman Ltd.

Dorr, A. (1983): 'No shortcuts to judging reality.' In J. Bryant and D. Anderson (eds), *Children's understanding of television: research on attention and comprehension*. New York: Academic Press,

Eron, L.D., Huesmann, L.K, Lefkowitz, M. M., and Walder, L, O. 1972: 'Does television violence cause aggression?' *American Psychologist*, 27, 253–63.

Freedman, J.L. 1984: 'The effect of television violence on aggressiveness.' *Psychological Bulletin*, 96, 227–46.

Hearold, S. 1986: 'A synthesis of 1043 effects of television on social behaviour.' In G. Comstock (ed.), *Public communications and behaviour: Volume 1* (pp. 65–133). New York: Academic Press.

Hennigan. K.M., Delrosario, M.L., Heath, L., Cook, T.D., Wharton, J,D., and Calder, B.J. 1982: 'Impact of the introduction of television crime in the United States. Empirical findings and theoretical implications.' *Journal of Personality and Social Psychology*, 42, 461–77.

Hicks, D.J. 1965: 'Imitation and retention of film-mediated aggressive peer and adult models.' *Journal of Personality and Social Psychology*, 2(1), 97–100.

Himmelweit, H. T., Oppenheim, A.N., and Vince, P. 1958: *Television and the child: An empirical study of the effect of television on the young.* London: Oxford University Press.

Hodge, R., and Tripp, D. 1986: *Children and television: A semiotic approach.* Cambridge: Polity Press.

Huesmann, L. R. 1982: 'Television violence and aggressive behaviour.' In D. Pearl, L. Bouthilet, and J. Lazar (eds), *Television and behaviour.* Washington DC: NIMH.

Huesmann. L.R., and Eron, L.D. (ed.). 1986: *Television and the aggressive child: a cross-national comparison.* Hillsdale, New Jersey: Lawrence Erlbaum Associates.

Huesmann, L. R., Eron. L.D., and Lefkowitz, M M. 1984: Stability of aggression over time and generation. *Developmental Psychology*, 20(6), 1120–34.

Huesmann, L R., Lagerspetz, K, and Eron, L.D. 1984: 'Intervening variables in the TV violence-aggression relation: Evidence from two countries.' *Developmental Psychology*, 20(5), 746–75.

Liebert, R. M., Sprafkin, J.N., and Davidson, E. S. 1982: *The early window: Effects of television on children and youth.* New York: Pergamon.

Noble, G. 1975: *Children in front of the small screen.* London: Sage.

Roberts, D.F., and Bachen, C.M. 1981: 'Mass communication effects.' *Annual Review of Psychology*, 32, 307–56.

Rubinstein, E.A., 1983: 'Television and behavior: research conclusions of the 1982 NIMH report and their policy implications.' *American Psychologist*, 38(7), 820–25.

Schramm. W., Lyle, J., and Parker, E.B. 1961: *Television in the lives of our children.* Stanford, CA: Stanford University Press.

Signorelli, N., and Morgan, M (ed.) 1990: *Cultivation analysis: new directions in media effects research.* Newbury Park, CA: Sage.

Turner, C.W, Hesse, B.W., and Peterson-Lewis, S. 1986: 'Naturalistic studies of the long-term effects of television violence.' *Journal of Social Issues*, 42(3), 51–73.

4.4 The sociology of moral panics
Stanley Cohen

Just as the Mods and Rockers did not appear from nowhere, so too must the societal reaction, the moral panic, be explained. Magistrates, leader writers and politicians do not react like laboratory creatures being presented a series of random stimuli, but in terms of positions, statuses, interests, ideologies and values. Their responsiveness to rumours, for example, is not just related to the internal dynamics of the rumour process as described earlier, but whether the rumours support their particular interests.

The foundations of this particular moral panic should be understood in terms of different levels of generality. At the lowest level, there were those peculiar to the Mods and Rockers phenomenon; at the highest, abstract principles which can be applied to the sociology of moral panics as a whole or (even more generally) to a theory of the societal reactions to deviance. [...]

The sixties began the confirmation of a new era in adult-youth relations. The Teddy Boys (and their European equivalents – *the halbstarke*, the *blouson noir*) were the first warnings on the horizon. What everyone had grimly prophesied had come true: high wages, the emergence of a commercial youth culture 'pandering' to young people's needs, the elevation of scruffy pop heroes into national idols (and even giving them MBEs), the 'permissive society', the 'coddling by the Welfare State' – all this had produced its inevitable results. As one magistrate expressed it to me in 1965, 'Delinquency is trying to get at too many things too easily ... people have become more aware of the good things in life ... we've thrown back the curtain for them too soon.' [...]

The Mods and Rockers symbolized something far more important than what they actually did. They touched the delicate and ambivalent nerves through which post-war social change in Britain was experienced. No one wanted depressions or austerity, but messages about 'never having it so good' were ambivalent in that some people were having it too good and too quickly: 'We've thrown back the curtain for them too soon.' Resentment and jealousy were easily directed at the young, if only because of their increased spending power and sexual freedom. When this was combined with a too-open flouting of the work and leisure ethic, with violence and vandalism, and the (as yet) uncertain threats associated with drug-taking, something more than the image of a peaceful Bank Holiday at the sea was being shattered.

One might suggest that ambiguity and strain was greatest at the beginning of the sixties. The lines had not yet been clearly drawn and, indeed, the reaction was part of this drawing of the line. The period can be seen as constituting what Erikson terms a 'boundary crisis', a period in which a group's uncertainty about itself is resolved in ritualistic confrontations between the deviant and the community's official agents.[1] One does not have to make any conspiratorial assumptions about deviants being deliberately 'picked out' to clarify normative contours at times of cultural strain and ambiguity, to detect in the response to the Mods and Rockers declarations about moral boundaries, about how much diversity can be tolerated. As Erikson notes about so-called 'crime waves', they dramatize the issues at stake when boundaries are blurred and provide a forum to articulate the issues more explicitly. Two things might be happening here:

> ...the community begins to censure forms of behaviour which have been present in the group for some time but have never attracted any particular attention before, and ... certain people in the group who have already acquired a disposition to act deviantly move into the breach and begin to test the boundary in question.[2]

Again, the notion of 'deviantly disposed' people actually 'moving in' to test the boundary should not be taken too literally. One only has to account for some autonomous potential for defiance from young people to see how the spiral of conflict develops. The real Devil, whose shapes the early Puritans were trying to establish, was the same devil that the Mods and Rockers represented.

It should be noted that scapegoating and other types of hostility are more likely to occur in situations of maximum ambiguity. The fact that it was not very clear what the Mods and Rockers had actually done, might have increased rather than decreased the chances of an extreme reaction. Groups such as the Northview sample had a very

unclear image of the behaviour, but supported fairly punitive sanctions. The message that did percolate through confirmed suspicions that little good would come from the new era. The threats posed by the Teddy Boys might now be realized and the situation was ripe for beliefs such as those expressed in the It's Not Only This theme.

As soon as the new phenomenon was named, the devil's shape could be easily identified. In this context, the ways in which the deviance was associated with a fashion style is particularly significant. Fashion changes are not always perceived simply as something novel, a desire to be different or attract attention or as fads which will ultimately die out. They might be seen as signifying something much deeper and more permanent – for example, 'the permissive society' – and historically, stylistic changes have often represented ideological commitments or movements. So, for example, the Sans Culottes in the French Revolution wore long pants instead of conventional breeches as a symbol of radicalism and the American beatnik style became identified with certain signs of disaffiliation.

Mod fashions were seen to represent some more significant departure than a mere clothing change. The glossiness of the image, the bright colours and the associated artefacts such as motor scooters, stood for everything resented about the affluent teenager. There were also new anxieties, such as the sexual confusion in clothing and hairstyles: the Mod boy with pastel-shaded trousers and the legendary make-up on his face, the girls with their short-cropped hair and sexless, flat appearance. The sheer uniformity in dress was a great factor in making the threat more apparent: the cheap mass-produced anoraks with similar colours, and the occasional small group riding their Vespas like a menacing pincer patrol, gave the appearance of greater organization than ever existed, and hence of a greater threat.

The way in which a single dramatic incident – or, at least, the reporting of this incident – served to confirm the actors' deviant identity is also important. To draw on the analogy already used, the situation was similar to that in which a natural disaster brings to the surface a condition or conflict that previously was latent. The requirement of visibility – and hooliganism is by definition public and visible – so essential for successful problem definition, was met right from the outset. Mass collective action which before was played out on a more restricted screen, now was paraded even to audiences previously insulated by geographical, age and social class barriers.

This leads on to another major reason for the form of the reaction. The behaviour was presented and perceived as something more than a delinquent brawl and the Mods and Rockers could not be classified very plausibly as the ordinary slum louts associated with such behaviour in the past. They appeared to be affluent, well clothed and groomed and, above all, highly mobile. They had moved out of the bomb-sites in the East End and the streets of the Elephant and Castle. The various forms which hooliganism had taken in the past were not of the same order. [...] The street gangs of the slums and housing estates could, if not tolerated, simply be allocated the traditional delinquent position. This was just how you expected kids from that sort of area/home/school to behave. But now, things were literally and metaphorically too close to home. These were not just the slum louts whom one could disown, but faintly recognizable creatures who had crawled out from under some very familiar rocks.

Allied to threats posed by the new mobility (the groups' motor-bikes and scooters were obsessively seen as important) and the wider stage on which the behaviour was now being played out, was the image of class barriers breaking down in the emergence of the teenage culture. Traditionally, the deviant role had been assigned to the lower class urban male, but the Mods and Rockers appeared to be less class tied: here were a group of impostors, reading the lines which everyone knew belonged to some other group. Even their clothes were out of place: without leather jackets they could hardly be distinguished from bank clerks. [...]

The Mod was unique in that his actual appearance was far away from the stereotypical hooligan personified by the Teddy Boy or the Rocker. He was also nowhere near as identifiable as the beatnik or hippy. Dave Laing attributes the Mods' subversive potential to this very ordinariness. With few exceptions, their dress was neat and not obviously extreme: 'The office boys, typists and shop assistants looked alright, but there was something in the way they moved which adults couldn't make out.'[3] His disdain for advancement in work, his air of distance, his manifest display of ingratitude for what society had given him (this appears strongly in the Boredom and Affluence themes): these were found more unsettling than any simple conformity to the folklore image of the yob. The detection of a new element in deviance is found more disturbing than

being presented with forms which society has already successfully coped with.

Such feelings were even more understandable and pronounced in places like Brighton. The town had not yet come to terms with the fact that the old type of summer visitors and day-trippers from London were no longer coming to Brighton, but spending their holidays on package trips to the Costa Brava. The respectable working-class couples in their twenties and thirties were no longer packing out the boarding-houses or spending money in the traditional avenues of entertainment which had remained basically unchanged for decades. The very old were still coming down, but a coach-load of pensioners down for the day were hardly big spenders. [...]

The Mods and Rockers just represented the epitome of these changes; to many local residents, as a Brighton editor put it ' ... they were something frightening and completely alien ... they were visitors from a foreign planet and they should be banished to where they came from'. When in 1965 the new Mayor of Brighton outlined his vision of the town's future as 'a popular holiday resort where the whelk stalls and the Mods and Rockers will be a thing of the past', a local newspaper's editorial comment was 'Mods and Rockers we would gladly be without – they are a pricey pest. But whelk stalls?...' (*Brighton and Hove Gazette*, 4 June 1965).

It was not surprising then, that at the local level, any 'solution' not based on the policy of total exclusion met with hostility. The early voices of the Seaview and Beachside groups were echoed in the sustained campaign against schemes such as the Brighton Archways Ventures[4] and later presences such as those of beatniks and hippies in resorts like St Ives. As a Brighton Alderman said about the beatniks, 'These are people who ought not to be in Brighton and if they are unfortunately here, they ought not to be catered for in any way' (*Evening Argus*, 24 November 1967). The rhetoric of moral panics – 'We won't allow our seafront/area/town /country to be taken over by hooligans/hippies/ blacks/ Pakistanis' is a firmly established one.

If the Mods and Rockers had done nearly all they were supposed to have done in the way of violence, damage to property, inconveniencing and annoying others (and clearly they did a lot of these things), it does not need a very sophisticated analysis to explain why such rule-breaking was responded to punitively. But threats need not be as direct as this and one must understand that the response was as much to what they stood for as what they did.

Coming to an end

The one more or less explicit way in which the emergence of the Mods and Rockers as folk devils and the generation of the moral panic around this have been related to each other, is via the model of deviancy amplification. A very truncated form of how one such sequence may have run is illustrated below.

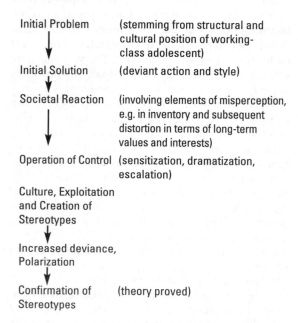

Initial Problem   (stemming from structural and cultural position of working-class adolescent)

Initial Solution   (deviant action and style)

Societal Reaction   (involving elements of misperception, e.g. in inventory and subsequent distortion in terms of long-term values and interests)

Operation of Control   (sensitization, dramatization, escalation)

Culture, Exploitation and Creation of Stereotypes

Increased deviance, Polarization

Confirmation of   (theory proved)
Stereotypes

Although it is not implausible to suggest that something like this sequence may have operated, one problem immediately apparent in any attempt to generalize too rigidly from it, is that no readily available explanation exists as to how and why the sequence ever ends. Putting the stages in some context – even as cursorily as this chapter has done – raises one defect of the amplification type of model, namely, that it is a-historical. This is paradoxical, because such processal models were put forward specifically to counteract static, canonical theories of deviance. Clearly, the use of cybernetic language such as feedback and stimuli is too automatic and mechanistic and does not allow for the range of meanings given to human action and the way in which the actor can move to shape his own passage. Both these elements can be examined if – taking the sequence merely as one typical movement in time – we try to answer the question of why it ever ended. What stopped the moral panic? Why do we still not have Mods and Rockers with us?

Looking firstly at the reaction from the public and the mass media, the answer is that there was simply a lack of interest. At no stage was there a simple one-to-one relationship between action and reaction: the Mod phenomenon developed before public attention branded it as evil, the attention continued ritualistically for a while even when the evil was subdued and finally the attention waned when other phenomena that were both new and newsworthy forced themselves into the public areas. While drugs, student militancy and hippies became the headline social problems of the later half of the sixties, 'traditional' fringe delinquency of the expressive type continued – even at seaside resorts – without much attention being paid to it. In northern resorts, less accessible places like the Isle of Sheppey or near certain cafes and roundabouts on inland roads, the same behaviour that took place in Clacton, Brighton or Margate was repeated. But the behaviour was too regular and familiar to be of note, it was not as visible as the original incidents and some of the original actors, particularly the Rockers, were leaving the stage. There were also the sorts of processes which occur in cases of mass delusion: a counter-suggestibility produced by the absurdity of some of the initial beliefs and a tailing off of interest when it was felt that 'something is being done about it'.

Like the last spurts of a craze or fashion style, the behaviour was often manifested with an exaggerated formalism. There was a conscious attempt to repeat what had been done two or three years before by actors who almost belonged to another generation. The media and the control agents sometimes seized on to this behaviour, gave it new names and attempted to elevate it to the Mods and Rockers position. In places like Skegness, Blackpool and Great Yarmouth, the new hooligans were called by the press or control agents, 'Greasers', 'Trogs' or 'Thunderbirds'. But such casting was not successful, even when there was an attempt to make the actors look even worse than the Mods and Rockers (as they, in turn) had been made to look worse than the Teddy Boys. At the end of 1966, for example, a Police Inspector told the Great Yarmouth court that the offenders were from '...the roughneck types who have come hell bent on causing trouble to everybody, including the police, but also the innocent youths who are trying to enjoy themselves ... – They are not the usual Mods and Rockers.' So already, the devils of three short years before were recast into relatively benign roles in the gallery of social types exhibited in the name of social control. It took another few years before the drug-taker and the student radical – destined, one thinks, for fairly permanent occupancy – were joined in the folk devil role by a more traditional working-class representative, the Skinhead.

Internal changes within the Mod phenomenon must also be appreciated. There was a straightforward generational change in which the original actors simply matured out. In 1966 one spoke to 19-year-olds who said that they used to be Mods but now it was 'dead' and anyway cost too much. Already by 1967, the major proportion of kids in towns like Brighton did not identify with, or even mention, either of the two groups. This sort of change is familiar to students of fads, crazes and fashions: an initial period of latency where the style or action is only followed by a few, is succeeded by a period of rapid growth and diffusion. There is, then, a phase of commercialization and exploitation, slackening off, resistance or lack of enthusiasm, followed by stagnation and the eventual preservation of the style in nostalgic memories. In his perceptive history of the pop explosion George Melly deduces the same basic pattern: 'What starts as revolt finishes as style – as mannerism.'[5] Thus – to use Melly's examples – the Monkees were plastic Beatles, Barry McGuire a plastic Bob Dylan. The cycle mirrors the stage of the adolescent breaking from his family; once this is through, the impetus is lost. The state is one of instant obsolescence.

The years of the Mod decline were actually more complicated than Melly's 'cycle of obsolescence' explanation suggests. By 1965 there were several strands within the Mod scene and the more extravagant Mods – who were too involved in the whole rhythm and blues, camp, Carnaby Street scene to really 'need' the weekend clashes – began merging into the fashion-conscious hippies and their music began to grow closer to underground sounds.[6] The others were never distinctive enough to maintain any generational continuity. Yet another curious and unpredictable twist was to take place:

It was not until the sixties had almost drawn to a close that the cool classic English tradition reasserted itself with the skinheads, whose formalisation of labouring clothes, braces, jeans, vests, heavy boots and orphanage haircuts was the most dourly anti-romantic style yet arrived at. It was a return to the position of the Ted, but in reverse. The Ted was striving to surmount his working-class family. The skinheads were and are striving to form a dissident group which enjoys all the security of a working-class identity. Thus they despise the strong bourgeois element in the underground and throw their lot in with their local football team and Enoch Powell. Armed, stoic, harrying the Pakistanis exactly as the Teds harried the West Indians in the Notting Hill riots in 1958. The simple clanging of reggae, ska and rock-steady swept away all the fancy arabesques of acid rock.[7]

Using parallels from the world of art and fashion though, is not enough. When more than a sheer aesthetic revolt is at stake, when the gesture is one that speaks of disgust, apathy, boredom and a sense of one's own obsolescence and lack of power, then the instrumental and expressive solutions are brought together. The power of the symbols to differentiate their users from those who accept defeat, becomes deflated. The sheer increases in what was familiar, standardized and routine, instead of – as the Mod's era often was – exciting and alive, accounts for much of this deflation. There is a striking parallel in Becker's account of the decline of the Alliance Youth (the Wandervogel) in the Germany of the twenties:

…the ways in which social objects, expected responses and reflected selves were defined had become relatively standard . . . it is a little hard to feel elation at its fullest intensity when thousands of others have undergone the same experience and have told all about it to everyone willing to lend an ear.[8]

It would, of course, be romantic in the extreme to talk of elation being the dominant mood of the Mods and Rockers. For much of the time any elation that a sense of action could bring, was submerged by the discomfort, unpleasantness and resentment caused by the treatment they received from nearly all the adults whom they encountered. This factor forces attention to another reason for the whole phenomenon coming to an end: the fact that social control might have its intended consequences. In the somewhat romantic eagerness of transactional theorists to point to the evil effects of social control in leading to yet more deviance, they have conveniently suppressed the possibility that potential deviants might, in fact, be frightened off or deterred by actual or threatened control measures. After being put off the train by the police before even arriving at your destination, and then being continually pushed around and harassed by the police on the streets and beaches, searched in the clubs, refused service in cafés, you might just give up in disgust. The game was simply not worth it. In a mass phenomenon such as the Mods and Rockers a form of de-amplification sets in: the amplification stops because the social distance from the deviants is made so great, that new recruits are put off from joining. The only joiners are the very young or the lumpen who have access to few other alternatives. These are the ones who might fight with the ferocity of a group who knows it is being left behind. In the meantime, the original hard-core might mature and grow out of deviance.

From S. Cohen, Folk Devils and Moral Panics, *3rd edn (London: Taylor & Francis), 2002, pp. 161–171.*

Notes

1 Kai T. Erikson, *Wayward Puritans: A Study in the Sociology of Deviance*, New York: John Wiley, 1966.
2 ibid. p.69.
3 D. Laing, *The Sound of Our Time*, London: Sheed and Ward, 1969, p.150.
4 The Brighton Archways Ventures Reports give a detailed chronicle of the opposition of the project by the local tradesmen and council. See particularly Volume 1, pp.15–25, and pp. 49–106, and Volume 3, pp. 167–70.
5 George Melly, *Revolt Into Style*, London: Allen Lane, The Penguin Press, 1970.
6 For one account of this transition, see J. Nuttall, 'Techniques of Separation' in Tony Cash (ed.) Anatomy of Pop, London: BBC Publications, 1970.
7 ibid, pp.127–8.
8 Howard Becker, *German Youth: Bond or Free?* London: Kegan Paul, 1946, p.147.

5

Classicism and positivism

5.1 **On crimes and punishment**
Cesare Beccaria   88

5.2 **The female born criminal**
Cesare Lombroso and Guglielmo Ferrero   93

5.3 **The positive school of criminology**
Enrico Ferri   99

Introduction

KEY CONCEPTS

born criminals; celerity; certainty; classicism; deterrence; positivism; severity

We are turning our attention now to criminological theory. This chapter covers two philosophical traditions that formed a key part of the basis for the emergence of criminology in the late nineteenth and early twentieth century. The first, classicism, is based on the assumption that as individuals we are able to exercise free will and rational choice. Reflecting this, classicism was highly critical of the often unpredictable and extreme forms of punishment that were largely typical of sixteenth- and seventeenth-century society and, rather, argued in favour of systems that were based on punishments that would be proportionate to the offence committed. By contrast, positivism was founded on the belief that there were other factors – either part and parcel of the individual or to be found in the immediate environment – which might be identified through study and observation and which would help distinguish the criminal from the non-criminal. It was these factors – rather than the expression of free will – which would explain criminality.

One of the most famous of writers in the classical tradition was Beccaria. In *On Crimes and Punishments* **(Reading 5.1)** Beccaria outlines a series of justifications for the imposition of various punishments. The basis for punishment by the sovereign (the monarch or government) is the necessity to defend those freedoms that we have willingly given up in order to live within a particular social group. However, this power must at all times be restrained, he argues. Crucially, there must be some proportionality between crimes and punishments. To be effective and justified, he argues, punishments should be prompt – delay in the imposition of punishment reduces its effectiveness. Second, 'punishment should, as far as possible, fit the nature of the crime'. That is, it should be sufficient to achieve its aims, but no more. Finally, rather than being harsh, punishment should be 'unerring'. Crimes are more likely to be prevented if potential offenders think a relatively mild punishment will almost certainly follow than if a very harsh punishment could follow, but the odds are against it.

Probably the most famous scholar associated with the early years of positivist criminology is the Italian, Cesare Lombroso, a man whose work though now largely discredited has had an enormous impact on the subject. In 'The Female Born Criminal' **(Reading 5.2)** Lombroso outlines his view of a particular type of female offender. They are, he argues, particularly perverse and are identified by two key characteristics, the variety of crimes they commit and the cruelty they display. There are fewer of them than male born criminals, but they are especially savage, he argues. Lombroso's particular approach to scientific method is also controversial: part of his work involved studying the facial features of 'criminals' as a means of distinguishing them from non-criminals, though he doesn't discuss this in detail in this excerpt. What he does outline is what he calls the female born criminal's 'moral physiognomy', in which he includes eroticism, weak maternal feelings and an inclination to dissipation.

The final excerpt in this chapter **(Reading 5.3)** comes from another mainstay of positivist criminology, Enrico Ferri. In discussing the main tenets of the positivist school of criminology, he argues that first and foremost is a concern with the causes of crime. Among these he identifies individual, personal factors, and causes found in the general environment. These he calls the anthropological (the factors that Lombroso was most concerned with), the telluric (aspects of the physical environment), and the social. It is in these three factors, in interaction, he suggests, that we can find an explanation for crime. Ferri ends on a positive (in a different sense of the word) note – and one that is often absent from discussions of positivist criminology – suggesting that 'In the society of the future, the necessity for penal justice will be reduced to the extent that social justice grows intensively and extensively'.

Questions for discussion

1. What did Beccaria mean by the idea of 'proportion between crimes and punishments'?

2. Why did he think such proportion important?

3. Why did Beccaria think torture and other extreme forms of punishment likely to be ineffective?

4. What do you think Lombroso and Ferrero meant by the term 'female born criminal'?

5. Why is the female born criminal described as 'doubly exceptional'?

6. What does Ferri mean by anthropological, telluric and social causes of crime? Give examples of each.

7. What are the main differences between classicism and positivism?

5.1 On crimes and punishments
Cesare Beccaria

The origin of punishment

Laws are the terms under which independent and isolated men come together in society. Wearied by living in an unending state of war and by a freedom rendered useless by the uncertainty of retaining it, they sacrifice a part of that freedom in order to enjoy what remains in security and calm. The sum of these portions of freedom sacrificed to the good of all makes up the sovereignty of the nation, and the sovereign is the legitimate repository and administrator of these freedoms. But it was insufficient to create this repository; it was also necessary to protect it from the private usurpations of each individual, who is always seeking to extract from the repository not only his own due but also the portions which are owing to others. What were wanted were sufficiently tangible motives to prevent the despotic spirit of every man from resubmerging society's laws into the ancient chaos. These tangible motives are the punishments enacted against law-breakers. I say *tangible motives* because experience shows that the common run of men do not accept stable principles of conduct. Nor will they depart from the universal principle of anarchy which we see in the physical as well as in the moral realm, unless they are given motives which impress themselves directly on the senses and which, by dint of repetition, are constantly present in the mind as a counterbalance to the strong impressions of those self-interested passions which are ranged against the universal good. Neither eloquence, nor exhortations, not even the most sublime truths have been enough to hold back for long the passions aroused by the immediate impact made by objects which are close at hand.

The right to punish

Every punishment which is not derived from absolute necessity is tyrannous, says the great Montesquieu, a proposition which may be generalised as follows: every act of authority between one man and another which is not derived from absolute necessity is tyrannous. Here, then, is the foundation of the sovereign's right to punish crimes: the necessity of defending the repository of the public well-being from the usurpations of individuals. The juster the punishments, the more sacred and inviolable is the security and the greater the freedom which the sovereign preserves for his subjects. If we consult the human heart, we find in it the fundamental principles of the sovereign's true right to punish crimes, for it is vain to hope that any lasting advantage will accrue from public morality if it be not founded on ineradicable human sentiments. Any law which differs from them will always meet with a resistance that will overcome it in the end, in the same way that a force, however small, applied continuously, will always overcome a sudden shock applied to a body.

No man has made a gift of part of his freedom with the common good in mind; that kind of fantasy exists only in novels. If it were possible, each one of us would wish that the contracts which bind others did not bind us. Every man makes himself the centre of all the world's affairs. [...]

Thus it was necessity which compelled men to give up a part of their freedom; and it is therefore certain that none wished to surrender to the public repository more than the smallest possible portion consistent with persuading others to defend him. The sum of these smallest possible portions constitutes the right to punish; everything more than that is no longer justice, but an abuse; it is a matter of fact not of right. Note that the word 'right' is not opposed to the word 'power', but the former is rather a modification of the latter, that is to say, the species which is of the greatest utility to the greatest number. And by 'justice' I mean nothing other than the restraint necessary to hold particular interests together, without which they would collapse into the old state of unsociability. Any punishment that goes beyond the need to preserve this bond is unjust by its very nature.

Consequences

The first consequence of these principles is that laws alone can decree punishments for crimes, and that this authority resides only with the legislator, who represents the whole of society united by the social contract. No magistrate (who is a member of society) can justly establish of his own accord any punishment for any member of the same society. A punishment which exceeds the limit laid down by law is the just punishment with another punishment superadded. Therefore, a magistrate may not, on any pretext of zeal or concern for the public good whatsoever, increase the punishment laid down by law for a miscreant citizen.

The second consequence is that whilst every individual is bound to society, society is likewise bound to every individual member of it by a pact which, by its very nature, places obligations on both parties. [...] The sovereign, as the representative of society, may only frame laws in general terms which are binding on all members. He may not rule on whether an individual has violated the social pact, because that would divide the nation into two parts: one, represented by the sovereign, who asserts the violation of the contract, and the other, represented by the accused, who denies it. There is, therefore, need of a third party to judge the truth of the matter. Herein lies the need for the magistrate, whose sentences admit of no appeal and consist in simply confirming or denying particular facts.

The third consequence is that, even if it could be shown that the extreme severity of some punishments, even if not directly contrary to the public good and the aim of discouraging crimes, is merely useless, even then, it will be contrary not only to those beneficent virtues which arise from an enlightened reason which prefers to govern happy men than a herd of slaves among whom timorous cruelty is rife, but also be contrary to justice and to the very nature of the social contract.

The interpretation of the laws

A fourth consequence. Nor can the authority to interpret the laws devolve upon the criminal judges, for the same reason that they are not legislators. The judges have not received the laws from our forefathers as if they were a family tradition or a will which leaves its inheritors no duty but that of obedience. Rather, they receive them from the living society or from the sovereign which represents it as the legitimate repository of the current sum of the will of the whole of society. The judges do not receive the laws as obligations of an ancient oath, which is void because it enchains the wills of those not yet born, and iniquitous because it reduces men from a state of society to the state of a herd. Rather, they receive them as the result of a tacit or express oath which the united wills of the subjects have made to the sovereign, as the bonds necessary to curb and control the domestic turbulence of particular interests. Such is the laws' physical and real authority. Who, then, shall be the rightful interpreter of the law? Shall it be the sovereign, that is the repository of the current will of all, or the judge, whose task is merely that of enquiring whether a given man has committed an unlawful act or not?

The judge should construct a perfect syllogism about every criminal case: the major premise should be the general law; the minor, the conformity or otherwise of the action with the law; and the conclusion, freedom or punishment. Whenever the judge is forced, or takes it upon himself, to construct even as few as two syllogisms, then the door is opened to uncertainty.

Nothing is more dangerous than the popular saw that we ought to consult the spirit of the law. This is a bulwark which, once breached, sets loose a flood of opinions. This truth, which seems paradoxical to common minds, which are more struck by a trivial present disorder than by the atrocious but remote consequences which grow out of a false principle's taking root in society, seems self-evident to me. There are mutual connections between all our knowledge and all our ideas; the more complex these connections are, the more ways there are by which we can arrive at or depart from any given idea. Every person has his own point of view, and at different times, every person has a different one. The spirit of the law, therefore, would be the upshot of good or bad logic on the part of the judge and of the state of his digestion, and would depend on the turbulence of his emotions, on the weakness of the aggrieved party, on the judge's relations with the plaintiff and on all those tiny pressures which, to the wavering mind of man, change the appearance of every object. Hence, we see the fate of a citizen changing many times as he progresses through the courts, and the lives of wretches falling victim to fallacious reasoning or the momentary turmoil of the mood of the judge, who takes for the legitimate interpretation of the law the haphazard upshot of this series of confused impulses which affect his mind. It is for this reason that we see the same court punish the same crime differently at different times, because it consults not the constant and fixed voice of the law, but the erring instability of interpretations.

The obscurity of the laws

If interpretation of the laws is an evil, it is obvious that the obscurity which makes interpretation necessary is another. And it is the greatest of evils if the laws be written in a language which is not understood by the people and which makes them dependent upon a few individuals because they cannot judge for themselves what will become of their freedom or their life and limbs, hindered by a language which turns a solemn and public book into what is almost a private and family affair. What are we to think of mankind, seeing that such is the long-standing practice of the greater part of educated and enlightened Europe? The more people understand the sacred code of the laws and get used to handling it, the fewer will be the crimes, for there is no doubt that ignorance and uncertainty of punishment opens the way to the eloquence of the emotions.

The proportion between crimes and punishments

It is in the common interest not only that crimes not be committed, but that they be rarer in proportion to the harm they do to society. Hence the obstacles which repel men from committing crimes ought to be made stronger the more those crimes are against the public good and the more inducements there are for committing them. Hence, there must be a proportion between crimes and punishments.

It is impossible to foresee all the mischiefs which arise from the universal struggle of the human emotions. They multiply at a compound rate with the growth of population and with the crisscrossing of private interests, which cannot be geometrically directed towards the public utility. In political arithmetic, we must substitute the calculus of probabilities for mathematical exactitude. [...]

That force which attracts us, like gravity, to our own good can be controlled only by equal and opposite obstacles. The effects of this force are the whole confused gamut of human actions: if these interfere with and obstruct one another, then the punishments, which we may call *political obstacles*, eliminate their evil effects, without destroying the moving cause, which is the very sensibility inalienable from man's nature. And the legislator behaves like the skilled architect, whose task is to counteract the destructive forces of gravity and to exploit those forces that contribute to the strengthening of the building.

Given men's need to come together, and given the compacts which necessarily arise from the very opposition of private interests, we can make out a scale of wrong actions, of which the highest grade consists in those which spell the immediate destruction of society, and the lowest those which involve the smallest possible injustice to its private participants. Between these two extremes are distributed in imperceptible gradations from the highest to the lowest, all the actions which are inimical to the public good and which can be called crimes. If it were possible to measure all the infinite and untoward combinations of human actions geometrically, then there should be a corresponding scale of punishments running from the harshest to the mildest. But it is enough that the wise lawgiver signposts the main stages, without confusing the order and not reserving for the crimes of the highest grade the punishments of the lowest. If there were an exact and universal scale of crimes and punishments, we should have an approximate and common measure of the gradations of tyranny and liberty, and of the basic humanity and evil of the different nations.

Any action which does not fall between the two limits noted above cannot be called a *crime*, nor be punished as such, unless by those who find it in their own interest so to call it. Uncertainty about where these limits lie has produced in nations a morality which is at odds with the law, enactments which are at odds with each other, and a mass of laws which expose the most sterling men to the most severe punishments, but which leave the words vice and virtue vague and afloat, raising those doubts about one's very existence which lead to the drowsiness and torpor fatal to the body politic. Anyone who reads the laws and histories of nations with a philosophical eye will see the changes which have always occurred over the centuries in the words *vice* and *virtue*, *good citizen* and *bad*, not as a result of changes in the countries' circumstances and so in the common interest, but as a result of the passions and false beliefs which at various times have motivated the different lawgivers. The reader will see often enough that the passions of one century are the basis of the morals of later centuries, that strong emotions, the offspring of fanaticism and enthusiasm, are weakened and, so to speak, gnawed away by time, which returns all physical and moral phenomena to equilibrium, and they become the common sense of the day and a powerful tool in the hands of the strong and the astute. In this way, the very obscure notions of virtue and honour were born, and they are so obscure because they change with the passage of time which preserves words rather than things, and they change with the rivers and mountains which so often form the boundaries not only of physical but also of moral geography.

If pleasure and pain are the motive forces of all sentient beings, and if the invisible legislator has decreed rewards and punishments as one of the motives that spur men even to the most sublime deeds, then the inappropriate distribution of punishments will give rise to that paradox, as little recognised as it is common, that punishments punish the crimes they have caused. If an equal punishment is laid down for two crimes which damage society unequally, men will not have a stronger deterrent against committing the greater crime if they find it more advantageous to do so.

Of prompt punishments

The swifter and closer to the crime a punishment is, the juster and more useful it will be. I say juster, because it spares the criminal the useless and fierce torments of uncertainty which grow in proportion to the liveliness of one's imagination and one's sense of one's own impotence. Juster because, loss of freedom being a punishment, a man should suffer it no longer than necessary before being sentenced. Remand in custody, therefore, is the simple safe-keeping of a citizen until he may be judged guilty, and since this custody is intrinsically of the nature of a punishment, it should last the minimum possible time and should be as lacking in severity as can be arranged. The minimum time should be calculated taking into account both the length of time needed for the trial and the right of those who have been held the longest to be tried first. The stringency of the detention ought not to be greater than what is necessary to prevent escape or to save evidence from being covered up. The trial itself ought to be brought to a conclusion in the shortest possible time. What crueller contrast could there be than that between the procrastination of the judge and the anguish of the accused? [...]

In general, the severity of a punishment and the consequence of crime ought to be as effective as possible on others and as lenient as possible on him who undergoes it, because a society cannot be called legitimate where it is not an unfailing principle that men should be subjected to the fewest possible ills. [...]

[T]he contiguity of crime and punishment is of the highest importance if we want the idea of punishment to be immediately associated in unsophisticated minds with the enticing picture of some lucrative crime. A long delay only serves to separate these two ideas further. [...]

There is another principle which serves admirably to draw even closer the important connection between a misdeed and its punishment. And that is that the punishment should, as far as possible, fit the nature of the crime. This sort of fit greatly eases the comparison which ought to exist between the incentive to crime and the retribution of punishment, so that the latter removes and redirects the mind to ends other than those which the enticing idea of breaking the law would wish to point it.

Lenience in punishing

One of the most effective brakes on crime is not the harshness of its punishment, but the unerringness of punishment. This calls for vigilance in the magistrates, and that kind of unswerving judicial severity which, to be useful to the cause of virtue, must be accompanied by a lenient code of laws. The certainty of even a mild punishment will make a bigger impression than the fear of a more awful one which is united to a hope of not being punished at all. For, even the smallest harms, when they are certain, always frighten human souls, whereas hope, that heavenly gift which often displaces every other sentiment, holds at bay the idea of larger harms, especially when it is reinforced by frequent examples of the impunity accorded by weak and corrupt judges. The harsher the punishment and the worse the evil he faces, the more anxious the criminal is to avoid it, and it makes him commit other crimes to escape the punishment of the first. The times and places in which the penalties have been fiercest have been those of the bloodiest and most inhuman actions. Because the same brutal spirit which guided the hand of the lawgiver, also moved the parricide's and the assassin's. He decreed iron laws from the throne for the savage souls of slaves, who duly obeyed them; and in secluded darkness he urged men to murder tyrants only to create new ones.

As punishments become harsher, human souls which, like fluids, find their level from their surroundings, become hardened and the ever lively power of the emotions brings it about that, after a hundred years of cruel tortures, the wheel only causes as much fear as prison previously did. If a punishment is to serve its purpose, it is enough that the harm of punishment should outweigh the good which the criminal can derive from the crime, and into the calculation of this balance, we must add the unerringness of the punishment and the loss of the good produced by the crime. Anything more than this is superfluous and, therefore, tyrannous. Men are guided by the repeated action on them of the harms they know and not by those they do not. Imagine two states, in which the scales of punishment are proportionate to the crimes and that in one the worst punishment is perpetual slavery, and that in the other it is breaking on the wheel. I maintain that there would be as much fear of the worst punishment in the first as in the second; and if there were cause to introduce in the first the worst punishments of the second, the same cause would produce an increase in the punishments of the second, which would gradually move from the wheel via slower and more elaborate torments to reach the ultimate refinements of that science which tyrants know all too well.

Two other disastrous consequences contrary to the very purpose of preventing crime follow from having harsh punishments. One is that it is not easy to sustain the necessary proportion between crime and punishment because, despite all the efforts of cruelty to devise all manner of punishments, they still cannot go beyond the limits of endurance of the human organism and feeling. Once this point has been reached, no correspondingly greater punishments necessary to prevent the more damaging and atrocious crimes can be found. The other consequence is that the harshness of punishments gives rise to impunity. Men's capacity for good or evil is confined within certain bounds, and a spectacle which is too awful for humanity cannot be more than a temporary upset, and can never become a fixed system of the sort proper to the law. If the laws are truly cruel, they must either be changed or they will occasion a fatal impunity.

What reader of history does not shudder with horror at the barbaric and useless tortures that so-called wise men have cold-bloodedly invented and put into operation? Who can fail to feel himself shaken to the core by the sight of thousands of wretches whom poverty, either willed or tolerated by the laws, which have always favoured the few and abused the masses, has dragged back to the primitive state of nature, and either accused of impossible crimes invented out of a cringing ignorance or found guilty of nothing but being faithful to their own principles, and who are then torn apart with premeditated pomp and slow tortures by men with the same faculties and emotions, becoming the entertainment of a fanatical mob?

How to prevent crimes

It is better to prevent crimes than to punish them. This is the principal goal of all good legislation, which is the art of guiding men to their greatest happiness, or the least unhappiness possible, taking into account the blessings and evils of life. [...] To forbid a large number of trivial acts is not to prevent the crimes they may occasion. It is to create new crimes, wilfully to redefine virtue and vice, which we are exhorted to regard as eternal and immutable. What a state would we be reduced to if we were forbidden everything which might tempt us to crime? It would be necessary to deprive a man of the use of his senses. [...]

Do you want to prevent crimes? Then make sure that the laws are clear and simple and that the whole strength of the nation is concentrated on defending them, and that no part of it is used to destroy them. (Make sure that the laws favour individual men more than classes of men.) Make sure that men fear the laws and only the laws.

Conclusion

From all I have written it is possible to draw a very useful general axiom, though it little conforms to custom – the most usual legislator of nations. It is: *In order that punishment should not be an act of violence perpetrated by one or many upon a private citizen, it is essential that it should be public, speedy, necessary, the minimum possible in the given circumstances, proportionate to the crime, and determined by the law.*

From C. Beccaria, On Crimes and Punishments and Other Writings, edited by Richard Bellamy and translated by Richard Davies *(Cambridge: Cambridge University Press), 1767/1995, pp. 9–113.*

5.2 The female born criminal
Cesare Lombroso and Guglielmo Ferrero

There is a perfect correspondence between the anthropology and the psychology of the female criminal. In the majority, degenerative traits are but few or weak, but there is a subgroup in which such traits are almost more marked and numerous than in male criminals. Similarly, while the majority of female criminals are merely led into crime by someone else or by irresistible temptation, there is a small subgroup whose criminal propensities are more intense and perverse than even those of their male counterparts. These are the female born criminals, whose evil is inversely proportionate to their numbers. 'Woman is rarely wicked, but when she is, she is worse than a man' (Italian proverb).

The extreme perversity of female born criminals manifests itself in two characteristics: the variety of their crimes and their cruelty.

Variety of crimes

Many female born criminals specialize in not just one but several types of crime and often in two types that in males are mutually exclusive, such as poisoning and murder. Bompard, for instance, was a prostitute, thief, swindler, slanderer, and murderer; Trossarello was a prostitute, adulterer, killer, abortionist, and thief. In history we find Agrippina, an adulterer, incest offender, and party to homicide, and Messalina, a prostitute, adulterer, accomplice in homicide, and thief.

Cruelty

Second, the female born criminal surpasses her male counterpart in the refined, diabolical cruelty with which she commits her crimes. Merely killing her enemy does not satisfy her; she needs to watch him suffer and experience the full taste of death.

In the band of assassins known as La Taille, the women were worse than the men in torturing captives, especially female captives. The woman Tiburzio, having killed a pregnant friend, bit her ferociously, tearing away pieces of flesh and throwing them to the dog. Chevalier killed a pregnant woman by driving a pair of scissors through her ear and into her brain. A certain D., when asked why she had not stabbed her lover instead of throwing

vitriol at him, answered by quoting a Roman tyrant: 'Because I wanted him to feel the misery of death.'

The very worst examples of such barbarity are provided by mothers in whom maternal affection – the most intense of all human sentiments – has been transformed into hatred. Hoegli beat her daughter and plunged her head into water to suffocate her cries. One day she kicked the girl downstairs, deforming her spine. Stakembourg, a loose woman, took to persecuting her daughter when she reached the age of forty-two and her lovers abandoned her. 'I do not like girls,' she used to say. She hung her daughter from the ceiling by the armpits, knocked her on the head with a brick, and burnt her with a hot iron. One day, having beaten the girl black with a shovel, she laughed and said, 'Now you are nothing but a little Negro.'

In short, while female born criminals are fewer in number than male born criminals, they are often much more savage. What is the explanation?

We have seen that the normal woman is by nature less sensitive to pain than a man. Because compassion is an effect of sensitivity, if one is lacking, the other will be too. We have also seen that women have many traits in common with children; that they are deficient in the moral sense; and that they are vengeful, jealous, and inclined to refined cruelty when they take revenge. Usually these defects are neutralized by their piety, maternity, sexual coldness, physical weakness, and undeveloped intelligence. However, when a morbid activity of the psychical centers intensifies their bad qualities, women seek relief in evil deeds. When piety and maternal feelings are replaced by strong passions and intense eroticism, muscular strength and superior intelligence, then the innocuous semicriminal who is always present in the normal woman is transformed into a born criminal more terrible than any male counterpart.

What awful criminals children would be if they had strong passions, physical strength, and intelligence, and if, moreover, their evil tendencies were aggravated by morbid psychical activity! And women are big children; their evil tendencies are more numerous and varied than men's, but usually these remain latent. When awakened and excited, however, these evil tendencies lead to proportionately worse results.

In addition, the female born criminal is, so to speak, doubly exceptional, first as a woman and then as a criminal. This is because criminals are exceptions among civilized people,[1] and women are exceptions among criminals, women's natural form of regression being prostitution, not crime. Primitive woman was a prostitute rather than a criminal. As a double exception, then, the criminal woman is a true monster. Honest women are kept in line by factors such as maternity, piety, and weakness; when a woman commits a crime despite these restraints, this is a sign that her power of evil is immense.

Eroticism and virility

We saw how sexuality can be exaggerated in female born criminals; this is one of the traits that makes them similar to men. Due to it, all women born criminals are prostitutes. While prostitution may be their least significant offense, it is never absent. Eroticism is the nucleus around which their other characteristics revolve.

This exaggerated eroticism, which is abnormal in most women, forms the starting point for vices and crimes. It turns female born criminals into unsociable beings preoccupied entirely with the satisfaction of their own desires, like lustful savages whose sexuality has not been tamed by civilization and necessity.

Affections and passions/maternity

One strong proof of degeneration in many born criminals is their lack of maternal affection. Lyons, the celebrated American thief and swindler, abandoned her children when she fled her country, leaving them dependent on public charity even though she was wealthy. Often female criminals will force their own children to become accomplices.

This lack of maternal feeling becomes comprehensible if we keep in mind the female criminal's masculine qualities, which prevent her from being more than half a woman, and her love of dissipation, which prevents her from carrying out her maternal duties. She feels few maternal impulses because psychologically and anthropologically she belongs more to the masculine than the feminine sex. Her exaggerated sexuality alone would be enough to render her a bad mother; it makes her egotistical and redirects her energies toward satisfying her pressing and multiple sexual needs. How, then, could she be capable of the abnegation, patience, and altruism that constitute maternity? While in the normal woman sexuality is subordinate to maternity, and a normal mother will unhesitatingly put a child before a lover or husband, among criminal women the opposite is true. Such women turn their daughters into prostitutes in order to keep a lover.

Another factor contributing to the female criminal's lack of maternal feeling is the organic anomaly of moral insanity stemming from epilepsy. This underlying cause of innate criminality tends to deflect women's feelings from their normal course, extinguishing maternal impulses first of all. Similarly, it extinguishes religiosity in nuns, turning them into blasphemers; and among military men it extinguishes loyalty, inspiring formerly loyal soldiers to savagely attack their superiors.[2]

Paradoxically, in some cases maternity and sexuality, instead of working against one another as usual, join together in incest, and the mother becomes the lover of the son, adoring him partly as a son and partly as a lover. This mixture of sexual and maternal love can be explained by the fact, established earlier, that maternal love has a sexual foundation; when nursing, the mother feels a little sexual pleasure and usually prefers a male baby. This factor, usually of little importance, becomes exaggerated in an intensely erotic woman.

Here is proof of the anticriminogenic influence of maternity on women. In those in whom it has not been entirely extinguished, maternity works, at least for certain periods, as a potent moral antidote.[3] Thus Thomas, a vicious woman who passed only six honest months in her entire life, was transformed during that period by bearing a child. But when her daughter died, she fell back into the gutter.

Maternity never inspires crime, even among female born criminals. The sentiment is too noble to coexist with degeneration. But the sorrows of maternity can lead to madness and suicide.

Vengeance

The chief motive for female crime is vengeance. The inclination toward revenge that we noted even in normal women becomes extreme in criminals. Because their psychic centers are irritated, the smallest stimulus can provoke an enormous reaction. But usually the female born criminal revenges herself more slowly than men. She has to develop her plan little by little because her physical weakness and fearful nature restrain her even when her reason does not.

Hatred

In certain very serious cases, female born criminals have no motive whatsoever other than a small and distant complaint. These crimes originate in an innate and blind savagery. Adulterers and poisoners, in particular, tend to commit oddly pointless crimes.

A passion for evil for evil's sake is a characteristic of born criminals, epileptics, and hysterics. It is an automatic hatred, one that springs from no external cause such as an insult or offense, but rather from a morbid irritation of the psychical centers which relieves itself in evil action. Driven by continuous irritation, such women need to discharge their aggravation on someone. Thus some unfortunate with whom they frequently come in contact becomes, for some trifling defect or difference, the object of their loathing and victim of their savagery.

Love

Although the female born criminal has intensely erotic tendencies, love is rarely a cause of her crimes. For her love, like hatred, is just another form of insatiable egotism. There is no self-abnegation or altruism in her love, only a drive for self-satisfaction.

The impulsivity and casualness of these women's passions are extraordinary. When they fall in love, they need to satisfy their desire immediately, even if that means committing a crime. Monomaniacal, as if hypnotized by desire, they think of nothing but how to satisfy themselves and rush to commit crimes even though if they were patient they might achieve the same goal without risk. Their affection is like that of children – intense but incapable of disinterested sacrifice or noble resignation. It can result in the kind of jealous tyranny more often found in the love of a man for a woman.

Greed and avarice

Greed is a cause of crime in women, though less often than vengeance. Among dissolute female offenders, who need a great deal of money for their orgies and other pleasures but do not care to work for it, avarice takes the same form as in male criminals: both want to have large sums of money to waste. This inspires them to attempt or instigate crimes which can reap a rich harvest. Thus Bompard encouraged Eyraud to kill the porter, and thus Messalina had the richest citizens of Rome killed so she could appropriate their villas and wealth.

Dress

Another factor that pushes women into crime is a passion for objects of clothing and ornament. Madame Lafarge stole her friend's diamonds, not to sell them, but only to possess them, even though doing so involved grave risks.[4] According to Tarnowsky, many Russian thieves steal not out of need (they have jobs and are earning wages) but to obtain small luxury objects.[5]

In the psychology of normal women, dress and personal adornment play a role of immense significance. A poorly dressed woman feels she has disgraced herself. Children and savages have similar reactions. Among savages, dress is the earliest form of property, and thus we should not be surprised that it is also a frequent cause of crime

Religiosity

Religiosity is neither rare nor weak in these born criminals. While Parency was killing an old man, his wife prayed to God that all would end well. G., when setting fire to her lover's house, cried out, 'May God and the Holy Virgin do the rest.' Pompilia Zambeccari vowed to light a candle to the Virgin if she succeeded in poisoning her husband.

Contradictions

The female born criminal does not lack a paradoxical and intermittent goodness which contrasts strangely with her usual depravity. Madame Lafarge was extremely kind to her servants. In her own neighborhood she was called the godsend of the poor, and she gave succor to the sick. Jegado was deeply affectionate to her fellow servants, but poisoned them the moment they offended her. Thomas gave alms to the poor, wept when they described their miseries, and bought presents and clothes for their children.

Such altruism is intermittent, however, and it does not last long. The kindness of criminal women is of an inferior sort, growing as it does out of selfishness. Charitable acts enable them to feel that others are at their feet; for once, their love of power is gratified by good behavior.

Sentimentalism

Although these women lack strong and true feelings, they do exhibit a kind of mawkish sentimentality, especially in correspondence. Trossarello wrote her lover letters full of affection and declarations of fidelity, even while betraying him. Criminal women are moral lunatics; having no noble, deep affections, they lapse easily into showy substitutes.

Intelligence

Criminal women exhibit many levels of intelligence. Some are extremely intelligent, while others are ordinary in this respect. As a rule, however, their minds are alert; this is evidently why, relative to men, they commit few impulsive crimes. To kill in a bestial rage requires no more than the mind of a Hottentot; but to plot out a poisoning requires ability and sharpness. The crimes of women are almost always deliberate.

M. (a case described by Ortolenghi) was capable of rapid and rich thinking despite her lack of schooling; in addition (and this is important given women's backwardness in the development of writing abilities), she felt a deep need to record the ideas that flooded her, scribbling some down, dictating others to her companions. Although she was only seventeen years old, she amply demonstrated her intelligence by organizing a vast and profitable prostitution ring.

Lyons, the famous American adventurer and thief, must have had a very superior intelligence. After enriching herself through burglary in America, she came to Europe to pursue the same system, solely out of love for her trade. Arrested *in flagrante* in Paris, she managed to get free through apologies and the intercession of the British and American ambassadors. Another example is Bell-Star, who for many years led a band of outlaws in Texas, organizing raids against the US government itself.

More evidence that female born criminals are often strong intellectually lies in the frequently original nature of their offenses. For example, M. (Ottolenghi's case) enriched herself through a remarkable combination of prostitution, pandering, and blackmail. The superior intelligence of these criminals can be explained by the fact that they are often physically incapable of satisfying their perverse instincts. With sufficient cleverness, they can still achieve their ends; if not, they become prostitutes.

Writing and painting

These two accomplishments are almost totally lacking in female born criminals. I have never found a drawing or tattoo alluding to crime and made by a female born criminal – not even an embroidery, a medium one might expect such women to favor. Nor are there many examples of their writing. We have found only three examples of memoirs by female born criminals: those of Madame Lafarge, of X, and of Bell-Star. Male criminals, on the other hand, are greatly addicted to these egotistical outpourings.

Method of committing crimes/deliberation

More evidence of the mental ability of female born criminals lies in the deliberation with which many of them plan their offenses. The means they use to reach a goal, even a relatively simple goal, are often very complicated.

To kill her husband, Rosa Bent ... prepared, in his room while he was sleeping, a great caldron of boiling water. When he suddenly woke up, she said that people were calling to him from the street, and when he rushed to the window, still half asleep, she pushed him into the caldron. Clearly, such complicated plans require a certain amount of imagination, which may take the place of physical force.

However, this deliberation often trips up even the cleverest criminals. Their elaborate plans turn out to be absurd and impossible, not to mention mad. Buisson, for example, was scratched by an old man while murdering him; as soon as she got home, she hanged her cat and proceeded to announce angrily to friends that the beast had clawed her face.

Instigation

The female born criminal does not always commit her crimes herself. Courage may fail her unless she has a man's strength, or her victim is another woman, or her crime is secretive as in poisoning or arson. It is not that such a woman shrinks morally from crime, but rather that she instigates an accomplice to commit it. Characteristically, her part in a joint crime is that of an *incubus*, to use Sighele's term; she incites her partner, deploying him with calculated evil.

Lasciviousness

Lasciviousness often plays a part in the crimes of these offenders, who tend to be lustful and immodest. It is natural that, in planning a crime, they often decide to use sexuality to achieve their ends.

Often the female criminal instigates her accomplice by promising sex. D...., who gave herself to everyone, refused only one admirer, the weakest and most suggestible. When she had in this way reinforced his desire, she promised to give herself to him if he killed her husband.

Obstinacy in denial

One peculiarity of female criminals, especially female born criminals, is the obstinacy with which they deny their crimes, no matter how strong the evidence against them. Male criminals confess when there is no longer any reason for denial; but women protest their innocence more strenuously as their claims increase in absurdity.

Madame Lafarge maintained her innocence to the end, proclaiming it in her memoirs. Jegado, despite the wealth of evidence against her, continued to assert that she knew nothing about arsenic and that her only fault lay in being too kind. She persisted in these claims to the end.

In court, these women sometimes change their defense argument completely, two or three times. Apparently unaware that such mutations raise doubts in judges' minds, they continue to assert their innocence with undampened ardor.

Revelation of crime

In yet another of those contradictions that turn up in the study of criminal women, we find that while they often obstinately deny their guilt, they also often spontaneously reveal it. This complex psychological phenomenon is caused in part by that need to gossip and that inability to keep a secret which are characteristic of females. Gabriella Bompard, for instance, when she was traveling with Garanger, started telling him many things about Eyraud, and when they arrived in Paris, where all the newspapers were full of news about Fyraud and herself, she could not refrain from revealing her own and her accomplice's identity. In a different case, Faure, a woman who threw vitriol at her lover, would never have been discovered if she had not confessed to a female friend. When the crime is one of vengeance, there is of course an additional temptation to confess, beyond that of confiding in someone, because avengers take joy in their deeds. Another factor here is the typical foolishness and imprudence of criminals, who speak openly of their deeds without recognizing the risks.

Particularly curious is the way a woman will confess to her lover. She will tell him of her crime even if he himself is honest, unsuspecting, and incurious. Sometimes she forces him to accept written proof of her guilt, proof that can convict her and that, when her intense but fleeting love has cooled, can constrain her to commit another and even more serious crime to get rid of an inconvenient witness. Here again we have an example of the habitual recklessness of the female criminal. Failing to realize that her loves are always brief, she believes that this time it will be as lasting as it is intense. This blindness, together with that lack of morality that causes her to regard the worst crimes as insignificant lapses, is the only way to explain her behavior.

But in other cases, driven by jealousy and a desire to revenge herself on a lover who has abandoned her, the female criminal will accuse her accomplice. Or, if she fears detection, she may betray her partner in hope of cutting a deal for herself. Female fickleness also plays a role here. A woman adores a man as if he is a god and is willing to die for him – for a few months. But then her affection turns to hatred, and she hands him over to justice without hesitation.

Summary

In general, the moral physiognomy of the born female criminal is close to that of the male. The atavistic diminution of secondary sexual characteristics which shows up in the anthropology of the subject appears again in the psychology of the female offender, who is excessively erotic, weak in maternal feelings, inclined to dissipation, and both astute and audacious. She dominates weaker people, sometimes through suggestion, sometimes through force. Her love of violent exercise, her vices, and even her clothing increase her resemblance to a man. These virile traits are often joined by the worst qualities of woman: her passion for revenge, her cunning, cruelty, love of finery, and dishonesty, which can combine to form a type of extraordinary wickedness.

It goes without saying that these characteristics are not found in the same proportion in every case. However, when muscular strength and intellectual power come together in the same individual, we have a female criminal of an indeed terrible type. A typical example is offered by Bell-Star, the female outlaw who several years ago terrorized all of Texas. Her education had developed her natural proclivities: as the daughter of a guerrilla chief who had fought for the South during the Civil War, she had grown up in the midst of fighting. At the age of eighteen she became head of her own gang, ruling her companions partly through superior intelligence, partly through courage, and to some extent through womanly charm. She organized attacks of great daring against cities and government troops; nor did she hesitate, the day after one of these raids, to enter a nearby town unaccompanied, dressed (as usual) like a man. Once she slept in the same hotel as the district judge without him suspecting her identity or even her sex. Her wish to die in her boots was granted when she fell in battle against government soldiers, directing the action until her final moment.

Bell-Star exemplifies the law we have formulated: that the female born criminal, when a full type, is more terrible than the male.[6]

From C. Lombroso and G. Ferrero, 'The Female Born Criminal', in Criminal Woman, the Prostitute and the Normal Woman *(translated, and with a new introduction by M. Gibson and N.H. Rafter) (Durham, NC: Duke University Press), 1893/2004, pp. 182–192.*

Notes

1 Lombroso means that criminals, as atavistic throwbacks to an earlier evolutionary stage, are exceptions among well-evolved, civilized people.

2 Here Lombroso is referring to the case of the soldier Misdea, who in 1884, unhinged by what seemed to him unfair treatment by a corporal, opened fire in a barracks in Naples, killing and wounding many fellow soldiers. Called in to examine Misdea, Lombroso concluded that his underlying problem was epilepsy.

3 Lombroso here anticipates the late twentieth-century 'control' theory of crime, according to which people who are bonded to society through relationships, religion, commitment to work, and so on are less likely than poorly bonded people to commit crimes.

4 The woman to whom Lombroso refers may have been the Madame Lafarge who was put on trial in 1840 for poisoning her husband with arsenic. This famous trial, in which experts battled over the physical evidence, is today cited as the origin of forensic toxicology. Madame Lafarge's memoirs, published in 1841 and frequently reprinted thereafter, provided one of the few first-person accounts by a notorious woman offender.

5 Similarly, a twentieth-century study identified a group of shoplifters who steal not out of dire necessity but because they are too poor to afford small luxuries for themselves. They feel obligated to spend the family's income on other family members; with nothing left over, the only way they can treat themselves to small 'extras' is by pilfering. See Cameron, 1964. However, Cameron does not draw biological conclusions from her findings.

6 Although Lombroso uses the outlaw Bell-Star to exemplify the moral ghastliness of the female born criminal, he is clearly captivated by her as a romantic, adventurous, cross-dressing hero.

5.3 The positive school of criminology
Enrico Ferri

The classic cycle of the science of crime and punishment, originated by Cesare Beccaria more than a century ago, was followed in our country, some twenty years since, by the scientific movement of the positive school of criminology. [...]

When a crime is committed in some place, attracting public attention either through the atrocity of the case or the strangeness of the criminal deed – for instance, one that is not connected with bloodshed, but with intellectual fraud – there are at once two tendencies that make themselves felt in the public conscience. One of them, pervading the overwhelming majority of individual consciences, asks: How is this? What for? Why did that man commit such a crime? This question is asked by everybody and occupies mostly the attention of those who do not look upon the case from the point of view of criminology. On the other hand, those who occupy themselves with criminal law represent the other tendency, which manifests itself when acquainted with the news of this crime. This is a limited portion of the public conscience, which tries to study the problem from the standpoint of the technical jurist. The lawyers, the judges, the officials of the police, ask themselves: What is the name of the crime committed by that man under such circumstances? Must it be classed as murder or patricide, attempted or incompleted manslaughter, and, if directed against property, is it theft, or illegal appropriation, or fraud? And the entire apparatus of practical criminal justice forgets at once the first problem, which occupies the majority of the public conscience, the question of the causes that led to this crime, in order to devote itself exclusively to the technical side of the problem which constitutes the juridical anatomy of the inhuman and antisocial deed perpetrated by the criminal.

In these two tendencies you have a photographic reproduction of the two schools of criminology. The classic school, which looks upon the crime as a juridical problem, occupies itself with its name, its definition, its juridical analysis, leaves the personality of the criminal in the background and remembers it only so far as exceptional circumstances explicitly stated in the law books refer to it: whether he is a minor, a deaf-mute, whether it is a case of insanity, whether he was drunk at the time the crime was committed. Only in these strictly defined cases does the classic school occupy itself theoretically with the personality of the criminal. But ninety times in one hundred these exceptional circumstances do not exist or cannot be shown to exist, and penal justice limits itself to the technical definition of the fact. But when the case comes up in the criminal court, or before the jurors, practice demonstrates that there is seldom a discussion between the lawyers of the defense and the judges for the purpose of ascertaining the most exact definition of the fact, of determining whether it is a case of attempted or merely projected crime, of finding out whether there are any of the juridical elements defined in this or that article of the code. The judge is rather face to face with the problem of ascertaining why, under what conditions, for what reasons, the man has committed the crime. This is the supreme and simple human problem. But hitherto it has been left to a more or less perspicacious, more or less gifted, empiricism, and there have been no scientific standards, no methodical collection of facts, no observations and conclusions, save those of the positive school of criminology. This school alone makes an attempt to solve in every case of crime the problem of its natural origin, of the reasons and conditions that induced a man to commit such and such a crime.

For instance, about 3,000 cases of manslaughter are registered every year in Italy. Now, open any work inspired by the classic school of criminology, and ask the author why 3,000 men are the victims of manslaughter every year in Italy, and how it is that there are not sometimes only as many as, say, 300 cases, the number committed in England, which has nearly the same number of inhabitants as Italy; and how it is that there are not sometimes 300,000 such cases in Italy instead of 3,000?

It is useless to open any work of classical criminology for this purpose, for you will not find an answer to these questions in them. No one, from Beccaria to Carrara, has ever thought of this problem, and they could not have asked it, considering their point of departure and their method. In fact, the classic criminologists accept the phenomenon of criminality as an accomplished fact. They analyze it from the point of view of the technical jurist, without asking how this criminal fact may have been produced, and why it repeats itself in greater or smaller numbers from year to year, in every country. The theory of a free will, which is their foundation, excludes the possibility of this scientific question, for according to it the crime is the product of the fiat of the human will. And if that is admitted as a fact, there is nothing left to account for. The manslaughter was committed, because the criminal wanted to commit it; and that is all there is to it. Once the theory of a free will is accepted as a fact, the deed depends on the fiat, the voluntary determination, of the criminal, and all is said.

But if, on the other hand, the positive school of criminology denies, on the ground of researches in scientific physiological psychology, that the human will is free and does not admit that one is a criminal because he wants to be, but declares that a man commits this or that crime only when he lives in definitely determined conditions of personality and environment which induce him necessarily to act in a certain way, then alone does the problem of the origin of criminality begin to be submitted to a preliminary analysis, and then alone does criminal law step out of the narrow and arid limits of technical jurisprudence and become a true social and human science in the highest and noblest meaning of the word. It is vain to insist with such stubbornness as that of the classic school of criminology on juristic formulæ by which the distinction between illegal appropriation and theft, between fraud and other forms of crime against property, and so forth, is determined, when this method does not give to society one single word which would throw light upon the reasons that make a man a criminal and upon the efficacious remedy by which society could protect itself against criminality.

It is true that the classic school of criminology has likewise its remedy against crime – namely, punishment. But this is the only remedy of that school, and in all the legislation inspired by the theories of that school in all the countries of the civilized world there is no other remedy against crime but repression. [...]

The method which we, on the other hand, have inaugurated is the following: Before we study crime from the point of view of a juristic phenomenon, we must study causes to which the annual recurrence of crimes in all countries is due. These are natural causes, which I have classified under the three heads of anthropological, telluric and social. Every crime, from the smallest to the most atrocious, is the result of the interaction of these three causes, the anthropological condition of the criminal, the telluric environment in which he is living, and the social environment in which he is born, living and operating. It is a vain beginning to separate the meshes of this net of criminality. There are still those who would maintain the one-sided standpoint that the origin of crime may be traced to only one of these elements, for instance, to the social element alone. So far as I am concerned, I have combatted this opinion from the very inauguration of the positive school of criminology, and I combat it today. It is certainly easy enough to think that the entire origin of all crime is due to the unfavorable social conditions in which the criminal lives. But an objective, methodical, observation demonstrates that social conditions alone do not suffice to explain the origin of criminality, although it is true that the prevalence of the influence of social conditions is an incontestable fact in the case of the greater number of crimes, especially of the lesser ones. But there are crimes which cannot be explained by the influence of social conditions alone. If you regard the general condition of misery as the sole source of criminality, then you cannot get around the difficulty that out of one thousand individuals living in misery from the day of their birth to that of their death only one hundred or two hundred become criminals, while the other nine hundred or eight hundred either sink into biological weakness, or become harmless maniacs, or commit suicide without perpetrating any crime. If poverty were the sole determining cause, one thousand out of one thousand ought to become criminals. If only two hundred become criminals, while one hundred commit suicide, one hundred end as maniacs, and the other six hundred remain honest in their social condition, then poverty alone is not sufficient to explain criminality. We must add the anthropological and telluric factor. Only by means of these three elements of natural influence can criminality be explained. Of course, the influence of either the anthropological or telluric or social element varies from case to case. If you have a case of simple theft, you may have a far greater influence of the social factor than of the anthropological factor. On the other hand, if you have a case of murder, the anthropological element will have a far greater influence than the social. And so on in every case of crime, and every individual that you will have to judge on the bench of the criminal.

The anthropological factor. It is precisely here that the genius of Cesare Lombroso established a new science, because in his search after the causes of crime he studied the anthropological condition of the criminal. This condition concerns not only the organic and anatomical constitution, but also the psychological, it represents the organic and psychological personality of the criminal. Every one of us inherits at birth, and personifies in life, a certain organic and psychological combination. This constitutes the individual factor of human activity, which either remains normal through life, or becomes criminal or insane. The anthropological factor, then, must not be restricted, as some laymen would restrict it, to the study of the form of the skull or the bones of the criminal. Lombroso had to begin his studies with the anatomical conditions of the criminal, because the skulls may be studied most easily in the museums. But he continued by also studying the brain and the other physiological conditions of the individual, the state of sensibility, and the circulation of matter. And this entire series of studies is but a necessary scientific introduction to the study of the psychology of the criminal, which is precisely the one problem that is of direct and immediate importance. It is this problem which the lawyer and the public prosecutor should solve before discussing the juridical aspect of any crime, for this reveals the causes which induced the criminal to commit a crime. At present there is no methodical standard for a psychological investigation, although such an investigation was introduced into the scope of classic penal law. But for this reason the results of the positive school penetrate into the lecture rooms of the universities of jurisprudence, whenever a law is required for the judicial arraignment of the criminal as a living and feeling human being. And even though the positive school is not mentioned, all profess to be studying the material furnished by it, for instance its analyses of the sentiments of the criminal, his moral sense, his behavior before, during and after the criminal act, the presence of remorse which people, judging the criminal after their own feelings, always suppose the criminal to feel, while, in fact, is seldom present. This is the anthropological factor, which may assume a pathological form, in which case articles 46 and 47 of the penal code remember that there is such a thing as the personality of the criminal. However, aside from insanity, there are thousands of other organic and psychological conditions of the personality of criminals, which a judge might perhaps lump together under the name of extenuating circumstances, but which science desires to have thoroughly investigated. This is not done today, and for this reason the idea of extenuating circumstances constitutes a denial of justice.

This same anthropological factor also includes that which each one of us has: the race character. Nowadays the influence of race on the destinies of peoples and persons is much discussed in sociology, and there are one-sided schools that pretend to solve the problems of history and society by means of that racial influence alone, to which they attribute an absolute importance. But while there are some who maintain that the history of peoples is nothing but the exclusive product of racial character, there are others who insist that the social conditions of peoples and individuals are alone determining. The one is as much a one-sided and incomplete theory as the other. The study of collective society or of the single individual has resulted in the understanding that the life of society and of the individual is always the product of the inextricable net of the anthropological, telluric and social elements. Hence the influence of the race cannot be ignored in the study of nations and personalities, although it is not the exclusive factor which would suffice to explain the criminality of a nation or an individual. Study, for instance, manslaughter in Italy, and, although you will find it difficult to isolate one of the factors of criminality from the network of the other circumstances and conditions that produce it, yet there are such eloquent instances of the influence of racial character, that it would be like denying the existence of daylight if one tried to ignore the influence of the ethnical factor on criminality.

In Italy there are two currents of criminality, two tendencies which are almost diametrically opposed to one another. The crimes due to hot blood and muscle grow in intensity from northern to southern Italy, while the crimes against property increase from south to north. In northern Italy, where movable property is more developed, the crime of theft assumes a greater intensity, while crimes due to conditions of the blood are decreasing on account of the lesser poverty and the resulting lesser degeneration of the people. In the south, on the other hand, crimes against property are less frequent and crimes of blood more frequent. Still there also are in southern Italy certain cases where criminality of the blood is less frequent, and you cannot explain this in any other way than by the influence of racial character. [...]

There are, furthermore, the telluric factors, that is to say, the physical environment in which we live and to which we pay no attention. It requires much philosophy, said Rousseau, to note the things with which we are in daily contact, because the habitual influence of a thing makes it more difficult to be aware of it. This applies also to the immediate influence of the physical conditions on human morality, notwithstanding the spiritualist prejudices which still weigh upon our daily lives. For instance, if it is claimed in the name of supernaturalism and psychism that a man is unhappy because he is vicious, it is equivalent to making a one-sided statement. For it is just as true to say that a man becomes vicious because he is unhappy. Want is the strongest poison for the human body and soul. It is the fountain head of all inhuman and antisocial feeling. Where want spreads out its wings, there the sentiments of love, of affection, of brotherhood, are impossible.

Take a look at the figures of the peasant in the far-off arid Campagna, the little government employe, the laborer, the little shopkeeper. When work is assured, when living is certain, though poor, then want, cruel want, is in the distance, and every good sentiment can germinate and develop in the human heart. The family then lives in a favorable environment, the parents agree, the children are affectionate. And when the laborer, a bronzed statue of humanity, returns from his smoky shop and meets his white-haired mother, the embodiment of half a century of immaculate virtue and heroic sacrifices, then he can, tired, but assured of his daily bread, give room to feelings of affection, and he will cordially invite his mother to share his frugal meal. But let the same man, in the same environment, be haunted by the spectre of want and lack of employment, and you will see the moral atmosphere in his family changing as from day into night. There is no work, and the laborer comes home without any wages. The wife, who does not know how to feed the children, reproaches her husband with the suffering of his family. The man, having been turned away from the doors of ten offices, feels his dignity as an honest laborer assailed in the very bosom of his own family, because he has vainly asked society for honest employment. And the bonds of affection and union are loosened in that family. Its members no longer agree. There are too many children, and when the poor old mother approaches her son, she

reads in his dark and agitated mien the lack of tenderness and feels in her mother heart that her boy, poisoned by the spectre of want, is perhaps casting evil looks at her and harboring the unfilial thought: 'Better an open grave in the cemetery than one mouth more to feed at home!'

It is true, that want alone is not sufficient to prepare the soil in the environment of that suffering family for the roots of real crime and to develop it. Want will weaken the love and mutual respect among the members of that family, but it will not be strong enough alone to arm the hands of the man for a matricidal deed, unless he should get into a pathological mental condition, which is very exceptional and rare. But the conclusions of the positive school are confirmed in this case as in any other. In order that crime may develop, it is necessary that anthropological, social and telluric factors should act together. [...]

We have now demonstrated that crime has its natural source in the combined interaction of three classes of causes, the anthropological (organic and psychological) factor, the telluric factor, and the social factor. And by this last factor we must not only mean want, but any other condition of administrative instability in political, moral, and intellectual life. Every social condition which makes the life of man in society insincere and imperfect is a social factor contributing towards criminality. [...]

This scientific deduction gives rise to a series of investigations which satisfy the mind and supply it with a real understanding of things, far better than the theory that a man is a criminal because he wants to be. No, a man commits crime because he finds himself in certain physical and social conditions, from which the evil plant of crime takes life and strength. [...]

We have thus exhausted in a short and general review the subject of the natural origin of criminality. To sum up, crime is a social phenomenon due to the interaction of anthropological, telluric, and social factors. This law brings about what I have called criminal saturation, which means that every society has the criminality which it deserves, and which produces by means of its geographical and social conditions such quantities and qualities of crime as correspond to the development of each collective human group. [...]

The truth is that the balance of crime is determined by the physical and social environment. But by changing the condition of the social environment, which is most easily modified, the legislator may alter the influence of the telluric environment and the organic and psychic conditions of the population, control the greater portion of crimes, and reduce them considerably. It is our firm conviction that a truly civilized legislator can attenuate the plague of criminality, not so much by means of the criminal code, as by means of remedies which are latent in the remainder of the social life and of legislation. And the experience of the most advanced countries confirms this by the beneficent and preventive influence of criminal legislation resting on efficacious social reforms.

We arrive, then, at this scientific conclusion; In the society of the future, the necessity for penal justice will be reduced to the extent that social justice grows intensively and extensively.

From Enrico Ferri, The Positive School of Criminology *(Chicago: H. Kerr and Co.), 1913, pp. 49–94.*

6

Biological positivism

6.1 Criminal anthropology in the United States
Nicole Hahn Rafter
108

6.2 The increasing appropriation of genetic explanations
Troy Duster
113

6.3 Biosocial studies of antisocial and violent behaviour in children and adults
Adrian Raine
119

6.4 Evolutionary psychology and crime
Satoshi Kanazawa
127

Introduction

KEY CONCEPTS	biosocial explanations; biosocial interaction; degeneration; eugenics; evolutionary psychology; genetics; natural and sexual selection; positivism

We have already encountered positivism as a general idea in chapter 5. Here we focus on criminological work that examines biological or physiological character-istics and, in a variety of differing ways, links these to criminal propensities. Such work varies from early forms which now often seem rather naïve in approach to more modern work that focuses on things like individual genetic make-up and how such factors interact with social environment to influence behaviour. In the background to much of this work, rightly or wrongly, there is the spectre of eugenics which, in its extreme form, is itself associated with policies such as segregation and sterilization (in an attempt to regulate those of inferior physical make-up).

Nicole Hahn Rafter **(Reading 6.1)** explores the history of criminal anthro-pology in the United States. Early work in this field in the late nineteenth century presented itself as a new science. It was positivist in the sense that it was based on methods using direct observation of phenomena and that work should not be influenced by the values of the observer. Moreover, it was founded on the assumption that the nature of the body could reveal facts about the moral make-up of the individual. Like Lombroso (see chapter 5), these scientists believed criminals to be different from other people but their work differed from Lombroso's in a number of important respects – in particular being sceptical about the existence of the 'natural born criminal' (again see chapter 5). At the end of the excerpt Rafter considers the relationship of American criminal anthro-pology to eugenics, finding that a number of authors went much further down this road than Lombroso, advocating policies ranging from restrictions on mar-riage to sterilization.

Picking up on this strand in socio-biological work, Troy Duster **(Reading 6.2)** looks at the vast expansion of interest in genetic explanations for crime, mental illness, intelligence and alcoholism. He challenges the idea that such work repre-sents 'hard science' as distinct from the 'soft science' of much traditional (i.e. sociological) criminology. In doing so he examines some of the classic studies based on studies of twins and adopted children and points to their reliance on institutional records for many of the claims that they make. If you have read the excerpts in chapter 1 then you will not be surprised to find perhaps that one of the complicated issues is what we mean when we use the terms 'crime' and 'criminal', or that there is dispute over whether populations identified by the criminal justice system can be used as the basis for broader generalizations.

There are those who would dismiss all work in this tradition as being crudely positivist, or reductionist, or because of the assumed link with eugenics. Much scholarship in this area is, however, very sophisticated and bears close scrutiny. Adrian Raine **(Reading 6.3)** reviews recent work on biosocial explana-tions for antisocial and violent behaviour in both children and adults. He begins with the bold statement that there 'is now clear evidence … to support the notion that there are genetic influences on antisocial and aggressive behaviour'. The key word here is *influences*, and this gives a clue to what comes later. Thus, for example, in reviewing work on obstetric influences, Raine argues that such factors – say complications in childbirth – interact with psychological risk factors to increase propensity to violence in adulthood. Any explanation offered is very far from some simple cause–effect model.

In the final excerpt Satoshi Kanazawa **(Reading 6.4)** outlines his view of the contribution evolutionary psychology can make to the understanding of crime. Processes of natural and sexual selection, he suggests, have led to the development of a number of psychological mechanisms which are species-typical and distinct to men and women. From this Kanazawa seeks to explain the patterning of various forms of criminal activity – including the predominance of males in such activity, and younger rather than older males. Thus, the age-crime curve, which we meet in a number of the other theory chapters, is linked to the reproductive benefits that are held to emanate from the rivalry between males, particularly at an early age when competition for mates is at its most intense.

Questions for discussion

1. Why might someone influenced by crude biological positivism advocate policies such as restrictions on marriage or sterilization of certain people as a means of reducing crime?

2. Discuss the ethics of eugenics.

3. Identify some of the potential methodological shortcomings in biological explanations for criminality based on studies of twins.

4. In what ways might genetics influence behaviour?

5. What are the main 'obstetric' factors in helping explain patterns in antisocial and violent behaviour?

6. According to Kanazawa, 'why do criminals have lower intelligence than the general population?' Can you see any difficulties with this argument?

7. Kanazawa speculates that 'lower-class men who are physically more attractive should be less criminal than lower-class men who are physically unattractive'. Following the other arguments in his excerpt, why might this be the case, and what difficulties do you see in such a suggestion?

6.1 Criminal anthropology in the United States
Nicole Hahn Rafter

The substance of US criminal anthropology

US criminal anthropologists wrote in a context in which the primary experts on criminal matters were legal authorities and penologists. Their own work was not as unprecedented as they claimed, for a tradition of positivist criminological research had been accumulating throughout the nineteenth century, built up by alienists who analyzed the connections between mental disorders and crime (e.g., Ray, 1838), phrenologists who investigated the organic causes of crime (e.g., Farnham, 1846; also see Davies, 1955: Ch. 8; Savitz *et al.*, 1977), and degenerationists, such as Richard Dugdale (1877), who associated criminal behavior with bad heredity. But these forerunners did not present their work as 'criminology' nor themselves as 'criminologists.' Lombroso's followers had to identify a new jurisdiction (Abbott, 1988) – to stake out professional territory, separate from jurisprudence and penology – over which criminologists would have authority. To accomplish this task they used two tactics, first claiming that their approach constituted an entirely new science and then producing information on criminal types that confirmed that claim.

Criminal anthropology as a science

Echoing Lombroso, the Americans insisted that criminal anthropology had for the first time carried the study of crime across the divide between idle speculation and true science. Noyes's (1887:32) early article heralds the advent of a 'new science, which considers the criminal rather than the crime'; Drahms, calling crime a 'social disease,' claims that 'Criminology reaches the dignity of a science by the same right of necessity that gives to the medical profession its place' (1900:xxi-xxii). They did not always label this science 'criminology,' however. Because the field was just beginning to emerge, through their work, they sometimes preferred to fold the study of criminal man into better accepted sciences – 'scientific sociology' (MacDonald, 1893:173), 'the science of penology' (Boies, 1901), or the 'scientific' investigation of degeneracy (Talbot, 1 898:viii). But all considered their work 'scientific,' by which they meant that unlike earlier

commentators on crime, who had included God and free will in the causational picture, they would be materialists examining only phenomena anchored in the natural world of matter. [...]

From their materialism, two methodological conclusions followed. First, criminal anthropologists would use only empirical methods, starting with direct observation instead of theory or metaphysics. They would report on measurements of criminals' bodies made with scientific equipment, such as callipers, the dynamometer, and the esthesiometer; they would collect information on criminal jargon and tattoos, excerpt passages from confessions, and gather 'proverbs expressing distrust of the criminal type' (Lombroso-Ferrero, 1911:50). All such data would be recorded dispassionately. [...]

Materialism led criminal anthropologists to their central assumption – that the body must mirror moral capacity. They took for granted a one-to-one correspondence between the criminal's physical being and ethical behavior. [...] Nature had made the investigator's task relatively simple: To detect born criminals, one needed only the appropriate apparatus. Degree of criminality could be determined by charting the offender's deformities.

The born criminal

At criminal anthropology's heart lay Lombroso's perception of 'the congenital criminal as an anomaly, partly pathological and partly atavistic, a revival of the primitive savage' (Lombroso-Ferrero 1911:xxii) .... 'Criminals,' Talbot (1898:18) writes in a typical passage,

> form a variety of the human family quite distinct from law-abiding men. A low type of physique indicating a deteriorated character gives a family likeness due to the fact that they form a community which retrogrades from generation to generation.

Most of the US criminal anthropologists repeat Lombroso's descriptions of the born criminal's physical anomalies – his pointed head, heavy jaw, receding brow, scanty beard, long arms, and so on. They also adhere closely to Lombroso by enumerating the criminal's 'psychical' anomalies – his laziness and frivolity, his use of argot and tendency to inscribe both his cell and his body with hiero-glyphics, his moral insensibility and emotional instability. Seemingly the most scientific aspect of criminal anthropology, these were also its most sensational findings.

But five of the eight American authors express doubts about the born criminal's existence even while devoting entire chapters to his stig-mata. Apparently unable to resist reporting Lombroso's galvanizing findings, these five simul-taneously qualify their reports, often without reconciling their enthusiasm for the 'new science' with their uneasiness about it. After filling many pages with such statements as 'Flesch, out of 50 brains of criminals, did not find one without anomalies,' MacDonald (1893:58, 65) confesses that little is known about the relation of 'psychical' to organic peculiarities. Henderson (1893:113) lauds Lombroso while warning that his views 'are by no means universally accepted as final.' Lydston (1904:25–26) masks his ambivalence by mocking the 'ultra-materialism' of 'so-called criminal anthropologists' and aligning himself with the doctrine's true practitioners. But Drahms (1900) and Parsons (1909) completely fail to harmonize their misgivings about born-criminal theory with their desire to advance it. These first criminologists lacked confidence in the scientific centerpiece of their doctrine. They endorsed a science that even to them seemed shaky.

Insofar as they deviated from Lombroso's teach-ings about born criminals, the Americans did so not by rejecting his theory but by supplementing it, par-ticularly by placing greater emphasis on the criminal's weak intelligence. In *Criminal Man*, Lombroso pays little attention to the criminal's men-tality aside from stating that '*Intelligence* is feeble in some and exaggerated in others' (Lombroso-Ferrero, 1911:41 (emphasis in original); also see Lombroso and Ferrero, 1895:170–171). Four of the eight US criminal anthropologists, in contrast, carry Lombroso's implications to their logical conclusion by finding that criminals are intellectually as well as ethically weak, mental as well as moral imbeciles. Talbot (1898:18), for example, draws on evolutionism to explain that 'there is truly a brute brain within the man's, and when the latter stops short of its charac-teristic development, it is natural that it should manifest only its most primitive functions.' Lydston (1904:946), noting that 'a defective moral sense is

most likely to be associated with defective develop-ment of the brain in general,' concludes that it is 'not surprising that the typic or born criminal should lack intelligence' (also see MacDonald, 1893:Ch. 4; Drahms, 1900:72–75). The American concern with the criminal's poor intelligence formed the bridge between criminal anthropology and its successor, defective delinquency theory, which identified crimi-nality with 'feeble-mindedness.'

The US authors further supplemented Lombroso's work by thoroughly integrating criminal anthropology with degeneration theory. Popular on both sides of the Atlantic, degenerationism attrib-uted the genesis of socially problematic groups – paupers and the insane and feeble-minded, as well as the criminalistic – to an inherited tendency toward organic devolution ('degeneracy,' 'depraved heredity,' 'innate viciousness,' and other syn-onyms). (On degenerationism, see, generally, Chamberlin and Oilman, 1985; Pick, 1989.) Lombroso did not immediately realize that degener-ation could explain the criminal's bad heredity; at first he relied on the notion of atavism (Parmelee, 1911:xxix; Wolfgang, 1972:247, 249). His American followers, writing after degeneration theory had had more time to mature, made it the basis for their hereditarianism. Aside from MacDonald (who depends most heavily on European sources), the US authors emphasize that the born criminal comes 'of a degenerate line, and that if he have offspring some measure of his innate viciousness will be transmit-ted' (McKim, 1900:23).

American criminal anthropologists stress the close connections among degenerate types; poverty, mental disease, and crime were but inter-changeable symptoms of the underlying organic malaise. 'The Degenerate Stock,' Henderson (1893:114) explained, 'has three main branches, organically united – Dependents, Defectives and Delinquents. They are one blood.' It followed that 'vice, crime, and insanity may be regarded as merely different phases of degeneracy which so resemble one another that we are often at a loss when we would distinguish between them' (McKim, 1900:64). The term 'criminal anthropol-ogy,' Haller (1963:16) has pointed out, was 'in a sense a misnomer,' for the doctrine 'was concerned with the nature and causes of all classes of human defects.' This was especially true of US criminal anthropology. Wedded to degenerationism, the first American criminologists had no interest in defining the study of crime as a field apart from the study of other social problems.

Other criminal types

Lombroso eventually opened his science to the investigation of a range of criminal types by distinguishing between born criminals and 'criminaloids,' such as habitual criminals, who do not inherit but acquire the habit of offending; juridical criminals, who violate the law accidentally; and the handsome, sensitive criminal-by-passion, who is motivated by altruism (Lombroso-Ferrero, 1911: Ch. 4). These were, in large part, etiological distinctions: Heredity alone determines the behavior of born criminals, whereas environmental and sociological factors increasingly shape the criminality of higher offender types. Six of the nine US books include substantial material on the etiology of criminal types (there is little or none in MacDonald, 1893; Talbot, 1898; or McKim, 1900). The Americans' typologies, like that of Lombroso, ultimately imply a close correlation between degree of criminality and social class. The positivist approach began by promoting a theory heavy with class content, and the founders of US criminology were unable to separate their methodological assumptions from the substance of their message.

The Americans' commentaries on criminal types fall along a continuum that starts with the very crude typification of one of their first books, Boies's *Prisoners and Paupers* (1893), and ends with the highly developed typology of the series' last work, Parsons' *Responsibility for Crime* (1909). *Prisoners and Paupers* reviews the causes of degeneration at length but does not relate them to a subsequent discussion of degrees of criminality. Boies had not yet realized that he could explain differences among criminal types in terms of varying causes of crime (cf. Boies, 1901). His typology, moreover, is rudimentary, identifying merely two sorts of criminals. On the one hand are the 'born' or 'incorrigible' offenders, who have 'inherited criminality' and constitute 40% of the 'criminal class' (Boies, 1893:172–183); the remaining 60% are 'the victims of heteronomy [multiple factors], the subjects of evil associations and environment' (p. 184). Only the latter can be reformed. Boies vaguely indicates that incorrigibles can be identified by number of convictions and offense seriousness (pp. 178, 185), but in this book he

mostly avoids the issue of how to distinguish the hereditary from the heteronomic criminal.

Chronologically and substantively, Drahms's *The Criminal* (1900) marks a midpoint in the process by which US criminal anthropologists articulated a hierarchy of criminal types differentiated by the causes of their offenses. Drahms recognizes three kinds of criminals. The *instinctive criminal's* 'biological, moral, and intellectual equipments are the results of hereditary entailment from prenatal sources' (p. 56). The *habitual criminal* 'draws his inspirational forces from... environment rather than parental fountains' (p. 57). And the 'essentially social misdemeanant,' whom Drahms labels not a 'criminal' but rather a *single offender*, is 'possibly as free from the antisocial taint as the average man' (p. 55). 'He is a criminal because the law declares it' (p. 57).

Parsons' *Responsibility for Crime* (1909) culminates this typification process by identifying a plethora of criminal types. Parsons starts with the most abnormal, the *insane criminal*, after which he describes the *born criminal* ('His normal condition is abnormal ... he is born to crime. It is his natural function' (p. 35); the *habitual criminal* ('he is capable of something else, at least in one period of his life. The born criminal never is' (p. 36)); and the *professional criminal* ('frequently of a high order of intelligence, – often a college graduate. His profession becomes an art in which he sometimes becomes a master' (p. 37)). Of the next type, the *occasional criminal*, Parsons informs us that, 'Here, for the first time, environment plays an important part in the nature of the crime committed'; the occasional criminal, moreover, 'frequently possesses a keen sense of remorse' and is 'frequently a useful citizen' (p. 41). Parsons' typology ends with the *criminal by passion or accident*, who is characterized by a high 'sense of duty' and 'precise motive,' unmarred by anomalies, and in need of neither cure nor punishment (pp. 42–44).

Whereas Boies (1893) had trouble explaining how to differentiate between criminal types, Parsons (1909) uses explicit criteria, including the frequency of physical and mental anomalies; degrees of reformability, intelligence, skill, and remorse; the extent to which environment influences behavior; and the offender's ability to exercise free will. These criteria, putatively derived from biology and then used to establish gradations within the criminal class, are in fact derived from social class and then attributed back to biology.

Criminal anthropology has finally unraveled the implications latent in Boies's distinction between hereditary and heteronomic criminals, arriving at a hierarchy of criminal types that corresponds to the social class hierarchy. At the bottom of the scale is the born criminal, rough in appearance and manners, a foreigner or Negro (Boies, 1893: Chs. 6 and 7), uneducated, of poor background, a drinker. At the top stands Parsons' gentlemanly normal offender, anomaly free, a product of not heredity but environment, intelligent and skilled, conscience stricken and reformable.

Criminal anthropologists' 'upper' groups, Zeman (1981:390) points out, 'made it possible to maintain a sharp separation, not just of degree, but of essence, between the motivation and character of the ordinary respectable citizen and that of the lower-class offender.' One can extend Zeman's insight by observing that that 'essence' was what criminal anthropologists called 'heredity.' In the process of distinguishing among types of criminal bodies, they established a biological hierarchy in which worthiness was signified by class attributes.

The criminal anthropologists' biologism had two long-term effects: It gave positivism a bad name, and it slowed the development of sociological approaches to the study of crime. Positivism suffered no immediate harm by making its criminological debut through criminal anthropology, but its initial confirmation of class biases helped make it suspect to mid-twentieth-century criminologists, some of whom rejected any methods that seemed remotely positivistic (see Gottfredson and Hirschi, 1987: esp. 9–10 and 14–17). Moreover, the biologistic and individualistic emphases of the criminal anthropologists, together with their wide-net degenerationism, attracted nonsociological specialists into criminology's domain. Even when they used a multifactorial approach, criminal anthropologists located 'the causes of human conduct in the physiological and mental characteristics of the individual' (Parmelee, 1911:xii). This set the stage for the heavy involvement of psychologists, armed with intelligence tests, in the articulation and application of the next criminological theory, that of defective delinquency (e.g., Gould, 1981: Ch. 5), and of physicians and psychiatrists in the subsequent theory of psychopathy. In the long run, criminal anthropology dampened development of sociological approaches to crime and legitimated those associated with biology

and psychology. This is one reason why, even today, criminology draws researchers from a variety of disciplines.

Criminal anthropology and eugenics

Advocating that punishments be tailored to fit the offender types they had identified, criminal anthropologists aimed at making justice as well as criminology a 'science' based on the lawbreaker's biology (Parsons, 1909:194). Much as some Americans had gone beyond Lombroso in developing aspects of criminal anthropology, so too did some outdo the master in deriving from the doctrine social defense conclusions of the sort that became known as *eugenics*.

According to eugenics theory, a nation can save its stock from degeneration by preventing reproduction of the unfit (negative eugenics) and simultaneously encouraging the fit to produce more offspring (positive eugenics). US criminal anthropologists did not use the term *eugenics*, which had not yet entered the American vocabulary. But some joined the ranks of Americans who had been calling for eugenic measures since the 1870s (e.g., Lowell, 1879; also see Hailer, 1963; Rafter, 1992; Tyor and Bell, 1984), employing such synonyms as 'the selection of the fittest and/the rejection of the unfit' (McKim, 1900:185).

In *Criminal Man and Crime: Its Causes and Remedies*, Lombroso argues merely for individualization of consequences: 'Punishments should vary according to the type of criminal' (Lombroso–Ferrero, 1911:185). Criminals of passion and political offenders should 'never' be imprisoned. For criminaloids, probation and indeterminate sentencing are appropriate (Lombroso–Ferrero, 1911:186–187). Even habitual and born criminals may be improved under the indeterminate sentence but those who continue to demonstrate incorrigibility should be kept in 'perpetual isolation in a penal colony' or, in extreme cases, executed (Lombroso – Ferrero, 1911:198, 208; also see Lombroso, 1911, Pt. III: Chs. 2 and 3). Lombroso makes these last recommendations not to prevent reproduction but 'to realise the supreme end – social safety' (Lombroso–Ferrero, 1911:216; cf. Lombroso, 1912:59–60).

Like Lombroso, half of the major US criminal anthropologists show little or no interest in eugenics.[1] The other four, however, champion eugenic solutions. Two support life sentences on the grounds that they will prevent criminals from breeding (Boies, 1893; Parsons, 1909). Several recommend marriage restriction. 'The marriages of all criminals should be prohibited, but the utmost vigilance should be exercised to prevent the marriage of the instinctive' (Boies, 1901:49; also see Boies, 1893:280; Lydston, 1904:55–562; and Parsons, 1909:198–199). And some advise sterilization (Boies, 1893, 1901; Lydston 1904).

The most extreme eugenic solution came from McKim (1900), who objected to perpetual detention due to its costliness and to sterilization partly because it 'could not be repeated' (p. 24). For 'the *very* weak and the *very vicious who fall into the hands of the State*,' McKim proposes 'a *gentle, painless death*' (p. 188; emphasis in original). Execution by 'carbonic acid gas' is the 'surest, the simplest, the kindest, and most humane means for preventing reproduction among those whom we deem unworthy of this high privilege' (pp. 193, 188). Their disappearance would result in 'a tremendous reduction in the amount of crime' (p. 255).[2]

Although there was no necessary connection between criminal anthropology and eugenics, some of the major US Lombrosians endorsed eugenic applications for their doctrine. In McKim's case in particular, advocacy of eugenic solutions is clearly the author's main purpose (1900:iii – v); Boies's two treatises and that of Lydston are also suffused with eugenic rationales. In these works, science becomes the servant of not just crime control but a highly charged ideology. Their authors treat criminology as a means to an end rather than a science of value in its own right. While most of today's criminologists would be appalled by such overt partisanship (not to mention eugenics theory itself), we remain divided over whether our field can or should even try to produce agenda-free information.

> *From N.H. Rafter 'Criminal anthropology in the United States',* Criminology, *(1992) 30(4): 525–546.*

References

Abbott, Andrew (1988) *The System of Professions.* Chicago: University of Chicago Press.

Boies, Henry M. (1893) *Prisoners and Paupers.* New York: G.P. Putnam's Sons.

— (1901) *The Science of Penology: The Defence of Society Against Crime.* New York: G.P. Putnam's Sons.

Chamberlin, J. Edward and Sander L. Gilman (eds.) (1985) *Degeneration: The Dark Side of Progress.* New York: Columbia University Press.

Davies, John D. (1955) *Phrenology: Fad and Science.* New Haven: Yale University Press.

Drahms, August (1900) *The Criminal: His Personnel and Environment – A Scientific Study, with an Introduction by Cesare Lombroso.* 1971. Montclair, N.J.: Patterson Smith.

Dugdale, Richard L. (1877) *'The Jukes': A Study in Crime, Pauperism, Disease and Heredity; also Further Studies of Criminals.* New York: G.P. Putnam's Sons.

Farnham, E.W. (1846) 'Introductory preface' to M.D. Sampson, *Rationale of Crime.* New York: D. Appleton & Company.

Gottfredson, Michael R. and Travis Hirschi (1987) The positivist tradition. In Michael R. Gottfredson and Travis Hirschi (eds.), *Positive Criminology*, Newbury Park, Calif.: Sage.

Gould, Stephen J. (1981) *The Mismeasure of Man.* New York: W.W. Norton.

Haller, Mark (1963) *Eugenics: Hereditarian Attitudes in American Thought.* New Brunswick, N.J.: Rutgers University Press.

Henderson, Charles R. (1893) *An Introduction to the Study of the Dependent, Defective and Delinquent Classes.* Boston: D.C. Heath.

Lombroso, Cesare (1895) Criminal anthropology: Its origin and application. *The Forum* 20:33–49.

— (1911) *Crime: Its Causes and Remedies.* 1918. Boston: Little, Brown.

— (1912) Crime and insanity in the twenty-first century. *The Journal of Criminal Law and Criminology* 3:57–61.

Lombroso, Cesare and William Ferrero (1895) *The Female Offender.* 1915. New York: D. Appleton.

Lombroso-Ferrero, Gina (1911) *Criminal Man According to the Classification of Cesare Lombroso.* 1972. Montclair, N.J: Patterson Smith.

Lowell, Josephine Shaw (1879) One means of preventing pauperism. National Conference of Charities, 6th Proceedings 1879:189–200.

Lydston, George F. (1904) *The Diseases of Society (The Vice and Crime Problem).* 1905. Philadelphia: LB. Lippincott.

MacDonald, Arthur (1893) *Criminology, with an Introduction by Dr. Cesare Lombroso*. New York: Funk & Wagnalls.

McKim, W. Duncan (1900) *Heredity and Human Progress*. New York: G.P. Putnam's Sons.

Noyes, William (1887) The criminal type. *American Journal of Social Science* 24:31–42.

Parmelee, Maurice (1911) Introduction to the English version of Cesare Lombroso, *Crime: Its Causes and Remedies* (1918). Boston: Little, Brown.

Parsons, Philip A. (1909) *Responsibility for Crime*. New York: Columbia University; Longmans, Green, agents.

Pick, Daniel (1989) *Faces of Degeneration: A European Disorder, c.1848–c.1918*. New York: Cambridge University Press.

Rafter, Nicole Hahn (1992) Claims-making and socio-cultural context in the first US eugenics campaign. *Social Problems* 39:17–34.

Ray, Isaac (1838) *A Treatise on the Medical Jurisprudence of Insanity*. 1983. New York: Da Capo Press.

Savitz, Leonard D., Stanley H. Turner, and Toby Dickman (1977) The origin of scientific criminology: Franz Joseph Gall as the first criminologist. In Robert F. Meier (ed.), *Theory in Criminology: Contemporary Views*. Beverly Hills, Calif.: Sage.

Talbot, Eugene S. (1898) *Degeneracy: Its Causes, Signs, and Results*. New York and London: Walter Scott.

Tyor, Peter L. and Leland V. Bell (1984) *Caring for the Retarded in America: A History*. Westport, Conn.: Greenwood Press.

Wolfgang, Marvin E. (1972) Cesare Lombroso. In Herman Mannheim (ed.), *Pioneers in Criminology*. 2d ed. enlr. Montclair, N.J.: Patterson Smith.

Zeman, Thomas E. (1981) Order, crime, and punishment: The American criminological tradition. Ph.D. dissertation, University of California, Santa Cruz.

Notes

1 Talbot explicitly rejects eugenics (1898:347–348); MacDonald and Drahms recommend life imprisonment to incapacitate born criminals physically but not reproductively. Henderson (1893:ft29) proposes 'a life sentence for recidivists' for mildly eugenical reasons ('to reduce the supply of morally deformed offspring'), but merely in passing.

2 Boies and Parsons praised McKim's proposal while reluctantly rejecting it, Boies (1901:53) because he feared that 'public sentiment does not yet support the purely scientific plan of Dr. McKim,' and Parsons (1909:90) because it was too violent.

6.2 The increasing appropriation of genetic explanations
Troy Duster

In the mid- to late 1970s, both the popular media and scientific journals published an explosion of articles that staked a renewed claim to the genetic explanation of matters that the previous two decades had 'laid to rest' as social and environmental. A review of the *Reader's Guide to Periodical Literature* from 1976 to 1982 revealed a 231 percent increase in articles that attempted to explain the genetic basis for crime, mental illness, intelligence, and alcoholism during this brief six-year period. Even more remarkably, between 1983 and 1988, articles that attributed a genetic basis to crime appeared *more than four times* as frequently as they had during the previous decade. This development in the popular print media was based in part upon what was occurring in the scientific journals.

During this period, a new surge of articles (more than double the previous decade) appeared in the scientific literature,[1] making claims about the genetic basis of several forms of social deviance and mental illness.[2]

At first glance, it would appear that this was an outgrowth of what was happening in the field of molecular genetics. [M]any important breakthroughs were occurring during this period, including the increasing ability for intrauterine detection of birth defects. However, the resurgence of genetic claims just noted was not coming from those working at the vanguard laboratories in molecular biology or biochemistry. Indeed, given the requirements of up-to-the minute monitoring to keep abreast of technological and scientific breakthroughs in these fields, it is of special interest to note that the major data base for the resurgent claims was a heavy reliance upon Scandinavian institutional registries dating back to the early part of the century (Kety, 1968, 1976; Kringlen, 1968; Fischer, 1971; Mednick, 1985; Mednick *et al.*, 1984 Jensen, 1969). If the new claimants were not the researchers responsible for the new developments described in the previous chapters, who were they?

Who is making the 'genetic claims'?

Those making the claims about the genetic component of an array of behaviors and conditions (crime, mental illness, alcoholism, gender relations, intelligence) come from a wide range of disciplines, tenuously united under a banner of an increased role for the explanatory power of genetics. Relatively few of these claims come from molecular genetics. Edward Wilson is an entomologist who made his reputation studying insect societies (Wilson, 1971). Yet, he got the Pulitzer Prize for publishing a book applying a genetic theory to social life of humans (Wilson, 1978). Then, in *Genes, Mind, and Culture* (cowritten with Lumsden, 1981), he went on to argue that culture itself springs largely from genetics.

Arthur Jensen (1969), who vaulted to national fame with a claim on the relationship between genetics and intelligence, is an educational psychologist. Seymour Kety (1976) is a psychiatrist, and is one of the leading figures in the world espousing the genetics of schizophrenia. David Rowe (1986) and Sarnoff Mednick (1984), who argue the genetic basis of crime, and Eysenck (1975, 1971), who argues the genetic basis of psychopathology and intelligence, are all psychologists. Richard Herrnstein (1971) is a Harvard psychologist who has not only argued the genetics of intelligence, but has even speculated that someday 'the tendency to be unemployed may run in the genes.' Herrnstein recently teamed with James Q. Wilson (1985:103), a political scientist, to write a book that asks for a more sympathetic reading of the possible 'biological roots of an individual predisposition to crime.' And it is a sociologist, Robert Gordon (1987), who argues that race differences in delinquency are best explained by IQ differences between the races, not socioeconomic status. Each of these men lays considerable claim, and most have achieved consid-

erable attention in the popular media postulating the importance of heredity in the explication of human behavior.

Molecular geneticists, whether specialists with humans, animals, or plants, are themselves typically wary of making claims about the genetics of these forms of human behavior.[3] How can the relative modesty, scientific tentativeness, even quietude of these laboratory geneticists on these subjects be explained, while researchers in these other traditions of genetics tend to be the most passionate advocates for the biological or genetic component? It is the rare molecular geneticist who would stake his or her professional reputation on the genetics of 'altruism' or 'intelligence' or 'crime' or a host of other human concerns and behaviors.[4] Yet, these other researches have made remarkably effective claim to the territory. Before turning to a closer examination of the nature and substance and credibility of the claim, it will be instructive to review some of the halo effects of some of these 'genetic explanations'.

Is the issue really 'hard' vs. soft' science?

In the conventional wisdom and the popular media, genetics is 'hard' science with a precise data base and clearly defined empirical referents for its concepts, while sociology is 'soft' or, perhaps, not science at all.[5] That depends. If one compares the prediction and control in plant or animal genetics with prediction and control in affective social relations, this is unequivocally true. A basic difference, of course, is the availability of far more tightly controlled experiments in plant and animal genetics, unthinkable in human genetics or human behavioral research (Edlin, 1987). However, in the construction of a knowledge base about such matters as the causes of mental illness, crime, intelligence, and alcoholism, the distinction between the explanatory power of genetics and sociology fades completely. In the language of science, the dependent variable is equally complex for those seeking a genetic explanation as for those seeking a social structural account. However, the social scientists have been far more sophisticated in analyzing the contingencies and patterned variations that render a one-dimensional version of these 'dependent variables' scientifically meaningless. To illustrate this point, I will contrast the basic flaws in the assumptions around the 'genetics' of [. . .] crime.

The problematic of the genetics of criminals

In early January 1982, Sarnoff Mednick, a professor of psychology at the University of Southern California, presented results of his research on 'crime and heredity' to the annual meeting of the American Association for the Advancement of Science. Mednick reported on a study of 14,237 Danish men from the Danish adoption records for the years 1924–1927. He found that the rate of criminality among men whose natural parents had been criminals was nearly three times higher than it was among men whose natural parents were law-abiding. He said he found this to be the case even when sons of criminals were raised in law-abiding families.

On the recurrent theme from those who report such results from twin studies, Mednick also reported that identical twins are more likely to both be criminals (if one was a criminal) than were fraternal twins, even when reared apart.

Here is the print media's account of Mednick's claims of findings on the 'biology of crime':

> Criminals Mednick has studied also show strong biological 'markers' associated with their criminality, he said. Their 'galvanic skin responses' – the kind of response typically elicited by liars in lie detector tests – show a marked difference from non-criminals, Mednick said. Their brain wave patterns are different from non-criminals, and so are several other nervous system responses, he said.[6]

Mednick is then reported to have stated the following:

> 'If this small, active and highly disturbing group could be identified early it would have a marked effect on the crime rate,' Mednick said. 'But the form of intervention would have to be attractive and non-punitive'. [...]

The major methodological strategy in twin studies and related work comparing adopted children to blood relatives is based primarily upon already existing *institutional* records.[7] These institutional contacts with the criminal justice system almost universally represent the population from which one can take and make generalizable statements.

However, there are three basic reasons why studies of crime and genetics are so problematic that it is almost impossible to have much confidence in them. First, the very definition of what constitutes a crime is highly socially variable, depending upon the passage of law, on policing practices and the judicial system of a society, on the point in history, etc. [...]

Even inside a single culture, at a given moment, the social status of the offender is central to the process of determining whether a 'crime' has been committed. It is the social scientists of crime who have best articulated, researched, and documented this problem (Currie, 1985).[8] Moreover, studies of crime and genetics are based upon police records, but the records simply record the local customs. For example, if one looks at the record in 250 years of US history, no white man ever committed the crime of rape on a black woman in twelve southern states. If a Scandinavian came to the United States to study crime and genetics (to parallel Mednick's study) and the research was based upon records, this whole population of 'criminals' would be missed.[9]

Second, the term *criminal* lumps together the one-time offender with the career criminal, the professional and isolated con artist with a bureaucrat in organized crime; it lumps together the hit-and-run driver with the rapist; it even lumps together the inadvertent poacher on the land of the gentry with a deliberately adulterous member of the gentry (Hay *et al.*, 1975:189–253). What it typically does not do is lump together the crimes of corporate executives with the crimes of the common thief and burglar. The implications of this for a genetic explanation of crime have not escaped the Supreme Court of the United States. [I]n *Skinner* v. *Oklahoma*, the Supreme Court ruled in 1942 that the sterilization of a man because he was a third-generation criminal was in violation of the equal protection clause of the Constitution, unwarranted because the prosecution had not demonstrated that the more privileged classes could not similarly be prosecuted. The State of Oklahoma's *Habitual Criminal Sterilization Act* provided that one convicted of three felonies could be 'rendered sexually sterile'.

> Skinner had been convicted of stealing chickens in 1926 and had been found guilty of armed robbery in 1926 and 1929 . . . [The US Supreme Court] chose to overturn the law because it violated the Fourteenth Amendment's guarantee of

the equal protection of the laws. Oklahoma had exempted certain kinds of felons from its reach. Offenses against prohibition, revenue laws, embezzlement, and political crimes were deemed insufficient for sterilization. This clear bias in favor of white-collar criminals was judged by the Supreme Court to be 'unmistakable discrimination'. (Reilly, 1977:126–127)

I shall return shortly to this very matter of systematic distortion in the scientific literature on crime as it relates to privilege, power, and genetic explanations.

Finally, what constitutes a criminal is not as straightforward as it appears. One way of defining a criminal is to simply say that it is someone who has committed a crime. However, there is a competing definition, which characterizes a criminal as someone who has been *convicted* of a crime. Not all those who commit crimes are convicted.[10] Only a small percentage of such persons are arrested, fewer still are prosecuted, only a fraction of these are convicted, and even a smaller percentage incarcerated. [...]

To understand the sieve of the criminal justice system that produces the remarkable skew of human subjects that show up in prisons, it is necessary to move from the commission of the act characterized in law as a 'crime' to the point of conviction. Starting with the arbitrary figure of 1,000 burglaries, it is generous beyond the best empirical research now available to say that 700 will come to the attention of the police (Reiman, 1984). Of these, at most 300 will be 'cleared by arrest,' and a maximum of 180 would go to trial. Of these, at most 120 would be convicted (often plea bargaining lessens the 'crime' to a different category). Of these, no more than 75 will ever spend any time in prison. To designate this the 'criminal population' for purposes of research is obviously not a sound procedure. Yet, it is from these records that researchers come along to obtain their data on the 'genetics' or 'biology' of criminals.

The assumption lodged in the genetic explanation of criminals based upon prison incarceration studies is that the population 'in hand' (in contact with the institutional sieve) can be related to the putative genetics of the phenomena. Rates of incarceration vary from country to country). [...]

When reviewing the incarceration rates in the United States, the striking figure is the difference by race. For whites, 65 per 100,000 are locked up, which comes close to the European figure. But for blacks, the rate an astonishing 544 per 100,000 (Dunbaugh, 1979). [...]

If one were doing a correlational study looking for the 'genetic component' in imprisonment, one could find a 'significant' statistic that would show the importance of 'genes' (in this case, race). [...]

The racial domination of blacks in US prisons has only occurred in the last part of this century. The problem with genetic interpretations is that they are routinely based upon institutional practices at certain historical moments. During the last decades of this century, with blacks constituting about 12 percent of the US population and committing about 60 percent of the reported homicides, and with the incarceration rate reflecting the racial patterns noted above, and with our prisons getting darker and darker, it is only a matter of time before there is a convergence of the halo of the new genetics and the appropriation of that halo by other researchers. Robert Gordon (1987) concluded his research on race and delinquency as follows:

> black-white IQ difference exists even before pupils enter school, that it holds for tests whose content is related to the school curriculum only remotely at best, that it is not changed in the course of schooling, that it has not decreased over time despite the substantial reduction of black-white differences in the amount of schooling attained, and that the difference has been demonstrated not to depend on differences in the same underlying *g* that accounts for individual differences within each race. It is time to consider the black-white IQ difference seriously when confronting the problem of crime in American society. (Gordon, 1987:91–92)

Many years ago, two scholars enjoined social scientists to spend more of their time studying the deviance of those in power, to at least bring some balance to the study of those without power. In the late 1960 Martin Nicolas coined a popular phrase when he said that sociologists of deviance spent too much of their time with 'their eyes down, and their hands up.' He called attention to the warped imbalance of the vast amount of time, resources, and energy social scientists spend looking at people at the bottom of the social order (prostitutes, traditional criminal gangs, organized crime, drug addicts, etc.). [...] Nicolas pointed to the sharp contrast of the relatively few studies done on the deviance and criminal behavior of those in power.[11] Laura Nader (1972) made a similar point when she enjoined anthropologists to balance their studies of tribal peoples and do more research on power and privilege, what she called a requirement to 'study up.'

There has been a plethora of data collected and published in the last decade documenting the pervasive character of crime among the most privileged strata of the society (Simon and Eitzen, 1982; Simpson, 1987; Clinard and Yeager, 1980; Mokhiber, 1988). These crimes range from criminal homicide prosecution and conviction to the knowledgeable continued pollution of workplace air with a substance known at the time to be cancer-causing (Brodeur, 1985). [...] Yet [...] when researchers summarize the data on 'crime and genetics' (Wilson and Herrnstein, 1985:90:103), there is no conceptualization of the upper strata of the society as the subject matter. Indeed, the one time that Wilson and Herrnstein refer to white-collar crime is to note that blacks make up about one-third of those arrested for fraud, forgery, and counterfeiting, and for receiving stolen property, and one-quarter of those arrested for embezzlement. They note that blacks are therefore overrepresented even in these categories. But they follow this with an insidious conclusion that white overrepresentation in securities violations and tax fraud schemes is mainly a function of the fact that blacks lack access to high-status occupations (Wilson and Herrnstein, 1985:462). In other words, when whites commit more crimes at the top, they attribute this to opportunity structures; when blacks commit more crimes, it is implicitly more a feature of their race.

In all of the adoption and twin studies around crime, none addresses the possible criminal genetics of the privileged strata (Marsh and Katz, 1985). Indeed, it seems a jarring concept to even consider. And that is of course the point. 'Genetic explanations' of crime are appropriated to account for those at the base of the social order.

From T.Duster Backdoor to Eugenics *(New York: Routledge), 2003, pp. 92–101.*

Notes

1 More than twice the number that appeared in the previous decade.

2 Crime, mental illness, intelligence and alcoholism.

3 To characterize these as 'behaviors' is a short-hand, since mental illness and intelligence are arguably not 'human behaviors'. However, the only way that one makes an assessment of either is with some behavioral manifestation, then observation and, ostensibly, measurement. It is the behavioral component that is usually the source of disagreement as to its root causes.

4 It does not follow that the highly esteemed scientists in biological research then come forward with jewels of social and political wisdom. In the first chapter, a quote from Linus Pauling on genetic screening, a quote from Jonas Salk in this chapter on the stratification of the sciences, and Stern's comment (also in this chapter) on 'controls' in social science research all reveal how modesty is the best strategy as one steps into social analysis.

5 The *New York Times* editorial of April 4, 1981, captured the image well. The *Times* was sympathetic to social research, but tried to explain why Regan's budget cutters at the Office of Management and Budget had targeted the social sciences for specific surgery, while leaving the natural sciences intact. The editorial speculated that the image of the social sciences is that that they are imprecise, commonsensical, and not of particular or practical use.

6 *San Francisco Chronicle*, Nov. 26, 1981.

7 Rowe (1986) does use self-report mailed questionnaire for data for a twin study. In this article, his focus is upon 'anti-social' behavior.

8 An excellent example is Paul Bohannan's (1960) classical work on the extraordinary low rates of homicide in sub-Sahara Africa. No empirical research before or since has thrown into better relief how ludicrous is the argument (pre-Bohannan) that the higher rate of homicide among American blacks is genetic.

9 Those who would suggest that rape during slavery is a political concept are on a slippery slope of logic that leads not only to joining with an old Eldridge Cleaver formulation about rape during rebellious periods as politics, but even more radically, to then have to address a rhetorical question from the Marxists: When is crime not political?

10 It has been estimated that Americans steal $38,000,000 per day in shoplifting alone. The president's Crime Commission's survey of 10,000 households concluded that '91 percent of all Americans have violated laws that could have subjected them to a term of imprisonment at one time in their lives' (Reimen, 1984).

11 Nicolas said that sociologists should rearrange their priorities, and put 'their hands down and their eyes up'. In the last decades, things have improved somewhat, as indicated by the references provided in the discussion at a later point in this chapter.

References

Brodeur, P. (1985) *Outrageous Misconduct: The Asbestos Industry on Trial*. New York: Pantheon.

Clinard, M.B. and Yeager, P.C. (1980) *Corporate Crime*. New York: Free Press.

Currie, Elliot (1985) *Confronting Crime: An American Challenge*. New York: Pantheon.

Dunbaugh, Frank M. (1979) Racially disproportionate rates of incarceration in the United States. *Prison Law Monitor* 1:9.

Edlin, Gordon J. (1987) Inappropriate use of genetic terminology in medical research: A public health issue. *Perspectives in Biology and Medicine* 31, no. 1:47–56.

Eysenck, H.J. (1971) The *IQ Argument: Race, Intelligence, and Education*. London: Library Press.

Eysenck, H.J. (1975) *The Inequality of Man*. London: Temple Smith.

Fischer, M. (1971) Psychosis in the offspring of schizophrenic monozygotic twins and their normal co-twins. *British Journal of Psychiatry* 118:43–52.

Gordon, Robert A. (1987) SES versus IQ in the race-IQ-delinquency model. *International Journal of Sociology and Social Policy* 7, no. 3:30–92.

Hay, D. *et al.* (1975) *Albion's Fatal Tree: Crime and Society in Eighteenth Century England*. New York: Pantheon.

Herrnstein, Richard J. (1971) I.Q. *The Atlantic* (September): 63–64.

Jensen, Arthur R. (1969) How much can we boost IQ and scholastic achievement? *Harvard Educational Review* (Winter).

Kety, S., Rosenthal, D., Wender, P. and Schulsinger, F. (1968) An epidemiological-clinical twin study on schizophrenia. In D. Rosenthal and S. Kety, eds., *The Transmission of Schizophrenia*. Oxford: Pergamon.

Kety, S.D. (1976) Genetic aspects of schizophrenia. *Psychiatric Annals* 6:6–15.

Kringlen, E. (1968) An epidemiological twin study on schizophrenia. In D. Rosenthal and S. Kety, eds., *The Transmission of Schizophrenia*. Oxford: Pergamon Press.

Lumsden, Charles J. and Wilson, E.O. (1981) *Genes, Mind* and *Culture: The Coerolutionary Process*. Cambridge, Mass: Harvard University Press.

Mednick, Sarnoff A. (1985). Biosocial factors and primary prevention of antisocial behavior. In Frank H. Marsh and Janet Katz, eds., *Biology, Crime, and Ethics*. Cincinnati: Anderson.

Mednick, Sarnoff A., Gabrelli, W.F. Jr., and Hutchins, B. (1984) Genetic influences in criminal convictions: Evidence from an adoption cohort, *Science* 224:891–893.

Mokhiber, R. (1988) *Corporate Crime and Violence*. San Francisco: Sierra Club Books.

Nader, L. (1972) Up the anthropologist: Perspectives gained from studying up. In Dell Hymes, ed., *Re-Inventing Anthropology*. New York: Pantheon.

Reilly, P. (1977) *Genetics, Law, and the Social Policy*. Cambridge, Mass.: Harvard University Press.

Reiman, Jeffrey H. (1984) *The Rich Get Richer and the Poor Get Prison*. New York: Wiley.

Rowe, David C. (1986) Genetic and environmental components of antisocial behavior: A study of 265 twin pairs. *Criminology* 24, no. 3:513–532.

Simon, D.R., and Eitzen, S.D 1982. *Elite Deviance*. Boston: Allyn and Bacon.

Simpson, Sally S. (1987) Cycles of illegality: Antitrust violations in corporate America. *Social Forces*. 64:943-63.

Wilson, E.O. (1971) *Insect Societies*. Cambridge, Mass.: Harvard University Press.

Wilson, E.O. (1978) *On Human Nature*. Cambridge, Mass.: Harvard University Press.

6.3 Biosocial studies of antisocial and violent behaviour in children and adults Adrian Raine

Despite increasing knowledge of social and biological risk factors for antisocial and violent behavior, we know surprisingly little about how these two sets of risk factors interact. This paper documents 39 empirical examples of biosocial interaction effects for antisocial behavior from the areas of genetics, psychophysiology, obstetrics brain imaging, neuropsychology, neurology, hormones, neurotransmitters, and environmental toxins.[1] Two main themes emerge. First, when biological and social factors are grouping variables and when antisocial behavior is the outcome, then the presence of both risk factors exponentially increases the rates of antisocial and violent behavior. Second, when social and antisocial variables are grouping variables and biological functioning is the outcome, then the social variable invariably moderates the antisocial–biology relationship such that these relationships are strongest in those from benign home backgrounds. It is argued that further biosocial research is critical for establishing a new generation of more successful intervention and prevention research.

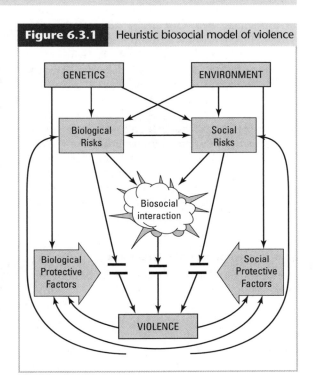

Figure 6.3.1 Heuristic biosocial model of violence

Introduction

Over the past 50 years, important progress has been made in delineating replicable psychosocial risk factors for antisocial and violent behavior (Farrington, 2000; Flinshaw and Anderson, 1996; Loeber and Farrington, 1998; McCord, 2001; Rutter, Giller, and Hagell, 1998). Within the past 15 years, important progress has also been made in uncovering biological risk factors that predispose to antisocial behavior (Lahey, McBurnett, Loeber, and Hart, 1995; Moffitt, 1990a; Rutter *et al.*, 1998; Susman and Finkelstein, 2001). Despite this progress, we know surprisingly little about how these different sets of risk factors *interact* in predisposing to antisocial behavior. [...]

To serve as a heuristic guide to this review, Fig. 6.3.1 illustrates a simple biosocial model of violent behavior that highlights the key influences of genetic and environmental processes in giving rise to social and biological risk factors that both individually and interactively predispose to antisocial behavior. The model also incorporates social

and biological protective factors, influences that will be touched upon briefly in this review. Inevitably, this model is overly simplistic, but it does provide a framework within which the research reviewed below can be viewed. It should also be noted that what constitutes a biological variable and what constitutes a social variable is open to question. There is much that is social about biological variables (e.g., head injuries leading to brain dysfunction are caused by the environment) and much that is biological about social variables (e.g., genetic factors, and their biological predispositions, contribute to bad parenting). Although 'biological' and 'social' are in strict terms false dichotomies, they are retained here for illustrative purposes.

Genetics

There is now clear evidence from twin studies, adoption studies, twins reared apart, and molecular genetic studies to support the notion that there are genetic influences on antisocial and aggressive behavior (Raine, 1993; Rowe, 2001; Rutter, 1997). The more challenging issue now concerns if and how genetic processes interact with environmental processes in predisposing to antisocial behavior. Twin studies find stronger evidence for heritability of antisocial behavior than adoption studies (Raine, 1993), and because interaction effects will influence heritability estimates from twin but not adoption designs, there is prima facie evidence that such interactions exist. Indeed, it is a truism that genetic processes need an environment in which to become expressed. As such, environmental changes will turn these genetic influences on and off across the life-span (Plomin and Rutter, 1998). Genetic factors likely give rise to biological risk factors for antisocial behavior such as low arousal, and if gene x environment interactions are found, this would suggest that interaction effects may well exist at the level of biological influences, a view that will be returned to later.

Gene by environmental interactions

One of the most striking examples of gene by environment interactions in genetic studies of crime is a cross-fostering analysis of petty criminality (Cloninger, Sigvardsson, Bohman, and von Knorring, 1982), results of which are illustrated in Fig. 6.3.2. Male Swedish adoptees (N = 862) were divided into four groups depending on the presence or absence of (a) a congenital predisposition (i.e., whether biological parents were criminal) and (b) a postnatal predisposition (how the children were raised by their adoptive parents). When both heredity and environmental predispositional factors were present, 40% of the adoptees were criminal compared to 12.1% with only genetic factors present, 6.7% for those with only a bad family environment, and 2.9% when both genetic and environmental factors were absent. The fact that the 40% rate for criminality when both biological and environmental factors are present is greater than the 18.8% rate given by a combination of 'congenital only' and 'postnatal only' conditions indicates that genetic and environmental factors interact. Further analyses indicated that occupational status of both biological and adoptive parents were the main postnatal variables involved in this non additive interaction.

Cloninger and Gottesman (1987) later analyzed data for females to compare with the findings for males. As would be expected, these crime rates in

female adoptees are much lower than for males, but the same interactive pattern is present: crime rates in adoptees are greatest when both heritable and environmental influences are present, with this interaction accounting for twice as much crime as is produced by genetic and environmental influences taken alone (see Fig. 6.3.2).

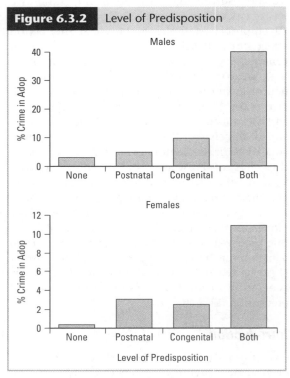

Figure 6.3.2   Level of Predisposition

Increased adult crime in adoptees when both genetic and environmental risk factors are present for both males (Cloninger *et al.*, 1982) and females (Cloninger & Gottesman, 1987).

Evidence for gene x environmental interactions is also provided by Cadoret, Cain, and Crowe (1983) who presented data from three adoption studies. When both genetic and environmental factors are present, they account for a greater number of antisocial behaviors than either of these two factors acting alone, Crowe (1974) also found some evidence for a gene x environment interaction in his analysis of adopted-away offspring of female prisoners, although this trend was only marginally significant (p < .10). Cadoret, Yates, Troughton, Woodworth, and Stewart (1995), in an adoption study of 95 male and 102 female adoptees whose parents had either antisocial personality and/or alcohol abuse showed that parental antisocial personality predicted increased aggression and conduct disorders in the offspring, illustrating evidence for genetic processes. But in addition, an adverse adoptive home environment was found to interact with adult antisocial personality in predicting increased aggression in the offspring, that is, a gene x environment interaction effect.

Gene by environmental correlation and the moderating effects of demographics

A related but different concept is that of gene-environment correlation. An interesting example is provided in a study by Ge, Conger, Cadoret, and Neiderhiser (1996) who showed that the adopted away offspring of biological parents who had antisocial personality/substance abuse were more likely to show antisocial and hostile behaviors in childhood compared to the adopted-away offspring of nonantisocial, nonsubstance abusing parents. This helps establish genetic transmission of childhood antisocial behavior, but in addition an association was found between antisocial behavior in the *biological* parent and the parenting behaviors of the *adoptive* parents. This can be explained by a transmission pathway in which the biological parent contributes a genetic predisposition toward antisocial behavior in the offspring. The antisocial offspring then in turn elicit negative parenting behaviors in the adoptive parents. This study provides direct evidence of an 'evocative' gene–environment correlation, and suggests that the association between negative parenting in the adoptive parent and antisocial behavior in the child is mediated by genetic processes. One of the goals of future behavior genetic studies should be to examine the interplay between genes and environment in this fashion further. More generally, there are likely to be future exciting developments with respect to identifying the specific genes which give rise to the risk factors that shape criminal behavior.

An interaction of a different kind was also reported by Christiansen (1977) in an analysis of Danish twin data on criminality. Although overall he found significant heritability for crime, he also found that such heritability was greater in (a) those from high socioeconomic backgrounds and (b) those who were rural born. In other words, these sociodemographic variables moderated heritability for criminal behavior. This finding is of interest because, as will be seen below, it has also been found on several occasions with respect to psychophysiological and brain imaging studies. This suggests that stronger biology–antisocial findings can be found in social contexts where social predispositions to crime are minimized. [...]

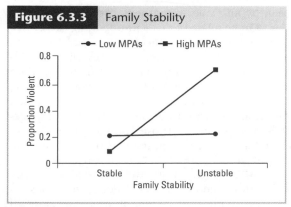

Figure 6.3.3   Family Stability

Interaction between family instability and high minor physical anomalies in the prediction of adult violence (Mednick & Kandel, 1988).

Obstetric factors

Of all the subfields of biological research on antisocial behavior, obstetric influences show the most compelling evidence for biosocial interactions, with at least 11 studies from five different countries finding evidence for statistical interactions. These obstetric studies fall into three domains: minor physical anomalies, prenatal nicotine exposure, and birth complications.

Pregnancy complications

Minor physical anomalies (MPAs)

At least six studies have found an association between increased MPAs and increased antisocial behavior in children (Raine, 1993). Minor physical anomalies have been associated with disorders of pregnancy and are thought to be a marker for fetal neural maldevelopment toward the end of the first 3 months of pregnancy. As such, they may be viewed as an indirect marker of abnormal brain development. MPAs are relatively minor physical abnormalities consisting of such features as low-seated ears, adherent ear lobes, and a furrowed tongue. Although MPAs may have a genetic basis, they may also be caused by environmental factors acting on the fetus such as anoxia, bleeding, and infection (Guy, Majorski, Wallace, and Guy, 1983).

At least three studies have found that MPAs interact with social factors in predicting antisocial and violent behavior. Mednick and Kandel (1988) assessed MPAs in a sample of 129 12-year-old boys seen by an experienced pediatrician. MPAs were found to be related to violent offending as assessed 9 years later when subjects were aged 21 years, although not to property offenses without violence. However, as illustrated in Fig. 6.3.3, when subjects were divided into those from unstable, nonintact homes and those from stable homes, a biosocial interaction was observed. MPAs only predicted violence in those individuals raised in unstable home environments. Similarly, Brennan, Mednick, and Raine (1997) found that those with both MPAs and family adversity had especially high rates of adult violent offending within a sample of 72 male offspring of psychiatrically ill parents. This interaction was again confirmed by Pine, Shaffer, Schonfeld, and Davies (1997) who found that MPAs in 7-year-olds combined with environmental risk in predisposing to conduct disorder at age 17. These findings are similar to those on birth complications reported above; in both cases the presence of a negative psychosocial factor is required to 'trigger' the biological risk factor, and in both cases the effects are specific to violent offending. In a study confirming specificity of MPAs to violence, Arseneault, Tremblay, Boulerice, Seguin, and Saucier (2000) found that MPAs assessed at age 14 predicted to violent delinquency at age 17 in 170 males, but not to nonviolent delinquency. In this study, effects were independent of family adversity.

Nicotine exposure

The effect of fetal exposure to alcohol in increasing risk for conduct disorders is well known (e.g., Fast, Conry, and Loock, 1999; Olson *et al.*, 1997; Streissguth, Barr, Bookstein, Sampson, and Olson, 1999), but recently a spate of studies has established beyond reasonable doubt a significant link between smoking during pregnancy and later conduct disorder and violent offending (see Raine, in press, for a review). Three of these studies have also observed interactions between nicotine exposure and psychosocial variables in the prediction of later violent offending, and are impressive in terms of their size, the prospective nature of data collection, long-term outcome, and control for third factors such as antisocial behavior in the parents, other drug use, and low social class. Brennan, Grekin, and Mednick (1999) using a birth cohort of 4,169 males found a twofold increase in adult violent offending in the offspring of mothers who smoked 20 cigarettes a day, and also found a dose-response relationship between increased number of cigarettes smoked and increased violence. However, a *fivefold* increase in adult violence was found when nicotine exposure was combined with exposure to delivery complications – there was no increase in violence in those who were nicotine-exposed but lacking delivery complications. Brennan *et al.* (1999) observed that effects were specific to persistent offending and did not apply to adolescent-limited offending. Similarly, Rasanen *et al.* (1999) found a twofold increase in violent criminal offending at age 26 in the offspring of women who smoked during pregnancy. In addition, nicotine exposure led to an 11.9-fold increase in recidivistic violence when combined with single-parent family, and a 14.2-fold increase when combined with teenage pregnancy, single-parent family, unwanted pregnancy, and developmental motor lags. Again, odds ratios were stronger for recidivistic violence than for violence in general or property offending. Gibson and Tibbetts (2000) also found that maternal smoking interacted with parental absence in predicting early onset of offending in a US sample.

Maternal smoking during pregnancy may be an important contributory factor to the brain deficits that have been found in adult offenders. Animal research has clearly demonstrated the neurotoxic effects of two constituents of cigarette smoke – carbon monoxide (CO) and nicotine (see Olds, 1997 for a detailed review). Prenatal nicotine exposure even at relatively low levels disrupts the development of the noradrenergic neurotransmitter system and disrupts cognitive functions (Levin, Wilkerson, Jones, Christopher, and Briggs, 1996). Reduction of noradrenergic functioning caused by smoking would be expected to disrupt sympathetic nervous system activity, consistent with evidence outlined earlier for reduced sympathetic arousal in antisocial individuals (Raine, 1996). Pregnant rats exposed to nicotine have offspring with an enhancement of cardiac M2-muscarinic cholinergic receptors that *inhibit* autonomic functions (Slotkin, Epps, Stenger, Sawyer, & Seidler, 1999). This would help to explain the well-replicated finding of *low* resting heart rate in antisocial individuals outlined above (Raine, 1993).

Birth complications

Several studies have shown that babies who suffer birth complications are more likely to develop conduct disorder, delinquency, and commit impulsive crime and violence in adulthood when other psychosocial risk factors are present. Specifically, obstetric factors interact with psychosocial risk factors in relation to adult violence. Werner (1987) found that birth complications interacted with a disruptive family environment (maternal separation, illegitimate child, marital discord, parental mental health problems, paternal absence) in predisposing to delinquency. Similarly, Raine, Brennan, and Mednick (1994) prospectively assessed birth complications and maternal rejection at age 1 year in 4,269 live male births in Copenhagen, Denmark. Birth complications significantly interacted with maternal rejection of the child in predicting to violent offending at age 18 years (see Fig. 6.3.4, upper half). Only 4% of the sample had both birth complications and maternal rejection, but this small group accounted for 18% of all the violent crimes committed by the entire sample.

In this latter study, the 4,269 babies were followed up to age 34 when outcome for violent crime was reassessed (Raine, Brennan, & Mednick, 1997). It was found that the biosocial interaction previously observed holds for violent but not nonviolent criminal offending. Furthermore, the interaction was found to be specific to more serious forms of violence and not threats of violence. The interaction held for early onset but not late onset violence, and was not accounted for by psychiatric illness in the mothers. Rearing in a public care institution in the first year of life and attempt to abort the fetus were the key aspects of maternal rejection found to interact with birth complications in predisposing to violence.

This finding from Denmark has recently been replicated in four other countries (Sweden, Finland, Canada, USA) in the context of a variety of psychosocial risk factors. Piquero and Tibbetts (1999) in a prospective longitudinal study of 867 males and females from the Philadelphia Collaborative Perinatal Project found that those with both pre/perinatal disturbances and a disadvantaged familial environment were much more likely to become adult violent offenders (see Fig. 6.3.4, lower half). Similarly, pregnancy complications interacted with poor parenting in predicting adult violence in a large Swedish sample of 7,101 men (Hodgins, Kratzer, and McNeil, 2001). In a Canadian sample of 849 boys, Arsenault, Tremblay, Boulerice, and Saucier (in press) found an interaction between increased serious obstetric complications and family adversity in raising the likelihood of violent offending at age 17 years. In a Finnish sample perinatal risk interacted with being an only child in raising the odds of adult violent offending by a factor of 4.4 in a sample of 5,587 males (Kemppainen, Jokelainen, Jaervelin, Isohanni, and Raesaenen, 2001). On the other hand, being an only child is not obviously linked to psychosocial adversity, and the meaning of this interaction requires further elucidation.

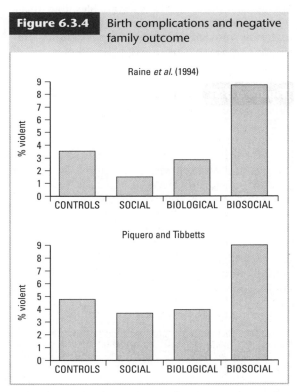

Figure 6.3.4 Birth complications and negative family outcome

Interaction between birth complications and negative family outcome in the prediction of adult violence in both Danish (Raine *et al.*, 1994) and US (Piquero & Tibbetts, 1999) samples.

A fifth study reported by Brennan, Mednick, and Mednick (1993) and also from Denmark showed that birth complications interacted with parental mental illness in predicting violent crime in the male offspring (see Fig. 6.3.5). On the other hand, no interaction between perinatal insult and family adversity was found for a smaller sample of German children (N = 322) where outcome was restricted to follow-up at age 8 years (Laucht *et al.*, 2000). This last failure may be due to the fact that neurological deficits stemming from birth complications may particularly influence the more severe outcome of life-course persistent antisocial behavior rather than the more common outcome of child antisocial behavior (Moffitt, 1993; Moffitt and Caspi, 2001). Indeed, several of the above studies find that interaction effects involving birth complications and family factors show evidence of linkage to what may be broadly termed life-course persistent violent behavior rather than adolescent-limited antisocial behavior. In addition to these interactions with psychosocial variables, low Apgar scores at birth have been found to interact with maternal smoking in the prediction of adult violent offending (Gibson and Tibbetts, 1998).

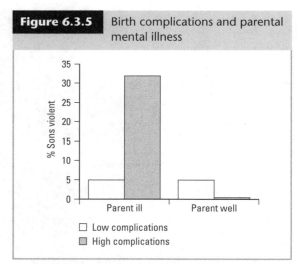

| **Figure 6.3.5** | Birth complications and parental mental illness |

Interaction between birth complications and parental illness in the prediction of violent crime in the offspring (Brennan *et al.*, 1993).

Birth complications such as anoxia (lack of oxygen), forceps delivery, and pre-eclampsia (hypertension leading to anoxia) are thought to contribute to brain damage, and they may be just one of a number of early sources of brain dysfunction observed in child and adult antisocial groups. On the other hand, as indicated above, birth complications may not by themselves predispose to crime, but instead may require the presence of negative environmental circumstance to trigger later adult crime and violence. Furthermore, although they are likely to contribute to prefrontal damage, their effects would not be specific to this brain area but would impact multiple brain sites, including the hippocampus. Interestingly, recent brain imaging studies have shown that the hippocampus shows abnormal functioning in murderers (Raine, Buchsbaum, and LaCasse, 1997), shows structural abnormalities in psychopaths (Laakso *et al.*, 2001) and is particularly susceptible to anoxia.

Conclusions and recommendations

Summarizing the key findings of this review, there has in recent years been growing evidence for replicable interactions between biological and social factors in relation to antisocial and violent behavior. [...]

Although these findings give reason to take biosocial perspectives on antisocial behavior seriously, study counts and documentation of findings by themselves will not advance knowledge within a field. The establishment of interaction effects is not an end process, but merely the end of a beginning in understanding antisocial behavior. Interaction effects need to be explained with respect to their underlying mechanisms. For example, birth complications consistently interact with negative home environments in predisposing to adult violence, and this effect seems specific to violence, and to violence with an early onset – but why? What are the processes that operate in negative home environments, which trigger the deleterious effects of birth complications? Do birth complications predispose to violence by mild impairment to brain functioning, or does family adversity instead predispose to both birth complications such as pregnancy-induced hypertension and also childhood conduct disorder? That is, are birth complications merely a marker of a third factor and are by themselves unrelated to violence? Although these questions are difficult to answer, the next generation of biosocial research needs to go beyond simple interaction effects and research the fundamental mechanisms and processes underlying the interactions. [...]

In analyzing the pattern of interaction effects observed above, there are two main conclusions that can be drawn and that can guide future hypothesis-testing. When the biological and social factors are the grouping variable and antisocial behavior is the outcome, then the presence of both risk factors appears to increase rates of antisocial and violent behavior. When social and antisocial variables are the grouping variables and biological functioning is the outcome, then the social variable invariably (but not always) moderates the antisocial–biology relationship such that these relationships are strongest in those from benign home backgrounds. A question for future biosocial studies is whether these two patterns of findings, which ask different questions, can be substantiated, or whether different patterns emerge.

> *From A. Raine, 'Biosocial studies of antisocial and violent behavior in children and adults',* Journal of Abnormal Child Psychology, *(2002), 30(4): 311–326.*

Note

1 Only genetics and obstetrics are included in this excerpt.

References

Arsenault, L., Tremblay, R.E., Boulerice, B., Seguin, J, R., and Saucier, J.F. (2000). Minor physical anomalies and family adversity as risk factors for violent delinquency in adolescence. *American Journal of Psychiatry*, 157, 917–923.

Brennan, P.A., Grekin, E.R., & Mednick, S.A. (1999). Maternal smoking during pregnancy and adult male criminal outcomes. *Archives of General Psychiatry*, 56, 215–219.

Brennan, P.A., Mednick, B.R., & Mednick, S.A. (1993). Parental paychopathology, congenital factors, and violence. In S. Hodgins (Ed.), *Mental disorder and crime* (pp. 244–261). Thousand Oaks: Sage.

Brennan, P.A., Mednick, S.A., & Raine, A. (1997). Biosocial interactions and violence: A focus on perinatal factors. In A. Raine, P.A. Brennan, D. Farrington, & S.A. Mednick (Eds.), *Biosocial bases of violence* (pp. 163–174). New York: Plenum.

Cadoret, R.J., Cain, C.A., & Crowe, R.R. (1983). Evidence for gene-environment interaction in the development of adolescent antisocial behavior. *Behavior Genetics*, 13, 301–310.

Cadoret, R.J., Yates, W.R., Troughton, F., Woodworth, G., & Stewart, M.A. (1995). Genetic-environmental interaction in the genesis of aggressivity and conduct disorders. *Archives of General Psychiatry*, 52, 916–924.

Christiansen, K.O. (1977). A preliminary study of criminality among twins. In S.A. Mednick & K. O. Christiansen (Eds.), *Biosocial bases of criminal behavior* (pp. 89–108). New York: Gardner Press.

Cloninger, C.R., & Gottesman, I.I. (1987). Genetic and environmental factors in antisocial behavior disorders. In S.A. Mednick, T.F. Moffitt, & S.A. Stack (Eds.), *The causes of crime: New biological approaches*. Cambridge: Cambridge University Press.

Cloninger, C.R., Sigvardsson, S., Bohman, M., & von Knorring, A.L. (1982). Predisposition to petty criminality in Swedish adoptees: II. Cross–fostering analysis of gene-environmental interactions. *Archives of General Psychiatry*, 39, 1242–1247.

Crowe, R.R. (1974). An adoption study of antisocial personality. *Archives of General Psychiatry*, 31, 785–791.

Farrington, D.P. (2000). Psychosocial predictors of adult antisocial personality and adult convictions. *Behavioral Sciences and the Law*, 18, 605–622.

Fast, D.K., Conry, J., & Loock, C.A. (1999). Identifying Fetal Alcohol Syndrome among youth in the criminal justice system. *Journal of Developmental and Behavioral Pediatrics*, 213, 370–372.

Ge, X., Conger, R.B., Cadoret, R.J., & Neiderhiser, J. M. (1996). The developmental interface between nature and nurture: A mutual influence model of child antisocial behavior and parent behaviors, *Developmental Psychology*, 32, 574–S 89.

Gibson, C.L., & Tibbetts, S.G. (1998). Interaction between maternal cigarette smoking and Apgar scores in predicting offending behavior. *Psychological Reports*, 83, 579–586.

Gibson, C.L., & Tibbetts, S.G. (2000). A biosocial interaction in predicting early onset of offending. *Psychological Reports*, 86. 509–518.

Guy, J.D., Majorski, L. V., Wallace, C.J., & Guy, M.P. (1983). The incidence of minor physical anomalies in adult male schizophrenics. *Schizophrenia Bulletin*, 9, 571–582.

Hinshaw, S. P., & Anderson, C.A. (1996). Conduct and oppositional defiant disorders. In E.J. Mash & R. A. Barkley (Eds.), *Child Psychopathology* (pp. 113–149). New York: Guilford Press.

Hodgins, S., Kratzer, L., & McNeil, T.F. (2001). Obstetric complications, parenting, and risk of criminal behavior. *Archives of General Psychiatry*, 58, 746–752.

Kemppainen, L., Jokelainen, J., Jaervelin, M.R., Isohanni, M., & Raesaenen, P. (2001). The one-child family and violent criminality: A 31-year follow-up study of the northern Finland 1966 birth cohort, *American Journal of Psychiatry*, 158, 960–962.

Laakso, M.P., Vaurio, O., Koivisto, E., Savolainen, L., Eronen, M., Aronen, H.J., *et al.* (2001). Psychopathy and the posterior hippocampus. *Behavioural Brain Research*, 118, 187–193.

Lahey, B. B., McBurnett, K., Loeber, R., & Hart, E.L. (1995). Psychobiology. In G.P. Shovelar (Ed.), *Conduct disorders in children and adolescents* (pp. 27–44). Washington, BC: American Psychiatric Press.

Laucht, M., Esser, G., Baving, L., Gerhold, M., Hoesch, I., Ihle, W., *et al.* (2000). Behavioural sequelae of perinatal insults and early family adversity at 8 years of age. *Journal of the American Academy of Child and Adolescent Psychiatry*, 39, 1229–1237.

Loeber, R., & Farrington, D.P. (1998). Never too early, never too late: Risk factors and successful interventions for serious and violent juvenile offenders. *Studies on Crime and Crime Prevention*, 7, 730.

McCord, J. (2001). Psychosocial contributions to psychopathy and violence. In A. Raine & I. Sanmartin (Eds.), *Violence and psychopathy* (pp. 141–170). New York: Kluwer Academic/ Plenum,

Mednick, S.A., & Kandel, E.S. (1988). Congenital determinants of violence. *Bulletin of the American Academy of Psychiatry and the Law*, 16, 101–109.

Moffitt, T.E. (1990a). The neuropsychology of delinquency: A critical review. In M. Tonry & N. Morris (Eds.), *Crime and justice: A review of research* (pp. 99–169). Chicago: University of Chicago Press.

Moffitt, T.E. (1993). Adolescence-limited and life-course-persistent antisocial behavior: A developmental taxonomy. *Psychological Review*, 100, 674–701.

Moffitt, T.E., & Caspi, A. (2001). Childhood predictors differentiate life-course persistent and adolescence-limited antisocial pathways among males and females. *Development and Psychopathology*, 13, 355–375.

Olds, B. (1997). Tobacco exposure and impaired development: A review of the evidence. *Mental Retardation and Developmental Disabilities Research Reviews*, 3, 257–269.

Olson, H.C., Streissguth, A.P., Sampson, P.D., Barr, H.M., Bookstein, F.L., & Thiede, K. (1997). Association of prenatal alcohol exposure with behavioral and learning problems in early adolescence. *Journal of the American Academy of Child and Adolescent Psychiatry*, 36, 1187–1194.

Pine, B.S., Shaffer, B., Schonfeld, I.S., & Davies, M. (1997). Minor physical anomalies: Modifiers of environmental risks for psychiatric impairment? *Journal of the American Academy of Child and Adolescent Psychiatry*, 36, 395–403.

Piquero, A. & Tibbetts, S. (1999). The impact of pre/perinatal disturbances and disadvantaged familial environment in predicting criminal offending. *Studies on Crime and Crime Prevention*, 8, 52–70.

Raine, A. (1993). *The psychopathology of crime: Criminal behavior as a clinical disorder*. San Diego: Academic Press,

Raine, A. (1996). Autonomic nervous system activity and violence. In D.M. Stoff & R.B. Cairns (Eds.), *Aggression and violence: Genetic, neurobiological, and biosocial perspectives* (pp. 145–168). Mahwah, NJ: Erlbaum.

Raine, A., Brennan, P., & Mednick, S.A. (1994). Birth complications combined with early maternal rejection at age 1 year predispose to violent crime at age 18 years. *Archives of General Psychiatry*, 51, 984–988.

Raine, A., Brennan, P., & Mednick, S.A. (1997). Interaction between birth complications and early maternal rejection in predisposing individuals to adult violence: Specificity to serious, early-onset violence. *American Journal of Psychiatry*, 154, 1265–1271.

Raine, A., Buchsbaum, M., & LaCasse, L. (1997). Brain abnormalities in murderers indicated by positron emission tomography. *Biological Psychiatry*, 42. 495–508.

Rasanen, F., Hakko, H., Isohanni, M., Hodgins, S., Jarvelin, M.R., & Tiihonen, J. (1999). Maternal smoking during pregnancy and risk of criminal behavior among adult male offspring in the northern Finland 1996 birth cohort. *American Journal of Psychiatry*. 156, 857–862.

Rowe, D.C. (2001). *Biology and crime*. Los Angeles: Roxbury Publishing.

Rutter, M.L. (1997). Nature–nurture integration: The example of antisocial behavior. *American Psychologist*, 52, 390–398.

Rutter M., Giller, H. & Hagell, A. (1998). *Antisocial behavior by young people*. Cambridge: Cambridge University Press,

Slotkin, T.A., Epps, T.A., Stenger, M.L., Sawyer, K.J. & Seidler, F.J. (1999). Cholinergic receptors in heart and brainstem of rats exposed to nicotine during development: Implications for hypoxia tolerance and perinatal mortality. *Brain Research*, 113, 1–12.

Streissguth, A.P., Barr, H.M., Bookstein, F.L., Sampson, P.D., & Olson, H. C. (1999). The long-term neurocognitive consequences of prenatal alcohol exposure: A 14-year study. *Psychological Science*, 113, 186–190.

Susman, E.J., & Finkelstein, J.W. (2001). Biology, development, and dangerousness. In G.F. Pinard & L. Pagani (Eds.), *Clinical assessment of dangerousness: Empirical contributions* (pp. 23–46). New York: Cambridge University Press.

Werner, E.E, (1987). Vulnerability and resiliency in children at risk for delinquency: A longitudinal study from birth to young adulthood. In J.D. Burchard & S.N. Burchard (Eds.), *Primary prevention of psychopathology* (pp. 16–43). Newbury Park, CA: Sage.

6.4 Evolutionary psychology and crime
Satoshi Kanazawa

Evolutionary psychology is the study of universal human nature, or the sex-specific male human nature and female human nature. Human nature consists of domain-specific evolved psychological mechanisms. A psychological mechanism is an information-processing procedure or 'decision rule' which evolution by natural and sexual selection has equipped humans to possess in order to solve an adaptive problem (problem of survival or reproduction). Unlike decision rules in decision theory or game theory, however, psychological mechanisms mostly operate behind our conscious thinking. Evolved psychological mechanisms produce values and preferences, which actors then pursue within their constraints; they also engender emotions (Kanazawa, 2001).

Figure 6.4.1 presents the basic theoretical structure of evolutionary psychology. Some adaptive problem during the course of human evolutionary history has led to the evolution of psychological mechanisms through natural and sexual selection.

eration after generation. Eventually, all individuals come to possess them, and they become part of universal (species-typical) human nature. Because men and women often faced different selection pressures through the course of evolution, especially in the area of sexual selection, men and women often have distinct evolved psychological mechanisms, and hence separate male and female human natures. Beyond the sex differences, however, evolved psychological mechanisms, and hence human nature they comprise, are species-typical, shared by all members of the species. Evolved psychological mechanisms then engender desires, values, preferences, emotions, and other internal states which serve as the proximate causes of behavior.

From an evolutionary psychological perspective, the ultimate (albeit unconscious) function of all biological organisms, including humans, is to increase reproductive success. We are designed to reproduce by evolution by natural and sexual selection. [...]

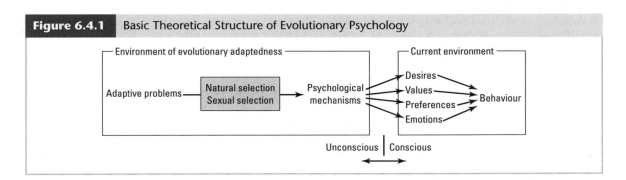

Figure 6.4.1   Basic Theoretical Structure of Evolutionary Psychology

Natural selection refers to the process of differential survival; sexual selection refers to the process of differential reproductive success.[1] Individuals who possess certain psychological mechanisms live longer (because the psychological mechanisms help them survive) and reproduce more successfully (because the psychological mechanisms help them find and keep mates). Those with such psychological mechanisms outreproduce those without them in each generation, and more and more individuals come to possess the psychological mechanisms gen-

Evolutionary psychological perspective on crime

In their comprehensive study of homicide from an evolutionary psychological perspective, Daly and Wilson (1988:137–161) note that humans throughout their evolutionary history were effectively polygynous. Even in nominally monogamous societies, such as the United States, many men practice serial **polygyny**, through a sequence of divorce and remarriage; in other words, they can have multiple wives, not simultaneously, but sequentially, and thereby exclude other men from access to these women during their reproductive years. Only societies that prohibit simultaneous polygyny, divorce, and extramarital affairs are strictly monogamous, and no human society falls into this category. In a polygynous breeding system, some males monopolize reproductive access to all females while other males are left out; in such a system, some males do not get to reproduce at all while almost all females do. This inequality of reproductive success (or fitness variance) between males and females makes males of species with polygynous breeding systems (such as humans) highly competitive, in their effort not to be left out of the reproductive game. This intrasexual competition among men leads to a high level of violence among them, and the large number of homicides between men (compared to the number of homicides between women or between the sexes) is a direct result of this intrasexual competition and violence.

In particular, Daly and Wilson (1988:123–136) note that most homicides between men originate from what Wolfgang (1958) calls 'trivial altercations.' A typical homicide begins as a fight about trivial matters of honor, status, and reputation between men (such as when one man insults another). Fights escalate because neither is willing to back down, until they become violent and one of the disputants ends up dead. Because women prefer to mate with men of high status and good reputation (Buss, 1989), men's status and reputation correlate directly with their reproductive success. Men are therefore highly motivated to protect their honor, and often go to extreme lengths to do so, compelled by their evolved psychological mechanisms. Daly and Wilson thus explain homicides between men in terms of their (largely unconscious) desire to protect their status and reputation in their attempt to gain reproductive access to women.

One can easily extend this analysis to other forms of interpersonal violence among men. Less serious violent crimes, such as assault and battery, can have the same underlying motive to protect one's status and reputation in an effort to gain reproductive access. Whether the violence results in a death (making the crime homicide) or an injury (making the crime serious assault) is often beyond the conscious control of the offender. It crucially depends on the reaction of the victim and what transpires between the offender and the vic-

tim in the course of the conflict, as well as other fortuitous circumstances such as the presence and reactions of others, distance to the nearest hospital and the physical strength of the victim. If men can be driven to kill in order to protect their status and reputation, they can easily be driven to commit less serious acts of violence.

Rape appears to be an exception to this reasoning, because, unlike murder and assault, the victims of rape are women and there is therefore no intrasexual competition for status and reputation. However, the same psychological mechanism that inclines men to gain reproductive access to women can motivate men to rape. Predatory rapists are overwhelmingly men of lower class and status, who have very dim prospects to gain legitimate access to women (Thornhill and Thornhill, 1983). While it is not a manifestation of intrasexual competition and violence, rape might also be motivated by men's psychological mechanism that inclines them to gain reproductive access to women when they do not have the legitimate means to do so.

One can also extend the same analysis to property crimes. If women prefer to mate with men with more resources, then men can increase their reproductive success by acquiring material resources. Material resources in traditional societies, which are usually gerontocratic, however, tend to be concentrated in the hands of elder men. Younger men are often excluded from attaining them through legitimate means and must therefore resort to illegitimate means. One method of doing so is to appropriate someone else's resources by stealing them. Thus the same psychological mechanism that creates the motive for violent crime can also induce men to commit property crimes. [...]

Note that it is immaterial to an evolutionary psychological perspective on crime that most criminals do not cite reproductive success as a motive for their crimes. For, as noted already, psychological mechanisms usually operate at the unconscious level. My contention is that men under some circumstances commit crimes because they want to (making then highly criminal), and they want to commit crimes because something inclines them to. I contend that that something is the evolved psychological mechanism that predisposes all men to seek reproductive success. The men themselves are often unaware of the evolutionary logic behind their motives.

Empirical puzzles

In addition to providing a comprehensive explanation of all criminal behavior, an evolutionary psychological perspective on crime can solve some of the persistent empirical puzzles within criminology.

Why men, not women?

In every human society, men commit an overwhelming majority of both violent and property crimes (Brown, 1991; Kanazawa and Still, 2000). Worldwide, men commit more than 90 percent of all crimes. Why is this?

One relatively unusual feature of the human mating system can account for the overwhelming male bias toward criminality. Unlike most other species in nature, human males make a large amount of parental investment in the offspring. The unusually high degree of *male parental investment* among humans leads to universal human female mate preference for men with a large amount of resources (Buss, 1989). The more resources a potential mate has, the more parental investment he can make in their joint children. Men's resources increase their children's chances of survival and their future reproductive prospects.

Because women prefer men with greater resources as their long-term mates, men fiercely compete with one another to accumulate resources and attain higher status. The more resources they possess and the higher the status they occupy, the greater the reproductive opportunities they have. Wealthier men of high status have more sex partners and copulate more frequently than poorer men of low status (Kanazawa, 2003a; Pérusse, 1993). Wealth and status do not affect women's desirability as long-term mates (Buss, 1989).

From an evolutionary psychological perspective, this is why men comprise an overwhelming majority of criminals worldwide. Material resources and status improve men's reproductive prospects much more than women's. We would therefore expect men to be much more motivated to accumulate material resources, either through legitimate or illegitimate means, than women. In fact, not only do men commit an overwhelming majority of theft and robberies worldwide, but they also make more money and attain higher status through legitimate means because they are more motivated to do so (Browne, 2002; Kanazawa, 2005a). Men are much more motivated to accumulate resources and attain status, whether through legitimate or illegitimate means, in order to attract mates.

Why younger men, not older men?

One of the advantages of an evolutionary psychological perspective on crime is that it can explain the universal age–crime curve. In their highly influential 1983 article 'Age and explanation of crime', Hirschi and Gottfredson claim that the relationship between age and crime is invariant across all social and cultural conditions at all times. In every society, for all social groups, for all races and both sexes, at all historical times, the tendency to commit crimes and other analogous, risk-taking behavior rapidly increases in early adolescence, peaks in late adolescence and early adulthood, rapidly decreases throughout the 20s and 30s, and levels off during middle age. Although there have been minor variations observed around the 'invariant' age–crime curve (Greenberg, 1985; Hirschi and Gottfredson, 1985), the essential shape of the curve for serious and interpersonal crimes remains uncontested in the criminological literature. For empirical examples of the invariant age–crime curve, see Campbell (1995: Figure 1), Daly and Wilson (1990: Figure 1) and Hirschi and Gottfredson (1983: Figures 1–8).

While Hirschi and Gottfredson claim that the age–crime curve is invariant and holds in all societies at all times, they provide no explanations for this universal observation. They instead argue that no theoretical or empirical variable then available in criminology (in 1983) could explain it. If the age–crime curve is truly constant across all populations, any factor that varies across such populations cannot explain it. Just as a constant cannot explain a variable, a variable cannot explain a constant. The invariant age–crime curve must be explained by something that is constant across all societies and cultures at all times. An evolutionary psychological perspective suggests just such a constant factor (Kanazawa, 2003b; Kanazawa and Still, 2000; Rowe, 2002:53–55).

There are reproductive benefits for men of intense competition. Those who are highly competitive act violently toward their male rivals. Their violence serves the dual function of protecting their status, honor, and reputation, and of discouraging or altogether eliminating their rivals from competition for mates (Daly and Wilson, 1988, 1990). Their competitiveness also predisposes them to accumulate resources to attract mates by stealing from others (either via theft or robbery). The same psychological mechanism induces men who cannot gain legitimate access to women to do so illegitimately through forcible rape (Thornhill and Thornhill, 1983). Figure 6.4.2(a) represents a hypothetical curve, depicting the relationship between men's age and their benefit from competition. There are no reproductive benefits from competition (violence and theft) before puberty because prepubertal males are not able to translate their competitive edge into reproductive success. With puberty, however, the benefits of competition skyrocket. Once the men are reproductively capable, every act of violence and theft can potentially increase their reproductive success. The benefits of competition stay high after puberty for the remainder of their lives since human males are reproductively capable for most of their adult lives.

This is not the whole story, however. There are also costs associated with competition. Acts of violence can easily result in their own death or injury, and acts of resource malappropriation can trigger retaliation from the rightful owners of the resources and their family and allies. Men's reproductive success is obviously reduced if the competitive acts result in their death or injury. Figure 6.4.2(b) presents a hypothetical curve depicting the costs of competition as a function of age. Before men start reproducing (before their first child), there are few costs of competition. True, being competitive might result in death or injury, and they might therefore lose in the reproductive game. However, they also lose by not competing. If they don't compete for mates in a polygynous breeding system (which all human societies are; Daly and Wilson, 1988:140 – 142), they'll be left out of the reproductive game altogether and end up losing as a result. In other words, young men *might* lose if they were competitive, but they will *definitely* lose if they are not competitive. So there is little cost to being competitive even at the risk of death or injury; the alternative – total reproductive failure – is even worse in reproductive terms.

The cost of competition, however, rises dramatically with the birth of the first child and subsequent children. True, men still benefit from competition (as Figure 6.4.2(a) shows) because such acts of competition might attract additional mates and mating opportunities. However, men's energies and resources are put to better use by protecting and investing in their existing children. In other words, with the birth of children, men should shift their reproductive effort away from *mating effort* and toward *parenting effort*, in the equation: Total reproductive effort = mating effort + parenting effort. If men die or get injured in their

acts of competition, their existing children will suffer; without sufficient parental investment and protection, they might starve or fall victim to predation or exploitation by others. The costs of competition, therefore, rapidly increase after the birth of the first child, which usually happens several years after puberty because men need some time to accumulate sufficient resources to attract their first mate. Nonetheless, in the absence of artificial means of contraception, reproduction probably began at a much earlier age than it does today. There is thus a gap of several years between the rapid rise in the benefits of competition, and the similarly rapid rise in its costs.

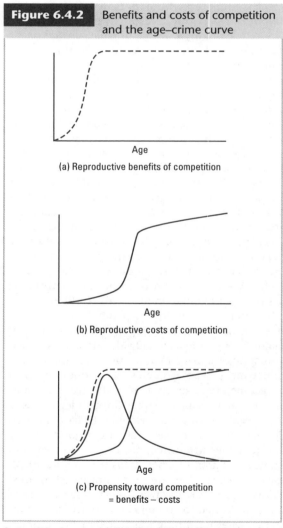

| **Figure 6.4.2** | Benefits and costs of competition and the age–crime curve |

(a) Reproductive benefits of competition

(b) Reproductive costs of competition

(c) Propensity toward competition = benefits – costs

Source: Kanazawa and Still (2000). Copyright by the American Sociological Association. Reprinted with permission.

Figure 6.4.2(c) depicts a curve that represents the mathematical difference between the benefits and the costs of competition. The curve (in the solid bold line) closely resembles the typical age–crime curve. An evolutionary psychological perspective suggests that male criminality varies as it does over the life-course because it represents the difference between the benefits and the costs of competition. It is important to note, however, that, unlike actors in decision theories in microeconomics (Grogger, 1998), men from an evolutionary psychological perspective do not make these calculations consciously. The calculations have already been performed by natural and sexual selection, so to speak, which then equips men's brains with appropriate psychological mechanisms to incline them to be increasingly competitive in their immediate postpubertal years and to make them less competitive right after the birth of the first child. Men simply do not *feel like* acting violently or stealing, or they just *want* to settle down, after the birth of their first child, but they do not necessarily know why.

Fluctuating levels of testosterone may provide the biochemical microfoundation for this psychological mechanism. David Gubernick's unpublished experiment (discussed in Blum, 1997:116) demonstrates that expectant fathers' testosterone levels fall precipitously immediately after the birth of their child. If high levels of testosterone predispose men to be more competitive, then the sudden drop in testosterone after the birth of their children may provide the biochemical reason why men's psychological mechanisms to commit crime 'turn off' when they become fathers. Mazur and Michalek's (1998) finding that marriage decreases and divorce increases testosterone levels in men provide a similar microfoundation for the commonly observed negative effect of marriage on criminality (Kanazawa, 2003b; Laub et al., 1998). Further consistent with this perspective, McIntyre et al. (2006) show that married men who actively seek extrapair copulations retain high levels of testosterone characteristic of single men.

Given that human society was always mildly polygynous, there were many men who did not succeed in finding a mate and reproducing. These men had everything to gain and nothing to lose by remaining competitive for their entire lives. However, *we are not descended from these men*. As noted above, all of us are disproportionately descended from men and women who were very successful at reproduction. Contemporary men, therefore, did not inherit a psychological mecha-

nism that forces them to stay competitive and keep trying to secure mates for their entire lives. An evolutionary psychological perspective can thus explain why criminal behavior is largely represented by younger men.

Why the less intelligent, not the more intelligent?

Criminologists have long known that criminals on average have lower intelligence than the general population (Herrnstein and Murray, 1994; Hirschi and Hindelang, 1977; Wilson and Herrnstein, 1985). Juvenile delinquents are less intelligent than nondelinquents (Wolfgang et al., 1972; Yeudall et al., 1982), and a significant difference in IQ between delinquents and nondelinquents appears as early as ages 8 and 9 (Gibson and West, 1970). Chronic offenders are less intelligent than one-time offenders (Moffitt, 1990; Wolfgang et al., 1972), and serious offenders are less intelligent than less serious offenders (Lynam et al., 1993; Moffitt et al 1981). The negative correlation between intelligence and criminality is not an artifact of a selection bias, whereby less intelligent criminals are more likely to be caught than more intelligent criminals, because the correlation exists even in self-report studies that do not rely on official police statistics (Moffitt and Silva, 1988).

Why is this? Why do criminals have lower intelligence than the general population? And why do more chronic and serious criminals have lower intelligence than their less chronic and serious counterparts? A new hypothesis in evolutionary psychology called the Savanna-IQ Interaction Hypothesis (Kanazawa, 2005b, 2006a, 2006b, 2007a) suggests one possible answer.

Relying on earlier observations made by pioneers of evolutionary psychology (Crawford, 1993; Symons, 1990; Tooby and Cosmides, 1990), Kanazawa (2004a) proposes what he calls the Savanna Principle, which states that *the human brain has difficulty comprehending and dealing with entities and situations that did not exist in the ancestral environment*. For example, individuals who watch certain types of TV show are more satisfied with their friendships, just as they are if they had more friends or socialized with them more frequently (Kanazawa, 2002). This may be because realistic images of other humans, such as television, movies, videos, and photographs, did not exist in the ancestral environment, where all realistic images of other humans were other humans. As a result, the human brain may have implicit difficulty distinguishing their 'TV friends' (characters they repeatedly see on TV shows) and their real friends, and may tend to respond similarly to both.

In an entirely separate line of research, Kanazawa (2004b) proposes an evolutionary psychological theory of the evolution of general intelligence. In contrast to views expressed by Chiappe and MacDonald (2005) and Cosmides and Tooby (2000, 2002), Kanazawa (2004b) suggests that what is now known as general intelligence may have originally evolved as a domain-specific adaptation to deal with evolutionarily novel, non-recurrent problems. The human brain consists of a large number of domain-specific evolved psychological mechanisms to solve recurrent adaptive problems. In this sense, our ancestors did not really have to think in order to solve such recurrent problems. Evolution has already done all the thinking, so to speak, and equipped the human brain with appropriate psychological mechanisms, which engender preferences, desires, cognitions and emotions, and motivate adaptive behavior in the context of the ancestral environment.

Even in the extreme continuity and constancy of the ancestral environment, however, there were occasional problems that were evolutionarily novel and nonrecurrent, which required our ancestors to think and reason in order to solve. To the extent that these evolutionarily novel, non-recurrent problems happened frequently enough in the ancestral environment (different problem each time) and had serious enough consequences for survival and reproduction, any genetic mutation that allowed its carriers to think and reason would have been selected for, and what we now call '(general intelligence' could have evolved as a domain-specific adaptation for the domain of evolutionarily novel, nonrecurrent problems.

General intelligence may have become universally important in modern life (Herrnstein and Murray, 1994) only because our current environment is almost entirely evolutionarily novel. The new theory suggests, and available empirical data confirm, that more intelligent individuals are better than less intelligent individuals at solving problems *only if* they are evolutionarily novel but that more intelligent individuals are *not better* than less intelligent individuals at solving evolutionarily familiar problems, such as those in the domain of mating, parenting, interpersonal relationships, and wayfinding (Kanazawa, 2007b).

The logical conjunction of the Savanna Principle and the theory of the evolution of general intelligence suggests a qualification of the Savanna Principle. If general intelligence evolved to deal with evolutionarily novel problems, then the human brain's difficulty in comprehending and dealing with entities and situations that did not exist in the ancestral environment (proposed in the Savanna Principle) should interact with general intelligence, such that the Savanna Principle holds stronger among less intelligent individuals than among more intelligent individuals. More intelligent individuals should be better able to comprehend and deal with evolutionarily novel (but *not* evolutionarily familiar) entities and situations than less intelligent individuals. [...]

Now, what does the Savanna-IQ Interaction Hypothesis have to do with crime? How can it explain the empirical observation that criminals tend to be less intelligent on average than the general population?

From the perspective of the hypothesis, there are two important points to note. First, much of what we now call interpersonal crime today was a routine means of intrasexual competition and resource acquisition and accumulation in the ancestral environment. This is most obvious from the fact that our primate cousins engage in what we call theft and robbery if perpetrated by humans (de Waal, 1989, 1992; de Waal *et al.*, 1993). More than likely, ancestral men competed with each other for resources and mating opportunities by stealing from each other if they could get away with it. In other words, most forms of criminal behavior are evolutionarily familiar.

Second, the institutions that deter, control, detect, and punish criminal behavior today – CCTV cameras, the police, the courts, and the prisons – are all evolutionarily novel; there was no third-party enforcement of norms in the ancestral environment, only second-party enforcement (by the victims and their kin and allies). In other words, the modern criminal justice system is an evolutionarily novel institution to deal with evolutionarily familiar criminal behavior.

Thus it makes perfect sense from the perspective of the Savanna-IQ Interaction Hypothesis that men with lower intelligence are more likely to resort to evolutionarily familiar means of competition for resources, status, and mating opportunities than to evolutionarily novel means (theft rather than full-time employment in a capitalist economy, forcible rape rather than long courtship), possibly because they are less likely to recognize or comprehend the evolutionarily novel alternatives. It also makes perfect sense from the perspective of the hypothesis that men with lower intelligence fail fully to comprehend the consequences of their criminal behavior imposed by evolutionarily novel entities of law enforcement and the criminal justice system. Hence the Hypothesis can explain why less intelligent individuals are more likely to engage in criminal behavior than more intelligent individuals.

The Savanna-IQ Interaction Hypothesis can also suggest a novel hypothesis with regard to intelligence and criminality. As mentioned earlier, while third-party enforcement (the police and the criminal justice system) are evolutionarily novel, second-party enforcement (retaliation and vigilance by the victims and their kin and allies) is not. Thus the hypothesis would predict that the difference in intelligence between criminals and noncriminals disappears in situations where third-party enforcement of norms is weak or absent, and criminal behavior is controlled largely via second-party enforcement, such as situations of prolonged anarchy and statelessness, in fact, any situation that resembles the ancestral environment.

Conclusion

By focusing on the importance of status and material resources for survival and reproductive success, and by underscoring the ultimate reproductive functions of all human behavior, an evolutionary psychological perspective can shed new theoretical light on crime. In particular, it can simultaneously explain why all interpersonal and property crimes are an overwhelmingly male enterprise; why young men are far more likely to engage in crime than older men (the age–crime curve); why social class and criminality are negatively correlated (the association being far from a 'myth'); and why criminals in general tend to be less intelligent than noncriminals. It can also elucidate the causal mechanism behind *why* lower class men are more likely to engage in crime than upper class men and *why* less intelligent men are more likely to engage in crime than more intelligent men.

At the same time, by focusing on individual characteristics that traditional criminologists and social scientists tend to overlook, such as physical attractiveness, height, and general intelligence, an evolutionary psychological perspective on crime can suggest novel hypotheses. For example, lower class men who are physically more attractive should be less criminal than lower class men who are physically unattractive, and the difference in intelligence between criminals and noncriminals should weaken to the extent that third-party enforcement (characteristic of modern society but not the ancestral environment) is absent. These and other novel hypotheses from an evolutionary psychological perspective on crime await empirical tests.

From S. Kanazawa, 'Evolutionary Psychology and Crime', in A. Walsh and K. Beaver (eds) Biosocial Criminology, (New York: Routledge), 2009, pp. 90–110.

Note

1 This is how Darwin originally defined natural and sexual selection, as two separate processes. That's why he wrote two separate books – *On the Origin of Species by Means of Natural Selection* (1859) to explain natural selection, and *The Descent of Man, and Selection in Relation to Sex* (1871) to explain sexual selection. In the 1930s, however, biologists redefined natural selection to subsume sexual selection, and began to contend that differential reproductive success was the currency of natural selection. This is now the orthodox in all biology textbooks. I concur with Millet (2000:8–12), Campbell (2002:34–35) and others in the current generation of evolutionary psychologists and believe that we should return to Darwin's original definitions and treat natural and sexual selection as two distinct processes. I am fully aware that this view is still controversial and in the minority, but I firmly believe that the conceptual separation of natural and sexual selection will bring theoretical clarity in evolutionary biology and psychology.

References

Blum, D. (1997). *Sex on the brain: the biological differences between men and women*. New York: Penguin.

Brown, D.E. (1991). *Human universals*. New York: McGraw-Hill.

Browne, K.R. (2002). *Biology at work: rethinking sexual equality*. New Brunswick: Rutgers University Press.

Buss, D.M. (1989). Sex differences in human mate preferences: evolutionary hypotheses tested in 37 cultures. *Behavioral and Brain Sciences*, 12:–49.

Campbell, A. (1995). A few good men: evolutionary psychology and female adolescent aggression. *Ethology and Sociobiology*, 16:99–123.

Campbell, A. (2002). *A mind of her own: the evolutionary psychology of women*. Oxford: Oxford University Press.

Chiappe, D. and K. MacDonald (2005). The evolution of domain-general mechanisms in intelligence and learning. *Journal of General Psychology*, 13:25–40.

Cosmides, L. and J. Tooby (2000). Consider the source: the evolution of adaptations for decoupling and metarepresentasion In Sperber, D. (Ed.), *Metarepresentations: a multidisciplinary perspective*. Oxford: Oxford University Press.

Cosmides, L. and J. Tooby (2002). Unraveling the enigma of human intelligence: evolutionary psychology and the multimodolar mind. In Sternberg, R. and J.C. Kaufman (Eds.). *The evolution of intelligence*. Mahwah, NJ: Lawrence Erlbaum Associates, Inc.

Crawford, C.B. (1993). The future of sociobiology: counting babies or proximate mechanisms? *Trends in Ecology and Evolution*, 8:183–186.

Daly, M. and M. Wilson (1988). *Homicide*. New York: Aldine De Gruyter.

Daly, M. and M. Wilson (1990). Killing the competition: female/female and male/male homicide. *Human Nature*, 1:81–107.

Darwin, C. (1859). *On the origin of species by means of natural selection*. London: John Murray.

Darwin, C. (1871). *The descent of man, and selection in relation to sex*. London: John Murray.

Gibson, H.B. and D.J. West (1970). Social and intellectual handicaps as precursors of early delinquency. *British Journal of Criminology*, 10:21–32.

Greenberg, D.E. (1985). Age, crime, and social explanation. *American Journal of Sociology*, 91:1–21.

Grogger, J. (1998). Market wages and youth crime. *Journal of Labor Economics*, 16:756–791,

Herrnstein, R.J. and C. Murray (1994). *The bell curve: intelligence and class structure in American life*. New York: Free Press,

Hirschi, T. and M. Gottfredson (1983). Age and the explanation of crime. *American Journal of Sociology*, 89:552–584.

Hirschi, T. and M. Gottfredson (1985). Age and crime, logic and scholarship: comment on Greenberg. *American Journal of Sociology*, 91:22–27.

Hirschi, T. and M. J. Hindelang (1977). Intelligence and delinquency: a revisionist review. *American Sociological Review*, 42:571–567.

Kanazawa, S. (2001). De gustibus *est* disputandum. *Social Forces*, 79:1131–1163.

Kanazawa, S. (2002). Bowling with our imaginary friends. *Evolution and Human Behavior*, 23:167–171.

Kanazawa, S. (2003a). Can evolutionary psychology explain reproductive behavior in the contemporary United States? *Sociological Quarterly*, 44:291–302.

Kanazawa, S. (2003b). Why productivity fades with age: the crime–genius connection. *Journal of Research in Personality*, 37:257–272.

Kanazawa, S. (2004a). The Savanna Principle. *Managerial and Decision Economics*, 25:41–54.

Kanazawa, S. (2004b). General intelligence as a domain-specific adaptation. *Psychological Review*, 111:512–523.

Kanazawa, S. (2005a). Is 'discrimination' necessary to explain the sex gap in earnings? *Journal of Economic Psychology*, 26:269–287.

Kanazawa, S. (2005b). An empirical test of a possible solution to 'the central theoretical problem of human sociobiology.' *Journal of Cultural and Evolutionary Psychology*, 3:249–260.

Kanazawa, S. (2006a). Why the less intelligent may enjoy television more than the more intelligent. *Journal of Cultural and Evolutionary Psychology*, 4:27–36.

Kanazawa, S. (2006b). Mind the gap... in intelligence: reexamining the relationship between inequality and health. *British Journal of Health Psychology*, 11: 623–642.

Kanazawa, S. (2007a). Dc gustibus *est* disputandum II: why liberals and atheists are more intelligent. London: London School of Economics and Political Science, Interdisciplinary Institute of Management.

Kanazawa, S. (2007b). Mating intelligence and general intelligence as independent constructs. In Gehec, G. and G.F. Miller (Eds.). *Mating intelligence: sex, relationships, and the mind's reproductive system*. Mahwah, NJ: Lawrence Erlbaum Associates, Inc.

Kanazawa, S. and M.C. Still (2000). Why men commit crimes (and why they desist). *Sociological Theory*, 18:434–447.

Laub, J.H., D.S. Nagin, and R.J. Sampson (1998). Trajectories of change in criminal offending: good marriages and the desistance process. *American Sociological Review*, 63:225–238.

Lynam, D., T.E. Moffitt, and M. Stouthamer – Loeber (1993). Explaining the relation between IQ and delinquency: class, race, test motivation, school failure, or self control? *Journal of Abnormal Psychology*, 102:187–196.

Mazur, A. and J. Michalek (1998). Marriage, divorce, and male testosterone. *Social Forces*, 77:315–330.

McIntyre, M., S.W. Gangestad, P.B. Gray, J.F. Chapman, T.C. Burnham, M.T. O'Rourke, *et al.* (2006). Romantic involvement often reduces men's testosterone levels – but not always: The moderating role of extrapair sexual interest. *Journal of Personality and Social Psychology*, 91:642–651.

Miller, G.F. (2000). *The mating mind: how sexual choice shaped the evolution of the human mind*. New York: Doubleday.

Moffitt, T.E. (1990). The neuropsychology of delinquency: a critical review of theory and research. *Crime and Justice: An Annual Review of Research*, 12:99–169.

Moffitt, T.E. and P.A. Silva (1988). IQ and delinquency: a direct test of the differential detection hypothesis. *Journal of Abnormal Psychology*, 97:330–333.

Moffitt, T.E., W.F. Gabrielli, S.A. Mednick, and E. Schulsinger (1981). Socioeconomic status, IQ, and delinquency. *Journal of Abnormal Psychology*, 90:152–156.

Pérusse, D. (1993). Cultural and reproductive success in industrial societies: testing the relationship at the proximate and ultimate levels. *Behavioral and Brain Sciences*, 16:267–322.

Rowe, D.C. (2002). *Biology and crime*. Los Angeles: Roxbury.

Symons, D. (1990), Adoptiveness and adaptation. *Ethology and Sociobiology*. 11: 427–444.

Thornhill, R. and N.W. Thornbill (1983). Human rape: an evolutionary analysis. *Ethology and Sociobiology*. 4: 137–173.

Tooby, J. and L. Cosmides (1990). The past explains the present: emotional adaptations and the structure of ancestral environments. *Ethology and Sociobiology*, 11:375–424.

de Waal, F.B.M. (1989). Food sharing and reciprocal obligations among chimpanzees. *Journal of Human Evolution*, 18:433–459.

de Waal, F.B.M. (1992). Appeasement, celebration, and food sharing in the two *Pan* species. In Nishida, T., W. C. McGrew, and P. Marler (Eds.). *Topics in primatalogy: human origins*. Tokyo: University of Tokyo Press.

de Waal, F.B.M., L.M. Luttrell, and M.F. Canfield (1993). Preliminary data on voluntary food sharing in brown capuchin monkeys. *American Journal of Primatology*, 29:73–78.

Wilson, J.Q. and R.J. Herrnstein (1985). *Crime and human nature: the definitive study of the causes of crime*. New York: Touchstone.

Wolfgang, M.E. (1958). *Patterns in criminal homicide*. Philadelphia: University of Pennsylvania Press.

Wolfgang, M.E., R.M. Figlio, and T. Sellin (1972). *Delinquency in a birth cohort*. Chicago: University of Chicago Press.

Yeudall, L.T., D. Fromm-Auch, and P. Davies (1982). Neuropsychological impairment of persistent delinquency. *Journal of Nervous and Mental Diseases*, 170:257–265.

7

Psychological positivism

7.1 Differential association
Edwin H. Sutherland and Donald R. Cressey   140

7.2 Social structure and social learning
Ronald L. Akers   142

7.3 Crime as choice
James Q. Wilson and Richard J. Herrnstein   149

**7.4 The link between cognitive ability
and criminal behavior**
Richard J. Herrnstein and Charles Murray   154

Introduction

Where biological positivism focused on the biological or biosocial bases for criminality, predictably enough psychological positivism is concerned with psychological and psychosocial explanations. This covers such matters as personality and learning processes and how these factors might be used to distinguish those involved in particular types of criminality from others.

The excerpts in this chapter begin with a piece that might seem slightly out of place – an excerpt from Sutherland and Cressey's work on 'differential association' **(Reading 7.1)**. This is a deeply sociological piece of work and thus, on one level, is strangely placed in a chapter on 'psychological positivism'. At heart, however, it contains a series of arguments about how ideas, values etc are learned and transmitted and, consequently, has had a fairly profound effect on subsequent psychological theorising in the field of criminology – as well as an enormous influence on sociological criminology. At the heart of Sutherland's theory was the idea that behaviour is learned through coming into contact with social norms (received expectations about standards of conduct). How one behaves is therefore influenced by the particular norms in the groups with which one comes into regular contact. Through learning and imitation such contact moulds individual behaviour and attitudes, including those toward law-breaking. For Sutherland, therefore, a crucial factor in explaining criminality was the balance of influences upon individuals.

A second learning theory is proposed by Ron Akers **(Reading 7.2)**. Like Sutherland and Cressey, Akers proposes a theory which combines the psychological with the sociological. As he puts it, the 'main proposition is that variations in the social structure, culture and locations of individuals and groups in the social system explain variations in crime rates'. They do this, in the main, through their influence on social learning, including but not limited to differential association. Centrally, Akers distinguishes between differential association and differential reinforcement, and argues that criminal behaviour is a direct function of the amount, frequency and probability of its reinforcement.

The next two excerpts take a somewhat different approach and one that caused a certain amount of controversy in criminological circles. The first, by James Q. Wilson and Richard Herrnstein **(Reading 7.3)** is drawn from their book, *Crime and Human Nature*. Their ideas are based on a form of weak rational choice theory: the assumption that when making decisions about what to do we are influenced by what we think the costs and benefits will be. They suggest that human behaviour is shaped by what they call primary (innate drives) and secondary (derived from learning) reinforcers. They then introduce another term – conditioning – to help explain the link between these different types of reinforcement. In essence these are a variety of processes through which we internalize particular rules or mores. Part of the explanation for criminality therefore may lie in the ease with which, or the willingness with which, people internalize rules.

In an excerpt from a book called *The Bell Curve* Richard Herrnstein and Charles Murray **(Reading 7.4)** explore the connection that they suggest exists between cognitive ability and criminal behaviour. They open with the intriguing – and you may think problematic – question: 'How big is the difference between criminals and the rest of us?' The difference they are referring to is in measured I.Q. This, they suggest, is quite sizeable and, moreover, is a very significant difference in explaining criminal conduct. What then is the link? To find out, you must read on!

Questions for discussion

1. How do 'norms' affect standards of behaviour?

2. What are the key components of the theory of differential association?

3. What are Akers' main criticisms of differential association theory?

4. In his social learning theory what other factors, in addition to differential association, does Akers identify?

5. What is the difference between primary and secondary reinforcers? Give examples of each and suggest how they might affect criminal conduct.

6. How do Wilson and Herrnstein suggest that the process of conditioning works?

7. What difficulties, if any, do you see in asking the question: 'How big is the difference between criminals and the rest of us?'

8. How many ways can you think of that intelligence might be linked to criminality? How strong and direct do you think these links might be?

7.1 Differential association
Edwin H. Sutherland and Donald R. Cressey

Scientific explanations of criminal behavior may be stated either in terms of the processes which are operating at the moment of the occurrence of crime or in terms of the processes operating in the earlier history of the criminal. In the first case the explanation may be called 'mechanistic,' 'situational,' or 'dynamic'; in the second, 'historical' or 'genetic.' Both types of explanation are desirable. The mechanistic type of explanation has been favored by physical and biological scientists, and it probably could be the more efficient type of explanation of criminal behavior. However, criminological explanations of the mechanistic type have thus far been notably unsuccessful, perhaps largely because they have been formulated in connection with the attempt to isolate personal and social pathologies among criminals. Work from this point of view has, at least, resulted in the conclusion that the immediate determinants of criminal behavior lie in the person-situation complex.

The objective situation is important to criminality largely to the extent that it provides an opportunity for a criminal act. A thief may steal from a fruit stand when the owner is not in sight but refrain when the owner is in sight; a bank burglar may attack a bank which is poorly protected but refrain from attacking a bank protected by watchmen and burglar alarms. A corporation which manufactures automobiles seldom or never violates the Pure Food and Drug Law, but a meat-packing corporation might violate this law with great frequency. But in another sense, a psychological or sociological sense, the situation is not exclusive of the person, for the situation which is important is the situation as defined by the person who is involved. That is, some persons define a situation in which a fruit-stand owner is out of sight as a 'crime-committing' situation, while others do not so define it. Furthermore, the events in the person-situation complex at the time a crime occurs cannot be separated from the prior life experiences of the criminal. This means that the situation is defined by the person in terms of the inclinations and abilities which the person has acquired up to date. For example, while a person could define a situation in such a manner that criminal behavior would be the inevitable result,

his past experiences would for the most part determine the way in which he defined the situation. An explanation of criminal behavior made in terms of these past experiences is an historical or genetic explanation.

The following paragraphs state such a genetic theory of criminal behavior on the assumption that a criminal act occurs when a situation appropriate for it, as defined by the person, is present. The theory should be regarded as tentative, and it should be tested by the factual information presented in the later chapters and by all other factual information and theories which are applicable.

Genetic explanation of criminal behavior.

The following statement refers to the process by which a particular person comes to engage in criminal behavior.

1 *Criminal behavior is learned.* Negatively, this means that criminal behavior is not inherited, as such; also, the person who is not already trained in crime does not invent criminal behavior, just as a person does not make mechanical inventions unless he has had training in mechanics.

2 *Criminal behavior is learned in interaction with other persons in a process of communication.* This communication is verbal in many respects but includes also 'the communication of gestures.'

3 *The principal part of the learning of criminal behavior occurs within intimate personal groups.* Negatively, this means that the impersonal agencies of communication, such as movies and newspapers, play a relatively unimportant part in the genesis of criminal behavior.

4 *When criminal behavior is learned, the learning includes (a) techniques of committing the crime, which are sometimes very complicated, sometimes very simple; (b) the specific direction of motives, drives, rationalizations, and attitudes.*

5 *The specific direction of motives and drives is learned from definitions of the legal codes as favorable or unfavorable.* In some societies an individual is surrounded by persons who

invariably define the legal codes as rules to be observed, while in others he is surrounded by persons whose definitions are favorable to the violation of the legal codes. In our American society these definitions are almost always mixed, with the consequence that we have culture conflict in relation to the legal codes.

6 *A person becomes delinquent because of an excess of definitions favorable to violation of law over definitions unfavorable to violation of law.* This is the principle of differential association. It refers to both criminal and anti-criminal associations and has to do with counteracting forces. When persons become criminal, they do so because of contacts with criminal patterns and also because of isolation from anti-criminal patterns. Any person inevitably assimilates the surrounding culture unless other patterns are in conflict; a Southerner does not pronounce 'r' because other Southerners do not pronounce 'r.' Negatively, this proposition of differential association means that associations which are neutral so far as crime is concerned have little or no effect on the genesis of criminal behavior. Much of the experience of a person is neutral in this sense, e.g., learning to brush one's teeth. This behavior has no negative or positive effect on criminal behavior except as it may be related to associations which are concerned with the legal codes. This neutral behavior is important especially as an occupier of the time of a child so that he is not in contact with criminal behavior during the time he is so engaged in the neutral behavior.

7 *Differential associations may vary in frequency, duration, priority, and intensity.* This means that associations with criminal behavior and also associations with anti-criminal behavior vary in those respects. 'Frequency' and 'duration' as modalities of associations are obvious and need no explanation. 'Priority' is assumed to be important in the sense that lawful behavior developed in early childhood may persist throughout life, and also that delinquent behavior developed in early childhood may persist throughout life. This tendency, however, has not been adequately demonstrated, and priority seems to be important principally through its selective influence. 'Intensity' is not precisely defined but it has to do with such things as the prestige of the source of a criminal or anti-criminal pattern and with emotional reactions related to the associations. In a precise description of the criminal behavior of a person these modalities would be stated in quantitative form and a mathematical ratio be reached. A formula in this sense has not been developed, and the development of such a formula would be extremely difficult.

8 The process of learning criminal behavior by association with criminal and anti-criminal patterns involves all of the mechanisms that are involved in any other learning. Negatively, this means that the learning of criminal behavior is not restricted to the process of imitation. A person who is seduced, for instance, learns criminal behavior by association, but this process would not ordinarily be described as imitation.

9 *While criminal behavior is an expression of general needs and values, it is not explained by those general needs and values since non-criminal behavior is an expression of the same needs and values.* Thieves generally steal in order to secure money, but likewise honest laborers work in order to secure money. The attempts by many scholars to explain criminal behavior by general drives and values, such as the happiness principle, striving for social status, the money motive, or frustration, have been and must continue to be futile since they explain lawful behavior as completely as they explain criminal behavior. They are similar to respiration, which is necessary for any behavior but which does not differentiate criminal from non-criminal behavior.

It is not necessary, at this level of explanation, to explain why a person has the associations which he has; this certainly involves a complex of many things. In an area where the delinquency rate is high a boy who is sociable, gregarious, active, and athletic is very likely to come in contact with the other boys in the neighborhood, learn delinquent behavior from them, and become a gangster; in the same neighborhood the psychopathic boy who is isolated, introvert, and inert may remain at home, not become acquainted with the other boys in the neighborhood, and not become delinquent. In another situation, the sociable, athletic, aggressive boy may become a member of a scout troop and not become involved in delinquent behavior. The person's associations are determined in a general context of social organization. A child is ordinarily reared in a family; the place of residence of the family is determined largely by family income; and the delinquency rate is in many respects related to the rental value of the houses. Many other factors enter into this social organization, including many of the small personal group relationships.

The preceding explanation of criminal behavior is stated from the point of view of the person who engages in criminal behavior. As indicated earlier, it is possible, also, to state sociological theories of criminal behavior from the point of view of the community, nation, or other group. The problem, when thus stated, is generally concerned with crime rates and involves a comparison of the crime rates of various groups or the crime rates of a particular group at different times. The explanation of a crime rate must be consistent with the explanation of the criminal behavior of the person, since the crime rate is a summary statement of the number of persons in the group who commit crimes and the frequency with which they commit crimes. One of the best

explanations of crime rates from this point of view is that a high crime rate is due to social disorganization. The term 'social disorganization' is not entirely satisfactory and it seems preferable to substitute for it the term 'differential social organization.' The postulate on which this theory is based, regardless of the name, is that crime is rooted in the social organization and is an expression of that social organization. A group may be organized for criminal behavior or organized against criminal behavior. Most communities are organized both for criminal and anti-criminal behavior and in that sense the crime rate is an expression of the differential group organization. Differential group organization as an explanation of variations in crime rates is consistent with the differential association theory of the processes by which persons become criminals.

> From E. Sutherland and D. Cressey, 'Differential association', in Principles of Criminology (5th ed.) (Chicago: J.P. Lippincott and Company), 1955, pp. 75–81.

7.2 Social structure and social learning
Ronald L. Akers

[The] basic assumption [of the Social Structure and Social Learning (SSL) theory of crime] is that social learning is the primary process linking social structure to individual behavior. Its main proposition is that variations in the social structure, culture, and locations of individuals and groups in the social system explain variations in crime rates, principally through their influence on differences among individuals on the social learning variables – mainly, differential association, differential reinforcement, imitation, and definitions favorable and unfavorable and other discriminative stimuli for crime. The social structural variables are indicators of the primary distal macro-level and meso-level causes of crime, while the social learning variables reflect the primary proximate causes of criminal behavior by individuals that mediate the relationship between social structure and crime rates. Some structural variables are not related to

crime and do not explain the crime rate because they do not have a crime-relevant effect on the social learning variables.

Deviance-producing environments have an impact on individual conduct through the operation of learning mechanisms. The general culture and structure of society and the particular communities, groups, and other contexts of social interaction provide learning environments in which the norms define what is approved and disapproved, behavioral models are present, and the reactions of other people (for example, in applying social sanctions) and the existence of other stimuli attach different reinforcing or punishing consequences to individuals' behavior. Social structure can be conceptualized as an arrangement of sets and schedules of reinforcement contingencies and other social behavioral variables. The family, peers, schools, churches, and other groups provide the more immediate contexts that promote or discourage the criminal or conforming behavior of the individual. Differences in the societal or group rates of criminal behavior are a function of the extent to which cultural traditions, norms, social organization, and social control systems provide socialization, learning environments, reinforcement schedules, opportunities, and immediate situations conducive to conformity or deviance.

I have made assertions like these over a great many years, and I have sketched out ways in which social learning is congruent with and could be integrated with social structural theories of crime rates (Burgess and Akers, l966b; Akers, 1968; Akers, 1973; 1977; 1985; Akers *et al.*, 1979; Akers, 1992b; 1994). Both these earlier statements and the current SSSL model harken back to the theme introduced by Sutherland fifty years ago.

It is not necessary at this level of explanation, to explain why a person has the associations which he has; this certainly involves a complex of many things .... The person's associations are determined in the general context of social organization .... Many other factors enter into this social organization, including many of the small personal group relationships.

The preceding explanation of criminal behavior [differential association theory] was stated from the point of view of the person who engages in criminal behavior. It is possible, also, to state theories of criminal behavior from the point of view of the community, nation, or other group. The problem, when thus stated, is generally concerned with crime rates and involves a comparison of the crime rates of various groups or the crime rates of a particular group at different times. One of the best explanations of crime rates from this point of view is that a high crime rate is due to social disorganization. The term 'social disorganization' is not entirely satisfactory and it seems preferable to substitute for it the term 'differential social organization.' The postulate on which this theory is based, regardless of the name, is that crime is rooted in the social organization and is an expression of that social organization. A group may be organized for criminal behavior or organized against criminal behavior. Most communities are organized both for criminal and anti-criminal behavior and in that sense the crime rate is an expression of the differential group organization. Differential group organiza-

tion as an explanation of a crime rate must be consistent with the explanation of the criminal behavior of the person, since the crime rate is a summary statement of the number of persons in the group who commit crimes and the frequency with which they commit crimes. (Sutherland, 1947:8–9)

This is a concise statement of the relationship between differential association as a causal process in criminal behavior at the individual level and social disorganization (or differential social organization) as an explanation of crime at the structural level. However, Sutherland did not develop this link systematically. Rather, he came back to it occasionally with brief references to the connection between differential association and social organization in his chapters on social disorganization and culture conflict. He also came back to it indirectly by pointing to the operation of differential association in various 'factors' in crime, such as family, age, sex, class, and race. Sutherland also referred to associations and value codes in his chapter dealing with behavior systems in crime, which can be taken as well as a discussion of differential social organization and association (Sutherland, 1947).

Cressey developed the connection between differential social organization (epidemiology) and differential association (individual conduct) more clearly, noting that, 'for example, a high crime rate in urban areas can be considered the end product of social conditions that lead to a situation in which relatively large proportions of persons are presented with an excess of criminal behavior patterns' (Sutherland and Cressey, 1960:55). In his revisions of *Principles of Criminology*, Cressey stressed that a general theory must be evaluated on the basis of its 'capacity to "make sense" of the facts' about the 'variations of crime and delinquency rates with age, sex, race, poverty, educational status, urbanization, and other variables, as well as the incidence among criminals and delinquents of various biological, psychological, and social traits, characteristics, and processes' (Sutherland and Cressey, 1960:v; 1970:v). This is sometimes mistakenly taken to mean that differential association is a theory of group-level crime rates and does not really apply to individual behavior. Neither Sutherland nor Cressey proposed that differential association was a theory of crime rates rather than a theory of individual criminal behavior. Rather, they proposed that when combined consistently with an explanation such as differential social organization, differential association as an explanation of individual criminality was more capable of 'making sense' of these group variations in crime than any other theory.

> Certain of these ratios, and variations in ratios, seem to be crucial for the explanation of criminal behavior. These may be called definitive facts; that is, facts which define or limit the explanations which can be regarded as valid. Some of the ratios and variations in ratios may be explained by one or another of the general theories of criminal behavior, but the differential association theory seems to explain *all* of these ratios and variations more adequately than the other theories. Although this theory has many defects, it seems to fit general facts better than does any other general theory. (Sutherland and Cressey, 1960:149; emphasis in original)

This is a clear-cut reiteration and elaboration by Cressey of Sutherland's view that differential association can make sense of the widely known correlates of crime and that it does so in a way that is consistent with a structural explanation of crime rates – for example, differential social organization or social disorganization. But Cressey's position does not offer a systematic statement of the theory of differential social organization or of an integrated theory of social organization and association.

In the Burgess and Akers (1966b) article, we stressed that our task was to revise Sutherland's processual theory of differential association *only*; we left undone connecting that process with the social structure. But we made it equally clear that this was something that should be undertaken later. [...]

I followed up [...] with remarks showing the general thrust of how social learning and structural theories can be integrated.

> The structural theories contend that more people in certain groups, located in certain positions in, or encountering particular pressures created by the social structure, will engage in deviancy than those in other groups and locations.
>
> The differential association–reinforcement theory formulated by Burgess and Akers avoids some of the problems of Sutherland's original formulation and describes the general process (consistently and integrally with a broader theory of behavior) of deviant behavior. It is capable of identifying the common elements in the separate processual theories and provides the groundwork for integrating structural and processual explanations. By conceptualizing groups and social structure as learning environments which structure the patterns of associations and reinforcement, a long step is taken in the direction of bringing the two together. Differential association-reinforcement spells out the mechanisms by which environmental stimuli produce and maintain behavior and the structural theories explicate the type of *environments* most likely to sustain norm and law-violating behavior. (Akers, 1968:457–58; emphasis in original)

Social structure, social correlates, and individual behavior: issues in cross-level integration of explanations of crime

Purely social structural theories of crime of the form shown in Figure 7.2.1 can stand on their own without the necessity of positing the mediating or intervening variables or of specifying the mechanisms by which the social structure produces higher or lower rates of crime, delinquency, or deviance. It is perfectly legitimate to hold that the question of 'by what mechanism' or 'by what mediating process' is outside the explanatory intent of the theory. This would not deny the importance of asking the question, but simply would define it as a question the theory was not designed to answer. Thus, differences in anomie, social disorganization or other conditions of the social structure may be posited as structural sources of differences in crime rates across societies, among subparts of the same society, or through time for the same society or group. Such an explanation would be sufficient to identify the macro-level causes of differences in crime rates, without the necessity of also explaining what micro-level mechanisms are involved in producing criminal acts. However, the question of how anomie produces crime rates is a good one, and a formulation that explicitly inserts elements into the theory that show how this occurs is a more complete explanation.

Similarly, purely social psychological (or purely biological or psychological) explanations, either of differences between individuals or variations in the behavior of the same individuals by time, place, and situation (shown in simplified form in Figure 7.2.1), can legitimately be formulated without also offering an answer to the question of what social structural conditions differentially distribute the processual variables in society. But it is a fuller explanation if the process can be tied to social structural sources of the variations.

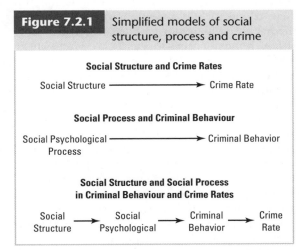

Figure 7.2.1 Simplified models of social structure, process and crime

Social Structure and Crime Rates

Social Structure ⟶ Crime Rate

Social Process and Criminal Behaviour

Social Psychological ⟶ Criminal Behavior
Process

**Social Structure and Social Process
in Criminal Behaviour and Crime Rates**

Social ⟶ Social ⟶ Criminal ⟶ Crime
Structure   Psychological   Behavior   Rate

Theories emphasizing social structure propose that the proportions of crimes among groups, classes, communities, or societies differ because of variations in their social or cultural makeup. Most structural theories, however, also include assumptions, and sometimes more explicit statements, regarding the process by which these structural conditions produce high or low crime rates. For instance, although variations in individual perceptions of the social structure are not an explicit part of Merton's anomie theory, most researchers, myself included, have operationalized the theory as if such perceptions were at least implicit in it. In order for objective differential opportunities to have an effect on deviant adaptations, the reasoning goes, individuals must perceive a discrepancy between their educational/occupational aspirations (goals) and realistic expectations of achieving those aspirations legitimately (perceived access to socially approved means). Therefore, the greater the perceived discrepancy, the greater the chance of deviant involvement. Indeed, this micro-level perceptual counterpart of the macro-level condition of anomie has become such a routine part of later interpretations and research on Merton's anomie theory that some have protested that the structural version of anomie theory has never really been tested (Bernard, 1987; Messner, 1988). Similarly, microlevel theories assert that an individual commits criminal acts because he or she has experienced a particular life history, possesses a particular set of individual characteristics, or has encountered a particular situation. Such theories imply something about the deviance-producing structures that an individual must encounter in order to increase the probability of his or her committing a crime.

Thus, theories of criminal behavior are neither purely structural nor processual. Nevertheless, structural variables are clearly separable from social psychological variables, regardless of how they are folded into a particular theory. In spite of its frequent operationalization at the social psychological level, for instance, anomie theory is still clearly and rightly classified as a structural theory. And the structural conditions of anomie are clearly separable from the social psychological process by which those conditions affect perceptions and individual behavior.

None of the structural approaches makes assumptions or produces hypotheses that would run counter to the basic, empirically sound, premise of the social learning approach that both conforming and deviant behavior are learned in the same way; the substance and direction of the learning is different, but the general process is the same for both. All would agree that the individual's behavior is shaped by the situations experienced in life. In fact, as I have noted, the primary burden of these theories, whatever social psychological processes they imply, is to show what kinds of social structures lead to high levels of delinquent, deviant, or criminal behavior. It is the burden of social learning theory to specify the process by which social structure produces variations in individual behavior. Thus, social learning is complementary to, not in competition with, any of the empirically validated structural theories.

Social structure and social learning in crime and deviance

Main components of the SSSL model

The SSSL model is diagrammed in Figure 7.2.2. The social learning variables in the model have been extensively defined, measured, and discussed in previous chapters. and the dependent variables of criminal behavior and crime rates are self-explanatory. The other sets of variables need further definition and comment. There are four dimensions, contexts, or elements of social structure that are expected to be related to social process and individual behavior and hence to crime rates in the SSSL model. The first two of these have to do with the social correlates or 'structural covariates' of crime, that is, the often-studied and well-known distributions of crime by age, sex, gender, community, inequality, population density and composition, and so on (Land *et al.*, 1990). These can be and have been identified on purely empirical grounds without regard to their theoretical relevance in explaining crime. In fact, they are routinely entered into tests of theoretical models as nontheoretical control variables. The third has to do with the conceptually defined features or conditions of social structure that sociological theories of social disorganization, anomie, and conflict hypothesize to be the cause(s) of crime. The fourth has to do with the small group level of social structure.

Social structural correlates: differential social organization. First, there are the known ecological, community, or geographical differences across systems (urban versus rural communities, cross-national comparisons, regional variations in rates,

differences by ecological areas of the city, differences in population size or density, etc.). The empirical variations in rates of crime and delinquency can be established, with or without specification of the causative structural or cultural characteristics of these systems. From this point of view, it makes little difference what the specific theoretical explanations of the variations are, although a particular set of authors or researchers may conceptualize them as operational measures of theoretical constructs. But the measure could be tapping some unspecified combination of the features of the social organization, culture, or social backgrounds of the people who form the community or society. I see these differences across social systems or areas as indicating in part what Sutherland meant by groups 'organized for and against crime.' That is, there are some known or unknown characteristics of the social structure and/or culture of the society, community, or group that lean it toward relatively high or relatively low crime rates. Following Sutherland, I identify these variations in structural conditions by the general

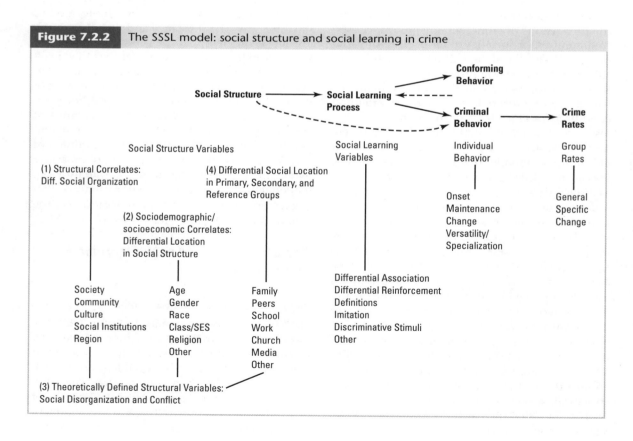

Figure 7.2.2　The SSSL model: social structure and social learning in crime

label of differential social organization, and I reiterate his view that 'crime is rooted in the social organization.' However, I do not agree with Sutherland that this term is essentially synonymous with, and should substitute for, the 'less satisfactory' concept of social disorganization.

Sociodemographic/socioeconomic correlates: differential location in the social structure. Second, there are the known or probable variations in crime rates by sociodemographic characteristics, groupings, aggregates, collectivities, or categories, such as race/ethnicity, class, gender, age, marital status, religion, occupation, and other dimensions of social differentiation that exist in societies, regions, and communities. These may be viewed as the direct causes of crime (e.g., there is something inherent in being male that makes men more prone to crime than women), but more frequently the relationship between them and crime is viewed as the thing to be explained. For instance, one may attempt to account for the high ratio of male to female crime by explaining that crime-proneness reflects gender-role expectations in society. At one level these are descriptive characteristics of individuals and may be measured as sources of variation in individual behavior. At the structural level, however, I conceptualize them as direct indicators of the differential location of groups or categories of individuals in the social structure. They are commonly conceptualized as defining sociocultural categories or collectivities. Many structural variables incorporated into empirical models of crime are simply the aggregation or proportional composition of social systems of individuals with these characteristics (e.g., racial and class composition of the population of a city or proportion of males aged 15 to 24).

Theoretically defined structural causes: social disorganization and conflict. Third, there are the conceptually defined structural variables that have been captured in particular theoretical formulations that propose them as structural causes of crime. I am referring here to the well-known structural theories of crime and deviance that propose elevated rates in those societies, or segments of societies, that are hypothesized to have higher levels of some abstractly defined condition like anomie, conflict, social disorganization, patriarchy, or class oppression. The explanatory variables in these theories typically do not simply reiterate the correlates of crime. Rather, the structural theories offer explanations for one or more of the known or assumed correlations between general or offense-specific crime rates and race, class, gender, region, city, neighborhood, and population size, density, and composition. Often the sociodemographic or socioeconomic variables are taken as empirical indicators of the explanatory concepts in these theories.

In the SSSL model, the most relevant of these explanatory concepts are drawn primarily from anomie, social disorganization, and conflict theories. Although they have evolved from different theoretical and research traditions in sociology, social disorganization and anomie theories propose essentially the same explanation for crime. Both view social order, stability, and integration as conducive to conformity, and disorder and malintegration as conducive to crime and deviance. A social system (a society, community, or subsystem within a society, such as a family) is socially organized and integrated if there is an internal consensus on its norms and values, a strong cohesion exists among its members, social interaction proceeds in an orderly way, and there is a low level of disruptive conflict. Conversely, the system is disorganized or anomic if there is a disruption in its social cohesion or integration, weakened formal or informal social control, or malalignment or disjuncture between its social and cultural elements. The greater the homogeneity and common loyalties to shared values and norms or functional interdependence, the lower the crime rate. The less solidarity, cohesion, or integration there is within a group, community, or society, the higher will be the rate of crime and deviance. The more disorganized or weakened the institutions of conventional formal and informal control and socialization (family, education, religion, government), the higher the crime rate. Social, political, and economic disparities and inequalities that produce group and culture conflict relate to crime both as indicators of general social disorganization and as indicators that some of the groups in the conflict, while they may be internally organized, have interests or normative expectations that violate the social and legal norms of the larger society.

Differential social location in primary, secondary, and reference groups. Fourth, there are the more immediate primary, secondary, and reference groups comprising the small-group and personal networks that impinge directly on the individual. These are the agents of informal and semiformal social control and socialization and are referred to specifically in social learning theory's concept of differential association. These are the groups to which the individual relates and which provide or filter the social environments, situations, and opportunities that promote or discourage his or her criminal or conforming behavior. Real and symbolic (through utilization of communications media) as well as direct and indirect participation, interaction, and identification with these groups provide the immediate social context in which differential social organization, differential social location, and social disorganization and conflict impinge on the individual and the operation of the social learning variables. Families, peers, schools, and other groups may be incomplete, disorganized, or ineffective agents of social control. They reflect the differential social organization and conflicts of the larger society or community and are the social locations for the operation of statuses and roles indicated by age, sex, race, and class. They provide the small-group, meso- or micro-level social contexts. From the perspective of the individual they are closely linked to the concept of differential association and entangled with the other social learning variables.

Please note that I am writing here about all of the social learning variables and primary groups, including the family. I am not postulating that peer group association is the only thing that counts. Sampson and Laub (1993:122) mistakenly believe that differential association theory hypothesizes that 'family, school, and other effects are *fully mediated by learning in delinquent groups'* (emphasis added). They incorrectly cite Matsueda (1982) on this point. Social learning theory would not hypothesize that only delinquent peer groups mediate the effects of family and school or that such delinquent groups 'fully' mediate other effects of these other groups. Rather, these are all primary and secondary groups that define the immediate social contexts within which the behavioral mechanisms operate.

From R. L. Akers, Social Learning and Social Structure: A general theory of crime and deviance *(Boston: Northeastern University Press), 1998, pp. 322–413.*

References

Akers, R.L. (1968) 'Problems in the sociology of deviance: social definitions and behavior,' *Social Forces*, 46:455–465.

Akers, R.L. (1973) *Deviant Behavior: A Social Learning Approach.* Belmont, CA: Wadsworth.

Akers, R.L. (1977) *Deviant Behavior: A Social Learning Approach.* Second edition. Belmont, CA: Wadsworth.

Akers, R.L. (1985) *Deviant Behavior: A Social Learning Approach.* Third edition. Belmont, CA: Wadsworth. Reprinted 1992. Fairfax, VA: Techbooks.

Akers, R.L. (1992b) *Drugs, Alcohol, and Society: Social Structure, Process, and Policy.* Belmont, CA: Wadsworth.

Akers, R.L. (1994) *Criminological Theories: Introduction and Evaluation.* Los Angeles: Roxbury.

Akers, R.L., Krohn, M.D., Lanza-Kaduce, L. and Radosevich, M. (1979) 'Social learning and deviant behavior: a specific test of a general theory,' *American Sociological Review*, 44:635–655.

Bernard, T.J. (1987) 'Testing structural strain theories,' *Journal of Research in Crime and Delinquency*, 24:262–272.

Burgess, R.L. and Akers, R.L. (1966b) 'A differential association-reinforcement theory of criminal behavior,' *Social Problems*, 14:128–147.

Matsueda, R.L. (1982) 'Testing control theory and differential association,' *American Sociological Review*, 47:489–584.

Messner, S.F. (1988) 'Merton's 'Social structure and anomie': the road not taken,' *Deviant Behavior*, 9:33–53.

Sampson, R.J. and Laub, J.H. (1993) *Crime in the Making: Pathways and Turning Points through Life.* Cambridge, MA: Harvard University Press.

Sutherland, E.H. (1947) *Principles of Criminology.* Fourth edition. Philadelphia: J.P. Lippincott.

Sutherland, E.H. and Cressey, D.R. (1960) Principles of *Criminology*. Sixth edition. Philadelphia: J.P. Lippincott.

Sutherland, E.H. and Cressey, D.R. (1970) *Criminology.* Eighth edition. Philadelphia: J.P. Lippincott.

7.3 Crime as choice
James Q. Wilson and Richard J. Herrnstein

Our theory rests on the assumption that people, when faced with a choice, choose the preferred course of action. This assumption is quite weak; it says nothing more than that whatever people choose to do, they choose it because they prefer it. In fact, it is more than weak; without further clarification, it is a tautology. When we say people 'choose,' we do not necessarily mean that they consciously deliberate about what to do. All we mean is that their behavior is determined by its consequences. A person will do that thing the consequences of which are perceived by him or her to be preferable to the consequences of doing something else. What can save such a statement from being a tautology is how plausibly we describe the gains and losses associated with alternative courses of action and the standards by which a person evaluates those gains and losses.

These assumptions are commonplace in philosophy and social science. Philosophers speak of hedonism or utilitarianism, economists of value or utility, and psychologists of reinforcement or reward. We will use the language of psychology, but it should not be hard to translate our terminology into that of other disciplines. Though social scientists differ as to how much behavior can reasonably be described as the result of a choice, all agree that at least some behavior is guided, or even precisely controlled, by things variously termed pleasure, pain, happiness, sorrow, desirability, or the like. Our object is to show how this simple and widely used idea can be used to explain behavior.

At any given moment, a person can choose between committing a crime and not committing it (all these alternatives to crime we lump together as 'noncrime'). The consequences of committing the crime consist of rewards (what psychologists call 'reinforcers') and punishments; the consequences of not committing the crime (i.e., engaging in noncrime) also entail gains and losses. The larger the ratio of the net rewards of crime to the net rewards of noncrime, the greater the tendency to commit the crime. The net rewards of crime include, obviously, the likely material gains from the crime, but they also include intangible benefits, such as obtaining emotional or sexual gratification, receiving the approval of peers, satis-fying an old score against an enemy, or enhancing one's sense of justice. One must deduct from these rewards of crime any losses that accrue immediately – that are, so to speak, contemporaneous with the crime. They include the pangs of conscience, the disapproval of onlookers, and the retaliation of the victim.

The value of noncrime lies all in the future. It includes the benefits to the individual of avoiding the risk of being caught and punished and, in addition, the benefits of avoiding penalties not controlled by the criminal justice system, such as the loss of reputation or the sense of shame afflicting a person later discovered to have broken the law and the possibility that, being known as a criminal, one cannot get or keep a job.

The value of any reward or punishment associated with either crime or noncrime is, to some degree, uncertain. A would-be burglar can rarely know exactly how much loot he will take away or what its cash value will prove to be. The assaulter or rapist may exaggerate the satisfaction he thinks will follow the assault or the rape. Many people do not know how sharp the bite of conscience will be until they have done something that makes them feel the bite. The anticipated approval of one's buddies may or may not be forthcoming. Similarly, the benefits of noncrime are uncertain. One cannot know with confidence whether one will be caught, convicted, and punished, or whether one's friends will learn about the crime and as a result withhold valued esteem, or whether one will be able to find or hold a job.

Compounding these uncertainties is time. The opportunity to commit a crime may be ready at hand (an open, unattended cash register in a store) or well in the future (a bank that, with planning and preparation, can be robbed). And the rewards associated with noncrime are almost invariably more distant than those connected with crime, perhaps many weeks or months distant. The strength of reinforcers tends to decay over time at rates that differ among individuals. As a result, the extent to which people take into account distant possibilities – a crime that can be committed only tomorrow, or punishment that will be inflicted only in a year – will affect whether they choose crime or noncrime. All of these factors – the strength of rewards, the problems of uncertainty and delay, and the way in which our sense of justice affects how we value the rewards – will be examined in the remainder of this chapter.

Reinforcers

All human behavior is shaped by two kinds of reinforcers: primary and secondary. A primary reinforcer derives its strength from an innate drive, such as hunger or sexual appetite; a secondary reinforcer derives its strength from learning. The line dividing reinforcers that are innate from those that are learned is hard to draw, and people argue, often passionately, over where it ought to be drawn. When we disagree over whether people are innately altruistic, men are innately more aggressive than women, or mankind is innately warlike or competitive, we are disagreeing over whether behavior responds to primary or to secondary reinforcers.

In fact, most reinforcers combine primary and secondary elements. Part of the benefit that comes from eating either bread or spaghetti must derive from the fact that their common ingredient, wheat, satisfies an innate drive – hunger. In this sense, both are primary reinforcers. But bread and spaghetti differ in texture, flavor, and appearance, and the preferences we have for these qualities are in part learned. These qualities constitute secondary reinforcers. The diversity of the world's cuisines shows, to some extent, how extraordinarily varied are the secondary aspects of even a highly biological reinforcer such as food.

The distinction between primary and secondary reinforcers is important in part because it draws attention to the link between innate drives and social conventions. For example, in every society men and women adorn themselves to enhance their sexual appeal. At the same time, styles in clothing and cosmetics vary greatly among societies and throughout history. As we are all immersed in the fashions of our place and time, we may suppose that fashion is purely arbitrary. But we are probably wrong, for these conventions of personal beauty are dependent on primary sexual reinforcers. But what constitutes acceptable adornment changes within broad limits. Once, for a woman to appear nude in a motion picture meant that she was wanton and the film was trash. Today, female nudity, though it is still offensive to some, is not construed by most viewers as an indication of the moral worth of the woman.

Not only do innate primary reinforcers become blended with learned secondary ones, the strength of even primary reinforcers (and of course of secondary reinforcers) will vary. Bread that we eat hungrily at seven o'clock in the morning may have no appeal to us at one o'clock in the afternoon, right after lunch. In fact, many forms of food may appeal to us before breakfast even though none may appeal after lunch. A class of reinforcers whose strengths vary together allows us to speak of a 'drive' – in this case, the hunger drive.

Drives vary in strength. The various food drives can be depended on to assert themselves several times a day, but the sexual drive may be felt much less frequently and then in ways powerfully affected by circumstances. The aggressive drive (to be discussed later in this chapter) may occur very rarely in some of us and frequently in others, and it may appear suddenly, in response to events, and blow over almost as quickly. We repeat these commonplace observations because we wish to emphasize that though much behavior, including criminal behavior, is affected by innate drives, this does not mean that crime is committed by 'born criminals' with uncontrollable, antisocial drives. We can, in short, include innate drives (and thus genetic factors) in our theory without embracing a view of the criminal as an atavistic savage or any other sort of biological anomaly.

Secondary reinforcers change in strength along with the primary reinforcers with which they are associated. Those secondary reinforcers that change the least in strength are those associated with the largest variety of primary reinforcers. Money is an especially powerful reward, not because it is intrinsically valuable (paper currency has almost no intrinsic worth), but because it is associated with so many primary reinforcers that satisfy innate drives. Money can buy food, shelter, relief from pain, and even sexual gratification. (It can also buy status and power, but we will not discuss here the interesting question of whether the desire for these things is innate.) The reinforcing power of money is relatively steady because the many primary rewards with which it is connected make it somewhat impervious to fluctuations in the value of any one drive.

Because of the constant and universal reinforcing power of money, people are inclined to think of crimes for money gain as more natural, and thus more the product of voluntary choice and rational thought, than crimes involving 'senseless' violence or sexual deviance. Stealing is an understandable, if not pardonable, crime; bestiality, 'unprovoked' murder, and drug addiction seem much less understandable, and therefore, perhaps, less voluntary or deliberate. People sometimes carry this line of thought even further: These 'senseless' crimes are the result of overpowering compulsions or irrational beliefs. But this is a false distinction. Certain reinforcers may have a steadier, more predictable effect, but all behavior, even the bizarre, responds to reinforcement. It is sometimes useful to distinguish between crimes that arise out of long-lasting, hard-to-change reinforcers (such as money) from those that stem from short-acting, (possibly) changeable drives (such as sexual deviance), but we must always bear in mind that these are distinctions of degree, not of kind.

Conditioning

Thus far, we have spoken of the 'association' between primary and secondary reinforcers. Now we must ask how that association arises. The answer is the process known as conditioning. The simplest form of conditioning is the well-known experiment involving Pavlov's dog. The dog repeatedly heard a buzzer a few moments before receiving some dried meat powder in its mouth. Soon, the dog salivated at the mere sound of the buzzer. Two different stimuli – meat and buzzers – were associated. The meat elicited an innate tendency to salivate; the buzzer came to elicit salivation through learning. Pavlov's successors extended his discovery to much more complex responses than salivation and to many other species, including man. These Pavlovian experiments involved what psychologists now call 'classical conditioning,' which typically involves the autonomic nervous system (that part of our neural structure controlling reflexive behavior, such as heartbeats, salivation, and perspiration, and internal emotional states, such as fear, anxiety, and relaxation) and in which the behavior of the subject (the dog or the man) does not affect the stimulus being administered.

Classical (or Pavlovian) conditioning can make an arbitrary stimulus reinforce behavior by associating the stimulus with either a primary (i.e., innate) reinforcer or some already-learned secondary reinforcer. As we have seen, money is an arbitrary stimulus (a collection of scraps of paper and bits of metal) that has become one of the most universal and powerful secondary reinforcers. But

there are many other examples. If a child is regularly praised for scrubbing his or her hands before dinner, then (provided that the praise is already felt to be rewarding), the child will in time scrub his hands without being told or praised. The satisfaction he feels in having scrubbed hands is now the internal feeling of reinforcement. In the same way, hand-scrubbing can be taught by scolding a child who does not wash up. If the scolding is already felt by the child to be punishing, in time the child will feel uncomfortable whenever he has dirty hands.

Classical conditioning does not produce only secretions or muscle twitches. These external responses may be accompanied by a complex array of internalized dispositions. The child who learns to scrub his hands, because of either parental praise or parental disapproval, will have learned things on which his mind and his subsequent experience will come to work in elaborate ways. In time, the satisfaction he feels from having clean hands may merge with other similar satisfactions and become a general sense of cleanliness, which he may eventually believe is next to godliness. He imputes virtue to cleanliness and regards filth with great distaste, even when he finds it in the world at large rather than simply on his own hands. Of course, all this presupposes growing up in a society in which neighbors, friends, and even the government regularly praise cleanliness and condemn slovenliness.

Although it does not do justice to the subtlety and generality of the process or the way in which its outcome is linked to social settings, H.J. Eysenck's remark that 'conscience is a conditioned reflex' is not far off the mark.[1] And it calls attention to the intriguing possibility that individuals may differ in their susceptibility to classical conditioning. As we will show, people are not alike in how readily they internalize rules, and thus they are not alike in the value they attach to the costs in conscience of a prospective crime. For some people, the benefits of a crime are not reduced as much by a 'conscience decrement' as they are for persons who have been more successfully subjected to classical conditioning.

Many people have a conscience strong enough to prevent them from committing a crime some of the time but not all of the time. In ways that will become clearer later in the chapter, a reasonably strong conscience is probably sufficient to prevent a person from committing a crime that would have only a modest yield *and* that could not take place for, say, two days. This would be true even if the person was confident he would not be caught. But now suppose the opportunity for committing the offense is immediately at hand – say, your poker-playing friends have left the room after the hand was dealt and you have a chance to peek at their cards, or the jewelry salesman has left the store with a tray of diamond rings open on the counter. Now, if the bite of conscience is not sufficient by itself to prevent the offense, the would-be offender will calculate, however roughly or inarticulately, the chances of being caught. He will know that if the friends suddenly return or the jewelry salesman is watching, he will lose things – in the first instance, reputation, and in the second, his freedom. People differ in how they calculate these risks. Some worry about any chance, however slight, of being caught and would be appalled at any loss of esteem, however small or fleeting; others will peek at the cards or grab a ring if they think they have any chance at all of getting away with it.

When present actions are governed by their consequences, 'instrumental' (or operant) conditioning is at work. Unlike classically conditioned responses, instrumental conditioning involves behavior that affects the stimulus (e.g., not peeking at the cards or not taking the ring avoids the costs of the offense). Instrumental behavior affects the stimuli we receive and this, in turn, affects subsequent behavior.

The distinction between classical and instrumental conditioning is by no means as clear as our simple definitions may make it appear. But if we bear in mind that behavior cannot be neatly explained by one or the other process, we can use the distinction to help us understand individual differences in criminality. Persons deficient in conscience may turn out to be persons who for various reasons resist classical conditioning – they do not internalize rules as easily as do others. Persons who, even with a strong conscience, commit crimes anyway may be persons who have difficulty imagining the future consequences of present action or who are so impulsive as to discount very heavily even those consequences they can foresee, and hence will resist the instrumental conditioning that might lead them to choose noncrime over crime.

The theory as a whole

We began by asserting that the chief value of a comprehensive theory of crime is that it will bring

to our attention all the factors that explain individual differences in criminality and thus prevent us from offering partial explanations or making incomplete interpretations of research findings.[2] The larger the ratio of the rewards (material and nonmaterial) of noncrime to the rewards (material and nonmaterial) of crime, the weaker the tendency to commit crimes. The bite of conscience, the approval of peers, and any sense of inequity will increase or decrease the total value of crime; the opinions of family, friends, and employers are important benefits of noncrime, as is the desire to avoid the penalties that can be imposed by the criminal justice system. The strength of any reward declines with time, but people differ in the rate at which they discount the future. The strength of a given reward is also affected by the total supply of reinforcers.

Some implications of the theory are obvious: Other things being equal, a reduction in the delay and uncertainty attached to the rewards of noncrime will reduce the probability of crime. But other implications are not so obvious. For instance, increasing the value of the rewards of noncrime (by increasing the severity of punishment) may not reduce a given individual's tendency to commit crime if he believes that these rewards are not commensurate with what he deserves. In this case, punishing him for preferring crime to noncrime may trigger hostility toward society in retaliation for the shortfall. The increased rewards for noncrime may be offset by an increased sense of inequity and hence an increased incentive for committing a crime. Or again: It may be easier to reduce crime by making penalties swifter or more certain, rather than more severe, if the persons committing crime are highly present-oriented (so that they discount even large rewards very sharply) or if they are likely to have their sense of inequity heightened by increases in the severity of punishment. Or yet again: An individual with an extroverted personality is more likely than one with an introverted one to externalize his feelings of inequity and act directly to correct then.

In laboratory settings involving both human and animal subjects, each element of the theory has received at least some confirmation and the major elements have been confirmed extensively.[3] Extrapolating these findings outside the laboratory, into real-world settings, is a matter on which opinions differ. In this book, we propose to bring together evidence from a variety of disciplines bearing on the connection between elements of the theory and the observed characteristics of crime and criminals.

The connection between crime and impulsiveness has been demonstrated as has the link between (low) intelligence and crime. Those features of family life that produce stronger or weaker internalized inhibitions will be seen to have a connection to the presence or absence of aggressiveness and criminality. Certain subcultures, such as street-corner gangs, appear to affect the value members attach to both crime and noncrime. The mass media, and in particular television, may affect both aggressiveness directly and a viewer's sense of inequity that can affect crime indirectly. Schooling may affect crime rates by bringing certain persons together into groups that reinforce either crime or noncrime and by determining the extent to which children believe that their skills will give them access to legitimate rewards. The condition of the economy will have a complex effect on crime depending on whether the (possibly) restraint-weakening impact of affluence dominates the restraint-strengthening influence of employment opportunities.

Though we will be using, for the most part, examples of rather common criminality to illustrate our argument, the theory is quite consistent with the more bizarre and unusual forms of crime. Psychopathic personalities lack to an unusual degree internalized inhibitions on crime. Persons possessed by some obsessive interest – for example, pyromania – attach an inordinately high value to the rewards of certain crimes. If everyone loved fire too much, society would try hard to teach the moral evil of fire, as well as its practical danger. As it is, what society does teach is sufficient to overcome whatever slight tendency toward pyromania every average person may have, but it is insuffi-cient to inhibit the rare pyromaniac. One reason society punishes arsonists is not only to make it more costly for persons to use fire for material gain but also to provide extra moral education to the occasional person who loves fire for its own sake.

In addition to pathological drives, there are ordinary ones that can, under certain conditions, become so strong as to lead to crime. History and literature abound with normal men and women in the grip of a too powerful reinforcement. Many people have broken the law for love, honor, family, and country, as well as for money, sex, vengeance, or delusion. Such criminals may be psychologically unremarkable; they transgressed because as they perceived the situation the reward for crime exceeded that for noncrime, and an opportunity presented itself. The legal system often tries to minimize the punishment inflicted on such people.

From J. Q. Wilson and R.J. Herrnstein, Crime and Human Nature *(New York: Simon and Schuster)*, *1985, pp. 43–63.*

Notes

1 Eysenck, H. J., 1977
2 There is an advantage to stating the theory mathematically. We thereby make it easier in principle to deal simultaneously with the interaction of several variables, and thus we resist the tendency in thinking about crime to keep only two or three things in mind at one time and to treat those few things as either-or propositions. But the essence of the theory can be grasped without the mathematical notation, and so we have put that in the Appendix.
3 For example, Bradshaw, Szabadi, and Lowe, 1981; Commons, Herrnstein and Rachlin, 1982.

7.4 The link between cognitive ability and criminal behavior Richard J. Herrnstein and Charles Murray

The size of the IQ gap

How big is the difference between criminals and the rest of us? Taking the literature as a whole, incarcerated offenders average an IQ of about 92, 8 points below the mean. The population of non offenders averages more than 100 points; an informed guess puts the gap between offenders and nonoffenders at about 10 points.[1] More serious or more chronic offenders generally have lower scores than more casual offenders.[2] The eventual relationship between IQ and repeat offending is already presaged in IQ scores taken when the children are 4 years old.[3]

Not only is there a gap in IQ between offenders and nonoffenders, but a disproportionately large fraction of all crime is committed by people toward the low end of the scale of intelligence. For example, in a twenty-year longitudinal study of over 500 hundred boys in an unidentified Swedish community, 30 percent of all arrests of the men by the age of 30 were of the 6 percent with IQs below 77 (at the age of 10) and 80 percent were of those with IQs below 100.[4] However, it stands to reason (and is supported by the data) that the population of offenders is short of very low-scoring persons – people whose scores are so low that they have trouble mustering the competence to commit most crimes.[5] A sufficiently low IQ is, in addition, usually enough to exempt a person from criminal prosecution.[6]

Do the unintelligent ones commit more crimes – or just get caught more often?

Some critics continue to argue that offenders whose IQs we know are unrepresentative of the true criminal population; the smart ones presumably slipped through the net. Surely this is correct to some degree. If intelligence has anything to do with a person's general competence, then it is not implausible that smart criminals get arrested less often because they pick safer crimes or because they execute their crimes more skillfully?[7] But how much of a bias does this introduce into the data? Is there a population of uncaught offenders with high IQs committing large numbers of crimes? The answer seems to be no. The crimes we can trace to the millions of offenders who do pass through the criminal justice system and whose IQs are known

account for much of the crime around us, particularly the serious crime. There is no evidence for any other large population of offenders, and barely enough crime left unaccounted for to permit such a population's existence.

In the small amount of data available, the IQs of uncaught offenders are not measurably different from the ones who get caught.[8] Among those who have criminal records, there is still a significant negative correlation between IQ and frequency of offending.[9] Both of these kinds of evidence imply that differential arrests of people with varying IQs, assuming they exist, are a minor factor in the aggregate data.

Intelligence as a preventative

Looking at the opposite side of the picture, those who do not commit crimes, it appears that high cognitive ability protects a person from becoming a criminal even if the other precursors are present. One study followed a sample of almost 1,500 boys born in Copenhagen, Denmark, between 1936 and 1938.[10] Sons whose fathers had a prison record were almost six times as likely to have a prison record themselves (by the age of 34–36) as the sons of men who had no police record of any sort. Among these high-risk sons, the ones who had no police record at all had IQ scores one standard deviation higher than the sons who had a police record.[11]

The protective power of elevated intelligence also shows up in a New Zealand study. Boys and girls were divided on the basis of their behavior by the age of 5 into high and low risk for delinquency. High-risk children were more than twice as likely to become delinquent by their mid-teens as low-risk children. The high-risk boys or girls who did not become delinquent were the ones with the higher IQs. This was also true for the low-risk boys and girls: The nondelinquents had higher IQs than the delinquents.[12]

Children growing up in troubled circumstances on Kauai in the Hawaiian chain confirm the pattern. Several hundred children were followed in a longitudinal study for several decades.[13] Some of the children were identified by their second birthday as being statistically 'vulnerable' to behavioral disorders or delinquency. These were children suffering from two or more of the following circumstances: they were being raised in troubled or impoverished families; had alcoholic, psychologically disturbed, or unschooled (eight years or less of schooling) parents; or had experienced prenatal or perinatal physiological stress. Two-thirds of these children succumbed to delinquency or other psychological disturbances. But how about the other third, the ones who grew up without becoming delinquents or disturbed psychologically? Prominent among the protective factors were higher intellectual ability scores than the average for the vulnerable group.[14]

The link between cognitive ability and criminal behavior: white men in the NLSY

In the United States, where crime and race have become so intertwined in the public mind, it is especially instructive to focus on just whites. To simplify matters, we also limit the NLSY [National Longitudinal Surrey of Youth] sample to males. Crime is still overwhelmingly a man's vice. Among whites in the sample, 83 percent of all persons who admitted to a criminal conviction were male.

Interpreting self-report data

In the 1980 interview wave, the members of the NLSY sample were asked detailed questions about their criminal activity and their involvement with the criminal justice system. These data are known as *self-report data*, meaning that we have to go on what the respondent says. One obvious advantage of self-reports is that they presumably include information about the crimes of offenders whether or not they have been caught. Another is that they circumvent any biases in the criminal justice system, which, some people argue, contaminate official criminal statistics. But can self-report data be trusted? Criminologists have explored this question for many years, and the answer is yes, but only if the data are treated gingerly. Different racial groups have different response patterns, and these are compounded by differences between the genders.[15] Other issues are discussed in the note.[16]

Our use of the NLSY self-report data sidesteps some of the problems by limiting the analysis to one ethnic group and one gender: white males. Given the remaining problems with self-report data, we will concentrate in this analysis on events that are on the public record (and the respondent knows are on the public record): being stopped by the police, formal charges, and convictions. In doing so, we are following a broad finding in crime research that official contacts with the law enforcement and criminal justice system are usefully accurate reflections of the underlying level of criminal activity.[17] At the end of the discussion, we show briefly that using self-report data on undetected crimes reinforces the conclusions drawn from the data on detected crimes.

IQ and types of criminal involvement

The typical finding has been that between a third and a half of all juveniles are stopped by police at some time or another (a proportion that has grown over the last few decades) but that 5 to 7 percent of the population account for about half the total number of arrests.[18] In the case of white males in the NLSY, 34 percent admitted having been stopped at some time by the police (for anything other than a minor traffic violation), but only 3 percent of all white males accounted for half of the self-reported 'stops.'

Something similar applies as we move up the ladder of criminal severity. Only 18 percent of white males had ever formally been charged with an offense, and a little less than 3 percent of them accounted for half the charges. Only 13 percent of white males had ever been convicted of anything, and 2 percent accounted for half of the convictions. Based on these self-reports, a very small minority of white males had serious criminal records while they were in this 15 to 23 age range.

Like studies using all races, the NLSY results for white males show a regular relationship between IQ and criminality. The table below [7.4.1] presents the average IQs of white males who had penetrated to varying levels of the criminal justice system as of the 1980 interview.[19] Those who reported they had never even been stopped by the police (for anything other than a minor traffic violation) were above average in intelligence, with a mean IQ of 106, and things went downhill from there. Close to a standard deviation separated those who had never been stopped by the police from those who went to prison.

A similar pattern emerges when the criminal involvements are sorted by cognitive class, as shown in the next table [7.4.2] Involvement with the criminal justice system rises as IQ falls from Classes I through IV. Then we reach Class V, with IQs under 75. If we take the responses at face value, the Class Vs are stopped, charged, and convicted at lower rates than the Class IVs but are sentenced to correctional facilities at rates almost exactly the same rate. We noted earlier that people at the lowest levels of intelligence are likely to be underrepresented in

Figure 7.4.1	Criminality and IQ among white males

Deepest Level of Contact with the Criminal Justice System	Mean IQ
None	106
Stopped by the police but not booked	103
Booked but not convicted	101
Convicted but not incarcerated	100
Sentenced to a correctional facility	93

criminal statistics, and so it is in the NLSY. It may be that the offenses of the Class Vs are less frequent but more serious than those of the Class IVs or that they are less competent in getting favorable treatment from the criminal justice system. The data give us no way to tell.

In addition to self-reports, the NLSY provides data on criminal behavior by noting where the person was interviewed. In all the interviews from 1979 to 1990, was the young man ever interviewed in a correctional facility? The odds shown in the table below [7.4.3] (computed from the unrounded results) that a white male had ever been interviewed in jail were fourteen times greater for Class V than for white males anywhere in the top quartile of IQ.

Being incarcerated at the time of the interview signifies not just breaking the law and serving time but also something about the duration of the sentence, which may explain the large increase at the bottom of the ability distribution. The NLSY sample of white males echoes the scientific litera-

ture in general in showing a sizable IQ gap between offenders and nonoffenders at each level of involvement with the criminal justice system.

Figure 7.4.3	The odds of doing time for young white males

Cognitive Class	Percentage Ever Interviewed in a Correctional Facility
I Very bright	1
II Bright	1
III Normal	3
IV Dull	7
V Very dull	12
Overall	3

The role of socioeconomic background

We will use both self-reports and whether the interviewee was incarcerated at the time of the interview as measures of criminal behavior. The self-reports are from the NLSY men in 1980, when they were still in their teens or just out of them. It combines reports of misdemeanors, drug offenses, property offenses, and violent offenses. Our definition of criminality here is that the man's description of his own behavior put him in the top decile of frequency of self-reported criminal activity.[20] The other measure is whether the man was ever interviewed while being confined in a correctional facility between 1979 and 1990. When we run our standard analysis for these two different measures, we get the results in the next figure.

Both measures of criminality have weaknesses but different weaknesses. One relies on self-reports but has the virtue of including uncaught criminality; the other relies on the workings of the criminal justice system but has the virtue of identifying people who almost certainly have committed serious offenses. For both measures, after controlling for IQ, the men's socioeconomic background had little or nothing to do with crime. In the case of the self-report data, higher socioeconomic status was associated with *higher* reported crime after controlling for IQ. In the case of incarceration, the role of socioeconomic background was close to nil after controlling for IQ, and statistically insignificant. By either measure of crime, a low IQ was a significant risk factor.

Figure 7.4.2	The odds of getting involved with the police and courts for young white males

	Percentage Who in 1980 Reported Ever Having Been:			
Cognitive Class	Stopped by the Police	Booked for an Offense	Convicted of an Offense	Sentenced to Incarceration
I Very bright	18	5	3	0
II Bright	27	12	7	1
III Normal	37	20	15	3
IV Dull	46	27	21	7
V Very dull	33	17	14	7
Overall	34	18	9	3

| **Figure 7.4.4** | The probability of meeting either of two criteria of criminality |

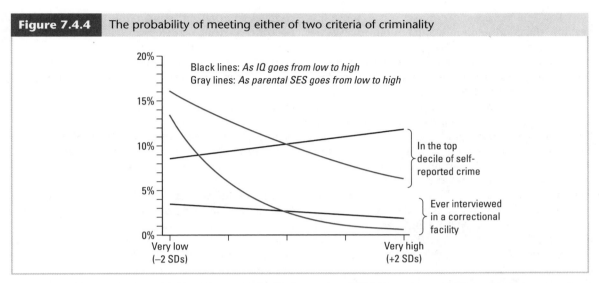

Note: For computing the plot, age and either SES (for the black curves) or IQ (for the gray curves) were set at their mean values.

The role of a broken home

When people think about the causes of crime, they usually think not only of the role of juvenile delinquent's age and socioeconomic background but also of what used to be called 'broken homes.' It is now an inadequate phrase, because many families do not even begin with a married husband and wife, and many broken homes are reconstituted (in some sense) through remarriage. But whatever the specific way in which a home is not intact, the children of such families are usually more likely to get in trouble with the law than children from intact families.[21] This was true for the NLSY white males. An intact family consisting of the biological mother and father was associated with better outcomes for their children than any of the other family arrangements. Was the young man ever stopped by the police? Thirty-two percent of white males from intact families compared to 46 percent of all others. Booked for an offense? Fifteen percent compared to 29 percent. Convicted of an offense? Eleven percent compared to 21 percent. Sentenced to a correctional facility? Two percent compared to 7 percent.

Although, family setting had an impact on crime, it did not explain away the predictive power of IQ. For example, a young man from a broken family and an average IQ and socioeconomic background had a 4 percent chance of having been interviewed in jail. Switch his IQ to the 2d centile, and the odds rise to 22 percent. (Switch his socioeconomic background to the 2d centile instead, and the odds rise only from

4 to 5 percent.) The same conclusions apply to the measure of self-reported crime.

The role of education

Scholars have been arguing about the relationship of education to crime and delinquency for many years without settling the issue. The case of the NLSY white males is a classic example. Of those who were ever interviewed in jail, 74 percent had not gotten a high school diploma. None had a college degree. Clearly something about getting seriously involved in crime competes with staying in school. Low IQ is part of that 'something' in many cases, but the relationship is so strong that other factors are probably involved – for example, the same youngster who is willing to burglarize a house probably is not the most obedient of pupils; the youngster who commits assaults on the street probably gets in fights on the school grounds; the youngster who is undeterred by the prospect of jail time probably is not much motivated by the prospect of getting a high school degree; and so forth.

Does high school dropout actually cause the subsequent crime? Many people assumed so until Delbert Elliott and Harwin Voss published a study in 1974 that concluded the opposite: Crime diminished after school dropout.[22] Since then, everyone has agreed that eventual dropouts tend to have high levels of criminal activity while they are in school, but disputes remain about whether the rates fall or rise after the dropout occurs.[23]

For our purposes, it makes little sense to examine the continuing role of IQ in our usual educational samples when the action is so conspicuously concentrated among those who fall neither in the high school nor the college graduate samples. Running our standard analysis on white males who did not get a high school diploma did not shed much more light on the matter.[24] Given the restriction of range in the sample (the mean IQ of the white male dropout sample was 91, with a standard deviation of only 12.5), not much can be concluded from the fact that the ones at the very bottom of the cognitive ability distribution were less likely to report high levels of criminal activity. For these school dropouts, the likelihood of having been interviewed in jail rose as IQ fell, but the relationship was weaker than for the unrestricted sample of white males.

Crime, cognitive ability, and conscience

By now, you will already be anticipating the usual caution: Despite the relationship of low IQ to criminality, the great majority of people with low cognitive ability are law abiding. We will also take this opportunity to reiterate that the increase in crime over the last thirty years (like the increases in illegitimacy and welfare) cannot be attributed to

changes in intelligence but rather must be blamed on other factors, which may have put people of low cognitive ability at greater risk than before.

The caveats should not obscure the importance of the relationship of cognitive ability to crime, however. Many people tend to think of criminals as coming from the wrong side of the tracks. They are correct, insofar as that is where people of low cognitive ability disproportionately live. They are also correct insofar as people who live on the right side of the tracks – whether they are rich or just steadily employed working-class people – seldom show up in the nation's prisons. But the assumption that too glibly follows from these observations is that the economic and social disadvantage is in itself the cause of criminal behavior. That is not what the data say, however. In trying to understand how to deal with the crime problem, much of the attention now given to problems of poverty and unemployment should be shifted to another question altogether: coping with cognitive disadvantage.

> From R.J. Herrnstein and C. Murray, The Bell-Curve: Intelligence and class structure in American life (New York: The Free Press), 1994, pp. 241–251.

Notes

1   D. Besharov and S. Besharov, quoted in Pelton 1978, p. 608.
2   Parke and Collmer 1975.
3   Coser 1965; Horowitz and Liebowitz 1969.
4   Jensen and Nicholas 1984; Osborne et al. 1988.
5   Leroy H. Pelton's literature review is still excellent on the studies through the mid-1970s, as is Garbarino's. See Garbarino and Crouter 1978; Pelton 1978. Also see Straus and Gelles 1986; Straus et al. 1980; Trickett et al. 1991. Unless otherwise noted, the literature review in this section is not restricted to whites.
6   U.S. Department of Health and Human Services 1988; Wolfe 1985.
7   Gil 1970.
8   Reported in Pelton 1978.
9   Young and Gately 1988, pp. 247, 248.
10 Reported in Pelton 1990–1991.
11 Klein and Stern 1971; Smith 1975.
12 Baldwin and Oliver 1975.
13 Cohen et al. 1966; Johnson and Morse 1968.
14 Smith et al. 1974.
15 Brayden et al. 1992.
16 Crittenden 1988, p. 179.
17 Drotar and Sturm 1989.
18 Azar et al. 1984. See Steele 1987 for supporting evidence and Kravitz and Driscoll 1983 for a contrary view.

19 Bennie 1969.
20 Dekovic and Gerris 1992. For findings in a similar vein, see Goodnow et al. 1984; Keller et al. 1984; and Knight and Goodnow 1988. For studies concluding that parental reasoning is not related to social class, see Newberger and Cook 1983.
21 Polansky 1981, p. 43.
22 Most tantalizing of all was a prospective study in Minnesota that gave an extensive battery of tests to young, socioeconomically disadvantaged women before they gave birth. In following up these mothers, two groups were identified: one consisting of thirty-eight young women with high-stress life events and adequate care of their children (HS-AC), and the other of twelve young women with high-stress life events and inadequate care (HS-NC). In the article, data on all the tests are presented in commendable detail, except for IQ. In the 'method' section that lists all the tests, an IQ test is not mentioned. Subsequently, there is this passage, which contains everything we are told about the mentioned test: 'The only prenatal measure that was not given at 3 months [after birth] was the Shipley-Hartford IQ measure. The mean scores on this measure were 26.9 for the HS-AC group and 23.5 for the HS-NC group (p=.064).' Egeland 1980, p201. A marginally statistically significant difference with samples of 12 and 38 suggests a sizeable IQ difference.
23 Friedman and Morse 1974; Reid and Tablin 1976; Smith and Hanson 1975.
24 Wolfe 1985.

8

Durkheim, anomie and strain

8.1 The normal and the pathological
Emile Durkheim   162

8.2 Social structure and anomie
Robert K. Merton   165

8.3 Why do individuals engage in crime?
Robert Agnew   169

**8.4 Crime and the American Dream:
an institutional analysis**
Richard Rosenfeld and Steven F. Messner   174

8.5 The vertigo of late modernity
Jock Young   181

Introduction

This chapter contains readings that reflect some of the earlier sociological origins of criminology. The first excerpt, from Emile Durkheim **(Reading 8.1)**, contains a number of enormously important insights about crime. Moreover, at first blush some of them may seem slightly odd. First, he describes crime as 'normal' – that is to say it is, in his view, 'an inevitable, although regrettable phenomenon'. Once you've got your head around that one, Durkheim then proceeds to say that crime is 'necessary'. Indeed, it is a factor in public health. In a few short pages, published over a century ago, one of the great sociological thinkers seeks to overturn a number of long-standing assumptions about crime.

Much influenced by Durkheim and, in particular, his notion of 'anomie', Robert Merton **(Reading 8.2)** sought to discover 'how some social structures exert a definite pressure upon certain persons in the society to engage in non-conforming rather than conforming conduct'. Merton was deeply critical of a number of aspects of American culture, especially its emphasis on consumption and what he perceived as the tendency toward greed and ever increasing desires and, consequently, dissatisfaction. In short, Merton argues that there is greater emphasis placed upon success, especially material success, in American society than there is upon the legitimate means by which such success might be achieved. This leads to a breakdown in the regulatory structure and what Merton calls a 'strain to anomie'. Citizens respond to this in a number of ways – what Merton refers to as 'modes of adaptation' – some of which will involve deviance.

A more recent reworking of what has become known as 'strain theory' is provided by Robert Agnew **(Reading 8.3)**. Agnew's 'General Strain Theory' (GST) says, very straightforwardly, that 'people engage in crime because they experience strains or stressors'. These strains may consist of various things – conflict, shortage of money, anger and so on. He distinguishes between 'objective' and 'subjective' strains: the former being things that are disliked by most people in a particular group; the latter being something that is more particularly disliked by an individual. The big question, of course, is what is the link between strains and crime? Agnew offers a number of possible connections. Crime may offer a release from particular strains, or may offer an opportunity for revenge or to do something about their negative feelings or emotions. Most audaciously, Agnew claims that this particular form of strain theory is broadly applicable to most types of crime – hence being called *General* Strain Theory.

A variant on this approach is provided by Richard Rosenfeld and Steven Messner **(Reading 8.4)** and is called 'institutional anomie theory'. In essence they argue that contemporary society is dominated by free-market economics, and that these conditions breed an over-emphasis on material success and a cultural tendency to anomie. So far, so Durkheim. What distinguishes their work is its emphasis on the institutional structure of societies and how these differ in their ability to mitigate the strain toward anomie. Societies differ, they argue, in the extent to which their institutional structures are able to exert a strong regulatory force on their members. Societies in which economic and financial institutions are valued much more highly than noneconomic institutions are less effective at constraining individual desires. Under such circumstances criminal temptations are less likely to be resisted.

The final excerpt, from Jock Young's book *The Vertigo of Late Modernity* **(Reading 8.5)**, takes a neo-Durkheimian look at our late modern world. You will come across a number of words and phrases – such as 'disembeddedness', 'ontological insecurity', 'hollowness', 'fluidity' – which you may well think are resonant of some of the ideas you have met in the other readings in this chapter. Young's immediate concern is less with anomie and more with the insecurities – moral and economic – of the contemporary world. The sense created by his writing is of a world in which old certainties and securities have been undermined and not yet replaced with anything else sufficiently solid to anchor our lives.

Questions for discussion

1. In Durkheim's terms, what is the distinction between what he called the 'normal' and the 'pathological'?

2. In what senses does Durkheim describe crime as 'normal'?

3. What are the main modes of adaptation identified by Merton, and what does each consist of?

4. What are the shortcomings of Merton's anomie theory?

5. When Agnew talks of strains or stressors, to what is he referring? Give half a dozen examples and explain how each might lead to crime.

6. Following Messner and Rosenfeld's argument, what institutional structures do you think promote high levels of criminality and what might be done at an institutional level to reduce crime?

7. What do you think Jock Young is referring to when he uses the word 'vertigo' when discussing the nature of modern life?

8. To what extent do you think it is accurate to say that 'a feeling of unsteadiness permeates the structure of [contemporary] society'? Offer illustrations to support your argument .

8.1 The normal and the pathological
Emile Durkheim

If there is any fact whose pathological character appears incontestable, that fact is crime. All criminologists are agreed on this point. Although they explain this pathology differently, they are unanimous in recognizing it. But let us see if this problem does not demand a more extended consideration.

We shall apply the foregoing rules. Crime is present not only in the majority of societies of one particular species but in all societies of all types. There is no society that is not confronted with the problem of criminality. Its form changes; the acts thus characterized are not the same everywhere; but, everywhere and always, there have been men who have behaved in such a way as to draw upon themselves penal repression. If, in proportion as societies pass from the lower to the higher types, the rate of criminality, i.e., the relation between the yearly number of crimes and the population, tended to decline, it might be believed that crime, while still normal, is tending to lose this character of normality. But we have no reason to believe that such a regression is substantiated. Many facts would seem rather to indicate a movement in the opposite direction. From the beginning of the [nineteenth] century, statistics enable us to follow the course of criminality. It has everywhere increased. In France the increase is nearly 300 per cent. There is, then, no phenomenon that presents more indisputably all the symptoms of normality, since it appears closely connected with the conditions of all collective life. To make of crime a form of social morbidity would be to admit that morbidity is not something accidental, but, on the contrary, that in certain cases it grows out of the fundamental constitution of the living organism; it would result in wiping out all distinction between the physiological and the pathological. No doubt it is possible that crime itself will have abnormal forms, as, for example, when its rate is unusually high. This excess is, indeed, undoubtedly morbid in nature. What is normal, simply, is the existence of criminality, provided that it attains and does not exceed, for each social type, a certain level, which it is perhaps not impossible to fix in conformity with the preceding rules.[1]

Here we are, then, in the presence of a conclusion in appearance quite paradoxical. Let us make no mistake. To classify crime among the phenomena of normal sociology is not to say merely that it is an inevitable, although regrettable phenomenon, due to the incorrigible wickedness of men; it is to affirm that it is a factor in public health, an integral part of all healthy societies. This result is, at first glance, surprising enough to have puzzled even ourselves for a long time. Once this first surprise has been overcome, however, it is not difficult to find reasons explaining this normality and at the same time confirming it.

In the first place crime is normal because a society exempt from it is utterly impossible. Crime, we have shown elsewhere, consists of an act that offends certain very strong collective sentiments. In a society in which criminal acts are no longer committed, the sentiments they offend would have to be found without exception in all individual consciousnesses, and they must be found to exist with the same degree as sentiments contrary to them. Assuming that this condition could actually be realized, crime would not thereby disappear; it would only change its form, for the very cause which would thus dry up the sources of criminality would immediately open up new ones.

Indeed, for the collective sentiments which are protected by the penal law of a people at a specified moment of its history to take possession of the public conscience or for them to acquire a stronger hold where they have an insufficient grip, they must acquire an intensity greater than that which they had hitherto had. The community as a whole must experience them more vividly, for it can acquire from no other source the greater force necessary to control these individuals who formerly were the most refractory. For murderers to disappear, the horror of bloodshed must become greater in those social strata from which murderers are recruited; but, first it must become greater throughout the entire society. Moreover, the very absence of crime would directly contribute to produce this horror; because any sentiment seems much more respectable when it is always and uniformly respected.

One easily overlooks the consideration that these strong states of the common consciousness cannot be thus reinforced without reinforcing at the same time the more feeble states, whose violation previously gave birth to mere infraction of convention – since the weaker ones are only the prolongation, the attenuated form, of the stronger. Thus robbery and simple bad taste injure the same single altruistic sentiment, the respect for that which is another's. However, this same sentiment is less grievously offended by bad taste than by robbery; and since, in addition, the average consciousness has not sufficient intensity to react keenly to the bad taste, it is treated with greater tolerance. That is why the person guilty of bad taste is merely blamed, whereas the thief is punished. But, if this sentiment grows stronger, to the point of silencing in all consciousnesses the inclination which disposes man to steal, he will become more sensitive to the offenses which, until then, touched him but lightly. He will react against them, then, with more energy; they will be the object of greater opprobrium, which will transform certain of them from the simple moral faults that they were and give them the quality of crimes. For example, improper contracts, or contracts improperly executed, which only incur public blame or civil damages, will become offenses in law.

Imagine a society of saints, a perfect cloister of exemplary individuals. Crimes, properly so called, will there be unknown; but faults which appear venial to the layman will create there the same scandal that the ordinary offense does in ordinary consciousnesses. If, then, this society has the power to judge and punish, it will define these acts as criminal and will treat them as such. For the same reason, the perfect and upright man judges his smallest failings with a severity that the majority reserve for acts more truly in the nature of an offense. Formerly, acts of violence against persons were more frequent than they are today, because respect for individual dignity was less strong. As this has increased, these crimes have become more rare; and also, many acts violating this sentiment have been introduced into the penal law which were not included there in primitive times.[2]

In order to exhaust all the hypotheses logically possible, it will perhaps be asked why this unanimity does not extend to all collective sentiments without exception. Why should not even the most feeble sentiment gather enough energy to prevent all dissent? The moral consciousness of the society would be present in its entirety in all the individuals, with a vitality sufficient to prevent all acts offending it – the purely conventional faults as well as the crimes. But a uniformity so universal and absolute is utterly impossible; for the immediate physical milieu in which each one of us is placed, the hereditary antecedents, and the social influences vary from one individual to the next, and consequently diversify consciousnesses. It is impossible for all to be alike, if only because each one has his own organism and that these organisms occupy different areas in space. That is why, even among the lower peoples, where individual originality is very little developed, it nevertheless does exist.

Thus, since there cannot be a society in which the individuals do not differ more or less from the collective type, it is also inevitable that, among these divergences, there are some with a criminal character. What confers this character upon them is not the intrinsic quality of a given act but that definition which the collective conscience lends them. If the collective conscience is stronger, if it has enough authority practically to suppress these divergences, it will also be more sensitive, more exacting; and, reacting against the slightest deviations with the energy it otherwise displays only against more considerable infractions, it will attribute to them the same gravity as formerly to crimes. In other words, it will designate them as criminal.

Crime is, then, necessary; it is bound up with the fundamental conditions of all social life, and by that very fact it is useful, because these conditions of which it is a part are themselves indispensable to the normal evolution of morality and law.

Indeed, it is no longer possible today to dispute the fact that law and morality vary from one social type to the next, nor that they change within the same type if the conditions of life are modified. But, in order that these transformations may be possible, the collective sentiments at the basis of morality must not be hostile to change, and consequently must have but moderate energy. If they were too strong, they would no longer be plastic. Every pattern is an obstacle to new patterns, to the extent that the first pattern is inflexible. The better a structure is articulated, the more it offers a healthy resistance to all modification; and this is equally true of functional, as of anatomical, organization. If there were no crimes, this condition could not have been fulfilled: for such a hypothesis presupposes that collective sentiments have arrived at a degree of intensity unexampled in history. Nothing is good indefinitely and to an unlimited extent. The authority which the moral conscience enjoys must not be excessive; otherwise no one would dare criticize it, and it would too easily congeal into an immutable form. To make progress, individual originality must be able to express itself. In order that the originality of the idealist whose dreams transcend his century may find expression, it is necessary that the originality of the criminal, who is below the level of his time, shall also be possible. One does not occur without the other.

Nor is this all. Aside from this indirect utility, it happens that crime itself plays a useful role in this evolution. Crime implies not only that the way remains open to necessary changes but that in certain cases it directly prepares these changes. Where crime exists, collective sentiments are sufficiently flexible to take on a new form, and crime sometimes helps to determine the form they will take. How many times, indeed, it is only an anticipation of future morality – a step toward what will be!

According to Athenian law, Socrates was a criminal, and his condemnation was no more than just. However, his crime, namely, the independence of his thought, rendered a service not only to humanity but to his country. It served to prepare a new morality and faith which the Athenians needed, since the traditions by which they had lived until then were no longer in harmony with the current conditions of life. Nor is the case of Socrates unique; it is reproduced periodically in history. It would never have been possible to establish the freedom of thought we now enjoy if the regulations prohibiting it had not been violated before being solemnly abrogated. At that time, however, the violation was a crime, since it was an offense against sentiments still very keen in the average conscience. And yet this crime was useful as a prelude to reforms which daily became more necessary. Liberal philosophy had as its precursors the heretics of all kinds who were justly punished by secular authorities during the entire course of the Middle Ages and until the eve of modem times.

From this point of view the fundamental facts of criminality present themselves to us in an entirely new light. Contrary to current ideas, the criminal no longer seems a totally unsociable being, a sort of parasitic element, a strange and unassimilable body, introduced into the midst of society.[3] On the contrary, he plays a definite role in social life. Crime, for its part, must no longer be conceived as

an evil that cannot be too much suppressed. There is no occasion for self-congratulation when the crime rate drops noticeably below the average level, for we may be certain that this apparent progress is associated with some social disorder. Thus, the number of assault cases never falls so low as in times of want.[4] With the drop in the crime rate, and as a reaction to it, comes a revision, or the need of a revision in the theory of punishment. If, indeed, crime is a disease, its punishment is its remedy and cannot be otherwise conceived; thus, all the discussions it arouses bear on the point of determining what the punishment must be in order to fulfil this role of remedy. If crime is not pathological at all, the object of punishment cannot be to cure it, and its true function must be sought elsewhere.

> *From E. Durkheim,* The Rules of Sociological Method, *translated by Sarah A. Solovay and John H. Mueller and edited by George E.G Caitlin (New York: The Free Press), 1985/1964, pp. 65–73.*

Notes

1 From the fact that crime is a phenomenon of normal sociology, it does not follow that the criminal is an individual normally constituted from the biological and psychological points of view. The two questions are independent of each other. This independence will be better understood when we have shown, later on, the difference between psychological and sociological facts.

2 Calumny, insults, slander, fraud, etc.

3 We have ourselves committed the error of speaking thus of the criminal, because of a failure to apply our rule (*Division du travail social*, pp. 395–96).

4 Although crime is a fact of normal sociology, it does not follow that we must not abhor it. Pain itself has nothing desirable about it; the individual dislikes it as society does crime, and yet it is a function of normal physiology. Not only is it necessarily derived from the very constitution of every living organism, but it plays a useful role in life, for which reason it cannot be replaced. It would, then, be a singular distortion of our thought to present it as an apology for crime. We would not even think of protesting against such an interpretation, did we not know to what strange accusations and misunderstandings one exposes oneself when one undertakes to study moral facts objectively and to speak of them in a different language from that of the layman.

8.2 Social structure and anomie
Robert K. Merton

Patterns of cultural goals and institutionalized norms

Among the several elements of social and cultural structure, two are of immediate importance. These are analytically separable although they merge in concrete situations. The first consists of culturally defined goals, purposes, and interests, held out as legitimate objectives for all or for diversely located members of the society. The goals are more or less integrated – the degree is a question of empirical fact – and roughly ordered in some hierarchy of value. Involving various degrees of sentiment and significance, the prevailing goals comprise a frame of aspirational reference. They are the things 'worth striving for.' They are a basic, though not the exclusive, component of what Ralph Linton has called 'designs for group living.' And, though some but not all of these cultural goals are directly related to the biological drives of man, they are not determined by them.

A second element of the cultural structure defines, regulates, and controls the acceptable modes of reaching out for these goals. Every social group invariably couples its cultural objectives with regulations, rooted in the mores or institutions, of allowable procedures for moving toward those objectives. These regulatory norms are not necessarily identical with technical or efficiency norms. Many procedures which from the standpoint of particular individuals would be most efficient in securing desired values – the exercise of force, fraud, power – are ruled out of the institutional area of permitted conduct. At times, the disallowed procedures include some which would be efficient for the group itself – such as historic taboos on vivisection, on medical experimentation, on the sociological analysis of 'sacred' norms – since the criterion of acceptability is not technical efficiency but value-laden sentiments (supported by most members of the group or by those able to promote these sentiments through the composite use of power and propaganda). In all instances, the choice of expedients for striving toward cultural goals is limited by institutionalized norms. [...]

No society lacks norms governing conduct. But societies differ in the degree to which the folkways, mores, and institutional controls are effectively integrated with the goals which stand high in the hierarchy of cultural values. The culture may be such as to lead individuals to center their emotional convictions about the complex of culturally acclaimed ends, with far less emotional support for prescribed methods of reaching out for these ends. With such differential emphases upon goals and institutional procedures, the latter may be so vitiated by the stress on goals as to have the behavior of many individuals limited only by considerations of technical expediency. In this context, the sole significant question becomes, which of the available procedures is most efficient in netting the culturally approved value? The technically most effective procedure, whether culturally legitimate or not, typically becomes preferred to institutionally prescribed conduct. As this process of attenuation continues, the society becomes unstable and there develops what Durkheim called 'anomie' (or normlessness).

The workings of this process eventuating in anomie can be easily glimpsed in a series of familiar and instructive, though perhaps trivial, episodes. Thus, in competitive athletics, when the aim of victory is shorn of its institutional trappings and success becomes construed as 'winning the game' rather than 'winning under the rules of the game,' a premium is implicitly set upon the use of illegitimate but technically efficient means. The star of the opposing football team is surreptitiously slugged; the wrestler incapacitates his opponent through ingenious but illicit techniques; university alumni covertly subsidize 'students' whose talents are confined to the athletic field. The emphasis on the goal has so attenuated the satisfactions deriving from sheer participation in the competitive activity that only a successful outcome provides gratification. Through the same process, tension generated by the desire to win in a poker game is relieved by successfully dealing oneself four aces or, when the cult of success has truly flowered, in a game of solitaire by sagaciously shuffling the cards. The faint twinge of uneasiness in the last instance and the surreptitious nature of public delicts indicate clearly that the institutional rules of the game are *known* to those who evade them. But cultural (or idiosyncratic) exaggeration of the success goal leads men to withdraw emotional support from the rules.

This process is of course not restricted to the realm of competitive sport, which has simply provided us with microcosmic images of the social macrocosm. The process by which exaltation of the end generates a literal *demoralization* – that is, a de-institutionalization – of the means occurs in many groups where the two components of the social structure are not highly integrated.

Contemporary American culture appears to approximate the polar type in which great emphasis upon certain success goals occurs without equivalent emphasis upon institutional means. It would of course be fanciful to assert that accumulated wealth stands alone as a symbol of success, just as it would be fanciful to deny that Americans assign it a place high in their scale of values. In some large measure, money has become consecrated as a value in itself, over and above its expenditure for articles of consumption or its use for the enhancement of power. Money is peculiarly well adapted to become a symbol of prestige. [...]

To say that the goal of monetary success is entrenched in American culture is only to say that Americans are bombarded on every side by precepts which affirm the right or, often, the duty of retaining the goal even in the face of repeated frustration. [...]

Coupled with this positive emphasis upon the obligation to maintain lofty goals is a correlative emphasis upon the penalizing of those who draw in their ambitions. Americans are admonished 'not to be a quitter' for in the dictionary of American culture, as in the lexicon of youth, 'there is no such word as "fail." The cultural manifesto is clear: one must not quit, must not cease striving, must not lessen his goals, for 'not failure, but low aim, is crime.'

Thus the culture enjoins the acceptance of three cultural axioms: first, all should strive for the same lofty goals, since these are open to all; second, present seeming failure is but a way station to ultimate success; and, third, genuine failure consists only in the lessening or withdrawal of ambition.

In rough psychological paraphrase, these axioms represent, first, a symbolic 'secondary reinforcement' of incentive; second, a curbing of the threatened extinction of a response through an associated stimulus; and, third, an increasing of the motive strength to evoke continued responses despite the continued absence of reward.

In sociological paraphrase, these axioms represent, first, the deflection of criticism of the social structure onto oneself among those so situated in the society that they do not have full and equal access to opportunity; second, the preservation of a given structure of social power by having individuals in the lower social strata identify themselves, not with their compeers, but with those at the top (whom they will ultimately join); and, third, the providing of pressures for conformity with the cultural dictates of unslackened ambition by the threat of less than full membership in the society for those who fail to conform.

It is in these terms and through these processes that contemporary American culture continues to be characterized by a heavy emphasis on wealth as a basic symbol of success, without a corresponding emphasis upon the legitimate avenues on which to march toward this goal. How do individuals living in this cultural context respond?

Types of individual adaptation

Five types of adaptation will be considered, as these are schematically set out in the following table, where (+) signifies 'acceptance,' (–) signifies 'rejection,' and (±) signifies 'rejection of prevailing values and substitution of new values.' [...]

Table 8.2.1 A typology of modes of individual adaptation

Modes of adaptation	Culture goals	Institutionalized means
I. Conformity	+	+
II. Innovation	+	–
III. Ritualism	–	+
IV. Retreatism	–	–
V. Rebellion	±	±

I. Conformity

To the extent that a society is stable, adaptation type I – conformity to both culture goals and institutionalized means – is the most common and widely diffused. Were this not so, the stability and continuity of the society could not be maintained. The mesh of expectancies constituting every social order is sustained by the modal behavior of its members representing conformity to the established, though perhaps secularly changing, culture patterns. In fact, it is only because behavior is not typically oriented toward the basic values of the society that we are permitted to speak of a human aggregate as comprising a society.

II. Innovation

Great cultural emphasis upon the success goal invites the second mode of adaptation, innovation, through the use of institutionally proscribed but often effective means of attaining at least the simulacrum of success – wealth and power. This response occurs when the individual has assimilated the cultural emphasis upon the goal without equally internalizing the institutional norms governing ways and means for its attainment.

From the standpoint of psychology, great emotional investment in an objective may be expected to produce a readiness to take risks, and this attitude may be adopted by people in all social strata. From the standpoint of sociology, the following question arises: Which features of our social structure predispose toward this type of adaptation, thus producing greater frequencies of deviant behavior in one social stratum than in another?

On the top economic levels, the pressure toward innovation not infrequently erases the distinction between businesslike strivings this side of the mores and sharp practices beyond the mores. [...]

A study of some 1,700 prevalently middle-class individuals found that 'off-the-record crimes' were common among wholly 'respectable' members of society. Ninety-nine per cent of those questioned confessed to having committed one or more of 49 offenses under the penal law of the state of New York, each of these offenses being sufficiently serious to draw a maximum sentence of not less than one year's imprisonment. The mean number of offenses in adult years – this excludes all offenses committed before the age of sixteen – was 18 for men and 11 for women. Fully 64 per cent of the men and 29 per cent of the women

acknowledged their guilt on one or more counts of felony, which under the law of New York is ground for depriving them of all rights of citizenship. [...]

Despite our persisting open-class ideology, advance toward the success goal is relatively rare and notably difficult for those armed with little formal education and few economic resources. The dominant pressure leads toward the gradual attenuation of legitimate, but by and large ineffectual, strivings and toward the increasing use of illegitimate, but more or less effective, expedients.

Of those located in the lower reaches of the social structure, the culture makes incompatible demands. On the one hand, they are asked to orient their conduct toward the prospect of large wealth – 'every man a king,' said Marden and Carnegie and Long – and on the other, they are largely denied effective opportunities to do so institutionally. The consequence of this structural inconsistency is a high rate of deviant behavior. The equilibrium between culturally designated ends and means becomes highly unstable with progressive emphasis on attaining the prestige-laden ends by any means whatsoever. Within this context, Al Capone represents the triumph of amoral intelligence over morally prescribed 'failure,' when the channels of vertical mobility are closed or narrowed *in a society which places a high premium on economic affluence and social ascent for* all *its members*. [...]

This last qualification is of central importance. It implies that other aspects of the social structure, besides the extreme emphasis on pecuniary success, must be considered if we are to understand the social sources of deviant behavior. A high frequency of deviant behavior is not generated merely by lack of opportunity or by this exaggerated pecuniary emphasis. A comparatively rigidified class structure, a feudalistic or caste order, may limit opportunities far beyond the point which obtains in American society today. It is only when a system of cultural values extols, virtually above all else, certain *common* success goals *for the population at large*, while the social structure rigorously restricts or completely closes access to approved modes of reaching these goals *for a considerable part of the same population*, that deviant behavior ensues on a large scale.

III. Ritualism

The ritualistic type of adaptation can be readily identified. It involves the abandoning or scaling down of the lofty cultural goals of great pecuniary success and rapid social mobility to the point where the individual's aspirations can be satisfied. But though he rejects the cultural obligation to attempt 'to get ahead in the world,' though he draws in his horizons, he continues to abide by institutional norms.

It is something of a terminological quibble to ask whether this represents 'genuinely deviant behavior.' Since the adaptation, in effect, is an internal decision and since the overt behavior is institutionally permissive, though not culturally preferred, it is not generally considered to represent a 'social problem.' Intimates of individuals making this adaptation may pass judgment in terms of prevailing cultural emphases and may 'feel sorry for them'; they may, in the individual case, feel that 'old Jonesy is certainly in a rut.' Whether this is described as deviant behavior or not, it clearly represents a departure from the cultural model in which men are obliged to strive actively, preferably through institutionalized procedures, to move onward and upward in the social hierarchy.

We should expect this type of adaptation to be fairly frequent in a society which makes one's social status largely dependent upon one's achievements. For, as has so often been observed, this ceaseless competitive struggle produces acute status anxiety. One device for allaying these anxieties is to lower one's level of aspiration – permanently. Fear produces inaction, or, more accurately, routinized action.

IV. Retreatism

Just as Adaptation I (conformity) remains the most frequent, Adaptation IV (the rejection of cultural goals and institutional means) is probably the least common. People who 'adapt' (or maladapt) in this fashion are, strictly speaking, *in* the society but not *of* it. Sociologically these constitute the true 'aliens.' Not sharing the common frame of values, they can be included as members of the *society* (in distinction from the *population*) only in a fictional sense.

In this category fall some of the adaptive activities of psychotics, autists, pariahs, outcasts, vagrants, vagabonds, tramps, chronic drunkards, and drug addicts. They have relinquished culturally prescribed goals and their behavior does not accord with institutional norms. [...]

In public and ceremonial life, this type of deviant behavior is most heartily condemned by conventional representatives of the society. In contrast to the conformist, who keeps the wheels of society running, this deviant is a nonproductive liability; in contrast to the innovator, who at least is 'smart' and actively striving, he sees no value in the success goal which the culture prizes so highly; in contrast to the ritualist, who at least conforms to the mores, he pays scant attention to the institutional practices.

Nor does the society lightly accept these repudiations of its values. To do so would be to put those values into question. Individuals who have abandoned the quest for success are relentlessly pursued to their haunts by a society insistent upon having all its members orient themselves to striving for success.

V. Rebellion

This adaptation leads men outside the environing social structure to envisage and seek to bring into being a new, that is to say, a greatly modified social structure. It presupposes alienation from reigning goals and standards, which come to be regarded as purely 'arbitrary.' And the arbitrary is precisely that which can neither exact allegiance nor possess legitimacy, for it might just as well be something else. In our society, organized movements for rebellion apparently aim to introduce a social structure in which the present cultural standards of success would be sharply modified and provision would be made for a closer correspondence between merit, effort, and reward. [...]

When the institutional system is regarded as the barrier to the satisfaction of legitimized goals, the stage is set for rebellion as an adaptive response. To pass into organized political action, allegiance not only must be withdrawn from the prevailing social structure but also must be transferred to new groups possessed of a new myth. The dual function of the myth is to locate the source of large-scale frustrations in the social structure and to portray an alternative structure which would not, presumably, give rise to frustration of the deserving. It is a charter for action.

The strain toward anomie

The social structure we have examined produces a strain toward anomie and deviant behavior. The pressure of such a social order is toward outdoing one's competitors. So long as the sentiments supporting this competitive system are distributed throughout the entire range of activities and are not confined to the final result of 'success,' the choice of means will remain largely within the ambit of institutional control. When, however, the cultural emphasis shifts from the satisfactions deriving from competition itself to almost exclusive concern with the outcome, the resultant stress makes for the breakdown of the regulatory structure. With this attenuation of institutional controls, there occurs an approximation to the situation erroneously held by the utilitarian philosophers to be typical of society – a situation in which calculations of personal advantage and fear of punishment are the only regulating agencies.

This strain toward anomie does not operate evenly throughout the society. Some effort has been made in the present analysis to suggest the strata most vulnerable to the pressures for deviant behavior and to set forth some of the mechanisms operating to produce these pressures.

From America Sociological Review, *1938, 3: 672–682.*

8.3 Why do individuals engage in crime?
Robert Agnew

Why do individuals engage in crime? Below are several explanations for individual offending. All are quotes from criminals who were asked why they engaged in crime or were thinking about doing so.

> [The idea of committing an armed robbery] comes into your mind when your pockets are low; it speaks very loudly when you need things and you are not able to get what you need. (Quote from an armed robber (Wright and Decker, 1997:33))

> My stepfather... used to sexually assault me a lot. And uh, I got fed up with it, and once I turned 13, I started running away. (Quote from a runaway living on the street (Hagan and McCarthy, 1997:29))

> I worked as a busboy for a week once. It was like being a pig in everyone else's slop. Why should I put up with that shit?.. . Doing crime is a lot more fun and pays a lot better. (Quote from a criminal (Fleming, 2003:101))

> I get depressed. Things start to pile up and I start shoplifting. Sometimes it's at finals [final exams] or when I have a fight with my boyfriend. One time when I thought I was pregnant. Who knows why. It's like I take out my feelings on them [the stores]. (Quote from a shoplifter (Cromwell, Parker, and Parker, 2003:117)) [...]

These quotes illustrate the central ideas behind general strain theory (GST), one of the leading theories of crime. *According to GST, people engage in crime because they experience strains or stressors. For example, they are in desperate need of money or they believe they are being mistreated by family members, teachers, peers, employers, or others. They become upset, experiencing a range of negative emotions, including anger, frustration, and depression. And they cope with their strains and negative emotions through crime. Crime may be a way to reduce or escape from strains.* For example, individuals engage in theft to obtain the money they desperately need or they run away from home to escape their abusive parents. *Crime may be a way for individuals to seek revenge against those who have wronged them.* For example, individuals assault those who have mistreated them. *And crime may be a way to alleviate the negative emotions that result from strains.* For example, individuals use drugs to make themselves feel better.

Not all individuals respond to strains with crime. If someone steps on your foot, for example, you are probably unlikely to respond by punching the person. *Some people are more likely than others to cope with strains through crime. Criminal coping is more likely when people lack the ability to cope in a legal manner.* For example, crime is more likely when people do not have the verbal skills to negotiate with those who mistreat them or do not have others they can turn to for help. *Criminal coping is more likely when the costs of crime are low.* For example, crime is more likely when people are in environments where the likelihood of being sanctioned for crime is low. *And criminal coping is more likely when people are disposed to crime.* For example, assault is more likely when people believe that violence is an appropriate response to being treated in a disrespectful manner.

What are strains?

Strains refer to events or conditions that are disliked by individuals. There are three major types of strains. *Individuals may lose something they value (lose something good).* Perhaps their money or property is stolen, a close friend or family member dies, or a romantic partner breaks up with them. *Individuals may be treated in an aversive or negative manner by others (receive something bad).* Perhaps they are sexually or physically abused by a family member, their peers insult or ridicule them, or their employer treats them in a disrespectful manner. Finally, *individuals may be unable to achieve their goals (fail to get something they want).* Perhaps they have less money, status, or autonomy than they want.

I sometimes ask the students in my juvenile delinquency and criminology classes to list the strains or stressors they have recently experienced. The strains they list are generally less severe than those listed at the start of this chapter, but they nevertheless illustrate the three major types of strains. A few examples follow:

I lost the paper that I was working on on my computer. I was almost done.

My roommate took my ethernet card with him to New Jersey without asking.

I got into a huge fight with my best friend and completely terminated our relationship.

My cheating ex is now engaged to the person he cheated with.

The strains examined in other versions of strain theory

General strain theory was not created 'out of thin air.' GST draws quite heavily on the work of others, especially the work of other strain theorists. [...]

Robert Merton (1938), Albert Cohen (1955), and Richard Cloward and Lloyd Ohlin (1960) pioneered the development of strain theory in criminology. They focus on that type of strain involving the inability to achieve the goal of monetary success or, in the case of Cohen, the somewhat broader goal of middle-class status. They argue that everyone in the United States – poor as

well as rich – is encouraged to pursue the goal of monetary success or middle-class status. They are encouraged by family members, teachers, friends, politicians, the mass media, and others. But at the same time, significant segments of the population are prevented from achieving those goals through legal channels, like getting a good education and then a good job. This is especially true of the lower class. Lower-class families are often unable to provide their children with the skills and resources necessary to do well in school. Such families also lack the money and connections to set their children up in business. And lower-class individuals often live in communities with poor schools and a lack of decent jobs. As a consequence, lower-class individuals often find that they are unable to achieve monetary success or middle-class status through legal channels. Some of these individuals respond with crime; for example, they attempt to achieve their monetary goals through theft, prostitution, or drug selling.

Greenberg (1977) focuses on the inability of some adolescents to (a) get the money they need to finance their social activities, and (b) achieve the freedom or autonomy they desire, especially from school authorities (also see Moffitt, 1993; Tittle, 1995). Such adolescents may cope with these strains by committing income-generating crimes like theft, and by skipping school, flouting school rules, and vandalizing school property. [...]

Messerschmidt (1993) and others focus on the inability of some males to 'accomplish masculinity.' or act in a 'manly manner' in particular settings. [...] When males have trouble 'acting manly' in a particular setting, they may attempt to 'accomplish masculinity' through crime. [...]

Finally, Colvin (2000) focuses on that type of strain involving coercion, where people are compelled to act in a certain way through force or the threat of unpleasant consequences. Those types of coercion that are related to crime include harsh, excessive, and erratic discipline by parents; demeaning treatment by teachers; physical and verbal abuse by peers; and abusive treatment at work, including threats of dismissal. Such coercion may lead to crime for several reasons, including the anger it provokes.

General strain theory examines all of these types of strain and more. [...] The fact that GST examines such a broad range of strains is the primary reason for the term general in general strain theory.

Objective and subjective strains

Some events and conditions are disliked by *most* people, or at least by most people in a given group. For example, most people dislike being physically assaulted or deprived of adequate food and shelter. And it has been argued that most males dislike having their masculine status called into question (Messerschmidt, 1993). I refer to these events and conditions as *objective strains*, because they are generally disliked. It is possible to measure the objective strains for a group of people in several ways (see Agnew, 2001). Perhaps the best method is to interview a carefully selected sample of group members or people familiar with the group [...].

It is important to keep in mind, however, that people sometimes differ in their subjective evaluation of the same events and conditions – even those events and conditions classified as objective strains. So a given objective strain, like a death in the family, may be strongly disliked by one person, but only mildly disliked by another. This is because the subjective evaluation of objective strains is influenced by a range of factors, including people's personality traits, goals and values, and prior experiences (see Dohrenwend, 1998; Kaplan, 1996; Lazarus, 1999). [...]

I therefore make a distinction between objective and *subjective strains*. While an objective strain refers to an event or condition that is disliked by most people or most people in a given group, a subjective strain refers to an event or condition that is disliked by the particular person or persons being examined (see Agnew, 2001). As just suggested, there is only partial overlap between objective and subjective strains.

Most of the research on strain theory focuses on objective strains.

Experienced, vicarious, and anticipated strains

Strain theory focuses on individuals' *personal experiences with strains*; that is, did they personally experience disliked events or conditions? For example, were they physically assaulted? Personal experiences with strains should bear the strongest relationship to crime. However, it is sometimes important to consider the individual's vicarious and anticipated experiences with strains as well (see Agnew, 2002; Eitle and Turner, 2003).

Vicarious strains refer to the strains experienced by others around individuals, especially close others like family members and friends. For example, were any of their family members or friends physically assaulted? Vicarious strains can also upset individuals and lead to criminal coping. Agnew (2002), for example, found that individuals were more likely to engage in crime if they reported that their family members and friends had been victims of serious assaults (also see Eitle and Turner, 2002; Maxwell, 2001; Mullins *et al.*, 2004). This held true even after Agnew took into account other factors, like individuals' own victimization experiences and prior criminal history. Agnew argued that vicarious strains may have increased the likelihood of crime for several reasons. For example, perhaps individuals were seeking revenge against those who had victimized their families and friends, or perhaps they were seeking to prevent the perpetrators from causing further harm. [...]

It is also sometimes important to consider anticipated experiences with strains. *Anticipated strains* refer to individuals' expectations that their current strains will continue into the future or that new strains will be experienced. For example, individuals may anticipate that they will be the victims of physical assault. Like vicarious strains, anticipated strains may upset individuals and lead to criminal coping. Individuals may engage in crime to prevent anticipated strains from occurring, to seek revenge against those who might inflict such strains, or to alleviate negative emotions. To illustrate, many adolescents, particularly in high-crime communities, anticipate that they will be the victims of violence. They often (illegally) carry weapons as a result, and may even engage in violence against others in an effort to reduce their own likelihood of victimization. In this area, Anderson (1999) argues that the young men in very poor, high-crime communities often try to reduce the likelihood they will be victimized by adopting a tough demeanor and responding to even minor shows of disrespect with violence. As Anderson (1999:92) states, they do this to 'discourage strangers from even thinking about testing their manhood .... [One] builds a reputation that works to prevent future challenges' (also see Baron *et al.*, 2001).

Why do strains increase the likelihood of crime?

Strains, by definition, are disliked events and conditions. Not surprisingly, then, the experience of strains often makes people *feel bad*. That is, strains contribute to one or more negative emotions, like anger, frustration, depression, or hopelessness. These negative emotions create pressure for corrective action. Individuals feel bad and they want to do something about it. As indicated above, *crime is one way to cope with strains*.

Crime may allow individuals to reduce or escape from their strains, at least temporarily

In particular, crime may allow individuals to protect or retrieve those things that they value. For example, individuals may assault those who try to take their possessions, or they may threaten romantic partners in an effort to prevent them from leaving. Crime may allow individuals to reduce or escape from negative treatment. For example, individuals may assault the peers who harass them or run away from the parents who abuse them. Crime may also allow individuals to achieve their goals. For example, individuals may engage in theft, drug-selling, or prostitution to achieve monetary goals. Crime is not always a successful strategy for reducing strains, and some evidence suggests that crime may create more problems than it solves *in the long run* (see Agnew, 2005b:90–93). For example, crime often leads to poor relations with parents and teachers, rejection by conventional peers, and problems with employers. But many individuals, especially those prone to crime, do not consider the long-term consequences of their behavior. They are merely looking for some way to alleviate their strain, even if only temporarily. A heroin-addicted offender illustrates this point when he explains why he committed a carjacking:

> I didn't have no money and I was sick and due some heroin so l knew I had to do something.... I just had to kill this sickness.... One way or another, I was going to get me some money to take me off this sickness. I just seen him and I got it [the car]. (Topalli and Wright, 2004:74)

Crime allows individuals to obtain revenge against those who have wronged them or, if this is not possible, against more vulnerable targets

Individuals may believe that certain of their strains are the result of accidents or 'bad luck' (e.g., losing a paycheck, place of employment going out of business). They may believe that they are to blame for other of their strains (e.g., receiving a low grade as a result of failing to study, being punished for misbehavior). But they often believe that some of their strains are the result of unjust treatment by others. For example, they may believe that someone has insulted or assaulted them for no good reason. This unjust treatment usually makes them angry and creates a desire for revenge. They want to right the wrong that has been done to them, even if doing so does little or nothing to reduce their strains (see Carey, 2004; Mullins *et al.*, 2004; Neergaard, 2004). And crime is often a good vehicle for revenge. Individuals can do such things as directly threaten or assault the person who wronged them, damage the person's property or related targets or steal from the person. [...]

Angered individuals, however, may sometimes be reluctant to seek revenge against the source of their strain. This source may be a powerful person who can punish them. A student who is mistreated by a teacher, for example, may be afraid to retaliate directly. The same may be true of an employee who is mistreated by an employer. In such cases, studies suggest that angered individuals may behave aggressively against other, more vulnerable targets (De Coster and Kort-Butler, 2004). Mistreated employees, for example, may sometimes 'take out' their anger on their spouses and children.

Crime may allow individuals to alleviate their negative emotions

Individuals may not be able to reduce or escape from their strains, and they may not be able to obtain revenge against those who have wronged them. But they may still be able to reduce the negative emotions that result from their strains. One way to do this is through crime, especially illegal alcohol and drug use. Individuals often drink excessively and use illegal drugs in an effort to seek relief from the strains they are experiencing (e.g., Aseltine and Gore, 2000; Cerbone and Larison, 2000; Hoffmann, 2000; Hoffmann *et al.*, 2000).

Is general strain theory able to explain all types of crime?

Most of the examples presented above refer to what are called 'street crimes.' Such crimes include homicide, assault, rape, robbery, burglary, larceny-theft, vandalism, and drug use. Certain of these examples also deal with 'status offenses,' or acts which are illegal for juveniles but not adults. Status offenses include running away from home, drinking alcohol, and truancy. The research on GST has focused on street crimes and status offenses, as has the research on most other theories of crime. GST, however, has the potential to help explain a wide range of crimes, including organized crime, white-collar crime, and terrorism (Bryant, 2001; Miethe and McCorkle, 2001).

GST can help explain any act which is condemned by most others in the society or that carries more than a trivial risk of punishment – including but not limited to punishment by the state. Almost all crimes meet these criteria. Most individuals refrain from engaging in such crimes unless they are under some pressure to do so. Strains provide the pressure to engage in these crimes, with the crimes providing some relief from the strains or negative emotions associated with the strains. GST, then, can help explain a broad range of criminal acts. Take, for example, a white-collar crime like embezzlement, where employees steal from their employers. This crime is often committed by employees who have serious financial problems that cannot be resolved through legal channels (Weisburd and Waring, 2001). So embezzlement is often used to cope with monetary strains. To give another example, terrorist acts are frequently used to cope with strains – as reflected in this journalistic account about the violence in Iraq:

Moneer Munthir is ready to kill Americans. For months he has been struggling to control an explosion of miserable feelings: humiliation, fear, anger, depression. 'But in the last two weeks these feelings blow up inside me,' said Munthir, a 35-year-old laborer. 'The Americans are attacking Shiite and Sunni at the same time. They have crossed a line. I had to get a gun.' (Gettleman, 2004:A14)

Saying that a wide range of crimes are committed in response to strains is not, of course, to justify or excuse such crimes. Rather, it is an effort to better understand the causes of such crimes in the hope that we can prevent them. Future research should attempt to broaden the scope of GST by applying it to crimes such as terrorist acts and white-collar crime. Among other things, researchers should examine whether particular types of strains are especially relevant to these types of crimes (for further discussion, see Agnew, 2004; Langton and Piquero, 2004).

> *From Robert Agnew,* Pressured into Crime: An overview of general strain theory *(Los Angeles: Roxbury), 2006, pp. 1–17.*

References

Agnew, Robert. 2001. 'Building on the foundation of general strain theory: Specifying the types of strain most likely to lead to crime and delinquency.' *Journal of Research in Crime and Delinquency* 38:319–361.

Agnew, Robert. 2002. 'Experienced, vicarious, and anticipated strain: An exploratory study focusing on physical victimization and delinquency.' *Justice Quarterly* 19:603–632.

Agnew, Robert. 2004. 'A general strain theory approach to violence.' In *Violence: From Theory to Research*, eds. Maraget A. Zahn, Henry H. Brownstein, and Shelly L. Jackson. Cincinnati: Anderson and LexisNexis.

Agnew, Robert. 2005b. *Why Do Criminals Offend? A General Theory of Crime and Delinquency*. Los Angeles: Roxbury.

Anderson, Elijah. 1999. *Code of the Street*. New York: W. W. Norton.

Aseltine, Robert H., Jr., and Susan L. Gore. 2000. 'The variable effects of stress on alcohol use from adolescence to early adulthood.' *Substance Use & Misuse* 35:643–668.

Baron, Stephen W., David R. Forde, and Leslie W. Kennedy. 2001. 'Rough justice: Street youth and violence.' *Journal of Interpersonal Violence* 16:662–678.

Bryant, Clifton D. 2001. *The Encyclopedia of Criminology and Deviant Behavior*. Philadelphia: Brunner Routledge.

Carey, Benedict, 2004. 'Payback time: Why revenge tastes so sweet.' *New York Times*, July 27, D1, 6.

Cerbone, Felicia Gray, and Cindy L. Larison. 2000. 'A bibliographic essay: The relationship between stress and substance use.' *Substance Use & Misuse* 35:757–786.

Cloward, Richard, and Lloyd Ohlin. 1960. *Delinquency and Opportunity*. Glencoe, IL: Free Press.

Cohen, Albert K. 1955. *Delinquent Boys*. Glencoe, IL: Free Press.

Colvin, Mark. 2000. *Crime & Coercion*. New York: St. Martin's Press.

Cromwell, Paul, Lee Parker, and Shawna Parker. 2003. 'The five-finger discount.' In *In Their Own Words: Criminals on Crime*, ed. Paul Cromwell. Los Angeles: Roxbury.

De Coster, Stacy, and Lisa Kort-Butler. 2004. 'How general is general strain theory? Assessing the specific domains of strains and delinquent responses.' Paper presented at the annual meeting of the American Society of Criminology, Nashville.

Dohrenwend, Bruce P. 1998. *Adversity, Stress, and Psychopathology*. New York: Oxford University Press.

Eitle, David J., and R. Jay Turner. 2003. 'Stress exposure, race, and young adult crime.' *Sociological Quarterly* 44:243–269.

Fleming, Zachary. 2003. 'The thrill of it all: Youthful offenders and auto theft.' In *In Their Own Words: Criminals on Crime*, ed. Paul Cromwell. Los Angeles: Roxbury.

Gettleman, Jeffrey. 2004. 'Anti-U.S. outrage sends Iraqis into militancy.' *Atlanta Journal-Constitution*, April 11, A14.

Greenberg, David F. 1977. 'Delinquency and the age structure of society.' *Contemporary Crisis* 1:189–223.

Hagan, John, and Bill McCarthy. 1997. *Mean Streets*. Cambridge, England: Cambridge University Press.

Hoffman, John P. 2000. 'Introduction to the special issue on stress and substance use.' *Substance Use and Misuse* 35: 635–641.

Hoffmann, John P., Felicia Gray Cerbone, and Susan S. Su. 2000. 'A growth curve analysis of stress and adolescent drug use.' *Substance Use & Misuse* 35:687–716.

Kaplan, Howard B. 1996. 'Psychosocial stress from the perspective of self theory.' In *Psychosocial Stress*, ed. Howard B. Kaplan. San Diego, CA: Academic Press.

Langton, Lynn, and Nicole Leeper Piquero. 2004. 'Can general strain theory explain white-collar crime? A preliminary investigation.' Paper presented at the annual meeting of the American Society of Criminology, Nashville.

Lazarus, Richard S. 1999. *Stress and Emotion: A New Synthesis*. New York: Springer.

Maxwell, Shelia Royo. 2001. 'A focus on familial strain: Antisocial behavior and delinquency in Filipino society.' *Sociological Inquiry* 71:265–292.

Merton, Robert K. 1938. 'Social structure and anomie.' *American Sociological Review* 3:672–682.

Messerschmidt, James W. 1993. *Masculinities and Crime*. Lanham, MD: Rowman and Littlefield.

Miethe, Terance D., and Richard C. McCorkle. 2001. *Crime Profiles*. Los Angeles: Roxbury.

Moffitt, Terrie E. 1993. 'Adolescence-limited and life-course persistent antisocial behavior: A developmental taxonomy.' *Psychological Review* 100:674–701.

Mullins, Christopher, Richard Wright, and Bruce Jacobs. 2004. 'Gender, streetlife, and criminal retaliation.' *Criminology* 42:911–940.

Neergaard, Lauran. 2004. 'Brain scan shows revenge has its thrills.' *New York Times*, August 27, A11.

Tittle, Charles R. 1995. Control Balance: *Toward a General Theory of Deviance*. Boulder, CO: Westview.

Topalli, Volkon, and Richard Wright. 2004. 'Dubs and dees, beats and rims: Carjackers and urban violence.' In *About Criminals*, ed. Mark Pogrebin. Thousand Oaks, CA: Sage.

Weisburd, David, and Elin Waring. 2001. *White-Collar Crime and Criminal Careers*. Cambridge, England: Cambridge University Press.

Wright, Richard T., and Scott H. Decker. 1997. *Armed Robbers in Action*. Boston: Northeastern University Press.

8.4 Crime and the American Dream: an institutional analysis Richard Rosenfeld and Steven F. Messner

In our view, the transformation of anomie theory into strain theory has had two unfortunate consequences. First, by reinforcing the dominance of individual-level perspectives in criminology, it has contributed to the neglect of the general question of why crime rates vary across social systems, as well as the specific question of why rates of serious crime are so high in the United States. Second, widespread acceptance of the individualistic version of SS&A [Social Structure and Anomie, henceforward SS&A] has fostered an underappreciation of those aspects of Merton's arguments that are of greatest assistance in answering macrolevel questions. Most important, criminologists have largely

ignored Merton's incisive critique of the anomic tendencies of American culture.

The anomic tendencies of the American Dream

In SS&A, Merton advances the provocative argument that there are inherent features of American culture, of the American Dream itself, that ultimately contribute to the high rates of crime and deviance observed in the United States. Although Merton does not provide a formal definition of 'the American Dream,' it is possible to formulate a reasonably concise characterization of this cultural orientation on the basis of his discussion of American culture in general and his scattered references to the American Dream. The American Dream refers to a commitment to the goal of material success, to be pursued by everyone in society, under conditions of open, individual competition.

Merton proposes that the American Dream has been highly functional for society in certain respects. This cultural ethos is particularly effective in satisfying motivational requirements because it encourages high levels of 'ambition' (Merton 1968: 200). At the same time, there is a dark side to the American Dream. It tends to promote an anomic imbalance wherein the importance of using the legitimate means is de-emphasized relative to the importance of attaining the desired cultural goals.

Merton explains that this anomic tendency derives ultimately from the very same basic value commitments upon which the American Dream rests. One such commitment is a strong *achievement orientation*. In American society, personal worth tends to be evaluated on the basis of what people have achieved rather than who they are or how they relate to others in social networks. 'Success' is to a large extent the ultimate measure of social worth. Quite understandably, then, there are pervasive cultural pressures to achieve at any cost. A strong achievement orientation, at the level of basic cultural values, thus cultivates and sustains a mentality that 'it's not how you play the game; it's whether you win or lose.'

A second basic value orientation that contributes to the anomic balance in American culture is *individualism*. In the pursuit of success, people are encouraged to 'make it' on their own. Fellow members of society are thus competitors in the struggle for achievement and the ultimate validation of personal worth. This intense, individual competition to succeed further encourages a tendency to disregard normative restraints on behavior when these restraints interfere with the realization of goals. [...]

A third component of American culture that is conducive to anomie imbalance is its *universalism*. Everyone is encouraged to aspire to social ascent, and everyone is susceptible to evaluation on the basis of individual achievements. As a consequence, the pressures to 'win' are pervasive; no one is exempt from the pursuit of success (Merton, 1968: 200; Orru, 1990: 234).

Finally, in American culture, success is signified in a special way: by the accumulation of *monetary rewards*. Merton is keenly aware of the high priority awarded to money in American culture. He observes that 'in some large measure, money has been consecrated as a value in itself, over and above its expenditure for articles of consumption or its use for the enhancement of power' (1968: 190). Merton's key point is not that Americans are uniquely materialistic; a strong interest in material well-being can be found in most societies. Rather, the distinctive feature of American culture is the preeminent role of money as the 'metric' of success. As Orru puts it, 'money is literally, in this context, a *currency* for measuring achievement' (1990: 235).

Merton points to an important implication of the signification of achievement with reference to monetary rewards. Monetary success is inherently open-ended. Because it is always possible in principle to have more money, 'in the American Dream there is no final, stopping point' (1968: 190). Cultural prescriptions thus mandate 'never-ending achievement' (Passas, 1990: 159); Relentless pressures to accumulate money, in turn, encourage people to disregard normative restraints when they impede the pursuit of personal goals.

In sum, dominant value patterns of American culture, specifically its achievement orientation, its competitive individualism, its universalism in goal orientations and evaluative standards – when harnessed to the preeminent goal of monetary success – give rise to a distinctive cultural ethos: the American Dream. The American Dream, in turn, encourages members of society to pursue ends, in Merton's words, 'limited only by considerations of technical expediency' (1968: 189). One consequence of this open, widespread, competitive and anomic quest for success by any means necessary is high levels of crime. [...]

Merton's critique of American culture goes a long way to explain high rates of crime in the United States. In the view of one highly influential critic, it goes too far. Ruth Kornhauser maintains that Merton's cultural account is sufficient by itself to explain high levels of crime in American society. If the culture is characterized by a generalized disregard for normative means, high levels of crime and deviance are likely to be observed regardless of the nature of social structural relationships (Kornhauser, 1978: 145–146). [...]

Kornhauser's criticism contains a kernel of truth but is overstated. Merton certainly attends to social structure in his account of the distribution of deviance and crime in the United States. His well-known hypothesis is that the anomic pressures responsible for deviance vary depending on access to legitimate means to attain economic success, which is determined by location in the stratification system. [...]

We agree with Kornhauser's criticism that SS&A does not provide a comprehensive account of the impact of social structure on crime rates. Her comment that 'there is much more to social structure than stratification' (1978: 178) is particularly relevant to our purposes. Merton's cultural critique represents only a partial explanation of the high levels of crime in the United States considered in comparative perspective. A complete explanation requires identification of the social structural underpinnings of American culture and its associated strains toward anomie. Merton's analysis stops short of an explication of the ways in which specific features of the institutional structure – beyond the class system – interrelate to generate the anomic pressures that are held to be responsible for crime (cf. Cohen, 1985: 233). As a consequence, the anomie perspective is best regarded as a 'work in progress.' In Cohen's words, Merton 'has laid the groundwork for an explanation of deviance [and crime] on the sociological level, but the task, for the most part, still lies ahead' (1985: 233).

The institutional dynamics of crime

The normal functions of social institutions

Social institutions are the building blocks of whole societies. As such, they constitute the fundamental units of macrolevel analysis. Institutions are 'relatively stable sets of norms and values, statuses and roles, and groups and organizations' that regulate human conduct to meet the basic needs of a society (Bassis, Gelles, and Levine, 1991: 142). These social needs include the need to adapt to the environment, to mobilize and deploy resources for the achievement of collective goals, and to socialize members in the society's fundamental normative patterns. [...]

Any given society will be characterized by a distinctive arrangement of social institutions that reflects a balancing of the sometimes competing claims and requisites of the different institutions, yielding a distinctive institutional balance of power. Further, the nature of the resulting configuration of institutions is itself intimately related to the larger culture. Indeed, our basic premise about social organization is that culture and the institutional balance of power are mutually reinforcing.

On the one hand, culture influences the character of institutions and their positions relative to one another. Culture is in a dense 'given life' in the institutional structure of society. On the other hand, the patterns of social relationships constituting institutions, which Parsons (1964: 239) terms the 'backbone' of the social system, reproduce and sustain cultural commitments. This is, ultimately, where culture 'comes from.'

In the macrocriminological analysis of a concrete social system, then, the task is to describe the interpenetration of cultural and institutional patterns, to trace the resulting interconnections among institutions that constitute the institutional balance of power, and finally, to show how the institutional balance of power influences levels of crime. In the following sections, we apply this kind of analysis to the relationships among culture, institutional functioning and crime in the United States.

The American Dream and the institutional balance of power

The core elements of the American Dream – a strong achievement orientation, a commitment to competitive individualism, universalism, and most important, the glorification of material success – have their institutional underpinnings in the economy. The most important feature of the economy of the United States is its capitalist nature. The defining characteristics of any capitalist economy are private ownership and control of property, and free market mechanisms for the production and distribution of goods and services.

These structural arrangements are conducive to, and presuppose, certain cultural orientations. For the economy to operate efficiently, the private owners of property must be profit-oriented and eager to invest, and workers must be willing to exchange their labor for wages. The motivational mechanism underlying these conditions is the promise of financial returns. The internal logic of a capitalist economy thus presumes that an attraction to monetary rewards as a result of achievement in the marketplace is widely diffused throughout the population (cf. Passas, 1990: 159).

A capitalist economy is also highly competitive for all those involved, property owners and workers alike. Firms that are unable to adapt to shifting consumer demands or to fluctuations in the business cycle are likely to fail. Workers who are unable to keep up with changing skill requirements or who are unproductive in comparison with others are likely to be fired. This intense competition discourages economic actors from being wedded to conventional ways of doing things and instead encourages them to substitute new techniques for traditional ones if they offer advantages in meeting economic goals. In short, a capitalist economy naturally cultivates a competitive, innovative spirit.

These structural and cultural conditions are common to all capitalist societies. What is distinctive about the United States, however, is the *exaggerated* emphasis on monetary success and the *unrestrained* receptivity to innovation. The goal of monetary success overwhelms other goals and becomes the principal measuring rod for achievements. The resulting proclivity and pressures to innovate resist any regulation that is not justified by purely technical considerations. The obvious question that arises is why cultural orientations that express the inherent logic of capitalism have evolved to a particularly extreme degree in American society. The answer, we submit, lies in the inability of other social institutions to tame economic imperatives. In short, the institutional balance of power is tilted toward the economy.

The historical evidence suggests that this distinctive institutional structure has always existed in the United States. In his analysis of American slavery, the historian Stanley Elkins observes that capitalism emerged 'as the principal dynamic force in American society,' free to develop according to its own institutional logic without interference from 'prior traditional institutions, with competing claims of their own' (Elkins, 1968: 43). Whereas capitalism developed in European societies (and later in Japan) within powerful preexisting institutional frameworks, the institutional structure of American society emerged simultaneously with, and was profoundly shaped by, the requirements of capitalist economic development. American capitalism thus took on a 'purity of form' unknown in other capitalist societies (Elkins, 1968: 43). Moreover, other institutions were cast in distinctly subsidiary positions in relation to the economy. [...]

Elkins's portrait of the barren institutional landscape of early American society may be somewhat overdrawn, and aspects of his analysis of the North American slave system are controversial (see Lane, 1971). Nonetheless, we accept his basic argument that capitalism developed in the United States without the institutional restraints found in other societies. As a consequence, the economy assumed an unusual dominance in the institutional structure of society from the very beginning of the nation's history. This economic dominance, we argue, has continued to the present and is manifested in three somewhat different ways: (1) in the *devaluation* of noneconomic institutional functions and roles; (2) in the *accommodation* to economic requirements by other institutions; and (3) in the *penetration* of economic norms into other institutional domains.

Consider the relative devaluation of the distinctive functions of education and of the social roles that fulfill these functions. Education is regarded largely as a means to occupational attainment, which in turn is valued primarily insofar as it promises economic rewards. The acquisition of knowledge and learning for its own sake is not highly valued. Effective performance of the roles involved with education, accordingly, do not confer particularly high status. The 'good student' is not looked up to by his or her peers; the 'master teacher' receives meager financial rewards and public esteem in comparison with those to be gained by success in business. [...]

The relative devaluation of the family in comparison with the economy is not an inevitable consequence of the emergence of a modern, industrial society, whether capitalist or socialist. Adler (1983: 131) points to nations such as Bulgaria, the (then) German Democratic Republic, Japan, Saudi Arabia, and Switzerland to illustrate the possibilities for maintaining a strong commitment to the family despite the profound social changes that accompany the transformation from agriculturally based economics to industrial economies. Each of these countries has made extensive, and sometimes costly, efforts to preserve the vitality of the family. Furthermore, these are precisely the kinds of societies that exhibit low crime rates and are not, in Adler's words, 'obsessed with crime.'

The distinctive function of the polity, providing for the collective good, also tends to be devalued in comparison with economic functions. The general public has little regard for politics as an intrinsically valuable activity and confers little social honor on the role of the politician: Perhaps as a result, average citizens are not expected to be actively engaged in public service, which is left to the 'career' politician. The contrast with economic activity is illuminating. The citizen who refuses to vote may experience mild social disapproval; the 'able-bodied' adult who refuses to work is socially degraded. Economic participation is obligatory for most adults. In contrast, even the minimal form of political participation entailed in voting (which has more in common with shopping than with work) is considered discretionary, and useful primarily to the extent that it leads to tangible economic rewards (e.g., lower taxes).

Moreover, the very purpose of government tends to be conceptualized in terms of its capacity to facilitate the individual pursuit of economic prosperity. [...]

Interestingly, one distinctive function of the polity does not appear to be generally devalued, namely, crime control. There is widespread agreement among the American public that government should undertake vigorous efforts to deal with the crime problem. If anything, Americans want government to do more to control crime. Yet, this apparent exception is quite compatible with the claim of economic dominance. Americans' 'obsession' with crime is rooted in fears that crime threatens, according to political analyst Thomas Edsall (1992: 9), 'their security their values, their rights, and their livelihoods and the competitive prospects of their children.' In other words because crime control bears directly on the pursuit of the American Dream, this particular function of the polity receives high priority.

A second way in which the dominance of the economy is manifested is in the *accommodations* that emerge in those situations in which institutional claims are in competition. Economic conditions and requirements typically exert a much stronger influence on the operation of other institutions than vice versa. For example, family routines are dominated by the schedules, rewards, and penalties of the labor market. [...]

The most important way that family life is influenced by the economy, however, is through the necessity for paid employment to support a family. Joblessness makes it difficult for families to remain intact and to form in the first place. In the urban underclass, where rates of joblessness are chronically high, so too are rates of separation, divorce, single-parent households, and births to unmarried women (Wilson, 1987).

Educational institutions are also more likely to accommodate to the demands of the economy than is the economy to respond to the requirements of education. The timing of schooling reflects occupational demands rather than intrinsic features of the learning process or personal interest in the pursuit of knowledge. People go to school largely to prepare for 'good' jobs, and once in the labor market, there is little opportunity to pursue further education for its own sake. When workers do return to school, it is almost always to upgrade skills or credentials to keep pace with job demands, to seek higher-paying jobs, or to 'retool' during spells of unemployment. [...]

The polity likewise is dependent on the economy for financial support. Governments must accordingly take care to cultivate and maintain an environment hospitable to investment. If they do not, they run the risk of being literally 'downgraded' by financial markets. [...]

A final way in which the dominance of the economy in the institutional balance of power is manifested is in the *penetration* of economic norms into other institutional areas. Schools rely on grading as a system of extrinsic rewards, like wages, to insure compliance with goals. Learning takes place within the context of individualized competition for these external rewards, and teaching inevitably tends to become oriented toward testing. Economic terminology permeates the very language of education, as in the recent emphasis in higher education on 'accountability' conceptualized in terms of the 'value-added' to students in the educational production process.

Within the polity, a 'bottom-line' mentality develops. Effective politicians are those who deliver the goods. Moreover, the notion that the government would work better if it were run more like a business continues to be an article of faith among large segments of the American public.

The family has probably been most resistant to the intrusion of economic norms. Yet even here, pressures toward penetration are apparent. Contributions to family life tend to be measured against the all-important 'breadwinner' role, which has been extended to include women who work in the paid labor force. [...]

In sum, the social organization of the United States is characterized by a striking dominance of the economy in the institutional balance of power. As a result of this economic dominance, the inherent tendencies of a capitalist economy to orient the members of society toward an unrestrained pursuit of economic achievements are developed to an extreme degree. These tendencies are expressed at the cultural level in the preeminence of monetary success as the overriding goal – the

American Dream – and in the relative deemphasis placed on the importance of using normative means to reach this goal – anomie. The anomic nature of the American Dream and the institutional structure of American society are thus mutually supportive and reinforcing. The key remaining question is the impact of this type of social organization on crime.

Anomie, weak social controls, and crime

The American Dream contributes to high levels of crime in two important ways, one direct and the other indirect. It has a direct effect on crime through the creation of an anomic normative order, that is, an environment in which social norms are unable to exert a strong regulatory force on the members of society. It has an indirect effect on crime by contributing to an institutional balance of power that inhibits the development of strong mechanisms of external social control. The criminogenic tendencies of the American Dream are thus due in part to the distinctive content of the cultural values and beliefs that comprise it and in part to the institutional consequences of these values and beliefs.

One criminogenic aspect of the specific content of the American Dream is the expression of the primary success goal in monetary terms. Because monetary success is inherently open-ended and elusive, the adequacy of the legitimate means for achieving this particular cultural goal is necessarily suspect. No matter how much money someone is able to make by staying within legal boundaries, illegal means will always offer further advantages in pursuit of the ultimate goal. There is thus a perpetual attractiveness associated with illegal activity that is an inevitable corollary of the goal of monetary success.

This culturally induced pressure to 'innovate' by using illegitimate means is exacerbated by the dominance of the economy in the institutional balance of power. There are, of course, important noneconomic tasks carried out in other institutional arenas, tasks associated with. goals that might in fact be readily attainable within the confines of the legal order. However, as we have suggested, roles effectively performed in the capacity of being a parent or spouse, a student or scholar, an engaged citizen or public servant are simply not the primary bases upon which success and failure are defined in American society. The dominance of the economy continuously erodes the structural supports for functional alternatives to the goal of economic success.

Nor does the ethos of the American Dream contain within it strong counterbalancing injunctions against substituting more effective illegitimate means for less effective legitimate means. To the contrary, the distinctive cultural 'value' accompanying the monetary success goal in the American Dream is the *devaluation* of all but the most technically efficient means.

The American Dream does not completely subsume culture. There are other elements of culture that define socially acceptable modes of behavior and that affirm the legitimacy of social norms, including legal norms. In principle, these other cultural elements could counterbalance the anomic pressures that emanate from the American Dream. However, the very same institutional dynamics that contribute to the pressures to innovate in the pursuit of economic goals also make it less likely that the anomic pressures inherent in the American Dream will in fact be counterbalanced by other social forces.

As noneconomic institutions are relatively devalued, are forced to accommodate to economic needs, and are penetrated by economic standards, they are less able to fulfill their distinctive functions effectively. These functions include socialization into acceptance of the social norms. Weak families and poor schools are handicapped in their efforts to promote allegiance to social rules, including legal prohibitions. As a result, the pressures to disregard normative constraints in the pursuit of the goal of monetary success also tend to undermine social norms more generally. In the absence of the cultivation of strong commitments to social norms, the selection of the means for realizing goals of any *type* is guided mainly by instrumental considerations.

In addition, the relative impotence of noneconomic institutions is manifested in a reduced capacity to exert external social control. The government is constrained in its capacity to provide public goods that would make crime less attractive and in its efforts to mobilize collective resources – including moral resources – to effectively deter criminal choices. Single-parent families or those in which both parents have full-time jobs, all else equal, are less able to provide extensive supervision over children. All families must rely to some extent on other institutions, usually the schools, for assistance in social control. Yet poorly funded or crowded schools also find it difficult to exert effective supervision, especially when students see little or no connection between what is taught in the classroom and what is valued outside of it.

Finally, weak institutions invite challenge. Under conditions of extreme competitive individualism, people actively resist institutional control. They not only fall from the insecure grasp of powerless institutions, sometimes they deliberately, even proudly, push themselves away. The problem of 'external' social control, then, is inseparable from the problem of the 'internal' regulatory force of social norms, or anomie. Anomic societies will inevitably find it difficult and costly to exert social control over the behavior of people who feel free to use whatever means that prove most effective in reaching personal goals. Hence the very sociocultural dynamics that make American institutions weak also enable and entitle Americans to defy institutional controls. If Americans are exceptionally resistant to social control – and therefore exceptionally vulnerable to criminal temptations – it is because they live in a society that enshrines the unfettered pursuit of individual material success above all other values. In the United States, anomie is a virtue.

Conclusion

This reformulation of Merton's classic theory of social structure and anomie is intended to chal-lenge criminologists and policymakers alike to think about crime in America as a macrolevel product of widely admired cultural and social structures with deep historical roots. Criminological theories that neglect the ironic interdependence between crime and the normal functioning of the American social system will be unable to explain the preoccupation with crime that so dramatically separates the United States from other developed societies. Significant reductions in crime will not result from reforms limited to the criminal justice system, which is itself shaped in important ways by the same cultural and social forces – the same desperate emphasis on ends over means – that produce high rates of crime. Nor will social reforms, whatever their other merits, that widen access to legitimate opportunities for persons 'locked out' of the American Dream bring relief from the crimes of those who are 'locked in' the American Dream, exposed to its limitless imperatives in the absence of moderating social forces. Reducing these crimes will require fundamental social transformations that few Americans desire, and a rethinking of a dream that is the envy of the world.

> *From Richard Rosenfeld and Steven F. Messner, 'Crime and the American Dream', in F. Adler and W. Laufer (eds)* The Legacy of Anomie Theory *(New Brunswick: Transaction), 1995, pp. 159–181.*

References

Adler, F. 1983. *Nations Not Obsessed with Crime.* Littleton, CO: Fred. B. Rothman.

Bassis, M.S., R.J. Gelles, and A. Levine. 1991. Sociology: *An Introduction.* 4th ed. New York: McGraw-Hill.

Cohen, A.K. 1985. 'The Assumption That Crime Is a Product of Environments: Sociological Approaches.' In *Theoretical methods in criminology*, ed. R.F. Meier, 223–243. Beverly Hills, CA: Sage Publications.

Edsall, T.B. 1992, February 13. 'Willie Horton's Message.' *New York Review*, pp. 7–11.

Elkins, S.M. 1968, Slavery. 2d ed. Chicago: University of Chicago Press.

Kornhauser, R.R. 1978. *Social Sources of Delinquency: An Appraisal of Analytic Models.* Chicago: University of Chicago Press.

Lane, A.J., ed. 1971. *The Debate over Slavery: Stanley Elkins and His Critics.* Urbana, IL: University of Illinois Press.

Merton, R.K. 1968. *Social Theory and Social Structure.* New York: Free Press.

Orru, M. 1990. 'Merton's Instrumental Theory of Anomie.' In *Robert K. Merton: Consensus and Controversy*, ed. J. Clark, C. Modgil, and S. Modgil, 231–40. London: Falmer Press.

Parsons, T. 1964. *Essays in Sociological Theory.* Rev, ed. New York: Free Press.

Passas, N. 1990. 'Anomie and Corporate Deviance.' *Contemporary Crises* 14: 157–78.

Wilson, W.J. 1987. *The Truly Disadvantaged.* Chicago: University of Chicago Press.

8.5 The vertigo of late modernity
Jock Young

Eric Hobsbawm, in his magisterial *Age of Extremes* (1994), characterises the late-twentieth century as experiencing a cultural revolution of an unparalleled nature. The American Dream of material comfort and the suburbs becomes replaced with a First World Dream extending across the world – harbouring the desires of the privileged and the envy of the rest. Here the point is not brute comfort and material success, but self-discovery and expression, it is not so much arrival as becoming and self-fulfilment, not of hard work rewarded, but of spontaneity and expressivity anew. The comfort-seeking creature of post-war modernity is replaced by the striving subject of late modernity. And if Durkheim's warnings of the *mal d'infiniti* in the late nineteenth century, or Merton's admonition of the incessant nature of material goals in the America of the 1930s (an aspect of his work sadly neglected), conveyed the notion of the human spirit always striving but never fulfilled, heightened individualism in an era of mass consumerism has granted it an even greater resonance today. We are therefore confronted with a combination of factors, some long existing yet unique in their combination, others pre-existent yet transformed in the present period. The impact revolves around three axes, the disembeddedness of everyday life, the awareness of a pluralism of values, and an individualism which presents the achievement of self-realisation as an ideal.

Liquid modernity generates a situation of disembeddedness. This has dual levels: social and individual. Culture and norms become loosened from their moorings in time and place: normative borders blur, shift, overlap, detach. And this precariousness is experienced on a personal level. The individual feels disembedded from the culture and institutions he or she finds themselves in. And to such a situation is presented a pluralism of values: migration, tourism, the mass media and most importantly the variety of indigenous subcultures within society that carry with them the constant nagging awareness that things could be done differently, that we could make different choices. And here it is often small differences, differences of a minor kind which are more disconcerting than norms which are manifestly distinct and somewhat alien. Finally, self-realisation, the notion of constructing one's own destiny and narrative, becomes a dominant ideal. There is, overall, a sense of detachment from the taken for granted social settings and with it an awareness of a situation of choice and freedom. So that which was once experienced as a thing – monumental and independent of human artifice – becomes de-reified and the social construction of reality is glimpsed particularly poignantly in everyday life, especially alarmingly at moments of personal crisis or sudden change.

All of this creates great potentialities for human flexibility and reinvention. Yet it generates at the same time considerable ontological insecurity – precariousness of being. To start with, the bases of identity are less substantial: work, family, community, once steadfast building blocks, have become shaky and uncertain. At no stage in history has there been such a premium on identity, on constructing a narrative of development and discovery, yet where the materials to construct it are so transient and insubstantial. But it is not merely the instability of work, family and community which make the writing of such a narrative difficult, it is the nature of the building blocks themselves. Work in particular is a locus of disappointment – it is the site of meritocratic ideals, of notions of reward and social mobility commensurate with effort, which very frequently it fails to deliver. It is the supposed font of self-realisation yet all too usually a mill of tedium. It is the workhorse of a consumerism which evokes self-realisation and happiness, but which all too frequently conveys a feeling of hollowness, and neverending extravagance, where commodities incessantly beguile and disappoint. Even the real thing seems a fake.

Work does not merely sustain family life, it manifestly intrudes upon it. It is the long commute which cuts into both ends of the day, and where the family becomes the place of tiredness and worn nerves. For the middle class, work is the price to pay for the sparkling family home and the help to clean it and take care of the children while the dual career family is out at work, yet in a strange sense it is often more of an image than a reality.

It is real in the glossy magazines of home and garden, it is a caricature in reality. For the working poor, it is the two jobs which make life sustainable, while curtailing family and community; it is time off from seeing one's own children and very often it is the time taken to look after the children of others. None of this should deny for an instant the perennial human joys of companionship of work, marriage and partnership, raising children and the comforts of neighbourliness. It is simply to note that it is precisely these parts of human fulfilment that suffer most ... the shoe pinches where it is needed most.

What one finds in late modernity is a situation of contradiction and of paradox. The major institutions have both repressive and liberative potentials. The mass media, for example, carries hegemonic messages justifying the status quo of power – yet constantly in news story and fiction points to the blatant failure and unfairness of the world (see Young, 1981). Cultural globalisation propagates the tinsel values of Hollywood, yet it also carries notions of meritocracy, equality, and female emancipation, while in its global reach and its implosiveness, it serves to stress the interconnections and commonality of the world across economic and social borders (see Thompson, 1995). Even consumerism, as Paul Willis has so ably argued in *Common Culture* (1990) not only sells lifestyle but generates a popular and autonomous demand for individualism and lifestyle of choice which develops, so to speak, on the back of the market place.

Disembeddedness, fluidity, can create the possibilities of seeing through the present institutional set up, of discarding the old traditions, of respect for authority which justify the status quo, of wealth and social division. It thus holds the possibility of a redistributionist approach to social justice and deconstructive approach to identity, yet it can paradoxically offer just the opposite: an acceptance of the world as it is, a mode of 'realism' and an essentialist notion of identity built around one's position of class, gender, ethnicity, place and nation. The outcome is not inevitable or, for that matter, random, but is a product of particular social and political configurations. Of great importance here are perceptual factors, that is the degree to which the basis of economic and social differentials are transparent. In particular I focus upon what I call the chaos of reward and the chaos of identity. As I will argue, the decline of manufacturing industries, the phenomenon of out-sourcing, of

core and peripheral work personnel, of freelance consultants and advisors, of a proliferating service industry of small restaurants, cafes, childcare and housework – all of these together make the comparison of rewards less obvious. The awareness of class distinction and inequalities was more obvious in the large Fordist bureaucracies of the post-war period, it becomes less tangible in late modernity – all that remains is a generalised feeling of unfairness, a failure of meritocracy which is underscored by widespread redundancies and changes in career. As for identity, the ideal of self-development, of a narrative of self-discovery and personal achievement is difficult in a world where the building blocks seem so insubstantial and contested. All of this makes the creation of a personal narrative difficult. It breeds a feeling of incoherence, of half-realised awareness and contradiction. It is not surprising then that at no time in human history has such a recourse been made to fictionalised narratives – the worlds of the soap opera, the thriller, and the romantic novel, a world where there is a beginning, a middle and an end, a story of substance and fulfilment albeit in a virtual reality.

The genesis of othering

In real life the narrative of life pales beside the narrative of fiction or the ideals of meritocracy, self-fulfilment – the First World Dream. Our narratives seem unfair – they are frequently broken and discontinuous, they have no ending. None of this adds up to a satisfying account, a good story – rather it makes for a feeling of incoherence and bitterness, edged with strong emotions of unfairness both in terms of just reward and social recognition. Note also, it does not make for a neat narrative to be discovered by the diligent researcher: a clear, crisp story to be uncovered and revealed. Yet the longing for existential security, for certainty and solidity often exacerbated by the experience of denigration and stigmatisation remains. So, just as barriers are demolished and rendered permeable, new barriers are erected in the false hope of creating rigidity and secure difference. Such a generation of hiatus of rigid distinctions is seen in many spheres of human activity. Most clearly it is seen in cultural essentialism where, in the process of othering, the self is granted a superior ontology, whether based on class, gender, race, nationality, or religion, and is valorised, given certainty in contrast with the other. Two modes of othering are prevalent: the first is a conservative demonisation which projects negative attributes on the other and thereby grants positive attributes to oneself. The second, very common yet rarely recognised, is a liberal othering where the other is seen to lack our qualities and virtues. Such a *lacking* is not seen, as in the conservative version, as an essential and qualitative difference so much as a deficit which is caused by a deprivation of material or cultural circumstances or capital. They would be *just like us* if these circumstances improved. Thus, whereas for the conservative difference is rendered a perversion, or perhaps an inversion, of normality, for the liberal it is rendered a deviance from a lacking of the normal.

Liberal othering focuses largely on the poor constituted as an underclass, who are seen as being a fairly homogenous group. The poor are seen as disconnected from us, they are not part of our economic circuit: they are an object to be pitied, helped, avoided, studied, but they are not in a social relationship with us. The poor are perceived as a residuum, a superfluity; a dysfunction of a system. Their lives are a product of material or moral determinism, which accentuates the miserable and unsatisfactory nature of their lives. They are not a site of creativity, joy or expressivity – but of a bleak and barren scenario which contrasts with the taken-for-granted satisfactions of the mainstream world.

Let me summarise the key components of liberal othering. 'They' – which is predominantly constituted as 'the poor' – are not so much different from us as suffering from a material or moral deficit, so rather they are a lacking from us. Their crime and deviance is the main focus of the othering, their 'normal' activities, for example their pattern of work and legal informal economies, are rendered invisible (e.g. the working poor). Their deviance is seen as a product of this deficit that can be remedied through education and the opportunity of work so as to make up the shortfall of the deficit. Our response to them is therefore not that of demonisation but of actuarial avoidance and judicious help. They are not connected to us either materially or symbolically, rather they are a residuum, separate from us spatially, socially and morally. There are therefore two moments in othering: diminishing (they are less than us) and distancing (we have no direct social relationship with them). Both conservative and liberal othering have in common the notion of a gulf between 'them' and 'us', a distancing, and both gain strength for the centre by diminishing the moral nature of the margins. The difference is that conservative othering involves the notion of suggesting that the deviant is alien – an inversion of 'our' values while liberal othering stresses a lacking, a deficit of value. Correspondingly, whereas conservatives focus on policies which are punitive or exclusionary, liberals focus on inclusionary measures which are educational and rehabilitative. However, importantly, in both modes the deviant does not threaten order, rather the deviant – whether internal or external to our society – helps to shore up order. Othering, then, is a key process which maintains order. I wish to argue that this late modern binary, in either of these modes, permeates public thinking and official discourse about deviants in our midst and extends to images of other cultures, countries, nationalities and religions and, with it, notions of immigration and population movement. Further, that such a binary is pivotal in much social scientific thinking, not only in the conceptualisation of the other and the deviant, but in the production of knowledge itself.

Ontological insecurity then gives rise to the search for clear lines of demarcation, crisp boundaries in terms of social groups (both in terms of the othering of deviants and conventional notions of multiculturalism and ethnic distinctions). On the level of the social sciences, this is reproduced in the search for clear definitions and in the assertion of an objectivity which suggests a gulf between the investigator and the investigated, together with the denial that any social relationship occurs across this hiatus with the implication or the rationality and integrity of the culture of the investigator and the relative irrationality and unsubstantiveness of the investigated.

The vertigo of late modernity

Imagine a society of saints, a perfect cloister of exemplary individuals. Crimes, properly so called, will there be unknown; but faults which appear venial to the layman will create there the same scandal that the ordinary offense does in ordinary consciousnesses. If, then, this society has the power to judge and punish, it will define these acts as criminal and will treat them as such. For the same reason, the perfect and upright man judges his smallest failings with a severity that the majority reserve for acts more truly in the nature of an offense. Formerly, acts of violence against persons were more frequent than they are today, because respect for individual dignity was less strong. As this has increased, these crimes have become more rare; and also many acts violating this sentiment have been introduced into the penal law which were not included there in primitive times. (Calumny, insults, slander, fraud, etc.)

(Emile Durkheim, *The Rules of Sociological Method*, 1964 [1895], pp. 68–9)

I have talked of how insecurities in economic position and status, coupled with feelings of deprivation in both these spheres, engender widespread feelings of ressentiment both in those looking up the class structure and those peering down. Such insecurities can be experienced as a sense of vertigo and, outside of the charmed sphere of the contented minority, such uncertainties are tinged with anger and dislike. Further, that such processes have a wide resonance throughout society, underscoring many of the anxieties and obsessions of contemporary life.

Vertigo is the malaise of late modernity: a sense of insecurity, of insubstantiality and of uncertainty, a whiff of chaos and a fear of falling. The signs of giddiness, of unsteadiness, are everywhere, some serious, many minor; yet once acknowledged, a series of separate seemingly disparate facts begin to fall into place. The obsession with rules, an insistence on clear uncompromising lines of demarcation between correct and incorrect behaviour, a narrowing of borders, the decreased tolerance of deviance, a disproportionate response to rule-breaking, an easy resort to punitiveness and a point at which simple punishment begins to verge on the vindictive. Some of these things are quite blatant, they are the major signposts of our times, the rise in the United States of a vast Gulag of 2.2 million people in prison and 1 in 34 of the population in prison, on probation, or parole at any one time, the draconian drug laws, the use of terrorist legislation to control everything from juvenile gangs to freedom of speech. Some are quite banal, the obsession with the politically correct, the attempt to fit the population into rigid but ever-changing ethnic categories, the policies of zero-tolerance in the United States: the move from policing felonies to the policing of misdemeanours, the shenanigans of New Labour over the control of undesirable behaviour, ASBO enters the English language (even becoming a verb: 'to be ASBO'd'), Anti-Social Behaviour Coordinators are advertised in the job columns of *The Guardian* (an anarchist's dream I would have imagined) while a

British Home Secretary stands up at the 2005 Labour Party Conference and announces his intention 'to eliminate anti-social behaviour' by 2010 (a statement of Canute-like munificence – goodness knows what he would make of Durkheim's society of saints). Moral panics abound, as I write, in Britain the media are obsessed with binge drinking, as if public drunkenness were some new phenomenon to these islands (see Hayward, 2006), while the concept of 'binge' shrinks palpably, now consuming four drinks in a row becomes considered a pariah act of wanton debauchery. The model Kate Moss is publicly pilloried for snorting a line of cocaine, an activity which a very large part of the upper middle class of London (including, of course, journalists and very many MPs) have got up to at some time or another. Journalists lurk in toilets with cocaine testing kits in order to hound those celebrities who have got beyond themselves. The great fashion houses and perfume makers withdraw their contracts and sponsorship, although as the fashion editor of *The Guardian*, Jessica Cartner-Morley (2005) has pointed out – make a great play on their edginess: of being risqué, of peddling the forbidden (witness the perfumes Opium, Poison, Obsession, the aesthetics of anorexia, juvenile sexuality, belts, buckles, bondage, etc.). Moss goes into rehab, like a penitent to a nunnery in the Middle Ages, although not for half a lifetime but for two weeks. And, spurred on by her newsworthiness, the sponsorship of the model near the end of her career is quickly renewed. Redemption is so much quicker in late modernity.

The sources of late modern vertigo are twofold: insecurities of status and of economic position. Although such a feeling of unsteadiness permeates the structure of society, it is particularly marked in the middle classes in the American sense of everyone from the middle level manager to the skilled worker, it is less so among upper middle class professionals, whose skills and professional organisations protect them from threat, or from the working poor and below who have precious little distance to fall. This involves, as all commentators concur, a wide swathe of workers, but particularly those whose status is closely welded to economic position. That is those whose lifestyle (holidays abroad, car, house, private education for children, domestic help, etc.) is so dependent on standard of living. Those for whom the realms of class and status are rightly fused. Here fear of falling is fear of total loss of everything – it threatens their loss of narrative, of a sense of modernity where life involves personal progress in career, in marriage, and in the community they choose to live in.

Pluralism, the shock of the different; the encounter with diversity face to face in the cities, on tourist visits abroad and through the global implosion of media imagery and actual realities, produces at the most a sense of disorientation. It points to the possibility that things could be different and that rational discourse need not lead to the same conclusions as in one's own culture; it de-reifies and de-familiarises – making the familiar no longer obvious and taken for granted. But disorientation alone does not precipitate feelings of anger and resentment. Indeed, among the secure and contented middle class, pluralism brings out the sense of the international flâneur; for the sophisticate well versed in the cultures of Europe and the frisson and energies of the United States, the awareness and enjoyment of diversity is an integral part of one's lifestyle. And, of course, so too is the sampling of the myriad cultures and cuisines of the city. This is a key factor behind gentrification, the move back into the city – just as those more threatened moved out in the evacuation of the inner cities subsequently known as 'white flight'. Thus, for the secure middle class, such encounters with diversity corroborate rather than threaten their ontology, their way of life, their sense of themselves. But this is not so for a wide swathe of the middle class whose jobs are threatened and who feel resentment towards those that they perceive as an underclass detached from decent society yet living on their taxes and making none of the daily sacrifices that they have to make.

From J. Young, The Vertigo of Late Modernity (London: Sage), *2007, pp. 2–14.*

References

Cartner-Morley, J. (2005) Beauty and the Bust, *The Guardian*, 23 September.

Hayward, K (2006) Beyond the Binge in Booze Britain: Market-led criminality and the spectacle of binge drinking, 34th Conference European Group for the Study of Deviance and Social Control, University of the Peloponnese, Corinth, Greece, August.

Hobsbawn, E. (1994) *The Age of Extremes*, London: Michael Joseph.

Thompson, J. (1995) *The Media and Modernity*, Cambridge: Polity.

Willis, P. (1990) *Common Culture*, Milton Keynes: Open University Press.

Young, J. (1981) Beyond the consensual paradigm, in S. Cohen and J. Young. (eds) *The Manufacture of News*, revised ed. London: Constable.

9

The Chicago School, culture and subcultures

9.1 Juvenile delinquency and urban areas
Clifford R. Shaw and Henry D. McKay   190

**9.2 Delinquent boys:
the culture of the gang**
Albert K. Cohen   194

**9.3 Subcultural conflict
and working-class community**
Phil Cohen   198

9.4 Subcultures, cultures and class
John Clarke, Stuart Hall, Tony Jefferson
and Brian Roberts   201

9.5 Cultural criminology
Jeff Ferrell   203

Introduction

KEY CONCEPTS cultural criminology; cultural transmission; differential social organization; 'magical' solutions; moral panic; reaction formation; subculture; zonal hypothesis

For much of the middle half of the twentieth century criminology was dominated by sociologists and sociological thought. The greatest initial influence in that century was undoubtedly the Sociology Department of the University of Chicago which housed and trained some of the most famous names in sociology/criminology including: Edwin Sutherland, Herbert Blumer, Erving Goffman, and Howard Becker. Their activities stimulated a remarkable body of criminological theorizing between the 1930s and 1960s in the United States and, in turn, had a very substantial impact on emergent British criminology from the 1960s onward. More recently, there has emerged a body of work styled as 'cultural criminology' which itself owes an enormous debt to the Chicago School and much of the work that followed in its train.

Two of the most famous early names, Clifford Shaw and Henry McKay **(Reading 9.1)** studied the social patterning of delinquency in Chicago and developed what they called their 'zonal hypothesis'. Not only was delinquency distributed differentially across various parts of the city but they argued that these areas or neighbourhoods were also characterized by different value systems: crudely, areas of high economic status and with low delinquency tend to have fairly uniform value systems and vice versa. In an argument that you may find familiar if you have read the excerpt from Sutherland and Cressey **(Reading 7.1)** they stress the importance of transmission of values through social groups. Here they introduce the term 'differential social organization' and explore the links between this, value systems, and the ability to curb desire and control behaviour.

Much attention in American sociology at this time was focused upon juvenile delinquency generally and gangs more particularly. One of the better known works is Albert Cohen's *Delinquent Boys* **(Reading 9.2)** in which he suggests that much activity of this kind is a response to the contradictions or strains experienced by young working-class men, especially in the absence of educational success. These 'corner boys' are generally ill-equipped for competition in the labour market and experience problems of adjustment. Repudiation of middle-class standards is a typical response. Delinquency, in Cohen's terms, is to be understood as an element of the corner boys' 'reaction formation' to the position they find themselves in.

There follow two excerpts from British subcultural theory. In the first, Phil Cohen **(Reading 9.3)** examines what he calls the 'latent function' of subculture. This, he says, is 'to express and resolve, albeit "magically", the contradictions which remain hidden or unresolved in the parent culture'. Cohen uses a number of examples – including mods and skinheads – to illustrate the ways in which youth subcultures offer a form of symbolic resolution of structural and material difficulties. John Clarke and colleagues **(Reading 9.4)** look at the social reaction to youthful subcultures. They note that social reaction tended to focus on working-class groupings – essentially the UK equivalent of Al Cohen's 'corner boys' – and coalesced into moral panics about such varied subjects as delinquency, truancy, permissiveness, drugs and pornography. Increasingly, they argue, there was recourse to the law as part of such panics and the end of the period they cover sees the birth of what they called a 'Law 'N Order' society – something that we have arguably become much more familiar with in recent decades.

Finally, Jeff Ferrell **(Reading 9.5)** takes a closer look at what in recent times has become known as 'cultural criminology'. Most straightforwardly, he says, it is a body of work that attempts to integrate criminology and cultural studies (not unlike much of the work of the 'Birmingham School' as illustrated in 9.3 and 9.4). Because of this approach it tends to depend on qualitative methods, particularly ethnography, and to take particular interest in subcultural matters. There is also an especial emphasis on the social construction of 'crime' and in these regards there is much about contemporary cultural criminology that harks back to the concerns of some of the radical critiques of the 1960s and 1970s.

Questions for discussion

1. What did Shaw and McKay mean by the phrase 'differential social organization'?

2. What are the links between 'differential social organization' and Sutherland's idea of 'differential association'?

3. According to Albert K. Cohen, what are the main characteristics of a delinquent subculture?

4. What does Phil Cohen mean by the idea that subcultures offer a means for 'magically' resolving contradictions in the parent culture?

5. In discussing how to understand youthful delinquency, Phil Cohen uses the phrase 'what can a poor boy do?' What do you think he means?

6. What was contradictory about the moral panics of the 1960s and 1970s according to Clarke *et al*?

7. Why are qualitative methods, particularly ethnography, argued to be particularly suited to cultural criminology?

8. What would you identify as the main characteristics of cultural criminology?

9.1 Juvenile delinquency and urban areas
Clifford R. Shaw and Henry D. McKay

Differential systems of values

In general, the more subtle differences between types of communities in Chicago may be encompassed within the general proposition that in the areas of low rates of delinquents there is more or less uniformity, consistency, and universality of conventional values and attitudes with respect to child care, conformity to law and related matters, whereas in the high-rate areas systems of competing and conflicting morals have developed. Even though in the latter situation conventional traditions and institutions are dominant, delinquency has developed as a powerful competing way of life. It derives its impelling force in the boy's life from the fact that it provides a means of securing economic gain, prestige, and other human satisfactions and is embodied in delinquent groups and criminal organizations, many of which have great influence, power and prestige.

In the areas of high economic status where the rates of delinquents are low there is, in general, a similarity in the attitudes of the residents with reference to conventional values, as has been said, especially those related to the welfare of children. This is illustrated by the practical unanimity of opinion as to the desirability of education and constructive leisure-time activities and of the need for a general health program. It is shown, too, in the subtle, yet easily recognizable, pressure exerted upon children to keep them engaged in conventional activities, and in the resistance offered by the community to behavior which threatens the conventional values. It does not follow that all the activities participated in by members of the community are lawful; but, since any unlawful pursuits are likely to be carried out in other parts of the city, children living in the low rate communities are, on the whole, insulated from direct contact with these deviant forms of adult behavior.

In the middle-class areas and the areas of high economic status, moreover, the similarity of attitudes and values as to social control is expressed in institutions and voluntary associations designed to perpetuate and protect these values. Among these may be included such organizations as the parent-teachers associations, women's clubs, service clubs, churches, neighborhood centers, and the like. Where these institutions represent dominant values, the child is exposed to, and participates in a significant way in one mode of life only. While he may have knowledge of alternatives, they are not integral parts of the system in which he participates.

In contrast, the areas of low economic status, where the rates of delinquents are high, are characterized by wide diversity in norms and standards of behavior. The moral values range from those that are strictly conventional to those in direct opposition to conventionality as symbolized by the family, the church, and other institutions common to our general society. The deviant values are symbolized by groups and institutions ranging from adult criminal gangs engaged in theft and the marketing of stolen goods, on the one hand, to quasi-legitimate businesses and the rackets through which partial or complete control of legitimate business is sometimes exercised, on the other. Thus within the same community, theft may be defined as right and proper in some groups and as immoral, improper, and undesirable in others. In some groups wealth and prestige are secured through acts of skill and courage in the delinquent or criminal world, while in neighboring groups any attempt to achieve distinction in this manner would result in extreme disapprobation. Two conflicting systems of economic activity here present roughly equivalent opportunities for employment and for promotion. Evidence of success in the criminal world is indicated by the presence of adult criminals whose clothes and automobiles indicate unmistakably that they have prospered in their chosen fields. The values missed and the greater risks incurred are not so clearly apparent to the young.

Children living in such communities are exposed to a variety of contradictory standards and forms of behavior rather than to a relatively consistent and conventional pattern.[1] More than one type of moral institution and education are available to them. A boy may be familiar with, or exposed to, either the system of conventional activities or the system of criminal activities, or both. Similarly, he may participate in the activities of groups which engage mainly in delinquent activities, those concerned with conventional pursuits, or those which alternate between the two worlds. His attitudes and habits will be formed largely in accordance with the extent to which he participates in and becomes identified with one or the other of these several types of groups.

Conflicts of values necessarily arise when boys are brought in contact with so many forms of conduct not reconcilable with conventional morality as expressed in church and school. A boy may be found guilty of delinquency in the court, which represents the values of the larger society, for an act which has had at least tacit approval in the community in which he lives. It is perhaps common knowledge in the neighborhood that public funds are embezzled and that favors and special consideration can be received from some public officials through the payment of stipulated sums; the boys assume that all officials can be influenced in this way. They are familiar with the location of illegal institutions in the community and with the procedures through which such institutions are opened and kept in operation; they know where stolen goods can be sold and the kinds of merchandise for which there is a ready market; they know what the rackets are; and they see in fine clothes, expensive cars, and other lavish expenditures the evidences of wealth among those who openly engage in illegal activities. All boys in the city have some knowledge of these activities; but in the inner-city areas they are known intimately, in terms of personal relationships, while in other sections they enter the child's experience through more impersonal forms of communication, such as motion pictures, the newspaper, and the radio. [...]

The heavy concentration of delinquency in certain areas means, therefore, that boys living in these areas are in contact not only with individuals who engage in proscribed activity but also with groups which sanction such behavior and exert pressure upon their members to conform to standards. Examination of the distribution map reveals that, in contrast with the areas of concentration of delinquents, there are many other communities where the cases are so widely dispersed that the chances of a boy's having intimate contact with other delinquents or with delinquent groups are comparatively slight.

The importance of the concentration of delinquents is seen most clearly when the effect is viewed in a temporal perspective. The maps representing distribution of delinquents at successive periods indicate that, year after year, decade after decade, the same areas have been characterized by these concentrations. This means that delinquent boys in these areas have contact not only with other delinquents who are their contemporaries but also with older offenders, who in turn had contact with delinquents preceding them, and so on back to the earliest history of the neighborhood. This contact means that the traditions of delinquency can be and are transmitted down through successive generations of boys, in much the same way that language and other social forms are transmitted. [...]

[The available research evidence indicates] that most delinquent acts are committed by boys in groups, that delinquent boys have frequent contact with other delinquents, that the techniques for specific offenses are transmitted through delinquent group organization, and that in his officially proscribed activity the boy is supported and sustained by the delinquent group to which he belongs.

Differential social organization

Other subtle differences among communities are to be found in the character of their local institutions, especially those specifically related to the problem of social control. The family, in areas of rates of delinquents, is affected by the conflicting systems of values and the problems of survival and conformity with which it is confronted. Family organization in high-rate areas is affected in several different ways by the divergent systems of values encountered. In the first place, it may be made practically impotent by the existing interrelationships between the two systems. Ordinarily, the family is thought of as representing conventional values and opposed to deviant forms of behavior. Opposition from families within the area to illegal practices and institutions is lessened, however, by the fact that each system may be contributing in certain ways to the economic well-being of many large family groups. Thus, even if a family represents conventional values, some member, relative, or friend may be gaining a livelihood through illegal or quasi-legal institutions – a fact tending to neutralize the family's opposition to the criminal system.

Another reason for the frequent ineffectiveness of the family in directing boys' activities along conventional lines is doubtless the allegiance which the boys may feel they owe to delinquent groups. A boy is often so fully incorporated into the group that it exercises more control than does the family. This is especially true in those neighborhoods where most of the parents are European born. There the parents' attitudes and interests reflect an Old World background, while their children are more fully Americanized and more sophisticated, assuming in many cases the role of interpreter. In this situation the parental control is weakened and the family may be ineffective in competing with play groups and organized gangs in which life, though it may be insecure, is undeniably colorful, stimulating, and enticing.

A third possible reason for ineffectiveness of the family is that many problems with which it is confronted in delinquency areas are new problems, for which there is no traditional solution. An example is the use of leisure time by children. This is not a problem in the Old World or rural American communities, where children start to work at an early age and have a recognized part in the system of production. Hence, there are no time-honored solutions for difficulties which arise out of the fact that children in the city go to work at a later age and have much more leisure at their disposal. In the absence of any accepted solution for this problem, harsh punishment may be administered; but this is often ineffective, serving only to alienate the children still more from family and home.

Other differences between high-rate and low-rate areas in Chicago are to be seen in the nature of the existing community organization. Thomas and Znaniecki[2] have analyzed the effectively organized community in terms of the presence of social opinion with regard to problems of common interest, identical or at least consistent attitudes with reference to these problems, the ability to reach approximate unanimity on the question of how a problem should be dealt with, and the ability to carry this solution into action through harmonious co-operation.

Such practical unanimity of opinion and action does exist, on many questions, in areas where the rates of delinquents are low. But, in the high-rate areas, the very presence of conflicting systems of values operates against such unanimity. Other factors hindering the development of consistently effective attitudes with reference to these problems of public welfare are the poverty of these high-rate areas, the wide diversity of cultural backgrounds represented there, and the fact that the outward movement of population in a city like Chicago has resulted in the organization of life in terms of ultimate residence. Even though frustrated in his attempts to achieve economic security and to move into other areas, the immigrant, living in areas of first settlement, often has defined his goals in terms of the better residential community into which he hopes some day to move. Accordingly, the immediate problems of his present neighborhood may not be of great concern to him. [...]

Economic segregation in itself does not furnish an explanation for delinquency. Negative cases are too numerous to permit such a conclusion. But in the areas of lowest economic status and least vocational opportunity a special setting is created in which the development of a system of values embodied in a social, economic, and prestige system in conflict with conventional values is not only a probability but an actuality. [...]

Briefly summarized, it is assumed that the differentiation of areas and the segregation of population within the city have resulted in wide variation of opportunities in the struggle for position within our social order. The groups in the areas of lowest economic status find themselves at a disadvantage in the struggle to achieve the goals idealized in our civilization. These differences are translated into conduct through the general struggle for those economic symbols which signify a desirable position in the larger social order. Those persons who occupy a disadvantageous position are involved in a conflict between the goals assumed to be attainable in a free society and those actually attainable for a large proportion of the population. It is understandable, then, that the economic position of persons living in the areas of least opportunity should be translated at times into unconventional conduct, in an effort to reconcile the idealized status and their practical prospects of attaining this status. Since, in our culture, status is determined largely in economic terms, the differences between contrasted areas in terms of economic status become the most important differences. Similarly, as might be expected, crimes against property are most numerous.

The physical, economic, and social conditions associated with high rates of delinquents in local communities occupied by white population exist in exaggerated form in most Negro areas. Of all population groups in the city, the Negro people occupy the most disadvantageous position in relation to the distribution of economic and social values. Their efforts to achieve a more satisfactory and advantageous position in the economic and social life of the city are seriously thwarted by many restrictions with respect to residence, employment, education, and social and cultural pursuits. These restrictions have contributed to the development of conditions within the local community conducive to an unusually large volume of delinquency.

The problems of education, training and control of children and youth are further complicated by the economic, social, and cultural dislocations that have taken place as a result of the transition from the relatively simple economy of the South to the complicated industrial organization of the large northern city. [...]

The development of divergent systems of values requires a type of situation in which traditional conventional control is either weak or nonexistent. It is a well-known fact that the growth of cities and the increase in devices for transportation and communication have so accelerated the rate of change in our society that the traditional means of social control, effective in primitive society and in isolated rural communities, have been weakened everywhere and rendered especially ineffective in large cities. Moreover, the city, with its anonymity, its emphasis on economic rather than personal values, and its freedom and tolerance, furnishes a favorable situation for the development of devices to improve one's status, outside of the conventionally accepted and approved methods. This tendency is stimulated by the fact that the wide range of secondary social contacts in modern life operates to multiply the wishes of individuals. The automobile, motion pictures, magazine and newspaper advertising, the radio, and other means of communication flaunt luxury standards before all, creating or helping to create desires which often cannot be satisfied with the meager facilities available to families in areas of low economic status. The urge to satisfy the wishes and desires so created has helped to bring into existence and to perpetuate the existing system of criminal activities.

It is recognized that in a free society the struggle to improve one's status in terms of accepted values is common to all persons in all social strata. And it is a well-known fact that attempts are made by some persons in all economic classes to improve their positions by violating the rules and laws designed to regulate economic activity.[3] However, it is assumed that these violations with reference to property are most frequent where the prospect of thus enhancing one's social status outweighs the chances for loss of position and prestige in the competitive struggle. It is in this connection that the existence of a system of values supporting criminal behavior becomes important as a factor in shaping individual life-patterns, since it is only where such a system exists that the person through criminal activity may acquire the material goods so essential to status in our society and at the same time increase, rather than lose, his prestige in the smaller group system of which he has become an integral part.

From C.R. Shaw and H.D. McKay, Juvenile Delinquency and Urban Areas (*Chicago: University of Chicago Press*), *1972, pp. 170–189.*

Notes

1   Edwin H. Sutherland has called this process 'differential association.' See E. H. Sutherland, *Principles of Criminology* (Chicago: J. B. Lippincott Co., 1939), chap. i.

2   W.I. Thomas and Florian Znaniecki, *The Polish Peasant in Europe and America* (New York: Alfred A. Knopf, 1927), II, 1171.

3   See Edwin H. Sutherland, 'White Collar Criminality,' *American Sociological Review,* V (February, 1940), 1–12.

9.2 Delinquent boys: the culture of the gang
Albert K. Cohen

Every society is internally differentiated into numerous sub-groups, each with ways of thinking and doing that are in some respects peculiarly its own, that one can acquire only by participating in these sub-groups and that one can scarcely help acquiring if he is a full-fledged participant. These cultures within cultures are 'subcultures.' Thus, within American society we find regional differences in speech, cookery, folklore, games, politics and dress. Within each age group there flourish subcultures not shared by its juniors or elders. The rules of marbles and jackstones live on, long after you and I have forgotten them, in the minds of new generations of children. Then there are subcultures within subcultures. There is the subculture of a factory and of a shop with the factory; the subculture of a university and of a fraternity within the university; the subculture of a neighborhood and of a family, clique or gang within the neighborhood. All these subcultures have this in common: they are acquired only by interaction with those who already share and embody, in their belief and action, the culture pattern.

When we speak of a delinquent subculture, we speak of a way of life that has somehow become traditional among certain groups in American society. These groups are the boys' gangs that flourish most conspicuously in the 'delinquency neighborhoods' of our larger American cities. The members of these gangs grow up, some to become law-abiding citizens and others to graduate to more professional and adult forms of criminality, but the delinquent tradition is kept alive by the age-groups that succeed them. [...]

Now we may ask: Why is there such a subculture? Why is it 'there' to be 'taken over'? Why does it have the particular content that it does and why is it distributed as it is within our social system? Why does it arise and persist, as it does, in such dependable fashion in certain neighborhoods of our American cities? Why does it not 'diffuse' to other areas and to other classes of our population? Similar questions can be asked about any subculture: the values and argot of the professional dance band musician, social class differences in religious beliefs and practice, the distinctive subcultures of college campuses. Any subculture calls for explana-

tion in its own right. It is never a random growth. It has its characteristic niche in our social structure; elsewhere it does not 'catch on.' It has its characteristic flavor, qualities, style. Why these and not others?

The content of the delinquent subculture

The common expression, 'juvenile crime,' has unfortunate and misleading connotations. It suggests that we have two kinds of criminals, young and old, but only one kind of crime. It suggests that crime has its meanings and its motives which are much the same for young and old: that the young differ from the old as the apprentice and the master differ at the same trade; that we distinguish the young from the old only because the young are less 'set in their ways,' less 'confirmed' in the same criminal habits, more amenable to treatment and more deserving because of their tender age, of special consideration.

The problem of the relationship between juvenile delinquency and adult crime has many facets. To what extent are the offenses of children and adults distributed among the same legal categories, 'burglary,' 'larceny,' 'vehicle-taking,' and so forth? To what extent, even when the offenses are legally identical, do these acts have the same meaning for children and adults? To what extent are the careers of adult criminals continuations of careers of juvenile delinquency? We cannot solve these problems here, but we want to emphasize the danger of making facile and unproven assumptions. If we assume that 'crime is crime,' that child and adult criminals are practitioners of the same trade, and if our assumptions are false, then the road to error is wide and clear. Easily and unconsciously, we may impute a whole host of notions concerning the nature of crime and its causes, derived from our knowledge and fancies about adult crime, to a large realm of behavior to which these notions are irrelevant. It is better to make no such assumptions; it is better to look at juvenile delinquency with a fresh eye and try to explain what we see.

What we see when we look at the delinquent subculture (and we must not even assume that this describes *all juvenile crime*) is that it is *non-utilitarian, malicious* and *negativistic*. [...]

Another characteristic of the subculture of the delinquent gang is *short-run hedonism*. There is little interest in long-run goals, in planning activities and budgeting time, or in activities involving knowledge and skills to be acquired only through practice, deliberation and study. The members of the gang typically congregate, with no specific activity in mind, at some street corner, candy store or other regular rendezvous. They 'hang around,' 'rough-housing,' 'chewing the fat,' and 'waiting for something to turn up.' They may respond impulsively to somebody's suggestion to play ball, go swimming, engage in some sort of mischief, or do something else that offers excitement. They do not take kindly to organized and supervised recreation, which subjects them to a regime of schedules and impersonal rules. They are impatient, impetuous and out for 'fun,' with little heed to the remoter gains and costs. [...]

Another characteristic not peculiar to the delinquent gang but a conspicuous ingredient of its culture is an emphasis on *group autonomy*, or intolerance of restraint except from the informal pressures within the group itself. Relations with gang members tend to be intensely solidary and imperious. Relations with other groups tend to be indifferent, hostile or rebellious. Gang members are unusually resistant to the efforts of home, school and other agencies to regulate, not only their delinquent activities, but any activities carried on within the group, and to efforts to compete with the gang for the time and other resources of its members.

Action is problem-solving

Our point of departure is the 'psychogenic' assumption that all human action – not delinquency alone – is an ongoing series of efforts to solve problems. By 'problems' we do not only mean the worries and dilemmas that bring people to the psychiatrist and the psychological clinic. Whether or not to accept a proffered drink, which of two ties to buy, what to do about the unexpected guest or the 'F' in algebra are problems too. They all involve, until they are resolved, a certain tension, a disequilibrium and a challenge. We hover between doing and not doing, doing this or doing that, doing it one way or doing it another. Each choice is an act, each act is a choice. Not every act is a *successful* solution, for our choice may leave us with unresolved tensions or

generate new and unanticipated consequences which pose new problems, but it is at least an attempt at a solution. On the other hand, not every problem need imply distress, anxiety, bedevilment. Most problems are familiar and recurrent and we have at hand for them ready solutions, habitual modes of action which we have found efficacious and acceptable both to ourselves and to our neighbors. Other problems, however, are not so readily resolved. They persist, they nag, and they press for novel solutions.

Pressures toward conformity

In a general way it is obvious that any solution that runs counter to the strong interests or moral sentiments of those around us invites punishment or the forfeiture of satisfactions which may be more distressing than the problem with which it was designed to cope. We seek, if possible, solutions which will settle old problems and not create new ones. A first requirement, then, of a wholly acceptable solution is that it be acceptable to those on whose cooperation and good will we are dependent. This immediately imposes sharp limits on the range of creativity and innovation. Our dependence upon our social milieu provides us with a strong incentive to select our solutions from among those already established and known to be congenial to our fellows. [...]

We see then why, both on the levels of overt action and of the supporting frame of reference there are powerful incentives not to deviate from the ways established in our groups. Should our problems be not capable of solution in ways acceptable to our groups and should they be sufficiently pressing, we are not so likely to strike out on our own as we are to shop around for a group with a different subculture, with a frame of reference we find more congenial. One fascinating aspect of the social process is the continual realignment of groups, the migration of individuals from one group to another in the unconscious quest for a social milieu favorable to the resolution of their problems of adjustment.

How subcultural solutions arise

Now we confront a dilemma and a paradox. We have seen how difficult it is for the individual to cut loose from the culture models in his milieu, how his dependence upon his fellows compels him to seek conformity and to avoid innovation. But these models and precedents which we call the surrounding culture are ways in which other people think and other people act, and these other people are likewise constrained by models in their milieus. *These models themselves, however, continually change.* How is it possible for cultural innovations to emerge while each of the participants in the culture is so powerfully motivated to conform to what is already established? This is the central theoretical problem.

The crucial condition for the emergence of new cultural forms is the existence, *in effective interaction with one another, of a number of actors with similar problems of adjustment.* These may be the entire membership of a group or only certain members, similarly circumstanced, within the group. Among the conceivable solutions to their problems may be one which is not yet embodied in action and which does not therefore exist as a cultural model. This solution, except for the fact that it does not already carry the social criteria of validity and promise the social rewards of consensus, might well answer more neatly to the problems of this group and appeal to its members more effectively than any of the solutions already institutionalized. For each participant, this solution would be adjustive and adequately motivated provided that he could anticipate a simultaneous and corresponding transformation in the frames of reference of his fellows. Each would welcome a sign from the others that a new departure in this direction would receive approval and support. But how does one *know* whether a gesture toward innovation will strike a responsive and sympathetic chord in others or whether it will elicit hostility, ridicule and punishment? *Potential* concurrence is always problematical and innovation or the impulse to innovate a stimulus for anxiety.

The paradox is resolved when the innovation is broached in such a manner as to elicit from others reactions suggesting their receptivity; and when, at the same time, the innovation occurs by increments so small, tentative and ambiguous as to permit the actor to retreat, if the signs be unfavorable, without having become identified with an unpopular position. Perhaps all social actions have, in addition to their instrumental, communicative and expressive functions, this quality of being *exploratory gestures.* For the actor with problems of adjustment which cannot be resolved within the frame of reference of the established culture, each response of the other to what the actor says and does is a clue to the directions in which change

may proceed further in a way congenial to the other and to the direction in which change will lack social support. And if the probing gesture is motivated by tensions common to other participants it is likely to initiate a process of mutual exploration and *joint* elaboration of a new solution. My exploratory gesture functions as a cue to you; your exploratory gesture as a cue to me. By a casual, semi-serious, noncommittal or tangential remark I may stick my neck out just a little way, but I will quickly withdraw it unless you, by some sign of affirmation, stick *yours* out. I will permit myself to become progressively committed but only as others, by some visible sign, become likewise committed. The final product, to which we are jointly committed, is likely to be a compromise formation of all the participants to what we may call a cultural process, a formation perhaps unanticipated by any of them. Each actor may contribute something directly to the growing product, but he may also contribute indirectly by encouraging others to advance, inducing them to retreat, and suggesting new avenues to be explored. The product cannot be ascribed to any one of the participants; it is a real 'emergent' on a group level.

Subcultural solutions to status problems

One variant of this cultural process interests us especially because it provides the model for our explanation of the delinquent subculture. Status problems are problems of achieving respect in the eyes of one's fellows. Our ability to achieve status depends upon the criteria of status applied by our fellows, that is, the standards or norms they go by in evaluating people. These criteria are an aspect of their cultural frames of reference. If we lack the characteristics or capacities which give status in terms of these criteria, we are beset by one of the most typical and yet distressing of human problems of adjustment. One solution is for individuals who share such problems to gravitate toward one another and jointly to establish new norms, new criteria of status which define as meritorious the characteristics they *do* possess, the kinds of conduct of which they *are* capable. It is clearly necessary for each participant, if the innovation is to solve his status problem, that these new criteria be shared with others, that the solution be a group and not a private solution. If he 'goes it alone' he succeeds only in further estranging himself from his fellows. Such new status criteria would represent new subcultural values different from or even antithetical to those of the larger social system.

What the delinquent subculture has to offer

The delinquent subculture, we suggest, is a way of dealing with the problems of adjustment we have described. These problems are chiefly status problems: certain children are denied status in the respectable society because they cannot meet the criteria of the respectable status system. The delinquent subculture deals with these problems by providing criteria of status which these children *can* meet. [...]

What does the delinquent response have to offer? Let us be clear, first, about what this response is and how it differs from the stable corner-boy response. The hallmark of the delinquent subculture is the explicit and wholesale repudiation of middle-class standards and the adoption of their very antithesis. *The corner-boy culture is not specifically delinquent.* Where it leads to behavior which may be defined as delinquent, e.g., truancy, it does so not because nonconformity to middle-class norms *defines* conformity to corner-boy norms but because conformity to middle-class norms *interferes with* conformity to corner-boy norms. The corner-boy plays truant because he does not like school, because he wishes to escape from a dull and unrewarding and perhaps humiliating situation. But truancy is not defined as intrinsically valuable and status-giving. The member of the delinquent subculture plays truant because 'good' middle-class (and working-class) children do not play truant. Corner-boy resistance to being herded and marshalled by middle-class figures is not the same as the delinquent's flouting and jeering of those middle-class figures and active ridicule of those who submit. The corner-boy's ethic of reciprocity, his quasi-communal attitude toward the property of in-group members, is shared by the delinquent. But this ethic of reciprocity does not sanction the deliberate and 'malicious' violation of the property rights of persons outside the in-group. We have observed that the differences between the corner-boy and the college-boy or middle-class culture are profound but that in many ways they are profound differences in emphasis. We have remarked that the corner-boy culture does not so much repudiate the value of many middle-class achievements as it emphasizes certain other values which make such achievements improbable. In short, the corner-boy culture temporizes with middle-class morality; the full-fledged delinquent subculture does not.

It is precisely here, we suggest, in the refusal to temporize, that the appeal of the delinquent subculture lies. Let us recall that it is characteristically American, not specifically working-class or middle-class, to measure oneself against the widest possible status universe, to seek status against 'all comers,' to be 'as good as' or 'better than' anybody – anybody, that is, within one's own age and sex category. As long as the working-class corner-boy clings to a version, however attenuated and adulterated, of the middle-class culture, he must recognize his inferiority to working-class and middle-class college-boys. The delinquent subculture, on the other hand, permits no ambiguity of the status of the delinquent relative to that of anybody else. In terms of the norms of the delinquent subculture, defined by its negative polarity to the respectable status system, the delinquent's very nonconformity to middleclass standards sets him above the most exemplary college boy.

Another important function of the delinquent subculture is the legitimation of aggression. We surmise that a certain amount of hostility is generated among working-class children against middle-class persons, with their airs of superiority, disdain or condescension and against middle-class norms, which are, in a sense, the cause of their status-frustration. [...]

It seems to us that the mechanism of 'reaction-formation' should also play a part here. We have made much of the corner-boy's basic ambivalence, his uneasy acknowledgement, while he lives by the standards of his corner-boy culture, of the legitimacy of college-boy standards. May we assume that when the delinquent seeks to obtain unequivocal status by repudiating, once and for all, the norms of the college-boy culture, these norms really undergo total extinction? Or do they, perhaps, linger on, underground, as it were, repressed, unacknowledged but an ever-present threat to the adjustment which has been achieved at no small cost? There is much evidence from clinical psychology that moral norms, once effectively internalized, are not lightly thrust aside or extinguished. If a new moral order is evolved which offers a more satisfactory solution to one's life problems, the old order usually continues to press for recognition, but if this recognition is granted, the applecart is upset. The symptom of this obscurely felt, ever-present threat is clinically known as 'anxiety,' and the literature of psychiatry is rich with devices for combatting this anxiety, this threat to a hard-won victory. One such device is reaction-formation. Its hallmark is an 'exaggerated,' 'disproportionate,' 'abnormal' intensity of response, 'inappropriate' to the stimulus which seems to elicit it. The unintelligibility of the response, the 'overreaction,' becomes intelligible when we see that it has the function of reassuring the actor against an inner threat to his defenses as well as the function of meeting an external situation on its own terms.

From *A.K. Cohen*, Delinquent boys: the culture of the gang (*New York: The Free Press*), *1955, pp. 12–133.*

9.3 Subcultural conflict and working-class community
Phil Cohen

It seems to me that the latent function of subculture is this: to express and resolve, albeit 'magically', the contradictions which remain hidden or unresolved in the parent culture. The succession of subcultures which this parent culture generated can thus all be considered so many variations on a central theme – the contradiction, at an ideological level, between traditional working-class Puritanism and the new hedonism of consumption; at an economic level, between a future as part of the socially, mobile elite or as part of the new lumpen proletariat. Mods, parkas, skinheads, crombies, all represent in their different ways, an attempt to retrieve some of the socially cohesive elements destroyed in their parent culture, and to combine these with elements selected from other class fractions, symbolizing one or other of the options confronting it.

It is easy enough to see this working in practice if we remember, first, that subcultures are symbolic structures and must not be confused with the actual young people who are their bearers and supports. Secondly, a given life-style is actually made up of a number of symbolic subsystems, and it is the way in which these are articulated in the total life-style that constitutes its distinctiveness. There are four subsystems, which can be divided into two basic types. There are the relatively 'plastic forms' – dress and music – which are not directly produced by the subculture but which are selected and invested with subcultural value in so far as they express its underlying thematic. Then there are the more infrastructural forms – argot and ritual – which are more resistant to innovation but, of course, reflect changes in the more plastic forms. I'm suggesting here that mods, parkas, skinheads, and so on, are a succession of subcultures which all correspond to the same parent culture and which attempt to work out, through a system of transformations, the basic problematic or contradiction which is inserted in the subculture by the parent culture.

So one can distinguish three levels in the analysis of subcultures; one is historical, which isolates the specific problematic of a particular class fraction – in this case, the respectable working class; the second is a structural and semiotic analysis of the subsystems, the way in which they are articulated and the actual transformations which those subsystems undergo from one moment to another; and the third is the phenomenological analysis of the way the subculture is actually 'lived out' by those who are the bearers and supports of the subculture. No real analysis of subculture is complete without all those levels being in place.

To go back to the diachronic string we are discussing, the original mod life-style could be interpreted as an attempt to realize, *but in an imaginary relation*, the conditions of existence of the socially mobile white-collar worker. While the argot and ritual forms of mods stressed many of the traditional values of their parent culture, their dress and music reflected the hedonistic image of the affluent consumer. The life-style crystallized in opposition to that of the rockers (the famous riots in the early 1960s testified to this), and it seems to be a law of subcultural evolution that its dynamic comes not only from the relations to its own parent culture, but also from the relation to subcultures belonging to *other class fractions*, in this case the manual working class.

The next members of our string – the parkas or scooter boys – were in some senses a transitional form between the mods and the skinheads. The alien elements introduced into music and dress by the mods were progressively de-stressed and the indigenous components of argot and ritual reasserted as the matrix of subcultural identity. The skinheads themselves carried the process to completion. Their life-style, in fact, represents a systematic inversion of the mods – whereas the mods explored the upwardly mobile option, the skinheads explored the lumpen. Music and dress again became the central focus of the life-style; the introduction of reggae (the protest music of the West Indian poor) and the 'uniform' (of which more in a moment) signified a reaction against the contamination of the parent culture by middle-class values and a reassertion of the integral values of working-class culture through its most recessive traits – its puritanism and chauvinism. This double movement gave rise to a phenomenon of 'machismo' – the deployment of masculinities associated with manual labour against groups perceived to threaten the status of both. A dramatic example of this was the epidemic of 'queer-bashing' around the country in 1969–70. The skinhead uniform itself could be interpreted as a kind of caricature of the model worker – the self-image of the working class as distorted through middle-class perceptions, a metastatement about the whole process of cultural emasculation. Finally, the skinhead life-style crystallized in opposition both to the greasers (successors to the rockers) and the hippies – both subcultures representing a species of hedonism which the skinheads rejected.

Following the skinheads there emerged another transitional form, variously known as crombies, casuals, suedes and so on (the proliferation of names being a mark of transitional phases). They represent a movement back towards the original mod position, although this time it is a question of incorporating certain elements drawn from a middle-class subculture – the hippies – which the skinheads had previously ignored. But even though the crombies have adopted some of the external mannerisms of the hippy life-style (dress, soft drug use), they still conserve many of the distinctive features of earlier versions of the subculture.

If the whole process, as we have described it, seems to be circular, forming a closed system, then this is because subculture, by definition, cannot break out of the contradiction derived from the parent culture; it merely transcribes its terms at a microsocial level and inscribes them in an imaginary set of relations.

But there is another reason. Apart from its particular thematic contradiction, all subcultures share a general contradiction which is inherent in their very conditions of existence. Subculture invests the weak points in the chain of socialization between the family/school nexus and integration into the work process which marks the resumption of the patterns of the parent culture for the next generation. But subculture is also a compromise solution to two contradictory needs: the need to create and express *autonomy* and *difference* from parents and, by extension, their culture, and the need to maintain the security of existing ego defences and the *parental identifications* which support them. For the initiates the subculture provides a means of 'rebirth' without having to undergo the pain of symbolic death. The autonomy it offers is thus both real (but partial) and illusory as a total 'way of liberation'. Far from constituting an improvised *rite de passage* into adult society, as some anthropologists have claimed, it is a collective and highly ritualized defence against just such a transition. Because defensive functions predominate, ego boundaries become cemented into subcultural boundaries. In a real sense, subcultural conflict (greasers *versus* skinheads, mods *versus* rockers) serves as a displacement of generational conflict, both at a cultural level and at an interpersonal level within the family. One consequence of this is to artificially foreclose the natural trajectory of adolescent revolt. For the kids who are caught up in the internal contradictions of a subculture, what begins as a break in the continuum of social control can easily become a permanent hiatus in their lives. Although there is a certain amount of subcultural mobility (kids evolving from mods to parkas or even switching subcultural affiliations, greasers 'becoming' skinheads), there are no career prospects! There are two possible solutions: one leads out of subculture into early marriage, and, as we've said, for working-class kids this is the normal solution; alternatively, subcultural affiliation can provide a way into membership of one of the delinquent groups which exist in the margins of subculture and often adopt its protective coloration, but which nevertheless are not structurally dependent on it (such groups as pushers, petty criminals or junkies).

This leads us into another contradiction inherent in subculture. Although as a symbolic structure it *does* provide a diffuse sense of identity in terms of a common life-style, it does not in itself prescribe any crystallized group structure. It is through the function of *territoriality* that subculture becomes anchored in the collective reality of the kids who are its bearers, and who in this way become not just its passive support but its conscious agents. Territoriality is simply the process through which environmental boundaries (and foci) are used to signify group boundaries (and foci) and become invested with a subcultural value. This is the function of football teams for the skinheads, for example. Territoriality is thus not only a way in which kids 'live' subculture as a collective behaviour, but also the way in which the subcultural group becomes rooted in the situation of its community. In the context of the East End, it is a way of retrieving the solidarities of the traditional neighbourhood destroyed by redevelopment. The existence of communal space is reasserted as the common pledge of group unity – you belong to the Mile End mob in so far as Mile End belongs to you. Territoriality appears as a magical way of expressing ownership; for Mile End is not owned by the people but by the property developers. Territorial division therefore appears within the subculture and, in the East End, mirrors many of the traditional divisions of sub-communities: Bethnal Green, Hoxton, Mile End, Whitechapel, Balls Pond Road and so on. Thus, in addition to conflict between subcultures, there also exists conflict within them, on a territorial basis. Both these forms of conflict can be seen as displacing or weakening the dynamics of generational conflict, which is in turn a displaced form of the traditional parameters of class conflict.

A distinction must be made here between subcultures and delinquency. Many criminologists talk of delinquent subcultures. In fact, they talk about anything that is not middle-class culture as subculture. From my point of view, I do not think the middle class produces subcultures, for subcultures are produced by a dominated culture, not by a dominant culture. But have subcultures altered the pattern of working-class delinquency?

For during this whole period there was a spectacular rise in the delinquency rates in the area, even compared with similar areas in other parts of the country. The highest increase was in offences involving attacks on property – vandalism, hooliganism of various kinds, the taking and driving away of cars. At the simplest level this can be interpreted as some kind of protest against the general dehumanization of the environment, an effect of the loss of the informal social controls generated by the old neighbourhoods. The delinquency rate also, of course, reflected the level of police activity in the area and the progressively worsening relations between young people and the forces of law and order.

There are many ways of looking at delinquency. One way is to see it as the expression of a system of transactions between young people and various agencies of social control, in the subcultural context of territoriality. One advantage of this definition is that it allows us to make a conceptual distinction between delinquency and deviancy, and to reserve this last term for groups (for example, homosexuals, professional criminals, revolutionaries) which crystallize around a specific counter-ideology, and even career structure, which cuts across age grades and often community or class boundaries. While there is an obvious relation between the two, delinquency often serving as a means of recruitment into deviant groups, the distinction is still worth making.

Delinquency can be seen as a form of communication about a situation of contradiction in which the 'delinquent' is trapped but whose complexity is excommunicated from his perceptions by virtue of the restricted linguistic code which working-class culture makes available. This is especially critical when the situations are institutional ones, in which the rules of relationship are often contradictory, denied or disguised but nevertheless binding on the speaker. For the working-class kid this applies to the family, where the positional rules of extended kinship reverberate against the personalized rules of its new nuclear structure; in the school, where middle-class teachers operate a whole series of linguistic and cultural controls which are 'dissonant' with those of family and peers, but whose mastery is implicitly defined as the index of intelligence and achievement; at work, where the mechanism of exploitation (extraction of surplus value, capital accumulation) are screened off from perception by the apparently free exchange of so much labour time for so much money wage. In the absence of a working-class ideology which is both accessible and capable of providing a concrete interpretation of such contradictions, what can a poor boy do? Delinquency is one way he can communicate, can represent by analogy and through non-verbal channels the dynamics of some of the social configurations he is locked into.

From P. Cohen, 'Subcultural conflict and working-class community', Working Papers in Cultural Studies, No. 2 *(University of Birmingham: CCCS), reprinted as Chapter 2 in P. Cohen (ed.)* Rethinking the Youth Question *(Basingstoke: Macmillan), 1972, pp. 48–63.*

9.4 Subcultures, cultures and class
John Clarke, Stuart Hall, Tony Jefferson and Brian Roberts

The social reaction to youth

As we have already hinted, the dominant society did not calmly sit on the sidelines throughout the period and watch the subcultures at play. What began as a response of confused perplexity – caught in the pat phrase, 'the generation gap' became, over the years, an intense and intensified struggle. In the 1950's, 'youth' came to symbolise the most advanced point of social change: youth was employed as a *metaphor* for social change. The most extreme trends in a changing society were identified by the society's taking its bearings from what youth was 'up to': youth was the *vanguard* party – of the classless, post-protestant, consumer society to come. This displacement of the tensions provoked by social change on to 'youth' was an ambiguous manoeuvre. Social change was seen as generally beneficial ('you've never had it so good'); but also as eroding the traditional landmarks and undermining the sacred order and institutions of traditional society. It was therefore, from the first, accompanied by feelings of diffused and dispersed social anxiety. The boundaries of society were being redefined, its moral contours redrawn, its fundamental relations (above all, those class relations which for so long gave a hierarchical stability to English life) transformed. As has been often remarked (cf: Erikson, 1966; Cohen, 1973, etc.), movements which disturb a society's normative contours mark the inception of troubling times – especially for those sections of the population who have made an overwhelming commitment to the continuation of the status quo. 'Troubling times', when social anxiety is widespread but fails to find an organised public or political expression, give rise to the displacement of social anxiety on to convenient scapegoat groups. This is the origin of the 'moral panic' – a spiral in which the social groups who perceive their world and position as threatened, identify a 'responsible enemy', and emerge as the vociferous guardians of traditional values: moral entrepreneurs. It is not surprising, then, that youth became the focus of this social anxiety – its displaced object. In the 1950's, and again in the early 1960's, the most visible and identifiable youth groups were involved in dramatic events which triggered off 'moral panics', focussing, in displaced form, society's 'quarrel with itself'. Events connected with the rise of the Teds, and later, the motor-bike boys and the Mods, precipitated classic moral panics. Each event was seen as signifying, in microcosm, a wider or deeper social problem – the problem of youth as a whole. In this crisis of authority, youth now played the role of *symptom* and *scapegoat*.

'Moral panics' of this order were principally focussed to begin with, around 'Working-class youth'. The tightly organised sub-cultures – Teds, Mods, etc. – represented only the most visible targets of this reaction. Alongside these, we must recall the way youth became connected, in the 1958 Notting Hill riots, with that other submerged and displaced theme of social anxiety – race; and the general anxiety about rising delinquency, the rising rate of juvenile involvement in crime, the panics about violence in the schools, vandalism, gang fights, and football hooliganism. Reaction to these and other manifestations of 'youth' took a variety of forms: from modifications to the Youth Service and the extension of the social work agencies, through the prolonged debate about the decline in the influence of the family, the clamp-downs on truancy and indiscipline in the schools, to the Judge's remarks, in the Mods vs. Rockers trial, that they were nothing better than 'Sawdust Caesars'. The waves of moral panic reached new heights with the appearance of the territorial-based Skinheads, the football riots and destruction of railway property.

To this was added, in the mid-1960's, a set of 'moral panics' of a new kind, this time focussing around middle-class youth and 'permissiveness'. Working-class youth groups were seen as symptomatic of deeper civil unrest. But middle-class groups, with their public disaffiliation, their ideological attack on 'straight society', their relentless search for pleasure and gratification, etc., were interpreted as action, more consciously and deliberately, to undermine social and moral stability: youth, now, as the active *agents* of social breakdown. The first wave of social reaction in this area crystallised around social, moral and cultural issues: drugs, sexuality, libertinism, pornography, the corruption of the young – the key themes of the 'permissive revolution'. (This produced, in response, the first organised anti-permissive 'backlash' amongst the moral guardians – Mrs Whitehouse, the Longford Report, the Festival of Light, SPUC., etc.) The second wave crystallised around the 'politicisation' of this counter-culture – student protest, the new street politics, demonstrations, etc. Here 'youth' was cast, not simply as the conscious agents of change, but as deliberately pushing society into anarchy: youth as the *subversive minority*. And now The Law, which had been mobilised from time to time, in its 'normal' routine way, to deal with hooliganism and vandalism, was brought more formally and actively into play. This shift inside the control culture, from informal outrage and moral crusading to formal constraint and legal control, had wider origins (which we cannot enter into here: see the Law and Order Sections of the forthcoming study of Mugging, CCCS.). But it came to bear heavily and directly on youth: the succession of trials and legal actions (the trials of *OZ* and *IT*, the arrests of prominent counter-culture figures for drug possession, the Little Red School Book affair, the drug and pornography 'clean-ups' instituted by the police, etc.) were matched by equally dramatic legal controls against youth's more political wing (the Garden House trial, the trials of Peter Hain and the Springbok Tour protesters, the Angry Brigade Trial and the widespread use of conspiracy charges).

When these are taken together with the much-augmented activity of the police and Special Branch, the extension of the law to industrial relations, strikes and picketing, the affairs of the five dockers and the Shrewsbury pickets, it makes sense, from about 1970 onwards (not surprisingly, in step with the return of the Heath government to power), to speak of a qualitative shift in the nature and activities of the control culture, a sharp movement towards 'closure' – the birth of a 'Law 'N Order' society. Though youth was, in this polarising climate, by no means the only object of attack and control, it continued to provide one of the pivots of more organised and orchestrated public campaigns. In these campaigns, politicians, chief constables, judges, the press and media joined hands and voices with the moral guardians in a general 'crack-down' on 'youth' and 'the permissive society'. The sharpening of control was nowhere so evident as in the activities of police and courts, local councillors and residents, against black youth – a moral panic which yielded, in 1972–3, the near conspiracy of the 'Mugging' scare. (But in fact, from about 1969 onwards, the black community, and especially black youth, is being constantly 'policed' in the ghetto areas.)

The contradictoriness of this 'control' response to youth must not be neglected. In the 1950's, the press publicised and patronised the 'Teds' in the very same moment that the fire hoses were brought up to control the crowds queuing to see 'Rock Around The Clock'. 'Mods' appeared, simultaneously, in court and on the front pages of the colour supplements. The date of the Mods vs. Rockers show-down coincided with the 'Mod' fashion explosion, with the 'takeover' by 'mod' styles of the Kings Road and the birth of 'Swinging London'. Hippies trailed their flowered gear all the way across the television screen to the addict centres. Mick Jagger was flown by helicopter, virtually straight from the Old Bailey to meet venerable figures of the Establishment to discuss the state of the world. There is a continuing, and characteristically twofaced musing in the high-brow press over the fate and fortunes of pop music throughout the period. We cannot examine either the detail or the roots of this ambivalence here, though we hope we have said enough to indicate that the two faces of the social reaction to youth – patronising publicity and imitation versus moral anxiety and outrage – *both* had their roots in a deeper social and cultural crisis in the society. However, as the disaffiliation of working-class youth became more pronounced, more traditionally 'delinquent' in form, as the counter-culture became organised and politicised, and as other sources of political dissent (especially from the organised working class movement) moved into greater visibility, above all, as the first flush of economic 'affluence' gave way to crisis and stagflation, the bloom faded. Whenever the 'Law and Order' society went campaigning as it did with increasing frequency in the late 1960's and 70's – some section of youth was never very far from the centre of social concern, and of social control, yet, looking across the whole span of the period, it is difficult to estimate firmly whether the more overt 'attack' on youth was of greater or lesser significance than the tendency, throughout the period as a whole, of the dominant culture to seek and find, in 'youth', the folk-devils to people its nightmare: the nightmare of a society which, in some fundamental way, had lost its sway and authority over its young, which had failed to win their hearts, minds and consent, a society teetering towards 'anarchy', secreting, at its heart, what Mr. Powell so eloquently described as an unseen and nameless 'Enemy'. The whole collapse of hegemonic domination to which this shift from the 1950's to the 1970's bears eloquent witness, was written – etched – in 'youthful' lines.

> *From J. Clarke, S. Hall, T. Jefferson and B. Roberts, 'Subcultures, cultures and class', in S. Hall and T. Jefferson,* Resistance Through Rituals *(London: Hutchinson), 1976, pp. 71–74.*

References

Cohen, S. (1973) *Folk Devils and Moral Panics*, London: Paladin.

Erikson, K.T. (1966) *Wayward Puritans*, New York: Wiley.

9.5 Cultural criminology
Jeff Ferrell

Foundations of cultural criminology

Historical and theoretical frameworks

At its most basic, cultural criminology attempts to integrate the fields of criminology and cultural studies or, put differently, to import the insights of cultural studies into contemporary criminology. Given this, much scholarship in cultural criminology takes as its foundation perspectives that emerged out of the British/Birmingham School of cultural studies, and the British 'new criminology' (Taylor *et al.* 1973), of the 1970s. The work of Hebdige (1979, 1988), Hall & Jefferson (1976), Clarke (1976), McRobbie (1980), Willis (1977, 1990), and others has attuned cultural criminologists to the subtle, situated dynamics of deviant and criminal subcultures, and to the importance of symbolism and style in shaping subcultural meaning and identity. Similarly, the work of Cohen (1972/1980), Cohen & Young (1973), Hall *et al.* (1978), and others has influenced contemporary understandings of the mass media's role in constructing the reality of crime and deviance, and in generating new forms of social and legal control. [...]

Grounded as it is in the frameworks of cultural studies and postmodernism, cultural criminology is at the same time firmly rooted in sociological perspectives. Perhaps because of its emergence out of sociological criminology, though, cultural criminology has to this point drawn less on the sociology of culture than it has on various other sociological orientations more closely aligned, historically, with criminology. Central among these is the interactionist tradition in the sociology of deviance and criminology (Becker 1963, Pfohl 1986). In examining the mediated networks and discursive connections noted above, cultural criminologists also trace the manifold interactions through which criminals, control agents, media producers, and others collectively construct the meaning of crime. In so doing, cultural criminologists attempt to elaborate on the 'symbolic' in 'symbolic interaction' by highlighting the popular prevalence of mediated crime imagery, the interpersonal negotiation of style within criminal and deviant subcultures, and the emergence of larger symbolic universes within which crime takes on political meaning. [...]

Finally, cultural criminology emerges in many ways out of critical traditions in sociology, criminology, and cultural studies, incorporating as it does a variety of critical perspectives on crime and crime control. Utilizing these perspectives, cultural criminologists attempt to unravel the politics of crime as played out through mediated anticrime campaigns; through evocative cultural constructions of deviance, crime, and marginality; and through criminalized subcultures and their resistance to legal control.

Methodological frameworks

Cultural criminology's melange of intellectual and disciplinary influences also surfaces in the methodologies that cultural criminologists employ. In exploring the interconnections of culture and crime, researchers utilize ethnographic models rooted in sociology, criminology, cultural studies, and anthropology; modifications of these models suggested by recent developments in feminist, postmodern, and existentialist thought; and a range of methods geared toward media and textual analysis. [...]

Ethnographic research in cultural criminology reflects the long-standing attentiveness of cultural studies researchers to precise nuances of meaning within particular cultural milieux. Willis (1977:3), for example, notes that his use of ethnographic techniques was 'dictated by the nature of my interest in "the cultural." These techniques are suited to record this level and have a sensitivity to meanings and values .....' [...]

In addition, the practice of field research within cultural criminology incorporates recent reconsiderations of field method among sociologists, criminologists, and anthropologists (Burawoy *et al.* 1991, Ferrell & Hamm 1998, Van Maanen 1995a), and among feminists, postmodernists, and existentialists (Fonow & Cook 1991, Clough 1992, Denzin 1997, Sanders 1995, Adler & Adler 1987) inside and outside these disciplines. Together, these works suggest that field research operates as an inherently personal and political endeavor, profoundly engaging researchers with situations and subjects of study. These works thus call for reflex-

ive reporting on the research process, for an 'ethnography of ethnography' (Van Maanen 1995b), which accounts for the researcher's own role in the construction of meaning. [...]

Alternatively, other bodies of research in cultural criminology are based not in researchers' deep participatory immersion in criminal worlds, but in their scholarly reading of the various mediated texts that circulate images of crime and crime control. The range of substantive scholarship that has recently emerged is itself remarkable, exploring as it does both historical and contemporary texts, and investigating local and national newspaper coverage of crime and crime control (Brownstein 1995, Websdale & Alvarez 1998, Perrone & Chesney-Lind 1997, Howe 1997); filmic depictions of criminals, criminal violence, and criminal justice (Newman 1998, Cheatwood 1998, Niesel 1998); television portrayals of crime and criminals (Tunnell 1998, Fishman & Cavender 1998); images of crime in popular music (Tunnell 1995); comic books, crime, and juvenile delinquency (Nyberg 1998, Williams 1998); crime depictions in cyberspace (Greek 1996); and the broader presence of crime and crime control imagery throughout popular culture texts (Barak 1995, Marx 1995, Surette 1998, Kidd-Hewitt & Osborne 1995, Kooistra 1989).

Contemporary areas of inquiry

Framed by these theoretical and methodological orientations, cultural criminological research and analysis have emerged in the past few years within a number of overlapping substantive areas. The first two of these can be characterized by an overly simple but perhaps informative dichotomy between 'crime as culture' and 'culture as crime.' The third broad area incorporates the variety of ways in which media dynamics construct the reality of crime and crime control; the fourth explores the social politics of crime and culture and the intellectual politics of cultural criminology.

Crime as culture

To speak of crime as culture is to acknowledge at a minimum that much of what we label criminal behavior is at the same time subcultural behavior, collectively organized around networks of symbol, ritual, and shared meaning. Put simply, it is to adopt the subculture as a basic unit of criminological analysis. While this general insight is hardly a new one, cultural criminology develops it in a number of directions. Bringing a postmodern sensibility to their understanding of deviant and criminal subcultures, cultural criminologists argue that such subcultures incorporate – indeed, are defined by – elaborate conventions of argot, appearance, aesthetics, and stylized presentation of self and thus operate as repositories of collective meaning and representation for their members. Within these subcultures as in other arenas of crime, form shapes content, image frames identity. Taken into a mediated world of increasingly dislocated communication and dispersed meaning, this insight further implies that deviant and criminal subcultures may now be exploding into universes of symbolic communication that in many ways transcend time and space. For computer hackers, graffiti writers, drug runners, and others, a mix of widespread spatial dislocation and precise normative organization implies subcultures defined less by face-to-face interaction than by shared, if second-hand, symbolic codes (Gelder & Thornton 1997:473–550).

Understandably, then, much research in this area of cultural criminology has focused on the dispersed dynamics of subcultural style.

Culture as crime

The notion of 'culture as crime' denotes the reconstruction of cultural enterprise as criminal endeavor – through, for example, the public labeling of popular culture products as criminogenic, or the criminalization of cultural producers through media or legal channels. In contemporary society, such reconstructions pervade popular culture and transcend traditional 'high' and 'low' cultural boundaries. Art photographers Robert Mapplethorpe and Jock Sturges, for example, have faced highly orchestrated campaigns accusing them of producing obscene or pornographic images; in addition, an art center exhibiting Mapplethorpe's photographs was indicted on charges of 'pandering obscenity,' and Sturges's studio was raided by local police and the FBI (Dubin 1992). Punk and heavy metal bands, and associated record companies, distributors, and retail outlets, have encountered obscenity rulings, civil and criminal suits, high-profile police raids, and police interference with concerts. Performers, producers, distributors, and retailers of rap and 'gangsta rap' music have likewise faced arrest and conviction on obscenity charges, legal confiscation of albums, highly publicized protests, boycotts, hearings organized by political figures and police officials, and ongoing media campaigns and legal proceedings accusing them of promoting – indeed, directly causing – crime and delinquency (Hamm & Ferrell 1994).

More broadly, a variety of television programs, films, and cartoons have been targeted by public campaigns alleging that they incite delinquency, spin off 'copycat' crimes, and otherwise serve as criminogenic social forces (Ferrell 1998, Nyberg 1998).

Media constructions of crime and crime control

The mediated criminalization of popular culture exists, of course, as but one of many media processes that construct the meanings of crime and crime control. As noted in earlier discussions of textual methodologies, cultural criminology incorporates a wealth of research on mediated characterizations of crime and crime control, ranging across historical and contemporary texts and investigating images generated in newspaper reporting, popular film, television news and entertainment programming, popular music, comic books, and the cyberspaces of the Internet. Further, cultural criminologists have begun to explore the complex institutional interconnections between the criminal justice system and mass media. [...]

In a relatively nonconspiratorial but nonetheless powerful fashion, media and criminal justice organizations thus coordinate their day-to-day operations and cooperate in constructing circumscribed understandings of crime and crime control.

A large body of research in cultural criminology examines the nature of these understandings and the public dynamics of their production. Like cultural criminology generally, much of the research here (Adler & Adler 1994, Goode & Ben-Yehuda 1994, Hollywood 1997, Jenkins 1992, Sparks 1995, Thornton 1994) builds on the classic analytic models of cultural studies and interactionist sociology, as embodied in concepts such as moral entrepreneurship and moral enterprise in the creation of crime and deviance (Becker 1963), and the invention of folk devils as a means of generating moral panic (Cohen 1972/1980) around issues of crime and deviance. [...]

Through all of this, cultural criminologists further emphasize that in the process of constructing crime and crime control as social concerns and political controversies, the media also construct them as entertainment. Revisiting the classic cultural studies/new criminology notion of 'policing the crisis' (Hall et al. 1978), Sparks (1995; see 1992), for example, characterizes the production and perception of crime and policing imagery in television crime dramas as a process of 'entertaining the crisis.'

The politics of culture, crime, and cultural criminology

Clearly, a common thread connects the many domains into which cultural criminology inquires: the presence of power relations, and the emergence of social control, at the intersections of culture and crime. The stylistic practices and symbolic codes of illicit subcultures are made the object of legal surveillance and control or, alternatively, are appropriated, commodified, and sanitized within a vast machinery of consumption. Sophisticated media and criminal justice 'culture wars' are launched against alternative forms of art, music, and entertainment, thereby criminalizing the personalities and performances involved, marginalizing them from idealized notions of decency and community and, at the extreme, silencing the political critiques they present. Ongoing media constructions of crime and crime control emerge out of an alliance of convenience between media institutions and criminal justice agencies, serve to promote and legitimate broader political agendas regarding crime control, and in turn function to both trivialize and dramatize the meaning of crime. [...]

At the same time, cultural criminologists emphasize and explore the various forms that resistance to this complex web of social control may take. As Sparks (1992, 1995) and others argue, the audiences for media constructions of crime are diverse in both their composition and their readings of these constructions; they recontextualize, remake, and even reverse mass media meanings as they incorporate them into their daily lives and interactions. Varieties of resistance also emerge among those groups more specifically targeted within the practice of mediated control. Artists and musicians caught up in contemporary 'culture wars' have refused governmental awards, resigned high-profile positions, won legal judgments, organized alternative media outlets and performances, and otherwise produced public counterattacks (Ferrell 1998). [...]

Moreover, cultural criminology itself operates as a sort of intellectual resistance, as a diverse counter-reading and counter-discourse on, and critical 'intervention' (Pfohl & Gordon 1986:94) into, conventional constructions of crime. In deconstructing moments of mediated panic over crime, cultural criminologists work to expose the political processes behind seemingly spontaneous social concerns and to dismantle the recurring and often essentialist metaphors of disease, invasion, and decay on which crime panics are built (Brownstein 1995, 1996, Reinarman 1994, Reinarman & Duskin 1992, Murji 1999).

Conclusions

As an emerging perspective within criminology, sociology, and criminal justice, cultural criminology draws from a wide range of intellectual orientations. Revisiting and perhaps reinventing existing paradigms in cultural studies, the 'new' criminology, interactionist sociology, and critical theory; integrating insights from postmodern, feminist, and constructionist thought; and incorporating aspects of newsmaking, constitutive, and other evolving criminologies, cultural criminology seek less to synthesize or subsume these various perspectives than to engage them in a critical, multifaceted exploration of culture and crime. Linking these diverse intellectual dimensions, and their attendant methodologies of ethnography and media/textual analysis, is cultural criminology's overarching concern with the meaning of crime and crime control.

> From J. Ferrell, 'Cultural criminology', Annual Review of Sociology, 1999, *25: 395–418*.

References

Adler P.A., Adler P. 1987. *Membership Roles in Field Research*. Newbury Park, CA: Sage.

Adler P.A., Adler F, eds. 1994. *Constructions of Deviance: Social Power, Context, and Interaction*. Belmont, CA: Wadsworth.

Barak G. 1995. Media, crime, and justice: a case for constitutive criminology. In Ferrell & Sanders *Cultural Criminology* 1995, Boston: Northeastern University Press. pp. 142–66.

Barak G., ed. 1996. *Representing O.J: Murder, Criminal Justice, and Mass Culture*. Guilderland, NY; Harrow & Heston.

Becker H.S. 1963. *Outsiders: Studies in the Sociology of Deviance*. New York: Free Press.

Brownstein H.H. 1995. The media and the construction of random drug violence. In Ferrell & Sanders *Cultural Criminology* 1995, Boston: Northeastern University Press. pp. 45–65.

Brownstein H.H., 1996. *The Rise and Fall of a Violent Crime Wave: Crack Cocaine and the Social Construction of a Crime Problem*. Guilderland, NY: Harrow & Heston.

Burawoy M., Burton A., Ferguson A.A., Fox K.J., Gamson J., *et al.* 1991. *Ethnography Unbound: Power and Resistance in the Modern Metropolis*. Berkeley: Univ. Calif. Press.

Cheatwood D. 1998. Prison movies: films about adult, male, civilian prisons: 1929–1995. In Bailey & Hale *Popular Culture, Crime and Justice*. 1998, Belmont, CA: West/Wadsworth. pp. 20–31.

Clarke J. 1976. Style. See Hall & Jefferson 1976, pp. 175–91.

Clough P. 1992. *The End(s) of Ethnography. From Realism to Social Criticism*. Newbury Park, CA: Sage.

Cohen S. 1972/1980. *Folk Devils and Moral Panics*. London: Macgibbon & Kee.

Cohen S., Young J., eds. 1973. *The Manufacture of News: Deviance, Social Problems, and the Mass Media*. London: Constable.

Denzin N.K., 1997. *Interpretive Ethnography*. Thousand Oaks, CA: Sage.

Dubin S. 1992. *Arresting Images: Impolitic Art and Uncivil Actions*. London: Routledge.

Ferrell J. 1998. Criminalizing popular culture. In Bailey & Hale *Popular Culture, Crime and Justice*. 1998, Belmont, CA: West/Wadsworth. pp. 71–83.

Ferrell J., Hamm M.S., eds. 1998. *Ethnography at the Edge: Crime, Deviance, and Field Research*. Boston: Northeastern Univ. Press.

Fishman M, Cavender G., eds. 1998. *Entertaining Crime: Television Reality Programs*. Hawthorne, NY: Aldine de Gruyter.

Fonow M., Cook J., eds. 1991. *Beyond Methodology: Feminist Scholarship as Lived Research*. Bloomington, IN: Indiana Univ. Press.

Gelder K., Thornton S., eds. 1997. *The Subcultures Reader*. London: Routledge.

Goode E., Ben-Yehuda N. 1994. *Moral Panics*. Cambridge, MA: Blackwell.

Greek C. 1996. O.J. and the internet: the first cybertrial. See Barak 1996, pp. 64–77.

Hall S., Critcher C., Jefferson T., Clarke J., Roberts B. 1978. *Policing the Crisis: Mugging, the State, and Law and Order*. Houndmills, UK: Macmillan.

Hall S., Jefferson T., eds. 1976. *Resistance Through Rituals: Youth Subcultures in Post-War Britain*. London: Hutchinson.

Hamm M.S., Ferrell J. 1994. Rap, cops and crime: clarifying the 'cop killer' controversy, *ACJS Today* 13:1,3,29.

Hebdige D. 1979. *Subculture: The Meaning of Style*. London: Methuen.

Hebdige D. 1988. *Hiding in the Light*. London: Routledge.

Hollywood B. 1997. Dancing in the dark: ecstasy, the dance culture, and moral panic in post ceasefire Northern Ireland. *Crit. Criminol.* 3:62–77.

Howe A. 1997. 'The war against women': media representations of men's violence against women in Australia. *Violence Against Women* 3:59–75.

Jenkins P. 1992. *Intimate Enemies: Moral Panics in Contemporary Great Britain*. Hawthorne, NY: Aldine de Gruyter.

Kidd-Hewitt D., Osborne R., eds. 1995. *Crime and the Media: The Post-Modern Spectacle*. London: Pluto.

Kooistra P. 1989. *Criminals as Heroes: Structure. Power, and Identity*. Bowling Green: Bowling Green State Univ. Popular Press.

Marx G.T. 1995. Electric eye in the sky: some reflections on the new surveillance and popular culture. In Ferrell & Sanders *Cultural Criminology*. 1995, Boston: Northeastern University Press. pp. 106–41.

McRobbie A. 1980. Settling accounts with subcultures: a feminist critique. *Screen Ed.* 34:37–49.

Murji K. 1999. Wild life: constructions and representations of yardies, In Ferrell & Websdale *Making Trouble: Cultural Constructions of Crime, Deviance and Control*. 1999, Hawthorne, NY: Aldine de Gruyter. pp. 179–201.

Newman G. 1992. Popular culture and violence: decoding the violence of popular movies. In Bailey & Hale *Popular Culture, Crime and Justice* 1998, Belmont, CA: West/Wadsworth. pp. 40–56.

Niesel J. 1998. The horror of everyday life: taxidermy, aesthetics, and consumption in horror films. In Anderson & Howard *Interrogating Popular Culture: Deviance, Justice and Social Order*. 1998, Guilderland, NY: Harrow & Heston. pp. 16–31.

Nyberg A.K. 1998. Comic books and juvenile delinquency: a historical perspective. In Bailey & Hale *Popular Culture, Crime and Justice*. 1998, Belmont, CA: West/Wadsworth. pp 61–70.

Perrone P.A., Chesney-Lind M. 1997. Representations of gangs and delinquency: wild in the streets? *Soc. Justice* 24:96–116.

Pfohl S., Gordon A. 1986. Criminological displacements: a sociological deconstruction. *Soc. Probl.* 33:9–113.

Reinarman C. 1994. The social construction of drug scares. See Adler & Adler 1994, pp. 92–104.

Reinarman C., Duskin C. 1992. Dominant ideology and drugs in the media. *Intern. J. Drug Pol.* 3:6–15

Sanders C.R. 1995. Stranger than fiction: insights and pitfalls in post-modern ethnography. *Stud. Symb. Interact.* 17:89–104.

Sparks R. 1992. *Television and the Drama of Crime: Moral Tales and the Place of Crime in Public Life*. Buckingham, UK: Open Univ. Press.

Sparks R. 1995. Entertaining the crisis: television and moral enterprise. See Kidd-Hewitt & Osborne 1995, pp. 49–66.

Surrete B. 1998. *Media, Crime, and Criminal Justice: Images and Realities*. Belmont, CA: West/Wadsworth 2nd ed.

Taylor I., Walton P., Young J. 1973. *The New Criminology: For a Social Theory of Deviance*. New York: Harper & Row.

Thornton S. 1994. Moral panic, the media, and British rave culture, *In Microphone Fiends: Youth Music and Youth Culture*, eds. A Ross, T Rose, pp. 176–92. New York: Routledge.

Tunnell K.D. 1995. A cultural approach to crime and punishment, bluegrass style. In Ferrell & Sanders *Cultural Criminology*. 1995, Boston: Northeastern University Press. pp. 80–105.

Tunnell K.D. 1998. Reflections on crime, criminals, and control in newsmagazine television programs. In Bailey & Hale *Popular Culture, Crime and Justice*. 1998, Belmont, CA: West/Wadsworth. pp. 111–22.

Van Maanen J, ed. 1995a. *Representation in Ethnography*. Thousand Oaks, CA: Sage.

Van Maanen J. 1995b. An end to innocence: the ethnography of ethnography, See Van Maanen 1995a, pp. 1–35.

Websdale N. Alvarez A. 1998. Forensic journalism as patriarchal ideology: the newspaper construction of homicide-suicide. In Bailey & Hale *Popular Culture, Crime and Justice* 1998, Belmont, CA: West/Wadsworth. pp. 123–141.

Williams J. 1998. Comics: a tool of subversion? In Anderson & Howard *Interrogating Popular Culture: Deviance, Justice and Social Order*. 1998, Guilderland, NY: Harrow & Heston. pp. 97–115.

Willis P. 1977. *Learning to Labor: How Working Class Kids Get Working Class Jobs*. New York Columbia Univ. Press.

10

Interactionism and labelling theory

10.1 Primary and secondary deviation
Edwin M. Lemert   212

10.2 Notes on the sociology of deviance
Kai T. Erikson   214

10.3 Outsiders
Howard S. Becker   216

10.4 Misunderstanding labelling perspectives
Ken Plummer   220

10.5 The social reaction against drugtaking
Jock Young   224

Introduction

In the 1960s, the view that the response to crime might itself be criminogenic became a popular source of enquiry. Work beginning from this premise explored the ways in which reactions to deviance became a crucial factor in understanding the behaviour itself. Indeed, in some extreme versions of what became known as 'labelling theory' there was little to distinguish deviant behaviour from the social reaction. This work was much influenced by the Chicago School, the social psychology of George Herbert Mead, and the sociology of Herbert Blumer. The sociologists in this tradition were particularly concerned to understand the meaning of social interaction.

Edwin Lemert **(Reading 10.1)** distinguishes between what he calls primary and secondary deviance. I won't explain this distinction in detail here – you should read the extract yourself – except to say that it relates to personal identity and the point at which we consider ourselves to be 'deviant' in some regard. It is an important distinction for it places social reactions to behaviour at the centre of our understanding of criminology's subject-matter. Picking up on this theme, Kai Erikson **(Reading 10.2)** notes that deviance is not a property inherent in certain forms of behaviour; it is a property conferred upon these forms by audiences which witness them. Picking up on Durkheim's observation that crime has a social utility **(Reading 8.1)** Lemert asks whether we can assume that society as a whole actively tries to promote such a resource?

The third excerpt in this chapter comes from one of the most famous books in twentieth-century criminology, Howard Becker's *Outsiders* **(Reading 10.3)**. Becker begins by making the distinction between how behaviour that is defined as 'wrong' is seen by those doing the defining and by those whose behaviour it is that is being judged. He goes on to examine various possible ways of defining deviant behaviour and concludes that its most important characteristic is that it is 'created by society'. Becker's important insight is that it is social groups that create the rules that, when broken, mean something deviant has occurred. Much of what we can therefore understand of deviance is bound up in the social reaction to such behaviour.

Given the importance of labelling theory much has been written about its nature and relevance within criminology, some of which, of course, has been critical. Ken Plummer **(Reading 10.4)** responds to some of these criticisms – the alleged biases and limitations of labelling theory – assessing their worth and pointing out some frequently made misconceptions. The most serious and telling criticism, he suggests, is that labelling theorists have tended to neglect the powerful and focus their attention on the relatively powerless. He accepts, at least in part, elements of this criticism but argues that there are important and valid reasons why this particular perspective gravitates toward the powerless.

The final excerpt in this chapter comes from Jock Young's book *The Drugtakers* **(Reading 10.5)**, a classic study in this tradition. Young begins by examining the process of deviancy amplification wherein the social reaction against some form of deviance serves to increase that deviance and sets off a spiral of increasing deviance and societal reaction. However, there is more than one type of deviancy amplification spiral and Young describes – graphically and in the text – the core elements of five different forms. Though similar, they have differing impacts on the opportunities, abilities and desires of the drugtaker, he argues, and may occur to varying extents in different types of drugtaking. Following Matza he goes on to suggest that, reflecting on the societal reaction to their conduct, the deviant (in this case, the drugtaker) adopts one of three possible attitudes – these attitudes being very similar to Sykes and Matza's 'techniques of neutralization' **(Reading 11.3)**.

Questions for discussion

1. What is the distinction between primary and secondary deviance, and why is the distinction important?

2. What is meant by 'deviance is not a property inherent in certain forms of behaviour'?

3. What is Erikson's answer to his own question of whether, given deviant behaviour performs an important social function, we should assume that society tries to promote this resource?

4. What is a 'self-fulfilling prophecy?

5. What does Becker mean when he uses the term 'outsiders'?

6. Describe the process outlined by Becker by which people become 'deviant'.

7. What have been the main criticisms of labelling theory and how valid are they?

8. Describe at least two different types of deviancy amplification spiral.

10.1 Primary and secondary deviation
Edwin M. Lemert

Primary and secondary deviation

There has been an embarrassingly large number of theories, often without any relationship to a general theory, advanced to account for various specific pathologies in human behavior. For certain types of pathology, such as alcoholism, crime, or stuttering, there are almost as many theories as there are writers on these subjects. This has been occasioned in no small way by the preoccupation with the origins of pathological behavior and by the fallacy of confusing *original* causes with *effective* causes. All such theories have elements of truth, and the divergent viewpoints they contain can be reconciled with the general theory here if it is granted that original causes or antecedents of deviant behaviors are many and diversified. This holds especially for the psychological processes leading to similar pathological behavior, but it also holds for the situational concomitants of the initial aberrant conduct. A person may come to use excessive alcohol not only for a wide variety of subjective reasons but also because of diversified situational influences, such as the death of a loved one, business failure, or participating in some sort of organized group activity calling for heavy drinking of liquor. Whatever the original reasons for violating the norms of the community, they are important only for certain research purposes, such as assessing the extent of the 'social problem' at a given time or determining the requirements for a rational program of social control. From a narrower sociological viewpoint the deviations are not significant until they are organized subjectively and transformed into active roles and become the social criteria for assigning status. The deviant individuals must react symbolically to their own behavior aberrations and fix them in their sociopsychological patterns. The deviations remain primary deviations or symptomatic and situational as long as they are rationalized or otherwise dealt with as functions of a socially acceptable role. Under such conditions normal and pathological behaviors remain strange and somewhat tensional bedfellows in the same person. Undeniably a vast amount of such segmental and partially integrated pathological behavior exists in our society and has impressed many writers in the field of social pathology.

Just how far and for how long a person may go in dissociating his sociopathic tendencies so that they are merely troublesome adjuncts of normally conceived roles is not known. Perhaps it depends upon the number of alternative definitions of the same overt behavior that he can develop; perhaps certain physiological factors (limits) are also involved. However, if the deviant acts are repetitive and have a high visibility, and if there is a severe societal reaction, which, through a process of identification is incorporated as part of the 'me' of the individual, the probability is greatly increased that the integration of existing roles will be disrupted and that reorganization based upon a new role or roles will occur. (The 'me' in this context is simply the subjective aspect of the societal reaction.) Reorganization may be the adoption of another normal role in which the tendencies previously defined as 'pathological' are given a more acceptable social expression. The other general possibility is the assumption of a deviant role, if such exists; or, more rarely, the person may organize an aberrant sect or group in which he creates a special role of his own. *When a person begins to employ his deviant behavior or a role based upon it as a means of defense, attack, or adjustment to the overt and covert problems created by the consequent societal reaction to him, his deviation is secondary.* Objective evidences of this change will be found in the symbolic appurtenances of the new role, in clothes, speech, posture, and mannerisms, which in some cases heighten social visibility, and which in some cases serve as symbolic cues to professionalization.

Role conceptions of the individual must be reinforced by reactions of others

It is seldom that one deviant act will provoke a sufficiently strong societal reaction to bring about secondary deviation, unless in the process of introjection the individual imputes or projects meanings into the social situation which are not present. In this case anticipatory fears are involved. For example, in a culture where a child is taught sharp distinctions between 'good' women and 'bad' women, a single act of questionable morality might conceivably have a profound meaning for the girl so indulging. However, in the absence of reactions by the person's family, neighbors, or the larger community, reinforcing the tentative 'bad-girl' self-definition, it is questionable whether a transition to secondary deviation would take place. It is also doubtful whether a temporary exposure to a severe punitive reaction by the community will lead a person to identify himself with a pathological role, unless, as we have said, the experience is highly traumatic. Most frequently there is a progressive reciprocal relationship between deviation of the individual and the societal reaction, with a compounding of the societal reaction out of the minute accretions in the deviant behavior, until a point is reached where ingrouping and outgrouping between society and the deviant is manifest.[1] At this point a stigmatizing of the deviant occurs in the form of name calling, labeling, or stereotyping.

The sequence of interaction leading to secondary deviation is roughly as follows: (1) primary deviation; (2) social penalties; (3) further primary deviation; (4) stronger penalties and rejections; (5) further deviation, perhaps with hostilities and resentment beginning to focus upon those doing the penalizing; (6) crisis reached in the tolerance quotient, expressed in formal action by the community stigmatizing of the deviant; (7) strengthening of the deviant conduct as a reaction to the stigmatizing and penalties; (8) ultimate acceptance of deviant social status and efforts at adjustment on the basis of the associated role.

As an illustration of this sequence the behavior of an errant schoolboy can be cited. For one reason or another, let us say excessive energy, the schoolboy engages in a classroom prank. He is penalized for it by the teacher. Later, due to clumsiness, he creates another disturbance and again he is reprimanded. Then, as sometimes happens, the boy is blamed for something he did not do. When the teacher uses the tag 'bad boy' or 'mischief maker' or other invidious terms, hostility and resentment are excited in the boy, and he may feel that he is blocked in playing the role expected of him. Thereafter, there may be a strong temptation to assume his role in the class as defined by the teacher, particularly when he discovers that there are rewards as well as penalties deriving from such a role. There is, of course, no implication here that such boys go on to become delinquents or criminals, for the mischief-maker role may later become integrated with or retrospectively rationalized as part of a role more acceptable to school authorities.[2] If such a boy continues this unacceptable role and becomes delinquent, the process must be accounted for in the light of the general theory of this volume. There must be a spreading corroboration of a sociopathic self-conception and societal reinforcement at each step in the process.

The most significant personality changes are manifest when societal definitions and their subjective counterpart become generalized. When this happens, the range of major role choices becomes narrowed to one general class.[3] This was very obvious in the case of a young girl who was the daughter of a paroled convict and who was attending a small Middle Western college. She continually argued with herself and with the author, in whom she had confided, that in reality she belonged on the 'other side of the railroad tracks' and that her life could be enormously simplified by acquiescing in this verdict and living accordingly. While in her case there was a tendency to dramatize her conflicts, nevertheless there was enough societal reinforcement of her self-conception by the treatment she received in her relationship with her father and on dates with college boys to lend it a painful reality. Once these boys took her home to the shoddy dwelling in a slum area where she lived with her father, who was often in a drunken condition, they abruptly stopped seeing her again or else became sexually presumptive.

> From E. Lemert, 'Primary and secondary deviance', Social Pathology (New York: McGraw Hill), 1951, pp. 75–78.

Notes

1 Mead, G., 'The Psychology of Punitive Justice,' *American Journal of Sociology*, 23, March 1918, pp. 577–602.
2 Evidence for fixed or inevitable sequences from predelinquency to crime is absent. Sutherland, E.H., *Principles of Criminology*, 1939, 4th ed., p. 202.
3 Sutherland seems to say something of this sort in connection with the development of criminal behavior. *Ibid.*, p. 86.

10.2 Notes on the sociology of deviance
Kai T. Erikson

From a sociological standpoint, deviance can be defined as conduct which is generally thought to require the attention of social control agencies – that is, conduct about which 'something should be done.' Deviance is not a property *inherent* in certain forms of behavior; it is a property *conferred* upon these forms by the audiences which directly or indirectly witness them. Sociologically, then, the critical variable in the study of deviance is the social *audience* rather than the individual *person*, since it is the audience which eventually decides whether or not any given action or actions will become a visible case of deviation.

This definition may seem a little indirect, but it has the advantage of bringing a neglected sociological issue into proper focus. When a community acts to control the behavior of one of its members, it is engaged in a very intricate process of selection. Even a determined miscreant conforms in most of his daily behavior – using the correct spoon at mealtime, taking good care of his mother, or otherwise observing the mores of his society – and if the community elects to bring sanctions against him for the occasions when he does act offensively, it is responding to a few deviant details set within a vast context of proper conduct. Thus a person may be jailed or hospitalized for a few scattered moments of misbehavior, defined as a full–time deviant despite the fact that he had supplied the community with countless other indications that he was a decent, moral citizen. The screening device which sifts these telling details out of the individual's overall performance, then, is a sensitive instrument of social control. It is important to note that this screen takes a number of factors into account which are not directly related to the deviant act itself: it is concerned with the actor's social class, his past record as an offender, the amount of remorse he manages to convey, and many similar concerns which take hold in the shifting moods of the community. This is why the community often overlooks behavior which seems technically deviant (like certain kinds of white collar graft) or takes sharp exception to behavior which seems essentially harmless (like certain kinds of sexual impropriety). It is an easily demonstrated fact, for example, that working class boys

who steal cars are far more likely to go to prison than upper class boys who commit the same or even more serious crimes, suggesting that from the point of view of the community lower class offenders are somehow more deviant. To this extent, the community screen is perhaps a more relevant subject for sociological research than the actual behavior which is filtered through it.

Once the problem is phrased in this way, we can ask: how does a community decide what forms of conduct should be singled out for this kind of attention? And why, having made this choice, does it create special institutions to deal with the persons who enact them? The standard answer to this question is that society sets up the machinery of control in order to protect itself against the 'harmful' effects of deviance, in much the same way that an organism mobilizes its resources to combat an invasion of germs. At times, however, this classroom convention only seems to make the problem more complicated. In the first place, as Durkheim pointed out some years ago, it is by no means clear that all acts considered deviant in a culture are in fact (or even in principle) harmful to group life.[1] And in the second place, specialists in crime and mental health have long suggested that deviance can play an important role in keeping the social order intact – again a point we owe originally to Durkheim.[2] This has serious implications for sociological theory in general. [...]

This raises a serious theoretical question. If we grant that deviant behavior often performs a valuable service in society, can we then assume that society as a whole actively tries to promote this resource? Can we assume, in other words, that some kind of active recruitment process is going on to assure society of a steady volume of deviance? Sociology has not yet developed a conceptual language in which this sort of question can be discussed without a great deal of circularity, but one observation can be made which gives the question an interesting perspective – namely, that deviant activities often seem to derive support from the very agencies designed to suppress them. Indeed, the institutions devised by human society for guarding against deviance sometimes seem so poorly equipped for this task that we might well ask why this is considered their 'real' function at all.

It is by now a thoroughly familiar argument that many of the institutions built to inhibit deviance actually operate in such a way as to perpetuate it. For one thing, prisons, hospitals, and other agencies of control provide aid and protection for large numbers of deviant persons. But beyond this, such institutions gather marginal people into tightly segregated groups, give them an opportunity to teach one another the skills and attitudes of a deviant career, and even drive them into using these skills by reinforcing their sense of alienation from the rest of society.[3] This process is found not only in the institutions which actually confine the deviant, but in the general community as well.

The community's decision to bring deviant sanctions against an individual is not a simple act of censure. It is a sharp rite of transition, at once moving him out of his normal position in society and transferring him into a distinct deviant role.[4] The ceremonies which accomplish this change of status, usually, have three related phases. They arrange a formal *confrontation* between the deviant suspect and representatives of his community (as in the criminal trial or psychiatric case conference); they announce some *judgment* about the nature of his deviancy (a 'verdict' or 'diagnosis,' for example); and they perform an act of social *placement*, assigning him to a special deviant role (like that of 'prisoner' or 'patient') for some period of time. Such ceremonies tend to be events of wide public interest and ordinarily take place in a dramatic, ritualized setting.[5] Perhaps the most obvious example of a commitment ceremony is the criminal trial, with its elaborate ritual and formality, but more modest equivalents can be found almost anywhere that procedures are set up for judging whether or not someone is officially deviant.

An important feature of these ceremonies in our culture is that they are almost irreversible. Most provisional roles conferred by society – like those of the student or citizen soldier, for instance – include some kind of terminal ceremony to mark the individual's movement back out of the role once its temporary advantages have been exhausted. But the roles allotted to the deviant seldom make allowance for this type of passage. He is ushered into the special position by a decisive and dramatic ceremony, yet is retired from it with hardly a word of public notice. As a result, the deviant often returns home with no proper license to resume a normal life in the community. From a ritual point of view, nothing has happened to cancel out the stigmas imposed upon him by earlier commitment ceremonies: the original verdict or diagnosis is still formally in effect. Partly for this reason, the community is apt to place the returning deviant on some form of probation within the group, suspicious that he will return to deviant activity upon a moment's provocation.

A circularity is thus set into motion which has all the earmarks of a 'self-fulfilling prophecy,' to use Merton's fine phrase. On the one hand, it seems obvious that the apprehensions of the community help destroy whatever chances the deviant might otherwise have for a successful return to society. Yet, on the other hand, everyday experience seems to show that these apprehensions are altogether reasonable, for it is a well-known and highly publicized fact that most ex-convicts return to prison and that a large proportion of mental patients require additional treatment after once having been discharged. The community's feeling that deviant persons cannot change, then, may be based on a faulty premise, but it is repeated so frequently and with such conviction that it eventually creates the facts which 'prove' it correct. If the returned deviant encounters this feeling of distrust often enough, it is understandable that he too may begin to wonder if the original verdict or diagnosis is still in effect – and respond to this uncertainty by resuming deviant activity. In some respects, this solution may be the only way for the individual and his community to agree what forms of behavior are appropriate for him.

From K.T. Erikson, 'Notes on the sociology of deviance', Social Problems, *1962, 9: 307–314.*

Notes

1 Emile Durkheim, *The Division of Labor in Society* (translated by George Simpson), Glencoe: The Free Press, 1952. See particularly Chapter 2, Book 1.
2 Emile Durkheim, *The Rules of Sociological Method,* (translated by S.A. Solovay and J.H. Mueller), Glencoe: The Free Press, 1958.
3 For a good description of this process in the modern prison, see Gresham Sykes, *The Society of Captives*, Princeton: Princeton University Press, 1958. For views of two different types of mental hospital settings, see Erving Goffman, *The Characteristics of Total Institutions*, Symposium on Preventive and Social Psychiatry, Washington, D.C.: Walter Reed Army

Institute of Research, 1957; and Kai T. Erikson. 'Patient Role and Social Uncertainty: A Dilemma of the Mentally Ill,' *Psychiatry*, 20 (1957), pp. 263–74,

4   Talcott Parsons, has given the classical description of how this role transfer works in the case of medical patients. *The Social System*, Glencoe: The Free Press, 1951.

5   Cf. Harold Garfinkel, 'Successful Degradation Ceremonies.' *American Journal of Sociology*, 61 (1956), pp. 420–24.

10.3 Outsiders
Howard S. Becker

All social groups make rules and attempt, at some times and under some circumstances, to enforce them. Social rules define situations and the kinds of behavior appropriate to them, specifying some actions as 'right' and forbidding others as 'wrong.' When a rule is enforced, the person who is supposed to have broken it may be seen as a special kind of person, one who cannot be trusted to live by the rules agreed on by the group. He is regarded as an *outsider*.

But the person who is thus labeled an outsider may have a different view of the matter. He may not accept the rule by which he is being judged and may not regard those who judge him as either competent or legitimately entitled to do so. Hence, a second meaning of the term emerges: the rule–breaker may feel his judges are *outsiders*.

In what follows, I will try to clarify the situation and process pointed to by this double-barrelled term: the situations of rule-breaking and rule-enforcement and the processes by which some people come to break rules and others to enforce them.

Definitions of deviance

The outsider – the deviant from group rules – has been the subject of much speculation, theorizing, and scientific study. What laymen want to know about deviants is: why do they do it? How can we account for their rule-breaking? What is there about them that leads them to do forbidden things? Scientific research has tried to find answers to these questions. In doing so it has accepted the common-sense premise that there is something inherently deviant (qualitatively distinct) about acts that break (or seem to break) social rules. It has also accepted the common-sense assumption that the deviant act occurs because some characteristic of the person who commits it makes it necessary or inevitable that he should. Scientists do not ordinarily question the label 'deviant' when it is applied to particular acts or people but rather take it as given. In so doing, they accept the values of the group making the judgment.

It is easily observable that different groups judge different things to be deviant. This should alert us to the possibility that the person making the judgment of deviance, the process by which that judgment is arrived at, and the situation in which it is made may all be intimately involved in the phenomenon of deviance. [...]

Our first problem, then, is to construct a definition of deviance. Before doing this, let us consider some of the definitions scientists now use, seeing what is left out if we take them as a point of departure for the study of outsiders.

The simplest view of deviance is essentially statistical, defining as deviant anything that varies too widely from the average. When a statistician analyzes the results of an agricultural experiment, he describes the stalk of corn that is exceptionally tall and the stalk that is exceptionally short as deviations from the mean or average. Similarly, one can describe anything that differs from what is most common as deviation. In this view, to be left-handed or redheaded is deviant, because most people are right–handed and brunette.

So stated, the statistical view seems simple-minded, even trivial. Yet it simplifies the problem by doing away with many questions of value that ordinarily arise in discussions of the nature of deviance. In assessing any particular case, all one need do is calculate the distance of the behavior involved from the average. But it is too simple a solution. Hunting with such a definition, we return with a mixed bag – people who are excessively fat or thin, murderers, redheads, homosexuals, and traffic violators. The mixture contains some ordinarily thought of as deviants and others who have broken no rule at all. The statistical definition of deviance, in short, is too far removed from the concern with rule-breaking which prompts scientific study of outsiders.

A less simple but much more common view of deviance identifies it as something essentially pathological, revealing the presence of a 'disease.' This view rests, obviously, on a medical analogy. The human organism, when it is working efficiently and experiencing no discomfort, is said to be 'healthy.' When it does not work efficiently, a disease is present. The organ or function that has become deranged is said to be pathological. Of course, there is little disagreement about what constitutes a healthy state of the organism. But there is much less agreement when one uses the notion of pathology analogically, to describe kinds of behavior that are regarded as deviant. For people do not agree on what constitutes healthy behavior. It is difficult to find a definition that will satisfy even such a select and limited group as psychiatrists; it is impossible to find one that people generally accept as they accept criteria of health for the organism.[1]

Sometimes people mean the analogy more strictly, because they think of deviance as the product of mental disease. The behavior of a homosexual or drug addict is regarded as the symptom of a mental disease just as the diabetic's difficulty in getting bruises to heal is regarded as a symptom of his disease. But mental disease resembles physical disease only in metaphor. [...]

The medical metaphor limits what we can see much as the statistical view does. It accepts the lay judgment of something as deviant and, by use of analogy, locates its source within the individual, thus preventing us from seeing the judgment itself as a crucial part of the phenomenon.

Some sociologists also use a model of deviance based essentially on the medical notions of health and disease. They look at a society, or some part of a society, and ask whether there are any processes going on in it that tend to reduce its stability, thus lessening its chance of survival. They label such processes deviant or identify them as symptoms of social disorganization. They discriminate between those features of society which promote stability (and thus are 'functional') and those which disrupt stability (and thus are 'dysfunctional'). Such a view has the great virtue of pointing to areas of possible trouble in a society of which people may not be aware.[2]

But it is harder in practice than it appears to be in theory to specify what is functional and what dysfunctional for a society or social group. [...] The functional view of deviance, by ignoring the political aspect of the phenomenon, limits our understanding.

Another sociological view is more relativistic. It identifies deviance as the failure to obey group rules. Once we have described the rules a group enforces on its members, we can say with some precision whether or not a person has violated them and is thus, on this view, deviant.

This view is closest to my own, but it fails to give sufficient weight to the ambiguities that arise in deciding which rules are to be taken as the yardstick against which behavior is measured and judged deviant. A society has many groups, each with its own set of rules, and people belong to many groups simultaneously.

Deviance and the responses of others

The sociological view I have just discussed defines deviance as the infraction of some agreed-upon rule. It then goes on to ask who breaks rules, and to search for the factors in their personalities and life situations that might account for the infractions. This assumes that those who have broken a rule constitute a homogeneous category, because they have committed the same deviant act.

Such an assumption seems to me to ignore the central fact about deviance: it is created by society. I do not mean this in the way it is ordinarily understood, in which the causes of deviance are located in the social situation of the deviant or in 'social factors' which prompt his action. I mean, rather, that *social groups create deviance by making the rules whose infraction constitutes deviance*, and by applying those rules to particular people and labeling them as outsiders. From this point of view, deviance is not a quality of the act the person commits, but rather a consequence of the application by others of rules and sanctions to an 'offender.' The deviant is one to whom that label has successfully been applied; deviant behavior is behavior that people so label.[3]

Since deviance is, among other things, a consequence of the responses of others to a person's act, students of deviance cannot assume that they are dealing with a homogeneous category when they study people who have been labeled deviant. That is, they cannot assume that these people have actually committed a deviant act or broken some rule, because the process of labeling may not be infallible; some people may be labeled deviant who in fact have not broken a rule. Furthermore, they cannot assume that the category of those labeled deviant will contain all those who actually have broken a rule, for many offenders may escape apprehension and thus fail to be included in the population of 'deviants' they study. Insofar as the category lacks homogeneity and fails to include all the cases that belong in it, one cannot reasonably expect to find common factors of personality or life situation that will account for the supposed deviance.

What, then, do people who have been labeled deviant have in common? At the least, they share the label and the experience of being labeled as outsiders. I will begin my analysis with this basic similarity and view deviance as the product of a transaction that takes place between some social group and one who is viewed by that group as a rule-breaker. I will be less concerned with the personal and social characteristics of deviants than with the process by which they come to be thought of as outsiders and their reactions to that judgment. [...]

Whether an act is deviant, then, depends on how other people react to it. [...] The point is that the response of other people has to be regarded as problematic. Just because one has committed an infraction of a rule does not mean that others will respond as though this had happened. (Conversely, just because one has not violated a rule does not mean that he may not be treated, in some circumstances, as though he had.) The degree to which other people will respond to a given act as deviant varies greatly. Several kinds of variation seem worth noting. First of all, there is variation over time. A person believed to have committed a given 'deviant' act may at one time be responded to much more leniently than he would be at some other time. The occurrence of 'drives' against various kinds of deviance illustrates this clearly. At various times, enforcement officials may decide to make an all-out attack on some particular kind of deviance, such as gambling, drug addiction, or homosexuality. It is obviously much more dangerous to engage in one of these activities when a drive is on than at any other time. [...]

The degree to which an act will be treated as deviant depends also on who commits the act and who feels he has been harmed by it. Rules tend to be applied more to some persons than others. Studies of juvenile delinquency make the point

clearly. Boys from middle-class areas do not get as far in the legal process when they are apprehended as do boys from slum areas. The middle-class boy is less likely, when picked up by the police, to be taken to the station; less likely when taken to the station to be booked; and it is extremely unlikely that he will be convicted and sentenced.[4] This variation occurs even though the original infraction of the rule is the same in the two cases. Similarly, the law is differentially applied to Negroes and whites. It is well known that a Negro believed to have attacked a white woman is much more likely to be punished than a white man who commits the same offense; it is only slightly less well known that a Negro who murders another Negro is much less likely to be punished than a white man who commits murder.[5] This, of course, is one of the main points of Sutherland's analysis of white-collar crime: crimes committed by corporations are almost always prosecuted as civil cases, but the same crime committed by an individual is ordinarily treated as a criminal offense.[6]

Some rules are enforced only when they result in certain consequences. The unmarried mother furnishes a clear example. Vincent[7] points out that illicit sexual relations seldom result in severe punishment or social censure for the offenders. If, however, a girl becomes pregnant as a result of such activities the reaction of others is likely to be severe. (The illicit pregnancy is also an interesting example of the differential enforcement of rules on different categories of people. Vincent notes that unmarried fathers escape the severe censure visited on the mother.)

Why repeat these commonplace observations? Because, taken together, they support the proposition that deviance is not a simple quality, present in some kinds of behavior and absent in others. Rather, it is the product of a process which involves responses of other people to the behavior. The same behavior may be an infraction of the rules at one time and not at another; may be an infraction when committed by one person, but not when committed by another; some rules are broken with impunity, others are not. In short, whether a given act is deviant or not depends in part on the nature of the act (that is, whether or not it violates some rule) and in part on what other people do about it.

Whose rules?

I have been using the term 'outsiders' to refer to those people who are judged by others to be deviant and thus to stand outside the circle of 'normal' members of the group. But the term contains a second meaning, whose analysis leads to another important set of sociological problems: 'outsiders,' from the point of view of the person who is labeled deviant, may be the people who make the rules he had been found guilty of breaking.

Social rules are the creation of specific social groups. Modern societies are not simple organizations in which everyone agrees on what the rules are and how they are to be applied in specific situations. They are, instead, highly differentiated along social class lines, ethnic lines, occupational lines, and cultural lines. These groups need not and, in fact, often do not share the same rules. The problems they face in dealing with their environment, the history and traditions they carry with them, all lead to the evolution of different sets of rules. Insofar as the rules of various groups conflict and contradict one another, there will be disagreement about the kind of behavior that is proper in any given situation.

Italian immigrants who went on making wine for themselves and their friends during Prohibition were acting properly by Italian immigrant standards, but were breaking the law of their new country (as, of course, were many of their Old American neighbors). [...]

While it may be argued that many or most rules are generally agreed to by all members of a society, empirical research on a given rule generally reveals variation in people's attitudes. Formal rules, enforced by some specially constituted group, may differ from those actually thought appropriate by most people.[8] Factions in a group may disagree on what I have called actual operating rules. Most important for the study of behavior ordinarily labeled deviant, the perspectives of the people who engage in the behavior are likely to be quite different from those of the people who condemn it. In this latter situation, a person may feel that he is being judged according to rules he has had no hand in making and does not accept, rules forced on him by outsiders.

To what extent and under what circumstances do people attempt to force their rules on others who do not subscribe to them? Let us distinguish two cases. In the first, only those who are actually members of the group have any interest in making and enforcing certain rules. If an orthodox Jew disobeys the laws of kashruth only other orthodox Jews will regard this as a transgression; Christians or nonorthodox Jews will not consider this deviance and would have no interest in interfering. In the second case, members of a group consider it important to their welfare that members of certain other groups obey certain rules. Thus, people consider it extremely important that those who practice the healing arts abide by certain rules; this is the reason the state licenses physicians, nurses, and others, and forbids anyone who is not licensed to engage in healing activities.

To the extent that a group tries to impose its rules on other groups in the society, we are presented with a second question: Who can, in fact, force others to accept their rules and what are the causes of their success? This is, of course, a question of political and economic power. [...] Here it is enough to note that people are in fact always forcing their rules on others, applying them more or less against the will and without the consent of those others. By and large, for example, rules are made for young people by their elders. Though the youth of this country exert a powerful influence culturally – the mass media of communication are tailored to their interests, for instance – many important kinds of rules are made for our youth by adults. [...]

In the same way, it is true in many respects that men make the rules for women in our society (though in America this is changing rapidly). Negroes find themselves subject to rules made for them by whites. The foreign–born and those otherwise ethnically peculiar often have their rules made for them by the Protestant Anglo–Saxon minority. The middle class makes rules the lower class must obey – in the schools, the courts, and elsewhere.

Differences in the ability to make rules and apply them to other people are essentially power differentials (either legal or extralegal). Those groups whose social position gives them weapons and power are best able to enforce their rules. Distinctions of age, sex, ethnicity, and class are all related to differences in power, which accounts for differences in the degree to which groups so distinguished can make rules for others.

In addition to recognizing that deviance is created by the responses of people to particular kinds of behavior, by the labeling of that behavior as deviant, we must also keep in mind that the rules created and maintained by such labeling are not universally agreed to. Instead, they are the object of conflict and disagreement, part of the political process of society.

From *H.S. Becker,* Outsiders *(New York: The Free Press), 1963, pp. 1–18.*

Notes

1 See the discussion in C. Wright Mills, 'The Professional Ideology of Social Pathologists,' *American Journal of Sociology*, XLIX (September, 1942).165–180.
2 See Robert K. Merton, 'Social Problems and Sociological Theory,' in Robert K. Merton and Robert A. Nisbet, editors, *Contemporary Social Problems* (New York: Harcourt, Brace and World, Inc., 1961), pp. 697–737; and Talcott Parsons, *The Social System* (New York: The Free Press of Glencoe, 1951), pp. 249–325.
3 The most important earlier statements of this view can be found in Frank Tannenbaum, *Crime and the Community* (New York: McGraw–Hill Book Co., Inc.,

951), and E. M. Lemert, *Social Pathology* (New York: McGraw–Hill Book Co., Inc., 1951). A recent article stating a position very, similar to mine is John Kitsuse, 'Societal Reaction to Deviance: Problems of Theory and Method,' *Social Problems*, 9 (Winter, 1962), 247–256.
4 See Albert K. Cohen and James F. Short, Jr., 'Juvenile Delinquency,' in Merton and Nisbet, *op. cit.*, p. 87.
5 See Harold Garfinkel, 'Research Notes on Inter– and Intra–Racial Homicides,' *Social Forces*, 27 (May, 1949), 369–381.
6 Edwin H. Sutherland, 'White Collar Criminality,' *American Sociological Review*, V (February, 1940), 1–12.
7 Clark Vincent, *Unmarried Mothers* (New York: The Free Press of Glencoe, 1961), pp. 3–5.
8 Arnold M. Rose and Arthur E. Prell, 'Does the Punishment Fit the Crime? – A Study in Social Valuation,' *American Journal of Sociology*, LXI (November, 1955), 247–259.

10.4 Misunderstanding labelling perspectives
Ken Plummer

The biases and limitations of labelling theory

A number of biases and limitations have been detected in labelling theory to date. It ignores the sources of deviant action; has too deterministic a conception of the labelling process; has relevance to only a limited range of deviant activities (cf. Reiss, 1970, pp. 80–2; Schur, 1971) ignores power [and] neglects structure.

The neglect of becoming deviant[1]

The first and most frequently cited limitation of labelling theory is that it fails to provide any account of the initial motivations towards deviance; it ignores the origins of deviant action and thereby frequently denudes the behaviour of meaning (Gibbs, 1966; Bordua, 1967; Mankoff, 1971; Taylor, Walton and Young, 1973a; Davis, 1972). These criticisms seem to be both fair and unfair. They are unfair in so far as they attack the perspective for not doing what it manifestly does not set out to do. [...]

However, a number of the criticisms are fairer, because while labelling theorists do not have to account for the initial deviance *in principle*, they very often do it *in practice*. [...]

The two accounts most frequently criticised seem to be ones in which:

1 the labels themselves are seen as the initiator of deviant behaviour; in other words, the deviance is created by societal reaction alone;
2 the impulse towards deviant activities is regarded as ubiquitous and widespread in society; in other words, all people would be deviant if there were not good reasons to be otherwise.

The first proposition is one frequently used by critics for the purpose of attack, but I do not think any labelling theorist would endorse it (cf. Schur, 1971, p. 5; Rock, 1973a, p. 66). Yet despite the fact that no labeling theorist seems to espouse the 'label creates behaviour' view, it is very often developed by critics. [...]

Lemert, Becker and Schur have all denied that careers necessarily start with societal reactions, although it remains unclear where, according to their argument, careers do commence (cf. Stebbins, 1971).

It is, I think, gross misreading of the interactionist version of labelling theory to impute the initiation of deviant careers to labelling. It is also a misreading to believe that labelling can only be evidenced by direct formal labelling. While, however, the critics' first attack on labelling theory's account of initial motivation can be faulted because no labellist would argue that position, the butt of the second criticism can certainly be evidenced in labellist writings.

This proposition is built right into the very heart of Becker's account. As Becker says: 'There is no reason to assume that only those who finally commit a deviant act actually show the impulse to do so. It is much more likely that most people experience deviant impulses frequently' (Becker, 1963, p. 26). [...]

While it may be true that in some parts of his writing Becker seems to imply a randomness of initial motivations towards deviance, I do not think this should be seen as a necessary feature of labelling theory. [...]

In sum I do not find the criticisms of labelling theory, on the ground of its neglect of initial motivation, very convincing, since there is no reason of internal consistency why it should address itself to the problem of initial motives. However; (a) in practice, labelling theorists have often implicitly addressed themselves to these problems in the past, and these theories do need critical examination and elaboration; (b) some researchers (though not necessarily labelling theorists) need to focus more directly upon the possible range of links between initial motives and labels (cf. Turner, 1972).

The 'man on his back' bias: a determinism of societal reactions

Closely linked to the above is the argument that labelling theorists have rescued the deviant from the deterministic constraints of biological, psychological and social forces only to enchain him again in new determinism of societal reactions. Thus Bordua suggests that labelling theory 'assumes an essentially empty organism or at least one with little or no autonomous capacity to determine conduct' (Bordua, 1967, p. 154), and Gouldner comments that it has 'the paradoxical consequence of inviting us to view the deviant as a passive nonentity who is responsible neither for his suffering nor its alleviation – who is more sinned against than sinning' (Gouldner, 1968, p. 106). [...]

I do not think that the 'man–on–his–back' criticism is particularly well–founded.

First, even those studies which *seem* to provide the most crude model of labelling ('no deviance → slam label → deviance') are often firmly within a humanist tradition which sees the labelled person as sensitively playing a part under

the weight of the deviant label. Goffman's mental patients are classic examples of people who have a label which is not internalised thrust upon them (Goffman, 1968). Secondly, there are a number of instances in the labelling literature of members working to fight off labels and neutralize their possible impact. [...] In other words, although there may be instances of 'passive labelling' both in the literature and in the empirical world, there are also many instances where the passive picture of the man on his back simply does apply.

I find this criticism an especially curious one when it is levied against the interactionists' account of labelling, for it is so clearly antithetical to some of the basic tenets of interactionist theory. To take a theory that is sensitive to self, consciousness and intentionality and render it as a new determinism of societal reaction could only be possible if the theory were totally misunderstood in the first place.

The irrelevance of labelling theory to certain problem areas

A third, and much less frequent, argument against labelling theory is raised by those who suggest that it is simply inapplicable to large areas of deviant behaviour. Thus the labelling model is not suitable for the analysis of impulsive crime such as violence, physical deviance such as blindness or mild deviations which involve few overt labellers and low normative and physical visibility, such as premarital intercourse (cf. Reiss, 1970, pp. 80–2). These criticisms are generally based upon crude models of labelling, arguing either that the behaviour exists in the first place, before the application of a societal reaction (whereas presumably in areas where labelling theory is applicable, the behaviour has to be caused by labels), or that the non-existence of specific others to react to the deviance makes the model inappropriate (whereas presumably in areas where labelling theory is applicable, there have to exist specific others, like control agents, who respond to the deviance). These criticisms are based upon misconceptions of labelling theory. No labelling theorist argues that societal reactions bring about the behaviour: only that labels alter the nature, shape and incidence of the experience. And few labelling theorists believe that all the labelling has to flow from specific others: it may also stem from abstract rules and self-reactions. Labelling theory is, in principle, applicable to any area of social life, deviant or non-deviant.

The neglect of power

The most serious objection to the labelling perspective which 'radical' or 'critical' criminologists have raised appears to be that it is insufficiently political. Their arguments, made forcefully in the early 1970s, take two major forms.

First, it is argued that labelling perspectives 'tend to incline sociologists toward focusing on deviance committed by the powerless rather than deviance committed by the powerful' (Thio, 1973, p. 8). Most notably, they concentrate upon the 'sociology of nuts, sluts and perverts' at the expense of 'covert institutional violence' (Liazios, 1972, p. 11). [...]

Secondly, it is argued that while many labelling theorists 'mention the importance of power in labelling people deviant', 'this insight is not developed' (Liazios, 1972, pp. 114–15). In particular, labelling theorists focus upon interpersonal relationships and so-called 'caretaker institutions', but fail to look at the broader economic structures in which deviance emerges. [...]

The consequence of these criticisms can only be viewed positively. It is important that sociologists should study the crimes of the powerful and the political economy of deviance. But while the consequences of the criticisms are sound, the criticisms themselves are weak. Both of the criticisms mentioned above flow from an ignorantly insensitive and dogmatically assertive assumption of the rightness of an absolutist position. The criticisms come close to denying the rightness of any theoretical posture or problematic other than their own. They generally imply that sociologists who look at these 'powerless' areas do so out of blindness, stupidity, ignorance or plain conservatism rather than reason. I will consider these two objections in turn.

First, the issue of a focus on the powerless. At first sight this criticism would seem to have great force. Almost without exception sociologists have focused upon the deviance of the powerless. This granted, however, it still seems to me that 'radical' critics have failed to comprehend four things: the sociology of deviance is *not* criminology; the study of deviance is the study of the powerless; the symbolic interactionist problematic is *not* the Marxist problematic; and the politics of libertarianism *directs* one to work with the victims of state power. These four statements are interconnected, but I will unpack each one separately.

First, the sociology of deviance is *not* criminology. This is a distinction that was much discussed during the mid–sixties, with the advent of the 'new deviance' theories. The rejection of so-called positivistic criminology ushered in the sociology of deviance; but this sociology not only changed the theoretical base for the study of criminals, it also brought in its wake a dramatic restructuring of empirical concerns. Sociologists turned their interests to the world of expressive deviance: to the twilight, marginal worlds of tramps, alcoholics, strippers, dwarfs, prostitutes, drug addicts, nudists; to taxi-cab drivers, the blind, the dying, the physically ill and handicapped, and even to a motley array of problems in everyday life. Whatever these studies had in common, it was very clear that it was not criminology. Of course, some of these same students continued to study crime, but only as one instance of deviance – an uneasy coexistence was established. [...]

Now this is not nit-picking. Of course, I do not want to defend the arbitrary construction of academic boundaries and the creation of sterile demarcation disputes. But is it vital to recognise that the concerns of the sociology of deviance (and I am not here particularly concerned with what the concerns of criminology are – I am no criminologist) send one *necessarily* on a mission to study powerless groups. It is not capricious whimsy but theoretical necessity that leads the sociology of deviance to study powerlessness. And the reason should be so obvious that one wonders how the attacks could ever have been so seriously accepted. *For the study of deviance is the study of devalued groups, and devalued groups are groups which lack status and prestige.* Now, of course, it may be useful – for a full account of deviance – to study 'top dogs' who maintain their prestige in order to understand the mechanisms by which prestige and stigma gets allocated. It is theoretically relevant to understand why it was so long before Nixon was placed in a devalued role. But a sociology of deviance which does not focus centrally on powerless groups is likely to be a very odd sociology of deviance. [...]

Understanding of why the powerless have frequently been the topic of labelling theory lies, finally, in recognition of the liberal-to-libertarian sympathies of many of its practitioners. They have been concerned with the excessive encroachment of technology, bureaucracy and the state upon the personal life – often in its grossest forms (the increasing criminalisation and medicalisation of deviance; the bureaucratisation of the control agencies and the concomitant dehumanisation of the lives of their 'victims'; and the direct application of technology in the service of control), but also in its more subtle forms – daily alienation, meaninglessness, despair and fragmentation (with the concomitant 'theory and practice of resistance to everyday life' (Cohen and Taylor, 1976)). Now, although critical criminologists deride such sympathies, they must at least agree that there is a political rationale behind the study of many powerless groups and that sometimes such concerns have had important practical, political payoffs (decriminalisation, deinstitutionalisation, demedicalisation, deprofessionalisation and the creation of movements concerned with such activities).

In summary, then, the labelling perspective gravitates toward the powerless because (a) the sociology of deviance generally directs them to devalued groups: (b) symbolic interactionism directs them to areas where ambiguity, marginality and precarious identities are readily available for study; and (c) libertarianism directs them to work with groups who are seriously 'up against the state'. Theoretically, sociologically and practically there are good reasons for a concern with the powerless.

The neglect of structure

To accuse symbolic interactionism of neglecting structural concerns is to misread the interactionist enterprise. Every social science theory brings with it its own distinctive problematic and set of concerns, and to accuse theories of failing to deal with what they do not intend to deal with is unfair. A Marxist concern with the mode of production cannot be faulted for failing to deal with an account of heart disease, any more than a Freudian account of the unconscious can be faulted for failing to explain reinforcement contingencies. [...]

The central concern of symbolic interactionism is not with structural matters; it does, however, need to acknowledge such concerns if it is to be a remotely adequate *social* psychology. Any adequate interactionist account will firmly acknowledge that the action of persons does not take place in social limbo, although it is through the actions of persons that any wider social order becomes historically constituted. Further, it is also true that the interactionist generally has a conception of persons wrestling with this wider order. [...] Most of the interactionist accounts of deviance portray

the labelled deviant as someone who employs multiple patterns of resistance (Goffman's mental patients. Cohen and Taylor's prisoners, Matza's delinquents, Humphrey's liberated homosexuals, Scott's blind, etc., etc.), and the wider interactionist portrayals of everyday life in society are overwhelmingly full of themes of the self in struggle with a wider 'abstract', 'homeless', 'paramount Reality' (Zijderveld, 1972; Berger *et al.*, 1974; Cohen and Taylor, 1976).

However, even given that the interactionists acknowledge the existence of a wider social order and demonstrate the persistent struggles of individuals with that wider order, it would be correct to say that they lack a conception of this totality as a *structure*, But they do not neglect the conception of structure out of ignorance (they speak to many of the same concerns as structuralists); rather they deny its importance and relevance for the interactionist task. The notion of structure, they argue, is a reification which does not do justice to the central interactionist concerns of emergence, process and negotiation.

From K. Plummer, 'Misunderstanding labelling perspectives', in D. Downes and P. Rock (eds) Deviant Interpretations *(Oxford: Martin Robertson), 1979, 85–121.*

Note

1 This criticism occurs on both an individual motivation level and on a structural level. Labelling theory does not explain why people commit deviant acts (Sagarin, 1975), or why there exist different 'objective' rates of deviance (cf. Gibbs, 1972). The latter objection has the merit of being a sociological objection but the former is curiously misplaced. Why *should* a sociologist seek to explain individual motives? It is hard to imagine an industrial sociologist seeking the motives of a striker or a political sociologist those of a working–class voter. Yet sociologists of deviance are still supposed to seek such explanations. Paradoxically, the major attempt at a sociology of motivation has actually come from those who are broadly sympathetic to the labelling/interactional approach (cf. Taylor and Taylor, 1972).

References

Becker, H.S. (1963), *Outsiders: Studies in the Sociology of Deviance*; New York, Free Press.

Berger, P., Berger, B. and Kellner, H. (1974), *The Homeless Mind*; Harmondsworth, Penguin.

Bordua, D.J. (1967), 'Recent Trends: Deviant Behavior and Social Control;, The *Annals of the American Academy of Political and Social Science*, 57, 149–63. p. 102–3, 106.

Cohen, S. and Taylor, L. (1976), *Escape Attempts: The Theory and Practice of Resistance to Everyday Life*; London, Allen Lane.

Davis, N.J. (1972), 'Labelling Theory in Deviance Research', *Sociological Quarterly*, 13, 4, 447–74. pp. 89, 102–3.

Gibbs, J. (1966), 'Conception of Deviant Behavior: The Old and the New', *Pacific Sociological Review*, 8, 1, 9–14 pp. 96, 103, 119.

Goffman, E. (1968), *Asylums*; Harmondsworth, Penguin.

Gouldner. A. (1968), 'The Sociologist as Partisan: Sociology and the Welfare State', *American Sociologist*, 103–16. pp. 4, 5, 59, 89, 106.

Liazios. A. (1972), 'The Poverty of the Sociology of Deviance: Nuts, Sluts and Perverts', *Social Problems*, 20, No 1, 103–19. pp. 97, 100, 108.

Mankoff, M. (1971), 'Societal Reaction and Career Deviance: A Critical Analysis', *Sociological Quarterly*, 12, Spring, 204–18. pp. 89, 100, 103–4.

Reiss, I.L. (1970), 'Premarital Sex as Deviant Behavior', *American Sociological Review*, 35, l,78–87 pp. 102, 107.

Rock, P. (1973a), *Deviant Behaviour*; London, Hutchinson.

Schur, E. (1971), *Labelling Deviant Behaviour: Its Sociological Implications*; London, Harper and Row.

Stebbins, R.(1971), *Commitment to Deviance: The Non–Professional Criminal in the Community*; Westport, Conn., Greenwood Press.

Taylor, I., Walton, P. and Young, J. (1973a), *The New Criminology: For a Social Theory of Deviance*; London, Routledge and Kegan Paul.

Thio, A. (1973), 'Class Bias in the Sociology of Deviance', *American Sociologist*, 8, 1, 1–12 pp. 100, 108.

Turner, R. (1972), 'Deviance Avowal as Neutralisation of Commitment', *Social Problems*, 19(3), 308–21.pp. 90, 106, 118.

Zijderveld, A.C. (1972), *The Abstract Society: A Cultural Analysis of Our Time*; Harmondsworth, Penguin.

10.5 The social reaction against drugtaking
Jock Young

The present solution

The individual, because of problems which he is unable to resolve via culturally approved ways, adopts illicit drug-taking as a solution. Now the way society, or, to be specific, significant and powerful groups within society, reacts to this initial deviance determines the nature of the environment within which the drug user must survive. Every solution creates its own problems, and new difficulties arise because of social reaction and contradictions within the emerging culture itself, which must in their turn be solved.

It is not a question merely of the forces of social order acting against the drug user and his being buffeted once and for all by this reaction. The relationship between society and the deviant is more complex than this. It is a tightknit interaction process which can most easily be understood in terms of a myriad of changes on the part of both society and the drug user. To take, for example, the relationship between the community and the bohemian marihuana smoker:

1 A group of young people face a problem of anomie (i.e., their aspirations cannot be realized in a culturally approved manner).

2 They begin, therefore, to evolve a bohemian culture in order to solve their problem.

3   Marihuana smoking is chosen as a vehicle for achieving the ends of this new subculture.

4   Significant groups in the wider community face the problem of controlling undesirable behaviour. That is, behaviour which either threatens their direct interests or offends their moral code.

5   They perceive the bohemian subculture as just such a threat and attempt to solve this problem by, first, creating support through the mass media and personal contact and, then, by pressurizing the police and courts into taking action against marihuana use amongst bohemians.

6   The social reaction against the marihuana user creates new problems for the group.

7   The group adapts and changes in an attempt to solve these problems.

8   The community reacts against the slightly changed group.

9   This either increases or decreases the problems of the group and they change and adapt once more.

10 The community reacts against the new changes and so on. [See Table 10.5.1]

Now one of the most common sequences of events in such a process is what has been termed deviancy amplification, the major exponent of which is the criminologist Leslie Wilkins. This is where the social reaction against the initial deviancy of a group serves to increase this deviance; as a result, social reaction increases even further, the group becomes more deviant, society acts increasingly strongly against it, and a spiral of deviancy amplification occurs.[1] There are four mechanisms by which such a process can come about. The social reaction against the deviant can progressively increase his problems and therefore demand even more deviant solutions than before. Thus, young people may form bohemian groups because of the meaninglessness and boredom of conventional jobs. After a period of dropout, however, they will find it even more difficult than before to obtain passably interesting work. For their aspirations will have risen and their possibilities declined. They are 'beatniks' with bad work

records, whom no one will employ. In terms of drug use this increase in anomie may lead to experimentation with drugs other than marihuana in order to solve their rising problems and perhaps eventual escalation to heroin.[2]

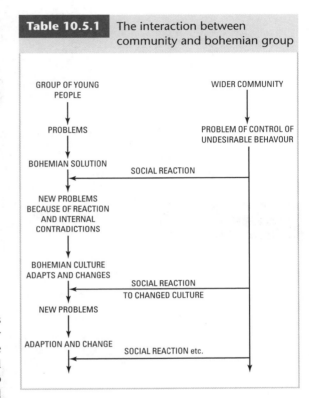

Table 10.5.1	The interaction between community and bohemian group

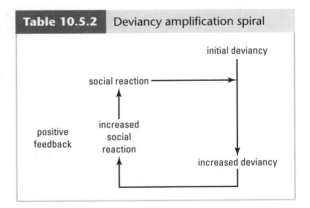

Table 10.5.2	Deviancy amplification spiral

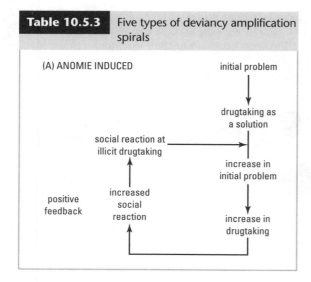

Table 10.5.3   Five types of deviancy amplification spirals

(A) ANOMIE INDUCED

placate.[3] W. and J. McCord[4] in their classic study on alcoholism invoke a similar process to this, suggesting that drinking is often engaged upon in order to buttress feelings of masculinity but that constant use serves to undermine the two criteria of male proficiency: marriage and occupation. This leads to a vicious circle where the alcoholic attempts to drown his own inadequacy with the very substance that is making him more inadequate.

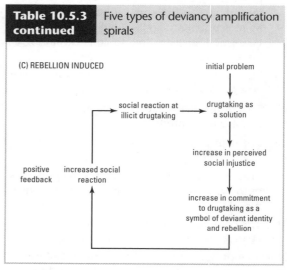

Table 10.5.3 continued   Five types of deviancy amplification spirals

(C) REBELLION INDUCED

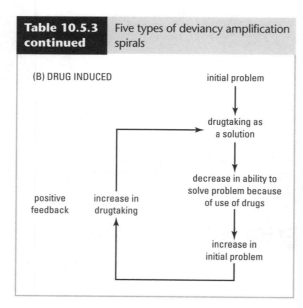

Table 10.5.3 continued   Five types of deviancy amplification spirals

(B) DRUG INDUCED

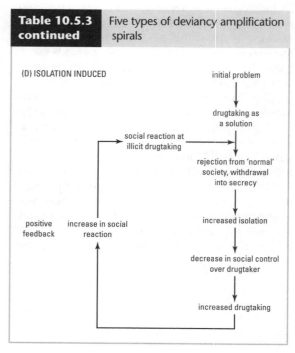

Table 10.5.3 continued   Five types of deviancy amplification spirals

(D) ISOLATION INDUCED

Drugtaking is a peculiar form of deviancy, in that the activity itself may make it impossible for the individual to re-enter normal society, it is not merely the social reaction against him as a drugtaker. Thus the alcoholic finds that the constant high concentration of alcohol in his bloodstream prohibits his engagement in work where any high degree of conscientiousness and regularity is demanded. His sexual relations with his wife will also suffer. Now, if either his work or marriage was the initial problem which sparked off his heavy drinking, then alcohol may well be a false solution in that it merely aggravates what it was used to

Table 10.5.3 continued   Five types of deviancy amplified spirals

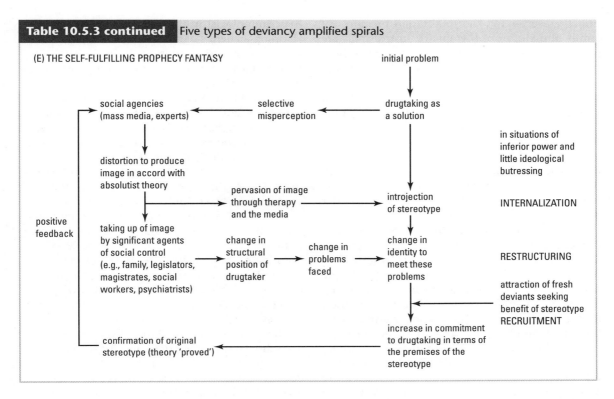

(E) THE SELF-FULFILLING PROPHECY FANTASY

Social reaction against illicit drug use can merely serve to inspire the drugtaker with a sense of gross social injustice. This happens in the case of bohemian marihuana use where the drug is perceived as innocuous, and police action as uninformed and predatory. The drug comes to be taken subsequently not only for its effects per se but as a symbol of righteous protest. Such commitment to marihuana merely serves to increase public alarm and an amplification of drug use occurs.[5]

The fourth type of deviancy amplification spiral is the one utilized by Leslie Wilkins.[6] He notes that when a society defines a group of people as deviant, it tends to react against them so as to isolate and alienate them from the company of 'normal' people. In this situation of isolation the deviant is not under the immediate control of the 'normal'. He is able to develop his own norms and values unimpeded, and, when this occurs, elicits even greater reaction from society with consequent increases in isolation and deviancy in an amplifying spiral.[7] Such a situation is, of course, a pre-condition rather than a cause of further deviancy: it allows the possibility of increased drug-taking, it does not necessitate it.

The last spiral is the self-fulfilling prophecy. Here significant social agencies, such as schools of psychiatry or the mass media, misperceive the nature of a specific form of drugtaking. They construct an image of it, hewn and distorted to fit their theoretical preconceptions. We have discussed the typical configuration of such absolutist premises in the last chapter. When these agencies have considerable prestige, in the sense of their opinions being accepted as reasonably accurate, and power, in the form of ability to influence legislators, the police, magistrates and therapeutic personnel, these images can have self-fulfilling effects. For if there is an imbalance of power, and the illicit group is unable to withstand the social and ideological onslaughts against it, its behaviour and interpretation of itself can be radically altered. There are three processes which can occur here: *internalization*, *restructuring* and *recruitment*.

The isolated drugtaker or culturally dependent group may have such insufficient desire or ability to create counter-definitions of themselves that they end up by *internalizing* the prevailing stereotypes. The housewife who finds herself grossly dependent on barbiturates will turn to her doctor – for want of other alternatives – to find an explanation for her own actions. But society cannot only interpret the actions of others: it can also change these actions by *restructuring* the social situations that individuals find themselves in. The totalitarian pressures of family and kin, or of therapeutic institutions, are particularly adept at achieving such a metamorphosis. The wife who treats her heavy-drinking husband as 'inadequate' may squeeze him into an 'alcoholic' role. The mental hospital which shears the heroin user of all autonomy will end up creating infantile behaviour similar to the therapeutic conception of the 'addict'. Finally, the stereotypes may reach such a degree of public currency that individuals who fit the descriptions are *recruited* into drug use. In all these instances the *fantasy* stereotypes of the powerful and the *reality* of the illicit drug user become identical.

Each of the five amplification processes acts differently on the opportunities, abilities and desires of the drugtaker. Anomie acts by restricting his opportunities to conform, drug use by reducing his ability to conform, and rebellion by removing his desire to conform. Isolation is a pre-condition for the development of deviant opportunities, abilities and motivations and the self-fulfilling prophecy occurs where opportunities are forcefully restricted and the individual's identity, and with it his notions of both his desires and abilities, are radically altered in a deviant direction. As to their theoretical status, amplification models are typical sequences of events which state that in such and such conditions A will be followed by B, C, D, E, etc., and which link the stages in terms of established generalizations derived from the sociology of deviant behaviour, e.g., anomie leads to deviant behaviour, or when groups are ideologically and socially weak they will take their identities from powerful surrounding groups. The major advantage of such models is that they do not limit themselves to a notion of linear causality but stress the mutual interaction and feedback between relevant variables. Thus, deviant behaviour does not cause social reaction; rather both increase with increments in each other. A common and misplaced criticism of the deviancy amplification approach is that it makes increased deviancy seem inevitable. This is widely off the mark, however, for by showing in what conditions, in terms of which principles, amplification occurs, they illustrate inevitably the circumstances in which the reverse process is generated. Thus, if society, instead of reacting to increase the anomie of the drugtaker, provides (for example) interesting and remunerative jobs, the individual's problems will be on the way to being solved and a process of deviancy de-escalation will take place. It is only the interest of

the criminologist in the 'serious' deviant, and the alarming tendency of modern societies to label permanently offenders after a certain threshold has been reached, which has led to the primary focus on amplification processes.

The different modes of amplification occur to varying extents in different types of drugtaking: it is of prime importance that such processes are separated and understood. It should not be thought, however, that deviant drugtaking groups are, so to speak, pinballs inevitably propelled in an increasingly deviant direction, nor that social agencies of control are like cushions of a machine that will inevitably reflex into action, phased to each minutiae of deviance. To view human action in such a light would be to reduce it to the realm of the inanimate, the non-human. As David Matza has forcefully argued in *Becoming Deviant*, the human condition is characterized by the ability of people to stand outside of, to exist apart from, the circumstances which impinge upon them: 'A subject actively addresses or encounters his circumstances; accordingly, his distinctive capacity is to reshape, strive towards creating and actually *transcend* circumstances.'[8] The drugtaking group creates its own circumstances to the extent that it interprets and makes meaningful the reactions of society against it. There are three possible attitudes of the taker of illicit drugs towards social reaction. He can neutralize his position by insisting that the drug is in fact innocuous; that it is compatible with respectable values and ought to be legalized. He therefore interprets repressive measures as being due to ignorance on the part of the authorities and actively avoids deviancy amplification by identifying with normal society as much as possible. In particular, he actively rejects attempts at isolation, holds his drug use at a level which does not interfere with 'normal' behaviour, and disdains the images purveyed by experts and the media. He avoids anomie by compartmentalizing his deviancy in the secrecy of his leisure time with a close circle of friends. His position is not that of the rebel but that of the reformer. Thus all five modes of amplification are mollified. An example of such a position would be the growing number of young middle-class professionals who smoke marihuana and hold respectable jobs.

In contrast, the *ideological* drug user insists that attempts to suppress the use of his particular drug is a significant indicator of the essentially repressive nature of society. The drug represents for him an alternative way of life; legalization, then, is irrelevant, for it is the deviant culture surrounding the drug which is all important. He is especially prone to deviancy amplification, courting rather than regretting the process. Rebellion then is the most important mode of amplification but other mechanisms also operate. Anomie is inevitably raised by virtue of his stance, the cult erected around the drug impairs his ability to act normally, and isolation into deviant communities lessens the impact of conventional forces of social control. The images held by the wider society are, however, scorned and self-fulfilling prophecies occur only if the culture is weak and the impact of social control especially overriding.

The *sick* drugtaker we have discussed in detail already; he believes the drug to be dangerous and its use contrary to the values of the wider society, which he himself upholds. His position in terms of deviancy amplification is interesting in that he is rejected from society and then held at a distance, ossified into a position which allows neither re-entry nor escape. In the therapeutic situation he is told that either he has deep-rooted personality problems for which he uses drugs as a solution, or he has been infected by the virus of addiction. I have argued that this expert estimation of the problem is often deluded. Its consequences, however, are far from illusory. His aspirations from the social world are regarded as mere surface manifestations of the underlying problem. He is told that he must cure himself; not attempt to change the social structure that he finds himself in. Anomie is therefore successfully mystified and therapeutic attempts are made to reduce it to zero. Rebellion is regarded as misguided and is similarly placated. Neither anomie nor rebellion therefore play a significant role in amplification. Drug-induced amplification does, however, for the sick role emphasizes the individual's inability to control his own actions. This results in an increase in drug use which lowers his actual ability to control his actions, confirming his notions of himself; and entering a spiral similar to Type B in Table 10.5.3. The sick drug user is not, however, allowed to deviate beyond certain limits: he is maintained within the parameters of the current stereotype. This is achieved usually within a hospital or treatment centre, buttressed by the ready acceptance of the medical metaphor by family and friends. It is thus in terms of self-fulfilment, underscored by drug-induced amplification and facilitated by clinical isolation, that the social forces impinging on the sick drug user must be understood.

From J. Young, The Drugtakers (*London: Paladin*), *1971, pp. 107–119.*

Notes

1 See Table 10.5.2.
2 See Type A in Table 10.5.3.
3 Type B in Table 10.5.3.
4 W. and J. McCord, *Origins of Alcoholism*, Stanford University Press, Stanford, 1960.
5 See Type C in Table 10.5.3.
6 L. Wilkins, 'Some Sociological Factors in Drug Addiction Control', in *Narcotics*, D. Wilner and G. Kassebaum (ed.), McGraw-Hill, New York, 1965.
7 See Type D in Table 10.5.3.
8 D. Matza, *Becoming Deviant*, Prentice-Hall, New Jersey, 1969, p. 93.

11

Control theories

11.1 Techniques of neutralization: a theory of delinquency
Gresham M. Sykes and David Matza   234

11.2 A control theory of delinquency
Travis Hirschi   236

11.3 A general theory of crime
Michael R. Gottfredson and Travis Hirschi   241

11.4 Charles Tittle's control balance and criminological theory
John Braithwaite   246

Introduction

KEY CONCEPTS control-balance theory; control ratios; immediate gratification; self-control; social bond theory; techniques of neutralization

Control theories, of various sorts, are not only central to criminological thinking, they permeate everyday conversations and assumptions about crime and its control. Control theories differ from much of the rest of criminological theory because they pay relatively little attention to the question of the *causes* of crime. Rather, put at its simplest, at the heart of control theories is the assumption that we would all commit crimes if we weren't in some way prevented from doing so. The sources of such inhibition can be external – the presence of laws, police officers, courts and punishments for example – or internal – the fact that we internalize moral prohibitions, i.e. we develop a conscience.

One hugely important body of work that builds on strain theory (see chapter 8) but also informs elements of a particular form of control theory, is Gresham Sykes' and David Matza's theory of 'techniques of neutralization' **(Reading 11.1)** and Matza's subsequent work on delinquency and drift. Sykes and Matza explore some of the ways in which individuals who engage in deviant activity justify and legitimize their behaviour. Their work begins by distancing itself from the assumption made by many previous criminological theorists that deviant behaviour is somehow necessarily a reflection of an attachment to a deviant value system. In fact, for most of their lives young delinquents, for example, are well embedded in the law-abiding world and quite often exhibit guilt or shame when their delinquency is revealed. In fact, they deploy a series of rationalizations, Sykes and Matza argue, that allow them to drift into and out of delinquency, and it is these that they term 'techniques of neutralization'.

There then follow two excerpts, both of which involve the American criminologist Travis Hirschi, but which contain a somewhat different take on control theory. In the first, Hirschi **(Reading 11.2)** outlines his 'social bond theory'. In some respects the starting point is outlined at the end of the excerpt in which Hirschi says: 'The question "Why do they do it?" is simply not the question the theory is designed to answer. The question is, "Why don't we do it?" There is much evidence that we would if we dared.' What Hirschi's theory is trying to explain, therefore, is conformity and he suggests that there are four major types of social bond – attachment, commitment, involvement and belief – that help to explain the typical situation and mindset of the non-deviant.

Some years later, writing with Michael Gottfredson, Hirschi **(Reading 11.3)** outlined a rather different theory – in fact what they referred to as a 'general theory of crime' – though still containing strong elements of control theory (many criminological theories do, as you will discover). At the heart of this theory is the idea of 'self-control' and, more particularly, the suggestion that unless this is instilled early in life then later deviant or delinquent activity is much more likely. Because of the need for early learning of self-control the family plays an important function in this theory, for it is parental failure to instil the necessary attributes in children that leads them to be impulsive, risk-taking and short-sighted. These characteristics are associated with seeking immediate gratification and in having a reduced or limited ability to consider the possible painful or negative consequences of one's actions.

The final excerpt in this chapter is from a review article by John Braithwaite **(Reading 11.4)** in which he assesses Charles Tittle's 'control-balance theory'. He begins by suggesting that it is 'one of the more important theoretical contributions to the sociology of deviance' but indicates that he also has some reservations about it. It is a control theory because at its core is the assumption that too little control, or too much, leads to criminality. As Braithwaite notes, what is intriguing about the theory is that it acknowledges that it can be too much as well as too little control that can conduce to crime. The central idea in the theory is that conformity requires a 'balance' between the amount of control a person is subject to and the amount of control that person can exert on the things around them. When this is out of kilter they are likely to engage – for a variety of reasons – in various forms of misconduct.

Questions for discussion

1. What are the main techniques of neutralization as outlined by Sykes and Matza?

2. What are the implications of Sykes' and Matza's theory for our understanding of 'delinquent values'?

3. Why is the question 'Why don't we do it?' the important one for the control theorist?

4. Outline and explain the four elements of the social bond as described by Hirschi.

5. What are the main elements and characteristics of self-control?

6. In what ways might self-control be related to criminal activity?

7. Using the idea of control-balance, explain how both too *little* and too *much* control can lead to crime.

8. Tittle attempts to link different types of deviance with different levels of control-balance. Why does Braithwaite suggest he would reject this?

11.1 Techniques of neutralization: a theory of delinquency
Gresham M. Sykes and David Matza

In attempting to uncover the roots of juvenile delinquency, the social scientist has long since ceased to search for devils in the mind or stigma of the body. It is now largely agreed that delinquent behavior, like most social behavior, is learned and that it is learned in the process of social interaction.

The classic statement of this position is found in Sutherland's theory of differential association, which asserts that criminal or delinquent behavior involves the learning of (a) techniques of committing crimes and (b) motives, drives, rationalizations, and attitudes favorable to the violation of law.[1] Unfortunately, the specific content of what is learned – as opposed to the process by which it is learned – has received relatively little attention in either theory or research. Perhaps the single strongest school of thought on the nature of this content has centered on the idea of a delinquent sub-culture. The basic characteristic of the delinquent sub-culture, it is argued, is a system of values that represents an inversion of the values held by respectable, law-abiding society. The world of the delinquent is the world of the law-abiding turned upside down and its norms constitute a countervailing force directed against the conforming social order. [...]

The difficulties in viewing delinquent behavior as springing from a set of deviant values and norms – as arising, that is to say, from a situation in which the delinquent defines his delinquency as 'right' – are both empirical and theoretical. [...]

In short the theoretical viewpoint that sees juvenile delinquency as a form of behavior based on the values and norms of a deviant sub-culture in precisely the same way as law-abiding behavior is based on the values and norms of the larger society is open to serious doubt. The fact that the world of the delinquent is embedded in the larger world of those who conform cannot be overlooked nor can the delinquent be equated with an adult thoroughly socialized into an alternative way of life. Instead, the juvenile delinquent would appear to be at least partially committed to the dominant social order in that he frequently exhibits guilt or shame when he violates its proscriptions, accords approval to certain conforming figures, and distinguishes between appropriate and inappropriate targets for his deviance. It is to an explanation for the apparently paradoxical fact of his delinquency that we now turn. [...]

It is our argument that much delinquency is based on what is essentially an unrecognized extension of defenses to crimes, in the form of justifications for deviance that are seen as valid by the delinquent but not by the legal system or society at large.

These justifications are commonly described as rationalizations. They are viewed as following deviant behavior and as protecting the individual from self-blame and the blame of others after the act. But there is also reason to believe that they precede deviant behavior and make deviant behavior possible. [...]

Social controls that serve to check or inhibit deviant motivational patterns are rendered inoperative, and the individual is freed to engage in delinquency without serious damage to his self image. In this sense, the delinquent both has his cake and eats it too, for he remains committed to the dominant normative system and yet so qualifies its imperatives that violations are 'acceptable' if not 'right.' Thus the delinquent represents not a radical opposition to law-abiding society but something more like an apologetic failure, often more sinned against than sinning in his own eyes. We call these justifications of deviant behavior techniques of neutralization. [...] In analyzing these techniques, we have found it convenient to divide them into five major types.

The Denial of Responsibility. In so far as the delinquent can define himself as lacking responsibility for his deviant actions, the disapproval of self or others is sharply reduced in effectiveness as a restraining influence. As Justice Holmes has said, even a dog distinguishes between being stumbled over and being kicked, and modern society is no less careful to draw a line between injuries that are unintentional, i.e., where responsibility is lacking, and those that are intentional. As a technique of neutralization, however, the denial of responsibility extends much further than the claim that deviant acts are an 'accident' or some similar negation of personal accountability. It may also be asserted that delinquent acts are due to forces outside of the individual and beyond his control such as unloving parents, bad companions, or a slum neighborhood. In effect, the delinquent approaches a 'billiard ball' conception of himself in which he sees himself as helplessly propelled into new situations. [...]

The Denial of Injury. A second major technique of neutralization centers on the injury or harm involved in the delinquent act. The criminal law has long made a distinction between crimes which are *mala in se* and *mala prohibita* – that is between acts that are wrong in themselves and acts that are illegal but not immoral – and the delinquent can make the same kind of distinction in evaluating the wrongfulness of his behavior. For the delinquent, however, wrongfulness may turn on the question of whether or not anyone has clearly been hurt by his deviance, and this matter is open to a variety of interpretations. Vandalism, for example, may be defined by the delinquent simply as 'mischief' – after all, it may be claimed, the persons whose property has been destroyed can well afford it. Similarly, auto theft may be viewed as 'borrowing,' and gang fighting may be seen as a private quarrel, an agreed upon duel between two willing parties, and thus of no concern to the community at large. [...]

Just as the link between the individual and his acts may be broken by the denial of responsibility, so may the link between acts and their consequences be broken by the denial of injury. Since society sometimes agrees with the delinquent, e.g., in matters such as truancy, 'pranks,' and so on, it merely reaffirms the idea that the delinquent's neutralization of social controls by means of qualifying the norms is an extension of common practice rather than a gesture of complete opposition.

The Denial of the Victim. Even if the delinquent accepts the responsibility for his deviant actions and is willing to admit that his deviant actions involve an injury or hurt, the moral indignation of self and others may be neutralized by an insistence that the injury is not wrong in light of the circumstances. The injury, it may be claimed, is not really an injury; rather, it is a form of rightful retaliation or punishment. By a subtle alchemy the delinquent moves himself into the position of an avenger and the victim is transformed into a wrong-doer. Assaults on homosexuals or suspected homosexuals, attacks on members of minority groups who are said to have gotten 'out of place,' vandalism as revenge on an unfair teacher or school official, thefts from a 'crooked' store owner – all may be hurts inflicted on a transgressor, in the eyes of the delinquent. [...]

To deny the existence of the victim, then, by transforming him into a person deserving injury is an extreme form of a phenomenon we have mentioned before, namely, the delinquent's recognition of appropriate and inappropriate targets for his delinquent acts. In addition, however, the existence of the victim may be denied for the delinquent, in a somewhat different sense, by the circumstances of the delinquent act itself. Insofar as the victim is physically absent, unknown, or a vague abstraction (as is often the case in delinquent acts committed against property), the awareness of the victim's existence is weakened. Internalized norms and anticipations of the reactions of others must somehow be activated, if they are to serve as guides for behavior; and it is possible that a diminished awareness of the victim plays an important part in determining whether or not this process is set in motion.

The Condemnation of the Condemners. A fourth technique of neutralization would appear to involve a condemnation of the condemners or, as McCorkle and Korn have phrased it, a rejection of the rejectors.[2] The delinquent shifts the focus of attention from his own deviant acts to the motives and behavior of those who disapprove of his violations. His condemners, he may claim, are hypocrites, deviants in disguise, or impelled by personal spite. This orientation toward the conforming world may be of particular importance when it hardens into a bitter cynicism directed against those assigned the task of enforcing or expressing the norms of the dominant society. Police, it may be said, are corrupt, stupid, and brutal. Teachers always show favoritism and parents always 'take it out' on their children. By a slight extension, the rewards of conformity – such as material success – become a matter of pull or luck, thus decreasing still further the stature of those who stand on the side of the law-abiding. The validity of this jaundiced viewpoint is not so important as its function in turning back or deflecting the negative sanctions attached to violations of the norms. The delinquent, in effect, has changed the subject of the conversation in the dialogue between his own deviant impulses and the reactions of others; and by attacking others, the wrongfulness of his own behavior is more easily repressed or lost to view.

The Appeal to Higher Loyalties. Fifth, and last, internal and external social controls may be neutralized by sacrificing the demands of the larger society for the demands of the smaller social groups to which the delinquent belongs such as the sibling pair, the gang, or the friendship clique. It is important to note that the delinquent does not necessarily repudiate the imperatives of the dominant normative system, despite his failure to follow them. Rather, the delinquent may see himself as caught up in a dilemma that must be resolved, unfortunately, at the cost of violating the law. [...]

If the juvenile delinquent frequently resolves his dilemma by insisting that he must 'always help a buddy' or 'never squeal on a friend,' even when it throws him into serious difficulties with the dominant social order, his choice remains familiar to the supposedly law-abiding. The delinquent is unusual, perhaps, in the extent to which he is able to see the fact that he acts in behalf of the smaller social groups to which he belongs as a justification for violations of society's norms, but it is a matter of degree rather than of kind.

'I didn't mean it.' 'I didn't really hurt anybody.' 'They had it coming to them.' 'Everybody's picking on me.' 'I didn't do it for myself.' These slogans or their variants, we hypothesize, prepare the juvenile for delinquent acts. [...]

Techniques of neutralization may not be powerful enough to fully shield the individual from the force of his own internalized values and the reactions of conforming others, for as we have pointed out, juvenile delinquents often appear to suffer from feelings of guilt and shame when called into account for their deviant behavior. And some delinquents may be so isolated from the world of conformity that techniques of neutralization need not be called into play. Nonetheless, we would argue that techniques of neutralization are critical in lessening the effectiveness of social controls and that they lie behind a large share of delinquent behavior.

> *From G.M. Sykes and D. Matza, 'Techniques of neutralization: A theory of delinquency'*, American Sociological Review, *1957, 22: 664–670.*

Notes

1 E.H. Sutherland, *Principles of Criminology*, revised by D.R. Cressey, Chicago: Lippincott, 1955, pp. 77–80.
2 Lloyd W. McCorkle and Richard Korn, 'Resocialization Within Walls,' *The Annals of the American Academy of Political and Social Science*, 293, (May, 1954), pp. 25–93.

11.2 A control theory of delinquency
Travis Hirschi

'The more weakened the groups to which [the individual] belongs, the less he depends on them, the more he consequently depends only on himself and recognizes no other rules of conduct than what are founded on his private interests.'[1]

Control theories assume that delinquent acts result when an individual's bond to society is weak or broken. Since these theories embrace two highly complex concepts, the *bond* of the individual to *society*, it is not surprising that they have at one time or another formed the basis of explanations of most forms of aberrant or unusual behavior. It is also not surprising that control theories have described the elements of the bond to society in many ways, and that they have focused on a variety of units as the point of control. I begin with a classification and description of the elements of the bond to conventional society. I try to show how each of these elements is related to delinquent behavior and how they are related to each other. I then turn to the question of specifying the unit to which the person is presumably more or less tied, and to the question of the adequacy of the motivational force built into the explanation of delinquent behavior.

Elements of the bond

Attachment

Durkheim said it many years ago: 'We are moral beings to the extent that we are social beings.'[2] This may be interpreted to mean that we are moral beings to the extent that we have 'internalized the norms' of society. But what does it mean to say that a person has internalized the norms of society? The norms of society are by definition shared by the members of society. To violate a norm is, therefore, to act contrary to the wishes and expectations of other people. If a person does not care about the wishes and expectations of other people – that is, if he is insensitive to the opinion of others – then he is to that extent not bound by the norms. He is free to deviate.

The essence of internalization of norms, conscience, or superego thus lies in the attachment of the individual to others.[3] This view has several advantages over the concept of internalization. For one, explanations of deviant behavior based on attachment do not beg the question, since the extent to which a person is attached to others can be measured independently of his deviant behavior. Furthermore, change or variation in behavior is explainable in a way that it is not when notions of internalization or superego are used. For example, the divorced man is more likely after divorce to commit a number of deviant acts, such as suicide or forgery. If we explain these acts by reference to the superego (or internal control), we are forced to say that the man 'lost his conscience' when he got a divorce; and, of course, if he remarries, we have to conclude that he gets his conscience back.

Commitment

'Of all passions, that which inclineth men least to break the laws, is fear. Nay, excepting some generous natures, it is the only thing, when there is the appearance of profit or pleasure by breaking the laws, that makes men keep them.'[4] Few would deny that men on occasion obey the rules simply from fear of the consequences. This rational component in conformity we label commitment. What does it mean to say that a person is committed to conformity? In Howard S. Becker's formulation it means the following:

First, the individual is in a position in which his decision with regard to some particular line of action has consequences for other interests and activities not necessarily [directly] related to it. Second, he has placed himself in that position by his own prior actions. A third element is present though so obvious as not to be apparent: the committed person must be aware [of these other interests] and must recognize that his decision in this case will have ramifications beyond it.[5]

The idea, then, is that the person invests time, energy, himself, in a certain line of activity – say, getting an education, building up a business, acquiring a reputation for virtue. When or whenever he considers deviant behavior, he must consider the costs of this deviant behavior, the risk he runs of losing the investment he has made in conventional behavior.

If attachment to others is the sociological counterpart of the superego or conscience, commitment is the counterpart of the ego or common sense. To the person committed to conventional lines of action, risking one to ten years in prison for a ten-dollar holdup is stupidity, because to the committed person the costs and risk obviously exceed ten dollars in value. (To the psychoanalyst, such an act exhibits failure to be governed by the 'reality-principle.') In the sociological control theory, it can be and is generally assumed that the decision to commit a criminal act may well be rationally determined – that the actor's decision was not irrational given the risks and costs he faces. Of course, as Becker points out, if the actor is capable of in some sense calculating the costs of a line of action, he is also capable of calculational errors: ignorance and error return, in the control theory, as possible explanations of deviant behavior.

The concept of commitment assumes that the organization of society is such that the interests of most persons would be endangered if they were to engage in criminal acts. Most people, simply by the process of living in an organized society, acquire goods, reputations, prospects that they do not want to risk losing. These accumulations are society's insurance that they will abide by the rules. Many hypotheses about the antecedents of delinquent behavior are based on this premise. For example, Arthur L. Stinchcombe's hypothesis that 'high school rebellion . . . occurs when future status is not clearly related to present performance'[6] suggests that one is committed to conformity not only by what one has but also by what one hopes to obtain. Thus 'ambition' and/or 'aspiration' play an important role in producing conformity. The person becomes committed to a conventional line of action, and he is therefore committed to conformity.

Most lines of action in a society are of course conventional. The clearest examples are educational and occupational careers. Actions thought to jeopardize one's chances in these areas are presumably avoided. Interestingly enough, even nonconventional commitments may operate to produce conventional conformity. We are told, at least, that boys aspiring to careers in the rackets or professional thievery are judged by their 'honesty' and 'reliability' – traits traditionally in demand among seekers of office boys.[7]

Involvement

Many persons undoubtedly owe a life of virtue to a lack of opportunity to do otherwise. Time and energy are inherently limited: 'Not that I would not, if I could, be both handsome and fat and well dressed, and a great athlete, and make a million a year, be a wit, a bon vivant, and a lady killer, as well as a philosopher, a philanthropist, a statesman, warrior, and African explorer, as well as a 'tone-poet' and saint. But the thing is simply impossible.'[8] The things that William James here says he would like to be or do are all, I suppose, within the realm of conventionality, but if he were to include illicit actions he would still have to eliminate some of them as simply impossible.

Involvement or engrossment in conventional activities is thus often part of a control theory. The assumption, widely shared, is that a person may be simply too busy doing conventional things to find time to engage in deviant behavior. The person involved in conventional activities is tied to appointments, deadlines, working hours, plans, and the like, so the opportunity to commit deviant acts rarely arises. To the extent that he is engrossed in conventional activities, he cannot even think about deviant acts, let alone act out his inclinations.[9]

This line of reasoning is responsible for the stress placed on recreational facilities in many programs to reduce delinquency, for much of the concern with the high school dropout, and for the idea that boys should be drafted into the Army to keep them out of trouble. So obvious and persuasive is the idea that involvement in conventional activities is a major deterrent to delinquency that it was accepted even by Sutherland: 'In the general area of juvenile delinquency it is probable that the most significant difference between juveniles who engage in delinquency and those who do not is that the latter are provided abundant opportunities of a conventional type for satisfying their recreational interests, while the former lack those opportunities or facilities.'[10]

The view that 'idle hands are the devil's workshop' has received more sophisticated treatment in recent sociological writings on delinquency. David Matza and Gresham M. Sykes, for example, suggest that delinquents have the val-

ues of a leisure class, the same values ascribed by Veblen to the leisure class: a search for kicks, disdain of work, a desire for the big score, and acceptance of aggressive toughness as proof of masculinity.[11] Matza and Sykes explain delinquency by reference to this system of values, but they note that adolescents at all class levels are 'to some extent' members of a leisure class, that they 'move in a limbo between earlier parental domination and future integration with the social structure through the bonds of work and marriage.'[12] In the end, then, the leisure of the adolescent produces a set of values, which, in turn, leads to delinquency.

Belief

Unlike the cultural deviance theory, the control theory assumes the existence of a common value system within the society or group whose norms are being violated. If the deviant is committed to a value system different from that of conventional society, there is, within the context of the theory, nothing to explain. The question is, 'Why does a man violate the rules in which he believes?' It is not, 'Why do men differ in their beliefs about what constitutes good and desirable conduct?' The person is assumed to have been socialized (perhaps imperfectly) into the group whose rules he is violating; deviance is not a question of one group imposing its rules on the members of another group. In other words, we not only assume the deviant *has* believed the rules, we assume he believes the rules even as he violates them.

How can a person believe it is wrong to steal at the same time he is stealing? In the strain theory, this is not a difficult problem. (In fact, as suggested in the previous chapter, the strain theory was devised specifically to deal with this question.) The motivation to deviance adduced by the strain theorist is so strong that we can well understand the deviant act even assuming the deviator believes strongly that it is wrong.[13] However, given the control theory's assumptions about motivation, if both the deviant and the nondeviant believe the deviant act is wrong, how do we account for the fact that one commits it and the other does not?

Control theories have taken two approaches to this problem. In one approach, beliefs are treated as mere words that mean little or nothing if the other forms of control are missing. 'Semantic dementia,' the dissociation between rational faculties and emotional control which is said to be characteristic of the psychopath, illustrates this way of handling the problem.[14] In short, beliefs, at least insofar as they are expressed in words, drop out of the picture; since they do not differentiate between deviants and nondeviants, they are in the same class as 'language' or any other characteristic common to all members of the group. Since they represent no real obstacle to the commission of delinquent acts, nothing need be said about how they are handled by those committing such acts. The control theories that do not mention beliefs (or values), and many do not, may be assumed to take this approach to the problem.

The second approach argues that the deviant rationalizes his behavior so that he can at once violate the rule and maintain his belief in it. Donald R. Cressey has advanced this argument with respect to embezzlement;[15] and Sykes and Matza have advanced it with respect to delinquency.[16] In both Cressey's and Sykes and Matza's treatments, these rationalizations (Cressey calls them 'verbalizations,' Sykes and Matza term them 'techniques of neutralization') occur prior to the commission of the deviant act. If the neutralization is successful, the person is free to commit the act(s) in question. Both in Cressey and in Sykes and Matza, the strain that prompts the effort at neutralization also provides the motive force that results in the subsequent deviant act. Their theories are thus, in this sense, strain theories. Neutralization is difficult to handle within the context of a theory that adheres closely to control theory assumptions, because in the control theory there is no special motivational force to account for the neutralization. This difficulty is especially noticeable in Matza's later treatment of this topic, where the motivational component, the 'will to delinquency' appears *after* the moral vacuum has been created by the techniques of neutralization.[17] The question thus becomes: 'Why neutralize?

In attempting to solve a strain theory problem with control theory tools, the control theorist is thus led into a trap. He cannot answer the crucial question. The concept of neutralization assumes the existence of moral obstacles to the commission of deviant acts. In order plausibly to account for a deviant act, it is necessary to generate motivation to deviance that is at least equivalent in force to the resistance provided by these moral obstacles. However, if the moral obstacles are removed, neutralization and special motivation are no longer required. We therefore follow the implicit logic of control theory and remove these moral obstacles by hypothesis. Many persons do not have an attitude of respect toward the rules of society; many persons feel no moral obligation to conform regardless of personal advantage. Insofar as the values and beliefs of these persons are consistent with their feelings, and there should be a tendency toward consistency, neutralization is unnecessary; it has already occurred.

Does this merely push the question back a step and at the same time produce conflict with the assumption of a common value system? I think not. In the first place, we do not assume, as does Cressey, that neutralization occurs in order to make a specific criminal act possible.[18] We do not assume, as do Sykes and Matza, that neutralization occurs to make many delinquent acts possible. We do not assume, in other words, that the person constructs a system of rationalizations in order to justify commission of acts he *wants* to commit. We assume, in contrast, that the beliefs that free a man to commit deviant acts are *unmotivated* in the sense that he does not construct or adopt them in order to facilitate the attainment of illicit ends. In the second place, we do not assume, as does Matza, that 'delinquents concur in the conventional assessment of delinquency.'[19] We assume, in contrast, that there is *variation* in the extent to which people believe they should obey the rules of society, and, furthermore, that the less a person believes he should obey the rules, the more likely he is to violate them.[20]

In chronological order, then, a person's beliefs in the moral validity of norms are, for no teleological reason, weakened. The probability that he will commit delinquent acts is therefore increased. When and if he commits a delinquent act, we may justifiably use the weakness of his beliefs in explaining it, but no special motivation is required to explain either the weakness of his beliefs or, perhaps, his delinquent act.

The keystone of this argument is of course the assumption that there is variation in belief in the moral validity of social rules. This assumption is amenable to direct empirical test and can thus survive at least until its first confrontation with data. For the present, we must return to the idea of a common value system with which this section was begun.

The idea of a common (or, perhaps better, a single) value system is consistent with the fact, or presumption, of variation in the strength of moral beliefs. We have not suggested that delinquency is based on beliefs counter to conventional morality; we have not suggested that delinquents do not believe delinquent acts are wrong. They may well believe these acts are wrong, but the meaning and efficacy of such beliefs are contingent upon other beliefs and, indeed, on the strength of other ties to the conventional order.[21]

Where is the motivation?

The most disconcerting question the control theorist faces goes something like this: 'Yes, but *why* do they do it?' In the good old days, the control theorist could simply strip away the 'veneer of civilization' and expose man's 'animal impulses' for all to see. These impulses appeared to him (and apparently to his audience) to provide a plausible account of the motivation to crime and delinquency. His argument was not that delinquents and criminals alone are animals, but that we are all animals, and thus all naturally capable of committing criminal acts. It took no great study to reveal that children, chickens, and dogs occasionally assault and steal from their fellow creatures; that children, chickens, and dogs also behave for relatively long periods in a perfectly moral manner. Of course the acts of chickens and dogs are not 'assault' or 'theft,' and such behavior is not 'moral'; it is simply the behavior of a chicken or a dog. The chicken stealing corn from his neighbor knows nothing of the moral law; he does not *want* to violate rules; he wants merely to eat corn. The dog maliciously destroying a pillow or feloniously assaulting another dog is the moral equal of the chicken. No motivation to deviance is required to explain his acts. So, too, no special motivation to crime within the human animal was required to explain his criminal acts.

In the end, then, control theory remains what it has always been: a theory in which deviation is not problematic. The question 'Why do they do it?' is simply not the question the theory is designed to answer. The question is, 'Why don't we do it?' There is much evidence that we would if we dared.

> *From T. Hirschi,* Causes of Delinquency *(Berkeley: University of California Press), 1969, pp. 16–34.*

Notes

1 Emile Durkheim, *Suicide*, trans. John A. Spalding and George Simpson (New York: The Free Press, 1951), p. 209.
2 Emile Durkheim, *Moral Education*, trans. Everett K. Wilson and Herman Schnurer (New York: The Free Press, 1961), p. 64.
3 Although attachment alone does not exhaust the meaning of internalization, attachments and beliefs combined would appear to leave only a small residue of 'internal control' not susceptible in principle to direct measurement.
4 Thomas Hobbes, *Leviathan* (Oxford: Basil Blackwell, 1957), p. 195.
5 Howard S. Becker, 'Notes on the Concept of Commitment,' *American Journal of Sociology*, LXVI (1960), 35–36.
6 Arthur L. Stinchcombe, *Rebellion in a High School* (Chicago: Quadrangle, 1964), p. 5.
7 Richard A. Cloward and Lloyd E. Ohlin, *Delinquency and Opportunity* (New York: The Free Press, 1960), p. 147, quoting Edwin H. Sutherland, ed., *The Professional Thief* (Chicago: University of Chicago Press, 1937), pp. 211–213.
8 William James, *Psychology* (Cleveland: World Publishing Co., 1948), p. 186.
9 Few activities appear to be so engrossing that they rule out contemplation of alternative lines of behavior, at least if estimates of the amount of time men spend plotting sexual deviations have any validity.
10 *The Sutherland Papers*, ed. Albert K. Cohen *et al.* (Bloomington: Indiana University Press, 1956), p. 37.
11 David Matza and Gresham M. Sykes, 'Juvenile Delinquency and Subterranean Values,' *American Sociological Review*, XXVI (1961), 712–719.
12 *Ibid.*, p. 718.
13 The starving man stealing the loaf of bread is the image evoked by most strain theories. In this image, the starving man's belief in the wrongness of his act is clearly not something that must be explained away. It can be assumed to be present without causing embarrassment to the explanation.
14 McCord and McCord, *The Psychopath*, pp. 12–15.
15 Donald R. Cressey, *Other People's Money* (New York: The Free Press, 1953).
16 Gresham M. Sykes and David Matza, 'Techniques of Neutralization: A Theory of Delinquency,' *American Sociological Review*, XXII (1957), 664–670.
17 David Matza, *Delinquency and Drift* (New York: Wiley, 1964), pp. 181–191.
18 In asserting that Cressey's assumption is invalid with respect to delinquency, I do not wish to suggest that it is invalid for the question of embezzlement, where the problem faced by the deviator is fairly specific and he can reasonably be assumed to be an upstanding citizen. (Although even here the fact that the embezzler's nonshareable financial problem often results from some sort of hanky-panky suggests that 'verbalizations' may be less necessary than might otherwise be assumed.)
19 *Delinquency and Drift*, p. 43.
20 This assumption is not, I think, contradicted by the evidence presented by Matza against the existence of a delinquent subculture. In comparing the attitudes and actions of delinquents with the picture painted by delinquent subculture theorists, Matza emphasizes – and perhaps exaggerates – the extent to which delinquents are tied to the conventional order. In implicitly

comparing delinquents with a supermoral man, I emphasize – and perhaps exaggerate – the extent to which they are not tied to the conventional order.

21 The position taken here is therefore somewhere between the 'semantic dementia' and the 'neutralization' positions. Assuming variation, the delinquent is, at the extremes, freer than the neutralization argument assumes. Although the possibility of wide discrepancy between what the delinquent professes and what he practices still exists, it is presumably much rarer than is suggested by studies of articulate 'psychopaths?'

11.3 A general theory of crime
Michael R. Gottfredson and Travis Hirschi

Self-control and alternative concepts

Our decision to ascribe stable individual differences in criminal behavior to self-control was made only after considering several alternatives, one of which (criminality) we had used before (Hirschi and Gottfredson 1986). A major consideration was consistency between the classical conception of crime and our conception of the criminal. It seemed unwise to try to integrate a choice theory of crime with a deterministic image of the offender, especially when such integration was unnecessary. In fact the compatibility of the classical view of crime and the idea that people differ in self-control is, in our view, remarkable. As we have seen, classical theory is a theory of social or external control, a theory based on the idea that the costs of crime depend on the individual's current location in or bond to society. What classical theory lacks is an explicit idea of self-control, the idea that people also differ in the extent to which they are vulnerable to the temptations of the moment. Combining the two ideas thus merely recognizes the simultaneous existence of social and individual restraints on behavior.

An obvious alternative is the concept of criminality. The disadvantages of that concept, however, are numerous. First, it connotes causation or determinism, a positive tendency to crime that is contrary to the classical model and, in our view, contrary to the facts. Whereas self-control suggests that people differ in the extent to which they are restrained from criminal acts, criminality suggests that people differ in the extent to which they are compelled to crime. The concept of self-control is thus consistent with the observation that criminals do not require or need crime, and the concept of criminality is inconsistent with this observation. By the same token, the idea of low self-control is

compatible with the observation that criminal acts require no special capabilities, needs, or motivation; they are, in this sense, available to everyone. In contrast, the idea of criminality as a special tendency suggests that criminal acts require special people for their performance and enjoyment. Finally, lack of restraint or low self-control allows almost any deviant, criminal, exciting, or dangerous act; in contrast, the idea of criminality covers only a narrow portion of the apparently diverse acts engaged in by people at one end of the dimension we are now discussing.

The concept of conscience comes closer than criminality to self-control, and is harder to distinguish from it. Unfortunately, that concept has connotations of compulsion (to conformity) not, strictly speaking, consistent with a choice model (or with the operation of conscience). It does not seem to cover the behaviors analogous to crime that appear to be controlled by natural sanctions rather than social or moral sanctions, and in the end it typically refers to how people feel about their acts rather than to the likelihood that they will or will not commit them. Thus accidents and employment instability are not usually seen as produced by failures of conscience, and writers in the conscience tradition do not typically make the connection between moral and prudent behavior. Finally, conscience is used primarily to summarize the results of learning via negative reinforcement, and even those favorably disposed to its use have little more to say about it (see, e.g., Eysenck 1977; Wilson and Herrnstein 1935).

We are now in position to describe the nature of self-control, the individual characteristic relevant to the commission of criminal acts. We assume that the nature of this characteristic can be derived directly from the nature of criminal acts. We thus infer from the nature of crime what people who refrain from criminal acts are like before they reach the age at which crime becomes a logical possibility. We then work back further to the factors producing their restraint, back to the causes of self-control. In our view, lack of self-control does not require crime and can be counteracted by situational conditions or other properties of the individual. At the same time, we suggest that high self-control effectively reduces the possibility of crime – that is, those possessing it will be substantially less likely at all periods of life to engage in criminal acts.

The elements of self-control

Criminal acts provide *immediate* gratification of desires. A major characteristic of people with low self-control is therefore a tendency to respond to tangible stimuli in the immediate environment, to have a concrete 'here and now' orientation. People with high self-control, in contrast, tend to defer gratification.

Criminal acts provide *easy or simple* gratification of desires. They provide money without work, sex without courtship, revenge without court delays. People lacking self-control also tend to lack diligence, tenacity, or persistence in a course of action.

Criminal acts are *exciting, risky, or thrilling*. They involve stealth, danger, speed, agility, deception, or power. People lacking self-control therefore tend to be adventuresome, active, and physical. Those with high levels of self-control tend to be cautious, cognitive, and verbal.

Crimes provide *few or meager long-term benefits*. They are not equivalent to a job or a career. On the contrary, crimes interfere with long-term commitments to jobs, marriages, family, or friends. People with low self-control thus tend to have unstable marriages, friendships, and job profiles. They tend to be little interested in and unprepared for long-term occupational pursuits.

Crimes require *little skill or planning*. The cognitive requirements for most crimes are minimal. It follows that people lacking self-control need not possess or value cognitive or academic skills. The manual skills required for most crimes are minimal. It follows that people lacking self-control need not possess manual skills that require training or apprenticeship.

Crimes often result *in pain or discomfort for the victim*. Property is lost, bodies are injured, privacy is violated, trust is broken. It follows that people with low self-control tend to be self-centered, indifferent, or insensitive to the suffering and needs of others. It does not follow, however, that people with low self-control are routinely unkind or antisocial. On the contrary, they may discover the immediate and easy rewards of charm and generosity.

Recall that crime involves the pursuit of immediate pleasure. It follows that people lacking self-control will also tend to pursue immediate pleasures that are *not* criminal: they will tend to smoke, drink, use drugs, gamble, have children out of wedlock, and engage in illicit sex.

Crimes require the interaction of an offender with people or their property. It does not follow that people lacking self-control will tend to be gregarious or social. However, it does follow that, other things being equal, gregarious or social people are more likely to be involved in criminal acts.

The major benefit of many crimes is not pleasure but relief from momentary irritation. The irritation caused by a crying child is often the stimulus for physical abuse. That caused by a taunting stranger in a bar is often the stimulus for aggravated assault. It follows that people with low self-control tend to have minimal tolerance for frustration and little ability to respond to conflict through verbal rather than physical means.

Crimes involve the risk of violence and physical injury, of pain and suffering on the part of the offender. It does not follow that people with low self-control will tend to be tolerant of physical pain or to be indifferent to physical discomfort. It does follow that people tolerant of physical pain or indifferent to physical discomfort will be more likely to engage in criminal acts whatever their level of self-control.

The risk of criminal penalty for any given criminal act is small, but this depends in part on the circumstances of the offense. Thus, for example, not all joyrides by teenagers are equally likely to result in arrest. A car stolen from a neighbor and returned unharmed before he notices its absence is less likely to result in official notice than is a car stolen from a shopping center parking lot and abandoned at the convenience of the offender. Drinking alcohol stolen from parents and consumed in the family garage is less likely to receive official notice than drinking in the parking lot outside a concert hall. It follows that offenses differ in their validity as measures of self-control: those offenses with large risk of public awareness are better measures than those with little risk.

In sum, people who lack self-control will tend to be impulsive, insensitive, physical (as opposed to mental), risk-taking, shortsighted, and nonverbal, and they will tend therefore to engage in criminal and analogous acts. Since these traits can be identified prior to the age of responsibility for crime, since there is considerable tendency for these traits to come together in the same people, and since the traits tend to persist through life, it seems reasonable to consider them as comprising a stable construct useful in the explanation of crime.

The many manifestations of low self-control

Our image of the 'offender' suggests that crime is not an automatic or necessary consequence of low self-control. It suggests that many noncriminal acts analogous to crime (such as accidents, smoking, and alcohol use) are also manifestations of low self-control. Our image therefore implies that no specific act, type of crime, or form of deviance is uniquely required by the absence of self-control.

Because both crime and analogous behaviors stem from low self-control (that is, both are manifestations of low self-control), they will all be engaged in at a relatively high rate by people with low self-control. Within the domain of crime, then, there will be much versatility among offenders in the criminal acts in which they engage.

Research on the versatility of deviant acts supports these predictions in the strongest possible way. The variety of manifestations of low self-control is immense. In spite of years of tireless research motivated by a belief in specialization, no credible evidence of specialization has been reported. In fact, the evidence of offender versatility is overwhelming (Hirschi 1969; Hindelang 1971; Wolfgang, Figlio, and Sellin 1972; Petersilia 1980; Hindelang, Hirschi, and Weis 1981; Rojek and Erickson 1982; Klein 1984).

By versatility we mean that offenders commit a wide variety of criminal acts, with no strong inclination to pursue a specific criminal act or a pattern of criminal acts to the exclusion of others.

The causes of self-control

We know better what deficiencies in self-control lead to than where they come from. One thing is, however, clear: low self-control is not produced by training, tutelage, or socialization. As a matter of fact, all of the characteristics associated with low self-control tend to show themselves in the absence of nurturance, discipline, or training. Given the classical appreciation of the causes of human behavior, the implications of this fact are straightforward: the causes of low self-control are negative rather than positive; self-control is unlikely in the absence of effort, intended or unintended, to create it. (This assumption separates the present theory from most modern theories of crime, where the offender is automatically seen as a product of positive forces, a creature of learning, particular pressures, or specific defect. We will return to this comparison once our theory has been fully explicated.)

At this point it would be easy to construct a theory of crime causation, according to which characteristics of potential offenders lead them ineluctably to the commission of criminal acts. Our task at this point would simply be to identify the likely sources of impulsiveness, intelligence, risk-taking, and the like. But to do so would be to follow the path that has proven so unproductive in the past, the path according to which criminals commit crimes irrespective of the characteristics of the setting or situation.

We can avoid this pitfall by recalling the elements inherent in the decision to commit a criminal act. The object of the offense is clearly pleasurable, and universally so. Engaging in the act, however, entails some risk of social, legal, and/or natural sanctions. Whereas the pleasure attained by the act is direct, obvious, and immediate, the pains risked by it are not obvious, or direct, and are in any event at greater remove from it. It follows that, though there will be little variability among people in their ability to see the pleasures of crime, there will be considerable variability in their ability to calculate potential pains. But the problem goes further than this: whereas the pleasures of crime are reasonably equally distributed over the population, this is not true for the pains. Everyone appreciates money; not everyone dreads parental anger or disappointment upon learning that the money was stolen.

So, the dimensions of self-control are, in our view, factors affecting calculation of the consequences of one's acts. The impulsive or shortsighted person fails to consider the negative or painful consequences of his acts; the insensitive person has fewer negative consequences to consider; the less intelligent person also has fewer negative consequences to consider (has less to lose).

No known social group, whether criminal or noncriminal, actively or purposefully attempts to reduce the self-control of its members. Social life is not enhanced by low self-control and its consequences. On the contrary, the exhibition of these tendencies undermines harmonious group relations and the ability to achieve collective ends. These facts explicitly deny that a tendency to crime is a product of socialization, culture, or positive learning of any sort.

The traits composing low self-control are also not conducive to the achievement of long-term individual goals. On the contrary, they impede educational and occupational achievement, destroy interpersonal relations, and undermine physical health and economic well-being. Such facts explicitly deny the notion that criminality is an alternative route to the goals otherwise obtainable through legitimate avenues. It follows that people who care about the interpersonal skill, educational and occupational achievement, and physical and economic well-being of those in their care will seek to rid them of these traits.

Two general sources of variation are immediately apparent in this scheme. The first is the variation among children in the degree to which they manifest such traits to begin with. The second is the variation among caretakers in the degree to which they recognize low self-control and its consequences and the degree to which they are willing and able to correct it. Obviously, therefore, even at this threshold level the sources of low self-control are complex.

There is good evidence that some of the traits predicting subsequent involvement in crime appear as early as they can be reliably measured, including low intelligence, high activity level, physical strength, and adventuresomeness (Glueck and Glueck 1950; West and Farrington 1973). The evidence suggests that the connection between these traits and commission of criminal acts ranges from weak to moderate. Obviously, we do not suggest that people are born criminals, inherit a gene for criminality, or anything of the sort. In fact, we explicitly deny such notions. What we do suggest is that individual differences may have an impact on the prospects for effective socialization (or adequate control). Effective socialization is, however, always possible whatever the configuration of individual traits.

Other traits affecting crime appear later and seem to be largely products of ineffective or incomplete socialization. For example, differences in impulsivity and insensitivity become noticeable later in childhood when they are no longer common to all children. The ability and willingness to delay immediate gratification for some larger purpose may therefore be assumed to be a consequence of training. Much parental action is in fact geared toward suppression of impulsive behavior, toward making the child consider the long-range consequences of acts. Consistent sensitivity to the needs and feelings of others may also be assumed to be a consequence of training. Indeed, much parental behavior is directed toward teaching the child about the rights and feelings of others, and of how these rights and feelings ought to constrain the child's behavior. All of these points focus our attention on child-rearing.

Child-rearing and self-control: the family

The major 'cause' of low self-control thus appears to be ineffective child-rearing. Put in positive terms, several conditions appear necessary to produce a socialized child. Perhaps the place to begin looking for these conditions is the research literature on the relation between family conditions and delinquency. This research (e.g., Glueck and Glueck 1950; McCord and McCord 1959) has examined the connection between many family factors and delinquency. It reports that discipline, supervision, and affection tend to be missing in the homes of delinquents, that the behavior of the parents is often 'poor' (e.g., excessive drinking and poor supervision (Glueck and Glueck 1950: 110–11)); and that the parents of delinquents are unusually likely to have criminal records themselves. Indeed, according to Michael Rutter and Henri Giller, 'of the parental characteristics associated with delinquency, criminality is the most striking and most consistent' (1984: 182).

Such information undermines the many explanations of crime that ignore the family, but in this form it does not represent much of an advance over the belief of the general public (and those who deal with offenders in the criminal justice system) that 'defective upbringing' or 'neglect' in the home is the primary cause of crime.

To put these standard research findings in perspective, we think it necessary to define the conditions necessary for adequate childrearing to occur. The minimum conditions seem to be these: in order to teach the child self-control, someone must (1) monitor the child's behavior; (2) recognize deviant behavior when it occurs; and (3) punish such behavior. This seems simple and obvious enough. All that is required to activate the system is affection for or investment in the child. The person who cares for the child will watch his behavior, see him doing things he should not do, and correct him. The result may be a child more capable of delaying gratification, more sensitive to the interests and desires of others, more independent, more willing to accept restraints on his activity, and more unlikely to use force or violence to attain his ends.

When we seek the causes of low self-control, we ask where this system can go wrong. Obviously, parents do not prefer their children to be unsocialized in the terms described. We can therefore rule out in advance the possibility of positive socialization to unsocialized behavior (as cultural or subcultural deviance theories suggest). Still, the system can go wrong at any one of four places. First, the parents may not care for the child (in which case none of the other conditions would be met); second, the parents, even if they care, may not have the time or energy to monitor the child's behavior; third, the parents, even if they care *and* monitor, may not see anything wrong with the child's behavior; finally, even if everything else is in place, the parents may not have the inclination or the means to punish the child. So, what may appear at first glance to be nonproblematic turns out to be problematic indeed. Many things can go wrong. According to much research in crime and delinquency, in the homes of problem children many things have gone wrong: 'Parents of stealers do not track ([they] do not interpret stealing ... as 'deviant'); they do not punish; and they do not care' (Patterson 1980: 88–89; see also Glueck and Glueck 1950; McCord and McCord 1959; West and Farrington 1977).

From M.R. Gottfredson and T. Hirschi, A General Theory of Crime *(Stanford, CA: Stanford University Press), 1990, pp. 87–91.*

References

Eysenck, Hans. 1977, *Crime and Personality*. Revised ed. London: Paladin.

Glueck, Sheldon, and Eleanor Glueck. 1950. *Unraveling Juvenile Delinquency*. Cambridge, Mass.: Harvard University Press.

Hindelang, Michael J. 1971. 'Age, Sex, and the Versatility of Delinquent Involvements.' *Social Problems*, 18: 522–35.

Hindelang, Michael, Travis Hirschi, and Joseph Weis. 1981. *Measuring Delinquency*. Beverly Hills, Calif.: Sage.

Hirschi, Travis. 1969. *Causes of Delinquency*. Berkeley: University of California Press.

Hirschi, Travis, and Michael Gottfredson. 1983. 'Age and the Explanation of Crime.' *American Journal of Sociology*, 89: 552–84.

Klein, Malcolm. 1984. 'Offense Specialization and Versatility Among Juveniles.' *British Journal of Criminology*, 24: 185–94.

McCord, William, and Joan McCord. 1959. *Origins of Crime: A New Evaluation of the Cambridge-Somerville Study*. New York: Columbia University Press.

Patterson, Gerald R. 1980. 'Children Who Steal.' In *Understanding Crime*, edited by T. Hirschi and M. Gottfredson (pp. 73–90). Beverly Hills, Calif.: Sage.

Petersilia, Joan. 1980. 'Criminal Career Research: A Review of Recent Evidence.' In *Crime and Justice: An Annual Review of Research*, vol. 2, edited by M. Tonry and N. Morris (pp. 321–79). Chicago: University of Chicago Press.

Rojek, Dean, and Maynard Erickson. 1982. 'Delinquent Careers.' *Criminology*, 20: 5–28.

Rutter, Michael, and Henri Giller. 1984. *Juvenile Delinquency*: Trends and Perspectives. New York: Guilford.

West, Donald, and David Farrington. 1973. *Who Becomes Delinquent?* London: Heinemann.

West, Donald, and David Farrington. 1977. *The Delinquent Way of Life*. London: Heinemann.

Wilson, James Q., and Richard Herrnstein. 1985. *Crime and Human Nature*. New York: Simon and Schuster.

Wolfgang, Marvin, Robert Figlio, and Thorsten Sellin. 1972. *Delinquency in a Birth Cohort*. Chicago: University of Chicago Press.

11.4 Charles Tittle's control balance and criminological theory John Braithwaite

In *Control Balance: Toward a General Theory of Deviance*, Charles Tittle (1995) has given us one of the more important theoretical contributions to the sociology of deviance. Tittle advances in a bold way Jack Gibbs' (1989) idea that control should become the central organizing concept of the discipline of sociology. The objectives of this article are to show why the theory of control balance is a major advance, yet to show how it could and should be simplified into a theory that has at once more explanatory power and greater parsimony.

The importance of Tittle's contribution

The variable to be explained in Tittle's theory is 'deviance' defined as 'any behavior that the majority of a given group regards as unacceptable or that typically evokes a collective response of a negative type' (Tittle, 1995: 124). The crucial independent variable is the 'control ratio'. The control ratio is the degree of control that one can exercise relative to that which one experiences. If by virtue of the roles and statuses one occupies and the personal strengths one has, one has the potential to exert more control over others and their environment than others (and the environment) do in fact exert over oneself, then one has a control surplus. Obversely, a person who by virtue of lowly status has little potential to control but who actually experiences enormous control has a control deficit.

The interesting theoretical move Tittle makes is to suggest that either kind of control imbalance – surplus or deficit – conduces to deviance. To see why this is an important move, consider one of the most influential sentences in the history of criminology, first uttered by Edwin Sutherland in his 1939 Presidential address to the American Sociological Society: 'If it can be shown that white collar crimes are frequent, a general theory that crime is due to poverty and its related pathologies is shown to be invalid' (Sutherland, 1983: 7). In light of *Control Balance*, a riposte to Sutherland is: If it can be shown that both control surpluses and control deficits explain deviance, it may be that crime in the suites can be explained by control surplus, crime in the streets by control deficit, so that control imbalance structured into a society

becomes a common cause of both types of crime. Another of what Kathleen Daly (1995) describes as the central paradoxes of crime and justice that Tittle's theory enables us to tackle is why women and girls in all societies we know commit much less crime than men and boys, while it is the latter who enjoy the greater wealth and power. If both control surplus and control deficit are involved in the explanation of crime, then as we will see below, we might come to grips with this paradox as well. And a good many more which are compellingly documented in Tittle's monograph.

Another attractive feature of Tittle's theory is that it manages synthesis of explanation by rational choice, virtuous choice and sociology of the emotions mechanisms. Unlike almost all traditional criminological theories, Tittle's theory includes an account of why people are motivated to commit crime. For present purposes, the crucial part of that motivational story is that the pursuit of autonomy is more or less a learned human universal. This is true to the point where when people enjoy a control surplus, they are still motivated to extend it. When they suffer a control deficit, they are motivated to eliminate it. Deviance results when *motivation* is triggered by *provocation* and enabled by the presence of *opportunity* and absence of *constraint*. Building opportunity and constraint into the theory brings into play the explanatory power of rational choice. Provocation is built into the theory in a way that brings the sociology of the emotions in. A person highly motivated to deviate by virtue of a control deficit, who is exposed to an opportunity with low risk that constraint would be mobilized may be virtuous enough not to deviate until there is a provocation – a racial insult or some other discourtesy, challenge or display of vulnerability that elicits resentment or shame over a control deficit (or temptation to exploit in the case of a control surplus). Provocations are 'contextual features that cause people to become more keenly cognizant of their control ratios and the possibilities of altering them through deviant behavior' (Tittle, 1995: 163). *Virtue* (or 'moral commitment' as Tittle prefers in his more normatively neutral approach) is snuck into the theory here not as a causal mainspring (like motivation, provocation, opportunity and constraint) but as a limiting contingency on the operation of those mainsprings of the theory (Tittle, 1995: 208–9). At least it is there.

Tittle's core contention that control imbalance motivates and explains rates and types of deviance seems a powerful and testable explanation for a lot of things we know from the sociology of deviance. Equally, his claim that control imbalance affects patterns of provocation, opportunity and constraint, which in turn affect deviance, adds to the power of the theory, if not to its testability. Tittle suggests in various places (e.g. pp. 170, 177, 182, 276) that deviance is a result of a desire to rectify a control imbalance. This is odd because while those with a control deficit may do this, those with control surpluses pursue ever bigger surpluses. It is both simpler and more plausible to assert that most people want more control, however much they have, than that they seek to 'rectify the [control] imbalance' (p. 177).[1] Elsewhere, Tittle is more careful on this matter, if more convoluted, where he speaks of 'motivation to correct a control imbalance or to extend a control surplus' (p. 182).

Why control deficits should stimulate deviance will be intuitively clear to most readers. The claim taps into a long tradition of writing in criminology about how powerlessness engenders resentment, envy, hopelessness, need, loss of stake in conformity and humiliation that can be acted out through either violent or property crime (Braithwaite, 1979). But why do control surpluses stimulate deviance? Tittle has a kind of 'power corrupts' explanation here. One effect of having a control surplus is that other people recognize this and subordinate themselves to you; most people with a control surplus take advantage of this proffered subordination. Because it is harder to control someone with a control surplus (by definition), deviance carries lower risk for persons with control surpluses. Therefore, they can and do take advantage of the subordination preferred to them in deviant ways when this is gratifying. This picks up one of the earliest insights of feminist theory; in the words of Mary Wollstonecraft (1995: 9): '…hereditary property – hereditary honours. The man has been changed into an artificial monster by the station in which he was born, and the consequent homage that benumbed his faculties like the torpedo's touch.' According to Tittle, the iterated subordination experienced by persons with control surpluses renders them ungrateful for the things subordinates are subordinate about. They

come to presume subordination to the point where any resistance to it becomes an insult and a provocation to deviance. An illustrative repeated observation from the literature on domestic violence is the dominating husband who is infuriated by the failure of his wife to have dinner ready for him at the time he expects (Hopkins and McGregor, 1991). Hence, in different ways, both subordination and resistance become provocations to deviance for those with control surpluses.

Moreover, Tittle contends that there is a reciprocal relationship between the deviance engendered by control surpluses and that engendered by control deficits. Domination and ingratitude at the hands of actors with control surpluses is humiliating for those with control deficits. This humiliation engenders defiant deviance among the powerless. Defiance in turn is reciprocated (with deviance of domination) to further extend the control of the actor with the surplus. Obversely, 'Efforts to extend control surpluses are likely to lead to efforts to overcome control deficits' (deviance of the dominated) (Tittle, 1995: 182).

Effects of redistributing control

Tittle's control ratio idea seems a more fruitful way of reconceptualizing my own work on why reducing inequality based on class, race, sex, age and political power (slavery, totalitarianism) might simultaneously reduce crimes of exploitation and crimes of the exploited, crimes of the powerful and crimes of the powerless (Braithwaite, 1979, 1991). A materialist and then a sociology of the emotions argument will be reformulated into Tittle's framework here. The first is an opportunity theory argument that: (1) crime is motivated in part by needs, often transient, episodic needs (Wright and Decker, 1994: 36–48); (2) needs are more likely to be satisfied as control ratios increase; (3) policies to foster control balance will do more to increase the need satisfaction of those with control deficits than to decrease the need satisfaction of those with control surpluses. The latter is true because of a standard welfare economics point that marginal gains from satisfying needs decline as need satisfaction increases. The value of one's millionth dollar is less than one's first. A billion dollars of GDP spent on housing for the homeless will increase need satisfaction more than the reduction of need satisfaction from reducing the value of mansions for the rich by a billion dollars. When people feel that few of their needs are met, they are more likely to perceive that they have little to lose through a criminal conviction, little stake in conformity. In contrast, a person with basic needs satisfied will suffer more from a prison sentence that deprives him of a comfortable home, a loving family life and a stimulating job.

Because people with large control surpluses are likely to be in a position where most of their needs are met, they are most unlikely to steal in order to increase need satisfaction. Their theft is more likely to be motivated by greed. The reformulated materialist argument becomes therefore that control imbalance increases:

Crimes of *poverty* (control deficit)	Crimes of *wealth* (control surplus)
motivated by *need*	motivated by *greed*
for goods for *use*	for goods for *exchange* (that are surplus to those required for use)

People with control surpluses tend to steal to gratify greed; in Marxist terms, not to acquire goods for use, but acquisition of goods for exchange that are surplus to what is required for use. Control surpluses result in the accumulation of economic surpluses to control. Surplus can be disposed of in a variety of ways such as inheritance, charitable contributions and conspicuous consumption to signify status. The important application of surpluses from a criminological point of view, however, is through exchanges which constitute new illegitimate opportunities. The best way to rob a bank is to own it. But that in turn requires a large quantity of capital. Elsewhere I have documented a variety of ways that the possession of goods for exchange beyond those required for use enables the constitution of a wide variety of extremely lucrative criminal opportunities that are not available to those of us still struggling to acquire the goods and services we would like to use (Braithwaite, 1991). The point is an old one, explicated in Cicero's prosecution of Verres, the corrupt governor of Sicily in 70 BC: 'The people who have reason to fear prosecution, Verres assures his friends, are those who have only stolen just enough for their own use: whereas what he, on the contrary, has stolen is enough to satisfy many people!' (Cicero, 1971: 38). Cicero's republican analysis of unchecked accumulation and corruption is

revived in the 18th-century feminism of Mary Wollstonecraft (1995: 234): 'The preposterous distinctions of rank, which render civilization a curse, by dividing the world between voluptuous tyrants and cunning envious dependants, corrupt, almost equally, every class of people...'

In terms of Cohen and Machalek's (1988) evolutionary ecological approach to expropriative crime, the returns to an expropriative strategy vary inversely with the number of others who are engaging in the same strategy. Extreme control surpluses foster extraordinarily lucrative minority strategies. People and organizations that control large surpluses can pursue criminal strategies that are novel and that excel because they cannot be contemplated by those without extreme surpluses.

It follows from Cohen and Machalek's (1988) analysis that those with extreme control surpluses will rarely resort to the illegitimate means which are the deviant staples of those with control deficits, because they can secure much higher returns by pursuing strategies to which those with control deficits have no access. There will be little direct competition between the control deficit criminal and the control surplus criminal. Yet it would be a mistake to conclude that separate explanations are required simply because these worlds of deviance take such different forms. On the contrary, Tittle's theory shows how there can be a common explanation for the two patterns of deviance in the form of the extent of control balance or imbalance.

Just as greed fetishizes money for its value for exchange rather than use, so control itself can be fetishized. Control can be exchanged, invested to generate more control. Hence, the crimes of J. Edgar Hoover (Geis and Goff, 1990) might be understood in terms of an insatiable desire to accumulate more power for exchange. In this way, the purchase of the materialist analysis can be extended beyond property crime to many other forms of deviance. The most terrible crimes of our history, of Hitler against the Jews, Cortez and the Conquistadors, the genocides in Rwanda and Cambodia,[2] are explained by the pursuit of power by actors whose lust to dominate was insatiable, who would never have been satisfied by a balance of control.

The second argument to be reconceptualized from Braithwaite (1991) is directly adopted by Tittle. This is a sociology of the emotions account about control ratios and humiliation. Tittle reads the criminal episodes analysed by Jack Katz (1988) rather as I do, and somewhat differently from the way Katz himself reads them, since Katz eschews general explanation. 'The latent argument' in Katz, according to Tittle (Tittle, 1995: 278), is that 'deviant behavior is attractive because it puts the person in control'. Indeed, the argument is not very latent when Katz characterizes the 'badass', for example, as one who takes pride in defiance at being bad:

> The badass, with searing purposiveness, tries to scare humiliation off; as one ex-punk explained to me, after years of adolescent anxiety about the ugliness of his complexion and the stupidness of his every word, he found a wonderful calm in making 'them' anxious about his perceptions and understandings. (Katz 1988: 312–3)

Beyond Katz, Tittle quotes ethnographies of burglars, for example: 'As I rifled through those people's most private possessions, I felt a peculiar power over them, even though we'd never met' (Tittle, 1995: 193). Katz does see violence as 'livid with the awareness of humiliation' (Katz, 1988: 23). Rage transcends the offender's humiliation by taking him to dominance over a proximate person. Just as humiliation of the offender is implicated in the onset of his rage, so the need to humiliate the victim enables her humiliation. Similar conclusions have been reached by psychiatric scholars (Kohut, 1972; Lewis, 1971; Lansky, 1984, 1987) and other scholars working in the sociology of the emotions tradition (Scheff, 1987; Scheff and Retzinger, 1991).

Katz rejects structural explanations for the cycles of humiliation, rage and assertion of domination that he documented. In contrast, Braithwaite (1991: 49) asserted:

> [S]ome societies are structurally more humiliating than others. For a black, living in South Africa [under Apartheid at the time] is structurally more humiliating than living in Tanzania. Living in a prison is structurally more humiliating than living in a nursing home and the latter is more humiliating than dwelling in a luxury apartment. Slavery is structurally more humiliating than freedom. School systems such as I experienced as a child, where children are linearly ordered in their classroom according to their rank, 'dunces' sitting at the front, are structurally more humiliating for those who fail .... More generally, *inegalitarian societies are structurally humiliating*. When patents cannot supply the most basic needs of their children, while at the same time they are assailed by the ostentatious consumption of the affluent, this is structurally humiliating for the poor. (Braithwaite, 1991: 49)

Now I might want to reformulate all this using Tittle's more general and elegant account: societies with large control imbalances will be structurally more humiliating than those with modest control imbalances. Much crime, particularly violent crime, is motivated by the humiliation of the offender and the offender's perceived right to humiliate the victim, by the offender being dominated and by the offender's domination of a victim. Like the materialist argument, the sociology of the emotions argument applies with as much force to crimes of control surplus as to those of control deficit. Hitler, as I have already said, enjoyed a control surplus. His fascism was structurally humiliating. In *Mein Kampf* he explained how the German people had been humiliated at Versailles, tricked and betrayed by Jews for generations. His was an appeal to a humiliated people, an appeal to transcend it through the violent assertion of world domination, and along the way to assert a right to humiliate the Jews. The historical stupidity of the Allies at Versailles was to saddle the Germans with a control imbalance which was an emotional as well as a material burden they were bound to defy (Scheff, 1994). It was the emotional dynamics of that control imbalance that handed the world the holocaust. An enormous appeal of Tittle's theory is the sweep of its relevance – from the most fragmentary domestic altercation to explaining global conflicts.

Control ratios and types of deviance

The aspect of Tittle's theory I would want to abandon is his account of how different types of deviance are associated with different levels of control imbalance. Consider his account of the effect of different levels of control surplus. When individuals exercise slightly more control than that to which they are subject, *exploitation* is said to be the most common form of deviance, examples of which are price-fixing, shake-down schemes by gang leaders who sell protection to merchants, bribery and extortion. In the zone of medium control surplus, the modal type of deviance shifts from exploitation to *plunder* –

selfish acts – forms of plunder – that include things like environmental pollution inflicted by imperialist countries whose leaders are in search of scarce resources in underdeveloped countries, programs of massive destruction of forests or rivers for the personal gain of corporate owners or executives, unrealistic taxes or work programs imposed by autocratic rulers, enslavement of natives by invading forces for the benefit of military commanders, pillage of communities by hoods doing the bidding of crime bosses, pogroms... (Tittle, 1995: 191)

When control surpluses are very large, *decadence* becomes the characteristic form of deviance, of which Nero, Howard Hughes and perhaps Michael Jackson are proffered as exemplars. The distinctions between exploitation, plunder and decadence are not clearly defined. Nor do they seem distinctions worth making. Tittle gives no empirical evidence to suggest that there might be some correspondence between the three zones of control surplus and these three types of deviance. So why render the theory more complex in this way? Why not adopt the more parsimonious and one might add more plausible, view that the larger the control surplus the more likely exploitation, plunder and decadence all become?

On the control deficit side, there are some suggestive empirical grounds for taking Tittle's partition into zones of deficit more seriously. Here *predation* is said to be associated with marginal control deficits. The classic instances of predation involve directly taking things from others, directly inflicting violence on them or directly forcing them to do things they do not want to do (e.g. rape). In the moderate zone of control deficit, *defiance* is said to be the modal form of deviance. Defiance means deviant acts of protest against the control to which they are subjected such as mocking authority or sullen conformity. Withdrawn or escapist deviance, such as 'alcoholism, drug abuse, suicide, family desertion, mental illness, or countercultural involvement' (Tittle, 1995: 190), is also a possibility in this intermediate zone of control deficit, though it is not clear how or whether most of this is classified as defiance. In the extreme zone of control deficit submissive deviance is said to be typical. Perhaps controversially, Tittle suggests that most people find slavish submission or grovelling compliance deviant. People in this zone are so dominated, according to Tittle, that they are too afraid of countercontrol to engage in either predation or defiance.

Again, the distinctions among predation and defiance are not especially clear, though they are sharply distinguished from submissive deviance. But then one wonders that many withdrawn forms of deviance such as mental illness or drug abuse might not be submissive. While the categorization across the zones of control deficit is not very compelling, Tittle is on to an underlying insight. This is that more predatory forms of deviance require a certain degree of autonomy; they require that one not be so dominated as to be afraid of standing up to others. When control deficits are extreme, people may be so terrified of countercontrol that they are beyond predation and even beyond sullen forms of defiance. This core insight is not only plausible; in contrast with the control surplus distinctions there is some empirical evidence which suggests that plausibility. Tittle points out that submission or defiance was more common than predation among black Americans during the period of slavery (Tittle, 1995: 250). With emancipation, predation became more possible because the countercontrol they feared reduced as their domination became less total. Indeed, Tittle could have gone further here. There are empirical grounds for believing that the civil rights progress of the 1960s in the US did more to increase than to reduce black violence (McDonald, 1972). The concept of resistance to domination increasing at the time when that domination is reduced has been a recurrent one in political theory since de Tocqueville (1856: 214), reaching its most developed form in Davies's (1962) theory, which associates revolution with a prolonged period of economic and social development followed by a short, sharp reversal.

Another form of support for Tittle's key insight here comes from experimental psychological research organized under Brehm's (1966) theory of psychological reactance as revised by Wortman and Brehm (1975). The key idea of the theory is that a threat to a freedom motivates the individual to restore that freedom. The psychological reactance literature supports a nonmonotonic relationship between the magnitude of a threat of control and a reaction by the controlled person to re-exert control or to give up (Brehm and Brehm, 1981: 58–97). Threat up to a certain point progressively increases psychological reactance; beyond that point, the subject of control gives up on the idea that she enjoys any control, ceasing resistance to the control. Empirical work derived from the 'learned helplessness' research program (Seligman,

1975) led to a modification of Brehm's (1966) original reactance theory to accommodate the finding that extended experience with uncontrollable outcomes leads to passivity.

The learned helplessness and psychological reactance literatures do highlight a problem with Tittle's theory. When there is a control deficit, deviance for Tittle is a way that people restore some sort of control. Yet submission, the form of deviance associated with the most extreme deficits, is hardly a means of restoring control; on the contrary, it amounts to yielding to a downward spiral into helplessness. As with the effect of control surpluses, there is therefore a need on the deficit side to reformulate the theory of control balance. The reformulation proposed is that as control deficits increase, predatory deviance increases up to a point where people become so dominated that the fear of countercontrol eventually throws this trend into reverse. Domination increases predation until people become so dominated that they are afraid to reassert their own control through predation (or even less predatory forms of defiance). Resistance is reinterpreted as pointless in the face of utter domination. At extremes of control deficit, people submit undefiantly or they withdraw, giving up on the mainstream of life, retreating into drugs, depression or even suicide. In summary, as control deficits become large, predatory deviance increases until a point is reached where predation declines in favour of retreatist forms of deviance. To this control deficit reformulation, we can add the simplified surplus reformulation: as control surpluses increase, exploitation, plunder and decadence all increase.

Indeed, we can simplify the two reformulations by pondering whether there is really a clear distinction between predation on the deficit side of control balance and exploitation on the surplus side. James Q. Wilson notwithstanding (1975), there is no problem with conceiving of shakedowns, bribery, extortion and price fixing as predation. Most of the world's antitrust laws actually incorporate a notion of 'predatory pricing' (e.g. Section 46 of the Australian Trade Practices Act). So we might consider abandoning the notion that Tittle's theory of control balance is a theory of deviance in general, conceiving it instead as a theory of predation.

The following simpler theory has attractions. Predatory deviance is least likely in societies where high proportions of citizens are in control balance and low proportions in control deficit or surplus. Predatory deviance increases monotonically with

increasing control surpluses; predatory deviance increases with rising control deficits up to the point where people give up on resistance (see Figure 11.4.1).[3] Beyond this turning point, predatory deviance declines, submission increases, as does the deviance of disengagement – drug abuse, alcoholism, depressive disorders and suicide. The simplified theory is not meant to suggest that there is no difference between the predatory deviance on the surplus side compared with the deficit side of balance. While predatory deviance is enabled both by having nothing to lose (high deficit) and by having little likelihood of losing it (high surplus), the power dynamics of being in surplus enable forms of deviance which are impossible for those with little control, as we saw in the discussion of Cohen and Machalek (1988). In their choices of predation, the powerless must make the best of a bad job, while those with control surpluses can take advantage of a good job. Where there is competition between the two over the same predatory strategies, it is fragile. The small drug dealer can be crushed by a powerful organized criminal unless she finds a way of complementing him or picking up his crumbs.

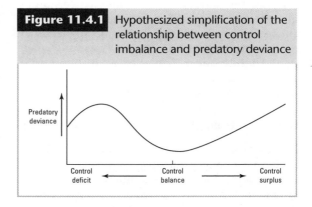

Figure 11.4.1 Hypothesized simplification of the relationship between control imbalance and predatory deviance

There is no way of saying anything clear about the specific forms of deviance that will attract those with extreme control surpluses. According to the evolutionary ecological understanding of crime, as in nature, a strategy of predation is more likely to persist if it is different from that used by other predators. Predation flourishes on the basis of innovation to discover niches untouched by competitors. For this reason, criminologists do not even know about the most lucrative forms of crime among the powerful; they are lucrative precisely because so few have the knowledge and resources to exploit them. Similarly, as control is exerted to further narrow the predations available to the powerless, they innovate by trying new scams on people less powerful than themselves (either permanently or momentarily).

This simplified formulation salvages the really important aspects of the explanatory power of Tittle's theory. It explains why the retired elderly should engage in little predatory deviance – their control deficit is so high that they generally have given up on resistance to control. Similarly, the very young, those under 10, generally have yet to imagine that they might have the power for predatory deviance in response to the enormous control deficit they suffer. Yet it explains why by the time young people pass adolescence, they have rounded the turning point and are near the maximum risk of predatory deviance. It explains why women in circumstances of extreme family and workplace domination can be beyond feeling the power for predation, why the ratio of submissive and withdrawn deviance to predatory deviance is so high for them. It explains why 18th and 19th century African Americans might have been dominated beyond predation, while late 20th century African Americans can imagine predation as within their grasp. At the same time, the simplified version of the theory avoids some predictions that are unlikely to be sustained. For example, the fact that control ratios are higher for men than for women should imply under Tittle's original theory that both predation and defiance are more common for women than for men.

Control ratios, provocation and opportunity

Part of Tittle's theory is that control imbalance explains deviance, not only because it increases motivation and emotional commitment to reclaim or extend control in ways such as those demonstrated by Katz (1988). The explanatory power of control imbalance also comes from the fact that people with control imbalances, according to Tittle, are exposed to greater provocation and opportunity for deviance. Hence, people who are dominated because of their race are also more likely to be *provoked* by racial insults and subtle forms of disrespect and as young people, they are exposed to the illegitimate *opportunities* constituted by stigmatized subcultures or criminal gangs that are organized in slums. Note the role of stigmatization in the constitution of criminal subcultures (Braithwaite, 1989: 65–8, 127–33); put another

way, criminal subculture formation maps the social structuring of provocation. Powerful men are provoked to predation and exploitation by the submission proffered by potential targets of their domination, by the way they experience power as unchecked, and by the opportunities (e.g. surplus capital for investment in scams) their control imbalance generates. On gender, the theory gives an interesting account of why men care more about loss or extension of control than women and how this engenders provocation (Tittle, 1995: 239):

> Traditionally, and to some extent continuing into the present, the male role was defined by active subjugation of the forces of nature and protection of his domain...These role distinctions made sense in primitive environments because they meshed with the superior physical strength of males and the relative confinement and dependency of females handicapped by child-bearing and nursing...Because of these role distinctions calling for dominance, males are more concerned about their relative control ratios. Consequently, they suffer much anxiety about whether they are living up to expectations, and uncertainty stimulates tests. Recurring challenges within male culture (Luckenbill, 1977, 1984) produce more potentially demeaning situational provocations than are faced by females. (Sanders, 1981; Short and Strodtbeck, 1974)

Similarly, it seems plausible that by the time people are old, they are resigned to not caring so much about the things they cannot control. Conversely, from adolescence to age 25, young people care enormously about establishing an independent identity, breaking free from the strictures of youth, such as family and school control. Because young people spend more of their time in public space, while the old spend more of theirs in private space, it is the young who encounter more provocation, more debasement by police and other superordinates and more of the opportunities for predation located at the 'hot spots' of public space (Sherman *et al.*, 1989).

The extent to which people in different structural locations care about their domination is important because of the considerable experimental evidence that psychological reactance is greater when people care most about the freedoms under threat (Brehm and Brehm, 1981: 58–63). Not only do crime-prone demographic groups such as adolescents, young adults and men care more about loss of control than others, those who select themselves into power-exerting vocations, such as politics, policing and the military, are likely to care more about debasement, humiliation and domination than those who have not been so socially selected. It is a recurrent tragedy of the human condition that those who are socially selected into the power-exerting vocations are so predisposed to predation and exploitation. This is one reason why throughout human history we have had so much rape in war, police violence, so much political corruption and war-mongering.

So the theory gives redundantly strong grounds for predicting some of the strongest correlates of predatory deviance we have – with age, gender, race and business and political elite status, plus a number of others that are discussed in the book itself.

From J. Braithwaite, 'Charles Tittle's Control Balance and criminological theory', Theoretical Criminology, 1997, 1(1): 77–97.

Notes

1 My hypothesis would be that when people are in perfect control balance, they will pursue the imbalance that will come from greater control.
2 Here I am indebted to the research of my PhD student, Jennifer Balint who is studying these genocides.
3 Note that Figure 11.4.1 differs from the (admittedly simpler) inverted-U in Tittle's (1995: 183) Figure 7.2 because submission is defined as deviance in the Tittle model, but not as predatory deviance in my model.

References

Braithwaite, John (1979) *Inequality, Crime and Public Policy*. London: Routledge & Kegan Paul.

Braithwaite, John (1989) *Crime, Shame and Reintegration*. Cambridge: Cambridge University Press.

Braithwaite, John (1991) 'Poverty, Power, White-Collar Crime and the Paradoxes of Criminological Theory', *Australian and New Zealand Journal of Criminology* 24: 40–50.

Brehm, J.W. (1966) *A Theory of Psychological Reactance*. New York: Academic Press.

Brehm, Sharon S. and Jack W. Brehm (1981) *Psychological Reactance: A Theory of Freedom and Control*. New York: Academic Press.

Cicero (1971) *Selected Works*. Translated by Michael Grant. Harmondsworth: Penguin.

Cohen, Lawrence E. and Richard Machalek (1988) 'A General Theory of Appropriative Crime: An Evolutionary Ecological Approach', *American Journal of Sociology* 94: 465–501.

Daly, Kathleen (1995) 'Crime and Justice: Paradoxes for Theory and Action', paper presented at the conference 'Advancing the Feminist Agenda: Law, Politics, Civil Society', Australian National University.

Davies, J.C. (1962) 'Toward a Theory of Revolution', *American Sociological Review* 27: 5–8, 15–18.

De Toqueville, A. (1856) *The Old Regime and the French Revolution*. New York: Harper & Row.

Geis, Gilbert and Colin Goff (1990) 'Edwin Sutherland and the FBI: The Evil of Banality', paper presented at the 'Edwin Sutherland Conference on White-Collar Crime', Indiana University.

Hopkins, Andrew and Heather McGregor (1991) *Working for Change: The Movement Against Domestic Violence*. Sydney: Allen & Unwin.

Katz, Jack (1988) *The Seductions of Crime: Moral and Sensual Attractions in Doing Evil*. New York: Basic Books.

Kohut, H. (1972) 'Thoughts on Narcissism and Narcissistic Rage', *The Psychoanalytic Study of the Child* 27: 360–400.

Lansky, M. (1984) 'Violence, Shame and the Family', *International Journal of Family Psychiatry* 5: 21–40.

Lansky, M. (1987) 'Shame and Domestic Violence', in D. Nathanson (ed.) *The Many Faces of Shame*, pp. 335–62. New York: Guilford.

Lewis, Helen (1971) *Shame and Guilt in Neurosis*. New York: International Universities Press.

Luckenbill, David F. (1977) 'Criminal Homicide as a Situated Transaction', *Social Problems* 25: 176–86.

Luckenbill, David F. (1984) 'Character Coercion, Instrumental Coercion and Gun Control', *Journal of Applied Behavioral Science* 20: 181–92.

McDonald, T.D. (1972) 'Correlates of Civil Rights Activity and Negro Intra-Racial Violence', PhD thesis, Southern Illinois University.

Sanders, William B. (1981) 'Delinquent Occasions', in William B. Sanders (ed.) *Delinquency: Causes, Patterns and Reactions*, pp. 81–95. Dallas: Holt, Rinehart & Winston.

Scheff, Thomas (1987) 'The Shame-Rage Spiral: A Case Study of an Interminable Squabble', in H.B. Lewis (ed.) *The Role of Shame in Symptom Formation*, pp. 109–49. Hillsdale, NJ: LEA.

Scheff, Thomas (1994) *Bloody Revenge: Emotions, Nationalism and War*. Boulder, CO: Westview Press.

Scheff, Thomas and Suzanne Retzinger (1991) *Emotions and Violence: Shame and Rage in Destructive Conflicts.* Lexington, MA: Lexington Books.

Seligman, M.E.P. (1975) *Helplessness: On Depression, Development and Death.* San Francisco: W.H. Freeman.

Sherman, L.W., P.R. Gartin and M.E. Buerger (1989) 'Hot Spots of Predatory Crime: Routine Activities and the Criminology of Place', *Criminology* 27: 27–55.

Short, James F., Jr and Fred L. Strodtbeck (1974) *Group Process and Gang Delinquency.* Chicago: University of Chicago Press.

Sutherland, Edwin (1983) *White Collar Crime: The Uncut Version.* New Haven: Yale University Press.

Tittle, Charles (1995) *Control Balance: Toward a General Theory of Deviance.* Boulder, CO: Westview Press.

Wilson, James Q. (1975) *Thinking About Crime.* New York: Random House.

Wollstonecraft, Mary (1995) *A Vindication of the Rights of Man with A Vindication of the Rights of Woman and Hints.* Cambridge: Cambridge University Press.

Wortman, C.B. and J.W. Brehm (1975) 'Responses to Uncontrollable Outcomes: An Integration of Reactance Theory and the Learned Helplessness Model', *Advances in Experimental Social Psychology* 8: 278–336.

Wright, Richard T. and Scott Decker (1994) *Burglars on the Job.* Boston: Northeastern University Press.

12

Radical and critical criminology

12.1 Toward a political economy of crime
William J. Chambliss   258

**12.2 The theoretical and political priorities of
critical criminology**
Phil Scraton and Kathryn Chadwick   261

12.3 Radical criminology in Britain
Jock Young   267

12.4 Abolitionism and crime control
Willem de Haan   271

Introduction

The work in this chapter was much influenced by the political movements of the 1960s and thereabouts. This was a time when some more radically-oriented criminologists began to look beyond ideas of anomie and strain and, rather, were more preoccupied with the structural inequalities they saw around them and the impact of these on crime and criminalization. They built on some of the insights of interactionism and labelling theory and focused on the ways in which people are identified as criminal and what such processes have to tell us about the nature of contemporary social relations.

Radical criminological work was much influenced by the writings of Karl Marx and in the opening excerpt William Chambliss **(Reading 12.1)** focuses on Marx's identification of the contradictions at the heart of capitalist societies and how these relate to criminal activity. At heart, Chambliss suggests that everyone, at some time, commits crime. The fundamental issue is therefore not *why* people commit crime, but who becomes identified – or if you like, labelled – as criminal. The reality, he goes on to argue, is that it is the poor, the working classes, who are most likely to be criminalized and this reflects the fact that it is the powerful and wealthy in our society that are able to control the use of discretion in law and criminal justice.

By no means dissimilar arguments are offered by Phil Scraton and Kathryn Chadwick **(Reading 12.2)** in their manifesto for 'critical criminology'. At its heart, they argue, lies a class analysis and the notion of 'criminalization': 'a process which has been employed to underpin the repressive or control functions of the state'. The issues they highlight go beyond class relations to take in racism and neo-colonialism, and feminism and patriarchy. The marginalization of ethnic minorities within conditions of neo-colonialism, and women within patriarchy, are further reinforced by differential policing and targeting and by a variety of forms of social exclusion and oppression.

In the third excerpt Jock Young **(Reading 12.3)** provides an overview of radical criminology in Britain. This body of work, he argues, emerged when 'social democratic positivism' reached something of crisis in the late 1960s. He summarizes the perspective as seeing 'the causes of crime as being at core the class and patriarchial relations endemic to our social order'. In exploring its development, he identifies what he refers to as an 'exterior history' (the political economy which prompted and provided the context for such work) and an 'interior history' (an aetiological crisis stemming from improving social conditions and rising crime). Young concludes by examining both the flaws and the advantages of radical criminology. Its advantages, he suggests, lie in its critical stance toward the criminogenic features of social structures and the operation of criminal justice and law, and in its moral and normative stance. These features, among others, distinguish it from the other body of work to emerge as a result of the aetiological crisis: administrative criminology. This Young identifies as a governmental, establishment approach to criminology, little interested in causes and largely uncritical in its approach to crime and justice.

At the radical fringe lies what has generally been termed 'abolitionism'. On the surface, as Willem de Haan **(Reading 12.4)** points out, abolitionist crime control appears oxymoronic – a contradiction in terms. However, as he goes on to explain, there is much that abolitionists potentially have to offer within criminology. At heart, he says, abolitionists argue for 'a minimum of coercion and interference with the personal lives of those involved [in the criminal justice and penal systems] and a maximum amount of care and service for all members of society'. He then goes on to outline abolitionism in a number of forms: notably as a social movement, as a theoretical perspective and as a political strategy. At a time when there are record numbers in prison it may seem something of a busted flush. However, one might reasonably take the opposite view and argue that with ever larger numbers of people being criminalized, the values and priorities of abolitionism have ever greater resonance and relevance.

Questions for discussion

1. What, according to Chambliss, are the main contradictions in capitalist society and how do they relate to crime?

2. What are the main assumptions in a Marxist view of crime and the criminal law?

3. What are the main priorities of 'critical criminology'?

4. What does Jock Young mean when he uses the term 'aetiological crisis'?

5. What are the main flaws of radical criminology and how serious do you think these are?

6. Outline three different types of 'abolitionism'.

7. Is abolitionism possible?

8. If yes, in what ways?

9. If no, why not? (And does this mean abolitionist ideas have no purpose?)

12.1 Toward a political economy of crime
William J. Chambliss

Capitalist societies, where the means of production are in private hands and where there inevitably develops a division between the class that rules (the owners of the means of production) and the class that is ruled (those who work for the ruling class), create substantial amounts of crime, often of the most violent sort, as a result of the contradictions that are inherent in the structure of social relations that emanate from the capitalist system.

The first contradiction is that the capitalist enterprise depends upon creating in the mass of the workers a desire for the consumption of products produced by the system. These products need not contribute to the well being of the people, nor do they have to represent commodities of any intrinsic value; nonetheless, for the system to expand and be viable, it is essential that the bulk of the population be oriented to consuming what is produced. However, in order to produce the commodities that are the basis for the accumulation of capital and the maintenance of the ruling class, it is also necessary to get people to work at tedious, alienating and unrewarding tasks. One way to achieve this, of course, is to make the accumulation of commodities dependent on work. Moreover, since the system depends as it does on the desire to possess and consume commodities far beyond what is necessary for survival, there must be an added incentive to perform the dull meaningless tasks that are required to keep the productive process expanding. This is accomplished by keeping a proportion of the labor force impoverished or nearly so.[1] If those who are employed become obstreperous and refuse to perform the tasks required by the productive system, then there is a reserve labor force waiting to take their job. And hanging over the heads of the workers is always the possibility of becoming impoverished should they refuse to do their job.

Thus, at the outset the structure of capitalism creates both the desire to consume and – for a large mass of people – an inability to earn the money necessary to purchase the items they have been taught to want.

A second fundamental contradiction derives from the fact that the division of a society into a ruling class that owns the means of production and a subservient class that works for wages *inevitably* leads to conflict between the two classes. As those conflicts are manifest in rebellions and riots among the proletariat, the state, acting in the interests of the owners of the means of production will pass laws designed to control, through the application of state sanctioned force, those acts of the proletariat which threaten the interests of the bourgeoisie. In this way, then, acts come to be defined as criminal.

It follows that as capitalism develops and conflicts between social classes continue or become more frequent or more violent (as a result, for example, of increasing proletarianization), more and more acts will be defined as criminal.

The criminal law is thus not a reflection of custom (as other theorists have argued), but is a set of rules laid down by the state in the interests of the ruling class, and resulting from the conflicts that inhere in class structured societies; criminal behavior is, then, the inevitable expression of class conflict resulting from the inherently exploitative nature of the economic relations. What makes the behavior of some criminal is the coercive power of the state to enforce the will of the ruling class; criminal behavior results from the struggle between classes whereby those who are the subservient classes individually express their alienation from established social relations. Criminal behavior is a product of the economic and political system, and in a capitalist society has as one of its principal consequences the advancement of technology, use of surplus labor and generally the maintenance of the established relationship between the social classes. Marx says, somewhat facetiously, in response to the functionalism of bourgeois sociologists:

> ...crime takes a part of the superfluous population off the labor market and thus reduces competition among the laborers – up to a certain point preventing wages from falling below the minimum – the struggle against crime absorbs another part of this population. Thus the criminal comes in as one of those natural 'counterweights' which bring about a correct balance and open up a whole perspective of

'useful' occupation…the criminal…produces the whole of the police and of criminal justice, constables, judges, hangmen, juries, etc.; amid all these different lines of business, which form equally many categories of the social division of labor, develop different capacities of the human spirit, create new needs and new ways of satisfying them. Torture alone has given rise to the most ingenious mechanical inventions, and employed many honorable craftsmen in the production of its instruments.[2]

Paradigms, as we are all well aware, do much more than supply us with specific causal explanations. They provide us with a whole set of glasses through which we view the world. Most importantly, they lead us to emphasize certain features of the world and to ignore or at least de-emphasize others.

The following propositions highlight the most important implications of a Marxian paradigm of crime and criminal law.[3]

A. On the content and operation of criminal law

1 Acts are defined as criminal because it is in the interests of the ruling class to so define them.

2 Members of the ruling class will be able to violate the laws with impunity while members of the subject classes will be punished.

3 As capitalist societies industrialize and the gap between the bourgeoisie and the proletariat widens, penal law will expand in an effort to coerce the proletariat into submission.

B. On the consequences of crime for society

1 Crime reduces surplus labor by creating employment not only for the criminals but for law enforcers, locksmiths, welfare workers, professors of criminology and a horde of people who live off of the fact that crime exists.

2 Crime diverts the lower classes' attention from the exploitation they experience, and directs it toward other members of their own class rather than towards the capitalist class or the economic system.

3 Crime is a reality which exists only as it is created by those in the society whose interests are served by its presence.

C. On the etiology of criminal behavior

1 Criminal and non-criminal behavior stem from people acting rationally in ways that are compatible with their class position. Crime is a reaction to the life conditions of a person's social class.

2 Crime varies from society to society depending on the political and economic structures of society.

3 Socialist societies should have much lower rates of crime because the less intense class struggle should reduce the forces leading to and the functions of crime. […]

Sutherland asked why some *individuals* became involved in criminal behavior while others did not. My contention is that this question is meaningless. Everyone commits crime. And many, many people whether they are poor, rich or middling are involved in a way of life that is criminal; and furthermore, no one, not even the professional thief or racketeer or corrupt politician commits *crime all the time*. To be sure, it may be politically useful to say that people become criminal through association with 'criminal behavior patterns,' and thereby remove the tendency to look at criminals as pathological. But such a view has little scientific value, since it asks the wrong questions. It asks for a psychological cause of what is by its very nature a socio-political event. Criminality is simply *not* something that people have or don't have; crime is not something some people do and others don't. Crime is a matter of who can pin the label on whom, and underlying this socio-political process is the structure of social relations determined by the political economy. It is to Sutherland's credit that he recognized this when, in 1924, he noted that:

> An understanding of the nature of Criminal law is necessary in order to secure an understanding of the nature of crime. A complete explanation of the origin and enforcement of laws would be, also, an explanation of the violation of laws.[4]

But Sutherland failed, unfortunately, to pursue the implications of his remarks. He chose instead to confront the prevailing functionalist perspective on crime with a less class-biased but nonetheless inevitably psychological explanation.

The argument that criminal acts, that is, acts which are a violation of criminal law, are more often committed by members of the lower classes is not tenable. Criminal acts are widely distributed throughout the social classes in capitalist societies. The rich, the ruling, the poor, the powerless and the working classes all engage in criminal activities on a regular basis. It is in the enforcement of the law that the lower classes are subject to the effects of ruling class domination over the legal system, and which results in the appearance of a concentration of criminal acts among the lower classes in the official records. In actual practice, however, class differences in rates of criminal activity are probably negligible. What difference there is would be a difference in the type of criminal act, not in the prevalence of criminality.

The argument that the control of the state by the ruling class would lead to a lower propensity for crime among the ruling classes fails to recognize two fundamental facts. First is the fact that many acts committed by lower classes and which it is in the interests of the ruling class to control (e.g., crimes of violence, bribery of public officials, and crimes of personal choice, such as drug use, alcoholism, driving while intoxicated, homosexuality, etc.) are just as likely – or at least very likely – to be as widespread among the upper classes as the lower classes. Thus, it is crucial that the ruling class be able to control the discretion of the law enforcement agencies in ways that provide them with immunity. For example, having a legal system encumbered with procedural rules which only the wealthy can afford to implement and which, if implemented, nearly guarantees immunity from prosecution, not to mention more direct control through bribes, coercion and the use of political influence.

The Marxian paradigm must also account for the fact that the law will also reflect conflict between members of the ruling class (or between members of the ruling class and the upper class 'power elites' who manage the bureaucracies). So, for example, laws restricting the formation of trusts, misrepresentation in advertising, the necessity for obtaining licenses to engage in business practices are all laws which generally serve to reduce competition among the ruling classes and to concentrate capital in a few hands. However, the laws also apply universally, and therefore apply to the ruling class as well. Thus, when they break these laws they are committing criminal acts. Again, the enforcement practices obviate the effectiveness of the laws, and guarantee that the ruling class will rarely feel the sting of the laws, but their violation remains a fact with which we must reckon.

It can also be concluded that law enforcement systems are not organized to reduce crime or to enforce the public morality. They are organized rather to manage crime by cooperating with the most criminal groups and enforcing laws against those whose crimes are minimal. In this way, by cooperating with criminal groups, law enforcement essentially produces more crime than would otherwise be the case. Crime is also produced by law enforcement practices through selecting and encouraging the perpetuation of criminal careers by promising profit and security to those criminals who engage in organized criminal activities from which the political, legal and business communities profit.

Thus, the data from this study generally support the Marxian assertion that criminal acts which serve the interests of the ruling class will go unsanctioned while those that do not will be punished. The data also support the hypothesis that criminal activity is a direct reflection of class position. Thus, the criminality of the lawyers, prosecuting attorneys, politicians, judges and policemen is uniquely suited to their own class position in the society. It grows out of the opportunities and strains that inhere in those positions just as surely as the drinking of the skidrow derelict, the violence of the ghetto resident, the drug use of the middle class adolescent and the white collar crimes of corporation executives reflect different socializing experiences.

> From W. Chambliss, 'Toward a political economy of crime', Theory and Society, *1975, 2(1): 149–170.*

Notes

1   Primary source materials for Marx's analysis of crime and criminal law are: *Capital, v .1,* pp: 231–298, 450–503, 556–557, 574, 674–678, 718–725, 734–741; *The Cologne Communist Trial,* London: Lawrence and Wishart; *The German Ideology (1845-6),* London: Lawrence and Wishart 1965, pp: 342–379; *Theories of Surplus Value, v. 1,* pp: 375–376; 'The State and the Law,' in T. B. Bottomore and Maxmillien Rubel (eds.), *Karl Marx: Selected Writings In Sociology and Social Philosophy,* New York: McGraw-Hill, 1965, pp: 215–231.

2   *Ibid., Theories of Surplus Value,* pp. 375–376.

3   For an excellent statement of differences in 'order and conflict' theories, see John Horton, 'Order and Conflict Approaches to the Study of Social Problems' *American Journal of Sociology,* May 1966; see also Gerhard Lenski, *Power and Privilege,* New York: McGraw-Hill, 1966; William J. Chambliss, *Sociological Readings in the Conflict Perspective,* Reading, Mass: Addison-Wesley, 1973.

4   Edwin H. Sutherland, *Criminology,* Philadelphia: J. P. Lippincott, 1924, p. 11.

12.2 The theoretical and political priorities of critical criminology Phil Scraton and Kathryn Chadwick

Establishing a framework for critical analysis

Gouldner's (1969, 1973) devastating indictment of Western sociology established that the 'domain assumptions' of academic disciplines and their pre-eminent theoretical perspectives had been influenced massively by those powerful vested interests who commissioned research. Academic research was identified as essential to the management of advanced capitalism's inherent contradictions and conflicts. For Foucault, however, power is not uni-dimensional nor is it restricted to those formal relations of dominance in the economic or political spheres. As Sim (1990: 9) remarks, power is 'dispersed through the body of society' and exercised through the processes of 'discipline, surveillance, individualization and normalization'. Crucially the power–knowledge axis permeates all formal or official discourses, their language, logic, forms of definition and classification, measurement techniques and empiricism as essential elements in the technology of discipline and the process of normalization. 'Professionals', as key interventionists in societal relations and in the political management of social arrangements, pursue a 'logic and language of control' revealing a daunting 'power to classify' with clear consequences for the reproduction of 'bodies' of knowledge and for the maintenance of dominant power relations (Cohen, 1985: 196).

Foucault's work demonstrates that the challenges to mainstream theoretical traditions have adopted the agendas of those traditions, taking their premises as legitimate points of departure. While starting with 'knowledge-as-it-stands', that which is 'known', a radical alternative must also contextualize knowledge – its derivation, consolidation and recognition – within dominant structural relations. Undoubtedly professionals, be they employed in the caring agencies, the military, the criminal justice system or private industry, operate on the basis of professional training and work experience enjoying discretionary powers in accord with their rank and status. Yet whatever the quality and implications of decisions formulated and administered at the interpersonal level of 'agency', their recognition and legitimacy are rooted in the determining contexts of 'structure' and their manifestation in the professional ideologies of control and political management (Giddens, 1979, 1984).

The dynamics and visibility of power, however, are not always so obvious. For, 'power may be at its most alarming, and quite often at its most horrifying, when applied as a sanction of force' but it is 'typically at its most intense and durable when running through the repetition of institutionalized practices' (Giddens, 1987: 9). As power is mediated through the operational practices of institutions their daily routines become regularized, even predictable. It is important to establish that the routine world of 'agency', of interpersonal relations, is neither spontaneous nor random. Personal reputations and collective identities are ascribed and become managed via official discourses, themselves derived within the dominant social relations of production, reproduction and neocolonialism. For these represent the primary determining contexts which require and reproduce appropriate relations of power and knowledge.

The structural contradictions of advanced capitalist patriarchies require political management. While grassroots resistance has remained a persistent feature in Western social democracies their great achievement has been to contain opposition through relying on 'consensus' rather than 'coercion'. Relations of domination and exploitation, both material and physical, have become redefined and broadly accepted as the justifiable pursuit of competing interests. The smooth and successful operation of power in this context is dependent on social arrangements, forms of political management and cultural traditions which together contribute towards hegemony (Gramsci, 1971). Dissent and disorder are regulated by social forces and cultural transmission rather than by physical coercion. To challenge orthodoxy, to question the established order or to raise doubts concerning formal authority are not perceived as acts of progression towards worthwhile change but are presented in official discourses as acts of subversion which undermine shared identities and common interests.

While 'power', 'regulation' or 'control' can be identified in personal action and social reaction as part and parcel of the daily routine of agency, critical analysis seeks to bring to the fore structural relations, involving the economy, the state and ideology, in explaining the significance of the power–knowledge axis and relating it to the processes by which dominant ideas gain political legitimacy. Discrimination on the basis of class, gender, sexuality and perceived ethnicity clearly operates at the level of attitude, on the street, in the home, at the workplace or at social venues. Once institutionalized, however, classism, sexism, heterosexism and racism become systematic and structured. They become the taken-for-granted social histories and contemporary priorities which constitute state institutions, informing policies and underwriting practices, and which provide legitimacy to interpersonal discrimination. Through the process of institutionalization, relations of dominance and subjugation achieve structural significance. Critical analysis of crime and the criminal justice process must be grounded in these theoretical imperatives.

Class analysis and the determining context of production

Much of the post-war optimism over capital reconstruction and economic growth was derived in the 'Butskellite' compromises which married Keynesian principles concerning state management of the economy to a protected programme of capital investment and development in the private sector (Taylor-Gooby, 1982; Gamble, 1981). This programme was made possible through the initiation of effective, albeit often illusory, programmes of state welfare and social justice. Through initiatives in public housing, access to health care and medicine, new educational priorities and state benefits the popular assumption, also embodied in academic accounts of welfarism, was that benevolent reformism and its commitment to social justice had broken the hold of the free enterprise economy and its market forces over the social well-being of the nation. The era of 'welfare capitalism' had arrived, led by entrepreneurs of conscience who claimed 'people before profit'.

A cursory glance, however, at the relationship between the public and private sectors which emerged during this period reveals the grand illusion through a series of ambiguities and contradictions. In all sections of public service and

ownership – schooling, housing, health and medicine – a strong and privileged private sector, bolstered by the inheritance of wealth, was maintained. Property ownership continued to become more centralized and concentrated within fewer hands. The expansion of state interventionism, local and central, ensured that the state became the largest employer and also the primary customer of private capital. Those industries which came under 'state ownership' were those essential to the reconstruction and consolidation of private manufacturing capital yet those deemed to be the least profitable or in need of the most reinvestment: coal, roads, railways, steel, communications, etc. The optimistic portrayal of this new pluralist society – based on equality of opportunity and access, on cradle-to-grave welfarism – disguised the structural contradictions inherent within the social arrangements and relations of the new dawn of economic expansionism. [...]

The 'attack on poverty' meant the virtual end of widespread destitution and starvation and there were major advances in housing, health care, schooling and the general 'quality of life' – but the divisions remained. [...]

The broadsides fired by stratification theorists and 'grand theorists' such as Parsons led to the reappraisal of Marxist analysis. Ten years after Dahrendorf's requiem for Marxism, Miliband (1969) and Quinney (1970) published their influential analyses of the advanced capitalist state. There followed a decade of important commentary on the state which picked up and developed the complexities of Miliband's central thesis. [...]

The reaffirmation of class analysis produced important work on class location (Poulantzas, 1973, 1975; Wright, 1976, 1978; Carchedi, 1977; Miliband, 1977; Hunt, 1977) in which the process by which classes were conceptualized and class location established was explored. [...]

Marginality, and the process of marginalization, is an important concept in the structural analysis of contemporary class location, clan fragmentation and Wright's discussion of contradictory class locations. Implicit in this analysis is the premise that during periods of economic recession part of the total workforce is used as the disposable surplus of wage-labour essential to the reconstruction of capital. [...]

Set within the context of the structural location of class the concept of marginality is both rigorous and significant. Marginality is manifested not only in terms of economic relations but also in terms of the subsequent political and ideological responses to those relations. Just as certain groups occupy 'contradictory class locations' so groups are pushed beyond the marginal locations of the relative surplus population. A range of identifiable groups and individuals, while relying on the capitalist mode of production and social democracy to provide them with an economic opportunity structure, live outside the 'legitimate' social relations of production. [...]

The link – unemployment, destitution, crime – has provided an important starting point for research which has developed the 'surplus population' thesis and its relevance in explaining not only certain categories of crime but also the process of criminalization of certain groups of people. [...]

Criminalization, the application of the criminal label to an identifiable social category, is dependent on how certain acts are labelled and on who has the power to label, and is directly limited to the political economy of marginalization. The power to criminalize is not derived necessarily in consensus politics but it carries with it the ideologies associated with marginalization and it is within these portrayals that certain actions are named, contained and regulated. This is a powerful process because it mobilizes popular approval and legitimacy in support of powerful interests within the state. As Hillyard's (1987) discussion of Northern Ireland illustrates clearly, public support is more likely to be achieved for state intervention against 'criminal' acts than for the repression or suppression of a 'political' cause. Further, even where no purposeful political intention is involved, the process of criminalization can divert attention from the social or political dynamics of a movement and specify its 'criminal' potential. If black youth is portrayed exclusively as 'muggers' (Hall *et al.*, 1978) there will be less tolerance of organized campaigns which emphasize that they have legitimate political and economic grievances (Gilroy, 1987a). The marginalization of women who campaign for rights or for peace and the questioning of their sexuality is a further example of the process by which meaningful and informed political action can be undermined, de-legitimized and criminalized (Chadwick and Little, 1987; Young, 1990). Fundamental to the criminalization thesis is the proposition that while political motives are downplayed, the degree of violence involved is emphasized. In industrial relations, for example, it is the violence of the pickets which is pinpointed (Scraton and Thomas, 1985; Fine and Millar, 1985; Beynon, 1985), rather than the importance, for the success of a strike, of preventing supplies getting through to a factory. The preoccupation with the 'violence' of political opposition makes it easier to mobilize popular support for measures of containment.

In many of these examples, 'criminalization' is a process which has been employed to underpin the repressive or control functions of the state. This compounds further the difficult distinction between 'normal' and 'social' crime, since criminalization fuses the categories. The problem remains that even when violence is only used tactically it is double-edged. It breaks the assumed agreement to pursue conflicts by 'democratic', 'parliamentary' means which is the basis of the social contract and the legitimacy of the liberal–democratic state. The state is then certain to react, by fair means or foul (Poulantzas, 1975). Consequently it becomes difficult to disentangle those instances in which criminalization is part of the maintenance of social order, and where it is not. Theoretically, however, it highlights a significant function of the law in the ideological containment of class conflict. Married to the process of marginalization, through which identifiable groups systematically and structurally become peripheral to the core relations of the political economy, criminalization offers a strong analytical construct. Taken together these theses provide the foundations to critical analyses of the state, the rule of law and social conflict in advanced capitalist society.

Racism, crime and the politics of neocolonialism

> ...if you were to ask a taxi driver, hotel clerk or news vendor in London they would explain the increase in violent crime, especially robbery, by the presence of West Indians. (Wilson, 1977: 69)

This statement, made by one of the leading New Right criminologists in the USA, directly attributes the escalation of street crime – and other 'predatory' crime – to the behaviour of a clearly identifiable group. It consolidated the media-hyped imagery of the 1970s which first named 'mugging' and then located it within the actions of black Afro Caribbean youth. What this confirmed, according to Gilroy (1987b: 108), was a generally held assumption that 'undesired immigrants' are infected by a 'culture of criminality and inbred inability to cope with that highest achievement of civilization – the rule of law'. That these views are prevalent in popular culture, the media coverage of 'hard news' and political commentaries is sufficient evidence of the breadth and depth of racism in Britain, but it is their institutionalization as all-pervasive (Gordon, 1983) which transforms imagery into ideology. The ideological construction of the race–crime–black criminality debate has been an essential condition upon which the differential policing and discriminatory punishment afforded to specific neighbourhoods has been based. [...]

In constructing an analysis of the social relations of neocolonialism as a determining context, clearly the connection has to be made with class and the relations of production. Advanced capitalism persistently has required relations based on national domination as well as the provision of a ready supply of cheap materials, fuel and labour power. Central to this is the historical development of class fragmentation, particularly the use and abuse of immigrant or migrant labour as 'reserve armies'. Ironically named 'guest workers', the exploitation of cheap labour from the colonies has been a key feature in the construction of European and US labour forces throughout the twentieth century. [...]

What has become clear during the 1980s, however, is the simple proposition that the differential policing and targeting of particular communities has not only led to rebellion (Scraton, 1987) but has also completed the process of marginalization. [...]

The shift from labour-intensive production and the uneven distribution of the effects of economic crisis in Britain have contributed significantly to the imposition of long-term, structural unemployment. The inevitable consequences of the economic, political and ideological location of black communities is that they are overrepresented in this surplus population.

> As with the late nineteenth century constructions of moral degeneracy and social contagion, black people have found themselves on the wrong end of the rough–respectable and nondeserving–deserving continua. This series of factors have created the preconditions in which black communities can be identified as the new 'dangerous classes'. (Sim *et al.*, 1987)

The feminist critiques and the determining context of patriarchy

The marginalization of women within patriarchies takes a variety of political and economic forms: the unwaged and unrecognized domestic mode of production (Delphy, 1984); the 'control of women's labour power' (Hartmann, 1979: 14) and the all-pervasiveness of masculine values and processes in paid work (Cockburn, 1986; Walby, 1986); the threat and reality of physical violence (Stanko, 1985; Kelly, 1988). [...]

Within criminology, as Carol Smart first noted in 1976, the 'wider moral, political, economic and sexual spheres which influence women's status and position in society' has been neglected or seen as irrelevant to the priority of studying men and crime (Smart, 1976: 185). More recent feminist research and publication has posed 'fundamental questions about the adequacy' of criminological analyses which has taken for granted the 'exclusion of women' (Gelsthorpe and Morris, 1990: 7). The substantive debates have prioritized: the relationship between patriarchy, the rule of law and the underpinnings of theoretical criminology (Smart, 1989); the universality of violence against women and the persistent reluctance of the state to intervene (Kelly and Radford, 1987); women's incarceration in prisons (Carlen, 1983) and in mental institutions (Showalter, 1987); family law and its 'role in enforcing women's position in society' (Bottomley, 1985:184).

In addition to this work there has been further critical research into women and crime (Carlen, 1988; Carlen and Worrall, 1987; Heidensohn, 1985). Hilary Allen's (1987: 1) work, for example, confirmed previous research in showing that women are 'twice as likely as a man to be dealt with by psychiatric rather than penal means'. Further, the trend – first reported in 1988 – of a sharp increase in the imprisonment of women, more readily and for longer sentences, has consolidated as courts have become more severe on women offenders. [...]

What this range of work has achieved has been to locate these issues within the material base of patriarchy demonstrating the diversity of women's oppression and the dynamics of male dominance. This includes 'women's access to production' and 'control over biological reproduction' but also through 'control of women's sexuality through a particular form of heterosexuality' (Mahony, 1985: 70). For 'male identity' and 'male sexuality' are 'crucial to the maintenance of male power' (Mahony, 1985). The determining context of patriarchal relations is based on the material and physical power appropriated by – but also ascribed to – men, and this is supported by a 'hegemonic form of masculinity in the society as a whole' with women 'oriented to accommodating the interests and desires of men' (Connell, 1987: 183). While women fight back individually and collectively, 'emphasized feminity' internalizes the ideology of servicing and use-value, and feeds the politics of dependency. It is within this process that gender divisions and ascribed sexualities become legitimated as 'natural' and, therefore, inevitable.

As with Connell's work, Brittan (1989) and Segal (1990) have explored the importance of hegemonic masculinity or masculinism in its subordination not only of women's sexuality, but also other male sexualities. [...]

Clearly all women are controlled by the public and private realities and fears inherent within male power relations but when they assert their rights, contest their oppression or organize against the discriminatory practices of the law, they become the threat. These are the women, already economically marginalized by the dependency relations of advanced capitalist patriarchy, who are further marginalized by their politics of opposition. Ultimately, as Chadwick and Little (1987) show, they are criminalized. The feminist critiques of criminology, both old and new, have demonstrated that critical criminology must have at its core the marginalization and criminalization of women, women's experiences of the criminal justice process and relationship of women to crime. They provide not only an essential contribution to critical analysis but also to the realization of a critical methodology which interprets the interpersonal experiences of women within the broader structural relations of advanced capitalist patriarchy.

Conclusion

What this discussion has pursued is the central argument that critical criminology recognizes the reciprocity inherent in the relationship between *structure* and *agency* but also that structural relations embody the primary determining contexts of production, reproduction and neocolonialism. In order to understand the dynamics of life in advanced capitalist societies and the institutionalization of ideological relations within the state and other key agencies it is important to take account of the historical, political and economic contexts of classism, sexism, heterosexism and racism. These categories do not form hierarchies of oppression, they are neither absolute nor are they totally determining, but they do carry with them the weight and legitimacy of official discourse. They reflect and succour the power–knowledge axis both in popular culture and in academic endeavour.

From P. Scraton and K. Chadwick, 'The theoretical and political priorities of critical criminology', in K. Stenson and D. Cowell (eds) The Politics of Crime Control (London: Sage), 1991, pp. 161–185.

References

Allen, H. (1987) *Justice Unbalanced: Gender, Psychiatry and Judicial Decisions*. Milton Keynes: Open University Press.

Beynon, H. (1985) *Digging Deeper: Issues in the Miners' Strike*. London: Verso.

Bottomley, A. (1985) 'What is happening to family law? A feminist critique of conciliation', in J. Brophy and C. Smart (eds), *Women in Law*. London: Routledge & Kegan Paul.

Brittan, A. (1989) *Masculinity and Power*. Cambridge: Polity.

Carchedi, G. (1977) *On the Economic Identification of Social Classes*. London: Routledge & Kegan Paul.

Carlen, P. (1983) *Women's Imprisonment*. London: Routledge & Kegan Paul.

Carlen, P. (1988) *Women, Crime and Poverty*. Milton Keynes: Open University Press.

Carlen, P. and Worrall, A. (1987) *Gender, Crime and Justice*. Milton Keynes: Open University Press.

Chadwick, K. and Little, C. (1987) 'The criminalisation of women', in P. Scraton (ed.), *Law, Order and the Authoritarian State*. Milton Keynes: Open University Press.

Cockburn, C. (1986) *Machineries of Dominance*. London: Pluto.

Cohen, S. (1985) *Visions of Social Control*. Cambridge: Polity.

Connell, R.W. (1987) *Gender and Power*. Cambridge: Polity.

Delphy, C. (1984) *Close to Home: A Materialist Analysis of Women's Oppression*. London: Hutchinson.

Fine, B. and Millar, R. (eds) (1985) *Policing the Miners' Strike*. London: Lawrence & Wishart.

Gamble, A. (1981) *Britain in Decline*. London: Papermac.

Gelsthorpe, L. and Morris, A. (1990) *Feminist Perspectives in Criminology*. Milton Keynes: Open University Press.

Giddens, A. (1979) *Central Problems in Social Theory*. London: Macmillan.

Giddens, A. (1984) *The Constitution of Society*. Cambridge: Polity.

Giddens, A. (1987) *The Nation-State and Violence*. Cambridge: Polity.

Gilroy, P. (1987a) *There Ain't No Black in the Union Jack*. London: Hutchinson.

Gilroy. P. (1987b) 'The myth of black criminality', in P. Scraton (ed.), *Law, Order and the Authoritarian State*. Milton Keynes: Open University Press.

Gordon, P. (1983) *White Law*. London: Pluto Press.

Gouldner, A.W. (1969) *The Coming Crisis in Western Sociology*. London: Heinemann.

Gouldner, A.W. (1973) 'Foreword' in I. Taylor, P. Walton and J. Young, *The New Criminology*. London: Routledge & Kegan Paul.

Gramsci, A. (1971) *Selections from the Prison Notebooks*. London: Lawrence & Wishart.

Hall, S. *et al.* (1978) *Policing the Crisis*. London: Macmillan.

Hartmann, H. (1979) 'The unhappy marriage of Marxism and feminism: towards a progressive union', *Capital and Class*, 8.

Heidensohn, P. (1985) *Women and Crime*. London: Macmillan.

Hunt, A. (ed.) (1977) *Class and Class Structure*. London: Lawrence & Wishart.

Kelly, L. (1988) *Surviving Sexual Violence*. Cambridge: Polity.

Kelly, L. and Radford, J. (1987) 'The problem of men: feminist perspectives on sexual violence', in P. Scraton (ed.), *Law, Order and the Authoritarian State*. Milton Keynes: Open University Press.

Mahony, P. (1985) *Schools for the Boys? Co-education Reassessed*. London: Hutchinson.

Miliband, R. (1969) *The State in Capitalist Society*. London: Weidenfeld & Nicholson.

Miliband R. (1977) *Class and Politics*. London: Macmillan.

Poulantzas, N. (1973) 'On social classes', *New Left Review*, 78.

Poulantzas, N. (1975) *Political Power and Social Classes*. London: New Left Books.

Quinney, R. (1970) *The Social Reality of Crime*. New York: Little Brown.

Scraton, P. (1987) 'Unreasonable force: policing, punishment and marginalisation', in P. Scraton (ed.), *Law. Order and the Authoritarian State*. Milton Keynes: Open University Press.

Scraton, P. and Thomas, P. (1985) *The State v The People: Lessons from the Coal Dispute (Journal of Law and Society*, special issue). Oxford: Blackwell.

Segal, L. (1990) *Slow Motion: Changing Masculinities, Changing Men*. London: Virago.

Showalter, E. (1987) *The Female Malady. Women, Madness and English Culture, 1830–1890*. London: Virago.

Sim, J. (1990) *Medical Power in Prisons: The Prison Medical Service in England 1774–1989*. Milton Keynes: Open University Press.

Sim, J., Scraton, P. and Gordon, P. (1987) 'Crime, the state and critical analysis: an introduction', in P. Scraton (ed.), *Law, Order and the Authoritarian State*. Milton Keynes: Open University Press.

Smart, C. (1976) *Women, Crime and Criminology*. London: Routledge & Kegan Paul.

Smart, C. (1989) *Feminism and the Power of Law*. London: Routledge.

Stanko, E. (1985) *Intimate Intrusions*. London: Routledge & Kegan Paul.

Taylor-Gooby, P. (1982) *The Welfare State from the Second World War to the 1980s*. D355 Social Policy and Social Welfare, Milton Keynes: Open University Press.

Walby, S. (1986) *Patriarchy at Work*. Cambridge: Polity.

Wilson, J.Q. (1977) 'Crime and punishment in England', in R.E. Tyrrell Jr. (ed.), *The Future that Doesn't Work: Social Democracy's Failures in Britain*. New York: Doubleday.

Wright, E.O. (1976) 'Class boundaries in advanced capitalist societies', *New Left Review*, 98.

Wright, E.O. (1978) *Class, Crisis and the State*. London: New Left Books.

12.3 Radical criminology in Britain
Jock Young

British criminology in the late 1960s was at a cross roads. The social democratic positivism which had been dominant in the post-war period entered into a period of prolonged crisis, out of which emerged the two major contending paradigms: radical criminology and administrative criminology. Of course, parallel processes occurred in other Western countries, but the exceptional success of radical criminology in this country, together with the particular flair of the state-centred administrative criminology, are a product of specific political and social conditions in Britain. It goes without saying that criminology does not occur in a vacuum. The central problem for social democratic or Fabian positivism was that a wholescale improvement in social conditions resulted, not in a drop in crime, but the reverse. I have termed this the aetiological crisis, and it was, of course, accompanied by grave problems in the prisons and within policing (Young, 1986).

What is radical criminology?

It is that part of the discipline which sees the causes of crime as being at core the class and patriarchial relations endemic to our social order and which sees fundamental changes as necessary to reduce criminality. It is politically at base socialist, libertarian/anarchist, socialist or radical feminist. It quarrels amongst itself – as such a radical mix has throughout history – but it is quite distinct from those parts of the discipline which see crime as a marginal phenomenon solvable with technical adjustments by control agencies which are, in essence, all right and in need of no fundamental changes.

The process of change in British criminology

In order to more systematically understand this process of change it is necessary to first create a structure which can adequately deal with the history of the development of paradigms in the social sciences. A central insight to this is the division between the *interior* and the *exterior* histories of a discipline.[1]

The interior history is the *material* and the intellectual problems which a discipline confronts in terms of its ability to sustain practitioners in the world and the way in which the paradigm generates problems and faces anomalies. The exterior history is the *material* and *political/cultural* context in which the discipline exists.

Exterior history

The most immediate material problem was a rising crime rate coupled with an increasing prison population, recidivism and declining police clear-up rates.

The political context of the emergence of radical criminology, both in Britain and the United States was, of course, the emergence of the New Left in the late sixties and early seventies. Radical criminology was as much part and parcel of this train of thought as were the anti-psychiatry movement, the prison support groups and community action groups in the inner cities and sit-ins on campuses. The specific problem of some part of radical criminological theory may be explained within itself, in terms of its particular debates and controversies, but its flavour, its essence and its care core propositions were indelibly coloured by its New Left origins and this is as true today as it was in the seventies. Central to New Left thinking of the time was a critique of the extension of the state. It is important to underline the extent to which the Welfare State itself was seen as a source of oppression.[2]

Interior history

The major problem facing positivism was what I have termed the aetiological crisis. That is, the contention that bad conditions lead to bad behaviour was undermined by the fact that as income levels rise, educational standards improved, slums were knocked down and unemployment levels dropped, crime continued to rise.

The most immediate response of positivism to the aetiological crisis was:

a an increased emphasis on individual rather than social reasons for crime. Important here were notions of maternal and paternal deprivation, the greater acceptance of biological factors and the obviously short-lived explanation of 'delinquent generations': children ill-socialised because of the war years;

b bifurcation: that is an explanation of only a minority of crime and delinquency as being a product of deep-seated individual causes and the rest due to individual choice and capriciousnesses. The problem of the rapid increase was thus cut down to size and explained away as a product of causes which were not endemic to the society as a whole. (See Greenwood and Young, 1980; J. Clarke, 1980; A. Bottoms, 1977.)

Radical criminology confronted the aetiological crisis in a dramatic fashion. It deemed that there was no rise in crime. In a situation worthy of Galileo the positivists looking through the telescope at crime saw an alarming increase and invoked further and further complexities to their paradigm. The radicals blamed the telescope. They argued that the rise of crime was largely epiphenomenal: it was a social construction produced by increased police time, less tolerant courts and a moral panic of the public swelled up by the mass media. The criminal statistics were held to be an index more at the disposal of police forces than that of crime and, indeed, the causal link between crime and, for example, poverty was cast into grave doubt. Crime was, after all, ubiquitous. The rich engaged in crime just as much as the poor – they were simply too powerful to be apprehended. And the same was true for middle and working class juvenile delinquents and black and white crime differentials.

Radical criminology: a developing paradigm

I want to look first at the flaws and advantages of the radical paradigm and discuss how development has occurred according to the interior and exterior histories of the subject. It is important to note at this juncture that just as establishment criminology developed into the new administrative criminology, radical criminology developed from an early left idealist to a realist phase. (See J. Young, 1986.)

I have detailed how the particular social and political context which gave birth to radical criminology impressed on the paradigm certain flaws. Important of these are:

1 *The unflawed underdog*

There is a tendency to idealise oppressed groups and an inability to see anti-social behaviour and divisions within them. This has led to an underplaying of the problem of crime and the creation of taboos about such areas as inter-racial crime. This is being countered recently by the increased political focus on crimes such as domestic violence, racist attacks and child abuse.

2 *Unwillingness to deal with positivism.*

The original unwillingness to come to terms with sociological rather than biological positivism which is displayed in the above incapacity to see how outside determination causes internal divisions, is to an extent obviated, although not solved, by the passing of the aetiological crisis. That is as unemployment in Britain has risen fast over the period, it is less of a problem to relate this to higher working-class crime rates, anti-social behaviour, heroin addiction, etc.

3 *Unwillingness to deal with statistics*

The tendency to see crime and other social problem rates as an epiphenomenon of social control is a widespread legacy of the early days of the paradigm. It is seen in, for example, in the seminal text of British radical criminology, *Policing the Crisis* (Hall *et al.*, 1978), as it is seen in social constructionism in the United States and abolitionism on the Continent. Once again, the worsening of social conditions makes such arguments much more low keyed.

4 *Unwillingness to deal with reform*

The radical emphasis on the genesis of crime in the core nature of the system and its values tends to preclude reform, and the New Left heritage is, as we have seen, very critical of the interventions of the Welfare State. (See Hood, 1987.) The predicament of Britain under the 'cuts' inflicted by a Thatcherite Government intent on rolling back the Welfare State has quickly reversed the attitudes of many British radicals! The importance of retaining the gains of the Welfare State and making local and national reforms becomes paramount. All of these left idealist tendencies we have discussed elsewhere (Lea and Young, 1984; Kinsey *et al.*, 1986; Young, 1986) and, of course, it would be wrong to suggest that such a position had disappeared (witness, e.g. P. Scraton, 1987). But there has been a distinct movement which attempts to cope with these problems and respond to the demands of this present period as was well charted by Tony Bottoms in his recent inaugural professorial lecture at the Cambridge Institute (A. Bottoms, 1987). But, contrary to Bottoms, there has also been a continuity in radical criminology from its early days through left idealism into realism (Young, 1988). I have written enough of the flaws of the paradigm: let us look at its continuing advantages.

The advantages of radical criminology

Let us spell out the advantages that radical crimi-nology has over its establishment competitors:

1 It is not politically constrained so that it is possible to trace the line of causality of crime to situations endemic in the social structure. That is to relationships of class and patriarchy.

2 It is not politically constrained so that it is able to point to endemic problems in the administration of justice. It can, for example, engage in a fullblown critique of policing and the need for genuine public accountability.

3 It is sensitised to the fact that crime statistics are social constructs and that their reality is not something 'out there' as positivism and administrative criminology would have it, but a product of behaviour and evaluation. At heart the extent of crime is a political as well as a behavioural matter. If there is one single fact that the radicals can tell a student of deviance, it is that the figures for crime, for alcoholism, for heroin addiction, for mental illness, etc. are not 'hard' facts in the sense that this is true of the height and weight of physical bodies. They are moral not physical statistics.

4 It is committed to the notion that the understanding of human behaviour and hence the aetiology of crime has a subjective component and that the central dynamic of this is the experience of justice and injustice. Because of this it is against generalisations about human behaviour in terms of mechanistic laws irrespective of culture and country, whether of a positivistic or an administrative kind.

5 Radical criminology introduces politics and morality into criminology and it sites the essential causes of crime in the injustice and immorality of the system. That is, it does not believe we can understand the causes of crime, the construction of criminal statistics or the basis

of successful intervention without consideration of politics and morality. It is a sense of injustice that moves the criminal actor (however unjust his or her actions), a sense of justice that creates the moral yardstick by which crime is variously measured and which determines the effect of interventions: whether to exacerbate (if unjust) or ameliorate (if judicious). It is the inability of administrative criminology to deal with the moral and political basis of crime which is its most fundamental flaw.

The emergence of administrative criminology

I have detailed elsewhere the emergence of the new administrative criminology as the major paradigm in establishment approaches to crime (1986, 1988). What is important to note is that its main thrust has been to sidestep the aetiological crisis by suggesting that the causes of crime are either relatively unim-portant or politically impossible to tackle. There is no need to explain the rise in crime: it is obvious that there is a rise. Rather we must find ways of stemming its impact. The question becomes what is the most cost-effective way of making control inter-ventions, an emphasis 'on the purely technical cost-benefit ratio aspects of crime: the opportunities for crime available in the environment, and the high risks attached to criminal activity' (Downes and Rock, 1982, p. 194). It is important to note how administrative criminology, both in Britain and the United States, was a result of the double failure of orthodox criminology. That is, not only was posi-tivism seen to be not working but, a little later – in the 1970s, particularly with the publication of a series of devastating police studies in the United States – neo-classicism was palpably not working either. If there was a crisis in aetiology there was also a crisis in penalty. Conventional police work simply did not seem effective against crime (see Skolnick and Bayley, 1986), and, of course, the pris-ons were the havens of crisis and the harbours of recidivism. This double crisis was quite clearly per-ceived in the research of Ron Clarke and his co-workers at the Home Office. (See especially, Clarke and Mayhew, 1980, chapter one.) The con-cept of situational crime prevention coupled with rational choice theory which they have pioneered to meet this challenge is – whatever its theoretical limitations – an innovative paradigm of great importance (Cornish and Clarke, 1986). [...]

I have no quarrel with the fact that the Government – on both a national and local level – should commission applied research on a customer-contract principle. The problem is, as Tony Bottoms has trenchantly pointed out, the national budgeting for research is so overwhelmingly in the bestow of such an orientation that there is a drastic lack of balance against basic criminological work of an explanatory character operating without political restrictions in its conceptualisation. (See A. Bottoms, 1987.) As Roger Hood has indicated, the emphasis on policy relevant research as set out by central government 'raises the question – what does policy relevance mean, as defined by the administrator? A short term administrative problem? Or the exploration of radical alternatives? One must at least recognise the natural defensiveness of all organisations when threatened with critical scrutiny, or even survival. Are there not problems in leaving them to set their own research agendas?' (1987, p. 537).

> *From J. Young, 'Radical criminology in Britain',* British Journal of Criminology, *1988, 28: 159–183.*

Notes

1 I am developing here the analysis first used by Ian Hacking (1981) in his seminal article on the history of statistics as used by Alan Phipps (1987) in his history of victimisation studies in Britain and the United States.

2 A re-read of the famous Becker – Gouldner debate, for example, reveals not merely that Becker was critical of the middle management of deviancy (the 'zoo-keepers'), whilst Gouldner was critical of the master institutions of society (the 'zoo'), but that both were opposed to the Welfare interventions of the State in a way which would make most present-day British radicals feet distinctly uneasy.

References

Bottoms, A. (1977). 'Reflections on the Renaissance of Dangerousness'. *Howard Journal*. 16, 70–96.

Bottoms, A. (1987). 'Reflections on the Criminological Enterprise'. *The Cambridge Law Journal*. 46, Part 2.

Clarke, J. (1980). 'Social Democratic Delinquents and Fabian Families' in National Deviancy Conference (1980).

Clarke, R. and Mayhew, P. (eds.) (1980), *Designing Out Crime*. London, HMSO.

Cornish, D. and Clarke, R. (1986). *The Reasoning Criminal*. New York: Springer Verlag.

Downes, D. and Rock, P. (1982). *Understanding Deviance*. Oxford, Clarendon Press.

Greenwood, V. and Young, J. (1980). 'Ghettoes of Freedom' in National Deviancy Conference (1980).

Hacking, I. (1981). 'How should we do a History of Statistics'. *Ideology and Consciousness*. 8.

Hall, S., *et al.*, (1978). *Policing the Crisis*. London, Macmillan.

Hood, R. (1987). 'Some Reflections on the Role of Criminology in Public Policy'. *Criminal Law Review*. 527–538.

Kinsey, R., Lea, J. and Young, J. (1986). *Losing the Fight Against Crime*. Oxford, Blackwell.

Lea, J. and Young, J. (1984). *What is to be done about Law and Order*. London, Penguin.

Phipps, A. (1987). *Criminal Victimization, Crime Control and Political Action*. PhD Thesis: Centre for Criminology, Middlesex Polytechnic.

Scraton, P. (1987). *Law, Order and the Authoritarian State*. Milton Keynes, Open University Press.

Skolnick, J. and Bayley, D. (1986). *The New Blue Line*. New York, The Free Press.

Young, J. (1986). 'The Failure of Criminology: The Need for Radical Realism', in R. Matthews and J. Young (eds). *Confronting Crime*. London, Sage.

Young, J. (1988). 'The Tasks of a Realist Criminology'. *Contemporary Crises*. II.

12.4 Abolitionism and crime control
Willem de Haan

An abolitionist perspective on crime control might seem like a contradiction in terms not unlike a peace research approach to waging a war. Abolitionism is based on the moral conviction that social life should not and, in fact, cannot be regulated effectively by criminal law and that, therefore, the role of the criminal justice system should be drastically reduced while other ways of dealing with problematic situations, behaviours and events are being developed and put into practice. Abolitionists regard crime primarily as the result of the social order and are convinced that punishment is not the appropriate reaction. Instead a minimum of coercion and interference with the personal lives of those involved and a maximum amount of care and service for all members of society is advocated. [...]

The term 'abolitionism' stands for a social movement, a theoretical perspective, and a political strategy.

Abolitionism as a social movement

Abolitionism emerged as an anti-prison movement when, at the end of the 1960s, a destructuring impulse took hold of thinking about the social control of deviance and crime among other areas (Cohen, 1985). In Western Europe, anti-prison groups aiming at prison abolition were founded in Sweden and Denmark (1967), Finland and Norway (1968), Great Britain (1970), France (1970), and the Netherlands (1971). Their main objective was to soften the suffering which society inflicts on its prisoners. This implied a change in general thinking concerning punishment, humanization of the various forms of imprisonment in the short run and, in the long run, the replacement of the prison system by more adequate and up-to-date measures of crime control.

It has been suggested that abolitionism typically emerged in small countries or countries with little crime and 'would never have been "invented" in a country like the United States of America with its enormous crime rate, violence, and criminal justice apparatus' (Scheerer, 1986: 18). However, in Canada and the United States family members of (ex-)convicts, church groups and individuals were

also engaged in prisoners' support work and actively struggling for prison reform. More specifically, these prison abolitionists in the United States considered their struggle for abolition of prisons to be a historical mission, a continuation and fulfilment of the struggle against slavery waged by their forebears. Imprisonment is seen as a form of blasphemy, as morally objectionable and indefensible and, therefore, to be abolished (Morris, 1976: 11). To this aim, a long-term strategy in the form of a three-step 'attrition model' is proposed, consisting of a total freeze on the planning and building of prisons, excarceration of certain categories of lawbreakers by diverting them from the prison system and decarceration, or the release of as many inmates as possible.

Originating in prison reform movements in the 1960s and 1970s in both Western Europe and North America, abolitionism developed as a new paradigm in (critical) criminology and as an alternative approach to crime control. As academic involvement increased and abolitionism became a theoretical perspective, its focus widened from the prison system to the penal system, thereby engaging in critical analyses of penal discourse and, in particular, the concepts of crime and punishment, penal practices, and the penal or criminal justice system.

Abolitionism as a theoretical perspective

As a theoretical perspective abolitionism has a negative and a positive side. Negatively, abolitionism is deeply rooted in a criticism of the criminal justice system and its 'prison solution' to the problem of crime. Positively, on the basis of this criticism an alternative approach to crime and punishment is offered both in theory and in practice. Thus, the abolitionist approach is essentially reflexive and (de)constructivist. We will first take a look at the negative side of abolitionism which will be followed by a brief exposé of its positive side.

From the abolitionist point of view, the criminal justice system's claim to protect people from being victimized by preventing and controlling crime, seems grossly exaggerated. Moreover, the notion of controlling crime by penal intervention is ethically problematic as people are used for the purpose of 'deterrence', by demonstrating power and domination. Punishment is seen as a self-reproducing form of violence. The penal practice of blaming people for their supposed intentions (for being bad and then punishing and degrading them accordingly) is dangerous because the social conditions for recidivism are thus reproduced. Morally degrading and segregating people is especially risky when the logic of exclusion is reinforced along the lines of differences in sex, race, class, culture or religion.

For the abolitionist, current crime policies are irrational in their assumptions that: crime is caused by individuals who for some reason go wrong; that crime is a problem for the state and its criminal justice system to control; and that criminal law and punishment or treatment of individual wrong-doers are appropriate means of crime control (Steinert, 1986). Crime control is based on the fallacy of taking *pars pro toto* or, as Wilkins (1984) has put it, crime control policy is typically made by reference to the dramatic incident, thereby assuming that all that is necessary is to get the micro-model right in order for the macro-model to follow without further ado. According to Wilkins, we must consider not only the specific criminal act but also the environment in which it is embedded. It could be added that the same argument holds for punishment and, more specifically, for imprisonment as an alleged solution to the problem of crime.

Abolitionism as a political strategy

Initially, a political strategy had been developed on the bases of the experiences of prison reform groups in their political struggle for penal and social reform. This 'politics of abolition' (Mathiesen, 1974, 1986) consistently refuses to offer 'positive' alternatives or solutions. It restricts itself to advancing open-ended, 'unfinished', 'negative' reforms, such as abolishing parts of the prison system. This requires that they be conceptualized in terms alien to current criminal justice discourse.

More recently, positive alternatives to punishment are also being considered. Various proposals have been made by abolitionists and others to decentralize or even completely dismantle the present penal system in order to create forms of 'informal justice' as an addition to or replacement of the present criminal justice system.

Their implementation also raises many questions, however, concerning allegations about widening the net of social control and, at the same time, thinning the mesh, extending and blurring the boundaries between formal penal intervention and other, informal forms of social control, thereby masking the coercive character of alternative interventions (Abel, 1982; Cohen, 1985).

Fundamental reform of the penal system requires not only imaginative alternatives but, at the same time, a radical change in the power structure. Thus a 'politics of abolition' aims at a negative strategy for changing the politics of punishment by abolishing not only the criminal justice system but also the repressive capitalist system part by part or step by step (Mathiesen, 1986).

A fundamental reform of the penal system presupposes not only a radical change of the existing power structure but also of the dominant culture. However, currently there is no appropriate social agency for any radical reform of the politics of punishment. There seems no immediate social basis upon which a progressive, let alone an abolitionist, strategy of crime control might be spontaneously constructed (Matthews, 1987: 389). Abolitionists tend to refer to the re-emergence of the subcultures of the new social movements with their own infrastructure of interaction and communication and their new ethics of solidarity, social responsibility, and care (Steinert, 1986: 28–9; see also Christie, 1982: 75–80). As Harris argues, the inadequacy of virtually all existing reform proposals lies in the failure to stop outside the traditional and dominant ways of framing the issues. To explore alternative visions of justice we need to consider 'philosophies, paradigms, or models that transcend not only conventional criminological and political lines, but also natural and cultural boundaries and other limiting habits of the mind' (Harris, 1987: 11). According to Harris a wide range of visions of a better world and a better future offer a rich resource for a fundamental rethinking of our approach to crime and justice. The new social movements, in particular the women's movement, have pointed out fundamental weaknesses or biases in criminology's background assumptions, conceptual frameworks, methodology and tacit morality (Gelsthorpe and Morris, 1990). However, the relationship between abolitionism and, for example, feminism is not without stress (van Swaaningen, 1989).

Abolitionism on crime control

Abolitionism calls for decriminalization, depenalization, destigmatization, decentralization and deprofessionalization, as well as the establishment of other, informal, participator, (semi-)autonomous ways of dealing with social problems. Problematic events may just as well be defined as social troubles, problems or conflicts due to negligence or caused by 'accident' rather than by purpose or criminal intent. What is needed is a wide variety of possible responses without a priori assuming criminal intent and responsibility.

Prison abolition, let alone penal abolition, requires an imaginative rethinking of possible ways of handling problematic situations as social problems, conflicts, troubles, accidents, etc, as well as reconceptualizing punishment and developing new ways of managing 'deviance' on the basis of, at least partial, suspension of the logic of guilt and punishment. [...]

This way of looking at crime and crime control is, of course, controversial. The abolitionist perspective is sometimes criticised for being naive and idealistic. In practice, however, the abolitionist approach turns out to be realistic in that social problems and conflicts are seen as inherent to social life. Since it is illusory that the criminal justice system can protect us effectively against such unfortunate events, it seems more reasonable to deal with troubles pragmatically rather than by approaching them in terms of guilt and punishment. Effectively to prevent and control unacceptable situations and behaviours requires a variety of social responses, one and only one of which is the criminal justice system. Its interventions are more of symbolic importance than of practical value. With some social, technical and organizational imagination 'crime' could be coped with in ways much more caring for those immediately involved. A variety of procedures could be established and institutionalized where social problems or conflicts, problematic events or behaviours could be dealt with through negotiation, mediation, arbitration, at intermediate levels. For dealing with the most common or garden varieties of crime, which is in any case the vast bulk of all recorded criminality, criminal prosecutions are simply redundant.

> *From W. de Haan, 'Abolitionism and crime control: a contradiction in terms', in K. Stenson and D. Cowell (eds)* The Politics of Crime Control *(London: Sage), 1991, 203–217.*

References

Abel, R. (ed.) (1982) *The Politics of Informal Justice*, Vols 1 and 2, New York: Academic Press.

Christie, N. (1986) 'Images of man in modern penal law', *Contemporary Crises*, 10: 95–106.

Cohen, S. (1985) *Visions of Social Control. Crime, Punishment and Classification*. Cambridge: Polity Press.

Gelsthorpe, L. and Morris, A. (eds) (1990) *Feminist Perspectives in Criminology*. Milton Keynes: Open University Press.

Harris, K. (1987) 'Moving into the new millennium: toward a feminist vision of justice', *The Prison Journal*, 67: 27–38.

Mathiesen, T. (1974) 'The politics of abolition. Essays', in *Political Action Theory*. London: Martin Robertson.

Mathiesen, T. (1986) 'The politics of abolition', *Contemporary Crises*, 10: 81–94.

Matthews, R. (1987) 'Taking realist criminology seriously', *Contemporary Crises*, 11: 371–401.

Morris, M. (ed.) (1976) *Instead of Prisons: A Handbook for Abolitionists*. Syracuse, New York: Prison Research Action Project.

Scheerer, S. (1986) 'Towards abolitionism', *Contemporary Crises*, 10: 5–20.

Steinert, H. (1986) 'Beyond crime and punishment', *Contemporary Crises*, 10: 21–39.

Swaaningen, R. van (1989) 'Feminism and abolitionism as critiques of criminology', *International Journal of the Sociology of Law*, 17: 287–306.

Wilkins, L. (1984) *Consumerist Criminology*. London: Heinemann.

13

Left and right realism

13.1 **Reflections on realism**
Roger Matthews and Jock Young   278

13.2 **The failure of criminology: the need for a radical realism**
Jock Young   282

13.3 **The emerging underclass**
Charles Murray   288

13.4 **Broken windows**
James Q. Wilson and George L. Kelling   295

Introduction

The Reagan and Thatcher governments, and their successors, which dominated American and British politics for much of the 1970s and 1980s, represented a significant break with the past. Both favoured free-market economics and were highly critical of the 'Great Society' and welfare programmes that had developed in previous decades. This political shift in turn gave rise to a new range of social policy commentators, including on the subject of crime and justice. Such observers differed politically, from those on the right who were broadly support-ive of the free-market criticisms of previous arrangements, through to those on the left who were critical both of free-market economics and associated political ideas and also of what they saw to be the unhelpful, increasingly irrelevant ideas of their radical predecessors.

Left realism, particularly in its influential British form, is interesting not least for the role played by Jock Young. In the previous chapter we saw how central Young was to early radical British criminology. Much of the critique of radical criminology which gave rise to left realism also emanates from Young. In the first excerpt Roger Matthews and Jock Young **(Reading 13.1)** outline some of the contrasts between left and right realism and also between left realism and radical criminology. Crucially, they say, whilst radical criminology produced an important critique of conventional criminology 'it was never able to offer a competing alter-native'. In outlining the building blocks of realism they introduce what they call the 'square of crime' – a graphic illustration designed to remind us that crime and criminalization are the product of a variety of competing institutional forces and that none of this can be reduced to the actions of the state.

A key element of the left realist critique of radical criminology was the suggestion that the latter, in its emphasis on processes of criminalization, tended to underplay the impact of crime on its victims. In the second excerpt, Jock Young **(Reading 13.2)** outlines the way in which the recognition that 'crime really is a problem' is central to left realism. It is vital, he argues, that realism should 'neither succumb to hysteria nor relapse into a critical denial of the severity of crime'. At its heart there should be an accurate victimology. Simultaneously a realist criminol-ogy, he argues, must combat what he calls 'impossibilism': the sense of being unable to do anything about crime without some form of social revolution.

One of the most visible of the commentators in a body of work that has subsequently become known as 'right realism' is Charles Murray **(Reading 13.3)**. His concern here is with the idea of an 'underclass'. Writing in 1990, he argued that the US has seen the emergence in recent times of an 'underclass' and that similar trends were visible and under way in the UK. The best indicator of an underclass in the making, he says, is illegitimacy. Children tend to behave like the adults around, he argues, and the absence of male role models produces a breeding ground for misconduct of various sorts. The second place to look for an underclass according to Murray is crime. Crime has been getting worse, he says, and it is time we stopped denying it. Moreover, the chances of being punished have declined and, even when punished, the penalties are now less. All these things need to be reversed is the argument – difficult though this is to do.

The final piece in this chapter is one of the most widely cited articles in criminology in recent decades. Written by James Q. Wilson and George Kelling, 'Broken Windows' **(Reading 13.4)** is frequently referred to but, I guess, read by relatively few of those that talk about it. Here is your chance to read it and make your own mind up. The article picks up on arguments that were particularly influential at the time ('Broken Windows' was published in 1982) which suggested that criminal justice agencies generally, and the police in particular, had relatively little impact on overall crime rates. The article is a strong attempt at refuting such arguments (actually what Jock Young in another context might have called 'impossibilism'). The heart of their thesis – and the source of both much of its influence and subsequent controversy – concerns the impact of policing (or its absence) on disorderly conduct and feelings of security. Their conclusion – in some respects an optimistic one – is that the police are 'plainly the key to order maintenance'.

Questions for discussion

1. Why, according to Matthews and Young, was radical criminology never much more than 'the bad conscience of conventional criminology'?

2. What do realists and abolitionists share?

3. What is meant by the 'square of crime'?

4. Why does left realism require an 'accurate victimology' and why might this distinguish it from other radical criminologies?

5. Why does Charles Murray think illegitimacy is the best indicator of an underclass in the making?

6. What is Murray's evidence for his argument that crime has become safer to commit? How satisfactory is his argument?

7. Explain why Wilson and Kelling's article is called 'Broken Windows'?

8. In what ways are the police 'plainly the key to order maintenance' according to Wilson and Kelling?

13.1 Reflections on realism
Roger Matthews and Jock Young

Left and right realism

Although there are some points of overlap between the 'new realists' and the 'radical realists', these two approaches represent distinctly different theoretical and political positions. They share a concern with the corrosive effects which crime can have on communities and with the formulation of workable policies, but they are ultimately oppositional and competing positions.

They differ in a number of important respects. First, the new realists tend to take conventional definitions of crime for granted. Radical realists on the other hand, although adopting the general categories of crime as their point of departure, are not constrained by either commonsensical definitions nor by official modes of prioritization. Rather, the issue of 'seriousness' and significance of different crimes is seen as the object of investigation. By the same token it employs a much wider frame of reference than 'new realism' which concentrates almost exclusively on 'street crime'. Radical realism has, through the use of victimization surveys, sought to broaden the parameters of enquiry and has more recently begun to examine a range of 'white-collar' and occupational offences (Pearce and Tombs, 1992).

Secondly, there are substantial differences in the type of explanations that are offered – particularly in relation to the question of causality. James Q. Wilson, for example, expresses reservations about what he sees as the search for 'deep' causes, offering instead in his book with Richard Herrnstein, *Crime and Human Nature* (1985), a behaviouristic theory of conditioning. Crime is, they maintain, ultimately a function of transhistorical 'human nature'. As a result their analysis lacks a social economic context and is excessively individualized. The relation between the individual and society and the role of socioeconomic processes in structuring choices and opportunities is conveniently played down.

The absence of a material context for social action and a lack of appreciation of the socioeconomic constituents of crime allows the 'new realists' to operate with a predominantly voluntaristic conception of the criminal and to embrace essentially punitive policies aimed at controlling the 'wicked'. Thus the import of the analysis offered by writers like Wilson and van den Haag is to encourage an overemphasis on control and containment to the exclusion of more thoughtful and constructive policies (Currie, 1985). [...]

Left realism then is the opposite of right realism. Whereas realists of the right prioritize order over justice, left realists prioritize social justice as a way of achieving a fair and orderly society. Whereas right realists descend to genetic and individualistic theories to blame the 'underclass', left realists point to the social injustice which marginalizes considerable sections of the population and engenders crime. If the two realisms have anything in common it is the rejection of utopianism: there are no magical solutions; all interventions in the control of crime have a social cost which must be weighed against their effectiveness.

Right realism is a new right philosophy: left realism stems from the current debates in democratic socialism. Thus it argues that only socialist intervention will fundamentally reduce the causes of crime, rooted as they are in social inequality, that only the universalistic provision of crime prevention will guard the poor against crime, that only a genuinely democratic control of the police force will ensure that community safety is achieved.

Thus on one hand, left realism takes an oppositional political and theoretical stance from that adopted by the realists of the right; while on the other it consciously avoids collapsing into the romanticism and idealism which has been evident in much of the radical and critical criminological literature of the 1970s.

Radical criminology and radical realism

It is easy to lose sight of the contribution which radical criminology played in shaping the nature of the debate in the 1960s and 1970s. Radical criminology provided many of the concepts and terms which were effective in opposing mechanistic conceptions of crime and deviance, while scrutinizing and exposing state (mal)practices. It offered a wider framework of analysis which was able to explore the social, political, ideological, economic and historical dimensions of crime and control. It challenged the dominant conceptions of crime and punishment, offered new perspectives, and attempted to develop a sustained critique of the operation of the criminal justice system.

Although radical criminology pointed to the weakness, omissions and errors of conventional criminology it was never able to offer a competing alternative. Its critique was essentially negative and reactive. Unable to offer a feasible alternative it was always destined to operate as the bad conscience of conventional criminology (Cohen, 1979). [...]

Central to the debates between radical criminologists is the notion of reform and in particular the meaning of progressive reform. For the realists the recognition that crime is largely intra- rather than inter-class, with the poor paying dearly for inadequate protection, the need to improve the effectiveness of criminal justice agencies seems obvious. For the abolitionists who believe that the notion of 'crime' is something of a fiction and that the criminal justice system is only capable of repression there is no justification for maintaining formal criminal justice agencies. Indeed they are even critical of the realists' emphasis on the need to create a more accountable and efficient system of policing and imprisonment (Mathiesen, 1990; Hulsman, 1986; Brown and Hogg, 1992).

Where realists and abolitionists do appear to share some common ground is in their belief that radical criminology should aim for the integration of theory and practice. How such integration should be achieved was one of the central themes in radical thinking throughout the 1960s and 1970s. The majority of radical criminologists during this period were never seriously interested in engaging in a detailed investigation of crime or in developing policies to control it. Instead they concentrated on the process of 'criminalization' and of providing a range of theoretical critiques of official policy (Young, 1988). Thus, in the area of criminology the relation between theory and practice was left largely unexplored and the balance tilted heavily in the direction of theory.

Realism and modernism

[...] Contemporary criminology is characterized by this lack of 'grand narratives' and has become increasingly fragmented and instrumentalist over the last decade or so. This, as left realists have argued, has impaired the coherence and value of criminological investigation (Young, 1986). At the same time, however, we have argued for specificity and warned against the dangers of 'globalism' (Matthews, 1987b). These aims are not incompatible. On the contrary, an adequate explanation of crime and control needs to incorporate the particular and the general, and to locate specific and discrete phenomena within a framework which locates and explains the relation between the parts. It is a serious error of the relativists and nominalists who argue that the divergent and contingent nature of crime makes a general theory of crime impossible. The aim of a general theory of crime is to explain the diversity and the apparently contingent nature of criminal events and to show how these apparently arbitrary events are linked within identifiable processes. [...]

The postmodernist critique of criminology melts into air. It offers deconstruction rather than reconstruction. By dismissing the 'essentialist' concept of 'crime' (everything has to be placed in parentheses) the principal object of criminology is removed and the subject is dissolved into larger 'essentialist' disciplines such as sociology. Even the subcategories of crime disappear (rape, murder, theft, etc) for the same reasons. Ultimately writers like Smart, having dispensed with 'criminology' and its modernist variants in the form of 'left realism', and proceed to deny the logic of a 'feminist criminology'. Not surprisingly, a number of feminists have distanced themselves from this position (Lovibond, 1989). Strangely enough, however, the postmodernist critique has indicated some points of overlap between left realist and feminist criminology.

Realism and feminist criminology

Although there is some uncertainty about exactly what is meant by 'feminist criminology', there can be little doubt that the impact of feminists on criminological thinking has been one of the most productive and progressive inputs into the subject over the last decade or so (Leonard, 1982; Gregory, 1986; Eaton, 1986; Stanko, 1985; Carlen, 1988; Daly and Chesney-Lind, 1988). [...]

If we begin with a discussion of epistemology it is with the group which Sandra Harding refers to as 'empiricist' that left realism most closely identifies. Some of the differences between postmodernism and left realism, with its commitment to a qualified modernism, have already been identified. In opposition to postmodernism, realism expounds an objectivism. It maintains that the processes of reasoned and rational debate are a necessary feature of any democratic social system, expresses a commitment to progress and, in particular, argues that the delivery of services on which the poor and powerless depend can, and should, be improved. [...]

An alternative to postmodernism is offered by what has become known as 'standpoint feminism'. This position has certain advantages in that it distances itself from the relativism and subjectivism of postmodernism and offers instead a sense of objectivism. [...]

The most prominent advocate of this position within the field of criminology and law is Maureen Cain, who has presented a version of standpoint feminism in opposition to the antiessentialism of postmodernism on one side and what is seen as the ultimate androcentrism of 'empiricist' feminism on the other. Standpoint feminism starts from the premise that different social groups speak from distinctly different social locations and experiences. Cain argues that 'knowing from a feminist standpoint is not the same and indeed precludes knowing from a working-class or a black standpoint' (Cain, 1990). This approach raises two immediate questions. The first is the objective problem of how to reconcile class, gender and racial determinants in terms of, say, criminal activity. The second is the subjective problem that a significant body of people transverse these various standpoints. Some people, for example, may want to speak as black working-class women. The overriding problem from this position is that people from the same standpoint do not only speak with the same voice but often speak with competing and oppositional voices. How do we know which voices are authentic? The problem is compounded when it is stated that some men can be feminists. It suggests that the relationship between knowledge and interests is not unmediated. The question then arises of explaining how people of different, and even oppositional, social locations and experiences can come to see the world in generally similar ways. The considerable degree of consensus which is repeatedly reported in relation to the question of the 'seriousness' of crime among all social groups would be difficult to explain from the 'standpoint' position. [...]

One issue which remains central to both realists and feminists is the definition of crime. The definitional issue has always been a stumbling block within criminology. Often criminologists have relied on simplistic definitions of crime and seen it as an 'act', or alternatively they have denied the significance of the act and claimed that it is a function of the 'reaction'. In attempting to move beyond these limited oppositions, realism has begun to examine the processes of action and reaction through what has become termed 'the square of crime'.

The square of crime

The notion of the square of crime is a shorthand which has emerged in the writings of criminological realism and is designed to serve as a reminder that 'crime' arises at the intersection of a number of lines of force. It is therefore an important antidote to those who see crime solely in terms of victims and offenders and ignore the role of the state and public opinion. At the same time it serves as a critique of those who see the process of 'criminalization' as a wholly state-generated process.

The growing interest in victimization and the recognition of the intimate relations which are often evident between victims and offenders has made this part of the equation a more accepted feature of the analysis. However, the role of the state and public opinion is less well understood. As we have seen with respect to radical criminology, when the state has been referred to it has been predominantly depicted as a repressive and essentially coercive instrument. But under the influence of writers like Foucault, the conception of the state and underlying notions of power have been challenged (Foucault, 1979). As a result there is now a greater sensitivity to the productive and constructive aspects of state control.

Within the square of crime the role and significance of public opinion has been generally neglected. Left realists, however, in arguing for a more democratic and responsive criminal justice system have begun to consider the role of public opinion and community controls in the construction and regulation of crime. The examination of police practices and crime figures indicates the critical role of public tolerance in defining and reporting incidents to the police (Kinsey et al., 1986). [...]

Realism argues against both the tendency of experts to tell the public what are its real problems and the 'subjectivist' approach, which believes that crime priorities can be simply deduced by reading off the computer printouts of public opinion surveys. It maintains that, particularly in the inner city, direct public experience of many crimes generates both rational priorities as to the problem faced and realistic fears. It sets its face against the conventional wisdom that women and the elderly are prone to irrational fears and that the fear of crime is more of a problem than crime itself (see Sparks, 1992).

Conclusion

We have tried to indicate that left realism does offer a distinctly different approach to the analysis of the processes through which crime is constructed, one which avoids the excesses of idealism and essentialism. Realism argues that previous criminological theories have been partial. That is, they only focus on one part of the square of crime: the state (as in labelling theory, neo-classicism), the public (as in control theory), the offender (as in positivism) or the victim (as in victimology). One of its major aims is to provide an analysis of crime on all levels and to develop where possible a range of policy recommendations. It does not aim, however, simply to synthesize the existing disparate range of criminologies, but rather to develop a coherent analysis which touches upon these diverse positions.

Realism is critical of the extremely simplistic notions of causality implicit in traditional social democratic theory, the inadequate theorization of the central categories of the state and 'public opinion', and the lamentable standards of evaluation used in monitoring interventions. It refuses to be drawn into the defeatism and pessimism associated with some current strands of 'radical' theorizing, particularly in the form of postmodernism, and expresses a qualified commitment to the modernist project, by attempting to develop a coherent and reasoned analysis which incorporates 'grand narratives' while recognizing the need for specificity. It retains a commitment to problem solving, to the improvement of service delivery and to the provision of a more equitable, responsive and accountable criminal justice system.

Finally, left realism involves the repoliticization of crime. It maintains that crime cannot be effectively reduced through individualistic, technicist or administrative policies as the neo-conservatives suggest. Rather, crime reduction requires, as radical criminology has always argued, an appreciation of a wide range of political and structural processes which go beyond the boundaries of conventional criminology. This does not mean that nothing can be done short of a fundamental transformation of the social structure, but that the effectiveness of particular strategies is likely to be conditioned by these wider processes. Criminology is drawn ineluctably, therefore, into the wider political realm, and crime control must inevitably become part of a comprehensive political programme. For too long we have pretended it could be otherwise.

From R. Matthews and J. Young, 'Reflections on realism', in J. Young and R. Matthews (eds) Rethinking Criminology: The Realist Debate *(London: Sage), 1992, pp. 1–23.*

References

Brown, D. and Hogg, R. (1992) 'Law and order politics', in R. Matthews and J. Young (eds), *Issues in Realist Criminology*. London: Sage.

Cain, M. (1990) 'Towards transgression: new directions in feminist criminology', *International Journal of the Sociology of Law*, 18(1): 1–18.

Carlen, P. (1988) *Women, Crime and Poverty*. Milton Keynes: Open University Press.

Cohen, S. (1979) 'Guilt, justice and tolerance: some old concepts for a new criminology', in D. Downs and P. Rock (eds), *Deviant Interpretations*. Oxford: Martin Robertson.

Currie, E. (1985) *Confronting Crime*. New York: Pantheon Books.

Daly, K. and Chesney-Lind, M. (1988) 'Feminism and criminology', *Justice Quarterly*, 5(4): 497–538.

Eaton, M. (1986) *Justice for Women? Family Court and Social Control*. Milton Keynes: Open University Press.

Foucault, M. (1979) *The History of Sexuality: An Introduction*. London: Allen Lane.

Gregory, J. (1986) 'Sex, class and crime: towards a non-sexist criminology', in R. Matthews and J. Young (eds), *Confronting Crime*. London: Sage.

Herrnstein, R. and Wilson, J. (1985) *Crime and Human Nature*. New York: Basic Books.

Hulsman, L. (1986) 'Critical criminology and the concept of crime', *Contemporary Crises*, 10: 63–90.

Kinsey, R., Lea, J. and Young, J. (1986) *Losing the Fight Against Crime*. Oxford: Blackwell.

Leonard, E. (1982) *Women, Crime and Society*. London: Longman.

Lovibond, S. (1989) 'Feminism and postmodernism', *New Left Review*, 178: 6–28.

Mathiesen, T. (1990) *Prison on Trial*. London: Sage.

Matthews, R. (1987b) 'Decarceration and social control: fantasies and realities', in J. Lowman *et al.* (eds), *Transcarceration*. Aldershot: Gower.

Pearce, F. and Tombs, S. (1992) 'Realism and corporate crime', in R. Matthews and J. Young (eds), *Issues in Realist Criminology*. London: Sage.

Sparks, R. (1992) 'Reason and unreason in 'left realism': some problems in the constitution of the fear of crime', in R. Matthews and J. Young (eds), *Issues in Realist Criminology*. London: Sage.

Stanko, E. (1985) *Intimate Intrusions. Women's Experience of Male Violence*. London: Virago.

Young, J. (1986) 'The failure of criminology: the need for radical realism', in R. Matthews and J. Young (eds), *Confronting Crime*. London: Sage.

13.2 The failure of criminology: the need for a radical realism Jock Young

The nature of left realism

The basic defect of pathology and of its romantic opposite is that both yield concepts that are untrue to the phenomenon and which thus fail to illuminate it. Pathology reckons without the patent tenability and durability of deviant enterprise, and without the subjective capacity of man to create novelty and manage diversity. Romance, as always, obscures the seamier and more mundane aspects of the world. It obscures the stress that may underlie resilience (Matza, 1969: 44).

The central tenet of left realism is to reflect the reality of crime, that is in its origins, its nature and its impact. This involves a rejection of tendencies to romanticize crime or to pathologize it, to analyse solely from the point of view of the administration of crime or the criminal actor, to underestimate crime or to exaggerate it. And our understanding of methodology, our interpretation of the statistics, our notions of aetiology follow from this. Most importantly, it is realism which informs our notion of practice: in answering what can be done about the problems of crime and social control.

It is with this in mind that I have mapped out the fundamental principles of left realism.

Crime really is a problem

It is unrealistic to suggest that the problem of crime like mugging is merely the problem of mis-categorization and concomitant moral panics. If we choose to embrace this liberal position, we leave the political arena open to conservative campaigns for law and order – for, however exaggerated and distorted the arguments conservatives may marshal, the reality of crime in the streets can be the reality of human suffering and personal disaster (Young, 1975: 89).

To be realistic about crime as a problem is not an easy task. We are caught between two currents, one which would grotesquely exaggerate the problems of crime, another covering a wide swathe of political opinion that may seriously underestimate the extent of the problem. Crime is a staple of news in the Western mass media and police fiction a major genre of television drama. We have detailed elsewhere the structured distortion of images of crime, victimization and policing which occur in the mass media (see Cohen and Young, 1981). It is a commonplace of criminological research that most violence is between acquaintances and is intra-class and intra-racial. Yet the media abound with images of the dangerous stranger. On television we see folk monsters who are psychopathic killers or serial murderers yet offenders who even remotely fit these caricatures are extremely rare. The police are portrayed as engaged in an extremely scientific investigative policy with high clear-up rates and exciting denouements although the criminologist knows that this is far from the humdrum nature of reality. Furthermore, it grossly conceals the true relationship between police and public in the process of detection, namely that there is an extremely high degree of dependence of the police on public reporting and witnessing of crime.

The nature of crime, of victimization and of policing is thus systematically distorted in the mass media. And it is undoubtedly true that such a barrage of misinformation has its effect – although perhaps scarcely in such a one-to-one way that is sometimes suggested. For example, a typical category of violence in Britain is a man battering his wife. But this is rarely represented in the mass media – instead we have numerous examples of professional criminals engaged in violent crime – a quantitatively minor problem when compared to domestic violence. So presumably the husband can watch criminal violence on television and not see himself there. His offence does not exist as a category of media censure. People watching depictions of burglary presumably get an impression of threats of violence, sophisticated adult criminals and scenes of desecrated homes. But this is of course not at all the normal burglary – which is typically amateurish and carried out by an adolescent boy. When people come home to find their house broken into there is no one there and their fantasies about the dangerous intruder are left to run riot. Sometimes the consequences of such fantastic images of criminals are tragic. For example, people buy large guard dogs to protect themselves. Yet the one most likely to commit violence is the man of the house against his wife, and there are many more relatives – usually children – killed and injured by dogs than by burglars!

In the recent period there has been an alliance between liberals (often involved in the new administrative criminology) and left idealists which evokes the very mirror image of the mass media. The chances of being criminally injured, however slightly, the British Crime Survey tells us is once in a hundred years (Hough and Mayhew, 1983) and such a Home Office view is readily echoed by left realists who inform us that crime is, by and large, a minor problem and indeed the fear of crime is more of a problem than crime itself. Thus, they would argue, undue fear of crime provides popular support for conservative law and order campaigns and allows the build up of further police powers whose repressive aim is political dissent rather than crime. For radicals to enter into the discourse of law and order is to further legitimize it. Furthermore, such a stance maintains that fear of crime has not only ideological consequences, it has material effects on the community itself. For to give credence to the fear of crime is to

divide the community – to encourage racism, fester splits between the 'respectable' and 'non-respectable' working class and between youths and adults. More subtly, by emptying the streets particularly at night, it actually breaks down the system of informal controls which usually discourage crime.

Realism must navigate between these two poles, it must neither succumb to hysteria nor relapse into a critical denial of the severity of crime as a problem. It must be fiercely sceptical of official statistics and control institutions without taking the posture of a blanket rejection of all figures or, indeed, the very possibility of reform.

Realism necessitates an accurate victimology. It must counterpose this against those liberal and idealist criminologies, on the one side, which play down victimization or even bluntly state that the 'real' victim is the offender and, on the other, those conservatives who celebrate moral panic and see violence and robbery as ubiquitous on our streets.

To do this involves mapping out who is at risk and what precise effect crime has on their lives. This moves beyond the invocation of the global risk rates of the average citizen. All too often this serves to conceal the actual severity of crime amongst significant sections of the population whilst providing a fake statistical backdrop for the discussion of 'irrational' fears.

A radical victimology notes two key elements of criminal victimization. Firstly, that crime is focused both geographically and socially on the most vulnerable sections of the community. Secondly, that the impact of victimization is a product of risk rate and vulnerability. Average risk rates across a city ignore such a focusing and imply that equal crimes impact equally. As it is, the most vulnerable are not only more affected by crime, they also have the highest risk rates.

Realism must also trace accurately the relationship between victim and offender. Crime is not an activity of latter day Robin Hoods – the vast majority of working class crime is directed within the working class. It is intra-class *not* inter-class in its nature. Similarly, despite the mass media predilection for focusing on inter-racial crime it is overwhelmingly intra-racial. Crimes of violence, for example, are by and large one poor person hitting another poor person – and in almost half of these instances it is a man hitting his wife or lover.

This is not to deny the impact of crimes of the powerful or indeed of the social problems created by capitalism which are perfectly legal. Rather, left realism notes that the working class is a victim of crime from all directions. It notes that the more vulnerable a person is economically and socially the more likely it is that *both* working class and white-collar crime will occur against them; that one sort of crime tends to compound another, as does one social problem another. Furthermore, it notes that crime is a potent symbol of the antisocial nature of capitalism and is the most immediate way in which people experience other problems, such as unemployment or competitive individualism.

Realism starts from problems as people experience them. It takes seriously the complaints of women with regards to the dangers of being in public places at night, it takes note of the fears of the elderly with regard to burglary, it acknowledges the widespread occurrence of domestic violence and racist attacks. It does not ignore the fears of the vulnerable nor recontextualize them out of existance by putting them into a perspective which abounds with abstractions such as the 'average citizen' bereft of class or gender. It is only too aware of the systematic concealment and ignorance of crimes against the least powerful. Yet it does not take these fears at face value – it pinpoints their rational kernel but it is also aware of the forces towards irrationality.

Realism is not empiricism. Crime and deviance are prime sites of moral anxiety and tension in a society which is fraught with real inequalities and injustices. Criminals can quite easily become folk devils onto which are projected such feelings of unfairness. But there is a rational core to the fear of crime just as there is a rational core to the anxieties which distort it. Realism argues with popular consciousness in its attempts to separate out reality from fantasy. But it does not deny that crime is a problem. Indeed, if there were no rational core the media would have no power of leverage to the public consciousness. Crime becomes a metaphor but it is a metaphor rooted in reality.

When one examines anxiety about crime, one often finds a great deal more rationality than is commonly accorded to the public. Thus, frequently a glaring discrepancy has been claimed between the high fear of crime of women and their low risk rates. Recent research, particularly by feminist victimologists, has shown that this is often a mere artefact of a low reporting of sexual attacks to interviewers – a position reversed when sympathetic women are used in the survey team (see Russell, 1982; Hanmer and Saunders, 1984; Hall,

1985). Similarly, it is often suggested that fear of crime is somehow a petit bourgeois or upper middle-class phenomenon despite the lower risk rates of the more wealthy. Yet the Merseyside Crime Survey, for example, showed a close correspondence between risk rate and the prioritization of crime as a problem, with the working class having far higher risk rates and estimation of the importance of crime as a problem. Indeed, they saw crime as the second problem after unemployment whereas in the middle class suburbs only 13 percent of people rated crime as a major problem (see Kinsey *et al.*, 1986). Similarly, Richard Sparks and his colleagues found that working class people and blacks rated property crimes more seriously than middle-class people and whites (Sparks *et al.*, 1977). Those affected by crime and the most vulnerable are the most concerned about crime.

Of course, there is a fantastic element in the conception of crime. The images of the identity of the criminal and his mode of operation are, as we have seen, highly distorted. And undoubtedly *fear displacement* occurs, where real anxieties about one type of crime are projected on another, as does *tunnel vision*, where only certain sorts of crime are feared, but the evidence for a substantial infrastructure of rationality is considerable.

The emergence of a left realist position in crime has occurred in the last five years. This has involved criminologists in Britain, Canada, the United States and Australia. In particular, the Crime and Justice Collective in California have devoted a large amount of space in their journal for a far-ranging discussion on the need for a left-wing programme on crime control (see e.g. *Crimes and Social Justice*, Summer, 1981). There have been also violent denunciations, as the English journalist Martin Kettle put it:

> For their pains the [realists] have been denounced with extraordinary ferocity from the left, sometimes in an almost paranoid manner. To take crime seriously, to take fear of crime seriously and, worst of all, to take police reform seriously, is seen by the fundamentalists as the ultimate betrayal and deviation (Kettle, 1984: 367).

This, apart, the basis of a widespread support for a realist portion has already been made. What remains now is the task of creating a realist *criminology*. For although the left idealist denial of crime is increasingly being rejected, the tasks of radical criminology still remain. That is, to create an adequate explanation of crime, victimization and the reaction of the state. And this is all the more important given that the new administrative criminology has abdicated all such responsibility and indeed shares some convergence with left idealism.

Conclusion

I have traced the extent of the crisis which has occurred within criminology in the last twenty years, attempting to place it in its empirical, social and political context. Central to this has been the demise of social democratic positivism, the major paradigm, within British and American criminology over the period. This has been primarily a response to what I have termed the aetiological crisis – the continued rise in the crime rate all the way through the affluence of the sixties wherein all the familiar 'causes' of crime were systematically diminished and ameliorated. And this was supplemented on a slightly different time scale by a collapse in positivist beliefs in rehabilitation within the prisons.

The most immediate response to this crisis was a remarkable creative ferment within the discipline. From different perspectives labelling theory, strain theory and to a lesser extent theories of social disorganization attempted to tackle the anomaly. It was out of these roots that the new deviancy theory and radical criminology emerged. What happened at that time was – despite widespread disagreements – the widening out of the subject. The need for placing crime in the context of the wider society, of relating macro- to micro-levels of analysis, of studying action and reaction, and of placing the discipline within the context of wider social theory had become paramount. For a period the often hidden philosophical and sociological underpinnings of the various currents in criminological thought were uncovered and there was a time of re-examination of the classic texts in terms of what light they would shed on the debate. Marx, Durkheim, Mead, Merton and the schools of symbolic interactionism, phenomenology and Chicago were all invoked and critically examined. It is no accident that criminology and the sociology of deviance during the 1960s and 1970s became a major focus of many of the debates within methodology and sociology.

The potentiality for a sophisticated radical criminology was, for a time, enormous. And indeed it expanded rapidly in influence within the expansion of higher education and the dissemination of New Left ideas. But there were substantial flaws both in its roots and in the social and political context which it developed. The old story of critique by inversion, which has dogged criminological thinking since the 1900s returned with a vengeance. The new deviancy theory gravitated towards an inverted positivism: its actors rendered too rational, and criminal action either minimized or romanticized, whilst social disorganization as a notion disappeared from its vocabulary. The dictates of 'really' radical thought inflicted a cauterization of the past. It became no longer fashionable to learn from structural functionalism or labelling theory – the process of Koshering had begun. Ironically, as Mertonian structural functionalism was shown to the door, Althusserian functionalism entered in the back way. Many thought that radical criminology was itself a conceptual impossibility and moved to the sociology of law, others that crime itself was a minor problem not worthy of consideration – the majority that the real concern must be with the state. All in all this created a one-sided, top-down type of theory, functionalist to its core, whose concern was not the causes of crime but the relation of state reaction to the political and economic needs of capitalism. And in such a functioning totality reform, whether it was in the streets or in the prisons, became an impossibility. Thus left idealism emerged, its dominance within socialist criminology confirmed by the recession. For as unemployment and poverty soared there no longer remained a problem of why the crime rate increased – the answer was obvious and unworthy of reflection. The aetiological crisis for the radicals had *temporarily* disappeared.

Meanwhile a silent palace revolution occurred within orthodox criminology with the emergence and rapid expansion of the new administrative criminology, whose dogged empiricism made it appear like positivism, yet nothing could be further from the case. For the historic search for causation had been abandoned and a neo-classicism had taken its place. No longer was there a notion of solving crime through increasing social justice; rather the emphasis became surveillance, policing and control.

A convergence between left idealism and the new administrative criminology unwittingly emerged. Both thought that investigation of causality was fruitless, both agreed that rehabilitation was impossible, both thought that crime control through the implementation of programmes of economic and social justice would not succeed, both focused on the reactions of the state, both were uninterested in past theory, both attempted to explain the effectiveness of crime control without explaining crime and both believed it was possible to generalize in a way which profoundly ignored the specificity of circumstances.

Thus a nadir has occurred within criminology. However, the discipline develops in a way which relates to changes in its empirical and social context. If the aetiological crisis was the empirical motor of the sixties, criminal victimization studies are the motor of the eighties. And whilst for radical criminology victimology is a veritable creator of anomalies, for the new administrative criminology it creates few surprises. There is little in the paradigm which is particularly jolted by asking the question who is the victim? Indeed by providing maps of the targets of crime it fits unabrasively into control theory. But the evidence for the high criminal victimization of the working class and its intra-class nature sets up real problems in left idealist theory – not the least that it inevitably highlights problems of community disorganization. And the pioneering work of feminist criminologists both in the field of women as victim and as offenders has been of prime importance in forcing radicals to re-examine their positions on punishment and the causes of crime. This has been underscored by a widespread concern over the problem of racist attacks within working class communities and the spread of heroin use to the working class of many European cities. Politically, this has combined with the need for socialist councils in the inner cities to develop a policy which tackles these problems and which cannot, with rising unemployment, depend on the traditional focus within the workplace. Thus all the prerequisites for the emergence of left realist criminology are now present.

This article has argued for the need for a systematic programme within radical criminology which should have theoretical, research and policy components. We must develop a realist theory which adequately encompasses the scope of the criminal act. That is, it must deal with both macro- and micro-levels with the causes of criminal action and social reaction, and with the triangular inter-

relationship between offender, victim and the state. It must learn from past theory, take up again the debates between the three strands of criminological theory and attempt to bring them together within a radical rubric. It must stand for theory in a time when criminology has all but abandoned theory. It must rescue the action of causality whilst stressing both the specificity of generalization and the existence of human choice and value in any equation of criminality.

On a research level we must develop theoretically grounded empirical work against the current of atheoretical empiricism. The expansion of radical victimology in the area of victimization surveys is paramount but concern should also be made with regard to developments in qualitative research and ethnography (see West, 1984). The development of sophisticated statistical analysis (see for example Box and Hale in this volume; Greenberg, 1984; Melossi, 1985) should not be anathema to the radical criminologist nor should quantitative and qualitative work be seen as alternatives from which the radical must obviously choose. Both methods, as long as they are based in theory, complement and enrich each other.

In terms of practical policy we must combat impossibilism: whether it is the impossibility of reform, the ineluctable nature of a rising crime rate or the inevitable failure of rehabilitation. It is time for us to *compete* in policy terms, to get out of the ghetto of impossibilism. Orthodox criminology with its inability to question the political and its abandonment of aetiology is hopelessly unable to generate workable policies. All commentators are united about the inevitability of a rising crime rate. Left idealists think it cannot be halted because without a profound social transformation nothing can be done; the new administrative criminologists have given up the ghost of doing anything but the most superficial containment job. Let us state quite categorically that the major task of radical criminology is to seek a solution to the problem of crime and that of a socialist policy is to substantially reduce the crime rate. And the same is true of rehabilitation. Left idealists think that it is at best a con-trick, indeed argue that unapologetic punishment would at least be less mystifying to the offender. The new administrative criminologists seek to construct a system of punishment and surveillance which discards rehabilitation and replaces it with a social behaviourism worthy of the management of white rats in laboratory cages. They both deny the moral nature of crime, that choice is always made in varying determining circumstances and that the denial of responsibility fundamentally misunderstands the reality of the criminal act. As socialists it is important to stress that most working class crime is intra-class, that mugging, wife battering, burglary and child abuse are actions which cannot be morally absolved in the flux of determinacy. The offender should be ashamed, he/she should feel morally responsible within the limits of circumstance and rehabilitation is truly impossible without this moral dimension.

Crime is of importance politically because unchecked it divides the working class community and is materially and morally the basis of disorganization: the loss of political control. It is also a potential unifier – a realistic issue, *amongst others*, for recreating community.

Bertram Gross, in a perceptive article, originally published in the American magazine *The Nation*, wrote: 'on crime, more than on most matters, the left seems bereft of ideas' (Gross, 1982: 51). He is completely correct, of course, in terms of there being a lack of any developed strategy amongst socialists for dealing with crime. I have tried to show, however, that it was the prevalence – though often implicit and frequently ill thought – of left idealist ideas which, in fact, directly resulted in the neglect of crime. There is now a growing consensus amongst radical criminologists that crime really is a problem for the working class, women, ethnic minorities: for all the most vulnerable members of capitalist societies and that something must be done about it. But to recognize the reality of crime as a problem is only the first stage of the business. A fully blown theory of crime must relate to the contradictory reality of the phenomenon as must any strategy for combatting it. And it must analyse how working class attitudes to crime are not merely the result of false ideas derived from the mass media and such like but have a rational basis in one moment of a contradictory and wrongly contextualized reality.

In a recent diatribe against radical criminology Carl Klockars remarked: 'Imagination is one thing, criminology another' (Klockars, 1980: 93). It is true that recent criminology has been characterized by a chronic lack of imagination – although I scarcely think that this was what Klockars lamented by his disparaging remark. Many of us were attracted to the discipline because of its theoretical verve, because of the centrality of the study of disorder to understanding society, because of the flair of its practitioners and the tremendous human interest of the subject. Indeed many of the major debates in the social sciences in the sixties and seventies focused quite naturally around deviance and social control. And this is as it should be – as it has been throughout history both in social science and in literature – both in mass media and the arts. What is needed now is an intellectual and political imagination which can comprehend the way in which we learn about order through the investigation of disorder. The paradox of the textbook in orthodox criminology is that it takes that which is of great human interest and transmits it into the dullest of 'facts'. I challenge anyone to read one of the conventional journals from cover to cover without having a desperate wish to fall asleep. Research grants come and research grants go and people are gainfully employed but crime remains, indeed it grows and nothing they do seems able to do anything about it. But is it so surprising that such a grotesquely eviscerated discipline should be so ineffective? For the one-dimensional discourse that constitutes orthodox criminology does not even know its own name. It is often unaware of the sociological and philosophical assumptions behind it. James Q. Wilson, for example, has become one of the most influential and significant of the new administrative criminologists. Yet his work and its proposals have scarcely been examined outside of the most perfunctory empiricist discussions. The discipline is redolent with a scientism which does not realize that its relationship with its object of study is more metaphysical than realistic, an apolitical recital of facts, more facts and even more facts then does not want to acknowledge that it is profoundly political, a paradigm that sees its salvation in the latest statistical innovation rather than in any ability to engage with the actual reality of the world. It is ironic that it is precisely in orthodox criminology, where practitioners and researchers are extremely politically constrained, that they write as if crime and criminology were little to do with politics. Radical criminology, by stressing the political nature of crime and social censure, and the philosophical and social underpinnings of the various criminologies is able to immediately take such problems aboard. The key virtue of realist criminology is the central weakness of its administrative opponent.

We are privileged to work in one of the most central, exciting and enigmatic fields of study. It is the very staple of the mass media, a major focus of much day to day public gossip, speculation and debate. And this is as it should be. But during the past decade the subject has been eviscerated, talk of theory, causality and justice has all but disappeared and what is central to human concern has been relegated to the margins. It is time for us to go back to the drawing boards, time to regain our acquaintanceship with theory, to dispel amnesia about the past and adequately comprehend the present. This is the central task of left realist criminology: we will need more than a modicum of imagination and scientific ability to achieve it.

> *From J. Young, 'The failure of criminology: the need for a radical realism', in R. Matthews and J. Young (eds)* Confronting Criminology, *(London: Sage), 1986, pp. 4–30.*

References

Box, S. and Hale, C. (1984) *Bibliography on Unemployment and Crime*. Unpublished, available from authors.

Cohen, S., and Young, J. (1981) *The Manufacture of News* (revised edition). London: Constable; Beverly Hills: Sage.

Greenberg, D.F. (1984) 'Age and Crime: in Search of Sociology'. Mimeo.

Gross, B. (1982) 'Some Anticrime Proposals for Progressives', *Crime and Social Justice*, Summer: 51–4.

Hall, R.E. (1985) *Ask Any Woman – A London Enquiry into Rape and Sexual Assault*. Falling Wall Press.

Hanmer, J. and Saunders, S. (1984) *Well-Founded Fears: A Community Study of Violence to Women*. London: Hutchinson.

Hough, M. and Mayhew, P. (1983) *The British Crime Survey: First Report*. London: Home Office Research and Planning Unit.

Kettle, M. (1984) 'The Police and the Left', *New Society*, 70 (1146): 366–7.

Kinsey, R., Lea, J. and Young, J. (1986) *Losing the Fight Against Crime*. Oxford: Blackwell.

Klockars, C. (1980) 'The Contemporary Crisis of Marxist Criminology', in Inciardi, J. (ed.) *Radical Criminology: The Coming Crisis*, Beverly Hills: Sage.

Matza, D. (1969) *Becoming Deviant*. Prentice Hall.

Melossi, D, (1985) 'Punishment and Social Action', in McNall (ed.) *Current Perspectives in Social Theory*. Greenwich, Conn: JAI Press.

Russell, D. (1982) *Rape in Marriage*. New York: Macmillan.

Sparks, R., Genn, H. and Dodd, D. (1977) *Surveying Victims: A Study of the Measurement of Criminal Victimisation*. Chichester: Wiley.

West, G. (1984) 'Phenomenon and Form', in Barton, L. and Walker, S. (eds.) *Educational Research and Social Crisis*. London: Croom Helm.

Young, J. (1976) 'Working Class Criminology', in Taylor, I., Walton, P. and Young J. (eds.) *Critical Criminology*. London: Routledge and Kegan Paul.

13.3 The emerging underclass
Charles Murray

The concept of 'underclass'

'Underclass' is an ugly word, with its whiff of Marx and the lumpen proletariat. Perhaps because it is ugly, 'underclass' as used in Britain tends to be sanitised, a sort of synonym for people who are not just poor, but especially poor. So let us get it straight from the outset: the 'underclass' does not refer to degree of poverty, but to a type of poverty.

It is not a new concept. I grew up knowing what the underclass was; we just didn't call it that in those days. In the small Iowa town where I lived, I was taught by my middle-class parents that there were two kinds of poor people. One class of poor people was never even called 'poor'. I came to understand that they simply lived with low incomes, as my own parents had done when they were young. Then there was another set of poor people, just a handful of them. These poor people didn't lack just money. They were defined by their behaviour. Their homes were littered and unkempt. The men in the family were unable to hold a job for more than a few weeks at a time. Drunkenness was common. The children grew up ill-schooled and ill-behaved and contributed a disproportionate share of the local juvenile delinquents.

British observers of the 19th century knew these people. To Henry Mayhew, whose articles in the *Morning Chronicle* in 1850 drew the Victorians' attention to poverty, they were the 'dishonest poor', a member of which was

> distinguished from the civilised man by his repugnance to regular and continuous labour – by his want of providence in laying up a store for the future – by his inability to perceive consequences ever so slightly removed from immediate apprehensions – by his passion for stupefying herbs and roots and, when possible, for intoxicating fermented liquors...

Other popular labels were 'undeserving', 'unrespectable', 'depraved', 'debased', 'disreputable' or 'feckless' poor. [...] Then came the intellectual reformation that swept both the United States and Britain at about the same time, in the mid-1960s, and with it came a new way of looking at the poor. Henceforth, the poor were to be homogenised. The only difference between poor people and everyone else we were told, was that the poor had less money. More importantly, the poor were all alike. There was no such thing as the ne'er-do-well poor person – he was the figment of the prejudices of a parochial middle class. Poor people, *all* poor people, were equally victims, and would be equally successful if only society gave them a fair shake.

The difference between the US and the UK

The difference between the United States and Britain was that the United States reached the future first. During the last half of the 1960s and throughout the 1970s something strange and frightening was happening among poor people in the United States. Poor communities that had consisted mostly of hardworking folks began deteriorating, sometimes falling apart altogether. Drugs, crime, illegitimacy, homelessness, drop-out from the job market, drop-out from school, casual violence – all the measures that were available to the social scientists showed large increases, focused in poor communities. As the 1980s began, the growing population of 'the other kind of poor peo-

ple' could no longer be ignored and a label for them came into use. In the US, we began to call them the underclass.

For a time, the intellectual conventional wisdom continued to hold that 'underclass' was just another pejorative attempt to label the poor. But the label had come into use because there was no longer any denying reality. What had once been a small fraction of the American poor had become a sizeable and worrisome population. An underclass existed, and none of the ordinary kinds of social policy solutions seemed able to stop its growth. One by one, the American social scientists who had initially rejected the concept of an underclass fell silent, then began to use it themselves.

By and large, British intellectuals still disdain the term. [...]

With all the reservations that a stranger must feel in passing judgement on an unfamiliar country, I will jump directly to the conclusion: Britain does have an underclass, still largely out of sight and still smaller than the one in the United States. But it is growing rapidly. Within the next decade, it will probably become as large (proportionately) as the United States' underclass. It could easily become larger. [...]

There are many ways to identify an underclass. I will concentrate on three phenomena that have turned out to be early-warning signals in the United States: illegitimacy, violent crime, and drop-out from the labour force. In each case I will be using the simplest of data, collected and published by Britain's Government Statistical Service. I begin with illegitimacy, which in my view is the best predictor of an underclass in the making.

Illegitimacy and the underclass

It is a proposition that angers many people. [...] The very world 'illegitimate' is intellectually illegitimate. Using it in a gathering of academics these days is a *faux pas*, causing pained silence.

I nonetheless focus on illegitimacy rather than on the more general phenomenon of one-parent families because, in a world where all social trends are ambiguous, illegitimacy is less ambiguous than other forms of single parenthood. It is a matter of degree. Of course some unmarried mothers are excellent mothers and some unmarried fathers are excellent fathers. Of course some divorced parents disappear from the children's lives altogether and some divorces have more destructive effects on the children than a failure to marry would have had. Being without two parents is generally worse for the child than having two parents, no matter how it happens. But illegitimacy is the purest form of being without two parents – legally, the child is without a father from day one; he is often without one practically as well. Further, illegitimacy bespeaks an attitude on the part of one or both parents that getting married is not an essential part of siring or giving birth to a child; this in itself distinguishes their mindset from that of people who do feel strongly that getting married is essential.

Call it what you will, illegitimacy has been sky-rocketing since 1979. [...]

The sharp rise is only half of the story. The other and equally important half is that illegitimate births are not scattered evenly among the British population. [...] The increase in illegitimate births is strikingly concentrated among the lowest social class.

'Children from single-parent households do just as well as children from two-parent households.'

The change in the received wisdom on this topic in the US has been remarkable. One example will serve to illustrate. In 1983, a statistic cited everywhere by those who would debunk the reactionaries was that 50 per cent of all US welfare mothers were off the welfare rolls within two years. The idea of 'welfare dependency' was a myth. Then, in 1986, David Ellwood, the scholar whose work had popularised the 50 per cent statistic, took a closer look at the same data (a large longitudinal study), separating welfare mothers into different categories. It turned out that one factor made a huge difference how quickly a woman left welfare: whether she had been married. The short-term welfare recipients were concentrated among those who had found themselves on welfare after a divorce. For the never-married woman, the average number of years on welfare was not the highly touted 2 years, but 9.3. [...]

Even after economic circumstances are matched, the children of single mothers do worse, often much worse, than the children of married couples. [...]

If we can be reasonably confident that the children of never-married women do considerably worse than their peers, it remains to explain why. Progress has been slow. Until recently in the United States, scholars were reluctant to concede that illegitimacy is a legitimate variable for study. Even as that situation changes, they remain slow

to leave behind their equations and go out to talk with people who are trying to raise their children in neighbourhoods with high illegitimacy rates.

Clichés about role models are true

It turns out that the clichés about role models are true. Children grow up making sense of the world around them in terms of their own experience. [...]

That's why single-parenthood is a problem for communities, and that's why illegitimacy is the most worrisome aspect of single-parenthood. Children tend to behave like the adults around them. A child with a mother and no father, living in a neighbourhood of mothers with no fathers, judges by what he sees. You can send in social workers and school teachers and clergy to tell a young male that when he grows up he should be a good father to his children, but he doesn't know what that means unless he's seen it. Fifteen years ago, there was hardly a poor neighbourhood in urban Britain where children did not still see plentiful examples of good fathers around them. Today, the balance has already shifted in many poor neighbourhoods. In a few years, the situation will be much worse, for this is a problem that nurtures itself.

Child-rearing in single-parent communities

We have only a small body of systematic research on child-rearing practices in contemporary low-income, single-parent communities; it's one of those unfashionable topics. But the unsystematic reports I heard in towns like Birkenhead and council estates like Easterhouse in Glasgow are consistent with the reports from inner-city Washington and New York: in communities without fathers, the kids tend to run wild. The fewer the fathers, the greater the tendency.

Crime and the underclass

Crime is the next place to look for an underclass, for several reasons. First and most obviously, the habitual criminal is the classic member of an underclass. He lives off mainstream society without participating in it. But habitual criminals are only part of the problem. Once again, the key issue in thinking about an underclass is how the community functions, and crime can devastate a community in two especially important ways. To the extent that the members of a community are victimised by crime, the community tends to become fragmented. To the extent that many people in a community engage in crime as a matter of course, all sorts of the socialising norms of the community change, from the kind of men that the younger boys choose as heroes to the standards of morality in general.

The intellectual conventional wisdom

The denial by intellectuals that crime really has been getting worse spills over into denial that poor communities are more violent places than affluent communities. To the people who live in poor communities, this doesn't make much sense. One man in a poor, high-crime community told me about his experience in an open university where he had decided to try to improve himself. He took a sociology course about poverty. The professor kept talking about this 'nice little world that the poor live in', the man remembered. The professor scoffed at the reactionary myth that poor communities are violent places. To the man who lived in such a community, it was 'bloody drivel'. A few weeks later, a class exercise called for the students to canvass a poor neighbourhood. The professor went along, but apparently he, too, suspected that some of his pronouncements were bloody drivel – he cautiously stayed in his car and declined to knock on doors himself. And that raises the most interesting question regarding the view that crime has not risen, or that crime is not especially a problem in lower-class communities: do any of the people who hold this view actually believe it, to the extent that they take no more precautions walking in a slum neighbourhood than they do in a middle-class suburb?

These comments will not still the battle over the numbers. But I will venture this prediction, once again drawn from the American experience. After a few more years, quietly and without anyone having to admit he had been wrong, the intellectual conventional wisdom in Britain as in the United States will undergo a gradual transition. After all the statistical artifacts are taken into account and argued over, it will be decided that England is indeed becoming a more dangerous place in which to live: that this unhappy process is not occurring everywhere, but disproportionately in particular types of neighbourhoods; and that those neighbourhoods turn out to be the ones in which an underclass is taking over. Reality will once again force theory to its knees.

Unemployment and the underclass

If illegitimate births are the leading indicator of an underclass and violent crime a proxy measure of its development, the definitive proof that an underclass has arrived is that large numbers of young, healthy, low-income males choose not to take jobs. (The young idle rich are a separate problem.) This decrease in labour force participation is the most elusive of the trends in the growth of the British underclass.

Economic inactivity and social class

The simple relationship of economic inactivity to social class is strong, just as it was for illegitimacy. According to the 1981 census data, the municipal districts with high proportions of household heads who are in Class V (unskilled labour) also tend to have the highest levels of 'economically inactive' persons of working age (statistically, the proportion of Class V households explains more than a third of the variance when inactivity because of retirement is taken into account).

This is another way of saying that you will find many more working-aged people who are neither working nor looking for work in the slums than in the suburbs.

A generation gap by class

My hypothesis – the evidence is too fragmentary to call it more than that – is that Britain is experiencing a generation gap by class. Well-educated young people from affluent homes are working in larger proportions and working longer hours than ever. The attitudes and behaviour of the middle-aged working class haven't changed much. The change in stance toward the labour force is concentrated among lower-class young men in their teens and twenties. It is not a huge change. I am not suggesting that a third or a quarter or even a fifth of lower-class young people are indifferent to work. An underclass doesn't have to be huge to become a problem.

That problem is remarkably difficult to fix. It seems simple – just make decent-paying jobs available. But it doesn't work that way. [...] It is an irretrievable disaster for young men to grow up without being socialised into the world of work.

Work is at the centre of life

The reason why it is a disaster is not that these young men cause upright taxpayers to spend too much money supporting them. That is a nuisance. The disaster is to the young men themselves and the communities in which they live. [...] By remaining out of the work force during the crucial formative years, young men aren't just losing a few years of job experience. They are missing out on the time in which they need to have been acquiring the skills and the networks of friends and experiences that enable them to establish a place for themselves – not only in the workplace, but vantage point from which they can make sense of themselves and their lives.

Furthermore, when large numbers of young men don't work, the communities around them break down, just as they break down when large numbers of young unmarried women have babies. The two phenomena are intimately related. [...] Young men who don't work don't make good marriage material. Often they don't get married at all; when they do, they haven't the ability to fill their traditional role. In either case, too many of them remain barbarians.

The size of the British underclass

How big is the British underclass? It all depends on how one defines its membership; trying to take a headcount is a waste of time. The size of the underclass can be made to look huge or insignificant, depending on what one wants the answer to be.

But it seems safe to conclude that as of 1989 the British underclass is still small enough not to represent nearly the problem that it does in the US. [...]

The question facing Britain is the same, haunting question facing the United States: how contagious is this disease? Is it going to spread indefinitely, or will it be self-containing?

Questions about causation

Here we reach controversial questions about causation. [...]

Let us think instead in common-sense terms. The topic is young people in their late teens and early twenties. The proposition is as simple as this: young people – not just poor young people, but all young people – try to make sense of the world around them. They behave in ways that reflect what they observe. In the 1960s and 1970s social policy in Britain fundamentally changed what makes sense. The changes did not affect the mature as much as the young. They affected the affluent hardly at all. Rather: the rules of the game changed fundamentally for low-income

young people. Behaviour changed along with the changes in the rules.

Crime has become safer

Consider how the world was changing at the time when the trendlines in crime and illegitimacy were changing. I begin with crime, assuming this common sense view of the situation: if the chances that one will get punished for a crime go down, then crime goes up. In every respect – the chances of getting caught, the chances of being found guilty and the chances of going to prison – crime has become dramatically safer in Britain throughout the post-war period, and most blatantly safer since 1960.

Clear-up rates provide an example. With a few crimes such as homicide, the clear-up rate has remained high and unchanged. But for a crime such as robbery, the clear-up rate has fallen from 61 per cent in 1960 to 21 per cent in 1987 – an extremely large change. Reductions for other crimes have been smaller but significant. [...]

Perhaps most importantly, the penalties imposed upon those convicted changed. [...] The obvious measure is not the number of people in prison, but rather the chances of going to prison if one commits a crime. That figure has plummeted. Prison sentences as a proportion of reported crimes fell by half during the period 1950 to 1970, and the 1970 figure had fallen again by half by 1987. [...]

But comparatively few offenders were sent to prison even in the tough old days. This statistic may be treated as an example, not the whole story. 'Penalty' doesn't mean simply 'prison', nor even 'the judge's sentence'.

The use of penalties has fallen

Even using simple measures, recent trends in penalties are at odds with the reputation of the Thatcher Government as tough, anti-crime and punitive. From 1982 to 1987, even as crime continued to rise, the number of convictions and prison sentences dropped – not just as a proportion of crimes, but in raw numbers. In 1982, 3.3 million indictable offences were known to the police, 475,000 persons were found guilty of them; of these, 50,300 received unsuspended prison sentences. In 1987, 3.9 million indictable offences were known to the police (up 19 per cent), 386,000 were found guilty of them (down 19 per cent); of these, 41,700 received unsuspended prison sentences (down 17 per cent). People who use the past few years as evidence that a 'get tough' policy doesn't work aren't defining 'get tough' from the criminal's point of view. [...]

I'm not claiming that the police have become lax (they've been overwhelmed), nor that one must ignore the complicated social forces associated with increases in crime. Just this: committing a crime has been getting safer for more than three decades, and the trend continues today.

The benefit system

At this point we come to the benefit system, and another source of great controversy and confusion. Conservatives in particular often misconstrue the problem, railing against the woman who goes out and gets pregnant so that she can get on the dole. It happens occasionally but, as far as anyone knows, the reason why single young women have babies is seldom specifically so that they can get income benefits. (Sometimes they have a second child specifically so that they can *remain* on benefit, but that constitutes a comparatively minor part of the problem.)

Rather, the problem in providing money to single women is that the income enables many young women to do something they would naturally like to do. Such benefits don't have much effect on affluent women – the benefit rate is so far below what they consider their needs, that they are not in any way 'enabled' to have babies by the level of support being provided. For poor women, however, the benefit level can be quite salient in deciding whether having a baby is feasible. And the simple economic feasibility of raising a baby without the support of a father has changed fundamentally since the end of the Second World War.

The Homeless Persons Act

During the first half of the 1970s the size of the benefit for single women began to rise more rapidly, increasing more than a third in purchasing power from 1970 to 1976. Then, in 1977 the Homeless Persons Act was passed. Before, a single mother had to wait in a queue for housing, but the new act stipulated that pregnant women and single mothers must get some sort of housing immediately – and go to the top of the queue for council housing – if they could demonstrate to the local authority's satisfaction that they couldn't live with their parents and were otherwise homeless.

I doubt that the Homeless Persons Act bribed many young women to have babies so that they could get their own flats. Rather, the increases in the benefits and the Homeless Persons Act were

steps in a quiet, commonsensical, cumulative process whereby having a baby as a single mother went from 'extremely punishing' to 'not so bad'. By 1977, poor young women looking at the world around them could see that single mothers in their neighbourhoods were getting along, whereas a similar young woman in the 1950s would have looked around and conclude that single motherhood was an awful state to be in. [...]

I'm not saying that single young women get pregnant for the money. I'm not chiding them for immorality. I'm not saying that they don't love their babies. I'm not saying that a 10 per cent cut in benefits will mean a 10 per cent reduction (or any reduction) in fertility among single women. Rather, a series of changes in the benefit rates and collateral housing benefits lifted a large portion of low-income young women above the threshold where having and keeping a baby became economically feasible.

It doesn't make any difference if the benefit level stops getting higher, or even if it diminishes somewhat. As long as the benefit level is well above the threshold, the dynamics of social incentives will continue to work in favour of illegitimacy as over time the advantages of legal marriage become less clear and its disadvantages more obvious. For men, the pressures to marry will continue to diminish. Given all this, I cannot see why the illegitimacy ratio should start to level off.

Social problems are interconnected

Everything interacts. When one leaves school without any job skills, barely literate, the job alternatives to crime or having a baby or the dole are not attractive. Young men who are subsisting in crime or the dole are not likely to be trustworthy providers, which makes having a baby without a husband a more practical alternative. If a young man's girl friend doesn't need him to help support the baby, it makes less sense for him to plug away at a menial job and more sense to have some fun – which in turn makes hustling and crime more attractive, marriage less attractive. Without a job or family to give life meaning, drugs become that much more valuable as a means of distraction. The cost of drugs makes crime the only feasible way to make enough money to pay for them. The interconnections go on endlessly, linking up with the reasons why community norms change, the role of older adults in the community changes, community bonds change.

Incremental changes won't solve the problem

The implication of these interconnections is that modest, incremental changes in one corner of the system are unlikely to have much effect. Everybody's pet solutions are wrong. People on the Right who think that they can reduce illegitimacy by snipping benefits are wrong. (Illegitimacy would be cut radically if you slashed benefits back to the 1970 level, but that's not under consideration.) The notion that giving the police more latitude or legislating longer prison sentences will reduce crime is wrong. (Crime would be cut radically if you enforced laws as strictly as you did in 1950, but in the short term that would mean tripling your prison population and vastly expanding your court system.)

What can Britain learn from the American experience?

So if the United States has had so much more experience with a growing underclass, what can Britain learn from it? The sad answer is – not much. The central truth that the politicians in the United States are unwilling to face is our powerlessness to deal with an underclass once it exists. [...]

Let me emphasise the words: *we do not know how*. It's not money we lack, but the capability to social-engineer our way out of this situation. Unfortunately, the delusions persist that our social engineering simply hasn't been clever enough, and that we must strive to become more clever.

Authentic self-government is the key

The alternative I advocate is to have the central government stop trying to be clever and instead get out of the way, giving poor communities (and affluent communities, too) a massive dose of self-government, with vastly greater responsibility for the operation of the institutions that affect their lives – including the criminal justice, educational, housing and benefit systems in their localities. My premise is that it is unnatural for a neighbourhood to tolerate high levels of crime or illegitimacy or voluntary idleness among its youth: that, given the chance, poor communities as well as rich ones will run affairs so that such things happen infrequently. And when communities with different values run their affairs differently, I want to make it as easy as possible for people who share values to live together. If people in one neighbourhood think marriage is an outmoded institutions, fine; let them run their neighbourhood as they see fit. But make it easy for the couple who thinks otherwise to move into neighbourhood where two-parent families are valued. There are many ways that current levels of expenditure for public systems could be sustained (if that is thought to be necessary) but control over them decentralised. Money isn't the key. Authentic self government is.

The bleak message

So, Britain, that's the bleak message. Not only do you have an underclass, not only is it growing, but, judging from the American experience, there's not much in either the Conservative or Labour agendas that has a chance of doing anything about it. A few years ago I wrote for an American audience that the real contest about social policy is not between people who want to cut budgets and people who want to help. Watching Britain replay our history, I can do no better than repeat the same conclusion. When meaningful reforms finally do occur, they will happen not because stingy people have won, but because generous people have stopped kidding themselves.

From C. Murray, The Emerging Underclass *(London: IEA), 1990, pp. 1–35.*

13.4 Broken windows
James Q. Wilson and George L. Kelling

In the mid-1970s the state of New Jersey announced a 'Safe and Clean Neighborhoods Program,' designed to improve the quality of community life in twenty-eight cities. As part of that program, the state provided money to help cities take police officers out of their patrol cars and assign them to walking beats. The governor and other state officials were enthusiastic about using foot patrol as a way of cutting crime, but many police chiefs were skeptical. Foot patrol, in their eyes, had been pretty much discredited. It reduced the mobility of the police, who thus had difficulty responding to citizen calls for service, and it weakened headquarters control over patrol officers.

Many police officers also disliked foot patrol, but for different reasons: it was hard work, it kept them outside on cold, rainy nights, and it reduced their chances for making a 'good pinch.' In some departments, assigning officers to foot patrol had been used as a form of punishment. And academic experts on policing doubted that foot patrol would have any impact on crime rates; it was, in the opinion of most, little more than a sop to public opinion. But since the state was paying for it, the local authorities were willing to go along.

Five years after the program started, the Police Foundation, in Washington, D.C., published an evaluation of the foot-patrol project. Based on its analysis of a carefully controlled experiment carried out chiefly in Newark, the foundation concluded, to the surprise of hardly anyone, that foot patrol had not reduced crime rates. But residents of the foot patrolled neighborhoods seemed to feel more secure than persons in other areas, tended to believe that crime had been reduced, and seemed to take fewer steps to protect themselves from crime (staying at home with the doors locked, for example). Moreover, citizens in the foot-patrol areas had a more favorable opinion of the police than did those living elsewhere. And officers walking beats had higher morale, greater job satisfaction, and a more favorable attitude toward citizens in their neighborhoods than did officers assigned to patrol cars.

These findings may be taken as evidence that the skeptics were right – foot patrol has no effect on crime; it merely fools the citizens into thinking that they are safer. But in our view, and in the view of the authors of the Police Foundation study (of whom Kelling was one), the citizens of Newark were not fooled at all. They knew what the foot-patrol officers were doing, they knew it was different from what motorized officers do, and they knew that having officers walk beats did in fact make their neighborhoods safer.

But how can a neighborhood be 'safer' when the crime rate has not gone down – in fact, may have gone up? Finding the answer requires first that we understand what most often frightens people in public places. Many citizens, of course, are primarily frightened by crime, especially crime involving a sudden, violent attack by a stranger. This risk is very real, in Newark as in many large cities. But we tend to overlook another source of fear – the fear of being bothered by disorderly people. Not violent people, nor, necessarily, criminals, but disreputable or obstreperous or unpredictable people: panhandlers, drunks, addicts, rowdy teenagers, prostitutes, loiterers, the mentally disturbed.

What foot-patrol officers did was to elevate, to the extent they could, the level of public order in these neighborhoods. Though the neighborhoods were predominantly black and the foot patrolmen were mostly white, this 'order-maintenance' function of the police was performed to the general satisfaction of both parties.

One of us (Kelling) spent many hours walking with Newark foot-patrol officers to see how they defined 'order' and what they did to maintain it. [...] The people on the street were primarily black; the officer who walked the street was white. The people were made up of 'regulars' and 'strangers.' Regulars included both 'decent folk' and some drunks and derelicts who were always there but who 'knew their place.' Strangers were, well, strangers, and viewed suspiciously, sometimes apprehensively. The officer – call him Kelly – knew who the regulars were, and they knew him. As he saw his job, he was to keep an eye on strangers, and make certain that the disreputable regulars observed some informal but widely understood rules. Drunks and addicts could sit on the stoops, but could not lie down. People could drink on side streets, but not at the main intersection. Bottles had to be in paper bags. Talking to, bothering, or begging from people waiting at the bus stop was strictly forbidden. [...] Noisy teenagers were told to keep quiet. These rules were defined and enforced in collaboration with the 'regulars' on the street. Another neighborhood might have different rules, but these, everybody understood, were the rules for *this* neighborhood. If someone violated them, the regulars not only turned to Kelly for help but also ridiculed the violator. Sometimes what Kelly did could be described as 'enforcing the law,' but just as often it involved taking informal or extralegal steps to help protect what the neighborhood had decided was the appropriate level of public order. Some of the things he did probably would not withstand a legal challenge.

A determined skeptic might acknowledge that a skilled foot-patrol officer can maintain order but still insist that this sort of 'order' has little to do with the real sources of community fear – that is, with violent crime. To a degree, that is true. But two things must be borne in mind. First, outside observers should not assume that they know how much of the anxiety now endemic in many big-city neighborhoods stems from a fear of 'real' crime and how much from a sense that the street is disorderly, a source of distasteful, worrisome encounters. [...] Second, at the community level, disorder and crime are usually inextricably linked, in a kind of developmental sequence. Social psychologists and police officers tend to agree that if a window in a building is broken and is left unrepaired, all the rest of the windows will soon be broken. This is as true in nice neighborhoods as in rundown ones. [...]

Philip Zimbardo, a Stanford psychologist, reported in 1969 on some experiments testing the broken-window theory. He arranged to have an automobile without license plates parked with its hood up on a street in the Bronx and a comparable automobile on a street in Palo Alto, California. The car in the Bronx was attacked by 'vandals' within ten minutes of its 'abandonment.' The first to arrive were a family – father, mother, and young son – who removed the radiator and battery. Within twenty-four hours, virtually everything of value had been removed. Then random destruction began – windows were smashed, parts torn off, upholstery ripped. Children began to use the car as a playground. Most of the adult 'vandals' were well-dressed, apparently clean-cut whites. The car in Palo Alto sat untouched for more than a week. Then Zimbardo smashed part of it with a sledge-hammer. Soon, passersby were joining in. Within a few hours, the car had been turned upside down and utterly destroyed. Again, the 'vandals' appeared to be primarily respectable whites.

Untended property becomes fair game for people out for fun or plunder and even for people who ordinarily would not dream of doing such things and who probably consider themselves law-abiding. Because of the nature of community life in the Bronx – its anonymity, the frequency with which cars are abandoned and things are stolen or broken, the past experience of 'no one caring' – vandalism begins much more quickly than it does in staid Palo Alto, where people have come to believe that private possessions are cared for, and that mischievous behavior is costly. But vandalism can occur anywhere once communal barriers – the sense of mutual regard and the obligations of civility – are lowered by actions that seem to signal that 'no one cares.'

We suggest that 'untended' behavior also leads to the breakdown of community controls. A stable neighborhood of families who care for their homes, mind each other's children, and confidently frown on unwanted intruders can change, in a few years or even a few months, to an inhospitable and frightening jungle. A piece of property is abandoned, weeds grow up, a window is smashed. Adults stop scolding rowdy children; the children, emboldened, become more rowdy. Families move out, unattached adults move in. Teenagers gather in front of the corner store. The merchant asks them to move; they refuse. Fights occur. Litter accumulates. People start drinking in front of the grocery; in time, an inebriate slumps to the sidewalk and is allowed to sleep it off. Pedestrians are approached by panhandlers.

At this point it is not inevitable that serious crime will flourish or violent attacks on strangers will occur. But many residents will think that crime, especially violent crime, is on the rise, and they will modify their behavior accordingly. They will use the streets less often, and when on the streets will stay apart from their fellows, moving with averted eyes, silent lips, and hurried steps. 'Don't get involved.' For some residents, this growing atomization will matter little, because the neighborhood is not their 'home' but 'the place where they live.' Their interests are elsewhere; they are cosmopolitans. But it will matter greatly to other people, whose lives derive meaning and satisfaction from local attachments rather than worldly involvement; for them, the neighborhood will cease to exist except for a few reliable friends whom they arrange to meet.

Such an area is vulnerable to criminal invasion. Though it is not inevitable, it is more likely that here, rather than in places where people are confident they can regulate public behavior by informal controls, drugs will change hands, prostitutes will solicit, and cars will be stripped. That the drunks will be robbed by boys who do it as a lark, and the prostitutes' customers will be robbed by men who do it purposefully and perhaps violently. That muggings will occur.

Among those who often find it difficult to move away from this are the elderly. [...] The prospect of a confrontation with an obstreperous teenager or a drunken panhandler can be as fear inducing for defenseless persons as the prospect of meeting an actual robber; indeed, to a defenseless person, the two kinds of confrontation are often indistinguishable. Moreover, the lower rate at which the elderly are victimized is a measure of the steps they have already taken – chiefly, staying behind locked doors – to minimize the risks they face. Young men are more frequently attacked than older women, not because they are easier or more lucrative targets but because they are on the streets more.

Nor is the connection between disorderliness and fear made only by the elderly. Susan Estrich, of the Harvard Law School, has recently gathered together a number of surveys on the sources of public fear. One, done in Portland, Oregon, indicated that three fourths of the adults interviewed cross to the other side of a street when they see a gang of teenagers; another survey, in Baltimore, discovered that nearly half would cross the street to avoid even a single strange youth. When an interviewer asked people in a housing project where the most dangerous spot was, they mentioned a place where young persons gathered to drink and play music, despite the fact that not a single crime had occurred there. In Boston public housing projects, the greatest fear was expressed by persons living in the buildings where disorderliness and incivility, not crime, were the greatest. Knowing this helps one understand the significance of such otherwise harmless displays as subway graffiti. [...]

In response to fear people avoid one another, weakening controls. Sometimes they call the police. Patrol cars arrive, an occasional arrest occurs but crime continues and disorder is not abated. Citizens complain to the police chief, but he explains that his department is low on personnel and that the courts do not punish petty or first-time offenders. To the residents, the police who arrive in squad cars are either ineffective or uncaring: to the police, the residents are animals who deserve each other. The citizens may soon stop calling the police, because 'they can't do anything.'

The process we call urban decay has occurred for centuries in every city. But what is happening today is different in at least two important respects. First, in the period before, say, World War II, city dwellers – because of money costs, transportation difficulties, familial and church connections – could rarely move away from neighborhood problems. When movement did occur, it tended to be along public-transit routes. Now mobility has become exceptionally easy for all but the poorest or those who are blocked by racial prejudice. Earlier crime waves had a kind of built in self-correcting mechanism: the determination of a neighborhood or community to reassert control over its turf. [...] Second, the police in this earlier period assisted in that reassertion of authority by acting, sometimes violently, on behalf of the community. Young toughs were roughed up, people were arrested 'on suspicion' or for vagrancy, and prostitutes and petty thieves were routed. 'Rights' were something enjoyed by decent folk, and perhaps also by the serious professional criminal, who avoided violence and could afford a lawyer. This pattern of policing was not an aberration or the result of occasional excess. From the earliest days of the nation, the police function was seen primarily as that of a night watchman: to maintain order against the chief threats to order – fire, wild animals, and disreputable behavior. Solving crimes was viewed not as a police responsibility but as a private one.

In the 1960s, when urban riots were a major problem, social scientists began to explore carefully the order maintenance function of the police, and to suggest ways of improving it – not to make streets safer (its original function) but to reduce the incidence of mass violence. Order maintenance became, to a degree, coterminous with 'community relations.' But, as the crime wave that began in the early 1960s continued without abatement throughout the decade and into the 1970s, attention shifted to the role of the police as crime-fighters. [...] A great deal was accomplished during this transition, as both police chiefs and outside experts emphasized the crime-fighting function in their plans, in the allocation of resources, and in deployment of personnel. The police may well have become better crime-fighters as a result. And doubtless they remained aware of their responsibility for order. But the link between order-maintenance and crime-prevention, so obvious to earlier generations, was forgotten.

That link is similar to the process whereby one broken window becomes many. The citizen who fears the ill-smelling drunk, the rowdy teenager, or the importuning beggar is not merely expressing his distaste for unseemly behavior; he is also giving voice to a bit of folk wisdom that happens to be a correct generalization – namely, that serious street crime flourishes in areas in which disorderly behavior goes unchecked. The unchecked panhandler is, in effect, the first broken window. Muggers and robbers, whether opportunistic or professional, believe they reduce their chances of being caught or even identified if they operate on streets where potential victims are already intimidated by prevailing conditions. If the neighborhood cannot keep a bothersome panhandler from annoying passersby, the thief may reason, it is even less likely to call the police to identify a potential mugger or to interfere if the mugging actually takes place.

Some police administrators concede that this process occurs, but argue that motorized-patrol officers can deal with it as effectively as foot patrol officers. We are not so sure. [...] Our experience is that most citizens like to talk to a police officer. Such exchanges give them a sense of importance, provide them with the basis for gossip, and allow them to explain to the authorities what is worrying them (whereby they gain a modest but significant sense of having 'done something' about the problem). You approach a person on foot more easily, and talk to him more readily, than you do a person in a car. Moreover, you can more easily retain some anonymity if you draw an officer aside for a private chat. [...] The essence of the police role in maintaining order is to reinforce the informal control mechanisms of the community itself. The police cannot, without committing extraordinary resources, provide a substitute for that informal control. On the other hand, to reinforce those natural forces the police must accommodate them. And therein lies the problem.

Should police activity on the street be shaped, in important ways, by the standards of the neighborhood rather than by the rules of the state? Over the past two decades, the shift of police from order-maintenance to law enforcement has brought them increasingly under the influence of legal restrictions, provoked by media complaints and enforced by court decisions and departmental orders. As a consequence, the order maintenance functions of the police are now governed by rules developed to control police relations with suspected criminals. [...] Once we begin to think of all aspects of police work as involving the application of universal rules under special procedures, we inevitably ask what constitutes an 'undesirable person' and why we should 'criminalize' vagrancy or drunkenness. A strong and commendable desire to see that people are treated fairly makes us worry about allowing the police to rout persons who are undesirable by some vague or parochial standard. A growing and not-so-commendable utilitarianism leads us to doubt that any behavior that does not 'hurt' another person should be made illegal. And thus many of us who watch over the police are reluctant to allow them to perform, in the only way they can, a function that every neighborhood desperately wants them to perform.

This wish to 'decriminalize' disreputable behavior that 'harms no one' – and thus remove the ultimate sanction the police can employ to maintain neighborhood order – is, we think, a mistake. Arresting a single drunk or a single vagrant who has harmed no identifiable person seems unjust, and in a sense it is. But failing to do anything about a score of drunks or a hundred vagrants may destroy an entire community. A particular rule that seems to make sense in the individual case makes no sense when it is made a universal rule and applied to all cases. It makes no sense because it fails to take into account the connection between one broken window left untended and a thousand broken windows. Of course, agencies other than the police could attend to the problems posed by drunks or the mentally ill, but in most communities – especially where the 'deinstitutionalization' movement has been strong – they do not.

The concern about equity is more serious. We might agree that certain behavior makes one person more undesirable than another but how do we ensure that age or skin color or national origin or harmless mannerisms will not also become the basis for distinguishing the undesirable from the desirable? How do we ensure, in short, that the police do not become the agents of neighborhood bigotry?

We can offer no wholly satisfactory answer to this important question. We are not confident that there is a satisfactory answer except to hope that by their selection, training, and supervision, the police will be inculcated with a clear sense of the outer limit of their discretionary authority. That limit, roughly, is this – the police exist to help regulate behavior, not to maintain the racial or ethnic purity of a neighborhood. [...]

It may be their greater sensitivity to communal as opposed to individual needs that helps explain why the residents of small communities are more satisfied with their police than are the residents of similar neighborhoods in big cities. Elinor Ostrom and her co-workers at Indiana University compared the perception of police services in two poor, all-black Illinois towns – Phoenix and East Chicago Heights – with those of three comparable all-black neighborhoods in Chicago. The level of criminal victimization and the quality of police-community relations appeared to be about the same in the towns and the Chicago neighborhoods. But the citizens living in their own villages were much more likely than those living in the Chicago neighborhoods to say that they do not stay at home for fear of crime, to agree that the local police have 'the right to take any action necessary' to deal with problems, and to agree that the police 'look out for the needs of the average citizen.' It is possible that the residents and the police of the small towns saw themselves as engaged in a collaborative effort to maintain a certain standard of communal life, whereas those of the big city felt themselves to be simply requesting and supplying particular services on an individual basis.

If this is true, how should a wise police chief deploy his meager forces? The first answer is that nobody knows for certain, and the most prudent course of action would be to try further variations on the Newark experiment, to see more precisely what works in what kinds of neighborhoods. The second answer is also a hedge – many aspects of order maintenance in neighborhoods can probably best be handled in ways that involve the police minimally if at all. A busy bustling shopping center and a quiet, well-tended suburb may need almost no visible police presence. In both cases, the ratio of respectable to disreputable people is ordinarily so high as to make informal social control effective.

Even in areas that are in jeopardy from disorderly elements, citizen action without substantial police involvement may be sufficient. Meetings between teenagers who like to hang out on a particular corner and adults who want to use that corner might well lead to an amicable agreement on a set of rules about how many people can be allowed to congregate, where, and when.

Where no understanding is possible – or if possible, not observed – citizen patrols may be a sufficient response. There are two traditions of communal involvement in maintaining order: One, that of the 'community watchmen,' is as old as the first settlement of the New World. Until well into the nineteenth century, volunteer watchmen, not policemen, patrolled their communities to keep order. They did so, by and large, without taking the law into their own hands – without, that is, punishing persons or using force. Their presence deterred disorder or alerted the community to disorder that could not be deterred. There are hundreds of such efforts today in communities all across the nation. [...]

The second tradition is that of the 'vigilante.' Rarely a feature of the settled communities of the East, it was primarily to be found in those frontier towns that grew up in advance of the reach of government. More than 350 vigilante groups are known to have existed; their distinctive feature was that their members did take the law into their own hands, by acting as judge, jury, and often executioner as well as policeman. Today, the vigilante movement is conspicuous by its rarity, despite the great fear expressed by citizens that the older cities are becoming 'urban frontiers.' But some community-watchmen groups have skirted the line, and others may cross it in the future. [...]

Though citizens can do a great deal, the police are plainly the key to order maintenance. For one thing, many communities... cannot do the job by themselves. For another, no citizen in a neighborhood, even an organized one, is likely to feel the sense of responsibility that wearing a badge confers... Ironically, avoiding responsibility is easier when a lot of people are standing about. On streets and in public places, where order is so important, many people are likely to be 'around,' a fact that reduces the chance of any one person acting as the agent of the community. The police officer's uniform singles him out as a person who must accept responsibility if asked. In addition, officers, more easily than their fellow citizens, can be expected to distinguish between what is necessary to protect the safety of the street and what merely protects its ethnic purity. [...]

Some neighborhoods are so demoralized and crime-ridden as to make foot patrol useless; the best the police can do with limited resources is respond to the enormous number of calls for service. Other neighborhoods are so stable and serene as to make foot patrol unnecessary. The key is to identify neighborhoods at the tipping point – where the public order is deteriorating but not unreclaimable, where the streets are used frequently but by apprehensive people, where a window is likely to be broken at any time, and must quickly be fixed if all are not to be shattered.

[T]he most important requirement is to think that to maintain order in precarious situations is a vital job. The police know this is one of their functions, and they also believe, correctly, that it cannot be done to the exclusion of criminal investigation and responding to calls. We may have encouraged them to suppose, however, on the basis of our oft-repeated concerns about serious, violent crime, that they will be judged exclusively on their capacity as crime-fighters. To the extent that this is the case, police administrators will continue to concentrate police personnel in the highest-crime areas (though not necessarily in the areas most vulnerable to criminal invasion),

emphasize their training in the law and criminal apprehension (and not their training in managing street life), and join too quickly in campaigns to decriminalize 'harmless' behavior (though public drunkenness, street prostitution, and pornographic displays can destroy a community more quickly than any team of professional burglars).

Above all, we must return to our long-abandoned view that the police ought to protect communities as well as individuals. Our crime statistics and victimization surveys measure individual losses, but they do not measure communal losses. Just as physicians now recognize the importance of fostering health rather than simply treating illness, so the police – and the rest of us – ought to recognize the importance of maintaining, intact, communities without broken windows.

From J. Q. Wilson and G.L. Kelling, 'Broken windows', Atlantic Monthly, *1982, March.*

14

Contemporary classicism

14.1 The new criminologies of everyday life
David Garland   304

**14.2 'Situational' crime prevention: theory
and practice**
Ronald V. Clarke   307

**14.3 Opportunity makes the thief:
practical theory for crime prevention**
Marcus Felson and Ronald V. Clarke   312

**14.4 Social change and crime rate trends:
a routine activity approach**
Lawrence E. Cohen and Marcus Felson   318

Introduction

At the heart of this approach to understanding crime is the general assumption that human beings are rational actors and that rational calculation plays an important part in decision-making, including decision-making about offending. From the late 1960s, and particularly in later decades, a number of criminological theories appeared which placed great emphasis upon the importance of the choices made by offenders in differing circumstances and locations. More particularly, such perspectives proceeded from the idea that if it were possible to manipulate circumstances and decision-making then crime might be prevented and reduced.

The excerpts in this chapter give some sense of the variety of work that can be found under the general rubric of 'contemporary classicism'. There is an obvious danger in such terms – not least that in putting things together (as of course has been the case in other chapters) the differences between them will be smoothed out. Nevertheless, there is much that they share and an influential analysis of the emergence and development of this general approach has been provided by David Garland **(Reading 14.1)**. He refers to the work in this general area as the 'new criminologies of everyday life'. He traces their emergence and argues that they proceed from the premise that crime is normal and commonplace. There is nothing abnormal or pathological about it. It is motivated in the same way other behaviours are. Crucially, this new perspective shifts the criminological gaze from being backward-looking to being forward-looking. It focuses on everyday interactions and seeks to manipulate them, in often small ways, to reduce criminal motivations or opportunities. A consequence of such an approach for punishment is to shift attention away from root causes and individual needs toward a greater concern with the swiftness and certainty of punishment (if you go back to the readings in chapter 5 you will see the connection here with 'classicism').

One particularly influential body of work in recent decades in criminology is what has become known as 'situational crime prevention'. In the second excerpt one of its best-known practitioners, Ron Clarke **(Reading 14.2)**, outlines both its theory and elements of its practice. In terms of practice, he discusses two key approaches: reducing physical opportunities and increasing the risks of being caught. He describes the approach as 'gradualist' – one offering small, incremental steps which might have small localized impacts – or occasionally greater ones – on crime. Put together, the argument goes (watch the pennies and the pounds will take care of themselves), and the impact can be sizeable. What Clarke outlines here has to be understood in part as a reaction to the 'nothing works' assumptions of the 1970s. For those of a more radical orientation, he notes, the lack of a concern with substantial social change, or with social justice in general, might be something of a sticking point.

As has already been alluded to, at the core of much of this work is the idea that 'opportunity' is the most important issue in crime and its prevention. In what is effectively a manifesto for such an idea, Marcus Felson and Ron Clarke

(Reading 14.3) outline what they suggest are the ten principles of opportunity and crime. These include such observations that opportunities occur in particular places and at particular times and that analysis of these may give rise to important insights into the nature of crime. One such insight is the concept of a 'hot spot': places, addresses, etc, in or around which particular crimes appear to be concentrated. One standard criticism of much criminology of this kind is that rather than *preventing* crime such activities merely *displace* it to other areas, people or places. Clarke and Felson mount a rigorous rebuttal of this idea and argue strongly that opportunity-based approaches really do prevent crime.

So far the excerpts have focused on what are largely individual-level analyses: how a rational-choice, opportunity theory can be used to understand crime in particular times and locations. In the final piece, Lawrence Cohen and Marcus Felson **(Reading 14.4)** apply what they term a 'routine activities approach' to crime rates over time. The routine activities approach suggests that three elements must come together for crime to occur: a motivated offender; a suitable target; and the absence of a capable guardian. In a startling thesis they argue that 'the dramatic increase in the reported crime rates in the US since 1960 is linked to changes in the routine activity structure of American society and a corresponding increase in target suitability and decrease in guardian presence'. In short, the changing nature of the labour market, of households and of consumer goods have combined to leave a greater number of attractive items unguarded and, consequently, to increasing crime levels.

Questions for discussion

1. What are the main characteristics, according to Garland, of the 'new criminologies of everyday life'?

2. What are the approaches here referred to as 'contemporary classicism'?

3. Give two examples in each case of how reducing opportunities or increasing risks might serve to reduce crime.

4. What are the main dangers of situational crime prevention?

5. Suggest five ways in which opportunity and crime are linked.

6. Is displacement the Achilles heel of situational crime prevention and related approaches?

7. What do Cohen and Felson identify as the main components of change giving rise to the substantial rise in crime in America since 1960?

8. What can these 'new criminologies of everyday life' tell us about criminal motivation?

14.1 The new criminologies of everyday life
David Garland

The new criminologies of everyday life

One of the most significant developments of the last two decades has been the emergence of a new style of criminological thinking that has succeeded in attracting the interest of government officials. With the fading of correctionalist rationales for criminal justice, and in the face of the crime-control predicament, officials have increasingly discovered an elective affinity between their own practical concerns and this new genre of criminological discourse. This new genre – which might be termed the *new criminologies of everyday life* – has barely impinged upon public attention, but it has functioned as a crucial support for much recent policy. One can trace its influence not just in the responsibilization strategy and in the new crime prevention apparatus, but also in recent policies of penal deterrence and incapacitation. This new way of thinking has, quite rapidly, become one of the key strands of official criminology, shaping government policies and organizational practice in both the USA and the UK. Despite its thoroughly practical and atheoretical character, this new way of thinking expresses very well some of the key ways in which the crime control field is currently being reconfigured.

The new criminologies of everyday life are a set of cognate theoretical frameworks that includes routine activity theory, crime as opportunity, lifestyle analysis, situational crime prevention, and some versions of rational choice theory.[1] The striking thing about these various criminologies is that they each begin from the premise that crime is a normal, commonplace, aspect of modern society. Crime is regarded as a generalized form of behaviour, routinely produced by the normal patterns of social and economic life in contemporary society. To commit an offence thus requires no special motivation or disposition, no abnormality or pathology. In contrast to earlier criminologies, which began from the premise that crime was a deviation from normal civilized conduct and was explicable in terms of individual pathology or faulty socialization, the new criminologies see crime as *continuous* with normal social interaction and explicable by reference to *standard* motivational patterns. Crime comes to be viewed as a routine risk to be calculated or an accident to be avoided, rather than a moral aberration that needs to be specially explained.

In the past, official criminology has usually viewed crime *retrospectively* and *individually*, in order to itemise individual wrongdoing and allocate punishment or treatment. The new criminologies tend to view crime *prospectively* and in *aggregate* terms, for the purpose of calculating risks and shaping preventative measures. This shift of perspectives is significant in its intellectual and practical consequences, since it opens up a whole series of new ways of understanding and acting upon crime. But it is also significant in institutional terms, as a sign of a changing field, because it entails a view of the crime problem that is no longer that of the criminal justice state. Up until this point, and in spite of intellectual arguments to the contrary, official criminology (and much academic criminology) viewed the problem of crime from the perspective of the criminal justice system, insisted on seeing crime as a problem of individual offenders, and tended to see offenders as typified by those in captivity. The new criminologies reject this institutional point of view, seeing crime in a social and economic perspective that owes nothing to process of law enforcement. The official endorsement of the new criminologies of everyday life thus represents a significant shift of perspective on the part of criminal justice administrators, and suggests the diminishing power of the institutional epistemology that previously shaped thinking and action in this field.

This new criminological approach emerges in a context where high crime rates are taken as a given, and where the data of self-report and victim studies testify to the normality of crime. Its emergence is testimony to the declining credibility of the criminal justice state, or at least of the myth of its sovereign capacity to control crime by itself. Many of the practical prescriptions that flow from these theories are addressed not to state agencies such as the police, the courts and the prisons, but *beyond* the state apparatus, to the organizations, institutions, and individuals of civil society. The theories simply take it for granted that the criminal justice state has a limited capacity, and they look to the everyday life world as the appropriate locus for action.

As well as empowering different agencies, these new theories identify different targets and new means of addressing them. Their programmes of action are directed not towards any and every individual offender, but instead towards the conduct of potential victims, to criminogenic situations, and to those routines of everyday life that create criminal opportunities as an unintended by-product. Where an older criminology concerned itself with disciplining delinquent individuals or punishing legal subjects, the new approach identifies recurring criminal opportunities and seeks to govern them by developing situational controls that will make them less tempting or less vulnerable. Criminogenic situations, 'hot products', 'hot spots' – these are the new objects of control. The assumption is that 'opportunity creates the thief' rather than the other way around. Such an approach promises to maximize the return for effort, since it focuses upon those elements of the criminal encounter that are most identifiable, fixed and predictable. As Nigel Walker puts it, 'potential offenders are numerous and by no means always recognisable. By contrast, we do at least know what property to protect, and where it is.'[2]

This is, in effect, 'supply side criminology', shifting risks, redistributing costs, and creating disincentives. It aims to embed controls in the fabric of normal interaction, rather than suspend them above it in the form of a sovereign command. Rather than rely upon the uncertain threat of deterrent sentences, or the dubious ability of the police to catch villains, it sets in place a more mundane set of reforms, designed not to change people but to redesign things and reshape situations. A thousand small adjustments are required. Replace cash with credit cards. Build locks into the steering columns of automobiles. Employ attendants in parking lots and use close circuit TV cameras to monitor city centre streets. Co-ordinate the closing times of rival clubs and discos. Lay on late night buses and special routes to and from football games. Advise retailers about security. Encourage local authorities to co-ordinate the various agencies that deal with crime. Remind citizens of the need to safeguard their property and supervise their neighbourhoods.

In contrast to correctionalist criminology, this approach no longer takes the state and its agencies to be the primary or proximate actors in the business of crime control. And to the extent that it depicts a criminal subject, this figure is no longer the poorly socialized misfit in need of assistance, but instead the opportunistic consumer, whose attitudes cannot be changed but whose access to social goods could be barred. This criminal figure – sometimes described as 'situational man' – lacks a strong moral compass or any effective internal controls, aside from a capacity for rational calculation and a healthy will to pleasure.[3] In the hands of other writers, this might be intended as a form of cultural critique or a commentary on contemporary consumerist mores. But there is no hint of irony in the flat, deadpan prose of the new criminological texts.

If the main effect of these criminologies has been to encourage new forms of action that go 'beyond the state', they have also helped revive some more traditional modes of action. Criminological discourses are always polyvalent in their relation to practical action, so it should not surprise us that the new criminologies of everyday life have influenced policy in more than one direction. As well as being put to use in strategies of prevention attuned to the new conditions of late modernity, these discourses have also played a part in the revival of older strategies that tend to ignore these conditions and rely upon the traditional penal powers of the sovereign state. The stripped down, skeletonized depiction of human motivation developed by rational choice theory has helped advocates of situational crime prevention to shift the focus of crime control away from individual disposition towards situational opportunity. But this rational choice conception also carries implications about the efficacy of penal threats that have made it useful in a quite different and much less innovative strategy: the renewed use of harsh penal sentences as a means to deter criminal conduct.[4]

Rational choice theories revive a simple utilitarian account of criminal conduct that had long since been displaced by positivist and sociological theories. Where correctional criminology took criminal conduct to be a product of social influences and psychological conflicts, and regarded the criminal as a deep subject, not altogether in control of his or her behaviour, the rational choice model regards criminal acts as calculated, utility-maximizing conduct, resulting from a straightforward process of individual choice. This model represents the problem of crime as a matter of supply and demand, with punishment operating as a price mechanism. It sees offenders as rational opportunists or career criminals whose conduct is variously deterred or disinhibited by the manipulation of incentives – an approach that makes deterrent penalties a self-evident means for reducing offending. Where correctionalist criminology treated crime as a problem with social, temporal and psychological dimensions, the rational choice model treats it as a function of price.

The penological corollary of this is that the concern with 'root causes', 'social problems' and 'individual needs' is displaced by a more singular focus upon 'pricing', and the effort to ensure that the penal consequences of criminal offending are sufficiently swift, certain, and severe to operate as an effective disincentive. After more than a century of social scientific research that complicated and refined the understanding of criminal offending; after a mass of evidence has been accumulated to show that criminal acts are typically embedded in, and produced by, definite social and psychological relations; rational choice analyses have, abruptly and without ceremony, swept aside all such complexity and empirical findings. With the certainty of armchair philosophers and economic modellers they insist that crime is, after all, simply a matter of individual choice – or anyway can be treated as if it were.[5] It would be wrong to say that the rational choice criminology had caused the shift towards harsher sentencing laws and a greater use of deterrent threats. But it is certainly plausible to argue that this kind of reasoning has functioned to legitimate these tougher policies and give them a gloss of respectability. Penal policy, like welfare assistance to the poor, has rediscovered market discipline and purity of coercive disincentives.

In the reactionary political context of the 1980s and 1990s, with its scepticism about welfare programmes and its emphasis upon individual responsibility, the simplicity of an account that blames the offender, silences excuses, ignores root causes, and sees the punishment of wrongdoers as the proper response, has a popular and a political appeal that runs well beyond its criminological merit. It is as if bestowing so much criminological attention upon the offender, and developing such exquisite analyses of criminal aetiology were suddenly deemed to be morally degenerate, as well as politically unacceptable. This cultural backlash against what Ronald Reagan called 'soft social theories' and 'pseudo-intellectual apologies for crime' is memorably encapsulated in James Q. Wilson's casual, reactionary insistence that 'Wicked people exist. Nothing avails except to set them apart from innocent people' – a claim that simultaneously re-asserts the most simplistic common sense, gives up on social and rehabilitative programmes, and dismisses the whole project of a social scientific criminology.[6] That such a position could be asserted by a prominent Harvard-based policy analyst, and repeatedly taken up as if it were an insight of great merit, attests to the political and cultural climate that formed around crime control policy in the 1980s.

From D. Garland, The Culture of Control *(Oxford: Oxford University Press), 2001, pp. 127–131.*

Notes

1 R.V. Clarke and D. Cornish (eds) *The Reasoning Criminal: Rational Choice Perspectives on Offending* New York: Springer-Verlag, 1986, M. Felson, *Crime and Everyday Life* London: Pine Forge Press/Sage, 1994; K. Heal and G. Laycock (eds) *Situational Crime Prevention: From Theory to Practice* London: HMSO, 1986; R.V. Clarke and P. Mayhew (eds) *Designing Out Crime* London: HMSO, 1980; M.J. Hindelang *et al.*, *Victims of Personal Crime: An Empirical Foundation for a Theory of Victimization* Cambridge MA: Ballinger, 1978.

2 N. Walker, 'Introduction', K. Heal and G. Laycock (eds) *Situational Crime Prevention: From Theory to Practice* London: HMSO, 1986, p. v.

3 R.V. Clarke and D. Cornish 'Introduction' to R.V. Clarke and D. Cornish (eds) *The Reasoning Criminal: Rational Choice Perspectives on Offending* New York: Springer-Verlag, 1986, 4.

4 J. Q. Wilson, *Thinking About Crime*, rev. edn New York: Vintage, 1983, ch. 7. 68. As van Dijk puts it: 'offenders are seen as the consumers of criminal gains and victims as the reluctant suppliers of criminal opportunities' and 'property offences are transactions completed by consumers without the suppliers' permission', J.J.M. van Dijk, 'Understanding Crime Rates: On the interactions between the rational choices of victims and offenders', *British Journal of Criminology* 1994, vol. 34, no 2, 105–21 at 105 and 106.

5 '[T]he policy analyst is led to act as if crime were the product of a free choice... The radical individualism of Bentham and Beccaria may be scientifically questionable but prudentially necessary', J.Q. Wilson, *Thinking About Crime*, 51.

6 This claim is stated in the concluding paragraph of ibid. 260.

14.2 'Situational' crime prevention: theory and practice
Ronald V. Clarke

Conventional wisdom holds that crime prevention needs to be based on a thorough understanding of the causes of crime. Though it may be conceded that preventive measures (such as bumps in the road to stop speeding) can sometimes be found without invoking sophisticated causal theory, 'physical' measures which reduce opportunities for crime are often thought to be of limited value. They are said merely to suppress the impulse to offend which will then manifest itself on some other occasion and perhaps in even more harmful form. Much more effective are seen to be 'social' measures (such as the revitalisation of communities, the creation of job opportunities for unemployed youth, and the provision of sports and leisure facilities), since these attempt to remove the root motivational causes of offending. These ideas about prevention are not necessarily shared by the man-in-the street or even by policemen and magistrates, but they have prevailed among academics, administrators and others who contribute to the formulation of criminal policy. They are also consistent with a preoccupation of criminological theory with criminal 'dispositions' (cf. Ohlin, 1970: Gibbons, 1971; Jeffery, 1971) and the purpose of this paper is to argue that an alternative theoretical emphasis on choices and decisions made by the offender leads to a broader and perhaps more realistic approach to crime prevention.

'Dispositional' theories and their preventive implications

With some exceptions noted below, criminological theories have been little concerned with the situational determinants of crime. Instead, the main object of these theories (whether biological, psychological, or sociological in orientation) has been to show how some people are born with, or come to acquire, a 'disposition' to behave in a consistently criminal manner. This 'dispositional' bias of theory has been identified as a defining characteristic of 'positivist' criminology, but it is also to be found in 'interactionist' or deviancy theories of crime developed in response to the perceived inadequacies of positivism. Perhaps the best known tenet of at least the early interactionist theories, which arises out of a concern with the social defi-

nition of deviancy and the role of law enforcement agencies, is that people who are 'labelled' as criminal are thereby prone to continue in delinquent conduct (see especially Becker, 1962).

Crime as the outcome of choice

Some of the above theoretical difficulties could be avoided by conceiving of crime not in dispositional terms, but as being the outcome of immediate choices and decisions made by the offender. This would also have the effect of throwing a different light on preventive options.

An obvious problem is that some impulsive offences and those committed under the influence of alcohol or strong emotion may not easily be seen as the result of choices or decisions. Another difficulty is that the notion of 'choice' seems to fit uncomfortably with the fact that criminal behaviour is to some extent predictable from knowledge of a person's history. This difficulty is not properly resolved by the 'soft' determinism of Matza (1963) under which people retain some freedom of action albeit within a range of options constrained by their history and environment. A better formulation would seem to be that recently expounded by Glaser (1977): 'both free will and determinism are socially derived linguistic representations of reality' brought into play for different explanatory purposes at different levels of analysis and they may usefully co-exist in the scientific enterprise.

Whatever the resolution of these difficulties – and this is not the place to discuss them more fully – commonsense as well as the evidence of ethnographic studies of delinquency (e.g. Parker, 1974) strongly suggest that people are usually aware of consciously choosing to commit offences. This does not mean that they are fully aware of all the reasons for their behaviour nor that their own account would necessarily satisfy a criminologically sophisticated observer, who might require information at least about (i) the offender's motives; (ii) his mood; (iii) his moral judgments concerning the act in question and the 'techniques of moral neutralisation' open to him (cf. Matza, 1963); (iv) the extent of his criminal knowledge and his perception of criminal opportunities; (v) his assessment of the risks of being caught as well as the likely consequences; and finally, as well as of a different order, (vi) whether he has been drinking. These separate components of subjective state and thought processes which play a part in the decision to commit a crime will be influenced by immediate situational variables and by highly specific features of the individual's history and present life circumstances in ways that are so varied and countervailing as to render unproductive the notion of a generalised behavioural disposition to offend. Moreover, as will be argued below, the specificity of the influences upon different criminal behaviours gives much less credence to the 'displacement' hypothesis; the idea that reducing opportunities merely results in crime being displaced to some other time or place has been the major argument against situational crime prevention.

In so far as an individual's social and physical environments remain relatively constant and his decisions are much influenced by past experience, this scheme gives ample scope to account not only for occasional offending but also for recidivism; people acquire a repertoire of different responses to meet particular situations and if the circumstances are right they are likely to repeat those responses that have previously been rewarding.

Preventive implications of a 'choice' model

In fact, just as an understanding of past influences on behaviour may have little preventive pay-off, so too there may be limited benefits in according greater explanatory importance to the individual's current life circumstances. For example, the instrumental attractions of delinquency may always be greater for certain groups of individuals such as young males living in inner city areas. And nothing can be done about a vast range of misfortunes which continually befall people and which may raise the probability of their behaving criminally while depressed or angry.

Some practicable options for prevention do arise, however, from the greater emphasis upon situational features, especially from the direct and immediate relationship between these and criminal behaviour. By studying the spatial and temporal distribution of specific offences and relating these to measurable aspects of the situation, criminologists have recently begun to concern themselves much more closely with the possibilities of manipulating criminogenic situations in the interests of prevention. [...] The suggestions for prevention arising out of the 'situational' research that has been done can be conveniently divided into measures which (i) reduce the physical opportunities for offending or (ii) increase the chances of an offender being caught. These categories are discussed separately below though there is some overlap between them; for example, better locks which take longer to overcome also increase the risks of being caught.

Reducing physical opportunities for crime and the problem of displacement

The potential for controlling behaviour by manipulating opportunities is illustrated vividly by a study of suicide in Birmingham (Hassal and Trethowan, 1972). This showed that a marked drop in the rates of suicide between 1962 and 1970 was the result of a reduction in the poisonous content of the gas supplied to householders for cooking and heating, so that it became much more difficult for people to kill themselves by turning on the gas taps. Like many kinds of crime, suicide is generally regarded as being dictated by strong internal motivation and the fact that its incidence was greatly reduced by a simple (though unintentional) reduction in the opportunities to commit it suggests that it may be possible to achieve similar reductions in crime by 'physical' means. Though suicide by other methods did not increase in Birmingham, the study also leads to direct consideration of the fundamental theoretical problem of 'displacement' which, as Reppetto (1976) has pointed out, can occur in four different ways: time, place, method, and type of offence. In other words, does reducing opportunities or increasing the risks result merely in the offender choosing his moment more carefully or in seeking some other, perhaps more harmful method of gaining his ends? Or, alternatively, will he shift his attention to a similar but unprotected target, for example, another house, car or shop? Or, finally, will he turn instead to some other form of crime?

For those who see crime as the outcome of criminal disposition, the answers to these questions would tend to be in the affirmative ('bad will out') but under the alternative view of crime represented above matters are less straightforward. Answers would depend on the nature of the crime, the offender's strength of motivation, knowledge of alternatives, willingness to entertain them, and so forth. In the case of opportunistic crimes (i.e.

ones apparently elicited by their very ease of accomplishment such as some forms of shoplifting or vandalism) it would seem that the probability of offending could be reduced markedly by making it more difficult to act. For crimes such as bank robbery, however, which often seem to be the province of those who make a living from crime, reducing opportunities may be less effective. [...]

It is the bulk of offences, however, which are neither 'opportunistic' nor 'professional' that pose the greatest theoretical dilemmas. These offences include many burglaries and instances of auto-crime where the offender, who may merely supplement his normal income through the proceeds of crime, has gone out with the deliberate intention of committing the offence and has sought out the opportunity to do so. The difficulty posed for measures which reduce opportunity is one of the vast number of potential targets combined with the generally low overall level of security. Within easy reach of every house with a burglar alarm, or car with an anti-theft device, are many others without such protection.

In some cases, however, it may be possible to protect a whole class of property, as the Post Office did when they virtually eliminated theft from telephone kiosks by replacing the vulnerable aluminium coin-boxes with much stronger steel ones (cf. Mayhew *et al.*, 1976). A further example is provided by the recent law in this country which requires all motor-cyclists to wear crash helmets. This measure was introduced to save lives, but it has also had the unintended effect of reducing thefts of motorcycles (Mayhew *et al.*, 1976). This is because people are unlikely to take someone else's motorbike on the spur of the moment unless they happen to have a crash helmet with them – otherwise they could easily be spotted by the police. But perhaps the best example comes from West Germany where, in 1963, steering column locks were made compulsory, on *all* cars, old and new, with a consequent reduction of more than 60 per cent, in levels of taking and driving away (Mayhew *et al.*, 1976). [...]

The question of whether, when stopped from committing a particular offence, people would turn instead to some other quite different form of crime is much more difficult to settle empirically, but many of the same points about motivation, knowledge of alternatives and so forth still apply. Commonsense also suggests, for example, that few of those Germans prevented by steering column locks from taking cars to get home at night are

likely to have turned instead to hijacking taxis or to mugging passers-by for the money to get home. More likely, they may have decided that next time they would make sure of catching the last bus home or that it was time to save up for their own car.

Increasing the risks of being caught

In practice, increasing the chances of being caught usually means attempting to raise the chances of an offender being seen by someone who is likely to take action. The police are the most obvious group likely to intervene effectively, but studies of the effectiveness of this aspect of their deterrent role are not especially encouraging (Kelling *et al.*, 1974; Manning, 1977; Clarke and Hough, 1980). The reason seems to be that, when set against the vast number of opportunities for offending represented by the activities of a huge population of citizens for the 24 hours of the day, crime is a relatively rare event. The police cannot be everywhere at once and, moreover, much crime takes place in private. Nor is much to be expected from the general public (Mayhew *et al.*, 1979). People in their daily round rarely see crime in progress: if they do they are likely to place some innocent interpretation on what they see; they may be afraid to intervene or they may feel the victims would resent interference; and they may encounter practical difficulties in summoning the police or other help in time. They are much more likely to take effective action to protect their own homes or immediate neighbourhood, but they are often away from these for substantial periods of the day and, moreover, the risks of crime in residential settings, at least in many areas of this country, are not so great as to encourage much vigilance. [...]

A recent Home Office Research report (Mayhew *et al.*, 1979) has argued, however, that there is probably a good deal of unrealised potential for making more deliberate use of the surveillance role of employees who come into regular and frequent contact with the public in a semi-official capacity. Research in the United States (Newman, 1973; Reppetto, 1974) and Canada (Waller and Okhiro, 1978) has shown that apartment blocks with doormen are less vulnerable to burglary, while research in this country has shown that vandalism is much less of a problem on buses with conductors (Mayhew *et al.*, 1976) and on estates with resident caretakers (Department of the Environment, 1977). There is also evidence (in Post Office records) that public telephones in places such as pubs or launderettes, which are given some supervision by staff, suffer almost no vandalism in comparison with those in kiosks; that car parks with attendants in control have lower rates of auto-crime (*Sunday Times*, April 9, 1978). Not everybody employed in a service capacity would be suited or willing to take on additional security duties, but much of their deterrent role may result simply from their being around. Employing more of them, for greater parts of the day, may therefore be all that is needed in most cases. In other cases, it may be necessary to employ people more suited to a surveillance role, train them better to carry it out, or even provide them with surveillance aids.

Some objections

Apart from the theoretical and practical difficulties of the approach advocated in this paper, it is in apparent conflict with the 'nothing works' school of criminological thought... But perhaps a panacea is being sought when all it may be possible to achieve is a reduction in particular forms of crime as a result of specific and sometimes localised measures. Examples of such reductions are given above and, while most of these relate to rather commonplace offences of theft and vandalism, there is no reason why similar measures cannot be successfully applied to other quite different forms of crime. [...] There are many crimes, however, when the offender is either so determined or so emotionally aroused that they seem to be beyond the scope of this approach. A further constraint will be costs: many shops, for example, which could reduce shoplifting by giving up self-service methods and employing more assistants or even store detectives, have calculated that this would not be worth the expense either in direct costs or in a reduction of turnover. Morally dubious as this policy might at first sight appear, these shops may simply have learned a lesson of more general application, i.e. a certain level of crime may be the inevitable consequence of practices and institutions which we cherish or find convenient and the 'cost' of reducing crime below this level may be unacceptable.

The gradualist approach to crime prevention advocated here might also attract criticism from some social reformers, as well as some deviancy theorists, for being unduly conservative. The former group, imbued with dispositional theory, would see the only effective way of dealing with crime as being to attack its roots through the reduction of inequalities of wealth, class and education – a solution which, as indicated above, has numerous practical and theoretical difficulties. The latter group would criticise the approach, not for its lack of effectiveness but – on the grounds that there is insufficient consensus in society about what behaviour should be treated as crime – for helping to preserve an undesirable status quo. Incremental change, however, may be the most realistic way of achieving consensus as well as a more equitable society. [...]

Many members of the general public might also find it objectionable that crime was being stopped, not by punishing wrong-doers, but by inconveniencing the law-abiding. The fact that opportunity reducing and risk-increasing measures are too readily identified with their more unattractive aspects (barbed wire, heavy padlocks, guard-dogs and private security forces) adds fuel to the fire. And in some of their more sophisticated forms (closed circuit television surveillance and electronic intruder alarms) they provoke fears, on the one hand, of 'big brother' forms of state control and, on the other of a 'fortress society' in which citizens in perpetual fear of their fellows scuttle from one fortified environment to another.

Expressing these anxieties has a value in checking potential abuses of power, and questioning the means of dealing with crime can also help to keep the problem of crime in perspective. But it should also be said that the kind of measures discussed above need not always be obtrusive (except where it is important to maximise their deterrent effects) and need not in any material way infringe individual liberties or the quality of life. Steel cash compartments in telephone kiosks are indistinguishable from aluminium ones, and vandal-resistant polycarbonate looks just like glass. Steering column locks are automatically brought into operation on removing the ignition key, and many people are quite unaware that their cars are fitted with them. 'Defensible space' designs in housing estates have the additional advantage of promoting feelings of neighbourliness and safety, though perhaps too little attention has been paid to some of their less desirable effects such as possible encroachments on privacy as a result of overlooking. And having more bus conductors, housing estate caretakers, swimming bath attendants and shop assistants means that people benefit from improved services – even if they have to pay for them either directly or through the rates.

Finally, the idea that crime might be most effectively prevented by reducing opportunities and increasing the risks is seen by many as, at best, representing an over-simplified mechanistic view of human behaviour... As shown above, however, it is entirely compatible with a view of criminal behaviour as predominantly rational and autonomous and as being capable of adjusting and responding to adverse consequences, anticipated or experienced. And as for being a pessimistic view of human behaviour, it might indeed be better if greater compliance with the law could come about simply as a result of people's free moral choice. But apart from being perilously close to the rather unhelpful dispositional view of crime, it is difficult to see this happening. We may therefore be left for the present with the approach advocated in this paper, time-consuming, laborious and, limited as it may be.

> *From R.V.G. Clarke, '"Situational" Crime Prevention: Theory and Practice'*, British Journal of Criminology, 1980, 20 (2): 136–47

References

Clarke, R.V.G. and Hough, J.M. (eds) (1980). *The Effectiveness of Policing.* Farnborough, Hants: Gower.

Department of the Environment (1977). *Housing Management and Design.* (Lambeth Inner Area Study). IAS/IA/I 8. London: Department of the Environment.

Gibbons, D.C. (1971). 'Observations on the study of crime causation.' *American Journal of Sociology*, 77, 262–278.

Glaser, D. (1977). 'The compatibility of free will and determinism in Criminology: comments on an alleged problem.' *Journal of Criminal Law and Criminology*, 67, 486–490.

Hassal, C. and Trethowan, W. H. (1972). 'Suicide in Birmingham.' *British Medical Journal*, 1, 717–718.

Jeffery, C.R. (1971). *Crime Prevention Through Environmental Design.* Beverly Hills: Sage Publications.

Kelling, G.L., Pate, T., Dieckman, D. and Brown, C. E. (1974). *The Kansas City Preventive Patrol Experiment.* Washington: Police Foundation.

Manning, P. (1977). *Police Work: The Social Organisation of Policing.* London: Massachusetts Institute of Technology Press.

Matza, D. (1963). *Delinquency and Drift.* New York: John Wiley and Sons.

Mayhew, P., Clarke, R.V.G., Sturman, A. and Hough, J.M. (1976). *Crime as Opportunity.* Home Office Research Study No. 34. London: HMSO.

Mayhew, P., Clarke, R.V.G., Burrows, J.N., Hough, J.M. and Winchester, S.W.C. (1979). *Crime in Public View.* Home Office Research Study No. 49. London: HMSO.

Newman, O. (1973). *Defensible Space: People and Design in the Violent City.* London: Architectural Press.

Ohlin, L.E. (1970). *A Situational Approach to Delinquency Prevention.* Youth Development and Delinquency Prevention Administration. U.S. Department of Health, Education and Welfare.

Parker, H. (1974). *View from the Boys.* Newton Abbot: David and Charles.

Reppetto, T.A. (1974). *Residential Crime.* Cambridge, Mass: Ballinger.

Reppetto, T.A. (1976). 'Crime prevention and the displacement phenomenon.' *Crime and Delinquency*, April, 166–177.

Waller, I. and Okihiro, N. (1978). *Burglary: The Victim and the Public.* Toronto: University of Toronto Press.

14.3 Opportunity makes the thief: practical theory for crime prevention Marcus Felson and Ronald V. Clarke

Ten principles of opportunity and crime

We have already stated the general principle of this publication, that opportunity causes crime. This has generated ten sub-principles of crime opportunity. We devote a section to each and offer illustrations within each section.

Ten principles of opportunity and crime

1 Opportunities play a role in causing all crime

2 Crime opportunities are highly specific

3 Crime opportunities are concentrated in time and space

4 Crime opportunities depend on everyday movements

5 One crime produces opportunities for another

6 Some products offer more tempting crime opportunities

7 Social and technological changes produce new crime opportunities

8 Opportunities for crime can be reduced

9 Reducing opportunities does not usually displace crime

10 Focussed opportunity reduction can produce wider declines in crime

---

1 Opportunities play a role in causing all crime

Many of the early examples linking opportunity to crime dealt with theft and burglary. As a result some observers mistakenly concluded that opportunity applies only to the more common property offences. We believe that opportunity has an important part to play in every class of offence, including violence.

Home Office research has already demonstrated how to reduce the opportunity for robbing post offices, and other research has applied similar principles to convenience stores and banks. A greater challenge is to explain why people get into foolish fights and attack others with no apparent gain. Why would such violent offences reflect crime opportunities? Theorists for many years explained such violence as irrational and expressive, hence not influenced by decisions or opportunities. More recently, theorists have begun to argue that all violence involves some sort of decision. Fights are not as senseless as they may seem later or to people not involved. To understand we need to look at the offender's viewpoint and to focus on the moment of the offence and just before it. At that time, the violent person may have a grievance and the attack may be made to remedy a perceived injustice. Or the offender may wish to preserve self esteem after a perceived insult. For example, someone in a pub goes to the toilet and comes back to find his chair taken. The person who took it has made him look weak in front of others. Having had too much to drink, he impolitely asks for his chair back and gets an equally impolite response. This escalates into a fight. Although the outcome may seem silly later, it makes sense at the time to those involved.

Studies of bars and pubs have shown that their design and management can lead to violence or its absence. Violent opportunities in pubs increase when they are larger in size; are dominated by young males; have clienteles that do not know each other; make it difficult to avoid jostling others; and have untrained and inexperienced bar staff. Liquor policy can have a major impact on the opportunity for violence within pubs and in the area outside. Happy hours, late closing, pub concentration and bar hopping – all of these have an impact on the opportunity for violence.

The structure of conflicts has been studied not only in bar-room settings but also in the laboratory, where researchers have shown that a young male insulting another in front of an audience will tend to receive back an insulting or aggressive response. Changing the composition of persons present – such as increasing the number of middle-aged persons and females – leads to less risk of an aggressive response. Other research confirms the commonsense notion that bigger people are more likely to hit little people, and that larger numbers of offenders are more likely to attack smaller numbers. In short, violence is strongly influenced by opportunity.

The same is also true of sexual offences. The opportunities that give rise to burglary may put occupants at risk of sexual assault, often unplanned. Children are most likely to be abused by adults who have access to them through everyday roles, and these adults need times and settings where guardians will not interfere with their crimes. Domestic violence also depends upon privacy, in particular, the absence of other family members or neighbours who might prevent the assault. Obscene and threatening phone calls depend upon telephone access and the ability of the caller to hide his own identity. Caller identification devices in the United States have removed much of this opportunity with demonstrated success. [...]

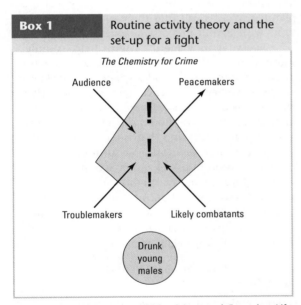

| Box 1 | Routine activity theory and the set-up for a fight |

The Chemistry for Crime

Source: Felson, Marcus. 1998. *Crime and Everyday Life*, Second edition. Thousand Oaks, CA: Pine Forge Press.

In sum the myth that opportunity is a cause only of theft and other common property crimes is rapidly being dispelled as environmental criminologists complete their studies into ever-widening categories of crime. Indeed, as every detective knows, opportunity plays a part in even the most carefully planned and deeply motivated offences of murder. There is no class of crime in which opportunity does not play a role.

2 Crime opportunities are highly specific

We do not believe in a single crime opportunity factor applying to all crimes. Indeed, our point is exactly the opposite. Crime opportunities are highly specific to each offence and offender subset. As a rule, crime analysts should not defuse the offence in legal terms, since that is not usually what the offender considers when making a decision about a crime. Thus an offender may walk down a street of bungalows for something to steal, leaving it open whether to take from the garden, the drive, the carport or the house itself. Even when committing a burglary, one offender may be interested mainly in cash, while others are seeking electronic goods, and still others jewellery. Among the latter, some use what they have stolen themselves, others sell it on to an acquaintance, others find second-hand stores, and yet others go to the pub or flea market to offload the stolen goods. As discussed earlier, several types of car thieves commit exactly the same legal offence but with very different goals in mind and hence different modus operandi. This is not to say that offenders are pure specialists, since they may go looking for crime opportunities and take whichever ones come up. Even those who have one thing in mind one day may shift their attention on another day.

In general, the opportunity for crime must be evaluated for very specific categories of offence. Thus robbery of post offices, banks, people on the streets or in the stairwells of council housing, are all different crimes from the standpoint of crime opportunity theory. Their modus operandi will differ, along with the methods for reducing the opportunity. Even within these categories, smaller opportunity categories are needed. Thus the 'inside-job' bank robbery must be distinguished from more common 'stick ups'. To be sure, some opportunity principles may fit all crimes. But even these need to be applied taking into account the specific setting and modus operandi.

Because offences differ, reductions in opportunity are also highly specific. Removing one crime opportunity may have no impact on another. For example, employing attendants to collect money at the exit of a multi-story car park may succeed in reducing the opportunity to steal a car. But this may have little effect on stealing goods left in cars parked on the higher levels. Devices that prevent stealing the car itself do not necessarily prevent breaking the window and taking the radio. Locks that prevent burglary have no impact on thefts of goods left outside in the back yard.

3 Crime opportunities are concentrated in time and space

Just because people and property are scattered throughout the city does not mean that crime opportunities are equally distributed; quite the contrary for the following reasons:

- Many people and things are not suitable targets for criminal attack.
- Many locations are unfavourable for crime to occur.
- A given location may be ideal for crime at one time but unfavourable for crime at another.
- Those who would discourage crime from happening, such as homeowners, concierges, receptionists, or security guards, cannot be everywhere.
- Nor can the most likely offenders be everywhere.

Indeed, the spatial and temporal distribution of people and things is highly uneven and sets the stage for crime to occur at particular times and places. This helps explain why a community bustling with activity does not necessarily generate crime everywhere and at every time. A street robber might be able to attack a weaker victim at daytime or dusk if he can find a moment when others are absent. But for attacking a stronger victim he might need a darker time and a more aggressive mode of attack. A residential burglar can find abandoned residential streets in the day and kick a door in, but at night he will have to be more quiet.

Researchers have recently begun to study crime 'hot spots,' namely addresses which draw many more calls for police service than others. Hot spots can drive up a local crime rate. Even though most people and places in the area are largely free from crime, their reputation is tarnished by the near-by hot spots. Removing one or two drug houses or badly-run pubs can thus change the whole complexion of a neighbourhood.

4 Crime opportunities depend on everyday movements of activity

If vendors of snacks and drinks seek crowds, so do pickpockets, luggage thieves, and bag snatchers. Other offenders pay closer attention to the absence of people. For example, the flow of people to work generates a counter flow of burglars to residential areas, taking advantage of their absence. The flow of workers home at night and on weekends produces a counter flow a few hours later of commercial and industrial burglars to take advantage of the situation. Those who use the Underground for trips to crime go to places they know using the lines they know, finding targets along the way or at the familiar destinations.

Changes in transportation lines can have a major impact on crime opportunities. Thus new roads or railway lines establish new crime risks in areas they touch, while closing down crime opportunities in areas they cut off. Pathways to and from school are essential features of crime opportunity in an area. If such pathways are not constructed or planned, youths will find their own routes, sometimes with significant consequences for crime.

Everyday movement patterns help us understand crime generators and crime attractors discussed above. Such nodes generate movements just as movements influence the nodes themselves. But movement patterns relevant to crime cannot be understood by taking nodes one at a time. People move among nodes and that is why their location with respect to one another is so important. The crucial question to ask is which activities and settings are adjacent and which ones are separate. Thus putting a secondary school next to a shopping area creates shoplifting, vandalism, and truancy. Adjacent schools may generate fights, if ages are the same, and bullying if ages are different.

5 One crime produces opportunities for another

Having embarked upon one crime, the offender can unwittingly be drawn into others simply because of the opportunities that unfold in the course of committing the act. The best example comes from a burglary, which can generate several types of crime on the spot, including a weapons charge, an assault or sexual attack inside the home. A burglary also generates such crimes as selling and receiving stolen goods or the fraudulent use of stolen credit cards. Finally, when more than one offender is involved, their conflicts over splitting up the loot can readily lead to violence.

Pimping and prostitution also set in motion a variety of other problems. These often lead to one party stealing from, robbing or assaulting the other, or selling illegal drugs. What if a prostitute's customer refuses to pay or if the two disagree on what he owes? This may lead to an attack. Prostitution can also involve trading sex for drugs or stolen goods, or repaying pimps or landlords with sex. Those engaging in illegal activities, no matter how small, immediately compromise their positions and may be impelled towards additional offences. Any offence can involve violence among the illegal parties, as they cannot go to a civil court and ask the judge to resolve their differences. [...]

In sum, individual offenders might dig themselves deeper into crime in at least eight ways:

- Blowing illegal gains on drugs or prostitutes.
- Repeating the offence later against the same victim or target.
- Spending time with co-offenders, who lead them into more crime.
- Spending time with dangerous people, who then victimise them.
- Spending more time in dangerous settings at dangerous hours.
- Provoking others to attack them.
- Developing expensive drug dependencies, leading to criminal acts.
- Impairing judgment through substance abuse, then taking more risks.

6 Some products offer more tempting crime opportunities

The VIVA [value, inertia, visibility and access] model offers a starting point for evaluating which things make better crime targets. For example videocassette players have made good targets because they are high in value and low in inertia, that is, they have high value per pound. They are also highly visible and accessible. Numerous other examples exist of such 'hot products', consumer items that seem particularly at risk of theft:

- Research in many countries, including recent Home Office work, has shown that particular

models of car are at much greater risk of theft than others.

- The cars most at risk of theft vary with the precise nature of the offence. Thus a few years ago the cars most taken for joyriding in the United States were 'macho' American-built vehicles, such as the Chevrolet Camaro, with plenty of acceleration. Those most likely to be stripped of parts were European cars such as Volkswagen Cabriolets with good radios easily interchanged between different models. Those most likely to be stolen for resale were very expensive models such as Porsche and Mercedes. (The increased popularity in America of high priced 'sport utility vehicles', such as the Toyota Land Cruiser or the Range Rover, has changed these patterns in recent years.)

- Lorries carrying cigarettes and liquor were most likely to be hijacked in the past, but electronic goods are now also frequently targeted.

- Studies in the retail industry, both of employee theft and shoplifting, have consistently shown that certain items are much more likely to be stolen than others. For example, a Home Office project of a few years ago showed that 'popular' records and tapes were much more likely to be stolen from the HMV store in Oxford Street than classical recordings.

- Residential burglars usually seek cash, jewellery and electronic goods (and guns in America). As discussed above, the increase in lightweight electronic goods in people's homes has been held partly responsible for the substantial increase of residential burglary in America during the 1970s.

- Cellular telephones, poorly-designed ticket machines on the London Underground, and aluminium cash compartments on public phones have all generated small crime waves.

This brief list suggests that hot products might help to explain patterns for many kinds of theft, as well as crime waves or increases in crime. These products might also help explain repeat victimization, as in cases where someone with a particular model of car has it repeatedly stolen or when shops carrying goods attractive to thieves are repeatedly burgled.

While we may know which products are hot, we know little about why they are hot. Studies are needed to understand why particular product brands attract more theft than other brands. For example, why are some brands of sneakers so much more likely to be stolen than other brands which sell equally well? Studies are also needed to elucidate the criminogenic properties of whole classes of products, such as cellular phones.

7 Social and technological changes produce new crime opportunities

Technology frequently works to produce new products, but many of these are not especially suitable for theft, since they have no mass market or are too difficult to use. Other products become targets for theft. Even these often go through a life cycle and may become no longer attractive to thieves. In general, mass-produced consumer goods pass through a life cycle of four stages:

- Innovation stage
- Growth stage
- Mass market stage
- Saturation stage

In the *innovation* stage, the product is sold to a special group of consumers. It may be expensive, difficult to use, relatively heavy and awkward. That explains why the early computers were not likely to be stolen. Even the early home video cassette players were not supported by a wide selection of available movies from nearby video stores. So why steal them? In the *growth* stage, products become easier to use, cheaper to buy, lighter and less awkward to carry. More people know how to use them and want one, and thefts therefore accelerate. That is just what happened as the desk computer became more popular and as video cassette players and CD players gained ground. In the *mass market* stage, the product gains further in appeal. More units are sold and theft becomes endemic. By the *saturation* stage most people who really want the product have it, and thefts decline. For example, video cassette and CD players are now so common that they cost relatively little and offer few rewards to the thief; hand calculators sell for a few dollars and are mostly safe on your desk with the door open.

Many products that once fed the crime wave are now in the saturation stage, offering little incentive to theft. As innovations occur, new products enter the same cycle. In addition, valuable items, such as airbags and laptop computers, provide valuable new targets for easy theft.

8 Crime can be prevented by reducing opportunities

If it were not true that reducing opportunities helps prevent crime, no-one would bother to take routine precautions such as locking their cars and houses, keeping their money in safe places, counselling their children to avoid strangers, and watching the neighbours' home when they are away. In fact, we all take these kinds of precautions every day of our lives.

These actions might sometimes displace the risk of criminal attack to others. To avoid this and achieve more general reductions in risks of crime, wider action to reduce opportunities must be taken by the police, by government and by other agencies. Similar thinking guides several approaches to crime prevention, including:

- problem-oriented policing
- defensible spare architecture
- crime prevention through environmental design
- situational crime prevention.

Despite their differences, each seeks to reduce opportunities for crime for particular kinds of targets, places, and classes of victims. Each is concerned with preventing very specific kinds of crime. None of the four attempts to improve human character. Most important, all four seek to block crime in practical, natural, and simple ways, at low social and economic costs.

9 Reducing opportunities does not usually displace crime

All these different ways of reducing opportunities for crime have met the same objection, that all they do is move crime around, not prevent it. This theory of 'displacement' sees crime as being shifted around in five main ways:

- crime can be moved from one location to another (geographical displacement);
- crime can be moved from one time to another (temporal displacement);
- crime can be directed away from one target to another (target displacement);
- one method of committing crime can be substituted for another (tactical displacement);
- one kind of crime can be substituted for another (crime type displacement).

In each case, it is assumed that offenders must commit crime whatever the impediments they face, or to put the point in colloquial terms, 'bad will out'. [...] Whatever the basis of the assumption, it neglects the important causal roles of temptation and opportunity. [...] Even in the case of more committed offenders, the displacement theory gives far too little importance to the causal role of opportunity. [...] Those who assume that displacement is inevitable overestimate its capacity to occur. This shown by the example of drug markets. It is frequently assumed that closing down a particular drug market will result in dealers simply moving to another nearby location where they can continue their trade. But this ignores the reasons why the original location was chosen in the first place. It might:

- be easy for drug purchasers to reach by car;

- be easy to find and to drive to from distant parts of the city or suburbs;

- be near a bus stop for those who have to travel by public transport;

- be near the dealers' homes and particularly convenient for them;

- be near a pub or corner store that provides dealers with refreshments and a betting shop that provides entertainment;

- have a public phone to facilitate contacts between dealers and purchasers.

Most nearby locations will lack these combined advantages for dealers and purchasers. When suitable locations exist nearby, they may already be drug sites whose dealers will fight to keep control.

This shows that the scope for displacement may be more limited than is often assumed, but it does not mean that it should be ignored. Rational choice theory predicts that:

Offenders will displace their prevented crimes when the benefits for doing so outweigh the costs. They will not displace their crimes when the costs outweigh their benefits. [...]

To sum up, displacement is always a threat to prevention, but there are strong theoretical reasons for believing that it is far from inevitable. In addition, the studies of displacement show that even when it does occur, it may be far from complete and that important net reductions in crime can be achieved by opportunity-reducing measures.

10 Focused opportunity reduction can produce wider declines in crime

Apart from showing that displacement is not the threat once thought, studies of displacement have yielded an additional dividend. They have found that sometimes the reverse of displacement can occur. Rather than crime being exported to other times and places by prevention measures, it is the benefits of focused prevention measures that can spread beyond the targets of intervention. Many examples now exist, including the following:

- When CCTV cameras were introduced to monitor three car parks at the University of Surrey, crime declined not only in these car parks but also in one other that was not given surveillance by the cameras.

- When CCTV cameras were installed on five double-decker buses belonging to a fleet of 80 in the North of England, vandalism by schoolchildren dropped for the whole fleet, not just those with cameras (three of which were fitted only with dummy cameras).

- When books in an University of Wisconsin library were electronically tagged to sound an alarm if they were removed illegitimately, not only did thefts of books decline but also of video-cassettes and other materials that had not been tagged.

- When a New Jersey discount electronic retailer introduced a regime of daily counting of valuable merchandise in the warehouse, not only did thefts of these items plummet, but also of those of other items not repeatedly counted.

- When 'red light' cameras were installed at certain junctions in Strathclyde, not only did fewer people 'run the lights' at these locations, but also at other traffic lights nearby.

- The implementation of a package of situational measures for houses that had been repeatedly burgled on the Kirkholt housing estate reduced burglaries for the whole of Kirkholt, not just for those houses given additional protection.

- When vehicle tracking systems were introduced in six large American cities, risks of theft declined not just for car owners who purchased the devices, but also city-wide.

These are all examples of what researchers call the 'diffusion of benefits' of crime prevention measures. Taken together, these examples suggest that potential offenders may be aware that new prevention measures have been introduced, but they are often unsure of the precise scope of these. They may believe the measures have been implemented more widely than they really have, and that the effort needed to commit crime or the risks incurred have been increased for a wider range of places, times or targets than in fact is the case.

> From M. Felson and R. V. G. Clarke, Opportunity Makes the Thief: Practical Theory for Crime Prevention (London: Home Office), 1998, pp. 9–35.

14.4 Social change and crime rate trends: a routine activity approach Lawrence E. Cohen and Marcus Felson

Introduction

In its summary report the National Commission on the Causes and Prevention of Violence (1969: xxxvii) presents an important sociological paradox:

> Why, we must ask, have urban violent crime rates increased substantially during the past decade when the conditions that are supposed to cause violent crime have not worsened – have, indeed, generally improved?
>
> The Bureau of the Census, in its latest report on trends in social and economic conditions in metropolitan areas, states that most 'indicators of well-being point toward progress in the cities since 1960.' Thus, for example, the proportion of blacks in cities who completed high school rose from 43 percent in 1960 to 61 percent in 1968; unemployment rates dropped significantly between 1959 and 1967 and the median family income of blacks in cities increased from 61 percent to 68 percent of the median white family income during the same period. Also during the same period the number of persons living below the legally-defined poverty level in cities declined from 11.3 million to 8.3 million.

Despite the general continuation of these trends in social and economic conditions in the United States, the Uniform Crime Report (FBI, 1975:49) indicates that between 1960 and 1975 reported rates of robbery, aggravated assault, forcible rape and homicide increased by 263%, 164%, 174%, and 188%, respectively. Similar property crime rate increases reported during this same period (e.g., 200% for burglary rate) suggest that the paradox noted by the Violence Commission applies to non-violent offenses as well.

In the present paper we consider these paradoxical trends in crime rates in terms of changes in the 'routine activities' of everyday life. We believe the structure of such activities influences criminal opportunity and therefore affects trends in class of crimes we refer to as direct-contact predatory violations. Predatory violations are defined here as illegal acts in which 'someone definitely and intentionally takes or damages the person or property of another' (Glaser, 1971:4). Further, this analysis is confined to those predatory violations involving direct physical contact between at least one offender and at least one person or object which that offender attempts to take or damage.

We argue that structural changes in routine activity patterns can influence crime rates by affecting the convergence in space and time of the three minimal elements of direct-contact predatory violations: (1) motivated offenders, (2) suitable targets, and (3) the absence of capable guardians against a violation. We further argue that the lack of any one of these elements is sufficient to prevent the successful completion of a direct-contact predatory crime, and that the convergence in time and space of suitable targets and the absence of capable guardians may even lead to large increases in crime rates without necessarily requiring any increase in the structural conditions that motivate individuals to engage in crime. That is, if the proportion of motivated offenders or even suitable targets were to remain stable in a community, changes in routine activities could nonetheless alter the likelihood of their convergence in space and time, thereby creating more opportunities for crimes to occur. Control therefore becomes critical. If controls through routine activities were to decrease, illegal predatory activities could then be likely to increase. [...]

Unlike many criminological inquiries, we do not examine why individuals or groups are inclined criminally, but rather we take criminal inclination as given and examine the manner in which the spatio-temporal organization of social activities helps people to translate their criminal inclinations into action. Criminal violations are treated here as routine activities which share many attributes of, and are interdependent with, other routine activities.

Changing trends in routine activity structure and parallel trends in crime rates

The main thesis presented here is that the dramatic increase in the reported crime rates in the U.S. since 1960 is linked to changes in the routine activity structure of American society and to a corresponding increase in target suitability and decrease in guardian presence. If such a thesis has validity, then we should be able to identify these social trends and show how they relate to predatory criminal victimization rates.

Trends in human activity patterns

The decade 1960–1970 experienced noteworthy trends in the activities of the American population. For example, the percent of the population consisting of female college students increased 118% (USBC, 1975: Table 225). Married female labor force participant rates increased 31% (USBC, 1975: Table 563), while the percent of the population living as primary individuals increased by 34% (USBC, 1975: Table 51; see also Kobrin, 1976). We gain some further insight into changing routine activity patterns by comparing hourly data for 1960 and 1971 on households *unattended* by persons ages 14 or over when U.S. census interviewers first called (see Table 14.4.1). These data suggest that the proportion of households unattended at 8 A.M. increased by almost half between 1960 and 1971. One also finds increases in rates of out-of-town travel, which provides greater opportunity for both daytime and nighttime burglary of residences. Between 1960 and 1970, there was a 72% increase in state and national park visits per capita (USBC, 1975), an 144% increase in the percent of plant workers eligible for three weeks vacation

(BLS, 1975: Table 116), and an 184% increase in overseas travellers per 100,000 population (USBC, 1975: Table 366). The National Travel Survey, conducted as part of the U.S. Census Bureau's Census of Transportation, confirms the general trends, tallying an 81% increase in the number of vacations taken by Americans from 1967 to 1972, a five-year period (USBC, 1973a: Introduction).

Table 14.4.1	Proportion of households unattended by anyone 14 years old or over by time of day during first visit by Census Bureau interviewer, 1960 and 1971

November, 1971 Time of day	1960 Census	Current Pop. Survey	Percent Change
8:00–8:59 a.m.	29%	43	+48.9%
9:00–9:59 a.m.	29	44	+58
10:00–10:59 a.m.	31	42	+36
11:00–11:59 a.m.	32	41	+28
12:00–12:59 p.m.	32	41	+28
1:00–1:59 p.m.	31	43	+39
2:00–2:59 p.m.	33	43	+30
3:00–3:59 p.m.	30	33	+10
4:00–4:59 p.m.	28	30	+7
5:00–5:59 p.m.	22	26	+18
6:00–6:59 p.m.	22	25	+14
7:00–7:50 p.m.	20	29	+45
8:00–8:59 p.m.	24	22	-8

Source: Calculated from USBC (1973b: Table A).

The dispersion of activities away from households appears to be a major recent social change. Although this decade also experienced an important 31% increase in the percent of the population ages 15–24, age structure change was only one of many social trends occurring during the period, especially trends in the circulation of people and property in American society.[1]

The importance of the changing activity structure is underscored by taking a brief look at demographic changes between the years 1970 and 1975, a period of continuing crime rate increments. Most of the recent changes in age structure relevant to crime rates already had occurred by 1970; indeed, the proportion of the population ages 15-24 increased by only 6% between 1970 and 1975, compared with a 15% increase during the five years 1965 to 1970. On the other hand, major changes in the structure of routine activities continued during these years. For example, in only five years, the estimated proportion of the population consisting of husband-present, married women in the labor force households increased by 11%, while the estimated number of non-husband-wife households per 100,000 population increased from 9,150 to 11,420, a 25% increase (USBC, 1976: Tables 50, 276: USBC, 1970–1975). At the same time, the percent of population enrolled in higher education increased 16% between 1970 and 1975.

Related property trends and their relation to human activity patterns

Many of the activity trends mentioned above normally involve significant investments in durable goods. For example, the dispersion of population across relatively more households (especially non-husband-wife households) enlarges the market for durable goods such as television sets and automobiles. Women participating in the labor force and both men and women enrolled in college provide a market for automobiles. Both work and travel often involve the purchase of major movable or portable durables and their use away from home.

Considerable data are available which indicate that sales of consumer goods changed dramatically between 1960 and 1970 (as did their size and weight), hence providing more suitable property available for theft. For example, during this decade, constant-dollar personal consumer expenditures in the United States for motor vehicles and parts increased by 71%, while constant-dollar expenditures for other durables increased by 105% (calculated from CEA, 1976: Table B-16). In addition, electronic household appliances and small houseware shipments increased from 56.2 to 119.7 million units (*Electrical Merchandising Week*, 1964; *Merchandising Week*, 1973), During the same decade, appliance imports increased in value by 681% (US13C, 1975: Table 1368).

This same period appears to have spawned a revolution in small durable product design which further feeds the opportunity for crime to occur. Relevant data from the 1960 and 1970 Sears catalogs on the weight of many consumer durable goods were examined. Sears is the nation's largest retailer and its policy of purchasing and relabeling standard manufactured goods makes its catalogs a good source of data on widely merchandised consumer goods. The lightest television listed for sale in 1960 weighed 38 lbs., compared with 15 lbs. for 1970. Thus, the lightest televisions were 2 ½ times as heavy in 1960 as 1970. Similar trends are observed for dozens of other goods listed in the Sears catalog. Data from *Consumer Reports Buying Guide*, published in December of 1959 and 1969, show similar changes for radios, record players, slide projectors, tape recorders, televisions, toasters and many other goods. Hence, major declines in weight between 1960 and 1970 were quite significant for these and other goods, which suggests that the consumer goods market may be producing many more targets suitable for theft. In general, one finds rapid growth in property suitable for illegal removal and in household and individual exposure to attack during the years 1960–1975.

Related trends in business establishments

Of course, as households and individuals increased their ownership of small durables, businesses also increased the value of the merchandise which they transport and sell as well as the money involved in these transactions. Yet the Census of Business conducted in 1958, 1963, 1967, and 1972 indicate that the number of wholesale, retail, service, and public warehouse establishments (including establishments owned by large organizations) was a nearly constant ratio of one for every 16 persons in the United States. Since more goods and money were distributed over a relatively fixed number of business establishments, the tempo of business activity per establishment apparently was increasing. At the same time, the percent of the population employed as sales clerks or salesmen in retail trade declined from 1.48% to 1.27%, between 1960 and 1970, a 14.7% decline (USBC, 1975: Table 589).

Though both business and personal property increased, the changing pace of activities appears to have exposed the latter to greater relative risk of attack, whether at home or elsewhere, due to the dispersion of goods among many more households, while concentrating goods in business establishments. However, merchandise in retail establishments with heavy volume and few employees to guard it probably is exposed to major increments in risk of illegal removal than is most other business property.

Figure 14.4.2	Offense analysis trends for robbery, burglary, larceny and murder; United States, 1960–1975

A. Robberies[a]	1960	1965	1970	
Highway robbery	52.6	57.0	59.8	
Residential robbery	8.0	10.1	13.1	
Commercial robbery	39.4	32.9	27.1	
Totals	100.0	100.0	100.0	
B. Burglaries	1960	1965	1970	1975
Residential	15.6	24.5	31.7	33.2
Residential nightime	24.4	25.2	25.8	30.5
Commercial	60.0	50.2	42.5	36.3
Totals	100.0	99.9	100.0	100.0
C. Larcenies	1960	1965	1970	1975
Shoplifting	6.0	7.8	9.2	11.3
Other	94.0	92.2	90.8	88.7
Totals	100.0	100.0	100.0	100.0
D. Murders	1963	1965	1970	1975
Relative killings	31.0	31.0	23.3	22.4
Romance, arguments[b]	51.0	48.0	47.9	45.2
Felon types[c]	17.0	21.0	28.8	32.4
Totals	100.0	100.0	100.0	100.0

Source: Offense analysis from UCR, various years.
[a] excluding miscellaneous robberies. The 1975 distribution omitted due to apparent instability of post-1970 data.
[b] Includes romantic triangles, lovers' quarrels and arguments.
[c] Includes both known and suspected felon types.

Composition of crime trends

If these changes in the circulation of people and property are in fact related to crime trends, the composition of the latter should reflect this. We expect relatively greater increases in personal and household victimization as compared with most business victimizations, while shoplifting should increase more rapidly than other types of thefts from businesses. We expect personal offenses at the hands of strangers to manifest greater increases than such offenses at the hands of nonstrangers.

Finally, residential burglary rates should increase more in daytime than nighttime.

The available time series on the composition of offenses confirm these expectations. For example, Table 14.4.2 shows that commercial burglaries declined from 60% to 36% of the total, while daytime residential burglaries increased from 16% to 33%. Unlike the other crimes against business, shoplifting increased its share. Though we lack trend data on the circumstances of other violent offenses, murder data confirm our expectations. Between 1963 and 1975, felon-type murders increased from 17% to 32% of the total. Compared with a 47% increase in the rate of relative killings in this period, we calculated a 294% increase in the murder rate at the hands of known or suspected felon types.

Thus the trends in the composition of recorded crime rates appear to be highly consistent with the activity structure trends noted earlier.

Discussion

In our judgment many conventional theories of crime (the adequacy of which usually is evaluated by cross-sectional data, or no data at all) have difficulty accounting for the annual changes in crime rate trends in the post-World War II United States. These theories may prove useful in explaining crime trends during other periods, within specific communities, or in particular subgroups of the population. Longitudinal aggregate data for the United States, however, indicate that the trends for many of the presumed causal variables in these theoretical structures are in a direction opposite to those hypothesized to be the causes of crime. For example, during the decade 1960–1970, the percent of the population below the low-income level declined 44% and the unemployment rate declined 186%. Central city population as a share of the whole population declined slightly, while the percent of foreign stock declined 0.1%, etc. (see USBC, 1975: 654, 19, 39).

On the other hand, the convergence in time and space of three elements (motivated offenders, suitable targets, and the absence of capable guardians) appears useful for understanding crime rate trends. The lack of any of these elements is sufficient to prevent the occurrence of a successful direct-contact predatory crime. The convergence in time and space of suitable targets and the absence of capable guardians can lead to large increases in crime rates without any increase or change in the structural conditions that motivate individuals to engage in crime. Presumably, had the social indicators of the variables hypothesized to be the causes of crime in conventional theories changed in the direction of favoring increased crime in the post-World War II United States, the increases in crime rates likely would have been even more staggering than those which were observed. In any event, it is our belief that criminologists have underemphasized the importance of the convergence of suitable targets and the absence of capable guardians in explaining recent increases in the crime rate. Furthermore, the effects of the convergence in time and space of these elements may be multiplicative rather than additive. That is, their convergence by a fixed percentage may produce increases in crime rates far greater than that fixed percentage, demonstrating how some relatively modest social trends can contribute to some relatively large changes in crime rate trends. [...]

Without denying the importance of factors motivating offenders to engage in crime, we have focused specific attention upon violations themselves and the prerequisites for their occurrence. However, the routine activity approach might in the future be applied to the analysis of offenders and their inclinations as well. For example, the structure of primary group activity may affect the likelihood that cultural transmission or social control of criminal inclinations will occur, while the structure of the community may affect the tempo of criminogenic peer group activity. We also may expect that circumstances favorable for carrying out violations contribute to criminal inclinations in the long run by rewarding these inclinations.

We further suggest that the routine activity framework may prove useful in explaining why the criminal justice system, the community and the family have appeared so ineffective in exerting social control since 1960. Substantial increases in the opportunity to carry out predatory violations may have undermined society's mechanisms for social control. For example, it may be difficult for institutions seeking to increase the certainty, celerity and severity of punishment to compete with structural changes resulting in vast increases in the certainty, celerity and value of rewards to be gained from illegal predatory acts.

It is ironic that the very factors which increase the opportunity to enjoy the benefits of life also may increase the opportunity for predatory violations. For example, automobiles provide freedom of movement to offenders as well as average citizens and offer vulnerable targets for theft. College enrollment, female labor force participation, urbanization, suburbanization, vacations and new electronic durables provide various opportunities to escape the confines of the household while they increase the risk of predatory victimization. Indeed, the opportunity for predatory crime appears to be enmeshed in the opportunity structure for legitimate activities to such an extent that it might be very difficult to root out substantial amounts of crime without modifying much of our way of life. Rather than assuming that predatory crime is simply an indicator of social breakdown, one might take it as a byproduct of freedom and prosperity as they manifest themselves in the routine activities of everyday life.

> *From L.E. Cohen and M. Felson, 'Social change and crime rate trends: a routine activity approach',* American Sociological Review, *1979. 44: 588–608.*

Note

1 While the more sophisticated treatments of the topic have varied somewhat in their findings, most recent studies attempting to link crime rate increases to the changing age structure of the American population have found that the latter account for a relatively limited proportion of the general crime trend (see, for example, Sagi and Wellford, 1968; Ferdinand, 1970; and Wellford, 1973).

References

Bureau of Labor Statistics (BLS) 1975 *Handbook of Labor Statistics 1975 – Reference Edition*. Washington, D.C.: U.S. Government Printing Office.

Council of Economic Advisors (CEA) 1976 *The Economic Report of the President*. Washington. D.C.: U.S. Government Printing Office.

Electrical Merchandising Week 1964 Statistical and Marketing Report (January). New York: Billboard Publications.

Federal Bureau of Investigation (FBI) 1975 *Crime in the U.S.: Uniform Crime Report*. Washington, D.C.: U.S. Government Printing Office.

Glaser, Daniel 1971 *Social Deviance*. Chicago: Markham.

Kobrin, Frances E. 1976 'The primary individual and the family: changes in living arrangements in the U.S. since 1940.' *Journal of Marriage and the Family* 38:233–9.

Merchandising Week 1973 Statistical and Marketing Report (February). New York: Billboard Publications.

National Commission on the Causes and Prevention of Violence 1969 *Crimes of Violence. Vol. 13*. Washington, D.C.: U.S. Government Printing Office.

U.S. Bureau of the Census (USBC) 1973a *Census of Transportation, 1972. U.S. Summary*. Washington, D.C.: U.S. Government Printing Office.

1975–1976 *Statistical Abstract of the U.S.* Washington D.C.: U.S. Government Printing Office.

15

Feminist criminology

15.1 The etiology of female crime
Dorie Klein   328

**15.2 Girls, crime and woman's place: toward
a feminist model of female delinquency**
Meda Chesney-Lind   335

15.3 Feminism and criminology
Kathleen Daly and Meda Chesney-Lind   340

**15.4 Feminist approaches to criminology or
postmodern woman meets atavistic man**
Carol Smart   347

Introduction

KEY CONCEPTS atavism; feminist empiricism; objectivity/subjectivity; patriarchy; postmodern feminism; standpoint feminism; status offences

The vast majority of criminologists you will have come across, and by now perhaps whose work you have read, are almost certainly men. Historically, this has been a male-dominated subject – not just in who its practitioners are, but also in much of its focus. By and large, deviance by women has just not interested (male) criminologists much. The feminist movement that emerged in the second half of the twentieth century has begun to change that, albeit slowly in some respects.

Dorie Klein **(Reading 15.1)** was one of a number of women at the forefront of this shift in criminological attention from the 1960s onward. In her article on the etiology of female crime she reviews some of the early work in the field, notably that of Cesare Lombroso, W.I. Thomas and Otto Pollak. As was suggested in chapter 5, although now widely discredited, Lombroso's work is of continuing importance. Crucially, she says, 'reading the work helps to achieve a better understanding of what kinds of myths have been developed for women in general and for female crime and deviance in particular'. In relation to Lombroso, these include passivity, amorality together with an inherent deceitfulness: 'bad women are whores, driven by lust for money or for men, often essentially *masculine* in their orientation'. Later, W.I. Thomas was to link women's deceitfulness to their physiology – in particularly to their sexuality. Old-fashioned it may be, but you may well find echoes (or something stronger than echoes) in some much more modern discussion of female offending.

Meda Chesney-Lind **(Reading 15.2)** offers a more modern take on female offending. She is highly critical of much criminological theorizing, such as that associated with the Chicago School (see chapter 9) for its preoccupation with boys (indeed its complete failure to even consider girls most of the time), and for strain theorists' identification of what are largely male opportunity structures and blockages. By contrast, she shows that the juvenile justice system in America paid much more attention to the female offender and how in the post-war years there was a particular preoccupation with girls' morals. As a consequence a large number of reformatories and training schools were developed for girls.

As feminist scholarship in criminology developed so a series of assumptions or, as Kathleen Daly and Meda Chesney-Lind **(Reading 15.3)** put it, 'myths', emerged. They tackle three of these: the idea that feminist analyses are problematically subjective; that feminism is only concerned with women and ignores men; and, finally, the implication that there is a *single* approach to feminist analysis. They go on to offer a definition of feminist analysis and then to distinguish such approaches from non-feminist analyses. Such approaches are or should be, central to criminology, they argue, in order to allow a fully-rounded explanation of female offending, victimization, and of criminal justice policy to emerge. It helps to reorient criminology away from its overarching focus on white, economically-privileged, male experience and to provide bridges to other social and political theory. However, it is not possible to produce a single, monolithic 'feminist criminology' for there will always, of necessity, be different perspectives.

A more critical approach to this latter question is offered by Carol Smart (**Reading 15.4**). As she puts it, 'I have argued that the core enterprise of criminology is profoundly problematic'. Smart uses Harding's distinction between 'feminist empiricism', 'standpoint feminism', and 'postmodern feminism'. Feminist empiricism, she notes, has been highly critical of traditional, empiricist models of scientific inquiry and for the way in which 'what has passed for science is in fact the world perceived from the perspective of men'. Standpoint feminism puts women's experiences and struggle at the heart of scholarly activity, and feminist postmodernism rejects the philosophical assumption of a single knowable reality. Taken together, these take feminism in very different directions from those she suggests are currently generally being pursued in criminology. To the question, therefore, of the nature of the future relationship between feminism and criminology she suggests that it is very difficult to see what the latter has to offer the former.

Questions for discussion

1. In what ways did Lombroso consider the female criminal to be 'atavistic'?

2. In what ways might an understanding of Lombroso's, W.I. Thomas' or Otto Pollak's ideas about female criminality be relevant today? Give examples.

3. What are the main feminist criticisms of the Chicago School, strain theory and subcultural theory?

4. Outline Chesney-Lind's argument in relation to the relevance and meaning of the post-war juvenile justice system's focus on girls' 'immorality' or 'waywardness'.

5. What are the main distinctions between feminist and non-feminist analyses?

6. What are the advantages of including a feminist perspective within criminology?

7. Why does Carol Smart argue that the 'core enterprise of criminology is profoundly problematic'?

8. What do you think the future relationship between feminist thought and criminology might look like, and why?

15.1 The etiology of female crime
Dorie Klein

Introduction

The criminality of women has long been a neglected subject area of criminology. Many explanations have been advanced for this, such as women's low official rate of crime and delinquency and the preponderance of male theorists in the field. Female criminality has often ended up as a footnote to works on men that purport to be works on criminality in general.

There has been, however, a small group of writings specifically concerned with women and crime. This paper will explore those works concerned with the etiology of female crime and delinquency, beginning with the turn-of-the-century writing of Lombroso and extending to the present. Writers selected to be included have been chosen either for their influence on the field, such as Lombroso, Thomas, Freud, Davis and Pollak [only Klein's overview of the works of Lombroso, Thomas and Pollak are included in this extract] because they are representative of the kinds of work being published, such as Konopka, Vedder and Somerville, and Cowie, Cowie and Slater. The emphasis is on the continuity between these works, because it is clear that, despite recognizable differences in analytical approaches and specific theories, the authors represent a tradition to a great extent. It is important to understand, therefore, the shared assumptions made by the writers that are used in laying the groundwork for their theories.

Lombroso: 'there must be some anomaly...'

Lombroso's work on female criminality (1920) is important to consider today despite the fact that his methodology and conclusions have long been successfully discredited. Later writings on female crime by Thomas, Davis, Pollak and others use more sophisticated methodologies and may proffer more palatable liberal theories. However, to varying degrees they rely on those sexual ideologies based on *implicit* assumptions about the physiological and psychological nature of women that are *explicit* in Lombroso's work. Reading the work helps to achieve a better understanding of what kinds of myths have been developed for women in general and for female crime and deviance in particular.

One specific notion of women offered by Lombroso is women's physiological immobility and psychological passivity, later elaborated by Thomas, Freud and other writers. Another ascribed characteristic is the Lombrosian notion of women's adaptability to surroundings and their capacity for survival as being superior to that of men. A third idea discussed by Lombroso is women's amorality: they are cold and calculating. This is developed by Thomas (1923), who describes women's manipulation of the male sex urge for ulterior purposes; by Freud (1933), who sees women as avenging their lack of a penis on men; and by Pollak (1950), who depicts women as inherently deceitful.

When one looks at these specific traits, one sees contradictions. The myth of compassionate women clashes with their reputed coldness; their frailness belies their capacity to survive. One possible explanation for these contradictions is the duality of sexual ideology with regard to 'good' and 'bad' women. Bad women are whores, driven by lust for money or for men, often essentially *'masculine'* in their orientation, and perhaps afflicted with a touch of penis envy. Good women are chaste, 'feminine,' and usually not prone to criminal activity. But when they are, they commit crime in a most *ladylike* way such as poisoning. In more sophisticated theory, all women are seen as having a bit of both tendencies in them. Therefore, women can be compassionate *and* cold, frail *and* sturdy, pious *and* amoral, depending on which path they choose to follow. They are seen as rational (although they are irrational, too!), atomistic individuals making choices in a vacuum, prompted only by personal, physiological/psychological factors. These choices relate only to the *sexual* sphere. Women have no place in any other sphere. Men, on the other hand, are not held sexually accountable, although, as Thomas notes (1907), they are held responsible in *economic* matters. Men's sexual freedom is justified by the myth of masculine, irresistible sex urges. This myth, still worshipped today, is frequently offered as a rationalization for the existence of prostitution and the double standard. As Davis maintains, this necessitates the parallel existence of classes of 'good' and 'bad' women.

These dual moralities for the sexes are outgrowths of the economic, political and social *realities* for men and women. Women are primarily workers within the family, a critical institution of reproduction and socialization that services such basic needs as food and shelter. Laws and codes of behavior for women thus attempt to maintain the smooth functioning of women in that role, which requires that women act as a conservative force in the continuation of the nuclear family. Women's main tasks are sexual, and the law embodies sexual limitations for women, which do not exist for men, such as the prohibition of promiscuity for girls. This explains why theorists of female criminality are not only concerned with sexual violations by female offenders, but attempt to account for even *nonsexual* offenses, such as prostitution, in sexual terms, e.g., women enter prostitution for sex rather than for money. Such women are not only economic offenders but are sexual deviants, falling neatly into the category of 'bad' women.

The works of Lombroso, particularly *The Female Offender* (1920), are a foremost example of the biological explanation of crime. Lombroso deals with crime as an atavism, or survival of 'primitive' traits in individuals, particularly those of the female and nonwhite races. He theorizes that individuals develop differentially within sexual and racial limitations which differ hierarchically from the most highly developed, the white men, to the most primitive, the nonwhite women. Beginning with the assumption that criminals must be atavistic, he spends a good deal of time comparing the crania, moles, heights, etc. of convicted criminals and prostitutes with those of normal women. Any trait that he finds to be more common in the 'criminal' group is pronounced an atavistic trait, such as moles, dark hair, etc., and women with a number of these tell-tale traits could be regarded as potentially criminal, since they are of the atavistic type. He specifically rejects the idea that some of these traits, for example obesity in prostitutes, could be the result of their activities rather than an indicator of their propensity to them. Many of the traits depicted as 'anomalies,' such as darkness and shortness, are characteristic of certain racial groups, such as the Sicilians, who undoubtedly comprise an oppressed group within Italy and form a large part of the imprisoned population.

Lombroso traces an overall pattern of evolution in the human species that accounts for the uneven development of groups: the white and nonwhite races, males and females, adults and children. Women, children and nonwhites share many traits in common. There are fewer variations in their mental capacities: 'even the female criminal is monotonous and uniform compared with her male companion, just as in general woman is inferior to man' (*ibid.*: 122), due to her being 'atavistically nearer to her origin than the male' (*ibid.*: 107). The notion of women's mediocrity, or limited range of mental possibilities, is a recurrent one in the writings of the twentieth century. Thomas and others note that women comprise 'fewer geniuses, fewer lunatics and fewer morons' (Thomas, 1907: 45); lacking the imagination to be at either end of the spectrum, they are conformist and dull ... not due to social, political or economic constraints on their activities, but because of their innate physiological limitations as a sex. Lombroso attributes the lower female rate of criminality to their having fewer anomalies, which is one aspect of their closeness to the lower forms of less differentiated life.

Related characteristics of women are their passivity and conservatism. Lombroso admits that women's traditional sex roles in the family bind them to a more sedentary life. However, he insists that women's passivity can be directly traced to the 'immobility of the ovule compared with the zoosperm' (1920: 109), falling back on the sexual act in an interesting anticipation of Freud.

Women, like the lower races, have greater powers of endurance and resistance to mental and physical pain than men. Lombroso states: 'denizens of female prisons ... have reached the age of 90, having lived within those walls since they were 29 without any grave injury to health' (*ibid.*: 125). Denying the humanity of women by denying their capability for suffering justifies exploitation of women's energies by arguing for their suitability to hardship. Lombroso remarks that 'a duchess can adapt herself to new surroundings and become a washerwoman much more easily than a man can transform himself under analogous conditions' (*ibid.*: 272). The theme of women's adaptability to physical and social surroundings, which are male initiated, male controlled, and often expressed by saying that women are actually the 'stronger' sex, is a persistent thread in writings on women.

Lombroso explains that because women are unable to feel pain, they are insensitive to the pain of others and lack moral refinement. His blunt denial of the age-old myth of women's compassion and sensitivity is modified, however, to take into account women's low crime rate:

> Women have many traits in common with children; that their moral sense is deficient; that they are revengeful, jealous ... In ordinary cases these defects are neutralized by piety, maternity, want of passion, sexual coldness, weakness and an undeveloped intelligence (*ibid.*: 151).

Although women lack the higher sensibilities of men, they are thus restrained from criminal activity in most cases by lack of intelligence and passion, qualities which *criminal* women possess as well as all *men*. Within this framework of biological limits of women's nature, the female offender is characterized as *masculine* whereas the normal woman is *feminine*. The anomalies of skull, physiognomy and brain capacity of female criminals, according to Lombroso, more closely approximate that of the man, normal or criminal, than they do those of the normal woman; the female offender often has a 'virile cranium' and considerable body hair. Masculinity in women is an anomaly itself, rather than a sign of development, however. A related notion is developed by Thomas, who notes that in 'civilized' nations the sexes are more physically different.

> What we look for most in the female is femininity, and when we find the opposite in her, we must conclude as a rule that there must be some anomaly ... Virility was one of the special features of the savage woman... In the portraits of Red Indian and Negro beauties, whom it is difficult to recognize for women, so huge are their jaws and cheekbones, so hard and coarse their features, and the same is often the case in their crania and brains (*ibid.*: 112).

The more highly developed races would therefore have the most feminized women with the requisite passivity, lack of passion, etc. This is a racist and classist definition of femininity – just as are almost all theories of *femininity* and as, indeed, is the thing itself. The ideal of the lady can only exist in a society built on the exploitation of labor to maintain the woman of leisure who can *be* that ideal lady.

Finally, Lombroso notes women's lack of *property sense*, which contributes to their criminality.

> In their eyes theft is... an audacity for which account compensation is due to the owner... as an individual rather than a social crime, just as

it was regarded in the primitive periods of human evolution and is still regarded by many uncivilized nations (*ibid.*: 217).

One may question this statement on several levels. Can it be assumed to have any validity at all, or is it false that women have a different sense of property than men? If it is valid to a degree, is it related to women's lack of property ownership and non-participation in the accumulation of capitalist wealth? Indeed, as Thomas (1907) points out, women are considered property themselves. At any rate, it is an interesting point in Lombroso's book that has only been touched on by later writers, and always in a manner supportive of the institution of private property.

Thomas: 'the stimulation she craves'

The works of W. I. Thomas are critical in that they mark a transition from purely physiological explanations such as Lombroso's to more sophisticated theories that embrace physiological, psychological and social-structural factors. However, even the most sophisticated explanations of female crime rely on implicit assumptions about the biological nature of women. In Thomas' *Sex and Society* (1907) and *The Unadjusted Girl* (1923), there are important contradictions in the two approaches that are representative of the movements during that period between publication dates: a departure from biological Social-Darwinian theories to complex analyses of the interaction between society and the individual, i.e., societal repression and manipulation of the 'natural' wishes of persons.

In *Sex and Society* (1907), Thomas poses basic biological differences between the sexes as his starting point. Maleness is 'katabolic,' the animal force which is destructive of energy and allows men the possibility of creative work through this outward flow. Femaleness is 'anabolic,' analogous to a plant which stores energy, and is motionless and conservative. Here Thomas is offering his own version of the age-old male/female dichotomy expressed by Lombroso and elaborated on in Freud's paradigm, in the structural-functionalist 'instrumental-expressive' duality, and in other analyses of the status quo. According to Thomas, the dichotomy is most highly developed in the more civilized races, due to the greater differentiation of sex roles. This statement ignores the hard physical work done by poor *white* women at home and in the factories and offices in 'civilized' countries, and accepts a *ruling-class* definition of femininity.

The cause of women's relative decline in stature in more 'civilized' countries is a subject on which Thomas is ambivalent. At one point he attributes it to the lack of 'a superior fitness on the motor side' in women (*ibid.*: 94); at another point, he regards her loss of *sexual freedom* as critical, with the coming of monogamy and her confinement to sexual tasks such as wifehood and motherhood. He perceptively notes:

> Women were still further degraded by the development of property and its control by man, together with the habit of treating her as a piece of property, whose value was enhanced if its purity was assured (*ibid.*: 297).

However, Thomas' underlying assumptions in his explanations of the inferior status of women are *physiological* ones. He attributes to men high amounts of sexual energy, which lead them to pursue women for their sex, and he attributes to women maternal feelings devoid of sexuality, which lead *them* to exchange sex for domesticity. Thus monogamy, with chastity for women, is the *accommodation* of these basic urges, and women are domesticated while men assume leadership, in a true market exchange.

Why, then, does Thomas see problems in the position of women? It is because modern women are plagued by 'irregularity, pettiness, ill health and inserviceableness' (*ibid.*: 245). Change is required to maintain *social harmony*, apart from considerations of women's needs, and women must be educated to make them better wives, a theme reiterated throughout this century by 'liberals' on the subject. Correctly anticipating a threat, Thomas urges that change be made to stabilize the family, and warns that 'no civilization can remain the highest if another civilization adds to the intelligence of its men the intelligence of its women' (*ibid.*: 3 14). Thomas is motivated by considerations of social integration. Of course, one might question how women are to be able to contribute much if they are indeed anabolic. However, due to the transitional nature of Thomas' work, there are immense contradictions in his writing.

Many of Thomas' specific assertions about the nature of women are indistinguishable from Lombroso's; they both delineate a biological hierarchy along race and sex lines.

> Man has, in short, become more somatically specialized an animal than women, and feels more keenly any disturbance of normal conditions with which he has not the same physiological surplus as woman with which to meet the disturbance ... It is a logical fact, however, that the lower human races, the lower classes of society, women and children show something of the same quality in their superior tolerance of surgical disease (*ibid.*: 36).

Like Lombroso, Thomas is crediting women with superior capabilities of survival because they are further down the scale in terms of evolution. It is significant that Thomas includes the lower classes in his observation; is he implying that the lower classes are in their position *because* of their natural unfitness, or perhaps that their *situation* renders them less sensitive to pain? At different times, Thomas implies both. Furthermore, he agrees with Lombroso that women are more nearly uniform than men, and says that they have a smaller percentage of 'genius, insanity and idiocy' (*ibid.*: 45) than men, as well as fewer creative outbursts of energy.

Dealing with female criminality in *Sex and Society* (1907), Thomas begins to address the issue of morality, which he closely links to legality from a standpoint of maintaining social order. He discriminates between male and female morality:

> Morality as applied to men has a larger element of the contractual, representing the adjustment of his activities to those of society at large, or more particularly to the activities of the male members of society; while the morality which we think of in connection with women shows less of the contractual and more of the personal, representing her adjustment to men, more particularly the adjustment of her person to men (*ibid.*: 172).

Whereas Lombroso barely observes women's lack of participation in the institution of private property, Thomas' perception is more profound. He points out that women *are* property of men and that their conduct is subject to different codes.

> Morality, in the most general sense, represents the code under which activities are best carried on and is worked out in the school of experience. It is preeminently an adult and male system, and men are intelligent enough to realize that neither women nor children have passed through this school. It is on this account that man is merciless to woman from the standpoint of personal behavior, yet he exempts her from anything in the way of contractual moral-

ity, or views her defections in this regard with allowance and even with amusement (*ibid.*: 234)

Disregarding his remarks about intelligence, one confronts the critical point about women with respect to the law: because they occupy a *marginal* position in the productive sphere of exchange commodities outside the home, they in turn occupy a marginal position in regard to 'contractual' law which regulates relations of property and production. The argument of differential treatment of men and women by the law is developed in later works by Pollak and others, who attribute it to the 'chivalry' of the system which is lenient to women committing offenses. As Thomas notes, however, women are simply not a serious *threat* to property, and are treated more 'leniently' because of this. Certain women do become threats by transcending (or by being denied) their traditional role, particularly many Third World women and political rebels, and they are *not* afforded chivalrous treatment! In fact, chivalry is reserved for the women who are least likely to ever come in contact with the criminal justice system: the ladies, or white middle-class women. In matters of *sexual* conduct, however, which embody the double standard, women are rigorously prosecuted by the law. As Thomas understands, this is the sphere in which women's functions *are* critical. Thus it is not a matter of 'chivalry' how one is handled, but of different forms and thrusts of social control applied to men and women. Men are engaged in productive tasks and their activities in this area *are* strictly curtailed.

In The *Unadjusted Girl* (1923), Thomas deals with female delinquency as a 'normal' response under certain social conditions, using assumptions about the nature of women which he leaves unarticulated in this work. Driven by basic 'wishes,' an individual is controlled by society in her activities through institutional transmission of codes and mores. Depending on how they are manipulated, wishes can be made to serve social or antisocial ends. Thomas stresses the institutions that socialize, such as the family, giving people certain 'definitions of the situation.' He confidently – and defiantly – asserts:

> There is no individual energy, no unrest, no type of wish, which cannot he sublimated and made socially useful. From this standpoint, the problem is not the right of society to protect itself from the disorderly and antisocial person, but the right of the disorderly and antisocial

person to be made orderly and socially valuable... The problem of society is to produce the right attitudes in its members (*ibid.*: 232–233).

This is an important shift in perspective, from the traditional libertarian view of protecting society by punishing transgressors, to the *rehabilitative* and *preventive* perspective of crime control that seeks to control *minds* through socialization rather than to merely control behavior through punishment. The autonomy of the individual to choose is seen as the product of his environment which the state can alter. This is an important refutation of the Lombrosian biological perspective, which maintains that there are crime-prone individuals who must be locked up, sterilized or otherwise incapacitated. Today, one can see an amalgamation of the two perspectives in new theories of 'behavior control' that use tactics such as conditioning and brain surgery, combining biological and environmental viewpoints.

Thomas proposes the manipulation of individuals through institutions to prevent antisocial attitudes, and maintains that there is no such person as the 'crime prone' individual. A hegemonic system of belief can be imposed by sublimating natural urges and by correcting the poor socialization of slum families. In this perspective, the *definition* of the situation rather than the situation *itself* is what should be changed; a situation is what someone *thinks* it is. The response to a criminal woman who is dissatisfied with her conventional sexual roles is to change not the roles, which would mean widespread social transformations, but to change her attitudes. This concept of civilization as repressive and the need to adjust is later refined by Freud.

Middle-class women, according to Thomas, commit little crime because they are socialized to sublimate their natural desires and to behave well, treasuring their chastity as an investment. The poor woman, however, 'is not immoral, because this implies a loss of morality, but amoral' (*ibid.*: 93). Poor women are not objectively driven to crime; they long for it. Delinquent girls are motivated by the desire for excitement or 'new experience,' and forget the repressive urge of 'security.' However, these desires are well within Thomas' conception of *femininity*: delinquents are not rebelling against womanhood, as Lombroso suggests, but merely acting it out illegally. Davis and Pollak agree with this notion that delinquent women are not 'different' from nondelinquent women.

Thomas maintains that it is not sexual desire that motivates delinquent girls, for they are no more passionate than other women, but they are *manipulating* male desires for sex to achieve their own ulterior ends.

> The beginning of delinquency in girls is usually an impulse to get amusement, adventure, pretty clothes, favorable notice, distinction, freedom in the larger world .. The girls have usually become 'wild' before the development of sexual desire, and their casual sex relations do not usually awaken sex feeling. Their sex is used as a condition of the realization of other wishes. It is their capital (*ibid.*: 109).

Here Thomas is expanding on the myth of the manipulative woman, who is cold and scheming and vain. To him, good female sexual behavior is a protective measure – 'instinctive, of course' (1907: 241), whereas male behavior is uncontrollable as men are caught by helpless desires. This is the common Victorian notion of the woman as seductress which in turn perpetuates the myth of a lack of real sexuality to justify her responsibility for upholding sexual mores. Thomas uses a market analogy to female virtue: good women *keep* their bodies as capital to sell in matrimony for marriage and security, whereas bad women *trade* their bodies for excitement. One notes, of course, the familiar dichotomy. It is difficult, in this framework, to see how Thomas can make any moral distinctions, since morality seems to be merely good business sense. In fact, Thomas' yardstick is social harmony, necessitating *control*.

Thomas shows an insensitivity to real human relationships and needs. He also shows ignorance of economic hardships in his denial of economic factors in delinquency.

> An unattached woman has a tendency to become an adventuress not so much on economic as on psychological grounds. Life is rarely so hard that a young woman cannot earn her bread; but she cannot always live and have the stimulation she craves (*ibid.*: 241).

This is an amazing statement in an era of mass starvation and illness! He rejects economic causes as a possibility at all, denying its importance in criminal activity with as much certainty as Lombroso, Freud, Davis, Pollak and most other writers.

Pollak: 'a different attitude toward veracity'

Otto Pollak's *The Criminality of Women* (1950) has had an outstanding influence on the field of women and crime, being the major work on the subject in the postwar years. Pollak advances the theory of 'hidden' female crime to account for what he considers unreasonably low official rates for women.

A major reason for the existence of hidden crime, as he sees it, lies in the *nature* of women themselves. They are instigators rather than perpetrators of criminal activity. While Pollak admits that this role is partly a socially enforced one, he insists that women are inherently deceitful for *physiological* reasons.

> Man must achieve an erection in order to perform the sex act and will not be able to hide his failure. His lack of positive emotion in the sexual sphere must become overt to the partner, and pretense of sexual response is impossible for him, if it is lacking. Woman's body, however, permits such pretense to a certain degree and lack of orgasm does not prevent her ability to participate in the sex act (*ibid.*: 10).

Pollak *reduces* women's nature to the *sex act*, as Freud has done, and finds women inherently more capable of manipulation, accustomed to being sly, passive and passionless. As Thomas suggests, women can use sex for ulterior purposes. Furthermore, Pollak suggests that women are innately deceitful on yet another level:

> Our sex mores force women to conceal every four weeks the period of menstruation ... They thus make concealment and misrepresentation in the eyes of women socially required and must condition them to a different attitude toward veracity than men (*ibid.*: 11).

Women's abilities at concealment thus allow them to successfully commit crimes in stealth.

Women are also vengeful. Menstruation, in the classic Freudian sense, seals their doomed hopes to become men and arouses women's desire for vengeance, especially during that time of the month. Thus Pollak offers new rationalizations to bolster old myths.

A second factor in hidden crime is the roles played by women which furnish them with opportunities as domestics, nurses, teachers and housewives to commit undetectable crimes. The *kinds* of crimes women commit reflect their nature: false accusation, for example, is an outgrowth of women's treachery, spite or fear and is a sign of neurosis; shoplifting can be traced in many cases to a special mental disease – kleptomania. Economic factors play a minor role; *sexual-psychological* factors account for female criminality. Crime in women is personalized and often accounted for by mental illness.

Pollak notes:

> Robbery and burglary ... are considered specifically male offenses since they represent the pursuit of monetary gain by overt action ... Those cases of female robbery which seem to express a tendency toward masculinization comes from ... [areas] where social conditions have favored the assumptions of male pursuits by women... The female offenders usually retain some trace of femininity, however, and even so glaring an example of masculinization as the 'Michigan Babes,' an all woman gang of robbers in Chicago, shows a typically feminine trait in the modus operandi (*ibid.*: 29).

Pollak is defining crimes with economic motives that employ overt action as *masculine*, and defining as *feminine* those crimes for sexual activity, such as luring men as baits. Thus he is using circular reasoning by saying that feminine crime is feminine. To fit women into the scheme and justify the statistics, he must invent the notion of hidden crime.

It is important to recognize that, to some extent, women *do* adapt to their enforced sexual roles and may be more likely to instigate, to use sexual traps, and to conform to all the other feminine role expectations. However, it is not accidental that theorists label women as conforming even when they are *not*; for example, by inventing sexual motives for what are clearly crimes of economic necessity, or by invoking 'mental illness' such as kleptomania for shoplifting. It is difficult to separate the *theory* from the *reality*, since the reality of female crime is largely unknown. But it is not difficult to see that Pollak is using sexist terms and making sexist assumptions to advance theories of hidden female crime. Pollak, then, sees criminal women as extending their sexual role, like Davis and Thomas, by using sexuality for ulterior purposes. He suggests that the condemnation

of extramarital sex has 'delivered men who engage in such conduct as practically helpless victims' (*ibid.*: 152) into the hands of women blackmailers, overlooking completely the possibility of men blackmailing women, which would seem more likely, given the greater taboo on sex for women and their greater risks of being punished.

The final factor that Pollak advances as a root cause of hidden crime is that of 'chivalry' in the criminal justice system. Pollak uses Thomas' observation that women are differentially treated by the law, and carries it to a sweeping conclusion based on *cultural* analyses of men's feelings toward women.

> One of the outstanding concomitants of the existing inequality ... is chivalry, and the general protective attitude of man toward woman. Men hate to accuse women and thus indirectly to send them to their punishment, police officers dislike to arrest them, district attorneys to prosecute them, judges and juries to find them guilty, and so on (*ibid.*: 151).

Pollak rejects the possibility of an actual discrepancy between crime rates for men and women; therefore, he must look for factors to expand the scope of female crime. He assumes that there is chivalry in the criminal justice system that is extended to the women who come in contact with it. Yet the women involved are likely to be poor and Third World women or white middle-class women who have stepped *outside* the definitions of femininity to become hippies or political rebels, and chivalry is *not* likely to be extended to them. Chivalry is a racist and classist concept founded on the notion of women as 'ladies' which applies only to wealthy white women and ignores the double sexual standard. These 'ladies,' however, are the least likely women to ever come in contact with the criminal justice system in the first place.

Conclusion

A good deal of the writing on women and crime being done at the present time is squarely in the tradition of the writers that have been discussed. The basic assumptions and technocratic concerns of these writers have produced work that is sexist, racist and classist; assumptions that have served to maintain a repressive ideology with its extensive apparatus of control. To do a new kind of research on women and crime – one that has feminist roots and a radical orientation – it is necessary to understand the assumptions made by the traditional writers and to break away from them. Work that focuses on human needs, rather than those of the state, will require new definitions of criminality, women, the individual and her/his relation to the state. It is beyond the scope of this paper to develop possible areas of study, but it is nonethe-less imperative that this work be made a priority by women and men in the future.

> *From D. Klein, 'The etiology of female crime: a review of the literature',* Issues in Criminology, *1973, 8: 3–30.*

References

Freud, S. (1933) *New Introductory Lectures on Psychoanalysis*. New York: W. W. Norton.

Lombroso, C. (1920) *The Female Offender*. (translation). New York: Appleton. Originally published in 1903.

Pollak, O. (1950) *The Criminality of Women*. Philadelphia: University of Pennsylvania Press.

Thomas, W.I. (1907) *Sex and Society*. Boston: Little, Brown and Company.

— (1923) *The Unadjusted Girl*. New York: Harper and Row.

15.2 Girls, crime and woman's place: toward a feminist model of female delinquency Meda Chesney-Lind

The romance of the gang or the West Side Story syndrome

From the start, the field of delinquency research focused on visible lower-class male delinquency, often justifying the neglect of girls in the most cava-lier of terms. Take, for example, the extremely important and influential work of Clifford R. Shaw and Henry D. McKay who, beginning in 1929, utilized an ecological approach to the study of juve-nile delinquency. Their impressive work, particularly *Juvenile Delinquency in Urban Areas* (1942) and inten-sive biographical case studies such as Shaw's *Brothers in Crime* (1938) and *The Jackroller* (1930), set the stage for much of the subcultural research on gang delinquency. In their ecological work, however, Shaw and McKay analyzed only the official arrest data on male delinquents in Chicago and repeatedly referred to these rates as 'delinquency rates' (though they occasionally made parenthetical reference to data on female delinquency) (see Shaw and McKay, 1942, p. 356). Similarly, their biographical work traced only male experiences with the law; in *Brothers in Crime*, for example, the delinquent and criminal careers of five brothers were followed for fifteen years. In none of these works was any justifi-cation given for the equation of male delinquency with delinquency.

Early fieldwork on delinquent gangs in Chicago set the stage for another style of delin-quency research. Yet here too researchers were interested only in talking to and following the boys. Thrasher studied over a thousand juvenile gangs in Chicago during roughly the same period as Shaw and McKay's more quantitative work was being done. He spent approximately one page out of 600 on the five of six female gangs he encoun-tered in his field observation of juvenile gangs. Thrasher (1927, p. 228) did mention, in passing, two factors he felt accounted for the lower number of girl gangs: 'First, the social patterns for the behavior of girls, powerfully backed by the great weight of tradition and custom, are contrary to the gang and its activities; and secondly, girls, even in urban disorganized areas, are much more closely supervised and guarded than boys and usually well incorporated into the family groups or some other social structure.'

Another major theoretical approach to delin-quency focuses on the subculture of lower-class communities as a generating milieu for delinquent behavior. Here again, noted delinquency researchers concentrated either exclusively or nearly exclusively on male lower-class culture. For example, Cohen's work on the subculture of delin-quent gangs, which was written nearly twenty years after Thrasher's, deliberately considers only boys' delinquency. His justification for the exclusion of the girls is quite illuminating:

> My skin has nothing of the quality of down or silk, there is nothing limpid or flute-like about my voice, I am a total loss with needle and thread, my posture and carriage are wholly lacking in grace. These imperfections cause me no distress – if anything, they are gratifying – because I conceive myself to be a man and want people to recognize me as a full-fledged, unequivocal representative of my sex. My wife, on the other hand, is not greatly embarrassed by her inability to tinker with or talk about the internal organs of a car, by her modest attainments in arithmetic or by her inability to lift heavy objects. Indeed, I am reliably informed that many women – I do not suggest that my wife is among them – often affect ignorance, frailty and emotional instability because to do otherwise would be out of keeping with a reputation for indubitable femininity. In short, people do not simply want to excel; they want to excel as a man or as a woman (Cohen, 1955, p. 138).

From this Cohen (1955, p. 140) concludes that the delinquent response 'however it may be condemned by others on moral grounds, has at least one virtue: it incontestably confirms, in the eyes of all concerned, his essential masculinity.' Much the same line of argument appears in Miller's influential paper on the 'focal concerns' of lower-class life with its emphasis on importance of trouble, toughness, excitement, and so on. These, the author concludes, predispose poor youth (particularly male youth) to criminal misconduct. However, Cohen's comments are notable in their candor and probably capture both the allure that male delinquency has had for at least some male theorists as well as the fact that sexism has rendered the female delinquent as irrelevant to their work.

Emphasis on blocked opportunities (sometimes the 'strain' theories) emerged out of the work of Robert K. Merton (1938) who stressed the need to consider how some social structures exert a definite pressure upon certain persons in the society to engage in nonconformist rather than conformist conduct. His work influenced research largely through the efforts of Cloward and Ohlin who discussed access to 'legitimate' and 'illegitimate' opportunities for male youth. No mention of female delinquency can be found in their *Delinquency and Opportunity* except that women are blamed for male delinquency. Here, the familiar notion is that boys, 'engulfed by a feminine world and uncertain of their own identification … tend to 'protest' against femininity' (Cloward and Ohlin, 1960, p. 49). Early efforts by Ruth Morris to test this hypothesis utilizing different definitions of success based on the gender of respondents met with mixed success. Attempting to assess boys' perceptions about access to economic power status while for girls the variable concerned itself with the ability or inability of girls to maintain effective relationships, Morris was unable to find a clear relationship between 'female' goals and delinquency (Morris, 1964).

The work of Edwin Sutherland emphasized the fact that criminal behavior was learned in intimate personal groups. His work, particularly the notion of differential association, which also influenced Cloward and Ohlin's work, was similarly male oriented as much of his work was affected by case studies he conducted of male criminals. Indeed, in describing his notion of how differential association works, he utilized male examples (e.g., 'In an area where the delinquency rate is high a boy who is sociable, gregarious, active, and athletic is very likely to come in contact with the other boys, in the neighborhood, learn delinquent behavior from them, and become a gangster' (Sutherland, 1978, p. 1311). Finally, the work of Travis Hirschi on the social bonds that control delinquency ('social control theory') was, as was stated earlier, derived out of research on male delinquents (though he, at least, studied delinquent behavior as reported by youth themselves rather than studying only those who were arrested).

Such a persistent focus on social class and such an absence of interest in gender in delinquency is ironic for two reasons. As even the work of Hirschi demonstrated, and as later studies would validate, a clear relationship between social class position and delinquency is problematic, while it is clear that gender has a dramatic and consistent effect on delinquency causation (Hagan, Gillis, and Simpson, 1985). The second irony, and one that consistently eludes even contemporary delinquency theorists, is the fact that while the academics had little interest in female delinquents, the same could not be said for the juvenile justice system. Indeed, work on the early history of the separate system for youth reveals that concerns about girls' immoral conduct were really at the center of what some have called the 'childsaving movement' (Platt, 1969) that set up the juvenile justice system.

'The best place to conquer girls'

The movement to establish separate institutions for youthful offenders was part of the larger Progressive movement, which among other things was keenly concerned about prostitution and other 'social evils' (white slavery and the like) (Schlossman and Wallach, 1978; Rafter, 1985, p. 54). Childsaving was also a celebration of women's domesticity, though ironically women were influential in the movement (Platt, 1969; Rafter, 1985). In a sense, privileged women found, in the moral purity crusades and the establishment of family courts, a safe outlet for their energies. As the legitimate guardians of the moral sphere, women were seen as uniquely suited to patrol the normative boundaries of the social order. Embracing rather than challenging these stereotypes, women carved out for themselves a role in the policing of women and girls (Feinman, 1980; Freedman, 1981; Messerschmidt, 1987). Ultimately, many of the early childsavers' activities revolved around the monitoring of young girls', particularly immigrant girls', behavior to prevent their straying from the path.

This state of affairs was the direct consequence of a disturbing coalition between some feminists and the more conservative social purity movement. Concerned about female victimization and distrustful of male (and to some degree female) sexuality, notable women leaders, including Susan B. Anthony, found common cause with the social purists around such issues as opposing the regulation of prostitution and raising the age of consent (see Messerschmidt, 1987). The consequences of such a partnership are an important lesson for contemporary feminist movements that are, to some extent, faced with the same possible coalitions.

Girls were the clear losers in this reform effort. Studies of early family court activity reveal that virtually all the girls who appeared in these courts were charged for immorality or waywardness (Chesney-Lind, 1971; Schlossman and Wallach, 1978; Shelden, 1981). More to the point, the sanctions for such misbehavior were extremely severe. For example, in Chicago (where the first family court was founded), one half of the girl delinquents, but only one-fifth of the boy delinquents, were sent to reformatories between 1899–1909. In Milwaukee, twice as many girls as boys were committed to training schools (Schlossman and Wallach, 1978, p. 72); and in Memphis females were twice as likely as males to be committed to training schools (Shelden, 1981, p. 70).

In Honolulu, during the period 1929–1930, over half of the girls referred to court were charged with 'immorality,' which meant evidence of sexual intercourse, in addition, another 30% were charged with 'waywardness.' Evidence of immorality was vigorously pursued by both arresting officers and social workers through lengthy questioning of the girl and, if possible, males with whom she was suspected of having sex. Other evidence of 'exposure' was provided by gynecological examinations that were routinely ordered in virtually all girls' cases. Doctors, who understood the purpose of such examinations, would routinely note the condition of the hymen: 'admits intercourse hymen rupture,' 'no laceration,' 'hymen ruptured' are typical of the notations on the forms. Girls during this period were also twice as likely as males to be detained where they spent five times as long on the average as their male counterparts. They were also nearly three times more likely to be sentenced to the training school (Chesney-Lind, 1971). Indeed, girls were half of those committed to training schools in Honolulu well into the 1950s (Chesney-Lind, 1973).

Not surprisingly, large numbers of girls' reformatories and training schools were established during this period as well as places of 'rescue and reform.' For example, Schlossman and Wallach note that 23 facilities for girls were opened during the 1910–1920 decade (in contrast to the 1850–1910 period where the average was 5 reformatories per decade (Schlossman and Wallach, 1985, p. 70)), and these institutions did much to set the tone of official response to female delinquency. Obsessed with precocious female sexuality, the institutions set about to isolate the females from all contact with males while housing them in bucolic settings. The intention was to hold the girls until marriageable age and to occupy them in domestic pursuits during their sometimes lengthy incarceration.

The links between these attitudes and those of juvenile courts some decades later are, of course, arguable; but an examination of the record of the court does not inspire confidence. A few examples of the persistence of what might be called a double standard of juvenile justice will suffice here.

A study conducted in the early 1970s in a Connecticut training school revealed large numbers of girls incarcerated 'for their own protection.' Explaining this pattern, one judge explained, 'Why most of the girls I commit are for status offenses. I figure if a girl is about to get pregnant, we'll keep her until she's sixteen and then ADC (Aid to

Dependent Children) will pick her up' (Rogers, 1972). For more evidence of official concern with adolescent sexual misconduct, consider Linda Hancock's (1981) content analysis of police referrals in Australia. She noted that 40% of the referrals of girls to court made specific mention of sexual and moral conduct compared to only 5% of the referrals of boys. These sorts of results suggest that all youthful female misbehavior has traditionally been subject to surveillance for evidence of sexual misconduct.

Gelsthorpe's (1986) field research on an English police station also revealed how everyday police decision making resulted in disregard of complaints about male problem behavior in contrast to active concern about the 'problem behavior' of girls. Notable, here, was the concern about the girl's sexual behavior. In one case, she describes police persistence in pursuing a 'moral danger' order for a 14-year-old picked up in a truancy run. Over the objections of both the girl's parents and the Social Services Department and in the face of a written confirmation from a surgeon that the girl was still premenstrual, the officers pursued the application because, in one officer's words, 'I know her sort . . . free and easy. I'm still suspicious that she might be pregnant. Anyway, if the doctor can't provide evidence we'll do her for being beyond the care and control of her parents, no one can dispute that. Running away is proof' (Gelsthorpe, 1986, p. 136). This sexualization of female deviance is highly significant and explains why criminal activities by girls (particularly in past years) were overlooked so long as they did not appear to signal defiance of parental control (see Smith, 1978).

In their historic obsession about precocious female sexuality, juvenile justice workers rarely reflected on the broader nature of female misbehavior or on the sources of this misbehavior. It was enough for them that girls' parents reported them out of control. Indeed, court personnel tended to 'sexualize' virtually all female defiance that lent itself to that construction and ignore other misbehavior (Chesney-Lind, 1973, 1977; Smith, 1978). For their part, academic students of delinquency were so entranced with the notion of the delinquent as a romantic rogue male challenging a rigid and unequal class structure, that they spent little time on middle-class delinquency, trivial offenders, or status offenders. Yet it is clear that the vast bulk of delinquent behavior is of this type.

Some have argued that such an imbalance in theoretical work is appropriate as minor misconduct, while troublesome, is not a threat to the safety and well-being of the community. This argument might be persuasive if two additional points could be established. One, that some small number of youth 'specialize' in serious criminal behavior while the rest commit only minor acts, and, two, that the juvenile court rapidly releases those youth that come into its purview for these minor offenses, thus reserving resources for the most serious youthful offenders.

The evidence is mixed on both of these points. Determined efforts to locate the 'serious juvenile offender' have failed to locate a group of offenders who specialize only in serious violent offenses. For example, in a recent analysis of a national self-report data set, Elliott and his associates noted 'there is little evidence for specialization in serious violent offending; to the contrary, serious violent offending appears to be embedded in a more general involvement in a wide range of serious and non-serious offenses' (Elliott, Huizinga, and Morse, 1987). Indeed, they went so far as to speculate that arrest histories that tend to highlight particular types of offenders reflect variations in police policy, practices, and processes of uncovering crime as well as underlying offending patterns.

More to the point, police and court personnel are, it turns out, far more interested in youth they charge with trivial or status offenses than anyone imagined. Efforts to deinstitutionalize 'status offenders,' for example, ran afoul of juvenile justice personnel who had little interest in releasing youth guilty of noncriminal offenses (Chesney-Lind, 1988). As has been established, much of this is a product of the system's history that encouraged court officers to involve themselves in the noncriminal behavior of youth in order to 'save' them from a variety of social ills.

Indeed, parallels can be found between the earlier Progressive period and current national efforts to challenge the deinstitutionalization components of the Juvenile Justice and Delinquency Prevention Act of 1974. These come complete with their celebration of family values and concerns about youthful independence. One of the arguments against the act has been that it allegedly gave children the 'freedom to run away' (Office of Juvenile Justice and Delinquency Prevention, 1985) and that it has hampered 'reunions' of 'missing' children with their parents (Office of Juvenile

Justice, 1986). Suspicions about teen sexuality are reflected in excessive concern about the control of teen prostitution and child pornography.

Opponents have also attempted to justify continued intervention into the lives of status offenders by suggesting that without such intervention, the youth would 'escalate' to criminal behavior. Yet there is little evidence that status offenders escalate to criminal offenses, and the evidence is particularly weak when considering female delinquents (particularly white female delinquents) (Datesman and Aickin, 1984). Finally, if escalation is occurring, it is likely the product of the justice system's insistence on enforcing status offense laws, thereby forcing youth in crisis to live lives of escaped criminals.

The most influential delinquency theories, however, have largely ducked the issue of status and trivial offenses and, as a consequence neg-

lected the role played by the agencies of official control (police, probation officers, juvenile court judges, detention home workers, and training school personnel) in the shaping of the 'delinquency problem.' When confronting the less than distinct picture that emerges from the actual distribution of delinquent behavior, however, the conclusion that agents of social control have considerable discretion in labeling or choosing not to label particular behavior as 'delinquent' is inescapable. This symbiotic relationship between delinquent behavior and the official response to that behavior is particularly critical when the question of female delinquency is considered.

> From M. Chesney-Lind, 'Girls, crime and woman's place: toward a feminist model of female delinquency', Crime and Delinquency, *1989, 35: 5–29.*

References

Chesney-Lind, Meda. 1971. *Female Juvenile Delinquency in Hawaii.* Master's thesis, University of Hawaii.

— 1973 'Judicial Enforcement of the Female Sex Role.' *Issues in Criminology* 3: 51–71.

— 1978. 'Young Women in the Arms of the Law.' In *Women, Crime and the Criminal Justice System,* edited by Lee H. Bowker. Boston: Lexington.

— 1988 'Girls and Deinstitutionalization: Is Juvenile justice Still Sexist?' *Journal of Criminal Justice Abstracts* 20: 144–165.

Cloward, Richard A. and Lloyd F. Ohlin. 1960. *Delinquency and Opportunity.* New York: Free Press.

Cohen, Albert K. 1955. *Delinquent Boys: The Culture of the Gang.* New York: Free Press.

Datesman, Susan and Mikel Aickin. 1984. 'Offense Specialization and Escalation Among Status Offenders,' *Journal of Criminal Law and Criminology* 75: 1246–1275.

Elliott, Delbert, David Huizinga, and Barbara Morse. 1987. 'A Career Analysis of Serious Violent Offenders.' In *Violent Juvenile Crime: What Can We Do About It?* edited by Ira Schwartz. Minneapolis, MN: Hubert Humphrey Institute.

Feinman, Clarice, 1980. *Women in the Criminal Justice System.* New York: Praeger.

Freedman, Estelle. 1981. *Their Sisters' Keepers.* Ann Arbor: University of Michigan Press.

Gelsthorpe, Loraine. 1986. 'Towards a Sceptical Look at Sexisms.' *International Journal of the Sociology of Law* 14: 125–152,

Hagan, John, A.R. Gillis, and John Simpson. 1985. 'The Class Structure of Gender and Delinquency: Toward

a Power-Control Theory of Common Delinquent Behavior.' *American Journal of Sociology* 90: 1151–1178.

Merton, Robert K. 1938. 'Social Structure and Anomie.' *American Sociological Review* 3 (October): 672–682.

Messerschmidt, James 1987. 'Feminism, Criminology, and the Rise of the Female Sex Delinquent, 1880–1930.' *Contemporary Crises* 11: 243–263.

Morris, Ruth. 1964. 'Female Delinquency and Relational Problems,' *Social Forces* 43: 82–89.

Office of Juvenile Justice and Delinquency Prevention. 1985. *Runaway Children and the Juvenile Justice and Delinquency Prevention Act: What is the impact?* Washington, DC: Government Printing Office.

— 1986. *America's Missing and Exploited Children. Report and Recommendations of the U. S. Attorney General's Advisory Board on Missing Children.* Washington, DC: Government Printing Office.

Platt, Anthony M. 1969. *The Childsavers.* Chicago: University of Chicago Press.

Rafter, Nicole Hahn. 1985. *Partial Justice.* Boston: Northeastern University Press.

Rogers, Kristine. 1972. 'For Her Own Protection ...': Conditions of Incarceration for Female Juvenile Offenders in the State of Connecticut', *Law and Society Review* (Winter): 223–246.

Schlossman, Steven and Stephanie Wallach. 1978. 'The Crime of Precocious Sexuality: Female Juvenile Delinquency in the Progressive Era.' *Harvard Educational Review* 4 8: 65–94.

Shaw, Clifford R. 1930. *The Jack-Roller.* Chicago: University of Chicago Press.

— 1938. *Brothers in Crime*. Chicago: University of Chicago Press.

— and Henry D. McKay. 1942. *Juvenile Delinquency in Urban Areas*. Chicago: University of Chicago Press.

Shelden, Randall. 1981. 'Sex Discrimination in the Juvenile Justice System: Memphis, Tennessee, 1900–1917.' *In Comparing Female and Male Offenders*, edited by Marguerite Q. Warren. Beverly Hills, CA: Sage.

Smith, Lesley Shacklady. 1978. 'Sexist Assumptions and Female Delinquency.' In *Women, Sexuality and Social Control*, edited by Carol Smart and Barry Smart. London: Routledge & Kegan Paul.

Sutherland, Edwin, 1978, 'Differential Association.' In *Children of Ishmael: Critical Perspectives on Juvenile Justice*, edited by Barry Krisberg and James Austin. Palo Alto, CA: Mayfield.

Thrasher, Frederic M. 1927. *The Gang*. Chicago: University of Chicago Press.

15.3 Feminism and criminology
Kathleen Daly and Meda Chesney-Lind

The last decade has seen an outpouring of feminist scholarship in the academy. Theories, research methods, and pedagogies have been challenged across the disciplines (e.g., Abel and Abel 1983; Bowles and Klein 1983; Cuiley and Portuges 1985; DuBois, Kelly, Kennedy, Korsmeyer, and Robinson 1985; Griffin and Hoffman 1986; Harding and Hintikka 1983; Klein 1987; Sherman and Beck 1979; Spender 1981; Stanley and Wise 1983). Feminist thought has deepened and broadened. Whereas in the early years of second-wave feminism[1] there was a collective sense of a 'we' to feminist theorizing, today postmodern thought and 'fractured identities' have decentered feminism (Ackoff 1988; Flax 1987; Harding 1986). Previously the emphasis was on women gaining equality with men within existing social institutions, but today feminist thought emphasizes a new vision of the social order in which women's experiences and ways of knowing are brought to the fore, not suppressed (Gross 1986). Theories and concepts rooted in men's experience formerly monopolized intellectual inquiry, but today disciplinary debates in some fields reflect the impact of feminist thought, albeit uneven, across the disciplines (Stacey and Thorne 1985).

How has criminology been affected by these developments? With the exception of feminist treatments of rape and intimate violence, the field remains essentially untouched. The time has come for criminologists to step into the world of feminist thought and for feminist scholars to move more boldly into all areas of criminology. This task will not be easy; we write as feminists interested in problems of crime and justice, and find that we lead a double life. As feminists,[2] we grapple with the many strands of feminist thought and activism, educate ourselves and others about the impact of gender relations on social life, and ponder our role as academics in a social movement. As criminologists, we grapple with the field's many theoretical and policy strands, educate ourselves and others on the conditions and social processes that make crime normal and deviant, and ponder the state's role in creating and reducing crime. All the while we wonder if it is possible to reconcile these double lives.

Myths about feminism

One difficulty in educating students and colleagues about feminism is that myths about the subject abound. We address three of these myths: feminist analyses are not objective, feminist analyses focus narrowly on women, and there is only one feminist perspective.

Myth 1: Lack of Objectivity
A major element of feminist thought centers on how gender constructs – the network of behaviors and identities associated with masculinity and femininity – are socially constructed from relations of dominance and inequality between men and women. Different natures, talents, and interests that define Western notions of manhood and womanhood rest on a number of male-centered oppositions to and negations of women and femininity. Masculinity and men are not only defined as not feminine, but also as superior to femininity and to women.

We will not discuss *why* gender relations took this form,[4] but instead will sketch some of the effects. In Western thought, depictions of men's and women's natures have been made almost exclusively by men (specifically by white, privileged men). As a consequence, these men's experience and intellectual stance have dominated explanations of gender difference and men's superiority. This situation led Poulain de la Barre, a seventeenth-century writer, to observe, 'All that has been written about women by men should be suspect, for the men are at once judge and party to the lawsuit' (cited in de Beauvoir 1961: xxi). It is plain that men can be no more objective than women (and nonfeminist views no more objective than feminist) about the character of gender relations, the qualities of gender difference, or the organization of social life. In fact, some thinkers argue that women's marginality affords them keener insights (Collins 1986; Rohrlich-Leavitt, Sykes and Weatherford 1975; Smith 1979), a perspective reminiscent of sociologists' (or other outsiders') claims to greater understanding because of their marginal status.

One consequence of male-centered (or androcentric) systems of knowledge is inaccurate readings of human history, evolution, and behavior, although these are presented as objective and authoritative depictions of the human condition. The central problem is that men's experiences are taken as the norm and are generalized to the population. For example, theories of the evolution of 'mankind' are precisely that: theories of how bipedalism and expanded brain size resulted from men's cooperation, toolmaking, and tool use in the hunting of large game. This approach led feminist anthropologists to ask, 'Have only men evolved?' (Hubbard 1982; Slocum 1975). Similarly, feminist historians questioned the basis for historical periodization by asking, 'Did women have a Renaissance?' (Kelly-Gadol 1977).

Some scholars propose a way to legitimate women's claims to knowledge with the concept of 'women's standpoint,' which Jaggar (1983: 370) argues is 'epistemologically advantageous' and 'provides the basis for a view of reality that is more impartial than that of the ruling class.' Other forms of knowledge seeking are used or advocated (see Harding 1986), but a major feminist project today is to expose the distortions and assumptions of androcentric science (e.g., Bleier 1984; Fee 1981; Keller 1984). These efforts reveal that an ideology of objectivity can serve to mask men's gender loyalties as well as loyalties to other class or racial groups. Thus when feminist analyses are dismissed because they are said to lack objectivity or to be biased toward women's viewpoints, we are bewildered and vexed. Bemused by other people's apparent inability to hear alternate accounts of social life, we wonder whether feminists can even be heard. Such frustration is compounded by knowing that the dominant paradigms and modes of inquiry are *a priori* accorded greater legitimacy.

Myth 2: The Narrow Focus on Women
When feminists analyze women's situation and the ways in which gender relations structure social life, they do not ignore men and masculinity, although they may displace men as the central (or sole) actors and may give more attention to women. This approach spawns a perception by men that they are being neglected, misunderstood, or cast as the ignominious 'other,' a reaction akin to that of white people toward critical analyses of race or ethnic relations. Both perceptions express a sense of entitlement about whose social reality is worthy of description and explanation, and who can be trusted to get it right.

Much feminist attention has been devoted to the ways in which men think, theorize, and collect and marshal evidence. It is impossible to understand women's situation and gender relations without examining masculinity, men's lives, and men's viewpoints. The irony is that feminist scholarship is characterized as being only about women or as hopelessly biased toward women, when in fact the project is to describe and change both men's and women's lives. By contrast, nonfeminist scholarship is more narrow, focusing as it does on the lives and concerns of men without problematizing gender relations or men as a social group. Moreover, *all* social institutions and social phenomena are 'women's issues' and thus subject to feminist inquiry. Furthermore, as we will argue, not all feminist analyses are put forth by women, nor is all research conducted on women or on gender difference *ipso facto* feminist.

Myth 3: The Feminist Analysis
To talk of *the* feminist analysis of a given social phenomenon is to talk nonsense. To assume that there is only one feminist analysis reveals a speaker's naiveté about the diverse views that characterize contemporary feminist thinking and strategies for social change. A more accurate way to describe feminist thought is as a *set of perspectives*,

which are linked in turn to different assumptions about the causes of gender inequality. These perspectives (or frameworks) include liberal, radical, Marxist, and socialist feminist. [...] There are other ways to categorize feminist thought (e.g., Banks 1981); some are humorous (Oakley 1981: 336-37), and differences exist within any one feminist perspective (see, e.g., Eisenstein 1983 on radical feminism; Sargeant 1981 on socialist feminism). Because the dominant voice of American feminism is white, middle-class, first-world, and heterosexual, modified feminisms (such as black, Chicana, Asian-American, Jewish, lesbian, and others) reflect racial, ethnic, cultural, and sexual specificities (Cole 1986; Darty and Potter 1984; Hooks 1981, 1984; Joseph and Lewis 1981; Moraga and Anzaldúa 1983; Smith 1983). In short, the ferment and debate among feminist scholars and activists today can no longer be contained within or characterized accurately as one perspective.

In assessing these myths about feminist thought, we offer a partial view of feminism and feminist inquiry by describing what they are not. Feminist investigations are not limited to women, nor are feminist analyses any less objective than nonfeminist. Different views of gender arrangements and the specific ways in which class, race and ethnicity, religion, sexuality, and so forth intersect in women's lives yield multiple analyses and visions for social change. Is there any common ground, then, to feminist thought? What distinguishes a feminist from a nonfeminist analysis?

Defining feminism

What is feminism?

In their introduction to *What is Feminism?* Mitchell and Oakley (1986: 3) suggest that it is 'easier to define feminism in its absence rather than its presence.' Delmar (1986) offers a 'baseline definition' on which feminists and nonfeminists might agree: a feminist holds that women suffer discrimination because of their sex, that they have needs which are negated and unsatisfied, and that the satisfaction of these needs requires a radical change. 'But beyond that,' Delmar says, 'things immediately become more complicated' (1986: 8).

This complication arises because feminism is a set of theories about women's oppression *and* a set of strategies for social change. Cott (1987) identifies the paradoxes of first-wave feminism (the 'woman movement' in the nineteenth and early twentieth centuries), which reflect the merging of

these theoretical and political impulses. These paradoxes include acknowledging diversity among women but claiming women's unity, requiring gender consciousness but calling for an eradication of gender-based distinctions and divisions, and aiming for individual freedom and autonomy by mobilizing a mass-based movement. The same paradoxical elements are seen in second-wave feminism (the contemporary women's movement beginning in the 1960s). Unfriendly interpretations of these contrary tendencies include, 'These women don't know what they want' or 'They want it both ways.' Yet as Harding (1986: 244) suggests, 'The problem is that we [feminists] do not know and should not know just what we want to say about a number of conceptual choices with which we are presented – except that the choices themselves create no-win dilemmas for our feminisms.' The task of describing and changing a spectrum of women's experiences, which have been formed by particular and often competing allegiances to class, race, and other social groups, is not straightforward but a blurred and contingent enterprise.

Distinguishing feminist from nonfeminist analyses

It is not easy to know when a work or action is feminist. Delmar asks, for example, 'Are all actions and campaigns prompted or led by women, feminist?' (1986: 11). 'Can an action be "feminist" even if those who perform it are not?' (1986: 12). She contrasts several views of feminism. It may be diffuse activity, any action motivated out of concern for women's interests, whether or not actors or groups acknowledge them as feminist. This view empties feminism of any meaning because all actions or analyses having women as their object fall into the same category. Delmar opts instead for another approach, which is to 'separate feminism and feminists from the multiplicity of those concerned with women's issues.' Feminism can be defined as a field – even though diverse – but feminists can 'make no claim to an exclusive interest in or copyright over problems affecting women' (1986: 13).

Neither a scholar's gender nor the focus of scholarship – whether women, gender difference, or anything else – can be used to distinguish feminist, nonfeminist, or even antifeminist works. Scholars' theoretical and methodological points of view are defined by the way in which they frame questions and interpret results, not by the social phenomenon alone. Thus to Morris's (1987: 15) question – 'Does feminist criminology include criminologists who are feminist, female criminologists, or criminologists who study women' – we reply that research on women or on gender difference, whether conducted by a male or a female criminologist, does not in itself qualify it as feminist. Conversely, feminist inquiry is not limited to topics on or about women; it focuses on men as well. For criminology, because most offenders and criminal justice officials are men, this point is especially relevant; allied social institutions such as the military have not escaped feminist scrutiny (Enloe 1983, 1987). When feminist, nonfeminist, or not-really-feminist distinctions are drawn, the main source of variation is how inclusively scholars (or activists) define a continuum of feminist thought.

Pateman (1986), for example, compares theories addressing 'women's issues' with those that are 'distinctly feminist.' She terms the former 'domesticated feminism' and sees it in liberal and socialist thought when scholars try to fit women or gender relations into existing theories, making 'feminism… safe for academic theory' (1986: 4). Such efforts deny that 'sexual domination is at issue, or that feminism raises a problem [patriarchy], which is repressed in other theories' (1986: 5). A more distinctive feminist approach assumes that individuals are gendered, and that 'individuality is not a unitary abstraction but an embodied and sexually differentiated expression of the unity of humankind' (1986: 9).

The implications of a distinctive feminist approach are profound – in Pateman's and others' words, 'subversive' – for social, political, criminological, and other theories. It is one thing to say that women have been excluded from general theories of social phenomenon. It is another matter to wonder how theories would appear if they were fashioned from women's experiences and if women had a central place in them. In addition, it is equally important to query the gender-specific character of existing theories fashioned from men's experiences.

Although some scholars (typically, liberal and Marxist feminists who do not accord primacy to gender or to patriarchal relations) assume that previous theory can be corrected by including women, others reject this view, arguing that a reconceptualization of analytic categories is necessary. Working toward a reinvention of theory is a major task for feminists today. Although tutored in 'male-stream' theory and methods,[5] they work within and against these structures of knowledge to ask new questions, to put old problems in a fresh light, and to challenge the cherished wisdom of their disciplines. Such rethinking comes in many varieties, but these five elements of feminist thought distinguish it from other types of social and political thought:

- Gender is not a natural fact but a complex social, historical, and cultural product; it is related to, but not simply derived from, biological sex difference and reproductive capacities.
- Gender and gender relations order social life and social institutions in fundamental ways.
- Gender relations and constructs of masculinity and femininity are not symmetrical but are based on an organizing principle of men's superiority and social and political-economic dominance over women.
- Systems of knowledge reflect men's views of the natural and social world; the production of knowledge is gendered.
- Women should be at the center of intellectual inquiry, not peripheral, invisible, or appendages to men.

These elements take different spins, depending on how a scholar conceptualizes gender, the causes of gender inequality, and the means of social change. Generally, however, a feminist analysis draws from feminist theories or research, problematizes gender, and considers the implications of findings for empowering women or for change in gender relations. Finally, we note that scholars may think of themselves as feminists in their personal lives, but they may not draw on feminist theory or regard themselves as feminist scholars. For personal or professional reasons (or both), they may shy away from being marked as a particular kind of scholar.

The relevance of feminist thought to criminology

What can feminist thought bring to studies of crime and justice? Sophistication in thinking about gender relations is one obvious contribution. Unfortunately, most criminologists draw on unexplicated folk models of gender and gender difference, or do not even consider the impact of gender relations on men's behavior. It is common to hear, for example, that because theories of crime exclude women, we can rectify the problem by adding women. It is even more common to find that theories are developed and tested using male-only samples without any reflection on whether concepts or results may be gender-specific. We suggest first that efforts to overcome these persistent problems must start with a conceptual framework for gender and gender relations. The four feminist perspectives (in addition to the traditional perspective) offer a comparative foothold. Each makes different assumptions about men's and women's relations to each other and to the social order; therefore each may pose different questions, use different methods, and offer distinctive interpretations. These perspectives have been applied in other areas of sociological, economic, psychological, and political philosophical inquiry (Andersen 1983; Jagger 1983; Kahn and Jean 1981; Sokoloff 1980; Tong 1984); thus why not in criminology, which borrows from these disciplines in varying degrees and combinations? In fact, we would put the case more strongly: we see no other means of comparing and evaluating efforts to include gender in theories of crime, to explain men's or women's crime, or to assess criminal justice policy and practices, among other foci of criminological inquiry, without explicit reference to these perspectives. We will give examples to illustrate our point throughout this essay.

Second, criminologists need not engage in surmise or guesswork about women's experiences. Again, it has become common to take the field to task for its distorted representations of women (this situation also holds true for men, but perhaps to a lesser extent). One obvious remedy is to read feminist journals[6] and books that offer studies of women's and men's lives and provide the structural and social contexts for their behavior. Criminologists must depart from the narrow confines of their discipline and its journals; otherwise we will continue to suffer from common-sense and *ad hoc* interpretations of data, as well as poorly informed research questions.

Third, criminologists should begin to appreciate that their discipline and its questions are a product of white, economically privileged men's experiences. We are not suggesting some simpleminded conspiracy theory; conscious intent would be hard to prove, and ultimately it is beside the point. Rather, we note simply who the scholars and practitioners have been over the last few centuries. Turning to the future, we wonder what will happen as increasing numbers of white women, as well as men and women of color, enter the discipline and try to find their place in it. One cannot expect that the first generation of new scholars will be confident or sure-footed after centuries of exclusion from the academy. One might expect,

however, that we will ask different questions or pursue problems which our discipline has ignored. These differences must be heard and nurtured, not suppressed. To be sure, the generational relations of elder and younger white men are also fraught with conflict, but that conflict occurs on a common ground of shared experiences and understandings. It is familiar terrain; the older men see bits of themselves in their younger male colleagues. By contrast, our differences with the mainstream of the discipline are likely to break new ground.

Finally, points of congruence exist between feminist perspectives and other social and political theories, and consequently between feminist perspectives and theoretical trajectories in criminology. Much of what is termed mainstream criminology easily embraces a liberal feminist perspective. The critical and Marxist criminologies have affinities with radical, Marxist, and socialist feminist perspectives. More can be done to exploit and contrast these points of affinity. Not surprisingly, the sharpest feminist critique today is leveled at the varieties of leftist criminology precisely because they hold the greatest promise for incorporating class, race, and gender relations in theories of crime and justice,

This feminist critique has been aired mostly, but not exclusively, in British criminology (see Gelsthorpe and Morris 1988; Heidensohn 1985, 1987; Messerschmidt 1986; Morris 1987); it may foster a larger coalition of men and women seeking a transformation, not simply a correction, of criminology.

Can there be a feminist criminology?

Morris (1987: 17) asserts that 'a feminist criminology cannot exist' because neither feminism nor criminology is a 'unified set of principles and practices.' We agree. Feminists engaged in theory and research in criminology may work within one of the feminist perspectives; thus, like feminist thought generally, feminist criminology cannot be a monolithic enterprise. We also agree with Morris's observation that 'the writings of Adler and Simon do not constitute a feminist criminology' (p. 16). Yet we think it important to identify Simon's and Adler's arguments as liberal feminist, to assess them on those terms, and to compare them with analyses adopting other feminist perspectives. Similarly, in the debates between radical and socialist feminists about controlling men's violence toward women, one can evaluate their different assumptions of gender and sexuality. A single feminist analysis across many crime and justice issues is not possible, but that fact does not preclude a criminologist who uses feminist theory or research from calling herself (or himself) a feminist criminologist. It's a convenient rubric, but only as long as criminologists appreciate its multiple meanings.

Feminist theories and research should be part of any criminologist's approach to the problems of crime and justice. They demonstrate that a focus on gender can be far more than a focus on women or sexism in extant theories. They offer an opportunity to study still-unexplored features of men's crime and forms of justice, as well as modes of theory construction and verification. In tracing the impact of feminist thought on studies of crime and justice, we find that the promise of feminist inquiry barely has been realized.

Notes

1   First-wave feminism (termed 'the woman movement') arose in the United States and in some European countries in conjunction with the movement to abolish slavery. Its beginning in the United States is typically marked by the Seneca Falls, New York, convention (1848), and its ending by the passage of the 19th Amendment to the United States Constitution (granting women's suffrage), coupled with the falling-out among women activists over the Equal Rights Amendment proposed in the early 1920s. See DuBois (1981) for the nineteenth-century context, Cott (1987) for the early twentieth-century context when the term 'feminist' was first used, Giddings (1984) for black women's social movement activity, Kelly-Gadol (1982) for 'pro-woman' writers in the four centuries before the nineteenth century, and Kimmell (1987) for men's responses to feminism. Second-wave American feminism emerged in the mid-1960s in conjunction with the civil rights

movement, the new left, and a critical mass of professional women (see Evans 1979; Hooks 1981, 1984). It has not ended (but see Stacey 1987 for an analysis of 'postfeminist' consciousness). Note that the conventional dating of the first- and second-wave is rightly challenged by several scholars who find greater continuity in feminist consciousness and action (Cott 1987; Delmar 1986; Kelly-Gadol 1982),

2   As we make clear later, the kind of feminist perspective we take is socialist feminist, which colors our commentary throughout this essay.

3   We focus primarily on criminology in the United States, although we include the work of feminist criminologists in other countries, especially Great Britain. See Gelsthorpe and Morris (1988) for an analysis of feminism and criminology in Britain.

4   There are different explanations for the emergence of patriarchy, as well as disputes over the definition of the term and over the degree of women's agency in and resistance to gender oppression; almost all are Eurocentric. We think it unlikely that any one set of 'causes' can be identified through many cultures and nation states, and across millennia. See Lerner (1986) for a recent bold effort and a discussion of central concepts in feminist thought.

5   We are uncertain who introduced the concept 'male-stream' because citations vary. *The Feminist Dictionary* (Kramarae and Treichler 1985: 244) says 'coined by Mary Daly,' but does not say where.

6   Some American feminist journals are *Signs: Journal of Women in Culture and Society, Feminist Studies, Gender and Society*, and *Women and Politics*; others, such as the *International Journal of Women's Studies* and *Women's Studies International Forum*, take a more international focus; a journal for 'pro-feminist' men is *Changing Men*. A new journal with an international and feminist focus on crime and justice, *Women and Criminal Justice*, will appear in 1989.

From K. Daly and M. Chesney-Lind, 'Feminism and criminology', Justice Quarterly, *1988, 5: 497–538.*

References

Abel, Elizabeth and Emily K. Abel, eds. (1983) *The Signs Reader: Women, Gender, and Scholarship*. Chicago: University of Chicago Press.

Ackoff, Linda (1988) 'Cultural Feminism versus Post-Structuralism.' *Signs: Journal of Women in Culture and Society* 13(3): 406–36.

Andersen, Margaret L. (1983) *Thinking About Women. Sociological and Feminist Perspectives*. New York: Macmillan.

Banks, Olive (1981) *Faces of Feminism*. Oxford, UK: Martin Robertson.

Beauvoir, Simone de (1949) *The Second Sex*. Translated and edited by H.M. Parshley, 1952 (Knopf). *Page reference to 1961 Bantam edition.* New York: Bantam.

Bleier, Ruth (1984) *Science and Gender: A Critique of Biology and Its Theories on Women*. New York: Pergamon.

Bowles, Gloria and Renate D. Klein, eds. (1983) *Theories of Women's Studies*, Boston: Routledge and Kegan Paul.

Cole, Johnnetta B., ed. (1986) *All American Women: Lines That Divide: Ties That Bind*. New York: Free Press.

Collins, Patricia Hill (1936) 'Learning from the Outsider Within: The Sociological Significance of Black Feminist Thought' *Social Problems* 33(6): 14–32.

Cott, Nancy (1987) *The Grounding of Modern Feminism*. New Haven: Yale University Press.

Culley, Margo and Catherine Portuges, eds. (1985) *Gendered Subjects: The Dynamics of Feminist Teaching*. Boston: Routledge and Kegan Paul.

Darty, Trude and Sandee Potter, eds. (1984) *Women-Identified Women*. Palo Alto: Mayfield.

Delmar, Rosalind (1986) 'What Is Feminism' In Juliet Mitchell and Ann Oakley (eds.), *What is Feminism?* New York: Pantheon, pp. 8–33.

Donovan, Josephine (1985) *Feminist Theory: The Intellectual Traditions of American Feminism*. New York: Ungar.

DuBois, Ellen Carol, Gail Paradise Kelly, Elizabeth Lapovsky Kennedy, Carolyn W. Korsmeyer, and Lillian S. Robinson (1985) *Feminist Scholarship: Kindling in the Groves of Academe*. Urbana: University of Illinois Press.

Eisenstein, Hester (1983) *Contemporary Feminist Thought*. Boston: G.K. Hall.

Enloe, Cynthia H. (1983) *Does Khaki Become You? The Militarization of Women's Lives*. Boston: South End.

Fee, Elizabeth (1981) 'Is Feminism a Threat to Scientific Objectivity?' *International Journal of Women's Studies* 4(4): 378–92.

Flax, Jane (1937) 'Postmodernism and Gender Relations in Feminist Theory?' *Signs: Journal of Women in Culture and Society* 12(4): 621–43.

Gelsthorpe, Loraine and Allison Morris (1288) 'Feminism and Criminology in Britain.' *British Journal of Criminology* 28(2): 223–40.

Griffin, Jean Thomas, and Nancy Hoffman, eds. (1986) 'Teaching About Women, Race, and Culture.' *Women's Studies Quarterly* 14(1–2).

Gross, Elizabeth (1986) 'What Is Feminist Theory?' In Carole Pateman and Elizabeth Gross (eds.), *Feminist Challenges: Social and Political Theory*. Boston: Northeastern University Press, pp. 190–204.

Harding, Sandra (1986) *The Science Question in Feminism*. Ithaca: Cornell University Press.

Harding, Sandra and Merrill Hintikka, eds. (1933) *Discovering Reality: Feminist Perspectives on Epistemology, Metaphysics, Methodology and Philosophy of Science*. Boston: Reidel.

Heidensohn, Frances M. (1985) *Women and Crime. The Life of the Female Offender*. New York: New York University Press.

—— (1987) 'Women and Crime: Questions for Criminology.' In Pat Carlen and Anne Worrall (eds.), *Gender, Crime and Justice*. Philadelphia Open University Press, pp. 16–21.

Hooks, Bell (1981) *Ain't I a Woman?* Boston: South End.

—— (1984) *Feminist Theory: From Margin to Center*. Boston: South End.

Hubbard, Ruth (1982) 'Have Only Men Evolved?' In Ruth Hubbard, M.S. Henifin, and Barbara Fried (eds.), *Biological Woman – The Convenient Myth*. Cambridge, MA: Schenkman, pp. 17–46.

Jaggar, Alison M. (1923) *Feminist Politics and Human Nature*. Totowa, NJ: Bowman and Allenheld.

Jaggar, Allison M. and Paula & Rothenberg, eds. (1984) *Feminist Frameworks: Alternative Theoretical Accounts of the Relations between Men and Women*. 2nd edition. New York: McGraw-Hill.

Joseph, Gloria I. and Jill Lewis (1981) *Common Differences: Conflicts in Black and White Feminist Perspectives*. Boston: South End.

Kahn, Arnold S. and Paula J. Jean (1983) 'Integration and Elimination or Separation and Redefinition: The Future of the Psychology of Women.' *Signs: Journal of Women in Culture and Society* 8(4): 659–71.

Keller, Evelyn Fox (1984) *Reflections on Gender and Science*. New Haven: Yale University Press.

Kelly-Gadol, Joan (1977) 'Did Women Have a Renaissance?' Reprinted 1987 in Renate Bridenthal, Claudia Koonz, and Susan Stuard, eds. *Becoming Visible: Women in European History*. 2nd edition. Boston: Houghton Mifflin, pp. 175–201.

Klein, Dorie (1973) 'The Etiology of Female Crime: A Review of the Literature.' *Issues in Criminology* 8: 3–30.

Kramarae, Cheris and Paula A. Treichler (1985) *A Feminist Dictionary*. Boston: Pandora/Routledge and Kegan Paul.

Messerschmidt, James W. (1986) *Capitalism, Patriarchy, and Crime: Toward a Socialist Feminist Criminology*. Totowa, NJ: Bowman and Littlefield.

Miller, Eleanor M. (1986) *Street Woman*. Philadelphia: Temple University Press.

Millman, Marcia (1975) 'She Did It All for Love: A Feminist View of the Sociology of Deviance.' In Marcia Millman and Rosabeth Moss Kanter (eds), *Another Voice: Feminist Perspectives on Social Life and Social Science*. Garden City, NY: Anchor Doubleday, pp. 25149.

Mitchell, Juliet and Ann Oakley, eds. (1986) *What is Feminism?* New York: Pantheon.

Moore, Joan W. (1978) *Homeboys: Gangs, Drugs, and Prison in the Barrios of Los Angeles*. Philadelphia: Temple University Press.

Moraga, Cherrie and Gloria Anzaldúa, eds. (1983) *This Bridge Called My Back': Writings by Radical Women of Color*. 2nd edition. New York: Kitchen Table/ Women of Color.

Morris, Allison (1987) *Women, Crime and Criminal Justice*. New York: Blackwell.

Oakley, Ann (1981) *Subject Women*. New York: Pantheon.

Pateman, Carole (1986) 'The Theoretical Subversiveness of Feminism.' In Carole Pateman and Elizabeth Gross (eds.), *Feminist Challenges: Social and Political Theory*. Boston: Northeastern University Press, pp. 1–10.

Rohrlich-Leavitt, Ruby, Barbara Sykes, and Elizabeth Weatherford (1975) 'Aboriginal Woman: Male and Female Anthropological Perspectives.' In Rayna R. Reiter (ed.), *Toward an Anthropology of Women*. New York: Monthly Review Press, pp. 110–26.

Sherman, Julia A. and Evelyn Torton Beck, eds. (1979) *The Prism of Sex: Essays in the Sociology of Knowledge*. Madison: University of Wisconsin Press.

Slocum, Sally (1975) 'Woman the Gatherer: Male Bias in Anthropology.' In Rayna R. Reiter (ed.), *Toward an Anthropology of Women*. New York: Monthly Review Press, pp. 36–50.

Smith, Barbara, ed. (1983) *Home Girls. A Black Feminist Anthology*. New York: Kitchen Table/Women of Color.

Smith, Dorothy E. (1979) 'A Sociology for Women.' In Julia A. Sherman and Evelyn Torton Beck (eds.), *The Prism of Sex. Essays in the Sociology of Knowledge*. Madison: University of Wisconsin Press, pp. 135–87.

Sokoloff, Natalie J. (1980) *Between Money and Love: The Dialectics of Women's Home and Market Work*. New York: Praeger.

Spender, Dale, ed. (1981) *Men's Studies Modified: The Impact of Feminism on the Academic Disciplines*. New York: Pergamon.

Stacey, Judith and Barrie Thorne (1285) 'The Missing Feminist Revolution in Sociology.' *Social Problems* 32(4): 301–16.

Stanley, Liz and Sue Wise (1983) *Breaking Out. Feminist Consciousness and Feminist Research*. Boston: Routledge and Kegan Paul.

Tong, Rosemary (1984) *Women, Sex, and the Law*. Totowa, NJ: Rowman and Allanheld.

15.4 Feminist approaches to criminology or postmodern woman meets atavistic man Carol Smart

The problem of criminology

The appliance of science

It is a story that has been told many times (although most effectively in *The New Criminology* (Taylor *et al.*, 1973)) that criminology is an applied discipline which searches for the causes of crime in order to eradicate the problem. Admittedly, criminology as a subject embraces much more than this. For example, it tends to focus also on the operations of the criminal justice system, the relationship between the police and communities or systems of punishment. However, such topics fit just as easily under the rubric of the sociology of law or even philosophy. What is unique about criminology, indeed its defining characteristic, is the central question of the causes of crime and the ultimate focus of the 'offender' rather than on mechanisms of discipline and regulation which go beyond the limits of the field of crime. It is this defining characteristic with which I wish to take issue here. Arguably, it is this which creates a kind of vortex in this area of intellectual endeavour. It is the ultimate question against which criminology is judged. Can the causes of

crime be identified and explained? Moreover, once identified, can they be modified?

Criminologies of the traditional schools have been unashamedly interventionist in aim if not always in practice. This goal was criticized by the radical criminologists of the 1970s for being oppressive, conservative and narrowly partisan (that is, on the side of the state and/or powerful). Moreover, the radicals argued that the traditional criminologists had, in any case, got their theories wrong. Crime, it was argued, could not be explained by chromosomal imbalance, hereditary factors, working-class membership, racial difference, intelligence and so on. So, among the many errors of traditional criminology, the two main ones to be identified were an inherent conservatism and inadequate theorization. The repudiation of these errors was condensed into the most critically damning term of abuse – positivist. To be positivist embodied everything that was bad. Positivism, like functionalism, had to be sought out, exposed and eliminated. Now, in some respects I would agree with this; but the problem we face is whether critical criminologies or the more recent left realist criminologies have transcended the problem of positivism or whether they have merely projected it on to their political opponents while assuming that they themselves are untainted.

I would argue that positivism is misconstrued if its main problem is seen as its connection to a conservative politics or a biological determinism. The problem of positivism is arguably less transparent than this and lies in the basic presumption that we can establish a verifiable knowledge or truth about events: in particular, that we can establish a causal explanation which will in turn provide us with objective methods for intervening in the events defined as problematic. Given this formulation, positivism may be, at the level of political orientation, either socialist or reactionary. The problem of positivism is, therefore, not redeemed by the espousal of left politics. Positivism poses an epistemological problem; it is not a simple problem of party membership.

It is this problem of epistemology which has begun to attract the attention of feminist scholarship (the postmodern woman of my title). Feminism is now raising significant questions about the status and power of knowledge (Weedon, 1987; Harding, 1986) and formulating challenges to modes of totalizing or grand theorizing which impose a uniformity of perspective and ignore the immense diversity of subjectivities of women and men. This has in turn led to a questioning of whether 'scientific' work can ever provide a basis for intervention as positivism would presuppose. This is not to argue that intervention is inevitably undesirable or impossible, but rather to challenge the modernist assumption that, once we have the theory ('master' narrative (Kellner, 1988)) which will explain all forms of social behaviour, we will also know what to do and that the rightness of this 'doing' will be verifiable and transparent.

The continuing search for the theory, the cause and the solution

It is useful to concentrate on the work of Jock Young as a main exponent of left realism in criminology. His work is particularly significant because, unlike many other left thinkers, he has remained inside criminology and, while acknowledging many of the problems of his earlier stance in critical criminology, has sustained a commitment to the core element of the subject. That is to say he addresses the question of the causes of crime and the associated problems of attempting to devise policies to reduce crime. For example, he states:

> It is time for us to *compete* in policy terms... the major task of radical criminology is to seek a solution to the problem of crime and that of a socialist policy is to substantially reduce the crime rate. (1986: 28, emphasis in the original)

This is compelling stuff but it is precisely what I want to argue is problematic about the new forms of radical criminology for feminism. It might be useful initially to outline Young's position before highlighting some of the problems it poses.

As part of his call for a left realist criminology, Young (1986) constructs a version of the recent history of post-war criminology. He sees it as a series of crises and failures (and in this respect we are at one). He points to the positivist heritage of post-war criminology in Britain which, in his account, amounts to a faith in medicine and cure and/or a reliance on biologically determinist explanations of crime. He sees the influence of North American criminology in a positive light (for example, Cohen, 1955; Cloward and Ohlin, 1961; Matza, 1969) and then turns to the work of the 'new criminologists' in Britain who constructed a political paradigm in which to reappraise criminal behaviour. He is, however, critical of the idealism of this work and interprets it as the 'seedbed' of more radical work to come rather than a real challenge to mainstream orthodoxy or an adequate account in and of itself.

The failures of the criminological enterprise overall which Young identifies are twofold. The first is the failure 'really' to explain criminal behaviour. The theories are always flawed either ontologically or politically. The second is the failure to solve the problem of crime or even to stem its rise. These are not two separate failures, however, as the failure to stop crime is 'proof' of the failure of the theories to explain the causes of crime. Young argues:

> All of the factors which should have led to a drop in delinquency if mainstream criminology were even half-correct, were being ameliorated and yet precisely the opposite effect was occurring. (1986: 5–6)

It is through this linkage between theory and policy that the positivism of the left realists comes to light. The problem is not that there is a commitment to reducing the misery to which crime is often wedded, nor is the problem that socialists (and feminists) want policies which are less punitive and oppressive. The problem is that science is held to have the answer if only it is scientific enough. Here is revealed the faith in the totalizing theory, the 'master' narrative which will eventually – when sufficient scales have fallen from our eyes or sufficient connections have been made – allow us to see things for what they really are.

To return to Young's story, we pick up the unfolding of criminology at the point of intervention by the new criminologists. Young points out that while this intervention may have excited the academic criminologists there was simultaneously another revolution in mainstream criminology. This revolution was the transformation of traditional criminology from a discipline concerned with causes and cures to one concerned with administrative efficiency and methods of containment. Young argues that mainstream criminology has given up the search for causes, the goal of the meta-narrative of criminal causation. It has gone wholeheartedly over to the state and merely provides techniques of control and manipulation. Again it is important to highlight the linkages in Young's argument. On the one hand, he is critical of what he calls administrative criminology because it has become (even more transparently?) an extension of the state (or a disciplinary mechanism). But the reason for this is identified as the abandonment of the search for the causes (a search which was, according to Young, in any case misdirected). The thesis, therefore, is that to abandon the search for the causes is to become prey to reactionary forces. This, it seems to me, is to ignore completely the debates which have been going on within sociology and cultural theory about the problems of grand and totalizing theories. And such ideas are coming not from the right but precisely from the subjects which such theoretical enterprises have subjugated, that is, lesbians and gays, black women and men, Asian women and men, feminists and so on. I shall briefly consider aspects of this debate before returning to the specific problem of feminism in criminology.

The debate over postmodernism

There is now a considerable literature on postmodernism and a number of scholars are particularly concerned to explore the consequences of this development for sociology (Bauman, 1988; Smart, 1988; Kellner, 1988) and for feminism (Fraser and Nicholson, 1988; Weedon, 1987; Harding, 1986). The concept of postmodernism derives from outside the social sciences, from the fields of architecture

and art (Rose, 1988). Bauman (1988) argues that we should not assume that postmodernism is simply another word for post-industrialism or post-capitalism. It has a specific meaning and a specific significance, especially for a discipline like sociology (and by extension criminology), one which challenges the very existence of such an enterprise. Postmodernism refers to a mode of thinking which threatens to overturn the basic premises of modernism within which sociology has been nurtured.

Briefly, the modern age has been identified by Foucault (1973) as beginning at the start of the nineteenth century. The rise of modernity marks the eclipsing of Classical thought and, most importantly, heralds the centring of the conception of 'man' as the knowing actor who is author of his own actions and knowledge (that is, the liberal subject) and who simultaneously becomes the object of (human) scientific enquiry. Modernism is, however, more than the moment in which the human subject is constituted and transformed. It is a world view, a way of seeing and interpreting, a science which holds the promise that it can reveal the truth about human behaviour. The human sciences, at the moment of constituting the human subject, make her knowable – a site of investigation. What secrets there are will succumb to better knowledge, more rigorous methodologies, or more accurate typologizing. Implicit in the modernist paradigm is the idea that there is progress. What we do not know now, we will know tomorrow. It presumes that it is only a matter of time before science can explain all from the broad sweep of societal change to the motivations of the child molester. And because progress is presumed to be good and inevitable, science inevitably serves progress. Knowledge becomes nothing if it is not knowledge for something. Knowledge must be applied or applicable – even if we do not know how to apply it now, there is the hope that one day we will find a use for it (space travel did after all justify itself for we do now have non-stick frying pans).

Modernity has now become associated with some of the most deep-seated intellectual problems of the end of the twentieth century. It is seen as synonymous with racism, sexism, Euro-centredness and the attempt to reduce cultural and sexual differences to one dominant set of values and knowledge. Modernism is the intellectual mode of Western thought which has been identified as male or phallogocentric (for example, by Gilligan, 1982 and Duchen, 1986) and as white or Eurocentric (for example, by Dixon, 1976 and Harding, 1987).

It is also seen as an exhausted mode, one which has failed to live up to its promise and which is losing credibility. As Bauman argues:

> Nobody but the most rabid of the diehards believes today that the western mode of life, either the actual one or one idealized ('utopianized') in the intellectual mode has more than a sporting chance of ever becoming universal ... The search for the universal standards has suddenly become gratuitous... Impracticality erodes interest. The task of establishing universal standards of truth, morality, taste does not seem that much important. (1988: 220–1)

Clinging to modernist thought, in this account, is not only antediluvian; it is also politically suspect. It presumes that sociology (which for brevity's sake I shall take to include criminology in this section) as a way of knowing the world is superior, more objective, more truthful than other knowledges. However, it is easier said than done to shake off the grip of a way of knowing which is almost all one knows. In turn, this reflects a dilemma which has always plagued sociology. If we say we do not know (in the modernist sense) then we seem to be succumbing to the forces of the right who have always said we knew nothing – or, at least, that we were good for nothing.

The irony is, as Bauman (1988) points out, that we are damned if we do and also if we do not. He points to the way in which sociology has little choice but to recognize the failure of its originating paradigm. On the one hand, doubts cannot be wished away and we cannot pretend that sociology produces the goods that the post-war welfare state required of it. On the other hand, governments already know this. We cannot keep it a secret. State funding of sociological research is already much reduced and what will be funded is narrowly restricted to meet governmental aims. It may have been possible in the past to claim that more money was necessary or that a larger study was imperative before conclusions could be drawn but now we know (and they know) that conclusions, in the sense of final definitive statements, cannot be drawn. The point is whether we argue that all the studies that have been carried out to date have been inadequate or whether we reappraise the very idea that we will find solutions. Young, for example, is scathing about a major study carried out on 400 schoolboys by West (1969). He points out that this was one of the largest and most expensive pieces of criminological work to be carried out in Britain. Yet, he argues disparagingly, it could only come up with a link between delinquency and poverty and no real causes. For Young the problem is the intellectual bankruptcy of the positivist paradigm. From where I stand he is right, but, as I shall argue below, the problem is that he locates himself inside exactly the same paradigm.

The vortex that is criminology

It is, then, interesting that Young acknowledges many of the problems outlined above, although he does not do so from a postmodern stance. Rather he is situated inside the modernist problematic itself. He acknowledges that mainstream criminology has given up the search for causes and the 'master' narrative. He also recognizes the power of governments to diminish an academic enterprise which they no longer have use for. Hence, to keep their jobs, criminologists have had to give up promising the solutions and knuckle down to oiling the wheels. He is rightly critical of this, but, rather than seeing the broad implications of this development, these *criminologists* are depicted as capitalist lackeys while criminology as an enterprise can be saved from such political impurity by a reassertion of a modernist faith. While applauding Young's resistance to the logic of the market which has infected much of criminology (and sociology), I am doubtful that a backward looking, almost nostalgic, *cri de coeur* for the theory that will answer everything is very convincing. Yet Young can see nothing positive in challenging the modernist mode of thought; he only sees capitulation. The way to resist is apparently to proclaim that suffering is real and that we still need a 'scientific' solution for it.

In so doing Young claims the moral high ground for the realists, since to contradict the intellectual content of the argument appears to be a denial of misery and a negation of the very constituencies for whom he now speaks. So, let me make it plain that the challenge to modernist thought, with its positivist overtones which are apparent in criminology, does not entail a denial of poverty, inequality, repression, racism, sexual violence and so on. Rather it denies that the intellectual can divine the answer to these through the demand for more scientific activity and bigger and better theories.

The problem which faces criminology is not insignificant, however, and, arguably, its dilemma is even more fundamental than that facing sociology.

The whole *raison d'être* of criminology is that it addresses crime. It categorizes a vast range of activities and treats them as if they were all subject to the same laws – whether laws of human behaviour, genetic inheritance, economic rationality, development or the like. The argument within criminology has always been between those who give primacy to one form of explanation rather than another. The thing that criminology cannot do is deconstruct crime. It cannot locate rape or child sexual abuse in the domain of sexuality or theft in the domain of economic activity or drug use in the domain of health. To do so would be to abandon criminology to sociology; but more importantly it would involve abandoning the idea of a unified problem which requires a unified response – at least, at the theoretical level. However, left realist criminology does not seem prepared for this: see, for example, Young, 1986: 27-8.

Feminist intervention into criminology

I have argued that the core enterprise of criminology is profoundly problematic. However, it is important to acknowledge that it is not just criminology which is inevitably challenged by the more general reappraisal of modernist thinking. My argument is not that criminology alone is vulnerable to the question of whether or not such a knowledge project is tenable. But criminology does occupy a particularly significant position in this debate because both traditional and realist criminological thinking are especially wedded to the positivist paradigm of modernism. This makes it particularly important for feminist work to challenge the core of criminology and to avoid isolation from some of the major theoretical and political questions which are engaging feminist scholarship elsewhere. It might, therefore, be useful to consider schematically a range of feminist contributions to criminology to see the extent to which feminism has resisted or succumbed to the vortex.

Feminist empiricism

Sandra Harding (1986 and 1987) has provided a useful conceptual framework for mapping the development of feminist thought in the social sciences. She refers to feminist empiricism, standpoint feminism and postmodern feminism. By feminist empiricism she means that work which has criticized the claims to objectivity made by mainstream social science. Feminist-empiricism points out that what has passed for science is in fact the world perceived from the perspective of men; what looks like objectivity is really sexism and that the kinds of questions social science has traditionally asked have systematically excluded women and the interests of women. Feminist empiricism, therefore, claims that a truly objective science would not be androcentric but would take account of both genders. What is required under this model is that social scientists live up to their proclaimed codes of objectivity. Under this schema, empirical practice is critiqued but empiricism remains intact. Such a perspective is not particularly threatening to the established order. It facilitates the study of female offenders to fill the gaps in existing knowledge; men can go on studying men and the relevances of men as long as they acknowledge that it is men and not humanity they are addressing.

In criminology there has been a growth in the study of female offenders (for example, Carlen, 1988; Heidensohn, 1985; Eaton, 1986). It would be unjust to suggest that these have merely followed the basic tenets of mainstream empirical work, but a motivating element in all of these has been to do studies on women. But, as Dorothy Smith pointed out in 1973, to direct research at women without revising traditional assumptions about methodology and epistemology can result in making women a mere addendum to the main project of studying men. It also leaves unchallenged the way men are studied.

Harding sees a radical potential in feminist empiricism, however. She argues that the fact that feminists identify different areas for study (for example, wife abuse rather than delinquency) has brought a whole range of new issues on to the agenda. It is also the case that feminists who subscribe to empiricism have challenged the way we arrive at the goal of objective knowledge. Hence different kinds of methods are espoused, note is taken of the power relationship between researcher and researched and so on (Stanley and Wise, 1983). The move towards ethnographic research is an example of this (although this is not, of course, peculiar to feminist work).

It is perhaps important at this stage to differentiate between empiricism and empirical work. Harding's categories refer to epistemological stances rather than practices (although the two are not unrelated). Empiricism is a stance which proclaims the possibility of objective and true knowledge which can be arrived at and tested against clearly identified procedures. Mainstream criminology, having followed these tenets, claimed to have discovered valid truths about women's criminal behaviour (and, of course, men's). The initial reaction of feminism to this claim was to reinterpret this truth as a patriarchal lie. It was argued that the methods used had been tainted with bias and so the outcome was inevitably faulty (Smart, 1986). This left open the presumption that the methods could be retained if the biases were removed because the ideal of a true or real science was posited as the alternative to the biased one.

Empirical research does not have to be attached to empiricism, however. To engage with women, to interview them, to document their oral histories, to participate with them, does not automatically mean that one upholds the ideal of empiricism. To be critical of empiricism is not to reject empirical work per se. However, some of the empirical studies, generated under the goal of collecting more knowledge about women, which feminist empiricism engendered presented a different sort of problem for the project of a feminist criminology.

This problem was the thorny question of discrimination. The early feminist contributions did not only challenge the objectivity of criminological thought; they challenged the idea of an objective judiciary and criminal justice system. Hence there grew up a major preoccupation with revealing the truth or otherwise of equality before the law in a range of empirical studies. Some studies seemed to find that the police or courts treated women and girls more leniently than men and boys. Others found the opposite. Then there were discoveries that much depended on the nature of the offence or the length of previous record or whether the offender was married or not (see, for example, Farrington and Morris, 1983). As Gelsthorpe (1986) has pointed out, the search for straightforward sexism was more difficult than anyone imagined at first. It was, of course, a false trail in as much as it was anticipated that forms of oppression (whether sexual or racial or other) could be identified in a few simple criteria which could then be established (or not) in following a ritual procedure. So in this respect the (with the benefit of hindsight) overly simplistic approach of early feminist work in this field has created an obstacle to further developments.

The other drawback to this type of research is the one which has been highlighted by MacKinnon (1987). She argues that any approach which focuses on equality and inequality always presumes that the norm is men. Hence studies of the criminal justice system always compare the treatment of women with men and men remain the standard against which all are judged. This has led to two problems. The first arouses a facile, yet widespread, reaction that if one has the audacity to compare women to men in circumstances where men are more favourably treated, then in those instances where they are treated less favourably one must, *ipso facto*, also be requiring the standard of treatment for women to be reduced. Hence, in comparing how the courts treat men and women, the response is inevitably the threat that if women want equality they must have it in full and so some feminists want women to be sent in their droves to dirty, violent and overcrowded prisons for long periods of time. This is what Lahey (1985) has called 'equality with a vengeance'.[1]

The second problem goes beyond the transparent difficulties of treating women as if they were men to the level of the symbolic. Basically the equality paradigm always reaffirms the centrality of men. Men continue to constitute the norm, the unproblematic, the natural social actor. Women are thus always seen as interlopers into a world already organized by others. This has been well established in areas like employment law where the equality argument has been seen unintentionally to reproduce men as the ideal employees, with women struggling to make the grade (Kenney, 1986). Underlying such an approach in any case is the presumption that law is fundamentally a neutral object inside a liberal regime, thus wholly misconstruing the nature of power and the power of law (Smart, 1989). Law does not stand outside gender relations and adjudicate upon them. Law is part of these relations and is always already gendered in its principles and practices. We cannot separate out one practice – called discrimination – and ask for it to cease to be gendered as it would be a meaningless request. This is not to say we cannot object to certain principles and practices but we need to think carefully before we continue to sustain a conceptual framework which either prioritizes men as the norm, or assumes that genderlessness (or gender-blindness) is either possible or desirable.

Standpoint feminism

The second category identified by Harding is standpoint feminism. The epistemological basis of this form of feminist knowledge is experience. However, not just any experience is deemed to be equally valuable or valid. *Feminist* experience is achieved through a struggle against oppression; it is, therefore, argued to be more complete and less distorted than the perspective of the ruling group of men. A feminist standpoint then is not just the experience of women, but of women *reflexively* engaged in struggle (intellectual and political). In this process it is argued that a more accurate or fuller version of reality is achieved. This stance does not divide knowledge from values and politics but sees knowledge arising from engagement.

Arguably, standpoint feminism does not feature strongly in feminist criminology except in quite specific areas of concern like rape, sexual assault and wife abuse. It is undoubtedly the influence of feminists engaged at a political level with these forms of oppression that has begun to transform some areas of criminological thinking. Hence the work of Rape Crisis Centres (for example, London Rape Crisis Centre, 1984) has been vital in proffering an alternative 'truth' about rape and women's experience of the criminal justice system. However, as far as mainstream criminology is concerned we should perhaps not be too optimistic about this since the accounts provided by such organizations have only been partially accepted and, even then, as a consequence of substantiation by more orthodox accounts (Blair, 1985; Chambers and Millar, 1983).

Taking experience as a starting point and testing ground has only made a partial entry into criminology and, interestingly, where it has entered has been in the domain of left realism. It is here we find the resort to experience (that is, women's experience of crime) a constant referent and justification. Women's fear of rape and violence is used in this context to argue that rape and violence must be treated as serious problems. The question that this poses is whether we now have a feminist realist criminology or whether left realism (and consequently criminology as a whole) has been revitalized by the energies and concerns of a politically active women's movement. If we consider texts like *Well Founded Fear* (Hanmer and Saunders, 1984) or *Leaving Violent Men* (Binney *et al.*, 1981), we find that the motivating drive is the desire to let women's experiences be told. These experiences are not meant to stand alongside the experiences of the police or violent men; they represent the expression of subjugation which will replace the dominant account. Hanmer and Saunders outline methodological procedures for tapping into this experience and produce what Harding has referred to as a 'successor science'. As

she argues, 'the adoption of this standpoint is fundamentally a moral and political act of commitment to understanding the world from the perspective of the socially subjugated' (1986: 149). In fact, it goes beyond this as the researchers, as feminists, also inhabit the world of the socially subjugated. It is not an act of empathy as such but a shared knowledge.

The real issue remains unresolved, however. For while feminist work is generating another sort of knowledge (for example, other ways of accounting for violence), feminist work which fits under the umbrella of left realist criminology does not embrace the full scope of what Young has called for (see, for example, Gregory, 1986).[2] This is because standpoint feminism has not taken masculinity as a focus of investigation. Precisely because standpoint feminism in this area has arisen from a grassroots concern to protect women and to reveal the victimization of women, it has not been sympathetic to the study of masculinity(ies). Indeed, it would argue that we have heard enough from that quarter and that any attempt by feminists to turn their attention away from women is to neglect the very real problems that women still face. So the feminist realists (if we can use this term for the sake of argument) are on quite a different trajectory from the left realists. It may be convenient to the left to support the work of feminists in this area but it is unclear to me where this unholy 'alliance' is going analytically. Like the protracted debate about the marriage of Marxism and feminism, we may find that this alliance ends in annulment.

Feminist postmodernism

It would be a mistake to depict feminist postmodernism as the third stage or synthesis of feminist empiricism and standpoint feminism. Feminist postmodernism does not try to resolve the problems of other positions; rather it starts from a different place and proceeds in other directions. Much postmodern analysis is rooted in philosophy and aesthetics (Rorty, 1985; Lyotard, 1986; Fekete, 1988) but in the case of feminism it started in political practice. It began with the separate demises of sisterhood and of Marxism.

By the demise of sisterhood, I mean the realization that women were not all white, middle class and of Anglo-Saxon, Protestant extract. Feminism resisted this realization by invoking notions of womanhood as a core essence to unite women (under the leadership of the said white, middle-class and Protestant women). However, black feminists, lesbian feminists, Third World feminists, aboriginal feminists and many others simply refused to swallow the story. To put it simply, they knew power when they saw it exercised. Feminism had to abandon its early framework and to start to look for other ways of thinking which did not subjugate other subjectivities. But at the same time, feminism came to recognize that individual women did not have unitary selves. Debates over sexuality, pornography and desire began to undo the idea of the true self and gave way to notions of fractured subjectivities. These developments were much influenced by the work of Foucault and psychoanalytic theory but they cannot be dismissed simply as a 'fad' because the recognition of the inadequacy of the feminist paradigm was not imposed by the intellectuals but arose out of a series of painful struggles for understanding combined with a progressive political stance.

The other key element in this development was the demise of Marxism as a rigorously policed grid of analysis, adherence to which had meant the promise of the total explanation or master narrative. Again, feminist practice revealed the inadequacy of the grand theoretical project of Marxism quite early in the second wave. But the struggle to retain the paradigm lasted much longer. None the less it is now realized that we cannot keep adding bits of Marxist orthodoxy to try to explain all the awkward silences. While many Marxian values may be retained, the idea and the promise of the totalizing theory have gradually loosened their grip.

The core element of feminist postmodernism is the rejection of the one reality which arises from 'the falsely universalizing perspective of the master' (Harding, 1987: 188). But unlike standpoint feminism it does not seek to impose a different unitary reality. Rather it refers to subjugated knowledges, which tell different stories and have different specificities. Thus the aim of feminism ceases to be the establishment of the feminist truth and becomes the deconstruction of truth and analysis of the power effects which claims to truth entail. So there is a shift away from treating knowledge as ultimately objective or, at least, the final standard and hence able to reveal the concealed truth, towards recognizing that knowledge is part of power and that power is ubiquitous. Feminist knowledge, therefore, becomes part of a multiplicity of resistances. Take, for example, feminist interventions in the area of rape. This is an area which I have explored in detail elsewhere (Smart, 1989) but for the sake of this discussion I wish to

rely on the work of Woodhull (1988). Woodhull, in an article on sexuality and Foucault, argues against a traditional feminist mode of explanation for rape. She concentrates on Brownmiller's (1975) approach which seeks to explain rape in terms of the physiological differences between men and women. Woodhull's argument is that in explaining rape in this way, Brownmiller puts sex and biology outside the social, as preceding all power relations. What is missing is an understanding of how sexual difference and the meanings of different bits of bodies are constructed. Woodhull argues:

> If we are seriously to come to terms with rape, we must explain how the vagina comes to be coded – and experienced – as a place of emptiness and vulnerability, the penis as a weapon, and intercourse as violation, rather than naturalize these processes through references to 'basic' physiology. (1988: 171)

So it becomes a concern of feminism to explore how women's bodies have become saturated with (hetero)sex, how codes of sexualized meaning are reproduced and sustained and to begin (or continue) the deconstruction of these meanings.

This is just one example of how postmodernism is influencing feminist practice (for others, see Diamond and Quinby, 1988; Jardine, 1985; Weedon, 1987; Fraser and Nicholson, 1988) and it is clear that the ramifications of the epistemological crisis of modernism are far from being fully mapped or exhaustively considered as yet. We are in no position to judge what shapes feminism will take in the next decade or so. However, it might be interesting to consider, albeit prematurely, what all this means for criminology.

Concluding remarks

It is a feature of postmodernism that questions posed within a modernist frame are turned about. So, for a long time, we have been asking 'what does feminism have to contribute to criminology (or sociology)?'. Feminism has been knocking at the door of established disciplines hoping to be let in on equal terms. These established disciplines have largely looked down their noses (metaphorically speaking) and found feminism wanting. Feminism has been required to become more objective, more substantive, more scientific, more anything before a grudging entry could be granted. But now the established disciplines are themselves looking rather insecure (Bauman, 1988) and, as the door is opening, we must ask whether feminism really does want to enter.

Perhaps it is now apt to rephrase the traditional question to read 'what has criminology got to offer feminism?' Feminism is now a broadly based scholarship and political practice. Its concerns range from questions of philosophy to representations to engagement; it is, therefore, no longer in the supplicant position of an Olivia Twist. On the contrary, we have already seen that a lot of feminist work has revitalized radical criminology. It might be that criminology needs feminism more than the converse. Of course, many criminologists, especially the traditional variety, will find this preposterous; but perhaps they had better look to who their students are and who their students are reading.

It is clear that if mainstream criminology remains unchanged it will follow the path that Young has outlined into greater and greater complicity with mechanisms of discipline. However, the path of radical criminology seems wedded to the modernist enterprise and is, as yet, unaffected by the epistemological sea changes which have touched feminism and other discourses. Under such circumstances, it is very hard to see what criminology has to offer to feminism.

> *From C. Smart, 'Feminist approaches to criminology or postmodern woman meets atavistic man', in L. Gelsthorpe and A. Morris (eds)* Feminist Perspectives in Criminology *(Milton Keynes: Open University), 1990, pp. 70–84.*

Notes

1   I have argued against equality feminism elsewhere (Smart, 1989). However, my criticism is that equality feminism misunderstands the nature of the law and the state and naively asks for equal treatment on the assumption that it will improve things. Evidence indicates that equality legislation only improves things for men (MacKinnon, 1987; Fudge, 1989).

2   Jeanne Gregory's paper in the Matthews and Young (1986) collection is an interesting example of what I mean here. Located alongside Young's call for a re-emphasis on criminology and deviance is Gregory's paper which starts within a criminological perspective but moves rapidly outside this field as she progresses on to a discussion of the future direction of feminist work.

References

Bauman, Z. (1988).'Is there a postmodern sociology?', *Theory, Culture and Society*, 5, 2/3, 217–38.

Binney, V., Harknell, G and Nixon, J. (1981). *Leaving Violent Men: A Study of Refuges and Housing for Battered Women. Leeds:* Woman's Aid Federation.

Blair, I. (1985). *Investigating Rape: A New Approach for the Police*. London: Croom Helm.

Brownmiller, S (1975). *Against Our Will: Men, Women and Rape*. London: Secker and Warburg.

Carlen, P. (1988). *Women, Crime and Poverty*. Milton Keynes: Open University Press.

Chambers, G and Millar, A. (1983). *Investigating Sexual Assault*. Edinburgh: HMSO, Scottish Office Social Research Study.

Cloward, R. and Ohlin, L. (1961). *Delinquency and Opportunity: A Theory of Delinquent Gangs*. London: Routledge and Kegan Paul.

Cohen, A. K. (1955). *Delinquent Boys: The Culture of the Gang*. New York: Free Press.

Diamond, I. and Quinby, L. (eds) (1988). *Feminism and Foucault*, Boston: Northeastern University Press.

Dixon, V. (1976) 'World views and research methodology', in L. King, V. Dixon and W. Nobles (eds), *African Philosophy: Assumptions and Paradigms for Research on Black Persons*. Los Angeles: Fanon Centre.

Duchen, C. (1986). *Feminism in France*. London: Routledge and Kegan Paul.

Eaton, M. (1986). *Justice for Women? Family, Court and Social Control*. Milton Keynes: Open University Press.

Farrington, D. and Morris, A. (1983). 'Sex, sentencing and reconviction', *British Journal of Criminolgy*, 23, 3, 229–48.

Fekete, J. (1988). *Life after Postmodernism: Essays on Value and Culture*. London: Macmillan.

Foucault, M. (1973). *The Order of Things*. New York: Vintage Books.

Fraser, N. and Nicholson, L. (1988). 'Social critisism without philosophy: an encounter between feminism and postmodernism'. *Theory, Culture and Society*, 5, 2/3, 373–94.

Gelsthorpe, L. (1986). 'Towards a sceptical look at sexism', *International Journal of the Sociology of Law*, 14, 2, 125–52.

Gilligan, C. (1982). *In a Different Voice*. London: Harvard University Press.

Gregory, J. (1986). 'Sex, class and crime: towards a non-sexist criminology', in R. Matthews and J. Young (eds), *Confronting Crime*. London: Sage.

Hanmer, J. and Saunders, S. (1984). *Well Founded Fear: A Community Study of Violence to Women*. London: Hutchinson in association with the Exploration in Feminism Collective.

Harding, S. (ed.) (1986). *The Science Question In Feminism*. Milton Keynes: Open University Press.

Harding, S. (ed.) (1987). *Feminism and Methodology*. Milton Keynes: Open University Press.

Heidensohn, F. (1985). *Women and Crime*. Basingstoke: Macmillan.

Jardine, A. (1985). *Gynesis*. London: Cornell University Press.

Kellner, D. (1988). 'Postmodernism as social theory: some challenges and problems'. *Theory, Culture and Society*, 5, 2/3, 239–70.

Kenney, S.J. (1986). 'Reproductive hazards in the workplace: the law and sexual difference', *International Journal of the Sociology of Law*, 14, 3/4, 393–44.

Lahey, K. (1985). '...until women themselves have told all that they have to tell...' *Osgoode Hall Law Journal*, 23, 3, 519–41.

London Rape Crisis Centre (1984). *Sexual Violence: The Reality for Women*. London: The Women's Press.

Lyotard, J. (1986). *The Postmodern Condition*. Manchester: Manchester University Press.

MacKinnon, C. (1987). *Feminism Unmodified: Discourse on Life and Law*. Cambridge, MA: Harvard University Press.

Matza, D. (1969). *Becoming Deviant*. Englewood Cliffs, NJ: Prentice Hall.

Rorty, B. (1985). 'Habermas and Lyotard on postmodernity', R. Bernstein (ed.), *Habermas and Modernity*. Cambridge: Polity Press.

Rose, G. (1988). 'Architecture to philosophy – the postmodern complicity', *Theory, Culture and Society*, 5, 2/3, 357–72.

Smart, B. (1988). 'Modernism, postmodernism and the present', unpublished paper: University of Auckland.

Smart, C. (1989). *Feminism and the Power of Law*. London: Routledge.

Stanley, L. and Wise, S. (1983). *Breaking Out: Feminist Consciousness and Feminist Research*. London: Routledge and Kegan Paul.

Taylor, I., Walton, P. and Young, J. (1973). *The New Criminology*. London: Routledge and Kegan Paul.

Weedon, C. (1987). *Feminist Practice and Poststructuralist Theory*. Oxford: Basil Blackwell.

West, D. (1969). *Present Conduct and Future Delinquency*. London: Heinemann.

Woodhull, W. (1988). 'Sexuality, power and the question of rape', in I. Diamond and L. Quinby (eds), *Feminism and Foucault*. Boston: Northeastern University Press.

Young, J. (1986). 'The failure of criminology: the need for a radical realism', in Zhana, (1989) (ed.) *Sojourn*. London: Methuen.

16

Late modernity, governmentality and risk

16.1 The new penology: notes on the emerging strategy for corrections
Malcom M. Feeley and Jonathan Simon   360

16.2 Actuarialism and the risk society
Jock Young   367

16.3 Risk, power and crime prevention
Pat O'Malley   373

16.4 Say 'Cheese!' The Disney order that is not so Mickey Mouse
Clifford D. Shearing and Philip C. Stenning   379

Introduction

KEY CONCEPTS actuarialism; late modernity; new penology; postmodernity; private security; reflexivity; risk; situational crime prevention

The work in this chapter all reflects the fact, and/or the perception, that the world appears to be changing remarkably quickly. The social and cultural revolution variously referred to by terms such as *globalization* and *postmodernity* among others, is held to be having its impact in the fields of crime and justice. At the heart of many of the changes discussed lie apparent shifts in the nature and role of the nation state, which are paralleled in shifts in policing and security, in the emphasis placed upon individual citizens in managing their own security, and in the emergence of new forms of punishment and control.

In the first excerpt, Malcolm Feeley and Jonathan Simon **(Reading 16.1)** develop their thesis about changes in the field of punishment which they refer to as 'new penology'. This influential thesis suggests that the new penology has a number of characteristics: its discourse replaces the language of rehabilitation or of clinical diagnosis with an actuarial, calculative language of probabilities. Second, the old objectives of rehabilitating individuals are gradually replaced by the new objectives of risk management, control. As a consequence new techniques for identifying and managing risk are developed. The aims of criminal justice and punishment, they argue, become increasingly short-term and prosaic.

The themes of risk and actuarialism are picked up by Jock Young **(Reading 16.2)**. He argues that the increasing centrality of risk in crime and deviance results in the rise of a 'calculative' or 'actuarial' attitude in individuals and institutions, as well as in criminal justice itself. In late modernity our society, he argues, is one in which citizens are much exposed (largely via the mass media) to revelations about crime and, simultaneously, through a general civilizing process our tolerance of misconduct is in decline. These, together with other attributes of the contemporary world, generate a sense of risk/riskiness which, in turn, leads to the emergence of an 'actuarial attitude'. Young goes on, in a critical manner, to link his thesis on this actuarial mentality to aspects of Wilson and Kelling's 'Broken Windows' thesis (see chapter 13) and to Feeley and Simon's notion of the new penology.

Further reflections on these and linked developments can be found in Pat O'Malley's discussion of situational crime prevention (see chapter 14) as risk management **(Reading 16.3)**. In fact, he suggests that situational crime prevention is 'quintessentially actuarial' in that it pays relatively little regard to individual offenders, is largely uninterested in the causes of crime, and is at best agnostic towards rehabilitative approaches. The fact that situational crime prevention has become so widespread and apparently popular in recent times, he argues, must be answered by looking at its relationship to political programmes and strategies. More specifically he goes on to argue that much of the answer is to be found in situational crime prevention's 'attractions to economic rationalist, neo-conservative and New Right programmes'. In particular, he suggests that social crime prevention's eschewal of interest in socio-economic causes and the shifting of responsibility away from the state and toward the individual citizen both resonate with the New Right's political and ideological priorities.

The final excerpt, by Clifford Shearing and Philip Stenning **(Reading 16.4)**, provides a glimpse of one aspect of late modern security by taking a trip to Disneyland. In this hugely influential article Shearing and Stenning outline a complex, but in ways almost invisible, blanket of ordering by which the Disney Corporation maintain order and control without recourse to uniformed officers or guards (at least not in the normal sense of what constitutes the social control agent's uniform). This is a world in which control strategies are 'embedded', in which self-control is inculcated and encouraged and where formal social control systems are ever-present but largely hidden. Disneyworld, they imply, is increasingly our neighbourhood, workplace, and leisure facility.

Questions for discussion

1. Briefly contrast the characteristics of the 'old penology' with those of the 'new penology'.

2. Give three examples of policy developments in recent years that appear to display some of the attributes of the new penology.

3. What are the six components of risk identified by Jock Young?

4. Outline Young's criticism of Feeley and Simon's discussion of the link between crime and fear of crime.

5. Why, according to O'Malley, is the New Right attracted by situational crime prevention?

6. How might situational crime prevention be compatible with political systems more concerned with equality and social justice?

7. How does social control work in Disneyland?

8. Why should we be interested in how security and control are organised at Disneyland?

16.1 The new penology: notes on the emerging strategy for corrections Malcolm M. Feeley and Jonathan Simon

Distinguishing features of the new penology

What we call the new penology is not a theory of crime or criminology. Its uniqueness lies less in conceptual integration than in a common focus on certain problems and a shared way of framing issues. This strategic formation of knowledge and power offers managers of the system a more or less coherent picture of the challenges they face and the kinds of solutions that are most likely to work. While we cannot reduce it to a set of principles, we can point to some of its most salient features.

The new discourse

A central feature of the new discourse is the replacement of a moral or clinical description of the individual with an actuarial language of probabilistic calculations and statistical distributions applied to populations. Although social utility analysis or actuarial thinking is commonplace enough in modern life – it frames policy considerations of all sorts – in recent years this mode of thinking has gained ascendancy in legal discourse, a system of reasoning that traditionally has employed the language of morality and been focused on individuals (Simon, 1988).[1] For instance, this new mode of reasoning is found increasingly in tort law, where traditional fault and negligence standards – which require a focus on the individual and are based upon notions of individual responsibility – have given way to strict liability and no-fault. These new doctrines rest upon actuarial ways of thinking about how to 'manage' accidents and public safety. They employ the language of social utility and management, not individual responsibility (Simon, 1987; Steiner, 1987).[2] [...]

Scholars of both European and North American penal strategies have noted the recent and rising trend of the penal system to target categories and subpopulations rather than individuals (Bottoms, 1983; Cohen, 1985; Mathieson, 1983; Reichman, 1986). This reflects, at least in part, the fact that actuarial forms of representation promote quantification as a way of visualizing populations.

Crime statistics have been a part of the discourse of the state for over 200 years, but the advance of statistical methods permits the formulation of concepts and strategies that allow direct relations between penal strategy and the population. Earlier generations used statistics to map the responses of normatively defined groups to punishment; today one talks of 'high-rate offenders,' 'career criminals,' and other categories defined by the distribution itself. Rather than imply extending the capacity of the system to rehabilitate or control crime, actuarial classification has come increasingly to define the correctional enterprise itself.

The importance of actuarial language in the system will come as no surprise to anyone who has spent time observing it. Its significance, however, is often lost in the more spectacular shift in emphasis from rehabilitation to crime control. No doubt, a new and more punitive attitude toward the proper role of punishment has emerged in recent years, and it is manifest in a shift in the language of statutes, internal procedures, and academic scholarship. Yet looking across the past several decades, it appears that the pendulum-like swings of penal attitude moved independently of the actuarial language that has steadily crept into the discourse.[3]

The discourse of the new penology is not simply one of greater quantification; it is also characterized by an emphasis on the systemic and on formal rationality. While the history of systems theory and operations research has yet to be written, their progression from business administration to the military and, in the 1960s, to domestic public policy must be counted as among the most significant of current intellectual trends.

The new objectives

The new penology is neither about punishing nor about rehabilitating individuals. It is about identifying and managing unruly groups. It is concerned with the rationality not of individual behavior or even community organization, but of managerial processes. Its goal is not to eliminate crime but to make it tolerable through systemic coordination.

One measure of the shift away from trying to normalize offenders and toward trying to manage them is seen in the declining significance of recidivism. Under the old penology, recidivism was a nearly universal criterion for assessing successor failure of penal programs. Under the new penology, recidivism rates continue to be important, but their significance has changed. The word itself seems to be used less often precisely because it carries a normative connotation that reintegrating offenders into the community is the major objective. High rates of parolees being returned to prison once indicated program failure; now they are offered as evidence of efficiency and effectiveness of parole as a control apparatus.[4]

It is possible that recidivism is dropping out of the vocabulary as an adjustment to harsh realities and is a way of avoiding charges of institutional failure. [...]

However, in shifting to emphasize the virtues of return as an indication of *effective* control, the new penology reshapes one's understanding of the functions of the penal sanction. By emphasizing correctional programs in terms of aggregate control and system management rather than individual success and failure, the new penology lowers one's expectations about the criminal sanction. These redefined objectives are reinforced by the new discourses discussed above, which take deviance as a given, mute aspirations for individual reformation, and seek to classify, sort, and manage dangerous groups efficiently.

The waning of concern over recidivism reveals fundamental changes in the very penal processes that recidivism once was used to evaluate. For example, although parole and probation have long been justified as means of reintegrating offenders into the community (President's Commission, 1967:165), increasingly they are being perceived as cost-effective ways of imposing long-term management on the dangerous. Instead of treating revocation of parole and probation as a mechanism to short-circuit the supervision process when the risks to public safety become unacceptable, the system now treats revocation as a cost-effective way to police and sanction a chronically troublesome population. In such an operation, recidivism is either irrelevant[5] or, as suggested above, is stood on its head and transformed into an indicator of success in a new form of law enforcement.

The importance that recidivism once had in evaluating the performance of corrections is now being taken up by measures of system functioning. Heydebrand and Seron (1990) have noted a tendency in courts and other social agencies toward decoupling performance evaluation from external social objectives. Instead of social norms like the elimination of crime, reintegration into the community, or public safety, institutions begin to measure their own outputs as indicators of performance. Thus, courts may look at docket flow. Similarly, parole agencies may shift evaluations of performance to, say, the time elapsed between arrests and due process hearings. In much the same way, many schools have come to focus on standardized test performance rather than on reading or mathematics, and some have begun to see teaching itself as the process of teaching students how to take such tests (Heydebrand and Seron, 1990:190–194; Lipsky, 1980:4–53).

Such technocratic rationalization tends to insulate institutions from the messy, hard-to-control demands of the social world. By limiting their exposure to indicators that they can control, managers ensure that their problems will have solutions. No doubt this tendency in the new penology is, in part, a response to the acceleration of demands for rationality and accountability in punishment coming from the courts and legislatures during the 1970s (Jacobs, 1977). It also reflects the lowered expectations for the penal system that result from failures to accomplish more ambitious promises of the past. Yet in the end, the inclination of the system to measure its success against its own production processes helps lock the system into a mode of operation that has only an attenuated connection with the social purposes of punishment. In the long term it becomes more difficult to evaluate an institution critically if there are no references to substantive social ends.

The new objectives also inevitably permeate through the courts into thinking about rights. The new penology replaces consideration of fault with predictions of dangerousness and safety management and, in so doing, modifies traditional individual-oriented doctrines of criminal procedure.

New techniques

These altered, lowered expectations manifest themselves in the development of more cost-effective forms of custody and control and in new technologies to identify and classify risk. Among them are low frills, no-service custodial centers; various forms of electronic monitoring systems that impose a form of custody without walls; and new statistical techniques for assessing risk and predicting dangerousness. These new forms of control are not anchored in aspirations to rehabilitate, reintegrate, retrain, provide employment, or the like. They are justified in more blunt terms: variable detention depending upon risk assessment.[6]

Perhaps the clearest example of the new penology's method is the theory of incapacitation, which has become the predominant utilitarian model of punishment (Greenwood, 1982; Moore *et al.*, 1984). Incapacitation promises to reduce the effects of crime in society not by altering either offender or social context, but by rearranging the distribution of offenders in society. If the prison can do nothing else, incapacitation theory holds, it can detain offenders for a time and thus delay their resumption of criminal activity. According to the theory, if such delays are sustained for enough time and for enough offenders, significant aggregate effects in crime can take place although individual destinies are only marginally altered.[7]

These aggregate effects can be further intensified, in some accounts, by a strategy of selective incapacitation. This approach proposes a sentencing scheme in which lengths of sentence depend not upon the nature of the criminal offense or upon an assessment of the character of the offender, but upon risk profiles. Its objectives are to identify high-risk offenders and to maintain long-term control over them while investing in shorter terms and less intrusive control over lower risk offenders.

The new penology in perspective

The correctional practices emerging from the shifts we identified above present a kind of 'custodial continuum.' But unlike the 'correctional continuum' discussed in the 1960s, this new custodial continuum does not design penal measures for the particular needs of the individual or the community. Rather, it sorts individuals into groups according to the degree of control warranted by their risk profiles.

At one extreme the prison provides maximum security at a high cost for those who pose the greatest risks, and at the other probation provides low-cost surveillance for low-risk offenders. In between stretches a growing range of intermediate supervisory and surveillance techniques. The management concerns of the new penology – in contrast to the transformative concerns of the old – are displayed especially clearly in justifications for various new intermediate sanctions.

What we call the new penology is only beginning to take coherent shape. Although most of what we have stressed as its central elements – statistical prediction, concern with groups, strategies of management – have a long history in penology, in recent years they have come to the fore, and their functions have coalesced and expanded to form a new strategic approach. Discussing the new penology in terms of discourse, objective, and technique, risks a certain repetitiveness. Indeed, all three are closely linked, and while none can be assigned priority as the cause of the others, each entails and facilitates the others.

Thus, one can speak of normalizing individuals, but when the emphasis is on separating people into distinct and independent categories the idea of the 'normal' itself becomes obscured if not irrelevant.[8] If the 'norm' can no longer function as a relevant criterion of success for the organizations of criminal justice, it is not surprising that evaluation turns to indicators of internal system performance. The focus of the system on the efficiency of its own outputs, in turn, places a premium on those methods (e.g., risk screening, sorting, and monitoring) that fit wholly within the bureaucratic capacities of the apparatus.

But the same story can be told in a different order. The steady bureaucratization of the correctional apparatus during the 1950s and 1960s shifted the target from individuals, who did not fit easily into centralized administration, to categories or classes, which do. But once the focus is on categories of offenders rather than individuals, methods naturally shift toward mechanisms of appraising and arranging groups rather than intervening in the lives of individuals. In the end the search for causal order is at least premature.

In the section below we explore the contours of some of the new patterns represented by these developments, and in so doing suggest that the enterprise is by now relatively well established.

New functions and traditional forms

Someday perhaps, the new penology will have its own Jeremy Bentham or Zebulon Brockway (Foucault, 1977:200; Rothman, 1980:33), some gigantic figure who can stamp his or her own sense of order on the messy results of incremental change. For now it is better not to think of it so much as a theory or program conceived in full by any particular actors in the system, but as an interpretive net that can help reveal in the present some of the directions the future may take. [...]

Below we reexamine three of the major features of the contemporary penal landscape in light of our argument – the expansion of the penal sanction, the rise of drug testing, and innovation within the criminal process – and relate them to our thesis.

The expansion of penal sanctions

During the past decade the number of people covered by penal sanctions has expanded significantly.[9] Because of its high costs, the growth of prison populations has drawn the greatest attention, but probation and parole have increased at a proportionate or faster rate. The importance of these other sanctions goes beyond their ability to stretch penal resources; they expand and redistribute the use of imprisonment. Probation and parole violations now constitute a major source of prison inmates, and negotiations over probation revocation are replacing plea bargaining as modes of disposition (Greenspan, 1988; Messinger and Berecochea, 1990).[10]

Many probation and parole revocations are triggered by events, like failing a drug test, that are driven by parole procedures themselves (Simon, 1990; Zimring and Hawkins, 1991). The increased flow of probationers and parolees into prisons is expanding the prison population and changing the nature of the prison. Increasingly, prisons are short-term holding pens for violators deemed too dangerous to remain on the streets. To the extent the prison is organized to receive such people, its correctional mission is replaced by a management function, a warehouse for the highest risk classes of offenders.

From the perspective of the new penology, the growth of community corrections in the shadow of imprisonment is not surprising.[11] The new penology does not regard prison as a special institution capable of making a difference in the individuals who pass through it. Rather, it functions as but one of several custodial options. The actuarial logic of the new penology dictates an expansion of the continuum of control for more efficient risk management. For example, the various California prisons are today differentiated largely by the level of security they maintain and, thus, what level risk inmate they can receive. Twenty years ago, in contrast, they were differentiated by specialized functions: California Rehabilitation Center, for drug users; California Medical Prison at Vacaville, for the mentally ill; Deuel Vocational Institute, for young adults.

Thus, community-based sanctions can be understood in terms of risk management rather than rehabilitative or correctional aspirations. Rather than instruments of reintegrating offenders into the community, they function as mechanisms to maintain control, often through frequent drug testing, over low-risk offenders for whom the more secure forms of custody are judged too expensive or unnecessary.[12]

Drugs and punishment

Drug use and its detection and control have become central concerns of the penal system. No one observing the system today can fail to be struck by the increasingly tough laws directed against users and traffickers, well-publicized data that suggest that a majority of arrestees are drug users, and the increasing proportion of drug offenders sent to prison.[13]

In one sense, of course, the emphasis on drugs marks a continuity with the past 30 years of correctional history. Drug treatment and drug testing were hallmarks of the rehabilitative model in the 1950s and 1960s. The recent upsurge of concern with drugs may be attributed to the hardening of social attitudes toward drug use (especially in marked contrast to the tolerant 1970s),[14] the introduction of virulent new drug products, like crack cocaine, and the disintegrating social conditions of the urban poor.

Without dismissing the relevance of these continuities and explanations for change, it is important to note that there are distinctive changes in the role of drugs in the current system that reflect the logic of the new penology. In place of the traditional emphasis on treatment and eradication, today's practices track drug use as a kind of risk indicator. The widespread evidence of drug use in the offending population leads not to new theories of crime causation but to more efficient ways of identifying those at highest risk of offending. With drug use so prevalent that it is found in a majority of arrestees in some large cities (Flanagan and Maguire, 1990:459), it can hardly mark a special type of individual deviance. From the perspective of the new penology, drug use is not so much a measure of individual acts of deviance as it is a mechanism for classifying the offender within a risk group.

Thus, one finds in the correctional system today a much greater emphasis on drug testing than on drug treatment. This may reflect the normal kinds of gaps in policy as well as difficulty in treating relatively new forms of drug abuse. Yet, testing serves functions in the new penology even in the absence of a treatment option. By marking the distribution of risk within the offender population under surveillance, testing makes possible greater coordination of scarce penal resources.

Testing also fills the gap left by the decline of traditional intervention strategies.

Innovation

Our description may seem to imply the onset of a reactive age in which penal managers strive to manage populations of marginal citizens with no concomitant effort toward integration into mainstream society. This may seem hard to square with the myriad new and innovative technologies introduced over the past decade. Indeed the media, which for years have portrayed the correctional system as a failure, have recently enthusiastically reported on these innovations: boot camps, electronic surveillance, high security 'campuses' for drug users, house arrest, intensive parole and probation, and drug treatment programs.

Although some of the new proposals are presented in terms of the 'old penology' and emphasize individuals, normalization, and rehabilitation, it is risky to come to any firm conviction about how these innovations will turn out. If historians of punishment have provided any clear lessons, it is that reforms evolve in ways quite different from the aims of their proponents (Foucault, 1977; Rothman, 1971). Thus, we wonder if these most recent innovations won't be recast in the terms outlined in this paper. Many of these innovations are compatible with the imperatives of the new penology, that is, managing a permanently dangerous population while maintaining the system at a minimum cost.

One of the current innovations most in vogue with the press and politicians are correctional 'boot camps.' These are minimum security custodial facilities, usually for youthful first offenders, designed on the model of a training center for military personnel, complete with barracks, physical exercise, and tough drill sergeants. Boot camps are portrayed as providing discipline and pride to young offenders brought up in the unrestrained culture of poverty (as though physical fitness could fill the gap left by the weakening of families, schools, neighborhoods, and other social organizations in the inner city).

The camps borrow explicitly from a military model of discipline, which has influenced penality

from at least the eighteenth century.[15] No doubt the image of inmates smartly dressed in uniforms performing drills and calisthenics appeals to long-standing ideals of order in post-Enlightenment culture. But in its proposed application to corrections, the military model is even less appropriate now than when it was rejected in the nineteenth century; indeed, today's boot camps are more a simulation of discipline than the real thing.

In the nineteenth century the military model was superseded by another model of discipline, the factory. Inmates were controlled by making them work at hard industrial labor (Ignatieff, 1978; Rothman, 1971). It was assumed that forced labor would inculcate in offenders the discipline required of factory laborers, so that they might earn their keep while in custody and join the ranks of the usefully employed when released. One can argue that this model did not work very well, but at least it was coherent. The model of discipline through labor suited our capitalist democracy in a way the model of a militarized citizenry did not.[16]

The recent decline of employment opportunities among the populations of urban poor most at risk for conventional crime involvement has left the applicability of industrial discipline in doubt. But the substitution of the boot camp for vocational training is even less plausible. Even if the typical 90-day regime of training envisioned by proponents of boot camps is effective in reorienting its subjects, at best it can only produce soldiers without a company to join. Indeed, the grim vision of the effect of boot camp is that it will be effective for those who will subsequently put their lessons of discipline and organization to use in street gangs and drug distribution networks. However, despite the earnestness with which the boot camp metaphor is touted, we suspect that the camps will be little more than holding pens for managing a short-term, mid-range risk population.

Drug testing and electronic monitors being tried in experimental 'intensive supervision' and 'house arrest' programs are justified in rehabilitative terms, but both sorts of programs lack a foundation in today's social and economic realities. The drug treatment programs in the 1960s encompassed a regime of coercive treatment: 'inpatient' custody in secured settings followed by community supervision and reintegration (President's Commission, 1967). The record suggests that these programs had enduring effects for at least some of those who participated in them (Anglin *et al.*, 1990). Today's proposals are similar, but it remains to be seen whether they can be effective in the absence of long-term treatment facilities, community-based follow-up, and prospects for viable conventional life-styles and employment opportunities.[17] In the meantime it is obvious that they can also serve the imperative of reducing the costs of correctional jurisdiction while maintaining some check on the offender population.

Our point is not to belittle the stated aspirations of current proposals or to argue that drug treatment programs cannot work. Indeed, we anticipate that drug treatment and rehabilitation will become increasingly attractive as the cost of long-term custody increases. However, given the emergence of the management concerns of the new penology, we question whether these innovations will embrace the long-term perspective of earlier successful treatment programs, and we suspect that they will emerge as control processes for managing and recycling selected risk populations. If so, these new programs will extend still further the capacity of the new penology. The undeniable attractiveness of boot camps, house arrest, secure drug 'centers,' and the like, is that they promise to provide secure custody in a more flexible format and at less cost than traditional correctional facilities. Indeed, some of them are envisioned as private contract facilities that can be expanded or reduced with relative ease. Further, they hold out the promise of expanding the range of low- and mid-level custodial alternatives, thereby facilitating the transfer of offenders now held in more expensive, higher security facilities that have been so favored in recent years. Tougher eligibility requirements, including job offers, stable residency, and promises of sponsorship in the community can be used to screen out 'higher risk' categories for non-custodial release programs (Petersilia, 1987). Thus, despite the lingering language of rehabilitation and reintegration, the programs generated under the new penology can best be understood in terms of managing costs and controlling dangerous populations rather than social or personal transformation.

From M. Feeley and J. Simon, 'The new penology: notes on the emerging strategy of corrections and its implications', Criminology, 1992, 30(4): 449–474.

Notes

1 A number of influential scholars have commented on this process, often calling attention to what they regard as the shortcomings of traditional individual-based legal language when applied to the problems of the modern organization-based society. See, e.g., dan-Cohen (1986), Stone (1975).

2 In contrasting the 'old' and the 'new' tort law, Steiner (1987:8) observes: 'They [judges with the new tort law] visualize the parties before them less as individual persons or discrete organizations and more as representatives of groups with identifiable common characteristics. They understand accidents and the social losses that accidents entail less as unique events and more as statistically predictable events. Modern social vision tends then toward the systemic-group-statistical in contrast with the vision more characteristic of the fault system, the dyadic-individual-unique.'

3 A good example of this is the President's Commission on Law Enforcement and Administration of Justice, created in 1966. Its report, *The Challenge of Crime in a Free Society* (1967), combined a commitment to the rehabilitative ideal with a new enthusiasm for actuarial representation. Indeed, that document represents an important point of coalescence for many of the elements that make up the new penology.

4 This is especially true for a number of new, intensive parole and probation supervision programs that have been established in recent years. Initially conceived as a way to reintegrate offenders into the community through a close interpersonal relationship between agent and offender, intensive supervision is now considered as an enhanced monitoring technique whose ability to detect high rates of technical violations indicates its success, not failure.

5 This does not mean that recidivism ceases to be a meaningful concept, but only that in its new mode of operation the penal system no longer accords it the centrality it once had. Recidivism remains a potent tool of criticism of the system, especially given its former significance. See, e.g., the California Legislative Analyst's *Report to the 1989/1990 Budget* (Sacramento), which contains a strong attack on the parole process for emphasizing the high rate of recidivism.

6 In recent years one of the authors has spent time with corrections officials in Japan and Sweden as well as the United States and found that significantly different language is used to characterize penal policies. In Sweden he heard the language of therapy and rehabilitation (the offender is not properly socialized and requires rehabilitative therapy). In Japan he heard the language of moral responsibility (the offender is morally deficient and needs instruction in responsibility to the community). In the United States, he heard the language of management (in a high-crime society, we need expanded capacity to classify offenders in order to incapacitate the most dangerous and employ less stringent controls on the less dangerous). Juxtaposed against each other, the differences are dramatic.

There is a similarity in approach between the new penology and the views expressed by Soviet legal theorist Eugenii Pashukanis (1978). He predicted that under socialism, law would 'wither away' and be replaced with management based upon considerations of social utility rather than traditional individualized considerations. See, e.g., Sharlet (1978).

7 Incapacitation then is to penology what arbitrage is to investments, a method of capitalizing on minute displacements in time, and like arbitrage it has a diminished relationship to the normative goal of enhancing the value of its objects.

8 The mean of a multinomial variable is incoherent.

9 In 1988, 3.7 million adults were under some form of correctional sanction in the United States, a 38.8% increase since 1984 (Bureau of Justice Statistics, 1989:5).

10 In 1988 there were 14 states in which more than a quarter of all prison admissions came from parole revocation (Bureau of Justice Statistics, 1989:69). In California, in 1988, 59% of admissions were from parole revocations (ibid.).

11 The importance of supervisory sanctions is all the more interesting given the effort of recent sentencing reform to remove discretion from corrections offices and establish juridical control through legislatures, judges, and prosecutors (Zimring and Hawkins, 1991).

12 The public remains interested in punishment for its own sake, and the expansion of parole and probation is tied in some degree to the ability of penal managers to convince the public that these supervisory sanctions can be punitive as well as managerial.

13 Incarceration for drug offenses grew at twice the rate of other offenses between 1976 and 1984 (Zimring and Hawkins, 1991:164),

14 Support for the legalization of marijuana, e.g., peaked among first year college students in 1977 at 52.9% and has since declined, reaching 16.7% in 1989 (Flanagan and Maguire, 1990:195).

15 The prison borrowed from the earlier innovations in the organization of spaces and bodies undertaken by the most advanced European military forces. See, e.g., Rothman (1971:105–108).

16 The model of industrial discipline was rarely fully achieved in prisons, but at least it had a clear referent in the real world, one that provided a certain coherence and plausibility to the penal project. The boot camp, like so much else in our increasingly anachronistic culture, is a signifier without a signified.

17 In his important 1966 essay 'Work and Identity in the Lower Class,' Rainwater suggested that members of the lower class often choose 'expressive' life-styles of deviance in the absence of opportunities for the most prestigious and desirable roles in the occupational structure. But he argued they also predictably burn out and accept the identification offered by 'even low-level employment of the good worker and provider. Rainwater urged that keeping entry-level employment available and tolerable was essential to fostering that transition. Today, when entry-level employment has shrunk to levels not imagined in the mid-1960s, the transition of those who are dissuaded or simply burn out on crime cannot be assumed (Duster, 1987).

References

Anglin, D., G. Speckhart, E.P. Deschenes (1990) *Examining the Effects of Narcotics Addiction*. Los Angeles: UCLA Neuropsychiatric Institute, Drug Abuse Research Group.

Bottoms, A. (1983) Neglected features of contemporary penal systems. In David Garland and Peter Young (eds.), *The Power to Punish*. London: Heinemann.

Cohen, S. (1985) *Visions of Social Control: Crime, Punishment and Classification*. Oxford: Polity Press.

dan-Cohen, M. (1986) *Persons, Rights and Organizations*. Berkeley: University of California Press.

Foucault, M. (1977) *Discipline and Punish*. New York: Pantheon.

Greenspan, R. (1988) The transformation of criminal due process in the administrative state. Paper prepared for delivery at the annual meeting of the Law and Society Association, Vail, Colo., June 1988.

Greenwood, P. (1982) *Selective Incapacitation*. Santa Monica, Calif.: Rand.

Heydebrand, W. and C. Seron (1990) *Rationalizing Justice: The Political Economy and Federal District Courts*. New York: State University of New York Press.

Ignatieff, M. (1978) *A Just Measure of Pain: The Penitentiary in the Industrial Revolution, 1750–1850*. London: Macmillan.

Jacobs, J.B. (1977) *Stateville: The Penitentiary in Mass Society*. Chicago: University of Chicago Press.

Lipsky, M. (1980) *Street Level Bureaucrats*. New York: Russell Sage Foundation.

Maguire, K. and T.J. Flanagan (1990) *Sourcebook of Criminal Justice Statistics 1989*. U.S. Department of Justice, Bureau of Justice Statistics, Washington, D.C.: U.S. Government Printing Office.

Mathieson, T. (1983) The future of control systems – The case of Norway. In David Garland and Peter Young (eds.), *The Power to Punish*. London: Heinemann.

Messinger, S. and J. Berecochea (1990) Don't stay too long but do come back soon. Proceedings, Conference on Growth and Its Influence on Correctional Policy, Center for the Study of Law and Society, University of California at Berkeley.

Moore, M.H., S.R. Estrich, D. McGillis, and W. Spelman (1984) *Dangerous Offenders: The Elusive Target of Justice*. Cambridge, Mass.: Harvard University Press.

Petersilia, J. (1987) *Expanding Options for Criminal Sentencing*. Santa Monica, Calif.: Rand.

President's Commission on Law Enforcement and the Administration of Justice (1967) *The Challenge of Crime in a Free Society*. Washington, D.C.,: Government Printing Office.

Reichman, N. (1986) Managing crime risks: Toward an insurance-based model of social control. *Research in Law, Deviance and Social Control* 8:151–172.

Rothman, D. (1971) *The Discovery of the Asylum: Social Order and Disorder in the New Republic*. Boston: Little, Brown.

— (1980) *Conscience and Convenience: The Asylum and its Alternative in Progressive America*. Boston: Little, Brown.

Simon, J. (1987) The emergence of a risk society: Insurance law and the state. *Socialist Review* 9561-89.

— (1988) The ideological effect of actuarial practices. *Law and Society Review* 22:771–800.

— (1990) From discipline to management: Strategies of control in parole supervision 1890–1990. Ph.D. dissertation, Jurisprudence and Social Policy Program, University of California at Berkeley.

Steiner, H.J. (1987) *Moral Vision and Social Vision in the Court: A Study of Tort Accident Law*. Madison: University of Wisconsin Press.

Stone, C. (1975) *Where the Law Ends*. New York: Harper & Row,

Zimring, F. and G. Hawkins (1991) *The Scale of Imprisonment*. Chicago: University of Chicago Press.

16.2 Actuarialism and the risk society
Jock Young

Actuarialism and the risk society

It is extraordinary that the academic discourse on actuarial justice develops separately from the rich vein of sociological scholarship concerning the nature of a 'risk society' (see Beck, 1992; Giddens, 1991). This is particularly so in that Jonathan Simon wrote an extremely prescient piece entitled 'The Emergence of the Risk Society' in 1987 which has a much wider compass than the now famous series of articles on the new penology and actuarial justice (Feeley and Simon, 1992, 1994; Simon, 1993; Simon and Feeley, 1995). But even the original article (quoted above) is concerned with the response to risk rather than risk itself, as its subtitle indicates: 'Insurance, Law and the State'.

For Anthony Giddens the concept of a risk society is concerned with the nature of risks in late modern society and with what he calls 'the calculative attitude' which individuals and collectivities develop in response to such risk:

> To live in the 'world' produced by high modernity has the feeling of riding a juggernaut. It is not just that more or less continuous and profound processes of change occur; rather, change does not consistently conform either to human expectation or to human control. The anticipation that the social and natural environments would increasingly be subject to rational ordering has not proved to be valid ....
>
> Providential reason – the idea that increased secular understanding of the nature of things intrinsically leads to a safer and more rewarding existence for human beings – carries residues of conceptions of fate deriving from pre-modern eras. Notions of fate may of course have a sombre cast, but they always imply that a course of events is in some way preordained. In circumstances of modernity, traditional notions of fate may still exist, but for the most part these are inconsistent with an outlook in which risk becomes a fundamental element. To accept risk as risk ... is to acknowledge that no aspects of our activities follow a predestined course, and all are open to contingent happenings. In this sense it is quite accurate to characterise modernity, as Ulrich Beck does, as a 'risk society', a phrase which refers to more than just the fact that modern social life introduces new forms of danger which humanity has to face. Living in the 'risk society' means living with a calculative attitude to the open possibilities of action, positive and negative, with which, as individuals and globally, we are confronted in a continuous way in our contemporary social existence. (1991, p. 28)

What I want to do is discuss the basis of such a notion of risk in the area of crime and deviance and how this results in a 'calculative' or 'actuarial' attitude in individuals, in institutions and in the criminal justice system itself.

Living with strangers: the six components of risk

A 'real' rise in risk

As I have documented throughout this book, the vast majority of countries in the developed world have experienced a rise in crime in the last 30 years. Such a crime rate has been accompanied by a penumbra of incivilities and crime has become increasingly internecine in its nature so that predatory behaviour and disorder is more and more implosive within each neighbourhood and social group.

Revelation

The mass media, the pressure group activities – and even the criminological researcher – have presented to the public a wider range of crime and on a greater scale than ever before. National crime surveys inform us that we can at least double (if not quadruple) the official crime rate, pressure groups indicate abuse occurring within the family often as much (if not more) than in the world outside, institutions which serve to protect and safeguard the vulnerable are seen to be sites of crime (from homes for the elderly to the orphanages of the Christian Brothers or the Sisters of Mercy), police and prisons are exposed as prime sites of corruption, violence and drug dealing. And on top of this, the illicit activities of white collar and corporate criminals are every day presented on our televisions and in our newspapers. No doubt some of this is inaccurate and a proportion misleading and mischievous, but the world which we *experience* as risky is *revealed* as risky on a wider and wider scale in all areas and parts of the social fabric.

Rising expectations

Risk is not a fixed objective thing: it rises or falls as our tolerance of a particular behaviour or practice changes. The change in public attitudes over the last 30 years has shown every indication of the 'civilizing influence' of a greater demand for a refinement in our behaviour towards each other and for an enhanced quality of life. Indeed the rising demand for law and order, which is often seen negatively as a sign of growing public authoritarianism may, more positively, be viewed as increasing demands for security, safety and civility in everyday life. One look at the area of violence confirms this, where a whole array of crimes have become a major focus of public concern: for example domestic violence, rape, child abuse and violence against animals. The entry of women into public life, consequent on their incorporation into the labour force, is no doubt a major influence on this, with rising demands being made on the level of civility both in public spaces and within the home. The area of public space is of interest in this respect in that it represents an area where women, because of increased economic and social equality, place themselves more at risk from male abuse but also demand more propriety. The greater use of pubs by women is a humdrum example of this two-way process, and is encouraged by the brewers for precisely these reasons.

Reserve

The greater mobility of people in modern society results in a decline of communities where people live most of their life and which centre around their workplace. This results in a significant drop in information, about neighbours, acquaintances, or chance encounters in the street. One has less direct knowledge of fellow citizens and this, together with living in a much more heterogeneous society, leads to much less *predictability* of behaviour. Unpredictability combined with risk generates a greater wariness in an actuarial stance towards others.

Reflexivity: the uncertainty of uncertainty

A key aspect of the late modern world, over and above the sensitization to risk, is the problematization of risk itself. Not only is the metropolis an uncertain world of dangers, but the level of risk itself is uncertain. In contrast to the modern world of predictable anxieties and dangers it is a world of uncertainty in that each level of risk will be questioned by experts and public alike. The fears come and go: carjacking, BSE, AIDS, road rage. They flicker on the screen of consciousness, something is going on but we are not sure who or what to believe. Whereas experts once concurred, they now seem to make a point of disagreement. From global warming to the ozone layer, from BSE to satanic child abuse, disagreement is the norm to an extent that the experts themselves begin to look shaky and to purvey just another opinion. But this is not a phantasmagoria, as some writers would have it (e.g. Furedi, 1997); city life is scarcely an Arcadian dream: if there was not a rational core of unease the images would not be able to find any purchase in the public consciousness.

Refraction

The mass media carry a plethora of images of crime and deviance gleaned from across the world. These media commodities are characterized like all news by their atypical nature – they are 'news' because they surprise and shock. Without doubt such imagery in its sheer quantity and in its garishness must cause 'fear' of crime disproportional to actual risk. Yet it is only one factor out of six, but it is often presented as *the* factor which determines public assessment of risk – as if fear were merely a metaphenomenon of television viewing.

Umwelt *and the management of risk*

The awareness of risk generates an actuarial attitude in the citizen of late modernity. This is an attitude of wariness, of calculation and of reflectiveness. Some of these calculations will involve seeking for opportunities: urban life is full of excitement and pleasure as well as risk. The citizens of all the great First World megalopolises – London, New York, Paris, for example – share the same habits of reserve, of abrasiveness with strangers, of 'ducking and diving': of avoiding trouble and seeking gain.

Anthony Giddens discusses the way in which human beings generate around themselves a feeling of bodily and psychic ease. 'If we mostly seem less fragile,' he notes, 'than we really are.. . it is because of long-term learning processes whereby potential threats are avoided or immobilized' (1991, p. 127). He builds on Goffman's notion of an *Umwelt*: a core of accomplished normality with which individuals and groups surround themselves. Taking inspiration from studies of animal behaviour, Goffman begins the section of *Relations in Public* designated 'normal appearances' with this remarkable imagery of the *Umwelt*:

> Individuals, whether in human or animal form, exhibit two basic modes of activity. They go about their business grazing, gazing, mothering, digesting, building, resting, playing, placidly attending to easily managed matters at hand, Or, fully mobilized, a fury of intent, alarmed, they get ready to attack or to stalk or to flee. Physiology itself is patterned to coincide with this duality.
>
> The individual mediates between these two tendencies with a very pretty capacity for dissociated vigilance. Smells, sounds, sights, touches, pressures – in various combinations, depending on the species – provide a running reading of the situation, a constant monitoring

of what surrounds. But by a wonder of adaptation these readings can be done out of the furthest corner of whatever is serving for an eye, leaving the individual himself free to focus his main attention on the non-emergencies around him. Matters that the actor has become accustomed to will receive a flick or a shadow of concern, one that decays as soon as he obtains a microsecond of confirmation that everything is in order; should something really prove to be 'up', prior activity can be dropped and full orientation mobilized, followed by coping behaviour .... (1971, p. 238)

The *Umwelt* has two dimensions: the area which one feels secure in and the area in which one is aware; the area of apprehension. The lioness sleeps tranquilly on the veldt, her eye every now and then taking in the activities in the distance. In human society it is a moving bubble which shrinks and expands wherever one is: whether, for example, one is at home or in the urban street. The nature of the *Umwelt* varies by social category. It is strongly gendered: Goffman noted that the *Umwelt* of women differed from men. Clearly, recognizing predatory sexual signs as well as signals of possible violence from men both in public and in the home is an important part of the social repertoire of women. Anyone who has conducted a criminal victimization survey knows that it is possible to identify and differentiate, 'blind', between women and men merely by looking at their avoidance behaviour patterns. Researchers talk of the 'curfew' at night of urban women (see Painter *et al.*, 1989). The *Umwelt* is strongly racialized: ethnic groups are aware of areas of safety and danger and in racist discourse, minorities are represented as signals of fear and danger to the majority population. It has strong dimensions of age: schoolchildren have a vivid sense of space and safety (see Anderson *et al.*, 1994); whilst street gangs and home boys actively police their turf, providing both security for themselves and alarm for others. Lastly, *Umwelt* is, of course, crucially constituted by class: the middle class by virtue of the cost of area, by the use of motor car, by private club and fancy restaurant seek to separate themselves from the undesirables, the 'dangerous classes', even when in transit through the busy city centres of Manhattan and London.

The signs of danger need not be crime itself or the threat of it, but more subtle perceptions of possible risk and the escalation of danger. Goffman was perhaps the first academic to note the problem of incivilities, way ahead of Wilson and Kelling's famous 'Broken Windows' [see p.295, this volume].

Thus:

> When an individual finds persons in his presence acting improperly or appearing out of place, he can read this as evidence that although the peculiarity itself may not be a threat to him, still, those who are peculiar in one regard may well be peculiar in other ways, too, some of which may be threatening. For the individual, then, impropriety on the part of others may function as an alarming sign. Thus, the minor civilities of every-day life can function as an early warning system; conventional courtesies are seen as mere convention, but non-performance can cause alarm. (1971, p. 241)

He cites an example of sexual harassment which graphically indicates the continuum nature of crime. This is from Meredith Tax's article in *Women's Liberation: Notes from the Second Year*:

> A young woman is walking down a city street. She is excruciatingly aware of her appearance and of the reaction to it (imagined or real) of every person she meets. She walks through a group of construction workers who are eating lunch in a line along the pavement. Her stomach tightens with terror and revulsion; her face becomes contorted into a grimace of self-control and fake unawareness; her walk and carriage become stiff and dehumanized. No matter what they say to her, it will be unbearable. She knows that they will not physically assault her or hurt her. They will only do so metaphorically. What they will do is impinge on her. They will use her body with their eyes. They will evaluate her market price. They will comment on her defects or compare them to those of other passers-by. They will make her a participant in their fantasies without asking if she is willing. They will make her feel ridiculous, or grotesquely sexual, or hideously ugly. Above all, they will make her feel like a thing. (Tax, 1970, p. 12)

Goffman is convinced that the condition of 'uneventfulness' is a moral right of a citizen (see 1971, p. 240); such a level of trust is part of the nature of civilized life. And he detects an overall deterioration in this quality of life:

> The vulnerability of public life is what we are coming more and more to see, if only because we are becoming more aware of the areas of intricacies of mutual trust presupposed in public order. Certainly circumstances can arise which undermine the case that individuals have within their *Umwelt*. Some of these circumstances are currently found in the semi-public places within slum housing developments . . . . Certainly the great public forums of our society, the downtown areas of our cities, can come to be uneasy places. Militantly sustained antagonisms between diffusely intermingled major population segments – young and old, male and female, white and black, impoverished and well-off – can cause those in public gatherings to distrust (and to fear they are distrusted by) the persons standing next to them. The forms of civil inattention, of persons circumspectly treating one another with polite and glancing concern while each goes about his own separate business, may be maintained, but behind these normal appearances individuals can come to be at the ready, poised to flee or to fight back if necessary. And in place of unconcern there can be alarm – until, that is, the streets are redefined as naturally precarious places, and a high level of risk becomes routine. (1971, pp. 331–2)

The area of security, of the Umwelt, shrinks apace as we enter the latter third of the twentieth century: it shrinks because of actual risk but also, as we saw in the last section, because sensitivity to risk rises whilst knowledge of others diminishes. But what can one say of the area of apprehension? Here the paradox of a drop in knowledge of immediates is associated with a globalization of knowledge of the wider outside world. *The area of security, of the* Umwelt, *thus decreases whilst at the same time the area of apprehension vastly increases.*

Lastly, there is another side of *Umwelt*, not touched upon by Goffman, but with obvious relevance and with parallels in animal behaviour. The lioness gazing fleetingly across the veldt is mapping out not only an area of security and one of apprehension but also looking for indications of prey and the possibilities of predation. In human terms the city is not only an area of security and insecurity but of opportunities for excitement, interest, gain and action. The *Soft City* of Jonathan Raban is an emporium of possibility as well as a labyrinth of danger.

Recalcitrant modernity and the critics of risk

There is a body of thought which sees fear of crime and perceptions of likely risk as a phenomenon quite separate from the actual risk of crime itself. Indeed 'fear' of crime is regarded sometimes as a problem autonomous from crime. Fear and concern about crime then become metaphors for other types of urban unease (e.g. urban development), or a displacement of other fears (e.g. racism, psychological difficulties). The 'real' or 'true' fears are separated from crime itself and this exercise is achieved by contrasting the 'gap' between the 'real' risk of crime and the evidence of 'disproportionate' fears. Women and old people are the most frequently cited examples of evidence that such a disproportionality exists. This is not the place to enter into a discussion of the concealment of risks of crime against these groups either by under-reporting or by avoidance behaviour which, so to speak, 'artificially' lowers the rates. I have analysed this extensively elsewhere (see Young, 1988, 1992). What is vital to reiterate, however, is that groups vary in their evaluation of the grossness of crime and that each item of risk is weighted differently by them. Women tend to view violence with greater abhorrence than men, but it is grotesque masculinism to suggest that because they worry more about violence, they are suffering from a form of irrationality which necessitates an expert unravelling their 'real' causes of discontent.

Crime, then, is refracted through the subculture of a group; it can never be perceived 'objectively' as naive 'realists' and their critics seem to believe. But there is more to it than this: within the notion of crime as a metaphor for other forms of urban unease is implicit the belief that crime is somehow separate from the other problems of society. Yet in fact, as numerous theorists have pointed out, crime is part of a continuum with other forms of antisocial behaviour and, indeed, as radical criminologists have never ceased to argue, the values which underlie much criminal behaviour are not distinct from conventional values but are closely related to them (see, e.g., Currie, 1997a). To talk, then, of crime as a metaphor for urban unease is a bit like saying that fire is a metaphor for heat; that it is somehow unrelated, but excessive heat is the real problem and that the fascination with these flames that flicker around us is merely a distraction brought upon us, no doubt, by the mass media and the crime control industry (e.g. Baer and Chambliss, 1997).

My argument is that because human behaviour is always a subject of evaluation and assessment there can be no one-to-one relationship between 'risk' and 'fear': arguments which are based simply on the level of correlation, for or against, are positivist blind alleys which lead

nowhere. What is necessary is to enter into the subculture in order to discover the significance of crime within it. To conduct qualitative research on the group is the only way to work outlines of causality (Sayer, 1984). In some cases almost metaphorical relationships will be found (but even here they are metaphors grounded in reality), in others the relationship will be stark and close (see Young, 1992).

Human evaluation takes time, it does not happen in an instant, as if we were talking of particles colliding with each other in the physical sciences. This mistake befuddles the debate about public attitudes to crime in the present period, particularly in the United States. Even such sophisticated commentators as Simon and Feeley can construct a false puzzle about public attitudes to crime:

What accounts for such intense fear? And what accounts for the dramatic increase in fear in recent years? Shifts in levels of fear of crime are not well-understood, and the answers to such questions are both complex and incomplete. But one important piece of the puzzle is well-charted if not well-understood: the intensity of public concern with crime is not directly or strongly related to the magnitude of crime. Indeed in recent years, concern about crime has increased despite a decline in overall rates of victimization. To be sure, some groups have experienced significant increases; young people from twelve to fifteen years of age, for example, experienced a 34 percent increase in violent crime victimizations during the 1980s. And citizens of our poorest inner-city neighborhoods, in particular young African-American males, have experienced significant increases in violence over the past decade. Still, the groundswell of support for more and more punitive crime measures in recent years has come after a decade of steady or declining crime rates for suburban middle-class whites, that segment of the population from which the strongest support for new get-tough measures comes. Why is this group which in other respects seems relatively insensitive to the well-being of people in communities distanced from themselves by poverty and race, and which is otherwise so sceptical of increases in government expenditures, so responsive to threats that in an objective sense affect them less now than at any time in recent memory? And why, when they generally resist increased

Figure 16.2.1   The murder rate in the US, 1995–93 (Archer and Gartner, 1984; Maguire and Pastore, 1995)

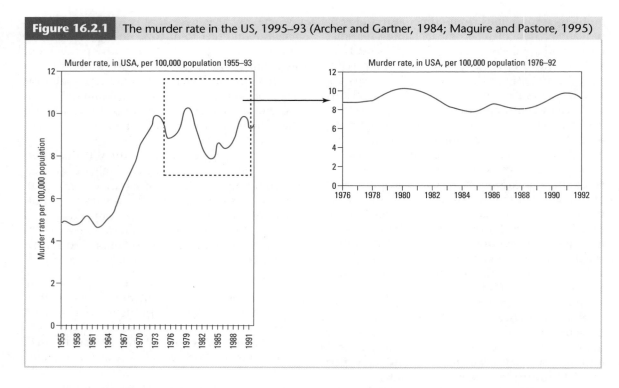

government spending, are they willing to support vast new expenditures for crime control measures of dubious efficacy?

Fear by itself is an inherently unsatisfying explanation for the formation of recent crime policy. Indeed, it is difficult to explain the fear itself, in its own right. And the very lack of any clear correspondence between objective risk and fear suggests that discourse, including the discourse of crime and penality, must be fundamental input to fear itself, along with factors such as neighborhood disorder, economic anxiety, and changes in racial demographics. (1995, p. 154)

I have quoted this at length, although such views are echoed regularly elsewhere (e.g. Chambliss, 1994a, 1994b; Platt, 1996) because it most thoroughly describes this perplexity. Briefly in response to this it should be noted that a central plank of the conundrum is that in the recent years the crime rate for the United States has levelled: for example the homicide rate (one of the more reliable statistics) was 10.2 per 100,000 in 1974 and 9.5 in 1993. In between this it has fluctuated, sometimes being as low as 8.0 (1985) (see Figure 16.2.1). William Chambliss quite correctly posited that the FBI has often capitalized on these fluctuations by claiming increases in violence when over

the longer period there was, if anything, a slight decline (see Chambliss, 1994b). This rosy positivistic vision is dependent on public memory being extremely short, yet it is undoubtedly longer than these authors allow for. Any middle-aged person in the United States will be only too aware that over the last third of the century (the period that concerns us here) there has been a dramatic increase in violence. In 1966, for example, the homicide rate was only 5.9 per 100,000 and the simple fact is that those who are careless enough to be mystified by public attitudes confine themselves to the plateau of the post-1973 period. For example, Chambliss' graph to illustrate this (1994a, Figure 2; 1994b, Figure 3) commences at this point but if he had started it just a few years earlier it would have shown a period of rapid growth up to this exceptionally high plateau (the present homicide rate is seven times that of England and Wales, and that of young men is a staggering 52 times). Could it not be that the American public is sick to its back teeth with this inordinate slaughter of its young people? Could it not be that they are willing to back intemperate policy and imprisonment in order, they hope, to achieve some abatement of the problem?

From J. Young, The Exclusive Society *(London: Sage), 1999, pp. 68–77.*

References

Baer, J. and Chambliss, W. (1997) 'Generating Fear: The Politics of Crime Reporting', *Crime, Law and Social Change* 27, pp. 87–107.

Beck, U. (1992) *Risk Society.* London: Sage.

Chambliss, W. (1994a) 'Profiling the Ghetto Underclass: The Politics of Law and Order Enforcement', *Social Problems* 41(2), pp. 177–194.

Chambliss, W. (1994b) 'Don't Confuse Me With Facts - 'Clinton Just Say No', *New Left Review* 204, pp. 113–128.

Currie, E. (1997a) 'Market, Crime and Community', *Theoretical Criminology* 1(2), pp. 147–172.

Feeley, M. and Simon, J. (1992) 'The New Penology: Notes on the Emerging Strategy of Corrections and its Implications', *Criminology* 30(4), pp. 449–474.

Feeley, M. and Simon, J. (1994) 'Actuarial Justice: The Emerging New Criminal Law' in D. Nelken (ed.) *The Futures of Criminology.* London: Sage.

Furedi, F. (1997) *The Culture of Fear.* London: Cassell.

Giddens, A. (1991) *Modernity and Self-Identity.* Cambridge: Polity.

Goffman, E. (1971) *Relations in Public.* London: Allen Lane.

Painter, K., Lea, J., Woodhouse, T. and Young, J. (1989) *The Hammersmith and Fulham Crime Survey.* Middlesex University: Centre for Criminology.

Platt, A. (1996) 'The Politics of Law and Order', *Social Justice* 21(3), pp. 3-13.

Sayer, A. (1984) *Method in Social Science: A Realist Approach.* London: Hutchinson.

Simon, J. (1987) 'The Emergence of a Risk Society: Insurance, Law and the State', *Socialist Review* 97, pp. 61-89.

Simon, J. (1993) *Poor Discipline.* Chicago: University of Chicago Press.

Simon, J. and Feeley, M. (1995) 'True Crime: The New Penology and Public Discourse on Crime' in T. Blomberg and S. Cohen (eds) *Punishment and Social Control.* New York: Aldine de Gruyter.

Tax, M. (1970) 'The Woman and Her Mind: The Story of Everyday Life' in A. Koedt and S. Firestone (eds) *Women's Liberation: Notes from the Second Year.* New York: Justice Books.

Young, J. (1988) 'Risk of Crime and Fear of Crime' in M. Maguire and S. Pointing (eds) *Victims of Crime: A New Deal.* Milton Keynes: Open University Press.

Young, J. (1992) 'Ten Points of Realism' in J. Young and R. Matthews (eds) *Rethinking Criminology.* London: Sage.

16.3 Risk, power and crime prevention
Pat O'Malley

Situational crime prevention as risk management

Situational crime prevention may be understood as quintessentially 'actuarial'. It deals hardly at all with individual offenders, is uninterested in the causes of crime, and generally is hostile or at best agnostic toward correctionalism. Its concern is with crime control as risk management (Reichman 1986). In a fairly aggressive self-description, the National Crime Prevention Institute outlines the following basic assumptions of what it grandly calls 'the contemporary perspective' in criminology:

- Prevention (and not rehabilitation) should be the major concern of criminologists;

- No one is sure how to rehabilitate offenders;

- Punishment and/or imprisonment may be relevant in controlling certain offenders;

- Criminal behaviour can be controlled primarily through the direct alteration of the environment of potential victims;

- Crime control programs must focus on crime before it occurs rather than afterward; and

- As criminal opportunity is reduced, so too will be the number of criminals,

(National Crime Prevention Institute 1986: 18)

As Cohen also indicates (but see too Bottoms 1990; O'Malley 1991; King 1989; Iadicola 1986; Hogg 1989) situational crime prevention is enjoying a period of extraordinary success in Britain, the United States, Australia and elsewhere – at least in the political sense of its influence as a program of crime control. Certainly it is tempting to follow earlier arguments and regard this as due to the increased efficiency of actuarial techniques. But the rapidity of its rise to prominence can scarcely be attributed to evidence of its superiority over correctionalism and causal/social criminologies. Rather what emerges, as might be expected from Cohen's (1985) original account of the 'politics of failure', is a political struggle over the definition and the criteria of failure and success. This may be seen in several ways.

First, advocates of situational crime prevention take inexorably rising crime rates as its evidence of the failure of criminology (e.g. Geason and Wilson 1988, 1989).[1] Yet while this may be a politically persuasive argument, it is scarcely an indisputable fact, since between the 1960s and 1980s social criminologies progressively undermined the validity of crime rates in this respect. The meaning and validity of crime rates in other words is part of the politics of failure rather than a neutral gauge for the measurement of efficiency.[2]

Second, the assault on social and causal criminologies' ineffectiveness, even where accepted, is readily turned aside by the argument that at no point have the insights of these theories been translated properly into policy. This point is one seized upon by Miller and Rose (1990) who point out that all policies 'fail' for this reason – because no policy is ever unadulterated in practice. Perhaps more to the point is the fact that no matter how 'pure' is the theoretical lineage of a policy, among adherents there will always be disputes over the 'correct' means of implementing the programs on which it is based. 'Failure' is always attributable to the mode of implementation rather than to the policy itself.

Third, situational crime prevention's own claims to success are undermined by counterclaims that it achieves merely the displacement of crime to softer targets (e.g. Wilson 1987; Cornish and Clarke 1986). More vitally, it is countered that it reacts only to symptoms, and thus fails to address the enduring social problems that crime merely manifests (King 1989; Bottoms 1990; MacNamara forthcoming). At this point, of course, the two approaches rather cease to converge – for the goals of each are regarded as misguided to the other, and the already disputed criteria of success and failure therefore lose the semblance of shared standards.

Such debates are endless. They reveal only that the politics of success and failure normally are struggles over the status of criteria, and can rarely be reduced to any universally accepted scale of efficiency. If this is the case, then the question of why situational crime prevention has proven so influential a technique will need to be answered in terms of its relationship to political programs and strategies, and especially to those currently in ascendance. I believe that the broader political and ideological effects of situational crime prevention reveal that its attractions to economic rationalist, neo-conservative and New Right programs provide such an answer (although not unrelated attractions to police forces are also significant). The primary attractions, I will argue, link directly with core ideological assumptions of the New Right, and through these with the two directions of population management – increasing punitiveness with respect to offenders, and with respect to victims, the displacement of socialized risk management with privatized prudentialism. While it is by no means the case that this is the only possible construction of situational crime prevention (others will be discussed briefly toward the end of this paper), for a variety of reasons it is a particularly durable and readily mobilized version under current conditions.

Neo-conservative readings of crime prevention

Situational crime prevention and the offender

Situational crime prevention destroys the disciplines' biographical individual as a category of criminological knowledge, but the criminal does not disappear. Opportunities only exist in relation to potential criminals who convert open windows into windows of opportunities for crime. To install such an agent, situational crime prevention replaces the biological criminal with a polar opposition – the abstract and universal 'abiographical' individual – the rational choice' actor (see also Geason and Wilson 1989; Heal and Laycock 1986; National Crime Prevention Institute 1986).

However, while abstract and abiographic, this rational choice individual nevertheless is clearly structured. It thinks in cost-benefit terms – weighing up the risks, potential gains and potential costs, and then committing an offence only when the benefits are perceived to outweigh the losses. This construction may be thought of as having a source very close to the foundations of actuarialism. It is of course the amoral rational choice individual beloved of classical economics, the *homo economicus* which inhabits the world of insurance – the home base of risk management discourses, and an industry closely connected with the promotion of situational crime prevention (O'Malley 1991).

This same being, but invested with additional moral and political characteristics is the denizen of neo-conservative and New Right discourses. It single-mindedly pursues the entrepreneurial ideal, as an atomistic being it is 'naturally free', self-reliant, and responsible (Gamble 1988). It is the underlying form of the human being that the Right would liberate from the debilitating 'public benefit' shackles of the welfare state which have progressively been imposed upon it especially since the end of the Second World War (Levitas 1986). Indeed, the demolition of socialized risk management and the restoration of social conditions approximating 'freedom' of the responsible individual is central to neo-conservative thinking about crime.

> When the traditional family is undermined, as it has been, self reliance tends to be lost and responsibility tends to disappear, both to be replaced by a dependence often long term, on the government and manipulation by social engineers. It also provides the setting which leads young people to the treadmill of drug abuse and crime. (Liberal Party of Australia 1988: 15)

Already it is possible to see how it might be that the neo-conservatives who are concerned to dismantle so much that Simon understands as actuarialism, might nevertheless embrace and foster the actuarialism of situational crime prevention. But there are other reasons as well.

Situational crime prevention's rejection of concern with biographical-causal approaches to understanding crime, and the focus on the targets of crime rather than on offenders, combine to deflect attention from the social foundations of offending. This effect is achieved in the case of the rational choice model by its rejection of or agnosticism toward conditions which may have given rise to the offenders' action, but also and especially by constructing the offender as abstract, universal and rational. Like the abstract legal subject explored by Pashukanis (1977) and Weber (1954), the abstract individual appears logically to be 'free' and thus a voluntary agent. Such abstract and universal, equal and voluntary individuals are free to act in a perfectly 'rational' self-interested fashion, maximizing gains and minimizing costs. They are free to commit crime or not to commit crime.

This latter point suggests that not only is the knowledge of the criminal disarticulated from a critique of society, but in turn, both of these may be disarticulated from the reaction to the offender. As Foucault made clear, what he saw as the 'criminological labyrinth' was constructed around the assumption that crime is caused, and that cause reduces responsibility (1977: 252). Elimination of cause from the discourse of crime obviously restores responsibility and this has its effects on punishment. Thus the logical corollary of situational crime prevention from the point of view of a New Right discourse, is a policy of punitive or just desserts sentencing, rather than a program of sentencing for reform. Compatibility of crime prevention thinking with these models is furthered by the argument that salutary punishment in the form of imprisonment incapacitates offenders and thus acts directly as a means of behavioural crime prevention.

Thus the criminal becomes individually responsible and our concern with offenders as such ceases with that knowledge. In consequence, any class, race, gender or similar foundations of crime, especially as identified by causal criminology, are automatically excluded from consideration except in their role as risk-enhancing factors. If bothered with at all they are taken to be predictive of behaviours, not explanatory of meaningful actions.

This shift in understanding eschews also the moral dimensions of the sociological criminologies, condemned to the status of 'failures' by situational crime prevention theorists (e.g. National Crime Prevention Institute 1986; Geason and Wilson 1989). Out with them go their respective agendas linking crime and social justice – for example that of strain theory and its concerns with relative deprivation and inequality of opportunity, and the appreciative recognition of cultural variability and of the impact of material degradation of the inner city poor that was the hallmark of ecological analysis. Academically as well as politically and administratively, it now becomes respectable to regard criminals as unconstrained agents, and to regard a crime control policy as divorced from questions of social justice.

Finally, the 'politics of failure' provide a technical gloss to justify punitiveness. If correction and deterrence do not work, then sanctions based on these ideas must be swept away. What is left for the offender but punishment, retribution and incapacitation?[3]

Situational crime prevention and the victim

If situational crime prevention short-circuits the link between criminality and social justice, then it might be expected that the victim of crime moves more into the centre of concern. In some sense this is undoubtedly the case, as the rhetoric of 'protecting the public' rings loud throughout this program (e.g. Home Office 1990).

However, just as the offenders are disconnected from the political dimensions of their existence, so too are the victims, for victims like offenders are to be understood as rational choice actors, responsible and free individuals.

Prevention now becomes the responsibility of the victim. This view is by no means the construct of academic reflection but permeates crime prevention thinking at all levels. At one level, this position emerges no doubt because it reduces pressure on police forces, which have not noticeably reduced crime victimization and which are therefore vulnerable to political pressure for this reason. Thus a senior official of the Australian Insurance Council has noted: 'Severely restricted police resources and the sheer frequency of crime, means that any improvement in the situation will rely heavily on property owners accepting responsibility for their own property and valuables' (Hall 1986: 243).

At broader political levels similar arguments are being presented for much the same reasons. Responding to news that crime rates in Britain have reached record levels, 'the Prime Minister, Mrs Thatcher, blamed a large portion of the crimes on the victims' carelessness. "We have to be careful that we ourselves don't make it easy for the criminal" she said' (*Age* 28 September 1990).

Not only does responsibility and thus critique shift, but so too do costs. Privatization of security practice and costs – to be seen in the trend toward private security agencies, security devices, domestic security practices, neighbourhood watch schemes (with attendant insurance underwriting) – generate the rudiments of a user pays system of policing security.[4] Closer to the heart of neo-conservatism, the rational choice public will come to see the justice in this:

> The general public's apathy about self-protection arises mainly from ignorance of the means of protection, and a perception that somebody else – 'the Government' or insurance companies – bears most of the cost of theft and vandalism. The community is beginning to realise however

that crime rates are rising despite increased penalties, that the judicial system cannot cope, and that it is the individual who eventually foots the bill for crime through increased taxes for expanded police forces and more jails, and through higher insurance premiums. (Geason and Wilson 1989: 9)[5]

In this process, security becomes the responsibility of the private individuals who through the pursuit of self interest, and liberated from enervating reliance on 'the state' to provide for them will participate in the creation of the new order.

Putting these points together, it can be seen that in this construction of situational crime prevention there is no conflict between risk management *per se* and punitiveness. Quite to the contrary, in the privatization of the actuarial techniques are the same notions of individual responsibility and rational choice that are present in the justification for expanding punitiveness. Reliance on the state, even for protection against crime, is not to be encouraged.[6] Quite literally therefore it represents the expression in one field of the New Right ideal of the Strong State and the Vice Market, combining to provide crime control in a period when the threat of crime generated by the Right's own market oriented practices can be expected to increase.

Crime prevention and social justice

The discussion of situational crime prevention thus far has been one-sided, for it has deliberately focused on developments illustrative of the ways in which risk-based and punitive techniques may be rendered compatible and mutually reinforcing under neo-conservatism. It will not have escaped recognition that situational crime prevention is by no means *necessarily* associated with neo-conservatism. The French Bonnemaison program for example incorporates much that is focused on social justice (King 1988). Likewise, in the Australian state of Victoria situational crime prevention is integrated quite explicitly with a government focus on social justice and is shaped accordingly (Sandon 1991a, 1991b; Victoria Police 1991). Thus with respect to the status of women, an issue on which situational crime prevention has been soundly criticized,[7] such policies have extended well beyond narrowly defensive and privatized risk bearing, and have embedded preventative techniques in socializing reforms, being 'concentrated on reducing violence against women by targeting the involvement of the community to change male behaviour and attitudes, empower women in unsafe situations and change community perceptions and understandings about violence toward women' (Thurgood 1991).

Clearly this social justice contextualization of situational crime prevention conflicts considerably with the behavioural regulation model reviewed above and criticized by Cohen. Not only is this because of the focus on changing people's attitudes and 'inner states', but also because it reflects a series of value assertions and policy directions which are remote from rational choice individualism. Such articulation between situational crime prevention and collective responses to crime as an issue of *social justice* of course reflects precisely that social risk-based model actively discarded by conservatives, and which was highlighted by the analyses of Simon *et al*. Articulation of situational crime prevention with social justice is intelligible in terms of the construction of risk as shared among large sectors of the populace – a precondition of socialized actuarialism. Thus with the welfare model, 'The concept of social risk makes it possible for insurance technologies to be applied to social problems in a way which can be presented as creative simultaneously of social justice and social solidarity' (Gordon 1991: 40).

It is therefore intelligible that risk-based techniques may be allied to socializing political programs through their discursive construction in terms of shared risk. Conversely it is equally clear that it may be articulated with a conservative political program through discursive construction in terms of rational choice individuals. As witnessed, this construction fosters the combination of a variety of disciplinary, punitive, and risk-based techniques in order to achieve effects consistent with neo-conservative programs.

Conclusions

Perhaps the central point in the argument of this paper is that history and the future are more contingent than is implied in the arguments of those theorizing the implications of risk-based social technologies. I have tried to argue that while such technologies undoubtedly have their own internal dynamics of development, these are neither perfectly autonomous nor do they have intrinsic effects which follow automatically from

their nature. Rather, the direction of development, the form in which they are put into effect in specific policies, their scope *vis-à-vis* that of other technologies, and the nature of their social impact are all quite plastic. Hopefully this will not be taken to imply that history is entirely contingent, for it should be clear that in the analysis above there are constants produced by the central place taken by risk in modern societies (cf. Giddens 1990). Thus I would not object to the assertion common to theorists of actuarialism that 'The concept of social risk makes it possible for insurance technologies to be applied to social problems in a way that can be presented as creative simultaneously of social justice and social solidarity'.

My point is simply to confirm that 'social risk' and 'insurance technologies' make this move *possible* rather than necessary. They make possible also a variety of other innovations with quite different implications, notably forms of privatized social risk management which have as their likely effects neither social justice nor solidarity. In addition these developments make possible many other hybrid developments with complex and varied possible effects – the nature of which has not yet been determined with any certainty by social research or theory. For example, state sponsored advertising campaigns concerning private property insurance against burglary may be linked to the development of neighbourhood-watch programs. Under some circumstances these may lead to vigilantism, victim-oriented pressure groups seeking harsher sentencing of offenders, and a fortress mentality. Under other circumstances they may lead to increased police responsiveness to community demands and a rise in levels of community solidarity and interaction. The point here is simply to reaffirm the openness of social forms based on risk management, and to question the extent to which any linear pattern can be discerned. If it is still the case after so many years that critical examination cannot lead to any definitive answers on the nature and direction of quite specific developments such as neighbourhood watch, why should it be anticipated that this task is less problematic when directed at developments at a broader level which are themselves conceptually distilled from a myriad of such specific programs?

Furthermore, one of the emergent outcomes of new social technologies is opposition, formed in important ways by the form and anticipated impact of the technology itself. Such opposition may never turn back the clock. The emergence of social technologies of risk mean that laissez-faire, for example, could never be resurrected in its original form, and the policies of neo-conservatism obviously reflect this. Nevertheless, the resurgence of neo-conservatism and economic rationalism has clearly created developments unanticipated by a previous generation of welfare state theorists. The difficulty, evidently, is working out the forms of oppositional resurrection and innovation which will be generated by new social technologies. Of even greater difficulty is working out what their degree of success will be, and how the struggle will change the nature of the emergent technology, and its place in the ensemble of technologies arrayed to deal with social problems.

From P. O'Malley, 'Risk, power and crime prevention', Economy and Society, 1992, *21(3): 252–275.*

Notes

1 Such a view for example recently has been promoted by the Australian Institute of Criminology.

> The traditional approach to crime prevention has been to identify the social and psychological causes of crime and to attempt to remedy these deficiencies by treating the individual offender and/or designing special educational, recreational and employment services for groups regarded as being at risk. The escalating crime rate suggests that this approach is not working.
> An alternative is 'situational crime prevention'. It rests on two assumptions: that the criminal is a rational decisionmaker who only goes ahead with a crime where the benefits outweigh the costs or risk; and the opportunity for crime must be there. (Geason and Wilson 1988: 1)

2 Such debates are extremely complex, and show no signs of resolving themselves. The position on the Left has been confused by the infusion of a qualified respect for crime rates as understood by Left realists (MacLean 1991), while more orthodox criminologists cannot agree even as to whether crime rates are rising or falling (Steffensmeier and Harer 1987) and many other Left commentators retain their very critical stance towards the entire exercise (Greenberg 1990).

3 The dimensions of this criminological stance no doubt are familiar, although of course all aspects and subtleties cannot be rehearsed here. Related matters concern the justification of punishment as respecting the dignity of the individual offender, and broader issues of 'truth in sentencing' and its relationship to the calculus of pleasure and pain thought to be intrinsic to the rational choice offender (see for example Van den Haag 1975).

4 A further element in emergent crime prevention practices consistent with the New Right credo is the focus on 'cool effectiveness' and 'cost-benefit' analysis. Thus for example *Young People and Crime* (Potas *et al.* 1990) produced by the Australian Institute of Criminology as part of its recently established series of publications dealing with crime prevention, ultimately asserts that no program of crime prevention should be established without prior and rigorous cost-effectiveness assessment (for which it duly provides a model). Indeed, for the more aggressively entrepreneurial versions of crime prevention

> this does not mean merely that it is important to keep the cost of security as low as possible (consistent with good security), it also means that he [i.e. the crime prevention analyst] should apply his knowledge of risk-management in as creative a way as possible, looking for opportunities for profit or other benefit as well as other ways to minimise loss. (National Crime Prevention Institute 1986: 51)

5 Of course, what this kind of argument tends to forget is that user pays models generally disadvantage the poor. In keeping with the tendency to abandon social justice, crime preventionism – through the progressive underdevelopment of public sector services – tends to leave the weak to fend for themselves (see O'Malley 1989).

6 Yet of course there is nothing in situational crime prevention that implies the diminution of police forces' powers and establishment. One of its major attractions for police is that it is an 'add-on' technique, augmenting traditional policing rather than replacing it. Moreover in many of its forms, for example neighbourhood watch, the police have been extremely active both in promoting it, in controlling the form of its development, and in maintaining control over its routine activities (e.g. O'Malley 1991).

7 Consider for example Lake (1990)

> In one sense women have gained a measure of freedom. A real measure of freedom. Yet...everywhere we are confined and I mean physically, mentally, psychologically confined. We know because we are told often enough that we must not walk on the streets at night. We must not now, it seems, travel on trains. Or public transport. Nor must we walk to dimly lit car parks. We must also every night securely lock ourselves up at home. And even then, of course, our security is illusory, for men force their way through windows into one's house or, they may already live in one's house...most domestic violence is committed on women known to the men who assault them, that is, it is committed on their wives, friends, daughters, sisters.

References

Bottoms, Anthony (1990) 'Crime prevention facing the 1990s,' *Police and Society* 1:32–2.

Cohen, Stanley (1985) *Visions of Social Control: Crime, Punishment and Classification*, London: Polity Press.

Cornish, Derek and Clarke, Robert (1986) 'Situational prevention: Displacement of crime and rational choice theory', in Kevin Heal and Gloria Laycock (eds) *Situational Crime Prevention: From Theory into Practice*, London: Home Office.

Geason, Susan and Wilson, Paul (1988) *Designing Out Crime*, Canberra: Australian Institute of Criminology.

— (1989) *Crime Prevention: Theory and Practice*, Canberra: Australian Institute of Criminology.

Giddens, Anthony (1990) *The Consequences of Modernity*, Stanford: Stanford University Press.

Gordon, Colin (1991) 'Governmental rationality: An introduction', in G. Burchell, C. Gordon and P. Miller (eds), *The Foucault Effect: Studies in Governmentality*, London: Harvester/Wheatsheaf.

Hall, John (1986) 'Burglary: the insurance industry viewpoint, in S. Mukherjee (ed.) *Burglary: A Social Reality*, Canberra: AIC.

Hogg, Russell (1089) 'Criminal justice and social control: Contemporary development in Australia', *Journal of Studies in Justice* 2: 89–122.

Home Office (1990) *Crime, Justice and Protecting the Public*, London: HMSO.

Iadicola, Peter (1986) 'Community crime control strategies', *Crime and Social Justice* 25: 140–57.

King, Michael (1988) *How to Make Social Crime Prevention Work: The French Experience*, London: NACRO Occasional Paper.

— (1989) Social crime prevention à la Thatcher', *Howard Journal of Penology* (October).

Macnamara, Luke (Forthcoming) 'Retrieving the law and order issue from the Right', *Law in Context*.

Miller, Peter and Rose, Nikolas, (1990) 'Governing economic life', *Economy and Society* 19: 131.

National Crime Prevention Institute (1986) *Crime Prevention*, Louisville: National Crime Prevention Institute.

O'Malley, Pat (1991) 'Legal networks and domestic security', *Studies in Law, Politics and Society* 11: 181–91.

Reichman, Nancy (1986) 'Managing crime risks: Toward an insurance based model of social control', *Research in Law and Social Control* 8: 151–72.

Sandon, Mal (1991a) *Safety and Society*, Melbourne: Ministry of Police and Emergency Services (Victoria).

— (1991b) *Ministerial Statement: Safety, Security and Women*, Melbourne: Parliament of Victoria.

Thurgood, Pat (1991) 'Safety, security and women', Paper presented at the Crime Prevention seminar, Ministry of Police and Emergency Services, Melbourne, 30 August.

16.4 Say 'Cheese!': The Disney order that is not so Mickey Mouse Clifford D. Shearing and Philip C. Stenning

One of the most distinctive features of that quintessentially American playground known as Disney World is the way it seeks to combine a sense of comfortable – even nostalgic – familiarity with an air of innovative technological advance. Mingled with the fantasies of one's childhood are the dreams of a better future. Next to the Magic Kingdom is the Epcot Center. As well as providing for a great escape, Disney World claims also to be a design for better living. And what impresses most about this place is that it seems to run like clockwork.

Yet the Disney order is no accidental by-product. Rather, it is a designed-in feature that provides – to the eye that is looking for it, but not to the casual visitor – an exemplar of modern private corporate policing. Along with the rest of the scenery of which it forms a discreet part, it too is recognizable as a design for the future.

We invite you to come with us on a guided tour of this modern police facility in which discipline and control are, like many of the characters one sees about, in costume.

The fun begins the moment the visitor enters Disney World. As one arrives by car one is greeted by a series of smiling young people who, with the aid of clearly visible road markings, direct one to one's parking spot, remind one to lock one's car and to remember its location and then direct one to await the rubber-wheeled train that will convey visitors away from the parking lot. At the boarding location one is directed to stand safely behind guard rails and to board the train in an orderly fashion. While climbing on board one is reminded to remember the name of the parking area and the row number in which one is parked (for instance, 'Donald Duck, 1'). Once on the train one is encouraged to protect oneself from injury by keeping one's body within the bounds of the carriage and to do the same for children in one's care. Before disembarking one is told how to get from the train back to the monorail platform and where to wait for the train to the parking lot on one's return. At each transition from one stage of one's journey to the next one is wished a happy day and a 'good time' at Disney World (this begins as one drives in and is directed by road signs to tune one's car radio to the Disney radio network).

As one moves towards the monorail platform the directions one has just received are reinforced by physical barriers (that make it difficult to take a wrong turn), pavement markings, signs and more cheerful Disney employees who, like their counterparts in other locations, convey the message that Disney World is a 'fun place' designed for one's comfort and pleasure. On approaching the monorail platform one is met by enthusiastic attendants who quickly and efficiently organize the mass of people moving onto it into corrals designed to accommodate enough people to fill one compartment on the monorail. In assigning people to these corrals the attendants ensure that groups visiting Disney World together remain together. Access to the edge of the platform is prevented by a gate which is opened once the monorail has arrived and disembarked the arriving passengers on the other side of the platform. If there is a delay of more than a minute or two in waiting for the next monorail one is kept informed of the reason for the delay and the progress the expected train is making towards the station.

Once aboard and the automatic doors of the monorail have closed, one is welcomed aboard, told to remain seated and 'for one's own safety' to stay away from open windows. The monorail takes a circuitous route to one of the two Disney locations (the Epcot Center or the Magic Kingdom) during which time a friendly disembodied voice introduces one briefly to the pleasures of the world one is about to enter and the methods of transport available between its various locations. As the monorail slows towards its destination one is told how to disembark once the automatic doors open and how to move from the station to the entrance gates, and reminded to take one's possessions with one and to take care of oneself, and children in

one's care, on disembarking. Once again these instructions are reinforced, in a variety of ways, as one moves towards the gates.

It will be apparent from the above that Disney Productions is able to handle large crowds of visitors in a most orderly fashion. Potential trouble is anticipated and prevented. Opportunities for disorder are minimized by constant instruction, by physical barriers which severely limit the choice of action available and by the surveillance of omnipresent employees who detect and rectify the slightest deviation.

The vehicles that carry people between locations are an important component of the system of physical barriers. Throughout Disney World vehicles are used as barriers. This is particularly apparent in the Epcot Center, the newest Disney facility, where many exhibits are accessible only via special vehicles which automatically secure one once they begin moving.

Control strategies are embedded in both environmental features and structural relations. In both cases control structures and activities have other functions which are highlighted so that the control function is overshadowed. Nonetheless, control is pervasive. For example, virtually every pool, fountain, and flower garden serves both as an aesthetic object and to direct visitors away from, or towards, particular locations. Similarly, every Disney Productions employee, while visibly and primarily engaged in other functions, is also engaged in the maintenance of order. This integration of functions is real and not simply an appearance: beauty is created, safety is protected, employees are helpful. The effect is, however, to embed the control function into the 'woodwork' where its presence is unnoticed but its effects are ever present.

A critical consequence of this process of embedding control in other structures is that control becomes consensual. It is effected with the willing co-operation of those being controlled so that the controlled become, as Foucault has observed, the source of their own control. Thus, for example, the batching that keeps families together provides for family unity while at the same time ensuring that parents will be available to control their children. By seeking a definition of order within Disney World that can convincingly be presented as being in the interest of visitors, order maintenance is established as a voluntary activity which allows coercion to be reduced to a minimum. Thus, adult visitors willingly submit to a variety of devices that increase the flow of consumers through Disney World, such as being corralled on the monorail platform, so as to ensure the safety of their children. Furthermore, while doing so they gratefully acknowledge the concern Disney Productions has for their family, thereby legitimating its authority, not only in the particular situation in question, but in others as well. Thus, while profit ultimately underlies the order Disney Productions seeks to maintain, it is pursued in conjunction with other objectives that will encourage the willing compliance of visitors in maintaining Disney profits. This approach to profit making, which seeks a coincidence of corporate and individual interests (employee and consumer alike), extends beyond the control function and reflects a business philosophy to be applied to all corporate operations (Peters and Waterman, 1982)

The coercive edge of Disney's control system is seldom far from the surface, however, and becomes visible the moment the Disney visitor consensus breaks down, that is, when a visitor attempts to exercise a choice that is incompatible with the Disney order. It is apparent in the physical barriers that forcefully prevent certain activities as well as in the action of employees who detect breaches of order. This can be illustrated by an incident that occurred during a visit to Disney World by Shearing and his daughter, during the course of which she developed a blister on her heel. To avoid further irritation she removed her shoes and proceeded to walk barefooted. They had not progressed ten yards before they were approached by a very personable security guard dressed as a Bahamian police officer, with white pith helmet and white gloves that perfectly suited the theme of the area they were moving through (so that he, at first, appeared more like a scenic prop than a security person), who informed them that walking barefoot was, 'for the safety of visitors', not permitted. When informed that, given the blister, the safety of this visitor was likely to be better secured by remaining barefooted, at least on the walkways, they were informed that their safety and how best to protect it was a matter for Disney Productions to determine while they were on Disney property and that unless they complied he would be compelled to escort them out of Disney World. Shearing's daughter, on learning that failure to comply with the security guard's instruction would deprive her of the pleasures of Disney World, quickly decided that she would prefer to further injure her heel and remain on Disney prop-

erty. As this example illustrates, the source of Disney Productions' power rests both in the physical coercion it can bring to bear and in its capacity to induce co-operation by depriving visitors of a resource that they value.

The effectiveness of the power that control of a 'fun place' has is vividly illustrated by the incredible queues of visitors who patiently wait, sometimes for hours, for admission to exhibits. These queues not only call into question the common knowledge that queueing is a quintessentially English pastime (if Disney World is any indication Americans are at least as good, if not better, at it), but provide evidence of the considerable inconvenience that people can be persuaded to tolerate so long as they believe that their best interests require it. While the source of this perception is the image of Disney World that the visitor brings to it, it is, interestingly, reinforced through the queueing process itself. In many exhibits queues are structured so that one is brought close to the entrance at several points, thus periodically giving one a glimpse of the fun to come while at the same time encouraging one that the wait will soon be over.

Visitor participation in the production of order within Disney World goes beyond the more obvious control examples we have noted so far. An important aspect of the order Disney Productions attempts to maintain is a particular image of Disney World and the American industrialists who sponsor its exhibits (General Electric, Kodak, Kraft Foods, etc.). Considerable care is taken to ensure that every feature of Disney World reflects a positive view of the American Way, especially its use of, and reliance on, technology. Visitors are, for example, exposed to an almost constant stream of directions by employees, robots in human form and disembodied recorded voices (the use of recorded messages and robots permits precise control over the content and tone of the directions given) that convey the desired message. Disney World acts as a giant magnet attracting millions of Americans and visitors from other lands who pay to learn of the wonders of American capitalism.

Visitors are encouraged to participate in the production of the Disney image while they are in Disney World and to take it home with them so that they can reproduce it for their families and friends. One way this is done is through the 'Picture Spots', marked with signposts, to be found throughout Disney World, that provide direction with respect to the images to capture on film (with cameras that one can borrow free of charge) for the slide shows and photo albums to be prepared 'back home'. Each spot provides views which exclude anything unsightly (such as garbage containers) so as to ensure that the visual images visitors take away of Disney World will properly capture Disney's order. A related technique is the Disney characters who wander through the complex to provide 'photo opportunities' for young children. These characters apparently never talk to visitors, and the reason for this is presumably so that their media-based images will not be spoiled.

As we have hinted throughout this discussion, training is a pervasive feature of the control system of Disney Productions, It is not, however, the redemptive soul-training of the carceral project but an ever-present flow of directions for, and definitions of, order directed at every visitor. Unlike carceral training, these messages do not require detailed knowledge of the individual. They are, on the contrary, for anyone and everyone. Messages are, nonetheless, often conveyed to single individuals or small groups of friends and relatives. For example, in some of the newer exhibits, the vehicles that take one through swivel and turn so that one's gaze can be precisely directed. Similarly, each seat is fitted with individual sets of speakers that talk directly to one, thus permitting a seductive sense of intimacy while simultaneously imparting a uniform message.

In summary, within Disney World control is embedded, preventative, subtle, co-operative and apparently non-coercive and consensual. It focuses on categories, requires no knowledge of the individual and employs pervasive surveillance. Thus, although disciplinary, it is distinctively non-carceral. Its order is instrumental and determined by the interests of Disney Productions rather than moral and absolute. As anyone who has visited Disney World knows, it is extraordinarily effective.

While this new instrumental discipline is rapidly becoming a dominant force in social control ... it is as different from the Orwellian totalitarian nightmare as it is from the carceral regime. Surveillance is pervasive but it is the antithesis of the blatant control of the Orwellian State: its source is not government and its vehicle is not Big Brother. The order of instrumental discipline is not the unitary order of a central State but diffuse and separate orders defined by private authorities responsible for the feudal-like domains of Disney World, condominium estates, commer-

cial complexes and the like. Within contemporary discipline, control is as fine-grained as Orwell imagined but its features are very different .... It is thus, paradoxically, not to Orwell's socialist-inspired Utopia that we must look for a picture of contemporary control but to the capitalist-inspired disciplinary model conceived of by Huxley who, in his *Brave New World*, painted a picture of consensually based control that bears a striking resemblance to the disciplinary control of Disney World and other corporate control systems. Within Huxley's imaginary world people are seduced into conformity by the pleasures offered by the drug 'soma' rather than coerced into compliance by threat of Big Brother, just as people are today seduced to conform by the pleasures of consuming the goods that corporate power has to offer.

The contrasts between morally based justice and instrumental control, carceral punishment and corporate control, the Panopticon and Disney World and Orwell's and Huxley's visions is succinctly captured by the novelist Beryl Bainbridge's observations about a recent journey she made retracing J. B. Priestley's celebrated trip around Britain. She notes how during his travels in 1933 the centre of the cities and towns he visited were defined by either a church or a centre of government (depicting the coalition between Church and State in the production of order that characterizes morally based regimes).

During her more recent trip one of the changes that struck her most forcibly was the transformation that had taken place in the centre of cities and towns. These were now identified not by churches or town halls, but by shopping centres; often vaulted glass-roofed structures that she found reminiscent of the cathedrals they had replaced both in their awe-inspiring architecture and in the hush that she found they sometimes created. What was worshipped in these contemporary cathedrals, she noted, was not an absolute moral order but something much more mundane: people were 'worshipping shopping' and through it, we would add, the private authorities, the order and the corporate power their worship makes possible.

> *From C. Shearing and P. Stenning, Say 'Cheese!': the Disney order that is not so Mickey Mouse, in C. Shearing and P. Stenning (eds)* Private Policing *(Newbury Park, CA: Sage), 1987, pp.317–323.*

References

Bainbridge, B. (1984) Television interview with Robert Fulford on 'Realities', Global Television, Toronto, October.

Foucault, M. (1977) *Discipline and Punish: The Birth of the Prison.* New York: Vintage.

Peters, T.J. and R.H. Waterman, Jr. (1982) *In Search of Excellence: Lessons from America's Best-run Companies.* New York: Warner.

Priestley, J.B. (1934) *English Journey: Being a Rambling but Truthful Account of What One Man Saw and Heard and Felt and Thought During a Journey Through England the Autumn of the Year 1933.* London: Heinemann & Gollancz.

Authors' note: This chapter is largely extracted from 'From the Panopticon to Disney World: The Development of Discipline:' pp. 335–349 in A. Doob and B. Greenspan (eds.) *Perspectives in Criminal Law: Essays in Honour of John Ll. J Edwards* (Aurora: Canada Law Book. 1984). We would like to thank the Canada Law Book company for granting permission to reprint part of this essay here.

17

Victims, victimization and victimology

17.1 On becoming a victim
Paul Rock   388

**17.2 Fiefs and peasants: accomplishing
change for victims in the criminal
justice system**
Joanna Shapland   397

**17.3 Violence against women and children:
the contradictions of crime control
under patriarchy**
Jill Radford and Elizabeth A. Stanko   402

**17.4 Multiple victimisation:
its extent and significance**
Graham Farrell   409

Introduction

KEY CONCEPTS   coercive sexuality; criminal justice fiefdom; domestic violence; Kirkholt burglary prevention project; patriarchy; multiple/repeat victimization; victimology

It is only relatively recently that criminology has begun to pay considerable attention to victims of crime. This is paralleled in formal criminal justice policy in which developments such as victim compensation, support schemes for people who have been victimized and discussions of the role of the victim in court have come to the fore only in recent decades. Indeed, the interest within criminology has given rise to its own subsidiary area of study, with its own journals and conferences, known as *victimology*.

As Paul Rock notes **(Reading 17.1)** the 'rediscovery of the victim' from around about the 1970s onward was stimulated by a number of developments – social, intellectual and political. Rock analyses the major shifts that led to greater criminal justice and criminological attention being paid to victims and to the experience of victimization. Despite the flourishing of scholarship in this area he goes on to outline some of the continuing limitations of our knowledge about victims. The major 'conceptual void', he suggests, concerns the problem of identity: the processes, psychological and otherwise, that are involved in 'becoming a victim'. Much scholarship has, for example, avoided the problem of 'interaction' – exploring and seeking to understand the fact that much victimization takes place between people who know each other and may be in close relationships with each other. At what point in these relationships do people come to see themselves as a 'victim'?

Rock's article encourages a set of changes in academic responses to, and analyses of, victims and victimization. The second excerpt, by Joanna Shapland **(Reading 17.2)** explores some of the difficulties in achieving change for victims of crime in the criminal justice system. One of the key problems she identifies is that criminal justice systems are in some respects best seen not as interconnected systems of agencies but, rather, as a series of semi-autonomous fiefdoms which guard their own territory jealously and are loath to work with others and to share resources. In circumstances where there is no agency which 'owns' victims, or where particular fiefdoms have other priorities, it can be highly problematic trying to achieve change.

One of the areas in which there has been perhaps the greatest development – both criminologically and within criminal justice – concerns violence against women. Jill Radford and Betsy Stanko **(Reading 17.3)** note how central violence is to women's lives and how hidden this remains. Their interpretation of this is that 'it is essential to a system of gender subordination', i.e. patriarchy. In the excerpt they examine some of the dangers inherent in the growing recognition by state agencies of women's victimization and argue strongly for the continued importance of feminist praxis and politics. Importantly, they argue, much of what women experience as coercive sexuality is not currently recognised in 'man-made law' and, even where recognized, old stereotypes tend to limit intervention and effectiveness. They are highly critical of official campaigns focusing on women's safety as, in essence, restricting women's freedoms at best and blaming women at worst.

One of the methodological developments that has increased our knowledge in this area is the victimization survey. This, perhaps, is of little surprise. One of the less predictable outcomes or results of such surveys, however, has been the identification of what has become known as 'multiple' or 'repeat victimization'. We have long known that some offenders tend to commit disproportionate numbers of offences. Graham Farrell **(Reading 17.4)** suggests that there is something of a parallel in the field of victimization. That is to say, some individuals, households or other targets are, repeatedly, disproportionately victimized. Thus, for example, the first British Crime Survey in 1982 found that over 70% of the offences that were reported to it had been experienced by just 14% of the population. This, like repeat offending, has some potentially sizeable policy implications – the challenges, as ever, are identification and prevention – and Farrell briefly discusses findings from a burglary prevention project in Kirkholt (that has subsequently become famous) in which these insights were successfully put into practice.

Questions for discussion

1. What, according to Paul Rock, were the main ways in which victims were dealt with in criminology prior to the 1970s and their 'rediscovery'?

2. What were the major changes which prompted increasing attention to be paid to victims of crime?

3. When Joanna Shapland describes the operation of the criminal justice system as 'feudal' what is she suggesting? And what are the implications for victims?

4. Is the creation of a set of institutions with victims at the heart of their concerns the solution to the problem of the relatively low profile of victims in criminal justice? What might be the difficulties with this?

5. What dangers do Radford and Stanko identify in what they describe as the moves to make women's studies respectable?

6. What, according to Radford and Stanko, is the heart of the contradiction facing feminists?

7. What is 'multiple victimization'?

8. What are the main policy implications of identifying multiple victimization?

17.1 On becoming a victim
Paul Rock

Introduction

Until the late 1970s, victims were almost wholly neglected in criminology and criminal justice. Crime and deviance were characteristically treated in the following ways:

- by the more positivistic, and especially by the more clinical, criminologist as discrete, material states inhering in individuals who could be examined independently of social context, relations and history (including any history of dealings with victims);

- by the more sociological as properties of structure and belief, and particularly of the larger structures of economic inequality and cultural difference, and victims were there analytically finessed;

- by the Marxist and radical, initially, as a facet of social disorganisation without reference to any victims other than deracinated industrial workers, then as the figments of a proletarian false consciousness that was turned towards the wrong objects[1] and, latterly, as the sometimes righteous, sometimes possessive, individualistic responses of the anomic poor and dispossessed to the pathologies of capitalism, and victims, by extension, were either undeserving or descriptively excluded;[2] and

- by the interactionist and phenomenologist as symbolic constructions manufactured in dialectical interchange with significant others, and with the powerful above all – control, not crime, was the problem – and victims did not seem to figure. [...]

The early victimologists themselves were often not much more than abstracted empiricists searching for a theory, a language and academic legitimacy. [...]

Much of the early, victim-free phase of criminology was the creature of what appears in retrospect to have been an innocent time and place, described by Young as the criminological 'Golden Age of the post-war period within the First World'.[3] The volume of recorded crimes in that English and Welsh Golden Age was small and diminishing in the early 1950s, although there were fears about youthful offending,[4] and about offences of violence above all.[5] [...]

Crime was taken to be a minor social problem the management of which could be entrusted to the expert – including the criminologist – who had a civilising mission to educate the public and politicians and reform the machinery of welfare, control and rehabilitation. [...]

Recorded crimes may have started rising again in the late 1950s, but cultural lag and an engrained scepticism about the State and its counting practices,[6] led influential members of the academic generations who were trained in the 1950s, 1960s and early 1970s to mistrust or ignore both government-generated crime rates and the State's analysis of what they portended.[7] [...]

It was as if some criminologists had decided that they did not wish to be associated with the discreditable victim, but, if they were obliged to be, the victim to be considered would be defined principally by the criminologists' criteria of eligibility as the deviant, offender, prisoner, proletarian or other neglected casualty of capitalism,[8] racism, imperialism and class exploitation.[9] [...]

Becker constructed one version of that argument in his metaphor of the hierarchy of credibility: the task of the sociologist of crime, he claimed, was to restore balance and challenge from below the seemingly authoritative accounts of crime and control and supplied by the powerful.[10] Hall and his colleagues constructed another: crime was a mystifiying diversion introduced to divide the subaltern and working classes in a capitalist state that was entering what could well be its terminal phase, and the criminal himself was a scapegoat in a politics of crisis.[11] Cohen constructed a third version:

> The [new] orientation is part of what might be called the sceptical revolution in criminology ... The older tradition was canonical in the sense that it saw the concepts it worked with as authoritative, accepted, given and unquestionable. The new tradition is sceptical in the sense that when it sees terms like 'deviant', it asks 'deviant to whom?' or 'deviant from what?... when certain conditions or behaviour are described as functional, embarassing, threatening or dangerous, it asks 'say who?' and 'why?'[12]

The sceptics did not speak with one voice, but for years they rejected the conventional politics of law and order, and, it may be presumed, rejected many of its themes, including talk of victims, in their turn (I write 'presumed' because there was almost no discussion of victims). [...]

It was only when criminology confronted a piecemeal battery of brute facts and criticisms that it somewhat grudgingly, raggedly and belatedly gave ground. Those facts and criticisms, it should be noted, almost invariably emanated from outside criminology.

The rediscovery of the victim

First, there was the question of the sheer volume of crime in the West, the problem it was supposed to represent, and, for a few, whether official talk about the nature and scale of offending was to be identified as part of a hegemonic project to divide and mislead the populace. Recorded crime in England and Wales grew ten-fold between the 1950s and the 1990s. [...] Reiner was moved to write at the end of 1994 (just when rates began to fall):

> So many people are rightly more cautious nowadays about saloon-bar pontifications on rising crime... Yet even with appropriate warnings most commentators – and I certainly include myself – feel this time things are really different. We are caught up in long-term expansion of crime and disorder, which has been with us for nearly forty years, and which has intensified greatly in the last year and a half.[13]

It had become more and more difficult to disparage crime as an over-inflated social problem.

Secondly, America saw lurid displays of violence in the assassination of politicians and the urban rioting of the 1960s especially in New York City, Philadelphia and Rochester, New York, in 1964; in Watts in 1965; Chicago, San Francisco, Dayton and Cleveland in 1966; and in over 150 cities in 1967. Politicians and lay commentators were jolted into suspending their belief in a social world that was safe, predictable and expertly-managed. [...] The third and fourth sentences of the President's Crime Commission report recited that: 'Every American is, in a sense, a victim of crime. Violence and theft have...injured, often irreparably, hundreds of thousands of citizens'.[14] It did not then pursue that line of reasoning much further, and neither did criminologists rush to talk about victims. But work for the Commission included some of the very first crime surveys[15] that were intended to enhance the analysis of crime by 'more rational ways... [of] measure[ment] than those currently in use',[16] and *they* led in their turn to the permanent establishment of national crime surveys in the United States from 1972 onwards and then, in different policy contexts in 1981, in Canada, the United Kingdom and elsewhere. Canadian surveys were initially presented as a means of preventing crime and violence in the heightened politics of debate about capital punishment.[17] In England and Wales, in the wake of Britain's own riots, and as a means of doing *something* about an abrupt crisis of public order, they were instituted in the name of 'improving the criminal justice database' (and it is revealing that surveys of victims are very generally called crime surveys).

Successive surveys in those different countries proceeded to illuminate new facts about the demography, epidemiology and geography of victims, their apprehensions about crime, and their encounters with the criminal justice system. [...] From the outset, they explored aspects of victimisation in ways that had been impracticable before. They revealed the distribution, scale, depth and injuries of crime and, in particular, its heavy impact on working class and minority ethnic groups, and the findings were not easily ignored. Crime, said Downes, had been shown to be a regressive tax on the poor. Although it was inevitable that diverse inferences were drawn about how they should be read, the surveys disarmed some of the sceptics. [...]

Lea and Young, radical criminologists who had once been prone to dismiss victimisation as an epiphenomenon of false consciousness, acknowledged on the heels of the first British Crime Survey:

> There was a schizophrenia about crime on the left where crimes against women and immigrant groups were quite rightly an object of concern, but other types of crime were regarded as being of little interest or somehow excusable. Part of this mistake stems from the belief that property offences are directed solely against the bourgeoisie and that violence against the person is carried out by amateur Robin Hoods in the course of their righteous attempts to redistribute wealth. All of this is, alas, untrue.[18]

There was, thirdly, a revelation of the abundant injuries inflicted by crime on vulnerable populations, and on children and women in particular. Clinicians and police discovered child abuse.[19] Feminism[20] and the feminist criminology of the 1970s and early 1980s[21] discovered widespread and ever multiplying incidents of domestic violence, rape and incest, transformed private troubles into public issues through 'speak-outs', marches and demonstrations,[22] and argued that the neglect of violence against women by practitioner and academic was insupportable – and the academics came in time to concur. Children and women were difficult to regard as either politically legitimate or inconsequential victims and they created new dilemmas for the campaigning criminologist and for left-wing criminologists especially. [...]

Fourthly, there was the so-called victims movement – very much more of a political and ideological movement in North America than in the United Kingdom – which declared angrily and at length that the victim was, as its members put it, 'the forgotten party of the criminal justice system' who was doubly victimised by the crime and by the State's response to crime. Their cry was 'what about the victim?' and it was to be timeously heard by the politician and practitioner[23] (if not at first by the more wary criminologist).[24] [...]

Fifthly, there was the work of Reiss,[25] Ericson[26] and others which showed that police work was not, as the academics, practitioners and politicians had tended to portray it, a technically competent, professional and self-reliant exercise in the detection of crime and enforcement of law, but, to the contrary, an activity which leaned heavily on the lay knowledge and observations of victims, witnesses and bystanders on the scene. [...] In the context of a rising volume of crime rates and a declining rate of detection, the emphasis grew on helping victims to *cope* with the effects of crime through victim support programmes rather than to expect arrests, punishment and the restoration of property. There was to be a new conception of community and multi-agency co-operation in which victims were enlisted to add informal social control to the armoury of a now less than confident State in the 'fight against crime.'

There was an accompanying administrative fear in North America,[27] but not in the United Kingdom, that the criminal justice system's alienation of lay witnesses and victims could jeopardise their willingness to report crime, give evidence and secure prosecutions, thereby endangering the system's very viability. [...]

There were, finally the victim–offender reconciliation projects designed (in the Canada[28] and United States[29] of the 1970s) to deal with the strained capacities and fiscal and administrative crises of overcrowded courts and prisons; replace the estranging polarities of the adversarial trial

process; and reinforce Christian themes of peace-making. They led into the reparative justice movement[30] which foundered on the economics of criminal justice in the mid-1980s, only to be revived in the 1990s as politicians and practitioners embraced John Braithwaite's 'big idea' of reintegrative shaming.[31]

The increasing scale and gravity of crime, and the growing prominence of the victim in many of the regions abutting their discipline, conspired to bring fractured images of victimisation more fully to the criminologist's attention. 'Victims, once on the margins of criminological research, are now a central focus of academic research'[32] and the consequence has been that we now know more, think differently and ask new questions. The rediscovery of the poor, proletarian, female and black victim galvanised those in and around radical criminology in the mid-1980s and led to left realism. [...]

The discovery of repeat victimisation transformed crime prevention policy and led to the idea of 'cocooning' and targeted strategies.[33] The revelation that crime has its spatial concentrations or 'hot spots'[34] led to new forms of intelligence-led or problem-oriented policing. We know that our earlier assumptions about the impact, quantity and spread of crime[35] have had to be replaced not only by an appreciation of its deep, persistent, pervasive and often unexpected[36] effects, but also by an awareness of its capacity to confound typifications of who the victim and offender might actually be. We no longer talk so glibly in the language of Christie's ideal victim,[37] the little old lady, as if she were a good enough ideal type.[38] We now know that victims are not always simon-pure but recruited in great measure from much the same demographic and geographical populations as offenders, bystanders and witnesses,[39] and that violent people are likely to become the victims of violence.[40] 'Generally,' Antilla remarked, 'one can say that the earlier stereotypes of "black and white" have been exchanged for "grey versus grey"'.[41]

Some limitations of knowledge about victims

All those images were prefabricated in sites outside criminology before they were imported.[42] They were not designed for academic criminology.[43] [...]

All frameworks have their opportunity-costs and the outcome of using these imported ones has been the creation of fuzzy areas at the heart of criminology that obscure scholarly understanding of who and what victims are. For some, perhaps, there was a distaste about the prospect of moving nearer to an ideologically uncongenial figure. For others, identification with the newly-defined victims nonetheless led to its own analytic taboos. And for a third group, methodology prevented any close examination of the nature of the victim at all.

I have already discussed how the more radical and political criminologists had been hesitant to talk about victims. But there have been countervailing hesitations. Take the more campaigning strands of victimology. They stemmed from an activism that sought to accomplish political objectives, and, however interlaced they may have become with academic work, that teleology remains a force, patrolling the moral standing, ontology and claims of the victim, editing what may be done and said, and erecting barriers around critical questions.[44] A number of radical criminologists have been somewhat disinclined to explore the newly-championed proletarian, minority-ethnic or female victim's role in crime. There has been, for instance, a marked nervousness about consideration of the black woman's exposure to domestic violence from what, in the main, could only have been a black partner.

More generally, the female victim has sometimes been represented in feminist analysis as an undeserving and innocent casualty of patriarchal relations who requires support and who is best described not in a language of victimisation at all but in that of survival. Pahl noted, for example, how the residents of a women's refuge were described as 'the women in the house' rather than as 'battered women'.[45] Some rape crisis centres preferred to talk of survivors or of 'raped women' rather than of victims: ' "Victims" cannot fight back,' it was said, but "raped women" will.[46]

Descriptions of female victims as people actively participating in evolving social relations have from time to time been dismissed as mere 'victim-blaming';[47] *blaming* itself being construed as almost any allusion to the victim's role in criminal transactions, from Mendelsohn's odd and freighted notion of a victim's 'guilty contribution to crime',[48] through Wolfgang's more neutral idea of victim-precipitation, to the argument that 'victim' is a social and rhetorical role fashioned collaboratively with others.[49] 'Innocent [female] victims', Kantor argued, 'continue to be blamed for the behavior of their attacker or for contributing to their own violent victimization.'[50] It was partly for that reason that Amir's *Patterns in Forcible Rape* was to be vilified for its discussion of victim-precipitated rape.

Alleged equivalencies between the plight of female and male victims[51] are held, at least in some texts, to neglect the distinctive and vitally gendered properties of violence under patriarchy. Stanko wrote:

> Creating a category 'victim' is one way of dealing with women's experiences of male violence. The role and status of 'victim' is separate from that of all women. 'Victimism', the practice of objectifying women's experiences of male violence, serves to deny the commonality among sexually and/or physically assaulted women and their oneness with all women.[52]

The third source of difficulty has been methodological. Take crime surveys: they have yielded abundant information that no other method could have produced and they have transformed the criminological landscape, but they were constructed (for precise policy and administrative ends) to count aggregations of somewhat atomised, deracinated and anonymous responses set in a limited context of social statics, rather than with appreciation of some of the more complicated and intertwined social relations that extend beyond the individual and evolve over time. They inevitably mask the existential elements in the development of victimisation.

The problem of identity

There is an ensuing conceptual void that has yet to be filled by an adequate description of the victim as a situated, reflective self in interaction with others, and it could be a useful description because much that is important in personal and collective conduct and belief in this area turns on what it is to be a victim. Any such examination must deal with how people cope with the here-and-now experience of crime; what sense they come to make of it; how they account to themselves and others about what has transpired (and, indeed, when and how accounting needs to be done); what materials are available to construct such accounts; what identities are implicated and how, if at all, they are acquired. The list could be extended but it does outline the kind of programme to be pursued, and what follows is a sketch of a framework in which it might be set.

A victim is one who is defined voluntarily or involuntarily, directly or indirectly, abruptly or gradually, consequentially or inconsequentially, by the proven or alleged criminal or crime-like actions of another. 'Victim', in other words, is an *identity*, a social artefact dependent, at the outset, on an alleged transgression and transgressor and then, directly or indirectly, on an array of witnesses, police, prosecutors, defence counsel, jurors, the mass media and others who may not always deal with the individual case but who will nevertheless shape the larger interpretative environment in which it is lodged.

Not all those who are transgressed against will evolve into full-blown victims. So abundant and varied is crime, and so contingent is its impact, that the mere fact that one has become or been made a victim lacks immediate predictive power about who one is, how one regards oneself or is regarded by others, or what one might do or become as a result. A *victim* could be little more than an item in an accounting system, a statistical entry with slight existential weight for one who has been so classified, a primary victim or victim *an sich*, as it were, whose experience is confined to a fleeting episode without significant aftermath. Some people might not even notice the transgression. [...] Other people might eschew the designation of victim or refrain from reflecting upon it. There are alternative frames which could enable a potential victim to be defined, say, as a disabled person, a claimant, survivor, patient, invalid or plaintiff instead. [...]

'Victim' itself is not then necessarily considered an appealing term. It is contradictory, connoting, in Downes's metaphor, images of pariah and saint, and those conflicting images have already been revealed in the stances of certain criminologists and campaigners. [...]

On the other hand, becoming a victim can have its rewards: sympathy; attention; being treated as blameless; the ability to bestow meaning and control on an untoward and disturbing experience; the receiving of exoneration, absolution, validation and credit, exemption from prosecution, mitigation of punishment and financial compensation. Those qualities are continuously refined and reinforced in the binary oppositions or 'opposing distortions'[53] that are fabricated in and about the adversarial trial, political speech and press reporting about crime, where innocent victims tend to be depicted as the very antithesis of wicked criminals. Becoming a secondary victim or a victim *für sich* can then supply a privileged moral place, a history, a present and a future, and there has been increasing competition in a more litigious, expressive and reflective[54] world to earn the title, and some policing of applicants by those who would regulate their admission and acceptance. There have been complaints about what is said to be a growing and unattractive culture of victimisation in which more and more people abjure responsibility for their own actions or refuse to accept that events may be beyond human control.[55] There have been disputes about whether the holocaust included Christians, communists and homosexuals. Legal definitions of genocide extend to race but not to the victims of mass killings based on politics and class, and powerful states, such as Turkey, can still withstand the charge. The classes of victims of rape and domestic violence have now been validated, but it is not clear whether they are always and everywhere permitted to include males. After agitation the relatives of homicide victims have only very recently been classified as victims proper for certain purposes in England and Wales,[56] but other groups are only uncertainly and unevenly acknowledged as casualties of crime: children in households that have been burgled;[57] the relatives of serious offenders who sometimes represent themselves as 'the other victims of crime';[58] those injured in, or related to people who have been injured or killed in, road crashes; offenders injured by their victims; prisoners injured whilst making their escape from prison; suspects and offenders injured or killed in custody; the police and ambulance staff who attend serious crime scenes; ushers and court staff who hear the harrowing testimony of victims every day; defendants who claim that they were the victims of food additives or bullying fathers; teenage prostitutes and 'trafficked' women;[59] defendants who claim the 'battered woman's defence' of 'slow burn provocation'[60] and women who plead that they were coerced into offending by dominant male partners.[61] Such a jostling for inclusion and exclusion repeatedly tests, delineates and, indeed, complicates what it is to be a victim.

The issue is complicated because becoming a victim can be a matter of contrasting claims made before disparate audiences with different powers to censure and reward, and the recognition of one victim may be secured only at the perceived cost to another. [...]

Victimisation is critically a process of alter-casting, and the victimisation of one can entail the criminalisation of another. [...] Intentionally or unintentionally, it establishes a frame in which networks of identities may be transformed. [...]

Becoming a 'victim', in short, is an emergent process of signification like many others, possibly involving the intervention and collaboration of others whose impact and meaning change from stage to stage, punctuated by benchmarks and transitions, and lacking any fixed end state. At an extreme pole, the existential consequences of being a homicide survivor, for instance, are not at first self-evident, but are built up step by step, over time, prompted by professionals and lay people engaged in the processing of crime and death, and embellished by readings provided by relatives, friends and the occasional fellow survivor. Such a process is an existential or moral career. [...]

Careers can be contingent, fluctuating in importance for the self and its others, and enlivened by its contrasts. Their development may be so gradual that it will only be the passing of some turning-point that enforces awareness.[62] But they may also be abrupt and traumatic – as in a rape, robbery or assault. Indeed, some forms of victimisation are *designed* by the offender to be disconcerting precisely because it is then that the victim is at his or her most defenceless and malleable.[63] It may only be by rendering a victim confused and helpless that an offence can be efficiently committed.[64]

Critical passages may be eased by pre-existing narratives supplied by 'status-coaches':[65] by texts, self-help manuals and agony columns; television programmes, films and newspapers; counselling and therapy; 'helplines', survivors' campaigns, 'speak-outs' and support groups, and the guiding procedures of police interrogation and prosecution examination-in-chief.[66] There are abundant scripts which lay out much of how to be a victim – what to do, feel and say, at a difficult juncture. [...]

It is perhaps about this point that understanding begins to falter. If becoming a victim depends in part on the borrowing or construction and application of frames to experience, more must be learned about how that process is negotiated. What remains is the progressive elaboration of the kinds of questions that might be asked.

There is, first, a problem of the substantial neglect of victimisation as *interaction*. We know, for instance, that much violence, and especially violence against females and children, is committed by members of the victim's intimate circle.[67] We may also surmise that much property crime is also committed by people known to the victim. Yet, despite work by Straus and his colleagues,[68] Hoyle,[69] Athens,[70] Katz,[71] Wright and Decker[72] and a few others, there has been very little description of crime as an embedded transaction unfolding in space and time. At best, there have been a few academic and lay descriptions of the stages of victimisation,[73] on the one hand, and of the stages

of criminal acts,[74] on the other, but we lack any unifying *Rashomon*-like analysis of crime in the round, as a process involving people in interaction, constituting themselves and one another, and deploying situated gestures, emergent meanings and changing identities. We have looked a little at strings of parts but not at larger wholes, and analysis is dismembered as a result, a collection of discrete monologues rather than of conversations.

Secondly, we need to describe the materials with which victimisation is construed in everyday life. When and how do people come to take it that they have been a *victim* of an act identified as a *crime*, and what is meant when they say that that is what has happened? What is victimisation supposed to be when it is invoked, and when is it considered to be a problem; what is the significance of being a victim (as opposed to being the occupant of some other or no well-defined role at all); how are identities distinguished, selected and enacted as, say, angry, campaigning, chastened, fearful, self-reproachful, cynical, nonchalant or resigned victims; how do those selves interplay with the wider biography of the victim and with retrospective and prospective readings of his or her identity; how much are they stereotyped and how much the result of reflective consideration and remodelling by the victim himself or herself; how are they shaped by readings of the offender and his or her motives and, reciprocally, of the offender's readings of the victim's behaviour; how do they sit with beliefs about fate and agency in human affairs; what practical, existential and moral consequences flow from the acquisition of victim selves; what parts do others play in formulating those interpretations; when and how would a victim seek their support, take action or call upon outsiders, amongst them the police; and when, most importantly, is victimisation an enduring signifier? In short, when and with what consequences does a person understand himself or herself to have *become* some existential entity called a victim?

Bittner argued that the police are summoned typically not to deal with precisely classified crimes but with loosely defined problems and troubles that are held to be beyond the immediate competence of people on the social scene.[75] Any initial common-sense understanding of victimisation and victim identity may be similarly nebulous, and interpretative work must sometimes be done to fix their character. Such work would presumably be shaped by everyday moralities of troubles, problems, disputes and dispute-resolution that point to how, when and by whom conflicts between people are deemed to be consequential or inconsequential, criminal or non-criminal, fair or unfair, provoked or unprovoked, avoidable or inevitable; soluble or insoluble; entailing proper chastisement or improper aggression?[76] 'Identical' acts of violence may be deemed to be no more than fun or rumbustuousness, but they may also be construed as bullying – a non-actionable but undesirable attack, or as an intolerably disturbing assault on the body and spirit that demands a response by the State. Crime is quite clearly context-dependant. [...]

What seems to be required, in the words of Girling, Loader and Sparks, is a more sophisticated understanding of the meanings-in-use of crime, of the:

> nuance, detail and variety of things that *people may be saying when they speak about crime* and ... the particularities of the contexts in which they are said.[77]

Girling and her colleagues did not themselves talk about the experience and construction of *victim* identity unless, perhaps, it was obliquely and inferentially. Their principal concern was with the spatially embedded character of the fear of crime, but, appropriately modified, their analysis could lead to an examination of forms of victim talk that are bound by the exigencies of space, time, relations, purposes, risk and, in Sparks's words, 'metaphors and narratives about social change'.[78]

The need for that examination would apply *a fortiori* to heavily-victimised populations. Something is known of their demographics and geography. [...] But they do not dwell overmuch on how victims constitute *themselves* in such places. [...] What, for example are the vocabularies of motive which permit one to victimise others but never the less condemn (if one does condemn) one's own victimisation or the victimisation of others close to one?[79] Other questions would centre on how and in what manner members of such groups can have become so disproportionately exposed to victimisation; how variegated are their experiences; how they move in and out of vulnerable situations and what their careers as victims might be;[80] whether and how, indeed, they define themselves as victims; what, if any, defensive strategies they adopt; how they mobilise informal controls; and what, if any, recourse they make to formal agencies such as the police.

Conclusion

This catalogue of unanswered questions could have been extended but it may now have achieved its object of underscoring how little exploration there has been of some of the principal actors and activities in criminal processes. If appreciating deviants was one of the big criminological projects of the 1960s, and appreciating control agents a project of the 1970s, it is now timely to enhance an appreciation of victims.

> *From P. Rock, 'On becoming a victim', in C. Hoyle and R. Young (eds)* New Visions of Victims, *3rd. ed. (Oxford: Hart Publishing) 2002, pp. 1–22.*

Notes

1 See F. Pearce, *Crimes of the Powerful* (Pluto Press, London, 1976).
2 Consider the rank indifference to victims displayed in I. Taylor, P. Walton and J. Young, *The New Criminology* (Routledge & Kegan Paul, London, 1973); I. Taylor, P. Walton and I. Young (eds), *Critical Criminology* (Routledge & Kegan Paul, London, 1975), or S. Hall *et al.*, *Policing the Crisis* (Macmillan, London, 1978).
3 J. Young, *The Exclusive Society* (Sage, London, 1999) 1.
4 See L. Wilkins, *Delinquent Generations* (HMSO, London, 1960).
5 See G. Pearson, *Hooligan* (Macmillan, London, 1983) esp 12.
6 See J. Kitsuse and A. Cicourel, 'A Note on the Uses of Official Statistics' (1963) 11 *Social Problems* 131.
7 Garland observed of the radical criminology of the 1960s and 1970s, '[a]lthough its appearance coincides with some of the fastest rising crime rates recorded in the twentieth century, many of its themes appear quite disconnected from that phenomenon.' Garland, *The Culture of Control*, 66.
8 See Pearce, *Crimes of the Powerful.*
9 See A. Platt, 'Prospects for a Radical Criminology in the USA' and H. Schwendinger and, J. Schwendinger, 'Defenders of Order or Guardians of Human Rights' both in I. Taylor, P. Walton and J. Young (eds), *Critical Criminology* (Routledge, London, 1975).
10 H. Becker, 'Whose Side Are We On?' (1967) 14 *Social Problems* 239.
11 Hall *et al.*, *Policing the Crisis*, n 2 above.
12 Cohen, *Folk Devils and Moral Panics* (Paladin, London 1973).
13 R. Reiner, 'The Mystery of the Missing Crimes' (1994) 1(2) *Policing Today* 16.
14 *The Challenge of Crime in a Free Society: A Report by the President's Commission on Law Enforcement and Administration of Justice* (US Government Printing Office, Washington DC, 1967) 1.
15 See A. Biderman and A. Reiss, 'On Explaining the 'Dark Figure' of Crime' (1967) 374 *Annals of the American Academy of Politics and Social Science* 1.
16 President's Commission on Law Enforcement and Administration of Justice, *Field Surveys III: Studies in*

Crime and Law Enforcement in Major Metropolitan Areas (US Government Printing Office, Washington, DC) Vol 1, 6.

17 Under the mandate provided by the Peace and Security Program of 1976.

18 J. Lea and J. Young, *What is to be Done about Law and Order?* (Penguin, London, 1984) 262.

19 See C. Kempe *et al.*, 'The Battered Child Syndrome' [1962] 181 *Journal of the American Medical Association* 17 and D. Griffiths and F. Moynihan, 'Multiple Epiphysical Injuries in Babies ('Battered Baby Syndrome')' (1963) 11 *British Medical Journal* 1558.

20 See S. Griffin, 'Rape: The All-American Crime' (1971) 10 *Ramparts* 26; M. Wasserman, 'Rape: Breaking the Silence', *The Progressive*, November 1973.

21 See C. Smart, *Women, Crime and Criminology* (Routledge & Kegan Paul, London, 1977); S.M. Edwards, *Female Sexuality and the Law* (M. Robertson, Oxford, 1981); and Z. Adler, *Rape on Trial* (Routledge & Kegan Paul, London, 1987).

22 See, for instance, L. Smith's judgement in *Concerns about Rape* (HMSO, London, 1989) 1.

23 In England, the former probation officer, Philip Priestley, published a NACRO Regional Paper with that very cry as its title in 1970.

24 Jan Van Dijk, a criminologist and a policy official in the Dutch Ministry of Justice, called them 'retribution with a human face.'

25 A. Reiss, *The Police and the Public* (Yale University Press, New Haven Conn, 1970).

26 R. Ericson, *Making Crime* (Butterworth, Toronto, 1981).

27 See R. Knudten, 'Will Anyone be Left to Testify?' in E. Flynn and J. Conrad (eds), *New and Old Criminology* (LEAA, US Department of Justice, Washington DC, 1978). See also R. Knudten *et al.*, *Victims and Witnesses: Their Experiences with Crime and the Criminal Justice System* (LEAA, US Department of Justice, Washington DC, 1977) and F. Cannavale and W. Falcon, *Improving Witness Cooperation* (Government Printing Office, Washington DC, 1976).

28 See W. MacPherson and M. Yantzi, *Victim-Offender Reconciliation Program* (Kitchener, Ontario, 1979).

29 See J. Hudson and B. Galaway (eds), *Restitution in Criminal Justice* (Lexington Books, Lexington Mass, 1977).

30 See J. Harding, *Victims and Offenders: Needs and Responsibilities* (Bedford Square Press, London, 1982); and T. Marshall and M. Walpole, *Bringing People Together: Mediation and Reparation Projects in Great Britain* (Home Office, London, 1985).

31 J. Braithwaite, *Crime, Shame and Reintegration* (Cambridge University Press, Cambridge, 1989).

32 L. Zedner, 'Victims' in M. Maguire *et al.* (eds), *The Oxford Handbook of Criminology* (Clarendon Press, Oxford, 1997) 577.

33 See, for example, K. Pease, 'Repeat Victimisation: Taking Stock' (Briefing note, Police Research Group, Home Office, London, undated) and J. Hanmer and S. Griffiths, 'Domestic Violence and Repeat Victimisation' (Briefing note, Police Research Group, Home Office, London, undated).

34 See L. Sherman, 'Hot Spots of Predatory Crime' (1989) 27 *Criminology* 27.

35 Exemplified most powerfully in I. Waller and N. Okihiro, *Burglary: The Victim and the Public* (University of Toronto Press, Toronto, 1974).

36 See M. Maguire, 'The Impact of Burglary on Victims' (1980) 20(3) *British Journal of Criminology* 261.

37 See N. Christie, 'The Ideal Victim' in E. Fattah (ed), *From Crime Policy to Victim Policy* (Macmillan, Basingstoke, 1986).

38 See R. Clarke *et al.*, 'Elderly Victims of Crime and Exposure to Risk' (1985) 24(1) *The Howard Journal of Criminal Justice* 1.

39 Smith remarked that 'people who tend to be repeatedly victims also have a much higher chance of being arrested'. D.J. Smith, *Police and People in London* (Policy Studies Institute, London, 1983) Vol 1, 124.

40 See W. Pedersen, 'Adolescent Victims of Violence in a Welfare State' (2001) 41(1) *British Journal of Criminology* 1.

41 I. Antilla, *Victimology – A New Territory in Criminology*, Scandinavian Studies in Criminology, vol 5 (M. Robertson, Oxford, 1974) 8.

42 For a more general discussion of the links between criminology, research and policy on victims, see L. Sebba, 'On the Relationship between Criminological Research and Policy' (2001) 1(1) *Criminal Justice* 27.

43 Thus Weed remarked of the United States, 'The victims-rights movement has developed outside of the academic disciplines of criminology and penology. The victim advocates, for the most part, have not been interested in social research.' F. Weed, *Certainty of Justice: Reform in the Crime Victim Movement* (Aldine de Gruyter, New York NY, 1995) 138.

44 See the chapter by Ann Grady in this volume.

45 J. Pahl, 'Refuges for Battered Women: Social Provision or Social Movement?' (1979) 8 *Journal of Voluntary Action Research* 25.

46 Rape Counselling and Research Project, *First Annual Report* (London, undated) i.

47 See L. Clark and D. Lewis, *Rape: The Price of Coercive Sexuality* (The Women's Press, Toronto, 1977).

48 B. Mendelsohn, 'Une nouvelle branche de la science bio-psycho-sociale' (1956) 18(2) *Revue internationale de la police technique* 95.

49 See J. Holstein and C. Miller, 'Rethinking Victimization: An Interactional Approach to Victimology' (1990) 13(1) *Symbolic Interaction* 103.

50 G. Kantor, 'Victim-Blaming and Victim-Precipitation, Concept of' in N. Rafter (ed), *Encyclopedia of Women and Crime* (Oryx Press, Phoenix Ariz, 2000) 266.

51 There was, for instance, some disquiet about the apparent implications of the 1995 British Crime Survey which showed that men suffered the same rate of domestic violence as women in the last year (although their injuries were less acute and the overall prevalence of violence in their lifetime was smaller).

52 E. Stanko, *Intimate Intrusions* (Routledge & Kegan Paul, London, 1985) 16.

53 M. McConville, 'Justice in the Dock' *The Times Higher Education Supplement*, 8 February 1990.

54 See A. Giddens, *Modernity and Self Identity* (Polity Press, Cambridge, 1991). 96: *The Decay of the American Charatcer.*

55 See C. Sykes, *A Nation of Victims: The Decay of the American Character* (St Martin's Press, New York, 1992).

56 They were acknowledged as victims in, for instance, the 1985 United Nations Declaration of Basic Principles of Justice for Victims of Crime and Abuse of Power which stated that: 'The term "victim" also includes, where appropriate, the immediate family or dependants of the direct victim and persons who have suffered harm to assist victims in distress or to prevent victimisation'. But they were excluded from the 'trialling' of what were to become called victim personal statements on the grounds that the real victims of homicide were the dead who could not speak.

57 See J. Morgan and L. Zedner, *Child Victims: Crime, Impact, and Criminal Justice* (Clarendon Press, Oxford, 1992).

58 See G. Howarth and P. Rock, 'Aftermath and the Construction of Victimisation: "The Other Victims of Crime" '(2000) 39(1) *Howard Journal of Criminal Justice* 58.

59 J. Doezema, 'Loose Women or Lost Women? The Re-emergence of the Myth of "White Slavery" in Contemporary Discourses of "Trafficking in Women" (Paper presented at the ISA Convention, Washington DC, February 1999).

60 J. Nadel, *Sara Thornton: The Story of a Woman who Killed* (Victor Gollancz, London, 1994) and S. Westervelt, *Shifting the Blame: How Victimization Became a Criminal Defense* (Rutgers University Press, New Brunswick NJ, 1998).

61 A. Matravers, *Justifying the Unjustifiable: Stories of Women Sex Offenders* (unpublished PhD thesis, University of Cambridge, 2000).

62 See, for instance, the diaries of Victor Klemperer, who was transformed little by little by the growth of Nazism from being a bourgeois, converted German professor into a fugitive Jew seeking to escape the death ramps. The second diary was published as *To the Bitter End* (Weidenfeld and Nicolson, London, 1999). Fictional accounts of the same process may be found in A. Appelfeld, *The Retreat* (Quartet Books, London, 1984) and M. Frisch, *The Fire Raisers* (Methuen, London, 1962).

63 See R. Wright and S. Decker, *Armed Robbers in Action* (Northeastern University Press, Boston, 1997).

64 See W. Einstadter, 'The Social Organization of Armed Robbery' (1969) 17(1) *Social Problems* 64.

65 See A. Strauss, *Minors and Masks* (Free Press, Glencoe Ill, 1959) ch IV.

66 See M. McConville, A. Sanders and R. Leng, *The Case for the Prosecution* (Routledge, London, 1991).

67 Only 12% of rapes recorded by the police in England and Wales in 1996 were committed by strangers, and 54% of male and 79% of female homicide victims in 1997 knew their killers: *Information on the Criminal Justice System in England and Wales: Digest 4* (Home Office, London, 1999).

68 M.A. Strauss *et al.*, *Behind Closed Doors: Violence in the American Family* (Anchor Books, Garden City NY 1981).

69 C. Hoyle, *Negotiating Domestic Violence: Police, Criminal Justice, and Victims* (Clarendon Press, Oxford, 1998).

70 L. Athens, *Violent Criminal Acts and Actors Revisited* (University of Illinois Press, Urbana Ill, 1997).

71 J. Katz, *Seductions of Crime* (Basic Books, New York NY, 1988).

72 Wright and Decker, *Armed Robbers in Action* (Northeastern University Press, Boston, 1997).

73 See, for example, J. Shapland, J. Willmore and P. Duff, *Victims in the Criminal Justice System* (Gower, Aldershot, 1985); P. Rock, *After Homicide: Practical and Political Responses to Bereavement* (Clarendon Press, Oxford, 1998).

74 Rational choice theorists like Cornish and Clarke are beginning to deconstruct ideal-typical crimes – and particularly organised crime – as scripts or patterned performances. See, for example, R.V. Clarke, 'Situational Crime Prevention' in M. Tonry and D. Farrington (eds), *Building a Safer Society: Strategic Approaches In Crime Prevention, Crime and Justice: A Review of Research* (University of Chicago Press, Chicago Ill, 1995) Vol 19,91–150.

75 E. Bittner, *The Functions of the Police in Modern Society* (National Institute of Mental Health, Chevy Chase MD, 1970).

76 We do know that some victims of violence tend to think that their assaults are purposive, meaningful and planned, whilst the perpetrators tend to dismiss the act as unplanned, spontaneous and lacking in significance. See R. Baumeister, A. Stillwell and S.R. Wotman, 'Victim and Perpetrator Accounts of Interpersonal Violence' (1990) 59(5) *Journal of Personality and Social Psychology* 994.

77 B. Girling, I. Loader and R. Sparks, *Crime and Social Change in Middle England* (Routledge, London, 2000) 2 (emphasis in original).

78 R. Sparks, 'Reason and Unreason in Left Realism: Some Problems in the Constitution of the Fear of Crime' in R. Matthews and J. Young (eds), *Issues in Realist Criminology* (Sage, London, 1992) 131.

79 They might well rest on the cynical metaphor of a feral world in which everyone preys on everyone else, in which the only moral imperative is not to be caught and not to be a sucker. See T. Parker, *The Courage of His Convictions* (Hutchinson, London, 1962).

80 Racial assault and domestic violence, for instance, are not discrete events but take some of their meaning and effect from their character as an interlocking sequence of acts taking place over time. See B. Bowling, *Violent Racism: Victimisation, Policing and Social Context* (Clarendon Press, Oxford, 1998).

17.2 Fiefs and peasants: accomplishing change for victims in the criminal justice system Joanna Shapland

The results of research into victims' reactions to their victimization and subsequent treatment by the criminal justice system now read almost like a litany, so universal are the findings. The studies emphasize the need for support and help to get over the effects of the offence, and for information from and for consultation with the agencies of the criminal justice system, notably the police and prosecution. It has been shown consistently that throughout the Anglo-American system of adversarial criminal justice – in England, Scotland, the United States and Canada – victims who are bewildered, angry or fearful, turn to the police and other officials for comfort and guidance, only to find them operating according to different priorities which place concern for victims low on the list (Shapland *et al.* 1985; Chambers and Millar 1983, 1986; Elias 1983c; Holstrom and Burgess 1978; Kelly 1982; Baril *et al.* 1984; Canadian Federal Provincial Task Force 1983). There are fewer research findings concerning the more inquisitorial systems of continental Europe, but questionnaire returns from member states of the Council of Europe – on which the Council's proposals for reform are substantially based – show little difference there (Council of Europe 1983, 1985, 1987).

Ideas and strategies to alleviate the plight of victims have come thick and fast over the last few years and, in contrast to the consistent way the problem has been defined, the response presents a varied picture. Victimologists in the United States have largely followed a 'rights'-based strategy – encouraging the passing of state and federal legislation to allow victims greater participation in the criminal justice process (see, for example, NOVA 1985). [...] In Europe, by contrast, the emphasis has been on training and/or commanding parts of the criminal justice system to take on duties relating to the provision of victim services (for example, van Dijk 1986a; Council of Europe 1985). In Britain, official action has been particularly low-key, and has been based on a perceived need to persuade agencies to devise their own responses and actions on behalf of victims.

These differences are unsurprising. Where action on behalf of victims has to involve the criminal justice system, it will tend to follow the criminal justice tradition of that country. Indeed, victims themselves will expect action within their own tradition. In complete contrast, however, the provision of victim support varies relatively little between different countries. If one looks through the summary of questionnaire returns made by member states of the Council of Europe, it is clear that the pattern of support and assistance is extremely similar throughout (Council of Europe 1987). State provision of social and medical services of course varies, but many countries also have generalist victim support services similar to those provided by VSS in the UK, as well as RCC and shelter homes for battered women.

The development of these services has been essentially a process of parallel evolution. Though there are personal and, on occasion, more formal links between those running services in different countries, these have tended to occur after the different services have become established. The trend towards cross-national associations, meetings and conferences is growing in strength now, mainly because quite a few countries have formed the kinds of networks or formal associations which make it easier to take part.

Does this similarity of organization, then, repudiate the assertion above that criminal justice traditions will compel different solutions to victim needs? I think not. The interesting fact about these victim support and assistance programmes is that they seem everywhere to have developed outside the realm of government and largely outside the ambit of the criminal justice agencies. They have their roots in the community or in voluntary associations, and rely heavily on voluntary workers and support. Governments have been hastening to try to catch up with and understand these mushrooming and popular voluntary bodies, not helped by their localization and hence the lack of central information about them. The problems of the associations are those of the voluntary sector: underfunding, lack of publicity about their services, inconsistency of approach in different parts of the same country, untrained personnel and shortage of specialist advice and support (see Maguire and Corbett 1987 for a comprehensive review of the position in England and Wales). The relative similarity of victims' services in different countries has resulted, I would argue, from their independence from criminal justice systems and governments.

Victim services involving the criminal justice system

Where the response to victim need has had to involve the criminal justice system, it has tended to be different in different countries. In North America, as mentioned above, it has often taken the form of legislated rights for individual victims or the drawing up of charters of such rights. These are essentially expressions of opinion or statements of values as to what the position of victims should be in a particular jurisdiction. They derive their strength from the future developments they may produce in concrete practices – through individual victims claiming and using those rights, or from the inspiration that practitioners in the system may derive from those statements of values to change their own practices. There is, however, very little *coercion* on either victim or practitioner to improve the lot of victims.

This is the problem with the use of a rights strategy to accomplish change. Success depends crucially on the willingness of individuals to institute legal action which will lead to judgments that enforce change. It has proved relatively successful in the field of prisoners' rights in England, where cases taken to the European Court of Human Rights in Strasbourg have led to a few changes in practices in prisons (see Maguire *et al.* 1985). However, even these changes have been patchy: an approach to change based on individual action cannot accomplish a wide-ranging review of current assumptions and practices. Moreover, individuals are often only successful in such cases if they are supported by a dynamic pressure group of their fellows, entirely committed to that strategy. This was the case, for example, with the campaign based upon legal action taken by MIND in England to change the 1959 Mental Health Act (cf. Gostin 1977).

While the national association in North America, NOVA, strongly supports the passing of legislation improving victim rights, the same is not true of its English counterpart, NAVSS. In England and Wales until recently, the language of individual rights has generally been seen as alien to the historical tradition of the criminal justice system (though one exception has been the right of the offender not be unlawfully detained). In order to explore how change might be accomplished here,

we need to digress in order to explore the nature of the English criminal justice system.

There has been considerable talk recently about interdependence and the benefits of cooperation among the various agencies of the criminal justice system (for example, Moxon 1985). By agencies, I am referring not only to those commonly seen as separate parts of the system – police, prosecution, judiciary, court administration, probation, prisons, and so on – but also to the various branches of the executive: the Home Office, the Lord Chancellor's Office and, now, the Attorney General's Department. Despite the obvious links between the agencies in terms of the numbers of offenders passing through from one to the other, 1 feel it is more apt to characterize the agencies not as part of an interconnected system, but as independent 'fiefs' under a feudal system. Each fief retains power over its own jurisdiction and is jealous of its own workload and of its independence. It will not easily tolerate (or in some cases even permit) comments from other agencies about the way it conducts its business. This tendency is exacerbated and continued by the separate education and training of the professional workers for each fief, by their separate housing and by the hierarchical structure of promotion within fiefs, with little or no transfer between them. Negotiations between adjacent fiefs do occur over boundary disputes (for example, in the form of Court User Groups), but these tend to be confined to the agencies directly affected which see themselves as entering the negotiations as equally powerful parties (Feeney 1985). Nor is there any 'Round Table' (such as a sentencing commission – see Ashworth 1983; Shapland 1981).

It is interesting that the recent construction of a new system of prosecution was accomplished by the production of yet another separate fief in the form of the Crown Prosecution Service, whose workers, premises and philosophy will again be separate from all the others, and which will be responsible to a different Minister (the Attorney General). This new fief, charged with producing a statement of its working practices, has responded naturally enough with one that concentrates almost entirely upon the central task – that of deciding upon prosecution. Its *Code of Conduct for Crown Prosecutors* appears to ignore the need to discuss and regulate relations with other fiefs and with those not represented by fiefs at all – victims and defendants (Crown Prosecution Service 1986).

This type of criminal justice system has the advantage that the necessary independence of its different parts is built into the structure. The structure does not need careful tending, since the natural tendencies of the fiefs will reinforce it in its current state. However, their separateness and pride in their independence are also likely to lead – and in my view have already led to a very great degree – to failures to perceive the need for control of the whole system and to an overall lack of consistency. The system breeds a reliance on individual decision making and on discretion by the fief's workers, which has been elevated by some into an absolute virtue. There is no corresponding stress upon the needs of the consumers of the fief's services, whether other fiefs or individuals. When individuals seriously question what is happening, as those espousing the needs of victims have done, their challenge is likely to be taken as a challenge to the autonomy and authority of the fief, rather than as a comment on its ways of working.

Taking again the advent of the Crown Prosecution System as an example, the negotiations that have taken place on the needs of victims – for information, for consultation and for the effective collection and presentation to the courts of information related to claims for compensation – seem to have been fraught with difficulty and demarcation disputes. The difficulty with victims is that their needs span several fiefs. For example, the police are the agency that will have both the most contact and the most ready contact with victims to ascertain losses and injuries; but with responsibility passing to the Crown Prosecution Service they can no longer ensure that this information is made available to the court. Again, as the police are now often not told the results of cases, they cannot notify victims of the outcome, even should they be willing to do so. In fact, the relatively simple and uncontroversial needs of victims in relation to the criminal justice system (advice, information, consultation, witness expenses, compensation – see Shapland *et al.* 1985) cannot be the subject of an instruction such as a Home Office Circular without negotiations taking place with at least six fiefs (three ministries and three other agencies).

The problem of producing change in such a system is one of either persuading an agency that its own view of its mandate and of the way it operates must change, or of imposing change from without. In other parts of Europe, the sectors of the criminal justice system are fewer in number and there is an acceptance that some are subordinate to others. For example, in the Netherlands, the police are under the direction of the prosecutors, who in turn are part of the Ministry of Justice. Changes in policy can be accomplished through convincing just one agency – the Ministry of Justice – of the need for them. For example, the Ministry has issued instructions to other agencies to support victim assistance schemes and to inform victims of the results of cases, and has affected sentencing levels by asking prosecutors to advocate different sentence lengths in court. Opposition from other, independent parts of the system, such as the judiciary, has been muted, owing partly to the similarity of outlook and frequency of communication between them. Another example is to be found in Scotland, where prosecutors have the power to influence police investigations and to talk directly to witnesses.

Even in these more co-ordinated systems, there are those who advocate a still greater degree of consistency and central co-ordination and communication (for example, Steenhuis 1986). In England and Wales, people have always railed at the criminal justice system for its inconsistencies and its diffusion of power. They have usually been answered with incantations about the need for independence of the various fiefs. It is not my purpose to advocate a centrally controlled, uniform system. Clearly, the separateness of its parts is one of its main strengths. On the other hand, there is also the danger that the checks and balances will become so 'perfectly' adjusted that stasis sets in. At that point, one which I think we have reached now, change becomes extremely difficult to produce without coercion (or popular revolt from those not enfranchised in a fief). Persuasion may not work because agencies see no need to change their current positions.

Legislation or persuasion?

There is little detailed information about how agencies in England and Wales have responded to the pressure for change to meet victims' needs. At the central government level, Rock (1987) has documented how the Home Office, in contrast to the relevant government agencies in Canada, has been slow to change its view. He shows how it has tended to follow belatedly, rather than produce policy to lead, on such issues as victim support. We still have no co-ordinated government policy on all matters affecting victims in the criminal justice system. Even where there have been relevant international documents, such as the Council of Europe Convention on state compensation for victims of violent crime (1983), these have not formed a central pivot of policy. Indeed, the Convention has not yet been ratified. This lack of a central policy lead for agencies, one suspects, partly reflects the division into fiefs at government, as well as at practitioner, level.

Nevertheless, certain agencies have become convinced of the need for change to take account of the problems of victims. Senior police officers have changed their attitudes markedly over the last ten years and, in certain cases, this has led to local initiatives to improve the lot of victims in practice. The most notable examples are the part played by the police in the rise of VSS (Maguire and Corbett 1987) and the provision of facilities for victims of sexual assault (Shapland and Cohen 1987). The police have not, however, been able to pass on this enthusiasm to other fiefs (and indeed would not see it as appropriate that they should exert such an influence).

We have already addressed the problems in respect of the Crown Prosecution Service. (In case it may be thought that this inactivity is an inevitable feature of the prosecutorial role, it is pertinent to mention initiatives involving prosecutors in other countries. These include the guidelines of South Australia (1985) promoted by the Attorney General and the right of victims in the Netherlands to appeal to an ombudsman – who may award damages – against the decision of the prosecutor.) Shapland and Cohen's (1987) survey also covered the administration of justice, in the form of justices' clerks from England and Wales. Here, it was apparent that a substantial minority of clerks were not only not trying to improve the lot of victims, but did not agree that to do so was part of their job. In other words, it may be concluded that where there is no agreement within a fief that a particular task, such as providing for victims, is part of its mandate, then persuasion will not work. Nor will guidelines or other manifestations of the service model be produced from within the profession. Pressure from without can be resisted.

Would legislated rights for individual victims, on the American model, break the deadlock? The problem is that, in order to claim them, victims have to be acknowledged as parties to the criminal justice system. If they are not, then again pressure can be ignored. A potential right of this kind was embodied in the Criminal Justice Bill 1986, although it was not legislated because of the intervention of the general election. This was a proposed requirement upon sentencers to give reasons if they decided not to make a compensation order. It is interesting to compare this with the obligation put upon magistrates under the Criminal Justice Act 1982 to give reasons before passing a custodial sentence upon a young adult. Burney's (1985) finding, that as many as 14 per cent of custodial disposals were not accompanied by a statement of reasons, does not lead one to believe that all judges and magistrates would comply with the comparable obligation proposed in the Criminal Justice Bill. Furthermore, an important difference between the two measures is that, while young adult defendants have a definite right of appeal in such cases, the position of victims is less clear. Could victims appeal if no reasons were given? What would then happen to the sentence if any appeal was allowed – would the defendant be re-sentenced? Would the victim obtain damages (on the Dutch model)?

More pertinently, even if these kinds of difficulties could be overcome, it appears that few, if any, young adult defendants have exercised their right of appeal in connection with the provisions of the 1982 Criminal Justice Act. Would victims exercise any equivalent right of appeal?

As a means of imposing change, then, such legislative provisions do not seem to be very effective. (They may be stimulating changes in attitudes, of course, but that is a long-term and stealthy process, not susceptible to research.) Given the lack of acknowledgement of the legal status of victims and the lack of a legally-inclined pressure group for victims, it is unlikely that this path will produce much change in the short term.

This is not to decry the need for individual, justiciable rights in some circumstances for victims. I have argued elsewhere (Shapland and Cohen 1987) that procedural duties backed up by victims' rights of appeal may well need to be enacted, for example, to ensure that details of victim injuries are placed before the court at the time of sentence (to allow the court to consider a compensation order). The need for rights as remedies, however limited the circumstances in which they apply, is a token of the difficulty of producing change in an unwilling system – a system which is unwilling both because parts of it do not appreciate the need for change and because it is insufficiently coherent to be able to produce change between its separate fiefs. The difficulty is that rights, by themselves, will be insufficient – they will need backing up by training and by codes of practice which bridge the gaps between the fiefs involved.

In essence, a package of measures is required to accomplish the changes in the criminal justice system that are necessary to ensure that victims are informed and consulted and that information about their losses and injuries is placed before the court at the appropriate time. To be effective, this package will need to contain some justiciable rights for individual victims and/or some legally enforceable duties upon particular fiefs of the criminal justice system. That implies new legislation. More pertinently, the package should include directives, codes of practice or circulars from Government departments to different fiefs and the promotion of training and different attitudes within fiefs.

There is only one body that can encourage the development of such a package – the same body that is able to enact its legislative elements – Parliament. But even Parliament cannot put together its own package with no other resources. There is a prior step to be taken: to produce a policy which attempts to address all the needs of victims in the context of a discussion of the balance to be struck between the needs of the various fiefs and of defendants and victims in the criminal justice system. Even the initiation of this policy will be difficult. The medieval solution to a plethora of independent fiefs was a Round Table committed to the pursuit of justice. Such a standing convention of fiefs could discuss relevant policy and likely practicalities before legislation is drafted.

The continued non-development of policy by the 'fiefs' raises another spectre: that of growing unrest by the 'peasants' – the victims – or by those who represent their interests. This unrest may, indeed, lead to the subsequent adoption of the only apparently successful formula for action within the system: in other words, the current stasis may be leading to the birth and growth of another small fief – that of victims, or of associations and people pressing on their behalf. Such a fief will have to distinguish its interests from those of other fiefs. It will become more adversarial in respect to other parties, including offenders, than the current groupings have been. The overall question is whether the English criminal justice system has within itself the ability and determination to discuss, and if necessary legislate, a package of rights, duties and services in respect of victims before such a fief is created.

From J. Shapland, 'Fiefs and peasants: accomplishing change for victims in the criminal justice system', in M. Maguire and J. Pointing (eds) Victims of Crime: A New Deal? *(Milton Keynes: Open University Press) 1988, pp. 187–194.*

References

Ashworth, A. (1983). *Sentencing and Penal Policy.* London: Weidenfeld and Nicholson.

Baril, M., Durand, S., Cousineau, M. and Gravel, S. (1984). *Victimes d'Actes Criminels: Mais Nous, les Temoins.* Canada: Department of Justice.

Burney, E. (1985), 'All Things to All Men: Justifying Custody under the 1982 Act.' *Criminal Law Review,* pp. 284–293.

Canadian Federal-Provincial Task Force (1983). *Justice for Victims of Crime: Report.* Ottawa: Canadian Government Publishing Centre.

Chambers, G. and Millar, A. (1983). *Investigating Sexual Assault.* Edinburgh: HMSO.

— (1986). *Prosecuting Sexual Assault.* Edinburgh: HMSO.

Council of Europe (1983). *European Convention on the Compensation of Victims of Violent Crimes.* Strasbourg: Council of Europe.

— (1985). *The Position of the Victim in the Framework of Criminal Law and Procedure. Recommendation No. R(85)11.* Strasbourg: Council of Europe.

— (1987). *Assistance to Victims and the Prevention of Victimization. Recommendation of the Council of Europe.* Strasbourg: Council of Europe.

Crown Prosecution Service (1986). *Code of Conduct for Crown Prosecutors.* London: Crown Prosecution Service.

Elias, R. (1983c). *Victims of the System.* New Brunswick: Transaction Books.

Feeney, F. (1985). 'Interdependence as a Working Concept,' in D. Moxon (ed.). *Managing Criminal Justice.* London: HMSO.

Gostin, L. (1977). *A Human Condition: Volume 2.* London: MIND.

Holmstrom, L. and Burgess, A. (1978). *The Victim of Rape: Institutional Reactions.* Chichester: John Wiley.

Kelly, D. (1982). 'Victims' Reactions to the Criminal Justice Response.' Paper delivered at the 1982 Annual Meeting of the Law and Society Association, Toronto, Canada.

Maguire, M., Vagg, J. and Morgan, R. (1985). *Accountability and Prisons: Opening Up a Closed World.* London: Tavistock.

Maguire, M. and Corbett, C. (1987). *The Effects of Crime and the Work of Victims Support Schemes*. Aldershot: Gower.

Moxon, D. (1985). *Managing Criminal Justice: A Collection of Papers*. London: HMSO.

NOVA (National Organisation for Victim Assistance) (1985). *Victim Rights and Services: A Legislative Directory*. Washington, DC: US Department of Justice.

Rock, P. (1987). 'Government, Victims and Policies in Two Countries.' *British Journal of Criminology*, Vol. 27, Autumn 1987.

Shapland, J. (1981). *Between Conviction and Sentence*. London: Routledge and Kegan Paul.

Shapland, J., Willmore, J. and Duff, P. (1985). *Victims in the Criminal Justice System*. Aldershot: Gower.

Shapland, J. and Cohen, D. (1987). 'Facilities for Victims: The Role of the Police and the Courts.' *Criminal Law Review* (January), pp. 28–38.

Steenhuis, D. (1986). 'Coherence and Coordination in the Administration of Criminal Justice,' in J. van Dijk, C. Haffmans, F. Ruter, J. Schutte and S. Stolwijk. *Criminal Law in Action*. Arnhem: Gouda Quint.

van Dijk, J. (1986a). *The Victims' Movement in Europe. Introductory Report 16th Criminological Research Conference, Research on Victimisation*. Strasbourg: Council of Europe.

17.3 Violence against women and children: the contradictions of crime control under patriarchy
Jill Radford and Elizabeth A. Stanko

Before engaging with our title subject, we will introduce ourselves and our relationship to the issue of violence against women and children and the academic debates about crime control. Jill Radford, a British feminist, has been active in researching, theorizing and campaigning against violence against women since the late 1970s. Betsy Stanko, an American feminist now working in Britain, founded, along with other women, a shelter for battered women and children in Worcester, Massachusetts in the late 1970s. Both of us are criminologists and have struggled with issues of men's violence in our own lives.

As feminists we argue that sexual violence is used by men as a way of securing and maintaining the relations of male dominance and female subordination, which are central to the patriarchal social order. We recognize that patriarchy is crossed through and is in interaction with other power structures, namely those of race, class, age and status regarding disability. These shape women's experience of sexual violence and the response of the police and others. We firmly believe that it is through challenging the patriarchal order by increasing women's autonomy that men's violence must be confronted. While this long term goal is central to our politics, we, like many feminists, are concerned with the need to address the problem in current society. It is these concerns which have drawn us into identifying, naming and working

around the problem of male sexual violence. Given that our work links both the immediate problems arising from ongoing sexual violence and the practical strategies to ease women's everyday lives with the longer term goal of eradicating sexual violence, we anticipate contradictions. This chapter addresses some of the contradictions arising in recent attempts to redefine and address the problem of sexual violence in England and Wales within the paradigms of crime control operant within the policing and legal process.

Violence against women: problems of definition

Over the past 20 years, feminists have once again named and addressed the problem of men's sexual violence from the perspective of women's experience. As has been documented previously:

through the process of naming, women have voiced their anger and expressed their commitment to struggle and survival. 'Men's violence', 'sexual violence', 'rape', 'incest', 'sexual abuse of women and children', 'woman battering', 'womanslaughter', 'woman killing', 'frawen [woman/wife] mishandling', 'the male peril', 'sexual terrorism', 'outrage', 'unspeakable horror', 'sexual harassment' – these are some of the words women in several cultures and at different times in this century have drawn upon to describe their experiences of men's violence. (Hanmer *et al.* 1989: 1–2)

Through listening to women's experiences of behaviour they found abusive, feminist definitions expanded as women named previously unnamed forms of abuse:

> The development of feminist research and discussion over the past fifteen years can in a very real sense be seen in terms of ever-widening definitions and naming of sexual violence in general and in particular forms. (Kelly and Radford 1987: 243)

A significant illustration of this is Ruth Hall's (1985) use of the concept 'racist sexual violence' to highlight the fact that for black women, racism and sexism are often inseparable.

Another strand in this work is the documentation of women's experience of sexual violence. Survey after survey documents the extent to which women endure various forms of male violence as everyday features of their lives (Stanko 1988). Sexual harassment, sexual assault, physical battering, childhood sexual abuse and intimidation, obscene phone calls, and the deluge of pornographic popular literature are the backdrop for women's relationships with men.

Kelly (1988) suggests that women's everyday lives exist along a continuum of sexual violence. Radford (1987) endorsed the 'circular spiral of violence', outlined earlier by Hanmer and Saunders (1984), which illustrates the ways in which dominant discourse about public violence impacts on women, often resulting in their becoming isolated within the wider community, retreating into their homes as ostensibly safe havens, where their resultant dependency on men makes them even more vulnerable to abuse.

Stanko (1985, 1990) concludes that women's understanding of physical and sexual safety is so tightly woven with their concern for sexual integrity as to render the concept of safety problematic for women. Rather than take safety for granted, women, she proposes, build strategies of precaution into their everyday lives and speak of situations as less *unsafe*. [...]

These and many other feminist studies over the past 15 years have consistently and persistently illustrated the endemic nature of violence within women's lives (Russell 1982, 1984, 1985; Scheppele

and Bart 1983). The central feminist explanation for the widespread existence of men's violence to women and children is that it is essential to a system of gender subordination (MacKinnon 1989). Much of violence against women, captured by the feminist surveys, remains outside the realm of criminological thinking about crime. This is a consequence of attempting to locate feminist definitions based on women's experiences into man-made legal categories. Basically they just don't fit. Legal definitions are drawn from dichotomies: lawful against unlawful; crime and no crime; innocence and guilt; the good polarized against the bad (Smart 1989). Women's experiences generally, and even more so in relation to violence, are much more complex. The 1970s debates around the limited legal concept of consent/nonconsent in the law of rape is one illustration.

While the most frequent and routinized forms of male sexual violence are shielded from public view, lost in the discourse of dysfunctional families and female inadequacies, what does come to the attention of the public are the crimes of the psychopathic stranger, the deranged rapist or the serial killer. The attention drawn to public danger to women is not however a commentary about the gendered nature of this danger (Cameron 1988; Caputi 1988), only that it is dangerous for women to be in public. Thus, the bulk of violence to women, that which occurs in private, rarely comes to public attention, is scorned by the police, and the women who ask for police intervention are left neglected and often abused by the very system financed by the state to protect them.

Criminological thinking about crime continues to revolve around the safety of the public and the traditional belief that the proper police role is the policing of public order. [...] The literature analysing risk of criminal victimization recognizes the important contribution made by the lifestyle of the 'victim' to their coming into contact with predatory crime, yet totally neglects how women are so often victimized by those they already know (Hindelang *et al.* 1978; Cohen and Felson 1979; Hough and Mayhew 1983, 1985; Gottfredson 1984; Mayhew *et al.* 1989).

What the changes in the police response to violence against women and children are about, is the pushing of some of what was classified as noncrime into the crime books.

Keeping feminism alive within debates about controlling violence

Our perspective is not that of dispassionate academics concerned with an anthropological or voyeuristic study of other women, that is with separating or distancing ourselves from our subject. We see the links between the provision of support and safe services, research, theorizing and campaigning as integral and necessary to confronting the oppression of patriarchy within women's everyday lives. Because we conduct our debates within the academic world as well as within the world of the everyday, we live out the contradictions in our social practice. At the same time we have a unique insight into processes through which issues feminists raised about male violence have sparked sudden interest on the part of academics, professional service providers (such as social services, psychologists, psychiatrists and counselling professionals) and also the Home Office (the central British ministry responsible for criminal justice in England and Wales), the police and the legal system.

Within academia, we have become aware of the move to make women's studies respectable, and as a part of this a growth of interest in the subject of violence against women and children. Once established on the agenda of acceptable academic issues, however, feminist concerns are often abandoned as academic success takes priority over feminist praxis. [...] Within the academy the personal is divorced from the political and both are divorced from the academic in the rush for academic success and recognition. In this process, we see every day how feminist work is appropriated, but without the feminist commitment which gave it its meaning.

A similar appropriation of feminist concerns can be identified in the belated recognition on the part of some in the caring professions that violence against women and children is a serious and a legitimate area of concern/intervention. While welcoming the fact that these professional carers are recognizing issues feminists have been highlighting as of urgent concern to women, we see very real problems in the form taken by this professional, so-called 'expert', intervention. [...]

We are particularly troubled by the professional redefinition of the problem. Rather than identifying male sexual violence as part of the backdrop of women's lives, conventional intervention models, using the paradigm of victimology, identify it as something that affects only a minority of women, who can then be held in some way responsible for it. This woman-blaming logic of victimology leads many social service providers to conduct support services on their own professional terms – counselling or family therapy directed at reintegrating women and children who have been abused back into active heterosexuality and family life with the abuser with minimum disruption. This is in contrast with feminist women-centred support services developed by and with survivors of male violence, whose response is unconditional support for women and children in whatever strategies they elect. Instead of forwarding women's and children's best interests, we see too many of these professionals containing women within the structures of heterosexuality and the family and building lucrative careers for themselves on the backs of male violence (Kelly 1989). These academic and professional interventions in the public discourse about violence against women mark two major ideological shifts.

A third major shift has become evident in the Home Office and police forces for England and Wales. Although feminist critiques in the UK and elsewhere through the 1970s and early 1980s constituted a continuing source of embarrassment to those responsible for law enforcement and the judicial process, the recent about-turn in UK policy, we argue, does not stem directly from the pressure of British feminists. Rather, the British police have sought advice and direction from their North American counterparts in dealing with modern management of inner-city riots as well as sexual violence and domestic assault against women. [...]

The work of North American feminists confronted police practices in relation to woman battering by lobbying for legislative mandates in many US states, and through filing class action law suits in New York and Oakland, condemning the practice of entire police forces. But the individual liability case against Torrington, Connecticut (which resulted in disastrous financial consequences for the municipal government) made police forces take notice; failing to take action in domestic situations could now cost police precious tax resources. These actions opened the doors to scrutinize US policing and police practice (Ferraro 1989). Changes in the US provided examples of 'good practice' that could be adopted by British police. But the importing of these ideas about 'good' practice left out any possibility of a feminist base.

Identifying women on the one hand as a vocal source of criticism and on the other as a needy target and by drawing on internal police debates on new softer 'community policing' styles of policing (Alderson 1979), police attention has turned to the long-neglected problem of violence against women. The change of heart has been rapid indeed. For instance, in 1984 Sir Kenneth Newman attempted to shed police responsibility for what he considered 'rubbish work', or non-police matters, naming domestic violence and stray dogs as two such examples. By 1990, police forces were competing with each other to find the most creative policy to deal with domestic violence!

But the new interest in violence against women does not include a commitment to promoting women's autonomy, nor does it recognize how policing policy affects women within varying race, class, ethnic and religious contexts. The location of London's first domestic violence units in Tottenham and Brixton, as Amina Mama (1989) states, raises questions about how policing differentially affects women and their communities:

> The establishment of domestic violence response units, staffed by women police officers and resourced to do proper monitoring and follow-up work may be a good idea, but we were concerned to note that these are an initiative so far restricted to areas of black concentration which are already heavily and oppressively policed. This raises the possibility that such units have a hidden agenda, concerned with convicting more black men, underpinning the publicly proclaimed agenda which stresses supporting and following up incidents in the interests of women being subjected to violence. (Mama 1989: 304–5)

The interest of the political heart of the British ministry in violence to women is widening. The Home Office now recognizes women's 'fear of crime' as a serious problem. [...]

Women's fear of crime, however unfounded to policy makers, has become the focus of a growing number of safety campaigns. The campaigns about safety attempt to reassure women by suggesting ways to minimize the potential threat of public space through the avoidance of dangerous strangers. Exemplified in their 'bolts and bars' approach to crime prevention, the Home Office's focus spotlights street crime, adding to the type of concern voiced by Amina Mama above. [...]

If feminism is to remain in the forefront of critiques of crime control, we must not lose sight of our politics. We must not lose sight of our starting point, the experiences of women and children; we must not separate women's experiences of violence and danger from unknown and known men; and we must not forget that men's sexual violence is part of the backdrop of all women's lives and not something experienced by a minority who can be labelled as inadequate and helpless victims. Managing sexual danger is an integral part of being female (Kelly 1988; Stanko 1990) and any understanding about crime control must place women's safety at the centre of the debate (see also MacKinnon 1989). Altering definitions of what is crime, such as changes to the law of rape and encouraging police to treat what comes to their attention as criminal violence are two approaches to confronting crime against women and children. Both strategies, we argue, may lead to some thorny contradictions in resulting approaches to crime prevention, women's safety and crime control.

Legislative change

An illustration of legislative change is the move towards outlawing rape in marriage in England and Wales. This was the subject of a concerted feminist campaign in the early 1980s in many countries, including the US, Canada, Australia and Sweden. Feminist arguments are arguments of principle, asserting that there could be no equality for married women while in law they could be subjected to sexual violence by their husbands without redress. From a feminist perspective this present state of law represented a clear statement about the nature of marriage and a woman's place within it, and the compulsory nature of heterosexuality itself. The British government in its decision in January 1990 to refer this matter to the Law Commission, under the supervision of Professor Brenda Hoggett, QC, has indicated its welcome for a change in law. [...]

What practical benefits this move will bring for women is difficult to know. We do know both that many women will welcome this legal reform and that many women are subjected to this form of abuse. The 1989 Granada Television *World in Action* survey designed by the Centre for Criminology at Middlesex Polytechnic showed that 96 per cent of the 1,000 women interviewed said there should be a law against rape in marriage. Further, 60 per cent reported there had been occasions when they had agreed with reluctance to have sex with their husbands; 15 per cent reported having been coerced by their husbands into having sex; 12 per cent reported that they had been forced into having sex, despite a clear refusal; and 5 per cent reported being beaten before being raped.

From these figures, it is clear that on the face of it there are real practical as well as ideological reasons for criminalizing rape in marriage. However, [...] in practice implementing such a law will be difficult. These difficulties were just one of the reasons why previous Law Commission reports have consistently rejected this change. The judiciary has systematically shown its reluctance to convict rapists when they are known to the abused woman. They are also reluctant to convict rapists on the testimony of women alone as shown in the corroboration warning, where judges in rape and sexual assault trials instruct juries to the effect that it is well known that women, like small children, are notorious liars. It seems again that a recommendation for change is largely symbolic. Perhaps the government is more concerned to improve the public image of marriage and heterosexuality, leaving all manner of practical difficulties in place to prevent large numbers of married men – practically one-third, taking the figures above in their most generous interpretation – being convicted of this crime. Removing the legal impediment will not automatically protect women from sexual abuse by their husbands.

Police practice

Feminist concern about the failure of police to protect them from violence is not new. The very inclusion of women within the police force, for instance, is grounded within the belief that women are best able to deal with women and their protection (Feinman 1986; Radford 1990). So when feminist criticism angrily attacked police treatment of women who reported rape or domestic violence during the 1970s in the US, the initial defensive reactions were followed by setting up special units in many forces to deal specifically with sexual assault.

Ian Blair's (1985) study of US police practices with respect to sexual assault provided the Metropolitan Police with a structure to ward off increasing public pressure about police treatment of women reporting rape. As the police began to reveal their private face to the public through Roger Graef's BBC documentary series (1982), a number of coterminous events, starkly illustrating the criminal justice insensitivity to women who had been raped, brought remarks even from (the then) Mrs Thatcher. Sir Nicholas Fairbairn, Lord Chancellor of Scotland, resigned over a decision not to prosecute three defendants in a horrendous and violent rape case (Jeffreys and Radford 1984).

Increasingly, the police turned to their US counterparts who had already begun to alter their practice. The establishment of special examination rooms for women victimized by sexual assault, the training of women police officers in taking initial statements from women reporting rape or sexual assault and, in some jurisdictions, the referring of women to Home Office-backed victim support schemes, are examples of recent UK initiatives.

For some feminists, this last point is a site of controversy and struggle. Rape crisis centres are consciously rooted in feminist principles, women-centred, and have a unique expertise working with women whether or not they rely on police intervention into the violence they experience from men. Victim Support, a voluntary organization, contacts victims of crime through police referrals. Their government support rose in 1991 to around £4.5 million, a 200 per cent increase over four years. As the funding to Victim Support increases, rape crisis centres and Women's Aid become starved of funding. At the same time, the majority of domestic physical and sexual assaults are never reported to police, and therefore would never be referred to Victim Support. Despite the commitment of some feminist volunteers within victim support, the philosophy of the national organization, Victim Support, is actively non-feminist. [...]

Attention has turned to police practice around domestic assault. Force orders in 1985 and Home Office guidelines concerning violence against women in 1986 and 1990, responded to criticisms from feminists. [...] Academic studies such as that by Susan Edwards (1989) in Islington, north London, showed that police response to complaints of violence within the home largely left women on their own with no legal recourse or protection against violent intimates or former intimates. In London alone, by 1991, over 40 jurisdictions have set up special units to monitor domestic violence and the Home Office guidelines of July 1990 recommend the establishment of such units in all police forces (Radford 1990).

Here also the British police looked to their American and Canadian colleagues to witness far-reaching change in policing practice. The studies of London, Ontario (Jaffe *et al.* 1982), and Minneapolis (Sherman and Berk 1984) pointed to a more aggressive policing policy to reduce violence in the home. A study by Horton and Smith (1988) of the Hampshire constabulary reinforced the need to do something about 'domestics': they reflected 10 per cent of police calls in citizen-initiated requests for assistance.

The new policing strategy is to treat the complaints they receive from women about sexual and physical violence more often as criminal violence. To this end, [...] specialist units have been established; some, but not all, staffed by women police officers to supervise officers' handling of 'domestics' and to provide follow up support services. In addition to recommending that all police forces establish such units, the July 1990 Home Office Guidelines also inform officers that their primary concern should be the safety of the woman and any children involved and that in relation to the man, their first concern should be the possibility of arrest. These measures are new. Their impact has still to be noted, researched and evaluated. [...] A vital and urgent task for feminists will be the monitoring of the impact of these new initiatives, particularly in terms of their class and race dynamics.

Criminal violence is private violence

The fact remains that many of women's experiences of coercive sexuality are not recognized in man-made law (Kelly 1988; Stanko 1990; Holland *et al.* 1990). Although the judicial authorities are now seeing more crime than previously, the problem of violence to women, largely located within their relationships with familiar and familial men, is still leading to some conceptual problems in relation to its redefinition in criminal discourse, and discourse concerning remedies and crime control strategies which still revolve around public, not private, violence.

When familial violence is recognized, the old stereotypes around race and class surface. Violence is assumed to be a characteristic of black and working-class families, which were then pathologized (see Ferraro 1989 on the US; Zoomer 1989 on Holland). If the violence is deemed the norm in 'pathological' families, then either no intervention is called for or alternatively black families are targeted for therapy to bring them into the white, nuclear family 'norm'. Conversely, in white middle-class families, the prevailing myth is that 'nice' professional men don't do it. The strength of this myth is such that some middle-class women find it hard to convince police and other state professionals that they need support.

What is interesting, however, is that the Home Office studies are now beginning to throw some light on the curious reality for women: that their attackers are most likely to be those near and dear rather than the shadowy stranger (Smith 1989a). [...]

Although there are moves within the Home Office to take this violence seriously, the policy on crime prevention has moved in the opposite direction. Crime prevention advice stems primarily from a perspective that rests prevention on situational deterrence. The 'locks and bolts' solution to crime suggests that adequate security, vigilance, and common sense reduce the likelihood of experiencing crime.

Moving the responsibility for crime prevention to the individual through adequate security and reasonable precaution means that approaches to preventing crime necessarily focus on the danger of the unpredictable stranger who awaits opportunities for criminal enterprise. (This approach leads to woman-blaming when protection fails. Not having taken self-defence classes is deemed provocation or negligence inviting attack.) [...]

If one assumes that it is women's safety that is important, then the Home Office campaign on crime prevention misses the mark by a wide margin. So too do the efforts of the newly arrived caring professionals in the field, because, we believe, they do not offer a gendered analysis about violence against women. Physical battering, according to this thinking, is either a reflection of bad marital relations, personality disputes, or intoxicating substances, not the manifestation of unequal power and a need for control. Sexual abuse, following the same line, arises because of some men's uncontrollable lust or miscommunication with women and children, not as an exercise of patriarchal power. Women, in the tradition of victimology, are often blamed as being inadequate wives or as colluding in their own harm and that of their children. The assumption, understandable in childhood, that mothers are all-knowing, is used by professionals to find mothers of abused children guilty of either collusion or 'failure to protect'. These explanations of men's violence succeed in keeping most of the violence against women outside officially used definitions of crime, and away from the only arm of the state mandated to protect – the police and the criminal justice apparatus (Stanko 1985). Instead diversion programmes, family therapy, and men's counselling groups are the new professional growth industry. [...]

This then is the heart of the contradiction facing feminists. On the face of it the police and caring professions have responded – albeit for a complex range of reasons – to feminist criticisms of the 1970s, but have done so in a way which has completely negated feminist definitions, politics, research and provision of support services. Not only this, but these interventions are part of a wider attempt on the part of an authoritarian right-wing populist government to win public support for their law and order policies, and these attempts are seductive to some white middle-class women. In terms of policing the velvet glove of a caring police force goes hand-in-hand with the iron fist of riot control and militaristic policing in the 'inner city'. One feminist response has been to monitor these moves, identify and bring together these developments, with a view to understanding at the level of practice as well as ideology. [...]

The family, and the institution of heterosexuality which underpins it, is a central institution in patriarchal society, one in which the private struggles around patriarchal power relations are enacted, and hence one in which violence frequently features as a form of control of the powerless by the powerful. It is not limited to the family, however, as in the public sphere and in paid employment women who are outside heterosexuality, or give the appearance of being marginal to it, are those primarily targeted for sexual violence, abuse and harassment, as the amount of violence experienced by lesbians and other women marginal to the white middle-class, ageist and able-bodied image of heterosexual 'normality' status. [...]

Controlling crime against women and children, as we see it, demands policy and practice that confronts men's licence to abuse. However,

the state's concern about male sexual violence in the family can be seen as an attempt at policing the family and heterosexuality in order to clean up its public face and to restore its legitimacy as a safe institution for women, by curbing that violence which it can no longer hide. So by moving towards curbing the excesses of male sexual violence within the family and heterosexuality, these sacred institutions of patriarchy are preserved intact and patriarchal gendered relations are reaffirmed, reproduced and represented as in the best interests of women and children. Achieving this requires a silencing of any feminist politics which asks disturbing questions about whether heterosexuality is the natural, normal and only possibility for women, whether it is indeed voluntary or compulsory for women living under conditions of patriarchy and whether it is in our best interests. We will continue to ask: is this new concern with violence to women on the part of the state's police and professional carers a concern with women's interests, a concern for women's autonomy, or is it a last ditch attempt at reinstating the patriarchal status quo by restoring an apparently respectable face to its central institutions, the family and heterosexuality?

From J. Radford and E.A. Stanko, 'Violence against women and children: the contradictions of crime control under patriarchy', in M. Hester, L. Kelly and J. Radford (eds) Women, Violence and Male Power *(Buckingham: Open University Press), 1996, pp. 65–80.*

References

Alderson, J. (1979) *Policing Freedom: a Commentary on the Dilemmas of Policing in Western Democracies.* Plymouth: McDonald and Evans.

Blair, I. (1985) *Investigating Rape.* London: Croom Helm.

Cameron, D. (1988) *Lust to Kill.* Oxford: Polity Press.

Caputi, J. (1988) *The Age of Sex Crime.* Ohio, NM: Bowling Green State University Press.

Cohen, L.E. and Felson, M. (1979) Social change and crime rate trends: a routine activity approach, *American Sociological Review*, 44(4): 588–608.

Edwards, S. (1989) *Policing Domestic Violence.* London: Sage.

Feinman, C. (1986) *Women and Criminal Justice.* New York: Pergamon.

Ferraro, K. (1989) The legal response to woman battering in the United States. In J. Hanmer, J. Radford and E.A. Stanko (eds) *Women, Policing and Male Violence.* London: Routledge.

Gottfredson, M. (1984) *Victims of Crime: Dimensions of Risk.* London: HMSO.

Hall, R. (1985) *Ask Any Woman.* London: Falling Wall Press.

Hanmer, J., Radford, J. and Stanko, E.A. (1989) *Women, Policing and Male Violence.* London: Routledge.

Hanmer, J. and Saunders, S. (1984) *Well Founded Fear.* London: Hutchinson.

Hindelang, M., Gottfredson, M. and Garofalo, J. (1978) *Victims of Personal Crime.* Cambridge, MA: Ballinger.

Holland, J., Ramazanoglu, C. and Scott, S. (1990) Managing risk and experiencing danger: Tensions between government AIDS educational policy and young women's sexuality, *Gender and Education*, July: 125–46.

Horton, C. and Smith, D. (1988) *Evaluating Police Work: An Action Research Project*. London: Policy Studies Institute.

Hough, M. and Mayhew, P. (1983) *The British Crime Survey*. London: HMSO.

Hough, M. and Mayhew, P. (1985) *Taking Account of Crime*. London: HMSO.

Jaffe, P., Wolfe, P., Telford, A. and Austin, C. (1982) The impact of police charges in incidents of wife abuse, *Journal of Family Violence*, 1(1): 37–49.

Jeffreys, S. and Radford, J. (1984) Contributory negligence: being a woman. In P. Scraton and P. Gordon (eds) *Causes for Concern*. London: Penguin.

Kelly, L. (1988) *Surviving Sexual Violence*. Cambridge: Polity Press.

Kelly, L. (1989) Bitter ironies: the professionalisation of child sex abuse, *Trouble and Strife*, 16, summer: 14–21.

Kelly, L. and Radford, J. (1987) The problem of men. In P. Scraton (ed.) *Law, Order and the Authoritarian State*. Milton Keynes: Open University Press.

MacKinnon, C.A. (1989) *Toward a Feminist Theory of the State*. Cambridge, MA: Harvard University Press.

Mama, A. (1989) *The Hidden Struggle: Statutory and Voluntary Sector Responses to Violence against Black Women in the Home*. London: The London Race and Housing Research Group.

Mayhew, P., Dowds, L. and Elliot, D. (1989) *The 1988 British Crime Survey*. London: HMSO.

Radford, J. (1987) 'Policing male violence – policing women'. In J. Hanmer and M. Maynard (eds) *Women, Violence and Social Control*. London: Macmillan.

Radford, J. (1990) Sorry, sir, it's domestic. You're nicked, *Rights of Women Bulletin*, autumn: 6–8.

Russell, D.E.H. (1982) *Rape in Marriage*. New York: Macmillan.

Russell, D.E.H. (1984) *Sexual Exploitation*. Beverly Hills, CA: Sage.

Russell, D.E.H. (1985) *Incest: The Secret Trauma*. New York: Basic Books.

Scheppele, K. and Bart P. (1983) Through women's eyes: defining danger in the wake of sexual assault, *Journal of Social Issues*, 39(2): 63–81.

Sherman, L. and Berk, R. (1984) The specific deterrent effects of arrest for domestic assault, *American Sociological Review*, 49(2): 261–72,

Smart, C. (1989) *Feminism and the Power of the Law*. London: Routledge.

Smith, L.J.F. (1989a) *Domestic Violence*. London: HMSO.

Stanko, E.A. (1985) *Intimate Intrusions*. London: Unwin Hyman.

Stanko, E.A. (1988) Hidden violence to women. In M. Maguire and J. Pointing (eds) *Victims of Crime: A New Deal?* Milton Keynes: Open University Press.

Stanko, E. (1990) *Everyday Violence*. London: Pandora.

Zoomer, O. (1989) Policing woman beating in the Netherlands. In J. Hanmer, J. Radford and E.A. Stanko (eds) *Women, Policing and Male Violence*. London: Routledge.

17.4 Multiple victimisation: its extent and significance
Graham Farrell

Introduction

It has long been suggested that some offenders repeatedly offend, (recidivist offending) and account for a disproportionately large amount of all offences committed. However, it has barely been recognised that some people, households, or other targets however defined, may, through being 'recidivist' or repeat victims, account for a large proportion of all offences experienced. (This is not necessarily to suggest a link between the two phenomena.) [...]

The term multiple victimisation is used in this paper to refer to multiple criminal incidents experienced by either a person or place. It is also called repeat victimisation, recidivist victimisation, or multi-victimisation. [...] One area of influence for multiple victimisation might be upon crime prevention strategy. [...] If a summary of the potential for developing a general crime prevention strategy around multiple victimisation had to be given, it might take the form given below, split into three parts:

- Reason: If multiple victimisation (using the broadest definition), could be prevented, most crimes would be prevented. That is, if a small proportion of the population are repeatedly victimised so that they experience a large proportion of *all* criminal offences, then preventing repeat victimisation would prevent a large proportion of *all* offences from being committed.[1,2]

- Illustration: The information gathered by the 1982 British Crime Survey suggests that over 70%, or over seven in ten, of the offences it covered, were experienced by just 14% of the total population.

- Method: The prevention of multiple victimisation might be developed through responses to victimisation. [...]

One of the major studies recognising repeat victimisation is also commonly accepted as one of the 'classics' of victim-survey based studies in victimology. *Surveying Victims* by Sparks *et al.* (1977) was based on work conducted in three London boroughs, from which Sparks went on to write a series of articles in the early 1980s (e.g. Sparks, 1981), and upon which Genn's article 'Multiple victimisation' (1988) is based. The 1977 book used mathematical modelling to observe the highly skewed distribution of victimisation through their sample. They found that a small percentage of the population, because they were repeatedly victimised, accounted for a substantial proportion of all types of crime in the survey. Initially they attempted to fit the spread of repeat victimisation to a Poisson distribution. The data did not fit this model, which suggested that repeat victimisation was not caused by 'bad luck', that is, it did not correspond to a chance distribution of independent, single-incident, victimisations in a population sampled with replacement. With the further dismissal of a 'contagion' effect Poisson model of victimisation, the attempt was made to fit a heterogeneous model. This was an attempt to fit a Poisson model to different sub-groups of the population characterised by, for example, socio-demographic characteristics such as age, sex and ethnicity, or by type of crime. Whilst this was found to be more accurate than the standard Poisson model, it was 'far from perfect'.

Hindelang *et al.* devoted a chapter of their 1978 book, *Victims of Personal Crime* (1978) to the analysis of multiple victimisation. They used data from eight US cities and over 165,000 interviews. The book is mainly known for developing the lifestyle/exposure theory of victimisation, which may have overshadowed their work on multiple victimisation. They established certain patterns of multiple victimisation which they summarised as follows:

'First, both once victimised persons and once victimised households were more likely to have suffered subsequent victimisation than were members of the population (persons or households respectively) selected at random. For personal victims, this is accounted for – but only in part – by the finding that repetitive victims were more likely than one-time victims to be victimised by persons known to them. Second, persons living in households in which another household member had been personally victimised had a greater risk of personal victimisation than persons living in households in which no other household member had been personally victimised. Third, persons living in households that had been victimised by a household crime had a higher risk of personal victimisation than persons living in households that had not been victimised by a household crime' (1978; p. 149). For Hindelang *et al.*, the implications of multiple victimisation were primarily to provide support for their lifestyle model of victimisation.

Since these three studies, other attempts have been made to investigate repeat victimisation through mathematical and statistical techniques. Albert Reiss (1980), using data from the US National Crime Survey (NCS) wrote: 'Evidence of repeat victimisation makes it clear that victimisation is not a random occurrence... Moreover, in repeat victimisation, there is a proneness to repeat victimisation by the same type of crime' (1980; p.52). [...]

Genn (1988) [...] provides a critique of victim surveys which impose a strict definition of 'a crime' and 'a victim' upon the interviewee. Most victim surveys have only a one year reporting period, limit the number of crimes which can be reported, and impose an artificial limit on those reported, before computer analysis. Genn suggests that, in particular for certain types of crime such as domestic violence, some people are forced to live with almost continual victimisation as part of their everyday lives. Based upon the findings of a victim survey (Sparks *et al.*, 1977) and the extent of victimisation in some households, Genn returned to the research site to conduct some follow-up interviews. Genn's participant observation study of multiple victimisation included spending several months with a group of victims on a high crime estate in north London. Genn reports that 'after some months of association with this group of people, I no longer found it surprising that a structured questionnaire administered to one household should uncover some thirteen incidents of "victimisation"' (1988; p.93). Genn argued that for some households, victim surveys often picked up only a fraction of the total incidents. Similar limitations of existing sources of knowledge about victimisation are suggested by Stanko (1988), who argues that most violence remains 'hidden' from official agencies like the police, as well as from victim surveys. This, it is argued, is one of the factors behind the commonly held belief, perpetuated by the media, that violence is usually between strangers. There is an increasing volume of literature to suggest that the majority of violence may take place between familiars, that is, people who know each other, whether as partners, neighbours, relatives, workplace acquaintances, 'friends' or known others (for example, Stanko 1988, 1990; and Smith, 1989 give an overview of some of the literature on domestic violence). The literature draws attention to the fact that a large proportion of familiars' violence is against women. [...]

Sherman *et al.* (1989) studied the spatial distribution of calls reported to the police. They found that in a major city in the US, 50% of all calls to the police for some types of crime came from 3% of locations. An analogy can be drawn between their locational 'hot-spots of predatory crime', and the phenomenon of repeat victimisation of certain people and households, with a similar potential for focusing crime prevention strategies.

Providing an additional quantitative perspective to the phenomenon of repeat victimisation, Trickett *et al.* (1991), using BCS data, suggest that repeat victimisation is more intense in 'high crime' areas. They broach the important question of whether certain areas have 'high' crime rates because more people are victimised, or because there is greater multiple victimisation of the same people. They suggest a positive correlation between the overall incidence of crime and the extent of repeat victimisation, from which it might be inferred that crime prevention may become more efficient as it becomes more 'focused'. Focusing on repeat victimisation within 'high crime' areas may be more efficient in terms of crimes prevented (as well, therefore, as per unit of labour and expenditure), even than focusing on repeat victimisation across all areas.

Multiple victimisation and the British crime survey

In 1984, Michael Gottfredson, in writing a Home Office report analysing aspects of the 1982 BCS [observed that]:

'of the victims of personal crime in the BCS, 72% were one time victims while 28% were repetitively victimised. For all crimes in the survey, the corresponding percentages are 56% one-time victims and 44% multiple victims...' (1984; p.42).

Further analysis of the data which Gottfredson presents suggests that over 70% of all criminal incidents reported by the 1982 BCS were experienced by multi-victims, who made up only 14% of the population. This is despite the fact that, as will be discussed later in this paper, the crimes against women which are under-represented in the BCS (see, for example, Stanko, 1983) may also be those most likely to result in repeat victimisation. The distribution of victimisation for 'all offences' in the 1982 BCS is shown in Table 17.4.1 below, calculated from Gottfredson (1984; p.41).

Table 17.4.1 Distribution of victimisation for all offences: 1982 British crime survey

Number of times victimised	Respondents (%)	Incidents (%)
0	68.1	0.0
1	17.8	29.1
2	6.2	20.3
3	3.1	15.2
4	1.8	11.8
5 or more	2.9	23.7
	99.9*	100.1*

* total percent not equal to 100 due to rounding

Table 17.4.1 shows the highly skewed distribution of victimisation revealed by the BCS. This is itself an extremely conservative estimate, given the current limitations of the BCS for the study of multiple victimisation (Genn, 1988). Those people who reported having been victimised on two or more occasions, that is with 'number of times victimised' between 2 and '5 or more' (left hand column) make up 14% of the population (summing the four corresponding percentages in the middle column). This 14% of the population who are multiple victims, in the year covered by the survey, reported 70.9% of all the incidents reported (summing the four percentages in the right hand column). Similar patterns of the distribution of victimisation for household offences and personal offences can also be generated.

Some inferences about the extent and nature of multiple victimisation might be made from Hough (1986). Hough presented both incidence and prevalence rates of victimisation for violent crimes (1986; p. 124). In his paper, the incidence rate represents the estimated average number of incidents per 100 respondents, here expressed as a percentage. The prevalence rate represents the estimated percentage of respondents who are victims. For all violent offences in the 1982 BCS, there is a prevalence of 4.5%, and an incidence of 8.02%, suggesting almost twice as many incidents as victims. There are variations within types of violence. The most prevalent crimes are not necessarily those with the highest average number of victimisations per victim. Thus the most prevalent crimes may not necessarily be those with the highest rates of repeat victimisation. (Sexual assaults are excluded here, which, as with other violence between familiars and against women, is largely unreported.) The rankings of incidence and prevalence are the same, with common assault the highest for each, followed by threat of assault, wounding and robbery. However, from the ratio of incidence to prevalence (which is, as discussed below, not a totally unambiguous indicator), robbery appears the most likely type of violence to be repeated. This is followed by assault, threat of assault and wounding. The suggestion is, therefore, that whilst a person is unlikely to be robbed, once robbed they may be the most likely to be robbed again in comparison to the recurrence of other types of violence. [...] For all types of violence, the ratio of incidence to prevalence for all types of crime is higher than would be expected if it were a sum of the individual types of crime. This suggests that victims report more than one type of violence. Multiple victimisation can therefore be by different types of violent crime as well as by the same type.

Incidence rates are always higher than prevalence rates, with there being more criminal incidents than victims. This is because some people are multiple victims. Presented side by side, incidence and prevalence rates do suggest the existence of multiple victimisation; however they serve as little more than an indicator and a generalisation.

Evidence from a local crime survey

A report by Alice Sampson (1991), presents information about multiple victims referred to the 'high crime' estate-based Victim Support scheme which mirror the patterns of repeat victimisation from victim surveys. Sampson found that out of 289 referrals to the scheme over two years, 46 households or residents (16%) were victims of more than one reported crime, and that '(t)hese victims accounted for 38% of the crimes' (1991; p.6). In addition, 20 of the multi-victim households suffered from both property and personal crimes, 20 from at least two property crimes, and 8 people were victims of interpersonal crime only. [...] The victim survey carried out on the estate on which the Victim Support office was based, found similar patterns of multiple victimi-sation (Sampson and Farrell, 1990; Farrell, 1990). [...] Six hundred people were interviewed in the survey. Multiple victims accounted for 78.8% of all crimes reported. This finding corresponds with the findings from the BCS where multiple victims accounted for 70% of all crimes. In addition, the higher rate of multiple victimisation on the 'high crime' estate corresponds with the findings of Trickett et al. (1991) that repeat victimisation is more intense in high crime areas. The survey also suggested that 5% of the respondents reported 62% of the personal crimes. Of the victims of personal crime, a third were multi-victims of personal crime, and one in six had experienced at least two different types of personal crime in the last year (corresponding with the suggestions from the re-analysis of Hough (1986)). A person or household reporting a burglary or attempted burglary was more than twice as likely to report a personal crime. The suggested link between personal and property crime found both in the survey and in the referrals to the Victim Support workers is also recognised by Hindelang et al. (1978) and by Gottfredson (1984). The intensity of victimisation of certain people may be even greater than this paper has suggested so far. In the 'high crime' estate victim survey, 15 people (2.5% of respondents) reported 141 incidents (30% of total incidents). The 1982 BCS data shows that 2.9% of the respondents reported 23.7% of the total incidents (see Table 17.4.1 above).

Preventing multiple and repeat victimisation

Whilst some of the implications of multiple victimisation for crime prevention policy have already been mentioned (Trickett et al., 1991), the only existing application of these practices is the Kirkholt Burglary Prevention Project (Forrester et *al.*, 1988a) which aimed to reduce burglary on a council housing estate in Rochdale, in the north west of England. The initial research phase combined interviews with known (detained) burglars, with burglary victims and their neighbours, and analysis of available burglary data, to find that,

> once a house had been burgled, its chance of further victimisation was four times the rate of houses that had not been burgled at all (Forrester *et al.*, 1988b; p.2289)

The strategy was developed to implement a combined package of opportunity reduction and situational crime prevention measures at those households which were burgled during the course of the project. These were the houses that were predicted to be the most likely victims in the near future, and the package of measures effectively stopped repeat victimisation. The final report of the project (Forrester *et al.*, 1990) states that burglary was reduced by 75% within three years. In addition, the project also implemented social crime prevention measures, such as initiatives in the local schools, to try to reduce the future levels of offending in the area. The project has been 'returned to the community' with the intention that its members will work to maintain its practices. As a crime prevention project, this provides the most persuasive indications to date that the targeting of repeat victimisation may be a successful, focused and economically viable means of general crime prevention. The perceived attractions of the prevention of repeat victimisation as a general strategy of crime prevention are summarised in Pease (1991; p.76):

- Attention to dwellings or people already victimised has a higher 'hit rate' of those likely to be victimised in the future.

- Preventing repeat victimisation protects the most vulnerable social groups, without having to identify those groups as such, which can be socially divisive. Having been victimised already probably represents the least contentious basis for a claim to be given crime prevention attention.

- Repeat victimisation is highest, both absolutely and proportionately, in the most crime-ridden areas (Trickett *et al.*, 1991), which are also the areas that suffer the most serious crime (Pease, 1988). The prevention of repeat victimisation is thus commensurately more important the

greater an area's crime problem.

- The rate of victimisation offers a realistic schedule for crime prevention activity. Preventing repeat victimisation is a way of 'drip-feeding' crime prevention.

- Even from the unrealistic view that crime is only displaced, avoiding repeat victimisation at least shares the agony around (see Barr and Pease, 1990).

Whilst the Kirkholt project focused solely on burglary prevention, Pease argues that its theoretical base provides a foundation for crime prevention of a general nature. This is not necessarily to argue that the opportunity reduction and situational measures used in the Kirkholt project are generally applicable – these were tailored for the specific project – rather that crime prevention in general might concentrate upon the phenomenon of repeat victimisation. [...]

The main objection to the prevention of repeat victimisation as it has so far been discussed might be that crimes perceived to be 'prevented' might instead be displaced. Barr and Pease (1990) suggest that whilst much of the literature on displacement is inconclusive, it is unlikely that all crime 'prevented' in one place will occur elsewhere, and that even if it does this may result in a more egalitarian distribution of crime.

The time interval between a victimisation and a further victimisation has significant implications for crime prevention policy. [...] The importance of Polvi *et al.*'s [1990] work lies in the time-course analysis, where it was found that:

> following a first burglary... the disporportionate risk is primarily encountered in the month following the first victimisation, and within that month in the first days following the first break-and-enter offense (1990; p.11).

Along similar lines, Farrell and Pease (1991) looked at the extent of crimes reported in 1990 by thirty-three schools in an area of Merseyside. Seven schools reported only one crime, and the most victimised school reported 28 crimes in 1990. Of the total of 296 crimes reported, 263 (97.6%) were repeat crimes. Of these, 208 or 79% were revictimisations occuring within one month of a prior victimisation. The implication for crime prevention is that responses to victimisation must be immediate, but that the necessary duration for a prevention strategy may be relatively short in order to prevent a large proportion of repeat victimisation.

A prevention strategy based upon repeat victimisation must have sources of information about crime. With respect to sources of information, property and personal crimes can again be contrasted. A large proportion of burglaries and car thefts are reported to the police (Hough and Mayhew, 1985), not least for insurance purposes. However, as already mentioned, much violence goes unreported. In order to have any chance of preventing repeat victimisation, knowledge of the occurrence of crime must be increased beyond that of recorded crime. Existing sources of information must be explored, and potential sources developed. One alternative to recorded crimes is police incident logs or message pads (which are mainly telephone calls to the police from the public). To give one concrete example, an ongoing Manchester University project researching violence has found that on one estate in Merseyside of about 1,300 houses, there were (the least estimate) 143 calls to the police about domestic violence in 1990 (Stanko, 1991). These calls came from 86 different addresses. One household made at least 15 calls! [...]

It is important to note that these are only incidents which, when received by the police, are 'coded' as domestic violence; it is possible for domestic violence to go unrecognised when it is logged as a disturbance or assault. With respect to repeat victimisation, these findings must also be taken in the context of the suggestion that a woman who calls the police has, on average, been the victim of 35 previous beatings by a male partner (cited in Horley, 1988; p.2).

Other potential sources of information about the nature of repeat victimisation might include hospital casualty departments (Shepherd, 1990) or General Practitioners' surgeries (Stanko, 1991).

Conclusions: looking to the fututre

[A] relatively small proportion of the population seems to experience a large proportion of all crime. There is a highly skewed distribution of crime in the population which is not due to chance. This observation would appear to hold up to rigorous testing from a variety of different sources. [...]

A multiple victim may experience many different types of crime. In addition, and not in contradiction, there is the suggestion of repeat victimisation by the same type of crime. These two phenomena might be termed inter-crime and intra-crime, or across-crime type and within-crime type multiple victimisation respectively. [...]

The Kirkholt project (Forrester et al., 1988a, 1988b, 1990; Pease, 1991) suggests that a combined package of opportunity reduction and situational and community crime prevention measures can be used to effectively reduce repeat household burglary in high crime areas, with comparatively low rates of displacement. [...] This could possibly be extended to such as the prevention of car theft and other motor vehicle crime; other possibilities for target hardening. [...]

The prevention of multiple victimisation might be developed through agency responses to victimisation. This is not to suggest that all crimes can be addressed through the same approach. Responses to victimisation will need to vary with agency, type of crime, circumstance, and the characteristics and resources of different areas. [...]

What becomes apparent from the literature are not only the crime prevention possibilities, but also the fact that criminology/victimology should only approach the study of victimisation when taking account of multiple victimisation. The perceived definition of 'victimisation' implicit in many criminological studies should adjust to include the phenomenon of multi-victimisation. Qualitative study is needed into the phenomenon of multiple victimisation. [...] Other theoretical implications may arise if multiple victimisation is recognised as significant. As well as questioning the accepted definitions of 'a victim' and 'a crime', these include implications for the study of fear of crime, and lifetime experiences of victimisation. For example, the disparity between reported fear of crime and reported experiences of crime may be a combination of hidden crime (Stanko, 1988) and past experiences of crime not picked up by the one year reporting period of victim surveys. Gender differences in fear might be linked to childhood victimisation experiences which, with the exception of the Edinburgh survey, remain marginalised. Sentencing policy and criminal injury compensation might need to take account of the perspective of the multiple victim.

From G. Farrell, *'Multiple victimisation: its extent and significance'*, International Review of Victimology, *1992, 2: 85–102.*

Notes

1 The summary used here generalises across types of crime, and assumes known and accepted (that is, often those used in law) definitions of what constitute 'a crime', 'a victim', and consequently a multiple victim.

2 The main reservation to crime prevention may be crime displacement, which will be touched on later.

References

Barr, R. and Pease, K. (1990). Crime placement, displacement and deflection. In: *Crime and Justice: An Annual Review of Research* (M. Tonry and N. Morris, eds) Vol. 12, pp. 277–315. University of Chicago Press; Chicago.

Farrell, G. (1990). *Multivictimisation*. Unpublished dissertation. University of Surrey; England.

Farrell, G. and Pease, K. (1991). *School Burglary, Criminal Damage and Other School Crime*, Unpublished report to Merseyside Police. August 1991.

Forrester, D., Chatterton, M. and Pease, K. with the assistance of Brown, R. (1988a). *The Kirkholt Burglary Prevention Project*, Rochdale. Home Office Crime Prevention Unit Paper no. 13. HMSO; London.

Forrester, D., Chatterton, M. and Pease, K. (1988b). Why it's best to lock the door after the horse has bolted. *Police Review*, 4 November 1988, 2288–2289.

Forrester, D., Frenz, S., O'Connell, M. and Pease, K. (1990). *The Kirkholt Burglary Prevention Project: Phase II*. Home Office Crime Prevention Unit Paper no. 23. HMSO; London.

Genn, H. (1988). Multiple victimisation. In: *Victims of Crime: a new deal?* (M. Maguire and J. Pointing, eds.) pp. 90–100. Open University Press; England.

Gottfredson, M.R. (1984). *Victims of Crime: The Dimensions of Risk*. Home Office Research Study 81. HMSO; London.

Hindelang, M., Gottfredson, M. R. and Garofalo, J. (1978). *Victims of Personal Crime: an Empirical Foundation for a Theory of Personal Victimisation*. Ballinger; Cambridge, Mass.

Horley, S. (1988). *Love and Pain: A Survival Handbook for Women*. Bedford Square Press; London.

Hough, M. and Mayhew, P. (1985). *Taking Account of Crime: Key Findings from the 1984 British Crime Survey*. Home Office Research Study 85. HMSO; London.

Hough, M. (1986). Victims of violent crime, findings from the British Crime Survey. In *From Crime Policy to Victim Policy; Reorienting the Justice System* (E. A. Fattah, ed.) pp. 117–132. Macmillan; Canada.

Pease, K. (1991). The Kirkholt Project: Preventing Burglary on a British Public Housing Estate. *Security Journal*, Vol. 2, No. 2, 73–77.

Polvi, N., Looman, T., Humphries, C. and Pease, K. (1990). Repeat break-and-enter victimisation: time course and crime prevention opportunity. *Journal of Police Science and Administration*, 17, 8–11.

Reiss, A.J. (1980). Victim proneness in repeat victimisation by type of crime. In *Indicators of Crime and Criminal Justice: Quantitative Studies* (S.E. Fienberg and A.J. Reiss, eds). US Dept. Bureau of Statistics.

Sampson, A. (1991). *Lessons from a Victim Support Crime Prevention Project*. Home Office Crime Prevention Unit, Paper No. 25. HMSO; London.

Sampson, A. and Farrell, G. (1990). *Victim Support and crime prevention in an Inner City setting*. Home Office Crime Prevention Unit Paper No. 21. HMSO; London.

Shepherd, J. (1990). Violent crime in Bristol; an accident and emergency department perspective. *British Journal of Criminology*, 30, 289–305.

Sherman, L.W., Gartin, P.R. and Buerger, M.E. (1989). Hot spots of predatory crime: routine activities and the criminology of place. *Criminology*, 27, 27–55.

Sparks, R., Genn, H. and Dodd, D. (1977). *Surveying Victims*. Wiley; London.

Stanko, E.A. (1988). Hidden violence against women, In *Victims of Crime: a new deal?* (M. Maguire and J. Pointing, eds) pp. 40–46. Open University Press; England.

Stanko, E.A. (1990). When precaution is normal: a feminist critique of crime prevention. In *Feminist Perspectives in Criminology* (L. Gelsthorpe and A. Morris, eds) pp. 173–183. Open University Press; England.

Stanko, E.A. (1991, unpublished) *Public Violence*. Summary of research findings, violent crime reduction project.

Trickett, A., Osborn, D.K., Seymour, J. and Pease, K. (1991). What is different about high crime areas? *British Journal of Criminology*, 32, 81–89.

18

White-collar and corporate crime

18.1 The problem of white-collar crime
Edwin H. Sutherland   420

18.2 Who is the criminal?
Paul W. Tappan   423

18.3 Defining white-collar crime
David O. Friedrichs   425

18.4 Iraq and Halliburton
Dawn Rothe   430

Introduction

If you have worked through any, or all, of the earlier theory chapters you will undoubtedly have discovered that the preoccupation of the scholars across almost all those bodies of work has been with youthful, male delinquency. Rarely does the gaze stray beyond such activities. Criminology traditionally has focused upon those activities that tend to fill our criminal courts: burglary, vandalism, theft and violence of various sorts. Much less attention is paid to fraud, embezzlement and corporate misconduct. This has been true throughout the history of criminology as an independent subject and remains largely true today.

There have been, however, those scholars who have sought to draw our attention to what variously is referred to as corporate or white-collar crime or, more generally, the crimes of the powerful. The earliest, and possibly most important, of these was Edwin Sutherland. As he suggests **(Reading 18.1)** 'criminal statistics show unequivocally that crime, as popularly understood and officially measured, has a high incidence in the lower socio-economic class and a low incidence in the upper socio-economic class'. One consequence of such information is that there has developed a set of theories of criminal behaviour that tend to focus on poverty and its related pathologies as the basis of explanation. This is inadequate, he argues, for such explanations rely upon biased statistics. Crucially, he says, 'persons of the upper socio-economic class engage in much criminal behaviour' and that this behaviour differs from other criminal behaviour largely in terms of how it is conducted, not in its essential nature.

Sutherland's arguments are picked up by Paul Tappan **(Reading 18.2, see also 1.1)** and he is largely content with the thesis so long as the offences concerned are confined to infractions of the criminal law. However, what he is less comfortable with is those criminological arguments which say that behaviour that is within the law but, say 'socially injurious', might be treated as the legitimate subject of criminological investigation. Who, he asks, should be considered the white-collar criminal? He argues in favour of a strict and narrow definition, for to allow otherwise would be to open up criminology to private values and biases and to give up on the possibility of social science. The arguments about definition are taken up by David Friedrichs **(Reading 18.3)** in which he explores the variety of attempts that have been made to define 'white-collar crime'. He proposes what he calls a 'multistage approach'. The three stages are: polemical (challenging popular conceptions of crime), typographical (setting out different forms of criminality each of which can be argued to come within the general rubric) and operational (which provides the basis for empirical investigation). Friedrichs then proceeds to analyse the relationship between three important dimensions of white-collar crime: trust, respectability and risk. The violation of trust, he argues, is central to white-collar crime, and although it may also be an element in other forms of criminality, the issue of trust tends to be higher in this arena. Similarly, respectability – itself defined in various ways – has an important role in understanding white-collar crime as, in complex ways, does risk.

The final excerpt, by Dawn Rothe **(Reading 18.4)**, shifts attention toward what is often referred to as state crime, or state-corporate crime. She focuses on the activities of the large private security conglomerate, Halliburton, in the second Iraq war. More particularly, she focuses on the role of Dick Cheney – one-time CEO of Halliburton and subsequently Vice-President to George W. Bush – in the contracting of the company to provide a variety of quasi-military services. The value of these contracts runs into billions of dollars and Rothe suggests that the company and its subsidiaries 'engaged in systematic and significant overcharging for services for contracts awarded in Iraq'. Moreover, the implication of her article is that the roles held by Cheney, albeit largely at different times, amount to a conflict of interest and a 'blatant misuse of public office'. This is not the usual subject-matter that concerns criminologists. However, those scholars concerned with white-collar, corporate and state crimes argue that such an oversight is hugely to the discredit of criminology.

Questions for discussion

1. Why, according to Sutherland, are poverty and related matters an inadequate basis for explaining crime?

2. Discuss, giving examples, four different types of white-collar criminality.

3. Why does Tappan argue in favour of a narrow definition of the 'white-collar criminal'?

4. What are the limitations of this approach?

5. What are the main components of Friedrichs' multistage approach to defining white-collar crime?

6. Explain the role of risk, respectability and trust in understanding white-collar crime.

7. In what ways, if any, might the activities of Dick Cheney and Halliburton be argued to be an appropriate focus for criminology?

18.1 The problem of white-collar crime
Edwin H. Sutherland

Criminal statistics show unequivocally that crime, as popularly understood and officially measured, has a high incidence in the lower socioeconomic class and a low incidence in the upper socioeconomic class. Crime, as thus understood, includes the ordinary violations of the penal code, such as murder, assault, burglary, robbery, larceny, sex offenses, and public intoxication, but does not include traffic violations. Persons who are accused or convicted of these ordinary crimes are dealt with by the police, juvenile or criminal courts, probation departments, and correctional institutions.

The concentration of crimes, as conventionally understood, in the lower socioeconomic class has been demonstrated by two types of research studies. First, the analysis of case histories of offenders and of their parents shows a high incidence of poverty in such cases. Sheldon and Eleanor Glueck studied 1,000 juvenile delinquents who had appeared before the juvenile courts of Greater Boston, 500 young-adult males who had been committed to the State Reformatory of Massachusetts, and 500 women who had been committed to the Massachusetts Reformatory for Women. [They found] that 76.3 percent of the offenders in one series and 91.3 percent in the series at the other extreme were below the level of comfort, which was defined as possession of sufficient surplus to enable a family to maintain itself for four months of unemployment without going on relief. Other data in these studies of the families of offenders show a high incidence of unemployment, of mothers engaged in remunerative occupations, of fathers in unskilled and semiskilled occupations, and of parents who lacked formal education; they show, also, that a large proportion of the offenders left school at an early age to engage in gainful occupations. [...]

The second method of demonstrating the concentration of crimes in the lower socioeconomic class is by statistical analysis of the residential areas of offenders; this is ordinarily called the 'ecological distribution of offenders.' Shaw and McKay have analyzed the data regarding residences of juvenile delinquents and adult criminals in twenty cities in the United States. In each of these cities the offenders are concentrated in areas of poverty. [...]

The scholars who have stated general theories of criminal behavior have used statistics such as those outlined above and individual case histories from which these statistics are compiled. Since these cases are concentrated in the lower socioeconomic class, the theories of criminal behavior have placed much emphasis on poverty as the cause of crime or on other social conditions and personal traits which are assumed to be associated with poverty. The assumption in these theories is that criminal behavior can be explained only by pathological factors, either social or personal. The social pathologies which have been emphasized are poverty and, related to it, poor housing, lack of organized recreations, lack of education, and disruptions in family life. The personal pathologies which have been suggested as explanations of criminal behavior were, at first, biological abnormalities; when research studies threw doubt on the validity of these biological explanations, the next explanation was intellectual inferiority, and more recently emotional instability. Some of these scholars believed that the personal pathologies were inherited and were the cause of the poverty as well as of the criminal behavior, while others believed that the personal pathologies were produced by poverty, and that this personal pathology contributed to the perpetuation of the poverty and of the related social pathologies.

[My] thesis is that these social and personal pathologies are not an adequate explanation of criminal behavior. The general theories of criminal behavior which take their data from poverty and the conditions related to it are inadequate and invalid, first, because the theories do not consistently fit the data of criminal behavior; and, second, because the cases on which these theories are based are a biased sample of all criminal acts. [...]

First, many of the facts regarding criminal behavior cannot be explained by poverty and its related pathologies. (a) The statistics of juvenile courts show at the present time that in the United States approximately 85 percent of the juveniles adjudged delinquent are boys and only 15 percent girls. The boys and girls of the United States are equally in poverty, come equally from homes with inadequate houses, are equally lacking in recreational facilities, are equal in intelligence tests and in emotional stability. With the approximate equality of the two sexes in these respects, poverty and its related pathologies obviously cannot explain the difference in the delinquency rates of the two sexes. (b) Many groups on the frontiers have been in extreme poverty but, nevertheless, have had low rates of juvenile delinquency and adult crime. (c) Many groups residing in slum areas of cities are in great poverty but have low rates of juvenile and adult delinquency, as illustrated by the Chinese colonies. (d) Certain immigrant groups have migrated from peasant communities in Europe, where they had high crime rates with perhaps less poverty than in their peasant communities. (e) Studies of the relation between crime rates and the business cycle have shown no significant association or a very slight association between depressions and crime rates in general, and no significant association between depressions and the crimes against property. These conclusions regarding crime and the business cycle, when considered in connection with the ecological studies, raise the question, Why does poverty, when distributed spatially by areas of a city, show a strikingly uniform and high association with crime, but when distributed chronologically in business cycles show a slight and inconsistent association with crime? The answer is that the causal factor is not poverty, in the sense of economic need, but the social and interpersonal relations which are associated sometimes with poverty and sometimes with wealth, and sometimes with both.

The second respect in which the conventional explanations of criminal behavior are invalid is their basis on biased statistics. This has two aspects: (a) Persons of the upper socioeconomic class are more powerful politically and financially and escape arrest and conviction to a greater extent than persons who lack such power. Wealthy persons can employ skilled attorneys and in other ways can influence the administration of justice in their own favor more effectively than can persons of the lower socioeconomic class. Even professional criminals, who have financial and political power, escape arrest and conviction more effectively than amateur and occasional criminals who have little financial or political power. This bias, while indubitable, is not of great importance from the theoretical point of view.

(b) And much more important is the bias involved in administration of criminal justice under laws which apply exclusively to business and the professions and which therefore involve only the upper socioeconomic class. Persons who violate laws regarding restraint of trade, advertising, pure food and drugs, and similar business practices are not arrested by uniformed policemen, are not tried in criminal courts, and are not committed to prisons; their illegal behavior receives the attention of administrative commissions and of courts operating under civil or equity jurisdiction. For this reason such violations of law are not included in the criminal statistics nor are individual cases brought to the attention of the scholars who write the theories of criminal behavior. The sample of criminal behavior on which the theories are founded is biased as to socioeconomic status, since it excludes these business and professional men. The bias is quite as certain as it would be if the scholars selected only red-haired criminals for study and reached the conclusion that redness of hair was the cause of crime.

[My] thesis, stated positively, is that persons of the upper socioeconomic class engage in much criminal behavior; that this criminal behavior differs from the criminal behavior of the lower socioeconomic class principally in the administrative procedures which are used in dealing with the offenders; and that variations in administrative procedures are not significant from the point of view of causation of crime. The causes of tuberculosis were not different when it was treated by poultices and bloodletting than when treated by streptomycin.

These violations of law by persons in the upper socioeconomic class are, for convenience, called 'white-collar crimes.' This concept is not intended to be definitive, but merely to call attention to crimes which are not ordinarily included within the scope of criminology. White-collar crime may be defined approximately as a crime committed by a person of respectability and high social status in the course of his occupation. Consequently it excludes many crimes of the upper class such as most cases of murder, intoxication, or adultery, since these are not a part of the occupational procedures. Also, it excludes the confidence games of wealthy members of the underworld, since they are not persons of respectability and high social status.

The significant thing about white-collar crime is that it is not associated with poverty or with social and personal pathologies which accompany poverty. If it can be shown that white-collar crimes are frequent, a general theory that crime is due to poverty and its related pathologies is shown to be invalid. Furthermore, the study of white-collar crime may assist in locating those factors which, being common to the crimes of the rich and the poor, are most significant for a general theory of criminal behavior.

A great deal of scattered and unorganized material indicates that white-collar crimes are very prevalent. The 'robber barons' of the last half of the nineteenth century were white-collar criminals, as practically everyone now agrees. Their behavior was illustrated by such statements as the following. Colonel Vanderbilt asked, 'You don't suppose you can run a railway in accordance with the statutes, do you?' A. B. Stickney, a railroad president, said to sixteen other railroad presidents in the home of J. P. Morgan in 1890, 'I have the utmost respect for you gentlemen individually, but as railroad presidents, I wouldn't trust you with my watch out of my sight.' Charles Francis Adams said, 'One difficulty in railroad management ... lies in the covetousness, want of good faith, low moral tone of railway managers, in the complete absence of any high standard of commercial honesty.' James M. Beck said in regard to the period 1905–17, 'Diogenes would have been hard put to it to find an honest man in the Wall Street which I knew as a corporation attorney.'

The present-day white-collar criminals are more suave and less forthright than the robber barons of the last century but not less criminal. Criminality has been demonstrated again and again in reports of investigations of land offices, railways, insurance, munitions, banking, public utilities, stock exchanges, the petroleum industry, the real estate industry, receiverships, bankruptcies, and politics. When the airmail contracts were canceled because of graft, Will Rogers said, 'I hope they don't stop every industry where they find crookedness at the top,' and Elmer Davis said, 'If they are going to stop every industry where they find crookedness at the top they will have to stop them all.' The Federal Trade Commission reported in 1920 that commercial bribery was a prevalent and common practice in many industries. In certain chain stores the net shortage in weight was sufficient to pay 3.4 percent on the investment, while no net shortage in weights was found in independent stores and cooperative stores. The Comptroller of the Currency reported in 1908 that violations of banking laws were found in 75 percent of the banks examined in a three-month period. Lie detector tests of all employees in certain Chicago banks, supported in almost all cases by subsequent confessions, showed that 20 percent of them had stolen bank property, and lie detector tests of a cross-section sample of the employees of a chain store showed approximately 75 percent had stolen money or merchandise from the store. Investigators for the *Reader's Digest* in 1941 drove into a garage with a defect in the car, artificially produced for this experiment, for which a proper charge would be 25 cents, and learned that 75 percent of the garages misrepresented the defect and the work which was done; the average charge was $4 and some garages charged as much as $25. Similar frauds were found in the watch-repair and the typewriter-repair businesses.

White-collar crime in politics, which is popularly supposed to be very prevalent, has been used by some persons as a rough gauge by which to measure white-collar crime in business. James A. Farley, who had experience both in business and in politics, said, 'The standards of conduct are as high among office-holders and politicians as they are in commercial life.' Cermak, mayor of Chicago and a businessman, said, 'There is less graft in politics than in business.' John Flynn wrote, 'The average politician is the merest amateur in the gentle art of graft compared with his brother in the field of business.' And Walter Lippmann wrote, 'Poor as they are, the standards of public life are so much more social than those of business that financiers who enter politics regard themselves as philanthropists.'

In the medical profession, which is used here as an example because it is probably less criminal than other professions, are found illegal sale of alcohol and narcotics, abortion, illegal services to underworld criminals, fraudulent reports and testimony in accident cases, extreme instances of unnecessary treatment and surgical operations, fake specialists, restriction of competition, and fee splitting. Fee splitting, for instance, is a violation of a specific law in many states and a violation of the conditions of admission to the profession in all states. The physician who participates in fee splitting tends to send his patients to the surgeon who will give the largest fee rather than to the surgeon who will do the best work. The report has been made that two-thirds of the surgeons in New York split fees and that more than half of the physicians in a central western state who answered a questionnaire on this point favored fee splitting.

The financial cost of white-collar crime is probably several times as great as the financial cost of all the crimes which are customarily regarded as the 'crime problem.' An officer of a chain grocery store in one year embezzled $800,000, which was six times as much as the annual losses from 500 burglaries and robberies of the stores in that chain. Public enemies numbered one to six secured $130,000 by burglary and robbery in 1938, while the sum stolen by Krueger is estimated at $250 million, or nearly 2,000 times as much. The *New York Times* in 1931 reported four cases of embezzlement in the United States with a loss of more than $1 million each and a combined loss of $9 million. Although a million dollar burglar or robber is practically unheard of, the million dollar embezzler is a small-fry among white-collar criminals. The estimated loss to investors in one investment trust from 1929 to 1935 was $580 million, due primarily to the fact that 75 percent of the values in the portfolio were in securities of affiliated companies, although the investment house advertised the importance of diversification in investments and its expert services

in selecting safe investments. The claim was made in Chicago about 1930 that householders lost $54 million in two years during the administration of a city sealer who granted immunity from inspection to stores which provided Christmas baskets for his constituents. This financial loss from white-collar crime, great as it is, is less important than the damage to social relations. White-collar crimes violate trust and therefore create distrust, and this lowers social morale and produces social disorganization on a large scale. Ordinary crimes, on the other hand, produce little effect on social institutions or social organization.

> *From E. Sutherland,* White-collar Crime: The Uncut Version *(New Haven, CT: Yale University Press) 1983, pp. 3–10.*

18.2 Who is the criminal?
Paul W. Tappan

Another increasingly widespread and seductive movement to revolutionize the concepts of crime and criminal has developed around the currently fashionable dogma of 'white-collar crime.' This is actually a particular school among those who contend that the criminologist should study antisocial behavior rather than law violation. The dominant contention of the group appears to be that the convict classes are merely our 'petty' criminals, the few whose depredations against society have been on a small scale, who have blundered into difficulties with the police and courts through their ignorance and stupidity. The important criminals, those who do irreparable damage with impunity, deftly evade the machinery of justice, either by remaining 'technically' within the law or by exercising their intelligence, financial prowess, or political connections in its violation. We seek a definition of the white-collar criminal and find an amazing diversity, even among those flowing from the same pen, and observe that characteristically they are loose, doctrinaire, and invective. When Professor Sutherland launched the term, it was applied to those individuals of upper socioeconomic class who violate the criminal law, usually by breach of trust, in the ordinary course of their business activities.[1] This original

usage accords with legal ideas of crime and points moreover to the significant and difficult problems of enforcement in the areas of business crimes, particularly where those violations are made criminal by recent statutory enactment. From this fruitful beginning the term has spread into vacuity, wide and handsome. We learn that the white-collar criminal, may be the suave and deceptive merchant prince or 'robber baron,' that the existence of such crime may be determined readily 'in casual conversation with a representative of an occupation by asking him, "What crooked practices are found in your occupation?"'[2]

Confusion grows as we learn from another proponent of this concept that, 'There are various phases of white-collar criminality that touch the lives of the common man almost daily. The large majority of them are operating within the letter and spirit of the law . . . .' and that 'In short, greed, not need, lies at the basis of white-collar crime.'[3] Apparently the criminal may be law obedient but greedy; the specific quality of his crimes is far from clear.

Another avenue is taken in Professor Sutherland's more recent definition of crime as a 'legal description of an act as socially injurious and legal provision of penalty for the act.'[4] Here he has deemed the connotation of his term too narrow if confined to violations of the criminal code; he includes by a slight modification conduct violative of any law, civil or criminal, when it is 'socially injurious.'

In light of these definitions, the normative issue is pointed. Who should be considered the white-collar criminal? Is it the merchant who, out of greed, business acumen, or competitive motivations, breaches a trust with his consumer by 'puffing his wares' beyond their merits, by pricing them beyond their value, or by ordinary advertising? Is it he who breaks trust with his employees in order to keep wages down, refusing to permit labor organization or to bargain collectively, and who is found guilty by a labor relations board of an unfair labor practice? May it be the white-collar worker who breaches trust with his employers by inefficient performance at work, by sympathetic strike or secondary boycott? Or is it the merchandiser who violates ethics by under-cutting the prices of his fellow merchants? In general these acts do not violate the criminal law. All in some manner breach a trust for motives which a criminologist may (or may not) disapprove for one reason or another. All are within the framework of the norms of ordinary business practice. One seeks in vain for criteria to determine this white-collar criminality. It is the conduct of one who wears a white collar and who indulges in occupational behavior to which some particular criminologist takes exception. It may easily be a term of propaganda. For purposes of empirical research or objective description, what is it?

Whether criminology aspires one day to become a science or a repository of reasonably accurate descriptive information, it cannot tolerate a nomenclature of such loose and variable usage. A special hazard exists in the employment of the term, 'white-collar criminal,' in that it invites individual systems of private values to run riot in an area (economic ethics) where gross variation exists among criminologists as well as others. The rebel may enjoy a veritable orgy of delight in damning as criminal most anyone he pleases; one imagines that some experts would thus consign to the criminal classes any successful capitalistic business man; the reactionary or conservative, complacently viewing the occupational practices of the business world might find all in perfect order in this best of all possible worlds. The result may be fine indoctrination or catharsis achieved through blustering broadsides against the 'existing system.' It is not

criminology. It is not social science. The terms 'unfair,' 'infringement,' 'discrimination,' 'injury to society,' and so on, employed by the white-collar criminologists cannot, taken alone, differentiate criminal and non-criminal. Until refined to mean certain specific actions, they are merely epithets.

Vague, omnibus concepts defining crime are a blight upon either a legal system or a system of sociology that strives to be objective. They allow judge, administrator, or – conceivably – sociologist, in an undirected, freely operating discretion, to attribute the status 'criminal' to any individual or class which he conceives nefarious. This can accomplish no desirable objective, either politically or sociologically.[5]

Worse than futile, it is courting disaster, political, economic, and social, to promulgate a system of justice in which the individual may be held criminal without having committed a crime, defined with some precision by statute and case law. To describe crime the sociologist, like the lawyer-legislator, must do more than condemn conduct deviation in the abstract. He must avoid definitions predicated simply upon state of mind or social injury and determine what particular types of deviation, in what directions, and to what degree, shall be considered criminal. This is exactly what the criminal code today attempts to do, though imperfectly of course. More slowly and conservatively than many of us would wish: that is in the nature of legal institutions, as it is in other social institutions as well. But law has defined with greater clarity and precision the conduct which is criminal than our anti-legalistic criminologists promise to do; it has moreover promoted a stability, a security and dependability of justice through its exactness, its so-called technicalities, and its moderation in inspecting proposals for change.

Having considered the conceptions of an innovating sociology in ascribing the terms 'crime' and 'criminal,' let us state here the juristic view: Only those are criminals who have been adjudicated as such by the courts. Crime is an intentional act in violation of the criminal law (statutory and case law), committed without defense or excuse, and penalized by the state as a felony or misdemeanor. In studying the offender there can be no presumption that arrested, arraigned, indicted, or prosecuted persons are criminals unless they also be held guilty beyond a reasonable doubt of a particular offense.[6] Even less than the unconvicted suspect can those individuals be considered criminal who have violated no law. Only those are criminals who have been selected by a clear substantive and a careful adjective law, such as obtains in our courts. The unconvicted offenders of whom the criminologist may wish to take cognizance are an important but unselected group; it has no specific membership presently ascertainable. Sociologists may strive, as does the legal profession, to perfect measures for more complete and accurate ascertainment of offenders, but it is futile simply to rail against a machinery of justice which is, and to a large extent must inevitably remain, something less than entirely accurate or efficient.

> From P.W. Tappan, 'Who is the criminal?', American Sociological Review, 1947, 12(1): 96–102.

Notes

1 E.H. Sutherland, 'Crime and Business,' 2,7 *The Annals of the American Academy of Political and Social Science* 112, (1941).
2 Sutherland, 'White-Collar Criminality,' 5 *American Sociological Review* I, (1940).
3 Harry Elmer Barnes and Negley K. Teeters, *New Horizons in Criminology*, p. 42–43, (1943).
4 Sutherland, 'Is 'White-Collar Crime' Crime?' 10 *American Sociological Review* 132, (1945).

5 In the province of juvenile delinquency we may observe already the evil that flows from this sort of loose definition in applied sociology. In many jurisdictions, under broad statutory definition of delinquency, it has become common practice to adjudicate as delinquent any child deemed to be anti-social or a behavior problem. Instead of requiring sound systematic proof of specific reprehensible conduct, the courts can attach to children the odious label of delinquent through the evaluations and recommendations of over-worked, undertrained case investigators who convey to the judge their hearsay testimony of neighborhood gossip and personal predilection. Thus these vaunted 'socialized tribunals' sometimes become themselves a source of delinquent and criminal careers as they adjudge individuals who are innocent of proven wrong to a depraved offender's status through an administrative determination of something they know vaguely as anti-social conduct. See Introduction by Roscoe Pound of Pauline V. Young, *Social Treatment in Probation and Delinquency*, (1937). See also Paul W. Tappan, *Delinquent Girls in Court*, (1947) and 'Treatment Without Trial,' 24 *Social Forces*, 306, (1946).
6 The unconvicted suspect cannot be known as a violator of the law: to assume him so would be in derogation of our most basic political and ethical philosophies. In empirical research it would be quite inaccurate, obviously, to study all suspects or defendants as criminals.

18.3 Defining white-collar crime
David O. Friedrichs

More than half a century, then, has passed since Sutherland formally introduced the concept of white-collar crime. Despite this extended passage of time, there is today more confusion than ever about the meaning and most appropriate application of this concept. [...]

First it must be recognized that a wide variety of terms have been used to characterize activities that could either be classified under the broad rubric of 'white-collar crime' or are closely linked with white-collar crime. Some of these terms include economic crime, commercial crime, business crime, marketplace crime, consumer crime, respectable crime, 'crime at the top,' 'suite' crime, elite crime and deviance, official crime and deviance, political crime, governmental crime,

state (or state-organized) crime, corporate crime, occupational crime, employee crime, avocational crime, technocrime, computer crime, and folk crime.

In some cases different terms refer to the same activity; in other cases the terms refer to very different types of activity. Obviously the invocation of so many different terms, interrelated in such a bewildering variety of ways, contributes to the general confusion about white-collar crime. Each term is likely to have some unique connotations, and each tends to emphasize a particular dimension of white-collar crime. [...]

Both *crime* and *deviance* have been used to describe many of [these] activities. The choice has been made to emphasize the term *crime*, because this term is more closely associated with doing harm to others than is *deviance*. Second, quite a bit of white-collar crime unfortunately does not deviate from typical patterns of behavior (e.g., deception in the marketplace). Third, many white-collar offenders avoid the stigma that is so central to the notion of deviance; they do not have a deviant self-identity or lifestyle.

Definitional clarity is, however, a precondition for any coherent theorizing about white-collar crime. The original debate on the concept, initiated by Tappan (1947), attacked Sutherland on the grounds that white-collar crime should refer to acts defined by the criminal law and adjudicated in a criminal proceeding. This issue continues to be debated in some form today, and in the intervening years other conceptual controversies arose: whether white-collar crime should refer to acts committed by higher-status individuals or institutions, or those committed in the context of a legitimate occupation, regardless of socioeconomic status; whether it should refer to acts involving economic and financial activities only, or other acts involving physical harm as well; and whether it should refer to acts of people only, or organizations only, or both.

More recent attempts to define white-collar crime and closely related concepts have emphasized a range of attributes, including commission in a legitimate occupational context, respectable social status of perpetrators, presence of calculation and rationality (with economic gain or occupational success a primary goal), absence of direct violence, offenders noncriminal self image, deterrence of, and a limited criminal justice system response (Coleman 1987; Edelhertz 1970; Geis 1974; Katz 1979; Shapiro 1980).

A multistage approach to defining white-collar crime

A coherent and meaningful understanding of white-collar crime must be approached in stages. The first (most general) definitional stage is polemical or presentational, the second stage is typological or taxonomic, and the third stage is operational or heuristic. The traditional, 'popular' conception of white-collar crime – the illegal and harmful actions of elites and repectable members of society carried out for economic gain in the context of legitimate organizational or occupational activity – has an important polemical and pedagogical purpose (as even such critics as

Shapiro (1990: 346) concede). This generalized conception, for all its operational deficiencies and logical contradictions, challenges a popular tendency to associate criminality with inner-city residents, minorities, young men, and conventional illegal activities such as homicide, robbery, and burglary. The more complex and qualified the concept, the less potent it is likely to be for challenging conventional crime consciousness. [...]

The second stage of conceptual development of white-collar crime is typological, but there has been some skepticism concerning whether criminological typologies correspond with reality. They may well put a disproportionate emphasis on more dramatic forms of criminality (Hartjen 1974: 69). The patterns of actual lawbreakers are so varied that a taxonomic classification (typology) may distort reality rather than clarify it (Clarke 1990: 3; Gibbons 1979: 92; Hagan 1986: 92). [...]

Despite the inevitably arbitrary and limited attributes of any classification scheme, typologies provide a necessary point of departure for any meaningful discussion of (and theorizing about) white collar crime. [...] The principal criteria for differentiating between the types of white-collar crime, broadly defined, are:

- Context in which illegal activity occurs, including the setting (e.g., corporation; government agency; professional service; etc.) and the level within the setting (e.g., individual; workgroup; organization)

- Status or position of offender (e.g., wealthy or middle class; chief executive officer or employee)

- Primary victims (e.g., general public or individual clients)

- Principal form of harm (e.g., economic loss or physical injury)

- Legal classification (e.g., antitrust; fraud; etc.)

The typology that follows includes activities that some students of white-collar crime would exclude, but at a minimum these activities have a close generic relationship with white-collar crime:

1 **Corporate crime**: Illegal and harmful acts committed by officers and employees of corporations to promote corporate (and personal) interests. Forms include corporate violence, corporate theft, corporate financial manipulation, and corporate political corruption or meddling.

2 **Occupational crime**: Illegal or harmful financially driven activity committed within the context of a legitimate, respectable occupation. Forms include retail crime, service crime, crimes of professionals, and employee crime.

3 **Governmental crime**: A cognate form of white-collar crime; a range of activities wherein government itself, government agencies, government office, or the aspiration to serve in a government office generates illegal or demonstrably harmful acts. Forms include the criminal state, state-organized crime, and political white-collar crime.

4 **State-corporate crime, finance crime and technocrime**: Major hybrid forms of white-collar crime that involve a synthesis of governmental and corporate crime, or of corporate and occupational crime. *Finance crime* specifically refers to criminal activity in the realm of high-level finance, from banking to the securities markets. *Technocrime* involves the intersection of computers and other forms of 'high technology' with white-collar crime.

5 **Enterprise crime, contrepreneurial crime and avocational crime**: 'Residual' forms of white-collar crime, or a variety of miscellaneous illegal activities that include more marginal forms of white-collar crime. *Enterprise crime* refers to cooperative enterprises involving syndicated (organized) crime and legitimate businesses; *contrepreneurial crime* refers to swindles, scams, and frauds that assume the guise of legitimate businesses; *avocational crimes* are illegal but nonconventional criminal acts committed by 'white-collar' workers outside a specifically organizational or occupational context, including income tax evasion, insurance fraud, loan/credit fraud, customs evasion, and the purchase of stolen goods.

The third stage for defining white-collar crime can be called operational or heuristic. On this level the objective of the definition is to provide a point of departure for focused empirical research or comparative critical analysis. [...]

The concept of white-collar crime is, in the final analysis, somewhat like a Chinese puzzle: Whichever way one turns with it, new difficulties and conundrums are encountered. Perhaps its least problematic or controversial definition is negative: It refers to illegal or harmful activity that is neither street crime nor conventional crime.

More generally, *white-collar crime* is a generic term for the whole range of illegal, prohibited and demonstrably harmful activities involving a violation of private or public trust, committed by institutions and individuals occupying a legitimate respectable status, and directed toward financial advantage or the maintenance and extension of power and privilege. But we should give up the illusion that *white-collar crime* can or – or even should – have a single meaning or definition.

Trust and white-collar crime

Trust – the confidence that the other party in such transactions or relationships will act with honor and integrity – has become much more problematic in the modern world.

The diffusion of impersonal trust into a broad range of relationships and transactions creates countless opportunities for corruption, misrepresentation, and fraud. Of course, in a complex society we develop many forms of monitoring and surveillance directed at overseeing these trust-based relationships and transactions. [...] Donald Cressey (1980), the distinguished early student of white-collar crime, argued that we must confront a fundamental paradox: If we attempt to curtail sharply the extension of trust in business relationships in the interest of reducing opportunities for white-collar crime, we will also severely jeopardize legitimate business relationships and other interpersonal transactions.

Trust and its violation are certainly key elements of white-collar crime. Sutherland (1940: 3; 1949: 152–58) characterized white-collar crime as involving a 'violation of delegated or implied trust.' [...] For lack of any other term that better captures the common links among the broad range of white-collar crimes, this book adopts the notion of 'trusted criminals,' even though focusing on the nature of their offenses may be more important than making sense of the offenders themselves. [...]

Trust and its violation are elements of other crimes, from confidence games to domestic violence. Conversely, the level of trust in white-collar relationships and transactions is hardly absolute, although it is typically higher than in many other realms, and this tends to broaden both the scope and the scale of possible crimes. Nevertheless, from a critical or progressive perspective, the essence of white-collar crime resides in the harm done, not simply in the violation of trust. [...]

The long-term consequences of violations of trust and the difficulties involved in restoring trusting relations once such violations occur are relatively understudied. Still, the harmful consequences of the erosion of trust are surely diffuse and many.

Respectability and white-collar crime

The idea of respectability has traditionally been closely associated with white-collar crime. As noted earlier, Sutherland's (1940: 1) initial characterization of white-collar crime identified it as 'crime in the upper or white-collar class, composed of respectable or at least respected business and professional men...'. This identification of white-collar crime with respectability has been criticized because 'respectability' is not so easily defined, can be faked, and is not linked with specific norms for acceptable behavior (Shapiro 1990). [...]

For our purposes, however, three different meanings of *respectable* must be distinguished: first, a normative meaning, or an assessment of moral integrity; second, a status-related meaning, that is to say a legitimate position or occupation; and third, a symptomatic meaning, or the outward appearance of acceptable or superior status. Obviously these different meanings are not synonymous. [...] When people object to the notion of 'respectable criminals,' they are, of course, focusing on the moral meaning. From this point of view, people who commit crimes and perpetrate harms are never respectable. Even if those who are exposed as criminals may indeed lose their respectable status, it is important to recognize that often it is precisely this status that enabled them to commit their crimes in the first place. [...]

Respectability is always a situational and contextual matter (Ball 1970). A variety of personal and impersonal attributes signify one's degree of respectability. Because many who enjoy a respectable status also have one or more obvious attributes more commonly associated with a non-respectable status, what matters is the overall configuration or balance of attributes. Those who are manifestly respectable enjoy many benefits: People will cash their checks, admit them to fine restaurants, employ them, and so on. The more respectable a person appears to be, the more likely (other things being equal) they are to be trusted. The more respectable a person appears to be, the less likely (other things being equal) that they will be suspected of committing serious crimes. [...]

Societies have ceremonies or rituals wherein respectable status is publicly acknowledged. Club inductions, commencement exercises, baptisms, and weddings are but a few of many ceremonies that confer a new or heightened status of respectability on the primary parties involved. Other ceremonies – Garfinkel (1956) has called them 'degradation ceremonies' – strip people of their respectable status. The criminal trial is perhaps the most obvious example; even though many who are brought to trial did not enjoy a truly respectable status to begin with, a criminal trial resulting in a conviction and a prison sentence formally transforms someone from a free citizen into an incarcerated felon. Commitment proceedings, formal expulsion processes, and other such rituals strip people of at least some measure of respectability. Some evidence of the advantages of a respectable status for those who are processed by the criminal justice system will be offered in subsequent chapters.

Risk and white-collar crime

The term *risk* has had a variety of meanings. Originally it was associated with a wager, or the probability of an event occurring; more recently it has come to mean great danger and alludes to negative outcomes exclusively (Douglas 1990). In the context of white-collar crime, risk can refer to either meaning.

Risk applies to white-collar crime in the original sense insofar as a calculated gamble is taken; the chances of being caught and punished are quite remote compared with the benefits that accrue from committing the crime. Although of course such calculation can play a role in most forms of crime, it is especially likely to be a central feature of much white-collar crime. Much evidence suggests that in most cases the risk strongly favors the offender because the probability of detection, prosecution, and sanctioning is typically very low.

Risk is also involved in an important class of white-collar crimes in the second, more recent sense: as the assessment of chances of dangerous (even catastrophic) consequences of corporate and professional decision making. One distinctive element of much white-collar crime is the absence of the *specific* intent to cause harm. Rather, the harm of much white-collar crime is a function of making the pursuit of profit or economic efficiency paramount over all other objectives. More to the point, corporations and professionals have often been prepared to put their workers, customers, and the general public at higher risk of harm if their course of action is seen to enhance profit or result in lower risk of loss.

Meier and Short (1985: 390), in a seminal article on crime and risk, argued that certain white-collar crimes are more similar to natural disasters than to ordinary crime, and thus are a subset of a broader category of hazards endangering human safety. The media play an important role in shaping perceptions of hazards and tend to portray them as natural rather than human-made (Spencer and Triche 1994). [...]

Charles Perrow (1984) coined the term *normal accident* to refer to the accidents that complex modern technological systems inevitably produce. Perrow insisted, however, that we recognize that the choices underlying high-risk systems are knowingly made in deference to organizational goals. The costs of such choices should not be simply dismissed as accidents dictated by the technology itself, or as human error. Rather, the nature of the risky choices built into these complex systems must be confronted. [...]

Recognition of the inherent risks of modern technology in particular has stimulated a number of questions. First, to what extent can science make reliable calculations of risk for a whole range of potential hazards? Second, what are 'acceptable' levels of risk, and who should make these determinations? Third, who should be held responsible for the harmful consequences – which may include the loss of human life – that result from decisions about risky technology, and, specifically, how should charges in these cases be processed? [...]

Although the use of risk analysis for various purposes has become a minor industry, the whole enterprise has been criticized on a number of grounds. From a methodological perspective, risk analysis has been criticized as excessively quantitative, technical, and psychological, and as failing to consider qualitative aspects of risk (i.e., how it is experienced), the social construction of risk (i.e., the social process of giving meaning to risk), and the organizational and interorganizational processes involved in making decisions about risk (Clarke 1988; Draper 1984; Freudenberg and Pastor 1992; Jacobs and Dopkeen 1990). Perrow (1984) bluntly characterized risk assessment as a pseudo-science that legitimates the status quo by persuading us to accept 'normal accidents.' [...]

Conversely, the cost-benefit analysis that plays such a central role in much risk assessment undertaken on behalf of corporations is seen by some as fundamentally immoral, especially when it dispassionately attempts to impose a monetary value on human lives and accepts the loss of a certain number of lives as an economic necessity (Teuber 1990). [...]

Some evidence suggests that corporations are more likely to take certain types of risks if they have reason to believe they can get away with it. For example, their concern for short-term financial gain means that they are more likely to reduce risks involving worker safety than those involving workers' long-term health (Felstiner and Siegelman 1989). Workers and regulatory inspectors alike tend to respond more readily to hazards that pose immediate risks of direct injury than to the uncertainties of long-term or latent injuries (Hawkins 1990). The short-term interests of corporations are not necessarily compatible with the months or years of trial and error often needed to reduce such risks (Short 1990: 185). Furthermore, corporations tend to accept higher levels of risk to employees than to the general public, because accidents involving the public are more likely to get media attention (Hutter and Lloyd-Bostock 1990). [...]

Some level of risk may be an inevitable feature of modern existence. Certainly no reasonable person imagines that all risk of harm (physical or financial) can be eliminated from modern corporate and professional activities, and it has been acknowledged that an excessive aversion to risks carries costs of its own. But a substantial amount of evidence also demonstrates that corporations (and professionals) have too often imposed excessive risks on vulnerable parties, such that the costs outweigh any possible benefits. Taking risks in the political and social realm (as opposed to corporate risk) that led to unsafe conditions and environmental damage is part of what made America great (Perrow 1984: 311). The risks created by corporations (and professionals) today are exceptionally harmful in many instances. Clearly, making decisions involving risk can cross a line and become a form of criminal conduct: white-collar crime.

From D. Friedrichs, Trusted Criminals: White-collar Criminals in Contemporary Society *(Belmont: Wadsworth), 1996, pp. 5–17.*

References

Ball, D. (1970) 'The problematics of respectability.' p. 326–371 in J.D. Douglas (Ed.) *Deviance and respectability: The social construction of moral meanings.* New York: Basic Books.

Clarke, L. (1988) 'Explaining choices among technological risks.' *Social Problems* 35: 22–35.

Clarke, M. (1990) *Business crime – Its nature and control.* New York: St. Martin's Press.

Coleman, J.W. (1987) 'Toward an integrated theory of white-collar crime.' *American Journal of Sociology* 93: 406–439.

Cressey, D.R. (1980) 'Management fraud, controls, and criminological theory.' p. 117–147 in R.K. Elliott and J.T. Willingham (Eds.) *Management fraud: Detection and deterrence.* New York: Petrocelli.

Douglas, M. (1990) 'Risk as a forensic resource.' *Daedalus* 119: 1–161.

Draper, E. (1984) 'Risk by choice? Knowledge and power in the hazardous workplace.' *Contemporary Sociology* 13: 688–691.

Felstiner, W.L.F. and Siegelman, P. (1989) 'Neoclassical difficulties: Tort and deterrence for latent injuries.' *Law & Policy* 11: 309–329.

Freudenburg, W.R. and Pastor, S.K. (1992) 'Public responses to technological risks: Toward a sociological perspective.' *Sociological Quarterly* 33: 389–412.

Garfinkel, H. (1956) 'Conditions of successful degradation ceremonies.' *American Journal of Sociology* 61: 420–424.

Geis, G. (1974) 'Avocational crime.' p. 272–298 in D. Glaser (Ed.) *Handbook of criminology.* New York: Rand McNally.

Gibbons, D.C. (1979) *The criminological enterprise – Theories and perspectives.* Englewood Cliffs, NJ: Prentice-Hall.

Hagan, F. (1986) *Introduction to criminology.* Chicago: Nelson Hall.

Hartjen, C. (1974) *Crime and criminalization.* New York: Praeger.

Hawkins, K. (1990) 'Compliance strategy, prosecution policy and Aunt Sally.' *British Journal of Criminology* 30: 444–466.

Hertz, H. (1970) *The nature, impact and prosecution of white-collar crime.* Washington, DC: National Institute for Law Enforcement and Criminal Justice.

Hutter, B.M. and Lloyd-Bostock, S. (1990) 'The power of accidents: The social and psychological impact of accidents and the enforcement of safety regulations', *British Journal of Criminology*, 30 409–422.

Jacobs, J. and Dopkeen, L. (1990) 'Risking the qualitative study of risk', *Qualitative Sociology* 13: 169–182.

Katz, J. (1979) 'Concerted ignorance: The social construction of cover-up.' *Urban Life* 8: 295–316.

Meier, R.P. and Short, J.F, Jr., (1985) 'Crime as hazard: Perceptions of risk and seriousness.' *Criminology* 23: 389–399.

Perrow, C. (1984) *Normal accidents – Living with high-risk technologies.* New York: Basic Books.

Shapiro, S.P. (1980) *Thinking about white-collar crime: Matters of conceptualization and research.* Washington, DC.: U.S. Department of Justice.

Shapiro, S.P. (1990) 'Collaring the crime, not the criminal: Reconsidering the concept of white-collar crime.' *American Sociological Review* 55: 346–365.

Short, J.F, Jr. (1990) 'Hazards, risks and enterprise: Approaches to science, law, and social policy.' *Law & Society Review* 24: 179–198.

Simon, R.J. (1990) 'Women and crime revisited.' *Criminial Justice Research Bulletin* 5:1–11.

Sutherland, E.H. (1940) 'White-collar criminality.' *American Sociological Review* 5:1–12.

Tappan, P. (1947) 'Who is the criminal?' *American Sociological Review* 12: 96–102.

Teuber, A. (1990) 'Justifying risk.' *Daedalus* 119: 235–254.

18.4 Iraq and Halliburton
Dawn Rothe

The intersection of state and corporate interests during times of war is a fundamental part of the war-making process. Every capitalist country must rely on private-sector production to produce the weapons of war. In the United States, for example, major auto manufacturers such as Chrysler, Ford, and Chevrolet retooled to produce tanks, guns, and missiles instead of cars during World War II, while many other companies refocused some or all of their production to serve the war effort. With the introduction of a permanent wartime economy after the end of World War II, amid concerns that the United States was coming to be dominated by a military-industrial complex (Melman 1974), major providers of weapons and logistical support such as General Electric, Boeing, Bechtel Group, and Lockheed Martin became regular recipients of government contracts. They were also repeatedly at the center of controversies concerning cost overruns and questionable charges (Johnson 2004; Greider 1998).

The close alignment of corporate and government interests in the production and procurement of the weapons of war is a vivid example of the 'revolving door' effect as described by C. Wright Mills (1954) in *The Power Elite*. As executives from major military contractors fill elected or appointed government positions, the interests of the state become increasingly entangled with prior corporate loyalties.

In recent years the integration of state interests with those of the private corporation has intensified. This integration began with efforts to adapt to a downsized military through increased reliance on just on time privatized logistic contracts. The move to an active war footing following the attacks of 9/11, including the wars in Afghanistan and Iraq and the permanent 'war on terror,' further cemented the private–public strategy for war making in the United States.

The controversy surrounding links between Vice President Dick Cheney and Halliburton, the company he formerly headed, provides a demonstration of the potential for state–corporate crime embedded in this new policy of war by subcontract.

Halliburton–Cheney connections

The connections between Halliburton and Cheney date back to the early 1990s. Dick Cheney, as Ronald Reagan's secretary of defense, assigned Halliburton subsidiary Brown & Root the task of conducting a classified survey detailing how private corporations such as itself could provide logistical support for U.S. military forces scattered around the world. At that time Halliburton prepared a report to implement the privatization of everyday military activities and logistical planning, for which it earned $3.9 million. During the latter part of 1992, Halliburton received an additional $5 million for a follow-up study to outline how private firms could supply the logistical needs of several contingency plans at the same time. This led to 'a five-year contract to be the U.S. Army's on-call private logistics arm,' what was known as the Logistics Civil Augmentation Program (LOGCAP) (Singer 2003:142–143). Halliburton held this contract until 1997, when Dyncorp, another private firm specializing in providing military logistical support, beat Halliburton's competitive bid.

When Cheney's term as secretary of defense ended in 1993, he and his deputy secretary of defense, David Gribbin, were hired by Halliburton: Cheney as acting CEO and Gribbin as the official go-between to obtain contracts from the U. S. government. [...]

Republican Party presidential nominee George W. Bush hired Cheney to oversee the selection process for a vice-presidential candidate. Just as Cheney was finding the right candidate (May–June 2000) to run on Bush's ticket, he sold 100,000 shares of Halliburton stock for 50.97 dollars a share for an approximate value of $5.1 million (Dean 2004). The first week of July 2000 the news was official: it would be a Bush-Cheney ticket. Cheney resigned from Halliburton in August 2000 with a retirement package on a future contract worth $45 to $62.2 million, which included stocks, options, and deferred income payments. Shortly after his role as CEO of Halliburton ended and he announced he was running for vice president, Cheney sold another 660,000 shares of stock (worth approximately $36 million). However, he continued to hold 433,000 stock options. [...]

Although it may appear to many that the Cheney–Halliburton marriage ended with the selling of stocks and options, the relationship continued. During his tenure as vice president, Cheney drew income both from U.S. taxpayers and from Halliburton. As Bivens (2004:1) stated, 'billions are slyly, secretively and controversially showered on the entity [Halliburton] that paid Dick Cheney 178,437 dollars this year, by the entity [the federal government] that paid him 198,600 dollars.' For the previous year, 2002, Cheney received $162,392 from Halliburton and $190,134 as vice presidential pay (White House 2004).

Halliburton contracts

Immediately after September 11, 2001, the neoconservatives and many corporations seized the moment for personal, political, and economic gain.[1] The 'war on terrorism' was announced, the long-sought plans to attack Iraq were jump-started, and Halliburton was ready to cash in on its relationship with its past CEO. In November 2001, Halliburton subsidiary Brown & Root received a contract worth $2 million to reinforce the U.S. embassy in Tashkent, Uzbekistan. By December 2001, Halliburton had won back the cost-plus LOGCAP contract to provide facilities, logistic support, and provisions for U.S. troops in places such as Afghanistan, Qatar, Kuwait, Georgia, Jordan, Djibouti, and Uzbekistan. The contract was originally won back through a competitive bid. However, additional no-bid contracts were awarded as the holder of the quick-response LOGCAP contract was already providing logistical help for the U.S. military and thus was ready at hand. 'Halliburton was the obvious choice,' said Army Corps of Engineers commander Lt. Gen. Robert Flowers. 'To invite other contractors to compete to perform a highly classified requirement that KBR [Halliburton] was already under a competitively awarded contract to perform would have been a wasteful duplication of effort' (Flowers 2003). Unlike the previous LOGCAP contract, the new contract extended over a ten-year period with an estimated value of $830 million to over $1 billion (Aljazeera 2003). Halliburton (KBR) also received contracts worth $110 million to build prison cells and other facilities at Guantanamo Bay. With the recent addition of Camp 5 (a permanent addition also built by KBR), the prison capacity grew to 1,100 detainees (Higham, Stephens, and Williams 2004).

In June 2002, Halliburton (KBR) was awarded a contract worth $22 million to run support services at Camp Stronghold and the Khanabad Air Base in Uzbekistan, the main U.S. base for the 'war on terrorism' in Afghanistan. This contract included serving the CIA paramilitary units, maintaining combat equipment, targeting aircraft, and providing logistical support. For example, Halliburton (KBR) employees operated the U.S. Air Force Global Hawks (unmanned surveillance planes) (Little 2002; Singer 2003).

During September 2002, 1,800 Halliburton employees were present in Kuwait and Turkey (under a contract for nearly $1 billion) to provide temporary housing (tents) and logistical support for the invasion into Iraq (Chatterjee 2003). Under the competitively bid contract, KBR provides for the support of the Reception, Staging, Onward Movement, and Integration (RSOI) process of U.S. forces as they enter or depart their theater of operation by sea, air, or rail. The post for the Halliburton employees, Camp Arifjan, includes a gymnasium and fast food outlets, including Burger King, Baskin-Robbins, and Subway, all paid for by U.S. taxpayers. While Halliburton employees are eating fast food, U.S. troops are served mess hall food and live in tents. Excessive U.S. taxpayer money is spent on cost-plus contracts allowing posh conditions for private contractors such as the one in Camp Arifjan while troops are left without the necessary equipment such as bullet-proof vests and armored vehicles. Moreover, Camp Arifjan is the same base in which a Saudi subcontractor hired by KBR billed for 42,042 meals a day on average but served only 14,053 meals a day (CNN Money 2004; Reuters 2004; *Wall Street Journal* 2004).

In the fall of 2002, Halliburton attained an additional no-bid contract to extinguish oil fires in Iraq, because 'the company was the only one in a position to implement the plan on time because it designed it' (Beelman 2004:2). (It was Halliburton who had constructed the contingency plans for what would be needed under these circumstances.) Several other corporations, however, had been contracted to do similar work in Kuwait after the Persian Gulf War. [...]

Not only has Halliburton received billions of dollars from the state through competitive and noncompetitive contracts, but most of these were cost-plus contracts. Cost-plus contracts are essentially blank checks that ensure that Halliburton is reimbursed for whatever it bills for its services as well as an additional percentage (between 2 percent and 7 percent) for the company's profits (fees). These types of open-ended contracts are incentives to maximize expenditures to attain an increase in the total value of the contract and profits. Moreover, the larger the contract, the more valuable becomes Halliburton's stock. In October 2002, for example, Halliburton's stock was $12.62 a share. When the KBR Iraq restructure contract was awarded, its stock rose to $23.90 a share (see Halliburton stock portfolios 2001–2004). According to Henry Bunting's testimony to the Democratic Policy Committee, the Halliburton motto in Iraq is 'don't worry about it, it's cost plus' (Bunting 2004). In essence, no one questioned pricing. [...]

To date, Halliburton has over 24,000 workers in Iraq and Kuwait alone, 11,000 more than the number of British soldiers deployed there (Chatterjee 2004; *Mother Jones* 2004a). By 2005 KBR had earned contracts worth over $2.2 billion from work in Iraq (of this, 42 percent was spent on combating oil fires and restoring pipelines and 48 percent for housing and transportation for troops) (Institute for Southern Studies 2004). Overall, it has been estimated that Halliburton has received more than $8 billion in contracts since Cheney became vice president.

Halliburton overcharges, kickbacks, and cost overruns

Halliburton and its subsidiaries have engaged in systematic and significant overcharging for services for contracts awarded in Iraq. This is not new behavior for the company. Thus it is not surprising that Halliburton would use 'war on terrorism' cost-plus contracts as an opportunity for overcharging. Previously, systemic overcharging by corporations potentially could have resulted in periods of ineligibility for new federal contracts. Specifically, some of the added language required a satisfactory record of integrity and business ethics, including satisfactory compliance with the relevant labor and employment, environmental, antitrust, and consumer protection laws (FAR (Federal Acquisitions Regulations) 9.104–1(d)).The burden of enforcement was on the contracting officers to consider all relevant credible information, with the greatest weight given to offenses adjudicated within the past three years. Thus it relied on the compliance of contracting officers for enforcement (FAR part 9, no. 65 FR 80255).

During the Clinton administration, requirements for contractors bidding on federal contracts were strengthened. New 'blacklisting' regulations would have barred contractors from future contracts if they had committed past labor, environmental, or violations of federal trade laws. On April 1, 2001, however, the Bush administration revoked this regulation (no. 65 FR 80255) with no. 66 FR 17754, thus undoing the tightening of regulations put forth by the Clinton administration. This change made it possible for Halliburton and other corporate criminals to obtain contracts regardless of previous or current allegations of illegal practices (Federal Register 2001; White House 2004). Moreover, although payments to corporations under investigation by a federal agency are supposed to be deferred, Halliburton continued to receive its pay as investigations were being carried out, thereby facilitating Halliburton's alleged illegal activities. For example, Halliburton was under investigation by the SEC for accounting fraud that was alleged to have occurred from 1999 to 2001, and the Justice Department was conducting an investigation on charges of bribery connected with the Nigerian official to attain an oil contract in Nigeria. After contracts were awarded to Halliburton in Iraq, the company continued to come under investigations by the Congressional Oversight Committee and the Department of Defense for overcharges, as we shall see.

In 2003 a Pentagon audit found that Halliburton (KBR) had overcharged the U.S. government for approximately fifty-seven million gallons of gasoline delivered to Iraqi citizens under a no-bid contract. These overcharges totaled nearly $61 million from May through September 2003. KBR was charging from $2.27 to $3.09 a gallon to import gasoline from Kuwait, while a different contractor delivered gas from Turkey to Iraq for $1.18 a gallon (Kelley 2003). Iraq's state oil company (SOMA) was charging 96 cents a gallon for gasoline delivered to the same depots in Iraq, utilizing the same military escorts (Southern Studies 2003/2004).

Further exacerbating the problem, part of the money for the KBR gas service contract came from the United Nation's oil-for-food program (now the Development Fund for Iraq). Under the terms of UN Security Resolution 1483, an independent board called the International Advisory and Monitoring Board was to be created to ensure that UN oil-for-food funds were spent for the benefit of Iraqi citizens. The purpose of this agency was to be 'the primary vehicle for guaranteeing the transparency of the DFI and for ensuring the DFI funds are used properly' (U.S. House 2003:6). As of the end of 2003, this body had not been created (U.S. House 2003:5).Thus the use of these funds to pay inflated prices to Halliburton ($600 million out of $1 billion in funds was transferred to Halliburton) by the U.S. Coalition Provisional Authority went uncontested. In this case the government's failure to provide the necessary oversight agency constitutes a case of state-facilitated wrongdoing.

After it won a ten-year contract worth $3.8 billion to provide food, wash clothes, deliver mail, and other basic services, Halliburton continued to systematically overcharge the government for services rendered (and unrendered). In one case Halliburton charged the government $67 million more for military dining services than the corporation had paid to the actual subcontractors who provided the service (Ivanovich 2004a). The *Wall Street Journal* reported that Pentagon auditors believed the corporation overcharged $16 million for meals served at Camp Arifjan (subcontracted to Tarnirni Global Company). Moreover, the military was already paying Halliburton $28 a day per soldier. In December 2003, Halliburton had estimated it served twenty-one million meals to 110,000 soldiers at forty-five sites in Iraq. Early in 2004 military auditors suspected the corporation was cooking the numbers and overcharging the government millions of dollars (Chatterjee 2004). The fact that these overcharges occurred in at least five of Halliburton's facilities suggests they were part of a systematic effort to increase profit margin.

Not only did Halliburton overcharge the government (nearly three times the number of meals than were actually provided to soldiers in Kuwait over a nine-month period), it had been repeatedly warned and audited for its dining service conditions by the Coalition Provisional Authority's inspector general Bowen. The claims were that the food was dirty, blood was consistently found on the kitchen floors, the utensils were dirty, and meats were rotting in four of the military messes the company operates in Iraq (*Boston Globe* 2004b; CBS 2003; Chatterjee 2004; *Washington Post* 2004). Moreover, Halliburton's promises of improvement in these messes were empty as they 'have not been followed through' (NBC News 2003). Regardless of the Pentagon report warning of 'serious repercussions,' no actions to date have been taken. The government has thus facilitated illegal and unethical profiteering by allowing charges for meals never provided and unsafe food handling and preparations (NBC News 2003).

Halliburton was also charged with improprieties surrounding a joint venture with Morris Corporation, an Australian catering company to which it has awarded a $100 million contract to supply meals to U.S. troops in Iraq. Halliburton canceled the contract six weeks after it was signed. An insider involved in the deal stated that the contract was canceled after a Halliburton employee sought kickbacks worth up to $3 million during the negotiations. A Pentagon report released in March 2004 stated that Halliburton failed to inform the military that the Morris contract to supply meals had been canceled while Halliburton continued to use the contract to estimate costs of more than $1 billion dollars for catering, including the site of Kuwait (Wilkinson 2004).

Halliburton initially agreed to credit the military $27.4 million and suspend billing on the remaining $141 million until the issue of overcharges had been satisfactorily addressed. In response to a criminal investigation by the Defense Criminal Investigation Service, in March 2004, Halliburton (while agreeing to suspend future billings to the government while under investigation) froze payments to its subcontractors totaling nearly $500 million in outstanding invoices (*Wall Street Journal* 2004). The first week of May 2004, however, Halliburton proceeded with billing the United States for the remaining $141 million. Pentagon experts reported that this billing violated a standing rule whereby contractors bill no more that 85 percent of costs until the corporation and military reach a consensus on a fair price (Ivanovich 2004). By mid-May 2004, the Pentagon suspended an additional $159.5 million payment after finding the company submitted incomplete paperwork (Chatterjee 2004).

Halliburton also acknowledged that it accepted up to $6 million in kickbacks taken by employees in return for granting a subcontract to a Kuwaiti firm pertaining to Iraq's rebuilding. Halliburton said it would repay the government $6.2 million to cover the overbilling by an unidentified Kuwaiti firm it contracted to as well as the kickbacks given to 'one or two' KBR employees (Ivanovich 2004).

The Coalition Provisional Authority (CPA) inspector general Bowen made allegations that Halliburton was claiming overexpenditures for the Hilton Kuwait Resort (where KBR houses employees while providing logistical support to U.S. military troops and while rebuilding Iraq's oil infrastructure) (Ivanovich 2004). Along with these charges, in early 2004 the CPA conducted an audit into the 'unnecessary' purchase of trucks and other costs associated with KBR's services.

Beyond overcharging and purchasing unnecessary and/or excessive products, Halliburton systematically billed for labor never performed. For example, Representative Henry Waxman posted whistleblower testimony on his Web site revealing systematic practices of overpaying employees for hours of labor never performed and billed to the U.S. government (Waxman 2004b). One of the testimonials, from Mike West, stated he was hired as a labor foreman at a salary of $130,000. Moreover, he stated he was paid despite the fact that he had no work; 'I only worked one day out of six in Kuwait' (West 2003:1). During his tenure at Al Asad he claimed to have worked one of every five days, although he was told by his supervisor to bill for twelve hours of labor every day (Chatterjee 2004). The failure of the House of Representatives Government Reform Committee to hear whistleblower testimony suggests that Halliburton's actions clearly fall in the category of state-facilitated corporate crime.

Halliburton's practice of billing for delivering supplies has amounted to systematic overcharges. The U.S. taxpayer has been billed nearly $327 million as of mid-2004 for these runs, and Halliburton was expecting to charge an additional $230 million more. Yet many of these runs have been unnecessary, because at least one in three trucks makes the three-hundred-mile trip empty while others may carry only one pallet of supplies (Chatterjee 2004). Moreover, of the fleet of trucks (Mercedes and Volvos), dozens have not been used (Wilson 2004).Trailers are left along the roadside when the slightest mechanical problem or flat tire occurs, or when the convoy lacks necessary maintenance items. It was also reported that one Halliburton employee took a video in January 2004 of fifteen empty trailers on the road and stated, 'This is just a sample of the empty trailers we're handling called sustainers. And there's more behind me .... this is fraud and abuse' (Chatterjee 2004:37).

As controversy continues to shroud the Bush-Cheney administration, little to no public outcry has occurred over the blatant misuse of a political office. In part this is due to the ideology of unquestioning patriotism during times of war, and also due to the lack of attention by news media to these issues. This has led to state-facilitated profiteering by Halliburton as an agent of the state. After all, Halliburton is the 'biggest contractor to the U.S. government in Iraq earning three times as much as Bechtel, its nearest competitor ... earning $3.9 billion dollars from the military in 2003, a dizzying 680% increase from 2002 when it earned $483 million' (Chatterjee 2004:39).

The Bush-Cheney team has achieved a level of secrecy and symbolic power unlike that of any other administration (Dean 2004). Criminologists and the public must delve into understanding how and why the Cheney–Halliburton marriage has been able to remain and prosper in the White House. Not doing so increases the probability of future abuses of power, corrupt relationships, and war profiteering.

From D. Rothe, 'Iraq and Halliburton', in R. Michalowski and R. Kramer (eds) State–Corporate Crime: Wrongdoing at the intersection of business and government *(New Brunswick, NJ: Rutgers University Press), 2006, pp. 215–228.*

Note

1 For more details on neocons and their ideology, see Dorrien (2004).

References

Bivens, M. 2004. 'Vice President Halliburton?' *The Nation*, April 14.
Boston Globe. 2004b. News. January 23. http://www.boston.com/globe/news/12304.
Bunting, H. 2004. *In Testimony given to Senate Democratic Policy Committee.* Session 12: Democratic Policy Committee on Iraq Contract Abuses. Washington, DC, February 13.
CBS News. 2003. News Report. December 12.
Chatterjee, P. 2004. *Iraq Inc.: A Profitable Occupation.* New York: Seven Stories Press.
CNN Money. 2004. 'Pentagon Puts Hold on Halliburton Pay.' March 17. http://money. cnn.com/2004/03/17/news/companies/halliburton/index.htm.
Dean, J. 2004. *Worse than Watergate: The Secret Presidency of George W Bush.* New York: Little, Brown and Company.
Federal Register. 2005. United States Government Printing Office. http://wais.access. gpo.gov [DOCID:fr27de01-31] (accessed March 12, 2005).
Greider, W. 1998. *Fortress America.* New York: Public Affairs Press.
Higham, S., J. Stephens, and M,Williams. 2004. 'Guantanamo – A Holding Cell in War on Terror.' *Washington Post*, May 2.
Institute for Southern Studies (2004) Campaign to Stop War Profiteers, http://southernstudies.org/reports/occupation (accessed October 30, 2004).
Ivanovich, D. (2004a) Houston Halliburton's Refunds $27 Million after Auditors check War Food Bills, *Houston Chronicle*, February 3.
Johnson, C. (2004) *The Sorrows of Empire: Militarism, Secrecy and the End of the Republic.* New York: Metropolitan/Holt
Little, R. 2002. 'American Civilians Go Off to War, Too.' *Baltimore Sun*, May 26.
Melman, S. 1974. *The Permanent War Economy: American Capitalism in Decline.* New York: Simon and Schuster, 1991.
Mother Jones. 2004a. 'Halliburton.' http://motherjones.com/ (accessed October 28, 2004).
NBC News. 2003. Pentagon Report News Coverage. September 14. Archived Transcripts. http://www.nbc.com.
Reuters. 2004. Reuters News Service. 2004. 'Halliburton in $16 Million Food Probe' February 2.
Singer, P W. 2003. *Corporate Warriors: The Rise of the Privatized Military Industry.* Ithaca, NY: Cornell University Press.
U.S. House of Representatives. 2003. See Waxman (2003).
Wall Street Journal. 2004. 'Halliburton Overcharged on Troops' Food.' February 2.
Washington Post. 2004. News Archive. January 21.
Waxman, H. 2004b. Memorandum: Congress of the United States, to Committee on Government Reform. March 10. http://www.house,gov/waxman/.

Waxman, H. 2003. House of Representatives. Letter to General Robert Flowers. October 20. http://www. house.gov/waxman/.

West, Mike. 2003. Whistleblower testimony. Online at Henry Waxman, http://www. house.gov/waxman.

White House. 2004. News Release. http://www.white-house.gov/news/releases/2004/04/print/20040413-5. html (accessed April 14, 2004).

Wilkinson, M. 2004. 'Corruption Stench as Company Loses Contract?' *Herald Correspondent* (DC), May 21, 2004.

Wilson, David, 2004. 'New Halliburton Whistleblowers Say Millions Wasted in Iraq.' Quoted in Pratap Chatterjee, Special to *Corp Watch*. June 16. www.cor-pwatch.org/ article.php?id= 11373.

19

Organised crime

19.1 Organized crime: the structural skeleton
Donald R. Cressey   440

**19.2 Fishy business: the mafia and
the Fulton Fish Market**
James B. Jacobs   444

19.3 The crime network
William J. Chambliss   449

19.4 The profession of violence: the Krays
John Pearson   453

19.5 Perspectives on 'organised crime'
Michael Levi   454

Introduction

KEY CONCEPTS   Cosa Nostra; organized crime; mafia; markets; professional crime; racketeering

Continually fascinating, but enduringly problematic, the whole area of organized crime has long been fraught with definitional difficulties and is, for some fairly obvious reasons, far from a straightforward area to study. In our globalized world there is increasing concern that organised crime is undertaken across national boundaries and that, consequently, it is ever more important to have cross-national means of responding to such problems or threats.

In a classic study, Donald Cressey **(Reading 19.1)**, who advised the President's Commission on Law Enforcement and the Administration of Justice in the late 1960s, argued that organized crime in America was dominated by a tightly-knit network of 'Mafia families'. Much of his work was based on the testimony of one individual, Joseph Valachi, and this model of organized crime has become part of our standard popular cultural presentation of such activity (largely through a series of famous mafia films from the 1970s onward). Cressey outlines the nature of a highly structured, hierarchical organization, in which a series of 'families' were headed by a 'Don' and had a clear line of command all the way down to 'good fellows' or 'wise guys'. The collection of these organized crime 'families' were known, he said, as the Cosa Nostra. Cressey's work has been much criticized, in part for its reliance on a highly dubious source of evidence, but has had a huge influence on our understanding, or at least our perception, of American organised crime.

The second excerpt, by James Jacobs **(Reading 19.2)**, takes another example of organized crime, this time in New York City. It concerns the Fulton Fish Market, the oldest fish market in the US. Jacobs details the racketeering undertaken by the Cosa Nostra – and in particular the Genovese and Bonanno crime families – from the 1920s onward. The Genoveses operated a series of cartels, specifically around the loading and unloading operations in the market, whilst the Bonannos were into loan sharking, gambling, and drugs. Their ability to operate as they did, Jacobs suggests, owed much to their influence over one of the local unions. As is almost always the case with stories of fraud and corruption, the ineffectiveness or, possibly, complicity of the authorities also forms an important part of the process. Relationships between organized crime figures and prominent politicians continued for decades, he notes.

A different picture of American crime networks from Cressey's, but picking up elements of Jacobs' story of Fulton market, is provided by William J. Chambliss **(Reading 19.3)** who studied a variety of criminal and corrupt activities in Seattle. However, here, rather than a study of organized crime families, we have a study of a city's elites – a network of people in powerful and apparently legitimate positions, involved in a variety of more or less dubious activities. His informants in Seattle deny that they are some branch of the Mafia. The highly structured picture produced by Cressey to convey the organizational structure was held not to apply in Seattle. As one respondent puts it: 'If you do diagram it, you can't read your diagram when you're done.' The picture he presents is perhaps closer to what Peter Reuter called 'disorganized crime'. One of the most

438

enduring images of British 'organized crime' is undoubtedly that of the Kray twins. In a short excerpt from his wonderful book, *The Profession of Violence*, John Pearson **(Reading 19.4)** offers some thoughts on the Krays and what set them apart.

As Michael Levi **(Reading 19.5)** notes, not only is organized crime inherently difficult to define but it brings with it 'an emotional kick'. It is talk of such things as 'mafia' and the like that is often sufficient to persuade politicians to find resources to fund new or expanded policing efforts or organizations. One approach to understanding organized crime is to look at its markets and the nature of its trade and trade links. Much of the literature, as you will see reading through the various extracts here, is about attempting to understand the ways in which criminal enterprises organize themselves and how they relate to each other. Finally, and this is both easier to make sense of and to research, is the whole issue of the nature of the control response to organized crime. There is, as Levi outlines, something of a tension (one of many) between those who see major risks and wish to create substantial and powerful new agencies to respond to these risks, and others who see much of this as overblown and as the exploitation of fears and opportunistic nest-feathering.

Questions for discussion

1. Where did Donald Cressey get his information from, and how reliable do you think this might have been?

2. Summarise Cressey's description of the structure of a typical 'Mafia family'.

3. Why are Chambliss' respondents critical of the idea of drawing a diagram of the racketeering enterprises in Seattle?

4. How does Chambliss suggest organized crime in Seattle works?

5. How significant is the absence of regulation to the story of organized crime at Fulton Fish Market?

6. What is significant about the 'ease' with which the Krays built their 'criminal empire'?

7. What connections do you see between the accounts provided by Cressey, Jacobs, Chambliss and Pearson? And what differences?

8. Do you think the nature of organized crime requires the creation of specialist law enforcement agencies?

19.1 Organized crime: the structural skeleton
Donald R. Cressey

Since 1963, when Joseph Valachi testified before the McClellan Committee, there has been a tendency to label America's nationwide criminal cartel and confederation 'Cosa Nostra' and then to identify what is known about Cosa Nostra's division of labor as the structure of 'organized crime' in the United States. I have followed this tendency, believing that the Cosa Nostra organization is so extensive, so powerful, and so central that precise description and control of it would be description of all but a tiny part of all organized crime. But this tendency has its attendant hazards.

In the first place, calling the entire apparatus 'Cosa Nostra' might lead to continuing misplaced skepticism about whether a dangerous organization of criminals exists in fact. Individual citizens do not necessarily find that their local bookie, lottery operator, or usurer is of Italian or Sicilian descent. When 'Cosa Nostra' is used as a synonym for 'organized crime,' these citizens might, then, believe that their local criminal purveyor of illicit goods and services has nothing to do with organized crime. The term directs attention to membership, rather than to the power to control and to make alliances. It should be understood that Cosa Nostra is the inner core, and that the only phrase adequately describing Cosa Nostra positions plus positions occupied by outsiders (of various national, ethnic, and religious backgrounds) is a rather clumsy one: 'nationwide criminal cartel and confederation.'

In the second place, using 'Cosa Nostra' as a capitalized noun implies that the economic and political structure of this secret society is as readily identifiable as that of associations such as the Elks, the Los Angeles Police Department, or the Standard Oil Company. This is obviously not the case. We know very little. Our knowledge of the structure which makes either Cosa Nostra or 'organized crime' organized is only a little bit better (thanks to taps and bugs) than the knowledge of Standard Oil which could be gleaned from interviews with gasoline-station attendants. [...]

But we do know enough about the structure of Cosa Nostra to conclude that it is indeed an organization with both formal and informal aspects. When there are specialized but integrated positions for a board of directors, presidents, vice presidents, staff specialists, works managers, foremen, and workers, there is an economic organization. When there are specialized but integrated positions for legislators, judges, and administrators of criminal justice, there is a political organization. Like the large legitimate corporations which it resembles, Cosa Nostra has both kinds of positions, making it both a business organization and a government. Further, Cosa Nostra exists independently of its current personnel, as does any big business or government. Business, government, and Cosa Nostra go on despite complete turnover in the personnel occupying the various positions making up the organization. If a president, vice president, or some other functionary resigns or dies, another person is recruited to fill the vacant position. No man is indispensable. Organization, or 'structure,' not persons, gives Cosa Nostra its self-perpetuating character.

As the former Attorney General's testimony before the McClellan Committee indicated (see p. 60), the highest ruling body in Cosa Nostra is the 'Commission,' sometimes called the 'High Commission,' the 'Grand Council,' the 'Administration,' 'Consiglio d'Amministrazione,' the 'Roundtable,' or the 'Inner Circle.' This body serves as a combination board of business directors, legislature, supreme court, and arbitration board, but most of its functions are judicial, as we will show later. Members look to the Commission as the ultimate authority on organizational disputes, and each Commission member is sometimes called a 'chairman' or an 'avvocato' (advocate, counsel). The Commission is made up of the rulers of the most powerful 'families,' which are located in large cities. At present, eight such 'families' are represented on the Commission, but the number of commissioners usually varies from nine to twelve. [...]

In some sections of the country, the next level of authority, below the Commission, is a 'council' made up of the more experienced members of each 'family' in a particular geographic area. New York, Detroit, and Chicago (at least) have councils. The patriarch of the council may be called a 'Don' or 'chairman,' and he might or

440

Figure 19.1.1 New York City Police Department chart of 'confederation families' in New York city from 1930 to 1965

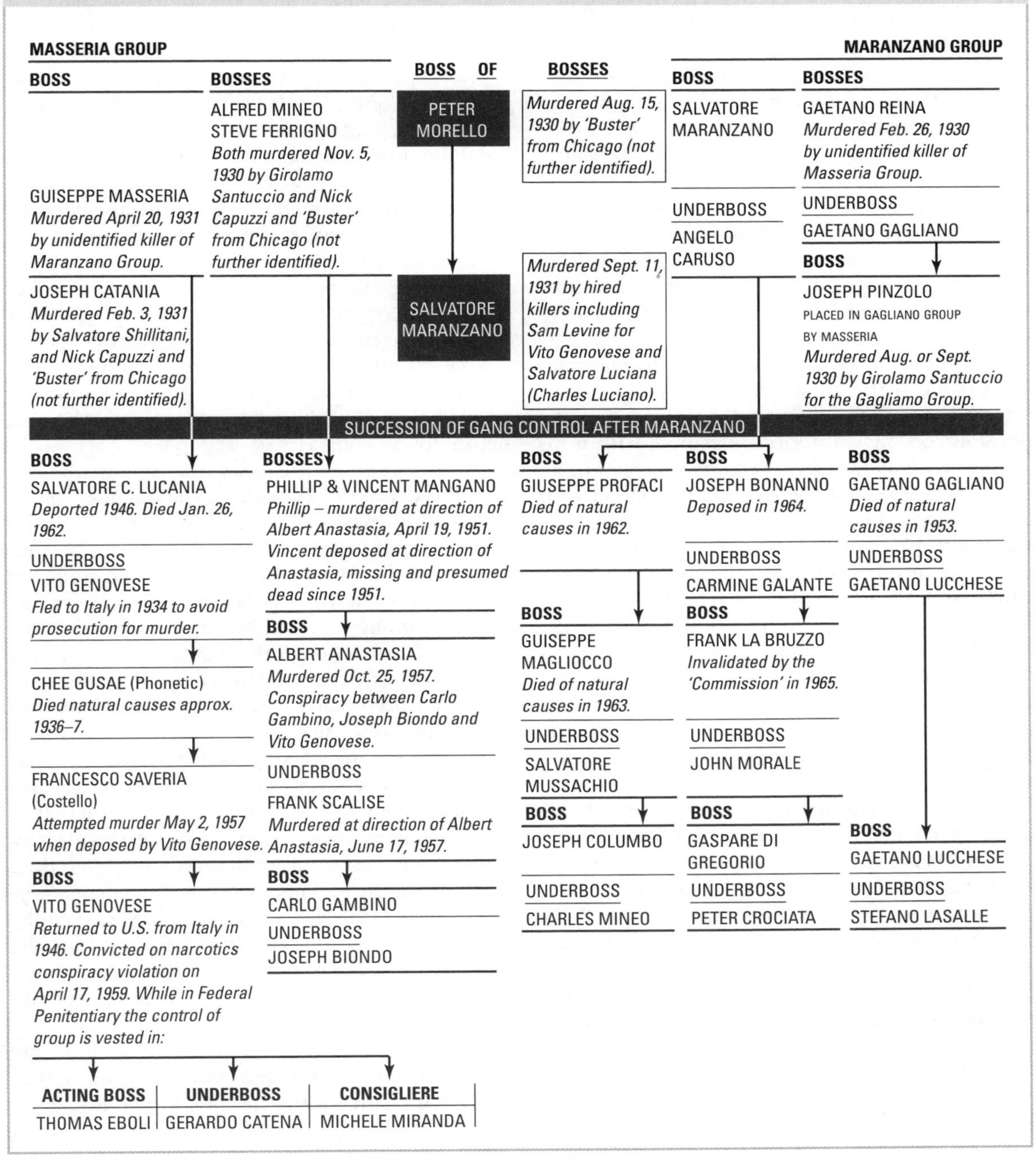

MASSERIA GROUP

BOSS	BOSSES	BOSS OF	BOSSES	MARANZANO GROUP

BOSS — PETER MORELLO

BOSSES:
ALFRED MINEO
STEVE FERRIGNO
Both murdered Nov. 5, 1930 by Girolamo Santuccio and Nick Capuzzi and 'Buster' from Chicago (not further identified).

BOSS — GUISEPPE MASSERIA *Murdered April 20, 1931 by unidentified killer of Maranzano Group.*

JOSEPH CATANIA *Murdered Feb. 3, 1931 by Salvatore Shillitani, and Nick Capuzzi and 'Buster' from Chicago (not further identified).*

BOSSES — *Murdered Aug. 15, 1930 by 'Buster' from Chicago (not further identified).*

SALVATORE MARANZANO — *Murdered Sept. 11, 1931 by hired killers including Sam Levine for Vito Genovese and Salvatore Luciana (Charles Luciano).*

MARANZANO GROUP

BOSS — SALVATORE MARANZANO

UNDERBOSS — ANGELO CARUSO

BOSSES:
GAETANO REINA *Murdered Feb. 26, 1930 by unidentified killer of Masseria Group.*

UNDERBOSS — GAETANO GAGLIANO

BOSS — JOSEPH PINZOLO
PLACED IN GAGLIANO GROUP BY MASSERIA
Murdered Aug. or Sept. 1930 by Girolamo Santuccio for the Gagliamo Group.

SUCCESSION OF GANG CONTROL AFTER MARANZANO

BOSS
SALVATORE C. LUCANIA
Deported 1946. Died Jan. 26, 1962.

UNDERBOSS
VITO GENOVESE
Fled to Italy in 1934 to avoid prosecution for murder.

CHEE GUSAE (Phonetic)
Died natural causes approx. 1936–7.

FRANCESCO SAVERIA (Costello)
Attempted murder May 2, 1957 when deposed by Vito Genovese.

BOSS
VITO GENOVESE
Returned to U.S. from Italy in 1946. Convicted on narcotics conspiracy violation on April 17, 1959. While in Federal Penitentiary the control of group is vested in:

ACTING BOSS	UNDERBOSS	CONSIGLIERE
THOMAS EBOLI	GERARDO CATENA	MICHELE MIRANDA

BOSSES
PHILLIP & VINCENT MANGANO
Phillip – murdered at direction of Albert Anastasia, April 19, 1951. Vincent deposed at direction of Anastasia, missing and presumed dead since 1951.

BOSS
ALBERT ANASTASIA
Murdered Oct. 25, 1957. Conspiracy between Carlo Gambino, Joseph Biondo and Vito Genovese.

UNDERBOSS
FRANK SCALISE
Murdered at direction of Albert Anastasia, June 17, 1957.

BOSS
CARLO GAMBINO
UNDERBOSS
JOSEPH BIONDO

BOSS
GIUSEPPE PROFACI
Died of natural causes in 1962.

BOSS
GUISEPPE MAGLIOCCO
Died of natural causes in 1963.

UNDERBOSS
SALVATORE MUSSACHIO

BOSS
JOSEPH COLUMBO
UNDERBOSS
CHARLES MINEO

BOSS
JOSEPH BONANNO
Deposed in 1964.

UNDERBOSS
CARMINE GALANTE

BOSS
FRANK LA BRUZZO
Invalidated by the 'Commission' in 1965.

UNDERBOSS
JOHN MORALE

BOSS
GASPARE DI GREGORIO
UNDERBOSS
PETER CROCIATA

BOSS
GAETANO GAGLIANO
Died of natural causes in 1953.

UNDERBOSS
GAETANO LUCCHESE

BOSS
GAETANO LUCCHESE
UNDERBOSS
STEFANO LASALLE

Source: Adapted from *Combating Organized Crime*, a report of the 1965 Oyster Bay, New York, Conferences on Combating Crime: pp.26–27.

might not be a member of the Commission. Council members are elected by the council. When a council member dies, the council chooses a new member from the men in his 'family.' [...]

Beneath the Commission and councils are at least twenty-four 'families,' each with its 'boss.' The wealthiest and most influential 'families' operate in New York, New Jersey, Illinois, Florida, Louisiana, Nevada, Michigan, and Rhode Island. The 'family' is the most significant level of organization and the largest unit of criminal organization in which allegiance is owed to one man, the boss. The number of members in a 'family' varies from about 800 to about 20. [...] Rather than 'boss,' the words '*il capo,*' '*don,*' '*capofanziglia,*' and '*rappresentante*' are used. [...]

The boss's primary function is to maintain order while at the same time maximizing profits. Subject to the possibility of being overruled by the Commission, his authority is absolute within his 'family,' geographical area, and any sphere of influence which does not bring him into conflict with another boss. He is the final arbiter in all matters relating to his branch of the confederation. Some bosses are members of the Commission. Each boss who is not a Commission member probably has his designated *avvocato* on the Commission.

The members of a 'family' are likely to believe that they elect their own boss, but this is only vaguely the case. The 'family' ordinarily submits the name of the man of its choice to the Commission, but the Commission makes the final decision. [...]

Each boss knows each of the other bosses personally. Accordingly, each 'family' is interrelated with every other 'family.' Alliances and agreements are usually formal, but sometimes they are merely based on the mechanism of 'respect' the bosses have for each other, and the fear they have of each other. The boss also initiates any alliances or other arrangements necessary for living in conditions of peaceful coexistence with any nonmember organized criminals permitted to operate in his community. [...]

Beneath each boss of the larger 'families,' at least, is an 'underboss,' or '*sottocapo,*' appointed by the boss. This position is, essentially, that of executive vice president and deputy director of the 'family' unit. The man occupying the position often collects information for the boss. He relays messages to him, and he passes his orders down to the men occupying positions below him in the hierarchy. He acts as boss in the absence of the boss.

On the same level as the underboss there is a position for a 'counselor,' or adviser, often referred to as '*consigliere,*' or in slang, '*consuliere.*' The person occupying this position is a staff officer rather than a line officer. He is likely to be an elder member who has partially retired after a career in which he did not quite succeed in becoming a boss. He is appointed by the boss, but he gives no commands or orders. He is something of a neutral adviser to all 'family' members, including the boss and underboss. The counselor also is a historian. Consistently, his advice is based on precedent, frequently reflecting the wishes of the boss, of whom he is a close confidant. He therefore enjoys considerable influence and power. Although the counselor has no subordinates reporting to him, he is given a piece of the action of many members, in return for his counsel.

Also at about the same level as underboss is another staff position, 'buffer.' The top members of the 'family' hierarchy, particularly the boss, avoid direct communication with the lower-echelon personnel, the workers. They are insulated from the police. To obtain this insulation, commands, information, money, and complaints generally flow back and forth through the buffer, who is a trusted and clever go-between. However, the buffer does not make decisions or assume any of the authority of his boss, as the underboss does.

To reach the working level, a boss usually goes through channels. For example, a boss's decision on the settlement of a dispute involving the activities of the 'runners' (ticket sellers) in a particular lottery game passes first to his underboss and buffer, then to the next level of rank, which is 'lieutenant,' 'captain,' 'head,' '*capodecina,*' '*ca-poregime,*' or, simply, '*capo.*' This position, considered from a business standpoint, is analogous to works manager or sales manager. The person occupying it is the chief of an operating unit. [...]

All lieutenants in a 'family' are of equal stature, no matter how many men each supervises. [...] Each lieutenant usually has one or two associates who work closely with him, serving as messengers and buffers. They carry orders, information, and money back and forth between the lieutenant and the men belonging to his regime. They do not share the lieutenant's administrative power.

Beneath the lieutenants there might be one or more 'section chiefs' or 'group leaders.' Messages and orders received from a boss's buffer by the lieutenant or his buffer are passed on to a section chief, who also may have a buffer. [...]

About five 'soldiers,' 'buttons,' 'button men,' 'good fellows,' 'wise guys' (meaning 'right guys'), or just 'members' report to each section chief or, if there is no section chief position, to a lieutenant. The number of soldiers in a 'family' varies from about twenty to over six hundred. [...]

Some members have retired from active crime, but one can leave the organization only by death. Theoretically, one could be boss of a 'family' and not engage directly in illegal activities. None of the twenty-four known bosses has chosen this course. The boss alone has the power to admit members, but he can do so only within limits set by the Commission, with the permission of the Commission, and at times designated by that body. 'Suspension' of membership (but not stripping of membership) has been used as a punishment for swindling another member and for excessive indebtedness to another member.

Partnerships between two or more soldiers, and between soldiers and men higher up in the hierarchy, including bosses, are common. The partnership could be in a usury operation, a dice game, a specific lottery, a specific bet-taking establishment, a vending-machine company, or any other enterprise, legal or illegal, making it possible to turn a fast buck. Most soldiers, like most upper-echelon 'family' members, have interests in more than one business.

'Family' membership ends at the soldier level. All members are of Italian descent. Members once had to be Italian by birth or by parentage on both sides of the family. This specification has, in one or two cases, recently been relaxed so as to admit men whose mothers are not of Italian descent. Similarly, a few men have been allowed to retain active membership despite the fact that they married women of non-Italian descent.

Membership in the Italian-Sicilian Mafia does not automatically make one a member of the American organization. This might not have been the case before World War II, but now even a Sicilian Mafia member must be recommended for membership. [...]

About five thousand men are known members of 'families' and, hence, of the cartel and confederation which is Cosa Nostra. But beneath the soldiers in the hierarchy of operations are large numbers of employees, sharecroppers, franchise holders, and commission agents who are not necessarily of Italian descent. These are the persons carrying on most of the work 'on the street.' They have no buffers or other forms of insulation from the police. [...]

The above sketch of the authority structure of Cosa Nostra is based on a variety of sources, most of them having their roots in information released at the time of the 1963 McClellan Committee hearings, including the testimony of Joseph Valachi. But the sketch based on this information was recently validated by publication of only ten FBI summaries of the sounds coming from a single electronic bug.

From, 'The structural skeleton', in D. Cressey, Theft of the Nation *(New York: Harper and Row), 1969, pp. 109–126.*

19.2 Fishy business: the mafia and the Fulton Fish Market
James B. Jacobs

[Operating] in a frontier atmosphere... the Fulton Fish Market is a sovereign entity where the laws of economic power and physical force, not the laws of New York City, prevail.[1]

Frank Wohl, court-appointed monitor of the Fulton Fish Market, 1990

How the fish market works

The Fulton Fish Market is the oldest and largest wholesale fish market in the United States. It was organized in 1833 to serve fishing fleets on the East River near Fulton Street. However, as early as 1924, some suppliers were trucking seafood to the market. Today, no seafood is delivered directly by ship; rather, refrigerated trucks bring seafood from around the world to the market in boxes of one hundred pounds or less, some of which is flown in from abroad. The market runs from 10:00 P.M. to 10:00 A.M., Sunday through Friday. It consists of approximately seventy 'stalls' – storefronts with stand space out front where most of the actual selling occurs. By morning, the stands are emptied and the buildings closed; only a few scattered fish and wooden wholesaler signs remain to hint at the overnight bustle. More than five hundred people work at the market. Approximately two hundred million pounds of seafood are delivered to the market annually. Estimates of the dollar amount of seafood sold annually vary from $200 million to $2 billion.[2] [...]

Wholesale seafood vendors at the Fulton Fish Market [...] are extremely vulnerable to threats of delay. Time is of the essence in selling fish. First, fishermen sell their catch to suppliers. The suppliers pack fish in boxes and use freight-hauling companies to transport it to the Fulton Fish Market. Fish from the West Coast and abroad is trucked in from area airports. Beginning at 10:00 P.M., truckers deliver frozen and fresh seafood in vehicles ranging from huge forty-foot refrigerated trailer trucks to small vans.[3] Each week, approximately four hundred vehicles belonging to dozens of trucking companies and suppliers transport seafood to the market. They line up along South Street north of the market and wait to be unloaded.[4]

Prior to the city's 1990s reforms, the unloaders had tremendous leverage over truckers and suppliers.[5] It is tiring, expensive, and frustrating for truckers to sit for hours waiting for a service that they could easily provide themselves. The time at which a truck is unloaded directly affects the day's profit because fish displayed at the wholesalers' stalls by 3:00 A.M. commands a higher price than fish displayed at 6:00 A.M. Thus, truckers were willing to pay to be accorded priority.

After the seafood is unloaded, it is delivered to wholesalers' stalls. The wholesalers employ approximately eight hundred workers, called 'journeymen,' who prepare the Seafood for display, sell it, and deliver it to their customers' vehicles. Many of these workers are members of Local 359 of the United Seafood Workers, Smoked Fish and Cannery Union.[6]

By 3:00 A.M., the deliveries are displayed and hundreds of 'retailers' from restaurants and retail seafood stores begin arriving at the market. Until the recent reforms, eleven loading companies, which were distinct entities from the unloading companies, assigned each retailer to a particular parking area in one of the eleven designated parking zones, located on public property. The retailers had no say in where they would be permitted to park and often were unable to change zones. The retailers leave their vehicles unlocked and walk from stall to stall, selecting seafood from the various wholesaler displays. The wholesalers' journeymen use hand trucks and 'hi-los' to take the fish to the retailers' parked vehicles. There the journeymen load the fish into the vehicles. Retailers paid fees ranging from $5 to $50 per night to the loaders to keep their vehicles and fish secure from vandalism or theft.

Suppliers are also somewhat dependent on the goodwill of the wholesalers, who sell their catch primarily for cash, at prices reached in on-the-spot negotiations with retailers and restaurant owners. Prices vary according to quality – quantity, and demand. The wholesalers, who – in effect – operate on consignment or commission, take a fee from each retailer's or restaurateur's payment and remit the remainder to the supplier.[7] Thus, the supplier does not know in advance the price his fish will command and must rely on the wholesaler's negotiating skills and honesty. Although the situation is changing, most of the market's sales involve cash.

How Cosa Nostra controlled the Fulton Fish Market

The Fulton Fish Market has been a revenue source and a power base for Cosa Nostra since the early twentieth century. The Genovese crime family has influenced every facet of the market's operations since the 1920s. This influence flowed from control of Local 359 of the United Seafood Workers, Smoked Fish and Cannery Union, which represents the four hundred journeymen and twenty wholesalers, managers, and supervisors. However, not all journeymen are union members, and the former loading and unloading crews were not unionized. The Genovese crime family created loading and unloading cartels, maintained interests in some wholesaling companies, operated 'security services,' and organized and charged for parking.[7] The Bonanno crime family played a lesser role in the market, through ownership of certain unloading companies and by conducting loan-sharking, gambling, drug sales, and protection services on premises.

As with the other mobbed-up industries examined in this book, Cosa Nostra functioned as a kind of legislature, court, and police force for the market. The rules covered competition, prices, labor relations, payoffs, and respect. Businesses and individuals faced threats of violence, property damage, and expulsion from the market for violating the rules.[8]

The Genovese crime family governed through two wholesaler associations, which represented many wholesalers at the market. The wholesalers located in the Old Market Building warehouse were represented by the Fulton Fishmongers Association, and those located in the New Market Building warehouse were represented by the New York Wholesale Fish Dealers Association. These organizations cooperated in market governance and defended market operations to the outside world. For example, the president of the Fulton Fishmongers explained that the low rent paid by the wholesalers was justified by the run-down accommodations in the Old Market Building.[9]

When problems such as theft of fish arose, the associations knew whom to contact. In 1975, the president of the Wholesale Fish Dealers Association asked Carmine Romano, an associate of the Genovese crime family and the secretary-treasurer of Local 359, for help in preventing thefts. Cosa Nostra established a watchmen's asso-ciation to patrol the market area; whether this was a protection service or a protection racket was unclear, even to those who paid the premiums. Years later, at Romano's trial on federal racketeering charges the president testified that 'if the thieves knew that the union was looking out for us...they wouldn't bother us...[b]ecause the thieves would be afraid of the Union.'[10]

Cosa Nostra's domination of Local 359

Given the perishability of seafood, the market required a reliable labor force. As federal prosecutors noted in a 1981 sentencing proceeding involving several convicted Local 359 officials, '[I]n the wholesale [fish] industry, where competition is fierce and time is of the essence, it is crucial for businesses to maintain the good will of the union and the men who run it. Organized crime recognizes this power and knows how to use it.'[11]

Cosa Nostra's influence in the Fulton Fish Market was rooted in its control of Local 359. That union had only 850 to 900 members including the four hundred journeymen at the market who set up the wholesalers' seafood displays and sold and delivered the fish.[12] The Genovese crime family controlled Local 359 since the 1920s; for decades, Joseph 'Socks' Lanza, a capo in the Genovese family, used his position as business agent of Local 359 as a power base. Known as the 'czar of Fulton Market,' Lanza determined who could transact business of any kind anywhere on market premises from the 1920s to the 1960s.[13] Lanza ran Local 359 for the benefit of the Genovese crime family. He accepted payoffs in exchange for the nonenforcement of certain contract terms and for not seeking increased wages and benefits for union members.[14] The result was labor peace and a smooth-running market.

Lanza found many ways to turn power into cash at the market. In the early 1930s, the Manhattan District Attorney's Office revealed that fishing-boat captains were forced to pay tribute in order to have their catch unloaded without problems. To obtain the ice needed to preserve their fish, boat crewmen were forced to hand over bags of scallops to the unloading crews.[15]

The watchman's association protection racket

As early as the 1920s, Lanza instructed his underlings to steal seafood from wholesalers, and then persuaded the victims to purchase theft insurance from him.[16] In 1931, Manhattan District Attorney Thomas C.T. Crain estimated that gangsters were shaking down fish merchants to the tune of $25,000 a year.[17] One wholesaler testified that he had paid $5,000 to Lanza's watchman's association for 'protection.' By 1981, the Fulton Patrol Association was collecting $700,000 ($1,180,000 in 1996 dollars) from businesses in the Fulton Fish Market.[18]

The wholesalers did not complain publicly about Lanza or market operations. They maintained that paying Lanza was cheaper and more efficient than other means of preventing thievery. The president of the Fulton Fishmongers Association (the trade association representing the Old Market Building wholesalers) explained that 'in almost every instance when someone has missed a barrel or a box of fish it has been returned within a few hours after we reported it' to the protection association.[19] Wholesalers declared that they were not victims of extortion but beneficiaries of theft insurance.

The Genovese crime family continued this racket through the years. For example, in 1975, Carmine Romano established the Fulton Patrol Association to protect the New Market Building wholesalers from thefts of seafood. For this 'insurance' the New Market Building wholesalers paid $1,300 ($3,720 in 1996 dollars) a week. Although the association employed only two watchmen, the number of thefts dropped significantly.[20] Perhaps the association instilled fear in would-be thieves; more likely, the wholesalers were paying off the very people who had been stealing from them. Tired of high theft rates, the Old Market Building wholesalers eventually purchased the association's services as well. The most lucrative scam was the association's special service of guarding unsold fish stored overnight for $2,800 weekly per wholesaler.[21]

Loading companies provided their own protection services to retailers. For a fee, the loading crews watched over the restaurateurs' and fish store-owners' unlocked vehicles while they shopped. According to the loading companies, it was not a protection scam. 'We help to stack the fish, we make sure it's not stolen, and we allow the retailers to go to all the wholesale stands without worrying about thousands of dollars of fish waiting in their vans.' Nevertheless, in a tax-evasion case one loader admitted that he encouraged retailers' payoffs with threats of violence; those who did not pay found their vehicles damaged and their fish stolen. In other words, the loaders were not typical security guards. For example, in 1995, one of the loaders was a Genovese family associate; two

others were awaiting trial on federal armed bank robbery and explosives charges.

The prosecution of the racketeers was impeded by witnesses' concerns that testifying would provoke violent retaliation against themselves and their families. Three wholesalers chose to serve six-month prison terms rather than testify against Romano and his associates.[22] Others committed perjury.[23] Local 359's longtime accountant admitted that he lied to a grand jury about Carmine Romano's participation in the Fulton Patrol Service scheme because he feared the Genovese crime family's retaliation.[24] Immediately following the trial, one witness was shot several times in front of union headquarters. No one ever was arrested. At the trial of Carmine Romano, the defense presented 350 letters from wholesalers, union members, and other market participants attesting to his integrity and good reputation.[25]

Coerced rental of union signs

Until the 1980s, Local 359 officials forced wholesalers to 'rent' cardboard signs stating that they employed union labor. The Romanos received more than $66,000 ($112,000 in 1996 dollars) in rent from this scam.[26] These sign rentals violated the Local 359 constitution.[27] In 1981, a federal court struck down the practice as violating the Taft-Hartley Act. Soon thereafter, the United Seafood Workers, Smoked Fish and Cannery Union placed Local 359 under trusteeship and ousted Carmine and Peter Romano from their union positions.[28] But the Genovese crime family retained its influence over Local 359 through Carmine and Peter's successor, their brother Vincent Romano.

Extorting Christmas payments

Fulton Fish Market wholesalers routinely gave Christmas presents to Local 359 officials. To insulate themselves from Taft-Hartley Act liabilities, union officers used middlemen to collect the funds; occasionally, however, they solicited directly. Throughout the 1970s, wholesalers were encouraged to make a holiday contribution 'to the boys in the union.' The union members never saw the money, which went directly into the coffers of the Genovese crime family.

Before 1975, this Christmas 'gift giving' was informal and irregular. After 1975, it became a systematic extortion scheme.[29] In *United States* v. *Romano*, the government alleged that from 1975 to

1979, union officials collected $300 per wholesaler each Christmas.[30] In 1979, the Fulton Fishmongers Association gave a lump sum donation of $2,400 ($5,000 in 1996 dollars) to the union, in lieu of individual contributions. The wholesalers apparently decided to overlook the illegality of such payments.

Defrauding suppliers

Wholesalers received fish from suppliers on consignment, sold it to retailers, deducted a 'commission,' and remitted the remainder to the supplier.[31] At the time the fish was delivered to the wholesaler, the supplier could not know what its ultimate payment would be because fish prices fluctuate daily. Thus, the suppliers risked being cheated.

The consignment system also made suppliers vulnerable to phantom wholesalers. Such corrupt wholesalers would order increasing amounts of seafood, eventually accepting large quantities with no intention of paying the supplier. The owner of the phantom company would then, often at the same location, establish a new wholesale business under another name and repeat the fraud. Although New York City had the authority to refuse licenses to unreliable wholesalers, it did not choose to exercise it.[32] [...]

In the late 1980s, officials estimated that suppliers lost $6 million as a result of fraud.

The unloading cartel

For decades, the Genovese crime family operated a lucrative unloading cartel at the market. Genovese soldiers ensured that no companies unaffiliated with the cartel worked at the market. In return, cartel members kicked back a portion of their revenues to the organized crime family. Throughout the 1970s, for example, the unloading companies made cash payments to Carmine Romano every Friday in the back room of a nearby Genovese social club.

The job of the unloading companies was to remove boxes of fish from the trucks and place them on the ground. This simple task required only basic equipment and unskilled labor. In the late 1980s and early 1990s approximately six unloading companies operated at the market; each one employed one 'unloading crew' or 'gang,' ranging in size from two to thirteen employees, to take the fish from the suppliers' trucks to the wholesalers' stalls. In 1992, the unloading companies had estimated

combined gross revenues of more than $2 million ($2.24 million in 1996 dollars).[33] [...]

There was no price competition among the unloading crews; to the contrary, there was a to-the-penny uniformity in the prices they charged the wholesalers: usually $1.35 per one-hundred-pound box and $0.65 per sixty-pound carton.[34] The power of the unloaders allowed them to extract supplemental charges ranging from $10 to $60 per truck. 'Jump-up' or 'man-on-truck' charges had to be paid in cash when an unloader entered the truck to unload cargo, and, often, even if the unloaders didn't enter the truck. Unloaders in other cities performed this service for the basic unloading fee.

Stealing seafood

Unloading crews and their associates had many opportunities to steal fish. Unloaders did not sign receipts for the products they handled. Moreover, there was no time to weigh shipments as they passed through the market. Stolen fish were easily diverted to mob-connected wholesalers.[35] Cosa Nostra 'skimmed' or 'tapped' money by taking a cut of seafood stolen by the unloaders. One undercover agent estimated that, as a group, wholesalers who were not mob controlled lost between two thousand and three thousand pounds of fish a night because of skimming; retailers had to purchase a 115-pound box of seafood to be sure of obtaining 90-pounds.[36] Wholesalers' annual losses added up to an estimated $1.5 million.[37]

The loading companies' parking racket

Through the loading companies, Cosa Nostra controlled parking at the market.[38] The parking areas varied in size, each operated by a different loading company. Some companies or their affiliates leased premises from the city for a nominal fee. Others simply appropriated the public streets for their private business without making any payments. The loading companies reaped lucrative profits. Circa 1990, the loading companies charged $20 a night or more for parking, depending on a variety of factors including the size of the retailer's vehicle and often the retailer's ethnicity. The loading companies reaped an estimated $5 million a year ($5.9 million in 1996 dollars) in fees from parking alone.[39] The Genovese crime family received a significant portion of this amount.

New York City's failure to regulate

In 1992, a government consultant reported that New York City received approximately $268,000 ($300,000 in 1996 dollars) annually in rent from the wholesalers in city-owned buildings, but that the annual market value of the leases was close to $3 million.[40] Politicians remained passive about this loss of potential revenue.

Conclusion

From the early twentieth century, the Fulton Fish Market served the Genovese crime family as a base of power and revenue. Businesses and individuals faced threats of violence and property damage if they did not follow the mob's dictates. The Genovese family used its influence over Local 359 to extort money through the collection of Christmas payments and union placards. Cosa Nostra established cartels of loading and unloading companies, controlled parking, and forced wholesalers to pay 'insurance' to prevent theft.

City regulation was practically nonexistent. In the 1930s, businesses at the market were required to obtain permits from the Department of Markets.[41] It was alleged that only the approval of 'Socks' Lanza, who maintained close friendships with many Tammany Hall politicians, was needed to obtain such permits.[42] Manhattan District Attorney Thomas C. T. Crain, facing removal from office in 1931, testified that he could not explain why he had been lax in investigating and prosecuting organized crime in the market.[43]

The relationship between top-ranking organized-crime figures and prominent politicians continued for decades, and no doubt had important implications for the lackluster efforts of law enforcement to crack down on mob domination of legitimate industries. While a few important mob figures were prosecuted and convicted of racketeering in the 1980s and court-appointed officials were put in place to root out corruption in the market, the overall results were unimpressive. Inaction by city officials and the inability of law enforcement agencies to weaken the Genovese crime family's lock on the market permitted racketeering to flourish. Suppliers, wholesalers, and retailers had no choice but to consider the payoffs as the cost of doing business, which they passed on to consumers through higher seafood prices. For decades, mob rule was an intractable fact of life at the Fulton Fish Market.

Participants in the Fulton Fish Market did not complain. Some observers attributed participants' silence to the fact that the costs of doing business with Cosa Nostra were passed on to consumers.[44] Mob rule had certain advantages. Cosa Nostra prevented competition in the provision of unloading, loading, and parking services. The lack of competition allowed cartel members to set prices higher than any fish market in the country, even controlling for the higher cost of living in New York City. With organized crime firmly in control of the union, labor relations remained peaceful. Other than a strike in 1987, there was no serious disruption of operations or a crisis in getting fish to restaurants and retail stores. It was not until the mid-1990s, under the Giuliani administration's organized-crime control campaign, that the city used its regulatory authority to attack organized-crime racketeering at the market.

> From J.B. Jacobs, Gotham Unbound (New York: New York University Press), 1999, pp. 33–47.

Notes

1 Frank Wohl, *Midterm Report of Administrator* (August 8, 1990), 11, pursuant to April 15, 1988, Consent Judgment in *United States* v. *Local 359*, 87 Civ. 7351 (S.D.N.Y. 1992).

2 Compare, e.g., *United States* v. *Local 359*, 705 1* Supp. 894, 899 (S.D.N.Y. 1989), with Selwyn Raab, 'Delay in Tackling Fish-Market Crime,' *New York Times*, February 17, 1991, 46.

3 Frank Wohl, *Notice of Imposition of Sanctions* (June 18, 1992), 5, pursuant to April 15, 1988, Consent Judgment in *United States* v. *Local 359*, 87 Civ. 7351 (S.D.N.Y 1992).

4 The description of market operations is based on an interview with Frank Maas, first deputy commissioner, New York City Department of Investigation, October 31, 1995.

5 *United States* v. *Romano*, 684 F.2d 1057, 1060 (2d Cit 1982).

6 See 'The Fulton Fish Market: Hearings Before the New York City Council Committee on Economic Development' (May 4, 1992).

7 See *United States* v. *Local 359*, 705 R Supp. 894,906 (S.D.N.Y. 1989).

8 Carroll, 'Combating Racketeering in the Fulton Fish Market,' 183, 192.

9 See Raab, 'Fish Market's Problems Revert to New York City'

10 *United States* v. *Romano*, 684 R2d at 1061 (2d Cit 1982).

11 John S. Martin, 'Sentencing Memorandum' (January 4, 1981), 24, following *United States* v. *Romano*, 81 Cr. 514 (S.D.N.Y 1981). In 1989, eight individuals, including a captain of the Bonanno crime family,

pled guilty to racketeering in connection with a gambling and loan-sharking ring that operated at the Fulton Fish Market. See Paul Moses, 'Guilty Pleas on Rackets Charges,' *Newsday*, December 21, 1989, 35.

12 *Danielson* v. *Local 359*,405 F. Supp. 396 (S.D.N.Y. 1975).

13 'Lanza Is Sentenced to Six Months More,' *New York Times*, March 19, 1938, 10.

14 Report of Judge Samuel Seabury to Honorable Governor Roosevelt Recommending Dismissal of Crain Charges, reprinted in *New York Times*, September 1, 1931.

15 See Carroll, 'Combating Racketeering in the Fulton Fish Market,' 185.

16 See Carroll, 'Combating Racketeering in the Fulton Fish Market,' 185.

17 See 'Crain Tells of Terrorism,' *New York Times*, April 9, 1931, 1.

18 See Martin, 'Sentencing Memorandum,' 11.

19 See 'Market Men 'Glad' to Buy Protection,' *New York Times*, January 16, 1934, 8.

20 *United States* v. *Romano*, 684 F.2d at 1060-61.

21 See James Cook, 'Fish Story,' *Forbes*, April 1982, 60.

22 *United States* v. *Romano*, 684 E2d at 1062; see also Arnold H. Lubasch, 'Organized Crime Said to Rule Fulton Fish Market,' *New York Times*, August 23, 1981, p. 46.

23 See, e.g., *United States* v. *Nunzio Leanzo*, 80 Cr. 808 (S.D.N.Y 1981) (sentencing owner of an unloading company to two years in prison for committing perjury before the grand jury).

24 *United States* v. *Romano*, 684 E2d at 1065.

25 See Arnold H. Lubasch, 'Union Heads Sentenced in Fulton Market Payoffs,' *New York Times*, February 6, 1982, 27.

26 See Martin, 'Sentencing Memorandum,' 13.

27 *United States* v. *Romano*, 684 F.2d at 1062.

28 See Martin, 'Sentencing Memorandum,' 14.

29 See *ibid*.

30 *United States* v. *Romano*, 684 F.2d at 1061.

31 See 'The Fulton Fish Market: Hearings Before the New York City Council Committee on Economic Development.'

32 See Wohl, *Midterm Report of Administrator*, 7-8.

33 See Wohl, *Notice of Imposition of Sanctions*, 6.

34 See Wohl, *Midterm Report of Administrator*, 16.

35 See Sentencing Memorandum, *United States* v. *Local 359*, 81 Cr. 514 at 24 (S.D.N.Y 1981).

36 Interview with Frank Maas.

37 See Cook, 'Fish Story,' 60.

38 See Martin, 'Sentencing Memorandum,' 25.

39 See Selwyn Raab, 'A Crackdown on Fees at Fulton Fish Market,' *New York Times*, January 11, 1987, 28.

40 See Selwyn Raab, 'To Fight Mob, Giuliani Proposes Takeover of Fulton Fish Market,' *New York Times*, February 1, 1995, A1.

41 *Russo* v. *Morgan*, 21 N.Y.S.2d 637 (1940). It was alleged that throughout the 1930s, only Joseph 'Socks' Lanza could obtain these permits. See Rebecca Rankin, *New York Advancing: A Scientific Approach to Municipal Government* (New York: Gallery Press, 1936), 282.

42 See 'Crain Tells of Terrorism.'

43 See 'Crain Denounces Accusers as Police Official Admits Racketeering City-Wide,' *New York Times*, April 14, 1931, 1.

44 See Cook, 'Fish Story,' 60.

19.3 The crime network
William J. Chambliss

There were over a thousand people in Seattle who profited directly from the rackets, bootleg whiskey, organized theft and robbery, drug traffic, abortion rings, gambling, prostitution, land transactions, arson, phony stock sales, and usury. Everyone who successfully engages in these criminal activities must share the profits with *someone* or some group of people. The more regulated the criminal activities and the more successful the participants, the more systematized the profit sharing. The entire system is simply a collection of independent operators who cooperate and compete according to their ability, their power, and their interests.

Disparate as it is, widely distributed among people in different walks of life, and changing all the time, there is nonetheless a hierarchy. Some people are more important than others. In times of crisis some people have the power to make critical decisions while others do not. Not surprisingly, those who profit the most from the rackets and who also have the power to take action are the most likely to meet and discuss problems and prospects. In Seattle the group of power-holders who controlled and set policy for the illegal business enterprises varied. Over the years the more active participants included a King County prosecutor, a Seattle city council president, an assistant chief of police, city police captains, the King County sheriff, the King County jail chief, undersheriffs, the president of the Amusement

Association of Washington (who had the only master's license for pinball machines in the county), a Seattle police major, and an official of the Teamsters Union. In addition there were persons from the business and professional community who were members of the network and who in a quiet, less conspicious way were as influential over illegal business activities as were the more visible operatives listed above. They included a leading attorney who defended network members and joined them in investments in illegal enterprises, a realtor who arranged real-estate transactions and shared investments, an officer of one of the state's leading banks, a board member of a finance company that loaned money exclusively to businesses or individuals who were either members of or under the control of the network, and various labor union officials – mostly in the Teamsters Union, but high-level officials of other labor unions were also involved from time to time.

One of the problems with determining the real power sources in an enterprise as inherently secretive and variable as a crime cartel is of course the line between active participant (or policymaker) and compliant benefactor. For example, a prosperous retail store-owner in the city often invested in and profited from illegal enterprises ranging from real-estate frauds to drug traffic. He also financed and arranged for the transportation of stolen jewelry out of the United States to Europe, where it could be recut and sold on the European market. He never set policy, never became involved in the day-to-day decisions, never allowed himself even to be consulted about the handling of a particular problem within the ongoing enterprises. Yet he knew of most of the problems and could well have been influential had he cared to make his wishes known. He preferred to remain silent. His decision, he told me, was based on the 'good old American tradition of self-preservation.' He felt that the less he was involved in 'administration' the more likely he was to remain unconnected publicly with the 'seamy side of business.' He acknowledged, however, that when a newspaper reported the death of a member of the network due to 'accidental drowning' he knew it was no accident.[...]

At one time (1963–65) it was fairly easy to identify seven people who constituted the backbone of the network. This group shifted, however, and some of the seven became less involved while some new people emerged as principals. Both composition and leadership are variable; success is determined by connections and profits. When drug trading becomes more precarious, the people involved may lose considerable influence; when cardrooms come under fire, those people whose profits or payoffs are principally in cardrooms lose their influence.

Whatever the composition, this coalition of shifting membership (but fairly constant leadership) persisted and had more to say about how the rackets were run than anyone else. It also met more or less regularly, but here too the pattern was not akin to a monthly board of directors' meeting but was more a series of meetings between key players from different walks of life. [...]

Some sense of the organized-disorganized nature of the rackets can be gleaned from a series of incidents in the mid 1960s which involved an attempt by Bill Bennett (P) to take over part of the pinball operation in the city. Bill's brother Frank was one of the prominent racketeers in town, a man generally believed to be involved in prostitution and the collection of payoffs for state officials (including the governor) as well as the police. Bill decided that he wanted a piece of the action in the pinball business. He tried at first to demand a territory but he met with resistance. Pinballs were at the time concentrated pretty much in the hands of several people. The only master license in the county was held by the Amusement Association. As president, Ben Cichy represented not only his own interests as the major pinball operator in the state, but also the interests of other pinball operators. Ben Cichy was well protected in his position. As president of the association that looked out for the pinball interests, he met regularly with and allegedly paid substantial sums of money to politicians, to Frank Bennett (P), and to members of the police department. In addition, the Amusement Association collected from all pinball operators a monthly fee that was used to ply state and local politicians with liquor, parties, and women for favors, not the least of which were large campaign contributions to politicians who worked in the interests of pinball owners. Thus Bill Bennett was taking on some formidable opponents when he tried to muscle into the pinball business. On the other hand, Bill and his brother Frank were well connected in political and business circles. Among others, Frank was closely allied with politicians who were the political and personal enemies of the county prosecutor and might well have been favorably disposed toward an attempt to undermine part of his political base.

When Bill's efforts to gain part of the pinball operation were turned down by Cichy and the other owners, he filed what is referred to as an 'underworld anti-trust suit.' He and some of his men began throwing Molotov cocktails through the windows of places containing Cichy's machines. Some restaurant owners were roughed up. This caused some attention in the press, so people were getting nervous. To calm things down, the pinball operators offered to let Bill in if he would agree to pay them twenty thousand dollars for the loss of their territory plus a fee of two dollars a month for each machine over and above the fifty cents per machine that went to the Amusement Association for lobbying.

The agreement reached by the other pinball operators was, however, not satisfactory to the chief of police, who saw Bill as a 'hoodlum.' This was one of the few occasions when the chief put his foot down. An informant in the police department said that 'in all likelihood' the chief vetoed the agreement as a result of support and instructions from the county prosecutor. Because of the trouble Bill had caused, the chief insisted that he leave the state, which he did.

Several features of this event are important. First, it underlines the competition between different persons acting primarily as individuals out to increase the size of their business and their profits. It also illustrates, however, that when the entire enterprise is threatened, it is possible for a coalition of the more powerful members of the rackets to force less powerful members to acquiesce. The incident also indicates an important element in the way any network protects itself. The two-fifty a month which Bill would have to pay for each machine was divided between protection (two dollars a month) and lobbying (fifty cents a month). The one activity is presumably criminal (by statute), the other legal.

Was this crime network, then, the local Mafia?

I talked with many people about the possibility that this network was a local branch of the Mafia. A professional thief who had also worked in the rackets (gambling, prostitution, drugs, etc.) told me, 'You can forget that Mafia stuff. We are Hoosiers out here. There is no organized crime like they have back east, like in Kansas City and Cleveland. We're too independent out here.'

This same feeling was expressed time and again by people at all levels. Virtually everyone in a position to know anything about the rackets in Seattle echoed these sentiments: 'Every time you check the Congressional Record and you see the FBI diagramming the Mafia families in San Francisco, you can tell them to shove it up their ass, because you can't diagram this. If you do diagram it, you can't read your diagram when you're done. It's all squiggly lines: the chain of command and who's in charge of any operation and who's entitled to what cut of the graft, it's all very changeable.' [...]

The people who are getting wealthy from the rackets are not the cafe, tavern, or cardroom owners. The people who are getting wealthy are the businessmen with capital to invest in an expanding, high-profit business, politicians and law-enforcement officers who can convert political or police power into wealth. It is an interesting, fascinating illustration of the two-faced nature of the adage that wealth is power. That is certainly true, but the other side is equally true: power makes wealth as well.

The network members who met regularly were more or less elected representatives of the business, political, and law-enforcement groups that profited most from the rackets. [...]

One feature of criminality that is almost always overlooked is the extent to which businessmen who operate a presumably legitimate and wholly legal enterprise are involved either overtly or covertly in criminal activities. More often than is ever acknowledged by law enforcers or investigators, businessmen are the financiers behind criminal operations. In Seattle one of the city's leading jewelers served simultaneously as a financier for large drug transactions and as a fence for stolen jewelry. Often businessmen are co-opted by business and friendship ties to members of the network. A vice-president of one of the city's leading banks was a close associate of the county prosecutor, lunched with him, contributed his personal endorsement to the prosecutor's political campaigns, invested in things the prosecutor recommended, supplied links to other businessmen for the prosecutor, arranged loans, and so forth. Both the vice-president of the bank and a jeweler were key members of the network. Their money financed criminal activities and they reaped huge profits from them.

Newsmen on the city's leading newspapers were also implicated. In one case it was principally through receiving gifts from various members of the network. There were also rumors that an editor received a monthly income from the network. This seems unlikely, for the editor was not only co-opted by friendship and small favors, but the newspaper was opposed to exposing any graft or corruption lest the city reassess the value of the newspaper's property. A local politician and one-time candidate for sheriff possessed information linking an editor of one of the newspapers with a national wire service that reported racing results. The police were also aware of these links. This information was never made public, perhaps because the keepers of the news are in the end the safest possible mediums for conducting illegal business activities.

There is clearly no 'godfather' in the crime network, no single man or group of men whose word is law and who control all the various levels and kinds of criminal activities. There is, nonetheless, a coalition of businessmen, politicians, law enforcers and racketeers (see diagram) who have a greater interest in the rackets than anyone else, who stand to lose the most if the operation is exposed, and who also have the power to do something when it is called for. These men do not have unlimited power, to be sure, and they must assess their power in each incident to see what is the best strategy to follow. [...]

At the root of the crime network's operation was the money that got shuffled from the people who operated the rackets – the bookie, the numbers man, the whorehouse operator, the drug trafficker, the cardroom manager, tavern owner, or pinball operator – to the politicians, law enforcers, and businessmen who protected the network and its enterprises.

The day-to-day decisions might have rested in the hands of seven, nine, or ten men who consulted regularly with the other principals in the network. But for such a widespread and profitable system to persist, a set of relations far more extensive than this and beyond mere payoffs had to develop, especially since the task of maintaining control over the various enterprises and the people involved was a task of major importance to everyone.

> *From W. Chambliss*, On the Take *(Bloomington: Indiana University Press)*, *1988, pp. 61–80.*

Table 19.3.1 Seattle's crime network

Financiers

Jewelers		Attorneys
Realtors		Businessmen
Contractors		Industrialists
	Bankers	

Organizers

Businessmen	**Politicians**	**Law-Enforcement Officers**
Restaurant Owners	City Councilmen	Chief of Police
Cardroom Owners	Mayors	Assistant Chief of Police
Pinball Machine License Holders	Governors	Sheriff
Bingo Parlor Owners	State Legislators	Undersheriff
Cabaret and Hotel Owners	Board of Supervisors Members	County Prosecutor
Club Owners	Licensing Bureau Chief	Assistant Prosecutor
Receivers of Stolen Property		Patrol Division Commanders
Pawnshop Owners		Vice Squad Commanders
		Narcotics Officers
		Patrolmen
		Police Lieutenants, Captains, and Sergeants

Racketeers

| Gamblers | Pimps | Prostitutes | Drug Distributors | Usurers | Bookmakers |

19.4 The profession of violence: the Krays
John Pearson

There had never been a pair of criminal twins like the Krays before, and only in recent years has the relationship between identical twins been understood. It seems indisputable that Reggie Kray could have built a powerful defence along the lines of diminished responsibility, had he chosen to. But this would have meant betraying Ronnie and denouncing him as his evil genius. It would also have meant the end of Ronnie's world, the destruction of the twins and of the violent dream that had sustained them both since childhood.

Gratefully the court was spared the task of settling responsibility for crimes committed when one disordered mind can dominate two separate bodies. Whatever may have been the truth, the twins were judged as separate and responsible individuals. This was what everybody wanted, themselves included. And it was as separate and responsible murderers that they were sentenced to life imprisonment, 'which I would recommend should not be less than thirty years', by Mr Justice Melford Stevenson on 8 March 1969. The twins were thirty-four. Their active life was over. [...]

But it would be wrong to allow the Kray twins to be forgotten. Their trial was concerned with cutting them down to size and left a picture of them both as blundering murderers duly defeated by the police. In fact they were more dangerous than this. More disturbing than the gruesome revelations from the witness-box was something that the prosecution and the court tended to overlook – the actual scale of their success. The Kray twins are important not as cheap murderers, but as professionals of violence, and it is their career and not their downfall that is significant.

The odds against their rise appear to have been enormous. They lacked finesse and had no education and no knowledge of the world. They were emotionally unstable, and most criminologists would probably dismiss them as anachronisms – the last of the old-style cockney villains acting out half-baked fantasies of Al Capone's Chicago. Yet despite this they came close to building a true empire of crime in Britain – and did it with extraordinary ease.

It is this ease that is disturbing. Any society that lets two cockney villains get away with what the Kray twins did must be quite frighteningly vulnerable and, if nothing else, their rise to power shows just how fragile the whole skin of order is in Britain. All they really did was bring the threat of violence into areas that had previously been relatively free from it – the fringes of big business, society and politics, the world of the suburban clubs and of the new legalized West End gambling. They had no startling techniques, and violence apart their one unerring instinct was for corruption. They could smell out the vulnerable as a pig smells truffles, and the corrupt became their victims. The violent will always feed on the corrupt, and it was not surprising that the twins found greater possibilities in society at large than in the poverty of Bethnal Green.

The use the Kray twins made of these new possibilities is something of an object lesson in what violence can achieve in Britain. They used it to create an area of freedom from the law. In different quarters it was the twins' name, not the law's, that kept the peace. People knew that they had more to lose from the twins' enmity than they would ever gain from the law's protection. The twins' power was a challenge to the authority of the State and for a long time it appeared as if the State were powerless against them. For they seemed to have stumbled on the formula for an independent, self-perpetuating criminal power in Britain.

Part of their secret was size, for with crime as with business, the profits increase with the scale of the operation. The twins were adroit users of bribery, blackmail and connections and could afford good lawyers and advisers and pay well for information. They manipulated the establishment; and used politicians, even to the extent of having questions asked on their behalf in Parliament. More important, they could always stay behind the scenes, organizing other men to do their bidding and ensuring that they themselves were never compromised. One of the lessons of the twins' career is the ease with which they built themselves a position of immunity. Paradoxically, the fact they were so widely known as organizing gangsters proved an advantage. It added to their reputation, made people fear them more and even brought them a status as celebrities. Journalists and public figures could be used, certain policemen had their price, trials could be fixed and prisons infiltrated.

The potentiality of power like this was vast. Protection rackets formed the largest single source of income, but on top of them the twins easily controlled a network of associated crime, part of which they initiated and from all of which they took their toll. They were already well into large-scale fraud, crooked share deals, organized intimidation and blackmail, and were thinking of extending to drugs, deals with foreign criminal networks and prostitution. Their contacts with the American Mafia in London showed what could be done. Control was easy to enforce through dele-gated violence. Profits would have been enormous and they would have found no difficulty investing overseas and building up legitimate businesses abroad. With power like this the twins could easily have become invulnerable.

That they did not was due entirely to their personal deficiencies. What limited them was not the law but their incompetence and instability. As criminals their major defect was lack of serious-ness. They proved incapable of exploiting the power they created and in the end became self-indulgent and erratic, soon bored and often surprisingly timid. Society was lucky; the twins destroyed themselves. Another time we may not be so fortunate.

> *From J. Pearson,* The Profession of Violence *(London: Panther), 1973, pp. 312–315.*

19.5 Perspectives on 'organised crime'
Michael Levi

General introduction

It has become commonplace to observe that the term 'organised crime' is frequently used but diffi-cult to define. It is generally applied to describe a group of people who act together on a long-term basis to commit crimes for gain though, as A. K. Cohen (1977) observed, it is important to separate out the distinction between structures of *associa-tion* and structures of *activity*. Maltz (1976) proposed that 'organised crime' was identifiable by means of a list of distinguishing features, of which four were considered essential characteristics: vio-lence, corruption, continuity, and variety in types of crime engaged in. However, smart people who avoid using violence and trade very competently and profitably in only one product – for example, ecstasy or cannabis production – thus cannot be described as organised criminals, which would doubtless please them if they thereby received less police attention and/or lighter sentences. Neither could professional full-time fraudsters (as discussed in the later article) be 'organised criminals'. In other words, one could sustain some distinction between people who make affluent livelihoods from crime – professional criminals – and those who do so according to Maltzist criteria – organ-ised criminals. But it is far from certain whether this would satisfy what I regard as the true *social* definition of 'organised criminals': a set of people whom the police and other agencies of the State, regard or wish us to regard as 'really dangerous' to its essential integrity. The notion of organised crime as a *continuing criminal enterprise* is embodied in the popularly accepted (in Europe) definition employed by the German Federal police, the *BundesKriminalAmt*.

> Organised crime is the planned violation of the law for profit or to acquire power, which offences are each, or together, of a major significance, and are carried out by more than two participants who co-operate within a division of labour for a long or undetermined time span using
> a commercial or commercial-like structures, or
> b violence or other means of intimidation, or
> c influence on politics, media, public adminis-tration, justice and the legitimate economy.

This BKA definition provides a baseline to deter-mine whether a criminal group ranks as 'organised crime'. Of course, there are shortcomings. The 'def-inition' does not delineate what counts as 'major importance', nor does it differentiate between vari-ous categories of organised crime. 'Organised crime' can mean anything from major Italian syndicates to three very menacing burglars and a window cleaning business who differentiate by having one as look-out, another as burglar and a third as money-launderer, and who sue every newspaper who suggests that their business is disreputable! Irony apart, this illustrates the difficulty that one has in defining the concept in a rigorous way, and the more sophisticated – who are well represented in this issue of the journal – have shifted towards the term 'enterprise crime', even though (or because) this shifts the focus away from the Red Menace or other alien groups.

But whatever the conceptual disadvantages – which did not occupy the UK Home Affairs Committee (1995) long, though the more prudent parliamentary draughtspeople preferred the perhaps even more flexible term 'serious crime' when drafting the Security Service Bill 1996 – one must appreciate that the term 'organised crime' has an emotional kick which makes it easier to get resources and powers, and sociologists of crime control ought to study this labelling process in its own right. Thus, the 'threat of organised crime' and 'the invasion of the Russian Mafia' were used to persuade British politicians and others to set up the National Criminal Intelligence Service and the National Crime Squad, described by the media (but denied by the Home Secretary) as being a 'British FBI', assisted by the Security Services (MI5) and the Secret Intelligence Services (MI6), which seek a social defence role after the collapse of the Soviet Union: the latter was publicly praised by the UK Foreign Secretary in April 1998 for its contribution to the fight against organised crime (though, not surprisingly, no details were released). In the wider European arena, there has been a flurry of activity in the European Union and the Council of Europe, accelerating since the 1996 EU Dublin Summit (itself stimulated by the Irish government's response to the high-profile contract killing of crime journalist Veronica Guerin), with high-level multi-disciplinary groups seeking areas of co-operation, implementing a High-Level Action Plan and finally getting Europol off the ground by 1999. Both the EU and the Council of Europe have extended their activities into EU applicant countries and others, training them in anti-laundering implementation and ensuring that legislation and some machinery for putting it into effect is in place before accession to the EU. Under EU review as I write are measures to criminalise membership of criminal organisations – influenced by the Italian legislation but harder to apply in less regimented settings – and tough action against criminal offshore finance centres. In the still wider international arena, the Financial Action Task Force (started only in 1989 by the G-7 – now G-8, including Russia – elite industrial countries) and the UN have vied for activism and prestige in anti-laundering and crime prevention, especially in the drugs issue but later on all-crime anti-laundering measures, as the boundaries between proceeds of different types of crime become increasingly blurred. The arrival in the top UN Drug Control and Crime Prevention post of Pino Arlacchi, a sociologist-turned-politician Mafia expert, placed organised crime at the top of the 1998 UN criminological agenda, with a rapidly devised draft UN Convention on the subject. This great political confluence has led to international pressure to harmonise the fight against organised crime, even if people do not always have a clear understanding of what 'it' is.

However, the nature of 'organised crime' remains deeply contested terrain, at least in academic circles and in those countries who are more worried about loss of independence and civil liberties than they are about subservience to organised crime. The role of intelligence agencies – regarding which the CIA is the best documented – in covert military operations overseas, especially in support of anti-communist military regimes or guerrilla movements, makes 'State-Organised Crime' often a more appropriate term. By contrast, the term 'organised crime' tends to focus us downwards towards the threat posed by some (usually alien) group of low-lifes, and one can see this in the work of the journalist Claire Sterling (1991, 1994), who appeared merely to reflect the ideological perspectives of US enforcement agencies. However, a note of caution. To explain the bureaucratic and ideological functions of the term 'organised crime' does not by itself demonstrate that the term is inappropriate, nor does it 'prove' that there are no long-term groups of criminals who commit serious offences or even begin to constitute the State. The epistemological difficulties are what sort of evidence one uses to account for the structuring of criminal behaviour; the range of criminal behaviours that come under the umbrella of any group of criminals; how far up the political chain one reaches in one's delineation of who are organised criminals (in Colombia and Mexico, for example); and how valid is the 'evidence' upon which one relies.

The nature of organised crime and 'its' markets

In north-western Europe, organised crime as a criminal economy is essentially a *cross-border* crime-trade (Van Duyne 1993, 1996). Despite the impact of modern horticulture on growing cannabis in the inclement weather of the UK, or of synthesising drugs – making importation from outside Europe or even the UK unnecessary – some element of cross-border trade is inevitable, even if it is only the importation of seeds and precursor chemicals and, perhaps, as a stage in the laundering of proceeds of crime.

The Italian (or rather, American-Italian) model has embedded itself in popular culture, mediated through Hollywood. Yet rather than being line-managerial, along the Cressey (1969) /Godfather model, most social scientists regard organised crime as less total in its ambit and as part of patron/client relationships. Thus, because of their reputation for violence and discipline, *Mafiosi* and other 'gangsters' play a key role in criminal dispute-settlement in the US and Italy. Indeed, Reuter (1983 and subsequently) has suggested that the principal function of the Mafia is in contract enforcement, and that one should separate out the people and groups involved in the commission of crime from those involved in dispute settlement (for which role high information is required). Similarly Gambetta (1994), in his book on the Sicilian Mafia, has suggested that the role of Mafia comes into play because of the absence of trust in underworld relationships.

Nowadays, there is hardly an Italian name in the FBI 'most wanted' list of targets. Cuban refugees, Colombians and, increasingly, Mexicans have come to dominate the distribution of narcotics in the Southern states, and other ethnic groups – Puerto-Rican, Japanese, and Chinese (particularly Fukinese) – as well as white motor-cycle gangs, also are involved in organised crime in the US. In the future, such groups will make less use than previously of Italian/ American Mafia dispute resolution services. Street-level criminals are normally independent of major crime syndicates. As Block and Chambliss (1981) suggest, rather than being viewed as an alien group of outsiders coming in and perverting society, organised crime in America is best viewed as a set of shifting coalitions between groups of gangsters, business people, politicians, and union leaders, normally local or regional in scope. Many of these people have legitimate jobs and sources of income. Similar

observations would apply in some Third World countries such as Mexico (*Geopolitical Drug Dispatch*, May 1998), where a small elite dominate the economy and political system and share favours out among themselves. Similarly, the privatisation of the economy has extended their opportunities in many former Communist countries, as well as providing easy avenues for money-laundering where the authorities are not too inquisitive about the source of the funds.

Among advanced industrial nations, the closest similarities to this 'political coalition' organisational model occur in Australia, where extensive narcotics, cargo theft, and labour racketeering rings have been discovered, and in Japan, where gangs such as Yakuza specialise in vice and extortion, including extortion on the part of separate groups of Sokaiya, by threatening embarrassment to large corporations at their Annual General Meetings. Both of these illustrations, however, also suggest that the coalition – in which campaign funds also play an important role – is not entirely by consent: business people would rather not pay the blackmail if they felt they had any realistic alternative, In Britain, by contrast, organised crime groups have not developed in this way, partly because of a more conservative social and political system but principally because the supply and consumption of alcohol, the opiates, gambling, and prostitution remain legal but partly regulated. This reduces the profitability of supplying them criminally. A host of ethnic groups (though see Stelfox's sceptical comments) are important in the supply of drugs to and via Britain. But except for narcotics importers and wholesalers, cargo thieves who work at airports, and local vice, protection, and pornography syndicates, British organised criminals tend to be relatively short-term groups drawn together for specific projects such as fraud and armed robbery, from a pool of long-term professional criminals on a within-force or regional basis (see McIntosh (1975) and Mack and Kerner (1975), for some early discussions along these lines).

Instead of such uncreative comparisons with the US, it may be better to look at organised crime in Europe from its own set of economic and social landscapes in which organised crime *trade* takes place. As Van Duyne (1996) observes, Europe has a large diversity of economies, extensive economic regulations, many loosely controlled borders to cross, and relatively small jurisdictions. This means that the largest illegal profits for European crime entrepreneurs are to be gained in the drug market and in the area of organised business crime. If the normal (licit) business nucleus in Southern Italy. Turkey or Pakistan is the (extended) family (Ianni and Reuss-Ianni 1972), in Northern Europe such socio-economic family units are much rarer and social bonds more restricted, for example to people bound by loyalties of place (Hobbs, this issue), though the very fracturing of the social fabric that has led to so much concern about social exclusion also paradoxically may inhibit *criminal* solidarity. The exceptions are the crime-enterprises of minorities in Europe whose businesses are family matters, which should not be equated with impersonal 'syndicates' (Ianni 1974).

No profits can be made if potential customers are not aware of the existence of the unlawful service, and this generally means that in the long run, the police will come to know about it too. To ensure freedom from the law, the criminals must therefore subvert the police and/or the courts, and this is a major reason for concern about the impact of organised crime. (Though in reality, it is a side-effect of the prohibition of goods and services in popular demand.) In the Italian case – though it is always difficult to know who controls whom – there are grounds for supposing that the State itself has in some sense been in league with organised crime groups: as the trial of former Prime Minister Giulio Andreotti for Mafia offences, the jailing (*in absentia*) of former PM Bettino Craxi for similar offences, and the conviction of recent PM Silvio Berlusconi for tax evasion and bribery might suggest. But arguably, whatever the patron-client relationships and the peculiar Italian 'professional politicians' that permeate Italian society (della Porta and Pizzorno 1996), few of these things could be done without the active complicity of US foreign policy, which consistently has been more concerned about defeating communism than about organised crime. It seems entirely plausible that without the collapse of Communism, the US would have continued to support the traditional Christian Democrat/Mafia coalition in Italy, and the *tangentopoli* scandal might never have developed in the way that it did (see Nelken 1996; della Porta and Pizzorno 1996).

Organised crime in Britain

Perceptive *Guardian* crime correspondent Duncan Campbell (1990, p. 1) starts one of his books on the changing face of professional crime by pointing to the shift in 25 years of two of the Great Train Robbers 'from teams of organised criminals in overalls grabbing large bundles of Bank of England notes to quiet, besuited drug-dealers selling white powders from Latin America'. However, in principle, this could just as easily be a function of their age: they were simply too old to go around threatening people with shotguns. According to Campbell, the age of the gangster/family firm was replaced by the age of the robber, as cash in transit became the strange object of desire, and, allegedly with some assistance from the Metropolitan Police, robbers were relatively free from arrest. However, the advent of supergrasses and reduction in corruption ended this in the early 1970s. As the Age of the Robber ended, the Age of the Dealer began. Yet though there is much in this as a general trend, we should not be seduced by this periodisation. There were twice as many robberies in the mid-1990s as in the mid-1980s, and considerably more than during the Age of the Robber. Although one might expect that the Age of the Fraudster represents the apotheosis of British organised crime, representing high profits and relatively low police interest and sentences, there appear to be cultural and skill barriers to entry into many areas of fraud which have stopped this transformation. Several armed robbers turned to long-firm (bankruptcy) frauds, credit card fraud, social security fraud, and even to fraud against the European Union – either alongside or subsequent to drug dealing – but this move into the moderately upmarket areas of fraud has hardly dented those other types of crime.

The haphazard development of criminological research in different parts of Europe means that our understanding of the way in which criminals organise themselves is very patchy. There is always a tendency to counterpoint North European forms of criminal organisation against the 'crime corporation' – like structures supposedly existing in North America and Southern Italy. British and German work from the 1970s was obsessed by distancing North European crime from American organised crime (Mack and Kerner 1975), implying that if crime is not syndicated (and supported by widespread police corruption), it cannot be 'organised'. McIntosh (1975) more usefully distinguishes methods of organising crime in terms of the technological and policing barriers the particular crime confronts: where prevention precautions are high, organisation shifts from routinised *craft* groups – pickpockets, and even safe-crackers – to looser, perhaps even one-off, alliances between *project* criminals.

My interview-based study of bankruptcy fraudsters found substantial variations in the organisation of that form of crime during the 1960s and 1970s, but since the 16th century, fraudsters in particular have found cross-border crime attractive because it creates problems of legal jurisdiction, investigative cost, and practical interest by police, prosecutors, and even creditors themselves (Levi 1981). European Union harmonisation does not itself make any difference to this, except: (i) in providing new pretexts or 'story lines' for fraudsters to use to get credit or investment, and (ii) inasmuch as it changes the structures of control, for example, reducing customs paperwork makes VAT evasion easier, or the UK's ratification of the European Convention on Mutual Assistance makes co-operation and conviction easier (see Passas and Nelken 1993).

The lack of a research base on patterns of criminal relationships in most European countries – including, regrettably, the UK – means that we have little information about how domestic criminals meet and decide what to do, let alone how and to what effect/lack of effect Euro-criminals meet. Major offenders do not advertise their services in the media, and apart from common holidays in Spain, marinas, and casinos, such contacts – mediated no doubt by language difficulties which British criminals may experience in more acute form than most – may often be tentative, hedged around with the problem of negotiating trust in an ambience in which betrayal (perhaps by an undercover agent, especially an American or British one) can have very serious consequence not just for freedom but for retention of proceeds of crime. Most plausible is the notion that Euro-criminals are either crime entrepreneurs who already exploit international trade for the purposes of fraud and/or smuggling, or money-launderers who put their clients in touch with each other. Beyond that, in the area of serious crime for gain, there is only speculation or the 'annual reports' compiled for the EU and the Council of Europe, largely on the basis of official police and intelligence sources. More recently, Ruggiero (1996) has argued that both corporate and organised crime can be understood as variations on the same theme.

The control of organised crime in the UK

There are two dimensions of shifts in approach to the control of organised crime in the UK. The first is substantive legislation, relating especially to money-laundering and proceeds of crime legislation (see Gold and Levi 1994: Levi and Osofsky 1995). Essentially, the unpopularity of bankers and of drugs traffickers has enabled the State to regulate certain areas of activity that otherwise might have been very difficult, and in this sense, the demonology of 'organised crime' has been very 'useful'. The second includes: (i) the more commonly understood area of 'policing powers', including the powers not only of the police but also of the security services and corporate crime investigation bodies such as the Department of Trade and Industry and the Serious Fraud Office: and (ii) the real resources devoted to controlling 'organised crime'. There is no space to discuss these in detail here, but despite some inhibiting effect from the European Court of Human Rights, the exchange of intelligence internationally and the depth of proactive surveillance – with the UK at the permissive extreme and Germany, because of its federal structure and data protection laws, at the other – have transformed the potential for intelligence-led policing (and disruption) of organised crime activity. However, apart from questions of demand for illegal goods and services, one factor acting as a brake upon this Panopticon is limited resources. National squads have to compete with a decentralised policing system which, at least in this respect, is well motivated and organised to resist the substantial 'top slicing' of their budgets to make room for measures against 'organised crime' about whose existence, rightly or wrongly, many senior police officers are deeply sceptical. The historic tension between the local and the central has bedevilled policing since its inception in England and Wales. During the 19th century, for example, it was commonplace for the resistance of the towns and boroughs to the establishment of modern police forces to be viewed by the Home Office as benighted parochialism, if not corruption. Many senior officers in police forces enjoy their feelings of autonomy from centralised control (and their prestige as chief officers of their 'patch'), and, whatever the merely ceremonial aspects may be of local police accountability in the 1990s, these interests promote resistance towards the concept of a 'British FBI' (usually displaying ignorance of that organisation's limited role even in the US Federal system, let alone State and local police forces), and a fortiori – given tabloid press Europhobia – a continental European force on French lines. It should not be forgotten that the 'bad example' of French centralisation under Napoleon was used as an argument against establishing a national or even local police force in England and Wales during the early and mid-19th centuries.

One of the consequences of this is that, though not quite to the same degree as in the 19th century, centralisers of the police have to approach their task with caution, addressing questions of ideology as well as of technical efficiency. Thus, although there has been frequent comment by detectives I have interviewed in the Metropolitan and other forces over the past 20 years to the effect that it is madness not to have a national force (particularly, as in fraud, when even routine investigations take them all over the country), this found few overt echoes at senior officer level. With the birth of 'organised crime' as a social problem, the time for such moves seemed propitious, and a crucial propellant was the report of the Home Affairs Committee (1995) on *Organised Crime*. Cynics may suggest that the proposers of a national force (and the Security Services, who arguably may need such an entity with whom to work) have simply invented the problem, but there is a difference between opportunism and invention. One could characterise much of the debate about how much organised crime there is 'in' the UK – and this is a conceptually important issue, for 'affecting the UK' might be a better way of looking at it – as being between 'believers' who see a risk (whether short or long term) and want to prepare our system to meet it and the 'unbelievers', who see simply a plot to undermine their local or regional autonomy by a Southern English clique of the National Criminal Intelligence Service (NCIS), City of London Commissioner and Metropolitan Police Assistant Commissioner (Special Operations), plus the Security Services. Thus, by analogy with the functional effects of Cressey (1969) in the US, the construction of 'the nature of the problem' is crucial to what one does about it. Though contrariwise, as with serial killings and rapes, the mode of organising knowledge has a key effect on whether one actually picks up patterns that 'objectively are there'.

The former Home Secretary Michael Howard observed (lunchtime BBC News, 2 July 1996):

> Organised Crime is a multi-million pound industry. The new National Crime Squad will be targeting drugs traffickers and other serious professional criminals who threaten the integrity of our financial system by fraud and money-laundering. We are not establishing a British equivalent of the FBI. There will be no federal crimes. Second, no direct recruitment: police officers will continue to be seconded from their local police forces. All crimes will still be reported locally. Tripartite accountability arrangements will remain.

The Liberal Democrats had great reservations about the proposals, and Labour, at least in opposition, wanted the same accountability authority for both NCIS and NCS, while agreeing that everything possible should be done about the menace of organised crime. So the future remains uncertain. It depends partly upon what resources the Security Services and the Secret Intelligence Service actually have available for this task (and how many 'problems' are caused in other areas, such as Northern Ireland), and how far any beefing up of the value of NCIS can achieve legitimacy in the eyes of operational police officers, in the internecine quarrels that are as prevalent among anti-organised crime agencies as they are elsewhere in the criminal justice system and academia. To this extent, the fears of many on the liberal left about the totalitarian dangers posed by the Organised Crime-fighting State are misconceived. On the other hand, these fights among organised crimefighters over 'rep' and 'turf' constitute a cost in terms of effectiveness for those who believe that the real enemy is the mixed set of crime entrepreneurs who are sometimes collected up under the label of 'organised crime'.

From M. Levi, 'Perspectives on 'organised crime': an overview', The Howard Journal, 1998, 37(4): 335–345.

References

Block, A. and Chambliss, W. (1981) *Organizing Crime*, New York: Elsevier.

Campbell, D. (1990) *That was Business, This is Personal*, London: Secker and Warburg.

Cohen, A.K. (1997) 'The concept of criminal organisation', *British Journal of Criminology*, 17, 97–111.

Cressey, D.R. (1969) *Theft of the Nation: The Structure and Operations of Organized Crime in America*, New York: Harper and Row.

della Porta, D. and Pizzorno, A. (1996) 'The business politicians: reflections from a study of political corruption', in: M. Levi and D. Nelken (Eds.). *The*

Corruption of Politics and the Politics of Corruption, Oxford: Blackwells (also in *Journal of Law and Society*, 23, 73–94).

Gambetta, D. (1994) *The Sicilian Mafia*, Cambridge, Mass: Harvard UP.

Gold, M. and Levi, M. (1994) *Money-Laundering in the UK: An Appraisal of Suspicion-Based Reporting*, London: The Police Foundation.

Home Affairs Committee (1995) *Organised Crime*, Report HC 18–1, London: HMSO.

Ianni, F.A. (1974) Authority, power and respect: the interplay of control systems in an organised crime 'family'', in: S. Rottenberg (Ed.), *The Economics of Crime and Punishment*, Washington DC: American Enterprise Institute for Public Policy Research,

Ianni, F.A. and Reuss-Ianni, E. (1972) *A Family Business: Kinship and Social Control in Organised Crime*, London: Routledge and Kegan Paul.

Levi, M. (1981) *The Phantom Capitalists: The Organisation and Control of Long-Firm Fraud*, Aldershot: Gower.

Levi, M. and Osofsky. L. (1995) *Investigating, Seizing and Confiscating the Proceeds of Crime* (Police Research Group Paper 61), London: Home Office.

McIntosh, M. (1975) *The Organisation of Crime*, London: Macmillan.

Mack, J. and Kerner, H. (1975) *The Crime Industry*, Lexington: Saxon House.

Maltz, M.D. (1976) 'On defining organised crime: the development of a definition and a typology', *Crime and Delinquency*, 22, 338–46.

Nelken, D. (1996) 'The judges and political corruption in Italy', in: M. Levi and D. Nelken (Eds.), *The Corruption of Politics and the Politics of Corruption*, Oxford: Blackwells (also in *Journal of Law and Society*, 23, 95–112).

Passas, N. and Nelken, D. (1993) 'The thin line between legitimate and criminal enterprises: subsidy frauds in the European Community', *Crime, Law and Social Change*, 3, 223–44.

Reuter, P. (1983) *Disorganized Crime: Illegal Markets and the Mafia*, Cambridge, Mass: MIT Press.

Ruggiero, V. (1996) *Organised and Corporate Crime in Europe*, Aldershot: Dartmouth.

Sterling, C. (1991) *The Mafia*, London: Grafton.

Sterling, C. (1994) *Crime without Frontiers*, London: Warner.

van Duyne, P. (1993) 'Organised crime and business-crime enterprises in the Netherlands', *Crime, Law and Social Change*, 19, 103–42.

van Duyne, P. (1996) 'The phantom and threat of organised crime.' *Crime, Law and Social Change*, 24, 341–77.

20

Violent and property crime

20.1 The social organization of burglary
Neal Shover   464

20.2 American lethal violence
Franklin E. Zimring and Gordon Hawkins   470

**20.3 Modernization, self-control
and lethal violence**
Manuel Eisner   476

**20.4 Racial harassment and the process
of victimization**
Benjamin Bowling   481

Introduction

KEY CONCEPTS civilizing process; cross-national comparisons; external social organization; fence; 'good burglar'; hate crime; internal social organization; levels and rates; racial harassment

The four readings in this chapter look at a range of studies of property and violent crime, covering both the present day as well as, in one case, a historical approach. In earlier chapters (chapters 1 and 4 in particular) when we discussed what we mean by the term 'crime', and how it is portrayed and represented by the mass media, we noted how fickle and easily misrepresented a notion it is. It is all the more vital, therefore, that one thinks carefully about how such crimes are understood, how we know how much there is of particular types of crime, and what this has to tell us about our society compared with others and compared with earlier eras.

In the first excerpt, Neil Shover **(Reading 20.1)** examines what he refers to as the 'internal' and 'external' organization of burglary. His work is based largely on interviews with convicted burglars and offers an interesting insight both about organization and method but also about the men's moral evaluation of themselves and their activities. Skilled burglary, Shover argues, is by necessity 'a social enterprise'. It involves lots of other people and cannot successfully operate without them. What he describes is the more or less complex series of networks – which will frequently include those in legitimate occupations/professions – that are required for the burglar to make his living. Though much of what he reports appears to be long-standing, his respondents end with a rather pessimistic sense that times are changing and that the old certainties no longer hold.

The other three readings all concern different aspects of violent crime. The first, by Franklin Zimring and Gordon Hawkins **(Reading 20.2)**, looks at lethal violence in the United States. The US has a reputation for high levels of violent crime. In the book from which this excerpt is drawn Zimring and Hawkins ask whether this reputation is deserved. Their answer is yes, but only in part. In fact, in relation to the less serious forms of violent crime America doesn't look all that different from other developed nations. It is the most serious forms, and lethal violence in particular, that really makes it stand out. Like all forms of crime, violence is not evenly distributed across the population (whether we are talking about victims or offenders) and Zimring and Hawkins go on to explore the demography of homicide (who kills and who gets killed).

Cross-national comparisons are one way of making some assessment of our society and its crime characteristics. Another method is to look historically and see how things have changed. However, as Manuel Eisner **(Reading 20.3)** shows, this is far from straightforward. Data are scarce, difficult to interpret and problematic to compare. Nevertheless, in an extraordinary article he looks at a period of several centuries (the excerpt covers England only, but the original article looked at other European countries also) and is able to provide a convincing argument that there is a fairly clear trend in violence that can be identified. Of course, one is then left with the major headache of trying to explain such a trend and, to do so, Eisner turns to the theory of the 'civilizing process' associated with Norbert Elias.

The final excerpt, by Ben Bowling **(Reading 20.4)**, considers the issue of racial harassment and, more particularly, how we assess levels of victimization. He begins, however, by looking at the emergence of racial violence as a social problem – that is to say, how and when it started to become treated as a serious problem worthy of discussion, legislation and a formal policing response. This is another area in which you will get a clear picture of how the process of labelling something a 'crime' can have a significant impact. Bowling argues that not only has racial violence generally not been recognised by criminal justice agencies but that it is generally systematically under-recorded even in our more sophisticated surveys such as the British Crime Survey. This, he says, has significant implications for criminal justice and for social policy.

Questions for discussion

1. What does Shover mean by the terms 'internal' and 'external social organization' in relation to burglary?

2. What is a 'good burglar' or 'good thief'?

3. What are some of the difficulties in making international comparisons in relation to levels of violence within particular societies?

4. Describe some of the main demographic trends in American homicide.

5. What are some of the main measurement difficulties in looking at trends in violent crime historically?

6. What is the main trend uncovered by Eisner and how does he relate this to the idea of a 'civilizing process'?

7. What were the main developments in the process by which racial violence was recognized as a social problem?

8. In what ways, according to Bowling, do victimization surveys such as the BCS tend to underestimate the extent of crimes such as racial harassment and violence?

20.1 The social organization of burglary
Neal Shover

One of the contributions of American sociologists to the analysis of crime was the early recognition that certain types of criminal pursuits could, like legitimate occupations, be studied as structured and collective activity (Sutherland, 1937; Hollingshead, 1939; Hall, 1952). It was recognized that these structures, or *behavior systems*, commonly consist of distinctive argot, an ideology of defense and legitimation, esoteric knowledge, behavioral norms, and more or less stable relationships between the occupational practitioners and a host of others on whom they are dependent for their successful work performance. Sutherland (1937) applied this sensitizing and organizing concept of the behavior system to theft, insightfully tracing the structure of *professional theft* and the crucial contingencies without which a career as a professional thief could not be realized. This analysis is intended as a continuation in the same tradition. It explicates some of the characteristics of the social relationships which enable one type of burglary offender, the 'good burglar,' to carry on his activities. The nature of the social relationships between working burglars, and also the relationships between burglars and quasi-legitimate members of the host society, are sketched.

Methods

Four different sources of materials were used for this study. First, I read 34 autobiographies of thieves – primarily, though not exclusively, burglars – in their entirety. In addition, 12 novels or journalistic accounts of crime and the activities of criminals were read (e.g., Davis, 1944). Second, a total of 47 interviews were conducted with men incarcerated in the various branches of the Illinois State Penitentiary system. Third, on the basis of these interviews, a lengthy questionnaire was constructed and administered to an additional 88 inmates, in small groups of from three to 12 men at a time. And fourth, interviews were conducted with seven unincarcerated burglars or former burglars, one former fence, and one very peripheral associate of a gang of former bank burglars. All nine of these men were contacted and interviewed without the assistance or cooperation of law enforcement or correctional agencies.

Findings

In the following discussion I present materials on both the *internal* and *external* social organization of burglary. I use the former to refer to the organization of burglary 'crews' (i.e., their division of labor) and how they actually operate when 'taking off' scores. By the external social organization of burglary, I refer to the relationships between burglars and those outside of their crews with whom they tend to maintain symbiotic social relationships. It is first necessary, however, to discuss the meaning of the concept *good burglar*, since the materials presented here are intended to apply to this type of offender.

The designation 'good thief' or 'good burglar' is one which is applied selectively by thieves themselves to those who (1) are technically competent, (2) have a reputation for personal integrity, (3) tend to specialize in burglary, and (4) have been at least relatively successful at crime; success in turn is determined by (1) how much money one has made stealing, and (2) how much time, if any, he has done. The good burglar, then, is the man who generally confines his stealing activities to burglary, has been relatively successful, has a reputation as 'good people,' and is technically competent. At times such a person would be referred to by the more generic designation as a good thief. But in either case the qualitative distinction is most important (cf. Morton, 1950:1819).[1]

Of the total number of respondents interviewed for this study, only ten men were considered to be good burglars. These determinations were made on the basis of peer evaluations and material elicited during the interview which indicated past success and sophistication in burglary. All of these men had, at some time, supported themselves solely by criminal activities, the shortest for one year and the longest for approximately 20 years without incarceration. Of the total questionnaire sample (88), only 20 men were classified as good thieves.

Internal social organization

Skilled burglary by necessity is a social enterprise. Successful good burglars rarely work alone. The problems simply of managing the act requires at least two persons, frequently more. The work is often physically demanding, very time consuming, and must be performed under the apprehension of potential discovery, injury, or arrest. All of these problems must be dealt with, typically by task specialization among members of the burglary crew or 'gang.' The membership of these crews is in a nearly constant state of flux, as some thieves are arrested, drop out of crime, or are discarded by their crime partners for one reason or another. [...]

The key to understanding the social world of the good burglar is found in the recognition that he and his associates form a *category* of individuals, not a society or organization. As Goffman (1963:23-24) defines it,

> The term category is perfectly abstract and can be applied to any aggregate, in this case, persons with a particular stigma. A good portion of those who fall within a given stigma category may well refer to the total membership by the term 'group' or to an equivalent, such as 'we' or 'our people', Those outside the category may similarly designate those within it in group terms. However, often in such cases the full membership will not be part of a single group, in the strictest sense; they will neither have a capacity for collective action, nor a stable and embracing pattern of mutual interaction. What one does find is that the members of a particular stigma category will have a tendency to come together into small social groups whose members all derive from the category, these groups themselves being subject to overarching organization to varying degrees. And one also finds that when one member of a category happens to come into contact with another, both may be disposed to modify their treatment of each other by virtue of believing that they each belong to the same 'group'. Further, in being a member of the category, an individual may have an increased probability of coming into contact with any other member, and even forming a relationship with him as a result. A category, then, can function to dispose its members to group-formation and relations, but its total membership does not thereby constitute a group.

Two men, occasionally three, are usually the largest number of men who will remain together in burglary activities over a relatively long period of time. They tend to confine their burglaries with this same 'partner,' crew or gang. Whenever the problems expected on some particular score necessitate additional manpower, a not uncommon

occurrence, someone who is known to them will be 'filled in' for the job. The person who is filled in will be selected on the basis of his trustworthiness, specialized competence, and availability at the time the score is being planned. If he performs well on one job, he may be asked in on other jobs where a person with his qualifications is needed.

As I have indicated, the locus of much of the contact between members of the category of thief or burglar is the hangout, usually a bar, lounge, or restaurant. Gould *et al.* (1968) have similarly called attention to these hangouts as the places where thieves may recruit partners. In these hangouts thieves spend much of their free time in drinking and socializing. Here they exchange technical information, gossip about one another, talk about 'old scores,' and plan future ones. [...]

As a consequence of these networks of relationships, even though the actual span of social organization is extremely limited, working thieves in even large cities often will know one another, although they may never have worked together.

> It's like everybody that is stealing – when you have several crews in a certain area – they generally know each other even though it's no big organization thing – 20 or 30 burglars and we all have some kind of conspiracy – it's just close knit groups and we all know each other. If you don't know them all you know two or three here and there, or one of your partners knows two or three, or a couple dudes you don't know. It's hard to explain. Over the years you get to know everybody (Prison interview, May 1, 1970).

Burglary crews, when working, usually function on a partnership basis (cf. Einstadter, 1969). Such differentiation of authority as does exist is usually grounded in marked internal differences in age, criminal experience, or skill. Rarely, however, is there a formally designated leader (cf. DeBaun, 1950). Tasks during scores are allocated on the basis of personal strengths and weaknesses, or personal preferences. An easy informally arrived at consensus seems to be the rule here. [...]

Potential scores are located through tips or direct personal selection. The burglar's various 'connections' or *occupational contacts* (cf. Katz, 1958) are the most important source of tips. Burglars themselves often locate potential scores in a number of different ways. During their free time, for example, they will often go on automobile trips for hundreds of miles into nearby cities and towns looking over a variety of places. On 'scouting trips' of this nature they will be especially alert for places similar to those they have made in the past (since chain stores, for example, will frequently purchase the same type of money safes for all of their stores).

Having once located a potential score, one or more of the crew will visit the place to make some preliminary observations. This can range from driving past a few times in an automobile to possibly walking around the place or even climbing to inspect the roof during non-business hours. During these early observations the location of the safe is of upmost importance. If it is located near a front window where there is no cover for anyone who would be trying to open it, and if it is also anchored to the floor, it represents a formidable challenge, one which will under most circumstances simply be passed up. On the other hand, if the safe is located in an area of the place which affords cover, the burglars will investigate further. In addition to providing cover from outsiders, the location of the place itself is extremely important. It should, ideally, provide privacy and more than one 'out' or avenue of escape. [...]

To get to and from the score, plans must be made for some kind of transportation. A 'work car' is used for this purpose. A stolen car or a used car, commonly purchased for cash under an assumed name, is kept hidden away until needed. A truck might be obtained and used in a similar manner. Occasionally, when the risks and stakes dictate, more than one car or truck will be used during a score; one vehicle might be a legitimate one – valid title and license plates – while one or more others are stolen.

The score itself, as I have emphasized, is planned so that each participant knows exactly what he is expected to do. Three or four men are the most typical size of a crew who take off a score; but here again there is variation, depending upon unique circumstances and conditions. One man is usually left 'on point' as a look-out.[2] [...]

Another man will 'sit on the calls,' listening to police calls on a portable radio, again so that instant warnings of detection can be provided. Another confederate might drive a 'pick-up car.' Occasionally both the 'radio man' and the 'point man' will be one and the same person. Most commonly, one or two others will actually make the entry and do the necessary work. This can involve opening a safe and/or preparing merchandise to be hauled away.

Preparations are frequently made in advance for the means and route of escape. The destination is fixed, especially if the burglary involves merchandise. Generally, in such a case, the first stop will be a 'drop' where the fence or one of his agents will inspect the proceeds and arrange for it to be cut up and moved on. If multiple vehicles are used in leaving the score, a legitimate car may be used as a 'crash car.' The driver of this car will follow the vehicle containing the merchandise and see to it that no one overtakes it from the rear. In the event of failure, and one or more of the participants are arrested, those who escaped are ready and expected immediately to post bail for them.

Members of the crew usually share equally in the proceeds of a score (even 'ends'). Any expenses incurred during the planning and carrying out of the score are also shared equally. (And it should be noted that the tools required are sometimes quite expensive.) If there is a 'tipster' involved, he will receive an agreed upon percentage of the gross proceeds, frequently a flat ten percent.

External social organization

The most important of the social relationships which the good burglar maintains with persons outside his group are closely related to the problems he faces in this work. Collectively these social relationships are known as one's 'connections'; the person who is 'well connected' has been fortunate in establishing and maintaining a particularly profitable set of such relationships. Systematic burglars face several problems in their work; and their connections are particularly important in helping them to cope with these problems.

First, the good burglar must know before burglarizing a place that it would be worth his while to do so. He wants, above all, to avoid unnecessary exposure to the 'bitch of chance' (Braly, 1967:233); so he tries, if possible, to assure himself in advance that a score will be rewarding. Second, if he steals a quantity of merchandise – or anything else that he cannot sell directly – he must have a safe outlet for it; he must be able to sell it without risk to himself of detection. And third, in the event of his arrest, he must be able to so thwart the criminal justice system, so that he either goes free or else receives an extremely light sentence for his crime(s). The first of these problems, the informational one, is handled by connections with 'tipsters;' the second problem, the merchandising problem, is handled by relationships with the 'fence;' the third is handled by attorneys, bondsmen, and occasionally, the 'fix.'[3]

The tipster

A tipster (also known as a 'spotter' or 'fingerman') is a person who conveys information to a burglar about some premises or its occupants which is intended to aid in burglarizing those premises.

Among even moderately successful burglars, tipsters represent an important connection and source of information.

> Your professional burglars depend on information. Any time you read about a darn good burglary, they didn't just happen to be walking along the street and say, Here's a good looking house, let's go in there. They depend upon information from strictly legitimate fellas (Martin, 1953:68).

Tipsters are of several types. Many of them (perhaps the majority) are fences who convey tips to thieves as a way of controlling their inventory. Another type is the ex-thief who holds legitimate employment but still maintains friendships with his old associates. A third type is the active thief who learns about some potentially lucrative score but cannot make it himself because the finger of suspicion would immediately be pointed at him. And finally, another type of tipster is what Hapgood (1903:262) referred to as the 'sure thing grafter.' This is a person, usually an older thief, who has become extremely selective in his scores. Whenever he hears about a score but does not want to make it himself, he may pass on the tip to some other thief of his acquaintance. [...]

There is reason to believe that the success of a burglar is directly related to the size of the geographical area over which he maintains connections such as relationships with tipsters (and fences). Some men scarcely know anyone outside of their own city, while others can count on receiving information and assistance from persons in widely separated parts of the United States – or even nearby countries such as Canada and Mexico.

The fence

A fence is a person who buys stolen merchandise, or some other type of commodities (e.g., a coin collection), generally for purposes of resale, which he knows or strongly suspects are stolen. As in the case of tipsters, fences are stratified such that some are better able than others to dispose of a more diversified line of products, a larger quantity of products, and to handle more frequent purchases of products. Additionally, fences can be ordered hierarchically on the basis of how deeply and heavily involved they are in the purchase of stolen goods (cf. Hall, 1952:155–64; 218–9). The lowest level of fence would be the 'square john,' who purchases an occasional item from a thief for his own use; the highest level fence would be the person who is able to dispose of nearly any type and quantity of merchan-

dise on the shortest of notices. If it were not for the existence of fences, thieves would have great difficulty disposing of the merchandise they steal. Indeed, systematic theft would be a quite different sort of enterprise without them.

Fences, as already suggested, are one of the most common sources of tips for good burglars. The reason for this is related to the fence's need to exercise some control over the nature and quantity of his inventory. 'Giving up scores' (tips) to burglars is one tested and proven technique for doing so. Evidence indicates that this is a very common practice on the part of fences (cf. Malcolm X, 1964:144). In fact, it is this practice which seems to be largely responsible for the fence's having a ready buyer for his products before the thief even 'takes off' the score. Giving up scores works, then, to the advantage of both the burglar and the fence. The latter must be seen as occupying a dual role in the behavior system of theft; he purchases stolen goods and simultaneously gathers information about future scores to which the good burglar can be tipped off. By searching out the kinds of merchandise he wants, and then giving the score to burglars, he is able to control his inventory.

But leaving aside the fence's role as a buyer of stolen merchandise, we find that sometimes their relationship with burglars is considerably more complex. Frequently, for example, the fence will be in a position to provide the burglar with several social services (cf. Martin, 1953:98-99). For example:

> I had...this one fence I was doing a lot of business with and he was giving me scores, too...He wasn't a nice man [loan shark] but if you needed $500 and you did a lot of business with him, if you sold to him regularly, there was no problem...If you had any problem and you needed money quick, say to go out of town to look at something, or if you got sort of short, he could come up with a G-note (Prison interview, March 13, 1970).

[...] With few exceptions fences maintain some sort of role in the legitimate business world. Most of them do appear, in fact, to be businessmen of one kind or another. According to burglars, there are primarily three reasons for this. First, it is usually only the businessman who has on hand at any given time the ready cash required in dealings with thieves. Second, businessmen can utilize the contacts and knowledge acquired in their legitimate business activities to evaluate and dispose of illicit merchandise (cf. Hall, 1952:156–57). And third, the fence can use his legitimate business transactions to mask his illicit dealings, thereby making it more difficult for law enforcement officials to build a case against him (cf. Yoder, 1954).

Bondsmen and attorneys

Bondsmen and attorneys occupy positions in legitimate society which carry with them the socially sanctioned approval to associate, at least to some extent, with persons who are known to be criminals. That some of them are corrupted in the process is common knowledge (cf. Goldfarb, 1965); of much more fundamental consequence, however, for the stability and perpetuation of the activities of professional criminals – and this includes the good burglar – are the routinized working relationships and understandings which have emerged out of this socially sanctioned link between the underworld and quasi-representatives of the criminal justice system.

For both the attorney and the bondsman there are two extremely important consequences of prolonged contact with members of the underworld. The first of these is a knowledge of the differences in personal integrity which exist among some of the criminal offenders with whom they have contact. The second is a recognition that there are constraints which operate so as to reduce the risks which are run by anyone, who in doing business with thieves, crosses the line of unethical or illegal behavior. Both the attorney and the bondsman learn rather quickly that some members of the underworld are more trustworthy than others. One result of this is recognition that they need not fear the consequences of unethical or illegal transactions so long as they are selective in the types of clients with whom they have potentially embarrassing dealings. Moreover, they learn that members of the underworld usually cannot divulge their guilty knowledge anyway because they themselves would stand to lose much by doing so. They would be sufficiently stigmatized by such disclosures as to make it difficult to acquire competent legal counsel and the services of bondsman on any subsequent criminal charges. This sets the stage for the emergence and flowering of a number of quasi-ethical practices and working relationships.

It must be noted that these practices are further stimulated, and possibly even generated, by certain characteristics of the problems faced by criminal lawyers and bondsmen generally in their work. The former, for example, unlike his corporate counterpart, routinely deals with clients who have little ready cash with which to compensate him for his services.

Now a criminal lawyer has to give credit, and the main reason for this is that burglars and armed robbers, if they had any money, they wouldn't be out stealing, they'd be partying. It's as simple as that. If they have money, they're partying, and when they're broke, they start to stealing again. If they get caught while they're stealing, they're broke (Jackson, 1969: 136).

One result of this is likely to be the attempt by his clients to obtain his services by offering other types of consideration (Carlin, 1966). Among these other kinds of consideration are such things as the sexual favors of wives or girl-friends, and property, both real and personal, some of which is almost certainly stolen. The good thief's ability to manipulate the criminal justice system cannot be comprehended unless it is recognized that he differs greatly from the petty thief and first time offender in his knowledge of the workings of the system. Unlike them, he has had a great deal of contact with the various actors which comprise it.

When the good burglar is arrested – as he frequently is – he can count upon receiving the services of both a bondsman and an attorney, even if he has virtually no ready cash. In lieu of a cash down payment the thief will be able to gain his release from confinement, and also preliminary legal representation, on the basis of his reputation and a promise to deliver the needed cash at a later date. He will then search for one or more suitable burglaries (or some other type of crime) which holds out the promise of a quick and substantial reward so that he can pay his attorney and bondsman. On occasion he will resort to high interest loan sharks ('juice loans') in order to quickly acquire the sums of cash which his attorney and bondsman demand for their services. [...]

The principal strategy which the good thief's attorneys use appears to be delay, in the hope that some kind of unforeseen contingency will arise which permits him to gain his client's release or, failing that, to strike a particularly favorable bargain. The fix, which once was relatively common in many American jurisdictions (cf. Byrnes, 1969), has become a much less predictable and available option for the good thief.[4] Admittedly, however, this is an area in which there has never been any thorough research. [...]

In addition to what has already been noted about the relationships between good burglars and bondsmen and attorneys, other matters should be briefly mentioned. The latter have been known on occasion to provide tips to burglars on places to burglarize. In addition, some of them are alleged occasionally to purchase stolen property from burglars. Finally, in those unusual cases in which the fix can be arranged, attorneys, of course, act as the go-between in working out the details.

Conclusion

It should be clear on the basis of what has been said here that an understanding of the activities of the systematic burglar must take into account the social matrix in which he carries on his work, indeed on which he is dependent. To this extent the burglar remains more like the professional thieves which Sutherland sketched, and less like the systematic check forgers studied by Lemert (1958). In some respects, then, the social organization of burglarly has continued *relatively* unchanged – at least in comparison with the considerable changes which have occurred in the social organization of check forgery.

Yet even as this is written there is reason to question how much longer it will remain so. For there seems to be near universal consensus that things are changing. In addition to interviews with burglars, the field work for this project included interviews with representatives of two large urban police departments, employees of two safe manufacturers, and a burglary underwriter for a large insurance company. One of the points which was made by all of these respondents was their belief that sophisticated burglary is a declining occupation (cf. Gould *et al.*, 1968). [...] Historical changes in the economy have made cash a declining medium of exchange. There simply is not that much cash in safes anymore. Instead, checks and credit cards are used, and it is in the fraudulent manipulation of these that future criminal opportunity will increasingly be found. To the extent that these changes in the economy do in fact produce changes in the attractiveness and social organization of burglary, it will parallel the changes which made check forgery a different kind

of offense from what it had been in the very early years of the 20th century (Lemert, 1958).

Another change which many of those interviewed mentioned spontaneously is the gradual erosion of 'the Code' among thieves. All seem to agree that the 'solid,' ethical career criminal seems to be giving way to the 'hustler,' an alert opportunist who is primarily concerned only with personal – as opposed to collective – security (cf. Irwin, 1970:8–15; and Gould *et al.*, 1968). It is always possible that the image of the past is more romance than reality and that this could account in part for the poor showing of our contemporaries (cf. Jackson, 1969:34–36).

From N. Shover, 'The social organization of burglary', Social Problems, 1973 *41(3): 813–839.*

Notes

1 An extended discussion of how the social organization of contemporary systematic burglars compares to the behavior system of professional theft as sketched by Sutherland is beyond the scope and space limitations of this paper. I touch upon this issue in the conclusion of this paper.
2 Cf. Einstadter (1969) for an excellent discussion of the social roles involved in heists. Einstadter, it should be noted, was only concerned with the internal social organization of armed robbery.
3 In many cities gamblers and loan-sharks are also important sources of support for working thieves. Because of their contacts in diverse social circles they are often instrumental in the integration of criminal networks, and in the integration of criminals with quasi-legitimate business and professional men.
4 Space precludes a discussion of the fix as it exists today; however, there is no doubt that the fix is still used in criminal cases. But there is real doubt about how often it is available to the burglar. My own views on the contemporary availability of the fix are quite similar to those expressed by Gould *et al.* (1968) and Jackson (1969).

References

Braly, M. (1967) *On the Yard*. Boston: Little, Brown.
Byrnes, T. (1969) *Professional Criminals of America*. New York: Chelsea House (original published in 1886).
Carlin, J. (1966) *Lawyer's Ethics*. New York: Russell Sage Foundation.
Davis, C.B. (1944) *The Rebellion of Leo McGuire*. New York: Farrar and Rinehart.

DeBaun, E. (1950) 'The heist: The theory and practice of armed robbery.' *Harpers* (February): 69–77.
Einstadter, W.J, (1969) 'The social organization of armed robbery.' *Social Problems* 17 (Summer): 64–82.
Goffman, E. (1963) *Stigma*. Englewood Cliffs, N.J.: Prentice-Hall.

Goldfarb, R. (1965) *Ransom*. New York: Harper and Row,

Gould, L., E. Bittner, S. Chaneles, S. Messinger, K. Novak, and F. Powledge (1968) *Crime As a Profession*. Washington, D.C.: U.S. Department of Justice, Office of Law Enforcement Assistance.

Hall, J. (1952) *Theft, Law and Society* (revised edition). Indianapolis: Bobbs-Merrill,

Hapgood, H. (1903) *Autobiography of a Thief*. New York: Fox, Duffield.

Hollingshead, A.B. (1939) 'Behavior systems as a field for research,' *American Sociological Review* 4 (October): 816–822.

Irwin, J. (1970) *The Felon*. Englewood Cliffs, N.J.: Prentice-Hall, Inc.

Jackson, B. (1969) *A Thief's Primer*. New York: Macmillan.

Katz, F.E. (1958) 'Occupational contact networks.' *Social Forces* 37 (October): 52–55.

Lemert, E. (1958) 'The behavior of the systematic check forger.' *Social Problems* 6 (Fall): 141–149.

Malcolm X (with the assistance of Alex Haley) (1964) *The Autobiography of Malcolm X*. New York: Grove Press.

Martin, J.B. (1953) *My Life in Crime*, New York: Signet Books.

Morton, J. (Big Jim) (with D. Witala) (1950) 'I was king of the thieves.' *Saturday Evening Post* (August 5, 12, and 19): 17–19, 78–81; 28, 92, 94–96; 30, 126, 128, 130–132.

Shover, N. (1971) 'Burglary as an occupation.' Unpublished Ph.D. Dissertation. University of Illinois (Urbana).

Sutherland, E. (1937) *The Professional Thief*. Chicago: University of Chicago Press.

Yoder, R.M. (1954) 'The best friend a thief ever had.' *Saturday Evening Post* 227 (December 25): 18–19; 72–73.

20.2 American lethal violence
Franklin E. Zimring and Gordon Hawkins

Other industrial democracies have rates of crime comparable to those found in the United States. Even rates of violent crime in European and Commonwealth nations are closer to U.S. levels than had been thought. But the death rates from all forms of violence are many times greater in the United States than in other comparable nations. Lethal violence is the distinctive American problem. [...]

The distinctive feature of the analysis [here] is the focus on risk of death as an organizing principle for examining all forms of violent crime. On this dimension, assault is the most life-threatening of all American crimes, no more common in the United States than in other nations but much more deadly. Robbery is the other major killer among American crimes. Burglary and rape are much less dangerous.

Does the American reputation for violence survive this new type of statistical analysis? For the most part, yes. The singular reputation of the United States for violence is justified, but requires qualification in two important respects. The first qualification is that rates of life-threatening violence in the United States are much higher than those of other nations of comparable industrial and social development. They are, however, not much higher and in some cases they are lower than the rates of violence experienced in some less developed nations. What is striking about the quantity of lethal violence in the United States is

that it is a third world phenomenon occurring in a first world nation.

The second major qualification is that the large difference between American rates of violence and those of other developed nations is most pronounced only in regard to the most serious forms of violence. Low-grade assaults, barroom brawls, the abusive disciplining of children, and the like are distributed broadly throughout the industrialized nations of the West. American rates of those behaviors place the United States at the higher end of the distribution for those events, but there is no pattern of singular predominance. It is for types of interpersonal violence likely to lead to death or serious bodily injury that the U.S. rate is four to ten times as high as other developed nations. That distinction between types of violence is a significant defining characteristic of the distinctively American violence problem.

Homicide: a profile

During 1990 the United States reported 23,438 criminal homicides, which represents a rate of 9.4 homicides per 100,000 citizens, or approximately one killing in that year for every 10,000 persons.

The American homicide rate is quite high by most international standards, but the relative position of the United States in terms of homicide varies substantially depending on the countries chosen for comparison. Homicide in the United States is greatly in excess of all the nations of Europe, averaging between three and ten times the homicide rates reported in Western European and more than three times the average homicide rates reported by the Eastern European nations. [...]

The moral to be drawn from international comparisons of lethal violence depends upon the standard of reference. When the comparison is made with nations of comparable social and economic development the contrast is dramatic. Figure 20.2.1 illustrates this by profiling rates of criminal homicide for the seven industrial and financial giants that constitute the Group of Seven (G7).

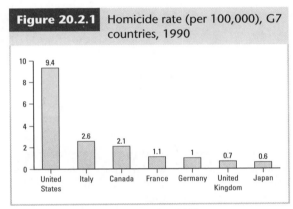

Figure 20.2.1 Homicide rate (per 100,000), G7 countries, 1990

Source: World Health Organization 1990.

When the basis for comparison is broadened, the national experience of the United States, while still not typical of any region or stage of development, is nevertheless less extreme than in the G7 frame of reference. Its current rates of intentional homicide place the United States in the upper third of the distribution of underdeveloped countries, but by no means at the top of that list.

Figure 20.2.2 begins the task of placing data on homicide in a public health context by showing the distribution of fatalities in the United States by cause of death for 1989. [...] Intentional homicide is the tenth leading cause of death in Figure 20.2.2 and accounts for a total of 1.1 percent of all the deaths that occurred in the United States in 1990. When compared with the major fatal diseases, such as heart disease and cancer, the death toll from homicide appears modest. All forms of heart disease were responsible for about thirty times as many deaths in the United States as intentional homicide.

But two related characteristics of homicide deaths increased the social costs of homicide: intentional killing usually strikes down persons without any major disease, and it also produces, disproportionally, the deaths of younger victims. In this regard homicide is similar to fatal automobile accidents and different from the major categories of disease.

Trends over time

Figure 20.2.3 attempts to put homicide rates in long-term perspective by reporting trends in intentional homicide throughout the twentieth century; This nine-decade range is not achieved without some sacrifice of the comparability and reliability of the data. Prior to 1933 the data on deaths in the United States are confined to a collection of death reporting states, while from 1933 onward the data are available for all states. Information provided after 1932 should thus be regarded as more representative of the country as a whole. Moreover the data for each year after 1932 should be regarded as more validly comparable with other post-1932 observations.

A long-range time series of homicide deaths in the United States produces some useful perspectives on recent trends. The first of these is the relatively narrow range within which criminal homicide rates have fluctuated. Putting aside the pattern for reporting states only from 1900–1909, rates of intentional homicide have fluctuated between a low of 4.5 per 100,000 population and a high of 10.7 per 100,000 over eight decades. Within this range, the death rate trended upward in the reporting states through the first third of the century, reached a peak in 1933 – the first year of comprehensive reporting – and fell off gradually to the end of the Second World War.

Homicide rates then remained stable to the early 1960s. From 1964 to 1974 the national homicide rate doubled, fell off slightly in the middle of the decade, then rose to its century high of 10.7 per 100,000 population in 1980. Through the first half of the 1980s the homicide rate fell back, but it then moved up again from 1986 to 1991.

Viewed in this long-term perspective, there are three significant eras in American homicide since 1933: a long downward drift to the century's lowest sustained homicide rate in the 1950s and early 1960s; a sharp and sustained increase during the period 1964 to 1974; and variations around the new high levels ever since.

The long-term perspective is both reassuring and discouraging. It is reassuring to note that one reason why the increases of the 1960s and 1970s looked so dramatic is because they were starting

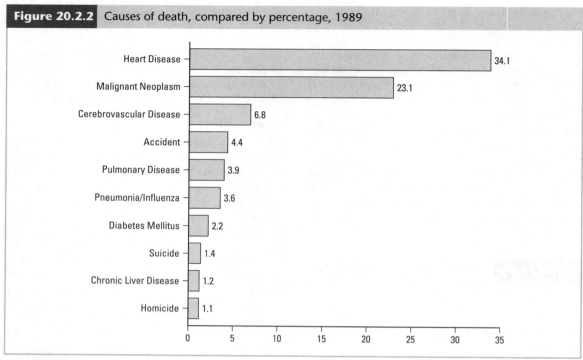

Figure 20.2.2 Causes of death, compared by percentage, 1989

Source: US Department of Health and Human Services 1991.

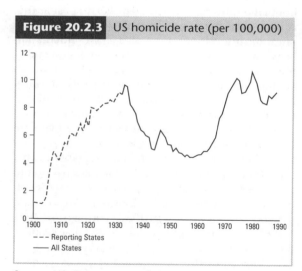

Figure 20.2.3 US homicide rate (per 100,000)

Source: US Department of Commerce, Bureau of the Census, 1976; US Department of Health and Human Serviecs 1991.

from historically low homicide rates. It is also reassuring to know that recent American homicide rates have not increased significantly when compared with previous peak periods: 1933, 1974, and 1980.

The discouraging feature of the long-range perspective is the absence of any sustained down-ward trend over time during the past three decades. Also, even the lower rate periods since 1974 have involved consistently high rates of homicide by historic standards.

The circumstances and demography of American lethal violence

Police statistics provide two types of information about the circumstances, motive and information about the prior relationship between the victim and the offender. Figure 20.2.4 provides the police classification of precipitating circumstances of homicide of the cases reported in the Supplementary Homicide Reports for 1992.

When the precipitating circumstances are known, the bulk of all homicides stem from conflicts that emerge from social relations. About 15 percent of the homicides are byproducts of collateral felonies where the homicide results from an interaction that began as a robbery, burglary, arson, or rape.

Does this mean that most homicides result from noncriminal social relations? In one sense, all attacks that result in criminal homicide are properly classified as criminal when the attack takes place. But the social processes that generate arguments that result in homicides are not distinctively criminal in most cases. Many of the same conflicts

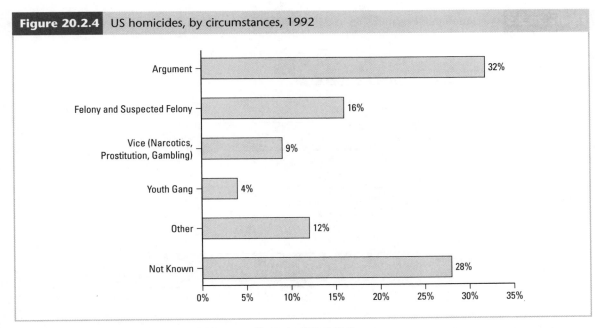

Figure 20.2.4 US homicides, by circumstances, 1992

Source: US Department of Justice, Federal Bureau of Investigation, 1994b.

that produce non life-threatening outcomes in most cases also lead to homicides.

In one sense then, social conflict is a cause of lethal violence. But this will rise and fall with the gross amount of social conflict. Arguments over money, sexual jealousy and male honor number in the millions in the United States, but also in every other industrial democracy. There is no reason to suppose that variations in the gross number of conflicts are a major explanation of variations in homicide. Our guess is that the rate of domestic argument is similar in England and in the United States, and that the rate of barroom arguments is as high in Sydney as in Los Angeles. [...]

One other routinely reported dimension of homicide circumstance is the relationship between victim and offender, as shown in Figure 20.2.5

The relationship between victim and offender can be specified by the police in six out of every ten cases when the Supplementary Homicide Reports are filed. Where the relationship is known, the offender and victim were acquainted in more than half the cases and were connected by family ties in an additional 15.3 percent of all homicides. The police judge that victim and offender were strangers in 13.5 percent of all cases or 23 percent of all cases where the police make a relationship classification.

What can we say from these data about the nature of victim–offender relationships in homi-

cide? To estimate the total volume of stranger homicides in the United States as about 14 percent is certainly an undercount because the police report that they cannot identify the relationship between victim and offender in 39 percent of all homicides. But a controversy has emerged regarding how to treat the 'relationship unknown' group of cases when estimating the total proportion of lethal violence that does not involve prior acquaintances.

One theory is that the police can usually specify the relationship in homicides involving domestic and romantic intimates. Since the 'relationship unknown' category will involve few such intimate homicides, it is best to add all 'relationship unknown' cases to the known stranger cases to estimate the true proportion of stranger cases. Such a procedure could produce an estimate that a majority of U.S. homicides involve strangers (Walinsky 1995; U.S. Department of Justice, Federal Bureau of Investigation, 1994b).

But the logical foundation on which this procedure rests is fallacious. There is no reason to doubt that killings by family members are not often included in the 'relationship unknown' category of homicides. But to conclude that all unsolved killings are committed by strangers is unwarranted because the largest category of homicides in the United States is killing where there is some prior acquaintance between victim and

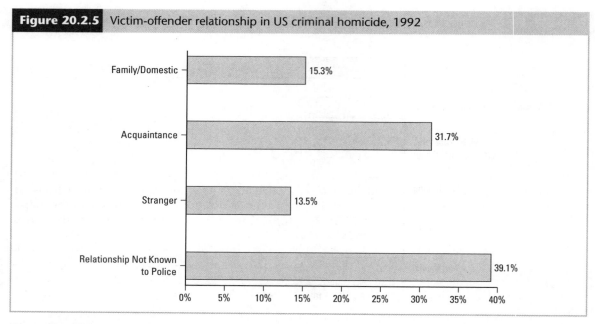

Figure 20.2.5 Victim-offender relationship in US criminal homicide, 1992

Source: US Department of Justice, Federal Bureau of Investigation, 1994b.

offender, and there is no reason to suppose that homicides involving friends or conflicts between casual acquaintances are easy for police authorities to solve. Perhaps the best provisional estimate of stranger killings can be obtained by distributing the unknown relationship killings according to the proportions of the known relationship cases other than those involving family and domestic disturbances. This would produce an estimate of 25 percent stranger killings in the United States when the 13.5 percent of confirmed stranger cases are added to the estimated 12 percent of cases that probably involve strangers.

The demography of homicide

The consistent theme in our account of the demography of violence is that the most lethal subtypes of violence are also the most concentrated in pockets of social disadvantage, while the less lethal forms of violence are more evenly distributed. [...]

Figure 20.2.6 begins the analysis by reporting rates of homicide separately by gender and race for Americans classified as white and black. Excluded from this analysis are some major racial and ethnic classifications, including Hispanic, Asian, and Pacific Islanders.

The aggregate homicide rate for the United States in 1989 was 9.4 per 100,000, but only one of

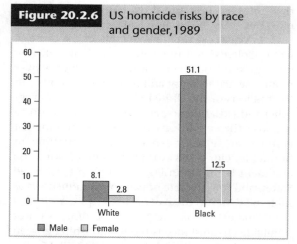

Figure 20.2.6 US homicide risks by race and gender,1989

Source: US Department of Justice, Federal Bureau of Investigation, 1994b.

the four groups represented in the figure has a rate close to that national average. Victimization rates for blacks are about five times those of whites, and victimization rates for males are about three times those of females. Thus the risks associated with being both black and male at 51 per 100,000 in 1989 are almost twenty times as great as the homicide experience of white women during the same years. Both gender and race are powerfully connected with the risk of homicide, but the predictive power of race appears to be slightly greater. Black women, the low-risk gender category within the high-risk racial group, have a 1989 homicide rate 50 percent higher than that of white males, the high-risk gender category within the low-risk racial group. [...]

In general, the risk of homicide is concentrated in the years of late adolescence and young adulthood with the median age of homicide death in the late twenties. Young children and middle-aged and older persons have much lower homicide rates. Again when considering age, the concentration of homicide offenders differs from the general population in the same way as for homicide victims only more so. A clear majority of all homicide offenders arrested are between the ages of fifteen and thirty. [...]

The concentration of homicide in race, gender, and age clusters produces dramatic contrasts. Homicide is the tenth leading cause of death in the U. S. population as a whole, but among young black males in the United States intentional homicide is the leading cause of death, and the death rate for young black males ages fifteen to twenty-nine per 1000 population is over forty times as great as for white females of all ages (U.S. Department of Health and Human Services 1991). [...]

Homicide is concentrated in the big cities of the United States, and in 1992 when the aggregate national homicide rate was 9.7 per 100,000, nineteen of the twenty largest cities had homicide rates that exceeded that figure with a median big city homicide rate of 27 per 100,000. Together, the twenty largest cities in the United States with 11.5 percent of the total population of the country had 34 percent of the criminal homicide reported to the police. [...]

The difference in homicide risk between high-risk and low-risk neighborhoods within each large city is much greater than the difference in homicide rate that is noted when big cities are compared with other population areas. New York City's aggregate homicide rate may be 27 per 100,000, but many residents of New York City live as safely on the borders of Central Park as do the residents of Sioux City, Iowa.

Conclusion: the multiple levels of U.S. violence

[...] American violence is a multiple-level phenomenon, an admixture of different kinds of behaviors that should be examined separately before coming to conclusions about causation or prevention. [...]

Much of the violent behavior present in the United States does not differ significantly from the patterns of violence found elsewhere in the industrial Western world. Most assaults in the United States grow out of conflicts of social life present in the United Kingdom, Western Europe, or in Australia: barroom fights, the battery of sexual intimates, the violent maltreatment of children, schoolyard extortions, and the like. These are chronic problems in most countries, and while the rates of many of these behaviors might be somewhat higher in the United States, there is a good deal of continuity between the kind of violence that makes up the bulk of reported assaults in the United States and the kind of conduct that observers find in other countries.

Using the broad categories developed in sample surveys of crime victimization, many, even most, of the violent acts reported in the United States resemble similar categories in other countries. But there are separate strands of high-death-risk violence present in the United States in much larger concentrations than in other countries, and these acts of high-death-risk violence are distributed among the U.S. population in patterns that are quite different from other types of violence.

From F. Zimring and G. Hawkins, Crime is not the problem: lethal violence in America *(New York: Oxford University Press), 1997, pp. 51–123.*

References

U.S. Department of Health and Human Services. 1991. *Vital Statistics of the United States; Volume II–Mortality.* Hyattsville, Md.: U.S. Department of Heath and Human Services.

U.S. Department of Justice, Federal Bureau of Investigation. 1994b. *Uniform Crime Reports: Supplementary Homicide Reports, 1976–1992.* 1st ICPSR version.

Walinsky, Adam. 1995. The Crisis of Public Order. *The Atlantic Monthly* (July): 39.

20.3 Modernization, self-control and lethal violence
Manuel Eisner

About 20 years ago, in an article that has become highly acclaimed among historians of crime, Ted Robert Gurr (1981: 295) examined empirical evidence on secular trends in lethal criminal violence. Gurr primarily reviewed a number of historical studies on homicide in medieval and early modern England, each based on detailed analyses of records for specific periods and specific jurisdictions. While not originally concerned with computing homicide rates, the studies did provide counts that could be used for estimating the rates. Gurr plotted the some 20 estimates for the period from about 1200 to 1800 on a graph, added the London homicide rates for the modern period, and fitted an elegant S-shaped trend curve to the data points. It starts at about 20 homicides per 100,000 population in the high and late Middle Ages and ends after an extended downswing at about one homicide per 100,000 in the twentieth century. Gurr interpreted this secular trend as 'a manifestation of cultural change in Western society, especially the growing sensitization to violence and the development of increased internal and external control on aggressive behavior' (Gurr 1981; also see Gurr 1989).

Since then, an impressive amount of research in the history of crime and criminal justice has greatly enlarged knowledge about historical manifestations of lethal violence. It has shown that the history of violence has to be firmly situated in the context of social and cultural history and the long-term development of the core institutions of modern society. Also, most historians of crime now agree on the notion of a long-term decline in lethal violence. Thereby, the work of Norbert Elias (1976, 1983) probably forms the most prominent theoretical framework discussed by those historians of crime who are interested in explaining this long-term trend. Elias's well-known theoretical model of the 'civilizing process' embraces long-term social dynamics at a macro level as well as changes in typical psychological traits and developments in characteristic modes of behaviour. In a nutshell, the theory of the civilizing process holds that over a period of several centuries a type of personality has come to prevail that is characterized by increasing affect control, decreasing impulsivity, and a rationalized manner of living – in brief: higher levels of *self-control*. Higher levels of self-control imply, in turn, the gradual pacification of

everyday interactions, which becomes manifest by lower levels of violent behaviour.'

Both in the 'civilizing process' and the 'courteous society' Elias develops a coherent theoretical framework for explaining the assumed secular increase of self-control in European societies. He argues that the most important cause of this psychological change is state formation processes. In particular, he emphasizes the gradual transition from the knightly warrior societies in the Middle Ages to the relatively pacified court societies in the sixteenth and seventeenth centuries, where violence comes to be monopolized by central authorities. According to Elias, the decisive factor was the rise of monarchic absolutism (Elias 1976:353). There, the state monopoly of power over a large territorial unit was accomplished in early modernity to the highest degree. Through this, the nobility lost its bellicose functions, which in turn facilitated the rise of complex economic and social chains of interdependency. As a result, courtly manners become increasingly differentiated, refined and civilized. This specific culture of the nobility then gradually diffuses from its very centre to other social groups and strata. As institutions enforcing the state monopoly of power become more stable, heightened levels of security in social life bring about more intense social interdependencies. The psychic corollary of this social process involves a personality structure, which emphasizes the inhibition of spontaneous emotions and the ability to distance oneself from open displays of aggression (Elias 1976: vol. 1, 320–5, 1978).

Some historians of crime, such as Spierenburg (1996), accept Elias's wide-ranging theoretical model of the rise of European modernity. Others refute the model as insufficient (Schuster 2000). Many, however, view the theory of the civilizing process as a fruitful point of departure for attempts at interpreting the secular trend first described by Ted R. Gurr (Osterberg 1996a; Sharpe 1996). Yet there have been only limited attempts at systematically integrating the vast knowledge accumulated since the early 1980s, which now covers far wider geographic areas than Ted Robert Gurr was able to include in his review (but see, e.g. Rousseaux 1999).

The present paper therefore presents the results of a systematic re-analysis of all available quantitative studies on pre-modern homicide. When combined with the more recent official statistics, the data allow us to follow homicide trends in several European regions for over as many as 800 years. The primary aim of this work is to tentatively develop a more detailed description of the long-term trends in lethal violence across parts of the European continent. More particularly, I will address questions such as: How universal was the secular decline in homicide? In what historical period did the decline begin and possibly end? Do geographic regions show differences in the timing of the decline?

The data

The data for this study come from two very different types of sources. As regards the *age of statistics*, I have primarily relied on the counts of victims of murder and manslaughter according to the national vital statistics. [...]

In any period prior to the invention of national statistics, however, any knowledge on homicides is based on local archival data of some sort, produced for widely varying purposes and not originally intended for statistical analyses. Therefore, as regards the pre-statistical period, the data used in this paper derive from a re-analysis of all available historical research that presents quantitative data on homicide frequencies prior to the beginning of national statistics. Due to the fragmented judicial structure of pre-modern Europe, and because there are large gaps in the surviving sources, we are here confronted with a patchwork of local historical studies on limited periods of time.

Results

For graphic display of the data, I follow the technique used by Gurr (1981). Each single local estimate is symbolized by a dot. This stands for the mean year of the investigated time period and the mean computed homicide rate if several population estimates were given. Lines show the continuous series based on the vital statistics as well as a few existing series for the pre-statistical period.

England

England constitutes the only region in Europe where estimates of homicide rates are available over several centuries for larger geographic areas. This is due to its early judicial unification, the exceptional richness of judicial archives, and a long tradition of research in criminal history. For the Middle Ages, most of the empirical evidence is based on the surviving eyre and coroners' rolls. Data start in the thirteenth century with the results presented by Given (1977). For the fourteenth century we then have Hanawalt's detailed

studies (1976, 1979) and Hammer (1978). Because the eyre courts ceased to function in the late fourteenth century and records of the county assize courts left sufficiently detailed records only from the Elizabethan age on, no data are available for the fifteenth and most of the sixteenth centuries. Extensive analyses based on the extant assize courts in several counties are presented in, for example, Beattie (1986) and Sharpe (1984). Cockburn (1991) presents a complete time series of indicted homicides in Kent from 1570 to 1985. From 1834 onwards, Gattrell *et al.* (1980) provides national homicide rates, and we can extend this series up to the present time using the crime statistics of the Home Office. Together with some additional single estimates of local pre-modern homicide rates, this yields the pattern shown in Figure 20.3.1.

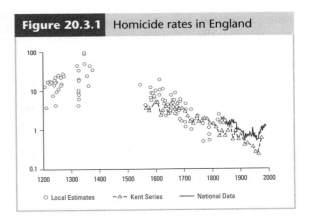

Figure 20.3.1 Homicide rates in England

○ Local Estimates   –△– Kent Series   —— National Data

Despite the limitations of the data mentioned above, an astonishingly clear picture emerges (also see Sharpe 1988). In the thirteenth and fourteenth century, the mean of almost 40 different estimates lies around 24 homicides per 100,000. The average homicide rates are higher for the late fourteenth century than for the thirteenth century, but it seems impossible to say whether this is due to the difference in the sources used or reflects a real increase related to the social and economic crises in the late Middle Ages. When estimates start again after a gap of some 150 years, the average calculated homicide rates are considerably lower with typical values of between 3–9 per 100,000. From then onwards, the data for Kent line up with surprising precision along a straight line that implies a long-term declining trend for more than 350 years. This impression is further corroborated by the other estimates of pre-modern regional homicide rates that cluster randomly around the Kent data.

Furthermore, the national data support the notion that homicide rates continued to decline until the 1960s, National estimates for the mid-nineteenth century are at about 1.8 and come to an all-time low of 0.6 per 100,000 in the early 1960s. Since then, an increasing trend prevails, which may well be underestimated because of drastically improved possibilities for medical intervention. Furthermore, there is evidence suggesting that there may have been at least two other periods of sustained tempo-rary increase in lethal violence. Sharpe (1984: 70) argues, for example, that serious crime including homicide increased considerably during between the 1580s and the 1620s. It also seems that there was some relevant increase between the late eigh-teenth century and the early decades of the nineteenth century (see also Emsley 1996).

Measurement issues

Some historians of crime have repeatedly cautioned that the comparison of quantitative data on pre-modern homicide is fraught with difficulties (see, e.g. Powell 1981; Stone 1983). First, some authors point out that the *legal concept* of inten-tional killing was not fully developed in earlier periods and that, hence, many recorded murder and manslaughter cases might have been accidents rather than intentional acts. However, my impres-sion from reading through a variety of mediaeval sources rather suggests that most cases would also be likely to qualify as a likely manslaughter in pres-ent society. Furthermore, a large proportion of recorded killings in pre-modern society were com-mitted by means of knives and there is no plausible reason why knives should have caused large num-bers of accidental deaths. Second, *population estimates* for pre-modern society are notoriously imprecise and one might assume that therefore the results might become distorted. Yet, substituting the mean population estimates used in the present fig-ures by either the lowest or highest population estimates quoted by historians does not significantly alter the overall trends. Some systematic distortion occurs, however, as a result of the changing age-structure of the population. Since young men have always committed most homicides and because their share of the total population has considerably declined throughout the twentieth century, the recent rise in lethal violence tends to be underesti-mated (Monkkonen 1999).

A third problem discussed by Spierenburg refers to the potential *incompleteness* of the extant data. More particularly, by comparing autopsy reports and conviction records in Amsterdam,

Spierenburg (1996) shows that in pre-modern soci-eties as few as 10–20 per cent of homicides may have resulted in the offender being arrested and convicted. He therefore assumes that data based on judicial records may seriously underestimate his-torical homicide rates. Given the lack of systematic findings, however, no attempt was made in this study to correct for potential bias due to the recording of homicides.

In my view, the potentially most serious sys-tematic distorting factor is the advance *in medical technology*. Undoubtedly, a significant proportion of people who died some time after having been wounded in pre-modern societies would be rescued by means of modern medical technology. Spierenhurg (1996) and Monkkonen (2000) have attempted to estimate the proportion of pre twenti-eth-century homicide victims who did not immediately die and who might therefore be res-cued nowadays. Spierenburg estimates that about a quarter of victims in Amsterdam around 1700 might have been saved by contemporary medical technol-ogy. Monkkonen (2000) finds that about half of the violent deaths in nineteenth-century New York could have been prevented by modern technology. Thus again, the increase of homicides since the 1960s may well underestimate the actual rise of vio-lence levels when compared to earlier historical periods. However, most scholars agree that medical technology is not a candidate for explaining the massive decline of homicide rates, which occurred mostly before the twentieth century.

The main patterns and secular trends

The quantitative data should not be regarded as precise measurements. However, they show that the huge amount of sophisticated historical work done over the past 30 years has resulted in a remarkable convergence as to a number of secular patterns in lethal violence that can not plausibly be interpreted as a result of systematic distortion.

First, the data confirm the notion, now hardly controversial among historians of crime, that homi-cide rates have declined in Europe over several centuries. Typical estimates referring to the late Middle Ages range between 20 and 40 homicides per 100,000, while respective data for the mid twen-tieth century are between 0.5 and 1 per 100,000. The notorious imprecision of population data, defi-ciencies of the sources, shifts in the legal definition of homicide, changes in the age structure as well as improved medical possibilities, surely have to be accounted for. But the evidence is so consistent, the

Table 20.3.2 Homicide rates in five European regions

Period	England	Netherlands and Belgium	Scandinavia	Germany and Switzerland	Italy
13th and 14th c.	23	47	–	37	(56)
15th c.	–	45	46	34	(73)
16th c.	7.0	25	21	11	47
17th c. First half	6.2	(6.0)	24	11	(32)
Second half	4.3	9.2	12	(2.4)	–
18th c. First half	2.3	7.1	2.8	(2.5)	(12)
Second half	1.4	4.1	0,7	5.5	9
1800–24	1.5	1,5	1,0	3.2	18
1825–50	1,7	–	1,4	4.1	15
1850–74	1,6	0,9	1,2	2.0	12
1875–99	1,3	1,5	0,9	2,2	5,5
1900–24	0,8	1,7	0,8	2,0	3,9
1925–49	0,8	1,3	0,6	1,4	2,6
1950–74	0,7	0,6	0,6	0,9	1,3
1975–94	1,2	1,2	1,2	1,2	1,7

Data are arithmetic means of all available estimates for a given period and region. Figures in brackets are particularly unreliable because they are based on less than five estimates. Figures in italics are based on national statistics.

secular decline so regular, and the differences in levels so large, that it seems difficult to refute the conclusion of a real and notable decline.

Second, the empirical evidence may help to narrow down the *historical period* in which unequivocal decline can be observed in large parts of Western Europe. Both the results of the meta-analysis and the judgments of experts in criminal history suggest that the early seventeenth century may be regarded as a decisive turning point. The average rates already decline somewhat from the fourteenth to the sixteenth centuries. But in view of the low precision of estimates it seems impossible to draw any firmer conclusions from this evidence. However, we are on much firmer ground as regards the considerable decline in homicide rates starting in the early seventeenth century and continuing well into the twentieth century.

Third, the data suggest that the secular trajectories of low homicide rates differ among large geographic areas. It appears that *English* homicide rates were already considerably lower in the late sixteenth century than during the late Middle Ages and that they declined continuously along a log-linear trend over several centuries. Extant estimates for the *Netherlands and Belgium* suggest a very simi-

lar secular trend in these areas. In the *Scandinavian countries*, the transition to the decreasing trend occurs notably later, namely in the first decades after 1600. Despite huge gaps in the data, the *German-speaking areas* may also be assumed to have joined the declining trend from the early seventeenth century onwards. For *Italy*, however, all the available data indicate that acts of individual-level lethal violence remained very frequent until the early nineteenth century. It is not until the mid-nineteenth century that the rate begins to decline, but then very steeply.

Finally, the data also reveal repeated *counter-trends*. Some of these counter-movements may reflect regional peculiarities, possibly related to phases of rapid social and political change. Others seem to occur simultaneously in several large geographic areas of Europe. It appears, for example, that lethal individual-level violence has increased during the last decades of the sixteenth and possibly the first two decades of the seventeenth century both in England, in Sweden, and in Switzerland. Also, there is some evidence suggesting that the late eighteenth and early nineteenth century may have seen another wave of augmenting homicide rates in several parts of Europe.

Finally, all European countries (with the exception of Finland) have experienced a period of unbroken increase in homicide rates between the early 1960s and the mid-1990s. While present rates in no way correspond to the frequencies of homicide in the pre-modern world, improvements in the field of medicine and the changed age structure of the population (smaller proportion of younger age cohorts) tend to lead to statistical underestimation of the magnitude of the increase.

The secular declining trend

Many of the trajectories described above broadly support Elias's concept of a long-term civilizing process. The gradual secular decline of homicide rates is precisely what the theory of the civilizing process had expected. Importantly too, other cultural and social processes signalling a growing sensitization to violence mirror the decline in homicide rates. Historians find consistent evidence suggesting a growing moral concern about cruelty and violence from the seventeenth century onwards. Infanticide becomes an important and severely punished crime (Soman 1980: 22). Throughout Western Europe, the number of public executions gradually declines, particularly cruel penal practices are progressively discontinued, and elite groups increasingly abhor the sight of the scaffold (Spierenburg 1997: 119).

Also, as Elias's theoretical framework would lead us to expect, several authors find that the decline in personal lethal violence occurred first among members of the upper classes and then gradually extended to other groups in early modern society (Osterberg 1996b: 55; Sharpe 1988: 129). Hammer (1978), for example, finds that academics in fourteenth-century Oxford may have been involved in lethal violence just as often as other groups in urban society. And Sharpe (1984) argues that gentry violence seems to have become less frequent since the late sixteenth century, while the poor and marginalized increasingly became perceived as the dangerous classes.

Finally, we find that the phases of accelerated decline in homicide rates often seem to coincide with periods of rapid expansion and stabilization of state structures. In Sweden, the decisive transition to lower rates as described above coincides most precisely with the triumph of monarchic absolutism and intensified, centralized, bureaucratic state control structures. And in Italy the spectacular decline in homicide rates from the 1870s onwards corresponds well with the triumph of the nation state and the withering away of local powers.

From M. Eisner, 'Modernization, self-control and lethal violence', British Journal of Criminology, 2001, 41 (4): 618–638.

References

Beattie, J.M. (1986), *Crime and the Courts in England 1660–1800*. Oxford: Clarendon.

Cockburn, J.S. (1991), 'Patterns of Violence in English Society: Homicide in Kent, 1560–1985', *Past and Present*, 130: 70–106.

Elias, N. (1976), *Über den Prozess der Zivilisation; Soziogenetische und psychogenetische Untersuchungen*. Frankfurt am Main: Suhrkamp.

— (1983), *Die höfische Gesellschaft; Untersuchungen zu einer Soziologie des Königtums und der höfischen Aristokratie*. Frankfurt am Main: Suhrkamp.

Gatrell, V.A.C. (1980), 'The Decline of Theft and Violence in Victorian and Edwardian England', in V.A.C. Gatrell, B. Lenman and C. Parker, eds., *Crime and the Law; The Social History of Crime in Western Europe since 1500*, 238–339. London: Europa Publications.

Given, J.B. (1977), *Society and Homicide in Thirteenth-Century England*. Stanford: University Press.

Gurr, T.R. (1981), 'Historical Trends in Violent Crime: A Critical Review of the Evidence', *Crime and Justice. An Annual Review of Research*, 3: 295–350.

Gurr, T.R. (1989), 'Historical Trends in Violent Crime: Europe and the United States', in T.R. Gurr, ed., *Violence in America, vol. 1: The History of Crime*, 21–54. Newbury Park: Sage.

Hammer, C.I., Jr. (1978), 'Patterns of Homicide in a Medieval University Town: Fourteenth-Century Oxford', *Past and Present*, 78: 3–23.

Hanawalt, B, A. (1976), 'Violent Death in Fourteenth- and Early Fifteenth Century England', *Comparative Studies in Society and History*, 18: 297–320.

— (1979), *Crime and Conflict in English Communities*, 1300–1348. Cambridge: Cambridge University Press.

Monkkonen, E. (1999), 'New York City Offender Ages; How Variable over Time?', *Homicide Studies*, 3/3: 256–69.

— (2000), American Homicide Rates: New Estimates (Contribution to the European Social Science History Conference, 12–15 April 2000, Amsterdam).

Österberg, E. (1996a), 'Criminality, Social Control, and the Early Modern State: Evidence and Interpretations in Scandinavian Historiography', in E.A. Johnson and E.H. Monkkonen, eds., *The Civilization of Crime: Violence in Town and Country since the Middle Ages*, 35-62. Urbana: Illinois University Press.

Powell, E. (1981), 'Social Research and the Use of Medieval Criminal Records', *Michigan Law Review*, 79: 967–78.

Rousseaux, X. (1999), 'From Case to Crime: Homicide Regulation in Medieval and Modern Europe', in D. Willoweit, D. ed., *Die Enstehung des öffentlichen Strafrechts; Bestandsaufnahme eines europäischen Forschungsproblems*, 143–75. Köln: Böhlau Verlag.

Schuster, P. (2000), *Eine Stadt vor Gericht: Recht und Alltag im spätmittelalterlichen Konstanz*. Paderborn: Schöningh.

Sharpe, J.A. (1984), *Crime in Early Modern England, 1550–1750*. London: Longman.

— (1988), 'The History of Crime in England c. 1300–1914', *British Journal of Criminology*, 28/2: 254–67.

Spierenburg, P. (1996), 'Long-Term Trends in Homicide: Theoretical Reflections and Dutch Evidence, Fifteenth to Twentieth Centuries', in E.A. Johnson and E.H. Monkkonen, eds., *The Civilization of Crime: Violence in Town and Country since the Middle Ages*, 63–108. Urbana: University of Illinois Press.

Stone, L. (1983), 'Interpersonal Violence in English Society, 1300–1980', *Past and Present*, 101: 22–33.

20.4 Racial harassment and the process of victimization
Benjamin Bowling

Racial violence: the emergence of a social problem

Some authors have argued that racial violence has for centuries formed an integral part of the experience of black- and brown-skinned people living in Britain (Gordon 1984; Fryer 1984). There is certainly evidence of violence directed specifically against ethnic minority individuals and communities in Britain since the 1950s (Klug 1982; Layton-Henry 1984). Several academic and journalistic accounts document outbreaks of racial violence in various parts of England during the 1950s and 1960s. There were, for example, 'anti-black riots' in Nottingham and London in 1958 (Layton-Henry 1984; Fryer 1984: 376-83; Solomos 1989) and in midland and northern towns such as Dudley, Smethwick, Wolverhampton, Middlesbrough, Accrington, Leeds, and elsewhere in the early 1960s (Pearson 1976; Reeves 1989: 44). Each of these outbreaks involved large gangs of white men targeting isolated black families and individuals. In some places the attackers belonged to 'racialist' youth cultures such as the Teddy Boys. Others involved far right, anti-immigration political movements such as Oswald Mosley's British Union of Fascists (Hall *et al.* 1978; Layton-Henry 1984).

During the 1970s what became known as 'Paki-bashing' was increasingly reported in numerous locations across the country (Layton-Henry 1984; Reeves 1989: 125–52; Gordon 1990). Gangs of white men targeted Afro-Caribbeans, Asians, and others who 'looked foreign'. Again, some attacks were perpetrated by youths allied to racist youth cultures such as the skinheads, while others involved racist political organizations such as the National Front (Gordon 1990; Tompson 1988). Towards the end of the 1970s it was widely believed that racial violence was escalating dramatically. There were some well-publicized violent episodes involving the NF, such as those in Brick Lane in 1978 and Southall in 1979. From around this time community organizations, trade unions, and anti-racist groups began to document racist outbursts, persistent campaigns of harassment, and the effects of violence on black communities (Bethnal Green and Stepney Trades Council 1978; Commission for Racial Equality 1979; Institute of Race Relations 1987).

Defining racial violence as crime

In February 1981, the Joint Committee Against Racialism (JCAR) presented a report on racial violence to the Home Secretary. In response, central government acknowledged the anxieties expressed by JCAR and commissioned the first official study of racial attacks and harassment (*Hansard*, 5 Feb. 1981, col. 393). The report of the Home Office study dramatically altered the status of racial violence as a policy issue. The study consisted of two complementary research strategies – a survey of reported incidents in selected police areas across the country and interviews with the police, local community organizations, and local officials in each area.

The information contained in the report which had the greatest impact was the quantitative '*factual* survey of racial attacks' based on incidents recorded by the police (Home Office 1981:6 emphasis added). [...]

The finding that has been most frequently cited by reports which followed (e.g. GLC 1984; Brown 1984; Kinsey *et al.* 1987) was that the rate of racially motivated victimization was 'much higher for the ethnic minority population, particularly the Asians, than for white people. Indeed the rate for Asians was 50 times that for white people and the rate for blacks was 36 times that for white people.' The report also commented on the types of incidents suffered by different ethnic groups: 'Figures for Asians were particularly suggestive: 12 of the 13 victims of arson were Asian, as were 16 of the 25 recipients of abusive telephone calls, and 57 of the 72 victims of racially motivated window-smashing. On the other hand, 20 of the 24 victims of handbag snatches or theft from persons, which were judged to be racially motivated, were white' (Home Office 1981: 12).

This statistical description overshadowed the qualitative 'views and opinions' gleaned from interviews with community groups and local officials. The primacy given to statistical 'fact' directed attention away from the subjective experience of racial harassment. [...]

A direct result of the production of this report was the introduction of an 'operational definitions' and recording and monitoring procedures within the Metropolitan Police (see House of Commons 1982). The publication of this report marks a dramatic increase in police and local and central government activity directed at controlling racial violence. Indeed, if one were to rely solely on police and central and local government sources of knowledge, it might appear that at the beginning of the 1980s a new form of crime emerged. This crime – termed variously racial (or racist) violence, racial attacks, racial harassment, and racial incidents – became, quite suddenly, a policy issue. It is only since 1981 that any local or central govern-

ment agency kept records of racist violence or began to develop policies to control it. It is only since this time that any have considered it necessary to ponder the definition of the problem and to carry out research on the extent and nature of the problem and the effectiveness of the statutory response to it.

Crime surveys and the prioritization of racial violence

During the 1980s, surveys contributed to the movement of racial violence from the margins to the centre of national and local political agendas. Now many statutory agencies have recording and monitoring procedures and operational guidelines. But despite these very real changes, there is little evidence that statutory policies directed at tackling perpetrators, assisting victims, or preventing racial violence have been effective. In 1989, the central government interdepartmental racial attacks group found 'few examples of effective multi-agency liaison . . . [and] ... relatively few examples of effective unilateral action by individual agencies' (Home Office 1989: para. 34). Despite a decade of statutory activity there is little evidence that racial violence is being controlled. There is little evidence indeed that it has decreased in incidence, prevalence, or in its effect on minority communities in Britain (FitzGerald 1989; Ginsburg 1989; Cutler and Murji 1990; Gordon 1990).

Criminal incidents and criminology

Until recently, criminology has been content to conceive of crime as a collection of criminal incidents – as events of norm violation (MacLean 1986). Although feminists and critical criminologists have developed more dynamic accounts of crime (of which more below), the dominant approach to the study of victimization is still events-oriented (Skogan 1986; Genn 1988). In this respect both conventional and 'left realist' surveys reflect the orientation of the criminal justice system. Criminal incidents are the stock-in-trade of the crime control sector of government and of administrative criminology. Estimates of the size of the problem, and descriptions of where it is located and who the actors are, are necessarily based on such counting exercises, as are measurements of police performance such as the clear-up rate. Indeed, the *modus operandi* of the criminal justice system is based upon and shaped by the processing of individual events.

The criminal justice system attempts to deal with racial violence as individual acts in the same way that it deals with other forms of crime. British law recognizes only the event defined as the criminal offence (Smith and Hogan 1983; Forbes 1988). The police definition of crime reflects the legal structure of police work (Grimshaw and Jefferson 1987), and, like the rest of the criminal justice system, is ordered around the reification of human experience into discrete events (Manning 1988). To become an object for policing or the courts, an aspect of human behaviour or interaction must be fixed in space and time and be definable as an offence (Young 1990). Police policy documents often stress that the object for policing is a *racial incident* rather than attack or harassment (e.g. House of Commons 1986: I). The policing systems, consisting of racial incident forms, incident report books, and methods for calculating response times and detection rates, reflect their concern with discrete events.

The orientation of the criminal justice system and of criminology towards counting individual events also reflects the quantitative emphasis of social science more generally. Qualitative data are often considered soft, anecdotal, or, as in the 1981 Home Office study on racial attacks, merely 'views and opinions'. Quantitative data, by contrast, are considered hard, objective, or 'factual'.

Racial victimization as a process

Despite the primacy of incident-based accounts of crime and racial violence, some authors have argued that crime should be seen not as an event, but as a process. As MacLean suggests, 'crime is not an *event* or "social fact", but a social *process* which includes a number of social events each of which is inextricably bound up with the other[s]' (1986: 4–5, emphases in original). Conceiving of racial violence and other forms of crime as processes implies an analysis which is dynamic; includes the social relationships between all the actors involved in the process; can capture the continuity across physical violence, threat, and intimidation; can capture the dynamic of repeated or systematic victimization; incorporates historical context; and takes account of the social relationships which inform definitions of appropriate and inappropriate behaviour.

Racial victimization is, like other social processes, dynamic and in a state of constant movement and change, rather than static and fixed. While individual events can be abstracted

from this process, fixed in time and place and recorded by individuals and institutions, the process itself is continuous. Much can be learned from studying criminal events; but, just as it is impossible to understand the content of a movie by looking at only one still frame, 'it is impossible for us to understand crime or any other process by looking at an individual event or moment' (MacLean 1986: 8).

The process of racial victimization involves a number of social actors, each of whom has a dynamic relationship with the others. It is usual, first, to look at victim and offender and at the relationship between them. Obviously, an investigation of racial violence should include an analysis of the characteristics of the people who set out to attack or harass ethnic minorities and of their motivation for doing so. Equally, it should include an analysis of the characteristics of the people under attack and of the effects that victimization has on them. But when an individual is attacked, the process of victimization is not confined to him or her alone, but may extend to immediate and extended families, friends, and 'community'. When a serious incident occurs – a racially motivated arson attack or murder, for example – the impact may be felt among people in locations far away from where the incident itself occurred. Similarly, there is a relationship between perpetrators of racial attacks and their families, friends, and community. The expression of racial violence and the victimization to which it gives rise is underpinned by the relationships between different *communities* in particular localities and within society as a whole. Exploring these relationships and the part they play in condoning or condemning racial outbursts seems crucial to an understanding of the process of racial victimization. As yet, however, we know much less about offenders in cases of racial violence than about victims.

Also of importance are the roles of the police and other state agents such as social workers and public housing managers. For those cases that come to be defined as crimes and for which a prosecution is initiated, criminal justice professionals (such as court officials, prosecutors, defence lawyers, magistrates, and judges) play their part. These actors intervene in the process of racial and other forms of victimization in ways which have the potential for escalation as well as amelioration of its effects. A dynamic account of the impact of state action and reaction is important for comprehending the totality of the process of victimization. Finally, local and national news media play their part in communicating knowledge of attacks or about the quality of the statutory response to various sections of the community.

Clearly, the notion of process applies to all forms of crime. Car theft is no less dynamic and bound up with wider social processes than is racial violence. However, the few qualitative accounts that exist point to racial violence often taking the form of multiple victimization (Sampson and Phillips 1992), repeated attacks (Home Office 1981), and a constant (Walsh 1987) or 'unrelenting barrage of harassment' (Tompson 1988). In this sense, racial victimization may be compared with wife battery, which is very often prolonged and habitual (Genn 1988; Stanko 1988). Victimization which constitutes repeated physical violence or continuous threat and intimidation may be distinguished by its enduring quality. As Stanko (1990) suggests, these forms of violence create 'climates of unsafety' which transcend individual instances of violence. Attempting to reduce multiple victimization to a series of incidents means that much of this experience will be lost (Genn 1988: 90; Farrell 1992; Sampson and Phillips 1992).

Thinking about how events may be connected so as to illuminate underlying social processes leads on to a consideration of the connections between different forms of violence in the experience of an individual who is being victimized. Kelly (1987) argues that women experience sexual violence as a continuum – 'a continuous series of events which pass into one another and which cannot be readily distinguished' (1987: 77). Making these connections seems equally important with regard to the experience of racial violence. As Pearson *et al.* suggest:

> For white people, for example, racial harassment and racial attacks are undoubtedly merely incidental, one-off events which are rarely, if ever, encountered. For black and minority ethnic groups, on the other hand, these are areas of experience which are part and parcel of everyday life. A black person need never have been the actual victim of a racist attack, but will remain acutely aware that she or he belongs to a group that is threatened in this manner. In much the same way that the high levels of 'fear of crime' among women can be better understood when experiences of subordination and daily harassments, from the subliminal to the blatant are reconnected (Stanko, 1987), so the re-connected experiences of racism from a black and minority ethnic perspective shift the ground of how to define a 'racial' incident and what it is to police 'racism'. (1989: 135)

Although the implications of such an approach have yet to be pursued in research practice, survey research has hinted at its importance. The authors of the first Islington Crime Survey, for example, concluded from one interview that: 'some segments of the population are so over-exposed to this kind of behaviour [racist assaults] that it becomes part of their everyday reality and escapes their memory in the interview situation' (Jones *et al.* 1986: 63).

The process of racial harassment: research and policy development

Implications for survey research

The problem facing those wishing to conduct survey research into racial violence is that of developing ways to capture victimization as a process from the events that surveys describe. This means developing ways of investigating repeat victimization, focusing on all the elements of the crime process and incorporating social context. Some aspects of the process of victimization may be captured by the creative use of the survey method. Capturing other aspects may require the use of supplementary or complementary methodologies. [...]

There is an urgent need for research to develop creative means of measuring and describing repeated, systematic, and enduring victimization (Farrell 1992). It may be that survey research can be adapted so that it is sensitive to this dynamic. Or it may be that surveys should be used for purposes for which they are better suited, leaving repeated victimization to be investigated by supplementary or alternative methods of research.

Surveys of racial violence have focused mainly on the experience of crime victims, and of their experiences of reporting to the police. There has been almost no research on perpetrators. [...] In order for a holistic account of victimization to be developed, account must be taken of all the actors in the process, and of the relationships among them. While they would be sensitive and difficult to conduct, surveys of perpetrators and their associates could be conducted in parallel with surveys of victims. It might be possible to conduct surveys of offending using the 'self-report method' in localities with high rates of racial victimization. Another approach would be to extend surveys of racist attitudes (e.g. Husbands 1983) to cover racially motivated violence and attitudes towards it.

Implications for policy development

Because surveys alone cannot capture the dynamic of crime as a social process, the policies to which they have given rise have tended to be one-dimensional, focusing on the event of norm violation. As a result, policies have tended to emphasize reactive police and local authority responses rather than community-based preventive measures. However, there seems to be a contradiction between the idea that racial victimization is a dynamic process and the idea that the problem may best be tackled by responding to a disconnected incident. [...] [This] perhaps explains why research studies report the police response to racial violence frequently to be inappropriate (e.g. Smith and Gray 1983: 409–12; Gordon 1990; Dunhill 1989: 68–79; Institute of Race Relations 1987; Newham Monitoring Project 1990; Hesse *et al.* 1992).

There is a similar contradiction between the experience of victimization and legal practice. Forbes has identified the limitations to tackling racial harassment imposed by a legal system which understands crime only as a single event: '[In presenting a case] only facts relevant to the particular offence which can be proved may be mentioned. Thus, it is not usually permissible to refer to other offences that have been committed by the perpetrator. This means that the offence cannot be set in context as part of a sustained campaign of racial harassment' (1988: 17–2). In court, as with policing, the focus on a single event renders the process of victimization invisible. It seems that reducing the complex processes of racial exclusion (Husbands 1983) and the expression of violence to a racial incident strips it of meaning for the victim and for those to whom the incident must be described (such as a police officer, judge, or jury). By rendering earlier episodes in the process of victimization 'inadmissible evidence' or irrelevant to police investigation, neither the effect on the victim nor the

implications for the rest of the 'community' can be described. This undermines the ability of statutory agents to understand the meaning of the event (from the victim's perspective in particular) and therefore to respond appropriately to it. Again, this point applies more broadly than to racially motivated crime. Indeed, it underlines one of the major dissatisfactions of victims and communities with criminal justice agencies – that they look only at the incident, not at its history and setting (Genn 1988; Shapland *et al.* 1985).

Ways forward

If racial victimization (and other forms of crime) may best be conceptualized processually, it follows that the social response to the problem must tackle the underlying processes as well as responding to the reported incidents to which these processes give rise (Goldstein 1990). In order to develop such a response, research is required that is dynamic, takes account of all moments in the crime process, can capture the dynamic of repeated victimization, and is set in geographical, social, historical, and political context. Some of these data may be provided by the next generation of crime, victimization, and offending surveys. However, as has been argued by many authors, qualitative as well as quantitative research methods are required to procure a holistic analysis (Bell and Newby 1977; Walklate 1989, 1990).

From B. Bowling, 'Racial harassment and the process of victimization', British Journal of Criminology, 1993, 33(2): 231–250.

References

Bell, C., and Newby, H. eds. (1977), *Doing Sociological Research*. London: Allen and Unwin.

Bethnal Green and Stepney Trades Council (1978) *Blood on the Streets*. London: Bethnal Green and Stepney Trades Council.

Brown, C. (1984), *Black and White Britain: The Third PSI Survey*. London: Heinemann.

CRE (1979), *Brick Lane and Beyond: An Inquiry into Racial Strife and Violence in Tower Hamlets*. London: Commission for Racial Equality.

Cutler, D., and Murji, K. (1990), 'From a Force into a Service? Racial Attacks, Policing and Service Delivery', *Critical Social Policy*, March/April.

Dunhill, C. (1989), 'Women, Racist Attacks and the Response from Anti-Racist Groups', in Dunhill, C., ed., *The Boys in Blue. Women's Challenge to the Police*. London: Virago.

Farrell, G. (1992), 'Multiple Victimisation: Its Extent and Significance', *International Review of Victimology*, 2: 85–102.

FitzGerald, M. (1989), 'Legal Approaches to Racial Harassment in Council Housing: The Case for Reassessment', *New Community*, 16/1: 93–106.

Forbes, D. (1988), *Action on Racial Harassment: Legal Remedies and Local Authorities*. London: Legal Action Group.

Fryer, P. (1984), *Staying Power: The History of Black People in Britain*. London: Pluto.

Genn, H. (1988), 'Multiple Victimization', in M. Maguire and J. Pointing, eds., *Victims of Crime: A New Deal?* 90–100. Milton Keynes: Open University Press.

Ginsburg, N. (1989), 'Racial Harassment Policy and Practice: The Denial of Citizenship', *Critical Social Policy*, 26: 66–81,

GLC (1984), *Racial Harassment in London: Report of a Panel of Inquiry Set Up by the GLC Police Committee*. London: Greater London Council.

Goldstein, H. (1990), *Problem-Oriented Policing*. New York: McGraw-Hill.

Gordon, P. (1984), *White Law*. London: Pluto.

Gordon, P. (1990), *Racial Violence and Harassment*, 2nd edn. Runnymede Research Report. London: Runnymede Trust.

Grimshaw, R., and Jefferson, T. (1987), *Interpreting Policework*. London: Allen and Unwin.

Hall, S., Critcher, C., Jefferson, T., Clarke, J., and Roberts, B. (1978), *Policing the Crisis: Mugging, the State, and Law and Order*. London: Macmillan.

Hesse, B., Rai, D.K., Bennett, C., and McGilchrist, P. (1992), *Beneath the Surface: Racial Harassment*. Aldershot: Avebury.

Home Office (1981), *Racial Attacks: Report of a Home Office Study*. London: Home Office.

— (1989), *The Response to Racial Attacks and Harassment: Guidance for the Statutory Agencies,* Report of the Inter-Departmental Racial Attacks Group. London: Home Office.

House of Commons (1982), Home Affairs Committee, 2nd Report, *Racial Attacks*. London: HMSO.

— (1986), Home Affairs Committee, 3rd Report, *Racial Attacks and Harassment*. London: HMSO.

Husbands, C. (1983), *Racial Exclusionism and the City: The Urban Support for the National Front*. London: Allen and Unwin.

Institute of Race Relations (1987), *Policing against Black People*. London: Institute of Race Relations.

Jones, T., MacLean, B.D., and Young, J. (1986), *The Islington Crime Survey: Crime, Victimisation and Policing in Inner-City London*, Aldershot: Gower.

Kelly, L. (1987), 'The Continuum of Sexual Violence', in J. Hanmer and M. Maynard, eds., *Women, Violence and Social Control*. 46–60. London: Macmillan.

Kinsey, R., Lea, J., and Young, J. (1987), *Losing the Fight Against Crime*. Oxford: Blackwell.

Klug, F. (1982), *Racist Attacks*. London: Runnymede Trust.

Layton-Henry, Z. (1984), *The Politics of Race in Britain*. London: Allen and Unwin.

MacLean, B.D. (1986), 'Critical Criminology and Some Limitations of Traditional Inquiry', in B.D. MacLean, ed., *The Political Economy of Crime: Readings for a Critical Criminology*. Scarborough, Ontario: Prentice-Hall.

Manning, P.K. (1988), *Symbolic Communication*. London: MIT Press.

Newham Monitoring Project (1990), *Newham Monitoring Project Annual Report 1989*. London: Newham Monitoring Project.

Pearson, G. (1976), '"Paki-bashing" in a North Eastern Lancashire Cotton Town: A Case Study and its History', in J. Mungham and G. Pearson, *Working Class Youth Culture*. London: Routledge.

Pearson, G., Sampson, A., Blagg, H., Stubbs, P., and Smith, D.J. (1989), 'Policing Racism', in R. Morgan and D.J. Smith, eds., *Coming to Terms with Policing: Perspectives on Policy*. London: Routledge.

Reeves, F. (1989), *Race and Borough Politics*. Aldershot: Avebury.

Rock, P. (1990), *Helping Victims of Crime*. Oxford: Oxford University Press.

Sampson, A., and Phillips, C. (1992), *Multiple Victimisation: Racial Attacks on an East London Estate*, Police Research Group Crime Prevention Unit Series Paper 36. London: Home Office Police Department.

Shapland, J., Willmore, J., and Duff, P. (1985), *Victims in the Criminal Justice System*. Aldershot: Gower.

Skogan, W.G. (1986), 'Methodological Issues in the Study of Victimisation', in E. Fattah, ed., *From Crime Policy to Victim Policy*. 80–116. London: Macmillan.

Smith, D.J., and Gray, J. (1983), *Police and People in London, vol. 4: The Police in Action*. London: Policy Studies Institute.

Smith, J.C., and Hogan, B. (1983), *Criminal Law*. London: Butterworth.

Solomos, J. (1989), *Race and Racism in Contemporary Britain*. London: Macmillan.

Stanko, E.A. (1987), 'Typical Violence, Normal Precautions: Men, Women and Interpersonal Violence in England, Wales, Scotland and the USA', in J. Hanmer and M. Maynard, eds., *Women, Violence and Social Control*. London: Macmillan.

— (1988), 'Hidden Violence Against Women', in Maguire and Pointing, eds.: 40–6.

— (1990), *Everyday Violence*. London: Pandora.

Tompson, K. (1988), *Under Siege. Racial Violence in Britain Today*. Harmondsworth: Penguin.

Walklate, S. (1989), *Victimology: The Victim and the Criminal Justice Process*. London: Unwin Hyman.

Walsh, D. (1987), *Racial Harassment in Glasgow*. Glasgow: Scottish Ethnic Minorities Research Unit.

Young, M. (1990), *An Inside Job*. Oxford: Clarendon Press.

21

Drugs and alcohol

21.1 Booze, the urban night and the human ecology of violence
Dick Hobbs, Phil Hadfield, Stuart Lister
and Simon Winlow   490

21.2 Heroin use and street crime
James A. Inciardi   496

21.3 Drug prohibition in the United States: costs, consequences and alternatives
Ethan A. Nadelmann   499

21.4 The war on drugs and the African American community
Marc Mauer   506

Introduction

Drugs and alcohol frequently appear in discussions of crime; either straightforwardly because purchase and sale of various substances is prohibited by law, or more indirectly as perceived causes of criminal activity. Criminological work in this area covers a broad range of issues ranging from the history of social policy in relation to the regulation of substance use and sale to explorations of the relationship between different substances and levels and types of crime.

Because of a preoccupation with illicit drugs in recent decades there has been, until relatively recently, much less discussion of alcohol, its consumption and its impact. This is changing, in part because of what appear to be changing patterns of consumption, many of which are linked to the changing nature of what has become known as the 'night-time economy'. Dick Hobbs and colleagues **(Reading 21.1)** explore the role of alcohol in the urban night and, in particular, what they refer to as the 'human ecology of violence'. They review some of the evidence from accident and emergency records that indicates what proportion of incidents resulting in injury appear to have involved alcohol and go on to explore those aspects of modern (post-industrial, they suggest) consumption that might plausibly be connected to high levels of violence.

If alcohol has an association with violence then it is often assumed that there is a connection between heroin use and acquisitive crime. James Inciardi **(Reading 21.2)** looks at the relationship between heroin use and street crime based on a study of 356 heroin users. He found that early involvement in criminal activity was common, with burglary being the most common initially committed crime. Most users had been arrested and a very substantial proportion had been incarcerated. According to Inciardi, the extensive criminal involvement tended to be connected to their drug habit. He outlines what seem to be very high numbers of offences committed by his sample of heroin users, but argues that a significant proportion of those crimes were 'crimes without victims'.

Attempting to control drug use is a major headache for governments. Ethan Nadelmann **(Reading 21.3)** looks at the history and some of the consequences of American drug prohibition policy. He examines American government policies in relation to overseas drug control and outlines the major barriers that exist, both practically and politically. Indeed, he argues that the major consequence of US drug interdiction policies has been the counterproductive one of increasing the availability of potent cocaine whilst limiting the availability of comparatively benign marijuana. Moreover, such action is extraordinarily expensive – the bill for drug enforcement over 20 years ago being as high as $10 billion. He concludes that the 'most unfortunate victims of drug prohibition policies have been the poor and law-abiding residents of urban ghettos'.

This argument is picked up by Mark Mauer **(Reading 21.4)** who looks at the impact of the so-called 'war on drugs' on the African-American community. He shows how it is African-Americans who have been disproportionately caught up in the huge increase in arrests as a result of drugs crackdowns – despite the fact that the data suggest that the ethnic differences in drug use are relatively minor. One of the best known, and most discriminatory, elements of American drugs policy is the extreme mandatory sentences linked to crack cocaine offences compared with the more liberal sentencing regime for powder cocaine offences. The outcome of these and other drugs policies has seen a very rapid expansion in the number of African-Americans in prison and gaol in the US. Indeed, it is drugs policy more than any other, Mauer suggests, that is responsible for so many Black Americans behind bars.

Questions for discussion

1. What are some of the main changes in the pattern of alcohol consumption outlined by Hobbs and colleagues?

2. In what ways might these changing patterns of consumption be linked with a tendency toward violence?

3. Describe the general characteristics of the criminal histories of Inciardi's sample of heroin users.

4. What does Inciardi mean by 'crimes without victims'? In what ways, if any, might this idea be problematic?

5. What have been the main barriers to American government attempts to prevent the export of drugs from other countries?

6. For what reason does Nadelmann argue that 'the greatest beneficiaries of the drug laws are organized and unorganized drug traffickers'?

7. How does the mandatory sentencing system for crack cocaine work, and how does it affect African-American communities disproportionately?

21.1 Booze, the urban night and the human ecology of violence Dick Hobbs, Phil Hadfield, Stuart Lister and Simon Winlow

> Truth be told, the drug that really did the business was *Stella Artois*.
>
> (Wilson, 2002:179)

Alcohol is the vital lubricant that aids the propulsion of young people into this carnivalesque and consumer-orientated world. It also frames the 'grounded aesthetic' (Willis, 1990:102) of possibilities that languish in young peoples' passionate embrace of risk. In purely commercial terms, alcohol is the commodity that draws people into our city centres after dark, and in addition, sustains associated, complementary markets. In cultural terms it provides an accepted means of altering the mundane, pressurized, regimented, and unattractive world of daylight comportment, realigning meaning and understanding to fit a more seductive and alluring world of hedonism and carnival.

Rather than alcohol consumption revealing a culture-free 'natural' self, the social element of drunkenness is learned behaviour like any other (MacAndrew and Edgerton, 1969), and the cultural expectation of alcohol's 'disinhibitor effect' (Room and Collins, 1983) aids consumers in abandoning their regulated and constrained daylight personas and immersing themselves in the comparatively ambiguous and chaotic culture of the night. Alcohol consumption provides both a culturally and legally sanctioned way of altering behaviour, and it is this opportunity to enjoy legitimized 'time out' in the form of hedonistic forms of experiential consumption and identification, that renders the night-time economy so alluring to young people. Indeed, without the acceptance of certain night-time forms of disorderly intoxicated behaviour, the night-time economy would be less attractive to contemporary youth; for it provides an excuse to 'start breaking down', loosen sensibilities, and abandon oneself to behaviour which would otherwise be contained.

The switch from industrial to post-industrial, from an emphasis on production to consumption, also marks a shift from the problematic producer to the problematic consumer (Ritzer, 2001:233–235). There is a wealth of evidence to suggest that violence is a major byproduct of this mass transgression in the form of 'cultural understandings of the connections between rowdy and violent group drinking, the construction and projection of empowered masculine identity, and the symbolic rejection of respectable social values' (Tomsen, 1997:100), which lie at the core of the enacted, as opposed to marketed night-time economy. Yet, this by-product is, in itself, far from a homogeneous phenomena, and any simplistic conception of 'alcohol-related violence' should be prefaced by a rider differentiating between context and pharmacology (Tierney and Hobbs, 2003).

However, evidence compiled from a huge sample of Accident and Emergency departments around the country (Hutchinson *et al.*, 1998), indicates that 24% of facial injuries were caused by assault, and that 90% of facial injuries in bars, and 45% of facial injuries in the street were associated with alcohol consumption. The busiest period for alcohol-related injuries was found to be between 21.00 hours to 03.00 hours. The 15–25 age group suffered the greatest number of assaults, and 79% of patients assaulted were male, although where injuries involving bottles or glasses had occurred, 83% of the victims were male. Most of the assaults took place in the street (43%), and pubs and bars were the sites of 21%. The peak times for assaults coincided with the closing times of licensed premises, with Friday and Saturday the busiest days. Assault with a blunt instrument (including parts of the body) was the most common form of interpersonal violence (89%), bottles or glasses were used in 8% of cases, and knives in 2%. Just over half of the assaults with bottles or glasses occurred in bars.

Much male violence is associated with drinking in bars (Homel *et al.*, 1992), and those most likely to become the victims of bar related violence are also young males (Langley *et al.*, 1996). In addition to these contextual relationships between alcohol and violence, an association has been established between alcohol and violent crime (Graham and West, 2001). For example, alcohol has been causally implicated in aggression (Bushman, 1997; Lipsey *et al.*, 1997), and the level of male intoxication has been associated with frequency of aggression (Homel and Clarke, 1994).

Crowded and smoky environments (Graham *et al.*, 1980; Homel and Clark, 1994), where large intoxicated groups mingle (ibid., 1994), are venues for displays of aggression (Lang *et al.*, 1995; Martin et al., 1998), and in terms of the compulsive dramas (Willis, 1990:105) ritually played out in the local night-time economy, alcohol inspires the drinker to focus upon the present (Graham *et al.*, 2000), to become impulsive (Berkowitz, 1986), and to overestimate personal power (Gibbs, 1986; Pernanem, 1976), while crucially eroding the ability to contrive non-violent resolutions to perceived provocations (Sayette *et al.*, 1993). Further, research indicates that some males have concerns with their personal power when they drink (McClelland *et al.*, 1972), are easily provoked (Guftanson, 1993), and become sensitive to the behaviour of third parties (Wells and Graham, 1999). Researchers have also found that retaliatory aggression often constitutes a means to settle grievances (Felson, 1982; Tedeschi and Felson, 1994) and is often linked to going to the aid of a friend (Archer *et al.*, 1995; Berkowitz, 1986).

The alcohol-fuelled night-time economy also provides an ideal environment for those who regard fighting as an expressive hobby (Burns, 1980; Dyck, 1980; Tomsen, 1997), providing a common thread linking current generations of drinkers to the hard case cobblestone fighters of yesteryear (Morton, 1993: chapter 1; Pearson, 1973: chapter 1; Samuel, 1981; Winlow, 2001). However, the key difference between these muscular urban legends of the past and the current crop of 'weekend warriors' (Marshall, 1979) is the scale, sheer power and pre-eminence in political and economic terms, that their arena, the night-time economy, has attained in contemporary Britain.

Drawing upon the concept of 'routine activities' (Cohen and Felson, 1979), quantitative research within the ecological tradition has long demonstrated the way in which various forms of crime have a tendency to be highly concentrated in space and time (Bottoms, 1994; Hope, 1985; Sherman *et al.*, 1989). Such studies have identified urban centres with a high density of licensed premises as the 'hot spots', and weekend evenings as the 'hot times' for incidents of assault and disorder (Felson, 1997; McClintock and Wikstrom, 1992; Phillips and Smith, 2000; Roncek and Maier, 1991). Clearly, the links between alcohol consumption and various forms of crime and disorder have long been acknowledged. However recent research has uncovered more about how, why, when, and where alcohol-related incidents in public places occur. In England and Wales, approximately 70% of crime audits published in 1998 and 1999 identified 'alcohol as an issue, particularly in relation to public order' (Home Office, 2001a:1). The majority of hot-spots for violence and disorder (in public) were located in areas containing high concentrations of licensed premises with the number of incidents peaking between 9 p.m. and 3 a.m. on Friday nights/Saturday mornings and Saturday nights/Sunday mornings.

Of course, whilst simple correlations do not explain causation, and the relationship between venue density/proliferation and associated violence and disorder is complex, evidence from deregulated city centre night-time economies such as Manchester, Hull, and the West End of London, many smaller English towns such as Oswestry, Worthing, Macclesfield, and Newcastle under Lyme, and also from Scotland would suggest that increases in the number of licensed premises and in their total capacities and terminal trading hours, are often accompanied by rises in assaults and public order offences, particularly in areas which have a high density of licensed premises.

In Manchester City Centre for example, the capacity of licensed premises increased by 240% between 1998 and 2001, whilst the number of assaults reported to the police increased by 225% between 1997 and 2001 (Home Office, 2001b:57). Manchester's 2001 crime audit recorded 1,277 assaults in and around the Gay Village (an area with a particularly high density of licensed premises); this figure was more than double the number recorded in any other part of the city centre (MCC, 2001). The same audit identified the Peter Street/Quay Street area as a hotspot for 'assault and wounding'. This area had not appeared in the two previous Manchester audits, however, during 2000 a large multi-leisure complex and a number of licensed premises opened in the vicinity, transforming a comparatively quiet street into an extremely busy drinking circuit. Similarly, the total number of recorded incidents of violence and disorder in Newcastle upon Tyne city centre fell between 1997 and 2001, however significant rises were recorded in the Quayside area which corresponded with the redevelopment of this area as the North East's most popular nightlife destination. Between 1997 and 2001 there was a 19% increase in the total capacity of Quayside licensed premises, a 38% increase in drunk and disorderly offences, a

38% increase in assaults and an 18% increase in criminal damage (McWilliams, 2002). Further, an 18-month survey of patients attending the Accident and Emergency department of Hereford General Hospital found that 44% of alcohol-related night-time assault victims received from the county of Herefordshire as a whole, were assaulted in just one street, known locally as 'alcohol alley' (Commercial Road, Hereford) which contains a small, but densely concentrated, number of licensed premises (Ballham, 2002). Evidence from the evaluation of a Home Office-funded Targeted Policing Initiative to reduce alcohol-related violence and disorder in Cardiff found that during the period July 1999 to June 2001, virtually all the rise in disorder 'was accounted for by one street (St Mary's Street) which contained the densest concentration of pubs and clubs and where a number of new premises opened over a short period' (Maguire and Nettleton, 2003:52). The evaluators note that.

> Where *violent* incidents were concerned, St Mary's Street showed a rise of 42 per cent, compared with a fall elsewhere of 15 per cent. And for incidents of *disorder*, St Mary's Street showed a rise of 99 per cent compared with a rise elsewhere of 38 per cent. Moreover, the increases were seen in all locations in this area – incidents inside premises here rose by 66 per cent, incidents outside named premises more than doubled (a rise of 151%), and incidents elsewhere in the street rose by 46 per cent. It is almost certainly relevant that the southern end of the street has seen the greatest growth and concentration of new licensed premises over the past few years. (Maguire and Nettleton, 2003:45)

The evaluators of a concurrent inter-agency initiative providing data to the project regarding the circumstances of violence obtained from assault patients attending the Accident and Emergency department University Hospital of Wales concluded that:

> There was a statistically significant, positively correlated, relationship between city centre licensed premise capacity and street assault... An increase in the number and particularly capacity of licensed premises on a particular street was associated with a disproportionate increase in the number of assaults in that street... There was a highly significant increase in assault in St Mary's Street, despite a well-funded targeted policing project, which focussed on alcohol-related vio-

lence during the study period... city centre violence prevention should be highly responsive to drinks licence applications, new licensed premises, levels of street violence and changes in character of existing licensed premises.
> (Warburton and Shepherd, 2002:27)

Our analysis of violent crime data recorded by the police in 'Eastville' (see Hobbs *et al.*, 2000) reveals a distinctly similar pattern. For example, one particular road in Eastville, 'Lager Street', had developed between 1996 and 1999 into an archetypal 'night-strip'. Within a stretch of two hundred yards there were two licensed nightclubs, one 'superpub' with a special hours licence, a further six pubs and a restaurant-bar, and also a further three applications pending for special hours certificates. Over this period, Lager Street witnessed an increase in recorded violent crime of 106% with 79% of recorded violence occurring between the hours 21.00 and 03.00.

Analysis of the above trends is hardly a matter of 'rocket science', the most obvious and simple explanation being that *when the activity levels of an intoxicated night-time consumer base increase, then, as one might expect, more crime and disorder will be generated* in the streets and public spaces of our night-time leisure zones. However, once a large intoxicated consumer base is formed, such problems do not remain restricted to these distinct leisure locales, but also impact upon late-night pedestrian and vehicular exit routes throughout the area, which become, in the early hours of the morning, the sites of further violence, disorder, anti-social behaviour, criminal damage, vandalism, and noise (Bromley and Nelson, 2002; Hadfield, forthcoming a; Nelson *et al.*, 2001). Further, as the tracing of such incident patterns is based primarily upon police-recorded crime statistics it will undoubtedly underestimate the total number of incidents that actually occur (Tierney and Hobbs, 2003).

Our research (interviews with doorstaff, observational fieldwork with police public order patrols, and examination of 'Eastville' Accident and Emergency records) indicates that recorded crimes represent only a fraction of the problem (see Lister *et al.*, 2000). However, as others have demonstrated (Cuthbert, 1990; Shepherd, 1990; Shepherd *et al.*, 1989; Shepherd and Lisles, 1998), medical data can reveal additional portions of the 'dark figure' of unrecorded violence and its relationship to alcohol consumption. Such statistics highlight the potential for violence that has long existed within our night-time leisure zones (Hope, 1985; Tuck, 1989). Nonetheless, they reveal little about the enacted environment of the night-time economy and its decidedly criminogenic situational and experiential dynamics. Whilst a small number of ethnographic accounts have served to highlight the 'recreational' or carnivalesque dimensions of alcohol-fuelled, night-time disorder (Dyck, 1980; Gofton, 1990; Tomsen, 1997), we would suggest that the problems of 'friction producing encounters between intoxicated strangers and acquaintances' often cited as central to the aetiology of alcohol-related violence (Homel *et al.*, 1992; Wikstrom, 1995), are being exacerbated within the contemporary night-time economy as the leisure industry targets a mainstream audience of young high-spending consumers.

A variety of promotional tools and marketing strategies are being employed which invite experiential transgression and are shrouded in promises of quasi-liminality (Hobbs *et al.*, 2000). The breakdown of old rules has been hastened by the marketing strategies of entrepreneurs who put together special offers and packages aimed at both attracting customers to their premises and keeping them there. Scantily-clad bar staff, striptease artistes, organized drinking games, hen nights, stag nights, and special nights for nurses, students, and even police officers (the wonderfully entitled '999 Disco') are offered, together with '£10-in – and-all-your-drinks-free' nights, and the inevitable three shots of whatever is not selling well for a pound.

Cheap drink and other bait are usually offered on mid-week evenings to maximize profits outside of the weekend deluge that signifies peak business, when drink prices can remain high without fear of dissuading custom. During the week custom must be attracted, and it is here that drinks' promotions work their charms. The promise of half-priced bottles of lager, or two or three shots of spirit for the price of one, a free Tequila with every pint, or a free cocktail upon admittance to a nightclub is often enough to seduce custom away from the television and mid-week hibernation, and back to the city centre to spend money. Bars often offer cheap drinks on the same night as their competitors, not as a form of direct competition, but to create a varied and cheap drinking environment, multiplying custom rather than competing for it, thus acknowledging the culturally informed attractions of circuit drinking. While selling drinks for half of their weekend price may seem like bad business, bars are boosting custom to premises which would in all likelihood remain relatively empty were it not for these marketing strategies.

Thus, consumers of the night-time leisure experience are encouraged to regard our urban centres as liminal zones: spatial and temporal locations within which the familiar protocols and bonds of restraint which structure routine social life loosen and are replaced by conditions of excitement, uncertainty, and pleasure (Turner, 1967, 1969). Within such milieux, interpersonal tensions and conflicts emerge (Arantes, 1996), aggressive hedonism and disorder is normalized (Gofton, 1990; Tomsen, 1997), and violence and intimidation become the blunt instruments of social control.

> *From D. Hobbs, P. Hadfield, S. Lister and S. Winlow* Bouncers: Violence and Governance in the Night-time Economy, *(Oxford: Oxford University Press), 2003, pp. 36–43*

References

Arantes, A.A. (1996) The war of places: Symbolic boundaries and liminalities in urban space. *Theory, Culture and Society*, 13(4): 81–92.

Archer, J., Holloway, R., and McLoughlin, K. (1995) Self-reported physical aggression among young men. *Aggressive Behaviour*, 21:325–342.

Ballham, A. (2002) Witness Statement by AED Consultant in Hereford General Hospital in Hereford Community Safety Partnership a. J.D.
Wetherspoon plc, Hereford Magistrates Court, 31 May 2002.

Berkowitz, L. (1986) Some varieties of human aggression: Criminal violence as coercion, rule-following, impression management and impulsive behavior. In Campbell, A. and Gibbs, J.J. (Eds.) *Violent Transactions. The Limits of Personality*. Oxford: Basil Blackwell, 87–103.

Bottoms, A. E. (1994) Environmental criminology. In Maguire, M., Morgan, K. and Reiner, K. (Eds.) *The Oxford Handbook of Criminology*, (1st edn.) Oxford: Clarendon Press.

Bromley, R. and Nelson, A. (2002) Alcohol-related crime and disorder across urban space and time: Evidence from a British city, *Geoforum*, 33:239–254.

Burns, T.F. (1980) Getting rowdy with the boys. *Journal of Drug Issues*, 10:273–286.

Bushman, B.J. (1997) Effects of alcohol on human aggression: Validity of proposed mechanisms. In Galanter, M. (Ed.) *Recent Developments in Alcoholism*. New York: Plenum Press, 13:227–244.

Cohen, L.E. and Felson, M. (1979) Social change and crime rate trends: A routine activity approach. *American Sociological Review*, 44(4):588–608.

Cuthbert, M. (1990) Investigation of the incidence and analysis of cases of alleged violence reporting to St. Vincent's Hospital. In Chappell, D., Grabosky, P. and Strang, H. (Eds.) *Australian Violence: Contemporary Perspectives*. Canberra: Australian Institute of Criminology.

Dyck, N. (1980) Booze, barrooms and scrapping: Masculinity and violence in a Western Canadian town. *Canadian Journal of Anthropology*, 1:191–8.

Felson, R.B. (1982) Impression management and the escalation of aggression and violence. *Social Psychology*, 45:245–254.

Felson, R.B. (1997) Routine activities and involvement in violence as actor, witness, or target. *Violence and Victims*, 12(3):209–221.

Gibbs, J.J. (1986) Alcohol consumption, cognition and context: examining tavern violence. In Campbell, A. and Gibbs, J.J. (Eds.) *Violent Transactions: The Limits of Personality*. Oxford: Blackwell.

Gofton, L. (1990) On the town: Drink and the 'new lawlessness'. *Youth and Policy*, 29, (April): 33–39.

Graham, K., LaRocquel, L, Yetman, R., Ross, T. J. and Guistra, E. (1980) Aggression in bar room environments. *Journal of Studies on Alcohol*, 41: 227–292.

Graham, K., West, P. and Wells, S. (2000) Evaluating theories of alcohol-related aggression using observations of young adults in bars. *Addiction*, 95(6): 847–863.

Graham, K. and West, P. (2001) Alcohol and crime: examining the link. In Heather, N., Peters, T.J. and Stockwell, T. (Eds) *International Handbook of Alcohol Dependence and Problems*. Sussex: Wiley & Sons, 439–470.

Guftanson, R. (1993) Alcohol-related expected effects and the desirability of these effects for Swedish college students measured with the Alcohol Expectancy Questionnaire (AEQ). *Alcohol and Alcoholism*, 28:469–475.

Hadfield, P. (forthcoming, a) Night as Contested Timespace, Unpublished PhD thesis, University of Durham.

Hobbs, D., Lister, S., Hadfleld, P., Winlow, S., and Hall, 5. (2000) Receiving shadows: Governance and liminality in the night-time economy. *British Journal of Sociology*, 51(4):701–717.

Home Office (2001a) *Assessing Local Alcohol-Related Crime: A Demonstration Project in Crime and Disorder Partnerships: Tender Document*. London: Home Office.

Home Office (2001b) *Fighting Violent Crime Together: An Action Plan*. London: Home Office.

Homel, R. and Clark, J. (1994) The prediction and prevention of violence in pubs and clubs. In Clarke, R.V. (Ed.) *Crime Prevention Studies*, vol 3, Monsey, New York: Criminal Justice Press.

Homel, R., Thomsen, S. and Thommeny, J. L.(1992) Public drinking and violence: Not just an alcohol problem. *Journal of Drug Issues*, 22(3):679–697.

Hope, T. (1985) Drinking and disorder in the city centre: A policy analysis. In *Implementing Crime Prevention Measures*. Home Office Research Study No. 86, London: HMSO.

Hutchinson, I.L., Magennis, P. Shepherd, J.P., and Brown, A.E. (1998) B.A.O.M.S United Kingdom survey of facial injuries, Pt 1: Aetiology and the association with alcohol consumption. *British Journal of Maxillofacial Surgery*, 36:3–13.

Lang E., Stockwell, T., Ryan, P. and Lockwood, A. (1995) Drinking settings and problems of intoxication. *Addiction Research*, 3:141–149.

Langley, J., Chalmers, D., and Fanslow, J. (1996) Incidence of death and hospitalization from assault occurring in and around licensed premises: A comparative analysis. *Addiction*, 91:985–993.

Lipsey, M.W., Wilson, O.B., Cohen, M.A. and Derzon, J.H. (1997) Is there a causal relationship between alcohol and violence? In Galanter, M. (Ed.) *Recent Developments in Alcoholism*. New York: Plenum Press, 13:245–282.

Lister, S., Hobbs, D., Hall, S. and Winlow, S. (2000) Violence in the night time economy: Bouncers: the reporting, recording and prosecution of assaults. *Policing and Society*, 10: 383–402.

McClelland, D.C., Davis, W.N., Kahn, R., and Wanner, E. (1972) *The Drinking Man: Alcohol and Human Motivation*. Toronto: Collier Macmillan.

McClintock, F.H. and Wikstrom, P-O. H. (1992) The comparative study of urban violence: Criminal violence in Edinburgh and Stockholm. *British Journal of Criminology*, 32(4):505–520.

McWilliams, T. (2002) An analysis of crime and disorder trends in Newcastle city centre 31.12.1997–31.12.2001, personal correspondence with the authors.

MacAndrew, C. and Edgerton, R.B. (1969) *Drunken Comportment: A Social Explanation*. London: Thomas Nelson and Sons Ltd.

Maguire, M. and Nettleton, H. (2003) *Reducing Alcohol-related Violence and Disorder: An Evaluation of the 'TASC' Project*. London: Home Office.

MCC(2001) *Crime and Disorder: Working in Partnership for a Safer Manchester*. Audit March 2001, Manchester: MCC.

Marshall, M. (1979) *'Weekend Warriors': Alcohol in a Micronesian Culture*, Palo Alto, C.A.: Mayfield.

Martin, J., Nada-Raja, S., Langley, J., Feehan, M., McGee, R., Clarke, J., Begg, D., Hutchinson-Cervantes, M., Moffit, T., and Rivara, F. (1998) Physical assault in New Zealand: The experience of 21 year old men and women in a community sample. *New Zealand Medical Journal*, 111:158–460.

Morton, J. (1993) *Gangland: London's Underworld*. London: Warner.

Nelson, A., Bromley, R., and Thomas, C. (2001) Identifying micro-spatial and temporal patterns of violent crime and disorder in a British city centre. *Applied Geography*, 21:249–274.

Pearson. J. (1973) *The Profession of Violence*. London: Granada.

Pernanem, K. (1976) Alcohol and crimes of violence. In Kissin, B. and Begleirer, H. (Eds.) *The Biology of Alcoholism*. New York: Plenum Press, 351–444.

Phillips, T. and Smith, P. (2000) Police violence occasioning police complaint: An empirical analysis of time-space dynamics, *British Journal of Criminology*, 40:480–496,

Ritzer, C. (2001) *Explorations in the Sociology of Consumerism*. California: Sage.

Roncek, D.W. and Maier, P.A. (1991) Bars, blocks, and crimes revisited: Linking the theory of routine activities to the empiricism of 'hot spots'. *Criminology*, 29(4):725–753.

Room, R. and Collins, G. (Eds.) (1983) *Alcohol and Disinhibition: Nature and Meaning of the Link*, Research Monograph No. 12, Rockville, MD.: National Institute of Alcohol Abuse and Alcoholism.

Samuel, R. (1981) *East End Underworld: The Life and Times of Arthur Harding*. London: Routledge and Kegan Paul.

Sayette, M.A., Wilson, T., and Elias, M.J. (1993) Alcohol and aggression: A social information processing analysis. *Journal of Studies on Alcohol*, 54:399–407.

Shepherd, J. (1990) Violent crime in Bristol: An Accident and Emergency perspective. *British Journal of Criminology*, 30 (3):289–305.

Shepherd, J. and Lisles, C. (1998) Towards multi-agency violence prevention and victim support. *British Journal of Criminology*, 38(3):351–370.

Shepherd, J.P., Shapland, M., and Scully, C. (1989) Recording of violent offences by the police: An Accident and Emergency department perspective. *Medicine, Science and the Law*, 29:251–257.

Sherman, L.W., Gartin, P.R., and Buerger, M.E. (1989) Hot spots of predatory crime: Routine activities and the criminology of place. *Criminology*, 27:27–55.

Tedeschi, J.T. and Felson, K.B. (1994) *Violence, Aggression and Coercive Actions*. Washington, DC: American Psychological Association.

Tierney, J. and Hobbs, D. (2003) *Alcohol-related Crime and Disorder Data: Guidance for Local Partnerships*. London: Home Office.

Tobias, J.J. (1979) *Crime and Police in England 1700–1900*. London: Gill and Macmillan.

Tomsen, S. (1997) A top night: Social protest, masculinity and the culture of drinking violence. *British Journal of Criminology*, 37(1):90–102.

Tuck, M. (1989) *Drinking and Disorder A Study of Non-Metropolitan Violence*. Home Office Research Study No. 108, London: HMSO.

Turner, V. (1967) *The Forest of Symbols*. Ithaca, NY: Cornell University Press.

Turner, V. (1969) *The Ritual Process*. London: Routledge and Kegan Paul.

Warburton, A.L. and Shepherd, J.P. (2002) *An Evaluation of the Effectiveness of New Policies Designed to Prevent and Manage Violence through an Interagency Approach* (a final report for WORD), Cardiff: Cardiff Violence Research Group.

Wells, S. and Graham, K. (1999) The frequency of third party involvement in incidents of barroom aggression. *Contemporary Drugs Problems*, 26:457-480.

Wikstrom, P.-O. (1995) Preventing city centre street crimes. In Tonry, M. and Farringron, D.P. (Eds.) *Building a Safer Society: Strategic Approaches to Crime Prevention, Crime and Justice: A Review of Research*. vol. 19, London: University of Chicago Press.

Willis, P. (1990) *Common Culture*. Milton Keynes: Open University Press.

Wilson, A.H. (2002) *24-Hour Party People: What the Sleeve Notes Never Tell You*. London: Channel 4 Books.

Winlow, S. (2001) *Badfellas: Crime, Tradition and New Masculinities*. Oxford:Berg.

21.2 Heroin use and street crime
James A. Inciardi

The relationship between heroin use and street crime represents an issue that has long been studied, argued, and reexamined – yet few definitive conclusions are apparent today. For more than six decades, researchers and opinion makers have addressed the subject, asking such questions as, Do heroin use and addiction cause crime? If so, what ought to be done to manage the problem? Much of the research on this has attempted to determine the sequence of heroin use and criminal activity. Does addiction per se lead the user into a life of crime, or do the demands of the addict's life-style force him into criminal behavior? Or, alternatively, is heroin use simply an additional pattern of deviant activity manifested by an already criminal population? [...] The present study focused during a twelve-month period ending in 1978 on the street community as an information source, using active cases in Miami, Florida.[1]

Method

The peculiar life-style, illegal drug-taking and drug-seeking activities, and mobility characteristics of active drug users preclude any examination of this group through standard survey methodology. [...]

In the field site, the author had established extensive contacts within the subcultural drug scene. These represented 'starting points' for interviewing. During or after each interview, at a time when the rapport between interviewer and respondent was deemed to be at its highest level, each respondent was requested to identify other current users with whom he or she was acquainted. These persons, in turn, were located and interviewed, and the process was repeated until the social network surrounding each respondent was exhausted. This method, as described, restricted the pool of users interviewed to those who were currently active in the given subcultural knit in the street community and who were 'at risk'. In addition, it eliminated former users as well as those who were only peripheral to the mainstream of the subcultural half world.

This selection plan does not guarantee a totally unbiased sample. However, the use of several starting points within the same locale eliminated the difficulty of drawing all respondents from one social network. Confidentiality was guaranteed to the respondents, interviewing was done in an anonymous fashion, and each respondent was paid a fee for participating.

This sampling technique resulted in an initial study population of 356 heroin users. [...] Not unlike other populations of drug users, most of the sample cases were males (67 percent), and the majority of both the males and females were unemployed whites, clustered in the 18 to 34-year-old age group. Males and females did, however, evidence many pronounced differences in their criminal career patterns.

Drug use patterns

The heroin users sampled in this study had long histories of multiple drug involvement, following clear sequential patterns of onset and progression. Both males and females began the use of drugs with alcohol. Their first experiences with alcohol intoxication occurred at median ages of 13.3 and 13.9 years, respectively, with 39.3 percent of the males and 21.4 percent of the females having such an experience before age 12. Furthermore, progression into the other major drugs followed identical sequential patterns for both sexes. For example, based on median ages of onset, alcohol use was followed by initial drug abuse experimentation at 15.2 years of age, followed by marijuana use, barbiturate use, heroin use, and cocaine use:

	Median onset age	
Substance	**Males**	**Females**
Alcohol use	12.8	13.8
Alcohol intoxication	13.3	13.9
First drug abuse	15.2	15.2
Marijuana use	15.5	15.4
Barbiturate use	17.5	17.0
Heroin use	18.7	18.2
Cocaine use	19.7	18.7

Curiously, while the females began their careers of substance use one year later than the males, their progression was more rapid and the extent of their drug involvement seemed to be greater.

Criminal histories

Early involvement in criminal activity was characteristic of the great majority of the sampled heroin users, and 99.6 percent of the males and 98.3 percent of the females reported having ever committed a crime, with the median age of the first criminal act preceding the sixteenth year. The first crimes committed were generally crimes against property, although the specific kind of property crime varied between males and females.

Burglary was cited most often by males as the first crime (25.1 percent), followed by shoplifting (20.1 percent), other larcenies (11.7 percent), and drug sales (10.0 percent). In contrast, 38.5 percent of the females reported shoplifting as their first offense, followed by prostitution (18.8 percent) and drug sales (12.8 percent). [...]

Most of the heroin users studied here had arrest histories, but these typically began more than two years after the initiation of criminal activity. Some 93.7 percent of the males reported having been arrested at least once, with the first arrest occurring at a median age of 17.2 years. Slightly fewer females (83.8 percent) had arrest histories, with the initiation into criminal justice processing beginning at a median age of 18.3 years. The data also indicate that the males had more frequent contacts with the criminal justice system. The median number of arrests for the males was 3.5, with 81.2 percent having histories of incarceration. In contrast, the females reported a median of 2.6 arrests, with 62.4 percent having been incarcerated. Such differences might be explained by the younger age at which the males initiated their criminal activity and arrest histories, or by the slightly younger age of the female group.

Current criminal activity

The data on current criminal activity clearly demonstrate not only that most of the heroin users were committing crimes, but also that they were doing so extensively and for the purpose of drug use support. Initially, some 98.7 percent of the males reported committing crimes during the twelve-month period prior to interviewer contact, with a median of 80.5 percent of such criminality undertaken for the purpose of supporting a drug habit.

The 239 male heroin users reported committing 80,644 criminal acts, averaging some 337 offenses per user. While this might be viewed as an astronomical sum, one must consider the relative proportions for each crime category. The violent crimes of robbery and assault, although reaching the considerable figure of almost 3,500, nevertheless represent only 4.3 percent of the total. Similarly, property crimes, while including some 17,846 thefts of various types, account for less than 25 percent of the total figure. On the other hand, a clear majority of the crimes by male heroin users were crimes without victims: almost 60 percent of the criminal behavior reported here was drug sales, prostitution, gambling, and alcohol offenses, with an additional 8.1 percent of criminal activity involving the buying, selling, or receiving of stolen goods – a secondary level of criminality resulting, in most instances, from the users' initial involvement in property crimes.

These comments are not intended to minimize the amount of serious crime among heroin users. Rather, they emphasize that such criminality is more often victimless crime than predatory crime. On the other hand, these data also indicate that male heroin users have diverse criminal careers. [...]

The level of criminal involvement among the female heroin users was also high, but with a different pattern. Some 96.6 percent of the females reported the commission of crimes during the twelve months preceding the interview, with a median of 87.7 percent of the criminal activity engaged in to support a drug habit. The 117 female heroin users admitted responsibility for 37,490 crimes, with prostitution and drug sales accounting for more than two-thirds (68.3 percent) of the total. Like the males, the female group manifested considerable diversity in their offense behavior, with 81.2 percent admitting drug sales, 72.6 percent engaging in prostitution, 70.1 percent reporting shoplifting, and 51.3 percent indicating prostitute theft. Fewer females participated in crimes of violence, and, while many engaged in burglaries and other types of theft, such larceny was notably less frequent than among males. Females, however, tended to be arrested more frequently than males during this twelve-month study period, with a ratio of 1 arrest for every 387 crimes committed. The highest rates of arrest involved assaults and alcohol; most arrests were for prostitution and drug sales; no arrests resulted from 1,345 cases of prostitution theft; and the ratio of shoplifting crimes to arrests was 398:1 for the more than 5,000 cases.

Discussion

These data suggest a number of considerations and implications relevant to the relationship between heroin use and crime, while at the same time indicating several areas for further research.

First, the data document a high incidence and diversity of criminal involvement among both male and female heroin users. The 356 persons studied here reported involvement in a total of 118,134 criminal offenses during a twelve month period, most of these offenses committed for the purpose of supporting the economic needs of a drug-using career. Furthermore, while most of the criminal offenses were what are often referred to as victimless crimes, the 356 respondents were nevertheless responsible for some 27,464 instances of what the Federal Bureau of Investigation designates as index, or serious, crimes.[2] Numerous differences are apparent between males and females in this regard, with the males manifesting a greater involvement in predatory crime, especially violent predatory crime; however, the data also demonstrate that heroin users of both sexes manifest considerable participation in many different levels of criminal activity.

Second, it is evident in these data that arrest rates among heroin users are low. The 118,134 criminal events reported here resulted in a total of only 286 arrests, or a ratio of 1 arrest for every 413 crimes committed; with respect to the more serious index crimes, there was a ratio of 1 arrest for every 292 crimes. This low level of arrest is also apparent in the overall arrest histories of the subjects studied. Among the males, whose careers in crime spanned a median of 12.8 years, the median number of arrests was 3.5. Similarly, the median career in crime among the female heroin users was 11.0 years, and the median number of arrests was only 2.6.

Third, the data described here provide some information pertinent to the question about drug use and crime; namely, is crime a pre- or post-drug-use phenomenon? What the data suggest is that the question phrased in these terms is an oversimplification of a very complex phenomenon. By examining the median ages of initiation into various stages of substance abuse and criminal careers, the complexity becomes evident. For example:

	Males	Females
First alcohol use	12.8	13.8
First alcohol intoxication	13.3	13.9
First criminal activity	15.1	15.9
First drug abuse	15.2	15.2
First marijuana use	15.5	15.4
First arrest	17.2	18.3
First barbiturate use	17.5	17.0
First heroin use	18.7	18.2
First continuous heroin use	19.2	18.4

Among the males, there seems to be a clear progression from alcohol to crime, to drug abuse, to arrest, and then to heroin use. But upon closer inspection, the pattern is not altogether clear. At one level, for example, criminal activity can be viewed as predating one's drug-using career, since the median point of the first crime is slightly below that of first drug abuse, and is considerably before the onset of heroin use. But, at the same time, if alcohol intoxication at a median age of 13.3 years were to be considered substance abuse, then crime is clearly a phenomenon that succeeds substance abuse. Among the females, the description is even more complex. In the population of female heroin users, criminal activity occurred after both alcohol and drug abuse and after marijuana use, but before involvement with the more debilitating barbiturates and heroin.

In summary, these preliminary data suggest that an alternative perspective for research on the link between drugs and crime may be in order. Although the findings here are descriptive of only one population, which could be unique, they suggest that the pursuit of some simple cause-and-effect relationship may be futile. It is clear that heroin users are involved extensively in crime, and that their involvement is largely for the purpose of supporting the desired level of drug intake. It is also clear that users' initiation into substance abuse and criminal activity occurs at a relatively early age. But there are several things that are not clear. Do substance abusers, for example, alter the nature, extent, and diversity of their criminal behaviors at the onset of marijuana use, at the onset of heroin use, or after their initial criminal justice processing? Do adolescent predatory criminals alter the nature and extent of their criminal involvement at various stages of drug abuse? Does drug abuse involve a shifting from primarily predatory crime to victimless crime? Does drug taking result in an increase or decrease in criminal activity? And finally, does a drug-taking career fix the criminal careers of adolescents who might otherwise shift into more law-abiding pursuits as they approach young adulthood.

From J.A. Inciardi, 'Heroin use and street crime', Crime and Delinquency, *1971, 25: 335–346.*

Notes

1 These data were generated by DHEW grant #I-RO1-DA-O-1527-02, from the Division of Research, National Institute on Drug Abuse.
2 The FBI index crimes include homicide, forcible rape, aggravated assault, robbery, burglary, larceny-theft, and motor vehicle theft.

21.3 Drug prohibition in the United States: costs, consequences, and alternatives Ethan A. Nadelmann

As frustrations with the drug problem and current drug policies rise daily, growing numbers of political leaders, law enforcement officials, drug abuse experts, and common citizens are insisting that a radical alternative to current policies be fairly considered: the controlled legalization (or decriminalization) of drugs[1].

Just as 'Repeal Prohibition' became a catchphrase that swept together the diverse objections to Prohibition, so 'Legalize (or Decriminalize) Drugs' has become a catchphrase that means many things to many people. [...]

There is no one legalization option. At one extreme, some libertarians advocate the removal of all criminal sanctions and taxes on the production and sale of all psychoactive substances – with the possible exception of restrictions on sales to children. The alternative extremes are more varied. Some would limit legalization to one of the safest (relatively speaking) of all illicit substances: marijuana. Others prefer a 'medical' oversight model similar to today's methadone maintenance programs. The middle ground combines legal availability of some or all illicit drugs with vigorous efforts to restrict consumption by means other than resort to criminal sanctions. Many supporters of this dual approach simultaneously advocate greater efforts to limit tobacco consumption and the abuse of alcohol as well as a transfer of government resources from anti-drug law enforcement to drug prevention and treatment. Indeed, the best model for this view of drug legalization is precisely the tobacco control model advocated by those who want to do everything possible to discourage tobacco consumption short of criminalizing the production, sale, and use of tobacco.

The limits of drug prohibition policies

Few law enforcement officials any longer contend that their efforts can do much more than they are already doing to reduce drug abuse in the United States. This is true of international drug enforcement efforts, interdiction, and both high-level and street-level domestic drug enforcement efforts.

The United States seeks to limit the export of illicit drugs to this country by a combination of crop eradication and crop substitution programs, financial inducements to growers to abstain from the illicit business, and punitive measures against producers, traffickers, and others involved in the drug traffic. These efforts have met with scant success in the past and show few indications of succeeding in the future. The obstacles are many: marijuana and opium can be grown in a wide variety of locales and even the coca plant 'can be grown in virtually any subtropical region of the world which gets between 40 and 240 inches of rain per year, where it never freezes, and where the land is not so swampy as to be waterlogged. In South

America this comes to [approximately] 2,500,000 square miles,' of which less than 700 square miles are currently being used to cultivate coca[2]. [...]

U.S. efforts to control drugs overseas also confront substantial, and in some cases well-organized, political opposition in foreign countries[3]. Major drug traffickers retain the power to bribe and intimidate government officials into ignoring or even cooperating with their enterprises[4]. [...]

Interdiction efforts have shown little success in stemming the flow of cocaine and heroin into the United States[5]. [...] The principal consequence of U.S. drug interdictions efforts, many would contend, has been a glut of increasingly potent cocaine and a shortage of comparatively benign marijuana.

Domestic law enforcement efforts have proven increasingly successful in apprehending and imprisoning rapidly growing numbers of illicit drug merchants, ranging from the most sophisticated international traffickers to the most common street-level drug dealers. The principal benefit of law enforcement efforts directed at major drug trafficking organizations is probably the rapidly rising value of drug trafficker assets forfeited to the government. There is, however, little indication that such efforts have any significant impact on the price or availability of illicit drugs. Intensive and highly costly street-level law enforcement efforts such as those mounted by many urban police departments in recent years have resulted in the arrests of thousands of low-level drug dealers and users and helped improve the quality of life in targeted neighborhoods[6]. In most large urban centers, however, these efforts have had little impact on the overall availability of illicit drugs.

The logical conclusion of the foregoing analysis is not that criminal justice efforts to stop drug trafficking do not work at all; rather, it is that even substantial fluctuations in those efforts have little effect on the price, availability, and consumption of illicit drugs. The mere existence of criminal laws combined with minimal levels of enforcement is sufficient to deter many potential users and to reduce the availability and increase the price of drugs. Law enforcement officials acknowledge that they alone cannot solve the drug problem but contend that their role is nonetheless essential to the overall effort to reduce illicit drug use and abuse. What they are less ready to acknowledge, however, is that the very criminalization of the drug market has proven highly costly and counterproductive in much the same way that the national prohibition of alcohol did 60 years ago.

The costs and consequences of drug prohibition policies

Total government expenditures devoted to enforcement of drug laws amounted to a minimum of $10 billion in 1987. Between 1981 and 1987, federal expenditures on anti-drug law enforcement more than tripled, from less than $1 billion per year to about $3 billion[7]. State and local law enforcement agencies spent an estimated $5 billion, amounting to about one-fifth of their total investigative resources, on drug enforcement activities in 1986[8]. Drug law violators currently account for approximately 10% of the roughly 550,000 inmates so state prisons, more than one-third of the 50,000 federal prison inmates, and a significant (albeit undetermined) proportion of the approximately 300,000 individuals confined in municipal jails[9]. [...]

The greatest beneficiaries of the drug laws are organized and unorganized drug traffickers. The criminalization of the drug market effectively imposes a de facto value-added tax that is enforced and occasionally augmented by the law enforcement establishment and collected by the drug traffickers. More than half of all organized crime revenues are believed to derive from the illicit drug business; estimates of the dollar value range between $10 and S50 billion per year[10]. [...]

The connection between drugs and crime is one that continues to resist coherent analysis both because cause and effect are so difficult to distinguish and because the role of the drug prohibition laws in causing and labelling 'drug-related-crime' is so often ignored. [...]

Perhaps the most unfortunate victims of the drug prohibition policies have been the poor and law-abiding residents of urban ghettos. Those policies have proven largely futile in deterring large numbers of ghetto dwellers from becoming drug abusers but they do account for much of what ghetto residents identify as the drug problem. In many neighborhoods, it often seems to be the aggressive gun-toting drug dealers who upset law-abiding residents far more than the addicts nodding out in doorways[11]. [...]

Among the most dangerous consequences of the drug laws are the harms that stem from the unregulated nature of illicit drug production and sale[12]. Many marijuana smokers are worse off for having smoked cannabis that was grown with dangerous fertilizers, sprayed with the herbicide paraquat, or mixed with more dangerous substances. Consumers of heroin and the various synthetic substances sold on the street face even more severe consequences, including fatal over-doses and poisonings from unexpectedly potent or impure drug supplies. [...]

Today, about 25% of all acquired immunode-ficiency syndrome (AIDS) cases in the United States and Europe, as well as the large majority of human immunodeficiency virus (HIV)-infected heterosex-uals, children, and infants, are believed to have contracted the dreaded disease directly or indi-rectly from illegal intravenous (IV) drug use[13]. [...]

Other costs of current drug prohibition poli-cies include the restrictions on using the illicit drugs for legitimate medical purposes[14]. Marijuana has proven useful in alleviating pain in some vic-tims of multiple sclerosis, is particularly effective in reducing the nausea that accompanies chemother-apy, and may well prove effective in the treatment of glaucoma[15–17]. [...] Heroin has proven highly effective in helping patients to deal with severe pain; some researchers have found it more effective than morphine and other opiates in treating pain in some patients[18]. [...]

Among the strongest arguments in favor of legalization are the moral ones. On the one hand, the standard refrain regarding the immorality of drug use crumbles in the face of most Americans' tolerance for alcohol and tobacco use. Only the Mormons and a few other like-minded sects, who regard as immoral any intake of substances to alter one's state of consciousness or otherwise cause pleasure, are consistent in this respect; they eschew not just the illicit drugs but also alcohol, tobacco, caffeinated coffee and tea, and even chocolate. 'Moral' condemnation by the majority of Americans of some substances and not others is lit-tle more than a transient prejudice in favor of some drugs and against others.

On the other hand, drug enforcement involves its own immoralities. Because drug law violations do not create victims with an interest in notifying the police, drug enforcement agents must rely heavily on undercover operations, electronic surveillance, and information provided by informants. [...]

Certainly every society requires citizens to assist in the enforcement of criminal laws. But soci-eties, particularly democratic and pluralistic ones, also rely strongly on an ethic of tolerance toward those who are different but do no harm to others. Overzealous enforcement of the drug laws risks undermining that ethic and propagating in its place a society of informants. Indeed, enforcement of drug laws makes a mockery of an essential prin-ciple of a free society, that those who do no harm

to others should not be harmed by others, and par-ticularly not by the state. Most of the nearly 40 million Americans who illegally consume drugs each year do no direct harm to anyone else; indeed, most do relatively little harm even to themselves. Directing criminal and other sanctions at them, and rationalizing the justice of such sanc-tions, may well represent the greatest societal cost of our current drug prohibition system.

Alternatives to drug prohibition policies

Repealing the drug prohibition laws clearly prom-ises tremendous advantages. Between reduced government expenditures on enforcing drug laws and new tax revenue from legal drug production and sales, public treasuries would enjoy a net bene-fit of at least $10 billion per year and possibly much more; thus billions in new revenues would be available, and ideally targeted, for funding much-needed drug treatment programs as well as the types of social and educational programs that often prove most effective in creating incentives for children not to abuse drugs. The quality of urban life would rise significantly. Homicide rates would decline. So would robbery and burglary rates. Organized criminal groups, particularly the up-and-coming ones that have yet to diversify into nondrug areas, would be dealt a devastating set-back. The police, prosecutors, and courts would focus their resources on combating the types of crimes that people cannot walk away from. More ghetto residents would turn their backs on crimi-nal careers and seek out legitimate opportunities instead. And the health and quality of life of many drug users and even drug abusers would improve significantly. Internationally, U.S. foreign policy-makers would get on with more important and realistic objectives, and foreign governments would reclaim the authority that they have lost to the drug traffickers.

All the benefits of legalization would be for naught, however, if millions more people were to become drug abusers. Our experience with alcohol and tobacco provides ample warnings. Today, alco-hol is consumed by 140 million Americans and tobacco by 50 million. All of the health costs asso-ciated with abuse of the illicit drugs pale in comparison with those resulting from tobacco and alcohol abuse. In 1986, for instance, alcohol was identified as a contributing factor in 10% of work-related injuries, 40% of suicide attempts, and about 40% of the approximately 46,000 annual traffic deaths in 1983. An estimated 18 million Americans are reported to be either alcoholics or alcohol abusers. The total coat of alcohol abuse to American society is estimated at over $100 billion annually[19]. Estimates of the number of deaths linked directly and indirectly to alcohol use vary from a low of 50,000 to a high of 200,000 per year[20]. The health costs of tobacco use are different but of similar magnitude. In the United States alone, an estimated 320,000 people die prematurely each year as a consequence of their consumption of tobacco. By comparison, the National Council on Alcoholism reported that only 3,562 people were known to have died in 1985 from use of all illegal drugs combined[21]. Even if we assume that thousands more deaths were related in one way or another to illicit drug use but not reported as such, we still are left with the conclusion that all of the health costs of marijuana, cocaine, and heroin combined amount to only a small fraction of those caused by either of the two licit substances. At the very least, this contrast emphasizes the need for a comprehensive approach to psychoactive substances involving much greater efforts to discourage tobacco and alcohol abuse.

The impact of legalization on the nature and level of consumption of those drugs that are currently illegal is impossible to predict with any accuracy. On the one hand, legalization implies greater availability, lower prices, and the elimination (particularly for adults) of the deterrent power of the criminal sanction – all of which would suggest higher levels of use. Indeed, some fear that the extent of drug abuse and its attendant costs would rise to those currently associated with alcohol and tobacco[22]. On the other hand, there are many reasons to doubt that a well-designed and implemented policy of controlled drug legalization would yield such costly consequences.

The logic of legalization depends in part upon two assumptions: that most illegal drugs are not as dangerous as is commonly believed; and that those types of drugs and methods of consumption that are most risky are unlikely to prove appealing to many people precisely because they are so obviously dangerous. Consider marijuana. Among the roughly 60 million Americans who have smoked marijuana, not one has died from a marijuana overdose[17], a striking contrast with alcohol, which is involved in approximately 10,000 overdose deaths annually, half in combination with other drugs[20]. Although there are good health reasons for people not to smoke marijuana daily,

and for children, pregnant women, and some others not to smoke at all, there still appears to be little evidence that occasional marijuana consumption does much harm at all. Certainly, it is not healthy to inhale marijuana smoke into one's lungs; indeed, the National Institute on Drug Abuse (NIDA) has declared that 'marijuana smoke contains more cancer-causing agents than is found in tobacco smoke'.[23] On the other hand, the number of 'joints' smoked by all but a very small percentage of marijuana smokers is a tiny fraction of the 20 cigarettes a day smoked by the average cigarette smoker; indeed, the average may be closer to one or two joints per week than one or two per day. Note that the NIDA defines a 'heavy' marijuana smoker as one who consumes at least two joints 'daily'. A heavy tobacco smoker, by contrast, smokes about 40 cigarettes per day.

Nor is marijuana strongly identified as a dependence-causing substance. A 1982 survey of marijuana use by young adults (18 to 25 years) found that 64% had tried marijuana at least once, that 42% had used it at least ten times, and that 27% had smoked in the last month. It also found that 21% had passed through a period during which they smoked 'daily' (defined as 20 or more days per month) but that only one-third of those currently smoked daily and only one-fifth (or about 4% of all young adults) could be described as heavy daily users (averaging two or more joints per day)[24]. This suggests in part that daily marijuana use is typically a phase through which people pass, after which their use becomes more moderate. By contrast, almost 20% of high school seniors smoke cigarettes daily.

The dangers associated with cocaine, heroin, the hallucinogens, and other illicit substances are greater than those posed by marijuana but not nearly so great as many people seem to think. Consider the case of cocaine. In 1986, NIDA reported that over 20 million Americans had tried cocaine, that 12.2 million had consumed it at least once during 1985, and that nearly 5.8 million had used it within the past month. Among 18- to 25-year-olds, 8.2 million had tried cocaine; 5.3 million had used it within the past year; 2.5 million had used it within the past month; and 250,000 had used it on the average weekly[25]. One could extrapolate from these figures that a quarter of a million young Americans are potential problem users. But one could also conclude that only 3% of those 18- to 25-year-olds who had ever tried the drug fell into that category, and that only 10% of those who had used cocaine monthly were at risk. (The NIDA survey did not, it should be noted, include persons residing in military or student dormitories, prison inmates, or the homeless.)

All of this is not to say that cocaine is not a potentially dangerous drug, especially when it is injected, smoked in the form of 'crack', or consumed in tandem with other powerful substances. Clearly, many tens of thousands of Americans have suffered severely from their abuse of cocaine and a tiny fraction have died. But there is also overwhelming evidence that most users of cocaine do not get into trouble with the drug. So much of the media attention has focused on the relatively small percentage of cocaine users who become addicted that the popular perception of how most people use cocaine has become badly distorted. [...]

With respect to the hallucinogens such as LSD and psilocybic mushrooms, their potential for addiction is virtually nil. The dangers arise primarily from using them irresponsibly on individual occasions[26]. Although many of those who have used hallucinogens have experienced 'bad trips,' far more have reported positive experiences and very few have suffered any long-term harm[26]. As for the great assortment of stimulants, depressants, and tranquilizers produced illegally or diverted from licit channels, each evidences varying capacities to create addiction, harm the user, or be used safely.

Until recently, no drugs were regarded with as much horror as the opiates, and in particular heroin. As with most drugs, it can be eaten, snorted, smoked, or injected. The custom among most Americans, unfortunately, is the last of these options, although the growing fear of AIDS appears to be causing a shift among younger addicts toward intranasal ingestion[27]. There is no question that heroin is potentially highly addictive, perhaps as addictive as nicotine. But despite the popular association of heroin use with the most down-and-out inhabitants of urban ghettos, heroin causes relatively little physical harm to the human body. Consumed on an occasional or regular basis under sanitary conditions, its worst side effect, apart from the fact of being addicted, is constipation[28]. That is one reason why many doctors in early 20th-century America saw opiate addiction as preferable to alcoholism and prescribed the former as treatment for the latter where abstinence did not seem a realistic option[29, 30].

It is both insightful and important to think about the illicit drugs as we do about alcohol and tobacco. Like tobacco, some illicit substances are highly addictive but can be consumed on a regular basis for decades without any demonstrable harm. Like alcohol, many of the substances can be, and are, used by most consumers in moderation, with little in the way of harmful effects; but like alcohol they also lend themselves to abuse by a minority of users who become addicted or otherwise harm themselves or others as a consequence. And like both the legal substances, the psychoactive effects of each of the illegal drugs vary greatly from one person to another. To be sure, the pharmacology of the substance is important, as is its purity and the manner in which it is consumed. But much also depends upon not just the physiology and psychology of the consumer but his expectations regarding the drug, his social milieu, and the broader cultural environment, what Harvard University psychiatrist Norman Zinberg called the 'set and setting' of the drug[31]. It is factors such as these that might change dramatically, albeit in indeterminate ways, were the illicit drugs made legally available.

It is thus impossible to predict whether or not legalization would lead to much greater levels of drug abuse. The lessons that can be drawn from other societies are mixed. China's experience with the British opium pushers of the 19th century, when millions reportedly became addicted to the drug, offers one worst-case scenario. The devastation of many native American tribes by alcohol presents another. On the other hand, the decriminalization of marijuana by 11 states in the United States during the mid-1970s does not appear to have led to increases in marijuana consumption[32]. In the Netherlands, which went even further in decriminalizing cannabis during the 1970s, consumption has actually declined significantly; in 1976, 3% of 15- and 16-year-olds and 10% of 17- and 18-year-olds used cannabis occasionally; by 1985, the percentages had declined to 2 and 6%, respectively[33]. The policy has succeeded, as the government intended, 'in making drug use boring'. Finally, late 19th-century America is an example of a society in which there were almost no drug laws or even drug regulations but levels of drug use were about what they are today[34]. Drug abuse was regarded as a relatively serious problem, but the criminal justice system was not regarded as part of the solution[35].

There are however, strong reasons to believe that none of the currently illicit substances would become as popular as alcohol or tobacco even if they were legalized. Alcohol has long been the principal intoxicant in most societies, including many in which other substances have been legally available. Presumably, its diverse properties account for its popularity; it quenches thirst, goes well with food, often pleases the palate, promotes appetite as well as sociability, and so on. The widespread use of tobacco probably stems not just from its powerful addictive qualities but from the fact that its psychoactive effects are sufficiently subtle that cigarettes can be integrated with most other human activities. None of the illicit substances now popular in the United States share either of these qualities to the same extent, nor is it likely that they would acquire them if they were legalized. Moreover, none of the illicit substances can compete with alcohol's special place in American culture and history, one that it retained even during Prohibition.

Much of the damage caused by illegal drugs today stems from their consumption in particularly potent and dangerous ways. There is good reason to doubt that many Americana would inject cocaine or heroin into their veins even if given the chance to do so legally. And just as the dramatic growth in the heroin-consuming population during the 1960s leveled off for reasons apparently having little to do with law enforcement, so we can expect, if it has not already occurred, a leveling off in the number of people smoking crack.

Perhaps the most reassuring reason for believing that repeal of the drug prohibition laws will not lead to tremendous increases in drug abuse levels is the fact that we have learned something from our past experiences with alcohol and tobacco abuse. We now know, for instance, that consumption taxes are an effective method for limiting consumption rates and related costs, especially among young people[36]. Substantial evidence also suggests that restrictions and bans on advertising, as well as promotion of negative advertising, can make a difference[37]. The same seems to be true of other government measures, including restrictions on time and place of sale[38], bans on vending machines, prohibitions of consumption in public places, packaging requirements, mandated adjustments in insurance policies, crackdowns on driving while under the influence[39], and laws holding bartenders and hosts responsible for the drinking of customers and guests. There is even some evidence that some education programs about the dangers of cigarette smoking have deterred many children from beginning to smoke[40]. At the same time, we also have come to recognize the great harms that can result when

drug control policies are undermined by powerful lobbies such as those that now block efforts to lessen the harms caused by abuse of alcohol and tobacco.

Legalization thus affords far greater opportunities to control drug use and abuse than do current criminalization policies. The current strategy is one in which the type, price, purity, and potency of illicit drugs, as well as the participants in the business, are largely determined by drug dealers, the peculiar competitive dynamics of an illicit market, and the perverse interplay of drug enforcement strategies and drug trafficking tactics. [...]

A drug control policy based predominantly on approaches other than criminal justice thus offers a number of significant advantages over the current criminal justice focus in controlling drug use and abuse. It shifts control of production, distribution, and, to a lesser extent, consumption out of the hands of criminals and into the hands of government and government licensees. It affords consumers the opportunity to make far more informed decisions about the drugs they buy than is currently the case. It dramatically lessens the likelihood that drug consumers will be harmed by impure, unexpectedly potent, or misidentified drugs. It corrects the hypocritical and dangerous message that alcohol and tobacco arc somehow safer than many illicit drugs. It reduces by billions of dollars annually government expenditures on drug enforcement and simultaneously raises additional billions in tax revenues. And it allows government the opportunity to shape consumption patterns toward relatively safer psychoactive substances and modes of consumption. [...]

The controlled drug legalization option is not an all-or-nothing alternative to current policies. Indeed, political realities ensure that any shift toward legalization will evolve gradually, with ample opportunity to halt, reevaluate, and redirect drug policies that begin to prove too costly or counterproductive. The federal government need not play the leading role in devising alternatives; it need only clear the way to allow state and local governments the legal power to implement their own drug legalization policies. The first steps are relatively risk-free: legalization of marijuana, easier availability of illegal and strictly controlled drugs for treatment of pain and other medical purposes, tougher tobacco and alcohol control policies, and a broader and more available array of drug treatment programs.

Remedying the drug-related ills of America's ghettos requires more radical steps. The risks of a more far-reaching policy of controlled drug legalization – increased availability, lower prices, and removal of the deterrent power of the criminal sanction – are relatively less in the ghettos than in most other parts of the United States in good part because drug availability is already so high, prices so low, and the criminal sanction so ineffective in deterring illicit drug use that legalization can hardly worsen the situation. On the other hand, legalization would yield its greatest benefits in the ghettos, where it would sever much of the drug-crime connection, seize the market away from criminals, deglorify involvement in the illicit drug business, help redirect the work ethic from illegitimate to legitimate employment opportunities, help stem the transmission of AIDS by IV drug users, and significantly improve the safety, health, and well-being of those who do use and abuse drugs. Simply stated, legalizing cocaine, heroin, and other relatively dangerous drugs may well be the only way to reverse the destructive impact of drugs and current drug policies in the ghettos. There is no question that legalization is a risky policy, one that may indeed lead to an increase in the number of people who abuse drugs. But that risk is by no means a certainty. At the same time, current drug control policies are showing little progress and new proposals promise only to be more costly and more repressive. We know that repealing the drug prohibition laws would eliminate or greatly reduce many of the ills that people commonly identify as part and parcel of the 'drug problem'. Yet that option is repeatedly and vociferously dismissed without any attempt to evaluate it openly and objectively. The past 20 years have demonstrated that a drug policy shaped by rhetoric and fear-mongering can only lead to our current disaster. Unless we are willing to honestly evaluate all our options, including various legalization strategies, there is a good chance that we will never identify the beat solutions for our drug problems.

> From E.A. Nadelmann, 'Drug prohibition in the United States: costs, consequences, and alternatives', Science, 1989, 245: 939–947.

References and Notes

1 The terms 'legalization' and 'decriminalization' are used interchangeably here. Some interpret the latter term as a more limited form of legalization involving the removal of criminal sanctions against users but not against producers and sellers.

2 Statement by Senator D.P. Moynihan, citing a U.S. Department of Agriculture report, in *Congr. Rec*, *134* (no. 77), p. S7049 (27 May 1988).

3 See, for example, K. Healy, *J. Interam. Stud. World Aff. 30* (no. 2/3), 105 (summer/fall 1988).

4 E.A. Nadelmann, *ibid. 29* (no. 4), 1 (winter 1987–88).

5 P. Reuter, *Public Interest* (no. 92) (summer 1988), p. 51,

6 *Street-Level Drug Enforcement: Examining the Issues*, M. R. Chaiken, Ed. (National Institute of Justice, Department of Justice, Washington, DC, September 1988).

7 National Drug Enforcement Policy Board, *National and International Drug Law Enforcement Strategy* (Department of Justice, Washington, DC, 1987).

8 *Anti-Drug Law Enforcement Efforts and Their Impact* (report prepared for the U.S. Customs Service by Wharton Econometric Forecasting Associates, Washington, DC, 1987), pp. 2 and 38–46.

9 *Sourcebook of Criminal Justice Statistics*, 1987 (Bureau of Justice Statistics, Department of Justice, Washington, DC, 1988), pp. 490, 494, and 518; and 'Prisoners in 1987' *Bur. Justice Stat. Bull.* (April 1988).

10 Wharton Econometric Forecasting Associates, The Impact: *Organized Crime Today* (President's Commission on Organized Crime, Washington, DC, 1986), pp. 413–494.

11 W. Nobles, L. Goddard, W. Cavil, P. George, *The Culture of Drugs in the Black Community* (Institute for the Advanced Study of Black Family Life and Culture, Oakland, CA, 1987).

12 C.L. Renfroe and T. A. Messinger, *Semin. Adolescent Med.* 1 (no. 4), 247 (1985).

13 D.C. Des Jarlais and S. R. Friedman, *J. AIDS* 1, 267 (1988).

14 See, for example, P. Fitzgerald, *St. Louis Univ. Public Law Rev.* 6, 371 (1987).

15 L. Grinspoon and J. B. Bakalar, in *Dealing with Drugs: Consequences of Government Control*, R. Hamowy, Ed. (Lexington Books, Lexington, MA, 1987), pp. 183–219.

16 T. H. Mikuriya, Ed., *Marijuana: Medical Papers*, 1839–1972 (Medi-Comp Press, Oakland, CA, 1973).

17 *In the Matter of Marijuana Rescheduling Petition*, Docket No. 86–22, 6 September 1988, Drug Enforcement Administration, Department of Justice.

18 A.S. Trebach, *The Heroin Solution* (Yale Univ. Press, New Haven, CT, 1982), pp. 59–84.

19 'Toward a national plan to combat alcohol abuse and alcoholism: A report to the United States Congress' (Department of Health and Human Services, Washington, DC, September 1986).

20 D.R. Gerstein, in *Alcohol and Public Policy: Beyond the Shadow of Prohibition*, M.H. Moore and D.R. Gerstein, Eds. (National Academy Press, Washington, DC, 1981), pp. 182–224.

21 Cited in T. Wicker, *New York Times*, 13 May 1987, p. 427.

22 M.M. Kondracke, *New Repub. 198* (no. 26), 16 (27 June 1988).

23 'Marijuana' (National Institute on Drug Abuse, Washington, DC, 1983).

24 J.D. Miller and I.H. Cisin, *Highlights from the National Survey on Drug Abuse, 1982* (National Institute on Drug Abuse, Washington, DC, 1983), pp. 1–10.

25 *Data from the 1985 National Household Survey on Drug Abuse (National Institute on Drug Abuse,* Rockville, MD, 1987).

26 Grinspoon and J. B. Bakalar, *Psychedelic Drugs Reconsidered* (Basic Books, New York, 1979).

27 J.F. French and J. Safford, *Lancet* I, 1082 (1989); D. C. Des Jarlais, S.R. Friedman, C. Casriel, A. Kott, *Psychol. Health* 1, 179 (1987).

28 J. Kaplan, *The Hardest Drug: Heroin and Public Policy* (Univ. of Chicago Press, Chicago, IL, 1983), p. 127.

29 S. Siegel, *Res. Adv. Alcohol Drug Probl.* 9, 279 (1986).

30 J.A. O'Donnell, *Narcotics Addicts in Kentucky* (Public Health Service Publ. 1881, National Institute of Mental Health, Chevy Chase, MD, 1969), discussed in *Licit and Illicit Drugs* [E. M. Brecher and the Editors of Consumer Reports (Little, Brown, Boston, 1972), pp. 8–10].

31 See N. Zinberg, *Drug, Set and Setting, The Basis for Controlled Intoxicant Use* (Yale Univ. Press, New Haven, CT, 1984).

32 L.D. Johnston, J.G. Bachman, P.M, O'Malley, 'Marijuana decriminalization: the impact on youth 1975–1980' (Monitoring the Future, Occasional Paper 13, Univ. of Michigan Institute for Social Research, Ann Arbor, MI, 1981).

33 'Policy on drug users' (Ministry of Welfare, Health, and Cultural Affairs, Rijswijk, the Netherlands, 1985).

34 D. Courtwright, *Dark Paradise, Opiate Addiction in America Before* 1940 (Harvard Univ. Press, Cambridge, MA, 1982).

35 E.M. Brecher and the Editors of Consumer Reports, *Licit and Illicit Drugs* (Little, Brown, Boston, 1972), pp. 1–41.

36 See P.J. Cook, in *Alcohol and Public Policy: Beyond the Shadow of Prohibition*, M.H. Moore and D.R. Gerstein, Eds. (National Academy Press, Washington, DC, 1981), pp. 255–285; D. Coate and M. Grossman, *J. Law Econ.* 31, 145 (1988); also see K.E. Warner, in *The Cigarette Excise Tax* (Harvard Univ. Institute for the Study of Smoking Behavior and Policy, Cambridge, MA, 1985), pp. 88–105.

37 J.B. Tye, K.E. Warner, S.A. Glantz, *J Public Health Policy* 8, 492 (1987).

38 O. Olsson and P.-O. H. Wikstrom, *Contemp. Drug Probl.* 11, 325 (fall 1982); M. Terris, *Am. J. Public Health* 57, 2085 (1967).

39 M. D. Laurence, J.R. Snortum, F.E. Zimring, Eds., *Social Control of the Drinking Driver* (Univ. of Chicago Press, Chicago, IL, 1988).

40 J.M. Polich, P.L. Ellickson, P. Reuter, J.P. Kahan, *Strategies for Controlling Adolescent Drug Use* (RAND, Santa Monica, CA, 1984), pp. 145–152.

21.4 The war on drugs and the African American community Marc Mauer

Since 1980, no policy has contributed more to the incarceration of African Americans than the 'war on drugs'. To say this is not to deny the reality of drug abuse and the toll it has taken on African American and other communities; but as a national policy, the drug war has exacerbated racial disparities in incarceration while failing to have any sustained impact on the drug problem.

Drug use and drug arrests

The drug war's impact on the African American community can be mapped by looking at two overlapping trends. First, there has been an enormous increase in the number of drug arrests overall; second, African Americans have constituted an increasing proportion of those arrests.

As seen in Figure 21.4.1, in 1980 there were 581,000 arrests for drug offenses, a number that nearly doubled to 1,090,000 by 1990. Although it appeared for a while that these trends might be leveling off in the early 1990s with a decline in arrests, that trend was quickly reversed: a record 1,476,000 drug arrests were made by 1995[1].

Did these arrests reflect rising rates of drug abuse nationally? No. In fact, the best data available show that the number of people using drugs had been declining since 1979, when 14.1 percent of the population reported using drugs in the past month. This proportion had halved to 6.7 percent by 1990, and it declined to 6.1 percent by 1995. Since fewer people were using drugs, and presumably fewer selling as well, then all things being

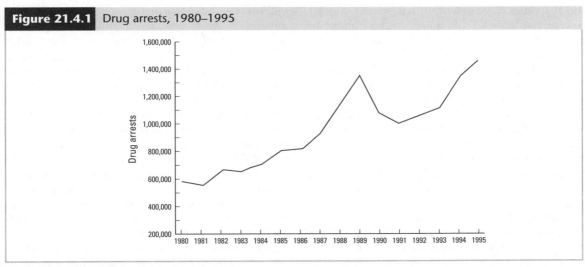

Figure 21.4.1 Drug arrests, 1980–1995

Source: FBI data provided to the author.

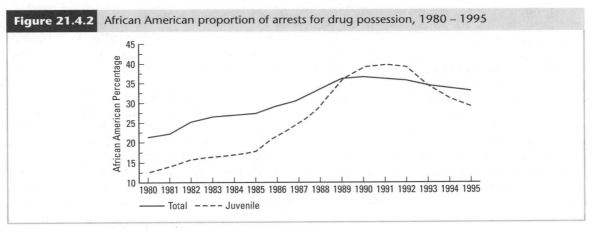

Figure 21.4.2 African American proportion of arrests for drug possession, 1980 – 1995

Source: FBI data provided to the author

equal, one would have thought that drug arrests would have declined as well.

But all things are not equal when it comes to crime and politics. Instead, heightened political and media attention, and increased budgets for law enforcement all contributed to a greater use of police resources to target drug offenders. At the same time, police increasingly began to target low-income minority communities for drug law enforcement.

We can see this most clearly by analyzing arrest data prepared annually by the FBI. As seen in Figure 21.4.2, in 1980, African Americans, who constitute 13 percent of the U.S. population, accounted for 21 percent of drug possession arrests

nationally. This number rose to a high of 36 percent in 1992 before dropping somewhat to 33 percent by 1995. For juveniles, the figures are even more stark: although blacks represented 13 percent of juvenile drug possession arrests in 1980, this proportion climbed to 40 percent by 1991, before declining to 30 percent in 1995. In looking at these statistics, we might conclude that blacks began using drugs in greater numbers during the decade of the 1980s, thereby leading to their being arrested more frequently. In fact no such drama can be detected. [...] Looking at the data for 1995, we find that while African Americans were slightly more likely to be monthly drug users than whites and Hispanics (7.9 percent vs. 6.0 percent and 5.1 percent respectively), the much greater number of whites in the overall population resulted in their constituting the vast majority of drug users. Thus, the SAMHSA data indicate that whites represented 77 percent of current drug users, with African Americans constituting 15 percent of users and Hispanics, 8 percent.[2] Even assuming that blacks may be somewhat undercounted in the household surveys, it is difficult to imagine that African American drug use is of a magnitude that could explain blacks representing 15 percent of current drug users yet 33 percent of arrests for drug possession.

Some observers have speculated that the higher arrest rates for drug possession may reflect the type of drug that is being used – in essence, law enforcement is more likely to target cocaine users or crack cocaine users. Unfortunately, FBI arrest data do not distinguish between powder cocaine and crack cocaine. Arrest data for all cocaine possession offenses for 1995 show that African Americans constituted 47 percent of all such arrests. Looking at data on cocaine use, though, we find that there are no dramatic differences in cocaine use by race or ethnicity. In 1995, 1.1 percent of blacks reported that they had used cocaine in the past month, compared to 0.7 percent of Hispanics and 0.6 percent of whites.[3] Overall, this translates into African Americans representing 15 percent of all recent cocaine users.

For users of crack cocaine, the disproportionate use among blacks is considerably higher than for cocaine overall, but it doesn't explain the arrest disparities. Data for 1995 show that although crack use is quite low for all groups, African Americans are six times as likely as whites to have used it in the past month and three times as likely as Hispanics (0.6 percent vs. 0.1 percent and 0.2 percent respectively).[4] Given the much greater proportion of whites in the overall population, though, these user rates translate into whites representing 54 percent of current crack users, blacks 34 percent and Hispanics 12 percent.

Are police arresting crack and cocaine users in general or preferentially going into black neighborhoods where some people are using these drugs?

Criminologists James Lynch and William Sabol analyzed data on incarceration rates, race, and class during the period 1979–91.[5] They identified inmates as either being 'underclass' or 'non-underclass' (working-class or middle class) based on educational levels, employment history, and income. They concluded that the most significant increase in incarceration rates was for working class black drug offenders, whose rates increased sixfold, from 1.5 per 1,000 in 1979 to match that of underclass blacks at 9 per 1,000 by 1991. The trend for whites, on the other hand, was just the opposite; the underclass drug incarceration rate was double that of the non-underclass by 1991.

Lynch and Sabol suggest that two factors may explain these trends. First, law enforcement targeting of inner-city neighborhoods may initially sweep many underclass blacks into the criminal justice system. Second, due to residential racial segregation patterns, there maybe a 'spillover' effect whereby police increase the number of arrests in the working-class black neighborhoods that border underclass communities.

Drug sales and arrests

Similar disproportionate arrest patterns can be seen for drug selling. In this area, the African American proportion rose from 35 percent in 1980 to 49 percent by 1995.

It is at least theoretically possible that the proportion of black drug traffickers has risen substantially in recent years, and that the arrest percentages reflect actual law-breaking behavior. [...]

One means of addressing this problem is to look at responses to parts of the SAMHSA surveys in which respondents are asked whether it is 'fairly or very easy' to obtain drugs in your neighborhood. Overall, 43 percent of the population in 1996 responded affirmatively regarding cocaine and 39 percent regarding crack. [...]

While blacks were more likely than whites to report that it was easy to obtain these drugs (57 percent vs. 4 percent for cocaine, and 58 percent vs. 8 percent for crack), the differences are still nowhere near the order of magnitude that would explain the arrest disparities.[6] [...]

A 1997 report of the National Institute of Justice lends support to the fact that whites are frequently involved in selling drugs. In an analysis of drug transactions in six cities, the researchers found that 'respondents were most likely to report using a main source who was of their own racial or ethnic background.'[7]

Table 21.4.1 State prison inmates by race and offense

Offence	White				Black			
	1985	1995	% Increase	%Total Increase	1985	1995	% Increase	% Total Increase
Total	224,900	471,100	109%	100%	211,100	490,100	132%	100%
Violent	111,900	214,800	92%	42%	124,800	228,600	83%	37%
Drug	21,200	86,100	306%	26%	16,600	134,000	707%	42%
Property	75,100	130,700	74%	23%	60,600	100,200	65%	14%
Public Order	14,900	39,000	162%	10%	7,600	25,000	229%	6%
Other	1,800	500	-72%	-1%	1,400	2,300	64%	0%

Source: Christopher J. Mumola and Allen J. Beck, 'Prisoners in 1996', Bureau of Justice Statistics, June 1997

Finally, consider the patterns of daily life in urban areas. If it were true that the overwhelming number of drug dealers are black, we would see large numbers of drug-seeking whites streaming into Harlem, South Central Los Angeles, and the east side of Detroit day after day. While some do visit these neighborhoods, there are few reports of massive numbers doing so on a regular basis.

Sentencing for drug offenses

The overrepresentation of African Americans in the criminal justice system has been exacerbated by changes in sentencing policy that coincided with the current drug war. Since 1975, every state has passed some type of mandatory sentencing law requiring incarceration for weapons offenses, habitual offenders, or other categories. These statutes have been applied most frequently to drug offenses, with two primary effects. First, they increase the proportion of arrested drug offenders who are sentenced to prison and, second, they increase the length of time that offenders serve in prison.

Data from the Bureau of Justice Statistics show that the chances of receiving a prison term after being arrested for a drug offense increased by 447 percent between 1980 and 1992.[8] [...]

From 1985 to 1995, drug offenders constituted 42 percent of the rise in the black state prison population (see Table 21.4.1). Note here that drug offenders in this case refers to individuals convicted only of a drug offense and not, for example, a drug-related assault or robbery. For white offenders, by contrast, drug offenders represented 26 percent of the increase and violent offenders 42 percent. Overall, the number of white drug offenders increased by 306 percent in the ten-year period, while for blacks the increase was 707 percent. [...]

The most discussed reason for the racial disparity in drug sentencing in recent years has been the issue of sentencing for crack cocaine offenses [...]. The mandatory sentencing laws passed by Congress provided for far harsher punishments for crack offenses than for powder cocaine crimes. Thus, the sale of 500 grams of cocaine powder resulted in a mandatory five-year prison term, while only 5 grams of crack was required to trigger the same mandatory penalty.

In addition to the other racial dynamics of the drug war, these laws have had a major impact on African Americans. The vast majority of persons charged with crack trafficking offenses in the federal system – 88 percent in 1992–93 – have been African American.[9] [...]

Given the severity of crack penalties in the federal system, the prosecutorial decision regarding whether to charge a drug offense as a state or federal crime has potentially significant consequences for sentencing. The results of a *Los Angeles Times* analysis, which examined prosecutions for crack cocaine trafficking in the Los Angeles area from 1988 to 1994, are quite revealing.[10] During that period, not a single white offender was convicted of a crack offense in federal court, despite the fact that whites comprise a majority of crack users. During the same period, though, hundreds of white crack traffickers were prosecuted in state courts, often receiving sentences as much as eight years less than those received by offenders in federal courts. As is true nationally, the *Times* analysis revealed that many of the African Americans charged in federal court were not necessarily drug kingpins, but rather low-level dealers or accomplices in the drug trade.

From M. Mauer, Race to Incarcerate *(New York: W.W. Norton), 1989, pp. 142–161.*

Notes

1 All figures on drug arrests in this chapter taken from data provided by the FBI to the author.
2 Substance Abuse and Mental Health Services Administration, *National Household Survey on Drug Abuse, Population Estimates 1995* (Washington, D.C.: Substance Abuse and Mental Health Services Administration, June 1996), pp. 18–19.
3 Ibid., pp. 30–31.
4 Ibid., pp. 36–37.
5 James P. Lynch and William J. Sahol, 'The Use of Coercive Social Control and Changes in the Race and Class Composition of U.S. Prison Populations,' paper presented at the American Society of Criminology, Nov. 9, 1994.
6 Substance Abuse and Mental Health Services Administration, 'Preliminary Results from the 1996 National Household Survey on Drug Abuse,' (Washington, D.C.: Substance Abuse and Mental Health Services Administration, July 1897), Tables 314B and 315B.
7 K. Jack Riley, *Crack, Powder Cocaine, and Heroin: Drug Purchase and Use Patterns in Six US. Cities*, National Institute of Justice, Dec. 1997, p. 1.
8 Allen J. Beck and Darrell K. Gilliard, *Prisoners in 1994* (Washington, D.C.: Bureau of Justice Statistics, August 1995), p. 13.
9 United States Sentencing Commission, *Cocaine and Federal Sentencing Policy* (Washington, D.C.: United States Sentencing Commission, February 1995), pp. 122–23.
10 Dan Weikel, 'War on Crack Targets Minorities over Whites,' *Los Angeles Times*, May 21, 1995.

22

Penology and punishment

22.1 The body of the condemned
Michel Foucault   514

**22.2 What works? Questions and answers
about prison reform**
Robert Martinson   517

22.3 Censure and proportionality
Andrew von Hirsch   520

**22.4 The largest penal experiment
in American history**
Franklin E. Zimring, Gordon Hawkins and Sam Kamin   524

Introduction

How are we to understand punishment? What are philosophical ideas and arguments that underpin and justify the ways in which we punish, and how have our systems of punishment changed over time? These are some of the more important questions we need to consider as criminologists.

The first excerpt comes from one the best known texts in the field of penology: Michel Foucault's *Discipline and Punish*. The extract is from the opening pages **(Reading 22.1)** in which Foucault contrasts two descriptions of very differing regimes of punishment. The first concerns an account of the punishment meted out to Robert Damiens, a man accused of the attempted murder of Louis XV. It is a horrific account and a rather chilling read even for those of the most hardened constitution. It is used by Foucault to give us a sense of the public and spectacular nature of much punishment in the eighteenth century and before. He follows this with some examples from the regime from the House of Young Prisoners in Paris some 80 years later. Despite the relatively short period between the two examples, they could not be more different. The (to modern eyes) violent excesses of the former have been replaced by a timetable of activities and a regime of work and prayer. Punishment has moved indoors and is not now characterised by extreme violence. Foucault's point here, in short, is not simply to note the reduction in 'penal severity', but to illustrate some of the ways in which the system of punishment was reorganised and to argue that this was indicative of broader changes in power relations.

In more recent times one of the bigger debates in criminal justice and penology has surrounded the question of 'what works'. In a famous article of that title, Robert Martinson **(Reading 22.2)** sought to summarise and evaluate the empirical evidence on the effectiveness of rehabilitative programmes. There was a lot of research to summarise and Martinson outlines how decisions were taken as to which studies to include and exclude and what measures of 'success' to use. One of his headline conclusions was that the evidence available gave 'us very little reason to hope that we have in fact found a sure way of reducing recidivism through rehabilitation'. One of the reasons for the fame that Martinson's article has achieved is that it subsequently became associated with the assumption that 'nothing works' in the rehabilitative field. This, like the Broken Windows piece in Chapter 13, is another work that is widely cited but much less frequently read. Here's your chance to get ahead of the game!

If we are to punish, how much should we punish? Often the answer is that we should impose a punishment that matches the offence; that is, in other words, proportionate. But why should it be proportionate? This, in essence, is the question that Andrew von Hirsch **(Reading 22.3)** asks and seeks to answer. In doing so he distinguishes between two elements of the punishment: the censure and the sanction, which have differing functions and audiences. Sanctions, he says, must express blame (censure) and their severity should convey the extent of that blame. This still leaves the practical question of 'how much'? Answering this question involves the introduction of another distinction: that between 'ordinal' and 'cardinal' proportionality – in effect grading punishments in relation to each other and determining where the overall scale should start and end.

The final extract, by Franklin Zimring and colleagues **(Reading 22.4)** examines the State of California's experiment with what have become known as 'three strikes and you're out' mandatory sentencing laws. The authors offer some quite extraordinary statistics reflecting the impact of this 'experiment'. One example will suffice. Using 1990 figures they show that the number of people in prison in California was more than twice the number in the whole of England and Wales. They go on to explore the legal rationale – the jurisprudence – for such sentencing and, in particular, the debates over the appropriateness of indeterminate sentencing and the emerging justification for determinate sentencing, and conclude by looking at the impact of the new sentencing regime in terms of sentence severity and proportionality.

Questions for discussion

1. In what way does Foucault suggest that the objective of punishment has changed?

2. When Foucault urges us in studying punishment not to concentrate on their 'repressive elements alone', what is he suggesting?

3. What were the main aim, and the core methods, of Martinson's study?

4. Why do you think that Martinson's article might have given rise to the assumption that 'nothing works'? Is it a reasonable conclusion to draw from the article?

5. What are the main reasons for supporting a principle of proportionality in punishment?

6. Explain the difference between cardinal and ordinal proportionality.

7. What is the underlying principle of 'three strikes' mandatory sentences and how have they affected the California prison population?

8. What are the pros and cons of indeterminate and determinate sentencing?

22.1 The body of the condemned
Michel Foucault

On 2 March 1757 Damiens the regicide was condemned 'to make the *amende honorable* before the main door of the Church of Paris', where he was to be 'taken and conveyed in a cart, wearing nothing but a shirt, holding a torch of burning wax weighing two pounds'; then, 'in the said cart, to the Place de Grève, where, on a scaffold that will be erected there, the flesh will be torn from his breasts, arms, thighs and calves with red-hot pincers, his right hand, holding the knife with which he committed the said parricide, burnt with sulphur, and, on those places where the flesh will be torn away, poured molten lead, boiling oil, burning resin, wax and sulphur melted together and then his body drawn and quartered by four horses and his limbs and body consumed by fire, reduced to ashes and his ashes thrown to the winds' (*Pièces originales...*, 372–4).

'Finally, he was quartered,' recounts the *Gazette d'Amsterdam* of 1 April 1757. 'This last operation was very long, because the horses used were not accustomed to drawing; consequently, instead of four, six were needed; and when that did not suffice, they were forced, in order to cut off the wretch's thighs, to sever the sinews and hack at the joints...

'It is said that, though he was always a great swearer, no blasphemy escaped his lips; but the excessive pain made him utter horrible cries, and he often repeated: "My God, have pity on me! Jesus, help me!" The spectators were all edified by the solicitude of the parish priest of St Paul's who despite his great age did not spare himself in offering consolation to the patient.'

Bouton, an officer of the watch, left us his account: 'The sulphur was lit, but the flame was so poor that only the top skin of the hand was burnt, and that only slightly. Then the executioner, his sleeves rolled up, took the steel pincers, which had been especially made for the occasion, and which were about a foot and a half long, and pulled first at the calf of the right leg, then at the thigh, and from there at the two fleshy parts of the right arm; then at the breasts. Though a strong, sturdy fellow, this executioner found it so difficult to tear away the pieces of flesh that he set about the same spot two or three times, twisting the pincers as he did so, and what he took away formed at each part a wound about the size of a six-pound crown piece.

'After these tearings with the pincers, Damiens, who cried out profusely, though without swearing, raised his head and looked at himself; the same executioner dipped an iron spoon in the pot containing the boiling potion, which he poured liberally over each wound. Then the ropes that were to be harnessed to the horses were attached with cords to the patient's body; the horses were then harnessed and placed alongside the arms and legs, one at each limb.

'Monsieur Le Breton, the clerk of the court, went up to the patient several times and asked him if he had anything to say. He said he had not; at each torment, he cried out, as the damned in hell are supposed to cry out, "Pardon, my God! Pardon, Lord." Despite all this pain, he raised his head from time to time and looked at himself boldly. The cords had been tied so tightly by the men who pulled the ends that they caused him indescribable pain. Monsieur le Breton went up to him again and asked him if he had anything to say; he said no. Several confessors went up to him and spoke to him at length; he willingly kissed the crucifix that was held out to him; he opened his lips and repeated: "Pardon, Lord."

'The horses tugged hard, each pulling straight on a limb, each horse held by an executioner. After a quarter of an hour, the same ceremony was repeated and finally, after several attempts, the direction of the horses had to be changed, thus: those at the arms were made to pull towards the head, those at the thighs towards the arms, which broke the arms at the joints. This was repeated several times without success. He raised his head and looked at himself. Two more horses had to be added to those harnessed to the thighs, which made six horses in all. Without success.

'Finally, the executioner, Samson, said to Monsieur Le Breton that there was no way or hope of succeeding, and told him to ask their Lordships if they wished him to have the prisoner cut into pieces. Monsieur Le Breton, who had come down from the town, ordered that renewed efforts be made, and this was done; but the horses gave up and one of those harnessed to the thighs fell to the ground. The confessors returned and spoke to him again. He said to them (I heard him): "Kiss me, gentlemen." The parish priest of St Paul's did not dare to, so Monsieur de Marsilly slipped under the rope holding the left arm and kissed him on the forehead. The executioners gathered round and Damiens told them not to swear, to carry out their task and that he did not think ill of them; he begged them to pray to God for him, and asked the parish priest of St Paul's to pray for him at the first mass.

'After two or three attempts, the executioner Samson and he who had used the pincers each drew out a knife from his pocket and cut the body at the thighs instead of severing the legs at the joints; the four horses gave a tug and carried off the two thighs after them, namely, that of the right side first, the other following; then the same was done to the arms, the shoulders, the arm-pits and the four limbs; the flesh had to be cut almost to the bone, the horses pulling hard carried off the right arm first and the other afterwards.

'When the four limbs had been pulled away, the confessors came to speak to him; but his executioner told them that he was dead, though the truth was that I saw the man move, his lower jaw moving from side to side as if he were talking. One of the executioners even said shortly afterwards that when they had lifted the trunk to throw it on the stake, he was still alive. The four limbs were untied from the ropes and thrown on the stake set up in the enclosure in line with the scaffold, then the trunk and the rest were covered with logs and faggots, and fire was put to the straw mixed with this wood.

'... In accordance with the decree, the whole was reduced to ashes. The last piece to be found in the embers was still burning at half-past ten in the evening. The pieces of flesh and the trunk had taken about four hours to burn. The officers of whom I was one, as also was my son, and a detachment of archers remained in the square until nearly eleven o'clock.

'There were those who made something of the fact that a dog had lain the day before on the grass where the fire had been, had been chased away several times, and had always returned. But it is not difficult to understand that an animal found this place warmer than elsewhere' (quoted in Zevaes, 201–14).

Eighty years later, Leon Faucher drew up his rules 'for the House of young prisoners in Paris':

'Art. 17. The prisoners' day will begin at six in the morning in winter and at five in summer.

They will work for nine hours a day throughout the year. Two hours a day will be devoted to instruction. Work and the day will end at nine o'dock in winter and at eight in summer.

Art. 18. *Rising.* At the first drum-roll, the prisoners must rise and dress in silence, as the supervisor opens the cell doors. At the second drum-roll, they must be dressed and make their beds. At the third, they must line up and proceed to the chapel for morning prayer. There is a five-minute interval between each drum-roll.

Art. 19. The prayers are conducted by the chaplain and followed by a moral or religious reading. This exercise must not last more than half an hour.

Art. 20. *Work.* At a quarter to six in the summer, a quarter to seven in winter, the prisoners go down into the courtyard where they must wash their hands and faces, and receive their first ration of bread. Immediately afterwards, they form into work-teams and go off to work, which must begin at six in summer and seven in winter.

Art. 21. *Meal.* At ten o'clock the prisoners leave their work and go to the refectory; they wash their hands in their courtyards and assemble in divisions. After the dinner, there is recreation until twenty minutes to eleven.

Art. 22. *School.* At twenty minutes to eleven, at the drum-roll, the prisoners form into ranks, and proceed in divisions to the school. The class lasts two hours and consists alternately of reading, writing, drawing and arithmetic.

Art. 23. At twenty minutes to one, the prisoners leave the school, in divisions, and return to their courtyards for recreation. At five minutes to one, at the drum-roll, they form into workteams.

Art. 24. At one o'clock they must be back in the workshops: they work until four o'clock.

Art. 25. At four o'clock the prisoners leave their workshops and go into the courtyards where they wash their hands and form into divisions for the refectory.

Art. 26. Supper and the recreation that follows it last until five o'clock: the prisoners then return to the workshops.

Art. 27. At seven o'clock in the summer, at eight in winter, work stops; bread is distributed for the last time in the workshops. For a quarter of an hour one of the prisoners or supervisors reads a passage from some instructive or uplifting work. This is followed by evening prayer.

Art. 28. At half-past seven in summer, half-past eight in winter, the prisoners must be back in their cells after the washing of hands and the inspection of clothes in the courtyard; at the first drum-roll, they must undress, and at the second get into bed. The cell doors are closed and the supervisors go the rounds in the corridors, to ensure order and silence' (Faucher, 274–82).

We have, then, a public execution and a time-table. They do not punish the same crimes or the same type of delinquent. But they each define a certain penal style. Less than a century separates them. It was a time when, in Europe and in the United States, the entire economy of punishment was redistributed. It was a time of great 'scandals' for traditional justice, a time of innumerable projects for reform. It saw a new theory of law and crime, a new moral or political justification of the right to punish; old laws were abolished, old customs died out. 'Modern' codes were planned or drawn up: Russia, 1769; Prussia, 1780; Pennsylvania and Tuscany, 1786; Austria, 1788; France, 1791, Year IV, 1808 and 1810. It was a new age for penal justice.

Among so many changes, I shall consider one: the disappearance of torture as a public spectacle Today we are rather inclined to ignore it; perhaps, in its time, it gave rise to too much inflated rhetoric; perhaps it has been attributed too readily and too emphatically to a process of 'humanization', thus dispensing with the need for further analysis. And, in any case, how important is such a change, when compared with the great institutional transformations, the formulation of explicit, general codes and unified rules of procedure; with the almost universal adoption of the jury system, the definition of the essentially corrective character of the penalty and the tendency, which has become increasingly marked since the nineteenth century, to adapt punishment to the individual offender? Punishment of a less immediately physical kind, a certain discretion in the art of inflicting pain, a combination of more subtle, more subdued sufferings, deprived of their visible display, should not all this be treated as a special case, an incidental effect of deeper changes? And yet the fact remains that a few decades saw the disappearance of the tortured, dismembered, amputated body, symbolically branded on face or shoulder, exposed alive or dead to public view. The body as the major target of penal repression disappeared.

By the end of the eighteenth and the beginning of the nineteenth century, the gloomy festival of punishment was dying out, though here and there it flickered momentarily into life. In this transformation, two processes were at work. They did not have quite the same chronology or the same *raison d'être*. The first was the disappearance of punishment as a spectacle. The ceremonial of punishment tended to decline; it survived only as a new legal or administrative practice. The *amende honorable* was first abolished in France in 1791, then again in 1830 after a brief revival; the pillory was abolished in France in 1789 and in England in 1837. [...]

At the beginning of the nineteenth century, then, the great spectacle of physical punishment disappeared; the tortured body was avoided; the theatrical representation of pain was excluded from punishment. The age of sobriety in punishment had begun. By 1830–48, public executions, preceded by torture, had almost entirely disappeared.

The reduction in penal severity in the last zoo years is a phenomenon with which legal historians are well acquainted. But, for a long time, it has been regarded in an overall way as a quantitative phenomenon: less cruelty, less pain, more kindness, more respect, more 'humanity'. In fact, these changes are accompanied by a displacement in the very object of the punitive operation. Is there a diminution of intensity? Perhaps. There is certainly a change of objective.

If the penality in its most severe forms no longer addresses itself to the body, on what does it lay hold? The answer of the theoreticians – those who, about 1760, opened up a new period that is not yet at an end – is simple, almost obvious. It seems to be contained in the question itself: since it is no longer the body, it must be the soul. The expiation that once rained down upon the body must be replaced by a punishment that acts in depth on the heart, the thoughts, the will, the inclinations. Mably formulated the principle once and for all: 'Punishment, if I may so put it, should strike the soul rather than the body' (Mably, 326). [...]

Beneath the increasing leniency of punishment, then, one may map a displacement of its point of application; and through this displacement, a whole field of recent objects, a whole new system of truth and a mass of roles hitherto unknown in the exercise of criminal justice. A corpus of knowledge, techniques, 'scientific' discourses is formed and becomes entangled with the practice of the power to punish. [...]

But from what point can such a history of the modern soul on trial be written? [...] This study obeys four general rules:

1 Do not concentrate the study of the punitive mechanisms on their 'repressive' effects alone, on their 'punishment' aspects alone, but situate

them in a whole series of their possible positive effects, even if these seem marginal at first sight. As a consequence, regard punishment as a complex social function.

2 Analyse punitive methods not simply as consequences of legislation or as indicators of social structures, but as techniques possessing their own specificity in the more general field of other ways of exercising power. Regard punishment as a political tactic.

3 Instead of treating the history of penal law and the history of the human sciences as two separate series whose overlapping appears to have had on one or the other, or perhaps on both, a disturbing or useful effect, according to one's point of view, see whether there is not some common matrix or whether they do not both derive from a single process of 'epistemologico-juridical' formation; in short, make the technology of power the very principle both of the humanization of the penal system and of the knowledge of man.

4 Try to discover whether this entry of the soul on to the scene of penal justice, and with it the insertion in legal practice of a whole corpus of 'scientific' knowledge, is not the effect of a transformation of the way in which the body itself is invested by power relations.

In short, try to study the metamorphosis of punitive methods on the basis of a political technology of the body in which might be read a common history of power relations and object relations. Thus, by an analysis of penal leniency as a technique of power, one might understand both how man, the soul, the normal or abnormal individual have come to duplicate crime as objects of penal intervention; and in what way a specific mode of subjection was able to give birth to man as an object of knowledge for a discourse with a 'scientific' status.

> *From M. Foucault,* Discipline and Punish, *translated by Alan Sheridan (Harmondsworth: Penguin), 1982, pp. 3–31.*

22.2 What works? Questions and answers about prison reform Robert Martinson

In the past several years, American prisons have gone through one of their recurrent periods of strikes, riots, and other disturbances. Simultaneously, and in consequence, the articulate public has entered another one of its sporadic fits of attentiveness to the condition of our prisons and to the perennial questions they pose about the nature of crime and the uses of punishment. The result has been a widespread call for 'prison reform', i.e., for 'reformed' prisons which will produce 'reformed' convicts. Such calls are a familiar feature of American prison history. American prisons, perhaps more than those of any other country, have stood or fallen in public esteem according to their ability to fulfill their promise of rehabilitation.

One of the problems in the constant debate over 'prison reform' is that we have been able to draw very little on any systematic empirical knowledge about the success or failure that we have met when we *have* tried to rehabilitate offenders, with various treatments and in various institutional and non-institutional settings. The field of penology has produced a voluminous research literature on this subject, but until recently there has been no comprehensive review of this literature and no attempt to bring its findings to bear, in a useful way, on the general question of 'What works?'. My purpose in this essay is to sketch an answer to that question. [...]

What we set out to do in this study was fairly simple, though it turned into a massive task. First we undertook a six-month search of the literature for any available reports published in the English language on attempts at rehabilitation that had been made in our corrections systems and those of other countries from 1945 through 1967. We then picked from that literature all those studies whose findings were interpretable – that is, whose design and execution met the conventional standards of social science research. Our criteria were rigorous but hardly esoteric: A study had to be an evaluation of a treatment method, it had to employ an independent measure of the improvement secured by that method, and it had to use some control group, some untreated individuals with whom the treated ones could be compared. We excluded studies only for methodological reasons: They presented insufficient data, they were only preliminary, they presented only a summary of findings and did not allow a reader to evaluate those findings, their results were confounded by extraneous factors, they used unreliable measures, one could not understand their descriptions of the treatment in question, they drew spurious conclusions from their data, their samples were undescribed or too small or provided no true comparability between treated and untreated groups, or they had used inappropriate statistical tests and did not provide enough information for the reader to recompute the data. Using these standards, we drew from the total number of studies 231 acceptable ones.

These treatment studies use various measures of offender improvement: recidivism rates (that is, the rates at which offenders return to crime), adjustment to prison life, vocational success, educational achievement, personality and attitude change, and general adjustment to the outside community. We included all of these in our study; but in these pages I will deal only with the effects of rehabilitative treatment on recidivism, the phenomenon which reflects most directly how well our present treatment programs are performing the task of rehabilitation. The use of even this one measure brings with it enough methodological complications to make a clear reporting of the findings most difficult. The groups that are studied, for instance, are exceedingly disparate, so that it is hard to tell whether what 'works' for one kind of offender also works for others. In addition, there has been little attempt to replicate studies; therefore one cannot be certain how stable and reliable the various findings are. Just as important, when the various studies use the term 'recidivism rate'. they may in fact be talking about different measures of offender behavior – i.e., 'failure' measures such as arrest rates or parole violation rates, or 'success' measures such as favorable discharge from parole or probation. And not all of these measures correlate very highly with one another. These difficulties will become apparent again and again in the course of this discussion.

With these caveats, it is possible to give a rather bald summary of our findings: *With few and isolated exceptions, the rehabilitative efforts that have been reported so far have had no appreciable effect on recidivism.* Studies that have been done since our survey was completed do not present any major grounds for altering that original conclusion.

The effects of community treatment

In sum, even in the case of treatment programs administered outside penal institutions, we simply cannot say that this treatment in itself has an appreciable effect on offender behavior. On the other hand, there is one encouraging set of findings that emerges from these studies. For from many of them there flows the strong suggestion that even if we can't 'treat' offenders so as to make them do better, a great many of the programs designed to rehabilitate them at least did not make them do *worse*. And if these programs did not show the advantages of actually rehabilitating, some of them did have the advantage of being less onerous to the offender himself without seeming to pose increased danger to the community. And some of these programs – especially those involving less restrictive custody, minimal supervision, and early release – simply cost fewer dollars to administer. The information on the dollar costs of these programs is just beginning to be developed but the implication is clear: *that if we can't do more for (and to) offenders, at least we can safely do less.*

There is, however, one important caveat even to this note of optimism: In order to calculate the true costs of these programs, one must in each case include not only their administrative cost but also the cost of maintaining in the community an offender population increased in size. This population might well not be committing new offenses at any greater rate; but the offender population might, under some of these plans, be larger in absolute numbers. So the total number of offenses committed might rise, and our chances of victimization might therefore rise too. We need to be able to make a judgment about the size and probable duration of this effect; as of now, we simply do not know.

Does nothing work?

Do all of these studies lead us irrevocably to the conclusion that nothing works, that we haven't the faintest clue about how to rehabilitate offenders and reduce recidivism? And if so, what shall we do?

We tried to exclude from our survey those studies which were so poorly done that they simply could not be interpreted. But despite our efforts, a pattern has run through much of this discussion – of studies which 'found' effects without making any truly rigorous attempt to exclude competing hypotheses, of extraneous factors permitted to intrude upon the measurements, of recidivism measures which are not all measuring the same thing, of 'follow-up' periods which vary enormously and rarely extend beyond the period of legal supervision, of experiments never replicated, of 'system effects' not taken into account, of categories drawn up without any theory to guide the enterprise. It is just possible that some of our treatment programs *are* working to some extent, but that our research is so bad that it is incapable of telling.

Having entered this very serious caveat, I am bound to say that these data, involving over two hundred studies and hundreds of thousands of individuals as they do, are the best available and give us very little reason to hope that we have in fact found a sure way of reducing recidivism through rehabilitation. This is not to say that we found no instances of success or partial success; it is only to say that these instances have been isolated, producing no clear pattern to indicate the efficacy of any particular method of treatment. And neither is this to say that factors *outside* the realm of rehabilitation may not be working to reduce recidivism – factors such as the tendency for recidivism to be lower in offenders over the age of 30; it is only to say that such factors seem to have little connection with any of the treatment methods now at our disposal.

From this probability, one may draw any of several conclusions. It may be simply that our programs aren't yet good enough – that the education we provide to inmates is still poor education, that the therapy we administer is not administered skillfully enough, that our intensive supervision and counseling do not yet provide enough personal support for the offenders who are subjected to them. If one wishes to believe this, then what our correctional system needs is simply a more full-hearted commitment to the strategy of treatment.

It may be, on the other hand, that there is a more radical flaw in our present strategies – that education at its best, or that psychotherapy at its best, cannot overcome, or even appreciably reduce, the powerful tendency for offenders to continue in criminal behavior. Our present treatment programs are based on a theory of crime as a 'disease' – that is to say, as something foreign and abnormal in the individual which can presumably be cured. This theory may well be flawed, in that it overlooks – indeed, denies – both the normality of crime in society and the personal normality of a very large proportion of offenders, criminals who are merely responding to the facts and conditions of our society.

This opposing theory of 'crime as a social phenomenon' directs our attention away from a 'rehabilitative' strategy, away from the notion that we may best insure public safety through a series of 'treatments' to be imposed forcibly on convicted offenders. These treatments have on occasion become, and have the potential for becoming, so draconian as to offend the moral order of a democratic society; and the theory of crime as a social phenomenon suggests that such treatments may be not only offensive but ineffective as well. This theory points, instead, to decarceration for low-risk offenders – and, presumably, to keeping high-risk offenders in prisons which are nothing more (and aim to be nothing more) than custodial institutions.

But this approach has its own problems. To begin with, there is the moral dimension of crime and punishment. Many low-risk offenders have committed serious crimes (murder, sometimes) and even if one is reasonably sure they will never commit another crime, it violates our sense of justice that they should experience no significant retribution for their actions. A middle-class banker who kills his adulterous wife in a moment of passion is a 'low-risk' criminal; a juvenile delinquent in the ghetto who commits armed robbery has, statistically, a much higher probabilty of committing another crime. Are we going to put the first on probation and sentence the latter to a long-term in prison?

Besides, one cannot ignore the fact that the punishment of offenders is the major means we have for *deterring* incipient offenders. We know almost nothing about the 'deterrent effect,' largely because 'treatment' theories have so dominated our research, and 'deterrence' theories have been relegated to the status of a historical curiosity. Since we have almost no idea of the deterrent functions that our present system performs or that future strategies might be made to perform, it is possible that there is indeed something that works – that to some extent is working right now in front of our noses, and that might be made to work better – something that deters rather than cures, something that does not so much reform convicted offenders as prevent criminal behavior in the first place. But whether that is the case and, if it is, what strategies will be found to make our deterrence system work better than it does now, are questions we will not be able to answer with data until a new family of studies has been brought into existence. As we begin to learn the facts, we will be in a better position than we are now to judge to what degree the prison has become an anachro-nism and can be replaced by more effective means of social control.

> *From R. Martinson, 'What works? Questions and answers about prison reform', The Public Interest, 1974, 35: 22–54.*

22.3 Censure and proportionality
Andrew von Hirsch

The principle of proportionality – that sanctions be proportionate in their severity to the gravity of offences – appears to be a requirement of justice. People have a sense that punishments which comport with the gravity of offences are more equitable than punishments that do not. However, appeals to intuition are not enough: the principle needs to be supported by explicit reasons. What are those reasons?

I. The 'unfair-advantage' theory

The unfair-advantage (or 'benefits-and-burdens') theory has been attributed to Kant, but whether Kant actually subscribed to it is debatable.[1] [...]

The unfair-advantage view offers a retributive, retrospectively-oriented account of why offenders should be made to suffer. The account focuses on the criminal law as a jointly beneficial enterprise. The law requires each person to desist from certain kinds of predatory conduct. By so desisting, the person benefits others; but he also benefits from their reciprocal self-restraint. The person who victimizes others while benefiting from their self-restraint thus obtains an unjust advantage. Punishment's function is to impose an offsetting disadvantage.

This theory has various perplexities.[2] It is arguable (although still debatable) that the offender, by benefiting from others' self-restraint, has a reciprocal obligation to restrain himself. It is much more obscure, however, to assert that – if he disregards that obligation and does offend – the unfair advantage he supposedly thereby gains can somehow (in other than a purely metaphorical sense) be eliminated or cancelled by punishing him. In what sense does his being deprived of rights *now* offset the extra freedom he has arrogated to himself *then* by offending? And why is preserving the balance of supposed advantages a reason for invoking the coercive powers of the state?

Even if such queries could be answered, the benefits-and-burdens theory has another difficulty: it provides little or no assistance for determining the quantum of punishment. [...]

The theory also provides little or no intelligible guidance on how much punishment an offence of any given degree of seriousness should receive. It is not concerned with literal advantage or disadvantage: what matters, instead, is the additional freedom of action that the offender has unfairly appropriated. But the notion of degrees of freedom is not helpful in making comparisons among crimes. It is one thing to say that the armed robber or the burglar permits himself actions that others refrain from taking, and thereby unfairly gains a liberty that others have relinquished in their (and his) mutual interest. It is different, and much more opaque, to say the robber deserves more punishment than the burglar because he somehow has arrogated to himself a greater degree of unwarranted freedom *vis-á-vis* others.

2. Censure-based justifications for punishment

Reprobative accounts of the institution of the criminal sanction are those that focus on that institution's condemnatory features, that is, its role as conveying censure or blame. The penal sanction clearly does convey blame. Punishing someone consists of visiting a deprivation (hard treatment) on him, because he supposedly has committed a wrong, in a manner that expresses disapprobation of the person for his conduct. Treating the offender as a wrongdoer is central to the idea of punishment. The difference between a tax and a fine does not rest in the kind of material deprivation (money in both cases). It consists, rather, in the fact that the fine conveys disapproval or censure, whereas the tax does not.[3]

An account of the criminal sanction which emphasizes its reprobative function has the attraction of being more comprehensible, for blaming is something we do in everyday moral judgements. A censure-based account is also easier to link to proportionality: if punishment conveys blame, it would seem logical that the quantum of punishment should bear a reasonable relation to the degree of blameworthiness of the criminal conduct.

Why the censure?

That punishment conveys blame or reprobation is, as just mentioned, evident enough. But why should there be a reprobative response to the core conduct with which the criminal law deals? Without an answer to that question, legal punishment might arguably be replaced by some other institution that has no blaming implications – a response akin to a tax meant to discourage certain behaviour.

P. F. Strawson provides the most straightforward account.[4] The capacity to respond to wrongdoing by reprobation or censure, he says, is simply part of a morality that holds people accountable for theft conduct. When a person commits a misdeed, others judge him adversely, because his conduct was reprehensible. Censure consists of the expression of that judgment, plus its accompanying sentiment of disapproval. It is addressed to the actor because he or she is the person responsible. One would withhold the expression of blame only if there were special reasons for not confronting the actor: for example, doubts about one's standing to challenge him.

While Strawson's account seems correct as far as it goes – blaming does seem part of holding people accountable for their actions – it may be possible to go a bit further and specify some of the positive moral functions of blaming.

Censure addresses the victim. He or she has not only been injured, but wronged through someone's culpable act. It thus would not suffice just to acknowledge that the injury has occurred or convey sympathy (as would be appropriate when someone has been hurt by a natural catastrophe).

Censure, by directing disapprobation at the person responsible, acknowledges that the victim's hurt occurred through another's fault.[5]

Censure also addresses the act's perpetrator. He is conveyed a certain message concerning his wrongful conduct, namely that he culpably has injured someone, and is disapproved of for having done so. Some kind of moral response is expected on his part – an expression of concern, an acknowledgement of wrongdoing, or an effort at better self-restraint. A reaction of indifference would, if the censure is justified, itself be grounds for criticizing him. [...]

The criminal law gives the censure it expresses yet another role: that of addressing third parties, and providing them with reason for desistence. Unlike blame in everyday contexts, the criminal sanction announces in advance that specified categories of conduct are punishable. Because the prescribed sanction is one which expresses blame, this conveys the message that the conduct is reprehensible, and should be eschewed. [...]

If persons are called upon to desist because the conduct is wrong, there ought to be good reasons for supposing that it *is* wrong; and the message expressed through the penalty about its degree of wrongfulness ought to reflect how reprehensible the conduct indeed is.

Why the hard treatment?

It is still necessary to address punishment's other constitutive element: deprivation or hard treatment. Some desert theorists (John Kleinig and Igor Primoratz,[6] for example) assert that notions of censure can account also for the hard treatment. They argue that censure (at least in certain social contexts) cannot be expressed adequately in purely verbal or symbolic terms; that hard treatment is needed to show that the disapprobation is meant seriously. For example, an academic department does not show disapproval of a serious lapse by a colleague merely through a verbal admonition; to convey the requisite disapproval, some curtailment of privileges is called for. This justification has plausibility outside legal contexts, where the deprivations involved are modest enough to serve chiefly to underline the intended disapproval. However, I doubt that the argument sustains the criminal sanction.

The criminal law seems to have preventive features in its very design. When the State criminalizes conduct, it issues a legal threat: such conduct is proscribed, and violation will result in the imposition of specified sanctions. The threat appears to be explicitly aimed at discouraging the proscribed conduct.[7] Criminal sanctions also seem too onerous to serve just to give credibility to the censure. Even were penalties substantially scaled down from what they are today, some of them still could involve significant deprivations of liberty or property. In the absence of a preventive purpose, it is hard to conceive of such intrusions as having the sole function of showing that the state's disapproval is seriously intended. [...]

The preventive function of the sanction should be seen, I think, as supplying a prudential reason that is tied to, and supplements, the normative reason conveyed by penal censure. The criminal law, through the censure embodied in its prescribed sanctions, conveys that the conduct is wrong, and a moral agent thus is given grounds for desistence. He may (given human fallibility) be tempted nevertheless. What the prudential disincentive can do is to provide him a further reason – a prudential one – for resisting the temptation. Indeed, an agent who has accepted the sanction's message that he ought not offend, and who recognizes his susceptibility to temptation, could favour the existence of such a prudential disincentive, as an aid to carrying out what he himself recognizes as the proper course of conduct.

A certain conception of human nature, of which I spoke in the previous chapter, underlies this idea of the preventive function as a supplementary prudential disincentive. Persons are assumed to be moral agents, capable of taking seriously the message conveyed through the sanction, that the conduct is reprehensible. They are fallible, nevertheless, and thus face temptation. The function of the disincentive is to provide a prudential reason for resisting the temptation.

3. The rationale for proportionality

So much, then, for the general justification for punishment. It is time to move from 'why punish?' to 'how much?'. Assuming a reprobative account of punishment's existence, how can the principle of proportionality be accounted for? The argument will reflect the idea that, if censure conveys blame, its amount should reflect the blameworthiness of the conduct; but it needs to be unpacked more carefully.

Stated schematically, the argument for proportionality involves the following three steps:

1 The State's sanctions against proscribed conduct should take a punitive form; that is, visit

deprivations in a manner that expresses censure or blame.

2 The severity of a sanction expresses the stringency of the blame.

3 Hence, punitive sanctions should be arrayed according to the degree of blameworthiness (i.e. seriousness) of the conduct.

Let us examine each of these steps. Step (1) reflects the claim made in the preceding pages: the response to harmful conduct with which the criminal law centrally deals should convey censure. A morally neutral sanction would not merely be a (possibly) less efficient preventive device; it would be objectionable on the ethical ground that it does not recognize the wrongfulness of the conduct, and does not treat the actor as a moral agent answerable for his or her behaviour.

Step (2) has also been touched upon: in punishment, deprivation or hard treatment is the vehicle for expressing condemnation. When a given type of conduct is visited with comparatively more hard treatment, that signifies a greater degree of disapprobation.

Step (3) – the conclusion – embodies the claim of fairness. When persons are (and should be) dealt with in a manner ascribing demerit, their treatment should reflect how unmeritorious theft conduct can reasonably be said to be. By punishing one kind of conduct more severely that another, the punisher conveys the message that it is worse – which is appropriate only if the conduct is indeed worse (i.e. more serious). Were penalties ordered in severity inconsistently with the comparative seriousness of crime, the less reprehensible conduct would, undeservedly, receive the greater reprobation.

The foregoing case for proportionality holds if my bifurcated justification for the criminal sanction's existence is adopted. It is not necessary to assert that punishment serves solely to express reprobation. In order for my three-step argument to work, it is necessary merely for its premise (Step (1)) to obtain: that the sanction should express reprobation. On my bifurcated view, it should, for I have been arguing why censuring is an essential (albeit not the exclusive) function of the institution of punishment.

Does my bifurcated account of punishment, however, create a Trojan Horse? If punishment's existence is justified even in part on preventive grounds, might prevention be invoked in deciding comparative severities of punishment? Were that permissible, proportionality would be undermined.

Relying on prevention to decide comparative severities is ruled out by the intertwining of punishment's reprobative and hard-treatment features. It is the threatened penal deprivation that expresses the censure as well as serving as the prudential disincentive. Varying the relative amount of the deprivation thus will vary the degree of censure conveyed. Consider a proposal to increase sanctions for a specified type of conduct (beyond the quantum that would be proportionate) in order to create a stronger inducement not to offend. Could such a step be justified under my theory of punishment on grounds that prevention is said to be part of the general aim of punishing and that this measure achieves prevention more efficiently? No, it could not. [...]

Any increase or decrease in the severity–ranking of a penalty on the scale alters how much censure is expressed – and hence needs to be justified by reference to the seriousness of the criminal conduct involved.

4. The criteria for proportionality

When we say sanctions should be 'proportionate', what does that mean? Is there any particular quantum of punishment that is the deserved penalty for crimes of a given degree of seriousness? If not, what guidance does the principle give?

To answer such questions, let me advert to the distinction between ordinal and cardinal proportionality. *Ordinal proportionality* relates to comparative punishments, and its requirements are reasonably specific. Persons convicted of crimes of like gravity should receive punishments of like severity. Persons convicted of crimes of differing gravity should receive punishments correspondingly graded in theft degree of severity. [...]

Ordinary proportionality involves three sub-requirements, which are worth summarizing briefly. The first is *parity*: when offenders have been convicted of crimes of similar seriousness they deserve penalties of comparable severity. This requirement does not necessarily call for the same penalty for all acts within a statutory crime category – as significant variations may occur within that category in the conduct's harmfulness or culpability. But it requires that once such within-category variations in crime–seriousness are controlled for, the resulting penalties should be of the same (or substantially the same) degree of onerousness.

A second sub-requirement is *rank-ordering*. Punishing crime Y more than crime X expresses more disapproval for crime Y, which is warranted only if it is more serious. Punishments should thus be ordered on the penalty scale so that their relative severity reflects the seriousness-ranking of the crimes involved.

The third sub-requirement concerns *spacing of* penalties. Suppose crimes X, Y, and Z are of ascending order of seriousness; but that Y is considerably more serious than X but only slightly less so than Z. Then, to reflect the conduct's gravity, there should be a larger space between the penalties for X and Y than for Y and Z. Spacing, however, depends on how precisely comparative gravity can be calibrated – and seriousness gradations are likely to be matters of rather inexact judgment.

Scaling penalties calls also for a starting point. If one has decided what the penalty should be for certain crimes, then it is possible to fix the sanction for a given crime, X, by comparing its seriousness with the seriousness of those other crimes. But no quantum of punishment suggests itself as the uniquely appropriate penalty for the crime or crimes with which the scale begins. Why not? Our censure-oriented account again provides the explanation. The amount of disapproval conveyed by penal sanctions is a convention. When a penalty scale has been devised to reflect the comparative gravity of crimes, altering the scale's magnitude by making *pro rata* increases or decreases represents just a change in that convention.

Not all conventions, however, are equally acceptable. There may be limits on the severity of sanction through which a given amount of disapproval may be expressed, and these constitute the limits of *cardinal* or non-relative proportionality. Consider a scale in which penalties are graded to reflect the comparative seriousness of crimes, but in which overall penalty levels have been so much inflated that even the lowest-ranking crimes are visited with prison terms. Such a scale would embody a convention in which even a modest disapproval appropriate to low-ranking crimes is expressed through drastic intrusions on offenders' liberties. If suitable reasons can be established for objecting to this, [...] a cardinal – that is, non-relative – constraint is established.

The cardinal–ordinary distinction explains why one cannot identify a unique 'proportionate' sanction for a given offence. Whether x months, y months, or somewhere in between is the appropriate penalty for (say) armed robbery depends on how the scale has been anchored and what punishments have been prescribed for other crimes. The distinction explains, however, why proportionality becomes a significant constraint on the ordering of penalties. Once the anchoring points and magnitude of the penalty scale have been fixed, ordinal proportionality will require penalties to be graded and spaced according to their relative seriousness, and require comparably-severe sanctions for equally reprehensible acts.

From A. von Hirsch, Censure and Sanctions (Oxford: Oxford University Press), 1993, pp. 115–132.

Notes

1 See e.g. D.B. Scheid, 'Kant's Retributivism' (1983); J. C. Murphy, 'Does Kant Have a Theory of Punishment?' (1987); B.S. Byrd, 'Kant's Theory of Punishment' (1989).
2 For critiques of the unfair-advantage theory, see, e.g., A. von Hirsch, *Past or Future Crimes* (1985), ch. 5; R. A. Duff, *Trials and Punishments* (1986), ch. 8; H. Bedau, 'Retribution and the Theory of Punishment' (1978); R. Burgh, 'Do the Guilty Deserve Punishment?' (1982).
3 For further discussion of the censuring character of punishment, and a response to some objections by Michael Davis, see von Hirsch, above n. 6, 270–1.
4 P.F. Strawson, 'Freedom and Resentment' (1974).
5 Joel Feinberg speaks of punishment's function in recognizing the wrongfulness of the conduct in his 'Expressive Function of Punishment' (1970). Uma Narayan points out, however, that censure not only recognizes that the conduct is wrong, but confronts the actor as the agent responsible for the wrongdoing. See U. Narayan, 'Adequate Responses and Preventive Benefits' (1993).
6 J. Kleinig, 'Punishment and Moral Seriousness' (1992); Primoratz, 'Punishment as Language' (1989), 198–202.
7 See N. Jareborg, *Essays in Criminal Law* (1988), 76–8.

22.4 The largest penal experiment in American history
Franklin E. Zimring, Gordon Hawkins and Sam Kamin

Three elements of the California initiative and legislation combine to make it a qualitatively different mandatory-sentencing regime. First, the scale of criminal justice in the state of California is by far the largest in the free world, much larger than the U.S. federal system. California's prisons incarcerate a larger volume of offenders than the penal systems of France and Germany combined (Zimring and Hawkins 1994). Therefore, any new wrinkle in criminal punishment will have a larger net effect in California than elsewhere because of the sheer size of the system. [...]

Second, Three Strikes legislation is much larger in scope than other experiments with mandatory imprisonment because of the lavish levels of imprisonment provided for. In California, defendants with one residential burglary or violent felony conviction must receive prison terms double those mandated for the triggering offense and must also serve a significantly larger fraction of their total sentence prior to release after good time. The doubling of the nominal sentence and the increase from 50% to 80% in required time served effectively triple the penalty for the triggering offense. A 25-year-to-life mandatory sentence is the response to conviction for any felony under the California scheme for defendants with two prior convictions for strike offenses. The eventual arithmetic of long mandatory sentences is obvious if they are actually served. One 25-year sentence has five times as much eventual impact on the prison population as one mandatory 5-year sentence. Add in the rule that requires 80% of the sentence to be served, and the Three Strikes sentence is seven times the size of a 5-year mandatory sentence with no special provisions. With such a heavy impact at the individual level, the aggregate impact on the prison system can be quite large even with a relatively small number of 25-year-to-life sentences. Only 1,000 25-year-minimum sentences are the eventual equivalent of 25,000 prison-man-years, more than that which 10,000 two-year terms would generate.

The third item that widens the impact of California's Three Strikes is the breadth of that law's coverage. Only one prior qualifying felony is necessary before expanded and mandatory imprisonment is required; and Three Strikes is invoked by any triggering felony conviction (including petty theft if a prior felony conviction is present). Other Three Strikes statutes only aggravate penalties after two prior strike convictions and also require a serious felony theft conviction to trigger draconian third-strike penalties (see Clark, Austin, and Henry 1997). [...]

The quantitative impact of all the California differences can be seen from some statistics gathered on the early performance of Three Strikes laws. The compound effects of California's extension of the law to all felony convictions and to sentence enhancements after one qualifying prior can be seen in a published comparison of California with the state of Washington, the first jurisdiction to enact Three Strikes in 1993. By the end of 1996, California had sentenced 26,074 offenders under its Three Strikes provisions, whereas Washington had sentenced 85 in the slightly longer effective span of its new legislation (Clark, Austin, and Henry 1997, p. 3). The ratio of the state populations of California and Washington was six to one; the ratio of sentences under Three Strikes was 307 to 1, or 50 times the population difference of the two states (U.S. Department of Commerce 1994). If the two-strike sentences in California are not counted, the ratio of those in California to Three Strikes sentences in Washington would shrink to 33 to 1, still more than five times the population difference between the two states.

The jurisprudence of imprisonment in California

Cycles of reform in criminal sentencing

Although California is only one of 50 states, debates surrounding its principles of punishment have played a prominent role in the intellectual and political history of criminal sentencing in the United States. The indeterminate sentencing scheme that governed imprisonment in California for the decades before 1976 was the iconic example of a rehabilitative philosophy that governed the terms of imprisonment in adult criminal sentencing, and the attack on that system in California was the major battle over sentencing reform in the United States during the 1970s (Zimring 1983). In the older California regime, when imprisonment was a part of the criminal sanction, formal sentencing authority was divided between superior court judges and the California Adult Authority.

Except where mandatory minimum penalties required imprisonment, the sentencing judge could choose between imprisonment and a sentence less than imprisonment. If imprisonment was selected, the judge would specify a minimum term and the law would provide a maximum term, typically greatly in excess of the minimum. The archetypal indeterminate sentence was not less than one year nor more than life, and the power to choose the actual term that an individual would serve resided with the adult authority.

The structure of indeterminate sentencing was such that both the sentencing judge and the adult authority had wide discretion, to be exercised individually on a case-by-case basis. The final authority for setting a term of imprisonment to be actually served resided in the adult authority, and the release date was set only after the offender had served a significant sentence of imprisonment. The formal rationale for setting release dates late in the prison term was the ability this gave the adult authority to take account of behavior in prison when considering the advisability of release. It was thought that conduct in prison was relevant to the progress of the inmate in rehabilitation programs and that in-prison behavior reflected the dangerousness of the offender if released to the community. [...]

The most popular criticism of indeterminate sentencing in the 1970s was of the tendency for parole power to produce disparity in sentences (see Fogel 1975; Messinger and Johnson 1977). The model case of sentencing disparity at that time was imagining two individuals who were convicted of exactly the same offense but ended up serving very different terms of imprisonment as a result of substantially different in-prison behavior. The power to choose widely different parole release dates, one case at a time, was rightly seen as pregnant with the potential to treat like cases in unlike ways.

There is an implication in this 1970s conception of disparity that deserves special emphasis. Whereas the system of indeterminate sentencing pays extensive attention to the nature of the individual offender in determining the appropriate term of imprisonment, the 1970s view demands more emphasis on the nature of the offense. Any criticism of sentencing disparity requires a conception of the moral currency of deserved punishment because cases cannot be judged similar until such criteria have been agreed upon. In the 1970s, what makes 'like cases alike' is for the most part the seriousness of the offense and the harm suffered by the victims. This is information that the legal system has at the time of the criminal trial; and if it should dominate the calculus of sentencing, no delay in coming to a conclusion about the appropriate length of a prison term is necessary.

The emphasis on the offense in the determination of just prison terms is explicit in the criticisms of the period.

The negative architecture of determinate sentencing

The radical restructuring of criminal sentencing passed by the California legislature in 1976 was designed only to negate the perceived injustices of indeterminate sentencing and parole board power. There was no pressure either to increase or to decrease the aggregate amount of imprisonment in California.

What the new sentencing structure did seek to change was the disparity in time served. The preamble to the reform legislation was forthright in announcing its purposes and priorities. In its singular emphasis it is one of the most noteworthy passages in all of penal legislation:

> (A) (1) The Legislature finds and declares that the purpose of imprisonment for crime is punishment. This purpose is best served by terms proportionate to the seriousness of the offense with provision for uniformity in the sentences of offenders committing the same offense under similar circumstances. [...]

What preoccupied the framers was not the correct sentence for robbery versus the correct sentence for burglary in the new California system, but rather to make sure that all of those offenders sent to prison for burglary received similar terms of imprisonment. The mechanism for achieving this objective was a presumptive 'middle term' for each offense and one greater and one lesser term that could be selected in appropriate circumstances; but the gap between the base term and its variations was deliberately much smaller than the range of sentences that had been served by persons convicted of the same offense under the previous indeterminate system. This was a negative theory of justice in the sense that the removal of one form of disparity was the preoccupying if not exclusive basis for the change.

Because the objective of the determinate system was the undoing of indeterminacy it should not be difficult to find sharp contrasts in the priorities and principles between the two regimes. Rehabilitation is a priority in indeterminate sentencing and is totally excluded from determinate regimes. Equality of punishment for crimes of equal

seriousness is a major emphasis in the new system but not in the old. However, the contrast in emphasis between the two regimes goes deeper than that: Indeterminate sentencing was an *offender-based* jurisprudence, with emphasis on the behavior and prospects of the individual offender. Commission of a serious offense is a necessary precondition of imprisonment; but the nature of the offense need not determine the term of imprisonment to be served. The jurisprudence of determinate sentencing is explicitly *offense-based*, so that the specific term of imprisonment should be dominated not by who the offender is but rather by what he or she has done. And major adjustments to terms of imprisonment based on the character of the individual offender are to be regarded with suspicion by a penal code that fixes sentences 'in proportion to the seriousness of the offense'.

This shift in emphasis downgrades the importance not only of amenability to rehabilitation but also of predictions of dangerousness. If the central justification for the prison term is the seriousness of the offense, the importance of differential predictions of the future conduct of individuals convicted of crime is correspondingly diminished. Thus the shift from offender to offense in the mid-1970s was an important step away from personal dangerousness as a significant influence on the appropriate length of penal confinement. [...]

The emphasis on seriousness and just deserts is thus vulnerable to the charge that it directs penal resources away from a priority on career criminals. In that sense, just as indeterminate sentences are a convenient target for the proponents of the determinate system, the priorities and impacts of determinate sentencing are a convenient target for the proponents of 'Three strikes and you're out'.

The jurisprudence of imprisonment in current California law

Current penal practice in California is a mixture of three distinct sentencing systems and more than three separate rationales for imprisonment. The old indeterminate sentencing system lives on only in sentencing provisions for murder and other crimes that carry high minimum prison terms and life as a maximum sentence. [...]

The great majority of all prison sentences imposed in California are determinate sentences with no parole board power for early release but with a mandatory period of postrelease parole supervision. The offense-based sentences remain the sentencing system most often used, and the time served under determinate sentences is fixed

Table 22.4.1 Severe outcomes of felony arrests before and after Three Strikes

Before Three Strikes		After Three Strikes	
Term	**Offense**	**Term**	**Offense**
20-years-to-life	Murder	Life	Murder
21 years	Robbery	Life	Rape
16 years	Burglary	61 years	Rape
11 years	Firearm assault (with prior felony conviction)	28-years-to-life	Murder
7 years	Robbery	25-years-to-life	Burglary[a]
7 years	Robbery	25-years-to-life	Burglary[a]
7 years	Assault with a deadly weapon	25-years-to-life	Receiving stolen property[a]
6 years	Drug possesion for sale	25-years-to-life	Motor vehicle theft[a]
6 years	Robbery	25-years-to-life	Grand theft[a]
6 years	Battery with great bodily harm	25-years-to-life	Burglary[a]
		15-years-to-life	Murder
		12 years	Robbery
		11 years	Robbery
		11 years	Voluntary manslaughter

[a]Three Strikes.

Source: Three-city sample, criminal sentencing data, 1993.

by the single period of imprisonment selected by the sentencing judge minus the allowable reduction for good time that the inmate earns.

'Three strikes and you're out' added two distinctly different principles of criminal sentencing to the statutory pattern in place in 1994. For offenders who were prosecuted under the second-strike provisions (and these are 9 out of 10 of all sentences under the law), the statutory approach is both offense-centered and offender-centered in an unprecedented mix. It is offense-centered because the defendant's current conviction provides the starting place for calculating his or her minimum punishment. Whatever the felony of the current conviction, the minimum prison sentence must be twice the standard sentence for that crime, and the maximum deduction for good time is reduced from 50% to 20% of the sentence. [...]

For offenders who qualify for third-strike treatment, the sentencing philosophy in California is almost completely offender-based. No matter what the crime, the appropriate sentence is 25-years-to-life and the minimum time served must be 20 years. The characteristics of the individual rather than the crime dominate the statutorily prescribed penal sentence even more in third-strike cases than in the indeterminate sentences of the period before 1977. For third-strike cases, the terms of the statute remove both the judges' power to avoid prison and sharply curtail the parole boards' ability to secure early release.

Proportionality and disparity in criminal sentencing

Table 22.4.1 provides a profile of the most severe sentences in our sample of 1,350 arrests before Three Strikes and 1,800 arrests in the same cities after the law went into effect. We compiled data on the most serious current conviction for the 10 most severe sentences in the pre-Three Strikes arrest sample and for the 14 most severe sentences identified in the Three Strikes sample. [...]

Two significant differences emerge when the most severe punishments imposed are compared before and after Three Strikes. The first difference is that the punishments are much more severe in the post-Three Strikes sample. The shortest sentence in the 'before' sample was 6 years, but almost double that in the 'after' sample. If the minimum number of years in a life term is estimated at 25, the mean minimum sentence at the most serious end of the scale in this cross section of urban arrests more than triples, from just over 10 years before the new law to 33 years after, and the median sentence increases from 7 to 25 years. Even these statistics understate the difference in actual prison stays because the legislation increased the amount of time that many defendants must serve, from 50% to 80% of the minimum. Thus the effective minimum sentence for the most serious end of the prison distribution increased more than threefold.

The second powerful effect concerns the nature of the crimes that produced the most serious sentences in our three-city sample. In the felony arrests before Three Strikes, 80% of the longest sentences handed down were for violent offenses and only one nonviolent offense produced a nominal prison sentence greater than 7 years. In the most serious sentences after Three Strikes, just under half of the longest prison terms were imposed for nonviolent crimes, and a majority of the sentences of more than 15 years were for property crimes that produced the 25-years-to-life sanction that had been selected for the third-strike category. Only two murder and two rape convictions produced nominal minimum sentences that were longer than the sentences handed down for grand theft, car theft, burglary, and receiving stolen property under the mandate of Three Strikes. And these sentences were significantly longer than the terms for murder, voluntary manslaughter, and robbery, which round out the group of the most severe sentences imposed after Three Strikes.

The problem with sandwiching burglars and car thieves in the middle of a distribution of murderers and robbers is the issue of proportionality in punishment.

From F. Zimring, G. Hawkins and S. Kamin, Punishment and Democracy: Three Strikes and You're Out in California *(New York: Oxford University Press), 2001, pp. 17–19, 109–119.*

References

Clark, J., J. Austin, and D.A. Henry. (1997) *Three Strikes and You're Out: A Review of State Legislation*. National Institute of Justice, U.S. Department of Justice, Office of Justice Programs. Washington, D.C.: U.S. Government Printing Office.

Fogel, D. (1975) 'We Are the Living Proof...' *The Justice Model for Corrections*. Cincinnati: W.H. Anderson.

Messinger, S., and P.E. Johnson. (1977) 'California's Determinate Sentencing Statute: History and Issues.' In *Determinate Sentencing: Reform or Regression*. Washington, D.C.: U.S. Government Printing Office.

Zimring, F.E. (1983) 'Sentencing Reform in the States: Lessons from the 1970s.' In *Reform and Punishment: Essays in Criminal Sentencing*. Michael Tonry and Franklin Zimring, eds. Chicago: University of Chicago Press.

Zimring, F.E., and G. Hawkins. (1994) 'The Growth of Imprisonment in California.' *British Journal of Criminology* 34:83–96.

23

Understanding criminal justice

23.1 Two models of the criminal process
Herbert L. Packer   532

23.2 Models of justice: Portia or Persephone? Some thoughts on equality, fairness and gender in the field of criminal justice
Frances Heidensohn   536

23.3 The antecedents of compliant behaviour
Tom R. Tyler   542

23.4 Defiance, deterrence and irrelevance: a theory of the criminal sanction
Lawrence W. Sherman   545

Introduction

In this and the following seven chapters we look at the criminal justice process and the main institutions in the criminal justice system. In relation to each of these it is important to have a sense of how particular institutions work, how they are governed and held accountable. In what follows we will also look at some of the key policy developments and government priorities.

The readings in this chapter cover two important themes: first, how we might best understand and evaluate systems of criminal justice and, second, why people obey the law and how criminal sanctions work. The first excerpt, by Herbert Packer **(Reading 23.1)** contains a brief overview of his famous distinction, or contrast, between two models of the criminal process. He suggests that these are normative models; that is to say, they illustrate the values that might be taken to underpin criminal justice. They are also ideal types: they are not descriptions of things as they are in reality but, rather, are constructs that are designed to allow us identify features of particular justice systems by the way the approximate elements of his two models. Packer calls his two models *due process* and *crime control* and they provide a means by which we can assess both the nature of, and developments in, our own system of criminal justice.

A contrasting approach to thinking about the nature of criminal justice systems is offered by Frances Heidensohn **(Reading 23.2)**. As a feminist scholar her concerns here are with the values of equality and fairness and, more particularly, how the treatment of women within the criminal justice system can be assessed. She also distinguishes two ideal typical models of criminal justice. The first she calls **Portia** after the heroine in Shakespeare's *The Merchant of Venice*; the second **Persephone** (the daughter of Demeter and Zeus in Greek mythology). Both models seek to capture particular values and characteristics of criminal justice, but the distinction between them is intended to convey the importance of recognising that men's and women's needs are different and criminal justice systems should, in some respects, treat them differently. At heart, this means thinking about and attempting to develop a woman-centred model of justice (we already have a male-centred one).

In different ways the two initial readings in this chapter were both partly concerned with issues of fairness and due process. In examining the antecedents of compliant behaviour, Tom Tyler **(Reading 23.3)** examines the idea of 'procedural justice': the idea that processes should be seen to be fair and just. This raises the question of how people define procedures as fair. The findings of his study are interesting for he suggests that consistency in processes is generally rated as being far less important than such factors as the ability to participate, to present arguments, and to be listened to. People also expect that decision-makers will be unbiased. Crucially he says that there is no single model of what is perceived to be 'fair' and that people will vary in the ways in which they evaluate their treatment. Central to understanding authority and compliance – essentially deciding to abide by norms and rules – are values he argues. Such a perspective suggests that self-interest is perhaps less important than other theories might imply.

Crudely put, when people engage in misconduct the criminal justice system may step in. The end point of the criminal justice process often involves the imposition of a criminal sanction – perhaps a fine, or probation, or even imprisonment. As we saw in the previous chapter in connection with Martinson's article, one long-standing question is of course 'what works'. In the final excerpt here, Lawrence Sherman **(Reading 23.4)** offers a theory of the criminal sanction – one he calls 'defiance theory'; in effect, examining the acts of resistance – ranging from anger to reoffending – that may (or may not) be stimulated by the imposition of some penalty. Our reaction to punishment, he suggests, is governed by a number of factors including whether we see it as 'fair', how well we are bonded to the community and to those imposing the sanction, and whether we are willing to acknowledge the shame the punishment makes us suffer. Sherman's theory is an attempt to get us to think about the complex relationships between people's behaviour and the punishments we impose upon them.

Questions for discussion

1. Describe the basic elements of each of Packer's two models of the criminal process.

2. Which of the models, or which elements of the two models, do you think best capture the nature of the criminal justice system you are most familiar with, and why?

3. What are the main distinctions between Heidensohn's two models of criminal justice?

4. What might a women-centred criminal justice process look like?

5. Explain the idea of procedural justice. What are its major characteristics?

6. In what ways does Tyler suggest that normative issues are central in understanding authority and compliance?

7. What does Sherman mean by 'defiance'?

8. What are the four conditions identified by Sherman as necessary for defiance to occur?

23.1 Two models of the criminal process
Herbert L. Packer

The kind of model we need is one that permits us to recognize explicitly the value choices that underlie the details of the criminal process. In a word, what we need is a *normative* model or models. It will take more than one model, but it will not take more than two. [...]

I call these two models the Due Process Model and the Crime Control Model. I shall sketch their animating presuppositions.

Values underlying the models

Each of the two models is an attempt to give operational content to a complex of values underlying the criminal law. [...]

Some Common Ground. However, the polarity of the two models is not absolute. [...] There are assumptions about the criminal process that are widely shared and that may be viewed as common ground for the operation of any model of the criminal process. Our first task is to clarify these assumptions.

First, there is the assumption, implicit in the ex post facto clause of the Constitution, that the function of defining conduct that may be treated as criminal is separate from and prior to the process of identifying and dealing with persons as criminals. How wide or narrow the definition of criminal conduct must be is an important question of policy that yields highly variable results depending on the values held by those making the relevant decisions. [...]

A related assumption that limits the area of controversy is that the criminal process ordinarily ought to be invoked by those charged with the responsibility for doing so when it appears that a crime has been committed and that there is a reasonable prospect of apprehending and convicting its perpetrator. Although police and prosecutors are allowed broad discretion for deciding not to invoke the criminal process, it is commonly agreed that these officials have no general dispensing power. [...]

Next, there is the assumption that there are limits to the powers of government to investigate and apprehend persons suspected of committing crimes. [...] I am talking about the general assump-tion that a degree of scrutiny and control must be exercised with respect to the activities of law enforcement officers, that the security and privacy of the individual may not be invaded at will.

Finally, there is a complex of assumptions embraced by terms such as 'the adversary system', 'procedural due process', 'notice and an opportunity to be heard', and 'day in court'. Common to them all is the notion that the alleged criminal is not merely an object to be acted upon but an independent entity in the process who may, if he so desires, force the operators of the process to demonstrate to an independent authority (judge and jury) that he is guilty of the charges against him. It is a minimal assumption. [...]

So much for common ground. There is a good deal of it, even in the narrowest view. Its existence should not be overlooked, because it is, by definition, what permits partial resolutions of the tension between the two models to take place. [...]

Crime Control Values. The value system that underlies the Crime Control Model is based on the proposition that the repression of criminal conduct is by far the most important function to be performed by the criminal process. The failure of law enforcement to bring criminal conduct under tight control is viewed as leading to the breakdown of public order and thence to the disappearance of an important condition of human freedom. If the laws go unenforced – which is to say, if it is perceived that there is a high percentage of failure to apprehend and convict in the criminal process – a general disregard for legal controls tends to develop. The law-abiding citizen then becomes the victim of all sorts of unjustifiable invasions of his interests. His security of person and property is sharply diminished, and, therefore, so is his liberty to function as a member of society. The claim ultimately is that the criminal process is a positive guarantor of social freedom. In order to achieve this high purpose, the Crime Control Model requires that primary attention be paid to the efficiency with which the criminal process operates to screen suspects, determine guilt, and secure appropriate dispositions of persons convicted of crime.

Efficiency of operation is not, of course, a criterion that can be applied in a vacuum. By 'efficiency' we mean the system's capacity to apprehend, try, convict, and dispose of a high proportion of criminal offenders whose offenses become known. [...] We use the criminal sanction to cover an increasingly wide spectrum of behavior thought to be antisocial, and the amount of crime is very high indeed, although both level and trend are hard to assess.[1] At the same time, although precise measures are not available, it does not appear that we are disposed in the public sector of the economy to increase very drastically the quantity, much less the quality, of the resources devoted to the suppression of criminal activity through the operation of the criminal process. These factors have an important bearing on the criteria of efficiency, and therefore on the nature of the Crime Control Model.

The model, in order to operate successfully, must produce a high rate of apprehension and conviction, and must do so in a context where the magnitudes being dealt with are very large and the resources for dealing with them are very limited. There must then be a premium on speed and finality. Speed, in turn, depends on informality and on uniformity; finality depends on minimizing the occasions for challenge. [...] The model that will operate successfully on these presuppositions must be an administrative, almost a managerial, model. The image that comes to mind is an assembly-line conveyor belt down which moves an endless stream of cases, never stopping, carrying the cases to workers who stand at fixed stations and who perform on each case as it comes by the same small but essential operation that brings it one step closer to being a finished product, or, to exchange the metaphor for the reality, a closed file. The criminal process, in this model, is seen as a screening process in which each successive stage – pre-arrest investigation, arrest, post-arrest investigation, preparation for trial, trial or entry of plea, conviction, disposition – involves a series of routinized operations whose success is gauged primarily by their tendency to pass the case along to a successful conclusion.

What is a successful conclusion? One that throws off at an early stage those cases in which it appears unlikely that the person apprehended is an offender and then secures, as expeditiously as possible, the conviction of the rest, with a minimum of occasions for challenge, let alone post-audit. By the application of administrative expertness, pri-

marily that of the police and prosecutors, an early determination of probable innocence or guilt emerges. Those who are probably innocent are screened out. Those who are probably guilty are passed quickly through the remaining stages of the process. The key to the operation of the model regarding those who are not screened out is what I shall call a presumption of guilt. [...]

The presumption of guilt is what makes it possible for the system to deal efficiently with large numbers, as the Crime Control Model demands. The supposition is that the screening processes operated by police and prosecutors are reliable indicators of probable guilt. Once a man has been arrested and investigated without being found to be probably innocent, or, to put it differently, once a determination has been made that there is enough evidence of guilt to permit holding him for further action, then all subsequent activity directed toward him is based on the view that he is probably guilty. The precise point at which this occurs will vary from case to case; in many cases it will occur as soon as the suspect is arrested, or even before, if the evidence of probable guilt that has come to the attention of the authorities is sufficiently strong. But in any case the presumption of guilt will begin to operate well before the 'suspect' becomes a 'defendant'.

The presumption of guilt is not, of course, a thing. Nor is it even a rule of law in the usual sense. It simply is the consequence of a complex of attitudes, a mood. If there is confidence in the reliability of informal administrative fact-finding activities that take place in the early stages of the criminal process, the remaining stages of the process can be relatively perfunctory without any loss in operating efficiency. The presumption of guilt, as it operates in the Crime Control Model, is the operational expression of that confidence.

It would be a mistake to think of the presumption of guilt as the opposite of the presumption of innocence that we are so used to thinking of as the polestar of the criminal process and that, as we shall see, occupies an important position in the Due Process model. [...]

The presumption of innocence is a direction to officials about how they are to proceed, not a prediction of outcome. The presumption of guilt, however, is purely and simply a prediction of outcome. The presumption of innocence is, then, a direction to the authorities to ignore the presumption of guilt in their treatment of the suspect. It tells them, in effect, to close their eyes to what will frequently seem to be factual probabilities. The reasons why it tells them this are among the animating presuppositions of the Due Process Model, and we will come to them shortly. It is enough to note at this point that the presumption of guilt is descriptive and factual; the presumption of innocence is normative and legal. The pure Crime Control Model has no truck with the presumption of innocence. [...]

In this model, as I have suggested, the center of gravity for the process lies in the early, administrative fact-finding stages. The complementary proposition is that the subsequent stages are relatively unimportant and should be truncated as much as possible. [...]

It might be said of the Crime Control Model that, when reduced to its barest essentials and operating at its most successful pitch, it offers two possibilities: an administrative fact-finding process leading (1) to exoneration of the suspect or (2) to the entry of a plea of guilty.

Due Process Values. If the Crime Control Model resembles an assembly line, the Due Process Model looks very much like an obstacle course. Each of its successive stages is designed to present formidable impediments to carrying the accused any further along in the process. Its ideology is not the converse of that underlying the Crime Control Model. It does not rest on the idea that it is not socially desirable to repress crime, although critics of its application have been known to claim so. [...] The ideology of due process is far more deeply impressed on the formal structure of the law than is the ideology of crime control; yet an accurate tracing of the strands that make it up is strangely difficult. What follows is only an attempt at an approximation.

The Due Process Model encounters its rival on the Crime Control Model's own ground in respect to the reliability of fact-finding processes. The Crime Control Model, as we have suggested, places heavy reliance on the ability of investigative and prosecutorial officers, acting in an informal setting in which their distinctive skills are given full sway, to elicit and reconstruct a tolerably accurate account of what actually took place in an alleged criminal event. The Due Process Model rejects this premise and substitutes for it a view of informal, nonadjudicative fact-finding that stresses the possibility of error. People are notoriously poor observers of disturbing events. [...] Considerations of this kind all lead to a rejection of informal fact-finding processes as definitive of factual guilt and

to an insistence on formal, adjudicative, adversary fact-finding processes in which the factual case against the accused is publicly heard by an impartial tribunal and is evaluated only after the accused has had a full opportunity to discredit the case against him. Even then, the distrust of fact-finding processes that animates the Due Process Model is not dissipated. The possibilities of human error being what they are, further scrutiny is necessary, or at least must be available, in case facts have been overlooked or suppressed in the heat of battle. How far this subsequent scrutiny must be available is a hotly controverted issue today. In the pure Due Process Model the answer would be: at least as long as there is an allegation of factual error that has not received an adjudicative hearing in a fact-finding context. The demand for finality is thus very low in the Due Process Model. [...]

The Due Process Model insists on the prevention and elimination of mistakes to the extent possible; the Crime Control Model accepts the probability of mistakes up to the level at which they interfere with the goal of repressing crime, either because too many guilty people are escaping or, more subtly, because general awareness of the unreliability of the process leads to a decrease in the deterrent efficacy of the criminal law. In this view, reliability and efficiency are not polar opposites but rather complementary characteristics. The system is reliable *because* efficient; reliability becomes a matter of independent concern only when it becomes so attenuated as to impair efficiency. All of this the Due Process Model rejects. If efficiency demands short-cuts around reliability, then absolute efficiency must be rejected. The aim of the process is at least as much to protect the factually innocent as it is to convict the factually guilty. It is a little like quality control in industrial technology: tolerable deviation from standard varies with the importance of conformity to standard in the destined uses of the product. The Due Process Model resembles a factory that has to devote a substantial part of its input to quality control. This necessarily cuts down on quantitative output.

All of this is only the beginning of the ideological difference between the two models. The Due Process Model could disclaim any attempt to provide enhanced reliability for the fact-finding process and still produce a set of institutions and processes that would differ sharply from those demanded by the Crime Control Model. Indeed, it may not be too great an oversimplification to assert that in point of historical development the doctrinal pressures emanating from the demands of the Due Process Model have tended to evolve from an original matrix of concern for the maximization of reliability into values quite different and more far-reaching. These values can be expressed in, although not adequately described by, the concept of the primacy of the individual and the complementary concept of limitation on official power.

The combination of stigma and loss of liberty that is embodied in the end result of the criminal process is viewed as being the heaviest deprivation that government can inflict on the individual. Furthermore, the processes that culminate in these highly afflictive sanctions are seen as in themselves coercive, restricting, and demeaning. Power is always subject to abuse – sometimes subtle, other times, as in the criminal process, open and ugly. Precisely because of its potency in subjecting the individual to the coercive power of the state, the criminal process must, in this model, be subjected to controls that prevent it from operating with maximal efficiency. According to this ideology, maximal efficiency means maximal tyranny. And, although no one would assert that minimal efficiency means minimal tyranny, the proponents of the Due Process Model would accept with considerable equanimity a substantial diminution in the efficiency with which the criminal process operates in the interest of preventing official oppression of the individual.

The most modest-seeming but potentially far-reaching mechanism by which the Due Process Model implements these anti-authoritarian values is the doctrine of legal guilt. According to this doctrine, a person is not to be held guilty of crime merely on a showing that in all probability, based upon reliable evidence, he did factually what he is said to have done. Instead, he is to be held guilty if and only if these factual determinations are made in procedurally regular fashion and by authorities acting within competences duly allocated to them. Furthermore, he is not to be held guilty, even though the factual determination is or might be adverse to him, if various rules designed to protect him and to safeguard the integrity of the process are not given effect.

From H.L. Packer, The Limits of Criminal Sanction (Stanford, CA: Stanford University Press), 1968, pp. 149–173.

Note

1 See President's Commission on Law Enforcement and Administration of Justice, *The Challenge of Crime in a Free Society* (Washington, D.C., 1967), chap. 2.

23.2 Models of justice: Portia or Persephone? Some thoughts on equality, fairness and gender in the field of criminal justice Frances Heidensohn

Criminal justice can be seen as a series of institutions and systems: (a) as a *moral* or value system where social norms are expressed, supported by penal sanctions and (b) as an *administrative* process, or processes, and also (c) as part of a system of *social control*; which has informal as well as formal structures and sanctions. In practice, of course, all these interact.

When we look at feminist critiques of criminal justice, the importance of stressing these interactions becomes apparent. Most criticisms focus initially on administrative practices: however, these are almost invariably linked to deep-seated assumptions about the roles of men and women and gender-appropriate behaviour. Often, there is a further crucial, socio-economic or other major dimension. [...]

We can, I would suggest, summarise modern criticisms of criminal injustice to women as having three main aspects. These are:

a that girls or women are not treated *equally* with men or boys – when they are prostitutes, for example, or receive harsher sentences for the same offence;

b that females are *unfairly* or unjustly treated in relation to a concept such as 'natural justice' or 'human rights' as in the stigmatising of 'common prostitutes';

c that girls or women are *inappropriately* treated in relation to their offence and degree of blame – when their treatment is medicalised, for example.

Now such criticisms seem to me to be located well within the traditional framework of criminal jurisprudence. Indeed the principles they imply correspond closely to those of the 'classical' school, I suggest calling this model 'Portia' because Shakespeare's heroine in *The Merchant of Venice* neatly encapsulates so many aspects of it. The focus of the 'Portia' model is clearly male and a rational, clear-thinking, procedurally competent male at that. The means of achieving justice are through laws and courts, in the present system, and there is only one world-view which is ulti-

mately valid, that of white middle-class males. The concept of justice is one of legal equity.

Although feminist views on injustice have taken this rational–legal form, I think there are also deeper issues involved, a more profound 'hidden agenda' which we also need to explore. In both academic accounts and even more noticeably, in the views of women defendants and victims in the criminal justice system there is a sense of outrage greater than that which the violation of rational principles would justify (see e.g. Peckham, 1985; Hayes, 1985; Carlen, 1985). Are we then justified in saying that there is a particularly female or feminist concept of justice which the criminal justice system of patriarchal society violates? If this is so, what would be special and distinctive about feminist justice: a just treatment of women?

Justice for women

'Women suffer from systematic social injustice because of their sex ... that proposition . . . (is) the essence of feminism and . . . anyone who accepts it (is) ... a feminist' argues Radcliffe Richards (1980, p. 14).

Radcliffe Richards, following the American philosopher John Rawls (1972), defines justice as fairness and tries in her book to lay down principles of sexual justice and practical rules derived from these. She is almost entirely concerned with distributive rather than retributive justice, i.e. with how resources are shared out in society, but she observes that: 'questions of retributive justice actually reduce to questions of distributive justice' (Radcliffe Richards, 1980, p. 354).

In the course of her discussion of justice, she argues that: 'a just society is one in which the least well off group is as well off as possible' and that 'justice,' in: 'this definition does not entail equality on average between men and women' (pp. 124–125).

As we have already noted, much even of the feminist criticism of criminal injustice to women is based on assumptions about equality: women are unfairly treated when they are more harshly punished than comparable men, for the same offence,

This is very much in accord with a long lineage of criminological and socio-legal thinking which assesses criminal justice within fairly narrow criteria. Baldwin & Bottomley for instance, define justice in terms of the rightness of objectives and the fairness and accountability of the procedures involved (Baldwin & Bottomley 1978, p. 5).

Even if the police, the courts and prisons operated with total fairness to women in their own terms (and I do not think that they do) they would still be part of a society which has fundamental injustices based on sex at its core. Three particular aspects are crucial: sexual inequality, the narrow stereotyping of women's behaviour and the distribution of power. Sex should not, in theory, need to be any woman's destiny today. In practice, being born a woman is likely to mean being poorer, less well-educated, having a more routine job, carrying a double burden of work in and out of the home; above all, having far less autonomy and far fewer real choices in life than being born to manhood.

Within the smaller social space and the lesser share of resources available to them, women are also confined to a narrow range of conventionally acceptable behaviours. Wives', 'mothers' and 'typical women' are alleged and supposed to act in certain ways. Sonic of the key assumptions behind sexual stereotypes are particularly relevant to criminality: thus males are said to be aggressive, females passive; women are thought of as 'naturally' devious and manipulative. Both these features of the social context in which justice is effected depend on a third: the power dimension. Ours is a society in which men are dominant and women subordinate its both private and public spheres – from Parliament to public houses, from the boardroom to the bedroom, power and control are vested its men and largely denied to women.

These features of society cannot be left outside the police station or courtroom when women confront the apparatus of criminal justice. Indeed, it is clear that they are present and pressing in many such situations. Carlen, for example, has pointed out the impossibility of fair and equal treatment for women offenders in her Scottish study because of the poverty, domestic violence and profoundly chauvinistic society they inhabit (Carlen, 1983), while Eaton has shown in London and Kruttschnitt in America that courts may take into account women's 'conventional' feminine behaviour and the informal social control which binds them in considering the sentencing tariff (Eaton, 1985).

Women who have been involved in crime do seem often to react to their experiences in distinctive ways which say a great deal about their perceptions of the 'fairness' of the system. Very few women offenders glory in their misdemeanours in the way some of their male colleagues do by, for example, writing self-justifying accounts of them. When women do recount their experiences, they are much more likely to deny their deviance and stress their virtues and conformity (see Heidensohn, 1985 for an analysis). [...]

I have already suggested that justice for women cannot simply be measured in terms of fair, open and rational treatment for them in the courts (i.e. the Portia model), although these are important dimensions, and our present arrangements do not always do women justice even on these terms. In addition, procedural justice has to be seen in its wider social context and in particular for women, in relation to the disadvantages they experience in society which makes them unequal to men even before they encounter the law. Now it can of course be argued that women are not the only social group to be so disadvantaged. Indeed it is very clear, for instance, that members of ethnic minorities, or unskilled workers or young people can often be in similarly disadvantaged positions. There have been protests and campaigns about injustice and bias, especially as these affect black people. There is however, I believe, a further and very specific way in which women are likely to experience and perceive the criminal justice system as unjust and that is because it is to them a peculiarly alien and unfamiliar world.

Few parts of our social world are quite so notably male than those of crime and its controlling agencies. Crime, according to official records and various other surveys and studies is overwhelmingly a male activity: over 80% of all serious offences are committed by men or boys. Females commit few serious offences and recidivism is far less common. Court appearances by girls and women are even less frequent: 90% of delinquent girls are cautioned even for serious offences. Men, too, predominate in the staffing and manning of the police and the courts. Women also have experience of the police and courts as victims as well as offenders and over several crimes are likely to feel some alienation and ambiguity. Thus in cases of rape and of domestic violence, police responses especially have been highly criticised as being unfair and unfeeling (Toner, 1982).

Women in general are not familiar with the criminal justice system, nor it with them. Indeed criminologists have coined the term 'doubly deviant' to describe courts' view of women offenders since they transgress two codes: legal rules about crime and society's approved pattern for proper, conforming womanhood. There is also evidence to suggest that women find their penal treatment unfair for similar reasons (Carlen, 1985), but also too because their lower crime rates do actually lead not to better prisons but to poorer: women are incarcerated further from home, there can be little segregation of offenders, or specialised programmes. Women clearly find prison a harsh punishment: their disciplinary offences and their intake of medicinal drugs are both high (Heidensohn, 1985). The penal system is designed to deal with male delinquencies and women fit uneasily into its patterns.

There is considerable support for the view that prison is a harsher and more unusual punishment for women than it is for men (Heidensohn, 1969, 1975: Giallombardo, 1966: Carlen, 1983, 1985; Expenditure Committee, 1978–1979). Among the reasons for this are that women lose more by imprisonment because their family lives are disrupted, their children separated from them and profoundly damaging stigma acquired. Regimes in women's prisons, while sometimes superficially 'softened' with cosmetic coverings of say, choice of clothing, are often: 'much more rigid than those imposed in the men's prisons' (Carlen, 1985, p. 182).

In particular, a form of repressive resocialisation appears to be attempted in some women's prisons, emphasising the need for conformity to good behaviour and conventional femininity, yet in the setting of a corrective institution. Carlen (1985) has pointed out how confusing this is: 'Women who have already rejected conventional and (for them) debilitating female roles are constantly enjoined "to be feminine"'. [...]

Perhaps the reason women are most likely to find the formal machinery of criminal justice harsh and unfair is that most of them unlike most men, are subject to elaborate and subtle informal social control. I have described elsewhere (Heidensohn, 1985) how pervasively this operates, with women being confined and controlled by their domestic ties, by patriarchal authority, by the division of public and private domains. In addition to this comprehensive and effective network of silken bonds, our society exhorts and prescribes good behaviour and conformity in women through magazines, films and television programmes, as well as the less ephemeral media of folk myth and legend, organised religion and popular culture, Women who confront the abstract system of formal justice are not only treated as 'doubly deviant' as women and offenders, they also experience 'double jeopardy' – they are likely already to have experienced the narrow confines and the informal, but formidable, system of sanctions which penalise deviant women.

Criminal justice is not only a matter of procedural propriety and fairness of tariff (although these are important); it also involves issues of social justice. This is true for all accused persons who may be disadvantaged by adverse social circumstances, but women experience two distinctive sorts of disadvantage, which markedly affect their rights and their treatment: they are greatly over-represented among the poor and the least powerful in our society while at the same time being rarely found to be officially criminal or as crime-control officials. Criminal injustice to women is, then, a compound of legal and administrative inequalities, such as in the treatment of prostitutes and of women who are role-deviant, and of social and sexual injustice. I am still measuring these on the scales derived earlier from traditional philosophical and legal notions, namely of equality, fairness and appropriateness, the assumed comparison always being with men. Now I want to look at whether this takes us far enough and answers the questions with which I began.

When men campaign for improvements in their rights whether political, social or economic, their object has always been to achieve parity with other, more privileged *men*. It is rather surprising that arguments about equal treatment with women have hardly ever been used by men seeking redress of grievances. The case made in the 1960s against the criminalising of private male homosexual activities was based on the concepts of privacy and lack of a victim. Comparisons were made with tolerance of adultery but not in terms of the rights of males and females. A few men have tried to use the Sex Discrimination Act in Britain, to equalise times for leaving work, for example. Women, too, have generally seen the rights of men to which they have aspired as being the same rights as men have had. This is the first, or 'Portia' model of rights and justice. There are other possibilities. One is to improve women's lot in relation to their present position but in a narrow and usually stereotyping fashion.

I suggest calling this the 'essentially feminine', or 'Persephone' approach, because it presupposes that women have certain inherent feminine characteristics different and requiring different treatment from the characteristics of men.

Table 23.2.1 Models of justice

Model	Values and Characteristics	Systems	Concept of Justice	Features
Portia	Masculine Rationality Individualism	Civic rights Rule of law	Legal, Equality Procedural	Norm is male
Persephone	Feminine Caring and personal	Networks Informal	Responsibilities Co-operation	Norm is female

Portia

Almost every feminist movement has sought to achieve the same rights for women as men enjoy. This is only realistic, for two major reasons. Firstly, as it is clear that men are the dominant, powerful group in all known societies, then obviously equality with the strongest is what anyone would seek. Secondly, domestically privatised and isolated as they are, women need access to the public sphere of politics and the market before they can achieve anything and this means access through and alongside men.

Even today, our judicial system is built round males, so that women who encounter it have to measure up to male-based norms and rules which may ignore for instance women's dependency on men or children's dependency on their mothers. Much recent public concern has focussed on the sense of injustice felt by men who have to support their former wives, and English law has even been changed in response to this.

Yet many women also have such feelings even if they have not been as fully articulated. Scutt, for example, writing of her study of marriage and divorce in Australia notes:

> Women base a sense that they are being treated unfairly because they cannot quantify the efforts that they have made, and think at times 'but I did do something that was worthwhile, didn't I?' Surely my efforts should be given some recognition in terms of the property division? (Scutt, pers. comm. and see Scutt & Graham, 1984)

Alternatively, women may be tested against norms about proper female behaviour which are derived from (man-made) stereotypes of femininity. Thus the definition of some forms of murder as infanticide by the mother, or the recent establishment of a defence plea based on premenstrual tension may give some relative leniency to some women, but at a considerable cost in paternalism and loss of

autonomy to them and many others. Thus, *if some women* are impelled to irrational behaviour by their hormonal urges, so the argument goes, then no women can be trusted to be rational and make major decisions. All female deviance can be then regarded as pathological, its source literally within the deviant herself This was clearly the thinking behind the plans for the new Holloway prison when they were first mooted in 1968 (Faulkner, 1971), Although these plans have long since been overtaken by other ideas about women's criminality, generations of women prisoners have had to suffer their consequences (Heidensohn, 1975; Carlen, 1985).

The alternative for women to the strict rationality of this model is likely to be the use of narrow stereotypes of femininity. Certain actions may be interpreted as explicable because of assumed female characteristics and punishment may be accordingly less (though it will probably be paternalistic and may still be stigmatising).

However, women who fail to conform to expectations of appropriate female behaviour may be treated very much more severely, because of their failure to weep or to show maternal love or even to look 'feminine'. (Such allegations have been made about, for example, the cases of Ruth Ellis (Delaney, 1985), of Christine Villemin (Smyth, 1985), the 'Dingo baby case' and of Karen Tyler (Toynbee, 1986). The 'Portia' model is the most familiar and the most widely accepted model of justice. It is the one that most feminists take for granted in measuring and pointing out deficiencies in present provision and practices. Its flaws are admirably summed up by Scutt:

> Women confront a legal system that professes to be attuned to the rights of all. It professes the ideals of fairness and equality. Many legal writers, judges and lawyers have concocted a jurisprudence that bolsters that false notion. Yet, as some men have recognised, 'fairness' is accorded only to those (that is, men) having the means to pay,

and having rights deemed worthy of protection. 'Equality' is judged according to the rule that 'some [men] are more equal than others'. It has taken women to press home the place patriarchal notions have in law (Scutt, 1985).

Persephone

If we reject the 'Portia' model and search for alternatives, we come of course into speculative realms. Modern feminist psychologists have proposed important changes in thinking about moral development. Several writers have worked particularly on new psychologies which could offer at least the basis of a new and better moral order. Miller, for example, argues that our present civilisation is built upon the historic subordination of women who became the 'carriers' of all the things: sexuality, emotion, creativity, managing bodily functions which men wished to repress and be dissociated from. In her 'new psychology' women have to recognise these qualities and functions as real strengths and add to them power and self-determination (Miller, 1978, p. 129). What is significant for our purposes in seeking new or alternative models in Miller's work is that she starts from a position of (re)valuing women and their experience and as a base for making moral judgments. As Eisenstein puts it:

> the goal for women ... should by no means be to learn to act like, think like and adopt the values of, men and the male-dominant culture. Rather, concepts such as autonomy, power, authenticity, self-determination – all of these should be re-examined and redefined by women ... (Miller takes) the condition of women as potentially normative for all human beings (Eisenstein, 1984, pp. 66–68).

Gilligan too seeks to redress the balance in studies of moral development by adding women back in. She describes men and women as having different maturing experiences. Men become detached, autonomous and individualised and take a: 'rights conception of morality ... geared to arriving at an objectively fair or just resolution to moral dilemmas upon which all rational persons could agree' (Gilligan, 1982, pp. 21–22).

Women, on the other hand, take part in a different cycle of growth and attachment as soon as they are adult, they become responsible for the care of others and help them in their turn to mature, thus perpetuating a cyclical pattern. In consequence, women see moral problems differ-

ently (she uses empirical studies to demonstrate this) and thus: 'the psychology of women that has consistently been described as distinctive in its greater orientation toward relationships and interdependence implies a *more contextual mode of judgment and a different moral understanding*' (Gilligan, 1982, p. 22).

Gilligan calls this approach Demeter/Persephone after the Homeric myth of mother and daughter whose story exemplifies the cycle of fertility of sowing and reaping, conception and birth. She goes on to stress that men have a 'justice' model of morality, based on rights while women have a 'caring' model. Both, she argues, must be recognised because the:

> two disparate modes of experience ... are in the end connected. While an ethic of justice proceeds from the premise of equality – that everyone should be treated the same – an ethic of care rests on the premise of nonviolence that no one should be hurt.

How might this translate into a new model of justice?

While women-centred approaches are obviously attractive and one can, on the basis of these writers' work begin to construct notions of justice and even practices, there are difficulties and dangers. The dangers, I think, lie partly in producing a version of justice which is welfare-based and individualised with the problems attendant upon it. However, the central problem is essentially one of *power*: it is possible, just, to envisage a separate, gentler, more sympathetic justice system exclusively reserved for women. That is, after all, what we already have broadly for juveniles: anonymity, informality, an emphasis on familial relationships and emotional maturity rather than strict notions of guilt. But just as adults control the juvenile court so would men still be in charge of female courts. Moreover, it strains credibility to believe that *men* would allow themselves or their peers to be subjected to a new, feminine morality and judgment. Women would thus, I am afraid, be two-fold losers: they might he 'infantilised' and they would also probably see what little influence they can exert over male behaviour through the courts lost. There are interesting avenues still to be explored within this model. It has also to be said that some recent developments in the criminal justice system do have Persephone aspects: community service orders for instance, exemplify an attachment and reparation approach, making the offender literally refurbish the social fabric. Again ideas of conciliation and of victim–offender contact and support schemes are 'outwith' traditional ideas of justice and stress 'caring' rather than 'rights' values.

Conclusion

There are in everyday practice, many questions faced by professionals, by policy makers, by lawyers and clients which may, I hope, be a little illuminated by this discussion. Is it fair for example, for non-delinquent girls to join Intermediate Treatment programmes? Is it fair for them not to? Should rape victim and accused both be anonymous? Should adult female offenders mix with youth custody cases for their own good?

There is also a list of sensible items to be considered when we face the real, sad everyday world:

1 Even in its own narrow terms, the 'Portia' model can be criticised and evaluated, procedurally and in principle. Courts, for example, have been imprisoning prostitutes for not paying fines. Edwards has criticised defence barristers whose questioning of rape victims is doubtful and seems designed to destroy the victim's character and, in her view, breaks the Bar's code of conduct.

2 A certain amount can be achieved by education and politics – 'consciousness raising' has clearly helped the introduction of different approaches to rape.

3 Any new criminal justice or penal measure should, as a matter of routine, be examined for its impact on gender.

4 While a separate *judicial* system for women is not feasible, and probably not viable, a separate and very different *penal* system is. This might involve small, well-scattered houses or hostels, with good community links and support.

Criminal justice for women involves, as it does for men, social justice too. Whichever model we take needs power and resources to make it work. What an exercise like this reminds us of is that women in our courts, police stations, etc. experience the stigma of 'double deviance' and risk the penalties of double jeopardy. They are fairly helpless before these hazards since they are not of their making or choosing. Little by little, grain of sand by grain of sand things may be changing. Nevertheless, while this is a man's world it will be his concept of justice which will prevail and his will be the one women have to use.

> From F. Heidensohn, 'Models of justice: Portia or Persephone? Some thoughts on equality, fairness and gender in the field of criminal justice', International Journal of the Sociology of Law, *1986, 14 (3): 287–298.*

References

Baldwin, J. & Bottomley. A.K. (1978) *Criminal Justice.* London: Martin Robertson.

Carlen, P. (1983) *Women's Imprisonment.* London: Routledge and Kegan Paul.

Carlen, P. (Ed.), (1985) *Criminal Women.* Oxford: Polity Press.

Delaney, S. (1985) *Observer,* 3 March 1985.

Eaton, M. (1985) Documenting the defendant: placing women in social inquiry reports. In *Women in Law* (Brophy, J. & Smart, C., Eds). London: Routledge and Kegan Paul.

Eisenstein H. (1981) *Contemporary Feminist Thought.* London: Unwin.

Expenditure Committee (1978–1979) *Education, Arts and Home Affairs Sub-Committee of the Expenditure Committee: Women and the Penal System.* Evidence in Vols 61-i to 61-xiv.

Faulkner D.E.R. (1971) The redevelopment of Holloway Prison. *Howard Journal of Penology and Crime Prevention 13(2).*

Giallombardo, R. (1966) *Society of Women: a Study of a Women's Prison.* Chichester: Wiley.

Gilligan, C. (1982) *In a Different Voice.* Cambridge: Harvard University Press.

Hayes, J. (1985) *My Story.* Kerry: Brandon.

Heidensohn, F. (1969) Prison for women, *Howard Journal.*

Heidensohn, F. (1975) The imprisonment of females. In *The Use of Imprisonment* (McConville, S.; Ed.) London: Routledge and Kegan Paul pp. 3–56.

Heidensohn, F. (1985) *Women and Crime.* London: Macmillan.

Peckham, A. (1985) *Women in Custody.* Fontana: London.

Radcliffe Richards, J. (1980) *The Sceptical Feminist.* Harmondsworth: Pelican.

Rawls, J. (1972) *A Theory of Justice.* Oxford: Oxford University Press.

Scutt, J. & Graham, D. (1984) *For Richer, for Poorer: Money, Marriage and Property Rights.* Ringwood: Penguin.

Scutt, J. (1985) In pursuit of equality: women and legal thought 1788–1984. *In Women, Social Science and Public Policy* (Goodnow, J, & Pateman, C. Eds) Australia: Academy of Social Science.

Smyth, R. (1985) *Observer,* 11 August 1985.

Toner, B. (1982) *The Facts of Rape.* London: Arrow Books.

Toynbee, P. (1986) *Guardian,* 17 March 1986.

23.3 The antecedents of compliant behaviour
Tom R. Tyler

Authorities in social groups recognize that their effectiveness depends on their ability to influence the behavior of the groups' members. In the case of legal authorities effectiveness depends on the extent to which they are able to influence the public's behaviors toward the law. Laws and the decisions of legal authorities are of little practical importance if people ignore them. Because of the centrality of compliance to effectiveness as a legal authority, understanding why people follow the law is a central issue in law and the social sciences.

Two theories of compliance with the law have been advanced: the instrumental and the normative. In this book I have emphasized the importance of the normative perspective, which focuses on the values that lead people to comply voluntarily with legal rules and the decisions of legal authorities. Such values, if they exist, form a basis for the effective functioning of legal authorities. This is especially true of legitimacy – the belief that one ought to obey the law. If normative values are absent, authorities must use the mechanisms of deterrence that stem from instrumental control over reward and punishments. Such mechanisms are costly and in many cases may be inadequate. The Chicago study supports the normative perspective on compliance. Both personal morality and legitimacy are found to have an effect on people's everyday behavior toward the law, whatever type of analysis is conducted.

Legitimacy is the normative factor of greatest concern to authorities. According to a variety of theories advanced by social scientists, legitimacy is crucial if the authorities are to have the discretionary power they need to fulfill their roles. In the case of legal authorities, legitimacy underlies their expectation that the public will generally obey the law. The Chicago study confirms that legitimacy plays an important role in promoting compliance.

The procedural basis of legitimacy

Given the centrality of legitimacy to compliance, it is important to understand how legitimacy is maintained or undermined among members of the public. The Chicago study explored this issue in the context of people's experiences with legal authorities, and examined the effects of experience with particular police officers and judges on views about the legitimacy of legal authorities. To be concerned with the impact of experiences on views about the legitimacy of legal authorities is to be concerned with the political impact of experience. If legitimacy diminishes, so does the ability of legal and political authorities to influence public behavior and function effectively.

Many aspects of experience could be important in determining the political impact of experience. The Chicago study contrasts the instrumental and normative perspectives on experience. The normative perspective that it emphasizes is represented by psychological theories of justice, according to which people react to social experiences in terms of the fairness of the outcomes they receive (distributive justice), and the fairness of the procedures by which those outcomes are arrived at (procedural justice). In contrast, according to an instrumental perspective people react to their experiences depending on the favorability of the outcomes of the experiences. The normative perspective is better able to account for people's reactions, especially when people use their experiences with particular police officers and judges to generalize about the overall legitimacy of legal authority. Procedural justice is the key normative judgment influencing the impact of experience on legitimacy. Similar evidence has been found in politics and the workplace (Lind and Tyler 1988; Tyler 1987c). Views about authority are strongly connected to judgments of the fairness of the procedures through which authorities make decisions.

That people are concerned with procedure is not a new idea. Past conceptions of the citizen have relied heavily on the principle that citizens evaluate government institutions and authorities in procedural terms (Anton 1967; Easton 1965; Edelman 1964; Engstrom and Giles 1972; Murphy and Tanenhaus 1969; Saphire 1978; Scheingold 1974; Wahlke 1971). The procedural effects found by the Chicago study may contradict the instrumental views now prevailing in legal studies, but they are consistent with a procedural school in the social sciences that is of long standing.

If one accepts the image of the person that is put forth by the Chicago study, one will look in a new way at how people react to decisions in political, legal, and work organizations. In the legal arena citizens will be seen as reacting to the procedures through which court decisions are made, as well as to the decisions themselves. In politics people will react to policies and politicians on procedural grounds. And in the workplace they will be concerned with how decisions are made about pay and promotions. Therefore, decision makers can gain public acceptance for their decisions and rules by making and implementing them in ways that the public thinks is fair.

One clear implication is that authorities are freer than they commonly believe to follow painful policies that are sound in the long term. Authorities often feel that their legitimacy is linked to their ability to deliver tangible positive outcomes to self-interested citizens. They reflect the assumptions of the economic model, and think that people affected by their decisions will react to the decisions based on the extent of their personal gain or loss. That people attend to matters of procedure gives authorities latitude to pursue long-term policies by stressing the fairness of the procedures through which they came about (Tyler, Rasinski, and Griffin 1986).

The meaning of procedural justice

Given the importance of procedural justice to legitimacy, it is crucial to understand how people define fair procedures. Again, an instrumental perspective contrasts with a normative one. According to the instrumental perspective of Thibaut and Walker (1975), people define fairness primarily by the extent to which they are able to influence the decisions made by the third party. According to a normative perspective, there are many other aspects to the fairness of a procedure, which have little or nothing to do with outcomes or the control of outcomes. The Chicago study reinforces the normative perspective on the meaning of fair process. Judgments of procedural justice are found to be multidimensional. They involve many issues besides favorability of outcome and control of outcome. In fact, the criterion of fair procedure most closely related to outcomes (that is, consistency) is found to be of minor importance. In contrast, judgments about the social dimensions of the experience, such as ethicality, weigh very heavily in assessments of procedural justice. In the context of people's experiences with police officers and judges, the Chicago study found that seven different aspects of procedure independently influenced judgments about whether the procedure was fair.

One important element in feeling that procedures are fair is a belief on the part of those involved that they had an opportunity to take part in the decision-making process. This includes having an opportunity to present their arguments, being listened to, and having their views considered by the authorities. Those who feel that they have had a hand in the decision are typically much more accepting of its outcome, irrespective of what the outcome is. An additional advantage of procedures that allow both sides to state their arguments is that each side is exposed to the other. Because a party to a dispute is often unaware of the feelings and concerns of the other party, this exposure is very important (Conley 1988; Tyler 1987b).

Judgments of procedural fairness are also linked to judgments about the neutrality of the decision-making process. People believe that decision makers should be neutral and unbiased. They also expect decision makers to be honest and to reach their decisions based on objective information about the case. As is true of questions of participation, these issues are linked to settling the dispute or policy issue involved. Procedural fairness is also related to interpersonal aspects of the decision-making procedure. People place great weight on being treated politely and having respect shown for their rights and for themselves as people. The way people are dealt with by legal and political authorities has implications for their connection with the social group and their position in the community. It therefore has important implications for self-esteem (Lane 1988) and group identification (Lind and Tyler 1988). People are unlikely to feel attached to groups led by authorities who treat them rudely or ignore their rights. The treatment accorded by public officials is also an indication of the likelihood that people will receive help if they have problems in the future, and so has important implications for feelings of security. People will not feel identified with officials whom they regard as unresponsive to their problems and unwilling to help and protect them.

The importance that people attach to their relationship to authorities is reflected in the importance of another criterion of procedural justice: inferences about the motives of the authorities. The way people assess procedural fairness is strongly linked to their judgments of whether the authority they are dealing with is motivated to be fair. Because motivational inferences require considerably more cognitive effort than assessments of such surface features as honesty and bias, one might expect them to be avoided. Why are they instead central to assessments of procedural fairness? One advantage of inferences of motive or intention is that they reflect dispositional characteristics, that is, features of the person that are likely to predict their future behavior (Heider 1958). The centrality of such inferences to issues of procedural justice reflects people's concern with knowing how authorities will act toward them in the future.

Finally, the fairness of procedures is linked to whether the procedures produce fair outcomes. Procedural issues are not independent of questions of outcome. Fair outcomes are one thing that people expect from a fair procedure, and a procedure that consistently produces unfair outcomes will eventually be viewed as unfair itself.

Although the factors outlined typically emerge as central to judgments about procedural justice, it is also important that the same issues are not used to judge the fairness of procedures with regard to all issues. In different situations people evaluate the fairness of procedures against different criteria of procedural justice: there is no universally fair procedure that can be used to resolve all types of problems and disputes. At the same time, different types of people do not evaluate the fairness of procedures against different criteria. Within the context of a particular type of problem or dispute, different types of people generally agree about the criteria that should be used to judge the fairness of the procedure. This finding is consistent with other recent evidence that there is a substantial consensus among Americans about what is fair (Merry 1985, 1986; Sanders and Hamilton 1987).

The normative perspective

The Chicago study makes clear that normative issues are central to any effort to understand authority and compliance. In three areas normative issues were found to be important: the legitimacy of leaders is directly related to compliance; justice affects reactions to personal experience; and people think about justice in non-instrumental terms.

The instrumental perspective is clearly insufficient to explain people's views about the legitimacy of authority and their behavioral compliance with the law. Citizens act as naive moral philosophers, evaluating authorities and their actions against abstract criteria of fairness. The instrumental conceptions of the person that have recently dominated discussions of legal issues are incomplete. Explanations based on the image of people as entirely rational beings who maximize utility are insufficient to account for their behavior in social groups. Further, procedural justice plays a crucial role in the political impact of experience. The legitimacy of authorities is closely intertwined with the procedures they use when dealing with the public. These findings of the Chicago study reinforce the importance of 'civic duty' in political science (Easton 1965), of normative issues in sociology (Gamson 1968; Schwartz 1978), and of distributive and procedural justice in psychology (Crosby 1976; Lind and Tyler 1988). Although issues of justice and legitimacy have long been given attention in each of these fields, more recently models of public choice emphasizing instrumental concerns have dominated. The Chicago study shows that a fuller description of citizens' behavior can be obtained by paying greater attention to normative questions.

A normative perspective can also give a differing approach to policy issues, such as the issue of how to implement public policies. In past discussions of policy implementation, it has been assumed that citizens' behavior is motivated by self-interest, and as a result the focus has been on the manipulation of behavior through the control of punishments and incentives. In light of the Chicago study, however, policymakers might also pay attention to the normative climate that surrounds legal authority and to citizens' conceptions of fair decision-making procedures in legal settings. The study does more than make the general suggestion that norms matter: it strongly supports a procedural orientation toward normative issues. Research on distributive justice has focused on fair outcomes, but people focus on fair procedure.

From T. Tyler, Why People Obey the Law *(New Haven: Yale University Press), 1990, pp. 161–166.*

References

Anton, T.J. (1967) Roles and symbols in the determination of state expenditures. *Midwest Journal of Political Science* 11: 27–43.

Conley, J. (1988) Ethnographic perspectives on informal justice: What litigants want. Paper presented at the annual meeting of the Law and Society Association, Vail, Colo., June.

Crosby, F. (1976) A model of egotistical deprivation. *Psychological Review* 83: 85–113.

Easton, D. (1965) *A systems analysis of political life.* Chicago: University of Chicago Press.

Edelman, M. (1964) *The symbolic uses of politics.* Urbana: University of Illinois Press.

Engstrom, R.L., and Giles, M.W. (1972) Expectations and images: A note on diffuse support for legal institutions. *Law and Society Review* 6: 631–636.

Gamson, W.A. (1968) *Power and discontent.* Homewood, Ill.: Dorsey.

Heider, F. (1958) *The psychology of interpersonal relations.* New York: John Wiley & Sons.

Lane, R.E. (1988) Procedural goods in a democracy: How one is treated versus what one gets. *Social Justice Research* 2:177–192.

Lind, E.A., and Tyler, T.R. (1988) *The social psychology of procedural justice.* New York: Plenum.

Merry, S.E. (1985) Concepts of law and justice among working-class Americans: Ideology as culture. *Legal Studies Forum* 9: 59–69.

Merry, S.E. (1986) Everyday understandings of law in working-class America. *American Ethnologist* 13: 253–270.

Murphy, W.F., and Tanenhaus, J. (1969) Public opinion and the United States Supreme Court: A preliminary mapping of some prerequisites for court legitimization of regime changes. In J. B. Grossman and J. Tanenhaus, (Eds), *Frontiers in judicial research.* New York: John Wiley & Sons.

Raainski, K.A., and Tyler, T.R. (1986) Social psychology and political behavior. In S. Long, (Ed), *Political behavior annual* 1: 103–128. Boulder: Westview.

Sanders, J., and Hamilton, L. (1987) Is there a 'common law' of responsibility? *Law and Human Behavior* 11: 277–297.

Saphire, R.B. (1978) Specifying due process values. *University of Pennsylvania Law Review* 127: 111–195.

Scheingold, S.A. (1974) *The politics of rights.* New Haven and London: Yale University Press.

Schwartz, R.D. (1978) Moral order and sociology of law: Trends, problems, and prospects. *Annual Review of Sociology* 4: 577–601.

Thibaut, J., and Walker, L. (1975) *Procedural justice: A psychological analysis.* Hillsdale, N.J.: Erlbaum.

Tyler, T.R. (1987b) The psychology of dispute resolution: Implications for the mediation of disputes by third parties. *Negotiation Journal* 3: 367–374.

Tyler. T.R. (1987c) Procedural justice: Future directions. *Social Justice Research* 1: 41–65.

Tyler, T.R., Rasinski, K., and Griffin, E. (1986) Alternative images of the citizen: Implications for public policy. *American Psychologist* 41: 970–978.

Wahlke, J. (1971) Policy demands and system support: The role of the represented. *British Journal of Political Science* 1: 271–290.

23.4 Defiance, deterrence and irrelevance: a theory of the criminal sanction Lawrence W. Sherman

Does punishment control crime? This question provokes fierce debates in criminology and public policy. Yet there is ample evidence that it is the wrong question. Widely varying results across a range of sanction studies suggest a far more useful question: under what conditions does each type of criminal sanction reduce, increase, or have no effect on future crimes? Answering that question is central to the future of research on crime and delinquency. [...]

Facts to be explained

Unlike the basic facts of crime (Braithwaite 1989, p. 44), the facts of sanction effects are not well established from repeated studies. Moreover, the causal linkage between sanctions and future crime is much more difficult to establish methodologically than descriptive facts about the distribution of crime. [...]

The key fact is this: *similar criminal sanctions have opposite or different effects in different social settings, on different kinds of offenders and offenses, and at different levels of analysis.* This pattern is found in different populations at the individual level of analysis as well as at the micro level (small group), macro level (large collectivity), and simultaneously across levels. It is true for both 'street' crime and more middle-class offenses (drunk driving and income tax evasion), suggesting that a general theory of sanctioning effects may be able to cut across many or most offense types.

Defiance theory

Defiance is the net increase in the prevalence, incidence, or seriousness of future offending against a sanctioning community caused by a proud, shameless reaction to the administration of a criminal sanction. Specific or individual defiance is the reaction of one person to that person's own punishment. General defiance is the reaction of a group or collectivity to the punishment of one or more of its members. Direct defiance is a crime committed against a sanctioning agent. Indirect defiance is the displaced just deserts committed against a target vicariously representing the sanctioning agents provoking the anger. Defiance is distinct from other hypothetical mechanisms by which sanctions increase crime, such as labeling (Lemert 1972), thrill seeking (Katz 1988), imitation, or brutalization (Bowers 1988). Defiance theory explains variation in criminal events, not criminality (Hirschi 1986). Defiance theory may encompass many types of crimes but may also be more powerful a predictor of predatory and competitive offenses than of mutualistic or retreatist offenses (Felson 1987).

Figure 23.4.1	Defiance Theory (Summary)

Dependent variable: criminal events by individuals and collectivities

Independent variable: criminal sanction content, certainty, dosage

Causal mechanism: emotions of shame and pride becoming rage.

Theories integrated:

    1 Braithwaite, reintegrative shaming

    2 Tyler, procedural justice

    3 Scheff and Retzinger, emotions with Black, crime as social control

Key concepts:

    1 legitimacy of governmental sanctioning

    2 offender social bonds to sanctioning community

    3 shame offender acknowledges or denies

    4 direct or displaced just deserts to victims

Necessary conditions for defiance (increase in crime caused by proud, angry reaction to sanctions):

    1 offender defines a criminal sanction as unfair

    2 offender is poorly bonded to community or agent

    3 offender defines sanction as stigmatizing personae

    4 offender refuses to acknowledge shame

Sufficient conditions for perceived unfairness:

    1 stylistic disrespect by sanctioning agent

    2 substantively arbitrary, discriminatory, excessive, or undeserved sanctions

Sufficient conditions for denial of shame:

    1 indignation chosen over impotence

    2 perceived weakness/ambivalence of sanctioning agents

Facts the theory fits:

    1 main effects of sanctions increasing crime

    2 interaction effects of sanctions with offender differences

    3 null effects of sanctions from countervailing influences

Defiance occurs under four conditions, all of which are necessary.

- The offender defines a criminal sanction as unfair.
- The offender is poorly bonded to or alienated from the sanctioning agent or the community the agent represents.
- The offender defines the sanction as stigmatizing and rejecting a person, not a lawbreaking act.
- The offender denies or refuses to acknowledge the shame the sanction has actually caused him to suffer.

Sanctions are defined as unfair under two conditions, either of which is sufficient:

- The sanctioning agent behaves with disrespect for the offender, or for the group to which the offender belongs, regardless of how fair the sanction is on substantive grounds.
- The sanction is substantively arbitrary, discriminatory, excessive, undeserved, or otherwise objectively unjust.

Offenders deny shame as one of two adaptive responses to alienation, as Karl Marx put it: 'impotence and indignation' (quoted in Scheff and Retzinger 1991, p. 64). The first response accepts shame and seeks escape through retreat or intoxicants, as in Anderson's (1978) 'wineheads.' The second denies shame and insulates against it by anger and rage in reaction to insult, as in Anderson's 'hoodlums'. We lack sufficient evidence or theory to specify the individual or social conditions under which alienated persons choose these alternative responses.[1]

Defiance theory therefore predicts three reactions to punishment defined as unfair.

- When poorly bonded offenders accept the shame an unfair stigmatizing sanction provokes, the sanction will be *irrelevant* or possibly even deterrent to future rates of offending.
- When poorly bonded offenders deny the shame they feel and respond with rage, the unfair stigmatizing sanction will *increase* their future rates of offending. This unacknowledged shame leads to an emotion of angry pride at defying the punishment. That pride predisposes the defiant offender to repeat the sanctioned conduct, symbolically labeling the sanctions or sanctioners, and not the offender's own acts, as truly shameful and morally deserving of

punishment. In the process, the victims or targets of the sanctioned acts become vicarious substitutes for the state or its sanctioning representatives.

- The full shame–crime sequence does not occur, however, when a well-bonded offender defines a sanction as unfair. The unfairness may weaken the deterrent effect of the sanction and make it irrelevant to future conduct. But even if the offender denies the shame, proud defiance is unlikely because it is less valued than the pride associated with social bonds.

In economic theory, the utility of defiance is generally less than the utility of social bonds. From this standpoint, there is no difference between a social control and rational choice theory of sanction effects (Berk et al. 1992), as distinct from crime causation (Hirschi 1986). Tyler (1990, p. 63) reports that when criminal justice loses legitimacy, peer disapproval of crime takes its place. Those who are bonded to peers (or for children, their handlers) who disapprove of crime would seem to be shielded from defiance.

Defiance as mainstream

Scheff and Retzinger (1991, p. 115) call the emotional reaction to unacknowledged shame a 'false' pride because it is founded on hidden shame at alienation from the sanctioning community's values. This is consistent with frequent descriptions of defiance as a subcultural reaction formation (Cohen 1955; Majors and Billson 1992). But if the sanctioning community perversely values both law-abiding and defiant behavior, there may be nothing false about defiant pride. In a mainstream culture that values defiance, the pride is legitimate as long as the sanctions can be labeled as illegitimate.

Defiance of authority runs deep in American history and culture, perhaps even deeper than pressures for financial success (cf. Merton 1938). From the American Revolution onward, the nation, symbolized by a snake saying 'Don't Tread on Me' (a revolutionary war flag) has held defiance in high esteem. Ohio even has a city by that name, founded as one of many forts with that name in revolutionary war times. The poetry of 'Bloodied but unbowed' Henley ([1875]1954) may have been written in nineteenth-century England, but the image is central to the Battle of the Alamo and the modern America of Rambo, Die Hard, and other popular movies worshiping heroic individual defiance of enormous opposition. [...]

Mainstream defiance of government requires both overwhelming odds and moral legitimation. The latter is readily found in accusations that basic principles have been violated: 'a government of laws, not of men', or more simply, 'playing by the rules'. Whenever the regime is seen to break its own rules, 'blowing the whistle' on injustice becomes legitimate (Westin 1981). And there is no shortage of mainstream opinion that criminal sanctions are administered unfairly. But the key question remains: by what process [...] do citizens define a governmental sanctioning decision as unfair?

Defining sanctions as unfair

Respect. The evidence suggests respect by punishers for the punished is a separate dimension from Braithwaite's (1989) distinction between reintegrative and stigmatic shaming. Rather, it is a more basic matter of treating people with human dignity. Reintegration can be done rudely, and stigma can be applied politely. As Braithwaite (1989, p. 101) points out, reintegrative shaming 'can be cruel, even vicious', as long as it has a finite end point and explicit ceremonies for accepting the offender back into the community administering the punishment. It seems reasonable to posit that unfair or disrespectful sanctions that are also stigmatizing are the most likely to provoke defiance, but that still presumes the two dimensions are distinct.

Fairness and respect is also not a simple matter of whether punishment is delivered or spared, as Tyler's (1990) findings show. What is more important in Tyler's evidence is that the offender's interpretation of events gets a fair hearing and that the sanctioning decision maker considers and respects that viewpoint. [...]

It is no accident that the demographic groups with the lowest opinion of the police – minorities and young men (Wilson 1983, p. 93; Clements 1993) – are also the most subject to police-initiated encounters (Sherman 1980) that lack the legitimacy of a citizen requesting police involvement (Reiss 1971, pp. 58-59). These are also situations in which police are more likely to encounter disrespect, get injured, make arrests, and have complaints filed against them. And although mutual respect characterizes most observed police encounters, inner-city police are somewhat more likely to be uncivil than the citizens they confront (Reiss 1971, p. 144). There is much evidence that police and poor young men are caught in a shame-

disrespect-anger spiral (Scheff and Retzinger 1991, p. 68). But the question for defiance theory is what effect that cycle has on the future offending of those caught up in it – on either the police (Skolnick and Fyfe 1993) or civilian side.

One answer is that the groups receiving the most disrespect from the police also have the highest participation rates in crime (Blumstein, Cohen, Roth, and Visher 1986). This fact might be dismissed as a mere artifact of measurement if arrest records were not confirmed by both self-report and victimization data. The fact is that young males, especially the poor and minorities, are much more exposed than lower crime groups to police disrespect and brutality, both vicariously and in person, *prior* to their peak years of first arrest and initial involvements in crime. This temporal order suggests a powerful role of police disrespect in sanction effects.

Substantive unfairness. Those who approach authority with defiant attitudes are often punished for their speech rather than for any substantive offense. When the criminal sanction is used in this fashion, it is substantively unjust and another potent source of defining police as illegitimate. There is no written law against 'contempt of cop', of course, but it is perhaps the most consistently enforced de facto law in the country. All systematic observation studies of police decision making (Sherman 1980; Smith and Visher 1981) have found that disrespect toward police powerfully increases the odds of being arrested. [...]

Other substantive sources of unfairness include the widespread non-enforcement of minor offenses (such as noise or public drinking), punctuated by arbitrary or discriminatory cases of enforcement (Reiss 1971, p. 51). 'Rounding up the usual suspects' implies police laziness in looking for the truly guilty, rather than efficiency in locating the probably guilty. Courts letting suspects go on 'technicalities' and juries not making the right decisions (Clements 1993) are other sources of perceived unfairness.

Remarkably, although most citizens feel unfairness is widespread, they do not feel courts or police discriminate against 'people like them' (Tyler 1990, p. 50). Thus, in comparing procedural to substantive unfairness, the former seems to do far more powerful harm to legitimacy. Personal experience with unfairness, most often in the form of perceived disrespect, may be the greatest spark of defiance.

Anger and displaced just deserts

Once a poorly bonded offender is punished unfairly and chooses to deny the shame of it all, he may or may not become angry at the punishers. Among the arrested suspects in the Milwaukee domestic violence experiment, 23% denied that it was immoral to hit your partner, but only 10% said the arrest had made them angry at the police (Sherman 1992, pp. 330–331). No matter what they say, we would expect almost none of them to attack the police in direct retaliation. Rather, their anger is displaced onto their present or future romantic partners or other citizens, who represent the clients police serve.

This displacement of just deserts for the wrong done to the sanctioned offender need not be a consciously articulated program. Rather, as Katz (1988) suggests, it can appear in the construction of a reputation for 'badness', a 'hardman' who will tolerate no disrespect and who will dominate anyone he chooses. When disrespect by another citizen is a precipitating situational cause of crime, it may actually reflect an underlying anger at the disrespect shown by police or courts in the last sanctioning encounter. Had that encounter been more respectful of the offender, perhaps the offender would be less sensitive to disrespect and less ready to punish anyone who accidentally or intentionally shows new disrespect to the offender.

Yet some defiance maybe a more explicit project of displaced just deserts. Much offending occurs in cyclical but brief, multi-offense crime 'sprees' or rampages, among both poor street robbers and middle-class adolescents (Katz 1988, p. 203). Such sprees might be touched off by episodes of disrespect, perhaps from authority figures other than criminal sanctioners: teachers, parents, employers.

The 1992 Rodney King verdict riot in Los Angeles illustrates this process for general defiance. The acquittal of the four accused officers symbolized the unfairness of criminal sanctions that allowed police to beat a Black man already in custody. But the riots that followed were not aimed at the police or Ventura County jurors. Rather, a major target was Korean and other Asian merchants operating in Black and Hispanic neighborhoods, 2,000 of whose businesses were destroyed (Kotkin 1993). These businesses had been repeatedly accused of disrespectful behavior toward neighborhood young people, including illegal use of deadly force against thieves (National Public Radio 1993). Those businesses thus substantively provoked the attacks on them, at least

---

Figure 23.4.2   Four Patterns of Defiance

I. Dimensions of Defiance

a. Specific vs. general

Specific defiance = individual reactions to sanctions

General defiance = collective reactions to sanctions

b. Direct vs indirect

Direct defiance = just deserts offending against a sanctioning agent

Indirect defiance = displaced just deserts against a vicarious agent

II. Two Dimensions Cross-Classified

	Specific	General
Direct	1	2
Indirect	3	4

Examples

1 = fighting police during arrest

2 = ambushing police in South Africa

3 = beating spouses more after a domestic violence arrest

4 = Rodney King verdict riots in Los Angeles

---

in the eyes of the attackers. But the attacks may never have occurred if the procedurally unfair beating and jury verdict had not sent the weakly bonded community into a spiral of proud defiance and rage.

Defiance theory thus calls attention to a problem that extends far beyond the criminal sanction: the conduct of everyday discourse with alienated persons who react with indignation to any hint of social disapproval. Schools, parents, employers, and fellow citizens increasingly recognize large numbers of highly 'touchy', angry people ready to punish any available target for the sins of their past insulters, starting with the shame they felt as children from rejection by caretakers (Scheff and Retzinger 1991, p. 64) or historical insults to their social category. Some of them are police, some of them are criminals, and some of them merely file lawsuits.

From L.W. Sherman, 'Defiance, deterrence and irrelevance: a theory of the criminal sanction', Journal of Research in Crime and Delinquency, *1993, 30: 445–473.*

Notes

1 John Braithwaite (personal communication, 1993) suggests that 'disengagement ' also predicts noncompliance with law in response to sanctions, and that the two reactions may vary by type of offense: although 'defiance theory would work better with male violence, disengagement theory will work better with drug use and female delinquency.'

References

Anderson, E. (1978) *A Place on the Corner*. Chicago: University of Chicago Press.

Berk, R.A., A. Campbell, R. Klap, and B Western, (1992). 'The Deterrent Effect of Arrest in Incidents of Domestic Violence: A Bayesian Analysis of Four Field Experiments.' *American Sociological Review* 57:698–708.

Blumstein, A., J. Cohen, J. Roth, and C. A, Visher. (1986) *Criminal Careers and 'Career Criminals'*. Washington, DC: National Academy of Sciences.

Bowers, W.J. (1988) 'The Effect of Executions Is Brutalization, Not Deterrence.' In *Challenging Capital Punishment: Legal and Social Science Approaches*, edited by K.C. Bass and J.A. Inciardi. Newbury Park, CA: Sage.

Braithwaite, J., (1989) *Crime, Shame and Reintegration*. Cambridge: Cambridge University Press.

Clements, M. (1993) National Survey on Law and Order. *Parade Magazine*, April 4, pp. 4–7.

Cohen, A.K. (1955) *Delinquent Boys: The Culture of the Gang*. New York: Free Press.

Felson, M. (1987) 'Routine Activities and Crime Prevention in the Developing Metropolis.' *Criminology* 25:911–32.

Henley, W.E. [1875] (1954) 'Invictus.' In *The Victorian Age: Prose, Poetry and Dream*. 2nd ed., edited by J.W. Bowyer and J.L. Brooks. New York: Appleton-Century-Crofts.

Hirschi, T. (1986) 'On the Compatibility of Rational Choice and Social Control Theories of Crime,' In *The Reasoning Criminal: Rational Choice Perspectives on Offending*, edited by D.B. Cornish and R.V. Clarke. New York: Springer-Verlag.

Katz, J. (1988) *Seductions of Crime: Moral and Sensual Attractions in Doing Evil*. New York: Basic Books.

Kotkin, J. (1993) 'How Not To Lose L. A.' *Washington Post*, April 18, p. C1.

Lemert, E. (1972) *Human Deviance, Social Problems and Social Control*. New York: Prentice-Hall.

Majors, R. and J. Mancini Bills. (1992) *Cool Pose: The Dilemmas of Black Manhood in America*. Lexington, MA: Lexington Books.

Merton, R.K. (1938) 'Social Structure and Anomie.' *American Sociological Review* 3:672–82.

National Public Radio (1993) 'All Things Considered.' Los Angeles segment, April 17.

Reiss, A.J., Jr. (1968) 'Police Brutality: Answers to Key Questions.' *Trans-action* July–August 12.

Reiss, A.J., Jr. (1971) *The Police and the Public*. New Haven: Yale University Press.

Scheff, T.J. and S.M. Retzinger (1991) *Emotions and Violence: Shame and Rage in Destructive Conflicts*. Lexington, MA: Lexington Books.

Sherman, L.W. (1980). 'Causes of Police Behavior: The Current State of Quantitative Research.' *Journal of Research in Crime and Delinquency* 17:69–100.

Sherman, L.W. (1992) *Policing Domestic Violence: Experiments and Dilemmas*. New York: Free Press.

Skolnick, J.H. and J.J. Fyfe. (1993) *Above the Law: Police and the Excessive Use of Force*. New York: Free Press.

Smith, D.A. and C.A. Visher. (1981) 'Street-Level Justice: Situational Determinants of Police Arrest Decisions.' *Social Problems* 29:167–78.

Tyler, T.R. (1990) *Why People Obey the Law*. New Haven: Yale University Press.

Westin, A.F. (1981), *Whistle-Blowing: Loyalty and Dissent in the Corporation*. New York: McGraw-Hill.

Wilson, J.Q. (1983) *Thinking About Crime*. Rev. ed New York: Basic Books.

24

Crime prevention and community safety

24.1 **A conceptual model of crime prevention**
Paul J. Brantingham and Frederic L. Faust   554

24.2 **The British gas suicide story and its
criminological implications**
Ronald V. Clarke and Pat Mayhew   559

24.3 **Neighborhoods and violent crime:
a multilevel study of collective efficacy**
Robert J. Sampson, Stephen W. Raudenbush
and Felton Earls   563

24.4 **The uses of sidewalks: safety**
Jane Jacobs   568

Introduction

One of the most substantial shifts in recent decades in criminology and criminal justice has been the emphasis placed upon crime prevention (see, for example, Reading 14.1 for a brief description of this shift). In part, this was a response to the apparently rapidly rising crime rates after the Second World War, together with the growing body of research evidence which raised doubts about the effectiveness of rehabilitative interventions (see Reading 22.2). As a consequence, increasing emphasis has more recently been placed on the role that criminal justice and other agencies, together with individual citizens, can play in the active prevention of criminal opportunity.

Crime prevention is, of course, a broad area of activities and there have been a variety of attempts to bring some order to this field. One of the best known, by Paul Brantingham and Frederic Faust **(Reading 24.1)**, draws a distinction between three 'levels' of activity: primary, secondary and tertiary prevention. The model, they suggest, has practical application as well as enabling us to conceptualise things more clearly. In practical terms, its purpose is to help arrange, organise and identify priorities in public policy. What are we attempting to achieve in the crime prevention arena and how should this be organised? The bulk of activity, they suggest, tends to be organised at the secondary level. By contrast, they argue, there has been little systematic study of primary prevention activity.

The second excerpt, from work by Ron Clarke and Pat Mayhew **(Reading 24.2)**, tells a fascinating story about the remarkable decline in the number of suicides in England and Wales and what this has to tell us about crime prevention. Historically, domestic gas in England contained high levels of carbon monoxide (which is highly toxic). Changes in the gas supply – primarily via a switch to natural gas – led to a very substantial drop in carbon monoxide levels in domestic gas and, in consequence, to a rapid decline in the number of suicides. If they are correct in their argument, the gas suicide story has important implications for the issue of displacement. As Clarke and Mayhew put it: 'faced with fewer opportunities to use gas, few potential gas suicides found some other way of killing themselves'.

Clarke and Mayhew's study focuses on social processes and individual decision-making. The next excerpt, by Robert Sampson and colleagues **(Reading 24.3)**, shifts attention to the neighbourhood level and asks how we might understand the very marked variation in rates of criminal violence between different areas? Their argument is that there are characteristics of local neighbourhoods – beyond the basic demographics of the area – that help to explain this variation. More particularly, they suggest that neighbourhoods vary in their ability to regulate the behaviour of their members – largely through informal social control. They then outline a model for assessing and measuring what they call the 'collective efficacy' of different neighbourhoods and the implications that an understanding of this factor might have for future crime control.

In an era when kids hanging about on street corners are as likely to give rise to ASBOs as they are to concerns that there may be insufficient local resources for young people, it is important to be reminded that strangers on the street might just be a good thing. In a classic study Jane Jacobs **(Reading 24.4)** offers a view of pavement/sidewalk life that is at variance with what has perhaps become the dominant discourse these days. Thus, she argues, that it is vital that we recognise that 'the public peace... of cities is not kept primarily by the police, necessary as the police are'. In effect, she says that the greatest source of crime prevention is the informal social control generated by groups of people occupying public spaces: 'a well used city street is apt to be a safe street'. Many current commentators see the growing complexity of our modern world as a source of danger and insecurity. By contrast, Jacobs' closing remark on the well-used and organised city street is that if it is full of activity then 'the more strangers the merrier'.

Questions for discussion

1. What are the main differences between the three types of prevention activity described by Brantingham and Faust? Give examples of each.

2. What do Clarke and Mayhew suggest are the most important lessons from the 'British gas suicide story'?

3. What other potential explanations might there be for the declining number of suicides in this period?

4. What do Sampson et al mean by the term 'collective efficacy'?

5. What are the main factors that affect collective efficacy?

6. How does informal social control operate within communities? Give examples.

7. What do Samson et al mean when they say, 'recognizing that collective efficacy matters does not imply that inequalities at the neighbourhood level can be neglected'?

8. What does Jane Jacobs mean when she says 'the public peace... of cities is not kept primarily by the police, necessary as the police are'? What are the implications of this for order on our local streets?

24.1 A conceptual model of crime prevention
Paul J. Brantingham and Frederic L. Faust

Prevention, probably the most overworked and least understood concept in contemporary criminology, might be defined simply as any activity, by an individual or a group, public or private, that precludes the incidence of one or more criminal acts. But caution is warranted here, for the simplicity is deceptive. Can crime prevention be logically conceived to encompass such divergent actions as long-term incarceration and pretrial diversion from the justice system? Solitary confinement and remedial reading instruction? The improvement of automotive antitheft devices and the development of neighborhood recreation centers? Or psychosurgery and the levying of fines? Considering the goal definition of crime prevention, the answer might well be 'yes'. But where means are concerned, the matter is heavily clouded by definitional ambiguity and theoretical contradiction.

A paradigm for analysis of crime prevention

Most of the time the preventive activities of non-criminal justice programs, police, courts, and correction are substantially different. The points of distinction may be identified most clearly by the level or stage in the development of criminal behavior at which intervening activity is implemented. Since it is similarly conceived as intervention at different developmental levels, the public health model of disease prevention is analogous and useful.[1]

The public health model posits three levels of activity.[2] *Primary* prevention identifies disease-creating general conditions of the environment and seeks to abate those conditions (e.g., sewage treatment, mosquito extermination, small-pox vaccination, job-safety engineering, personal hygiene education). *Secondary* prevention identifies groups or individuals who have a high risk of developing disease or who have incipient cases of disease and intervenes in their lives with special treatments designed to prevent the risk from materializing or the incipient case from growing worse (e.g., chest x-rays in poor neighborhoods, special diets for overweight executives, rubella vaccinations for prospective but not-yet-expectant mothers, dental examinations). *Tertiary* prevention identifies individuals with advanced cases of disease and intervenes with treatment to prevent death or permanent disability (e.g., stomach pumping for poisoning, open-heart surgery for defective heart valves, radiation therapy for some forms of cancer), provides rehabilitation services for those persons who must live under the constraints of permanent disability (e.g., Braille training for the blind, prosthetic limbs for amputees), and provides a measure of relief from pain and suffering for individuals with incurable diseases (e.g., opiate therapy for terminal cancer patients, leper colonies).[3]

Tertiary prevention, then, aims at three forms of prevention: (1) prevention of death or disability; (2) prevention of a decline to a less adequate level of social, economic, and physical activity; (3) prevention of more physical and social pain than necessary in an inevitable demise.

Crime prevention can be conceptualized as operating at these same three levels.[4] (See Figure 24.1.1).

Primary crime prevention identifies conditions of the physical and social environment that provide opportunities for or precipitate criminal acts. Here the objective of intervention is to alter those conditions so that crimes cannot occur. *Secondary* crime prevention engages in early identification of potential offenders and seeks to intervene in their lives in such a way that they never commit criminal violation. *Tertiary* crime prevention deals with actual offenders and involves intervention in their lives in such a fashion that they will not commit further offenses. With this classification in view, let is examine the relationship of these levels of crime prevention to contemporary issues in criminal justice. For the purpose of analysis, we will consider the three levels of crime prevention in reverse order.

Application of the model

The correctional subsystem within the criminal justice system is charged with tertiary prevention. The optimistic – perhaps heroic – assumption is made that, through effective intervention, the offender will be fully restored to a permanent, functional level of socially acceptable behavior. For those offenders whose behavior is not amenable to

Figure 24.1.1	Models of prevention

Public Health Paradigm

Primary		Secondary		Tertiary
Health Promotion	**Specific Protection**	**Early Diagnosis**	**Disability Limitation**	**Rehabilitation**
health education general social & physical well-being programs nutrition genetics periodic examinations	personal hygiene specific immunizations job safety engineering environmental sanitation	case finding screening selective examinations	treatment for advanced disease	retraining community placement and support

Criminological Paradigm

Primary	Secondary	Tertiary		
			Reform	**Rehabilitation**
environmental design general social and physical well-being programs crime prevention education	early identification pre-delinquent screening individual intervention neighborhood programs		community treatment institutional treatment punishment	training support surveillance
		Incapacitation		
		Institutional custody		

modification through known forms of punishment or treatment, tertiary prevention aims to provide such control of the offender's behavior as is necessary, to protect society and elicit the highest and most sustained level of conforming behavior possible.[5] The preventive aspect of intervention at this level may be found in the notion that such intervention keeps society from being placed at increased risk, keeps the offender from being placed at greater risk for his own harmful behavior and from the excessive retaliation of others,[6] and keeps conditions from occurring which offer no opportunity and encouragement for whatever higher level of conforming behavior the offender might be capable of achieving at some future time.

For offenders whose criminal behavior is not amenable to correction through known forms of punishment and treatment and who are seen as potentially dangerous to society, the traditional societal reaction has been incapacitation – the imposition of lifetime or long-term confinement in a secure setting. This confinement has been justified as societal protection.[7] Theoretically, it is assumed that the behavior of offenders in this category might improve to some degree but not sufficiently to warrant their release from custody in the near future. But still, any behavioral improvement is desirable. Toward this end, the President's Crime Commission recommended that offenders of this type be transferred to special institutions that would 'encourage the development of more imaginative programs for long-term prisoners – special industries, perhaps greater independence and self-sufficiency within the confines of a secure institution'.[8] For those offenders who are not seen as potentially serious threats to society, the correctional system combines rehabilitation and reform to elicit more conforming behavior. The hope is that the behavioral improvements for these prisoners will be sufficient to inhibit further illegal activities.

Effective tertiary prevention is the primary goal of the correctional subsystem. It is also one of the goals of the courts and the probation and parole service as these subsystems interact and interlink with correction. Effective tertiary prevention is, and always has been, more ideal than actual. But the justification of particular forms of both punishment and treatment is grounded on their efficacy in achieving this level of prevention. As a result, corporal punishment has been generally abolished because it fails to prevent recidivism rather than because it is inhumane, even though a case can be made for it on retributive grounds. Other forms of punishment such as imprisonment and other forms of treatment such as castration of sexual offenders are currently under attack because they fail to reduce recidivism below the levels attained by cheaper and less drastic methods. On the other hand, forms of punishment such as fines and forms of treatment such as psychosurgery, which promise improved tertiary prevention, are currently fashionable even though retributive and humanitarian problems are raised.[9]

Secondary prevention is the level at which crime prevention is most fervently pursued in research and program funding. Courts, probation and parole services, general social services, educational institutions, planners, private citizens, and police all engage in secondary prevention. It is argued that poverty, low educational level, lack of vocational skills, minority status and poor physical and mental health are all associated with criminal activity. The assumption is that these social and physical problems are causally related to crime, although most current research rejects the causal link.

Without question, the great hulk of intervention activities labeled 'crime prevention' must be categorized as secondary prevention – i.e., early identification of potential offenders, followed by action designed to reduce the risk of future involvement in more serious forms of antisocial behavior, particularly criminal behavior. For example, during the 1960s, massive federal, state, and local programs were mounted to identity and deal with problems of school drop-outs, vocationally untrained and economically disadvantaged youth,

physically and mentally handicapped individuals, minority group members, etc., with the assumption that such intervention would curb and reverse the increasing crime rates.[10] While these endeavors have been launched toward laudable objectives, they have frequently rested on the false assumption that they were striking at the root 'cause' of crime and delinquency when, instead, they were dealing only with observable symptoms.[11]

Primary prevention – identification of those conditions of the physical and social environment that provide opportunities for or precipitate criminal behavior and the alteration of those conditions so that no crimes occur – is clearly the ideal objective. In fact this is the objective that is posited as the justification for most secondary prevention activities, but obviously the identification of incipient cases implies that the opportunity for primary prevention (in those instances at least) has already passed. With a few notable exceptions, there has been little systematic study of primary prevention of criminal behavior.[12] The work accomplished at this level has been largely pursued along one of three lines: (1) psychological immunization from certain types of behavioral tendencies, (2) preclusion of criminal activity by redesign of the physical environment, and (3) general 'deterrence' of criminal activity by exemplary sentences and the presence of correctional facilities. The first two directions of inquiry have raised serious ethical and legal questions, to say nothing of the problem of resource allocation for implementation on a scale large enough to affect crime rates significantly.

Directions for crime prevention

Using the three-part model we can classify criminal justice system activities and noncriminal justice system activities designed to prevent crime. As can be seen by examining Figures 24.1.2 and 24.1.3, most crime prevention activity has occurred in secondary and tertiary prevention. Less effort has been spent on primary prevention.

Figure 24.1.2 Prevention activities of the criminal justice system

	Primary	Secondary	Tertiary
Police	General deterrence (through 'presence') Citizens education programs	Intelligence operators Social service operations (athletic programs, family crisis units, sensitive training) Patrol peace-keeping actions ('move-along' orders, stop-and-frisk contacts) Intervention and diversion (drunk detoxification, juvenile supervision)	Arrest and prosecution Misdemeanor correctional institutions
Courts	General deterrence (though 'exemplary' sentence)	Pre-adjudication diversion	Post-adjudication diversion, reform, rehabilitation, and incapacitation (through sentence)
Corrections	General deterrence (through existence)	Operation of diversion programs	Reform (through punishment, community treatment, institutional treatment) Rehabilitation (through aftercare support, training, and surveillance) Incapacitation (through custody)

Figure 24.1.3 Prevention activities outside the criminal justice system

	Primary	Secondary	Tertiary
Private citizens	Household and business Security precautions General charity	Big brother programs Delinquency specific Social activities	Correctional volunteers
Schools	General education	Pre-delinquent screening Educational intervention programs	Prosecution of truants and delinquents Institutional education programs
Business	Security provisions	Employee screening	Prosecution of offenders Hiring of ex-offenders
Planners	Modification of physical environment to reduce criminal opportunity Modification of social environment to reduce impulsions towards criminal behavior	Crime location anaylsis for neighborhood education and modification programs Criminal residence study for neighborhood social work	Institutional design
Religious and social agencies	Moral training Family education General social work	Welfare services: child protection programs for disadvantaged & pre-delinquent youth, crisis intervention	Aftercare services

From P. J. Brantingham and F. L. Faust, 'A conceptual model of crime prevention', Crime and Delinquency, *1976, 22: 284–296.*

Notes

1 We recognize the risk inherent in borrowing a conceptual model from medicine. Criminology is only just beginning to recover from the damage done by the Positivist School's use of the medical analogy of crime as disease. In borrowing from public health concepts here, we have modified the public health model to fit the criminological situation rather than vice versa.

2 Hugh R. Leavell and E. Gurney Clark, *Preventive Medicine for the Doctor in His Community: An Epidemiological Approach*, 3rd ed. (New York: McGraw-Hill, 1965), pp. 19-28. We are indebted to Jack Wright, of the Florida Department of Health and Rehabilitative Services, for bringing the public health paradigm to our attention.

3 We have modified the groups of activity within the primary, secondary, and tertiary classifications described above to facilitate their use for criminological purposes. See Leavell and Clark, *op. cit. supra* note 2, pp. 20–21. For an argument that an unmodified public health model is not useful to criminological thinking, even in the drug abuse area, see Richard Brotman and Frederic Suffet, 'The Concept of Prevention and Its Limitations,' *Annals of the American Academy of Political and Social Science*, January 1975, pp. 55–56.

4 Lejins has developed a tripartite classification of crime prevention which cuts orthogonally across our model. Thus, he describes (1) punitive prevention (a primary and tertiary form), (2) corrective prevention (a primary and secondary form), and (3) mechanical prevention (a primary and tertiary form). Peter Lejins 'The Field of Prevention,' *Delinquency Prevention: Theory and Practice*, William Amos and Charles Wellford, eds. (Englewood Cliffs, N.J. Prentice-Hall, 1967), pp. 1–21. Wolfgang's tripartite categorization of prevention appears to be a breakdown of secondary and tertiary forms of prevention. Marvin E. Wolfgang, 'Urban Crime,' *The Metropolitan Enigma*, James Q. Wilson, ed. (New York: Anchor Books, 1970) p. 299. The Florida State Bureau of Criminal Justice Planning has developed a typology of crime prevention programs which also cuts across our model. It defines programs of prevention aimed at (1) the initiating conditions of crime (primary prevention) and (2) the sustaining conditions of crime (secondary prevention). Florida Bureau of Criminal Justice Planning and Assistance, *The Florida Annual Action Plan for* 1974 (Tallahassee, Fla., 1974), pp1–21.

5 Capital punishment does not fall within this conceptual model without straining the analogy considerably since the legal and ethical tenets of public health medicine do not include the intentional infliction of death, regardless of the patient's medical threat to the health of others. If we do strain the analogy, however, the death penalty might be viewed as the most extreme form of tertiary prevention, with general deterrence feedback to the primary prevention level.

6 Canadian Committee on Correction, *The Basic Principles and Purposes of Criminal Justice* (Ottawa: Queen's Printer, 1969).

7 Capital punishment is excluded from consideration here and is not treated seriously within the general model of crime prevention, since the principal justification for imposition of the death penalty is retribution rather than any utilitarian judgment that the offender is not amenable to reform or rehabilitation and is too dangerous for less final methods of incapacitation.

8 President's commission on Law Enforcement and Administration of Justice, *Task Force Report: Corrections* (Washington, D.C.: U.S. Govt. Printing Office, 1967), p. 58. (Our italics.)

9 See generally, Alan. R. Mabe, ed., *New Techniques and Strategies for Social Control: Ethical and Practical Limits*, a special issue of *American Behavioral Scientist*, May-June 1975, for a group of articles probing state-of-the-art issues its behavioral control. Note that the ethical and legal issues surrounding such modes of behavioral control make them politically vulnerable as secondary and tertiary prevention techniques. See, e.g., 'Clockwork Orange Projects Banned,' *Crime & Delinquency*, July 1974, pp. 314–15

10 Peter Marris and Martin Rein, *Dilemmas of Social Reform*, 2nd ed. (Chicago: Aldine, 1973); Daniel P. Moynihan, *Maximum Feasible Misunderstanding* (New York: Free Press, 1968).

11 C. Ray Jeffery, *Crime Prevention through Environmental Design* (Beverly Hills, Calif.: Sage, 1971).

12 *Ibid.*; Oscar Newman, *Defensible Space* (New York: Macmillan, 1972).

24.2 The British gas suicide story and its criminological implications Ronald V. Clarke and Pat Mayhew

A few years ago, a proposal to erect an antisuicide barrier on San Francisco's Golden Gate Bridge is said to have been defeated through the combined opposition of environmentalists and psychiatrists. The former objected to the barrier's unsightliness; the latter said that potential suicides would find other ways to kill themselves, with no net saving in lives. Whatever the merits of the environmental position, the recent 35 percent drop in Britain's national rate of suicide suggests that the psychiatric objections were misplaced. It is now clear that this remarkable decline in suicide was brought about by removal of carbon monoxide from the domestic gas supply during the period. This was a by-product of the search for cheaper forms of gas and resulted from two separate developments: first, the adoption of new manufacturing processes for so-called town gas and, later, the wholesale replacement (between 1968 and 1977) of town gas by natural gas from the North Sea, Natural gas is free of carbon monoxide, and some of the new town gases contained as little as 2–7 percent carbon monoxide, whereas older town gas contained around 8–16 percent carbon monoxide. This means that, after being at highly lethal levels until the beginning of the 1960s, carbon monoxide was almost eliminated from the domestic gas supply by 1975. The decline in toxicity was accompanied by a fall in the number of gas suicides. Although these accounted for almost half of all suicide deaths in England and Wales in 1960, gas suicides had virtually disappeared by 1975. Faced with fewer opportunities to use gas, few potential gas suicides found some other way of killing themselves.

These facts have important implications for the prevention of suicide and, as long as the analogy with crime holds, also for the prevention of crime. If opportunity determines not merely the time, place, and method but the very occurrence of a behavior that is usually seen to be the outcome of strong internal motives, the same is likely to be true of crime, most of which seems less deeply motivated. That few people found other ways of killing themselves is especially instructive in that similar evidence of lack of displacement is difficult to obtain in the criminological field. The gas suicide story therefore considerably strengthens the case for opportunity-reducing, or 'situational'

(Clarke 1983), measures of crime prevention. Moreover, it suggests that the common assumption that criminality has drive-like properties may be false, supporting the need for theory that takes due account of both the objective and the subjective components of opportunity. [...]

Domestic gas and suicide in England and Wales, 1968–83

A. General features of suicide in England and Wales

From 1963, as will be shown in more detail below, rates of suicide for both men and women in England and Wales declined markedly until the mid-1970s. Only Scotland and Greece among eighteen European countries studied by Sainsbury, Jenkins, and Levey (1980) showed similar, though

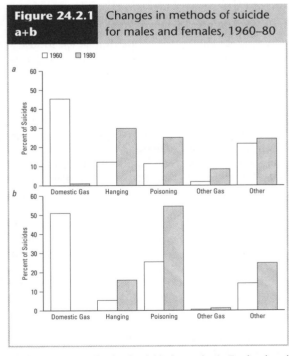

Figure 24.2.1 a+b Changes in methods of suicide for males and females, 1960–80

a: Changes in methods of suicide for males in England and Wales, 1960–80. **b**: Changes in methods of suicide for females in England and Wales, 1960–80. *Source*: Bulusu and Alderson (1984).

less pronounced, declines. Since the mid-1970s, female suicides in England and Wales have declined further, whereas those for males have risen, though not yet to the levels of the early 1960s (for commentary on long-term trends in suicide in Britain, see, e.g., Adelstein and Mardon [1975], Farmer [1979], and Low et al. [1981]).

Detoxification of gas has changed the distribution of different methods of suicide considerably, as Figure 24.2.1 shows. For example, in 1960, suicides by domestic gas accounted for, respectively, just under and just over half of all male and female suicides; but by 1980, only 0.2 percent of all suicides were committed by this method. The most frequently used method of suicide in 1980 for men was hanging (including strangulation and suffocation), which accounted for nearly a third of deaths; hanging was followed by poisoning with solid and liquid substances, which accounted for nearly one-quarter of deaths (Fig. 24.2.1a). Poisoning by gases other than ones in domestic use (mostly car exhaust fumes) accounted for roughly a further 17 percent of the total male suicides. There was little change during the period, however, in the proportion of suicides using a variety of other methods such as cutting, shooting, drowning, and jumping.

B. Detoxification of domestic gas

Following nationalization of the British gas industry in 1949, an extensive program of modernization was begun. [...] The average CO content of the public gas supply in Great Britain gradually declined, with minor fluctuations, from a high of about 13 percent in the late 1950s to about 7 percent in 1968 (Kreitman 1976), the year the second major change began to take effect. This was the replacement of manufactured 'town' gas by the then recently discovered natural gas from the North Sea. Natural gas consists largely of methane and is nonpoisonous. Because its combustion properties are different from those of manufactured gas, the two cannot be mixed, and natural gas had to be introduced area by area, as consumers' appliances were converted to burn natural gas. This massive conversion program, involving some 13.5 million consumers and 35 million appliances, took nine years and was completed in September 1977 (Elliott 1980). [...]

C. Detoxification and the decline in suicide: statistics

Table 24.2.1 shows the numbers of suicides by gas and by other methods in England and Wales for

Table 24.2.1 Suicides by domestic gas, England and Wales, 1958-77

Year	Total suicides	Suicides by domestic gas	Percent of total
1958	5,298	2,637	49.8
1959	5,207	2,594	49.8
1960	5,112	2,499	48.9
1961	5,200	2,379	45.8
1962	5,588	2,469	44.2
1963	5,714	2,368	41.4
1964	5,566	2,088	37.5
1965	5,161	1,702	33,0
1966	4,994	1,593	31.9
1967	4,711	1,336	28.4
1968	4,584	988	21.6
1969	4,326	790	18.3
1970	3,940	511	13.0
1971	3,945	346	8.8
1972	3,770	197	5.2
1973	3,823	143	3.7
1974	3,899	50	1.3
1975	3,693	23	.6
1976	3,816	14	.4
1977	3,944	8	.2

Source: Office of Population Censuses and Surveys (1959–78).

1958–77, and Figure 24.2.2 illustrates the relation between numbers of gas suicides and the annual average proportion of CO in the gas supply for England and Wales between 1960 and 1977. [...] The decline in gas suicides closely matches reduced levels of toxicity. These suicides, which numbered 2,499 in 1960, when CO concentrations were above 11 percent, declined to a mere 23 in 1975, when average CO concentrations were less than 1 percent. Although CO concentrations began to be reduced at the end of the 1950s (the peak year for gas suicides was 1958), overall rates of suicide did not begin to decline until 1963 because the reduction in gas suicides before then was masked by a general rise in other suicides.

The fit between toxicity and suicide could hardly have been any closer. [...]

Figure 24.2.2 Relation between gas suicides in England and Wales and CO content of domestic gas, 1960–77.

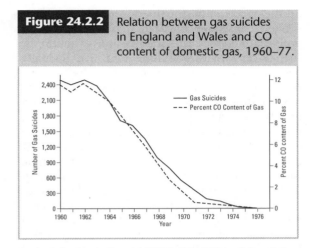

Sources: Registrar General (1959–73); Office of Population Census and Surverys (1974–85); unpublished estimates of CO content by British gas.

While there can be no doubt that detoxification of the gas supply caused the decline in gas suicides, the more important and interesting question concerns the effect of detoxification on the suicide rate as a whole. [...]

A number of conclusions can be drawn:

1 The overall decline in male suicides between the early 1960s and the early 1970s is accounted for largely by the halving of suicides by the oldest age group – brought about by the elimination of gas suicides. There is no evidence that other suicides increased for this age group as gas suicides declined.

2 The decline in gas suicides for the two younger groups of males during the same ten years is matched by increases in other kinds of suicide. However, these other suicides had been increasing before detoxification, which means that displacement from gas to other methods cannot wholly account for the observed pattern.

3 After 1975, when detoxification was all but complete, suicide rates for all three age groups of men show distinct rises.

4 For women, the decline in gas suicides is not matched by increases in other kinds of suicide for the two older age groups, though this is the case for those under 24 years of age.

5 Unlike the case for men, rates of suicide for women have shown very little increase since 1975.

While these facts indicate that, following detoxification, there was little displacement to other methods of suicide, especially by women and older men, and that thousands of lives were saved (6,700, according to the calculations made by Wells [1981]). [...]

It is clear that substantial reductions in the CO content of the public gas supply in Britain led to the virtual disappearance of suicide by domestic gas. Because few people stopped from using gas found another way of killing themselves, a substantial decline in the overall number of suicides resulted. Since the mid-1970s, suicides have gradually increased and, for men, have now surpassed the levels that held prior to detoxification of the gas supply. In light of the evidence concerning a general rise in suicidal behavior, and also because of the increased use of some more novel means of suicide (such as car exhaust gases), it is not unreasonable to think that these increases might have occurred even without detoxification. [...]

Criminological implications

A. The lessons for displacement

The gas suicide story is important precisely because it furnishes clear proof that the preventive gains of a reduction in opportunity were not merely dissipated through displacement. Even if some displacement occurred, particularly to less lethal methods, thousands of lives were still saved. This changes the balance of the argument about the value of situational measures. It is now more incumbent on the skeptic to show that displacement has defeated a crime prevention measure than for the advocate to prove beyond doubt that it has not. [...]

B. Practical difficulties of situational prevention

In our minds, at least, there is little doubt that limiting the availability of firearms in the United States would have a substantial effect on homicide and probably also on other violent crimes. We draw this conclusion from the fact that, for 1980-84, the non-gun homicide rate in the United States was only 3.7 times greater than that in England and Wales, while the rate for gun homicides was 63 times and for hand-gun homicides 175 times greater. [...]

The difficulties facing gun control signify a more general problem of implementation: opportunity-reducing measures with respect to crime encounter the same objections concerning individual freedoms, costs, inconvenience, and so forth as they do with respect to suicide. In addition, prevention of crime is frequently seen as less important than its punishment. These obstacles have become more apparent with attempts to implement situational prevention (see, esp., Hope 1985a), Indeed, just as some of the theoretical objections to situational prevention – concerning its alleged neglect of fundamental causes and the dangers of displacement – begin to lose their force, so the practical impediments are assuming greater importance. [...] The moral of this is not that there should be less investment in situational prevention since, unlike social prevention, there is much evidence that it works (Heal and Laycock 1986). Rather, it is that much more effort will have to be devoted to implementation and that the rate of progress is likely to be slower than originally anticipated. It takes time for the public to accept the need for change – to take an example from another field, it was long after the first convincing demonstration of the link between smoking and lung cancer that governments accepted the need to limit advertising of tobacco products and that people's smoking habits began to change.

C. The opportunity structure for crime

Suicide by gas was common in Britain, not merely because it was the easiest way to act out suicidal despair, but because the existence of this method may have encouraged more unhappy people to pursue the idea of killing themselves. In other words, gas suicide may have been as much a product of the particular opportunity structure pertaining in Britain as it was of social and psychological malaise. [...]

The relation between opportunity structure and crime is, however, far from straightforward: many more opportunities for crime exist than are acted on (Clarke 1984), and, unquestionably, there are important intervening variables relating to the perception and evaluation of opportunities. For example, as certain material goods become more widely owned, there may come a point at which their social value declines and they are less sought after by thieves (Gould 1969), even if given less protection by their owners. A further example is provided by the fact that fewer people killed themselves with domestic gas in Holland than expected from measures of its toxicity and availability, possibly because suicide in Holland really is associated in the public consciousness with drowning rather than with gas.

Some useful lessons for criminology follow from speculating about the effect of detoxification on the opportunity structure for suicide in Britain. A likely consequence will be that new cohorts of potential suicides will identify novel methods, such as car exhaust poisoning, that then gradually become established in public knowledge. This process is similar to displacement except that the new methods are not necessarily identified and used by individuals prevented from using toxic gas: many of those now availing themselves of car exhaust fumes may not even have known that domestic gas was once an option. A crime example would be the rise in convenience store robbery that may have resulted from increased bank security: many of those now obtaining cash in such robberies may not have considered robbing banks – they may have been too young when this was a feasible option. Another change in the criminal opportunity structure producing displacement-like effects would be the move to the 'cashless society'. While reducing opportunities for theft, this has presented new possibilities for computer crime, for instance – possibilities exploited by offenders who may never have entertained the idea of mugging or committing other forms of personal theft.

The gas suicide story permits one further comment on the importance of the opportunity structure at the stage of first entertaining the idea of committing a deviant act. Doubt has been cast on the notion that much crime is impulsively committed, following the sudden perception of a criminal opportunity (Maguire 1980; Bennett and Wright 1984), and this, in turn, has been used to question the value of situational prevention. However, just as the existence of an easy method might have encouraged some people to think about suicide, so, for example, the recognition that residential burglary is now easier because of lower occupancy levels and a greater amount of 'stealable' property might have tempted more individuals to try their hand at this crime (e.g., Cohen and Felson 1979). How this became recognized and how such knowledge about new criminal opportunities spreads would be a fruitful line of inquiry.

From R.V. Clarke and P. Mayhew, 'The British gas suicide story and its criminological implications', in N. Morris and M. Tonry (eds) Crime and Justice, *vol. 10 (Chicago: University of Chicago Press), 1988, pp. 79–116.*

References

Adelstein, A., and C. Macdon (1975), 'Suicides, 1961–74.' In *Population Trends*, vol. 2. London: H.M. Stationery Office.

Bennett, T., and R. Wright (1984) *Burglars on Burglary*. Farnsborough: Gower.

Clarke, R.V. (1983) 'Situational Crime Prevention: Its Theoretical Basis and Practical Scope.' In *Crime and Justice: An Annual Review of Research*, vol. 4, edited by M. Tonry and N. Morris. Chicago: University of Chicago Press.

Clarke, R.V. (1984) 'Opportunity-based Crime Rates: The Difficulties of Further Refinement.' *British Journal of Criminology* 24:74–83.

Cohen, L.E., and M. Felson (1979) 'Social Change and Crime Rate Trends: A Routine Activity Approach.' *American Sociological Review* 44:588–608.

Elliott, C. (1980) *The History of Natural Gas Conversion in Great Britain*. Royston and Cambridge: Cambridge Information and Research Services in association with the British Gas Corp.

Farmer, R.D.T. (1979) 'Suicide by Different Methods.' *Postgraduate Medical Journal* 55:775–79.

Gould, L.C. (1969) 'The Changing Structure of Property Crime in an Affluent Society.' *Social Forces* 48:50–59.

Heal, K. and Laycock, G. (1986) *Situational Crime Prevention: from Theory into Practice*. London: H.M. Stationery Office.

Hope, T. (1985a) *Implementing Crime Prevention Measures*. Home Office Research Study no. 86. London: H.M. Stationery Office.

Kreitman, N. (1976) 'The Coal Gas Story: United Kingdom Suicide Rates, 1960–71.' *British Journal of Preventive and Social Medicine* 30:86–93.

Low, A.A., R.D.T. Farmer, D.R. Jones, and J.R. Rohde (1981) 'Suicide in England and Wales: An Analysis of 100 Years, 1876–1975.' *Psychological Medicine* 11:359–68.

Maguire, M. (1980) 'Burglary as Opportunity.' *Home Office Research Unit Research Bulletin*, no. 10, pp. 6–9.

Sainsbury, P., J. Jenkins, and A. Levey (1980) 'The Social Correlates of Suicide in Europe.' In *The Suicide Syndrome*, edited by R. Farmer and S. Hirsch. London: Croom Helm.

Wells, N. (1981) *Suicide and Deliberate Self-Harm*. London: Office of Health Economics.

24.3 Neighborhoods and violent crime: a multilevel study of collective efficacy Robert J. Sampson, Stephen W. Raudenbush and Felton Earls

For most of this century, social scientists have observed marked variations in rates of criminal violence across neighborhoods of U.S. cities. Violence has been associated with the low socioeconomic status (SES) and residential instability of neighborhoods. Although the geographical concentration of violence and its connection with neighborhood composition are well established, the question remains: why? What is it, for example, about the concentration of poverty that accounts for its association with rates of violence? What are the social processes that might explain or mediate this relation[1–3]? In this article, we report results from a study designed to address these questions about crime and communities.

Our basic premise is that social and organizational characteristics of neighborhoods explain variations in crime rates that are not solely attributable to the aggregated demographic characteristics of individuals. We propose that the differential ability of neighborhoods to realize the common values of residents and maintain effective social controls is a major source of neighborhood variation in violence[4,5]. Although social control is often a response to deviant behavior, it should not be equated with formal regulation or forced conformity by institutions such as the police and courts. Rather, social control refers generally to the capacity of a group to regulate its members according to desired principles – to realize collective, as opposed to forced, goals[6]. One central goal is the desire of community residents to live in safe and orderly environments that are free of predatory crime, especially interpersonal violence.

In contrast to formally or externally induced actions (for example, a police crackdown), we focus on the effectiveness of informal mechanisms by which residents themselves achieve public order. Examples of informal social control include the monitoring of spontaneous play groups among children, a willingness to intervene to prevent acts such as truancy and street-corner 'hanging' by teenage peer groups, and the confrontation of persons who are exploiting or disturbing public space[5, 7]. Even among adults, violence regularly arises in public disputes, in the context of illegal markets (for example, prostitution and drugs), and in the company of peers[8]. The capacity of residents to control group-level processes and visible signs of social disorder is thus a key mechanism influencing opportunities for interpersonal crime in a neighborhood.

Informal social control also generalizes to broader issues of import to the well-being of neighborhoods. In particular, the differential ability of communities to extract resources and respond to cuts in public services (such as police patrols, fire stations, garbage collection, and housing code enforcement) looms large when we consider the known link between public signs of disorder (such as vacant housing, burned-out buildings, vandalism, and litter) and more serious crime[9].

Thus conceived, neighborhoods differentially activate informal social control. It is for this reason that we see an analogy between individual efficacy and neighborhood efficacy: both are activated processes that seek to achieve an intended effect. At the neighborhood level, however, the willingness of local residents to intervene for the common good depends in large part on conditions of mutual trust and solidarity among neighbors[10]. Indeed, one is unlikely to intervene in a neighborhood context in which the rules are unclear and people mistrust or fear one another. It follows that socially cohesive neighborhoods will prove the most fertile contexts for the realization of informal social control. In sum, it is the linkage of mutual trust and the willingness to intervene for the common good that defines the neighborhood context of collective efficacy. Just as individuals vary in their capacity for efficacious action, so too do neighborhoods vary in their capacity to achieve common goals. And just as individual self-efficacy is situated rather than global (one has self-efficacy relative to a particular task or type of task)[11], in this paper we view neighborhood efficacy as existing relative to the tasks of supervising children and maintaining public order. It follows that the collective efficacy of residents is a critical means by which urban neighborhoods inhibit the occurrence of personal violence, without regard to the demographic composition of the population.

What influences collective efficacy?

As with individual efficacy, collective efficacy does not exist in a vacuum. It is embedded in structural contexts and a wider political economy that stratifies places of residence by key social characteristics[12]. Consider the destabilizing potential of rapid population change on neighborhood social organization. A high rate of residential mobility, especially in areas of decreasing population, fosters institutional disruption and weakened social controls over collective life. A major reason is that the formation of social ties takes time. Financial investment also provides homeowners with a vested interest in supporting the commonweal of neighborhood life. We thus hypothesize that residential tenure and homeownership promote collective efforts to maintain social control[13].

Consider next patterns of resource distribution and racial segregation in the United States. Recent decades have witnessed an increasing geographical concentration of lower income residents, especially minority groups and female-headed families. This neighborhood concentration stems in part from macroeconomic changes related to the deindustrialization of central cities, along with the outmigration of middle-class residents[14]. In addition, the greater the race and class segregation in a metropolitan area, the smaller the number of neighborhoods absorbing economic shocks and the more severe the resulting concentration of poverty will be[15]. Economic stratification by race and place thus fuels the neighborhood concentration of cumulative forms of disadvantage, intensifying the social isolation of lower income, minority, and single-parent residents from key resources supporting collective social control[1,16].

Perhaps more salient is the influence of racial and economic exclusion on perceived powerlessness. Social science research has demonstrated, at the individual level, the direct role of SES in promoting a sense of control, efficacy, and even biological health itself[17]. An analogous process may work at the community level. The alienation, exploitation, and dependency wrought by resource deprivation act as a centrifugal force that stymies collective efficacy. Even if personal ties are strong in areas of concentrated disadvantage, they may be weakly tethered to collective actions.

We therefore test the hypothesis that concentrated disadvantage decreases and residential stability increases collective efficacy. In turn, we assess whether collective efficacy explains the association of neighborhood disadvantage and residential instability with rates of interpersonal violence. It is our hypothesis that collective efficacy mediates a substantial portion of the effects of neighborhood stratification.

Research design

This article examines data from the Project on Human Development in Chicago Neighborhoods (PHDCN). Applying a spatial definition of neighborhood – a collection of people and institutions occupying a subsection of a larger community – we combined 847 census tracts in the city of Chicago to create 343 'neighborhood clusters' (NCs). The overriding consideration in formation of NCs was that they should be as ecologically meaningful as possible, composed of geographically contiguous census tracts, and internally homogeneous on key census indicators. We settled on an ecological unit of about 8,000 people, which is smaller than the 77 established community areas in Chicago (the average size is almost 40,000 people) but large enough to approximate local neighborhoods. Geographic boundaries (for example, railroad tracks, parks, and freeways) and knowledge of Chicago's neighborhoods guided this process[18].

The extensive racial, ethnic, and social-class diversity of Chicago's population was a major criterion in its selection as a research site. At present, whites, blacks, and Latinos each represent about a third of the city's population. [...]

Measures

'Informal social control' was represented by a five-item Likert-type scale. Residents were asked about the likelihood ('Would you say it is very likely, likely, neither likely nor unlikely, unlikely, or very unlikely?') that their neighbors could be counted on to intervene in various ways if (i) children were skipping school and hanging out on a street corner, (ii) children were spray-painting graffiti on a local building, (iii) children were showing disrespect to an adult, (iv) a fight broke out in front of their house, and (v) the fire station closest to their home was threatened with budget cuts. 'Social cohesion and trust' were also represented by five conceptually related items. Respondents were asked how strongly they agreed (on a five-point scale) that 'people around here are willing to help their neighbors', 'this is a close-knit neighborhood', 'people in this neighborhood can be trusted', 'people in this neighborhood generally don't get along with each other', and 'people in this neighborhood do not share the same values' (the last two statements were reverse coded).

Responses to the five-point Likert scales were aggregated to the neighborhood level as initial measures. Social cohesion and informal social control were closely associated across neighborhoods

($r = 0.80$, P < 0.001), which suggests that the two measures were tapping aspects of the same latent construct. Because we also expected that the willingness and intention to intervene on behalf of the neighborhood would be enhanced under conditions of mutual trust and cohesion, we combined the two scales into a summary measure labeled collective efficacy[19].

The measurement of violence was achieved in three ways. First, respondents were asked how often each of the following had occurred in the neighborhood during the past 6 months: (i) a fight in which a weapon was used, (ii) a violent argument between neighbors, (iii) a gang fight, (iv) a sexual assault or rape, and (v) a robbery or mugging. The scale construction for perceived neighborhood violence mirrored that for social control and cohesion. Second, to assess personal victimization, each respondent was asked 'While you have lived in this neighborhood, has anyone ever used violence, such as in a mugging, fight, or sexual assault, against you or any member of your household anywhere in your neighborhood?'[20]. Third, we tested both survey measures against independently recorded incidents of homicide aggregated to the NC level[21]. Homicide is one of the most reliably measured crimes by the police and does not suffer the reporting limitations associated with other violent crimes, such as assault and rape.

Ten variables were constructed from the 1990 decennial census of the population to reflect neighborhood differences in poverty, race and ethnicity, immigration, the labor market, age composition, family structure, homeownership, and residential stability. [...]

Collective efficacy as a mediator of social composition

Past research has consistently reported links between neighborhood social composition and crime. We assessed the relation of social composition to neighborhood levels of violence, violent victimization, and homicide rates, and asked whether collective efficacy partially mediated these relations.

Perceived violence. Using a model that paralleled that for collective efficacy, we found that reports of neighborhood violence depended to some degree on personal background. Higher levels of violence were reported by those who were separated or divorced (as compared with those who were single or married), by whites and blacks (as opposed to Latinos), by younger respondents, and by those with longer tenure in their current neighborhood. Gender, homeownership, mobility, and SES were not significantly associated with responses within neighborhoods. When these personal background characteristics were controlled, the concentrations of disadvantage and immigrants were positively associated with the level of violence. Also, as hypothesized, residential stability was negatively associated with the level of violence. The model accounted for 70.5% of the variation in violence between neighborhoods. [...]

We found collective efficacy to be negatively related to violence net of all other effects. Hence, after social composition was controlled, collective efficacy was strongly negatively associated with violence. [...] As hypothesized, then, collective efficacy appeared to partially mediate widely cited relations between neighborhood social composition and violence. The model accounted for more than 75% of the variation between neighborhoods in levels of violence.

Violent victimization. Social composition, as hypothesized predicted criminal victimization, with positive coefficients for concentrated disadvantage and immigrant concentration and a negative coefficient for residential stability. [...] These estimates controlled for background characteristics associated with the risk of victimization. When added to the model, collective efficacy was negatively associated with victimization. [...]

Homicide. Although concentrated disadvantage was strongly positively related to homicide, immigrant concentration was unrelated to homicide, and residential stability was weakly positively related to homicide. However, when social composition was controlled, collective efficacy was negatively related to homicide. Collective efficacy can be viewed as partially mediating the association between concentrated disadvantage and homicide[22]

Control for prior homicide. Results so far were mainly cross-sectional, which raised the question of the possible confounding effect of prior crime. For example, residents in neighborhoods with high levels of violence might be afraid to engage in acts of social control[9]. We therefore reestimated all models controlling for prior homicide: the 3-year average homicide rate in 1988, 1989, and 1990. Prior homicide was negatively related to collective efficacy in 1995 and positively related to all three measures of violence in 1995, including a direct association with homicide. However, even after prior homicide was controlled, the coefficient for collective efficacy remained statistically significant and substantially negative in all three models.

Discussion and implications

The results imply that collective efficacy is an important construct that can be measured reliably at the neighborhood level by means of survey research strategies. In the past, sample surveys have primarily considered individual-level relations. However, surveys that merge a cluster sample design with questions tapping collective properties lend themselves to the additional consideration of neighborhood phenomena.

Together, three dimensions of neighborhood stratification – concentrated disadvantage, immigration concentration, and residential stability – explained 70% of the neighborhood variation in collective efficacy. Collective efficacy in turn mediated a substantial portion of the association of residential stability and disadvantage with multiple measures of violence, which is consistent with a major theme in neighborhood theories of social organization[1-5]. After adjustment for measurement error, individual differences in neighborhood composition, prior violence, and other potentially confounding social processes, the combined measure of informal social control and cohesion and trust remained a robust predictor of lower rates of violence.

There are, however, several limitations of the present study. Despite the use of decennial census data and prior crime as lagged predictors, the basic analysis was cross-sectional in design; causal effects were not proven. Indicators of informal control and social cohesion were not observed directly but rather inferred from informant reports. Beyond the scope of the present study, other dimensions of neighborhood efficacy (such as political ties) may be important, too. Our analysis was limited also to one city and did not go beyond its official boundaries into a wider region.

Finally, the image of local residents working collectively to solve their own problems is not the whole picture. As shown, what happens within neighborhoods is in part shaped by socioeconomic and housing factors linked to the wider political economy. In addition to encouraging communities to mobilize against violence through 'self-help' strategies of informal social control, perhaps reinforced by partnerships with agencies of formal social control (community policing), strategies to address the social and ecological changes that beset many inner-city communities need to be considered. Recognizing that collective efficacy matters does not imply that inequalities at the neighborhood level can be neglected.

From R. J. Sampson, S. W. Raudenbush and F. Earls, 'Neighborhoods and violent crime: a multilevel study of collective efficacy', Science, 1997, 277: 1–7.

References and notes

1 For a recent review of research on violence covering much at the 20th century, including a discussion at the many barriers to direct examination of the mechanisms explaining neighborhood-level variations, see P.J. Sampson and J. Lauritsen, in *Understanding and Preventing Violence: Social Influences*, vol. 3, A.J. Reiss Jr. and J. Roth, Eds. (National Academy Press, Washington, DC, 1994). pp, 1–114.

2 J.F. Short Jr., *Poverty, Ethnicity, and Violent Crime* (Westview, Boulder, CO. 1997).

3 For a general assessment of the difficulties facing neighborhood-level research on social outcomes, see S.E. Mayer and C. Jencks, *Science* 243, 1441 (1989).

4 R. Kornhauser, *Social Sources of Delinquency* (Univ. of Chicago Press, Chicago, IL, 1978); R. J. Bursik Jr., *Criminology* 26, 519 (1988); D. Elliott *et al.*, *J. Res. Crime Delinquency* 33, 389 (1996),

5 R.J. Sampson and W. B. Groves, *Am. J. Sociol.* 94, 774 (1989).

6 M. Janowitz, *ibid.* 81, 32 (1975).

7 E. Maccoby, J. Johnson, R. Church, *J. Social Issues* 14, 38 (1958); R. Taylor, S. Gottfredson, S. Brower, *J. Res. Crime Delinquency* 21, 303 (1983); J. Hacker, K. Ho, C. Ross, *Social Problems* 21, 328 (1974). A key finding from past research is that many delinquent gangs emerge from unsupervised spontaneous peer groups [F. Thrasher, *The Gang: A Study of 1,313 Gangs in Chicago* (Univ. of Chicago Press, Chicago, IL, 1963); C. Shaw and H. McKay, *Juvenile Delinquency and Urban Areas* (Univ. of Chicago Press. Chicago, IL. 1969), pp. 178–185; J. F. Short Jr. and F, Strodtbeck, *Group Process and Gang Delinquency* (Univ. of Chicago Press, Chicago, IL. 1965)].

8 For example, about half of all homicides occur among non-family members with a preexisting relationship: friends, neighbors, casual acquaintances, associates in illegal activities, or members of a rival gang. Illegal markets are especially high-risk settings for robbery, assault, and homicide victimization, whether by an associate or a stranger [A.J. Reiss Jr. and J. Roth, Eds. *Understanding and Preventing Violence* (National Academy Press, Washington, DC. 1993), pp. 18. 79; A.J, Reiss Jr., in *Criminal Careers and 'Career Criminals,'* A. Blumstein, J. Cohen. J. Roth, C Visher, Eds. (National Academy Press, Washington, DC, 1986]. pp. 121–160].

9 W. Skogan, *Disorder and Decline: Crime and the Spiral of Decay in American Neighborhoods* (Univ. of California Press, Berkeley, CA, 1990).

10 J. Coleman, *Foundations of Social Theory* (Harvard Univ. Press, Cambridge, MA, 1990); R. Putnam, *Making Democracy Work* (Princeton Univ. Press, Princeton, NJ, 1993).

11 A. Bandura, *Social Foundations of Thought and Action: A Social Cognitive Theory* (Prentice Hall, Englewood Cliffs, NJ, 1986).

12 See, generally. J. Logan and H. Molotch, *Urban Fortunes: The Political Economy of Place* (Univ. of California Press, Berkeley, CA, 1987).

13 See also J. Kasarda and N. Janowitz, *Am. Sociol. Rev.* 39, 328 (1974); R. Sampson, *ibid.* 53, 766 (1988).

14 W.J. Wilson. *The Truly Disadvantaged* (Univ. of Chicago Press, Chicago, IL, 1987).

15 D. Massey and N. Denton. *American Apartheid: Segregation and The Making of the Underclass* (Harvard Univ. Press, Cambridge, MA, 1993); D. Massey. *Am. J. Sociol.* 96. 329 (1990).

16 J. Brooks-Gunn, G. Duncan, P. Kato, N. Sealand. *Am. J. Sociol.* 99. 353 (1993); F.F. Furstenberg Jr., T.D. Cook, J. Eccles, G. H. Elder, A. Sameroff, *Urban Families and Adolescent Success* (Univ. of Chicago Press, Chicago, IL, in press), chap. 7. Research has shown a strong link between the concentration of female headed families and rates of violence [see (1)].

17 D. Williams, and C. Collins, *Annu. Rev Sociol.* 21, 349(1995].

18 Cluster analyses of census data also helped to guide the construction of internally homogenous NCs with respect to racial and ethnic mix, SES, housing density, and family organization. Random-effect analyses of variance produced intracluster correlation coefficients to assess the degree to which this goal had been achieved; analyses (37) revealed that the clustering was successful in producing relative homogeneity within NCs.

19 'Don't know' responses were recoded to the middle category of 'neither likely nor unlikely' (informal social control) or 'neither agree nor disagree' (social cohesion). Most respondents answered all 10 items included in the combined measure; for those respondents, the scale score was the average of the responses. However, anyone responding to at least one item provided data for the analysis; a person-specific standard error of measurement was calculated on the basis of a simple linear item response model that took into account the number and difficulty of the items to which each resident responded. The analyses reported here were based on the 7729 cases having sufficient data for all models estimated.

20 Respondents were also asked whether the incident occurred during the 6 months before the interview; about 40% replied affirmatively. Because violence is a rare outcome, we use the total violent victimization measure in the main analysis. However, in additional analyses, we examined a summary of the prevalence of personal and household victimizations (ranging from 0 to four) restricted to this 6-month window. This test yielded results very similar to those based on the binary measure of total violence.

21 The original data measured the address location of all homicide incidents known to the Chicago police (regardless of arrests) during the months of the community survey.

22 Although the zero-order correlation of residential stability with homicide was insignificant, the partial coefficient is significantly positive. Recall from that stability is positively linked to collective efficacy. But higher stability without the expected greater collective efficacy is not a positive neighborhood quality according to the homicide data. See (14).

24.4 The uses of sidewalks: safety
Jane Jacobs

Streets in cities serve many purposes besides carrying vehicles, and city sidewalks – the pedestrian parts of the streets – serve many purposes besides carrying pedestrians. These uses are bound up with circulation but are not identical with it and in their own right they are at least as basic as circulation to the proper workings of cities.

A city sidewalk by itself is nothing. It is an abstraction. It means something only in conjunction with the buildings and other uses that border it, or border other sidewalks very near it. The same might be said of streets, in the sense that they serve other purposes besides carrying wheeled traffic in their middles. Streets and their sidewalks, the main public places of a city, are its most vital organs. Think of a city and what comes to mind? Its streets. If a city's streets look interesting, the city looks interesting; if they look dull, the city looks dull.

More than that, and here we get down to the first problem, if a city's streets are safe from barbarism and fear, the city is thereby tolerably safe from barbarism and fear. When people say that a city, or a part of it, is dangerous or is a jungle what they mean primarily is that they do not feel safe on the sidewalks.

But sidewalks and those who use them are not passive beneficiaries of safety or helpless victims of danger. Sidewalks, their bordering uses, and their users, are active participants in the drama of civilization versus barbarism – in cities. To keep the city safe is a fundamental task of a city's streets and its sidewalks. […]

The bedrock attribute of a successful city district is that a person must feel personally safe and secure on the street among all these strangers. He must not feel automatically menaced by them. A city district that fails in this respect also does badly in other ways and lays up for itself, and for its city at large, mountain on mountain of trouble.

Today barbarism has taken over many city streets, or people fear it has, which comes to much the same thing in the end. 'I live in a lovely, quiet residential area,' says a friend of mine who is hunting another place to live. 'The only disturbing sound at night is the occasional scream of someone being mugged.' It does not take many incidents of violence on a city street, or in a city

district, to make people fear the streets. And as they fear them, they use them less, which makes the streets still more unsafe.

To be sure, there are people with hobgoblins in their heads, and such people will never feel safe no matter what the objective circumstances are. But this is a different matter from the fear that besets normally prudent, tolerant and cheerful people who show nothing more than common sense in refusing to venture after dark – or in a few places, by day – into streets where they may well be assaulted, unseen or unrescued until too late.

The barbarism and the real, not imagined, insecurity that gives rise to such fears cannot be tagged a problem of the slums. The problem is most serious, in fact, in genteel-looking 'quiet residential areas' like that my friend was leaving. […]

Some of the safest sidewalks in New York City, for example, at any time of day or night, are those along which poor people or minority groups live. And some of the most dangerous are in streets occupied by the same kinds of people. All this can also be said of other cities.

Deep and complicated social ills must lie behind delinquency and crime, in suburbs and towns as well as in great cities. This book will not go into speculation on the deeper reasons. It is sufficient, at this point, to say that if we are to maintain a city society that can diagnose and keep abreast of deeper social problems, the starting point must be, in any case, to strengthen whatever workable forces for maintaining safety and civilization do exist in the cities we do have. To build city districts that are custom made for easy crime is idiotic. Yet that is what we do.

The first thing to understand is that the public peace – the sidewalk and street peace -- of cities is not kept primarily by the police, necessary as police are. It is kept primarily by an intricate, almost unconscious, network of voluntary controls and standards among the people themselves, and enforced by the people themselves. In some city areas – older public housing projects and streets with very high population turnover are often conspicuous examples – the keeping of public sidewalk law and order is left almost entirely to the police and special guards. Such places are jungles. No amount of police can enforce civilization where the normal, casual enforcement of it has broken down.

The second thing to understand is that the problem of insecurity cannot be solved by spreading people out more thinly, trading the characteristics of cities for the characteristics of suburbs. If this could solve danger on the city streets, then Los Angeles should be a safe city because superficially Los Angeles is almost all suburban. It has virtually no districts compact enough to qualify as dense city areas. Yet Los Angeles cannot, any more than any other great city, evade the truth that, being a city, it is composed of strangers not all whom are nice. Los Angeles' crime figures are flabbergasting. [...]

Here we come up against an all-important question about any city street: How much easy opportunity does it offer to crime? [...]

Some city streets afford no opportunity to street barbarist. The streets of the North End of Boston are outstanding examples. They are probably as safe as any place on earth in this respect. Although most of the North End's residents are Italian or of Italian descent, the district's streets are also heavily and constantly used by people of every race and background. Some of the strangers from outside work in or close to the district; some come to shop and stroll; many, including members of minority groups who have inherited dangerous districts previously abandoned by others, make a point of cashing their paychecks in North End stores and immediately making their big weekly purchases in streets where they know they will not be parted from their money between the getting and the spending. [...]

A well-used city street is apt to be a safe street. A deserted city street is apt to be unsafe. But how does this work, really? And what makes a city street well used or shunned? Why is the sidewalk mall in Washington Houses, which is supposed to be an attraction, shunned? Why are the sidewalks of the old city just to its west not shunned? What about streets that are busy part of the time and then empty abruptly?

A city street equipped to handle strangers, and to make a safety asset, in itself, out of the presence of strangers, as the streets of successful city neighborhoods always do, must have three main qualities:

First, there must be a clear demarcation between what is public space and what is private space. Public and private spaces cannot ooze into each other as they do typically in suburban settings or in projects.

Second, there must be eyes upon the street, eyes belonging to those we might call the natural proprietors of the street. The buildings on a street equipped to handle strangers and to insure the safety of both residents and strangers, must be oriented to the street. They cannot turn their backs or blank sides on it and leave it blind.

And third, the sidewalk must have users on it fairly continuously, both to add to the number of effective eyes on the street and to induce the people in buildings along the street to watch the sidewalks in sufficient numbers. Nobody enjoys sitting on a stoop or looking out a window at an empty street. Almost nobody does such a thing. Large numbers of people entertain themselves, off and on, by watching street activity.

In settlements that are smaller and simpler than big cities, controls on acceptable public behavior, if not on crime, seem to operate with greater or lesser success through a web of reputation, gossip, approval, disapproval and sanctions, all of which are powerful if people know each other and word travels. But a city's streets, which must control not only the behavior of the people of the city but also of visitors from suburbs and towns who want to have a big time away from the gossip and sanctions at home, have to operate by more direct, straightforward methods. It is a wonder cities have solved such an inherently difficult problem at all. And yet in many streets they do it magnificently.

It is futile to try to evade the issue of unsafe city streets by attempting to make some other features of a locality, say interior courtyards, or sheltered play spaces, safe instead. By definition again, the streets of a city, must do most of the job of handling strangers for this is where strangers come and go. The streets must not only defend the city against predatory strangers, they must protect the many, many peaceable and well-meaning strangers who use them, insuring their safety too as they pass through. Moreover, no normal person can spend his life in some artificial haven, and this includes children. Everyone must use the streets.

On the surface, we seem to have here some simple aims: To try to secure streets where the public space is unequivocally public, physically unmixed with private or with nothing-at-all space, so that the area needing surveillance has clear and practicable limits; and to see that these public street spaces have eyes on them as continuously as possible.

But it is not so simple to achieve these objects, especially the latter. You can't make people use streets they have no reason to use. You can't make people watch streets they do not want to watch. Safety on the streets by surveillance and mutual policing of one another sounds grim, but in real life it is not grim. The safety of the street works best, most casually, and with least frequent taint of hostility or suspicion precisely where people are using and most enjoying the city streets voluntarily and are least conscious, normally, that they are policing.

The basic requisite for such surveillance is a substantial quantity of stores and other public places sprinkled along the sidewalks of a district; enterprises and public places that are used by evening and night must be among them especially. Stores, bars and restaurants, as the chief examples, work in several different and complex ways to abet sidewalk safety.

First, they give people – both residents and strangers – concrete reasons for using the sidewalks on which these enterprises face.

Second, they draw people along the sidewalks past places which have no attractions to public use in themselves but which become traveled and peopled as routes to somewhere else; this influence does not carry very far geographically, so enterprises must be frequent in a city district if they are to populate with walkers those other stretches of street that lack public places along the sidewalk. Moreover, there should be many different kinds of enterprises, to give people reasons for crisscrossing paths.

Third, storekeepers and other small businessmen are typically strong proponents of peace and order themselves; they hate broken windows and holdups; they hate having customers made nervous about safety. They are great street watchers and sidewalk guardians if present in sufficient numbers.

Fourth, the activity generated by people on errands, or people aiming for food or drink, is itself an attraction to still other people.

This last point, that the sight of people attracts still other people, is something that city planners and city architectural designers seem to find incomprehensible. They operate on the premise that city people seek the sight of emptiness, obvious order and quiet. Nothing could be less true. People's love of watching activity and other people is constantly evident in cities everywhere. [...]

In some rich city neighborhoods, where there is little do-it-yourself surveillance, such as residential Park Avenue or upper Fifth Avenue in New York, street watchers are hired. The monotonous sidewalks of residential Park Avenue, for example, are surprisingly little used; their putative users are populating, instead, the interesting store-, bar- and restaurant-filled sidewalks of Lexington Avenue and Madison Avenue to east and west, and the cross streets leading to these. A network of doormen and superintendents, of delivery boys and nursemaids, a form of hired neighborhood, keeps residential Park Avenue supplied with eyes. At night, with the security of the doormen as a bulwark, dog walkers safely venture forth and supplement the doormen. But this street is so blank of built-in eyes, so devoid of concrete reasons for using or watching it instead of turning the first corner off of it, that if its rents were to slip below the point where they could support a plentiful hired neighborhood of doormen and elevator men, it would undoubtedly become a woefully dangerous street.

Once a street is well equipped to handle strangers, once it has both a good, effective demarcation between private and public spaces and has a basic supply of activity and eyes, the more strangers the merrier.

From J. Jacobs, Death and Life of Great American Cities *(New York. Vintage Books), 1992, pp. 29–40.*

25

The police and policing

25.1 What do the police do?
David H. Bayley   574

**25.2 A sketch of the policeman's
'working personality'**
Jerome H. Skolnick   580

25.3 The rhetoric of community policing
Carl B. Klockars   585

25.4 The future of policing
David H. Bayley and Clifford D. Shearing   592

Introduction

The police are an apparently ubiquitous part of our modern landscape. They are an ever-present feature of drama. As a consequence, this is an institution about which most people probably feel that they have some knowledge. Yet, how accurate are dramatic portrayals of the police and policing? Moreover, to what extent do citizens generally come into contact with the police and how meaningful are their perceptions of policing likely to be? Finally, what do we mean by policing? Is it simply what the police do, or some broader set of tasks and activities in which a variety of organisations and agencies are involved?

What do the police do? David Bayley asks **(Reading 25.1)**. Using four years of empirical research he offers a number of potentially surprising findings. Predictably enough, patrolling is the biggest element in policing. However, relatively little patrol time is spent dealing with crime. When officers do deal with crime most of the time, he says, it is not serious and 'the trail is almost always cold'. Arrests are infrequent, but the threat of arrest is what makes their intervention authoritative. Finally, he suggests that policing doesn't vary all that much from country to country and (from his perspective in the early 1990s) had not changed a great deal in the previous 20 years.

What of police officers themselves? Jerome Skolnick **(Reading 25.2)** looks at the way in which the occupational realities of policework affect the outlook of those that do the job. This he refers to as the policeman's 'working personality', something found in its most developed form among those involved in patrol work. He argues that there are two principal variables in the policeman's role which affect the development of their 'personality'. These are danger and authority. The police officer is continually preoccupied, he suggests, with potential violence. The officer's world is shaped therefore by 'persistent suspicion'. In turn, the officer is socially isolated and highly bonded with fellow officers. Their authority, and the ever-present sense of danger, produce and reinforce both of these characteristics.

One of the most talked about and widespread reforms of policing in recent decades has involved the emergence of what has been termed 'community policing'. Variations on the theme of community, policing have spread across the globe. It is generally viewed very positively and, yet, Carl Klockars **(Reading 25.3)** argues that it should be understood 'as the latest in a fairly long tradition of circumlocutions whose purpose is to conceal, mystify, and legitimate police distribution of non-negotiably coercive force'. As a number of subsequent commentators have noted, the term 'community' implies common beliefs and understandings, and of reciprocity. This, Klockars says, is rather at variance with what policing involves and also of what we should reasonably expect from policing. Policing involves the use of force and, anyway, for most practitioners doesn't operate at the level of 'the community'. 'Community' is a means of wrapping the police in attractive and romantic, but largely unrealisable objectives he suggests. Community policing is, in effect, 'about some very good things we might gladly wish, but which, sadly, cannot be'.

Thus far the readings have focused on 'the police'. However, a quick look around modern urban environments suggests that there are lots of other agencies and individuals out there that are doing tasks that we would broadly understand as 'policing'. Indeed, David Bayley and Clifford Shearing **(Reading 25.4)** suggest that we are currently living through a period of remarkable change: one which can be seen as a 'watershed in the evolution of ... systems of crime control and law enforcement'. This can be seen in a variety of ways, not least in the apparently spectacular rise of private security but also in the changes that have given rise to new models of policing, such as community policing. We will be faced with some difficult choices in the future they suggest, not least in terms of how we ensure that policing (in its broadest sense) is democratically controlled and organised.

Questions for discussion

1. What, according to Bayley, are the major aspects of policework?

2. Which if any of Bayley's findings did you find surprising, and why?

3. What, according to Skolnick, are the main features of the policeman's 'working personality'?

4. How do danger and authority feed into, or produce, the key elements of the working personality?

5. What are the main ways in which community policing conceals, mystifies and legitimises according to Klockars?

6. What does Klockars mean when he says that 'the only reason to maintain police in modern society is to make available a group of persons with a virtually unrestricted right to use violent... means to bring certain types of situations under control'?

7. Why is community policing 'about some very good things we might gladly wish, but which, sadly, cannot be'?

8. What are the major reasons for Bayley and Shearing's argument that we are currently witnessing a watershed in the development of our systems of policing and law enforcement?

25.1 What do the police do?
David H. Bayley

Introduction

The research findings described here are based on four years, from 1989 to 1993, of intensive research with 28 police forces in five countries – 7 in Australia, 3 in England and Wales, 6 in Canada, 3 in Japan and 9 the United States. The countries were chosen because they are similar politically and economically and are accessible for research on the police. Each police force studied provided information on their performance from existing records and files and it is a reflection of what police managers themselves have at hand when they make decisions about police activities. I made a special point of visiting commands where something explicitly new or experimental was taking place. Within each police force I collected information about the activities of a cross section of police stations selected from urban, suburban and rural locations. Information on police performance was collected from 12 front-line stations in Australia, 8 in England and Wales, 3 in Canada, 12 in Japan and 11 in the United States. In addition, I observed police operations in the field and interviewed police managers and supervisors at all levels.

Patrolling

Patrolling is by far the biggest assignment in policing. In the United States 65 per cent of police officers are assigned to patrol work, 64 per cent in Canada, 56 per cent in England and Wales, 54 per cent in Australia, and 40 per cent in Japan. These officers work round the clock every day of the year, in uniform, usually in marked radio patrol cars.

Patrol work is determined almost entirely by what the public ask the police to do. Contrary to what most people think, the police do not enforce their own conception of order on an unwilling populace. Almost all they do is undertaken at the request of some member of the public. If the public stopped calling the police, the police would have to re-invent their job.

Driving slowly around their assigned beats, patrol officers wait for radio dispatchers to relay calls that have come over the well-publicised emergency telephone numbers. In cities, over 90 per cent of the work of patrol officers is generated by dispatch. Self-initiated, or proactive work in police jargon, occurs more frequently in less developed or rural areas.[1]

Stopping motor vehicles that have violated traffic law accounts for the largest proportion of self-generated work, at least, in Australia, Canada and the United States. Patrol officers spend the rest of their time discouraging behaviour that they view as disruptive or unseemly, such as drunks sleeping in front of doorways, teenage boys hanging around on street corners, prostitutes soliciting, or men urinating against a wall around the corner from a busy bar.

Very little of the work patrol officers do has to do with crime. British and US studies have consistently shown that not more than 25 per cent of all the calls to the police are about crime, more often the figure is 15–20 per cent.[2] Moreover, what is initially reported by the public as a crime is often found not to be a crime by the police who respond.[3] For example, lonely elderly people may report burglaries in progress so that police will come and talk to them for a while. Thus, the real proportion of requests to the police that involve crime may be more like 7–10 per cent.

Most of the genuine crime the police are called upon to handle is minor. In the United States, using the categories provided by the Uniform Crime Reports, one finds that from 1984 to 1990 violent crime (homicide, forcible rape, aggravated assault, robbery) averaged 13 per cent of all reported serious crime (violent crime plus burglary, larceny theft and auto theft). In Australia violent crime accounts for about 2 per cent of reported serious crime. The ratio of reported violent to serious crime tends to be higher in large cities, but violent crime still represents only 25 per cent of the total of reported crime in New York city, 12 per cent in Houston, 26 per cent in Los Angeles, 16 per cent in Montreal and 17 per cent in Toronto.

If one compares violent crime to all crime no matter how trivial, such as minor shoplifting, disturbing the peace, vandalism, minor property theft, and so on, the proportion is much lower. In 1990 violent crimes accounted for around 1 per cent of all reported crime in Australia, 9 per cent in Canada, 5 per cent in England and Wales, and 1 per cent in Japan.

Not only *is* crime a minor part of patrol work and often not especially serious, the trail is almost always cold by the time the police arrive, with the culprit having been gone for hours and often days. This is typical of crimes against property, the largest category of serious crimes.

If the majority of police officers are not directly fighting crime, what are they doing? The answer is they are restoring order and providing general assistance. In the apt words of Egon Bittner[4] the key function of the police is to stop 'something that ought not to be happening and about which someone had better do something now'. Police interrupt and pacify situations of potential or ongoing conflict. Typical instances are young men drinking beer on a street corner and making rude remarks, tenants refusing to leave an apartment from which they have been evicted, a dog barking persistently late at night, a truculent and inconsiderate neighbour obstructing a driveway with his car. Most of the time the police do not use the criminal law to restore calm and order. They rarely make arrests, though the threat of doing so always exists.

When officers are called to actual or potential conflicts they try to 'sort out', as the British say, what has been going on and to produce a truce that will last until the officer gets away. Is there an offence? Who is the victim? This searching for the truth is often very difficult. People lie brazenly, which explains in large part why the police become cynical and hard to convince. Or people tell self-serving, partially true stories. The police 'sort out' situations by listening patiently to endless stories about fancied slights, old grievances, new insults, mismatched expectations, infidelity, dishonesty and abuse. They hear all about the petty, mundane, tedious, hapless, sordid details of individual lives. Patient listening and gentle counselling are undoubtedly what patrol officers do most of the time.

The most common, as well as the most difficult, conflict situations the police handle are disputes within families. Officers round the world claim that such disturbances are more common on days when public assistance cheques are delivered, because then people have the money to drink.

Research into the handling of domestic disputes in the United States shows that the police routinely pursue eight different courses of action.[5]

Most commonly, they simply leave after listening, without doing anything at all (24 per cent). Next, they give friendly advice about how to avoid a repetition of the incident (16 per cent). Arrest is the next most commonly used action, occurring in 14 per cent of incidents. British police also make arrests in domestic disputes about 23 per cent of the time, they only 'advise' 50 per cent of the time.[6] Police also pointedly warn people what will happen if they are called back; promise future help if it is needed; give explicit advice to one or the other about what they should do to extricate themselves from the conflict; make sure one party leaves the scene; or suggest referral to third parties, professional or otherwise.[7]

The infrequency of arrests is not just true of police responses to disputes. In general, patrol officers, who are responsible for most contacts with the general population, rarely make arrests. In the United States in 1990, police officers made an average of 19 arrests a year.[8] That is less than one arrest per officer every 15 working days. In Canada, police officers make one criminal arrest a month and encounter a recordable criminal offence only once a week.[9]

Although police rarely enforce the law in their manifold encounters with the public, it would be wrong to suggest that the power to arrest is not important. The threat is potent, whatever the outcome of particular encounters. The power to arrest is what makes their intervention authoritative. Police can forcibly stop people from doing what they are doing; they can push people into bare cells with wet concrete floors and slam shut the heavy barred door behind them, As US police officers sometimes say 'Maybe I can't give 'em a rap (a conviction), but I sure can give them the ride'.

Disputes are not the only situations in which the police are called upon to intervene authoritatively. People come to the police with all sorts of urgent problems hoping they are able to help. These requests, which vastly outnumber disturbances, are as varied as the needs of the public. Such calls require service, not force or law enforcement. In the United States requests of this kind are referred to as 'cats-in-a-tree' situations and in Australia as 'frogs-in-the-drain' cases.

Most patrol work is boring, whether it involves restoring order or providing services. Most of the incidents to which patrol officers respond are routine and undramatic. Los Angeles police estimate that not more than 7 per cent of their dispatched calls require an emergency response.

Police in Edmonton, Canada, say 18 per cent, in Seattle 13 per cent, and in Kent, England, 4 per cent. Actually, officers soon learn that often what seems like an emergency probably isn't, so they often dawdle in situations that would seem to require a fast response. Patrol officers spend a lot of time simply waiting for something to happen. They spend most of the time driving methodically around, guided by their extensive knowledge of where incidents are likely to occur. Like tour guides in the museum of human frailty, they can point to houses where they are repeatedly called to mediate family disputes, up-market apartment complexes where young swingers frequently hold noisy parties, troublesome 'biker' bars where drugs are sold, business premises patrolled by a vicious dog, street corners where drug dealers collect, car parks often hit by thieves, warehouses with poor alarm systems and places where police officers have been shot and wounded.

By and large, the people police deal with are life's refugees. Uneducated, poor, often unemployed, they are both victims and victimisers. Hapless, befuddled, beaten by circumstances, people like these turn to the police for the help they can't give themselves. There is little the police can do for them except listen, shrug and move on. The police try to distinguish the few who are genuinely vicious from the majority who are not and treat them differently. Although patrol work is mostly trivial and non-criminal, it is nonetheless fraught with uncertainty. Officers can never forget that at any moment the boredom of a long shift can be shattered by a call that can be harrowing, traumatic, dangerous or life-threatening. The dilemma for patrol officers is that they must prepare for war even though they are rarely called upon to fight. To relax invites risk; to be constantly on guard invites over-reaction.

Criminal investigation

The next biggest job in policing after patrolling is criminal investigation. It accounts for 14 per cent of police personnel in Canada, 15 per cent in England and Wales and the United States, 16 per cent in Australia and 20 per cent in Japan. Criminal investigation is done by detectives, who do not usually work in uniform and have more flexible hours than patrol officers. Detectives in small police departments or those assigned to field stations tend to be generalists, investigating whatever crime occurs. The rest, usually working out of

headquarters, are assigned to speciality units, such as homicide, robbery, vice, narcotics, auto theft and burglary. In recent years some forces have added new specialities such as bias crime, child abuse, sexual assault and computer crime.

Like patrol, criminal investigation is overwhelmingly reactive. Whatever preventive effect detectives have comes primarily through deterrence – that is, by removing particular offenders from the streets or by demonstrating to would-be offenders that crime does not pay. Detectives rarely anticipate crime and prevent it from happening. They occasionally 'stake-out' the sites of likely criminal activity or clandestinely watch known criminals in order to catch them in the act. Both tactics have been shown to be costly relative to the amount of criminal activity discovered. Undercover penetration of criminal conspiracies, featured so often in films and television, is rare. A common tactic, especially during the 1980s, was for detectives to pose as people willing to do something illegal, such as buying drugs or receiving stolen property.[10]

What do the vast majority of detectives who investigate crime do? Basically, they talk to people – victims, suspects, witnesses – in order to find out exactly what happened in particular situations and whether there is enough evidence to arrest and prosecute suspects with a reasonable likelihood of conviction. In most cases detectives make very quick judgements about whether an investigation should be undertaken. It depends on two factors: first, whether a credible perpetrator has been fairly clearly identified and, second, whether the crime is especially serious or repugnant – the sort that attracts public attention. Except when forced to do so by public pressure, police do not invest resources in cases in which they have no idea who the criminal might be. Such cases are almost always burglaries and most robberies.

Detectives, quickly formulate a theory about who committed the crime and then set about collecting the evidence that will support arrest and prosecution. They know if perpetrators cannot be identified by people on the scene the police are not likely to find the criminals on their own. Nor is physical evidence especially important in determining whether a case is pursued, it is used as confirmation – to support testimony that identifies suspects. The absence of physical evidence might mean a case cannot be made; it may also disconfirm a theory. But it hardly ever leads to the identification of persons not already suspected by the police.

In short, criminal investigations begin with the identification, then collect evidence; they rarely collect evidence and then make an identification.

Like doctors in a war zone, criminal investigators employ a triage strategy. If a crime cannot be solved more or less on the spot, the case will probably be closed and the detectives will move on to more promising cases.

Because most crime suspects cannot be identified readily, most crimes go unsolved. Japan is the exception among developed democratic countries. There the police solve about 58 per cent of all crime reported to them. The United States has one of the worst records: only 22 per cent of even the most serious crimes are solved; in England and Wales 35 per cent, in Canada 45 per cent and in Australia 30 per cent. The likelihood of solving a crime varies with the nature of the offence, with higher rates for confrontational crimes and lower rates for property crimes. In the United States police solve 46 per cent of violent crimes against people and 18 per cent of property crimes. Amongst serious crimes, homicide is the most likely to be solved, 67 per cent, and motor vehicle theft the least likely, 15 per cent.[11]

Detectives spend most of their time talking to people strongly suspected of being involved in crimes in an attempt to get them to confess. Interrogations are generally fairly low key and straightforward. Detectives simply confront a suspect with the evidence they have. They do not have to be very clever because most of the time suspects do confess. Sometimes they make threats which have much more to do with the ability of the police to persist than with physical force. Sometimes they bluff and sometimes they cajole.

Detectives also work hard to get 'secondary clearances', that is, when a person who is prosecuted – or sometimes convicted – for one crime confesses to other crimes. Many burglaries are cleared up in this way. Studies in Britain and the United States indicate that the only sure way for a police force to increase a low clear-up rate is to give more attention to obtaining secondary clearances.[12]

Perhaps the most demanding part of a detective's job is developing expertise in the legal requirements for collecting and reporting evidence. Few have formal legal training, yet they need to understand how prosecutors will use their evidence and the challenges it will face in court. Detectives complain that paperwork is becoming increasingly more intricate and burdensome as a result of changes in court rulings and legislation. Research shows that for every hour detectives talk to people and search for evidence they spend half an hour on paperwork.

Although criminal investigation is regarded as the epitome of policing, it is not at all clear that it requires skills that are peculiar to the police. Many detectives admit off the record that investigation can be done by anyone who is intelligent, poised and willing to learn the intricacies of the criminal law. As one experienced detective chief inspector in England said, 'criminal investigation work is the sort of work any good Prudential Insurance man could do'.[13]

Traffic

The third big job the police undertake is the regulation of motor vehicle traffic. In Japan 17 per cent of police officers are assigned to traffic units, 10 per cent in Australia, 7 per cent in England and Wales and the United States and 6 per cent in Canada. Traffic regulation is important for two reasons; first, the number of people killed or injured in traffic accidents and the monetary value of damage to property are substantially higher than result from crime; second, a larger cross section of the populace comes into contact with the police through the enforcement of traffic laws than in any other way.

Traffic officers generally work in marked cars patrolling major roads for the purpose of preventing motor vehicle accidents. They do this by enforcing laws against dangerous driving as well as against defective vehicles and by controlling traffic flow in potentially hazardous circumstances, such as those associated with accidents, spillage of toxic substances, parades, sporting events and construction sites. Their work is more self-initiated than that of patrol officers or detectives. They go where the problems are.

Traffic officers tend to be zealous, convinced that what they are doing is very important. They also feel beleaguered, unappreciated and understaffed. Their reaction may have to do with the view among police officers that traffic regulation is peripheral to 'crime fighting'.

Enforcement of traffic laws is a means to an end – maintaining order and safety – not an end in itself. Traffic officers, like patrol officers, use the law as a tool for obtaining compliance. Traffic policing is highly discretionary, requiring officers to make a lot of decisions on the spot whether the law should be enforced. Traffic officers can almost always find an excuse to stop a vehicle, if not for speeding or driving mistakes then for mechanical vehicle defects.

When traffic officers stop a car for a driving violation, their options are not simply whether or not to impose a punishment. They can either apply an official penalty with or without a stern lecture, warn the driver, arrest the driver for being intoxicated or for another crime, or take no action. In England and Wales an official penalty is applied in only 25 per cent of traffic stops.[14]

Other work

Patrol, criminal investigation and traffic regulation are the largest areas of modern operational policing occupying about 85 per cent of all police personnel. Most of the rest is accounted for by administration: 11 per cent in Japan, 10 per cent in Canada, 9 per cent in the United States, 7 per cent in England and Wales and 6 per cent in Australia. Administration includes recruitment, training, public relations and all the housekeeping functions of purchasing, paying, supervising and so forth.

All the other operational units are very small, designed to support patrol, criminal investigation and traffic regulation in specialised ways. The most well known special units are probably the dog squad and the special weapons and tactics team (or SWAT) – these units are used in incidents such as hostage takings or barricaded suspects or rescue operations.

Large police forces may also have permanent formations of riot police – the *Kidotai* in Japan, the Mobile Reserves in England and Wales and the Task Force in New York City. Police forces in cities that are political centres, for example, Tokyo, London and New York are called upon to protect important persons.

The people who must give explicit attention to anticipating and preventing crime, apart from routine uniform patrolling and the undercover work of a few investigators, barely show up on most organisational charts. Specialised crime prevention units account for 6 per cent of personnel in Japan – by far the largest among the police forces studied. In Australia the figure is 4 per cent, in large United States forces 3 per cent, in Canada 1 per cent, and in England and Wales less than 1 per cent. These 'crime prevention' units are relatively new, dating generally from the 1980s.

Some police forces are also responsible for a number of other activities including inspection and licensing of firearms, bars, liquor stores and gaming parlours; serving of warrants and summonses; dealing with lost and found property; background checks on government employees; transporting emergency medical supplies. In short, police often perform a host of ancillary tasks given them by government, largely for reasons of convenience.

The point is that although the police are expected to prevent crime, people expect them to do many other things – things that are not noticed until they are not available.

Variations in police work

Policing is strikingly similar from place to place, at least as indicated by organisational assignments. Among the forces studied about 60 per cent of police personnel patrol and respond to requests for service, 15 per cent investigate crime, 9 per cent regulate traffic and 9 per cent administer. Within countries the proportion of officers assigned to different specialities varies considerably among forces – less in Japan and England and Wales, more in Australia and the United States.

These differences are not systematic, that is, related to features of social context, such as crime rates of population densities. Two factors are indicative. First, the proportions of officers on the major assignments differ very little among urban, suburban and rural police stations. Second, the proportion of officers assigned to different sorts of work has not changed significantly among the forces surveyed during the last 20 years. [...]

Although these data do not constitute a definitive test, they suggest that police forces are organised to do the same sorts of work regardless of the social circumstances they confront. Crime and social conditions certainly vary amongst urban, suburban and rural police jurisdictions but police organisations are staffed in almost exactly the same way everywhere. Although social conditions, particularly crime, changed between 1970 and 1990 in the five countries studied, police organisations did not. What the police are prepared to do does not change with what needs doing.

There are several reasons for this. The first is bureaucratic politics. Existing organisational units fight hard to maintain their share of resources. A second reason is that police forces are sometimes compelled to adhere to national standards for staffing. In England and Wales Her Majesty's Inspectorate of Constabulary, a central government agency, monitors force staffing patterns and recommends adjustments to fit the preferred model.

In Japan the National Police Agency has the same functions, In the United States so-far voluntary processes of accreditation exert the same homogenizing effect.

Finally, police officers are part of an international professional culture, reinforced by conferences, seminars and workshops, exchanges of personnel and trade publications. They continually look over their shoulders to determine whether their forces follow what the profession considers 'efficient, modern and progressive'. In

short, they copy one another, especially a few 'flagship' forces such as Los Angeles and New York City, the London Metropolitan Police and the Royal Canadian Mounted Police.

For all these reasons, police organisations do not adapt to the work they must do. Rather the work they must do is adapted to the police organisation.

From David Bayley, Police for the Future *(New York: Oxford University Press), 1994, pp 29–41.*

References

1 Bayley, D.H. (1985) *Patterns of Policing.* New Brunswick, NJ: Rutgers University Press.

2 Whitaker, G. *et al.,* (1981) *Measuring Police Agency Performance.* Washington, DC: Law Enforcement Assistance Agency. Mimeo. Morris, P. and Heal, K. (1981) *Crime Control and the Police. A Review of Research,* Home Office Research Study No, 67. London: HMSO. Thames Valley Police (1991) *Annual Report of the Chief Constable.*

3 Gilsinian, J.F. (1989) They is clowning tough: 911 and the social construction of reality. *Criminology,* 27, pp. 329–44. Reiss, A.J. (1971) *The Politics of the Police.* New Haven: Yale University Press.

4 Bittner, P. (1970) *The Functions of the Police in Modern Society: A Review of Background Factors, Current Practices and Possible Role Models.* Chevy Chase, MD: National Institute of Mental Health.

5 Bayley, D.H. (1986) The tactical choice of police patrol officers. *Journal of Criminal Justice,* 14, pp. 32–48.

6 Shapland, J. and Hobbs, D. (1989) Policing priorities on the ground. In Morgan, R. and Smith, D.H. (eds) *Coming to Terms with Policing.* London: Routledge.

7 McIver, J.P. and Parks, N.B. (1981) Evaluating police performance. In Bennett, K. (ed) *Police at Work: Policy Issues and Analysis.* Beverly Hills, CA: Sage Publications.

8 Bureau of Justice Statistics (1988, 1990, 1991) *Sourcebook of Criminal Justice Statistics.* Washington, DC: Government Printing Office.

9 Ericson, R.V. and Shearing, C.D. (1986) The scientification of police work. In Bohme, G. and Stehr, N. (eds) *The Knowledge Society.* Dordrecht: D. Reidel Publishing Company.

10 Marx, G,T. (1988) *Undercover Police Work: The Paradoxes and Problems of a Necessary Evil.* Berkeley CA: University of California Press.

11 Bureau of Justice Statistics (1988, 1990, 1991) *Sourcebook of Criminal Justice Statistics.* Washington, DC: Government Printing Office.

12 Eck, J.E. (1982) *Problem Solving: The Investigation of Residential Burglary and Robbery.* Washington, DC: Police Executive Research Forum. Burrows, J. (1986) *Investigating Burglary: The Measurement of Police Performance.* Home Office Research Study No. 88. London: HMSO.

13 McClure, J. (1980) *Spike Island: Portrait of a British Police Division.* New York: Pantheon Books.

14 Skogan, W.C. (1990) *Police and the Public in England and Wales: A British Crime Survey Report.* Home Office Research Study No. 117. London: HMSO.

25.2 A sketch of the policeman's 'working personality'
Jerome H. Skolnick

A recurrent theme of the sociology of occupations is the effect of a man's work on his outlook on the world.[1] Doctors, janitors, lawyers, and industrial workers develop distinctive ways of perceiving and responding to their environment. Here we shall concentrate on analyzing certain outstanding elements in the police milieu, danger, authority, and efficiency, as they combine to generate distinctive cognitive and behavioral responses in police: a 'working personality'. Such an analysis does not suggest that all police are alike in 'working personality', but that there are distinctive cognitive tendencies in police as an occupational grouping. Some of these may be found in other occupations sharing similar problems. [...]

The policeman's 'working personality' is most highly developed in his constabulary role of the man on the beat.

The symbolic assailant and police culture

In attempting to understand the policeman's view of the world, it is useful to raise a more general question: What are the conditions under which police, as authorities, may be threatened?[2] To answer this, we must look to the situation of the policeman in the community. One attribute of many characterizing the policeman's role stands out: the policeman is required to respond to assaults against persons and property. When a radio call reports an armed robbery and gives a description of the man involved, every policeman, regardless of assignment, is responsible for the criminal's apprehension. [...]

The policeman, because his work requires him to be occupied continually with potential violence, develops a perceptual shorthand to identify certain kinds of people as symbolic assailants, that is, as persons who use gesture, language, and attire that the policeman has come to recognize as a prelude to violence. This does not mean that violence by the symbolic assailant is necessarily predictable. On the contrary, the policeman responds to the vague indication of danger suggested by appearance. Like the animals of the experimental psychologist, the policeman finds the threat of random damage more compelling than a predetermined and inevitable punishment.

Nor, to qualify for the status of symbolic assailant, need an individual ever have used violence. A man backing out of a jewelry store with a gun in one hand and jewelry in the other would qualify even if the gun were a toy and he had never in his life fired a real pistol. To the policeman in the situation, the man's personal history is momentarily immaterial. There is only one relevant sign: a gun signifying danger. Similarly, a young man may suggest the threat of violence to the policeman by his manner of walking or 'strutting', the insolence in the demeanor being registered by the policeman as a possible preamble to later attack.[3] Signs vary from area to area, but a youth dressed in a black leather jacket and motorcycle boots is sure to draw at least a suspicious glance from a policeman. [...]

However complex the motives aroused by the element of danger, its consequences for sustaining police culture are unambiguous. This element requires him, like the combat soldier, the European Jew, the South African (white or black), to live in a world straining toward duality, and suggesting danger when 'they' are perceived. Consequently, it is in the nature of the policeman's situation that his conception of order emphasize regularity and predictability. It is, therefore, a conception shaped by persistent *suspicion*. [...]

Policemen are indeed specifically *trained* to be suspicious, to perceive events or changes in the physical surroundings that indicate the occurrence or probability of disorder. [...]

The individual policeman's 'suspiciousness' does not hang on whether he has personally undergone an experience that could objectively be described as hazardous. Personal experience of this sort is not the key to the psychological importance of exceptionality. Each, as he routinely carries out his work, will experience situations that threaten to become dangerous. Like the American Jew who contributes to 'defense' organizations such as the Anti-Defamation League in response to Nazi brutalities he has never experienced personally, the policeman identifies with his fellow cop who has been beaten, perhaps fatally, by a gang of young thugs.

Social isolation

The patrolman in Westville, and probably in most communities, has come to identify the black man with danger. James Baldwin vividly expresses the isolation of the ghetto policeman:

> The only way to police a ghetto is to be oppressive. None of the Police Commissioner's men, even with the best will in the world, have any way of understanding the lives led by the people they swagger about in twos and threes controlling. Their very presence is an insult, and it would be, even if they spent their entire day feeding gumdrops to children. They represent the force of the white world, and that world's criminal profit and ease, to keep the black man corraled up here, in his place. The badge, the gun in the holdster and the swinging club make vivid what will happen should his rebellion become overt ...

> It is hard, on the other hand, to blame the policeman, blank, good-natured, thoughtless, and insuperably innocent, for being such a perfect representative of the people he serves. He, too, believes in good intentions and is astounded and offended when they are not taken for the deed. He has never, himself, done anything for which to be hated – which of us has? And yet he is facing, daily and nightly, people who would gladly see him dead, and he knows it. There is no way for him not to know it: there are few things under heaven more unnerving than the silent, accumulating contempt and hatred of a people. He moves through Harlem, therefore, like an occupying soldier in a bitterly hostile country; which is precisely what, and where he is, and is the reason he walks in twos and threes.[4]

While Baldwin's observations on police–Negro relations cannot be disputed seriously, there is greater social distance between police and 'civilians' in general regardless of their color than Baldwin considers. Thus, Colin MacInnes has his English hero, Mr. Justice, explaining:

> The story is all coppers are just civilians like anyone else, living among them not in barracks like on the Continent, but you and I know that's just a legend for mugs. We *are* cut off: we're *not* like everyone else. Some civilians fear us and play up to us, some dislike us and keep out of our way but no one – well, very few

indeed – accepts us as just ordinary like them. In one sense, dear, we're just like hostile troops occupying an enemy country. And say what you like, at times that makes us lonely.[5]

MacInnes' observation suggests that by not introducing a white control group, Baldwin has failed to see that the policeman may not get on well with anybody regardless (to use the hackneyed phrase) of race, creed, or national origin. Policemen whom one knows well often express their sense of isolation from the public as a whole, not just from those who fail to share their colour. [...]

Although the policeman serves a people who are, as Baldwin says, the established society, the white society, these people do not make him feel accepted. As a result, he develops resources within his own world to combat social rejection.

Police solidarity

All occupational groups share a measure of inclusiveness and identification. People are brought together simply by doing the same work and having similar career and salary problems. As several writers have noted, however, police show an unusually high degree of occupational solidarity.[6] It is true that the police have a common employer and wear a uniform at work, but so do doctors, milkmen, and bus drivers. Yet it is doubtful that these workers have so close knit an occupation or so similar an outlook on the world as do police. Set apart from the conventional world, the policeman experiences an exceptionally strong tendency to find his social identity within his occupational milieu.

Police solidarity and danger

There is still a question, however, as to the process through which danger and authority influence police solidarity. The effect of danger on police solidarity is revealed when we examine a chief complaint of police: lack of public support and public apathy. The complaint may have several referents including police pay, police prestige, and support from the legislature. But the repeatedly voiced broader meaning of the complaint is resentment at being taken for granted. The policeman does not believe that his status as civil servant should relieve the public of responsibility for law enforcement. He feels, however, that payment out of public coffers somehow obscures his humanity and, therefore, his need for help.[7] As one put it:

Jerry, a cop, can get into a fight with three or four tough kids, and there will be citizens passing by, and maybe they'll look, but they'll never lend a hand. It's their country too, but you'd never know it the way some of them act. They forget that we're made of flesh and blood too. They don't care what happens to the cop so long as they don't get a little dirty.

Although the policeman sees himself as a specialist in dealing with violence, he does not want to fight alone. He does not believe that his specialization relieves the general public of citizenship duties. Indeed, if possible, he would prefer to be the foreman rather than the workingman in the battle against criminals.

The general public, of course, does withdraw from the workaday world of the policeman. The policeman's responsibility for controlling dangerous and sometimes violent persons alienates the average citizen perhaps as much as does his authority over the average citizen. If the policeman's job is to ensure that public order is maintained, the citizen's inclination is to shrink from the dangers of maintaining it. [...]

Thus, the element of danger contains seeds of isolation which may grow in two directions. In one, a stereotyping perceptual shorthand is formed through which the police come to see certain signs as symbols of potential violence. The police probably differ in this respect from the general middle-class white population only in degree. This difference, however, may take on enormous significance in practice. Thus, the policeman works at identifying and possibly apprehending the symbolic assailant; the ordinary citizen does not. As a result, the ordinary citizen does not assume the responsibility to implicate himself in the policeman's required response to danger. The element of danger in the policeman's role alienates him not only from populations with a potential for crime but also from the conventionally respectable (white) citizenry, in short, from that segment of the population from which friends would ordinarily be drawn.

Social isolation and authority

The element of authority also helps to account for the policeman's social isolation. Policemen themselves are aware of their isolation from the community, and are apt to weight authority heavily as a causal factor. When considering how authority influences rejection, the policeman typically singles

out his responsibility for enforcement of traffic violations.[8] Resentment, even hostility, is generated in those receiving citations, in part because such contact is often the only one citizens have with police, and in part because municipal administrations and courts have been known to utilize police authority primarily to meet budgetary requirements, rather than those of public order. Thus, when a municipality engages in 'speed trapping' by changing limits so quickly that drivers cannot realistically slow down to the prescribed speed or, while keeping the limits reasonable, charging high fines primarily to generate revenue, the policeman carries the brunt of public resentment. [...]

Closely related to the policeman's authority-based problems as *director* of the citizenry are difficulties associated with his injunction to *regulate public morality*. For instance, the policeman is obliged to investigate 'lovers' lanes', and to enforce laws pertaining to gambling, prostitution, and drunkenness. His responsibility in these matters allows him much administrative discretion since he may not actually enforce the law by making an arrest, but instead merely interfere with continuation of the objectionable activity.[9] Thus, he may put the drunk in a taxi, tell the lovers to remove themselves from the back seat, and advise a man soliciting a prostitute to leave the area.

Such admonitions are in the interest of maintaining the proprieties of public order. At the same time, the policeman invites the hostility of the citizen so directed in two respects: he is likely to encourage the sort of response mentioned earlier (that is, an antagonistic reformulation of the policeman's role) and the policeman is apt to cause resentment because of the suspicion that policemen do not themselves strictly conform to the moral norms they are enforcing. Thus, the policeman, faced with enforcing a law against fornication, drunkenness, or gambling, is easily liable to a charge of hypocrisy. Even when the policeman is called on to enforce the laws relating to overt homosexuality, a form of sexual activity for which police are not especially noted, he may encounter the charge of hypocrisy on grounds that he does not adhere strictly to prescribed heterosexual codes. The policeman's difficulty in this respect is shared by all authorities responsible for maintenance of disciplined activity, including industrial foremen, political leaders, elementary schoolteachers, and college professors. All are expected to conform rigidly to the entire range of norms they espouse.[10] The policeman, however, as a result of the unique combination of the elements of danger and authority, experiences a special predicament. It is difficult to develop qualities enabling him to stand up to danger, and to conform to standards of puritanical morality. The element of danger demands that the policeman be able to carry out efforts that are in their nature overtly masculine. Police work, like soldiering, requires an exceptional calibre of physical fitness, agility, toughness, and the like. The man who ranks high on these masculine characteristics is, again like the soldier, not usually disposed to be puritanical about sex, drinking, and gambling. [...]

More than that, a portion of the social isolation of the policeman can be attributed to the discrepancy between moral regulation and the norms and behavior of policemen in these areas. [...]

The policeman may be likened to other authorities who prefer to violate moralistic norms away from onlookers for whom they are routinely supposed to appear as normative models. College professors, for instance, also get drunk on occasions, but prefer to do so where students are not present. Unfortunately for the policeman, such settings are harder for him to come by than they are for the college professor. The whole civilian world watches the policeman. As a result, he tends to be limited to the company of other policemen for whom his police identity is not a stimulus to carping normative criticism.

Correlates of social isolation

The element of authority, like the element of danger, is thus seen to contribute to the solidarity of policemen. To the extent that policemen share the experience of receiving hostility from the public, they are also drawn together and become dependent upon one another. Trends in the degree to which police may exercise authority are also important considerations in understanding the dynamics of the relation between authority and solidarity. It is not simply a question of how much absolute authority police are given, but how much authority they have relative to what they had, or think they had, before. If, as Westley concludes, police violence is frequently a response to a challenge to the policeman's authority, so too may a perceived reduction in authority result in greater solidarity. Whitaker comments on the British police as follows:

> As they feel their authority decline, internal solidarity has become increasingly important to the

police. Despite the individual responsibility of each police officer to pursue justice, there is sometimes a tendency to close ranks and to form a square when they themselves are concerned.[11]

These inclinations may have positive consequences for the effectiveness of police work, since notions of professional courtesy or colleagueship seem unusually high among police.[12] When the nature of the policing enterprise requires much joint activity, as in robbery and narcotics enforcement, the impression is received that cooperation is high and genuine. Policemen do not appear to cooperate with one another merely because such is the policy of the chief, but because they sincerely attach a high value to teamwork. [...]

Finally, to round out the sketch, policemen are notably conservative, emotionally and politically. If the element of danger in the policeman's role tends to make the policeman suspicious, and therefore emotionally attached to the status quo, a similar consequence may be attributed to the element of authority. The fact that a man is engaged in enforcing a set of rules implies that he also becomes implicated in *affirming* them. Labor disputes provide the commonest example of conditions inclining the policeman to support the status quo. In these situations, the police are necessarily pushed on the side of the defense of property. Their responsibilities thus lead them to see the striking and sometimes angry workers as their enemy and, therefore, to be cool, if not antagonistic, toward the whole conception of labor militancy.[13] If a policeman did not believe in the system of laws he was responsible for enforcing, he would have to go on living in a state of conflicting cognitions, a condition which a number of social psychologists agree is painful.[14]

Conclusion

The combination of *danger* and *authority* found in the task of the policeman unavoidably combine to frustrate procedural regularity. If it were possible to structure social roles with specific qualities, it would be wise to propose that these two should never, for the sake of the rule of law, be permitted to coexist. Danger typically yields self-defensive conduct, conduct that must strain to be impulsive because danger arouses fear and anxiety so easily. Authority under such conditions becomes a resource to reduce perceived threats rather than a series of reflective judgments arrived at calmly. The ability to be discreet, in the sense discussed above, is also affected. As a result, procedural requirements take on a 'frilly' character, or at least tend to be reduced to a secondary position in the face of circumstances seen as threatening.

If this analysis is correct, it suggests a related explanation drawn from the realm of social environment to account for the apparent paradox that the elements of danger and authority are universally to be found in the policeman's role, yet at the same time fail to yield the same behavior regarding the rule of law. If the element of danger faced by the British policeman is less than that faced by his American counterpart, its ability to undermine the element of authority is proportionately weakened. Bluntly put, the American policeman may have a more difficult job because he is exposed to greater danger. Therefore, we would expect him to be less judicious, indeed less discreet, in the exercise of his authority. Similarly, such an explanation would predict that if the element of actual danger or even the perception of such in the British policeman's job were to increase, complaints regarding the illegal use of his authority would also rise.

> From J. Skolnick, Justice Without Trial *(New York: Wiley), 3rd edition, 1994, pp. 264–279.*

Notes

1 For previous contributions in this area, see the following: Ely Chinoy, *Automobile Workers and the American Oman* (Garden City: Doubleday and Company, Inc., 1955); Charles R. Walker and Robert H. Guest, *The Man on the Assembly Line* (Cambridge: Harvard University Press, 1952); Everett C. Hughes, 'Work and the Self', in his *Men and their Work* (Glencoe, Illinois: The Free Press, 1958), pp. 42–55; Harold L. Wilensky, *Intellectuals in Labor Unions: Organizational Pressures on Professional Roles* (Glencoe, Illinois: The Free Press, 1956); Wilensky, 'Varieties of Work Experience', in Henry Borow (ed.), *Man in a World at Work* (Boston: Houghton Mifflin Company, 1964), pp. 125–54; Louis Kriesberg, 'The Retail Furrier: Concepts of Security and Success', *American Journal of Sociology*, 57 (March, 1952), 478–85; Waldo Burchard, 'Role Conflicts of Military Chaplains', *American Sociological Review*, 19 (October, 1954), 528–35; Howard S. Becker and Blanche Gear, 'The Fate of Idealism in Medical School', *American Sociological Review*, 23 (1958), 50–6; and Howard S. Becker and Anselm L. Strauss, 'Careers, Personality, and Adult Socialization', *American Journal of Sociology*, 62 (November, 1956), 253–63.

2 William Westley was the first to raise such questions about the police, when he inquired into the conditions under which police are violent. Whatever merit this analysis has, it owes much to his prior insights, as all subsequent sociological studies of the police must. See his 'Violence and the Police', *American Journal of Sociology*, 59 (July, 1953), 34–41; also his unpublished Ph.D. dissertation *The Police: A Sociological Study of Law, Custom, and Morality*, University of Chicago, Department of Sociology, 1951.

3 See Irving Piliavin and Scott Briar, 'Police Encounters with Juveniles,' *American Journal of Sociology* 70 (September, 1964), 206–14.

4 James Baldwin, *Nobody Knows my Name* (New York: Dell Publishing Company, 1962), pp. 65–7.

5 McInnes, *op. cit.*, p. 20.

6 In addition to Banton, William Westley and James Q. Wilson have noted this characteristic of police. See Westley, *op. cit.*, p. 294; Wilson, 'The Police and their Problems: A Theory', *Public Policy*, 12, (1963), 189–216.

7 On this issue there was no variation. The statement 'the policeman feels' means that there was no instance of a negative opinion expressed by the police studied.

8 OW. Wilson, for example, mentions this factor as a primary source of antagonism toward police. See his 'Police Authority in a Free Society', *Journal of Criminal Law, Criminology and Police Science*, 54 (June, 1964), 175–7. In the current study, in addition to the police themselves, other people interviewed, such as attorneys in the system, also attribute the isolation of police to their authority. Similarly, Arthur L. Stinchcombe, in an as yet unpublished manuscript, 'The Control of Citizen Resentment in Police Work', provides a stimulating analysis, to which I am indebted, of the ways police authority generates resentment.

9 See Wayne R. La Fave, 'The Police and Nonenforcement of the Law', *Wisconsin Law Review* (1962), 104–37, 179–239.

10 For a theoretical discussion of the problems of leadership, see George Homans, *The Human Group* (New York: Harcourt, Brace and Company, 1950), especially the chapter on 'The Job of the Leader', pp. 415–40.

11 Ben Whitaker, *The Police* (Middlesex, England: Penguin Books., 1964), p. 137.

12 It would be difficult to compare this factor across occupations, since the indicators could hardly be controlled. Nevertheless, I felt that the sense of responsibility to policemen in other departments was on the whole quite strong.

13 In light of this, the most carefully drawn lesson plan in the 'professionalized' Westville police department, according to the officer in charge of training, is the one dealing with the policeman's demeanor in labor disputes. A comparable concern is now being evidenced in teaching policemen appropriate demeanor in civil rights demonstrations. See, e.g., Juby E. Towler, *The Police Role in Racial Conflicts* (Springfield: Charles C. Thomas, 1964).

14 Indeed, one school of social psychology asserts that there is s basic 'drive', a fundamental ten-

dency of human nature, to reduce the degree of discrepancy between conflicting cognitions. For the policeman, this tenet implies that he would have to do something to reduce the discrepancy between his beliefs and his behavior. He would have to modify his behavior, his beliefs, or introduce some outside factor to justify the discrepancy. If he were to modify his behavior, so as not to enforce the law in which he disbelieves, he would not hold his position for long. Practically, then, his alternatives are to introduce some outside factor, or to modify his beliefs. However, the outside fac-

tor would have to be compelling in order to reduce the pain resulting from the dissonance between his cognitions. For example, he would have to be able to convince himself that the only way he could possibly make a living was by being a policeman. Or he would have to modify his beliefs. See Leon Festinger, *A Theory of Cognitive Dissonance* (Evanston, Ill.: Row-Peterson, 1957). A brief explanation of Festinger's theory is reprinted in Edward F. Sampson (ed), *Approaches, Contexts, and Problems of Social Psychology* (Englewood Cliffs, N.J.: Prentice-Hall, 1964), pp. 9–15.

25.3 The rhetoric of community policing
Carl B. Klockars

The thesis of this [reading] is that the modern movement toward what is currently called 'community policing' is best understood as the latest in a fairly long tradition of circumlocutions whose purpose is to conceal, mystify, and legitimate police distribution of nonnegotiably coercive force.

The circumlocutions of community policing

There are many notions of what community policing is, what it means, and what it can mean (Kelling, 1985; Wilson and Kelling, 1982; Sykes, 1986; Klockars, 1985). Perhaps the most comprehensive attempt to identify the critical elements of the movement is to be found in Jerome Skolnick and David Bayley's *The New Blue Line* (1986). The chief virtue of that book from our perspective is that it is uniformly cheerful about the movement and wholly without critical reservations as to its capacities and limits. Conceding that a more measured advocacy of community policing might provoke a less-revealing analysis of the rhetoric of community policing, we will, nevertheless, focus on what Skolnick and Bayley identify as the four elements of community policing that make it the 'wave of the future' (p. 212): (1) police–community reciprocity, (2) areal decentralization of command, (3) reorientation of patrol, and (4) civilianization.

Police – community reciprocity

The first and most distinctive element of the community policing movement is what Skolnick and

Bayley term 'police–community reciprocity'. The term as Skolnick and Bayley employ it embodies practical, attitudinal, and organizational dimensions. Practically, it implies that 'the police must involve the community ... in the police mission'. Attitudinally, police–community reciprocity 'means that police must genuinely feel, and genuinely communicate a feeling that the public they serve has something to contribute to the enterprise of policing' (p.211). Organizationally, police–community reciprocity implies that 'the police and the public are co-producers of crime prevention. If the old professional leaned toward, perhaps exemplified, a 'legalistic' style of policing ... the new professionalism implies that the police serve, learn from, and are accountable to the community' (p.212).

Two central circumlocutions mark this vision of the relationship between police and the people they police. They are: (1) the mystification of the concept of community, and (2) the mixed metaphors of reduced crime. Although the two circumlocutions are heavily intertwined, let us begin by considering each of them separately.

The mystification of the concept of community

Sociologically, the concept of community implies a group of people with a common history, common beliefs and understandings, a sense of themselves as 'us' and outsiders as 'them', and often, but not always, a shared territory. Relationships of community are different from relationships of society. Community relationships are based upon status not contract, manners not morals, norms not laws, understandings not regulations. Nothing, in fact, is more different from community than those relationships that characterize most of modern urban life. The idea of police, an institution of state and societal relations, is itself foreign to relations of community. The modern police are, in a sense, a sign that community norms and controls are unable to manage relations within or between communities, or that communities themselves have become offensive to society. The bottom line of these observations is that genuine communities are probably very rare in modern cities, and where they do exist, have little interest in cultivating relationship of any kind with police. University communities, for example, have often behaved in this way, developed their own security forces and judicial systems, and used them to shield students (and faculty) from the scrutiny of police.

The fact that genuine communities do not exist or are very rare and are largely self-policing entities in modern society raises the question of just why it is that the community policing movement has chosen to police in their name. An hypothesis suggests itself. It is that nonexistent and uninterested communities make perfect partners for police in what Skolnick and Bayley have termed the 'co-production of crime prevention'. What makes them perfect partners is that while they lend their moral and political authority as communities to what police do in their name, they have no interest in and do not object to anything that might be done.

The flaw in this thesis is that it asks police to behave like good sociologists and use their concepts carefully. Of course, police do not behave in this way and it is probably unfair to ask them to do so. If we admit this flaw and excuse police for using the concept of 'community' in far too casual a sense, we are obliged to ask what 'police–community reciprocity' implies if it is not policing 'communities'. One answer is 'neighborhoods', 'districts', and 'precincts', each of which can often be spoken of as having legitimately identifiable characters and characteristics that police rightly and routinely take into account when working there.

There are, however, two major difficulties with substituting real entities like neighborhoods, districts, or interest groups for the concept of community. The first is that doing so misrepresents what working police officers in those places do. Those officers who actually work in those areas see themselves policing people and incidents, perhaps even 'corners', 'houses', 'parks', 'streets', or even a 'beat'. But the concept of a patrol officer policing an entire neighborhood, district, or precinct extends the notion of a police officer's sense of territorial responsibility beyond any reasonable limits.

The only persons in police departments who can be said to police entities as large as entire neighborhoods, districts, or precincts are police administrators. It is police administrators who can be pressured by representatives of groups or associations from those areas. In policing such areas, police captains, inspectors, and police chiefs have rather limited resources and a rather limited range of real things they can do for or offer to such groups. By and large, police administrators at captain rank or above, the only persons in police agencies who can be said to police areas of the size of communities, police those areas with words. Thus the idea of police–community reciprocity becomes a rhetorical device for high-command-rank police officers to speak to organizations or groups in areas that are at once, geographically, too large to be policed and, politically, too large to be ignored.

The second major difficulty with substituting a concept like neighborhood for the too casual police use of community is that such a term tends to belie the character of the entities with which police leaders interact. In speaking to traditional neighborhood groups, police community relations officers have always had their 'community-is-the-eyes-and-ears-of-the-police' speeches. But what is distinctive about the community policing movement is that it places the burden of bringing those groups into being and giving them an institutional or organizational reality on police. The typical strategy involves creating some form or organization that can act as a public forum for information exchange. In Santa Ana, California, the model community policing agency in Skolnick and Bayley's study, the department's organizational efforts are described as follows:

Each of the four community areas has 150-250 block captains who may be responsible for thirty or forty neighbors ... Block captains are actively involved as liaisons, communicating with the Police Department. The result is quite extraordinary. The Police Department has not only responded to the community it has, in effect, created a community – citywide – where formerly none existed. Neighbors who were strangers now know each other. A sociologist who wants to consider the 'positive functions' of the fear of crime need only look at the Santa

Ana team policing experience. Consider that up to 10,000 residents annually participate in a 'Menudo cook-off and dance' organized by participants in community-oriented policing programs. This sort of community support is obviously important for social adhesion. It is equally significant for the Police Department. Community support is not simply an abstraction. It is also a grassroots political base, assuring the department a generous portion of the city budget (of which in 1983 it received 30.7 percent) (pp. 28–9).

The city-wide community the Santa Ana police have created is, of course, not in any meaningful sense of the word a community at all. Nor is it a neighborhood, precinct, district, or any other form of indigenous, area-based entity. It is, rather, a grassroots political action organization, brought into being, given focus, and sustained by the Santa Ana police.

As such, it is a very new form of political organization and one that our review of the history of circumlocutions in U.S. policing has prepared us to understand. Historically, each of those circumlocutions has served to increase the autonomy and independence of police, making them not only less receptive to demands from indigenous neighborhood action and interest groups, but also less tractable to control by elected political leaders. Progressively, these movements eventually left a void in municipal government. For while they increased the autonomy of police, they robbed them of both their popular and political support.

From the police point of view, the type of organization Skolnick and Bayley describe in Santa Ana as a model for community-oriented policing fills the void perfectly. It does so because it creates a political base for police that not only is independent of other municipal political organizations – indeed it deems itself 'apolitical' in the case of the Santa Ana organization – but is totally dependent upon, organized by, and controlled by police themselves.

The mixed metaphors of reduced crime

Despite the fact that for the past 50 years the police have been promoting themselves as crime fighters, devoting enormous resources to the effort, taking credit for drops in the crime rate and criticism for rises in it, the best evidence to date is that no matter what they do they can make only marginal differences in it. The reason is that all of the major factors influencing how much crime there is or is not are factors over which police have no control whatsoever. Police can do nothing about the age, sex, racial, or ethnic distribution of the population. They cannot control economic conditions; poverty; inequality; occupational opportunity; moral, religious, family, or secular education; or dramatic social, cultural, or political change. These are the 'big ticket' items in determining the amount and distribution of crime. Compared to them what police do or do not do matters very little.

While all of this is true for police, it is equally true of the kind of political entities the community policing movement calls communities. This reality is not lost on Skolnick and Bayley. Unlike some authors in the community policing movement (Kelling, 1985; Wilson and Kelling, 1982; and Sykes, 1986) and some community action groups, Skolnick and Bayley have chosen poses with respect to the prospect of controlling crime that leave the community policing movement some important outs and may even have diversified sufficiently to withstand the depression that is inevitable when it is realized that they have failed once again.

The Skolnick and Bayley construction of the relationship of community-oriented policing to crime control appears to consist of three images. The first is the image of the police and the people working side by side as coproducers of crime prevention. Describing community-oriented policing as the 'new professionalism', Skolnick and Bayley (pp. 212-13) write: 'The new professionalism implies that the police serve, learn from, and are accountable to the community. Behind the new professionalism is a governing notion: that the police and the public are coproducers of crime prevention.' If ordinary citizens are actually to become crime prevention coproducers, reciprocity is a necessity. Communities cannot be mobilized for crime prevention from the top down. Members of the community have to become motivated to work with and alongside professional law enforcement agents.

Prevention. Historically, the most significant semantic shift in the relationship between police and crime is the shift from promises to reduce it to promises to prevent it. The difference is important because, practically speaking, failures of crime reduction are measurable while failures of crime prevention are not. It is possible, though difficult, to test promises of crime reduction by determining whether there is more or less crime today than last year or the year before. By contrast, the success of crime prevention can only be evaluated against a prediction of what would have happened had the crime prevention effort not been made. Given that such predictions are presently impossible and that prevention efforts of any kind are able to produce at least some anecdotal evidence of occasional successes, the promise of successful prevention is virtually irrefutable. Skolnick and Bayley (p. 48) write of Santa Ana:

> Measures of police department effectiveness continue to baffle those inside departments as well as those who try to write about them. One measure is the crime rate. Santa Ana Police Department statistics show crime rising less than had been projected between 1970 and 1982. It is possible, however, that the overall rise in reported crime rates is attributable to citizen willingness to report having been victimized. Another [sic!] indicator of Santa Ana success is the willingness of banks to provide loans to residents where they would not have been so willing a decade earlier.

Skolnick and Bayley do not report how the 12-year predicted rise in crime rates was arrived at, what the actual rise in crime rates was, nor how they arrived at measures of the 'not so' willingness of banks to provide loans a decade ago, or of their alleged willingness to do so today.

Coproduction. Even though prevention efforts will invariably be judged successful, a second rhetorical line of defense should prevention somehow be found to be slightly less successful than was hoped is provided by the contention that it is the product of the police and community coproduction. As this coproduction cannot be imposed from the top down, shortcomings in preventive efforts will be attributable to a lack of genuine community support. Although police may then step up their community organizing efforts, the blame for shortcomings will fall on the community.

The virtue of crime. Skolnick and Bayley lay atop the notions of prevention and coproduction a third theme to guard against the possibility that community-oriented policing might be judged a failure against some crime control standard. Even though controlling crime is the manifest justification for coproductive prevention efforts. Skolnick and Bayley suggest a line of argument that, if taken seriously, leads to the conclusion that even if such efforts failed completely, coproductive prevention efforts would in and of themselves be sufficient evidence of community-oriented policing's success (1986: 214):

We have spoken freely about 'neighborhoods' and 'communities'. In actuality, these forms of social organization – implying face-to-face interaction and a sense of communal identity may be weak... [T]he police may find they have to activate neighborhood and community associations. In our often anomic urban society, the transcendent identity of many city dwellers is that of crime victim. Their neighbors may be the very people they fear. In such circumstances, police departments can facilitate, even create, a sense of community where one did not previously exist or was faintly imprinted

Could it be that crime, like war and other disasters, might turn out to be America's best antidote to anomie in the United States?

It is with this third theme that Skolnick and Bayley's circumlocution of the idea of community-oriented policing comes full circle. Community-oriented policing is brought into being with the expectation that it will reduce crime. Political action groups are organized by police under that assumption. The assumption itself is converted into an untestable and irrefutable promise of prevention, coupled with an escape clause under which failure to achieve prevention becomes the fault of the 'community'. Finally, in the face of their failure to reduce crime, the organizations police created for the manifest purpose of reducing it become ends in themselves – success as antidotes to the problems of urban anomie. Indeed, such success would appear to be much like the success of war and often disasters.

Areal decentralization of command

After police–community reciprocity, understood as we have outlined it above, the second theme Skolnick and Bayley identify as crucial to community-oriented policing is 'areal decentralization of command'. It refers to the creation of ministations, substations, storefront stations, and the multiplication of precincts, each of which is given considerable autonomy in deciding how to police the area in which it is located. 'The purpose behind all of them,' explain Skolnick and Bayley (p. 214), 'is to create the possibility of more intensive police–community interaction and heightened identification by police officers with particular areas.'

As a symbolic gesture of police focus on a particular area, the ministation concept has considerable surface appeal. But as Skolnick and Bayley themselves admit, such decentralization does not automatically lead to the kind of community-oriented policing they advocate. They merely create conditions under which police assigned to these substations might engage in that type of behaviour if they were motivated to do so. For example, Detroit had over 100 ministations before 1980, which were considered a joke by local residents, an administrative nightmare by police administrators, and a rubber-gun assignment by police officers.

The Skolnick and Bayley position on ministations, which is that unless they are genuinely committed to and motivated to do neighborhood organization, they will not promote community-oriented policing, conceals an administrative paradox. The paradox is that the more latitude and autonomy one gives to ministations to decide what is best for their local area, the less capacity one has to ensure that those decisions are made in the genuine interest of that local area. Under such conditions, one simply has to trust that ministation crews embrace the community-oriented policing philosophy to a degree that will prevent them from perverting their autonomy for their own ends.

Perhaps the greatest danger in a police administrative structure in which command is radically decentralized to hundreds of ministations is corruption. Skolnick and Bayley (p. 215) are well aware of this problem and in acknowledgment of it they write:

> [T]here is a significant potential problem with the delegation of command to relatively small areas. Where a department has an unfortunate history of corruption, decentralization could prove to be a disaster, creating the exact conditions that facilitate further corruption. Where corruption prevails, however, it is unlikely that one would find much genuine interest in the sort of community crime prevention philosophy we have described here.

Their words are not, to say the least, very assuring. Their argument is that only a department with an 'unfortunate history' of corruption would be subject to the danger of corruption in their ministations. The fact is that such decentralization of command invites new corruption to develop as surely as it invites old corruption to spread. Their further argument that departments in which corruption prevails would not have much 'genuine' interest in developing an operating philosophy that creates the 'exact conditions that facilitate further corruption' is even less comforting.

Reorientation of patrol

The third rhetorical pillar in Skolnick and Bayley's construction of the idea of community policing is what they term the 'reorientation of patrol'. Practically speaking, the term means two things: increased use of foot patrol, and a reduction in police response to telephone calls for emergency service. Skolnick and Bayley offer four claims in favor of foot patrol, all of which they report are supported by their observations and other studies. According to Skolnick and Bayley, foot patrol: (1) prevents crime, (2) makes possible 'order maintenance' in ways motor patrol does not, (3) generates neighborhood goodwill, and (4) raises officer morale.

While it is not possible to refute Skolnick and Bayley's observational claims for these meritorious effects of foot patrol – except perhaps to say that they were made by observers who were categorically convinced of its virtues before they began their observations – at least some of those observations run directly counter to systematic, empirical evaluations of the effects of foot patrol. It is generally conceded that foot patrol can have some effect in reducing citizen fear of crime and in affecting positively citizen evaluations of the delivery of police service. It is also accepted that in certain very high-density urban areas foot patrol officers can engage in certain types of order maintenance policing that motor patrol officers cannot easily do. However, there is no evidence whatsoever that foot patrol can reduce or prevent crime (Police Foundation, 1981).

Moreover, it is of utmost importance to add to these observations on the effects of foot patrol that all of them are the product not of foot patrol alone, but of foot patrols added to areas already patrolled at normal levels by motor patrol. This fact is especially bothersome in light of the second theme in Skolnick and Bayley's idea of 'reorientation of patrol'. In *The New Blue Line* (pp. 216–17), they write:

> Police departments are also trying in various ways, though they don't like to admit it, to unplug the 911 emergency dispatch system selectively for patrol officers. By doing so, they free themselves for community development and crime prevention activities of their own devising. In many cities, the 911 system with its promise of emergency response has become a

tyrannical burden ... The pressure of 911 calls has become so great that few officers are available for proactive community development. Moreover, patrol personnel can exhaust themselves speeding from one call to another, using up the time needed for understanding the human situations into which they are injected.

So, cautiously, [community-oriented police departments] are experimenting with measures that have the effect of reducing 911 pressure. Some departments are directing officers to park patrol cars periodically and patrol on foot; ... others encourage patrol officers to take themselves 'out of service' and simply stop and talk to people; and still others help them to prepare individualized plans for meeting local crime problems, even if it means not responding to calls or going under cover.

We are obliged to point out that not one of the measures Skolnick and Bayley identified above has, as they claim, 'the effect of reducing 911 pressure'. The pressure remains constant. Only the level of police response to its changes when patrol officers take themselves out of service or otherwise make themselves unavailable to respond.

Civilianization

The fourth and final rhetorical dimension Skolnick and Bayley fashion into the circumlocution of community policing is 'civilianization' – the employment of nonsworn employees to do jobs that were formerly done by police officers. 'Where civilianization does not prevail – and it does not in most police departments – it is difficult to offer much more than lip service to crime prevention' (p. 219).

Of all the arguments in *The New Blue Line*, the argument linking civilianization to community policing may be the most puzzling. There is, of course, a simple, powerful, and straightforward argument in favor of civilianization. It is that it can be significantly cheaper to have civilian employees do certain types of tasks than to have full-fledged, sworn officers do them. This argument is well accepted in police agencies in the United States, virtually all of which are concerned with finding ways to save money. In fact, it is probably difficult to find a U.S. police department that has not already civilianized at least a portion of its traffic control, motor pool, maintenance, clerical, and communication functions. At present, about 20 percent of the employees of the typical U.S. police agency are civilians. Moreover, it is quite likely that

as the costs of police officers' salaries and benefits increase, police agencies will continue to civilianize certain routine tasks and duties that are unlikely to require the use of coercive force.

It is obvious that this economic argument in favor of civilianization is totally silent on the question of community-oriented policing. Its only premise is that police agencies have some interest in saving money and its only promise is that through civilianization they may do so. However, while Skolnick and Bayley accept this economic argument, they find that civilianization leads almost directly to the creation of successful community organization and crime prevention programs. '[O]ur investigations have persuaded us,' say Skolnick and Bayley, 'that the more a department is civilianized, the greater the likelihood that it will successfully introduce and carry out programs and policies directed toward crime prevention' (p. 219).

Skolnick and Bayley attempt to link the economic argument for civilianization to successful community crime prevention via two different but parallel arguments. The first argument holds that once some portion of their present duties are civilianized, police officers can be made available for crime prevention and community liaison activities. The second argument holds that by civilianizing the community liaison or crime prevention activities in a police officer's role, the officer can be freed to attend to genuine emergency situations.

Both arguments rest upon four highly questionable assumptions. The first assumption is that civilianization will be achieved by adding civilian employees to an agency's payroll rather than replacing sworn employees with civilians. No one is freed for any new forms of work if a department merely replaces retired police officer clerks, evidence technicians, or dispatchers with less costly civilian employees.

The second assumption is that new civilian employees performing tasks formerly assigned to police officers are not hired in lieu of needed additional police officers. If, for example, an agency concludes that it needs ten new police officers in its patrol division, but obtains them by hiring ten civilian employees who, in turn, free ten officers already employed for patrol duty, no one, neither sworn officer nor civilian, is freed for any new form of work.

The third assumption linking the economic argument for civilianization with the conclusion that it leads to community-oriented policing is the belief that any additional funds or personnel resources, police or civilian, gained by civilianization will be devoted to crime prevention and community organization. Needless to say, such additional funds and resources must compete with every other need for funds and resources in a modern police agency and there is no reason to believe that crime prevention will gain or merit first priority.

Fourth and finally, Skolnick and Bayley link civilianization with community-oriented policing with the assumption that civilian employees will be more sensitive, receptive, and responsive to community needs and values than sworn police officers. 'If civilians are drawn from within the inner-city communities that are being policed, they are likely to possess special linguistic skills and cultural understandings ... [which can] further contribute to strengthening mobilization efforts to prevent crime' (p. 219). This assumption pales quickly when one begins to examine its credibility in numerous other municipal government agencies. Consider it in light of urban education, transportation, social welfare, public housing, and sanitation, none of which are much appreciated for their sensitivity, receptivity, or responsiveness to the communities they serve, even though all of them are 100 percent civilianized.

Whither the circumlocution of community policing?

This [reading] attempts to point out the errors, in fact, logic, and judgment, that mark the modern movement that goes by the name of community policing. Whatever the merit of the arguments and observations advanced here, they will undoubtedly strike some readers as misdirected and perhaps even mean spirited. Its difficulties, exaggerations, misrepresentations, and shortcomings notwithstanding, some will find it offensive to be critical of a movement that aspires to diminish urban anomie, to prevent crime by enlisting local support for police, and to make police agencies more sensitive to the cultural complexities of the areas they police. This reaction is to be anticipated and its appearance is central to the core argument of the [reading].

The only reason to maintain police in modern society is to make available a group of persons with a virtually unrestricted right to use violent and, when necessary, lethal means to bring certain types of situations under control. That fact is as fundamentally offensive to core values of modern society as it is unchangeable. To reconcile itself to its police, modern society must wrap it in concealments and circumlocutions that sponsor the appearance that the police either are something other than what they are or are principally engaged in doing something else. Historically, the three major reform movements in the history of the U.S. police, their militarization, legalization, and professionalization, were circumlocutions of this type and all sought to accomplish just such concealments. To the extent that these circumlocutions worked, they worked by wrapping police in aspirations and values that are extremely powerful and unquestionably good.

The movement called community policing is precisely this type of concealment and circumlocution. It wraps police in the powerful and unquestionably good images of community, cooperation, and crime prevention. Because it is this type of circumlocution, one cannot take issue with its extremely powerful and unquestionably good aspirations. Who could be against community, cooperation, and crime prevention? To do so would not only be misdirected and mean spirited, it would be perverse.

This [reading] is not against any of these aspirations. What it does oppose is the creation of immodest and romantic aspirations that cannot, in fact, be realized in anything but ersatz terms. Police can no more create communities or solve the problems of urban anomie than they can be legalized into agents of the courts or depoliticized into pure professionals. There is no more reason to expect that they can prevent crime than to expect that they can fight or win a war against it.

Be that as it may, the circumlocution of community policing, like the circumlocutions of militarization, legalization, and professionalization before, enjoys a peculiar form of rhetorical immunity that it is likely to sustain in the face of even the most damaging criticism. At the International Conference on Community Policing at which an early draft of this [reading] was first presented, Chris Murphy of the Office of Canadian Solicitor General captured the sense of this immunity elegantly by observing that criticizing community policing was 'like criticizing the tune selection of the singing dog'. It is not that the police dog is singing well that is so remarkable, but that he is in fact singing.

What this [reading] attempts to show is that it is not all remarkable that we should find the new song of community policing being sung by or about police. We have heard the songs of militarization, legalization, and professionalization in the past and we will no doubt continue to hear the tunes of community policing in the future. An echo of the songs that preceded it, this tune also is about some very good things we might gladly wish, but which, sadly, cannot be.

> *From Carl B. Klockars 'The rhetoric of community policing' in J.R. Greene and S.D. Mastrofski (eds),* Community Policing: rhetoric or reality *(New York: Praeger) 1988, pp 442–449.*

References

Kelling, C.L. (1985) 'Order Maintenance, the Quality of Urban Life, and Police: A Line of Argument.' In W.A. Geller (ed.), *Police Leadership in America: Crisis and Opportunity*. New York: Praeger, pp. 296–308.

Klockars, C.B. (1985) 'Order and Maintenance, the Quality of Urban Life, and Police; a Different Line of Argument.' In W.A. Geller (ed.), *Police Leadership in America: Crisis and Opportunity*. New York: Praeger, pp. 309–21.

Skolnick, J.H., and D.H. Bayley (1986) *The New Blue Line: Police Innovation in Six American Cities*. New York: The Free Press.

Sykes, C. (1986) 'Street Justice: A Moral Defense of Order Maintenance.' *Justice Quarterly* 3(4).

Wilson, J.Q., and G.L. Kelling (1982) 'The Police and Neighborhood Safety: Broken Windows.' *Atlantic Monthly* 127(March): 29–38.

25.4 The future of policing
David H. Bayley and Clifford D. Shearing

Modern democratic countries like the United States, Britain, and Canada have reached a watershed in the evolution of their systems of crime control and law enforcement. Future generations will look back on our era as a time when one system of policing ended and another took its place. Two developments define the change – the pluralizing of policing and the search by the public police for an appropriate role.

First, policing is no longer monopolized by the public police, that is, the police created by government. Policing is now being widely offered by institutions other than the state, most importantly by private companies on a commercial basis and by communities on a volunteer basis. Second, the public police are going through an intense period of self-questioning, indeed, a true identity crisis. No longer confident that they are either effective or efficient in controlling crime, they are anxiously examining every aspect of their performance – objectives, strategies, organization, management, discipline, and accountability. These movements, one inside and the other outside the police,

amount to the restructuring of policing in contemporary democratic societies. [...]

It is very important to be clear about what we mean when we talk about policing. We are not concerned exclusively with 'the police', that is, with people in uniforms who are hired, paid, and directed by government. We are interested in all explicit efforts to create visible agents of crime control, whether by government or by nongovernmental institutions. So we are dealing with *policing*, not just *police*. At the same time, we say *explicit* attempts to create policing institutions so as not to extend our discussion to all the informal agencies that societies rely on to maintain order, such as parents, churches, employers, spouses, peers, neighbors, professional associations, and so forth. The activities of such people and institutions are undoubtedly critically important in crime control, but they have not been explicitly designed for this purpose. They are rarely objects of explicit crime policy. So the scope of our discussion is bigger than the breadbox of the police but smaller than the elephant of social control. Our focus is on the self-conscious process whereby societies designate and authorize people to create public safety.

The end of a monopoly

In the past 30 years the state's monopoly on policing has been broken by the creation of a host of private and community-based agencies that prevent crime, deter criminality, catch lawbreakers, investigate offenses, and stop conflict. The police and policing have become increasingly distinct. While the customary police are paid, the new policing agents come in both paid and unpaid forms. The former are referred to as private security; the latter as community crime prevention.

To complicate matters further, private security – the paid part of private policing – comes in two forms: people employed by commercial companies who are hired on contract by others and persons employed directly by companies to work as security specialists. Private police now outnumber the public police in most developed countries. In the United States, for example, there are three times more private security agents than public police officers (Bayley, 1994).[1] There are twice as many private police as public police in Canada and in Britain (Johnston, 1992). In all countries for which there is information, the private security sector is growing faster than the public. This has been true since the early 1960s, when the contemporary rebirth of private security began. Businesses and commercial firms, by the way, are not the only customers for private security. Private guards are now often used to guard many government buildings, including police stations.

The increase in the numbers of private police reflects a remarkable change in their status (Shearing, 1992). Through World War II, private security was looked on as a somewhat unsavory occupation. It had the image of ill-trained bands of thugs hired by private businesses to break strikes, suppress labor, and spy on one another. The police, as well as the public, viewed private security companies as a dangerous and unauthorized intrusion by private interests into a government preserve. Since World War II, however, a more tolerant attitude has developed, with private security seen as a necessary supplement to the overburdened public police. In the past few years especially, governments have gone beyond passive acceptance to active encouragement of commercial private security. There now seems to be a general recognition that crime is too extensive and complex to be dealt with solely by the police and that the profit motive is not to be feared in policing.

In recent years private policing has also expanded under noncommercial auspices as communities have undertaken to provide security using volunteered resources and people. A generation ago community crime prevention was virtually nonexistent. Today it is everywhere – citizen automobile and foot patrols, neighborhood watches, crime-prevention associations and advisory councils, community newsletters, crime-prevention publications and presentations, protective escort services for at-risk populations, and monitors around schools, malls, and public parks. Like commercial private security, the acceptability of volunteer policing has been transformed in less than a generation. While once it was thought of as vigilantism, it is now popular with the public and actively encouraged by the police. Because these activities are uncoordinated, and sometimes ephemeral, it is hard to say how extensive they are. Impressionistically, they seem to be as common as McDonald's golden arches, especially in urban areas.

Policing has become a responsibility explicitly shared between government and its citizens, sometimes mediated through commercial markets, sometimes arising spontaneously. Policing has become pluralized. Police are no longer the primary crime-deterrent presence in society; they have been supplanted by more numerous private providers of security.

Searching for identity

During the past decade, police throughout the developed democratic world have increasingly questioned their role, operating strategies, organization, and management. This is attributable to growing doubts about the effectiveness of their traditional strategies in safeguarding the public from crime.

The visible presence of the police seems to be stretched so thin that it fails to deter. Police devote about 60% of their resources to patrolling but complain about running from one emergency call to another, often involving noncriminal matters. The scarecrow has grown tattered in relation to the prevalence of crime. At the same time, regrettably few villains are caught in relation to crimes committed: 21% in the United States, 26% in Britain, and 16% in Canada (1992 statistics).[2] Even fewer receive any sort of punishment through the criminal justice system. Crime pays, as scarcely more than 5% of crimes committed in the United States result in the imprisonment of the criminals involved. Because the police know all this, they are desperately searching for new approaches, responding in part to the competition they face from private security whose strategies overwhelmingly favor prevention over detection and punishment. The central question underlying police soul-searching is whether they can become more effective in truly preventing crime.

One answer to this has been community policing. Its philosophy is straightforward: the police cannot successfully prevent or, investigate crime without the willing participation of the public, therefore police should transform communities from being passive consumers of police protection to active coproducers of public safety. Community policing changes the orientation of the police and represents a sharp break with the past. Community policing transforms police from being an emergency squad in the fight against crime to becoming primary diagnosticians and treatment coordinators. [...]

Although community policing has gotten most of the publicity in recent years, many police believe that law enforcement, their traditional tool in crime fighting, can be made more efficient. [...]

In addition to rethinking their standard strategies, the police are themselves helping to blur the line between government and nongovernment policing. For example, some police departments now sell the protective services they used to give away. Rather than considering police protection as a public good, free to all citizens, police are increasingly taking the view that people who derive a commercial benefit from police efforts should pay for it. Accordingly, ordinances have been enacted requiring private burglar-alarm companies to be fined or charged a fee if their electronic systems summon police to false alarms more than a specified number of times. Police are also beginning to charge fees for covering rock concerts, professional sporting events, and ethnic festivals. In some cities, businesses have banded together to pay for additional police patrols in order to get the protection they think they need.

In a development that is found across northern America, police not only sell their protective services but allow their own officers to be hired as private security guards – a practice known as 'moonlighting'. Many American police regularly work two jobs, one public, the other private. Indeed, moonlighting is considered a valuable perquisite of police employment. What this means is that the pluralizing of policing is being directly

subsidized in the United States by public funds. Private policing uses police that have been recruited, trained, and supported by government. When acting as agents of private entities, police retain their legal authority and powers.

Not only do public police work as private police but civilians – nonpolice people – increasingly share responsibilities within public policing. Special Constables in Great Britain and Cadets, Police Auxiliaries, and Reserves in the United States often work on the street alongside regular police personnel. Though they serve without pay, and often without weapons, they are virtually indistinguishable in appearance from police. Some communities in Britain have hired able-bodied unemployed persons to patrol the streets, and others have deployed partially trained police officers as community liaison officers (Johnston, 1994).

Furthermore, work traditionally performed by uniformed officers has increasingly been given to civilian employees. Usually these are jobs that don't require law enforcement, such as repairing motor vehicles, programming computers, analyzing forensic evidence, and operating radio-dispatch systems. Of all police employees, 27% in the United States are now civilians; 35% in Great Britain; 20% in Canada and Australia; and 12% in Japan (Bayley, 1994). A variation on this is to contract out – privatize – support functions altogether, such as publishing, maintaining criminal records, forensic analysis, auditing and disbursement, and the guarding of police premises. Police departments are also beginning to use senior citizen volunteers to provide specialized expertise as pilots, auditors, chemists, or computer programmers. [...]

The innovations that are being made in operational strategies as well as the increasing use of civilians in police work have important implications for the management and organization of the police. For example, police increasingly resent being used by government as an omnibus regulatory agency. So, in an effort to save money and focus on crime prevention, many departments are considering reducing the scope of regulatory activity, such as licensing bars and nightclubs, enforcing parking regulations, maintaining lost and founds, organizing neighborhood watches, conducting crime-prevention seminars, and advising property owners about protective hardware (Johnston, 1994; Bayley, 1985).

Police are also beginning to recognize that the traditional quasi-military management model, based on ranks and a hierarchical chain of command, may not accommodate the requirements of modern policing. Several forces have recently eliminated redundant supervisory ranks, and almost all are talking about the value of participative, collegial management. This involves decentralizing command and allowing subordinate commanders to determine the character of police operations in their areas. There is also a great deal of talk about treating the public as customers and about measuring performance by surveys of public satisfaction rather than exclusively by the number of crimes and arrests.

Finally, police are being subjected to more intense and rigorous supervision by both government and nongovernment agencies than has ever been true in the past. [...] Moreover, great attention is now being given to developing mechanisms for the systematic evaluation of the quality of police service. Checklists of performance indicators have been developed and national data bases assembled to assist the evaluation exercise. Private management consultant firms are now regularly hired to assist local governments in evaluating police. Accrediting organizations have been set up nationally as well as in several American states and Canadian provinces to develop standards of police performance and organization.

Taken together, the pluralizing of policing and the search by the public police for a new role and methodology mean that not only has government's monopoly on policing been broken in the late 20th century, but the police monopoly on expertise within its own sphere of activity has ended. Policing now belongs to everybody – in activity, in responsibility, and in overview.

What's at stake

Does it matter that policing is being reconstructed? Should we care that policing is pluralizing and that the public police are having an identity crisis? Yes, we should. These developments have fateful consequences for the level of public safety, for access to public security, for human rights, and for accountability. Let us examine restructuring's implications for each of these.

Safety

Expanding the auspices under which policing is provided increases the number of security agents. If visible policing deters, then communities should be safer if there are private uniformed security guards and designated civilian patrols and watchers to supplement the public police. If the expansion of private policing was occurring at the expense of public police, of course, then safety would not be enhanced. But that does not appear to be happening. Relative to population, there are more police in developed democracies in 1995 than in 1970 despite the growth in private security. It seems reasonable to conclude, therefore, that pluralizing has made communities safer.

Pluralizing the sources of policing affects not only the quantity of policing but its quality as well. Although both public and private police rely on visibility to deter criminality, private police emphasize the logic of security, while public police emphasize the logic of justice. The major purpose of private security is to reduce the risk of crime by taking preventive actions; the major purpose of the public police is to deter crime by catching and punishing criminals.

Arrest is the special competence and preferred tool of the public police. By using it quickly and accurately, they hope to deter criminality. Private police, on the other hand, both commercial and community based, have no greater enforcement powers than property owners and ordinary citizens. Thus, their special competence and preferred tool is anticipatory regulation and amelioration. By analyzing the circumstances that give rise to victimization and financial loss, they recommend courses of action that will reduce the opportunity for crime to occur. [...]

There is a closer connection between the end – safety – and the means-policing – with private police, both commercial and volunteer, than with public police. Governments protect communities by providing police and then limiting their authority; private institutions and informal communities protect themselves by determining what circumstances produce crime and then finding people who know how to change them (Shearing, 1996). Private police are more responsive than public police to the 'bottom line' of safety. If safety is not increased, private police can be fired. For public police the bottom line is not safety but clearance rates. But even here failure has few negative consequences. Police are not fired for not achieving this objective.

The public police are beginning to recognize the inherent limitations of their justice-based approach. Through community policing and order-maintenance policing, the public police are developing strategies for reducing disorder and the opportunities for crime that are similar to the practices readily accepted by commercial and informal communities from private police.

Both quantitatively and qualitatively, then, the pluralizing of policing should increase public safety.

The gains in public safety from the soul-searching currently unsettling public policing are less predictable. It depends on which way they go: more of the same, crime-oriented law enforcement, order maintenance, or community policing. Improvements in crime prevention will require commitment to experiment with new approaches and a willingness to subject them to rigorous evaluation. What is required is a shift in the logic of policing from one that conceives of it as remedying past wrongs to one that seeks to promote security.

Equity

The pluralizing of policing promises to increase public safety and has already done so in some places. The problem is that pluralizing under market auspices at present does not improve security equally across society. It favors institutions and individuals that are well-to-do. Commercial policing not balanced either by voluntary neighborhood crime prevention or by public policing following a preventive, presumptive logic leads to the inequitable distribution of security along class lines. If public safety is considered a general responsibility of government, perhaps even a human right, then increased reliance on commercial private policing represents a growing injustice.

The effects of pluralization under commercial auspices would be even more harmful if the prosperous sectors of the community who pay most of the taxes were to withdraw resources from the public sector, objecting that they were paying twice for security – once to the government and once again to hired private security. [...]

Some of the efforts the public police are making to restructure themselves may help to solve the equity issue, others will not. If police concentrate on law enforcement, the dualism between rich and poor will be exacerbated. The rich will be increasingly policed preventively by commercial security while the poor will be policed reactively by enforcement-oriented public police. Moreover, since there seems to be a qualitative difference in the efficacy of these approaches deterrence versus prevention – the poor will also be relatively less secure. There are three ways theoretically to prevent this inequitable dualism from arising, given the unavailability of market mechanisms for poor people.

First, the numbers of traditional police could be increased in poor high-crime areas. Unfortunately, this might be as unpleasant for the poor as the dualism itself, because it would lead to an intensification of traditional law enforcement.

Second, the public police could adopt the community policing model for economically poor high-crime areas. [...]

Third, communities themselves might spontaneously develop their crime-preventing capacities. The chances of community-based pluralizing offsetting the defects of public policing are difficult to predict. Mobilization takes place more easily where people trust one another, possess leadership skills, have a stake in their communities, and are organized politically to achieve it. Although such efforts are growing by leaps and bounds, their efficacy, especially in high-crime areas, is unproven (Rosenbaum and Heath, 1990; Skogan, 1990).

Human rights

Because government is deeply distrusted in Anglo-American tradition, the powers of the police are circumscribed; their activities closely monitored. Private commercial policing and community-based private security, on the other hand, are apt to be more intrusive, premonitory, and presumptive than public policing. They impose the more onerous and extensive obligations of custom and public opinion. The pluralizing of policing, therefore, increases the informal regulatory control of crime. This, indeed, is the strength of policing under non-state auspices: social pressure rather than law ensures discipline.

Seen in these terms, community policing, which is community-based crime prevention under governmental auspices, is a contradiction in terms. It requires the police, who are bound by law, to lead communities in informal surveillance, analysis, and treatment. Community policing is a license for police to intervene in the private life of individuals. It harnesses the coercive power of the state to social amelioration. This represents an expansion of police power, and is much more in keeping with the continental European than with the Anglo-American traditions of policing. Community policing may be an answer to the dualism brought by pluralizing but at the risk of encouraging the 'vigilantism of the majority' (Johnston, 1994).

Community policing, and its cousin community-based crime prevention, are attractive solutions to the problem of security inequity in a society where policing is being pluralized. But both impose costs. Community-based crime prevention, like commercial private policing, imposes social rather than governmental constraints. Community policing, on the other hand, couples social pressure with government direction. The mitigating factor is that community policing, as we note below, can provide for some measure of 'bottom-up' accountability if it is developed in ways that encourage and permit genuine citizen participation.

Democracy

Democratic principle requires that police be accountable so that they serve the interests of the people. This is surely no less true for policing generically, which, as we have just seen, determines in a practical way the balance between freedom, and order that people experience. At first glance, pluralization would not seem to pose a problem for accountability. Commercial private security is accountable to the market. If customers don't like what their security experts do, they can fire them. This alternative is not available for public police, who can only be fired by revolution. The problem with this view is that the accountability provided by markets accrues to buyers of private security and not to all the people who might be affected by it. Private security inevitably serves employers better than workers, owners better than patrons, and institutions better than individuals. The great advantage of public policing in democratic countries is that it is accountable to every citizen through the mechanisms of representative government. [...]

Commercial private policing provides accountability through the formal mechanism of contracts but on the basis of social interests that may exclude many citizens. Volunteer private security provides accountability through informal mechanisms organized on the basis of citizenship that may or may not include everybody. Public policing provides accountability through formal mechanisms organized on the basis of citizenship that, in principle, cover everyone. Unless new alternatives are developed, it follows that accountability is best achieved through public policing operating according to principles of community policing. Community policing supplements the customary accountability of representative political institutions with grassroots consultation, evaluation, and feedback.

Trade-offs

What trade-offs among these qualitatively different features – safety, equity, human rights, and accountability – does the current restructuring of policing present?

Broadening the auspices under which policing is organized, especially substituting private for governmental ones, probably raises the level of public safety because it increases the number of security agents and also substitutes a preventive security paradigm for a deterrent one. However, pluralizing increases safety at the cost of equity. This can be offset if community policing is strongly implemented in disorganized poor communities afflicted by crime.

Pluralized policing, however, is less constrained by formal rules and, therefore, puts the rights of the people it polices at risk. Pluralized policing is more security conscious than rights conscious.

Pluralized policing, under both commercial and community auspices, is only fictively consensual and democratic. Although it represents and empowers new groups, it does so on the basis of social interest rather than citizenship, and it provides haphazardly for the representation of all who might be affected by it. Pluralized policing inevitably shifts power away from government, but it does not necessarily distribute it to more people. Community policing, on the other hand, combines the traditional accountability of representative government with the informal accountability of volunteer crime prevention.

The point to underscore is that the changes occurring in policing are more than technical adjustments in the way policing is delivered. They represent the restructuring of government itself and the redistribution of power over one of government's core functions. By shifting policing to new auspices through markets, community action, and police reform, the nature of governance is changing.

The likely future

Recognizing that fundamental changes are being made in policing that have profound consequences for the quality of civic life, is it possible to predict what the future holds? What balance among the overlapping and competing movements of pluralization and reformation will emerge? Will a new and stable equilibrium be found between state and nonstate policing? Might the state reassert itself, once again dominating policing? Could the public police become increasingly marginalized, confined to the policing of poor inner cities? And what will the character of public policing become – enforcement oriented, community based, or some new combination?

Fateful choices

The fear of crime, the absence of ameliorative social policies, the ineffectiveness of deterrence, the rise of mass private property, and the commodification of security are powerful forces shaping the future of policing. The dualistic tendencies in policing are almost certain to be strengthened, with consequent distortions of equity, human rights, and accountability. In the face of these developments, can modern democratic, individualistic societies provide humane policing equitably for all their members? We believe they can, but only if two policies are adopted.

First, it is necessary to enable poor people to participate in markets for security. For this to happen it will be necessary to develop mechanisms to provide for the reallocation of public funding for security. The objective should be to provide poorer communities with the ability to sustain self-governing initiatives.

One way of achieving this would be through block grants to poor communities so that they can participate in the commercial market for security. Not only does this level up access to security, it vests directive authority in the people most affected. If appropriate mechanisms for community self-government are created, block grants raise the likelihood that policing will be responsive to the wishes of the community. Block grants would encourage poor communities to develop security regimes that fit their problems and mores in the same way that private security adapts to the goals of businesses. In effect, communities would be given security budgets that they could spend on various mixtures of public and private policing. Distributional problems between rich and poor might still arise, of course, particularly if the rich refused to pay. All policies that have any prospect of mitigating the growing class differences in public safety depend on the affluent segments of our societies recognizing that security is indivisible. The well-to-do are paying for crime now; but they have not learned that they will save more by leveling up security than by ghettoizing it.

Second, community policing must become the organizing paradigm of public policing. Through community policing governments can develop the self disciplining and crime-preventive capacity of poor, high-crime neighborhoods. Community policing incorporates the logic of security by forging partnership between police and public. Since safety is fundamental to the quality of life, co-production between police and public legitimates government, lessening the corrosive alienation that disorganizes communities and triggers collective violence. Community policing is the only way to achieve discriminating law enforcement supported by community consensus in high-crime neighborhoods.

Community policing faces substantial obstacles and will not be easy to achieve. Most police are still not convinced it is needed, and research so far is equivocal about its success. The latter may be attributable more to failures in implementation than defects in the program. Community policing requires substantial revision of organizational priorities within the police and is managerially demanding. It requires new styles of supervision and new methods of evaluating performance. Although community policing sounds appealing, few politicians have the nerve to force community policing on reluctant police departments. They would rather give unrestricted grants to police agencies, thereby earning credit for being tough on crime while not challenging standard operating procedures. Finally, as we have noted, community policing is hardest to achieve in the places that need it most. In terms of resources, it requires government to take the security problems of the poor as seriously as it does the security problems of the rich.

Both of these policies – community block grants and community policing – highlight a fundamental question: does government have the wisdom, even if it has the will, to guide the course of security's restructuring without making it worse? Vouchers and community policing will work to offset the socially divisive effects of restructuring only to the extent that they empower communities to take responsibility for themselves and, in some cases, to heal themselves. This requires government not only to reform the police but to redistribute political power with respect to one of the core functions of government. This is a lot to ask, because faced with shortcomings in public safety, governments will be tempted to enhance directiveness rather than encourage devolution. To avoid this, a radical rethinking of the role of government is required.

Fortunately, while the inclination of government to stipulate rather than facilitate remains strong, there is a widespread and growing movement to challenge this. Just as the past is prologue to the continued restructuring of policing, so, too, there seems to be a growing realization in democratic, individualistic societies that in order to create a more humane, safe, and civil society, government must be reinvented, specifically, that grassroots communities must be made responsible for central aspects of governance. The rethinking of security that our proposals require is consistent with this rethinking of governance. Restructuring is a problem that may contain the seeds of its own solution.

From David H. Bayley and Clifford D. Shearing, 'The future of policing', Law and Society Review, 1996, 30 (3): 585–606.

Notes

1 In the United States there are about 2 million private security people as opposed to about 650,000 sworn police.
2 These calculations are based on clearances for U.S. Index crimes or their near equivalents in Britain and Canada – homicide, rape, aggravated assault, robbery, burglary, larceny, and auto theft. US Bureau of Justice Statistics, 1993; United Kingdom Home Office, 1992; and Statistics Canada, 1993.

References

Bayley, D.H. (1985) *Patterns of Policing: A Comparative International Policing*. New Brunswick, NJ: Rutgers Univ. Press.

Bayley, D.H. (1994) *Police for the Future*. New York: Oxford Univ Press.

Johnston, L. (1992) *The Rebirth of Private Policing*. London: Routledge.

Johnston, L. (1994) 'Policing in Late Modern Societies.' Paper for the Workshop on Evaluating Police Service Delivery, Montreal (Nov.).

Rosenbaun, D.P. and Heath, L. (1990) 'The "Psycho-Logic" of Fear-Reduction and Crime-Prevention Programs,' in J. Edwards et al., eds. Social Influence Processes and Prevention. New York: Plenum Press.

Shearing, C. (1992) 'The Relation between Public and Private Policing, in M. Tonry and N. Morris, eds., *Modern Policing*. Chicago: Univ. of Chicago Press.

Shearing, C. (1996) 'Reinventing Policing: Policing as Governance,' in O. Marenin, ed., *Policing Change: Changing Police*. New York: Garland Press.

Skogan, W.G. (1990) *Disorder and Decline*. New York: Free Press.

26

Criminal courts and the court process

26.1 Conditions of successful degradation ceremonies
Harold Garfinkel   604

26.2 Materials of control
Pat Carlen   608

26.3 The adversarial system
Paul Rock   613

26.4 Understanding law enforcement
Doreen McBarnet   619

Introduction

After arrest and charge, the next stage in the criminal justice process generally involves an appearance in court. Rather like policing, however, whilst dramatic representations of courts are fairly common, they often given a rather false impression of what happens in a criminal court. What do these processes involve and how should we understand them? We begin with two readings that stress the symbolic and dramaturgical elements involved in court proceedings.

Harold Garfinkel **(Reading 26.1)** uses the term 'degradation ceremony' to capture an important element of social transactions that are intended to convey important messages about the changed or changing status of particular individuals. Degradation ceremonies are used in order to convey the idea that someone's social status has been lowered; their behaviour is contrasted with what is valued or desired and they are placed outside the legitimate order. Garfinkel's model might be applied to a variety of social situations, but the criminal trial might be argued to be a status degradation ceremony par excellence.

Traditional fictional representations of the criminal trial will usually involve a judge and a jury. And, yet, these constitute only a very small minority of criminal trials. The vast majority – in England and Wales those that occur in magistrates' courts – have neither judge nor jury but are adjudicated by a group of magistrates. Pat Carlen **(Reading 26.2)** explores the world of magistrates' justice and, more particularly, looks at its dramatic and symbolic aspects. In fact, she suggests that the dramatic processes undermine the ability of defendants to participate in the proceedings. There are many parallels, she suggests, with the theatre of the absurd. These include the architecture of the courtroom – with the positioning of the various participants – and the breaking of usual conversational assumptions in courtroom communication.

Moving to the Crown Court, Paul Rock **(Reading 26.3)** examines the nature of the adversarial system and what this means in practice. Trials are antagonistic, with the struggle played out through a variety of rituals. What is presented is inevitably a simplified version of events, designed with a particular end in mind. Cross-examination of witnesses requires the employment of a variety of tactics, the aim of which is to establish the likely veracity of one story, undermine another, or reinforce or challenge the credibility of the person being questioned. Beneath the surface, and sometimes very visible, there is often considerable emotion though, in the main, the adversarial contest was generally managed through the display of 'endemic good manners'.

Doreen McBarnet **(Reading 26.4)** examines the social processes underpinning conviction at court. She argues that there is a substantial gap between the rhetorical presentation of the justice process and its practice. In short, 'the process of conviction is easier than the rhetoric of justice would have us expect'. This has two implications, she suggests. First, it should make us think anew about many contemporary debates about law and order, not least the continual suggestion that new laws, new powers and so on are necessary. Second, her analysis suggests that it is not the way in which law and criminal justice is put into practice that leads to the problematic outcomes criminologists identify (discrimination, etc) but the very nature of law itself.

Questions for discussion

1. What is a 'status degradation ceremony'?

2. What are the features of a criminal trial that might qualify it as a status degradation ceremony?

3. In what ways, according to Carlen, does the use of space and time in the courtroom affect the nature of justice in the magistrates' court?

4. How might the dramatic rituals in the magistrates be changed and what impact do you think your proposed changes would have?

5. Outline some of the main tactics highlighted by Rock in his analysis of the questioning of witnesses in court.

6. What are the main gaps between the ideology and practice of justice according to McBarnet?

7. What does McBarnet mean by arguing that 'if the practice of criminal justice does not live up to its rhetoric one should look… to the law itself'?

26.1 Conditions of successful degradation ceremonies
Harold Garfinkel

Degradation ceremonies fall within the scope of the sociology of moral indignation. Moral indignation is a social affect. Roughly speaking, it is an instance of a class of feelings particular to the more or less organized ways that human beings develop as they live out their lives in one another's company. Shame, guilt, and boredom are further important instances of such affects.

Any affect has its behavioral paradigm. That of shame is found in the withdrawal and covering of the portion of the body that socially defines one's public appearance – prominently, in our society, the eyes and face. The paradigm of shame is found in the phrases that denote removal of the self from public view, i.e., removal from the regard of the publicly identified other: 'I could have sunk through the floor; I wanted to run away and hide; I wanted the earth to open up and swallow me.' The feeling of guilt finds its paradigm in the behavior of self-abnegation – disgust, the rejection of further contact with or withdrawal from, and the bodily and symbolic expulsion of the foreign body, as when we cough, blow, gag, vomit, spit, etc.

The paradigm of moral indignation is *public* denunciation. We publicly deliver the curse: 'I call upon all men to bear witness that he is not as he appears but is otherwise and *in essence*[1] of a lower species.'

The social affects serve various functions both for the person as well as for the collectivity. A prominent function of shame for the person is that of preserving the ego from further onslaughts by withdrawing entirely its contact with the outside. For the collectivity shame is an 'individuator.' One experiences shame in his own time.

Moral indignation serves to effect the ritual destruction of the person denounced. Unlike shame, which does not bind persons together, moral indignation may reinforce group solidarity. In the market and in politics, a degradation ceremony must be counted as a secular form of communion. Structurally, a degradation ceremony bears close resemblance to ceremonies of investiture and elevation. How such a ceremony may bind persons to the collectivity we shall see when we take up the conditions of a successful denuncia-

tion. Our immediate question concerns the meaning of ritual destruction.

In the statement that moral indignation brings about the ritual destruction of the person being denounced, destruction is intended literally. The transformation of identities is the destruction of one social object and the constitution of another. The transformation does not involve the substitution of one identity for another, with the terms of the old one loitering about like the overlooked parts of a fresh assembly, any more than the woman we see in the department store window that turns out to be a dummy carries with it the possibilities of a woman. It is not that the old object has been overhauled; rather it is replaced by another. One declares, '*Now*, it was otherwise in the first place.'

The work of the denunciation effects the recasting of the objective character of the perceived other: The other person becomes in the eyes of his condemners literally a different and new person. It is not that the new attributes are added to the old 'nucleus.' He is not changed, he is reconstituted. The former identity, at best, receives the accent of mere appearance. In the social calculus of reality representations and test, the former identity stands as accidental; the new identity is the 'basic reality.' What he is now is what, 'after all,' he was all along.[2]

The public denunciation effects such a transformation of essence by substituting another socially validated motivational scheme for that previously used to name and order the performances of the denounced. It is with reference to this substituted, socially validated motivational scheme as the essential grounds, i.e., the *first principles*, that his performances, past, present, and prospective, according to the witnesses, are to be properly and necessarily understood.[3] Through the interpretive work that respects this rule, the denounced person becomes in the eyes of the witnesses a different person.

How can one make a good denunciation?[4] To be successful, the denunciation must redefine the situations of those that are witnesses to the denunciation work. The denouncer, the party to be denounced (let us call him the 'perpetrator'), and the thing that is being blamed on the perpetrator (let us call it the 'event') must be transformed as follows:[5]

1 Both event and perpetrator must be removed from the realm of their everyday character and be made to stand as 'out of the ordinary.'

2 Both event and perpetrator must be placed within a scheme of preferences that shows the following properties:

A The preferences must not be for event A over event B, but for event of *type* A over event of *type* B. The same typing must be accomplished for the perpetrator. Event and perpetrator must be defined as instances of a uniformity and must be treated as a uniformity throughout the work of the denunciation. The unique, never recurring character of the event or perpetrator should be lost. Similarly, any sense of accident, coincidence, indeterminism, chance, or monetary occurrence must not merely be minimized. Ideally, such measures should be inconceivable; at least they should be made false.

B The witnesses must appreciate the characteristics of the typed person and event by referring the type to a dialectical counterpart. Ideally, the witnesses should not be able to contemplate the features of the denounced person without reference to the counter conception, as the profanity of an occurrence or a desire or a character trait, for example, is clarified by the references it bears to its opposite, the sacred. The features of the mad-dog murderer reverse the features of the peaceful citizen. The confessions of the Red can be read to teach the meanings of patriotism. There are many contrasts available, and any aggregate of witnesses this side of a complete war of each against all will have a plethora of such schemata for effecting a 'familiar,' 'natural,' 'proper,' ordering of motives, qualities, and other events.

From such contrasts, the following is to be learned. If the denunciation is to take effect, the scheme must not be one in which the witness is allowed to elect the preferred. Rather, the alternatives must be such that the preferred is morally required. Matters must be so arranged that the validity of his choice, its justification, is maintained by the fact that he makes it.[6] The scheme of alternatives must be such as to place constraints upon his making a selection 'for a purpose.' Nor will the denunciation succeed if

the witness is free to look beyond the fact that he makes the selection for evidence that the correct alternative has been chosen, as, for example, by the test of empirical consequences of the choice. The alternatives must be such that, in 'choosing,' he takes it for granted and beyond any motive for doubt that not choosing can mean only preference for its opposite.

3 The denouncer must so identify himself to the witnesses that during the denunciation they regard him not as a private but as a publicly known person. He must not portray himself as acting according to his personal, unique experiences. He must rather be regarded as acting in his capacity as a public figure, drawing upon communally entertained and verified experience. He must act as a bona fide participant in the tribal relationships to which the witnesses subscribe. What he says must not be regarded as true for him alone, not even in the sense that it can be regarded by denouncer and witnesses as matters upon which they can become agreed. In no case, except in a most ironical sense, can the convention of true-for-reasonable-men be invoked. What the denouncer says must be regarded by the witnesses as true on the grounds of a socially employed metaphysics whereby witnesses assume that witnesses and denouncer are alike in essence.[7]

4 The denouncer must make the dignity of the supra-personal values of the tribe salient and accessible to view, and his denunciation must be delivered in their name.

5 The denouncer must arrange to be invested with the right to speak in the name of these ultimate values. The success of the denunciation will be undermined if, for his authority to denounce, the denouncer invokes the personal interests that he may have acquired by virtue of the wrong done to him or someone else. He must rather use the wrong he has suffered as a tribal member to invoke the authority to speak in the name of these ultimate values.

6 The denouncer must get himself so defined by the witnesses that they locate him as a supporter of these values.

7 Not only must the denouncer fix his distance from the person being denounced, but the witnesses must be made to experience their distance from him also.

8 Finally, the denounced person must be ritually separated from a place in the legitimate order, i.e., he must be defined as standing at a place opposed to it. He must be placed 'outside,' be must be made 'strange.'

These are the conditions that must be fulfilled for a successful denunciation. If they are absent, the denunciation will fail. Regardless of the situation when the denouncer enters, if he is to succeed in degrading the other man, it is necessary to introduce these features.[8]

Not all degradation ceremonies are carried on in accordance with publicly prescribed and publicly validated measures. Quarrels which seek the humiliation of the opponent through personal invective may achieve degrading on a limited scale. Comparatively few persons at a time enter into this form of communion, few benefit from it, and the fact of participation does not give the witness a definition of the other that is standardized beyond the particular group or scene of its occurrence.

The devices for effecting degradation vary in the feature and effectiveness according to the organization and operation of the system of action in which they occur. In our society the arena of degradation whose product, the redefined person, enjoys the widest transferability between groups has been rationalized, at least as to the institutional measures for carrying it out. The court and its officers have something like a fair monopoly over such ceremonies, and there they have become an occupational routine. This is to be contrasted with degradation undertaken as an immediate kinship and tribal obligation and carried out by those who, unlike our professional degraders in the law courts, acquire both right and obligation to engage in it through being themselves the injured parties or kin to the injured parties.

Factors conditioning the effectiveness of degradation tactics are provided in the organization and operation of the system of action within which the degradation occurs. For example, timing rules that provide for serial or reciprocal 'conversations' would have much to do with the kinds of tactics that one might be best advised to use. The tactics advisable for an accused who can answer the charge as soon as it is made are in contrast with those recommended for one who had to wait out the denunciation before replying. Face-to-face contact is a different situation from that wherein the denunciation and reply are conducted by radio and newspaper. Whether the denunciation must be accomplished on a single occasion or is to be carried out over a sequence of 'tries,' factors like the territorial arrangements and movements of persons at the scene of the denunciation, the numbers of persons involved as accused, degraders, and witnesses, status claims of the contenders, prestige and power allocations among participants, all should influence the outcome.

In short, the factors that condition the success of the work of degradation are those that we point to when we conceive the actions of a number of persons as group-governed. Only some of the more obvious structural variables that may be expected to serve as predicters of the characteristics of denunciatory communicative tactics have been mentioned. They tell us not only how to construct an effective denunciation but also how to render denunciation useless.

> *From H. Garfinkel, 'Conditions of successful degradation ceremonies'*, American Journal of Sociology, *1956, pp. 420–424.*

Notes

1 The man at whose hands a neighbor suffered death becomes a 'murderer.' The person who passes on information to enemies is really, i.e., 'in essence,' 'in the first place,' 'all along,' 'in the final analysis,' 'originally,' an informer.

2 Two themes commonly stand out in the rhetoric of denunciation: (1) the irony between what the denounced appeared to be and what he is seen now really to be where the new motivational scheme is taken as the standard and (2) a re-examination and redefinition of origins of the denounced. For the sociological relevance of the relationship between concerns for essence and concerns for origins see particularly Kenneth Burke, *A Grammar of Motives*.

3 While constructions like 'substantially a something' or 'essentially a something' have been banished from the domain of scientific discourse, such constructions have prominent and honored places in the theories of motives, persons, and conduct that are employed in handling the affairs of daily life. Reasons can be given to justify the hypothesis that such constructions may be lost to a group's 'terminology of motives' only if the relevance of socially sanctioned theories to practical problems is suspended. This can occur where interpersonal relations are trivial (such as during play) or, more interestingly, under severe demoralization of a system of activities. In such organizational states the frequency of status degradation is low.

4   Because the paper is short, the risk must be run that, as a result of excluding certain considerations, the treated topics may appear exaggerated. It would be desirable, for example, to take account of the multitude of hedges that will be found against false denunciation; of the rights to denounce; of the differential apportionment of these rights, as well as the ways in which a claim, once staked out, may become a vested interest and may tie into the contests for economic and political advantage. Further, there are questions centering around the appropriate arenas of denunciation. For example, in our society the tribal council has fallen into secondary importance; among lay persons the denunciation has given way to the complaint to the authorities.

5   These are the effects that the communicative tactics of the denouncer must be designed to accomplish. Put otherwise, in so far as the denouncer's tactics accomplish the reordering of the definitions of the situation of the witnesses to the denunciatory performances, the denouncer will have succeeded in effecting the transformation of the public identity of his victim. The list of conditions of this degrading effect are the determinants of the effect. Viewed in the scheme of a project to be rationally pursued, they are the adequate means. One would have to choose one's tactics for their efficiency in accomplishing these effects.

6   Cf. Gregory Bateson and Jurgen Ruesch, *Communication: The Social Matrix of Psychiatry* (New York: W. W. Norton & Co., 1951), pp. 212–27.

7   For bona fide members it is not that these are the grounds upon which we are agreed but upon which we are *alike*, consubstantial, in origin the same.

8   Neither of the problems of possible communicative or organizational conditions of their effectiveness have been treated here in systematic fashion. However, the problem of communicative tactics in degradation ceremonies is set in the light of systematically related conceptions. These conceptions may be listed in the following statements:

1   The definition of the situation of the witnesses (for ease of discourse we shall use the letter S) always bears a time qualification.

2   The S at t_2 is a function of the S at t_1. This function is described as an operator that transforms the S at t_1.

3   The operator is conceived as communicative work.

4   For a successful denunciation, it is required that the S at t_2 show specific properties. These have been specified previously.

5   The task of the denouncer is to alter the S's of the witnesses so that these S's will show the specified properties.

6   The 'rationality' of the denouncer's tactics, i.e., their adequacy as a means for effecting the set of transformations necessary for effecting the identity transformation, is decided by the rule that the organizational and operational properties of the communicative net (the social system) are determinative of the size of the discrepancy between an intended and an actual effect of the communicative work. Put otherwise, the question is not that of the temporal origin of the situation but always and only how it is altered over time. The view is recommended that the definition of the situation at time 2 is a function of the definition at time 1 where this function consists of the communicative work conceived as a set of operations whereby the altered situation at time 1 is the situation at time 2. In strategy terms the function consists of the program of procedures that a denouncer should follow to effect the change of state $S\,t_1$ to $S\,t_2$. In this paper $S\,t_1$ is treated as an unspecified state.

26.2 Materials of control
Pat Carlen

You have to admit it; everyone enjoys it. It's dramatic. If it wasn't the court it would be the Old Vic. S

Senior probation officer (1973)

Staging justice: a celebration of ritual coercion

Metaphoric critiques of judicial proceedings have been done mainly by American writers: Garfinkel (1956), Emerson (1967) and Blumberg (1967), for instance, have all used dramaturgical or game imagery in analyses of courtroom interaction. In England, on the other hand, the concern has been different, and largely reformative. Here, analyses of sentencing patterns (Hood, 1962; King, 1972); surveys of the availability of Legal Aid (Patterson, 1971); and assessment of bailing procedures (Bottomley, 1970; Dell, 1970) have provided the major focal points for socio-legal research. [...]

This chapter will be devoted to the development of a two-tiered argument. At the level of irony I shall be describing the material geneses and symbolic forms of the coercive surrealism and absurdity which permeate the court. At the level of explanation, I shall argue:

1 that material arrangements in the magistrates' courts iconically index forms of superordination and subordination which must be realised if the ideal of adversary justice is to be successfully displayed;

2 that the courts' scenic, scheduling and categorising conventions translate the ideal of adversary justice into material forms whose ritual communications ensure that the staging of magistrates' justice in itself infuses the proceedings with a surreality which atrophies defendants' abilities to participate in them.

Staging the absurd

Traditionally and situationally, judicial proceedings are dramatic. Aristotle noted the importance of forensic oratory as a special device of legal rhetoric; playwrights have always appreciated the dramatic value of a trial scene; lawyers have always been cognisant of rhetorical presentations.

In 1950, nine years before Goffman's *The Presentation of Self in Everyday Life*, a lawyer, Jerome Frank, discussed the conventional ascription of character which occurs in law courts and which is dependent upon the tacit dimensions of interpersonal knowledge. Such analyses are nowadays the familiar stuff of the dramaturgical perspectives in sociology. But people do not only ascribe character to one another. Furniture, stage-props, scenic devices, tacit scheduling programmes, etiquettes of ritual address and reference – in short, all the paraphernalia of social occasions – are, both immediately and documentarily, indexed with consequential social meanings (Mannheim, 1968; Schutz, 1970). These meanings can be set up as being either mundane (i.e. constitutive of and reflecting everyday realities); or puzzling (i.e. constitutive of and reflecting intimations of alternative realities); or, less often, as being both mundane and puzzling (i.e. surreal). In hierarchically organised social institutions, however, certain people can monopolise and manipulate the scenic and scheduling arrangements of the most important public settings, so that a coercive control, often spurious to the professed aims of the institution, can be maintained. [...]

In magistrates' courts, as in the theatre of the absurd, mundane and conventional ways of organising and communicating the operative meanings of social occasions are simultaneously exploited and denied. Yet their outcomes are situationally authenticated, and the intermeshed structures of surreality and psychic coercion are difficult to locate. This is because police and judicial personnel systematically present their coercive devices as being nothing more than the traditional, conventional and commonsensical ways of organising and synchronising judicial proceedings. The authenticity of their rhetoric is hewn out of: the temporal and spatial conventions for the management of judicial action; the conventions for the rhetorical presentation of legal and judicial personnel; and the theatrical ascription of character to defendants.

Space

A magistrates' court is a very formal and ritualistic social setting. [...] In the courtroom spatial dominance is achieved by structural elevation, and the magistrate sits raised up from the rest of the court. The defendant is also raised up to public view but the dock is set lower than the magisterial seat, whilst the rails surrounding it are symbolic of the defendant's captive state. Of all the main protagonists the defendant is the one who is placed farthest away from the magistrate. Between the defendant and the magistrate sit clerk, solicitors, probation officers, social workers, press reporters, police, and any others deemed to be assisting the court in the discharge of its duties. Spatial arrangements, however, which might signify to the onlooker a guarantee of an orderly display of justice, are too often experienced by participants as being generative of a theatrical autism with all the actors talking past each other.

Difficulties of hearing are endemic to magistrates' courts. At one court where microphones are used they distort voices so badly that most people in the courtroom laughingly wince when they are turned on and visibly sympathise with the lady magistrate who always has them turned off because 'they make us sound like Donald Duck'. [...]

Acoustics, however, cannot bear total responsibility for the chronic breakdown of communication in magistrates' courts. The placing and spacing of people within the courtroom is a further cause of the series of 'pardons' and 'blank stares' which characterise and punctuate judicial proceedings.

It has already been stressed that defendants and magistrates are set well apart from each other. Distances between bench and dock vary from court to court but in all courts such distances are certainly greater than those usually, and voluntarily, chosen for the disclosure of intimate details of sexual habits, personal relationships and financial affairs. Certain communications are conventionally presented as intimate communications, and both their timing and situating are delicately arranged. Indeed, 'there are certain things which are difficult to talk about unless one is within the proper conversational zone' (Hall, 1959).

In magistrates' courts, where the vast majority of defendants do not have a solicitor as a 'mouthpiece', defendants are set up in a guarded dock and then, at a distance artificially stretched beyond the familiar boundaries of face-to-face communication, asked to describe or comment on intimate details of their lives; details which do not in themselves constitute infractions of any law but which are open to public investigation once a person has been *accused* of breaking the law. This ceremonial 'stripping of a man of his dignity' as a prelude to judicial punishment has been thoroughly explicated and analysed by Harold Garfinkel (1956); degradation or humiliation of the man in the dock was spontaneously mentioned by several solicitors and probation officers at Metropolitan Court. 'People laugh about something he says which may sound funny, or some aspect of his private life which comes out in court, you know? People *laugh*. It's treated without any respect at all.' (Mrs W, probation officer)

Further, during such sequences of interrogation, defendants' embarrassed stuttering is often aggravated by judicial violation of another taken-for-granted conversational practice. For in conventional social practice the chain-rule of question-answer sequence (Sacks, 1967; Schegloff, 1972) is also accompanied by the assumption that it is the *interrogator* who demands an answer. In magistrates' courts, however, defendants often find that they are continually rebuked, either for not addressing their answers to the magistrate or for directing their answers to their interrogators in such a way that the magistrate cannot hear them. As a result, defendants are often in the position of having to synchronise their answers and stances in a way quite divorced from the conventions of everyday life outside the courtroom.

For defendants who often do not immediately distinguish between magistrate and clerk, for defendants who do not comprehend the separate symbolic functions of dock and witness box, for defendants who may have already spent up to three hours waiting around in the squalid environs of the courtroom, the surreal dimensions of meaning, emanating from judicial exploitation of courtroom placing and spacing, can have a paralysing effect.

Time

Though it is unlikely that absolute control of the situation can be obtained in a cramped courtroom which may have thirty to forty people in its main area, and over that number in its public gallery, officials, as I have already argued, appear to be well aware of how to facilitate control through exploitation of the courtroom's physical dimensions. [...]

In the management of social occasions, time, like place, always belongs to somebody or some group. During formal social occasions certain persons are appointed to oversee the timing of events, to ensure both the continuity and punctuation of performances. During judicial proceedings in magistrates' courts the timing of events is monopolised by the police. They are the ones who set up the proceedings; it is their responsibility to see that all defendants arrive at court; it is their job to draw up the charge sheets; it is their job to ensure that all relevant documents are in the hands of the clerk of court. And policemen are very jealous of their competence in programming the criminal business. [...]

Policemen are well aware that concern with time-saving can influence their decision concerning the nature of the charge in the first place: 'Most of them you just charge with being drunk, because if you say "drunk and disorderly" they won't plead guilty. It's a waste of time.' (policeman, Court A) And at the hearing both solicitors and defendants experience police pressure to save time. At one court, a detective, telling a solicitor that he would not accept a surety who lived in Birmingham, said: 'It's not worth raising. *You* don't want to hang around while he's contacted and I'm sure I don't.' Similar dependence on an assumption of a consensual evaluation of time gives the police a lever in their pretrial negotiations with defendants. A policeman at Metropolitan Court with whom I had been discussing this topic turned to me after he had been speaking with a defendant in the gaoler's office, saying: 'He didn't have to give me *that*,' pointing to some written information he had just elicited from the defendant, 'so when he got a bit stroppy I said, "We could always put it over."' In courts where there are two or more stipendiary magistrates presiding over different courtrooms, the warrant officer will draw on his knowledge of their relative performing times when he does the court lists. At Court A the warrant officer showed me a very long list of cases, remarking:

> When I do the lists I know for instance that if I gave this list to *him* [points to the name of a magistrate at the top of the other list] he would take all day. So you get to know the slower magistrates, and you do the list accordingly. [...]

Time-saving is an organisation value, yet, for the majority of the *defendants*, the court experience is characterised by long periods of waiting, unpunctuated by any official explanations about the cause of the delays. 'Witnesses, defendants come at ten and their case may not be heard until twelve-thirty.' (Miss B, probation officer) This uncertainty is not diminished by the dearth of information available to them:

At present some of them turn up at court at ten o'clock, don't appear until half-past twelve. Two and a half hours could be agony. They could tell them why their case might be called last – guilty pleas to be dealt with, the police officer detained in another case. All these things are very practical, simple information which an official at the court *can* find out and convey to the client. [Mr G, senior probation officer]

Worse, because cases can be arbitrarily switched from courtroom to courtroom, a defendant can have his case heard in one courtroom while his friends (among them potential witnesses) sit unsuspectingly in the public gallery of an adjacent courtroom. During the long hours of waiting, many defendants become more and more nervous, harbouring fears (usually unfounded) that they will be sent to prison and, in the majority of courts, unable to get either refreshments or privacy in which to talk to their solicitors or probation officers.

The theatrical ascription of character

Dramaturgical discipline is imposed on every person in the courtroom. Magistrates who do not like the behaviour of policemen in court can, and do, instruct the Court Inspector to 'have a word'. Errant probation officers, 'particularly those who left college with a Che Guevara do-it-yourself outfit' (magistrate), can be 'spoken to' by their senior. Counsel who chatter in court can be told to be quiet by the warrant officer or even by the magistrate. *Anyone* whose interruptions threaten the court proceedings can be removed.

Most defendants cause no trouble in the courtroom. After a long wait in the corridors or waiting-room, many of them make an initial attempt to hear and follow the proceedings and then visibly give up the pretence of understanding and stare restlessly around the courtroom until the policeman, touching them on the arm, indicates that the formalities are over. [...]

Defendants come into court in all shapes and sizes. They are of all occupational classes, they are of all nationalities. They are representative of all religions, politics and educational systems. Cross-cutting the diversity of their backgrounds is the similarity of their demeanours towards the court. Indifference, fear, contempt or hatred are the most marked features of their in-court stances. Their corporate diversity and individual brands of unamenability are not conducive to the rhetoric of consensual control which provides the theatrical backcloth to the court proceedings. Policemen reduce the diversity of defendants to manageable proportions by categorising them into five main types: the 'villains'; the 'regulars'; the 'nuts'; the 'immigrants and foreigners'; the 'normal, ordinary person'.

'Villains' or 'regular villains' are the defendants whom the police see as 'your regular criminals'. They are those defendants who are seen to be making a living out of serious (i.e. lucrative) crime. The presence of villains in court is noted by magistrates and police and it presages the appearance of a specialised supporting cast. A magistrate at Metropolitan Court said that he only had to see certain counsel in court and he knew that a 'regular villain' would be coming up. Appearances of 'regular villains' may also draw in an audience whose interest in the proceedings is professional rather than merely supportive or casual. Accordingly, while the magistrate surveys the counsels' benches, the policemen scan the public gallery: 'The policeman stands in court and looks at the public gallery: he thinks, "I know him .... Oh yes." The policeman then sees him out in the street and thinks "I've seen you somewhere .... Oh, yes".' (Inspector, Metropolitan Court) Besides surveying the public gallery, policemen have to provide extra guard for those 'villains' who are 'runners' and who are likely to make an escape bid. Additional policemen are stationed near the dock when a 'runner' is in court, and sometimes, in courts where the cells are beneath the courtroom, policemen are stationed on the stairs leading down from the dock. The charges against 'villains' are usually serious enough to be heard at higher courts, and 'villains', having a justified faith in trial by jury, usually elect to go there. Their passage through the magistrates' courts is either marked by 'plenty of lip' (policeman) or by a jocular or aggressive insouciance. Policemen treat 'villains' with the malevolent respect accorded to stars.

'Regulars', of course, are characterised by the regularity with which they appear in the same or an adjacent court and by the previous knowledge which local police, magistrates and probation officers have of them. The crimes of 'regulars', unlike those of villains, are seen as constituting a nuisance. 'Regulars' can be further subdivided into the following categories: young, repeating offenders accused of a mixture of petty crimes, particularly petty theft and taking and driving away a motor vehicle; people following an occupation whose public manifestations are regulated by criminal laws, e.g. men and women soliciting in the street, gamers pursuing their skills in a public place; and people whose legally proscribed appetites bring them before the courts, e.g. – people who get drunk in the street or who are continually pleading guilty to charges of indecent exposure. Policemen often predict that the regular young offenders are on their way to becoming 'regular villains'. [...]

Mention of 'nuts' and 'nutcases' is a regular feature of talk in the gaoler's office. 'Nuts' are not defined by their offence but by their behaviour in the courtroom, the gaoler's office and the cells. Seemingly, they are divided into two categories, 'real nuts' and 'nuts'. 'Real nuts' are those whose situational title has already been trans-situationally legitimated by a psychiatric report. The 'nuts' are those defendants whose behaviour the police find bizarre, inconvenient or 'inappropriate' in court. In so far as 'nuts' break only the implicit rules of the court, policemen found it difficult to explicate what a nut is, except in terms of behaviour like 'stripping off' in the cells, behaviour which is an infraction of the regulative rules of many social activities and which would likewise be seen as deviant in many settings. It seemed, though, that the terse and frequent epithet of 'nut', bestowed on defendants who had just passed through the gaoler's office, was additionally used to give the warrant officer the final word in encounters which had not been entirely satisfactory from his point of view. [...]

'Nuts', like drunks, annoy the police. They are not 'serious' criminals and they are seen as wasting police time. As a result they tend to be known by reputation as well as by present behaviour: 'You get to know the nutcases. You go to a new place and someone comes in – and someone comes up to you behind the counter and nudges you: says "Nutcase!".' (Court Inspector, Metropolitan Court)

'Immigrants' or 'foreigners' were the most discussed category of offender at Metropolitan Court. In a situation fraught by potential breaches of control everybody has to be accounted for. Policemen are jealous of their skills of categorisation and in this area immigrants present them with many difficulties:

> You can usually tell what's coming through the door – counsel, CID, [*pause*] researcher! The only problem is with coloured people, then it's difficult to tell who's counsel and who's defendants. They all look the same. [warrant officer, Metropolitan Court]

Even when immigrant defendants have been identified, policemen often find it difficult to understand their style, and particular nationalities can be variously described by different officials as having completely opposing characteristics. So the Court Inspector at Metropolitan Court stressed to me: 'West Indians are often so aggressive. They are difficult'; whereas the policeman who called the cases complained: 'You get so much trouble from the West Indians. In court some of them seem in a dream. They're slow. You call out their name – they just look round – they don't jump to it.' Policemen did stress, 'Mind you, we only see the rubbish of any nationality.' But immigrants or foreigners in the court were, none the less, seen as a special source of trouble because of: (1) their reluctance to plead guilty; (2) their inability to understand the court procedure; (3) their recurrent accusations against the police; and (4) the incomprehensibility of their presentational style. Although this presentational style was described by policemen in contradictory terms, its main attribute appeared to be a failure to respond to the paternalistic attitude which policemen successfully adopt towards those defendants whom they categorise as the 'normal, ordinary type'.

The 'normal, ordinary person' in court is a non-villainous Britisher who is neither an 'immigrant' nor a 'nut'. He is either a first or very intermittent offender, visibly anxious about the outcome of his case and visibly anxious not to offend the court. His offence may be minor, like a motoring offence or the odd, petty dishonesty, or it may be a serious (but non-lucrative) offence like murder or manslaughter, the type of offence which might 'happen' to anyone and which can be seen as a circumstantial aberration rather than as indicative of an essential deviancy. Towards the 'normal, ordinary person' police are paternalistic; they tell him what will happen in court, they tell him what to say in court, they tell him after he has been sentenced that 'things could have been much worse'. Indeed a certain inability to understand the courtroom procedure is seen by the police as being indicative of the 'normal, ordinary person's' naivety about crime; 'The regular villains understand it all right – the other, ordinary type never understand all of it.' (warrant officer, Metropolitan Court) 'Normal, ordinary' defendants can easily be accounted for and dealt with by the police; by definition, they cause the police no trouble and are deferentially grateful for police sponsorship through the courts.

Beyond absurdity

A court of law, like the theatre, is an arena where both social values and the devices employed to choose between them can be studied. The law is both ritualistic and dramatic. Management of ritual occasions is always precarious because of the permanent threat that their prefabricated character will be revealed. In the theatre such prefabrication is overtly managed, and masks and costumes bridge the gap between realised art and artful reality. In legal proceedings, however, law, unlike drama, has to be portrayed as a natural, rather than artful, emanation from a recognisably consensual society.

Portrayal of an inviolate and necessary justice is aided in the higher courts by rigid rules of ceremony and by the traditional ceremonial costume. There, men and women well trained in legal rhetoric monopolise the stage, and the acting is often worthy of the best traditions of the theatre. In the lower courts it is different. Magistrates are not bewigged and enrobed; there are very few solicitors to mediate between the accused and their accusers; the daily presence of people whom the police variously call 'nuts', 'drunks' and 'rubbish' lends a farcical, rather than solemn, air to the whole proceedings. [...]

The court is not a theatre. It is an institutional setting charged with the maintenance and reproduction of existing forms of structural dominance. Courtworkers, unlike stage actors, have to account not only for the way they interpret their parts but also for the authorship and substance of the scripts. Aware of the written rules of law, courtworkers often claim that their script has been written elsewhere; proud of a judicial competence, courtworkers often claim that they write the script themselves; called to account for the mode and substance of their performance, courtworkers, using the imagery of the theatre, claim that they perennially tell a tale of possible justice. To conserve the rhetoric of justice in a capitalist society such a tale is as necessary as it is implausible.

Transformation of the ritual display of justice into the socio-legal technology of coercion is the first step in the manufacture and celebration of all magistrates' justice.

> From P. Carlen, Magistrates' Justice *(Oxford: Martin Robertson)*, 1976, pp. 18–38.

References

Blumberg, A.S. (1967a), *Criminal Justice*, Chicago, Quadrangle.

Blumberg, A.S. (1967b), 'The Practice of Law as a Confidence Game' *Law and Society Review* 1.

Bottomley, A. K. (1970), *Prison before Trial*, London, Bell.

Dell, S. (1970) *Silent in Court*, London, Bell.

Emerson, R.M. (1967) *Judging Delinquents*, Chicago, Aldine.

Garfinkel, H. (1956) 'Conditions of Successful Degradation Ceremonies', *American Journal of Sociology* LXIV pp 420–4.

Hall, E.T. (1959) *The Silent Language*, Garden City, NY, Doubleday.

Hood, R. (1962) *Sentencing in Magistrates' Courts*, London, Stevens.

King, M. (1972) *Bail or Custody*, London, Cobden Trust.

Mannheim, K. (1968) *Essays on the Sociology of Knowledge*, London, Routledge and Kegan Paul.

Patterson, A. (1971) *Legal Aid as a Social Service*, London, Cobden Trust.

Sacks, H. (1967) Transcribed Lectures (unpublished).

Schegloff, E.A. (1972) 'Notes on a Conversational Practice Formulating Place' in David Sudnow, *Studies in Social Interaction*, New York. Free Press.

Schutz, A. (1970) *Reflections on the Problems of Relevance*, New Haven, Yale University Press.

26.3 The adversarial system
Paul Rock

It is important neither to belittle nor yet to exaggerate the conflicts of the trial system. On one level, the contested trial was palpably adversarial: Weinreb called it 'a highly ritualized struggle between good and evil, the State and the Malefactor.'[1] and Neubauer argued that 'the basis of criminal law can be summarized in two words, human conflict'.[2] There was an antagonism that was so commonplace, widely presumed, and routine in the courtroom that it is almost necessary to be reminded of its significant features: that trials were fought by two opposing sides ('fight', 'side', and 'opponent' being words in common use), one prosecuting and one defending, and each having its own retinue and clients; that the system was conceived not as an inquiry into the final truth of a matter but as a struggle, a 'trial of strength',[3] between two competing, partial, and incomplete cases made out in public by advocates; and that judge and jury acted as arbiters rather than as inquisitors, necessarily leaving much that was unquestioned, unsaid, and unresolved.

The perennial issue was whether the Crown could prove its case to the satisfaction of jurors, not establish what might 'really' have happened. It was not how protagonists in their 'natural attitude' understood and presented their problems, but how matters could be reconstructed for purposes of a successful prosecution.[4] 'Dispute' perhaps best captured the character of such trials. Mather and Yngvesson defined a dispute as 'a particular stage in which conflict between two parties ... is asserted publicly – that is, before a third party', and, they continued, 'at a fundamental level, the transformation of a dispute involves a process of *rephrasing* – that is, some kind of reformulation into a public discourse.'[5] Disputes involved the deployment of a public language (a 'specialized legal discourse'[6]) and a narrowing of conflicts to formulate the few pivotal allegations that organized the presentation of a case.

A case was a deliberate simplification that obscured some issues, giving luminosity only to what were called the 'facts at issue', the facts that were deemed to be causally related to the commission of the offence. It was so constructed that it tended to strip away volumes of context and history (a recorder told a jury in his summing-up at Wood Green: 'the background to the incident is not the concern of the Court today. What is of concern is what took place on [a certain date]'). It was designed to ignore many of the tangled social relations, hurts, incidents, motives, and emotions that could be woven into personal disputes, concentrating on but a few matters.[7]

It was intended to shed greyness and ambiguity, severing the ties with what de Waele and Harré once called the 'unfolding processes'[8] of social life, amplifying the differences between protagonists, focusing on the circumstantial and situational, and offering a stark argument for fault-finding and judgment. A member of the branch CPS staff serving Wood Green said: 'our system is not designed to test the truth of anything. It's about pragmatics and fairness.'

At the core of a prosecution case were pointed allegations about wrongdoing, immorality, and mendacity whose acceptance would almost certainly lead to public disgrace and punishment. I have remarked how trials moved routinely, almost mechanically, through set stages. In their opening speech, prosecution counsel would make it evident to the jury that they were presenting what was, in essence, a chain of *assertions* about the offence, the victim, the defendant and the connections binding them together. In one very typical case, the prosecutor began by stating: 'The Crown say that this was an attack and it also says it was an unprovoked attack ... again the Crown say that ... piecing the picture together, the witnesses for the Crown will say ...' Note that the prosecution did not claim: 'This is what happened' but 'This is what the Crown *say* happened'. The prosecution case was a thesis to be defended in an argument that was substantially rhetorical.[9]

So the adversarial system brought it about that, even though they frequently alluded to what were called the 'facts of the case', the prosecution would, in effect, tell juries that they should not listen to what they said as if it were unproblematic and unchallenged. On the contrary, a prosecutor's speech was to be received as a piece of interpretation with which to frame *allegations* ('The suggestion in the prosecution evidence is that no-one had any business to hit Mr X ... I don't know whether it will be suggested that it didn't happen like that. It may be that it will be said that it wasn't Mr Y who did it'). Those allegations were a contestable construction placed on what may have been the rather murkier and muddlier events of the experienced world.

An opening statement would suggest to the jury what questions they might consider as the trial proceeded ('I don't propose to say more now than will enable you to make sense of the evidence when you hear it. When you hear the evidence, you will know what to listen for'). It would typically be described as a relatively slight thing, a preamble that should be brief,[10] especially in the kinds of case tried at Wood Green. It was presented as what could be expected of one who was paid to be persuasive, a suggestive account that was not

self-validating: 'You will decide the case on the evidence, not on counsel's speeches.' To become more, it was said, the prosecution case required substantiation of a special kind, evidence, and that could emanate only from one authority, witnesses of the facts in question ('What I have told you is not evidence. It is an outline. Evidence is what you hear from witnesses'). Evidence was the report of those who purported actually to have seen and heard what was alleged to have happened.[11] It elaborated and underpinned a case. It was memorable. Evidence was recorded by the shorthand writer, whilst opening statements were not. I shall describe evidence more fully below.

The prosecution would routinely promise to furnish witnesses to testify on behalf of each component stage of a version of events ('At that point, the defendants sought to assault X and you'll hear something about that .... To summarize, and you'll hear the evidence and you'll also hear ... You'll hear, members of the jury, that the defendants were employed .... You'll hear that the defendants were interviewed and I'm not going to go into those interviews at length. You'll hear from the police officers who did the interviews'). That then was the prosecution thesis, an explanatory frame of accusation to be girded by oral testimony from bystanders and participants on the scene at issue.

It was the job of defence counsel to supply a rival way of explaining what had occurred, what might be called the antithesis, although that term was not used in the courts. The defence case did not have to be as solid or imposing as that of the prosecution. It was an attack that sought chiefly to so puncture the impression achieved by the prosecution and prosecution witnesses that it became difficult for the jury to be sure of what had been said and, indeed, of what may have happened (and, in the relatively sealed world of the courtroom,[12] where stories and their tellers were all there was to judge, doubt did not seem very difficult to introduce). The defence would employ argument and questioning to reveal inconsistency, error, improper motives, forgetfulness, and falsehood in prosecution witnesses. The questions would often be searching. One counsel said: 'Anything that tends to mask the reality about the witnesses is hostile to the adversarial process. It should be stark. The choices that [the jury] have should be stark. The compulsion to tell the truth should be there.' The questions would probe minor contradiction after minor contradiction: 'You have to deal with things in detail, first of all to prevent anybody from saying that you didn't do that, but also ideally of giving a different account of even small details, raising a doubt as to the prosecution case ... because [the jury] have been told they have to be sure.'

Almost as a matter of course, counsel would, as a judge put it, so 'blackguard' the witnesses that they were no longer believable. Under cross-examination, victims and prosecution witnesses could be asked about matters touching on their 'title to credit': their way of life, their associations, their past convictions, their disinterestedness, and their integrity.[13] They could be vilified and shamed as they defended, in public and perhaps for the very first time, testimony about matters that were painful, embarrassing, and once personal. (Victim 20,[14] for instance, had been questioned about events before she had had a miscarriage: 'He was going on about me and X ... she was pregnant at the same time, going out together buying baby clothes. That upset me because I don't like talking about it.') At stake, wrote Ericson and Baranek, was the protection of valued aspects of identity.[15] Prosecution witnesses certainly experienced questioning by defence counsel as an assault on their identity. Those for whom public face was important (and it is important for most of us[16]) found it harrowing (Victim 6 called it 'nerve wracking ... I was shaking inside'). The techniques deployed were precisely those used by the prosecution in cross-examination of the defendant, and they seemed to put prosecution witnesses themselves on trial. Victim 20 told me after cross-examination, 'They made me feel like a criminal! It's the last time I'll come to court.' And Victim 17, a victim of assault by a cabdriver, said the worst thing about her routine cross-examination, in which she had been accused of lying, taking drugs, being drunk, and being provocative, was

> Being called a liar all the time, being accused of causing the affray. He asked me if I had been drinking ... I knew what [defence counsel] was trying to do. I'm not stupid. When he said I was smoking cannabis, that's when I went, 'No way! This is getting out of hand!' I just felt that I was the one being proved wrong .... How can he imply we were doing something with absolutely no proof!? How can he do that? Can he do that, suggest that we were taking drugs when we weren't? It's total rubbish! What was really upsetting was trying to convince them I was telling the truth. That's not fair.

In promoting that antithesis, and to sow uncertainty in the jury's minds, the defence might produce their own witnesses, who could be 'blackguarded' by the prosecution in turn.[17] Defence witnesses' motives, credibility, and creditability could be exposed to public examination, and that would be disagreeable for them too. A judge reflected: 'A close investigation of people's motives and actions may be very uncomfortable for those investigated.' So it was that advocates laid their tales and tale-bearers before jurors, inviting them to place a favoured construction on facts, arguments, and witnesses and deliver a verdict. The result, Pannick argued, was a choice between different constructions. 'The reality is that the adversary process of a trial more than leaves the truth mysteriously hidden, covered over by the evasions and half-truths of competing contentions.'[18]

Trials were intended to culminate in the unambiguous victory of one side or the other (unless, of course, there was an appeal), and very grave matters were at stake for those involved, the people formally called the 'alleged' defendants and victims. There was, on the one hand, liberty and reputation and, on the other, a vindication of wrongs. Trials supplied competing stories about the past, reconstructing all the indeterminacy and muddle of everyday life into what McConville once called 'opposing distortions'.[19] Juries would be given bleak choices between innocence and guilt, truth and falsehood, this or that account. Over and over again, they might have before them two quite plausible descriptions of the 'same' episode. Over and over again, they would be invited to choose between the credibility of one story and its train of witnesses and that of another. Only one version could prevail, and obstacles to its acceptance had to be explained by simple, corrigible error or dishonesty, not by the ineluctable ambiguity of a social world where multiple truths coexisted.[20]

Whatever lawyers and professionals might argue outside the courtroom,[21] witnesses tended to take it that defeat signified that they had been disbelieved, that they had been taken for liars. And that was not a view discouraged inside the courtroom itself. Of one very routine trial, the prosecutor said to the jury, 'It's quite clearly a case of whom you believe. If you believe the defendant, then ...', and a judge summed up in another such case: 'There it is, members of the jury, that's the evidence. That's the evidence on winch you've got to decide this case ... The prosecution say that unless you find all these police are telling lies, you'll have to find the defendant guilty.' Being publicly cast as tellers of untruths engendered distress. A barrister reflected that 'those who give their evidence orally are the most vulnerable. They don't expect their credibility to be challenged.' One witness, Victim 16, said: 'What really upset me was trying to convince them I was telling the truth. That's what upset me.' And another, Victim 1, said: 'I thought it would be straightforward. They kept asking me questions and trying to put them the other way around. It got confusing.' Even police officers who gave evidence regularly said, as one sergeant said, 'I don't think you ever get used to it...'

In delivering a verdict, there could be nothing of legal consequence between guilt and innocence (unless it was reintroduced afterwards, when greyness could be invoked by the defence in mitigation). After all, that was probably the chief purpose of the trial, to give an unambiguous and decisive resolution to disputes that could otherwise have continued interminably. The Court was the non-partisan third party confronting the dyad of victim and offender, accuser and accused, the party hitherto untouched by quarrels and passions.[22] And the prosecution's task would be confounded and the defendant would be aggrieved if the Crown tried to persuade jurors so that they were sure that a defendant might just *probably* be guilty. Certainty was the prosecution's province, doubt that of the defence. Whatever epistemological dilemmas might arise, the prosecution's simple polarized choice was a harder test to pass, and it could be argued that it was almost certainly better for purposes of justice: juries could not declare the defendant and victim both complicit in what had happened; the victim could not be just a little guilty or the defendant also wronged.

> The complexities ... are usually not apparent ... because police and prosecutors structure their accounts of cases to fit into accepted legal categories. These categories are simple, often dichotomous (guilty/not guilty; sane/insane; intentional/not intentional; reckless/not reckless; voluntary/involuntary) and deny the ambiguities and uncertainties of the world of experience.[23]

Only occasionally would lawyers protest about the starkness of such choices. In only one instance did I hear an advocate publicly criticize the feeding of a confused relationship into the adversarial system, and that was on the eve of the trial of a man on assault charges related to domestic violence. The defence counsel remonstrated with the prosecution that neither defendant nor victim was clearly blameless: 'This is the sort of case where the judge should take the two and bang their heads together!'[24] But the prosecution was adamant. 'We're fighting,' she said. All contested trials were called 'fights'. Ushers would ask counsel if a trial was to be a fight. The use of battle language was not fortuitous.

Conflict was not merely a matter of form. Although trials have been described in the vocabulary of a sporting contest, as if they were game-like, they were often suffused with the intense passion and pain of their civilian protagonists. There was an anger that could be ignited more than once as the Court reunited those who had fought, exploited, wronged, vilified, and oppressed one another; set them against each other again in public; interrogated them; judged them to be truthful or untruthful; exonerated or condemned them; and then inflicted punishment. And that anger was sometimes quite tangible. Crown Court buildings were the occasional targets of political and personal attack, being designed to withstand vandalism and bomb blasts.[25] They were witnesses to commotion as people hurled abuse at one another, furnishing a latter-day Greek chorus to comment on the performance of witnesses and defendants, and crying out in shock, lamentation, or triumph at verdicts and sentences. Those appearing in Court had often to be physically restrained and kept apart.[26] I shall describe just such a running display of wrath in the next chapter. Yet, on another level, conflict was quite controlled, and much of the remainder of this book will provide a description of just how it was made safe.

Very few lawyers and staff appeared surprised at outbursts. It was not considered professional to evince surprise at very much at all. The extraordinary anger and discomfort of witnesses, victims, and defendants were ordinary enough matters to those who worked in the courts every day. That is part of the business of being a professional, to translate the private and exceptional troubles of others into the recurrent and unremarkable materials of a specialized craft. (There were, nevertheless, moments that made counsel and other professionals apprehensive. One barrister told me of the lawyer's nervousness whenever a defendant was asked to examine a weapon.)

In effect, the antagonisms of private individuals were taken up and mediated by professionals who worked with the standard forms of conflict but did not experience its volatile contents as their own. It was not *their* distress and humiliation that counsel paraded before judge and jury. A barrister said: 'The professionals aren't allowed to show emotion, it's a big claim to make, but in fact they generally don't get emotional.'[27] In such a separation of form from content, of professional composure from the layman's anguish, counsel, staff, and others traced two domains: the calm, disciplined world of the insider and the wilder, angrier world of the civilian. That is a theme I shall pursue more than once, and especially in Chapter 5. Insider and outsider was the great organizing opposition of the Court.[28] Insiders necessarily shared a closer intimacy than any possible with an outsider. Whilst civilians moved in and out of the courtroom in great numbers, often never to be seen again, sometimes not even to be remembered (a judge remarked that 'witnesses are the fodder of the courts'), insiders were likely to meet day after day. They might know one another elsewhere in other courts, in police stations or chambers. They might begin to recognize one another, learn something about one another, and form patterns of dependency and collaboration that transcended the special features of an evanescent case. There was, observed Ericson and Baranek of the Canadian courts, a 'stake in future relationships that must be kept in mind in conducting transactions'.[29]

As they worked together in trial after trial, as counsel were seen sometimes defending, sometimes prosecuting, so the embedded adversarial roles of the trial system became detached from the selves of those who played them. Advocates were not to be confused wholly with the animosities they dramatised. They were, as the saying goes, 'only doing a job'. A probation officer remarked, 'They are just playing parts. They are lawyers just playing parts. It's a great big game with rules to be observed!' And, in doing that job, it would not do to lose the good will of an usher, a court clerk, or a colleague when so much in the courtroom rested on a friendly co-operativeness that was itself based on trust. A barrister said:

> One is obviously going to be pleasant to ushers and so forth on a mercenary level because if you want your case on quickly, then one will do ... But having said that – and it may sound a trite thing to say – but I always try and work with counsel as well ... I always try and make it as friendly as possible so you can have a laugh, simply because it's your working environment.

In the courtroom itself, there were endemic good manners that eased fraught and antagonistic relations that were always teetering on collapse. One counsel committed to defence work remarked, 'It can be quite civilized, counsel working very hard

for their side whatever it be, but we are all supposed to play by a set of rules ... There is no point in us getting into an argument...' Judges and counsel would say the most disagreeable things in the most agreeable way, the substance of conflict being presented in the forms of polite breeding.[30] Defendants were addressed by proper title and, until they were convicted, were always called 'gentlemen' and 'ladies'. Counsel did not menace witnesses bodily as their colleagues sometimes did elsewhere, in North America and Australia for example. They were rooted to their own small space in counsel's row, remaining physically remote from those whom they interrogated, reinforcing not only their own appearance of authority but also the formality and impersonality of their discourse. There was a tight control over the kind of talk that was permitted, and over the taking of discrete turns to speak in particular. People could usually be heard clearly, decorously, and one at a time. Their speech did not often collapse into shouting matches, although it sometimes seemed on the verge of doing so. And all that discipline and courteousness were enforced by judges.

In one case, the judge told a defence counsel to take his hand out of his pocket when he addressed the court. In another, counsel was repeatedly corrected in the courtroom itself, the judge telling him, 'Do things properly, it's not agreeable' and 'I may say, Mr X, that I would be grateful if you would take particular care to address witnesses with courtesy'. Witnesses themselves were rarely reproved. They were not expected to be disciplined or self-controlled. On the contrary: for reasons that I shall explain below, a candid, unbuttoned display of self could advance the Court's purposes.

From P. Rock, 'The adversarial system', in The Social World of an English Crown Court: Witness and Professionals in the Crown Court Centre at Wood Green *(Oxford: Oxford University Press), 1993, pp. 30–40.*

Notes

1 L. Weinreb, *Denial of Justice* (New York, Free Press, 1977), 98.

2 D. Neubauer, *America's Courts and the Criminal Justice System* (Pacific Grove, Calif, Brooks/Cole, 1988), 16.

3 P. Devlin, *The Judge* (Oxford, Oxford Univ. Press, 1979), 54.

4 See A. Sarat and W. Felstiner, 'Law and Social

Relations: Vocabularies of Motive in Lawyer/Client Interaction', *Law and Society Review*, 22(4) (1988), 739–40.

5 L. Mather and B. Yngvesson, 'Language, Audience, and the Transformation of Disputes', *Law and Society Review*, 15(3) (1981), 776, 777.

6 *Ibid*. 783.

7 Thus W. Felstiner, R. Abel, and A. Sarat observe that 'the early stages of naming, blaming and claiming are significant ... because the range of behaviour they encompass is greater than that involved in the later stages of disputes, where institutional patterns restrict the options open to disputants' ('the Emergence and Transformation of Disputes: Naming, Blaming, Claiming...', *Law and Society Review*, 15(3) (1981), 636).

8 See J. de Waele and R. Harré, *Personality* (Oxford, Basil Blackwell, 1979).

9 See Morison and Leith; *The Barrister's World and the Nature of Law*, 5.

10 Sec Mazengarb, *Advocacy in Our Time*, 146.

11 The prosecution may well decide not to call witnesses damaging to their case but they should disclose their names to the defence. See C. Emmins, *A Practical Approach to Criminal Procedure* (London, Financial Training Publications, 1987), 105.

12 A journalist, recalling his experience as a juror at Wood Green, wrote about 'a sense of watching a case from a position of fresh innocence, through a glass that filters out some of the surrounding "reality" (H. Young, 'An Indictment of Justice', *Guardian*, 1 Feb. 1992).

13 See *Archbold: Pleading, Evidence and Practice in Criminal Cases* (London, Sweet and Maxwell, 1988), 484.

14 A total of 33 victims were interviewed between Jan. and June 1990, 16 before the move to the new courthouse and the inauguration of the victim–witness project, 17 afterwards. They have been numbered in the order of interview.

15 See R. Ericson and P. Baranek, *The Ordering of Justice: A Study of Accused Persons as Dependants in the Criminal Process* (Toronto, Univ. of Toronto Press, 1982), 205.

16 For the importance of face, and particularly of presenting oneself as 'hard' in the everyday life of young working-class males, see P. Willis, *Common Culture* (Milton Keynes, Open Univ. Press, 1990), 103.

17 Such discrediting was not disfavoured. Those in the prosecutor's retinue tended to regard defence wit-

nesses with some suspicion. A police officer reflected: 'A lot of prosecution witnesses are there because they were in the wrong place at the wrong time a year ago, whereas the defence witness is there because they were a mate of the defendant's in the boozer.'

18 D. Pannick, *Judges* (Oxford, Oxford Univ. Press, 1987), 53.

19 M. McConville, 'Justice in the Dock', *Times Higher Education Supplement*, 8 Feb. 1990.

20 See M. Pollner, 'Mundane Reasoning', *Philosophy of the Social Sciences*, 4(1) (1974).

21 That argument characteristically took the form that failure to win a prosecution case reflected the heavy burden of proof, a burden that demanded that juries must be sure about the defendant's guilt. Witnesses were not necessarily to be seen as liars. Rather, it was said, the jury had probably been unable to arrive at a state of certainty about a case.

22 See G. Simmel, 'The Triad', in K. Wolff (ed.); *The Sociology of Georg Simmel* (New York, Free Press, 1950), 146–7.

23 M. McConville *et al.*, 'The Case for the Prosecution' TS, n.d., 22.

24 And it should be noted that that counsel had a reputation in the court for being unusually emotional and theatrical in her conduct.

25 See 'Liverpool Crown Court', *Construction*, July 1979, 30.

26 See K. Manasian, 'On Trial', *Interior Design*, Apr. 1981, 20–1.

27 A barrister was reported to have said of a trial lawyer's performance in the American case of William Smith, 'She became too emotionally engaged. The more professional you are, the more you keep that under wraps.' 'Kennedy's Verdict on Kennedy Case', *Sunday Times*, 15 Dec. 1991.

28 As it is of the criminal justice system at large. See e.g. M. Young, *An Inside Job* (Oxford, Oxford Univ. Press, 1991), esp. 111.

29 *The Ordering of Justice*, 14.

30 Giving a different inflection to much the same point, M Feeley observed of the American court: 'Language in the courtroom is extremely arcane and formal, and it can easily accommodate the most bitter denunciations and sarcasm in a way that does not unduly strain the rituals of court procedures', *The Process is the Punishment* (New York, Russell Sage Foundation, 1979), 68.

26.4 Understanding law enforcement
Doreen McBarnet

Understanding law enforcement: a new perspective

This study set out to analyse the role of legal forms, powers, privileges, limitations, and rulings on the process of constructing conviction in court – conviction in both the subjective sense of how a judge or jury comes to be convinced beyond reasonable doubt of its verdict, and in the legal sense of a finding of guilt; for that, statistically, is the likely outcome of a foray into the criminal courts. The problem for the sociologist is how that is possible when all the rhetoric of the democratic ideology of justice proclaims that in the battle between the state and the accused the system is heavily biased in favour of the latter. By examining the law not just in terms of the general principles of its own ideology, but in terms of the details of its specific structures, procedures, and decisions, this analysis has tried to show that the law governing the production, preparation, and presentation of evidence does not live up to its own rhetoric.

The rhetoric of justice requires incriminating evidence as the basis for arrest and search; the law allows arrest and search in order to establish it. Justice requires that no-one need incriminate himself; the law refuses to control the production of confessions and allows silence as a factor in proving guilt. Justice requires equality; the law discriminates against the homeless, the jobless, the disreputable. Justice requires each case be judged on its own facts; the law makes previous convictions grounds for defining behaviour as an offence and evidence against the accused. Justice places the burden of proof on the prosecutor; the law qualifies the standard and method of proof required and offers the prosecutor opportunities for making a case which the accused is denied. Justice proclaims the right to trial by one's peers; the legal system ensures that 91 per cent of all defendants plead guilty, and of the rest most are tried without a jury.

If, then, the process of conviction is easier than the rhetoric of justice would have us expect – and easier still the lower the status of the defendant – it is hardly surprising. A wide range of prosecution evidence can be legally produced and presented, despite the rhetoric of a system geared overwhelmingly to safeguards for the accused, precisely because legal structure, legal procedure, legal rulings, *not* legal rhetoric, govern the legitimate practice of criminal justice, and there is quite simply a distinct gap between the substance and the ideology of the law.

This conclusion has two direct and immediate implications. First it places the contemporary policy debate over law and order in a new light. The police demand for more powers, for the removal of the hamstrings of the right to silence, the limitations on arrest and search – and indeed the civil liberties camp's agitated response that the legal checks of British justice must be upheld – begin to appear rather odd. *Both* sides of the debate are framed in terms of the ideology of civil rights, not in terms of the realities of legal procedure and case law which, as I hope this analysis has amply shown, have all too often already given the police and prosecution the very powers they are demanding. The law does not need reform to remove hamstrings on the police: they exist largely in the unrealised rhetoric.

Second, more theoretically, this analysis has implications for the explanation of law-enforcement and its outcomes. A whole range of excellent sociological studies has pointed out situational, informal, non-legal factors in police–citizen encounters and courtroom interaction to explain *who* is arrested or convicted, and to explain why the system so often seems *in practice* to be weighted against the accused. Their answer lies essentially in the complex nature of social interaction and motivation; in the fact that people do not merely administer the law but act upon and alter it as they do so. This study offers a supplementary perspective, making the law rather than the activities of its administrators problematic. The conclusion is quite different. Given the formal procedures and rules of the law and the structure of arrest, investigation, plea and trial, one could not – even if human beings acted entirely as legal automatons – expect the outcomes to be other than they are. If the practice of criminal justice does not live up to its rhetoric one should not look only to the interactions and negotiations of those who put the law into practice but to the law itself. One should not look just to how the rhetoric of justice is subverted intentionally or otherwise by policemen bending the rules, by lawyers negotiating adversariness out of existence, by out-of-touch judges or biased magistrates: one must also look at how it is subverted *in the law*. Police and court officials need not abuse the law to subvert the principles of justice; they need only use it. Deviation from the rhetoric of legality and justice is institutionalised in the law itself.

Coming back to Packer's two polar types for describing law enforcement, due process and crime control, empirical analysis of the process reveals them as a false distinction. The law on criminal procedure in its current form does not so much set a standard of legality from which the police deviate as provide a licence to ignore it. If we bring due process down from the dizzy heights of abstraction and subject it to empirical scrutiny, the conclusion must be that due process is *for* crime control.

This perspective offers quite a different ideological gloss on the nature of criminal justice and a shift of focus for its study. Focusing on the subversion of justice by its petty administrators, on the gap between the law in the books and the law in action, in effect whitewashes the law itself and those who make it. Front-men like the police become the 'fall guys' of the legal system taking the blame for any injustices in the operation of the law, both in theory (in the assumption like Skolnick's that they break the rules) and indeed, in the law. The law holds the individual policeman personally responsible for contraventions of legality that are successfully sued, while at the same time refusing to make clear until after the event exactly what the police are supposed to do. It is no coincidence that the police themselves asked for the original Judges' Rules. Shifting the focus to the substance of law places responsibility for the operation of criminal justice – and the need for the spotlight of study – squarely on the judicial and political elites who make it.

Tracing a gap between the rhetoric of justice and the substance and structure of law is not, however, just the end of a piece of indignant exposé research (Taylor, Walton, and Young 1975, p. 29). It opens up a whole complex of further issues. If the contradictions between rhetoric and practice in law-enforcement cannot simply be explained away as the unintended consequences of the action of petty officials, then we are faced with contradictions within the core of the state between the ideology and substance of the law. Why does such institutionalised deviation occur? How is the ideo-

logical gap managed? What implications does it have for the idea of the rule of law? Though these are major issues which each require a full-scale study in themselves, the sections that follow offer some speculative beginnings.

Rhetoric and law: why the gap?

It is too simple to discuss the gap between the rhetoric of justice and the substance of law as unproblematic, as the inevitable and self-evident consequence of a class society in which the rhetoric of justice is necessarily mere illusion. Some more sophisticated analyses have been suggested. Hall and his colleagues (1978) have tried to offer a materialist explanation of a particular move in the 1970s to a more repressive crime-control oriented use of law and steady erosion of civil liberties by relating it to a crisis in the hegemony of the bourgeois state, and that in turn to economic crisis. At another level of contextual analysis a series of sociologists,[1] including indeed Hall *et al.*, have demonstrated how a moral panic and campaign for the repression of a particular social problem – mugging, football hooliganism, drugs, mods and rockers – can lead to more crime-control oriented judicial decisions, and so help explain why particular swings in the orientation of law to or away from the rhetoric of justice take place. It might also be possible, however, that a tendency one way or the other exists in the law itself. From examining the legal structure it would seem that there are also forces *within* the law which might well lead *routinely* – when there are no moral panics in either direction – to a development of case law that favours crime control rather than due process.

Case law and judicial discretion could as readily be used – and indeed have been – to condemn police practices as to condone them. But case law emanates, to state the obvious, from particular trials. There is no public interest law in Britain, no way in which a point of law can be brought to court as an abstract issue of public concern. A point of law can only be clarified in the context of a dispute in a real case, either directly at a High Court trial from the decision taken by the judge on a dispute over a point of law, or indirectly via appeal from the trial court to the Court of Appeal or House of Lords. Locating the dispute over law in the facts of a concrete case might well, despite the distinction drawn in legal theory between issues of fact and issues of law, mean that the facts of the case affect the finding in law by providing the context in which the decision has to be made. What this whole study has suggested is that that context, if the point of law is being raised in the course of a trial, is one in which the accused is likely to look guilty. If it is being raised on appeal, then he will already have been *found* guilty since, in the main, only defendants can appeal, and only defendants with a grievance – that is, those who have been convicted.[2] What is more, because re-trials of fact, or the introduction of new evidence, are rarely allowed on appeal, that defendant's case is often of necessity based on technicality rather than equity, on the means by which the evidence was acquired rather than the misleading or inaccurate nature of the evidence itself. Judges making case law on appeal are thus faced in effect with a guilty defendant trying to argue his way out of his due deserts through legal technicalities. Who would blame them for closing the escape route by removing the technicality, by seeing rights as loopholes that should in the name of justice be removed? If these hypotheses are correct, one can readily see why in particular cases judges may be likely to decide against the accused.

The problem is that judges are exercising a dual function in reaching their decision. They must not just ensure that justice is done in the sense of the accused getting his deserts; they must also ensure that the technical checks on *how* criminal justice is executed are upheld. They must not just uphold the substantive criminal law but the procedures of legality. They must think not only of the apparently guilty man before them but of the protection of the innocent in the future. But this duality of function sets up an impossible contradiction. The decision is a finding for *either* one party or the other. It has *either* to declare the methods illegitimate, the evidence inadmissible and quash the defendant's conviction, *or* uphold the conviction, but in doing so, inevitably legitimise the questionable methods – inevitably because of a second duality in the function of decisions. The judicial decision does not just resolve the particular case but sets a precedent for future cases. Provisos in civil rights introduced in the context of a particular case become abstracted and available for argument in all cases. Rejecting a technical defence may be quite understandable in the context of the black-and-white cases constructed through advocacy and procedure, but with every rejection of a technical defence case comes an extension of police and prosecution powers. Civil liberties cease to be legal rights and the control of crime is safeguarded at the expense of legality.[3]

In short, from the structure of trial and appeal, and from the functional dualities in the judicial decision – deciding on both the individual case and the law; upholding both substantive and procedural law – one can plausibly hypothesise a structural trend in case law towards crime control and away from due process. While contextual analysis is obviously vital, the legal system itself may also help explain why substantive law might routinely be upheld at the expense of procedural law and the rights of the rhetoric of justice gradually whittled away.

Managing the ideological gap

The gap between the rhetoric of justice and the substance and structure of law raises not only 'why' questions but 'how' questions. How is it possible for the law to deviate from the rhetoric, and how does the rhetoric survive the deviation? Much has been made of the tension between due process and crime control but the law seems to achieve crime control while keeping the ideology of due process in play;[4] it seems to achieve in some measure at least the impossible task of maintaining two contradictory ideas at once. How are the ideological gap and the ideological contradictions managed?

Part of the answer lies in the mystique and inaccessibility which protects the detail of law from the mass of people. It is the rhetoric rather than the law that is public knowledge. Indeed one can observe defendants losing their case precisely because they are arguing it on the basis of the rhetoric rather than the law. One needs a knowledge of both law and rhetoric before the gap between them becomes evident. What is more, a good deal of what occurs in the courts, [...] may appear to fit the rhetoric of justice only because the organisation of the facts into not only black-and-white cases but into black-and-white cases that are likely to persuade ordinary people of guilt has taken place *out* of the public eye. The ideological shutters around the magistrates' courts [...] and the difficulties attached even to getting leave to appeal, have the same effect. The division of the process into public and private faces helps in itself to maintain the ideology.

Part of the answer lies too in the techniques of judicial reasoning. Judges deciding a point of law routinely reiterate the rhetoric in resounding prose, yet decide the case in such a way that the rhetoric is, for this individual, effectively denied. Throughout we have seen examples of how this apparent contradiction is calmly and routinely accomplished. Judges may draw literal distinctions which reiterate the principle but make it simultaneously irrelevant or indeed uphold the principle but give such specific reasons that it cannot be generalised, as in *Lawrie v. Muir* or *H.M. Adv. v. Aitken*. They may avoid the applicability of the rhetoric by redefining the situation in such a way that it is no longer covered by the principle; for example, creating the limbo of the 'suspect' who was thus not protected by the rhetoric or law on arrest and interrogation. They may uphold the rhetoric by expressing dissatisfaction with the questionable means used to acquire evidence, but simultaneously allow that evidence to be used to convict on other grounds, maintaining that the trial judge has discretion in such matters as to precisely how it should be applied as in the *R.v. Lemsatef* case, or deciding – on no rational empirical grounds at all – that the conviction by the jury did not depend on that piece of evidence anyway. All kinds of techniques of reasoning allow the rhetoric to be both eulogised and denied.

But structural factors also provide some of the means of bridging the ideological gap. The doctrine of the separation of powers provides a multi-headed state and with it the potential to extol the rhetoric in one sector and deny it in another. Statutes may provide rights in general terms – the 1887 Act, for example, made provision for a defendant to consult a solicitor – only to have the judges refine the right out of existence. The rhetoric lives on in the statute but is routinely negated in the courts by judicial reasoning.

Beneath judicial reasoning itself structural factors are also at work. Just as the techniques of advocacy are themselves only adaptations to a particular form of proof, so the techniques of judicial reasoning are themselves significant only in a particular form of law. Law is made through the case law method both in the development of common law and the application of statutes. The rhetoric of justice in the form of general abstract rules is quite simply incompatible with the notion of case law. Levi notes that a general overall rule is useless in law because:

> It will have to operate at a level where it has no meaning … The legal system does not work with the rule but at a much lower level.
>
> (Levi, 1949, p. 9)

A legal system based on case law (and even the states that boast codified law also use case law in a modified form) operates at the level of the concrete case: is highly particularistic. Hence the justification of excepting the specific case from the application of the general rule without destroying the general rule *per se*. The rhetoric and the law operate at two different levels, the abstract and the concrete, and the contradiction is operationally negated and a clear clash prevented by each being pigeon-holed out of the other's realm of discourse. The rhetoric is rarely actually denied, it is simply whittled away by exceptions, provisos, qualifications.

Law in this form is rather like a Russian doll. You begin with the rhetoric and a single, apparently definite, condition which on closer inspection turns out to contain another less clear condition which in turn opens up to reveal even more ifs and buts and vaguenesses, reducing so often to the unpredictability of 'it all depends on the circumstances' – what criteria we use in your case depends on your case. This form provides an extremely potent way of maintaining the facade of civil rights ideology – the first doll – while in fact allowing extensive *legal* police powers. Cases can readily accommodate both statements of general principle and the exceptions of particular circumstances. Thus an appeal on the grounds of abuse of a legal right can be rejected because of the circumstances of the particular case, while at the same time a grand statement reiterating that right is made. The conflicting rhetoric of due process and practical demands for crime control are thus both simultaneously maintained and the gap between rhetoric and practice is managed out of existence. Lawyers may boast of the flexibility and individualised treatment afforded by case law but it also plays a potent role in maintaining the ideology of justice.[5]

This has implications for policy for it sets parameters on any possibility of lasting reform. Recommendations for changes in the law made by the Royal Commission on Criminal Procedure, the Fisher Report, committees on law reform, or whatever, must be seen as themselves subject to future change, future change which if the hypothesised development of case law noted in the previous section is anything to go by, all too often means a whittling away of the original principle. The spirit lingers in the rhetoric of justice but the qualifications and provisos of case law render it rather less effective. Lasting reform cannot be possible without some deeper change in the form of law itself.

But the nature of case law has implications not only for policy but for sociological understanding of the role of law in society, for the operation of dominant ideology and the democratic state. It has implications in particular for one area in which these three coalesce, in the idea of the rule of law.

From D. McBarnet, Conviction: law, the state and the construction of justice *(Basingstoke: Macmillan), 1981, pp. 154–162.*

Notes

1 Taylor *et al.* (1971); Young (1971); Cohen (1971).
2 The inevitable exceptions are: in England, the prosecutor's right of appeal from a magistrates' court where the magistrate has dismissed a case on a point of law; in Scotland the prosecutor may not appeal against the decision of a High Court or Sheriff Court with a jury but may appeal by stated case against a summary acquittal. In addition, Andrew Ashworth has kindly pointed out that the Criminal Justice Act 1972 s.36 introduced an opportunity to clear up disputed points of law even if the accused was acquitted, though he also notes that this is statistically insignificant.
3 Developed from a discussion in McBarnet 1978b.
4 Surveys may not suggest any overwhelming belief by the British public at large in the impartiality of justice, but there is sufficient indignation expressed by middle-class liberal camps, when crime control or *raison d'etat* too explicitly steamrolls over civil liberties, to suggest a belief on their part at least that the law is, or should normally be, geared to civil rights. Witness not just liberal reaction to the law and order campaign of the 1970s but to specific incidents like the Hosenball affair (in 1977) or jury vetting in 1979.
5 See McBarnet, 1978b; Kinsey, 1978; Picciotto, 1979.

References

Cohen, S. (1971) Mods, rockers and the rest. In Carson, W.G. and Wiles, P. (Eds) *Sociology of Crime and Delinquency*. Martin Robertson.

Hall, S., Critcher, C, Jefferson, T., Clarke, J. and Roberts, B. (1978) *Policing the Crisis: Mugging the State and Law and Order*. Macmillan.

Kinsey, R. (1978) Marxism and the law: Preliminary analyses. *British Journal of Law and Society*, 5 (2). Winter.

Levi, E.H. (1949) *An Introduction to Legal Reasoning*. University of Chicago Press.

McBarnet, D.J. (1978b) The Fisher Report on the Confait case: Four issues. *Modern Law Review*. May.

Picciotto, S. (1979) The theory of the state, class struggle and the rule of law. In NDC/CSE *Capitalism and the Rule of Law*. Hutchinson.

Taylor, I., Walton, P. and Young, J. (1975) *Critical Criminology*. Routledge & Kegan Paul.

Young, J. (1971) *The Drugtakers*. Paladin.

27

Sentencing and non-custodial penalties

27.1 Crime, inequality and sentencing
Pat Carlen   628

27.2 The punitive city: notes on the dispersal of social control
Stanley Cohen   633

27.3 The dispersal of discipline thesis
Anthony Bottoms   640

27.4 Understanding the growth in the prison population in England and Wales
Andrew Millie, Jessica Jacobson and Mike Hough   644

Introduction

KEY CONCEPTS

community corrections; corporal, juridical and carceral forms of punishment; correctional continuum; criminal justice; discipline; dispersal of social control; mesh-thinning; net-widening; penetration; rehabilitation; social justice

Here we turn to all those penalties available to the courts other than imprisonment. The readings deal with a number of issues ranging from concerns around equality and the differential use of courts' powers through to the history of the spread of non-custodial penalties.

Pat Carlen **(Reading 27.1)** looks at sentencing practice and questions of inequality. She begins by arguing that sentencing is likely to be ineffective – judged by its success in bringing about reductions in lawbreaking – unless the connection is drawn between criminal and social justice. To illustrate this point she outlines what she argues are four different models of sentencing, and how the emphasis has shifted in recent times between elements of these different models. One of these models – the justice model – she suggests continues to dominate and that this is a major blockage to social justice-oriented reform in the criminal justice system.

In a hugely influential article, Stanley Cohen **(Reading 27.2)** advances a radical argument in which he suggests that one reading of the spread of community-based punishment would be to see it as involving 'the dispersal of social control'. This process of dispersal blurs the boundaries between previously clearer distinctions such as 'inside/outside', 'guilty/innocent' and 'imprisoned/released'. This is the world of the 'correctional continuum'. The new structure also involves 'thinning the mesh' and 'widening the net' of social control. Finally, he suggests that the new mechanisms of formal control also penetrate more deeply into the informal networks of society. The overwhelming impression, he says, is 'one of bustling, almost *frenzied* activity', all of which is indicative of the creation of a broader, more subtle and insidious system of social control.

A challenge to aspects of this 'dispersal of discipline' thesis is offered by Anthony Bottoms **(Reading 27.3)**. In order to do so, Bottoms returns to the text that inspired much of Cohen's thesis, Michel Foucault's *Discipline and Punish* (see also Reading 22.1). In it, Foucault draws a distinction between three different types of punishment mechanism: the 'corporal', the 'juridical' and the 'carceral'. Cohen's argument, Bottoms suggests, rests on the idea that what we witnessed in the late twentieth century was largely a continuation of what was occurring in the nineteenth – identified by Foucault as the emergence of carceral forms of punishment. However, much of what has actually been occurring in the late twentieth century, Bottoms argues, is more resonant of other styles of punishment - or, using Foucault's terminology, many recent developments are not 'disciplinary' in character.

The final excerpt, by Andrew Millie and colleagues **(Reading 27.4)** asks why the prison population in England and Wales has increased so substantially in recent years. A number of possibilities are canvassed and rejected including the possibility that this is a reflection of changing crime rates or the increasing seriousness of the crimes that are coming to attention of the courts. In both cases there is no evidence to suggest that either has occurred. Rather, the changes are a reflection of changed sentencing practices and, more particularly, an increase in the use of imprisonment by the courts (for offences that would have been dealt with in other ways) and increasing terms of imprisonment. They conclude by briefly exploring the likely reasons for the changed sentencing practices they outline and by suggesting potential policy options for containing the prison population in the future.

Questions for discussion

1. Why does Carlen believe that the link between criminal justice and social justice is important?

2. Outline and differentiate the four models of sentencing described by Carlen.

3. What are the major barriers to a social justice-oriented criminal justice system?

4. What does Cohen mean by 'thinning the mesh' and 'widening the net' of social control?

5. Briefly summarise the differences between the three mechanisms of punishment identified by Foucault.

6. What is Bottoms' main line of criticism of Cohen's dispersal of discipline thesis?

7. What do Millie *et al.* suggest has led to tougher sentencing?

8. What do they suggest might be adopted as a strategy for containing the prison population? How realistic is each of these suggestions?

27.1 Crime, inequality and sentencing
Pat Carlen

Introduction

The fundamental implication [is] that, until there is a greater recognition of the relationships between crime, criminal justice and social justice, it is unlikely that sentences will be fashioned which will bring about reductions in lawbreaking. At the most general level the argument will be that the state's right to punish is based on a contractual obligation to attempt to rectify the particular 'social problems which both occasion, and are occasioned by, lawbreaking' (Carlen, 1983a: 213) and that forms of punishment which ignore that obligation, while they might fulfil other functions, will *not* reduce crime.

Four models of sentencing

1 The general rehabilitation model (fitting the punishment to the offender)

2 The justice model (making the punishment fit the crime)

3 The community corrections model (bringing the pains of imprisonment into the community)

4 The state-obligated rehabilitation model (obligation to society – denunciation

obligation to victim – restitution

obligation to offender – rehabilitation)

The general rehabilitation model

The general rehabilitation model of sentencing has traditionally been concerned both with punishment of the offender and with crime control. Unlike the classical theory of justice put forward by Beccaria (1963), the general rehabilitative model has always been less committed to making the punishment fit the crime and more concerned with fitting the punishment to the offender – in other words, with an individualized sentencing aimed at removing (or ameliorating) the conditions presumed to have been part-cause of the criminal behaviour.

Rehabilitationist penology was developed at the beginning of the twentieth century in England and was innovative in incorporating into sentencing a range of extra-legal criteria – medical, social, psychological and psychoanalytical. It reached its zenith with the 1969 Children and Young Persons' Act (CYPA, 1969) and it was the body of criticism subsequently directed at the working of CYPA which prepared the way for the decline of the general rehabilitation model in the 1970s and the rise of the justice model thereafter.

After 1969, rehabilitationism (called 'general' in this chapter because it embraces an eclectic mix of psychological, psychoanalytical and positivistic theories of crime) was strongly attacked by critics from both the left and the right. [...] [T]he attack on rehabilitationism united such powerful critiques from diverse political perspectives that the growing calls for a 'return to justice' in penology met with very little resistance. While conservative thinkers hoped that a 'just deserts' model would ensure that criminals would indeed be punished and not 'let off' with a rehabilitative sentence, more liberal proponents argued that the 'net-widening' effects (S. Cohen, 1985) of the preventive treatment of people 'at risk' could best be eliminated by a 'just deserts' model which would punish offenders for what they had done rather than for who they were. Even more importantly, it was contended on all sides that 'just deserts' sentencing would reduce crime. [...]

In the rush to renounce rehabilitationism, few supporters of the justice model appeared to suspect that the 1970s attack on welfare in criminal justice might be the thin edge of the wedge as far as welfare provision in general was concerned. In future, it was agreed, the state's role in the punishment of offenders was to be concerned primarily with 'doing justice' (Von Hirsch, 1976) arid only secondarily with 'doing good'.

The justice model

The major principles of the justice model of sentencing are desert, equivalence, determinacy and consistency. In 1986 the Home Office's handbook for the courts on the treatment of offenders (Home Office, 1986a) clearly stated that these principles were to be preferred over those of an individualized, rehabilitationist justice. Sentencers were advised that

a sentence should not normally be justified on merely deterrent or therapeutic grounds – either that the offender will be 'cured' or that others need to be discouraged from similar crimes. It may be that properly reflecting the relative gravity of the offence, and fairness between different offenders, are more important aims in the individual case. (Home Office, 1986a: 7)

By 1986 however, it had already become apparent that after a decade of sentencing dominated by the justice model, crime and imprisonment rates had increased while the sentences of the courts continued to reflect the inequalities of society at large – that is they still discriminated either against or in favour of certain categories of offenders regardless of the nature of their offences. [...]

Barbara Hudson, in a passionate and elegant denunciation of the justice model, has explained precisely why 'just deserts' sentencing is consistently unjust:

What deserts-based sentencing means...is building on class-based definitions of serious crime, ignoring class-differential vulnerability to the acquisition of a 'bad' record and imposing an arbitrary, blind 'fairness' at an advanced stage of the criminal justice process. Ignoring the 'non legal' factors in sentencing means ignoring the fact that in all its stages, criminal justice is a complex process of negotiation... . By modestly demurring that social injustices can be dealt with by the criminal justice system, justice model reformers are building those very injustices into the heart of the system, by privileging the factors they most strongly influence – the nature of the charge faced by a defendant, and the length of the previous criminal record – as the only factors relevant in sentencing.

(Hudson, 1987: 114)

The community corrections model

The government's Green Paper 'Punishment, Custody and the Community' (Home Office, 1988a) was published in July 1988. Its main proposals were that

1 more offenders convicted of less serious crimes should be 'punished in the community' rather than sent to prison

2 offenders should be made to pay as much as they can to provide financial compensation to their victims

3 to increase public confidence in court orders which leave offenders in the community, the regulations governing community service and

probation orders should be strengthened, while day centre projects should offer 'strict and structured regimes' aimed at reducing the offending of young adult offenders

4 a new sentence might be developed to include

– compensation to the victim
– community service
– residence at a hostel or other approved place
– prescribed activities at a day centre or elsewhere
– curfew or house arrest
– tracking an offender's whereabouts
– other conditions, such as staying away from particular places.

(Home Office, 1988a: 13)

The penal principles underlying the proposals were clearly stated. Retribution and general deterrence, still the dominant planks of what in effect remained a 'just deserts' policy, were in future to be buttressed by an individualized sentence designed to incapacitate offenders according to their circumstances. There was a new emphasis on reparation both to community and victim.

When an offence is so serious that a financial penalty alone is inadequate, the government considers that the penalty should, where possible, involve these three principles:

– restrictions on the offender's freedom of action – as a punishment
– action to reduce the risk of further offending; and
– reparation to the community and, where possible, compensation to the victim.

(Home Office, 1988a: 2)

Unfortunately, present inequalities of wealth and income will make it impossible to fashion each offender's penalty in accordance with the foregoing principles. Rather, it is likely that as far as non-custodial sentencing is concerned offenders will fall into three main groups. The largest will be comprised of those poorer people who, unable to pay a financial penalty or make compensation to the victim, will receive a tough punishment involving close surveillance in the community. In this group will be those whose social circumstances make them least able to cope with any further punishment in the community (punishment, that is, beyond that already inflicted by unemployment and poor to non-existent housing) and who are therefore the least likely to be deterred from crime by stiffer penalties. Another group will contain first-time or other 'not-at-risk of recidivism' offenders who will most probably not reoffend whatever noncustodial penalty is imposed. And a third will consist of better-off 'professional' or 'white-collar' criminals who, having paid a not-too-onerous fine (and maybe compensation) will either be excused 'punishment in the community' altogether, or discover that, within the comfort of their well-off homes and supportive environments, 'punishment in the community' is no punishment at all. [...] In short, although there was much to welcome in the government's proposals to reduce the prison population and fashion more socially productive penalties for crime, their implementation would be unlikely to produce the desired reductions in crime and imprisonment rates unless accompanied by other, more radical reforms.

State-obligated rehabilitation

The term 'state-obligated' rehabilitation (though not the model developed here) is taken from F. T. Cullen and K. E. Gilbert (1982) who, in their book *Reaffirming Rehabilitation*, were among the first to warn that a renaissance of the justice model of sentencing might not be the best way to reduce crime and prison populations. Arguing that where rehabilitationism had previously failed it had done so because of the state's lack of commitment to it, they suggested that

> Liberal interest groups should embark on efforts to transform enforced therapy, into a programme of state-obligated rehabilitation that takes seriously the betterment of inmates but legitimates neither coercion in the name of treatment nor neglect in the name of justice.
> (Cullen and Gilbert, 1982: 246)

In their programme of liberal reforms Cullen and Gilbert proposed that prison administrators should be obliged to offer treatment to every inmate and that 'all prisoners should be invited to enter a parole contract' whereby they 'agree to complete certain rehabilitation programmes and in exchange are given the exact date on which they will be paroled' (*ibid.*).

The notion of state-obligated rehabilitation could also be profitably extended to non-custodial penalties, though in the model developed below it

would be assumed that, in order to be rehabilitated, offenders would need to be convinced not only that their own behaviour had been reprehensible but also that the state's treatment of them had been *just* – in terms of impact in relation to their *offence* and in terms of sentence feasibility in relation to their *social circumstances*.

A fundamental assumption of state-obligated rehabilitation would posit that as both offender and state might be more or less responsible for the breakdown of social relations which had resulted in crime, both had an obligation (more or less) to take action to reduce the likelihood of similar rupture in future.

State-obligated rehabilitation: sentencing principles

The major principles of state-obligated rehabilitation should be

1 that imprisonment is an extreme form of punishment, to be used only in exceptional cases and *never* as back-up to a non-custodial court order;

2 that denunciation, crime-reduction, rehabilitation and reconciliation (between community, offender and victim) should be the major aims of sentencing (see Blom-Cooper, 1988);

3 that punishment should be a primary aim of sentencing only if offender and court are agreed that a rehabilitative element would be redundant in a particular case;

4 that so long as the state fulfilled its obligation to rehabilitate in a particular case the offender could be obliged to engage in any 'feasible' programme of rehabilitation or regulation (including, for instance, urine testing of drugtakers or electronic monitoring of other offenders). For no rehabilitative or regulatory programme would be rejected out of hand on the grounds of its being an essential violation of civil liberties or on the grounds of its being essentially lacking in feasibility. Rather, it would only be rejected on the grounds of its non-feasibility in a specific case;

5 that attempts to achieve greater equality of sentence impact should only be qualified by the court's recognition that in a specific case an offender's circumstances rendered the appropriate degree of punishment non-feasible.

Towards state-obligated rehabilitation: suggested sentencing reforms

Sentencing to promote good rather than to impede evil

The aim of judicial intervention into offenders' lives should be to help them create living conditions in which they will be more likely to choose to be law abiding in the future. Close surveillance, punitive work schemes, curfews and so on are not necessarily the types of interventions that will increase all offenders' capacity to change their behaviour. Indeed a radical approach to rehabilitative sentencing might not concentrate on the individual offender at all. Rather, it might see law-breaking as part and parcel of other social problems. [...]

When individual sentences *are* being considered, however, the notion that rehabilitation is only for poorer offenders should be abandoned. Every offender should have the chance to say if he or she thinks that there should be an element of rehabilitation in the sentence and in certain cases of recidivism an offender might even be coerced into accepting a rehabilitative order. [...] No order should be imposed, however, until the court has been assured by the probation service that, in the light of the offender's circumstances, such an order is *feasible*.

Sentence feasibility, social circumstances and the tariff

Whereas the principle of equality of impact raises questions about the possible inequality of pain or deprivation suffered by different offenders awarded the same punishment, the notion of sentence feasibility raises questions about the likelihood of extremely disadvantaged offenders being able successfully to complete *any* very demanding non-custodial order. [...]

The problem of sentence feasibility and social circumstances comes about primarily in two ways. First, because so many people are currently enduring domestic situations fractured by the pains of unemployment, low wages and poor housing. Second, because many areas of the country lack the communal facilities which provide for a decent standard of public life. Thus, while certain offenders might be perfectly willing to attempt compliance with specified non-custodial orders, their probation officers might rightly calculate that, given the tensions and frustrations already existing in their homes, the clients would be unlikely to complete

any order involving constant home calls, curfews or house arrest. Similarly, in other cases officers might know that while a lack of child-minding facilities would prevent some parents from doing community service, a dearth of public transport would equally prevent some other clients from getting to and from suitable schemes. Additionally it might also be unrealistic to expect emotionally and mentally damaged recidivist clients to complete a punitive, as opposed to a supportive, order. It would be desirable, therefore, that sentencers be obliged to accept a probation officer's assessment of the non-feasibility of a rigid non-custodial sentence in certain cases, and that, in the cases of offenders bearing multiple social disadvantage, they should attempt to do least harm by making orders that are totally supportive and non-punitive.

Equality of sentence impact

Even on a state-obligated model of corrections, many offenders, as well as being deemed suitable for some kind of rehabilitative element in their sentences, would also be judged as culpable and deserving of punishment. In some cases, moreover, the court would decide that though questions of rehabilitation did not arise, punishment would be necessary both to symbolize the state's abhorrence of the crime and to deter this offender and his/her potential imitators in the future. In such cases it is likely that the fine would remain the most favoured sentencing option and it is in relation to monetary penalties that questions of sentence impact are at their most difficult. [...]

A partial solution to the problem of differential sentence impact on offenders of differing means is to be found in the day fine system of some European countries. This could well be used in England to calculate fines in the cases of all but the very poor and the very rich. Andrew Ashworth (1983) gives a succinct description of the procedures involved.

For this system the courts must obtain information about the offender's annual income, together with information about his liabilities and any capital he may possess. In general the day fine is assessed at one thousandth of his annual income. Once this calculation has been completed the court can order him to pay so many day fines, the number being calculated according to the seriousness of the case. Thus the two factors, the seriousness of the case and the offender's means, are determined quite independently of each other, and both the number of day fines and the amount of each are announced in court.

(Ashworth, 1983: 288)

But, even if this system were to be introduced into the English courts, there would still be problems in relation to those too poor to pay a fine and those too rich to suffer deprivation as a result of any fine a court would be likely to impose. [...]

In reality, it is likely that offenders too poor to pay a fine are also those suffering from other social disadvantage and under a system of state-obligated rehabilitation, the court would have a duty to make an order that was at least in part rehabilitative, if in addition the court were to consider it desirable to include an element of retribution in the sentence, a community service order might be imposed with a condition of deferral until such time as the offender was receiving sufficient support to make the order feasible. At the other end of the scale, a progressive (rather than arithmetical) approach to day fines would help ensure that the final sum exacted would hurt the offender despite his or her great wealth (Ashworth, 1983:291).

A more democratic approach to sentencing

A state-obligated rehabilitation model [...] might specifically require

1 that prosecutors have the power to waive prosecution and ask for a rehabilitative order when an offender (having admitted guilt) is clearly in need of assistance and when no public good would be served by prosecution (see Carlen, 1983a)

2 that probation officers have the duty to object to the supervision of certain orders on grounds of their non-feasibility and that sentencers be required to justify in open court any over-ruling of a probation objection

3 that *all* sentences be justified in open court and that where a sentencer wishes to make a particular rehabilitative order but can not because of lack of facilities, a record to that effect be made and sent to a regional sentencing review committee.

Summary and conclusions

The major arguments of this chapter have been that

1 The criminal justice system should be used not only to punish criminals but also to redress some social injustices, or, failing that, to ensure that at least its sentencing policies do not increase social inequality.

2 Because fear of punishment is but one factor amongst many more positive ones which result in offenders becoming law-abiding, a purely punitive approach to sentencing (especially one involving imprisonment as the ultimate sanction) will do little to decrease crime and will certainly increase the prison population.

The specific reforms suggested in the latter part of the chapter have not been intended as a blueprint for a radically changed sentencing policy. They have merely been put forward to highlight four of the major impediments to a more rational approach. These impediments are

1 the continuing dominance of the justice model, even in the government's proposals for community-based punishments

2 the reluctance in practice for the courts to elevate sentence feasibility to a major sentencing principle

3 the similar reluctance, in practice, to ensure that the rich pay for their crimes; and the concomitant failure of courts to use to the full the already existing disabling measures that would limit the opportunities of rich business and other 'respectable' criminals to re-offend in future

4 the failure of governments to limit sentencing discretion and make criminal justice more democratic.

Implementation of a state-obligated rehabilitation model of sentencing would not be cheap. On the contrary, in the short term its full implementation would most likely cost as much as the present housing and maintenance of a prison population of over 50,000. But with a much reduced prison population, the initial costs of community schemes could be met. Once the initial capital outlay had been made, community projects would be much cheaper to run than the labour-intensive gaols. But there is no *very* cheap way of paying for the problems caused by the positive relationship between crime and inequality. The choice is between continuing to squander millions of pounds on prisons, or developing a rational system of criminal justice which could use the savings ensuing from a heavily reduced prison population to regenerate the communities where, too often,

victim and offender continue to live in fear, poverty and isolation long after the sentence of the court has been pronounced.

> *From P. Carlen, 'Crime, inequality and sentencing', in P. Carlen and D. Cook (eds)* Paying for Crime *(Milton Keynes: Open University Press), 1989, pp. 8–28.*

References

Ashworth, A. (1983) *Sentencing and Penal Policy*. London: Weidenfeld and Nicholson.

Beccaria, C. (1963) *On Crimes and Punishment*. Indianapolis, IN: Bobbs-Merrill.

Blom-Cooper, L. (1988) *The Penalty of Imprisonment*. London: Prison Reform Trust.

Carlen, P. (1983a) On rights and powers: Some notes on penal politics. In Garland, D. and Young, P. (Eds) *The Power to Punish*. London: Heinemann.

Cohen, S. (1985) Social control talk: Telling stories about correctional change. In Garland, D. and Young, P. (Eds) *The Power to Punish*. London: Heinemann.

Cullen, F. and Gilbert, K. (1982) *Reaffirming Rehabilitation*. Cincinatti, OH: Anderson Publishing.

Home Office (1986a) *The Sentence of the Court*. London: HMSO.

Home Office (1988a) *Punishment, Custody and the Community*, Cm 424. London: HMSO.

Hudson, B. (1987) *Justice Through Punishment*. London: Macmillan.

Von Hirsch, A. (1976) *Doing Justice*. New York: Hill & Wang.

27.2 The punitive city: notes on the dispersal of social control Stanley Cohen

What I want to do – largely for a sociological audience outside crime and justice professionals – is sort out some of the implications of the apparent changes in the formal social control apparatus over the last decade or so. I will concentrate on crime and juvenile delinquency though there are important tendencies – some parallel and some quite different – in such areas as drug abuse and mental illness which require altogether separate comment. I will be drawing material mainly from the United States and Britain – countries which have developed a centralized crime control apparatus embedded in a more (Britain) or less (United States) highly developed commitment to welfare and more (United States) or less (Britain) sophisticated ideologies and techniques of treatment and rehabilitation.

From prison to community

Our current system of deviancy control originated in those great transformations which took place from the end of the 18th to the beginning of the 19th centuries: firstly the development of a centralized state apparatus for the control of crime and the care of dependency; secondly the increasing differentiation of the deviant and dependent into separate types each with its own attendant corpus of 'scientific' knowledge and accredited experts; and finally the increased segregation of deviants and dependents into 'asylums': mental hospitals, prisons, reformatories and other such closed, purpose-built institutions for treatment and punishment. [...]

We are now living through what *appears* to be a reversal of this first Great Transformation. The ideological consensus about the desirability and necessity of the segregative asylum – questioned before but never really undermined[1] – has been broken. The attack on prisons (and more dramatically and with more obvious results on mental hospitals) became widespread from the mid 1960s, was found throughout the political spectrum and was partially reflected in such indices as declining rates of imprisonment. At the end of the 18th century, asylums and prisons were places of the *last* resort; by the mid-19th century they became places of the *first* resort, the preferred solution to problems of deviancy and dependency. By the end of the 1960s they looked like once again becoming places of the *last* resort. The extraordinary notion of abolition, rather than mere reform became common talk. With varying degrees of enthusiasm and actual measurable consequences, officials in Britain, the United States and some Western European countries, became committed to the policy labelled 'decarceration': the state-sponsored closing down of asylums, prisons and reformatories. This apparent reversal of the Great Incarcerations of the 19th century was hailed as the beginning of a golden age – a form of utopianism whose ironies cannot escape anyone with an eye on history: 'There is a curious historical irony here, for the *adoption* of the asylum, whose *abolition* is now supposed to be attended with such universally beneficent consequences, aroused an almost precisely parallel set of millenial expectations among its advocates'.[2]

The irony goes even further. For just at the historical moment when every commonplace critique of 'technological' or 'post-industrial' or 'mass' society mourned the irreplaceable loss of the traditional *Gemeinschaft* community, so a new mode of deviancy control was advocated whose success rested on this very same notion of community. [...]

In the literature on community treatment itself,[3] two sets of assumptions are repeated with the regularity of a religious catechism. The first set is seen either as a matter of common sense, 'what everybody knows' or the irrefutable result of empirical research: 1) prisons and juvenile institutions are (in the weak version) simply ineffective: they neither successfully deter nor rehabilitate. In the strong version, they actually make things worse by strengthening criminal commitment; 2) community alternatives are much less costly and 3) they are more humane than any institution can be – prisons are cruel, brutalizing and beyond reform.

Their time has come. Therefore: community alternatives 'must obviously be better', 'should at least be given a chance' or 'can't be worse'. [...]

I shall take the term 'community control' to cover almost any form of formal social control outside the walls of traditional adult and juvenile institutions. There are two separate, but overlapping strategies: firstly, those various forms of intensive intervention located 'in the community': sentencing options which serve as intermediate alternatives to being sent to an institution or later options to release from institutions and secondly, those programs set up at some preventive, policing or pre-trial stage to divert offenders from initial or further processing by the conventional systems of justice. Behind these specific policies lies an overall commitment to almost anything which sounds like increasing community responsibility for the control of crime and delinquency.

Blurring the boundaries

The segregated and insulated institution made the actual business of deviancy control invisible, but it did make its boundaries obvious enough. Whether prisons were built in the middle of cities, out in the remote countryside or on deserted islands, they had clear spatial boundaries to mark off the normal from the deviant. These spatial boundaries were reinforced by ceremonies of social exclusion. Those outside could wonder what went on behind the walls, those inside could think about the 'outside world'. Inside/outside, guilty/innocent, freedom/captivity, imprisoned/released – these were all meaningful distinctions.

In today's world of community corrections, these boundaries are no longer as clear. There is, we are told, a 'correctional continuum' or a 'correctional spectrum': criminals and delinquents might be found anywhere in these spaces. So fine – and at the same time so indistinct – are the gradations along the continuum, that it is by no means easy to answer such questions as where the prison ends and the community begins or just why any deviant is to be found at any particular point. Even the most dedicated spokesmen for the community treatment have some difficulty in specifying just what 'the community' is. [...]

Even the most cursory examination of the new programs, reveals that many varieties of the more or less intensive and structured 'alternatives' are virtually indistinguishable from the real thing.

A great deal of energy and ingenuity is being devoted to this problem of definition: just how isolated and confining does an institution have to be before it is a prison rather than, say a residential community facility? Luckily for us all, criminologists have got this matter well in hand and are spending a great deal of time and money on such questions. They are busy devising quantitative measures of indices such as degree of control, linkages, relationships, support – and we can soon look forward to standardized scales for assigning programs along an institutionalization – normalization continuum.[4]

But, alas, there are not just untidy loose ends which scientific research will one day tie up. The ideology of the new movement quite deliberately and explicitly demands that boundaries should not be made too clear. The metaphor of 'crumbling walls' implies an undifferentiated open space. The main British prison reform group, the Howard League, once called for steps to '... restore the prison to the community and the community to the prison' and less rhetorically, here is an early enthusiast for a model 'Community Correction Centre':

> The line between being 'locked up' and 'free' is purposely indistinct because it must be drawn differently for each individual. Once the client is out of Phase I, where all clients enter and where they are all under essentially custodial control, he may be 'free' for some activities but still 'locked up' for others.[5]

There is no irony intended in using inverted commas for such words as 'free' and 'locked up' or in using such euphemisms as 'essentially custodial control'. This sort of blurring – deliberate or unintentional – may be found throughout the complicated networks of 'diversion' and 'alternatives' which are now being set up. The half-way house might serve as a good example. These agencies called variously, 'residential treatment centers', 'rehabilitation residences', 'reintegration centers' or (with the less flowery language preferred in Britain) simply 'hostels', invariably become special institutional domains themselves. They might be located in a whole range of odd settings – private houses, converted motels, the grounds of hospitals, the dormitories of university campuses or even within the walls of prisons themselves. Their programs[6] reproduce rules – for example about security, curfew, permitted visitors, drugs – which are close to those of the institution itself. Indeed it becomes

difficult to distinguish a very 'open' prison – with liberal provisions for work release, home release, outside educational programs – from a very 'closed' half-way house. The house may be half-way *in* – for those too serious to be left at home, but not serious enough for the institution and hence a form of 'diversion' – or half-way *out* – for those who can be released from the institution but are not yet 'ready' for the open community, hence a form of 'after care'. To confuse the matter even further, the same center is sometimes used for both these purposes, with different rules for the half way in inmates and the half way out inmates. [...]

We are seeing, then, not just the proliferation of agencies and services, finely calibrated in terms of degree of coerciveness or intrusion or unpleasantness. The uncertainties are more profound than this: voluntary or coercive, formal or informal, locked up or free, guilty or innocent. Those apparently absurd administrative and research questions – when is a prison a prison or a community a community? is the alternative an alternative? who is half-way in and who is three-quarter way out? – beckon to a future when it will be impossible to determine who exactly is enmeshed in the social control system – and hence subject to its jurisdiction and surveillance – at any one time.

Thinning the mesh and widening the net

On the surface, a major ideological thrust in the move against institutions derives from a desire to limit state intervention. Whether arising from the supposed failures of the treatment model, or the legal argument about the over-reach of the law and the necessity to limit the criminal sanction, or the implicit non-interventionism of labelling theory, or a general disenchantment with paternalism, or simply the pragmatic case for easing the burdens on the system – the eventual message looked the same: the state should do less rather than more. It is ironical then – though surely the irony is too obvious even to be called this – that the major results of the new movements towards 'community' and 'diversion' have been to increase rather than decrease the *amount* of intervention directed at many groups of deviants in the system and, probably, to increase rather than decrease the total *number* who get into the system in the first place. In other words: 'alternatives' become not alternatives at all but new progams which supplement the existing system or else expand it by attracting new populations.

I will refer to these two overlapping possibilities as 'thinning the mesh' and 'widening the net' respectively. No one who has studied the results of such historical innovations as probation and parole should be surprised by either of these effects. [...]

Let us first examine community alternatives to incarceration. The key index of 'success' is not simply the proliferation of such programs, but the question of whether they are replacing or merely providing supplementary appendages to the conventional system of incarceration. The statistical evidence is by no means easy to decipher but it is clear, both from Britain and America, that rates of incarceration – particularly in regard to juveniles – are not at all declining as rapidly as one might expect and in some spheres are even increasing. Critically – as one evaluation suggests[7] – the 'alternatives' are not, on the whole, being used for juveniles at the 'deep end' of the system, i.e. those who really would have been sent to institutions before. When the strategy is used for 'shallow end' offenders – minor or first offenders whose chances of incarceration would have been slight – then the incarceration rates will not be affected. [...]

Leaving aside the question of the exact effects on the rest of the system, there is little doubt that a substantial number – perhaps the majority – of those subjected to the new programs, will be subjected to a degree of intervention higher than they would have received under previous non-custodial options like fines, conditional discharge or ordinary probation. [...]

The paradox throughout all this is that the more benign, attractive and successful the program is defined – especially if it uses the shallow end principle, as most do – the more it will be used and the wider it will cast its net. [...]

Turning now to the more explicit forms of diversion, it is once again clear that the term, like the term 'alternatives' is not quite what it implies. Diversion has been hailed as the most radical application of the non-intervention principle short of complete decriminalization. The grand rationale is to restrict the full force of the criminal justice process to more serious offences and to either eliminate or substantially minimize penetration for all others.[8] The strategy has received the greatest attention in the juvenile field: a remarkable development, because the central agency here, the juvenile court, was *itself* the product of a reform movement aimed at 'diversion'.

Clearly, all justice systems – particularly juvenile – have always contained a substantial amount of diversion. Police discretion has been widely used to screen juveniles: either right out of the system by dropping charges, informally reprimanding or cautioning, or else informal referral to social services agencies. What has now happened, to a large degree, is that these discretionary and screening powers have been formalized and extended – and in the process, quite transformed. The net widens to include those who, if the program had not been available would either not have been processed at all or would have been placed on options such as traditional probation. Again, the more benevolent the new agencies appear, the more will be diverted there by encouragement or coercion. And – through the blurring provided by the welfare net – this will happen to many not officially adjudicated as delinquent as well. There will be great pressure to work with parts of the population not previously 'reached'.

All this can be most clearly observed in the area of police diversion of juveniles. Where the police used to have two options – screen right out (the route for by far the *majority* of encounters) or process formally – they now have the third option of diversion into a program. Diversion can then be used as an alternative to screening and not an alternative to processing.[9] The proportion selected will vary. [...]

The key to understanding this state of affairs lies in the distinction between *traditional* or *true* diversion – removing the juvenile from the system altogether by screening out (no further treatment, no service, no follow up) – and the *new* diversion which entails screening plus program: formal penetration is minimized by referral to programs in the system or related to it.[10] Only traditional diversion is true diversion in the sense of diverting *from*. The new diversion diverts – for better or worse – *into* the system. [...]

Whatever the eventual pattern of the emergent social control system, it should be clear that such policies as 'alternatives' in no way represent a victory for the anti-treatment lobby or an 'application' of labelling theory. Traditional deviant populations are being processed in a different way or else new populations are being caught up in the machine.

Masking and disguising

The softness of the machine might also be more apparent than real. It became common place in historical analyses to suggest that the more benign parts of the system such as the juvenile court[11]

masked their most coercive intentions and consequences. This conclusion might apply with equal
force to the current strategies of diversion and
alternatives. Even more than their historical
antecedents, they employ a social work rather than
legalistic rationale; they are committed to the principle of blurring the boundaries of social control
and they use the all-purpose slogan of 'community' which cannot but sound benign.

There can be little doubt that the intentions
behind the new movement and – more to the
point – its end results, are often humane, compassionate and helpful. Most clients, deviants or
offenders would probably prefer this new variety to
the stark option of the prison. But this argument is
only valid if the alternatives are real ones. [...]

Even when the alternatives *are* real ones, it is
not self evident that they are always more humane
and less stigmatizing just because, in some sense,
they are 'in the community'. Community agencies,
for example, might use a considerable amount of
more or less traditional custody and often without
legal justification. [...]

Disguised detention, though, is probably not
a major overall source of masking. More important
is the bureaucratic generation of new treatment criteria which might allow for more unchecked
coercion than at first appears. In a system with low
visibility and low accountability, there is less room
for such niceties as due process and legal rights.
Very often, for example, 'new diversion' (mini-
mization of penetration) occurs by deliberately
avoiding due process: the client proceeds through
the system on the assumption or admission of
guilt. Indeed the deliberate conceptual blurring
between 'diversion' and 'prevention' explicitly calls
for an increase in this sort of non-legal discretion.

All this, of course, still leaves open the question of whether the end result – however
mystifying some of the routes that led to it – is
actually experienced as more humane and helpful
by the offender. There is little evidence either way
on this, beyond the rather bland common sense
assumption that most offenders would prefer not
to be 'locked up'. What is likely, is that deep end
projects – those that are genuine alternatives to
incarceration – have to make a trade-off between
treatment goals (which favour the integrated community setting) and security goals which favour
isolation. The trade-off under these conditions will
tend to favour security resulting in programs

which simulate or mimic the very features of the
institution they set out to replace.

Absorption, penetration, re-integration

The asylum represented not just isolation and confinement – like quarantining the infected – but a
ritual of physical exclusion. Without the possibility
of actual banishment to another society, the asylum had to serve the classic social function of
scapegoating. The scapegoat of ancient legend was
an animal driven to the wilderness, bearing away
the sins of the community.

In the new ideology of corrections, there is
no real or symbolic wilderness – just the
omnipresent community into which the deviant
has to be unobtrusively 'integrated' or 'reinte-
grated'. The blurring of social control implies both
the deeper penetration of social control into the
social body and the easing of any measures of
exclusion, or status degradation. [...]

In the most immediate sense, what is being
proposed is a greater direct involvement of the
family, the school and various community agencies
in the day to day business of prevention, treatment, and resocialization. This implies something
more profound than simply using more volunteers
or increasing reporting rates. It implies some sort
of reversal of the presumption in positivist criminology that the delinquent is a different and alien
being. Deviance rather is with us, woven into the
fabric of social life and it must be 'brought back
home'. Parents, peers, schools, the neighbourhood,
even the police should dedicate themselves to
keeping the deviant out of the formal system. He
must be absorbed back into the community and
not processed by official agencies.[12] [...]

Needless to say, there are profound limits to
the whole ideology of integration – as indeed there
are to all such similar patterns I have described.
The 'community' – as indicated by the standard
local reaction to say, half-way houses or day centers being located in their own neighbourhood – is
not entirely enthusiastic about such 'integration'.
In the immediate future the segregation of the
deviant will remain as the central part of the control apparatus. The established professionals,
agencies and service bureaucracies are not going to
give up so easily their hard won empires of 'expertise' and identity in the name of some vague
notion of integration. Nevertheless at the rhetori-

cal and ideological levels, the move to a new model of deviancy control has been signalled.

Conclusion – towards the punitive city

These emerging patterns of social control – dispersal, penetration, blurring, absorption, widening – must be seen as no more than patterns: representations of what is yet to be fully constructed. [...]

It is, eventually, the sheer proliferation and elaboration of these other systems of control – rather than the attack on prison itself – which impresses. What is happening is a literal reproduction on a wider societal level of those astonishingly complicated systems of classification – the 'atlases of vice' – inside the 19th century prison. New categories and subcategories of deviance and control are being created under our eyes. All these agencies – legal and quasi-legal, administrative and professional – are marking out their own territories of jurisdiction, competence and referral. Each set of experts produces its own 'scientific' knowledge: screening devices, diagnostic tests, treatment modalities, evaluation scales. All this creates new categories and the typifications which fill them: where there was once talk about the 'typical' prisoner, first offender or hardened recidivist, now there will be typical 'clients' of half-way houses, or community correctional centers, typical divertees or predelinquents. These creatures are then fleshed out – in papers, research proposals, official reports – with sub-systems of knowledge and new vocabularies; locking up becomes 'intensive placement', dossiers become 'anecdotal records', rewards and punishments become 'behavioural contracts'. [...]

The overwhelming impression is one of bustling, almost *frenzied* activity: all these wonderful new things are being done to this same old group of troublemakers (with a few new ones allowed in). [...]

The logic of this master pattern – dispersal, penetration, spreading out as opposed to its particular current forms, is not at all new. Its antecedents can be traced though, not to the model which its apologists cite – the idyllic pre-industrial rural community – but to a somewhat later version of social control, a version which *in theory* was an alternative to the prison. When, from the end of the 18th century, punishment started entering deeper into the social body, the alternative vision to the previous great concentrated spectacles of public torture, was of the dispersal of control through 'hundreds of tiny theatres of punishment'.[13] The 18th century reformers dreamed of dispersal and diversity but this vision of the punitive city was never to be fully realized. Instead punishment became concentrated in the coercive institution, a single uniform penalty to be varied only in length. The earlier 'projects of docility' which Foucault describes – the techniques of order, discipline and regulation developed in schools, monasteries, workshops, the army – could only serve as models. Panopticism (surveillance, discipline) began to spread: as disciplinary establishments increased, '...their mechanisms have a certain tendency to become "de-institutionalized", to emerge from the closed fortresses in which they once functioned and to circulate in a "free" state; the massive compact disciplines are broken down into flexible methods of control, which may be transferred and adapted'.[14]

This principle of 'indefinite discipline' – judgements, examinations and observations which would never end – represented the new mode of control as much as the public execution had represented the old. Only in the prison, though, could this utopia be realized in a pure, physical form. The 'new' move into the community is merely a continuation of the overall pattern established in the 19th century. The proliferation of new experts and professionals, the generation of specialized domains of scientific knowledge, the creation of complicated classification systems, the establishment of a network of agencies surrounding the court and the prison – all these developments marked the beginning a century ago of the widening of the 'carceral circle' or 'carceral archipelago'.

The continuous gradation of institutions then – the 'correctional' continuum' – is not new. What is new is the scale of the operation and the technologies (drugs, surveillance and information gathering techniques) which facilitate the blurring and penetration which I described. Systems of medicine, social work, education, welfare take on supervisory and judicial functions, while the penal apparatus itself becomes more influenced by medicine, education, psychology.[15] This new system of subtle gradations in care, control, punishment and treatment is indeed far from the days of public execution and torture – but it is perhaps not quite as far as Foucault suggests from that early reform vision of the punitive city. The ideology of community is trying once more to increase the visibility – if not the theatricality – of social control. True, we must not know quite what is happening – treatment or punishment, public or private, locked up or free, inside or outside, voluntary or coercive – but we must know that something is happening, here, in our very own community.

From S. Cohen, 'The punitive city: notes on the dispersal of social control', Contemporary Crises, 3(4): 339–363.

Notes

1 Scull, A. (1977) *Decarceration: Community Treatment and the Deviant.* London: Prentice Hall, documents both the presence at the end of the 19th century of the equivalent of today's liberal/social scientific critique of institutions and the reasons for the failure of this earlier attack. For him, the origins of current policy lie in certain changing features of welfare capitalism. Crudely expressed: it no longer 'suits' the state to maintain segregative modes of control based on the asylum. In relative terms (and hence the appeal to fiscal conservatives) such modes become costly, while the alternative of welfare payments allowing subsistence in the community, is easier to justify and can be sold on humanitarian and scientific grounds. Scull's argument is a useful corrective to accounts purely at the level of ideas, but it places too much importance on the supposed fiscal crisis, it is less relevant to Britain and America and far less relevant for crime and delinquency than mental illness. In regard to crime and delinquency the picture is not the non-interventionist one Scull implies but – as this paper suggests – the development of parallel systems of control.

2 Scull, op. cit., p.42.

3 The most informative sources in the United States would be journals such as *Crime and Delinquency* and *Federal Probation* from the mid-sixties onwards and the various publications from bodies such as the National Institute of Mental Health and, later, the Law Enforcement Assistance Administration. A representative collection of such material is Perlstein, G.R. and Phelps, T.R. (eds.) (1975) *Alternatives to Prisons: Community Based Corrections.* Pacific Palisades, CA: Goodyear Publishing Co. In Britain the ideology of community control has been slower and less obvious in its development, though it can be traced in various Home Office publications from the end of the 1960s. See also Blom-Cooper, L. (ed.)(1974) *Progress in Penal Reform.* Oxford: Oxford University Press and Tutt, N. (ed.) (1978) *Alternative Strategies for Coping with Crime.* Oxford: Basil Blackwell.

4 Coates, R.B., *et al.* (1976). Social Climate, Extent of Community Linkages and Quality of Community Linkages: The Institutionalisation Normalisation Continuum, unpublished Ms, Centre for Criminal Justice, Harvard Law School.

5 Bradley, H.B. (1969). Community based treatment for young adult offenders. *Crime and Delinquency*, 15(3): 369.

6 For a survey, see Seiter, R.P. *et al.* (1977) *Halfway House.* Washington, DC: National Institute of Law Enforcement and Criminal Justice, LEAA.

7 Rutherford, A. and Bengur, O. (1976). *Community Based Alternatives to Juvenile Incarceration.* Washington, DC: National Institute of Law Enforcement and Criminal Justice, LEAA.

8 A clear statement of this rationale and the legal problems in implementing it, is to be found in Law Reform Commission of Canada (1975) *Working Paper No. 7: Diversion*, Ottawa: Law Reform Commission of Canada.

9 Dunford, F.W. (1977) Police diversion – An illusion? *Criminology*, 15 (3): 135–352.

10 Rutherford, A. and McDermott, R. (1976) *Juvenile Diversion.* Washington, DC: National Institute of Law Enforcement and Criminal Justice, LEAA.

11 See, especially, Platt, A. M. (1969) *The Child Savers: The Invention of Delinquency.* Chicago: Chicago University Press.

12 For typical statements about absorption, see Carter, R.M. (1972) The diversion of offenders. *Federal Probation*, 36 (4): 31–36.

13 Foucault, M. (1977) *Discipline and Punish: The Birth of the Prison.* London: Allen Lane, p. 113.

14 *Ibid.*, p. 211.

15 *Ibid.*, p.306.

27.3 The dispersal of discipline thesis
Anthony Bottoms

The dispersal of discipline thesis

I shall begin with an analysis of Cohen's essay on 'The punitive city' (1979b). This starts from an acceptance of the existence of the so-called 'great transformation' of punishment from the corporal to the carceral at the end of the eighteenth century and into the nineteenth, as described by Rothman (1971), Foucault (1977a) and Rusche and Kirchheimer (1939). The thesis then argued by Cohen is essentially a more elaborated version of that which he put tersely in an earlier essay:

> Foucault described one historical take-off in terms of the move from 'simple' punishment to the concentrated surveillance of the asylum. We are living through another change: from the *concentration* to the *dispersal* of social control.
>
> (Cohen, 1977: 227, italics in original)

This 'dispersal of social control' of course refers to the community-corrections movement. Much of Cohen's concern, in his 1979 article, is to describe in detail (and, for the most part, very tellingly) some of the key features of this movement. These include:

1 *'Blurring'*. This is the breakdown between the old and simple institutional/non-institutional distinction, as institutions develop leave programmes, hostels, etc., and community agencies develop residential and day-attendance facilities. These developments 'beckon to a future when it will be impossible to determine who exactly is enmeshed in the social control system' (Cohen, 1979b: 346).

2 *'Widening the net'*. This concept brings within the ambit of an allegedly beneficial community programme not only those who would otherwise have been the subject of formal social control (for example, in institutions), but also others who would not (for example, who would have been given an informal warning). This development therefore acts 'to increase rather than decrease the total *number* who get into the system in the first place' (1979b: 347, italics in original).

3 *'Thinning the mesh'*. Although this fishing metaphor is more obscure than the previous one, its import is that the new community programmes may increase the *amount* of intervention directed at many deviants in the system. 'There is little doubt that a substantial number – perhaps the majority – of those subjected to the new programs will be subjected to a degree of intervention higher than they would have received under previous non-custodial options like fines, conditional discharge or ordinary probation' (1979b: 347).

4 *'Penetration'*. This concept essentially sums up Cohen's thesis: the *formal* social-control agencies of the state are seen as penetrating more deeply into the *informal* networks of society. In the end, it is 'the sheer proliferation and elaboration of these other systems of control – rather than the attack on the prison itself – which impresses' (1979b: 358). Moreover, these developments are throwing up whole new groups of professionals, and 'each set of experts produces its own "scientific" knowledge: screening devices, diagnostic tests, treatment modalities, evaluation scales' (1979b: 358).

In the last two pages of his article, Cohen relates his thesis to that of Foucault in *Discipline and Punish* (1977a). Just as Foucault had seen 'discipline' as the key concept in the emergence of the prison as the dominant form of punishment at the beginning of the nineteenth century, so Cohen, after speaking of 'indefinite discipline', asserts boldly that 'the 'new' move into the community is *merely* a continuation of the overall pattern established in the nineteenth century' (1979b: 359, my italics). [...]

Cohen recognises, of course, that Foucault in *Discipline and Punish* spoke of discipline as a new form of power, applied not only in the prison, but also in other areas of society: 'is it surprising that prisons resemble factories, schools, barracks, hospitals, which all resemble prisons?' (Foucault, 1977a: 228). Thus Cohen sees the new alleged 'dispersal of social control' as merely a continuation of this pattern into new areas. But this presupposes that all the dispersed forms of social control are *disciplinary*, in Foucault's sense; and this may be questioned.

In approaching this issue, it is important to be very clear about the concepts used. In one of the most illuminating passages of *Discipline and Punish*, Foucault (1977a: 130–1) draws some clear contrasts between three ideal types of punishment mechanisms (what he calls 'technologies of power') available at the end of the eighteenth century. These may be described as the *corporal*, that exemplified in the old punishment system of the *ancien régime*; then the *juridical*, that proposed by the classical reformers such as Beccaria (1764), but never generally implemented; and finally the *carceral*, or that which found expression in the prison, the overwhelmingly dominant punishment of the nineteenth century. In a summary sentence, Foucault expresses succinctly the main differences between these three mechanisms; these I have systematised and slightly elaborated to produce Table 27.3.1.

There are crucial differences between the juridical and the carceral systems. In the juridical system, just enough punishment is applied to act as a deterrent to the offender and to others; punishment must, as Beccaria firmly insisted, be always *preventive* in ultimate intent. But the intended preventive message of punishment is provided simply by representations and signs ('behave or you will be punished', etc.); there is no specific penal administrative apparatus designed to mould offenders into obedient subjects. Moreover, when the punishment is completed (and, of course, for the classical jurists it must be of a fixed duration,

proportionate to the seriousness of the offence), then the punished subject rejoins society as a full member. [...]

In the contemporary context, a seemingly trivial but nevertheless very instructive example of this kind of juridical punishment can be seen in the game of ice hockey. Here, a player who breaks the rules may be given a 'penalty'; this is a term of fixed duration (perhaps two minutes or five minutes) during which he must leave the ice. For this period, he is placed in a 'penalty box', a special spatial area at the side of the rink, in clear view of the public but symbolically placed on the opposite side of the ice from the other members of the offenders' team who are awaiting their turn to play. Thus by symbolic representation the infraction of the player is marked, both for himself and for others; and, since teams do not wish to lose players, the overall purpose of the system is clearly to prevent breaches of the rules of the game. Once the player has 'sat out' for the required period, however, he may return to the ice without disgrace: he is now a 'requalified subject'. As Foucault (1977a: 104 ff.) explains the project of the classical reformers, punishment was to be *school* rather than *ceremony* (for the offender, and especially others, to learn to obey); punishment should be public, the better to impress others; and punishment should be as unarbitrary as possible (to protect the liberties of the citizens in the social contract). To comply with all of these requirements, there must be a complex of punitive signs (or coded sets of representations) which both reduces the desire that makes crime attractive, and increases the interest that makes the penalty feared, to a just sufficient

Table 27.3.1 Central features of three mechanisms of punishment

	Corporal	Judicial	Carceral
(a) Locus of the power to punish	Sovereign and his force	Social body	Administrative apparatus
(b) Intended residual object of the power to punish	Ritual marks of vengance	Signs (coded sets of representations)	Traces (behavioural habits of obedience)
(c) Mode of penalty	Ceremony of power	Representation	Exercise
(d) Status of offender	Vanquished enemy	Juridical subject in process of requalification	Individual subject to immediate coercion
(e) Body/soul	Tortured body	Soul with manipulated representations	Body subjected to training (to produce compliance of the soul)

Source: Adaptation of passage in Foucault (1977a: 130–1).

extent (but no more) to preserve the overall social order. This message must be widely disseminated throughout society:

> This, then, is how one must imagine the punitive city. At the crossroads, in the gardens, at the side of roads being repaired or bridges built, in workshops open to all, in the depths of mines that may be visited, will be hundreds of tiny theatres of punishment.

(Foucault, 1977a: 113)

But none of this is *discipline*, in Foucault's sense. To return to the ice-hockey example, no one does anything to the offending player while he is in the penalty box; he just sits there. In the ideal project of the carceral system of punishment, on the other hand, there is an explicit apparatus of punishment established whereby the offender is intendedly *trained*. The forms of this prison training may vary, for example, from *religious exercises* to *work* to *schooling* to *quasi-medical treatment*; but in each case, specific exercises are performed with and upon the offender. Like the classicists' juridical punishment, all this is intendedly preventive; but 'what one is trying to restore in this technique of correction is not so much the juridical subject, who is caught up in the fundamental interests of the social pact, but the obedient subject, the individual subjected to habits, rules, orders, an authority that is exercised continually around him and upon him, and which he must allow to function automatically in him' (Foucault, 1977a: 128–9). Thus, in the carceral project, 'work on the prisoner's soul must be carried out as often as possible' (1977a: 125), for disciplinary punishment's intended corrective effect is *'obtained directly through the mechanics of a training'* (1977a: 180, my italics). It is this *training* which requires knowledge of the offender as a whole person (and not just as someone who can be placed into a penalty box), with the correlative apparatus of expertise, judgements, professionalism and so forth.

Cohen (1979b: 360) is aware that Foucault draws some distinctions between the classical reformers and the prison project, but he does not by any means fully explicate the presence of discipline (or coercive soul-training) in the one scheme and its absence from the other. Thus, although the main argument of his paper leads up to a description of the new community-corrections movement as 'indefinite *discipline*' and as '*merely* a continuation of the overall pattern established in the nineteenth century' (1979b: 359, my italics), Cohen nevertheless actually derives the title of his paper from Foucault's passage about the 'punitive city' of the classical reformers, as cited above. Indeed, he even (and most incongruously) places the passage itself in a place of honour at the beginning of his argument.

I have drawn particular attention to this contrast between the juridical and the carceral projects because of its relevance to an understanding of contemporary punishment. For when we juxtapose this juridical/carceral contrast with [contemporary] developments, immediate doubt is cast upon the universal applicability of Cohen's 'dispersal of discipline' thesis. Cohen nowhere mentions the growth of the fine, and the modern fine is clearly more of a classical than a disciplinary punishment.[1] Neither the rise of the fine, nor the growth of compensation, nor the general increase in penalties not involving supervision by a penal agent look remotely congruent with the general thesis of a thrust towards 'indefinite discipline'.

Community service, however, appears to be an altogether different case. [...] It therefore merits some close attention. Cohen says that 'the stress on community absorption has found one of its most attractive possibilities' in the community service order; it is attractive because it 'appeals not just to the soft ideology of community absorption but the more punitive objectives of restitution and compensation' (1979: 357). Mathiesen refers to the British experience with the community service order as tending, for a slight majority of recipients, to be imposed in place of another non-custodial sentence rather than in place of prison (citing here Pease *et al.*, 1977). Thus, argues Mathiesen, 'it constitutes an increase rather than a decrease of the total criminal justice control system' or in other words, in Cohen's terms, it is an example of 'thinning the mesh'.

Both authors undeniably have a point. Community service does sometimes have a 'thinning mesh' effect (for example, in replacing the fine); and some of its specific work projects ('helping in geriatric wards ...painting and decorating the houses of various handicapped groups, building children's playgrounds etc.' as Cohen puts it) do look like punishment penetrating deeply into the informal social fabric. Nevertheless, we do need to ask one crucial question: is this an extension of *discipline*, in Foucault's sense?

Here we must go back to *Discipline and Punish* once again. There we find Foucault noting that the juridical reformers 'almost always proposed public works as one of the best possible penalties' (1977a: 109). 'Public works' as a penalty meant two things;

it signified the collective interest in the punishment, and also its visible, verifiable character. Later, Foucault draws a sharp contrast between the classical reformers and the carceral project so far as the link between work and punishment is concerned. For the reformers, work in prison or in public works projects could be 'an example for the public or a useful reparation for society' (1977a: 240), but in the carceral project:

> Penal labour must be seen as *the very machinery that transforms* the violent, agitated, unreflective convict into a part that plays its role with perfect regularity. The prison is not a workshop; it is, it must be of itself, a machine whose convict-workers are both the cogs and the products.
>
> (Foucault, 1977a: 242, my italics)

When we look at community service against this background, to which model does it more closely approximate – that of public works or penal labour? A clue may be gleaned from considering a passage by Warren Young (1979) in which he notes three distinctions between what he describes as the respective 'modes of rehabilitation' attempted under a probation order and a community service order:

> First, the traditional approach of the probation service, based essentially on social casework principles (however they are for the time being defined) has been preoccupied with the offender's shortcomings and failures ... The community service order, on the other hand, is concerned with utilising the positive attributes of the offender. In essence, it is an ability-oriented rather than a problem-oriented approach... Secondly, while the requirements of the probation order are normally fulfilled within the sanctuary of the office or home interview, work under the community service order is usually performed in full view of the outside community... Thirdly, the community service order has a fixed and limited content directed towards the fulfilment of a clearly defined objective ordered by the court . . in stark contrast to the vague, diffuse and often global objectives of the probation order.
>
> (Young, 1979: 40-1)

This statement is probably rather too precise, for we know from elsewhere that community service is a concept sufficiently flexible to develop in a number of different directions in different local areas (Pease and McWilliams, 1980: esp. ch 9). Nevertheless, in the context of the present discus-

sion Young's statement is of great interest. Developments away from preoccupation with the offender's shortcomings, towards a more public penality and towards greater precision of punishment are *precisely* what one would expect, if a disciplinary project (in Foucault's terms) were being eroded and replaced by a more juridical one. This view is reinforced when one considers aspects of the choice of work placement in community service, as discussed by Pease and McWilliams (1980: 22–4). They note that in most local areas 'the work placement is largely chosen by the offender rather than by the organiser'; that in all areas the offender will be shown a list of tasks and asked which interests him most; and that there is everywhere an implication that his choice will be a reasoned one, consistent with a view of the offender as an autonomous moral actor. None of this looks much like 'discipline'.

The conclusion should not be overstated. In the first place, community service is still in its infancy and could yet be developed in a more disciplinary form. Secondly, there is known to be substantial local variation in the way this penalty is administered. Thirdly, it is possible that with rising unemployment levels magistrates will increasingly intend community service as disciplinary for unemployed offenders, even if the mechanism of the application of the penalty does not appear specifically disciplinary in its actual administration. Nevertheless, despite these caveats, it is safe to conclude that community service is rather less disciplinary than Cohen at least supposes.

If the foregoing is correct, the following conclusions may be drawn. First, none of the major penal developments [such as] the growth of the fine, compensation and community service are fully consistent with the 'dispersal of discipline' thesis, for none of them is primarily disciplinary. Secondly, although community service may not be primarily disciplinary, it does appear to involve some of the specific mechanisms which Cohen describes, namely, 'thinning the mesh' and 'community absorption'. [...] The juxtaposition of these two main conclusions suggests that we need a different kind of theoretical apparatus to the one Cohen employs, if we are successfully to explain some of the developments which he describes.

From A.E. Bottoms, 'Neglected features of contemporaray penal systems,' in D. Garland and P.Young (eds) The Power to Punish (Aldershot: Gower), 1983. pp 173–180).

Note

1 Because the fine is calculable, public and potentially free from arbitrariness, it accords well with the tenets of the classical school; hence it was attractive to the eighteenth century reformers, although they saw a number of practical difficulties in its administration.

I have, however, deliberately limited my comment to the 'modern fine', because in an earlier era the fine was often so closely connected with imprisonment through the default mechanism: in England and Wales, in 1910 almost 20 per cent of all persons fined were eventually imprisoned for default, but by 1940 this figure had dropped to 1 per cent.

References

Beccaria, C. (1764) *On Crimes and Punishments*, London: F. Newbery.

Cohen, S. (1977) Prisons and the future of control systems, in M. Fitzgerald, P. Halmos, J. Muncie and D. Zeldin (eds) *Welfare in Action*, London: RKP.

Cohen, S. (1979b) The punitive city: notes on the dispersal of social control, *Contemporary Crises*, 3: 339–63.

Foucault, M. (1977a) *Discipline and Punish*, Harmondsworth: Penguin.

Pease, K., Billingham, S. and Earnshaw, I. (1977) *Community Service Assessed in 1976*, London: Home Office.

Pease, K. and McWilliams, B. (1980) (eds) *Community Service by Order*, Edinburgh: Scottish Academic Press.

Rothman, D. (1971) *The Discovery of the Asylum*, Boston: Little Brown.

Rusche, G. and Kirchheimer, O. (1939) *Punishment and Social Structure*, New York: Columbia University Press.

Young, W. (1979) *Community Service Orders: The Development and Use of a New Penal Measure*, London: Heinemann.

27.4 Understanding the growth in the prison population in England and Wales
Andrew Millie, Jessica Jacobson and Mike Hough

Introduction

On 11 July 2003, the prison population in England and Wales topped 74,000 for the first time, an increase of more than 60 per cent on 1991 figures. The number of adults in prison – that is, excluding offenders aged 15 to 20 – has increased even more steeply by 73 per cent from a daily average of 36,246 in 1991 to 62,838 on 11 July 2003.[1] This unprecedented rate of increase has occurred against a backdrop of gradually declining crime rates since the mid-1990s, according to both recorded crime figures and the British Crime Survey (Simmons and colleagues, 2002).

England and Wales now have the highest prison rate in the European Union at 139 per 1000 population[2] (Walmsley, 2003).

Accounting for the growth in the prison population[3]

The most obvious explanation for the rise in the prison population – and one that the 'man in the street' would probably offer – is that crime has increased. This is clearly not the case. Crime levels, however measured, are lower now than in 1991.

Nor is it a function of increases in court workloads, which could occur even at a time of falling crime. The general trend in the number of convictions has been downward. For 1991 the recorded adult total was 1.2 million (Home Office, 1992: 101). By 2001 the figure was down 11 per cent to just under 1.1 million (Home Office, 2002a: 45). Over the same period the number of adults found guilty of indictable offences fell by 1 per cent from 220,000 to 217,400 (Home Office, 1992: 100, 2002a: 44).

One might argue that the overall fall in crime has masked rises in more serious categories of offences. We found little statistical support for this. For example, the proportion of convictions for violence against the person,[4] sexual offences and burglary – all of which tend to attract custody – has fallen substantially. The one notable exception is a large increase in the number of convictions for drugs offences (see also Corkery, 2002).

The use of remands has increased. The adult remand population grew by one-third, from 6665 in 1991 to 8890 in 2001. However, in absolute terms the increase of just over 2000 is dwarfed by the increase of 16,000 in the sentenced adult population; thus changes in the use of remand cannot be regarded as a significant factor behind the increase in the overall prison population.

This suggests that the main sources of the rise in the prison population are changes either in the proportion of people *sentenced* to prison (the 'flow' into prison) or changes in the length of time that people are *kept there* (which interacts with the 'flow' to create the 'stock' of people in prison).

Changes in courts' custody rates

There have been very marked changes since 1991 in the custody rate – that is, the proportion of those found guilty who are given a custodial sentence. As Table 27.4.1 shows, the adult custody rate in 2001 was approaching twice the 1991 level at 28 per cent. Over the same period the custody rate for magistrates' courts increased more than three times from 5 per cent to 16 per cent. Use of custody by Crown Courts similarly rose from 46 per cent to 64 per cent (Home Office, 2002a: 118).

These changes are not restricted to the adult courts. Using figures for all offenders, irrespective of age, increases in custody rates for selected offence categories are shown in Table 27.4.2.

Length of sentence passed by the courts

There have also been large changes in sentence length, though it is more complex to identify these than might be imagined. The sharp rise in the use of custody means that those who previously might have been given a community penalty are now serving short prison sentences, typically for six months or less. This has effectively masked increases in other sentence length categories. The average length of adult sentences fell from 19 months in 1991 to 15.4 months in 2001 (Home Office, 2003: 93).[5] In order to identify trends within different sentence length categories Table 27.4.3 divides adult sentences into three groups by length.

The rise in prisoners with short sentences was by far the steepest, showing an increase of 139 per cent from 1991 to 2001. Those with sentences of 12 months to less than four years increased by 13 per cent, while those with four years to life rose by 62 per cent (see Home Office, 2003: 28). It would be a misreading of Table 27.4.3 to suggest that the rise in the prison population can be attributed largely to increases in short sentences. Even if the number of short-sentence prisoners increased quickly, they may make a smaller contribution to the total prison population than those serving long sentences. A typical lifer will occupy a prison cell for the same amount of time as 100 short-sentence offenders.[6] Thus the rise of 62 per cent in sentences of four years or more will have had a very significant impact on the overall population.

Table 27.4.1 Adult custody rate at the courts[*]

Year	Magistrates' courts %	Crown court %	All courts %
1991	5	46	17
1996	10	61	24
1997	11	61	25
1998	13	61	25
1999	14	63	26
2000	16	64	28
2001	16	64	28

[*] Persons aged 21 and over sentenced to immediate custody as a percentage of all persons of relevant age group sentenced for indictable offences.

Source: Home Office (2002a: 118)

Table 27.4.2 Increase in custody rates for selected offences categories (all offenders)

Offence groups	1991 (%)	2001 (%)
Burglary in a dwelling	37	60
Burglary not in a dwelling	21	37
Wounding section 20 – Grievous bodily harm	28	54
Wounding section 47 – Actual bodily harm	10	27
Driving while disqualified (*magistrates' courts*)	18	47

Figures provided by Home Offices RDS

Table 27.4.3 Adult receptions into prison under sentence – by sentence length (% change on 1991)

Year	Short sentences – less then 12 months	Middle-range sentences – 12 months and less than 4 years	Long sentences – 4 years to life
1991	*N* = 19,311	*N* = 15, 112	*N* = 3889
	% change	*% change*	*% change*
1992	− 4	− 6	+ 4
1993	+ 9	− 17	− 3
1994	+ 46	− 6	0
1995	+ 71	+ 1	+ 13
1996	+ 81	+ 10	+ 36
1997	+ 100	+ 16	+ 50
1998	+ 120	+ 20	+ 46
1999	+ 136	+ 17	+ 49
2000	+ 142	+ 14	+ 49
2001	+ 139 (*N* = 46, 146)	+ 13 (*N* = 17,116)	+ 62 (*N* = 6,292)

Source: Home Office (2003: 28)

Analysis of Home Office statistics relating to sentence length and offence group revealed a complicated pattern (see Home Office, 1993: 85 and 97, 2003: 81). For some offence groups – e.g. theft and handling – short sentences have become proportionately more significant over the last decade. In these cases courts have probably become more likely to impose custodial rather than community penalties. Violence against the person offences showed no real change in sentence length. In this case the rise in custody has likely interacted with an increase in average sentence length, to cancel out any overall change.

Sentences have clearly become longer in cases of rape and other sexual offences. The proportion getting middle-range sentences has shrunk while the proportion getting long sentences has grown. There is a similar pattern for burglary, except that the shift has been from short sentences to middle-range ones. When all offence types are combined, the largest increase has been in long sentences at the expense of middle-range offences.

In terms of the sentencing court the most significant changes were in Crown Court decisions. For example, while the average length of male custodial sentences given by magistrates' courts showed an increase in the early 1990s, by 1997 this was back down to 1991 levels (2.6 months), and even fell slightly below this for 2000 and 2001 (2.5 months). Although magistrates' courts were sending more people to prison, the length of sentence was in fact slightly lower in 2001 than it was 10 years before. The average length of custodial sentence given by the Crown Court has generally been increasing over the past decade, but especially from 1995 onwards. The average sentence given to adult males has increased by one-third from 20.5 months in 1991 to 26 months in 2001 (Home Office, 2002a: 120-1). Such a large increase in Crown Court sentence length will have been a major factor in increasing the prison population. [...]

The growth in the use of imprisonment over the last 10 years has been at the expense not of community penalty but of the fine. Since 1991 there has been a fall of almost one-third in the use of fines. It is unclear whether this reflects declining confidence among sentencers about fine enforcement, a real reduction in offenders' ability to pay fines or the expansion of community penalties available to the courts. All three are probably implicated. Whatever the reasons, the decline in the use of fines has indirect but important consequences for the prison population. If offenders now receive community penalties earlier in their criminal careers than 10 years ago, they will exhaust the alternatives to imprisonment more rapidly than previously. The proportion of offenders given community penalties that have no previous convictions has steadily risen over the last decade. For example, in 1991 11 per cent of those given Community Rehabilitation Orders had no previous convictions. By 2001 this figure was 27 per cent. For those given Community Punishment Orders, the figure has risen from 14 per cent to 51 per cent (Home Office, 2002b: 25).

Explaining sentencers' greater use of custody

We have suggested that while there are also other factors at work, the main reasons for the rise in the prison population are that sentencers are sending a higher proportion of offenders to prison, and that when they use custody they are passing longer sentences. Why should this have occurred? There are two competing explanations:

1 defendants have longer records or have committed more serious crimes than hitherto;

2 sentencers have become more severe in their sentencing decisions.

Have cases appearing before the courts become more serious?

[T]here is some reason for thinking that sentencers are now faced with more serious cases – either in terms of criminal record or in terms of the gravity of the instant offence – than 10 years ago. Certainly it would be rash and arrogant to reject out-of-hand sentencers' contention that this is the case. However the statistical evidence is patchy and inconsistent. Some statistics suggests that the reverse may be true. The very absence of conclusive evidence about more serious or more persistent offending suggests that the worsening nature of offending is likely to be, at best, a secondary explanation for the growth in the prison population.

Tougher sentencing

By a process of elimination we have arrived at tougher sentencing as the most probable explanation for the increased use of imprisonment. The evidence is inferential, rather than direct. We have simply demonstrated that other possible explanations are insufficient to account for the size of the rise in the prison population. However we have some confidence in this claim, in that we can point to the various mechanisms that have led to increases in severity of sentence.

What has led to tougher sentencing?

[...] In summary, the argument presented here is that the rise in the prison population is due to sentencers passing more custodial sentences, and passing longer sentences when they opt for custodial sentences. The main factors behind this are likely to be the following:

> a more punitive climate of opinion; a more punitive legislative framework; guideline judgments and sentencing guidelines that counteract leniency; some changes in patterns of offending; sentencers' perceptions of changes in patterns of offending.

Can the ever-upward trend in the prison population be halted? Whether the growth of the prison population should be contained is a political decision that falls beyond the boundaries of this study. But if there is some political will to do so, then success in reducing prison numbers will depend on changes both to sentencing practice and to the context in which sentencing is carried out.

One approach that has been tried by successive governments is to provide sentencers with a wider and more attractive range of community penalties. This may go *some* way to reducing prison numbers. However sentencers in this study did not say that they were using prison for want of adequate non-custodial options. The enhancement of community penalties could simply result in 'net-widening' – where the new sentences are used with offenders who would previously have been fined, or served a conventional community penalty.

Encouraging the use of fines could prove a sensible option. This would relieve pressure on the probation service; in terms of outcomes it could at best deflect some offenders entirely from further offending without resort to imprisonment or community penalties; and at worst it could defer the point in their criminal career where prison becomes inevitable.

The analysis presented here suggests that policies to contain the prison population should involve three levels of intervention:

1 adjustment to the legal and legislative framework of sentencing, so as to bring down custody rates and sentence lengths;

2 softening of the climate of political and public opinion on crime and punishment, so that sentencers feel at liberty to make more sparing use of custody, and greater use of the alternatives to custody;

3 improving understanding of the range of non-custodial penalties – including the fine – both among sentencers and the wider public.

However, none of these interventions is likely to meet with much success unless there is clear political will to stop the uncontrolled growth in prison numbers, and visible, consistent, political leadership in stressing the need to do so.

> From A. Millie, J. Jacobson and M. Hough, *'Understanding the growth in the prison population in England and Wales'*, Criminology and Criminal Justice, *2003, 3(4): 369–387.*

Notes

1 Sources: 1991 (Home Office, 2003); 2003 (HM Prison Service, 2003: www.hmprisonservice.gov.uk/statistics).

2 Attempts have been made to compare different countries' use of imprisonment in relation to their crime rates, rather than their overall populations. These show England and Wales in a slightly more favourable light. However this is at least in part because the police in England and Wales tend to record crime more fully than in many other countries, artificially inflating the rate's denominator. The problems in deriving genuinely comparable statistics on this basis are considerable. Research reported in Tonry and Frase (2001) suggested that variations in the imprisonment rate in different countries are to be explained not by variations in crime rates but through differences in sentencing policy and practice.

3 A more detailed analysis of the available sentencing and prison statistics is provided in Hough *et al.* (2003).

4 Some of this will reflect a changing standard for assault introduced on 31 August 1994 which moved some offences to summary common assault.

5 Figures exclude those sentenced to life imprisonment.

6 Assuming that the lifer serves about 13 years, and that the average sentence in magistrates' courts is about three months, with six weeks actually served.

References

Corkery, J. (2002) *Drug Seizure and Offender Statistics. United Kingdom, 2000.* London: Home Office.

Home Office (1992) *Criminal Statistics England and Wales 1991.* London: HMSO.

Home Office (1993) *Prison Statistics England and Wales 1991.* London: HMSO.

Home Office (2002a) *Criminal Statistics England and Wales 2001.* London: TSO.

Home Office (2002b) *Probation Statistics England and Wales 2001.* London: Home Office.

Home Office (2003) *Prison Statistics England and Wales 2001.* London: TSO.

Hough, M., Jacobson, J. and Millie, A. (2003) *The Decision to Imprison: Sentencing and the Prison Population.* London: Prison Reform Trust.

Simmons, J. and colleagues (2002) *Crime in England and Wales 2001/2.* Home Office Statistical Bulletin 7/02. London: Home Office.

Tonry, M. and Frase, R. (2001) *Sentencing and Sanctions in Western Countries.* Oxford: Oxford University Press.

Walmsley, R. (2003) *World Prison Population List*, (4th ed.) Home Office Research Findings 188. London: Home Office.

28

Prisons and imprisonment

28.1 The 'disciplinary' origins of the prison
David Garland   652

**28.2 Prisons and the contested nature
of punishment**
Richard Sparks   657

28.3 The inmate world
Erving Goffman   664

28.4 Women in prison: the facts
Pat Carlen and Anne Worrall   669

Introduction

Our criminal courts send only a small minority of people that come before them to prison. Nevertheless, for a variety of reasons imprisonment is one of the most visible parts of our system of punishment. Moreover, we now have record numbers incarcerated in our jails, and the same is true in many other nations. The prison consequently has a special hold on our imagination and the readings in this chapter explore various aspects of the experience of incarceration and of government policy in this area.

In a number of previous sections in this volume (chapters 22 and 27 in particular) we have encountered aspects of the history of imprisonment. In the first excerpt, David Garland **(Reading 28.1)** examines what, following Foucault, he refers to as the 'disciplinary' origins of the prison (see also Reading 27.3). This refers to what he describes as the ways in which 'the prison seizes the body of the inmate, exercising it, training it, organizing its time and movement in order ultimately to transform the soul'. The system of sanctioning described by Foucault involves a process of 'normalization'; a corrective process involving surveillance and individualization. We are introduced to Jeremy Bentham's model Panopticon which Foucault presents as encapsulating in relatively pure form the system of discipline he describes. There are a number of features of this account that you might find surprising. The first is Foucault's view of power-knowledge and, more specifically, what this tells us about the rise of 'criminology'. The second is what is referred to as the 'failure' of the prison. In short, the prison has always failed penologically, but has been a success politically.

In the following reading Richard Sparks **(Reading 28.2)** takes us through some of the most important ideas in thinking about the philosophical justifications for punishment (some of which were also referred to in Chapter 22) and about the range of penalties available to the courts (also referred to in Chapter 27). He concludes this discussion by observing that we now tend to talk less about 'punishment' in the singular but, rather, 'to think instead about the varied ideologies, knowledges, professional specialisms and decisions involved in the field of penal practices'. It is this shift that is captured by the word 'penality'. In the closing section in the reading, Sparks discusses the important topic of legitimacy. The central questions that preoccupy him here are, first, what do we mean by 'legitimacy' and, second, to what extent can prisons be considered legitimate?

From the outside to the inside and the issue of how imprisonment is experienced. Erving Goffman **(Reading 28.3)** explores what he refers to as the 'inmate world'. According to Goffman, the new inmate 'comes into the establishment with a conception of himself made possible by certain stable social arrangements in his home world. Upon entrance, he is immediately stripped of the support provided by these arrangements.' Goffman describes the barriers that the prison places between the inmate and the wider social world and shows how some of the 'losses' that are experienced are irretrievable despite eventual release. He describes how admissions procedures and other aspects of the physical and social environment of the prison work to violate the territories of the inmate's self.

The bulk of the literature on prisons and imprisonment deals with men. On one level this is understandable as men form the vast majority of prison inmates. However, it also reflects (and continues to reinforce) the historic marginalization of women's imprisonment. Pat Carlen and Anne Worrall **(Reading 28.4)** examine a number of aspects of contemporary women's imprisonment. The first matter they explore is what we know about how women are sentenced by the courts and what this has to tell us about how women offenders are perceived and how we should assess their treatment. Then, having reviewed the available data on trends in women's imprisonment, they look at the characteristics of women in prison. Here they find a number of differences between male and female inmates and, disturbingly, of the consequences for some women in prison.

Questions for discussion

1. What did Foucault mean by the term 'discipline'? Outline some of the organizational principles that emerged to facilitate this form of control.

2. What is the Panopticon and which of its features illustrate the disciplinary system Foucault was outlining?

3. What is meant by the phrase the 'failure' of the prison?

4. What is meant by the term 'penality'? What does it signify about the way in which we talk and think about the field of punishment?

5. What do you think Goffman means when he says of the new inmate that 'his self is systematically, if often unintentionally, mortified'?

6. Goffman frequently uses the language of 'drama' to illustrate his arguments. Give some examples of the ceremonies he describes in prison and the effects they might have on the individuals at the heart of them.

7. In what ways do sentencers 'construct men and women differently'? Does this matter?

8. What are the main demographic differences between the male and female prison populations?

9. Carlen and Worrall conclude that although women represent a very small proportion of the prison population, 'there is no rational reason why that proportion should not be even smaller'. Do you agree (give reasons)?

28.1 The 'disciplinary' origins of the prison
David Garland

The 'disciplinary' origins of the prison

The usual explanation for the rise of the prison points to the prior existence of several great models of punitive confinement – the Rasphuis of Amsterdam, the *Maison de Force* at Ghent, the Gloucester Penitentiary in England, and the Walnut Street Prison in Philadelphia. These institutions, with their emphasis upon work and reformation, had developed regimes which to some extent converged with the reformers' programmes, in so far as they were correctionalist rather than punitive in design. But if prison regimes and the reformers' programme both aimed to reform the individual, they went about this in quite different ways, each using a quite different technology to get hold of the individual and transform him, each developing its own specific techniques for addressing 'the body' and gaining access to 'the soul'. The reformers approached the matter at the level of ideas – proposing signs, lessons, and representations as forms of persuasion or aids to calculation. In contrast to this the prison seizes the body of the inmate, exercising it, training it, organizing its time and movement in order ultimately to transform the soul, 'the seat of the habits'. It takes hold of the individual, manipulating and moulding him or her in a behaviouristic mode, rather than just attempting to influence his or her moral thinking from the outside. There is thus a major difference between the reformers' model and the prison-based system which came to be established – a difference which is primarily technological rather than legal or theoretical.

The major problem, then, around which the whole of *Discipline and Punish* actually turns, is why did the prison succeed in displacing the demands of the reformers and the logic of penal theory? Where did it come from and how did it come to be so quickly and universally accepted? At this point the text undergoes a sudden and rather disconcerting shift of focus, moving away from penal ideas and legal theory to examine a much wider, non-discursive, series of developments: the evolution of what Foucault calls the disciplinary techniques. This turns out to be the most original and interesting aspect of Foucault's historical argument. Where conventional accounts of penal history – and even the 'revisionist' accounts of Rothman and Ignatieff – give a central place to the 'ideological' genesis of modern punishment, locating it within the history of ideas and intellectual movements, Foucault shifts attention to the role of political technology in penal development. In doing so he allows us to come to terms with the physical materiality of the prison – and its political significance – to an extent which has never previously been achieved.[1]

Setting aside the historical narrative pursued in the first section of the book, the three central chapters of *Discipline and Punish* adopt a more structuralist mode in order to map out the techniques and principles of disciplinary power. They aim to produce a diagram of disciplinary technology reduced to its ideal form, the idea being to show its logic and operating principles rather than to give a history of its actual development and use.

Training the body

Discipline, for Foucault, is 'an art of the human body' and a method of mastering the body and rendering it both obedient and useful, and as such has a very long history.[2] However, it was in the classical age that the body came to be conceived as an object and target of power which could be controlled and improved without the costly use of violence. The techniques that provided these means of control and improvement were first generated in a variety of institutions – in the army, the monasteries, and in schools, hospitals, and workshops – but from the sixteenth century onwards these began to be consolidated and reproduced whenever and wherever they seemed applicable.

Foucault sets out a kind of blueprint of the general methods and principles of discipline, abstracting these from the practices and texts of the period. In his description, discipline is above all a 'political anatomy of detail'.[3] It operates on the smallest scale of control, paying attention not primarily to the whole body but to its individual movements and gestures. It aims to increase the efficiency of each movement and develop its co-ordination with others, exercising different forces and building them up together. It does this by bringing to bear a constant, uninterrupted supervision which is alert to the slightest deviation, thereby allowing a meticulous control of the body which is being disciplined.

In order to facilitate this kind of control, certain organizational principles were developed, adapted to particular institutions at first, but later generalized to suit other circumstances. Thus it was the army which did most to develop the art of distributing individuals in space – its ranks and files introducing a set orderliness into a mass of individuals, separating them one by one so that they could be individually viewed, supervised, and assessed. This same form of distribution was quickly adopted in the schoolroom, the workshops, the hospital, and so on. Similarly the monastery developed the timetable – a means of imposing set rhythms to organize time and movement, specify a series of occupations, and regulate the cycle of repetition. On a smaller scale, the concept of 'the manoeuvre' derives from both the barracks and the workshop. In this repeated routine the exact posture of the body, the positioning of the limbs, and the smallest of bodily movements were programmed to increase their efficiency and link them to the use of a weapon or the operation of a machine. By these means, bodies were to be put through their paces until they became docile, efficient, useful machines, programmed to carry out the functions to which they had been trained.

Normalizing deviance

Of course individuals are by nature recalcitrant, and so dealing with disobedience is a central problem for any method of control. Significantly, these disciplinary methods do not simply punish troublesome cases, but develop a whole new method of sanctioning which Foucault calls 'normalization'. This method is essentially corrective rather than punitive in orientation, concerned to induce conformity rather than to exact retribution or expiation. It involves, first of all, a means of assessing the individual in relation to a desired standard of conduct: a means of knowing how the individual performs, watching his movements, assessing his behaviour, and measuring it against the rule. Surveillance arrangements and examination procedures provide this knowledge, allowing incidents of non-conformity or departures from set standards to be recognized and dealt with, at the same time 'individualizing' the different subjects who fall under this gaze. And since the object is to correct rather than punish, the actual sanctions used tend to involve exercises and training, measures which in themselves help bring conduct 'into line' and help make individuals more self-controlled.

'The examination' is, for this system, a central method of control, allowing close observation, differentiation, assessment of standards, and the identification of any failure to conform. So too is the dossier or case record, which allows the characteristics of the individual to be assessed over time and in comparison with others. From this time onwards, writing about individuals ceases to be a form of worship fit only for notables, kings, and heroes, and becomes instead a form of domination to which the powerless are more and more subjected. Out of these practices emerges a detailed and systematic knowledge of individuals, a knowledge which gave rise, in turn, to the various 'human sciences' of criminology, psychology, sociology, and so on. And, as Foucault is at pains to point out, the procedures of observation, examination, and measurement which allow this knowledge to develop are, at the same time, exercising power and control over the individuals who are isolated – and in a sense, constituted – within their gaze.

Bentham's Panopticon

The 'Panopticon' or 'Inspection House' which Jeremy Bentham designed in 1791 is seen by Foucault as the very epitome of these power–knowledge principles. It takes the form of a circular building, with individual cells around its perimeter whose windows and lighting are arranged so as to make their occupants clearly visible to the central inspection tower, though it remains opaque to them. It is thus an architectural form designed to individualize bodies and to render these individuals constantly subject to the knowledge and power of the authorities who occupy its centre. In time, this constant visibility and vulnerability induces self-control on the part of the inmates of the cells. Power no longer needs to unleash its sanctions and instead its objects take it upon themselves to behave in the desired manner. Any remnant of physical repression is thus gradually replaced by a gentle but effective structure of domination. Moreover, the power relations involved are, in a sense, automated and objective. They are an effect of the distribution of places and visibility and do not depend upon the strength or intentions of those who occupy these positions: 'the perfection of power should tend to render its actual exercise unnecessary...this architectural apparatus should be a machine for creating and sustaining a power relation independent of the person who exercises it; in short...the inmates should be caught up in a power situation of which they are themselves the bearers.'[4]

According to Foucault, the usefulness of these panoptic, disciplinary principles was such that they were soon imitated in society's major institutions and eventually came to be generalized throughout the entire social body. However, the actual nature of this 'generalized panopticism' is not precisely detailed in Foucault's text. Sometimes the claim is relatively modest – that all modern forms of power have been affected by the development of disciplinary principles. At other times a more inflated rhetoric takes over and describes modern society as 'the disciplinary society' – a 'society of surveillance' in which we are all subjected to 'infinite examination' in 'the panoptic machine'.[5]

Discipline and democracy

Whatever the exact extent of these large claims, a number of points are clearly made regarding the genesis of the disciplines and their subsequent effects. First of all, although it was within the context of early European capitalism that the disciplines achieved their rapid development, their techniques and principles are transferable and may be operated elsewhere and under different regimes. However, they do have a special and interesting relationship to the development of democracy in the West, summed up in the aphorism that 'the "Enlightenment" which discovered the liberties, also invented the disciplines'.[6] According to Foucault, it was ultimately the generalization of discipline which underpinned and made possible the generalization of democratic constitutions and the expansion of liberal forms of freedom. Without this vast infrastructure of power relations which subjected the masses to an orderly, disciplined existence, the extension of 'liberty' could never have taken place. This echoes the Hobbesian argument that freedom under the law implies a prior process of subjugation, and it constitutes the meaning of Foucault's suggestion that discipline is 'the dark side' of democracy and its egalitarian laws.[7] Foucault argues that the effect of disciplinary relations is to undercut the fairness of exchange and the equalities of status provided for in law and legal doctrine, an effect which operates in an invisible and extra-legal fashion. The disciplines ensure that real constraints and controls are introduced into relationships which the law deems to be voluntary or contractual, thus permitting the coexistence of legal freedom and habitual domination. It is in this sense that the disciplines are said to be 'a sort of counter-law'.[8]

Returning now, after this long but crucial detour, to the problem of penal history, we are able to view the rise of the prison in a rather different light. Given the context in which Foucault has located it, the prison now appears as an aspect of that wider historical phenomenon, the development and generalization of the disciplines. And indeed, if one thinks of the specifically modern developments in penology which have been associated with the prison – the investigation of 'the criminal' behind the crime, the concern with correction and adjustment, the involvement of experts whose task it is to observe, to assess, and to cure – then one can see the extent to which disciplinary and normalizing concerns have indeed penetrated the judicial framework of the criminal justice system.

This genealogical argument – that the disciplines are the ancestors of the prison – is presented by Foucault in its strongest version when he argues that the 'general form' of the prison institution was prefigured in these wider disciplinary developments, and simply imported into the legal system from outside. To this extent, nineteenth-century penal history should not be seen as part of the history of moral ideas but rather as a chapter in the history of the body and its investment by power– knowledge techniques. Within these terms, the great model prisons of Ghent, Gloucester, Walnut Street, etc. must be seen as the first points of transition or imitation, not as innovations as such. This genealogy also serves as an explanation for the rapid acceptance of the prison as an 'obvious' or 'natural' institution. In a society which was already becoming inured to the operation of disciplinary mechanisms, the prison could appear to be self-evident right from the beginning.

A further consequence of this genealogical argument is that it changes the way we must think about the character and function of the prison. If it is conceived, from the start, as being a disciplinary institution, then its function of confinement and deprivation of liberty must always have been supplemented by a second, disciplinary function, namely the transformation of individuals. Foucault asserts that this is in fact the case: that the 'penitentiary techniques' of isolation, work, individualized treatment, and the adjustment of sentence to reflect reformatory progress are all hallmarks of the disciplinary process. Indeed he points out that one ironic consequence of the prison's disciplinary function is that it involves giving the prison authorities a degree of autonomy and discretion to carry out this task, thus re-creating in a new form all the arbitrariness and despotism which was so much criticized in the old penal systems.

'The criminal' and 'criminology'

The operation of the disciplinary prison also gave rise to a new body of information and knowledge about the criminal which was not previously available. Prison practices of isolation, observation, and individual assessment ensured that offenders were no longer thought of in the abstract, but were instead studied as individuals with their own characteristics, peculiarities, and differences. Whereas the law viewed offenders as being no different from anyone else, except in so far as they happened to have committed an offence, the prison aimed to individualize offenders, to find out what kind of people they were, and to determine the relationship between their character and their criminality. In this sense, the prison led to the discovery of 'the delinquent' of the criminal type whose biography, character, and environment mark him or her off as different from the non-delinquent. And from this point one can trace the rise of a science of criminology which takes up the task of investigating this criminal entity, and describing it in all its aspects.

In respect of this 'delinquent' and the 'criminology' to which it gives rise, Foucault makes a point of major importance. He argues that the prison did not 'discover' delinquents, but rather it *fabricated* them, and it did so in two distinct senses. First of all, it 'made' delinquents in a literal sense by creating the conditions for recidivism: offenders were so stigmatized, demoralized, and deskilled in prison that after their release they tended to re-offend, to be reconvicted and eventually be transformed into career criminals. Secondly, the prison produced the delinquent in a categorical or epistemological sense, by creating in the course of its practices, the category of 'the individual criminal': it was in the prison that the individual criminal first became a visible, isolated object of intense study and control. One implication of this is that criminology – that systematic knowledge of the delinquent suggested by and developed within the prison – owes its existence to a system of power and to that system's hold over individual bodies.

Criminology is founded on a particular power–knowledge regime, not an undeniable truth.[9]

The 'failure' of the prison

The final sections of *Discipline and Punish* return to the historical narrative and trace, rather too hurriedly, the actual impact of the prison and its position within the contemporary network of social control. In many ways this is the least satisfactory part of the book, but it does state a thesis which is clear and of considerable interest: namely, that the prison has always been a failure in penological terms, but that it successfully achieves important political effects at a wider social level, which is why it has never been abandoned.

Foucault shows that the defects of the prison – its failure to reduce crime, its tendency to produce recidivists, to organize a criminal milieu, to render prisoners' families destitute, etc. – have all been recognized and criticized from as early as the 1820s up to the present day. Moreover, each time this critique is restated, the official response has been to reassert the maxims of good penitentiary practice rather than to dispense with the institution itself. This historical pattern of constant failure and constant resistance to change leads Foucault to raise forcefully a question which is in many ways central to contemporary penal politics, namely: why does the prison persist? As usual the answer he gives to this familiar question is not at all the familiar one. Instead he offers explanations which are what one might call 'depth explanations' in so far as they refer to decisions and rationales which are neither apparent nor easily demonstrable. He suggests two such reasons; the first is that the prison is 'deeply rooted', by which he means that it is embedded in the wider disciplinary practices which he deems to be characteristic of modern society.[10] This, of course, refers back to his wider genealogical argument. The second is that the prison persists because it carries out 'certain very precise functions'.[11] This functional argument is pursued by reversing the problem of failure and asking if it can instead be understood as a covert form of success. In other words, he asks what interests could be served by the production of delinquency, recidivism, and a criminal milieu and could these 'interests' so act as to perpetuate these apparent defects?

The answer which he outlines here is placed not on a penological level but in the wider, political sphere and against the background of French politics in the 1840s and 1850s. What it amounts to is an argument that the creation of delinquency is useful in a strategy of political domination because it works to separate crime from politics, to divide the working classes against themselves, to enhance the fear of prison, and to guarantee the authority and powers of the police. He argues that in a system of domination which depends upon respect for law and for property it is essential to ensure that illegalities and lawbreaking attitudes do not become widespread or popular, and, above all, that they do not become linked with political objectives. In this context, the unintended creation of a delinquent class may be turned to advantage in a number of ways. Delinquency in itself is no great political danger – its attacks on property or authority are individualized and often petty, moreover its victims are usually from the lower classes – and it can therefore be tolerated by the authorities, at least within certain limits. And by creating a well-defined delinquent class, the prison ensures that habitual criminals are known to the authorities and can more easily be managed or kept under surveillance by the police.

What is more, the existence of a delinquent class can be used to curb other kinds of illegalities in a number of ways. First of all, the police measures and supervision which it necessitates can be used for wider political purposes. Secondly, the predatory nature of delinquency makes it unpopular with other members of the working classes, who tend to call upon the law as a protection and increasingly to shun law-breaking in itself. The myths of dangerousness which grow up around the criminal element add to this process of distancing and division. Finally, an awareness that imprisonment tends to bring about a subsequent identification with the criminal ranks gives people added reason to avoid taking any risks with the law and to distrust those who do. On this account then, the prison does not control the criminal so much as control the working class by creating the criminal, and, for Foucault, this is the unspoken rationale for its persistence. Clearly this is not a policy which is ever declared as such in public, but Foucault insists that it does in fact amount to a deliberate strategy. Consequences of imprisonment, which were unintended and thought of as detrimental at first, were subsequently recognized to be of some use. Consequently they were reinforced and deliberately employed in what might be termed a regrouped strategy.[12] The prison is thus retained for its failures and not in spite of them.

The carceral continuum

The closing section of the book is entitled, simply, 'the carceral'. It describes how the frontiers between judicial punishment and the other institutions of social life, such as the school, the family, the workshop, and the poor law came increasingly to be blurred by the development of similar disciplinary techniques in all of them, and the frequent transfers which take place from one institution to another. (Foucault cites the example of a reformatory for youth, which receives problem cases from families, schools, and prisons, and deals in the same disciplinary way with offenders and non-offenders alike.) According to Foucault, there exists a kind of carceral continuum which covers the whole social body, linked by the pervasive concern to identify deviance, anomalies, and departures from the relevant norms. This framework of surveillance and correction stretches from the least irregularity to the greatest crime and brings the same principles to bear upon each. The idea of the 'continuum' is important here, not just to describe the relations of one institution to another, but also to suggest the similarities that exist between societies. Foucault's description of Western liberal democracy as a society of surveillance, disciplined from end to end, is deliberately reminiscent of a totalitarianism which is usually ascribed to others. And in case anyone should miss this implied reference to the Gulag and its confinements, he coins the phrase 'carceral archipelago' to describe the chain of institutions which stretches out from the prison.

To return, finally, to punishment once more, all this has some very specific consequences for the way we think about penal practice. Within this overall framework, the process of punishing is not essentially different from that of educating or curing and it tends to be represented as merely an extension of these less coercive processes. This has two important results. First of all legal punishments come to be regarded as more legitimate and less in need of justification than when they were previously seen as forms of harm or coercion. Secondly, the legal restriction and limitations which once surrounded the power to punish – tying it to specific crimes, determining its duration, guaranteeing the rights of those accused, etc – tend to disappear. Penal law in effect becomes a hybrid system combining the principles of legality with the principles of normalization. Its jurisdiction is thus extended so that it now sanctions not just 'violations of the law' but also 'deviations from the norm'. In this system there are many areas where the traditional protections of 'the rule of law' and 'due process' are no longer operative, or even appropriate, but so far no new framework of review and limitation has been developed to deal with these new forms through which modern administrative power actually operates.

From D. Garland, Punishment and Modern Society *(Oxford: Oxford University Press), 1990, pp. 143–151.*

Notes

1 Rothman, *The Discovery of the Asylum*; Ignatieff, *A Just Measure of Pain*. For a discussion of how these 'revisionist' texts revised the orthodoxies of penal history, see S. Cohen and A. Scull (eds.), *Social Control and the State* (Oxford, 1983), chs. 3 and 4. On power as it operates in prisons and other 'total institutions', see Sykes, *The Society of Captives*, and Goffman, *Asylums*.
2 Foucault's *Discipline and Punish*, p. 137.
3 *Ibid*. 139.

4 Foucault's *Discipline and Punish*, p. 201.
5 *Ibid*. 209, 217, 189, 217 respectively.
6 *Ibid*. 222.
7 *Ibid*. 222. Here Foucault's argument closely parallels Marx's famous distinction between 'the two spheres' of capitalist society – the sphere of consumption or exchange, which is the realm of freedom and equality, contrasted with the sphere of production where despotism and exploitation are the order of the day. K. Marx, *Capital*, i (London, 1976), p. 280. See on this B. Fine *et al.* (eds.), *Capitalism and the Rule of Law* (London, 1979).
8 Foucault, *Discipline and Punish*, p. 222.
9 For an analysis of criminology conceived in similar terms see D. Garland, 'The Criminal and His Science', *The British Journal of Criminology*, 25 (1985), 109–37, and id., 'British Criminology Before 1935', *The British Journal of Criminology*, 28 (1988), 131–47.
10 Foucault, *Discipline and Punish*, p. 271.
11 *Ibid*.
12 A contemporary example of the unintended consequences of the prison being used in just this way is the 'Scared Straight' juvenile program developed in New Jersey, USA, in the early 1980s. Here the facts of intra-prisoner violence, rape, and brutality were explicitly used by the authorities to try to deter young offenders from becoming involved in crimes that might lead to imprisonment.

28.2 Prisons and the contested nature of punishment
Richard Sparks

Methods of punishment or correction have long been amongst the more vexed and contested aspects of public life. At different moments in their historical development modern Western societies have conceived of the causes of crime and disorder in distinct ways and have formulated their philosophies and practices of punishment variably, according to the dominant explanatory models, religious and other value systems and crime control priorities of the times. (If we were to extend this discussion to include non-Western or 'traditional' societies, the range of customs, practices and beliefs that could be termed 'punishments' would be seen to be even more bewilderingly wide.) Even within particular moments or periods, the historical record suggests sharp disagreement on matters of justification and of method, as the disputes between deterrence and reformation as aims of imprisonment in Victorian England indicate. Thus, although particular criteria for deciding

on questions of appropriate punishment and particular institutional arrangements for delivering it may predominate at any given time, we cannot assume that they ever achieve a consensus of support nor that they will not be subject to change. On one level this is because real institutions of punishment have never been 'perfected' in the way that their more visionary advocates (such as John Howard's ideal images of penitentiary imprisonment) imagined they could be. On quite another level, it is because matters of penal policy always broach some of the most basic questions of justice, order and social control that any society confronts, and on which settled agreement always seems elusive. This is why Garland comments that:

The punishment of offenders is a peculiarly unsettling and dismaying aspect of social life. As a social policy it is a continual disappointment, seeming always to fail in its ambitions and to be undercut by crises and contradictions of one sort or another. As a moral or political issue it provokes intemperate emotions, deeply conflicting interests, and intractable disagreements.

(Garland, 1990, p.1)

It would appear that whenever we discuss questions of penal policy we find ourselves in the presence of uncertainty and controversy. Even defining punishment (given the range of practices and penalties which have claimed justification in its name) is no easy matter. Perhaps, then, we must give up the idea that we will one day discover a form of punishment which is undeniably just and self-evidently effective. Rather, we may have to accept that any social practice that is so much caught up with issues of authority, legitimacy and compulsion is inevitably subject to what philosophers call 'the conflict of interpretations'. The morality of punishment is, as Lacey (1988, p14), puts it, 'incurably relative'.

Punishment as an 'essentially contested concept'

There is, of course, one overriding reason why punishment poses these sorts of problems in an especially acute way. By definition, punishing offenders is generally taken to imply the imposition of some form of 'hard treatment' (von Hirsch, 1993). It involves 'what are usually regarded as unpleasant consequences' (Lacey, 1988, p.9). Justifications for punishing may be offered on a number of grounds. Let us briefly outline some of the fundamental positions. For many philosophers, and perhaps most ordinary people, the justification for punishing resides simply in the view that the penalty is seen as *deserved* for the offence (in which case the punishment is described as *retributive*). For others the key question lies in a *practical* or *instrumental* benefit that is intended to follow. Thus it may be held that the principal aim of imposing a penalty for an offence is in order to *deter* its repetition, or to *incapacitate* the offender (that is, in some way to prevent them from repeating an action either by locking them up, placing them under supervision or removing their means of doing it). Still others propose that we punish mainly in order to express social disapproval ('denunciation').

The most ambiguous case is where the penalty is held also to do the offender good (to *rehabilitate* them through participation in a programme of counselling, education or training). Yet even in the mildest forms of rehabilitation offenders will be placed under a degree of compulsion. They can be required to do things that may inconvenience them and which they would not do voluntarily (attend appointments with a probation officer, spend Saturday afternoons at an attendance centre), usually with the threat of more severe penalties if they do not comply. The tensions which inevitably arise within such mixtures of helping and compelling may be even more acute where attempts to bring about rehabilitation occur *within* prisons. In liberal democratic societies like our own, punishment generally equates to some form of *deprivation*, whether of liberty, time or money (and, we might add, social standing or reputation).

It is because punishment usually implies compulsion, and often deliberately imposed hardship, that decisions to punish always pose problems of moral justification and call for the provision of reasons. When we punish we are using the legal authority of the state to do things which would otherwise (if we did them privately, or if they were done without a sufficient reason) be '*prima facie* morally wrongful' (Lacey, 1988, p.14). Yet it is very often unclear whether punishment does achieve the effects that are claimed for it. Moreover, the major justifications that are used do not always go easily together. Retribution looks back towards the original offence, and seeks to punish proportionately (it is generally *intuitionist* with regard to what is deserved). Deterrence looks forward to the prevention of future crimes (it is *consequentialist*; if it does not work it cannot claim justification). As one commentator puts it, these two principal justifications for punishing 'stand in open and flagrant contradiction' (Bean, 1981, p.1). The primary point is that we should never be complacent about our grounds for punishing. It is often far from self-evident in any given case just which objectives are being pursued, still less whether they will be successful, and debate is often further clouded by political contingencies (Prison Reform Trust, 1993).

In most criminal justice systems (and certainly in the famously 'eclectic' English case) the different rationales for punishing have often co-existed in various, more or less uneasy, combinations. Criminal sentencing is a complex intellectual and cultural phenomenon, capable of answering to a range of institutional and political demands. It tends, therefore, to resist codification, however many academic theorists of different stripes (be they pure retributivists or advocates of classical deterrence) insist that they have discovered the one true rationale for state punishment. Punishment is *overdetermined*: its aims may be simultaneously *instrumental* (concerned with the suppression of crime and the control of behaviour) and *symbolic* or *ideological* (concerned with the vindication of the law and its claims to exercise justice in the defence of the authority and legitimacy of the state). Historically, it is more common than not for retributive and deterrent principles to stand side by side in the armoury of possible sentences, even when purist advocates of each insist that they are logically incompatible.

The penal range and the choice of punishments

With the notable exception of the USA (see Zimring and Hawkins, 1986), the Western liberal democracies have abandoned the use of capital punishment. Even in the USA, where it is a highly politically charged issue, the death penalty is actually carried out only in a relative handful of cases each year (there were 14 executions in 1991), although the numbers executed have increased (31 in 1994); the number of persons under sentence of death, however, is very much larger (2,500 in 1991; 2,870 in 1994) (figures for 1991 from United States Department of Justice, 1992; for 1994 from Amnesty International, 1995, p.302). In other respects the 'penal range' (the variety of available penalties) in all such societies is broadly comparable, albeit organized and applied in very different ways. It extends from various forms of token penalty or admonition (in the UK, absolute and conditional discharges, binding over) through financial penalties (fines, compensation orders) and varieties of non-custodial or 'community' supervision (probation, community service, in some cases 'curfew orders') to imprisonment. In most systems, and certainly in the UK, financial penalties are by some margin the most commonly used. This has led some commentators (notably Young, 1989; see also Bottoms, 1983) to argue that in fact it is the 'cash nexus' of the fine that is the most characteristic form of contemporary punishment rather than the more drastic but more rarely used sanction of imprisonment.

Nevertheless, it is imprisonment which has probably received the lion's share of media debate, academic attention and political controversy. The reasons for this preoccupation are perhaps not too difficult to detect. The scale of punishment is organized hierarchically in the form of a 'tariff'. In most contemporary systems the prison is at the apex of this ordinal series of values. Although it is by no means the case that everyone who goes to prison has been convicted of grave offences, ordinary language (and judicial reasoning) generally sees a powerful connection between the severity of an offence and the likelihood or appropriateness of imprisonment. (This expectation was formalized in England and Wales in the sentencing structure of the 1991 Criminal Justice Act.) Moreover, imprisonment involves the deprivation of something on which most societies, and certainly ones in which liberalism is a dominant ideology, set a special value – liberty, freedom of movement and association. For this reason the general problems of justifying punishments are seen to apply in especially acute ways to imprisonment (witness the widespread public concern over 'miscarriage of justice' cases in England – most famously those of the Guildford Four and Birmingham Six; to be wrongfully imprisoned is acknowledged to be a very severe injustice: it is the wrongful application of the state's most draconian power over its citizens).

Plainly, other sanctions (such as community service orders and probation) also restrict liberty, but not in so obvious or readily understood a fashion. This leads to a number of ambiguities in the interpretation of such penalties. In much 'common-sense' discussion and in popular press imagery, non-custodial penalties are not regarded as 'proper' punishments at all. The equation between punishment and imprisonment for many people is so strong that for the offender to remain 'in the community' is for them to be 'let off'. Moreover, it is common for such measures to be described as 'alternatives to' imprisonment, implying that incarceration remains the central, perhaps the only 'real', sort of punishment.

We can therefore only really understand the uses of imprisonment within any particular criminal justice system in the context of the range of other measures that that system also applies. In recent times most Western penal systems have moved increasingly towards a stance of bifurcation (or 'twin tracking') in an explicit attempt to reserve imprisonment for the more serious offences, whilst providing an 'adequate' range of 'community penalties' for the rest. Certainly this philosophy underlay the British government's thinking in the formulation of the 1991 Criminal Justice Act which introduced the concept of a specific 'threshold' between custody and other penalties (see Wasik and Taylor, 1991, p. 17). Whilst this strategy has an obvious plausibility, its actual effects can be uncertain or even counterproductive. It presents itself as a *diversionary* measure. Yet sentence lengths for the 'hard core' who continue to receive imprisonment may increase, as average prison terms in the UK did incrementally throughout the 1980s (Home Office, 1993; Morgan, 1994). At the same time, non-custodial penalties may also be made consciously more severe in order to be made 'credible' to sentencers. In addition, such penalties may not always be strictly or appropriately applied: that is, they may move *down-tariff*, supplanting other 'lesser' penalties. This is now widely held to have been the fate of the suspended sentence in the UK since its introduction in 1967 (Bottoms, 1987). It may also be reflected in the increasing popularity amongst sentencers in the UK of community service orders which have tended to displace the longer established penalty of probation since about 1980 (Cavadino and Dignan, 1992, p.171). Such measures can serve to increase prison populations, either because imprisonment may follow when their conditions are breached (and the more demanding those conditions become the more likely this seems to be), or because courts treat subsequent offences in a more serious light. In either case the result is not so much 'twin tracking' as *punitive bifurcation*, in which both 'tracks' become more stringent (Cavadino and Dignan, 1992, pp.108–9). The relation between imprisonment and its 'alternatives' is thus a complicated one. The history of attempts to introduce additional sentencing options, especially where these are meant to divert offenders from prison, is littered with unintended (and sometimes actively 'perverse') consequences.

Two considerations may be paramount in explaining why non-custodial sanctions have not had a profound effect in displacing the use of imprisonment. The first concerns, once again, the prison's symbolic position at the summit of the ascending scale of penalties. There would appear to be a widely held view amongst some sentencers, in press discourse and, perhaps by extension, in 'public opinion', that no other penalty adequately conveys the degree of reproof or censure necessary in responding to offences regarded as highly morally culpable (Bishop, 1988; Zimring and Hawkins, 1991). (One alternative conception is that espoused by Braithwaite who argues that sanctions should embody the ritual expression of both 'shaming' and 'reintegration' (Braithwaite, 1989; Braithwaite and Mugford, 1994; see also Cragg, 1992)).

The second obstacle to decarceration includes a more practical dimension. A sanction is only likely to displace imprisonment to any marked degree if it is consistently used in cases where the offender *actually would otherwise* go to prison. But such cases do include a high proportion of offences involving demonstrable harm to others. Meanwhile, sentencers and members of the public tend to focus on one of the most obvious and salient features of imprisonment: self-evidently it does confine people and set them apart from the general community for the duration of their sentence. Despite many efforts and no little evidence to the contrary, it seems inherently difficult to persuade people either that prisons do not have a crime preventive function through incapacitation to anything like the extent that is sometimes claimed for them (Greenberg, 1991; Zimring and Hawkins, 1991; Mathiesen, 1990), or, conversely, that other means of supervision, support or remedial assistance 'in the community' can do so.

The activity of punishment is deeply involved in processes of social regulation and social change. It reflects changes in the distribution of power, in conceptions of individuals and their motivation, and in ideas of what is permissible or desirable in the defence of social order and legality. The reasons given by a judge when passing sentence are a 'vocabulary of motive' (Melossi, 1985). But as social scientists we may also wish to ask: Why does one such vocabulary, say deterrence or 'just deserts', come to predominate in one country or at one time rather than another? So, for instance, we might want to know why two neighbouring countries with very similar rates of recorded crime, such as England and Wales and The Netherlands, can come to differ markedly in their use of imprisonment. What might this reveal about differences in their political climates or intellectual culture? When we pose such questions we move from the traditional concerns of penology (Whom should we punish? How much? By what means?) towards what Garland and Young (1983b) have termed the 'social analysis of penality'. When we do this we will tend no longer to talk of 'punishment' in the singular (as an 'it'), but to think instead about the varied ideologies, knowledges, professional specialisms and decisions involved in the field of penal practices and about the relations between that 'penal realm' and other spheres of economic and political life. The resulting differences in the 'scale of imprisonment' (Zimring and Hawkins,

1991) may tell us something of importance about the 'sensibilities' towards punishment (Garland, 1990) that prevail in each country. More specifically, they may reveal both constant and variable aspects of the ways in which prisons are used. Such comparative knowledge can be useful in helping us to decide what level of imprisonment we are prepared to accept as necessary or legitimate.

Prisons and the problem of legitimacy

Prisons have a number of features that mark them out as unique amongst contemporary social institutions. Some of these are obvious but their implications are nonetheless important. Prisons confine people under conditions not of their own choosing, in close proximity with others whose company they may not desire, attended by custodians who are formally empowered to regulate their lives in intimate detail. It is true that prisons share some of these characteristics with other 'total institutions', if by 'total' we mean institutions that 'tend to encompass the whole of the lives of their inmates' (Goffman, 1961). Examples often cited of total institutions include barracks, boarding schools, children's homes and hospitals (see Cohen and Taylor, 1981); but the only really close analogy is probably with compulsory psychiatric confinement under mental health legislation. It is largely because of their 'total' character that prisons pose issues of *legitimacy* that are in some degree special. Why is this so? And why is it important? What is legitimacy anyway?

It has long been argued that prison administrators hold 'a grant of power without equal' (Sykes, 1958, p.42) in liberal democratic societies. Many political theorists argue that questions of legitimacy arise whenever states claim the right to exercise power over their citizens, especially when they support these claims with reference to the necessity of upholding the law or other aspects of the 'general good' (such as the maintenance of public safety through the suppression of crime). Legitimacy can thus be defined as a claim to justified authority in the use of power. It would seem to follow that the greater the power in question the more urgently it stands in need of legitimation. Consider the following definition, taken from David Beetham's book *The Legitimation of Power* (1991):

Power can be said to be legitimate to the extent that:

i   it conforms to established rules

ii the rules can be justified by reference to beliefs shared by both dominant and subordinate

iii there is evidence of consent by the subordinate to the particular power relation.

(Beetham, 1991, p.16)

Beetham argues that all systems of power relations seek legitimation. Such criteria are almost never perfectly fulfilled and each dimension of legitimacy has a corresponding form of non-legitimate power. Where power fails to conform to its own rules of legal validity it is illegitimate. Where it lacks justification in shared beliefs it experiences a legitimacy deficit. Where it fails to find legitimation through expressed consent it may finally experience a crisis of delegitimation (withdrawal of consent) (Beetham, 1991, p.20). Most pointedly for the present discussion of prisons: 'the form of power which is distinctive to [the political domain] – organized physical coercion – is one that both supremely stands in need of legitimation, yet is also uniquely able to breach all legitimacy. The legitimation of the state's power is thus both specially urgent and fateful in its consequences' (Beetham, 1991, p. 40).

Prisons, like other forms of punishment but in a particularly acute way, confront questions of legitimacy because they assume an especially high degree of power over the lives of their inmates, and that power is in the last instance buttressed by the right to use sanctions, including physical force, to secure prisoners' compliance. The question of legitimacy is also complicated by two further considerations.

First, to confine an individual is also to place them in a position of dependency. As Mathiesen (1965) puts it, prisoners are reliant on prison staff for the 'distribution of benefits and burdens' in both formal and discretionary ways. In this respect, in claiming the authority to imprison one of its citizens, a state is undertaking a responsibility for the prisoner's health, safety and physical and psychological well-being which is qualitatively greater than that which it owes to the free citizen. Questions thus arise concerning the scope of prisoners' rights or entitlements (Richardson, 1985; Livingstone and Owen, 1993) and of the mechanisms of legal accountability (Gearty, 1991), inspection (Morgan and Evans, 1994) and standards (Woolf, 1991) that govern the operation of prisons in complex modern societies.

Second, the question of legitimacy also arises in relation to the internal order and organization of the prison. It is notoriously true that prisons sometimes erupt in violent upheavals, protest and riots (most famously in the USA at Attica in 1971 and in England at Strangeways in 1990 – see Adams, 1992), Some would argue that this is a risk inherent in the process of confinement. King puts the matter succinctly:

> It is best to acknowledge at the outset that there is no solution to the control problem in prisons, nor can there be. The control problem – of how to maintain 'good order and discipline' – is inherent and endemic. For as long as we have prisons – and an institution that has become so entrenched in our thinking shows no sign whatever of becoming disestablished – then we will continue to hold prisoners against their will. At bottom that is what it is about.

> (King, 1985, p.187)

Yet, we also know that such endemic problems do not always and everywhere result in riots and major crises. It is intriguing and important to ask what marks the transition between a chronic background issue (in Beetham's terms a 'legitimacy deficit') and a serious breakdown of order (a 'crisis of delegitimation'). Answers to this question encompass a complex range of factors including levels of material provision in prison regimes (crowding, sanitation, food, work, education and so on – see King and McDermott, 1989) and procedural fairness (such as disciplinary and grievance procedures – see Woolf, 1991), as well as less readily quantifiable issues concerning the nature of social relationships between staff and prisoners (Sparks and Bottoms, 1995).

Since at least the late 1970s it has become commonplace to find references to the prison systems of a number of countries (the UK and the USA perhaps in particular, but latterly also coun-

tries such as Italy – see Pavarini, 1994) as being 'in crisis'. Increasingly, commentators on penal affairs have begun to think about such 'crises' – especially where they include serious problems of order or control – as being in the first instance problems of legitimation (Woolf, 1991; Sim, 1992; Cavadino and Dignan, 1992; Sparks, 1994; Sparks and Bottoms, 1995). We can thus regard legitimacy as a linking idea which runs throughout the apparently disparate questions of penal politics discussed in this chapter. Let us for the time being pose these issues as a series of open questions:

- Is the allocation of punishments in any given society justified by coherent principles? Is it consistent and procedurally fair? Do sentences in the main achieve their stated objectives? Is punishment legitimate in Beetham's first sense (conformity with established rules)?

- Do the system's present practices find widespread acceptance and support in the wider society or are they the subject of disagreement and ideological dispute? Are they therefore legitimate in Beetham's second and more 'external' sense (justification in terms of shared belief)?

- Can the system sustain itself over time in a relatively stable and orderly way or is it subject to repeated challenge and resistance? Can it secure the consent (or even simply compliance) of its own subordinate members – in this case prisoners and to some extent lower level staff? Or has it embarked upon a 'crisis of delegitimation' (withdrawal of consent)?

In our view these questions provide the framework for understanding what is meant by the term 'penal crisis' and for evaluating policy changes introduced with the aim of resolving or averting the most pressing problems.

From R. Sparks, 'Prisons, punishment and penality' in E. McLaughlin and J. Muncie (eds) Controlling Crime (London: Sage), 1996, pp. 199–207.

References

Adams, R. (1992) *Prison Riots in Britain and the US*. London: Macmillan.

Amnesty International (1995) *Amnesty International Report 1995*. London: Amnesty International.

Bean, P. (1981) *Punishment: A Philosophical and Criminological Inquiry*. Oxford: Martin Robertson.

Beetham. D. (1991) *The Legitimation of Power*. London: Macmillan.

Bishop, N. (1988) *Non-custodial Alternatives in Europe*. Helsinki: Institute for Crime Prevention and Control.

Bottoms, A. (1983) Neglected features of contemporary penal systems. In Garland and Young (1983a).

Bottoms. A. (1987) Limiting prison use. *Howard Journal of Criminal Justice*, 26, (3), 177–202.

Braithwaite, J. (1989) *Crime, Shame and Reintegration*. Cambridge and New York: Cambridge University Press.

Braithwaite, J. and Mugford, S. (1994) Conditions of successful reintegration ceremonies. *British Journal of Criminology*, 34, (2), 139–71.

Brody, S. (1976) *The Effectiveness of Sentencing*. London. HMSO.

Cavadino, M. and Dignan, J. (1992) *The Penal System: An Introduction*. London: Sage.

Cohen, S. and Taylor, L. (1981) *Psychological Survival* (2nd ed.), Harmondsworth: Penguin.

Cragg, W. (1992) *The Practice of Punishment*. London: Routledge.

Garland, D. (1990) *Punishment and Modern Society*. Oxford: Oxford University Press.

Garland, D. and Young, P.J. (Eds) (1983a) *The Power to Punish*. Aldershot: Gower.

Garland, D. and Young, P.J. (1983b) Towards a social analysis of penality. In Garland and Young (1983a).

Gearty, C. (1991) The prisons and the courts. In Muncie and Sparks (1991b) *Imprisonment: European Perpectives*. Hemel Hempstead: Harvester Wheatsheaf.

Goffman, E. (1961) On the characteristics of total institutions. In Cressey, D. (Ed.) *The Prison: Studies in Institutional Organization and Change*. New York: Holt, Rinehart and Winston.

Greenberg, D. (1991) The cost-benefit analysis of imprisonment. *Social Justice*, 17, (4), 49–75.

Home Office (1993) Digest 2: *Information on the Criminal Justice System in England and Wales*. Home Office Research and Statistics Department, London: HMSO.

King, R,.D. (1985) Control in prisons. In Maguire *et al.* (1985). *Accountability and Prisons*: London: Tavistock.

King, R.D. and McDermott, K. (1989) British prisons, 1970-1987: the ever deepening crisis. *British Journal of Criminology*, 29, 107–28.

Lacey, N. (1988) *State Punishment*. London: Routledge.

Livingstone, S. and Owen, T. (1993) *Prison Law*. Oxford: Oxford University Press.

Mathiesen, T. (1965) *The Defences of the Weak*. London: Tavistock.

Mathiesen, T. (1990) *Prison on Trial*. London: Sage.

Melossi, D. (1985) Punishment and social action: changing vocabularies of motive within a political business cycle. *Current Perspectives in Social Theory*, 6, 169–97,

Morgan, R. (1994) Imprisonment. In Maguire, M., Morgan, R. and Reiner, R. (Eds) *The Oxford Handbook of Criminology*. Oxford: Oxford University Press.

Morgan, R. and Evans, M. (1994) Inspecting prisons – the view from Strasbourg. *British Journal of Criminology*. 34, (1), 144–59.

Pavarini, M. (1994) The new penology and politics in crisis: the Italian case. *British Journal of Criminology*, 34, (1), 49–6 1.

Prison Reform Trust (1993) *Does Prison Work?* London: Prison Reform Trust.

Richardson, G. (1985) The case for prisoners' rights. In Maguire *et al.* (1985).

Sim, J. (1992) When you ain't got nothing you got nothing to lose: the Peterhead rebellion, the state and the case for prison abolition. In Bottomley, A.K., Fowles, A.J, and Reiner, R. (Eds) *Criminal Justice: Theory and Practice*. London: British Society of Criminology.

Sparks, J.R. (1994) Can prisons be legitimate? *British Journal of Criminology*, 34, (1), 14–28.

Sparks, J.R. and Bottoms, A.E. (1995) Legitimacy and order in prisons. *British Journal of Sociology*, 46, (1), 45–62.

Sykes, C. (1958) *The Society of Captives*. Princeton, NJ: Princeton University Press.

United States Department of Justice (1992) *Capital Punishment 1991*, Bureau of Justice Statistics Bulletin. Washington, DC: Department of Justice.

von Hirsch, A. (1993) *Censure and Sanction*. Oxford: Oxford University Press.

Wasik, M. and Taylor, R. (1991) *Blackstones Guide to the Criminal Justice Act 1991*. London: Blackstone Press.

Woolf, Lord Justice (1991) *Prison Disturbances, April 1990*. London: HMSO.

Young, P.J. (1989) Punishment, money and a sense of justice. In Carlen, P. and Cook, D. (Eds) *Paying for Crime*. Milton Keynes: Open University Press,

Zimring, F. and Hawkins, G. (1991) *The Scale of Imprisonment*. Chicago, IL: University of Chicago Press.

28.3 The inmate world
Erving Goffman

It is characteristic of inmates that they come to the institution with a 'presenting culture' (to modify a psychiatric phrase) derived from a 'home world' – a way of life and a round of activities taken for granted until the point of admission to the institution. (There is reason, then, to exclude orphanages and foundling homes from the list of total institutions, except in so far as the orphan comes to be socialized into the outside world by some process of cultural osmosis even while this world is being systematically denied him.) Whatever the stability of the recruit's personal organization, it was part of a wider framework lodged in his civil environment – a round of experience that confirmed a tolerable conception of self and allowed for a set of defensive manoeuvres, exercised at his own discretion, for coping with conflicts, discreditings, and failures.

Now it appears that total institutions do not substitute their own unique culture for something already formed; we deal with something more restricted than acculturation or assimilation. If cultural change does occur, it has to do, perhaps, with the removal of certain behaviour opportunities and with failure to keep pace with recent social changes on the outside. Thus, if the inmate's stay is long, what has been called 'disculturation'[1] may occur – that is, an 'untraining' which renders him temporarily incapable of managing certain features of daily life on the outside, if and when he gets back to it.

The full meaning for the inmate of being 'in' or 'on the inside' does not exist apart from the special meaning to him of 'getting out' or 'getting on the outside'. In this sense, total institutions do not really look for cultural victory. They create and sustain a particular kind of tension between the home world and the institutional world and use this persistent tension as strategic leverage in the management of men.

The recruit comes into the establishment with a conception of himself made possible by certain stable social arrangements in his home world. Upon entrance, he is immediately stripped of the support provided by these arrangements. In the accurate language of some of our oldest total institutions, he begins a series of abasements, degradations, humiliations, and profanations of self. His self is systematically, if often unintentionally, mortified. He begins some radical shifts in his *moral career*, a career composed of the progressive changes that occur in the beliefs that he has concerning himself and significant others.

The processes by which a person's self is mortified are fairly standard in total institutions;[2] analysis of these processes can help us to see the arrangements that ordinary establishments must guarantee if members are to preserve their civilian selves.

The barrier that total institutions place between the inmate and the wider world marks the first curtailment of self. In civil life, the sequential scheduling of the individual's roles, both in the life cycle and in the repeated daily round, ensures that no one role he plays will block his performance and ties in another. In total institutions, in contrast, membership automatically disrupts role scheduling, since the inmate's separation from the wider world lasts around the clock and may continue for years. Role dispossession therefore occurs. In many total institutions the privilege of having visitors or of visiting away from the establishment is completely withheld at first, ensuring a deep initial break with past roles and an appreciation of role dispossession. A report on cadet life in a military academy provides an illustration:

> This clean break with the past must be achieved in a relatively short period. For two months, therefore, the swab is not allowed to leave the base or to engage in social intercourse with non-cadets. This complete isolation helps to produce a unified group of swabs, rather than a heterogeneous collection of persons of high and low status. Uniforms are issued on the first day, and discussions of wealth and family background are taboo. Although the pay of the cadet is very low, he is not permitted to receive money from home. The role of the cadet must supersede other roles the individual has been accustomed to play. There are few clues left which will reveal social status in the outside world.[3]

I might add that when entrance is voluntary, the recruit has already partially withdrawn from his home world; what is cleanly severed by the institution is something that had already started to decay.

Although some roles can be re-established by the inmate if and when he returns to the world, is plain that other losses are irrevocable and may be painfully experienced as such. It may not be possible to make up, at a later phase of the life cycle, the time not now spent in educational or job advancement, in courting, or in rearing one's children. A legal aspect of this permanent dispossession is found in the concept of 'civil death'; prison inmates may face not only a temporary loss of the rights to will money and write cheques, to contest divorce or adoption proceedings, and to vote but may have some of these rights permanently abrogated.[4]

The inmate, then, finds certain roles are lost to him by virtue of the barrier that separates him from the outside world. The process of entrance typically brings other kinds of loss and mortification as well. We very generally find staff employing what are called admission procedures, such as taking a life history, photographing, weighing, fingerprinting, assigning numbers, searching, listing personal possessions for storage, undressing, bathing, disinfecting, haircutting, issuing institutional clothing, instructing as to rules, and assigning to quarters.[5] Admission procedures might better be called 'trimming' or 'programming' because in thus being squared away the new arrival allows himself to be shaped and coded into an object that can be fed into the administrative machinery of the establishment, to be worked on smoothly by routine operations. Many of these procedures depend upon attributes such as weight or fingerprints that the individual possesses merely because he is a member of the largest and most abstract of social categories, that of human beings. Action taken on the basis of such attributes necessarily ignores most of his previous bases of self-identification.

Because a total institution deals with so many aspects of its inmates' lives, with the consequent complex squaring away at admission, there is a special need to obtain initial cooperativeness from the recruit. Staff often feel that a recruit's readiness to be appropriately deferential in his initial face-to-face encounters with them is a sign that he will take the role of the routinely pliant inmate. The occasion on which staff members first tell the inmate of his deference obligations may be structured to challenge the inmate to balk or to hold his peace forever. Thus these initial moments of socialization may involve an 'obedience test' and even a will-breaking contest: an inmate who shows defiance receives immediate visible punishment, which increases until he openly 'cries uncle' and humbles himself. [. . .]

Admission procedures and obedience tests may be elaborated into a form of initiation that has been called 'the welcome', where staff or inmates, or both, go out of their way to give the recruit a clear notion of his plight.[6] As part of this rite of passage be may be called by a term such as 'fish' or 'swab', which tells him that he is merely an inmate, and, what is more, that he has a special low status even in this low group.

The admission procedure can be characterized as a leaving off and a taking on, with the midpoint marked by physical nakedness. Leaving off of course entails a dispossession of property, important because persons invest self feelings in their possessions. Perhaps the most significant of these possessions is not physical at all, one's full name; whatever one is thereafter called, loss of one's name can be a great curtailment of the self.[7]

Once the inmate is stripped of his possessions, at least some replacements must be made by the establishment, but these take the form of standard issue, uniform in character and uniformly distributed. These substitute possessions are clearly marked as really belonging to the institution and in some cases are recalled at regular intervals to be, as it were, disinfected of identifications. With objects that can be used up – for example, pencils – the inmate may be required to return the remnants before obtaining a reissue.[8] Failure to provide inmates with individual lockers and periodic searches and confiscations of accumulated personal property[9] reinforce property dispossession. Religious orders have appreciated the implications for self of such separation from belongings. Inmates may be required to change their cells once a year so as not to become attached to them. The Benedictine Rule is explicit:

> For their bedding let a mattress, a blanket, a coverlet, and a pillow suffice. These beds must be frequently inspected by the Abbot, because of private property which may be found therein. If anyone be discovered to have what he has not received from the Abbot, let him be most severely punished. And in order that this vice of private ownership may be completely rooted out, let all things that are necessary be supplied by the Abbot: that is, cowl, tunic, stockings, shoes, girdle, knife, pen, needle, handkerchief, and tablets; so that all plea of necessity may be

taken away. And let the Abbot always consider that passage in the Acts of the Apostles: 'Distribution was made to each according as anyone had need.'[10]

One set of the individual's possessions has a special relation to self. The individual ordinarily expects to exert some control over the guise in which he appears before others. For this he needs cosmetic and clothing supplies, tools for applying, arranging, and repairing them, and an accessible, secure place to store these supplies and tools – in short, the individual will need an 'identity kit' for the management of his personal front. He will also need access to decoration specialists such as barbers and clothiers.

On admission to a total institution, however, the individual is likely to be stripped of his usual appearance and of the equipment and services by which he maintains it, thus suffering a personal defacement. Clothing, combs, needle and thread, cosmetics, towels, soap, shaving sets, bathing facilities – all these may be taken away or denied him, although some may be kept in inaccessible storage, to be returned if and when he leaves. In the words of St Benedict's Holy Rule:

> Then forthwith he shall, there in the oratory, be divested of his own garments with which he is clothed and be clad in those of the monastery. Those garments of which he is divested shall be placed in the wardrobe, there to be kept, so that if, perchance, he should ever be persuaded by the devil to leave the monastery (which God forbid), he may be stripped of the monastic habit and cast forth.[11]

As suggested, the institutional issue provided as a substitute for what has been taken away is typically of a 'coarse' variety, ill-suited, often old, and the same for large categories of inmates. The impact of this substitution is described in a report on imprisoned prostitutes:

> First, there is the shower officer who forces them to undress, takes their own clothes away, sees to it that they take showers and get their prison clothes – one pair of black oxfords with cuban heels, two pairs of much-mended ankle socks, three cotton dresses, two cotton slips, two pairs of panties, and a couple of bras. Practically all the bras are flat and useless. No corsets or girdles are issued.

> There is not a sadder sight than some of the obese prisoners, who, if nothing else, have been managing to keep themselves looking decent on the outside, confronted by the first sight of themselves in prison issue.[12]

In addition to personal defacement that comes from being stripped of one's identity kit, there is personal disfigurement that comes from direct and permanent mutilations of the body such as brands or loss of limbs. Although this mortification of the self by way of the body is found in few total institutions, still, loss of a sense of personal safety is common and provides a basis for anxieties about disfigurement. Beatings, shock therapy, or, in mental hospitals, surgery – whatever the intent of staff in providing these services for some inmates – may lead many inmates to feel that they are in an environment that does not guarantee their physical integrity.

At admission, loss of identity equipment can prevent the individual from presenting his usual image of himself to others. After admission, the image of himself he presents is attacked in another way. Given the expressive idiom of a particular civil society, certain movements, postures, and stances will convey lowly images of the individual and be avoided as demeaning. Any regulation, command, or task that forces the individual to adopt these movements or postures may mortify his self. In total institutions, such physical indignities abound. In mental hospitals, for example, patients may be forced to eat all food with a spoon.[13] In military prisons, inmates may be required to stand at attention whenever an officer enters the compound.[14] In religious institutions, there are such classic gestures of penance as the kissing of feet,[15] and the posture recommended to an erring monk that he

> lie prostrate at the door of the oratory in silence; and thus, with his face to the ground and his body prone, let him cast himself at the feet of all as they go forth from the oratory.[16]

In some penal institutions we find the humiliation of bending over to receive a birching.[17]

Just as the individual can be required to hold his body in a humiliating pose, so he may have to provide humiliating verbal responses. An important instance of this is the forced deference pattern of total institutions; inmates are often required to punctuate their social interaction with staff by verbal acts of deference, such as saying 'sir'. Another instance is the necessity to beg, importune, or humbly ask for little things such as a light for a cigarette, a drink of water, or permission to use the telephone.

Corresponding to the indignities of speech and action required of the inmate are the indignities of treatment others accord him. The standard examples here are verbal or gestural profanations: staff or fellow inmates call the individual obscene names, curse him, point out his negative attributes, tease him, or talk about him or his fellow inmates as if he were not present.

Whatever the form or the source of these various indignities, the individual has to engage in activity whose symbolic implications are incompatible with his conception of self. A more diffuse example of this kind of mortification occurs when the individual is required to undertake a daily round of life that he considers alien to him – to take on a disidentifying role. In prisons, denial of heterosexual opportunities can induce fear of losing one's masculinity.[18] In military establishments, the patently useless make-work forced on fatigue details can make men feel their time and effort are worthless.[19] In religious institutions there are special arrangements to ensure that all inmates take a turn performing the more menial aspects of the servant role.[20] An extreme is the concentration-camp practice requiring prisoners to administer whippings to other prisoners.[21]

There is another form of mortification in total institutions; beginning with admission a kind of contaminative exposure occurs. On the outside, the individual can hold objects of self-feeling – such as his body, his immediate actions, his thoughts, and some of his possessions – clear of contact with alien and contaminating things. But in total institutions these territories of the self are violated; the boundary that the individual places between his being and the environment is invaded and the embodiments of self profaned.

There is, first, a violation of one's informational preserve regarding self. During admission, facts about the inmate's social statuses and past behaviour – especially discreditable facts – are collected and recorded in a dossier available to staff. Later, in so far as the establishment officially expects to alter the self-regulating inner tendencies of the inmate, there may be group or individual confession – psychiatric, political, military, or religious, according to the type of institution. On these occasions the inmate has to expose facts and feelings about self to new kinds of audiences. [...]

New audiences not only learn discreditable facts about oneself that are ordinarily concealed but are also in a position to perceive some of these facts directly. Prisoners and mental patients cannot prevent their visitors from seeing them in humiliating circumstances.[22] Another example is the shoulder patch of ethnic identification worn by concentration-camp inmates.[23] Medical and security examinations often expose the inmate physically, sometimes to persons of both sexes; a similar exposure follows from collective sleeping arrangements and doorless toilets.[24] An extreme here, perhaps, is the situation of a self-destructive mental patient who is stripped naked for what is felt to he his own protection and placed in a constantly lit seclusion room, into whose Judas window any person passing on the ward can peer. In general, of course, the inmate is never fully alone; he is always within sight and often earshot of someone, if only his fellow inmates.[25] Prison cages with bars for walls fully realize such exposure. [...]

A very common form of physical contamination is reflected in complaints about unclean food, messy quarters, soiled towels, shoes and clothing impregnated with previous users' sweat, toilets without seats, and dirty bath facilities.[26] [...]

Finally, in some total institutions the inmate is obliged to take oral or intravenous medications, whether desired or not, and to eat his food, however unpalatable. When an inmate refuses to eat, there may be forcible contamination of his innards by 'forced feeding'.

I have suggested that the inmate undergoes mortification of the self by contaminative exposure of a physical kind, but this must be amplified: when the agency of contamination is another human being, the inmate is in addition contaminated by forced interpersonal contact and, in consequence, a forced social relationship. (Similarly, when the inmate loses control over who observes him in his predicament or knows about his past, he is being contaminated by a forced relationship to these people – for it is through such perception and knowledge that relations are expressed.)

The model for interpersonal contamination in our society is presumably rape; although sexual molestation certainly occurs in total institutions, there are many other less dramatic examples. Upon admission, one's on-person possessions are pawed and fingered by an official as he itemizes and prepares them for storage. The inmate himself may be frisked and searched to the extent – often reported in the literature – of a rectal examination.[27] Later in his stay he may be required to undergo searchings of his person and of his sleeping quarters, either routinely or when trouble arises. In all these cases it is the searcher as well as the search that penetrates the private reserve of the individual and violates the territories of his self. [...]

I have suggested that authority in total institutions is directed to a multitude of items of conduct – dress, deportment, manners – that constantly occur and constantly come up for judgement. The inmate cannot easily escape from the press of judgemental officials and from the enveloping tissue of constraint. A total institution is like a finishing school, but one that has many refinements and is little refined. I would like to comment on two aspects of this tendency towards a multiplication of actively enforced rulings.

First, these rulings are often geared in with an obligation to perform the regulated activity in unison with blocks of fellow inmates. This is what is sometimes called regimentation.

Second, these diffuse rulings occur in an authority system of the *echelon* kind: *any* member of the staff class has certain rights to discipline *any* member of the inmate class, thereby markedly increasing the probability of sanction. (This arrangement, it may be noted, is similar to the one that gives any adult in some small American towns certain rights to correct any child not in the immediate presence of his parents and to demand small services from him.) On the outside, the adult in our society is typically under the authority of a *single* immediate superior in connexion with his work, or the authority of one spouse in connexion with domestic duties; the only echelon authority he must face – the police – is typically not constantly or relevantly present, except perhaps in the case of traffic-law enforcement.

Given echelon authority and regulations that are diffuse, novel, and strictly enforced, we may expect inmates, especially new ones, to live with chronic anxiety about breaking the rules and the consequence of breaking them – physical injury or death in a concentration camp, being 'washed out' in an officer's training school, or demotion in a mental hospital:

Yet, even in the apparent liberty and friendliness of an 'open' ward, I still found a background of threats that made me feel something between a prisoner and a pauper. The smallest offence, from a nervous symptom to

displeasing a sister personally, was met by the suggestion of removing the offender to a closed ward. The idea of a return to 'J' ward, if I did not eat my food, was brandished at me so constantly that it became an obsession and even such meals as I was able to swallow disagreed with me physically, while other patients were impelled to do unnecessary or uncongenial work by a similar fear.[28]

In total institutions staying out of trouble is likely to require persistent conscious effort. The inmate may forgo certain levels of sociability with his fellows to avoid possible incidents.

> *From E. Goffman,* Asylums *(Harmondsworth: Penguin), 1968, pp. 23–47.*

Notes

1 A term employed by Robert Sommer, 'Patients who grow old in a mental hospital', *Geriatrics*, XIV (1959), pp. 586–7. The term 'desocialization', sometimes used in this context, would seem to be too strong, implying loss of fundamental capacities to communicate and cooperate.

2 An example of the description of these processes may be found in Gresham M. Sykes, *The Society of Captives* (Princeton: Princeton University Press, 1958), ch. iv, 'The Pains of Imprisonment', pp. 63–83.

3 Sanford M. Dornbusch, 'The Military Academy as an Assimilating Institution', *Social Forces*, XXXIII (1955), p. 317. For an example of initial visiting restrictions in a mental hospital, see D. McI. Johnson and N. Dodds, eds., *The Plea for the Silent* (London: Christopher Johnson, 1957), p. 16. Compare the rule against having visitors which has often bound domestic servants to their total institution. See J. Jean Hecht, *The Domestic Servant Class in Eighteenth-Century England* (London: Routledge and Kegan Paul, 1956), pp. 127–8.

4 A useful review in the case of American prisons may be found in Paul W. Tappan, 'The Legal Rights of Prisoners', *The Annals*, CCXCIII (May 1954), pp. 99–111.

5 See, for example, J. Kerkhoff, *How Thin the Veil: A Newspaperman's Story of His Own Mental Crack-up and Recovery* (New York; Greenberg, 1952), p. 110; Elie A. Cohen, *Human Behaviour in the Concentration Camp*, (London: Jonathan Cape, 1954), pp. 118–22; Eugen Kogon, *The Theory and Practice of Hell* (New York: Berkley Publishing Corp., n.d.), pp. 63–8.

6 For a version of this process in concentration camps, see Cohen, *op. cit.*, p. 120. and Kogon, *op. cit.*, pp. 64–5. For a fictionalized treatment of the welcome

in a girls' reformatory see, Sara Harris, *The Wayward Ones* (New York: New American Library, 1952), pp. 31–4. A prison version, less explicit, is found in George Dendrickson and Frederick Thomas, *The Truth About Dartmoor* (London: Gollancz, 1954), pp. 42–57.

7   For example, Thomas Merton, *The Seven Storey Mountain* (New York: Harcourt, Brace and Company, 1948), pp. 290–91; Cohen, *op. cit.*, pp. 145–7.

8   Dendrickson and Thomas, *op. cit.*, pp. 83–4, also *The Holy Rule of Saint Benedict*, ch. 55.

9   Kogon, *op. cit.*, p. 69.

10   *The Holy Rule of Saint Benedict*, ch. 55.

11   *The Holy Rule of Saint Benedict*, ch. 58.

12   John M. Murtagh and Sara Harris, *Cast the First Stone* (New York: Pocket Books, 1958), pp. 239–40. On mental hospitals see, for example, Kerkhoff, *op. cit.*, p. 10. Ward, *op. cit.*, p.60, makes the reasonable suggestion that men in our society suffer less defacement in total institutions than do women.

13   Johnson and Dodds, *op. cit.*, p. 15; for a prison version see Alfred Hassler, *Diary of a Self-Made Convict* (Chicago: Regnery, 1954), p. 33.

14   L. D. Hankoff, 'Interaction Patterns Among Military Prison Personnel', *U.S. Armed Forces Medical Journal*, X (1959), p. 1419.

15   Kathryn Hulme, *The Nun's Story* (London: Muller, 1951), p. 52.

16   *The Holy Rule of Saint Benedict*, ch. 44.

17   Dendrickson and Thomas, *op. cit.*, p. 76.

18   Sykes, *op. cit.*, pp. 70–72.

19   For example, Lawrence, *op. cit.*, pp. 34–5.

20   *The Holy Rule of Saint Benedict*, ch. 35.

21   Kogon, *op. cit.*, p. 102.

22   Wider communities in Western society, of course, have employed this technique too, in the form of public floggings and public hangings, the pillory and stocks. Functionally correlated with the public emphasis on mortifications in total institutions is the commonly found strict ruling that staff is not to be humiliated by staff in the presence of inmates.

23   Kogon, *op. cit.*, pp. 41–2.

24   Behan, *op. cit.*, p. 23.

25   For example, Kogon, *op. cit.*, p. 128; Hassler, *op. cit.*, p. 16. For the situation in a religious institution, see Hulme, *op. cit.*, p. 48. She also describes a lack of aural privacy since thin cotton hangings are used as the only door closing off the individual sleeping cells (p. 20).

26   For example, Johnson and Dodds, *op. cit.*, p. 75; Heckstall-Smith, *op. cit.*, p. 1

27   For example, Lowell Naeve, *A Field of Broken Stones* (Glen Gardner, New Jersey: Libertarian Press, 1950), p. 17; Kogon, *op. cit.*, p. 67; Holley Cantine and Dachine Rainer, *Prison Etiquette* (Bearsville, NY: Retort Press, 1950), p. 46.

28   Johnson and Dodds, *op. cit.*, p. 36.

28.4 Women in prison: the facts
Pat Carlen and Anne Worrall

Introduction

Women in prison are sent there by courts. This may seem an obvious statement but it is easy to forget that there is no inevitable or direct link between the crime a woman commits and her imprisonment. There are a number of stages and factors that intervene between crime and sentence and a number of choices to be made by a number of different people.

Sentencing women: chivalry or double jeopardy?

Hedderman and Gelsthorpe argue that:

> equal treatment for men and women is a matter of approach not outcome. The underlying assumption is that fairness consists of people in similar circumstances being treated in similar ways, but it must be recognised that men and women do not necessarily appear in similar circumstances. (1997:1)

Despite periodic claims that women's offending is disproportionately under-reported (Pollak 1950; Mirrlees-Black 1999) there has never been any serious evidence to support this contention (see, for example, Gadd *et al.*'s (2002) attempt to follow up claims of domestic violence victimisation by men in the Scottish Crime Survey). In 2000, women accounted for 16 per cent of those arrested (Home Office 2002a). Within this small proportion, they tended to be over-represented in arrests for fraud and forgery (mainly falsely claiming social security) and theft and handling (mainly shoplifting). They were markedly under-represented in sexual offences and burglary.

Police decisions to proceed are influenced by a number of factors, including perceptions of the extent to which a woman fulfils gender role expectations and is therefore likely to respond to informal social controls, making formal controls unnecessary (Horn 1995). Over and above this consideration, women are more likely than men to admit their offences, making it easier for them to be cautioned (Phillips and Brown 1998). The reasons for women's apparent readiness to admit guilt may have less to do with an acceptance of legal guilt and more to do with, on the one hand, practical concerns about time and publicity and, on the other, an all-pervasive sense of guilt about being a failing wife and mother. [...] What is clear is that women feel – and, indeed, are – 'out-of-place' in the criminal justice system (Worrall 1981), unable to command the language and behaviour that will enable them to negotiate for themselves what passes for 'justice' in a male-dominated system.

On reaching court, women are more likely than men to receive conditional discharges and supervision, and less likely to receive fines and custody (Home Office 2002a). The overwhelming reasons for this apparent leniency are that women commit less serious offences and have fewer previous convictions than men. While one in three men is likely to have a conviction by the age of 40 years, this is true of only one in twelve women (Home Office 2002a). Women's criminal careers are also much shorter than men's, the vast majority lasting less than a year. Additionally, there has been a limited recognition in recent years of the 'criminalisation of female poverty' (Pantazis 1999) and women's relative inability to pay fines. There has been a consequent reluctance on the part of sentencers to burden women with fines (Hedderman and Gelsthorpe 1997) though the result has been that some women may experience the greater intrusiveness of supervision rather than the lesser sentence of a conditional discharge.

There may, however, be other 'non-legal' factors which influence the sentencing of women and these concern sentencers' perceptions of the women before them. These perceptions are, in turn, dependent on the kinds of information they have about the women and their own value judgements about what the woman 'needs' and/or 'deserves'. Only certain kinds of information are admissible in court. Most routinely, these kinds of information (or knowledge claims) are: lay 'commonsense' knowledge; legal knowledge; social

psychological knowledge and (occasionally) medical knowledge (Worrall 1990). Any other information or knowledge claim (such as the defendant's own explanation or socio-political analyses of the defendant's circumstances) are inadmissible unless re-presented in ways that are compatible with 'authorised' versions of events. This is what is meant when writers assert that 'women are socially constructed within discourses of femininity'. [...]

Sentencers tend to construct men and women differently, though it is arguable that those differences are diminishing and that it is this, rather than any changes in women's offending behaviour, that accounts for the increase in the numbers of women being sent to prison. This change has been termed the 'backlash' against feminist perspectives on women and crime, or the 'search for equivalence' (Worrall 2002a). Traditionally, sentencers have allowed considerations of women's domestic competence, sexual respectability and mental (in)stability (Eaton 1986; Allen 1987a; Worrall 1990; Hedderman and Gelsthorpe 1997) to inform their decisions to a greater extent than would be the case for men (where employment and general citizenship are considered to be more relevant) (Deane 2000; Horn and Evans 2000).

Not withstanding all of the above, Hedderman and Gelsthorpe (1997) identified two groups of women for whom these considerations appeared to play little or no part in sentencing – women who commit drugs or violent offences. Although women are less likely than men to be sent to prison for their first drugs offence, repeat offenders are equally likely to receive a custodial sentence, regardless of other factors. The pattern is reversed in the case of violent offences. First-time violent female offenders are as likely as men to be sent to prison, though this is not true for repeat offenders. One can speculate that this is because women who commit violent offences are most likely to commit one very serious offence such as either homicide (of a male partner following years of his abuse, for example) or cruelty to a child. Those who engage in repeat but lower level violence may invite concerns about their mental stability and thus be diverted away from custody towards treatment.

Thomas (2002) is convinced that a major explanation for the increase in women's immediate imprisonment can be found in the decline in the use of the suspended prison sentence. If he is correct (and his argument appears to make numerical sense) then one aim of the Criminal Justice Act 1991[1] – to reduce the prison population – has been undermined by the restrictions placed on the use of the suspended sentence by that same Act. Prior to the Act, it had become received wisdom that suspended sentences simply postponed imprisonment and had a net-widening effect. In the case of women, however, because of their low reoffending rates, its use might well have prevented imprisonment. The case on which Thomas comments appears to have been an excellent example of this – a first offender with responsibility for children, committing a serious offence of dishonesty.

Discrimination and Section 95 publications

Section 95 of the [Criminal Justice Act 1991] required the Secretary of State to 'publish such information as he considers expedient for the purpose of enabling persons engaged in the administration of justice to ... avoid discriminating against any persons on the ground of race or sex or any other improper ground'. Two publications now appear annually, on women and 'race' (Home Office 2002a, 2002b) which summarise, in an entirely descriptive but deliberately readable manner, selective statistical data on the experiences of women (and ethnic minorities) as offenders, victims and workers in the criminal justice system. The publications provide no new data, but are a useful supplement to the rather less accessible official statistics publications.

Counting women in prison

Average population

There are several ways of counting prisoners and this section will explain the main differences between the methods. The *average population* of prisoners derives from snapshots of all the people in prison on a given day. In England and Wales, the main day that is used for the production of annual prison statistics is 30 June. There are also monthly Prison Population Briefings which count prisoners on the last day of each month and the Prison Service now produces a weekly *average population* every Friday on its website (www.hmprisonservice.gov.uk). This method of counting will tell you how many people are in prison but it will not tell you how long they are in prison for. Counting the *average population* is a

method which is biased in favour of people serving long sentences. For example, if a person is in prison for ten years, they will be counted ten times in the annual count at the end of June – and 120 times in the monthly briefings. On the other hand, if 52 people are sent to prison for seven days each (for example, for fine default) and they are sent one after another, only one of them will be counted at the end of June and only 12 will be counted for the monthly briefings. Only weekly counts would ensure that they were all counted. So, long-term prisoners are over-represented in the *average population* count and short-term prisoners are under-represented.

Receptions

An alternative way of counting prisoners is by *receptions*. This method counts everyone who is sent to prison during a year, for whatever reason and for however long or short a term. This gives a much better picture of the number of people being sent to prison by the courts. However, this method is biased towards short-term prisoners, who are over-represented. To use the previous example, a person spending ten years in prison will only be counted as one reception in the first year and not counted at all in subsequent years. The 52 people serving seven days each will be counted 52 times. A good example of this difference can be found when considering *fine defaulters* and *life sentence prisoners*. Fine defaulters are people who fail to pay court fines and are subsequently sent to prison, often only for a few days until they pay the fine. On average, male fine defaulters spend six days in prison and female fine defaulters spend two days in prison (Home Office 2003a). In 2001, there were 1,460 *receptions* of fine defaulters, but an *average population* of only 43 (Home Office 2003a). At the opposite end of the spectrum from fine defaulters are *life sentence* prisoners, who serve indeterminate sentences for murder or other very serious offences of violence. In 2001, there were 512 receptions of life sentence prisoners but an *average population* of 4,810 (almost ten times more than the receptions). The difference between the figure for receptions and the figure for *average population* gives an indication of the length of prison sentences. The greater the difference in favour of *receptions*, the shorter will be the length of sentences; the greater the difference in favour of *average population*, the longer will be the length of the sentences.

Rates of imprisonment

A third method of counting prisoners has become increasingly popular in recent years, primarily because it allows for international comparisons. This method is known as *rates of imprisonment* and has become the internationally accepted method for comparing penal policy and practice. Absolute numbers of prisoners give no indication of the size of a country's overall population or the percentage of that population which is imprisoned. Normally based on the *average population* and the relevant overall population in a country, *rates of imprisonment* tell you how many people out of every 100,000 in a total population are sent to prison. This method allows for more accurate comparisons over time as well as comparisons across populations.

How many women are there in prison?

The statistics in this section are all taken from *Prison Statistics for England and Wales 2001* (Home Office 2003a) and the tables and figures in brackets refer to the tables and figures in that document. These tables can be downloaded from the Home Office website (www.homeoffice.gov.uk/rds/). Click on 'subjects', then 'prisons'.

In 2001, the *average population* in prison was 66,301. Of these prisoners, 3,740 – or 5.6 per cent – were women (Home Office 2003a: Table 1.2a). During the previous ten years, the female prison population doubled, while the male population increased by about 50 per cent. But if we take a much longer-term view, it is clear from this same table and the accompanying figures (Figure 1:2a-d) that the *trend* or pattern of imprisonment for men and women was very different during the twentieth century. For men, the population increased from around 16,000 in 1901 to 62,500 in 2001. For women, the population declined from around 3,000 in 1901 to under 700 in the mid-1930s, then increased steadily thereafter. So, in 1901, there were as many women in prison as there are now and they represented over 16 per cent of the prison population, the majority being imprisoned for offences of drunkenness and prostitution (Home Office 2003a: 4).

The increase in the *average population* masks a different pattern of imprisonment, namely, changes in sentence length and time on remand. For this to be revealed, we need to consider *receptions* (Home Office 2003a: Table 1.1). In 2001, a total of 141,395 people were sent to prison and of these 11,946 were women – or around 8 per cent. Overall, there has been a large increase in *receptions* over the past ten years, but a small decline between 1999 and 2001. Nevertheless, the higher proportion of female receptions indicates (see previous section) that women are more likely than men to receive short sentences – or to be on remand.

Characteristics of women in prison

Prisoners fall into a number of different categories within the prison system, according to their age, type of offence, whether or not they are on remand or sentenced, the length of their sentence, and so on. Male prisoners are also categorised into one of four security categories (A – D) according to their assessed likelihood of escaping and the danger they would pose if they did escape. Women are only categorised as being suitable for closed (high security) or open (low security) conditions. It is not considered practical to categorise women in any greater detail because the numbers are so small that it would not be possible to provide sufficiently varied regimes to cater for more than two security categories. Thus, in theory, women might be either over- or under-categorised in terms of their security risk. In practice, the tendency is towards over-categorisation. [...] Despite the overall increase in the number of women in prison, the number of 'open' places for women has declined from almost 500 prior to 2000 to fewer than 250. [...] Women are now held in 19 prisons, of which only 17 are designated as 'female establishments'. Two more women' prisons are due to be opened in 2004. The remainder are male establishments with separate female wings. In all, there are 139 prisons in England and Wales. Fewer than 10 per cent of women in prison are now in open conditions.

Age and motherhood

The age distribution of sentenced women in prison is similar to that of sentenced men (Home Office 2003a: Table 1.9). Over 80 per cent of the *average population* of both men and women in prison are under the age of 40 years. About 66 per cent of men and 70 per cent of women are aged between 21 and 40; about 4 per cent of men and 2.3 per cent of women are juveniles (under the age of 18). This distribution has not changed greatly over the past ten years. The significance of these figures is that at least 70 per cent of women in prison are of child-bearing age and, if we add those aged 18–20 and those aged 40–49, it is likely that 95 per cent of them could have dependent children. In fact, surveys show consistently (Caddle and Crisp 1997; HM Chief Inspector of Prisons 1997) that some two-thirds of women in prison have dependent children. While 90 per cent of fathers in prison expect their children to be cared for by the children's mother, only about 25 per cent of mothers in prison expect their children to be cared for by the children's father (Home Office 2002a), the remainder being cared for by grandmothers, female relatives and friends, or the local authority. There are currently around 70 places in four women's prisons (at Holloway, Styal, Askham Grange and New Hall prisons) for mothers to care for babies (HM Prison Service 1999) but the upper age limit for babies is 18 months. Provision for mothers to care for their babies in prison is a controversial issue.

Another feature of the age distribution of female prisoners is the very small number of young offenders – women aged between 15 and 20 years. In 2001 there were about 2,700 *receptions* in this age category (Home Office 2003a: Table 3.10) compared with about 39,000 young men. For both men and women, the *receptions* were divided half and half between remands and sentenced prisoners.

Ethnic group and nationality

In 2001, minority ethnic groups made up 21 per cent of the male and 26 per cent of the female *average population* in prison. In the general population of England and Wales, approximately 94 per cent is white, 23 per cent black, 2–3 per cent South Asian and 1 per cent Chinese and other ethnic groups (Home Office 2003a: Figure 6.2). However, the picture is complicated by the issue of *nationality*. In 2001, 10 per cent of the prison population was made up of foreign nationals, a few of whom would be classified as 'white', but most of whom would be from other ethnic groups. In total in 2001, there were 2,986 British national women in prison and 696 foreign national women. Of the former group, about 419 were black, South Asian, Chinese or other. Of the latter group, about 545 were in those categories. So, just under 1,000 'non-white' women are divided between British and foreign nationals in a ratio of roughly 45:55 (Home Office 2003a: Table 6.3).

Offences and previous convictions

Men and women are sent to prison for different offences (Home Office 2003a: Table 1.7). If we remove the 1,100 women in prison for drugs offences in 2001, the next largest group is the 439 in prison for violence, followed by the 434 in prison for theft and handling. This suggests that theft, handling and drugs offences account for over half the female prison population. For men, the picture is very different. The largest group of men in prison are there for violence (11,198), followed by burglary (8,361), with drugs accounting for the third largest group (7,936). Between them, these offences make up about 27,000 men, or half the sentenced population. Theft and handling come a long way down the list. The reason that women are sent to prison for different offences from men is because they *commit* different offences from men. Seventy per cent of all offences committed by women are for theft and handling, compared with less than half of those committed by men (Home Office 2002a). So it could be argued that the prison population is bound to reflect that difference. Nevertheless, it is important to recognise these differences when confronted with claims that 'women are getting more violent'. Even with the acknowledged concern about the increase in drugs offences committed by women, they still account for little more than 10 per cent of all drugs offenders in prison. [...]

Not only are women sent to prison for different offences from men, but they are also sent with fewer previous convictions. About one-third of women in prison are first offenders, compared with 13 per cent of men in prison (Home Office 2003a: Table 4.2). However, as many writers have pointed out (for example, Hedderman and Hough 1994) this does not mean that female first offenders are more likely than male first offenders to be sent to prison. The fact is that, because *most* women who appear in court are first offenders (Morgan 1997), first offenders will appear to be over-represented in *all* sentences on women.

Sentence lengths

On average, the sentences which women receive are shorter than those received by men (Home Office 2003a: Table 4.10), although both have increased steadily since 1995. In 2001 average sentences imposed on men by the Crown Court were 30 months and on women they were 26 months; sentences imposed by Magistrates' Courts were 4.4 months and 3.6 months respectively. However, this difference increases when one takes account of the fact that almost all short-term prisoners and many longer-term prisoners serve only half of their sentence in custody before being released on a supervised licence.[...] When these things are taken into account, women serve, on average, 50 per cent of their sentence length, while men serve 55 per cent (Home Office 2003a: Table 4.11). We have already seen that women serve, on average, two days for fine default, while men serve six days. In 2001, 73 women went to prison for fine default, compared with 1,380 men (Home Office 2003a: Table 1.14).

Suicide, disciplinary offences and reconvictions

Women prisoners don't riot – or so said Liebling (1994) after the Woolf Inquiry into the disturbances at Manchester prison in 1990. This, Liebling argued, is why they are so often overlooked. Women are more likely to self-harm and attempt suicide if they are distressed. Women are over-represented in self-inflicted deaths in prison, accounting for 9 per cent of such deaths (Home Office 2003a: Table 11.20) and, when one considers that, in the outside community, men commit suicide more than twice as frequently as women, this over-representation is even greater. Additionally, Liebling (1994, 1999) argues that women's apparent suicides in prison may attract verdicts such as 'misadventure', 'accidental' or 'open', due to assumptions of low intent (1999: 308).

However, it is certainly not true that women are not disruptive in response to the experience of imprisonment. They may not respond collectively in the way that men do, but they commit more disciplinary offences per head than men do (Home Office 2003a: Table 8.1). In 2001, they averaged 2.3 offences, compared with 1.6 for men. But what sort of behaviour are we talking about here? Disciplinary offences consist of five broad categories – violence, escape, disobedience and disrespect, damage and unauthorised transactions (stealing or possessing unauthorised items including drugs) (Home Office 2003a: Table 8.3). Because of increased security, there are virtually no escapes from either male or female prisons these days. In all other categories, women commit more offences than men and young women commit the most offences. [...]

It has already been stated that women have fewer convictions and shorter criminal careers than men (Home Office 2002a). Women's reconviction rates within two years of discharge from prison are also lower, though perhaps not as markedly lower as one might expect, given their lower levels of previous offending. Of the men released from prison in 1999, 58 per cent had been reconvicted by 2001 (though that includes 73 per cent of young male offenders). Of the women released in 1999, 53 per cent had been reconvicted by 2001 (including 58 per cent of young female offenders) (Home Office 2003a: Table 9.1). When considered alongside the high level of disciplinary offences among women, there would seem to be at least some evidence to support the view that prison exacerbates whatever prior offending problems women might have had and, to adapt a phrase from the Government (Home Office 1990) 'makes bad/sad/mad women worse'.

Drugs, sexual abuse and mental health

Leaving aside, for the moment, the numbers of women who are in prison specifically for drugs offences, the Prison Service now estimates that almost all prisoners have problems with alcohol, drugs and/or mental illness. Women in prison are more likely than men to report having had a drugs dependency before coming to prison and they are also more likely to report having had treatment for some form of mental ill-health prior to imprisonment. The latter is not a surprising observation since women not in prison are more likely than men in the community to seek help for mental ill-health (predominantly depression and anxiety) (Chesler 1974; Allen 1987a; Department of Health 2002). Having said this, one in five women in prison has spent some time as an in-patient in a psychiatric hospital (Prison Reform Trust 2000a), which is a higher proportion than in the population at large. Many writers (Carlen 1988; Howard League 1997; Prison Reform Trust 2000a) have pointed to the fact that many women in prison report having been sexually abused at some time in their childhood or adult lives. A high proportion have been subject to local authority care, thus moving from one institution to another on reaching adulthood (Carlen 1988). (For an analysis of the gender, ethnicity and vulnerability of young women in local authority care, see Lees 2002.)

It is clear from all the above that most women in prison have grown up in multiply disadvantaged environments and, given their relatively low levels of offending, have spent much of their lives struggling to live within the law. Although they still represent a very small proportion of the prison population, there is no rational reason why that proportion should not be even smaller. Instead, it is slowly but surely increasing and, as we shall see now, this is not a problem confined to England and Wales.

> *From P. Carlen and A. Worrall,* Analysing Women's Imprisonment *(Cullompton: Willan Publishing), 2004, pp. 28–42.*

References

Allen, H. (1987a) *Justice Unbalanced*. Buckingham: Open University Press.

Caddle, D. and Crisp, D. (1997) *Imprisoned Women and Mothers*. Home Office Research Study 162. London: Home Office.

Carlen, P. (1988) *Women, Crime and Poverty*. Buckingham: Open University Press.

Chesler, P. (1974) *Women and Madness*. London: Allen Lane.

Deane, H. (2000) The influence of pre-sentence reports on sentencing in a District Court in New Zealand. *The Australian and New Zealand Journal of Criminology*, 33(1): 91–106.

Department of Health (2002) *Women's Mental Health: Into the Mainstream*. London: Department of Health.

Eaton, M. (1986) *Justice for Women? Family, Court and Social Control*. Buckingham: Open University Press.

Gadd, D., Farrall, S., Dallimore, D. and Lombard, N. (2002) *Domestic Abuse Against Men in Scotland*. Edinburgh: Scottish Executive Central Research Unit.

Hedderman. C. and Gelsthorpe, L. (1997) *Understanding the Sentencing of Women*. Home Office Research Study 170. London: HMSO.

Hedderman, C. and Hough, M. (1994) Does the criminal justice system treat men and women differently? *Research Findings* 10. London: Home Office Research and Statistics Department.

HM Chief Inspector of Prisons (1997) *Women in Prison: A Thematic Review*. London: Home Office.

HM Prison Service (1999) *Report of a Review of Principles, Policies and Procedures on Mothers and Babies/Children in Prison*. London: HM Prison Service.

Home Office (1990) *Crime, Justice and Protecting the Public*. Cm 965. London: Home Office.

Home Office (2002a) *Statistics on Women and the Criminal Justice System* 2001. London: Home Office.

Home Office (2002b) *Statistics on Race and the Criminal Justice System* 2001. London: Home Office.

Home Office (2003a) *Prison Statistics England and Wales 2001*. Cm 5743, London: The Stationery Office.

Horn, R. (1995) Not real criminals – police perceptions of women offenders. In *Criminal Justice Matters*, 19: 17–18.

Horn, R. and Evans, M. (2000) The effect of gender on pre-sentence reports. *Howard Journal*, 39(2): 184–204.

Howard League (1997) *Lost Inside – the Imprisonment of Teenage Girls*. London: Howard League for Penal Reform.

Lees, S. (2002) Gender, ethnicity and vulnerability in young women in local authority care. *British Journal of Social Work*, 32: 907–22.

Liebling, A. (1994) Suicides amongst women prisoners. *Howard Journal*, 33(1): 1–9.

Liebling, A. (1999) Prison suicide and prison coping. In Tonry, M. and Petersilia, J. (Eds) Prisons, vol. 25 of *Crime and Justice: A Review of Research*. Chicago, IL: University of Chicago Press.

Mirrlees-Black, C. (1999) *Domestic Violence: Findings from a New British Crime Survey Self-Completion Questionnaire*, Home Office Research Study 191. London: Home Office.

Morgan, R. (1997) Prisons. In Morgan, Maguire, R.M. and Reiner, R. (Eds) *The Oxford Handbook of Criminology*. Oxford: Clarendon Press.

Pantazis, C. (1999) The criminalization of female poverty. In Watson, S. and Doyal, L. (Eds) *Engendering Social Policy*. Buckingham: Open University Press.

Phillips, C. and Brown, D. (1998) *Entry into the Criminal Justice System: A Survey of Police Arrests and their Outcomes*. Home Office Research Study 185. London: Home Office.

Pollak, O. (1950) *The Criminality of Women*. Philadelphia, PA: University of Pennsylvania Press.

Prison Reform Trust (2000a) *Justice for Women: The Need for Reform*, (The Wedderburn Report). London: Prison Reform Trust.

Thomas, D.A. (2002) Case comment. *Crim. L. R.* 2002, April, 331–3.

Worrall, A. (1981) Out of place: Female offenders in court. *Probation Journal*, 28(3): 90–3.

Worrall, A. (1990) *Offending Women: Female Lawbreakers and the Criminal Justice System*. London: Routledge.

Worrall, A. (2002a) Rendering them punishable. In Carlen, P. (Ed.) *Women and Punishment: The Struggle for Justice*. Cullompton: Willan.

29

Youth crime
and youth justice

29.1 Present tense: moderates and hooligans
Geoffrey Pearson   680

29.2 The coming of the super-predators
John J. Dilulio   684

**29.3 Penal custody: intolerance, irrationality
and indifference**
Barry Goldson   689

29.4 Comparative youth justice
Michael Cavadino and James Dignan   698

Introduction

In the last century or thereabouts we have developed a separate system of juvenile or youth justice, aimed at dealing with the specific needs or requirements of youthful offenders. The readings in this chapter examine various aspects of the social response to youth crime – both in terms of how it is constructed as a social problem and in relation to the nature of the institutions that we put in place to deal with this social problem.

Worrying about youthful behaviour seems to be pretty much a constant feature of our social life – almost irrespective of the era in which we live. Successive generations have generally found something in the conduct of the young people of the day about which to get concerned and to use as an indication that somehow 'things are not what they used to be'. In a marvellous book entitled *Hooligan: A History of Respectable Fears*, Geoffrey Pearson **(Reading 29.1)** examines this long-standing and rather unchanging feature of our social world. Pretty much wherever one starts, he says, it is implied that there was once something of a 'golden age' but we have lost it now. It is a story of national decline, and young people are deeply inscribed in it. The timescale employed by those bemoaning the lost golden age is often 'twenty years ago' and this sense of a generational shift perhaps tells us much about how young people become a key source of our concerns and fears. Once you have read Pearson's introductory analysis I urge you to borrow the book from your library and read any one of the subsequent chapters to get a flavour of how we have talked about young people at different periods in our history.

A commentator who recently caused quite a furore over his depiction of youthful criminality is the American political scientist, John Dilulio. In an article written in an American periodical called *The Weekly Standard* in 1995 **(Reading 29.2)** he coined the term 'super-predators'. In it he tells a story of social decline: although crime overall has been dropping, youthful violence has been remarkably on the increase, he suggests. Most worryingly, he argues, each generation of crime-prone boys has been about three times as dangerous as the one that preceded it. Part of the problem we need to tackle, he suggests, is the 'moral poverty' that these young men grow up in.

In the third excerpt Barry Goldson **(Reading 29.3)** examines the recent politics of youth justice and changing government responses to youthful offending. The last decade to decade and a half, he suggests, has seen a toughening up of youth justice with a consequent increase in the use of imprisonment for juveniles. He then goes on to examine the conditions and treatment of young people in custody. First and foremost, he notes that young people in prison are generally drawn from the most disadvantaged sectors of our society. Approximately half will be 'known' to social services and a substantial proportion will have spent some of their life in care. Moreover, he argues that custody 'can never be a neutral experience' given the very substantial human costs involved for those incarcerated.

In what ways is our system of youth justice similar to, or different from, those of other jurisdictions? This is the question explored by Michael Cavadino and James Dignan **(Reading 29.4)**. They identify five different general models of youth justice and then identify the core characteristics of each. Such models can be used not for the usual comparative purposes – i.e. between jurisdictions – but can also be applied to help make sense of how youth justice penal policies shift and alter within jurisdictions over time.

Questions for discussion

1. Why do you think young people are often the source of public concerns? Are these concerns realistic?

2. John DiIulio's article on 'super-predators' caused considerable controversy. Why do you think this might have been?

3. What is the basis for DiIulio's argument that each generation of crime-prone boys is roughly three times worse than the one that preceded it? Can you see any difficulties with this argument?

4. What do you think DiIulio meant by 'moral poverty'? If he is right, what are the sensible social policy responses to this?

5. What were the main features of juvenile justice in the 1980s and how has it changed subsequently?

6. In what way is it true to say that 'child prisoners are routinely drawn from some of the most structurally disadvantaged and impoverished families, neighbourhoods and communities'? Provide illustrative evidence.

7. What are the main distinguishing characteristics of the five models of justice systems identified by Cavadino and Dignan?

8. Which aspects of the five systems are currently visible in youth justice in the jurisdiction you are most familiar with?

29.1 Present tense: moderates and hooligans
Geoffrey Pearson

To think this is England. (*The Sun*, 6 July 1981)

People are bound to ask what is happening to our country...Having been one of the most law-abiding countries in the world – a byword for stability, order, and decency – are we changing into something else?

(*The Daily Express*, 6 July 1981)

Once upon a time, so the story runs in these characteristic responses to the summer riots of 1981, violence and disorder were unknown in Britain. The hallowed traditions of the 'British way of life' were founded upon civility, reasonableness and an unquestioning respect for law and authority. Violence was entirely foreign to the nation and its people who were renowned for fair play, *sang froid* and the stiff upper lip.

But all that is no more. Now violence and terror lurk in the once-safe streets. The family no longer holds its proper place and parents have abandoned their responsibilities. In the classroom, where once the tidy scholars applied themselves diligently in their neat rows of desks, there is a carnival of disrespect. The police and magistrates have had their hands tied by the interference of sentimentalists and do-gooders. A new generation is upon us of mindless bully boys, vandals, muggers, head-bangers, football rowdies, granny-murderers, boot boys, toughs and tearaways who laugh in the face of the law, as we stand before the rising tide of violence and disorder with a Canute-like impotence.

'Are we the same people that we were thirty, forty, fifty years ago?' Mr Enoch Powell asked himself only weeks before the riots erupted in the British cities in 1981.[1] Mr Powell, of course, has not been notably shy about declaring his belief that it is black people who are at the root of the decline and fall of the 'British way of life'. In the wake of the riots, while denouncing all sorts of 'sentiment, wishful-thinking and humbug', *The Daily Mail* also saw fit to editorialise on the black community who, it was said, 'must bear no small responsibility for the fear of the mob that has now returned after a century or more to haunt the cities of this land'.[2] Mr George Gale, on the other hand, sensed a more general deterioration in manners as

the fountain-head of Britain's troubles, while bringing a much abbreviated timescale to bear on their onset. 'Over the past twenty years or so', he announced in a *Daily Express* front-page splash, 'there has been a revulsion from authority and discipline...There has been a permissive revolution...and now we all reap the whirlwind.'[3]

'Permissive' rot: history lessons without dates

It was never seriously in dispute, of course, that black and white people alike were caught up in the summer disturbances of 1981. Nor did it need riots to provoke these swan-songs for the old traditions. Throughout the 1970s, in a gathering storm of discontent, the same accusations had become a dominant and characteristic feature of the social landscape. The decline of family life, the lowering of standards in the schools, the 'permissive' worm within, the irresponsibility of working mothers and their delinquent 'latch-key' children, the excessive leniency of the law, and the unwarranted interference of the 'softy-softy, namby-pamby pussyfooting' of the 'so-called experts'[4] – these were well trodden avenues of complaint by 'law-and-order' enthusiasts and 'anti-permissive' moralists, warning of a vast historical degeneration among the British people.

In 1974, for example, we learned that 'For the first time in a century and a half, since the great Tory reformer Robert Peel set up the Metropolitan police, areas of our cities are becoming unsafe for peaceful citizens by night, and some even by day' – from no less an authority than that great Tory reformer Sir Keith Joseph. Warning that 'the balance of our population, our human stock is threatened', Keith Joseph sensed truly momentous possibilities of decline. 'Rome itself fell,' he reminded us, 'destroyed from inside.' 'Are we to be destroyed from inside, too, a country which successfully repelled and destroyed Philip of Spain, Napoleon, the Kaiser, Hitler?'[5]

Tory politicians of the so-called New Right have undoubtedly been the most active in promoting these ways of thinking, and the 'law-and-order' question played a major part in Mrs Thatcher's victorious election campaign in 1979.[6] Rhodes Boyson, the trouble-shooting panjandrum of the new moral conservatism, has been particularly energetic in admonishing the 'mindless sociologists' and 'all that mush' which has corrupted the national character.[7] 'It has not gone unnoticed,' said Dr Boyson in 1978, 'that crime has increased parallel with the number of social workers.' 'It is equally true,' countered *The Daily Mirror* in a spirited editorial response, 'that crime has increased parallel with speeches from Dr Boyson.'[8]

Senior policemen have also queued up in numbers to deliver their judgements against the decline in public morals, and to warn of the imminent eclipse of the old standards and traditions. 'The freedom and way of life we have been accustomed to enjoy for so long will vanish', Kenneth Oxford, Chief Constable of Merseyside, prophesied in 1977; 'what we are experiencing is not a passing phenomenon but a continuing process of change in our way of life ... our customary ways of behaving and our traditional values are being radically modified.'[9] 'The mindless violence, the personal attacks and injury,' asserted Philip Knights, President of the Association of Chief Police Officers, 'and above all the use of violence in all its forms to further political creeds, are relatively new to the streets of this country.'[10] The allegations that such developments are somehow unprecedented, together with the feeling that they involve a massive historical shift, are entirely typical. The work of the police, according to Sir Robert Mark in 1978, now required 'not only as much physical courage and dedication as policing parts of Victorian London but a great deal more moral courage than has been required by the police at any time since Peel'.[11] Another senior police officer who more than once captured the headlines, James Anderton, Chief Constable of Greater Manchester, decrying 'the rot that has now taken a firm hold in the fabric of our society', was so moved as to describe crime as Britain's 'Top Growth Industry'.[12] So, too, if we consult the Report of Her Majesty's Chief Inspector of Constabulary, 1975 (or almost any other year for that matter) we find ourselves assailed within the space of only a few paragraphs with repeated references to

vicious and ugly attacks...becoming all too commonplace...anxiety about violence...this increasing resort to violence ... violent crime which is becoming an accepted part of day to day life...the trend of increased violence in our society...this menace to our way of life.

The report was generous enough to remind us that the personal violence over which so much ink had been spilled amounted to less than 4 per cent of known serious crime. Even so, without pause the report resumed its brooding concern over 'the apparent relaxation of standards of behaviour', 'the lowering of hitherto established values', 'the erosion of good standards, which were hitherto commonplace' and the necessity of 'reinforcing the values of what as a nation we had believed in for many years'. 'Without due care', it was feared that 'the all too common attitude of self-preservation and the growing general acceptance to do as one pleased without fear of retribution would ... lead the country to anarchy'.[13] Nor would it appear that these awful prophecies from her Majesty's Chief Inspector were calculated to depress the spirits of the royal household. For HRH Prince Philip is known to have entertained his own version of this 'law-and-order' jeremiad, warning in 1979 of 'this avalanche of lawlessness threatening to engulf our civilisation'.[14]

'Whatever achievements policemen can claim, the ability to communicate is certainly not one of them', said Sir Robert Mark in his 1973 Dimbleby Lecture. 'We share with another more famous service a tradition of silence.'[15] If so, then we must freely admit that another time-honoured tradition of British self-restraint has very recently bit the dust. In contemporary Britain it seems almost impossible to go a single day without hearing, from some quarter or another, a senior policeman hectoring us on the deteriorated condition of public morals, while assuming the right to deliver homespun history lessons in which the past is lovingly remembered as a time of harmony. A time, that is, when the traditions of the 'British way of life' held sovereign sway, and the policeman's lot was an extremely happy one.

Locating the golden age

Now, what I wish to ask is whether this way of thinking about Britain's decline is useful and accurate. And if it is not (and I will argue that it is not) then to what extent does this tradition of anguished regret for the past hinder our actions in the present and in the future? We must be careful not to place the entire blame upon the amateur historians in Britain's police force. While policemen freely peddle these cherished beliefs in the lost standards of the 'British way of life', they did not invent them. Nor when the Tory press informs us, as it does unceasingly, that 'Britain has a pro-found tradition of unregimented, tolerant order'[16] should we rush to indict the historical embroidery of newspaper editors. Professional historians, too, are not unknown to indulge in this kind of histori-cal reasoning, perhaps best exemplified by T. A. Critchley's raptures about 'the native self-discipline of Anglo-Saxon England' and 'this streak of national self-discipline'.[17]

This view of Britain's history as one founded on stability and decency is deeply ingrained in the self-understanding of the British people. The pres-ent, we hardly need to be told, is extremely tense. But the past, say the accumulated traditions of our national culture, was a 'golden age' of order and security. Nowadays we need the iron fist of polic-ing in order that we might sleep soundly in our beds. Whereas formerly we did not, and our love of tolerant freedom was spontaneous, unregimented and natural.

The extremity of these awful judgements against the moral deterioration of the British peo-ple, and the enormous vision of chaos and disorder which they conjure up, suggest the need for a cau-tious organisation of our thought and feeling as we approach these matters. Clearly, there is an impres-sive consistency in this line of thinking – both in terms of the belief in a pre-existing era of tranquil-ity, and in the agreement that the natural moderacy of the 'British way of life' has been eclipsed in the hooligan deluge. However, when we come to more detailed considerations – such as exactly where this 'golden age' is to be located in real historical time – then we are confronted with such a disorderly jumble of datemarks and vague historical allusion as to allow for wide margins of disagreement even among dedicated 'law-and-order' enthusiasts. Indeed, at the centre of the preoccupation with declining standards and mounting disorder, there is an immense historical 'black hole'.

There are various historical reference points made available to us, by which it is said we can chart Britain's fall from grace. One of the most popular slogans suggests that we need only look back to 'Before the War' in order to reach the solid ground of tradition and stability. The Society of Conservative Lawyers, for example, confidently announced in its report on Public Order (1970) that such things as gang fights between youths were 'a distinctively postwar phenomenon'.[18] Patrick Jenkin, as Conservative Social Services

Secretary, more recently described how he had been reliably informed that 'the increasing turbu-lence of modern life, with rising crime, industrial disruption, violence and terrorism, was rooted in the separation of children from their parents dur-ing the war'.[19] Sir Keith Joseph offers a flexi-time history according to which, in the same speech where he entertained the spectacular belief that Britain's streets had been plunged into insecurity 'for the first time in a century and a half', he also conjured with a more modest timescale whereby 'such words as good and evil, such stress on self-discipline and standards have been out of favour since the war'.[20] Finally, from its privileged vantage point to diagnose any deterioration in the national character, the National Front described its own understanding of pre-war social realities in a leaflet offering advice to schoolchildren on *How to Spot a Red Teacher* (1977): 'Tell the Red Teacher the poor whites during the Great Slump didn't commit muggings on defenceless old ladies.'[21] Well, we shall see.

If the Second World War is often regarded as the watershed of 'permissiveness', then those with more educated tastes – who perhaps remember the precipitating crisis of the Public Order Act of 1936 and Mosley's black shirts, or who might have read the descriptions of pre-war razor gangs in Graham Greene's *Brighton Rock* – look back beyond the war before that, to the slumbering golden years of Edwardian England which is one of the most authoritative versions of the true location of the 'British way of life'. Next in line is the Victorian era, which is commonly remembered as harbour-ing some kind of gold standard of untarnished moral worth. 'We need to get back towards the Victorian days of discipline' says Dr Boyson in one of his attacks on 'permissiveness', and he is cer-tainly not alone among Tory fundamentalists in fondly remembering the glories of empire, child labour and workhouse in Queen Victoria's reign.[22]

The idea that the past harbours a golden age of tranquillity also readily lends itself to the view that history might furnish us with effective meth-ods of commonsense crime control. So, one Member of Parliament's idea 'to have girl muggers whipped' would turn back the clock to the 1820s when corporal punishment for women was abolished, whereas another Parliamentary recom-mendation to 'Bring back stocks for hooligans' would presumably transport us into the Dark Ages.[23] Indeed, the powerful imagery of pastoral will often suggest that the true location of the golden age lies in pre-industrial Merrie England – a traditional lament that was already well established in Queen Victoria's golden era.[24]

But although devastating historical judgements such as these can be found in abundance amidst the speculations of the 'law-and-order' movement, the urgency of Britain's contemporary predicament insists that a much more abbreviated timescale is often used to describe the rapidity of the descent into lawlessness. 'Twenty Years Ago', which conveys the sense of a generational decline, is the slogan most commonly employed. Patricia Morgan plumps for this timescale in her critique of the 'New Establishment' of social workers, psychologists, teachers and other exponents of what she calls the 'New Socio-Psychological Expertise' of child care and education. The moral collapse of the younger generation, as she describes it, is 'the logical outcome of the theory and practice of the past couple of decades'.[25] From another quarter, Baroness Faithful took issue in 1979 with the 'simplistic belief' in the short-sharp-shock remedy which she viewed as no less foolish than 'the theories of those false prophets of permissiveness at whose door must be laid a considerable part of the blame for the rise in crime over the last two decades'.[26]

'Twenty years ago' has a ring of common sense about it. A typical letter in the correspondence columns of *The Daily Mail* in 1977 summed up the commonplace fears and aspirations which are arranged around this slogan:

> In the past two decades standards and values have so deteriorated that materialism and selfishness have become the norm. . . The general public are nostalgic for family life as depicted in the old days when love, concern and discipline were considered of greater importance... than wealth, permissiveness, 'doing one's own thing' regardless of the consequences to others. We don't need researchers to tell us what is wrong in this cynical 'anything goes' era. We see it all around us.[27]

This kind of commonsense reasoning, invariably linked to the perceived upsurge in crime and mischief, has become such a day-to-day feature of life in contemporary Britain that one hears complaints phrased in the idiom of 'Twenty Years Ago' amidst the gossip of bus queues, pubs and launderettes. Even so, when I stumbled across Miss Diana Dors – a 'permissive' sex-symbol of some notoriety twenty years ago – advancing its claims in a popular magazine and asking us to cast our minds towards 'my era back in the fifties', I was not immediately sure whose side she was supposed to be on. But it was business as usual. 'As an ex-sex symbol', Miss Dors confessed, 'I usually amaze those who pose the question by saying that I believe the permissive society HAS gone too far.'[28]

Nor has the Labour Party, which has traditionally kept its own counsel on 'law-and-order' matters, proved entirely immune to the surrounding clamour. Mr Merlyn Rees as Labour Home Secretary had given voice to the more usually reticent position early in 1978 when he charged Mrs Thatcher with 'an irresponsible and dangerous approach to law and order. . . whipping up people's fears in a "cynical" attempt to win votes'.[29] Later in the same year, however, appearing on television in a news item on vandalism, Mr Rees was to be found closing the commonsense consensus. 'You only have to look around,' he explained, 'and see that something has happened in the last twenty years.'[30]

It is a simple enough invitation, with no strings attached. So let us take a look around and see what is to be seen.

> *From G. Pearson,* Hooligan: A History of Respectable Fears *(Basingstoke: Macmillan), 1983, pp. 3–11.*

Notes

1 Enoch Powell, BBC Television, 28 May 1981.
2 *The Daily Mail*, 7 July 1981.
3 *The Daily Express*, 7 July 1981.
4 Austin Haywood, Deputy Chief Constable of West Yorkshire, *Bradford Telegraph and Argus*, 17 April 1976, and Mr James Jardine, Chairman of the Police Federation, *The Daily Telegraph*, 16 March 1978.
5 Sir Keith Joseph, *The Guardian*, 21 October 1974.
6 A. Clarke and I. Taylor, Vandals, Pickets and Muggers: Television Coverage of Law and Order in the 1979 Election, *Screen Education*, August 1980.
7 Quoted in *Social Work Today*, 29 April 1976; and *The Daily Mirror*, 11 October 1978.
8 *The Daily Mirror*, 28 June 1978.
9 *The Times*, 26 April 1978.
10 *The Daily Telegraph*, 31 May 1979.
11 R. Mark, *In the Office of Constable* (Collins, 1978) p.286.
12 *The Daily Telegraph*, 26 April 1978.
13 *Report of Her Majesty's Chief Inspector of Constabulary*, 1975 (HMSO, 1976) pp. 1–3, 38–9.

14 *The Guardian*, 4 July 1979.

15 R. Mark, *Minority Verdict* (Police Federation Occasional Papers, (1973) p. 1.

16 *The Daily Express*, 6 October 1977.

17 T.A. Critchley, *The Conquest of Violence* (Constable, 1970) pp. 193, 199.

18 Public Order (Conservative Political Centre, 1970) p. 26.

19 *The Guardian*, 22 September 1979.

20 *The Guardian*, 21 October 1974.

21 *How to Spot a Red Teacher* (National Front, 1977).

22 Quoted in *Social Work Today*, 29 April 1976. Cf. R. Boyson, *Down with the Poor* (Churchill Press, 1971); T. Russell, *The Tory Party* (Penguin, 1978) pp. 103ff.

23 Flog the Girl Thugs, *The Sun*, 13 February 1976; Bring back stocks for hooligans, MP says, *The Guardian*, 14 March 1981.

24 Cf. G. Pearson, *The Deviant Imagination* (Macmillan, 1975) ch. 7 and Chapters 4, 5, 7 and 8 of the present work.

25 P. Morgan, *Delinquent Fantasies* (Temple Smith, 1978) p. 191.

26 *The Daily Telegraph*, 25 October 1979.

27 *The Daily Mail*, 30 August 1977.

28 The Diana Dors Column, 'Sex is getting out of hand!', *Revue*, 8 February 1980.

29 Rees attacks 'dangerous' Maggie, *The Daily Mail*, 24 February 1978.

30 Merlyn Rees, BBC Television, 31 October 1978.

29.2 The coming of the super-predators
John J. Dilulio

Lynne Abraham doesn't scare easily. Abraham is the no-nonsense Democratic district attorney of Philadelphia. The city's late tough-cop mayor, Frank Rizzo, baptized her 'one tough cookie.' The label stuck, and rightly so. Abraham has sent more mafiosi to prison than Martin Scorsese, stood up (all 5'2" of her) to violent drug kingpins, won bipartisan support in this Congress for wrestling control of the city's jail system from an ACLU-brand federal judge, and, most recently, publicly shamed the know-nothing literati who want to free convicted copkiller Mumia Abu-Jamal. Today various of her colleagues at the non-partisan National District Attorneys Association describe her as 'suite smart and street smart,' 'a genuine law-and-order liberal,' and 'probably the best big-city D.A. in the country.'

All true. So pay attention, because Lynne Abraham is scared.

In a recent interview, Abraham used such phrases as 'totally out of control' and 'never seen anything like it' to describe the rash of youth crime and violence that has begun to sweep over the City of Brotherly Love and other big cities. We're not just talking about teenagers, she stressed. We're talking about boys whose voices have yet to change. We're talking about elementary school youngsters who pack guns instead of lunches. We're talking about kids who have absolutely no respect for human life and no sense of the future.

In short, we're talking big trouble that hasn't yet begun to crest.

And make no mistake. While the trouble will be greatest in black inner-city neighborhoods, other places are also certain to have burgeoning youth-crime problems that will spill over into upscale central-city districts, inner-ring suburbs, and even the rural heartland. To underscore this point, Abraham recounted a recent townhall meeting in a white working-class section of the city that has fallen on hard times: 'They're becoming afraid of their own children. There were some big beefy guys there, too. And they're asking me what am I going to do to control their children.'

I interviewed Abraham, just as I have interviewed other justice-system officials and prison inmates, as a reality check on the incredibly frightening picture that emerges from recent academic research on youth crime and violence. All of the research indicates that Americans are sitting atop a demographic crime bomb. And all of those who are closest to the problem hear the bomb ticking.

To cite just a few examples, following my May 1995 address to the district attorneys association, big-city prosecutors inundated me with war stories about the ever-growing numbers of hardened, remorseless juveniles who were showing up in the system. 'They kill or maim on impulse, without any intelligible motive,' said one. Likewise, a veteran beat policeman confided: 'I never used to be scared. Now I say a quick Hail Mary every time I get a call at night involving juveniles. I pray I go home in one piece to my own kids.'

On a recent visit to a New Jersey maximum-security prison, I spoke to a group of life-term inmates, many of them black males from inner-city Newark and Camden. In a typical remark, one prisoner fretted, 'I was a bad-ass street gladiator, but these kids are stone-cold predators.' Likewise, in his just-published book, Mansfield B. Frazier, a five-time convicted felon, writes of what he calls 'The Coming Menace': 'As bad as conditions are in many of our nation's ravaged inner-city neighbor-hoods, in approximately five years they are going to get worse, a lot worse.' Having done time side-by-side with today's young criminals in prisons and jails all across the country, he warns of a 'sharp, cataclysmic' increase in youth crime and violence.[...]

The numbers are as alarming as the anec-dotes. At a time when overall crime rates have been dropping, youth crime rates, especially for crimes of violence, have been soaring. Between 1985 and 1992, the rate at which males ages 14 to 17 committed murder increased by about 50 per-cent for whites and over 300 percent for blacks.

While it remains true that most violent youth crime is committed by juveniles against juveniles, of late young offenders have been committing more homicides, robberies, and other crimes against adults. There is even some evidence that juveniles are doing homicidal violence in 'wolf packs.' Indeed, a 1993 study found that juveniles committed about a third of all homicides against strangers, often murdering their victim in groups of two or more.

Violent youth crime, like all serious crime, is predominantly intra-racial, not interracial. The surge in violent youth crime has been most acute among black inner-city males. In 1992, black males ages 16 to 19 experienced violent crime at nearly double the rate of white males and were about twice as likely to be violent crime victims as were black males in 1973. Moreover, the violent crimes experienced by young black males tended to be more serious than those experienced by young white males; for example, aggravated assaults rather than simple assaults, and attacks involving guns rather than weaponless violence.

The youth crime wave has reached horrific proportions from coast to coast. For example, in Philadelphia, more than half of the 433 people murdered in 1994 were males between the ages of 16 and 31. All but 5 of the 89 victims under 20 were non-white. In Los Angeles, there are now some 400 youth street gangs organized mainly along racial and ethnic lines: 200 Latino, 150 black, the rest white or Asian. In 1994, their known members alone committed 370 murders and over 3,300 felony assaults.

But what is really frightening everyone from D.A.s to demographers, old cops to old convicts, is not what's happening now but what's just around the corner – a sharp increase in the number of super crime-prone young males.

Nationally, there are now about 40 million children under the age of 10, the largest number in decades. By simple math, in a decade today's 4 to 7-year-olds will become 14 to 17-year-olds. By 2005, the number of males in this age group will have risen about 25 percent overall and 50 percent for blacks.

To some extent, it's just that simple: More boys begets more bad boys. But to really grasp why this spike in the young male population means big trouble ahead, you need to appreciate both the sta-tistical evidence from a generation of birth-cohort studies and related findings from recent street-level studies and surveys.

The scientific kiddie-crime literature began with a study of all 10,000 boys born in 1945 who lived in Philadelphia between their tenth and eigh-teenth birthdays. Over one-third had at least one recorded arrest by the time they were 18. Most of the arrests occurred when the boys were ages 15 to 17. Half of the boys who were arrested were arrested more than once. Once a boy had been arrested three times, the chances that he would be arrested again were over 70 percent.

But the most famous finding of the study was that 6 percent of the boys committed five or more crimes before they were 18, accounting for over half of all the serious crimes, and about two-thirds of all the violent crimes, committed by the entire cohort.

This '6 percent do 50 percent' statistic has been replicated in a series of subsequent longitudi-nal studies of Philadelphia and many other cities. It is on this basis that James Q. Wilson and other leading crime doctors can predict with confidence that the additional 500,000 boys who will be 14 to 17 years old in the year 2000 will mean at least 30,000 more murderers, rapists, and muggers on the streets than we have today.

Likewise, it's what enables California officials to meaningfully predict that, as the state's population of 11 to 17-year-olds grows from 2.9 million in 1993 to 3.9 million in 2004, the number of juvenile arrests will increase nearly 30 percent.

But that's only half the story. The other half begins with the less well-known but equally important and well-replicated finding that since the studies began, each generation of crime-prone boys (the '6 percent') has been about three times as dangerous as the one before it. For example, crime-prone boys born in Philadelphia in 1958 went on to commit about three times as much serious crime per capita as their older cousins in the class of '45. Thus, the difference between the juvenile criminals of the 1950s and those of the 1970s and 80s was about the difference between the Sharks and Jets of West Side Story fame and the Bloods and Crips of Los Angeles County.

Still, demography is not fate and criminology is not pure science. How can one be certain that the demographic bulge of the next 10 years will unleash an army of young male predatory street criminals who will make even the leaders of the Bloods and Crips – as O.G.s, for 'original gangsters'- look tame by comparison? The answer centers on a conservative theory of the root causes of crime, one that is strongly supported by all of the best science as well as the common sense of the subject. Call it the theory of moral poverty.

Most Americans of every race, religion, socio-economic status, and demographic description grow up in settings where they are taught right from wrong and rewarded emotionally or spiritually (if not also or always materially) for deferring immediate gratification and respecting others. Most of us were blessed to be born to loving and responsible parents or guardians. And most of us were lucky enough to have other adults in our lives (teachers, coaches, clergy) who reinforced the moral lessons that we learned at home – don't be selfish, care about others, plan for the future, and so on.

But some Americans grow up in moral poverty. Moral poverty is the poverty of being without loving, capable, responsible adults who teach you right from wrong. It is the poverty of being without parents and other authorities who habituate you to feel joy at others' joy, pain at others' pain, happiness when you do right, remorse when you do wrong. It is the poverty of growing up in the virtual absence of people who teach morality by their own everyday example and who insist that you follow suit.

In the extreme, moral poverty is the poverty of growing up surrounded by deviant, delinquent, and criminal adults in abusive, violence-ridden, fatherless, Godless, and jobless settings. In sum, whatever their material circumstances, kids of whatever race, creed, or color are most likely to become criminally depraved when they are morally deprived.

Most predatory street criminals – black and white, adult and juvenile, past and present – have grown up in abject moral poverty. But the Bloods and Crips were so much more violent, on average, than their 50s counterparts, and the next class of juvenile offenders will be even worse, because in recent decades each generation of youth criminals in this country has grown up in more extreme conditions of moral poverty than the one before it.

The abject moral poverty that creates super-predators begins very early in life in homes where unconditional love is nowhere but unmerciful abuse is common. One of the best ethnographic accounts of this reality is Mark S. Fleisher's 1995 book on the lives of 194 West Coast urban street criminals, including several dozen who were juveniles at the time he did his primary field research (1988 to 1990). Almost without exception, the boys' families 'were a social fabric of fragile and undependable social ties that weakly bound children to their parents and other socializers.' Nearly all parents abused alcohol or drugs or both. Most had no father in the home; many had fathers who were criminals. Parents 'beat their sons and daughters – whipped them with belts, punched them with fists, slapped them, and kicked them.'

Such ethnographic evidence is mirrored by national statistics on the morally impoverished beginnings of incarcerated populations. For example, 75 percent of highly violent juvenile criminals suffered serious abuse by a family member; nearly 80 percent witnessed extreme violence (beatings, killings); over half of prisoners come from single-parent families; over one quarter have parents who abused drugs or alcohol; nearly a third have a brother with a prison or jail record.

Among other puzzles, the moral poverty theory explains why, despite living in desperate economic poverty under the heavy weight of Jim Crow, and with plenty of free access to guns, the churchgoing, two-parent black families of the South never experienced anything remotely like the tragic levels of homicidal youth and gang violence that plague some of today's black inner-city neighborhoods.

It also explains why once relatively crime-free white working-class neighborhoods are evolving into white underclass neighborhoods. The out-migration of middle-class types, divorce, out-of-wedlock births, and graffiti-splattered churches have spawned totally unsocialized young white males who commit violent crimes and youth gangs that prefer murder to mischief (Anyone who doubts it is welcome to tour my old Catholic blue-collar neighborhood in Philadelphia.)

Moral poverty begets juvenile super-predators whose behavior is driven by two profound developmental defects. First, they are radically present-oriented. Not only do they perceive no relationship between doing right (or wrong) now and being rewarded (or punished) for it later. They live entirely in and for the present moment; they quite literally have no concept of the future. As several researchers have found, ask a group of today's young big-city murderers for their thoughts about 'the future,' and many of them will ask you for an explanation of the question.

Second, the super-predators are radically self-regarding. They regret getting caught. For themselves, they prefer pleasure and freedom to incarceration and death. Under some conditions, they are affectionate and loyal to fellow gang members or relatives, but not even moms or grand-moms are sacred to them; as one prisoner quipped, 'crack killed everybody's "mama".' And they place zero value on the lives of their victims, whom they reflexively dehumanize as just so much worthless 'white trash' if white, or by the usual racial or ethnic epithets if black or Latino.

On the horizon, therefore, are tens of thousands of severely morally impoverished juvenile super-predators. They are perfectly capable of committing the most heinous acts of physical violence for the most trivial reasons (for example, a perception of slight disrespect or the accident of being in their path). They fear neither the stigma of arrest nor the pain of imprisonment. They live by the meanest code of the meanest streets, a code that reinforces rather than restrains their violent, hair-trigger mentality. In prison or out, the things that super-predators get by their criminal behavior – sex, drugs, money – are their own immediate rewards. Nothing else matters to them. So for as long as their youthful energies hold out, they will do what comes 'naturally': murder, rape, rob, assault, burglarize, deal deadly drugs, and get high.

What is to be done? I will conclude with one big idea, but my best advice is not to look for serious answers from either crowd in Washington. Earlier this year, I was among a dozen guests invited to a working White House dinner on juvenile crime. Over gourmet Szechwan wonton and lamb, the meeting dragged on for three-and-a-half hours. President Clinton took copious notes and asked lots of questions, but nothing was accomplished. One guest pleaded with him to declare a National Ceasefire Day. Wisely, he let that one pass. But another guest recommended that he form (you guessed it) a commission. In mid-July, the president named six members to a National Commission on Crime Control and Prevention. I didn't know whether to laugh or cry.

Meanwhile, Republicans have made some real improvements on the 1994 crime bill. But it is hard to imagine that block-granting anti-crime dollars will work (it never has before). And it is easy to see how the passion for devolution is driving conservatives to contradict themselves. For years they've stressed that drugs, crime, and welfare dependency are cultural and moral problems. Now, however, they talk as if perverse monetary incentives explained everything.

True, government policies helped wreck the two-parent family and disrupted other aspects of civil society. But how does the sudden withdrawal of government lead automatically to a rebirth of civil society, an end to moral poverty, and a check on youth crime? It doesn't, not any more than pulling a knife from the chest of a dead man brings him dancing back to life. Liberal social engineering was bad; conservative social re-engineering will prove worse.

My one big idea is borrowed from three well known child-development experts – Moses, Jesus Christ, and Mohammed. It's called religion. If we are to have a prayer of stopping any significant fraction of the super-predators short of the prison gates, then we had better say 'Amen,' and fast.

Why religion? Two reasons. First, a growing body of scientific evidence from a variety of academic disciplines indicates that churches can help cure or curtail many severe socioeconomic ills. For example, a 1986 study by Harvard economist Richard Freeman found that among black urban youth, church attendance was a better predictor of who would escape drugs, crime, and poverty than any other single variable (income, family structure) and that churchgoing youth were more likely than otherwise comparable youth to behave in socially constructive ways. Likewise, a study by a panel of leading specialists just published by the journal *Criminology* concluded that, while much work remains to be done, there is substantial empirical evidence that religion serves 'as an insulator against crime and delinquency.' And we have long known that many of the most effective substance abuse prevention and treatment programs, both in society and behind bars, are either explicitly religious or quasi-religious in their orientation.

Second, religion is the one answer offered time and again by the justice-system veterans, prisoners, and others I've consulted. With particular reference to black youth crime, for example, it is an answer proffered in recent books by everyone from liberal Cornel West to neoconservative Glenn Loury, Democrat Jesse Jackson to Republican Alan Keyes.

[...] To be sure. black churches are in decline in many needy neighborhoods. They are straining to stay open despite lost membership, near empty coffers, and increasing community demands. Still, they remain the last best hope for rebuilding the social and spiritual capital of inner-city America.

We must, therefore, be willing to use public funds to empower local religious institutions to act as safe havens for at-risk children (church-run orphanages, boarding schools, call them what you please), provide adoption out-placement services, administer government-funded 'parenting skills' classes, handle the youngest non-violent juvenile offenders, provide substance-abuse treatment, run day-care and preschool programs, and perform other vital social and economic development functions.

Although many government officials are reluctant to admit it – and while data on how much of each government social-services dollar already goes through religious institutions are incredibly sparse – in some places churches are already performing such tasks with direct or indirect public support. We should enable them to do even more.

Obviously, even with increased public support, churches could not come close to saving every child or solving every social problem. But I'd bet that the marginal return on public investments that strengthen the community-rebuilding and child-protection capacities of local churches would equal or exceed that of the marginal tax dollar spent on more cops, more public schools, and more prisons.

Such proposals raise all sorts of elite hackles. But most Americans believe in God (90 percent) and pray each day (80 percent). The trouble is that our faith in God and religion is not reflected in federal, state, and local social policies, courtesy of the anti-religious and non-religious liberal and conservative pseudo-sophisticates of both parties. [...]

No one in academia is a bigger fan of incarceration than I am. Between 1985 and 1991 the number of juveniles in custody increased from 49,000 to nearly 58,000. By my estimate, we will probably need to incarcerate at least 150,000 juvenile criminals in the years just ahead. In deference to public safety, we will have little choice but to pursue genuine get-tough law enforcement strategies against the super-predators.

But some of these children are now still in diapers, and they can be saved. So let our guiding principle be, 'Build churches, not jails' – or we will reap the whirlwind of our own moral bankruptcy.

From J.J. Dilulio, 'The coming of the super-predators', The Weekly Standard, *27 November 1995.*

29.3 Penal custody: intolerance, irrationality and indifference Barry Goldson

The contemporary politics of penal custody: from the 'reductionist agenda' to 'the rush to custody'

Newburn (1997: 642) described the 1979 Conservative Manifesto as 'the most avowedly "law and order" manifesto in British political history': it 'promised, among many other measures, to strengthen sentencing powers with respect to juveniles'. Indeed, the 1980 White Paper *Young Offenders* proposed the re-introduction of Detention Centres with tough regimes designed to deliver a 'short, sharp, shock' and William Whitelaw, the Home Secretary, warned that the children and young people 'who attend them will not ever want to go back' (cited in Newburn, 1997: 642; see also Muncie, 1990). Paradoxically, however, the decade that followed comprised 'one of the most remarkably progressive periods of juvenile justice policy' (Rutherford, 1995: 57) within which a 'reductionist agenda' (Rutherford, 1984) in respect of penal custody consolidated. A coincidence of four otherwise disparate (even contradictory) concerns combined to legitimise penal reduction. First, elements of academic research demonstrated the counter-productive consequences of disproportionate forms of criminal justice intervention generally, and custodial sanctions in particular (Goldson, 1997a). Second, developments in juvenile/youth justice practice, especially imaginative community-based 'alternative to custody' schemes (Haines and Drakeford, 1998). Third, specific policy objectives of Thatcherite Conservatism; as Pratt (1987: 429) observed: 'to reduce the custodial population on the grounds of cost effectiveness ... led to a general support for alternatives to custody initiatives'. Fourth, the stated imperatives of the police and the courts to reduce the incidence of juvenile crime; whilst some reservations remained, many senior police officers and court officials positively embraced the reductionist agenda (Gibson, 1995) in the light of 'the plethora of Home Office research ... that evidenced the discernible success of such policies' (Goldson, 1994: 5).

The combination of permissive statute[1] and innovatory 'alternative to custody' practice, was not insignificant. The number of custodial sentences imposed on children fell from 7,900 in 1981 to 1,700 in 1990 (Allen, 1991). Furthermore, the 'reductionist agenda' was effective not only in terms of substantially moderating the practice of child imprisonment but also, according to David Faulkner, the Head of the Home Office Crime Department between 1982 and 1990, it was 'successful in the visible reduction of known juvenile offending' (cited in Goldson, 1997b: 79). Indeed, faith in the effectiveness and rationality of decarceration was such that penal reform organisations confidently advocated 'phasing out prison department custody for juvenile offenders' and 'replacing custody' (Nacro, 1989a and 1989b). Government support for the 'reductionist agenda' was always contingent, however, and its fortunes ultimately depended upon the extent to which it continued to suit wider political priorities.

The size of the Conservatives' parliamentary majority and the strength of its electoral mandate throughout the 1980s, were such that the Party was both able and prepared to relax its long-established attachment to a punitive 'law and order' politics. Between 1989 and 1992, however, Britain experienced a major economic recession which indirectly, but no less dramatically, served to subvert political support for the 'reductionist agenda'. The opinion polls started to signal that public confidence in the Conservatives was abating and, as a consequence, the triumphalism of Thatcherism finally looked vulnerable. Downes (2001: 69) observed that: 'with ... a prison population falling from 50,000 to 42,000 ... the Conservative lead over Labour as the party best able to guarantee law and order [was seriously threatened] for the first time in over 30 years'. The Conservative Party reacted by deposing Margaret Thatcher and installing John Major as leader, and Prime Minister. Along with senior colleagues, Major set about restoring the Party's more traditional 'law and order' mantle.

By early 1993 juvenile crime came into sharp focus. In particular, the media drew attention to car crime, youth disorder, children and young people offending whilst on court bail, and those whom they described as 'persistent young offenders' with increasing regularity and developing force. Such phenomena were shrouded in vagueness and there was minimal effort to distinguish, and thus account for, the specificities of the various forms of 'anti-social behaviour', youth 'disorder' and/or the different 'types' of child 'offender'. Rather every troublesome child was portrayed as 'out of control' and a 'menace to society'. There was a developing sense that 'childhood' was in 'crisis' (Scraton, 1997) and any lingering doubts were seemingly extinguished by a single case in February 1993, in which two children aged ten were charged with the murder of two-year-old James Bulger. This imposed enormous symbolic purchase over the public imagination and activated processes of demonisation (Davis and Bourhill, 1997; Goldson 1997a), as 'myth and fantasy [began] to replace objectivity and detachment and conjure monsters that seem to lurk behind the gloss and glitter of everyday life' (Pratt, 2000: 431). Troublesome children were 'essentialised as other' (Young, 1999) and an 'ecology of fear' (Davis, 1998) was awakened and mobilised. The reaction from a government intent on re-establishing its traditional credentials with regard to law and order was predictable. The Prime Minister, John Major, argued that the time had come for society 'to condemn a little more and understand a little less' and the Home Secretary, Michael Howard, proclaimed that 'prison works' (cited in Goldson, 1997a: 130–1).

For its part, the re-styled New Labour project – emerging under the steadily increasing influence of Tony Blair – broke with its conventionally moderate position on questions of penal policy and 'pressed home (its) advantage ... by emphasising the .. leniency of sentencing' (Downes, 2001: 69). In January 1993, three days after returning from a visit to the USA, Tony Blair – as Opposition Home Secretary – coined what was to become a famous New Labour sound-bite in declaring his intention to be 'tough on crime, tough on the causes of crime'. Blair had been persuaded – by what he had seen and learnt in the US – to exploit the political vulnerabilities of the Major administration by following the example set by Bill Clinton's New Democratic Coalition. Clinton had repoliticised crime to positive electoral effect in the USA and Blair intended to do likewise in Britain (Tonry, 2004). The 'Americanisation' of criminal justice in general, and youth justice in particular, operated both at the symbolic level of political rhetoric and more significantly, at the material level of policy development (Jones and Newburn, 2004; Muncie, 2002; Pitts, 2000 and 2001).

Throughout the period 1993–97, New Labour policy-makers published a wide range of policy documents focusing on youth justice and related matters, within which a creeping punitivity was increasingly evident (Jones, 2002). It was not until the election of the first New Labour Government in May 1997, however, that the full weight of its 'toughness' agenda was felt. Within months of coming to office, the newly elected government produced a raft of consultative documentation in relation to youth justice (Home Office, 1997a; 1997b; 1997c), followed by a White Paper, ominously entitled *No More Excuses: A New Approach to Tackling Youth Crime in England and Wales* (Home Office, 1997d). Clinton adopted and applied the notion of 'zero tolerance' in the USA. Blair settled for 'no more excuses' in England and Wales. The 'reductionist agenda' had been abandoned and, instead, the 'rush to custody' (Rutherford, 2002: 102) was concretised. Political calculations and electoral ambitions served to usurp penological rationality.

Intolerance: enacting custodial punishment

From the early-1990s, both Conservative and New Labour governments translated 'tough' political rhetoric and symbolic posturing into legislation and youth justice policy. It is not practical in a chapter such as this to analyse the provisions of statute in detail, but there is value in sketching some of their defining characteristics with regard to the question of penal custody.

The Criminal Justice and Public Order Act 1994 ushered in new punitive powers in three particularly significant ways. First, the Act lowered the age threshold – from 14 to 10 – for the imposition of indeterminate sentences (14 years or more) in cases where children are convicted of 'grave crimes' in the Crown Court. Second, it doubled the length of the maximum determinate sentence of detention in a Young Offender Institution – for 15–17-year-old children from 12 to 24 months. Third, and perhaps most significant of all, section 1 of the 1994 Act created a new custodial sentence for 12–14-year-old children – the Secure Training Order – to be served in a private jail (a Secure Training Centre) for terms of up to 24 months. The legislation was implemented by a Conservative government with little tangible opposition from Labour. Although Labour opposed various aspects of the Bill at Parliamentary Committee stages, it abstained during the final vote (Howard League,

1995: 3). The significance of this should not be under-estimated; the Criminal Justice and Public Order Act 1994 effectively reversed the decarcerative provisions of youth justice law and policy – in respect of children aged 12-14 years – that dated back to the Children Act 1908 (Rutherford, 1995).

The Crime and Disorder Act 1998 (implemented by the first New Labour administration) is an extraordinarily wide-ranging piece of legislation. Whilst it served to abolish the Secure Training Order (for 12–14-year-old children) it substituted it with the Detention and Training Order (which also replaced the sentence of detention in a Young Offender Institution for children aged 15–17 years). The new custodial sentence became operational in April 2000 and the length of a Detention and Training Order is set at 4, 6, 8, 10, 12, 18 or 24 months. It is served half in penal custody and half in the community, although the Act allows for varying the balance of the sentence (including extending the custodial element) depending upon 'assessments' of the child's progress. Thus the courts' power to lock up children between the ages of 12 and 17 years for non-grave offences is now provided within the remit of a single custodial sentence, and there is provision in the Crime and Disorder Act 1998 to allow the Home Secretary to further extend the powers of the court to encompass children aged 10 and 11 years.

The Powers of the Criminal Courts (Sentencing) Act 2000 contained provisions (at sections 90–92) for the custodial sentencing of children convicted of 'grave crimes' and, according to Bateman (2002), when combined with the Detention and Training Order powers contained within the Crime and Disorder Act 1998, the legislation comprises a 'recipe for injustice'.

Finally, for the purposes here, section 130 of the Criminal Justice and Police Act 2001 significantly relaxes the penal remand criteria in respect of children. The Act empowers the courts to remand children to custodial institutions in cases where they have 'repeatedly' committed offences whilst on bail (including shoplifting, petty theft and criminal damage), irrespective of whether or not such offences are adjudged to expose the public to 'serious harm'. The term 'repeatedly' has been defined in case law as meaning 'on more than one occasion' (Monaghan et al., 2003: 31). Thus, section 130 of the Criminal Justice and Police Act 2001 effectively replaced the long-established 'seriousness' threshold with a 'nuisance' test: a perfect

exemplar of 'institutionalised intolerance'. Bearing in mind that in practice many penal remands are imposed upon children awaiting trial or sentence in respect of non-serious offences (Goldson and Peters, 2002), together with all that is known about the particular vulnerabilities of child remand prisoners (Goldson, 2002b), the provisions of the Criminal Justice and Police Act 2001 also convey penological irrationality and indifference to the welfare of child remand prisoners.

Hough et al. (2003) have noted that the combined practical effect of the above – together with similar developments in law and policy – has precipitated significant penal expansion:

> The increases in custody rates and sentence length strongly suggest that sentencers have become more severe. This greater severity undoubtedly reflects, in part, a more punitive legislative and legal framework of sentencing. Legislation, guideline judgements and sentence guidelines have all had an inflationary effect on sentences passed. At the same time, the climate of political and media debate about crime and sentencing has become more punitive, and is also likely to have influenced sentencing practice. (ibid.: 2)

Indeed, total rates of imprisonment in England and Wales have escalated significantly during the last decade or more. In 1994 the average prison population was 48,631 but by 1997 it had risen to 60,131 (Prison Reform Trust, 2004: 3). This 'inflationary effect' has continued since the first New Labour administration took office in 1997. In 2002, for example, the average prison population, at 70,860, was higher than in any previous year (Councell, 2003: 1; Home Office 2003a: 3), by March 2004, however, the total prison population exceeded 75,000 (Howard League for Penal Reform, 2004a) and, by May 2005, it had reached more than 76,000 for the first time in penal history (British Broadcasting Corporation, 2005). Between 1997 and 2005 there was 'an increase in prison numbers of 25 per cent' (Stern, 2005: 81). Expressed as a rate per 100,000 of the national population, the prison population in England and Wales is now the highest among countries of the European Union (Home Office, 2003b).

Contemporary statistical trends in relation to child prisoners follow similar contours. The total number of custodial sentences imposed upon children rose from approximately 4,000 per annum in 1992 to 7,600 in 2001, a 90 per cent increase

(Nacro, 2003 and 2005). During the same period the child remand population grew by 142 per cent (Goldson, 2002b). Whilst it is true to say that such trends were initiated prior to the election of the first New Labour government in 1997, they have simply consolidated since that time (Hagell, 2005). In March 2004 alone, there were 3,251 children and young people (10–17 years inclusive) in penal custody in England and Wales: 2,772 in Prison Service Young Offender Institutions; 290 in Local Authority Secure Children's Homes and 189 in privately managed Secure Training Centres (Youth Justice Board, 2005a: 78). Moreover, such trends appear to be unrelenting. The 'number of young people in custody rose in June and July (2005) causing concern [because] the secure estate is under severe pressure' (Youth Justice Board, 2005b: 8), and 'in August the overall under-18 population rose ... during a month when we would normally expect the custody level to fall slightly ... the increase is due to a surge in the remand population' (Youth Justice Board, 2005c: 5).

Furthermore, within the general trend of penal expansion in respect of child prisoners in England and Wales, a range of additional observations might be made. First, whilst comparative analyses of youth justice systems in general, and rates of child imprisonment in particular, are extraordinarily difficult (Muncie, 2003 and 2005; Muncie and Goldson, 2006), it appears that greater use of penal custody for children is now made in England and Wales than in most other industrialised democratic countries in the world (Youth Justice Board for England and Wales, 2004). Second, in addition to substantial increases in the numbers of children sent to custody, sentences have also increased in length (Home Office, 2003b), and proportionately more children are sentenced to long-term detention (Graham and Moore, 2004). Third, law and policy have provided for the detention of younger children and Nacro (2003: 12) has observed that: 'as a consequence the detention of children under the age of 15 years has become routine'. Fourth, the expansionist drift has been disproportionately applied in terms of gender and the rate of growth is higher for girls than boys (Nacro, 2003). Furthermore, girls are regularly detained alongside adult prisoners, a practice that has been seriously questioned by penal reform organisations (Howard League for Penal Reform, 2004b) and Her Majesty's Chief Inspector of Prisons (2004) alike. Fifth, racism continues to pervade youth justice sentencing processes and custodial regimes. For example, black boys are 6.7 times more likely than their white counterparts to have custodial sentences in excess of 12 months imposed upon them in the Crown Court (Feilzer and Hood, 2004), and black child prisoners are more likely than white detainees to encounter additional adversity within custodial institutions owing to racist practices (Cowan, 2005). Sixth, the expansionist drive bears virtually no relation to either the incidence or the seriousness of youth crime (Goldson and Coles, 2005; Nacro, 2005); it is purely an artefact of the 'new punitiveness'.

Irrationality and indifference: negating the evidence

Substantial penal expansion within the youth justice system in England and Wales, triggered by the Conservative government during the period between 1993 and 1997, and consolidated by three successive New Labour administrations thereafter, pays scant regard to the imperatives of 'evidence-based policy' and 'what works' priorities. Indeed, the penological irrationality of the 'new punitiveness' is expressed via its indifference to a wealth of evidence in at least three key respects: the corrosive nature of custodial regimes for children and young people; the failure of penal custody to prevent youth offending (the 'principal aim' of the youth justice system as provided by section 37 of the Crime and Disorder Act 1998); and the enormous financial burden that penal expansion imposes on the public purse.

Child imprisonment: conditions and treatment

Child prisoners are routinely drawn from some of the most structurally disadvantaged and impoverished families, neighbourhoods and communities in England and Wales (Goldson, 2002b; Goldson and Coles, 2005). Her Majesty's Chief Inspector of Prisons (1999: 3) has noted that penal custody often marks 'just one further stage in the exclusion of a group of children who between them, have already experienced almost every form of social exclusion on offer', later adding that:

> Before any work can be done to sensitise [child prisoners] to the needs of others and the impact of their offending on victims, their own needs as maturing adolescents for care, support and direction have to be met.
> (Her Majesty's Chief Inspector of Prisons, 2000: 25)

Approximately half of the children held in penal custody at any one time will be, or will have been, 'open cases' to statutory child welfare agencies as a result of neglect and/or other child protection concerns; a significant proportion will have biographies scarred by adult abuse and violation (Association of Directors of Social Services *et al.*, 2003; Challen and Walton, 2004; Holmes and Gibbs, 2004; Prison Reform Trust, 2004; Social Exclusion Unit, 2002; Social Services Inspectorate *et al.*, 2002). In a major review of the educational needs of children in penal custody, Her Majesty's Chief Inspector of Prisons and the Office for Standards in Education (2001: 10) found that: 84 per cent of child prisoners had been excluded from school; 86 per cent had regularly not attended school; 52 per cent had left school aged 14 years or younger; 29 per cent had left school aged 13 years or younger and 73 per cent described their educational achievement as 'nil'. Over 25 per cent of child prisoners have literacy and numeracy skills equivalent to a 7-year-old (Social Exclusion Unit, 2002) and 'most' have 'very significant learning needs and problems' (Social Services Inspectorate *et al.*, 2002: 70). The British Medical Association, commenting upon the relationship between poverty, disadvantage and poor health, observed:

...patients within prison are amongst the most needy in the country in relation to their health care needs. Over 90 per cent of patients who reside in our jails come from deprived backgrounds ... 17 per cent of young offenders were not registered with a general practitioner and generally the young people had a low level of contact with primary health care. (2001: 1 and 5)

Moreover, and not surprisingly, the experience of imprisonment itself has been identified as having a deleterious effect on the physical and mental well-being of children (Farrant, 2001; Goldson, 2002b; Goldson and Coles, 2005; Leech and Cheney, 2001; Mental Health Foundation, 1999). In sum, when taking account of the backgrounds and personal circumstances of child prisoners: 'it is evident that on any count this is a significantly deprived, excluded, and abused population of children, who are in serious need of a variety of services' (Association of Directors of Social Services *et al.*, 2003: 6) and the 'Juvenile Secure Estate' is 'not equipped to meet their needs' (Her Majesty's Chief Inspector of Prisons, 2000: 69–70).

In England and Wales, more than 80 per cent of child prisoners are detained in Young Offender Institutions (managed by the Prison Service)[2] and this raises important issues with regard to conditions and treatment:

One of the most important factors in creating a safe environment is size. The other places where children are held – Secure Units and Secure Training Centres – are small, with a high staff–child ratio. The Prison Service, however, may hold children in what we regard as unacceptably high numbers and units. Units of 60 disturbed and damaged adolescent boys are unlikely to be safe ... There are therefore already significant barriers to the Prison Service being able to provide a safe and positive environment for children; and the question whether it should continue to do so is a live one. Yet during the year the number of children has risen, to close to 3,000, and looks set to rise further. Promises to reduce unit size ... are further than ever from being delivered.

(Her Majesty's Chief Inspector of Prisons, 2002: 36–7)

The Children's Rights Alliance for England (2002: 49–137) undertook a detailed analysis of the conditions and treatment experienced by children in Young Offender Institutions, drawing on reports prepared by Her Majesty's Inspectorate of Prisons. The results were illuminating: widespread neglect in relation to physical and mental health; endemic bullying, humiliation and ill-treatment (staff-on-child and child-on-child); racism and other forms of discrimination; systemic invasion of privacy; long and uninterrupted periods of cell-based confinement; deprivation of fresh air and exercise; inadequate educational and rehabilitative provision; insufficient opportunities to maintain contact with family; poor diet; ill-fitting clothing in poor state of repair; a shabby physical environment; and, in reality, virtually no opportunity to complain and/or make representations. All of these negative and neglectful processes define the conditions within which children are routinely held in penal custody leading Mr Justice Munby, a High Court judge, to conclude that:

They ought to be – I hope they are – matters of the very greatest concern to the Prison Service, to the Secretary of State for the Home Department and, indeed, to society at large. For these are things being done to children by the State – by all of us – in circumstances where the State appears to be failing, and in some instances failing very badly, in its duties to vulnerable and damaged children ... [these are] matters which, on the face of it, ought to shock the conscience of every citizen. (Munby, 2002: paras. 172 and 175)

Penal custody for children, therefore, can never be a neutral experience. Bullying, in all of its forms, is a particular problem that exerts substantial human costs for child prisoners. Her Majesty's Chief Inspector of Prisons (2005: 56) surveyed children in one Young Offender Institution and found that: 56 per cent reported that they had felt 'unsafe'; 'nearly a quarter said they had been hit, kicked or assaulted' and there 'had been 150 proven assaults in eight months'. Physical assault – or physical abuse – is clearly commonplace in penal custody. Furthermore, children are also exposed to other forms of 'bullying' including sexual assault; verbal abuse (including name-calling; threats; racist, sexist and homophobic taunting); extortion and theft; and lending and trading cultures – particularly in relation to tobacco – involving exorbitant rates of interest that accumulate on a daily basis (Goldson, 2002). Staff–child ratios are so stretched within penal custody that levels of supervision inevitably are strained. Bullying is insufficiently 'managed': it is entrenched within the very fabric of prison life.

For all child prisoners, such harsh conditions and treatment perpetuate misery and/or fear and thousands are emotionally and psychologically damaged. For some, it is literally too much to bear. Between 1998 and 2002, for example, there were 1,659 reported incidents of self-injury or attempted suicide by child prisoners in England and Wales (Howard League for Penal Reform, 2005). At the sharpest extremes, 29 children died in penal custody in England and Wales between July 1990 and September 2005 (27 in state prisons and 2 in private jails), all but two of the deaths were apparently self-inflicted (Goldson and Coles, 2005).

The paradoxical fact about the corrosive effect of penal custody on children is that it is recognised comprehensively by government ministers and major state agencies alike. In answer to a Parliamentary question on 7 June 2004, for example, Paul Goggins, Home Office Minister, confirmed that the numbers of vulnerable children placed in Young Offender Institutions have followed upward trajectories each year since 2000. The figures given for children officially assessed as 'vulnerable' and yet still 'placed' in Prison Service establishments by the Youth Justice Board for

England and Wales were: 432 for 2000–01; 1,875 for 2001–02; 2,903 for 2002–03 and 3,337 for 2003–04 (cited in Bateman, 2004). Furthermore, the most senior personnel from eight major statutory inspectorates have concluded that 'young people in YOIs still face the gravest risks to their welfare' (Social Services Inspectorate *et al.* 2002: 72), and Her Majesty's Chief Inspector of Prisons (2005: 57) has observed that 'some young people are not safe ... simply because they should not be there'. In October 2002, the United Nations Committee on the Rights of the Child (2002: para. 57) formally reported its 'deep concern' at 'the high increasing numbers of children in custody' in England and Wales and its 'extreme concern' regarding 'the conditions that children experience in detention', including the 'high levels of violence, bullying, self-harm and suicide'. Three years later, the Council of Europe's Commissioner for Human Rights noted that: 'one can only conclude that the prison service is failing in its duty of care towards juvenile inmates' (Office for the Commissioner for Human Rights, 2005: para. 93).

Despite all of the evidence in respect of the damaging and harmful impositions of penal custody on children, excessive practices of child imprisonment in England and Wales continue. Such indifference towards evidence is curious. it implies, to paraphrase Cohen (2001: 1), that human suffering is being 'denied', 'evaded', 'neutralised' or 'rationalised away'.

Conclusion

The central line of argument and analysis within this chapter is that penal expansion is derived from a politics of intolerance and punitiveness that has come to frame contemporary youth justice policy in England and Wales. Custodial institutions for children are 'socially unproductive' (Stern, 2005: 82) and such expansion has no claim to penological rationality and legitimacy: it is actually indifferent to evidence.

Bateman (2005) detects an 'emerging consensus that the current number of children within penal establishments needs to be addressed as a matter of urgency'. He suggests that the Youth Justice Board for England and Wales and the Home Office appear to share this consensus. The fact that every Youth Offending Team has been issued with specific 'targets' to reduce the use of penal custody, and the Youth Justice Board is looking towards a 10 per cent reduction in the number of child prisoners by 2007 (Youth Justice Board, 2004), might be taken to indicate that such 'consensus' is consolidating. Indeed, within the 'professional' youth justice community there are few, if any people, who would choose to quarrel with this. Perhaps the conditions are emerging within which tolerance, penological rationality and responsible concern (for child 'offenders' in particular, and the interests of the 'community' more generally) might impact more positively upon youth justice policy and practice in coming years.

Such optimism has to be historically contextualised, however. A key lesson from history with regard to penal policy provides that, in itself, 'failure never matters' (Muncie, 1990). For penal reduction – if not abolition – to be realised, therefore, it will require more than legitimising evidence. Ultimately, it is precisely because the 'new punitiveness' is derived from political calculations, that the enduring imperative to be seen to be 'tough' always outweighs penological rationality. In this respect, Prime Minister Tony Blair's reported concerns that Charles Clarke, the current Home Secretary, is 'going soft in the fight against crime' (Hennessey, 2005), together with punitive posturing from each of the major political parties leading up to the General Election in 2005 (Conservative Party, 2005; Labour Party, 2005; Liberal Democratic Party, 2004), implies a rather different, less optimistic and almost certainly more powerful, 'consensus'.

Notes

1   For example: the Criminal Justice Act 1982 imposed tighter criteria for custodial sentencing and introduced the 'Specified Activities Order' as a direct alternative to custodial detention: the Criminal Justice Act 1988 tightened the criteria for custodial sentencing further: the Children Act 1989 abolished the Criminal Care Order and the Criminal Justice Act 1991 abolished prison custody for 14-year-old boys and provided for the similar abolition of penal remands for 15–17-year-olds (although this provision has never been implemented), for a fuller discussion, see Goldson (2002b) and Goldson and Coles (2005).
2   The remaining number are held in private jails (Secure Training Centres) or Local Authority Secure Children's Homes (see Goldson and Coles, 2005: 25–6).

From B. Goldson, 'Penal custody: intolerance, irrationality and indifference', in B. Goldson and J. Muncie (eds), Youth, Crime and Justice *(London: Sage), 2006, pp. 139–156.*

References

Allen, R. (1991) Out of jail: The reduction in the use of penal custody for male juveniles 1981–1988. *The Howard Journal of Criminal Justice*, 30(1): 30–52.

Association of Directors of Social Services, Local Government Association, Youth Justice Board for England and Wales (2003) *The Application of the Children Act (1989) to Children In Young Offender Institutions*. London: AOSS, LGA and YJB.

Bateman, T. (2002) A note on the relationship between the Detention and Training Order and Section 91 of the Powers of the Criminal Courts (Sentencing) Act 2000: A recipe for injustice. *Youth Justice*, 1 (3): 36–41.

Bateman, T. (2004) Vulnerable children routinely held in Prison Service custody. Youth Justice News, *Youth Justice*, 4(2):144–5.

Bateman, T. (2005) Reducing child imprisonment: A systemic challenge. *Youth Justice*, 5(2): 91–105.

British Broadcasting Corporation (2005) Prison Numbers Continue to Climb. BBC News Friday 27 May, http://news.bbc.co.uk/1/hi/uk/4586949.stm.

British Medical Association (2001) *Prison Medicine: A Crisis Waiting to Break*. London: BMA.

Challen, M. and Walton, T. (2004) *Juveniles in Custody*. London: Her Majesty's Inspectorate of Prisons.

Children's Rights Alliance for England (2002) *Rethinking Child Imprisonment: A Report on Young Offender Institutions*. London: Children's Rights Alliance for England.

Cohen, S. (2001) *States of Denial: Knowing about Atrocities and Suffering*. Cambridge: Polity Press.

Conservative Party (2005) Are you thinking what we're thinking? It's time for action. *Conservative Election Manifesto*, London: Conservative Party.

Councell, R. (2003) *The Prison Population in 2002*: A Statistical Review, Findings 226. London: Home Office.

Cowan, R. (2005) Juvenile jail staff accused of racism. *The Guardian*, 14 June.

Davis, H. and Bourhill, M. (1997) 'Crisis': The demonization of children and young people. In Scraton, P. (Ed.) *'Childhood' in 'Crisis'?* London: UCL Press.

Davis, M. (1998) *Ecology of Fear: Los Angeles and the Imagination of Disaster*. New York: Metropolitan Press.

Downes, D. (2001) The macho penal economy: mass incarceration in the United States – a European perspective. *Punishment and Society*, 3(1): 61–80.

Farrant, F. (2001) *Troubled Inside: Responding to the Mental Health Needs of Children and Young People in Prison*. London: Prison Reform Trust.

Feilzer, M. and Hood, R. (2004) *Differences or Discrimination?* London: Youth Justice Board for England and Wales.

Gibson, B. (1995) Young people, bad news, enduring principles. *Youth and Policy*, 48:64–70.

Goldson, B. (1994) The changing face of youth justice. *Childright*, 105: 5–6.

Goldson, B. (1997a) Children in trouble: State responses to juvenile crime. In Scraton, P. (Ed.) *'Childhood' in 'Crisis'?* London: UCL Press.

Goldson, B. (1997b) Children, crime, policy and practice: Neither welfare nor justice. *Children and Society*, 11(2): 77–88.

Goldson, B. (2002) *Vulnerable Inside: Children in Secure and Penal Settings*. London: The Children's Society.

Goldson, B. and Coles, D. (2005) *In the Care of the State? Child Deaths in Penal Custody in England and Wales*. London: INQUEST.

Goldson, B. and Peters, E. (2002) *The Children's Society National Remand Review Initiative: Final Evaluation Report* (1 December 1999 – 30 November 2001), Prepared for the Youth Justice Board for England and Wales. Unpublished.

Graham, J. and Moore, C. (2004) *Trend Report on Juvenile Justice in England and Wales, European Society of Criminology Thematic Group on Juvenile Justice*, http://www.esc-eurocrim.org/workgroups.shtml juvenile_justice accessed 24 August 2004.

Hagell, A. (2005) The use of custody for children and young people. In Bateman, T. and Pitts, J. (Eds) *The RHP Companion to Youth Justice*. Lyme Regis: Russell House Publishing.

Haines, K. and Drakeford, M. (1998) *Young People and Youth Justice*. Basingstoke: Macmillan.

Hennessey, P. (2005) Blair humiliates Clarke for going soft in the fight against crime. *The Sunday Telegraph*, July 3.

Her Majesty's Chief Inspector of Prisons (1999a) *Suicide is Everyone's Concern: A Thematic Review by HM Chief Inspector of Prisons for England and Wales*. London: Home Office.

Her Majesty's Chief Inspector of Prisons (1999b) *Report on an Announced Inspection of HMP YOI Portland 24 October–3 November 1999 by HM Chief Inspector of Prisons*. London: Home Office.

Her Majesty's Chief Inspector of Prisons (2000) *Unjust Deserts: A Thematic Review by HM Chief Inspector of Prisons of the Treatment and Conditions for Unsentenced Prisoners in England and Wales*. London: Her Majesty's Inspectorate of Prisons for England and Wales.

Her Majesty's Chief Inspector of Prisons (2002) *Annual Report of HM Chief Inspector of Prisons for England and Wales*, 2001–2002. London: The Stationery Office.

Her Majesty's Chief Inspector of Prisons (2004) *Report on an Announced Inspection of HMP Eastwood Park 22–26 September 2003 by HM Chief Inspector of Prisons*. London: Home Office.

Her Majesty's Chief Inspector of Prisons (2005) *Annual Report of HM Chief Inspector of Prisons for England and Wales*, 2003–2004, London: The Stationery Office.

Her Majesty's Chief Inspector of Prisons and The Office for Standards in Education (2001) *A Second Chance: A Review of Education and Supporting Arrangements within Units for Juveniles Managed by HM Prison Service*. London: Home Office.

Holmes, C. and Gibbs, K. (2004) *Perceptions of Safety: Views of Young People and Staff Living and Working in the Juvenile Estate*. London: Her Majesty's Prison Service.

Home Office (1997a) *Tackling Youth Crime: A Consultation Paper*. London: Home Office.

Home Office (1997b) *Tackling Delays in the Youth Justice System: A Consultation Paper*. London: Home Office.

Home Office (1997c) *New National and Local Focus on Youth Crime*: A Consultation Paper. London: Home Office.

Home Office (1997d) *No More Excuses – A New Approach to Tackling Youth Crime in England and Wales*. London: The Stationery Office.

Home Office (2003a) *Prison Statistics England and Wales*. London: The Stationery Office.

Home Office (2003b) *World Prison Population List, Findings* 234. London: Home Office.

Hough, M., Jacobson, J. and Millie, A, (2003) *The Decision to Imprison: Key Findings*. London: Prison Reform Trust.

Howard League for Penal Reform (1995) *Secure Training Centres: Repeating Past Failures*, Briefing Paper. London: The Howard League for Penal Reform.

Howard League for Penal Reform (2004a) *Prison Overcrowding: 75,000 Behind Bars*, Briefing Paper. London: The Howard League for Penal Reform.

Howard League for Penal Reform (2004b) 'Girls Held in Adult Prisons Against their Best Interests', Press Release 20 January. London: The Howard League for Penal Reform.

Howard League for Penal Reform (2005) *Children in Custody: Promoting the Legal and Human Rights of Children*. London: The Howard League for Penal Reform.

Jones, D. (2002) 'Questioning New Labour's Youth Justice Strategy: A Review Article', *Youth Justice*, 1(3): 14–26.

Jones, T. and Newburn, T. (2004) 'The Convergence of US and UK Crime Control Policy: Exploring Substance and Process', in T. Newburn and R. Sparks (eds) *Criminal Justice and Political Cultures: National and International Dimensions of Crime Control*. Cullompton: Willan.

Labour Party (2005) *Britain Forward not back: The Labour Party Manifesto*. London: The Labour Party.

Leech, M, and Cheney, D. (2001) *The Prisons Handbook*. Winchester: Waterside Press.

Liberal Democratic Party (2004) Tough Liberalism', speech presented by Rt. Hon. Charles Kennedy, 30 March, http://www.libdems.org.uk/parliament/feature.html?id=6453 – accessed 29 April 2005.

Mental Health Foundation (1999) *Bright Futures: Promoting Young People's Mental Health*. London: Salzburg-Wittenburg.

Monaghan, C., Hibbert, P. and Moore, S. (2003) *Children in Trouble: Time for Change*. London: Barnardo's.

Munby, The Honourable Mr Justice (2002) *Judgment Approved by the Court for Handing Down in R (on the application of the Howard League for Penal Reform) v. The Secretary of State for the Home Department*, 29 November London: Royal Courts of Justice.

Muncie, J. (1990) 'Failure Never Matters: Detention Centres and the Politics of Deterrence', *Critical Social Policy*: 28: 53–66.

Muncie, J. (2002) 'Policy Transfers and What Works: Some Reflections on Comparative Youth Justice', *Youth Justice*, 1(3): 27–35.

Muncie, J. (2003) 'Juvenile Justice in Europe: Some Conceptual, Analytical and Statistical Comparisons', *Childright*, 202: 14–17.

Muncie, J. (2005) 'The Globalization of Crime Control – The Case of Youth and Juvenile Justice: Neoliberalism, Policy Convergence and International Conventions', *Theoretical Criminology*, 9(1): 35–64,

Muncie, J. and Goldson, B. (eds) (2006) *Comparative Youth Justice: Critical Issues*. London: Sage.

Nacro (1989a) *Phasing Out Prison Department Custody for Juvenile Offenders*. London: Nacro.

Nacro (1989b) *Replacing Custody: Findings from Two Census Surveys of Schemes for Juvenile Offenders Funded Under the DHSS Intermediate Treatment Initiative Covering the Period January to December 1987*. London: Nacro.

Nacro (2003) *A Failure of Justice: Reducing Child Imprisonment*. London: Nacro.

Nacro (2005) *A Better Alternative: Reducing Child Imprisonment*. London: Nacro.

Newburn, T. (1997) 'Youth, Crime and Justice', in M. Maguire, R. Morgan and R. Reiner (eds) *The Oxford Handbook of Criminology*. (2nd edn) Oxford: Clarendon Press.

Office for the Commissioner for Human Rights (2005) *Report by Mr Alvaro Gil-Robles, Commissioner for Human Rights, on His Visit to the United Kingdom* 4–12 November 2004. Strasbourg: Council of Europe.

Pitts, J. (2000) 'The New Youth Justice and the Politics of Electoral Anxiety', in B. Goldson (ed.) *The New Youth Justice*. Lyme Regis: Russell House Publishing.

Pitts, J. (2001) *The New Politics of Youth Crime: Discipline or Solidarity*. Basingstoke: Palgrave.

Pratt, J. (1987) 'A Revisionist History of Intermediate Treatment', *British Journal of Social Work*, 17(4): 417–35.

Pratt, J. (2000) 'Emotive and Ostentatious Punishment: its Decline and Resurgence in Modern Society', *Punishment and Society*, 2(4): 417–39.

Prison Reform Trust (2004) *Prison Reform Trust Factfile: July 2004*. London: Prison Reform Trust.

Rutherford, A. (1984) *Prisons and the Process of Justice*. London: Heinemann.

Rutherford, A. (1995) 'Signposting the Future of Juvenile Justice Policy in England and Wales', in Howard League for Penal Reform, *Child Offenders: UK and International Practice*. London: Howard League for Penal Reform,

Scraton, P. (ed,) (1997) *'Childhood' In 'Crisis'?* London: UCL Press.

Social Exclusion Unit (2002) *Reducing Re-offending by Ex-prisoners*. London: Social Exclusion Unit.

Social Services Inspectorate, Commission for Health Improvement, Her Majesty's Chief Inspector of Constabulary, Her Majesty's Chief Inspector of the Crown Prosecution Service, Her Majesty's Chief Inspector of the Magistrates' Courts Service, Her Majesty's Chief Inspector of Schools, Her Majesty's Chief Inspector of Prisons and Her Majesty's Chief Inspector of Probation (2002) *Safeguarding Children: A Joint Chief inspectors' Report on Arrangements to Safeguard Children*. London: Department of Health Publications.

Stern, V (2005) 'The Injustice of Simple Justice', in D. Conway (ed.) *Simple Justice*. London: CIVITAS.

Tonry, M. (2004) *Punishment and Politics: Evidence and Emulation in the Making of English Crime Control Policy*. Cullompton: Willan.

United Nations Committee on the Rights of the Child (2002) *Concluding Observations of the Committee on the Rights of the Child: United Kingdom of Great Britain and Northern Ireland*. Geneva: United Nations.

Young, J. (1999) *The Exclusive Society*. London: Sage,

Youth Justice Board for England and Wales (2004) *Strategy for the Secure Estate for Juveniles. Building on the Foundations*. London: Youth Justice Board for England and Wales.

Youth Justice Board for England and Wales (2005a) *Youth Justice Annual Statistics* 2003/04. London: Youth Justice Board for England and Wales.

Youth Justice Board for England and Wales (2005b) *Secure Estate Bulletin: September 2005*. London: Youth Justice Board for England and Wales.

Youth Justice Board for England and Wales (2005c) *Secure Estate Bulletin: October 2005*. London: Youth Justice Board for England and Wales.

29.4 Comparative youth justice
Michael Cavadino and James Dignan

[Looked at comparatively] the origins, history and continuing development of 'youth justice' (or 'juvenile justice') systems have been particularly complex and often paradoxical and this presents a major challenge when seeking to compare them. One analytical aid that we propose to use seeks to differentiate between a number of distinct approaches that [. . .] encapsulate different philosophical assumptions, institutional arrangements and operational policies and processes. These five youth justice 'models' are presented in diagrammatic form in Table 29.4.1 and will be discussed more fully below. One very important preliminary observation, however, is that these models are intended to serve solely as 'conceptual tools' with a view to capturing some important distinctions between the different approaches to the treatment and processing of particular categories of young people. It should not be assumed that any of the youth justice systems we will be examining have ever corresponded exclusively and unequivocally to any of the models presented here.

The 'welfare model'

The 'welfare model' encapsulates a positivistic approach that is based on the assumption that juvenile wrongdoing is the product of social or environmental factors for which the young person cannot be held individually responsible. Accordingly, the primary goal of the youth justice system is to provide appropriate help or treatment for offenders; rather than punishment. Indeed, young people who are vulnerable or in trouble are considered to be in need of protection from the potentially harmful and corruptive influences of the adult world, including the adult criminal justice system. Consequently, the primary emphasis is on the 'needs' and 'best interests' of the child rather than the 'deeds' they may have committed.

These paternalistic assumptions are also reflected in the institutional arrangements that – in some jurisdictions at least – have come to be associated with the welfare model. The most distinctive of these arrangements has been the creation of a separate set of 'socialized welfare tribunals' as alternatives to the regular criminal courts, in which the state invokes the principle of *parens patriae* to assume the role and responsibilities of a surrogate parent in respect of troublesome and vulnerable children. Two aspects of the socialized welfare tribunal are particularly noteworthy. First, it combines two conceptually distinct jurisdictional strands: one relating to young offenders and the other to children in need of care and protection. And second, consistent with the fact that its proceedings are characterized as civil or welfare in nature, rather than criminal, the tribunal's jurisdiction encompasses not only conventional criminal offences but also so-called 'status offences'. The latter include 'dissolute' or 'wayward' behaviour on the part of young people, such as truancy, illicit sexual activity, and other forms of non-criminal 'delinquency'.

Consequently, one of the policies and processes that is associated with the welfare model involves the authorization of 'pre-delinquent interventions' in respect of a wide range of 'inappropriate' behaviour by young people. A second relates to the use of informal procedures that are designed to elicit the 'whole truth' about the child, unfettered by restrictive constructs such as the concept of legal relevance and the need to prove the commission of an offence. Indeed, there is a tendency to downplay the significance of the offence itself, and concentrate instead on the social facts and circumstances that have precipitated the child's appearance in court. This aspect is linked to a third characteristic which relates to the use of social scientific 'experts' (social workers, psychologists, psychiatrists, those trained in pedagogy), either as decision-makers in their own right or, more commonly, as advisers and report-writers to assist judges. Another closely related feature involves the conferral of wide-ranging discretion on the part of decision-makers who are responsible for determining and providing for the 'best interests' of the child. This is reflected in the use of a 'one-track' adjudication procedure for all 'troubled' children, whether they are offenders, non-criminal delinquents, or victims of abuse or neglect, since all are liable to be dealt with by means of 'ward

Table 29.4.1 Typology of youth justice models

Models	Philosophical assumptions	International arrangements	Policies and processes
Welfare model	Determinist: crime is 'caused' Paternalistic and protectionist Focus on 'needs' not 'deeds' Child as dependent Help/treatment or education, not punishment	'Socialized welfare tribunal' based on *parens patriae* Unified care/criminal jurisdiction	Pre-delinquent interventions Informal procedures 'One-track adjudication' Unfettered discretion Social science expertise Use of diagnostic custody Indeterminate, flexible orders
Justice	'Free will' and 'accountability' Child as responsible agent Focus on 'deeds' not 'needs' Young offender as 'bearer of rights' Focus on 'just deserts'	'Modified criminal court' Distinct care/criminal jurisdiction	'Two-track adjudication' Precedural safeguards in court Procedural formality Determinate sentencing Proportionality in punishment Treat all cases alike
Minimum intervention model	'Labelling perspective' Dangers of secondary deviance Avoidance of 'net-widening'	'Gate-keeping mechanisms' Alternatives to custody	Decriminalization Diversion from prosecution Decarceration Systems management approach Targeting, monitoring
Restorative justice model	Focus on restoration for victims Focus on reintegration (and accountability) of offenders Empowerment of parties New role for state: 'subsidiarity'	'Family group conference' Victim–offender mediation Changes in role of youth court Unified care/criminal jurisdiction	Diversion from courts combined with reparation Decarceration Flexible/innovative outcomes Need for cultural sensitivity
Neo-correctional model	Primacy of offending prevention 'Law and order' ideology 'Responsibilizaton' of offenders and their parents Young offender as bearer of responsibilities and obligations Offender accountability towards victims and community Efficiency and effectiveness Focus on community safety	Reform of court process Closer links with adult courts New 'civil' forms of punishment	Early interventionism Pre-delinquent interventions Relaxation of age limits 'Zero tolerance' Reparation by offenders Focus on persistence 'Progressive' sentencing Quasi-mandatory sentences 'Fast-tracking' Systems management approach

of court proceedings'. It frequently involves a willingness to use custody (or at least compulsory removal from home) both for diagnostic purposes and also to remove the child from its harmful environment. There is also a marked preference for court orders and disposals that are flexible, individualized, and open-ended or indeterminate in duration. Such disposals have the effect of investing a high degree of discretionary power over the young person's life in the practitioners who are charged with implementing them.

Turning now to the impact of the welfare model: aspects of the welfare approach have at various times influenced the youth justice systems in all of the countries in our study, though both the extent and duration of its influence have been highly variable. Generalizing very broadly, we will see that the welfare approach was adopted in its 'purest' form during the early part of the twentieth century in much of the USA and, somewhat later, in the Scandinavian countries (especially Sweden) and also Japan. Key elements of the welfare approach have also influenced the development of youth justice systems in most of the conservative corporatist countries, particularly Germany, but also Italy, France and (at least until recently) the Netherlands. The remaining common law countries have not been totally immune from its influence although in most of them, as we shall see, its impact has been far less pervasive, particularly with regard to the development of youth justice institutions and their associated jurisdictional arrangements.

However, it is also true to say that the impact of the welfare approach has considerably diminished since its heyday during the first two-thirds of the twentieth century. Nowhere is this more apparent than in the USA, which has since the 1960s comprehensively abandoned many aspects of its erstwhile welfare-oriented youth justice system. Elsewhere, the welfare approach has also come under pressure, but while the influence of other approaches has become more apparent, it shows no signs in these countries of being abandoned altogether. This is particularly true of Sweden, and it also applies to a lesser extent to several of the conservative corporatist countries (notably Germany and France) and to Japan, where the welfare approach still retains much of its former pre-eminence.

The 'justice model'

In contrast to the positivism of the welfare model, the 'justice model' espouses a 'classicist' approach that is based on the assumption that even young people are – with certain limited exceptions – reasoning agents who are endowed with free will. Because they are considered to be responsible for their actions, it is felt acceptable for them to be held accountable in law for what they have done, which means that the primary focus is on the 'deeds' of the child rather than their welfare 'needs'. Accordingly, the principal goal of the youth justice system – as of the adult criminal justice system – is initially to determine the suspect's legal guilt or innocence and next, if convicted, to assess the degree of culpability that they bear. Punishment should then be apportioned in accordance with the seriousness of the offence and the offender's corresponding 'just deserts'. Because the system is acknowledged to be unequivocally engaged in the administration of punishment that often entails a loss of liberty, and that cannot be assumed to be benign 'treatment' that is in the interests of the offender, there is a greater emphasis – formally at least – on the need for procedural rights of 'due process' and for appropriate constraints to be placed on the punitive power of the state.

Not surprisingly, perhaps, the institutional arrangements that are most closely associated with the justice model consist of modified 'junior criminal courts' rather than the socialized welfare tribunals that help to characterize 'pure' versions of the welfare approach. The notion that young people need to be protected from 'contamination' by mixing with older offenders is still present – albeit in highly attenuated form – but is addressed by introducing relatively minor modifications to the standard lower-tier criminal courts that deal with adult offenders. The most common modifications relate to the provision of separate juvenile court proceedings that are held either in a different building or at least at a different time from adult court proceedings; the restriction of access to the public; and the imposition of constraints on the freedom of the media to identify the young people who appear before the court. A second tendency is to introduce a much clearer differentiation between the two jurisdictional strands relating on the one hand to young offenders and on the other to those in need of care and protection. When taken to its logical conclusion, this might entail a complete separation between the two strands, and an institutional separation between children who are 'in trouble' for what they have done, and those who are vulnerable to abuse or neglect, with completely separate courts and procedures for each category. But even where the two strands are united, there is a tendency to adopt a 'two track' adjudication model, with different procedures for dealing with each group of children. In some jurisdictions (as we shall see) there has also been a tendency in practice for the 'criminal' strand to be prioritized (ideologically and, frequently also, numerically) in comparison with the 'care' jurisdiction of the juvenile court.

The procedural safeguards that are associated with the justice model include the following rights: to be notified in advance of the specific charges a young person is facing; to legal representation (paid for out of public funds if necessary); to a fair and impartial hearing; to confront and cross-examine witnesses and to be presumed innocent until proven guilty, which includes a privilege against self-incrimination). The range of sentencing 'outcomes' that are associated with the justice model more closely resemble those available in adult criminal courts, with a strong emphasis on the need for proportionate, finite and consistent penalties rather than the open-ended, indeterminate and highly individualized orders that are characteristic of the welfare model.

As for the impact of the justice model, its influence – particularly with regard to the adoption of 'modified criminal courts' as opposed to socialized welfare tribunals – may be seen in the early development of juvenile justice systems in many of the common law jurisdictions, with the notable exception, initially, of the USA. However, its most dramatic impact was subsequently to be felt in the USA itself, as we shall see, following a series of landmark decisions by the Supreme Court during the 1960s. The ultimate effect of these rulings was to transform the juvenile court 'from a nominally rehabilitative welfare agency into a scaled-down second-class criminal court for young offenders' (Feld, 1999), thereby paving the way for further, even more radical changes to come. The influence of the justice approach on youth justice systems has also been felt in many other jurisdictions, including conservative corporatist states and Nordic social democracies. But although it has moderated certain aspects of their predominantly 'welfare-based' systems notably with regard to the elimination of 'indeterminate' sentencing practices – it has failed to bring about a wholesale transformation of the systems themselves on anything like the scale experienced in the USA.

The 'minimum intervention model'

The philosophy that underpins the 'minimum intervention model' is derived in part from crimi-nological 'labelling theory', which suggests that all official forms of processing young offenders are potentially harmful to them since they 'label' and stigmatize them as criminals. This makes it more, rather than less, difficult for them to desist from crime in future since it may make it harder for them to engage in lawful activities, for example by rendering them unemployable. Indeed, it may also increase the risk of them participating in illicit activities, for example by confining them in custodial institutions where they can meet other offenders, learn from them and be drawn into criminal subcultures. Placement in custodial institutions could for this reason constitute the most harmful and counter-productive of all official interventions. There is indeed criminological evidence that lends support to the idea that official responses to crime may frequently promote 'secondary deviance' on the part of young offenders, thereby fuelling the 'deviancy amplification spiral' that they are ostensibly designed to prevent! Such considerations have given rise to a 'minimum intervention' strategy – particularly popular with certain youth justice practitioners – incorporating some or all of the following elements:

1 avoiding the use of custodial or residential institutions wherever possible because of the adverse effects they can have on the social development and criminal propensities of young people (linked with a policy of decarceration and deinstitutionalization);

2 using community-based alternatives to custody wherever possible in cases that do call for a punitive intervention (linked with a policy of diverting young offenders from custody);

3 avoiding prosecution altogether where possible, by encouraging prosecutors to discontinue proceedings and encouraging the police to 'caution' or warn young offenders instead (linked with a policy of diversion from prosecution);

4 taking care to avoid 'net-widening' by ensuring that the above interventions are never used for young people who would otherwise have been dealt with informally (linked with a policy of targeting and monitoring);

5 advocating a policy of 'decriminalization', certainly with regard to 'status' offences where they exist but also at the very least in respect of minor criminal offences which, when committed by young people, would no longer carry even the threat of criminal sanctions;

6   and advocating a policy of 'depenalization' whereby even young offenders who commit more serious offences would no longer come within the jurisdiction of the criminal courts, but would be dealt with instead by means of civil proceedings administered by an appropriate 'child-sensitive' institution or tribunal.

Another important feature of the minimum intervention philosophy is that it applies as much to interventions that are ostensibly 'welfare-based' as it does to those that are imposed with criminal justice objectives in mind. The 'helping' professions are seen as potentially just as harmful to young people as their more openly coercive criminal justice counterparts, since they are apt to pathologize young people and consequently they too are likely to intervene in their lives far too readily and too intensively, with damaging consequences. For this reason, the minimum intervention approach opposes the indiscriminate use of 'welfare' considerations, whether in respect of sentencing (or remand) decisions, or in deciding whether to prosecute or caution young people.

As for the institutional arrangements that might be expected to feature within a minimum intervention model, a distinction perhaps needs to be drawn between a 'pure' version of the model, which would incorporate the full range of policies itemized above, and the more limited version that is more likely to be encountered in practice. Different institutional methods have been adopted in order to instantiate the minimum intervention principle. In Canada, for example, a largely welfare-based system for dealing with young offenders was modified in 1984 by the introduction of criminal law based proportionality principles in order to reduce the intrusion of the justice system into the lives of young people in pursuit of welfare goals (Doob and Sprott, 2004: 190–8; Doob and Tonry 2004: 14). Scotland, on the other hand, has until now retained a relatively 'pure' welfare approach that is strongly committed to the principles of diversion and minimum intervention (Bottoms and Dignan, 2004). Indeed, perhaps one of the reasons for the continuing international interest that has been shown in the Scottish Children's Hearings system (which we describe below) since its inception in 1971 relates to the 'unique nature' of the Scottish youth justice system, one important feature of which is its commitment to implement-

ing such a radical minimum intervention model in practice (Bottoms, 2002: 455). In reality, however, most other youth justice systems continue to rely on either a modified criminal court or a more traditional form of socialized welfare tribunal, neither of which is fully committed to the principle of minimum intervention. In circumstances such as these the use of diverse 'gatekeeping' mechanisms is especially important, in order to secure the diversion of offenders from prosecution or custody, though the precise form they take varies widely within different jurisdictions, as we shall see. Another institutional feature that may often (though not invariably) be associated with a diversionary approach involves the adoption of various 'alternatives to custody'.

Apart from the various diversionary processes themselves, another policy that has often been associated with the minimum intervention model involves the use of a distinctive implementational strategy that is known in England as 'systems management'. This involves a number of managerialist techniques. They include the use of research and analysis in order to ascertain how the youth justice system is operating in a particular local area, the setting of targets and the adoption of appropriate procedures (for example 'gatekeeping' mechanisms) by criminal justice agencies. The latter work in collaboration with one another in pursuit of shared diversionary objectives, and monitor the outcomes of their interventions to ensure that these objectives are achieved.

In terms of its impact, the minimum intervention model came to prominence much more recently than either of the other two models we have looked at so far and was particularly influential during the 1970s and 1980s in a wide variety of penal jurisdictions. One of the key tenets of the minimum intervention model – that custody should by imposed on those under the age of eighteen only as a last resort and for the shortest possible period – was incorporated in Article 37 of the UN Convention on the Rights of the Child. The Convention was established in 1989 and has been ratified by 191 of the 193 members of the United Nations, the two exceptions being the USA and Somalia.

So potent was the model for a time that it almost assumed the status of 'the new orthodoxy' particularly when the practitioners who were often instrumental in promoting the 'minimum intervention' agenda succeeded for a time in gaining the interest and active support of governments. Despite these short-term successes, however, the influence of the model has waned more recently, especially in some of the neo-liberal countries, where it has lost ground to two even more recent models. Ironically, however, one specific feature of the minimum intervention model that seems destined to continue to shape the youth justice agenda in these countries – even after the eclipse of the 'new orthodoxy' itself – relates to its use of managerialist techniques, most notably in the sphere of inter-agency cooperation. The difference is that these techniques are increasingly being pressed into service in pursuit of other, sharply contrasting, youth justice objectives, as we shall see.

The 'restorative justice model'

The 'restorative justice model' is based on a radically different set of assumptions about the concept of crime itself, the relationship between offenders, victims, citizens and the state, and also about the most appropriate ways of responding to crime. Whereas traditional criminal justice theorists have portrayed crime first and foremost as an offence against the state, the restorative justice model places particular emphasis on the harm that is done to the victim, whose interests were for many years neglected by mainstream criminal justice agencies and policy-makers alike. Traditional approaches have tended to place the responsibility for dealing with crime firmly in the hands of state-appointed agencies, who are expected to deal with offenders (and almost exclusively with offenders) in accordance with 'the public interest'. In marked contrast, the restorative justice model advocates a policy based on involving those who are most directly affected by a particular offence – victims, offenders and their 'communities of care' – in decisions about how it should be resolved. Moreover, such a policy gives primacy to those interests as opposed to the more general and abstract 'public interest'.

The restorative justice model also advocates a very different set of goals for the criminal justice system instead of the predominantly offender-focused goals retribution, deterrence, rehabilitation, and incapacitation – that are associated with traditional approaches. With regard to victims, the aim is *restoration*, which encompasses the repairing of the physical, emotional and psychological harm that may have been experienced. With regard to offenders, the primary aims include the promotion of accountability towards those who have been harmed by an offence, and the active reintegration of offenders themselves back into the community. With regard to communities the goal is one of empowerment and a reinvigoration of civil society founded on a network of constructive and largely self-repairing social relationships. Many of those who favour the restorative justice model advocate a radical reformulation of the state's role and responsibilities with regard to crime, which can be expressed in terms of the 'principle of subsidiarity'. Instead of the state – or its representatives within the criminal justice agencies – assuming direct and primary responsibility for 'dealing with' crime and its aftermath, its chief function should be to act as facilitator, information giver, provider of resources and deliverer of services. Only in cases that cannot be satisfactorily resolved by the relevant communities of care should the state serve as the ultimate arbiter of fairness, and provide a court-based forum for delivering restorative outcomes.

In terms of criminal justice policies and processes, the restorative justice model – like the minimum intervention model – favours the diversion of (many not most) offenders from prosecution, and also strategies aimed at decarceration (since custodial interventions often make it very difficult to secure restorative outcomes). Moreover, in some jurisdictions, as we shall see, the approach has accorded a high priority to the need to develop culturally sensitive and appropriate procedures for dealing with particular categories of young offenders (notably those belonging to indigenous racial or ethnic minorities) and their victims. Not surprisingly, the emphasis on meeting the needs of victims while promoting the accountability and well-being of offenders – and at the same time securing the empowerment of victims, offenders and communities – has resulted in a quest for new and more suitable institutional arrangements and procedures. The best known of these procedural innovations include the use of 'family group conferencing', 'community conferencing' and other variants on the conferencing theme, which enable offenders, victims and their respective families to informally resolve matters by reaching an agreement as to how the offence should be dealt with. Another, very closely related, innovation involves the use of 'victim–offender mediation', which differs from conferencing mainly with regard to its more restricted focus on the principal 'stakeholders' themselves (victims and offenders) rather than their respective communities of care. The adoption of a 'full-blown' restorative justice model would clearly entail major changes in the role (and prominence) of the juvenile court, which would largely be confined to determining issues of guilt or innocence in contested cases, and providing a back-up in cases that could not be satisfactorily resolved by the standard restorative justice procedures. It might also be noted in passing that a conferencing approach need not be confined to young people who are in trouble with the law, but would in principle be equally appropriate for those in need of care and attention and, in this sense, the adoption of a restorative justice approach is compatible with a 'unified' jurisdiction dealing with both criminal and care matters.

The effects of the restorative justice model have so far been highly variable. Although the term 'restorative justice' itself did not come into widespread use until much later, victim–offender mediation schemes originated in North America (where they were initially known as 'Victim–Offender Reconciliation Projects', or 'VORPs') during the 1970s and 1980s. However, these are not in any sense integrated into the criminal justice system since they are not legislatively mandated and where they do operate it is solely on a 'stand-alone' basis. Elsewhere, as we shall see, notably in France and Germany, the use of victim–offender mediation forms an integrated part of the regular criminal justice system, since it is now authorized by law, though the extent to which it is used in practice in these countries remains patchy. The family group conferencing approach was initially introduced and pioneered in New Zealand which, as we shall see, remains unique in the extent to which it has adopted a reasonably 'pure' version of the restorative justice model as the basis of its youth justice system. Other forms of conferencing programmes have been developed elsewhere which differ from the New Zealand approach in a number of important respects, most notably insofar as they mainly involve the police rather than social workers as facilitators. This variant on the conferencing approach was originally pioneered in a number of Australian states, though most have now adopted the New Zealand model. However, police-led conferencing has also been introduced on a stand-alone, trial, basis in a number of other jurisdictions including the USA, England and Wales and also South Africa. In many of the countries in which restorative justice initia-

tives have been introduced, however, their restorative potential has been somewhat blunted by the emergence and growing predominance of a very different youth justice model, to which we now turn.

The 'neo-correctionalist model'

The 'neo-correctionalist model' resembles the justice model inasmuch as both adopt an uncompromisingly punishment-oriented approach, but in other respects they are very different. Whereas the justice approach views the offender as a bearer of rights – and therefore entitled to protection against excessive punitive interventions on the part of the state – the neo-correctionalist approach is more likely to emphasize the responsibilities that young offenders, and even their parents, owe towards others, including the victim, the community and the state. And whereas the justice model makes at best modest claims as regards its ability to achieve any reduction in the incidence of crime – preferring to ensure that offenders receive the punishment which is more just rather than the most effective in terms of crime reduction – the neo-correctionalist approach espouses a much more ambitious crime control goal for the youth justice system. The prevention of offending by young people is accorded primacy, and all other aims are subordinated to it. Thus, reparation – for victims and also the wider community – is favoured chiefly insofar as it may contribute to a reduction in reoffending rates rather than something to which recipients should be entitled as of right, as restorative justice proponents would advocate.

Another aim of the neo-correctionalist model is to improve the efficiency of the youth justice system, for example by co-ordinating the activities of the various criminal justice agencies, speeding up the criminal justice process and increasing the effectiveness of the various interventions that are directed at young offenders. In addition to these purely pragmatic considerations, however, the principal philosophical foundation for the neo-correctionalist approach derives from an unashamedly populist 'law and order' ideology that equates effectiveness with the imposition of tough, intensive and unashamedly punitive interventions. In certain other respects, the neo-correctionalist model more closely resembles the welfare model than the justice model with which it is more commonly compared. This is particularly true with respect to the type of behaviour it seeks to prevent, which is not confined to purely criminal behaviour but often extends also to acts of 'pre-delinquency', including truancy and other non-criminal forms of rowdy or anti-social behaviour. To some extent this change of focus reflects the adoption of a much broader agenda for the criminal justice system as a whole, which is no longer restricted to responding to crime *per se*, but has to do with the preservation of 'community safety' and public order in general.

These broad assumptions are reflected in a number of more specific policies and processes that help to characterize the neo-correctionalist model. They include a marked preference for strategies based on the principle of 'early intervention', which in this context can take a number of different forms. Firstly, there is a tendency to adopt various preventive measures for dealing with acts of predelinquency, including the creation of new quasi-criminal forms of 'civil' penalties to combat anti-social and related forms of behaviour. Secondly, there is a tendency to extend the principle of criminal responsibility to younger age groups. One way of doing this involves the abolition of the protective legal doctrine of *doli incapax* whereby children of a certain age are presumed to be incapable of committing a crime unless they can be shown to appreciate the difference between right and wrong. Another such strategy involves the use of 'transfer procedures', whereby young offenders may be subjected to the jurisdiction of adult criminal courts instead of dealing with them in juvenile courts, where the type and severity of any punishment to which they may be liable is likely to be limited. Thirdly, there is a tendency to adopt more intensive and punitive interventions even in respect of petty and first-time offending, in order to 'nip it in the bud': the policy of 'zero tolerance'. Other measures that are associated with the neo-correctionalist approach include the use of mandatory or semi-mandatory penalties for certain categories of offenders, and the adoption of so-called 'progressive' sentencing strategies whereby persistent offending is met by increasingly punitive responses regardless of the seriousness of the offences themselves. Finally, the emphasis on efficiency is reflected in the adoption of two related sets of measures. One involves the introduction of 'fast-tracking' procedures that are designed to reduce the time taken to deal with young offenders. The other involves the extension of 'systems management' techniques – such as inter-agency collaboration – that are intended to unite all criminal justice agencies in pursuit of a common set of preventive goals.

The institutional arrangements that are associated with the neo-correctionalist model include the adoption of the 'transfer' procedures mentioned above which enable certain young offenders to be dealt with in adult criminal courts, and also modifications of juvenile court proceedings in order to make them more meaningful to young people, thereby supposedly enhancing their preventive potential.

In terms of its effect, the first signs of an emergent neo-correctionalist model could be detected in the USA during the late 1970s, and during the next two decades the transformation of American juvenile courts from a nominally rehabilitative welfare agency into a modified criminal court for young offenders was increasingly influenced by an overtly neo-correctionalist agenda. Similar tendencies can also be discerned in most other neo-liberal countries during this period, with the notable and interesting exception of New Zealand. Beyond the neo-liberal sphere of influence however, as we shall see, the impact of the neo-correctionalist model has so far been much less pervasive.

One possible general explanation for this fairly pronounced 'pattern of penality' in the youth justice realm is that the emergence of the justice model in many neo-liberal societies coincided with a severe and widespread economic downturn. This resulted in high levels of unemployment in which the young, the poor and the disadvantaged were particularly badly affected by the disruption of one of the main socialization processes during the transitional period from childhood to adulthood. Perhaps not surprisingly, the same period also coincided with growing moral panics – by no means confined to neo-liberal countries – over various youth crime issues. In several neo-liberal countries, however, this disruption was compounded by attempts on the part of mainly right-wing governments to restructure the welfare state, notably by restricting young people's access to unemployment benefits and other forms of welfare support. Within this context, the prior (or in some instances contemporary) adoption of a justice model that was based on an explicitly punitive orientation – even though nominally tempered by just deserts principles – provided a fertile medium for the emergence of a still more punitive approach in pursuit of an openly neo-correctionalist agenda.

The fact that most conservative corporatist societies and social democracies appear not to have succumbed to the same tendencies despite their exposure to the same economic downturn, and in spite of their willingness to embrace at least some aspects of the justice model, may be attributable to two important sets of differences, operating respectively at the material and ideological levels.

Firstly, such countries did not set about the systematic dismantling of their welfare state provisions on anything like the scale experienced within the neoliberal camp. And secondly, they did not entirely reject the philosophy underlying the welfare model, which continued to provide an alternative and still vibrant mode of discourse to the harsher punitive rhetoric that underlies both the justice and, in particular, the neo-correctionalist models.

From M. Cavadino and J. Dignan, 'Comparative youth justice' in Penal Systems *(London: Sage), 2006, pp. 199–212.*

References

Alder, C. and Wundersitz, J. (Eds) (1994) *Family Conferencing and Juvenile Justice: The Way Forward or Misplaced Confidence?* Canberra: Australian Institute of Criminology.

Bottoms, A.E. and Dignan, J. (2004) Youth justice in Great Britain. In Tonry, M. and Doob, A. N. (Eds) *Crime and Justice: A Review of Research*, 31. Chicago: University of Chicago Press.

Bottoms, A.E., Brown, P., McWilliams, B., McWilliams, W. and Nellis, M. (1990) *Intermediate Treatment and Juvenile Justice*. London: HMSO.

Brody, S.R. (1976) *The Effectiveness of Sentencing*. Home Office Research Study No. 35. London: HMSO.

Cavadino, M. and Dignan, J. (2002) *The Penal System: An Introduction*. (3rd ed.) London: Sage.

Cavadino, M., Crow, I. and Dignan, J. (1999) *Criminal Justice 2000: Strategies for a New Century*. Winchester: Waterside Press.

Dignan, J. (2002) Restorative justice and the law: the case for an integrated, systemic approach. In Walgrave, L. (Ed.) *Restorative Justice and the Law*. Leuven: Leuven University Press.

Dignan, J. and Marsh, P. (2001) 'Restorative justice and family group conferences in England'. In A. Morris and G. Maxwell (eds), *Restorative Justice for Juveniles: Conferencing, Mediation and Circles*. Oxford: Hart Publications.

Doob, A.N. and Sprott, J.B. (2004) Youth justice in Canada. In Tonry, M. and Doob, A.N. (Eds) *Crime and Justice: A Review of Research*, 31. Chicago: University of Chicago Press.

Doob, A.N. and Tonry, M. (2004) Varieties of youth justice. In Tonry, M. and Doob, A.N. (Eds) *Crime and Justice: A Review of Research*, 31. Chicago: University of Chicago Press.

Dünkel, F. (1996a) Current directions in criminal policy. In McCarney, W. (Ed.), *Juvenile Delinquents and Young People in Danger in an Open Environment*. Winchester 1996, S. 38–74, 214–222 (Erweiterte and überarbeitete Fassung von Nr. 163).

Fagan, J. and Feld, B.C. (2001) Juvenile justice in the United States. Paper presented at a conference on 'Crime and Justice' – a review of research on comparative juvenile justice, held at Cambridge, 18–20 October 2001.

Faust, F.L. and Brantingham, P.J. (1979) *Juvenile Justice Philosophy: Readings, Cases and Comments*. (2nd ed.) St Paul, MN: West Publishing Co.

Feld, B (1999) *Bad Kids: Race and Transformation of the Juvenile Court*. New York: Oxford University Press.

Home Office, Lord Chancellor's Dept. and Youth Justice Board (2002) *Referral Orders and Youth Offender Panels: Guidance for Courts, Youth Offending Teams and Youth Offender Panels*. London: Home Office/Lord Chancellor's Dept./ Youth justice Board. Also available online at: www.homeoffice.gov.uk/docs/referral_orders_and_yop.pdf.

Jones, R. (1984) Questioning the new orthodoxy. *Community Care*, 11 October: 26–9.

Morris, A. (2004) Youth Justice in New Zealand. In Tonry, M. and Doob, A.N.(Eds) *Crime and Justice: A Review of Research*, 31., pp. 243–92. Chicago: University of Chicago Press.

Morris, A., Giller, H. Swed, E. and Geach, H. (1980) *Justice for Children*. London: Macmillan.

Muncie, J. and Hughes, G. (2002) Modes in youth governance: Political rationalities, criminalization and resistance. In Muncie, J., Hughes, G. and McLaughlin, E. (Eds) *Youth Justice: Critical Readings*. London: Sage.

O'Connor, I. (1998) Models of juvenile Justice. In Alder, C. (Ed.) *Juvenile Crime and Juvenile Justice*. Australian Institute of Criminology Research and Public Policy Series, no. 14.

Qvortrup, J. (1997) A voice for children in statistical and social accounting: a plea for children's rights to be heard. In James, A. and Prout, A. (Eds) *Constructing and Reconstructing Childhood*. London: Falmer.

Rutherford, A. (1992) *Growing Out of Crime: The New Era*. Winchester: Waterside Press.

Stang Dahl, T. (1985) *Child Welfare and Social Defence*. Oslo: Norwegian University Press.

Thorpe, D.H., Smith, D., Green, C.J. and Paley, J.H. (1980) *Out of Care: The Community Support of Juvenile Offenders*. London: Allen and Unwin.

West, D.J. (9182) *Delinquency: Its Roots, Careers and Prospects*. London: Heinemann.

30

Restorative justice

30.1 Conflicts as property
Nils Christie   712

30.2 Restorative Justice: an overview
Tony Marshall   719

**30.3 Responsibilities, rights
and restorative justice**
Andrew Ashworth   726

**30.4 Critiquing the critics: a brief response to
critics of restorative justice**
Allison Morris   732

Introduction

KEY CONCEPTS conflict; discrimination; legitimacy; net-widening; procedural safeguards; proportionality; reintegration; reintegrative shaming; restoration; victim-oriented court; victim rights/responsibilities; victims' needs

One of the most popular alternative approaches to criminal justice in recent times is what has become known as 'restorative justice'. Ideas and initiatives influenced by restorative justice are now regularly offered as holding out the prospect of a more civilized and efficient means of dealing with criminal conflicts. Despite the spread of practices that claim to be restorative in character there remains a certain amount of confusion about what restorative justice actually is about, what it aims to achieve, and whether there is evidence as to its effectiveness.

In a seminal article entitled 'Conflict as property', Norwegian criminologist Nils Christie **(Reading 30.1)** provides an argument in favour of overhauling the way in which we do 'justice' and which has been held to favour approaches such as those contained in restorative justice initiatives. The title of his article gives a clue to part of his argument. In short, it is that much of what comes before our courts involves conflicts between citizens. However, the legal system we have is an adversarial one (see Chapter 26) in which the contest is not between the victims and the offender but between the state and the offender. Conflicts are potentially valuable, he suggests, and the exclusion of the victim in the criminal justice process is to their general disbenefit.

There is much dispute as to what is meant by 'restorative justice'. Tony Marshall **(Reading 30.2)** provides an overview of the field, beginning with a definition and then setting out the basic objectives and assumptions of restorative justice interventions. One of the pitfalls in the literature in this area is that some commentators present what might be thought of as an overly-romantic picture of restorative justice or an overly-optimistic view of what it can achieve. Marshall seeks to dampen down some of the expectations of restorative justice by discussing its limitations. He ends by exploring some of the theoretical underpinnings of such approaches and concludes that, as things currently stand, 'restorative justice still lacks a definitive theoretical statement'. Nevertheless, despite this absence, it remains the case that the restorative justice 'movement' has been one of the most influential in contemporary criminal justice.

Restorative justice is very much presented as a contrast to state justice systems – and one that brings with it a number of potential benefits. However, there is also the question of whether there are dangers in promoting this alternative. Andrew Ashworth **(Reading 30.3)** argues that one potential danger lies in the reduced procedural safeguards within restorative justice models. His argument, in brief, is that there are potential benefits in having the state play a prominent role in the justice system and we should be cognisant of the dangers of tampering with this role. At the core of much restorative justice literature (including Christie's article) is the assumption that empowerment of victims is necessarily a positive development. Ashworth questions this and asks us to think through the implications of giving victims greater rights and responsibilities within the justice system. How do we ensure proportionality, for example, within such a system?

A defence of restorative justice and a reply to some of its critics is provided by Allison Morris **(Reading 30.4)**. She groups the most important criticisms under eleven headings and responds to each. The first of these concerns the issue of legal rights – in effect those criticisms made by Ashworth. She denies that restorative justice erodes legal rights, though concedes that such approaches place a different priority on the protection of them. In relation to Ashworth's argument about the dangers of unbridled community involvement, she argues that the solution here lies in the nature of the implementation of programmes. In effect, there are means for protecting against such unwanted outcomes. You will have to read the article yourself in order to decide how convincing you think the defence against these and other criticisms is.

Questions for discussion

1. Why does Nils Christie say, 'Maybe we should not have any criminology'?

2. Why does Christie argue that conflicts are valuable?

3. What would you say are the main features of restorative justice?

4. What are the main limitations of restorative justice?

5. What reasons does Ashworth advance in support of state control over punishment and official responses to offences?

6. What are the main dangers of enhanced community involvement in criminal justice decision-making?

7. What are the appropriate limits to the rights and responsibilities of victims in the criminal justice system?

8. What, according to Morris, have been the main criticisms of restorative justice?

30.1 Conflicts as property
Nils Christie

Introduction

Maybe we should not have any criminology. Maybe we should rather abolish institutes, not open them. Maybe the social consequences of criminology are more dubious than we like to think.

I think they are. And I think this relates to my topic – conflicts as property. My suspicion is that criminology to some extent has amplified a process where conflicts have been taken away from the parties directly involved and thereby have either disappeared or become other people's property. In both cases a deplorable outcome. Conflicts ought to be used, not only left in erosion. And they ought to be used, and become useful, for those originally involved in the conflict.

On happenings and non-happenings

Let us take our point of departure far away. Let us move to Tanzania. Let us approach our problem from the sunny hillside of the Arusha province. Here, inside a relatively large house in a very small village, a sort of happening took place. The house was overcrowded. Most grown-ups from the village and several from adjoining ones were there. It was a happy happening, fast talking, jokes, smiles, eager attention, not a sentence was to be lost. It was circus, it was drama. It was a court case.

The conflict this time was between a man and a woman. They had been engaged. He had invested a lot in the relationship through a long period, until she broke it off. Now he wanted it back. Gold and silver and money were easily decided on, but what about utilities already worn, and what about general expenses?

The outcome is of no interest in our context. But the framework for conflict solution is. Five elements ought to be particularly mentioned:

1 The parties, the former lovers, were in *the centre* of the room and in the centre of everyone's attention. They talked often and were eagerly listened to.

2 Close to them were relatives and friends who also took part. But they did not *take over*.

3 There was also participation from the general audience with short questions, information, or jokes.

4 The judges, three local party secretaries, were extremely inactive. They were obviously ignorant with regard to village matters. All the other people in the room were experts. They were experts on norms as well as actions. And they crystallised norms and clarified what had happened through participation in the procedure.

5 No reporters attended. They were all there.

My personal knowledge when it comes to British courts is limited indeed. I have some vague memories of juvenile courts where I counted some 15 or 20 persons present, mostly social workers using the room for preparatory work or small conferences. A child or a young person must have attended, but except for the judge, or maybe it was the clerk, nobody seemed to pay any particular attention. The child or young person was most probably utterly confused as to who was who and for what, a fact confirmed in a small study by Peter Scott (1959). In the United States of America, Martha Baum (1968) has made similar observations. Recently, Bottoms and McClean (1976) have added another important observation: 'There is one truth which is seldom revealed in the literature of the law or in studies of the administration of criminal justice. It is a truth which was made evident to all those involved in this research project as they sat through the cases which made up our sample. The truth is that, for the most part, the business of the criminal courts is dull, commonplace, ordinary and after a while downright tedious.'

But let me keep quiet about your system, and instead concentrate on my own. And let me assure you: what goes on is no happening. It is all a negation of the Tanzanian case. What is striking in nearly all the Scandinavian cases is the greyness, the dullness, and the lack of any important audience. Courts are not central elements in the daily life of our citizens, but peripheral in four major ways:

1 They are situated in the administrative centres of the towns, outside the territories of ordinary people.

2 Within these centres they are often centralised within one or two large buildings of considerable complexity. Lawyers often complain that they need months to find their way within these

buildings. It does not demand much fantasy to imagine the situation of parties or public when they are trapped within these structures. A comparative study of court architecture might become equally relevant for the sociology of law as Oscar Newman's (1972) study of defensible space is for criminology. But even without any study, I feel it safe to say that both physical situation and architectural design are strong indicators that courts in Scandinavia belong to the administrators of law.

3 This impression is strengthened when you enter the courtroom itself – if you are lucky enough to find your way to it. Here again, the periphery of the parties is the striking observation. The parties are represented, and it is these representatives and the judge or judges who express the little activity that is activated within these rooms. Honoré Daumier's famous drawings from the courts are as representative for Scandinavia as they are for France.

There are variations. In the small cities, or in the countryside, the courts are more easily reached than in the larger towns. And at the very lowest end of the court system – the so-called arbitration boards – the parties are sometimes less heavily represented through experts in law. But the symbol of the whole system is the Supreme Court where the directly involved parties do not even attend their own court cases.

4 I have not yet made any distinction between civil and criminal conflicts. But it was not by chance that the Tanzania case was a civil one. Full participation in your own conflict presupposes elements of civil law. The key element in a criminal proceeding is that the proceeding is converted from something between the concrete parties into a conflict between one of the parties and the state. So, in a modern criminal trial, two important things have happened. First, the parties are being *represented*. Secondly, the one party that is represented by the state, namely the victim, is so thoroughly represented that she or he for most of the proceedings is pushed completely out of the arena, reduced to the triggerer-off of the whole thing. She or he is a sort of double loser; first, *vis-à-vis* the offender, but secondly and often in a more crippling manner by being denied rights to full participation in what might have been one of the more important ritual encounters in life. The victim has lost the case to the state.

Professional thieves

As we all know, there are many honourable as well as dishonourable reasons behind this development. The honourable ones have to do with the state's need for conflict reduction and certainly also its wishes for the protection of the victim. It is rather obvious. So is also the less honourable temptation for the state, or Emperor, or whoever is in power, to use the criminal case for personal gain. Offenders might pay for their sins. Authorities have in time past shown considerable willingness, in representing the victim, to act as receivers of the money or other property from the offender. Those days are gone; the crime control system is not run for profit. And yet they are not gone. There are, in all banality, many interests at stake here, most of them related to professionalisation.

Lawyers are particularly good at stealing conflicts. They are trained for it. They are trained to prevent and solve conflicts. They are socialised into a sub-culture with a surprisingly high agreement concerning interpretation of norms, and regarding what sort of information can be accepted as relevant in each case. Many among us have, as laymen, experienced the sad moments of truth when our lawyers tell us that our best arguments in our fight against our neighbour are without any legal relevance whatsoever and that we for God's sake ought to keep quiet about them in court. Instead they pick out arguments we might find irrelevant or even wrong to use. My favourite example took place just after the war. One of my country's absolutely top defenders told with pride how he had just rescued a poor client. The client had collaborated with the Germans. The prosecutor claimed that the client had been one of the key people in the organisation of the Nazi movement. He had been one of the master-minds behind it all. The defender, however, saved his client. He saved him by pointing out to the jury how weak, how lacking in ability, how obviously deficient his client was, socially as well as organisationally. His client could simply not have been one of the organisers among the collaborators; he was without talents. And he won his case. His client got a very minor sentence as a very minor figure. The defender ended his story by telling me – with some indignation – that neither the accused, nor his wife, had ever thanked him, they had not even talked to him afterwards.

Conflicts become the property of lawyers. But lawyers don't hide that it is conflicts they handle. And the organisational framework of the courts underlines this point. The opposing parties, the judge, the ban against privileged communication within the court system, the lack of encouragement for specialisation – specialists cannot be internally controlled – it all underlines that this is an organisation for the handling of conflicts. *Treatment personnel* are in another position. They are more interested in *converting the image of the case from one of conflict into one of non-conflict*. The basic model of healers is not one of opposing parties, but one where one party has to be helped in the direction of one generally accepted goal – the preservation or restoration of health. They are not trained into a system where it is important that parties can control each other. There is, in the ideal case, nothing to control, because there is only one goal. Specialisation is encouraged. It increases the amount of available knowledge, and the loss of internal control is of no relevance. A conflict perspective creates unpleasant doubts with regard to the healer's suitability for the job. A non-conflict perspective is a precondition for defining crime as a legitimate target for treatment.

One way of reducing attention to the conflict is reduced attention given to the victim. Another is concentrated attention given to those attributes in the criminal's background which the healer is particularly trained to handle. Biological defects are perfect. So also are personality defects when they are established far back in time – far away from the recent conflict. And so are also the whole row of explanatory variables that criminology might offer. We have, in criminology, to a large extent functioned as an auxiliary science for the professionals within the crime control system. We have focused on the offender, made her or him into an object for study, manipulation and control. We have added to all those forces that have reduced the victim to a nonentity and the offender to a thing. And this critique is perhaps not only relevant for the old criminology, but also for the new criminology. While the old one explained crime from personal defects or social handicaps, the new criminology explains crime as the result of broad economic conflicts. The old criminology loses the conflicts, the new one converts them from interpersonal conflicts to class conflicts. And they are. They are class conflicts – also. But, by stressing this, the conflicts are again taken away from the directly involved parties. So, as a preliminary statement: Criminal conflicts have either become *other people's property* – primarily the property of lawyers – or it has been in other people's interests to *define conflicts away*.

Structural thieves

But there is more to it than professional manipulation of conflicts. Changes in the basic social structure have worked in the same way.

What I particularly have in mind are *two types of segmentation* easily observed in highly industrialised societies. First, there is the question of segmentation *in space*. We function each day, as migrants moving between sets of people which do not need to have any link – except through the mover. Often, therefore, we know our work-mates only as work-mates, neighbours only as neighbours, fellow cross-country skiers only as fellow cross-country skiers. We get to know them as roles, not as total persons. This situation is accentuated by the extreme degree of division of labour we accept to live with. Only experts can evaluate each other according to individual – personal – competence. Outside the speciality we have to fall back on a general evaluation of the supposed importance of the work. Except between specialists, we cannot evaluate how good anybody is in his work, only how good, in the sense of important, the role is. Through all this, we get limited possibilities for understanding other people's behaviour. Their behaviour will also get limited relevance for us. Role-players are more easily exchanged than persons.

The second type of segmentation has to do with what I would like to call our re-establishment of caste-society. I am not saying class-society, even though there are obvious tendencies also in that direction. In my framework, however, I find the elements of caste even more important. What I have in mind is the segregation based on biological attributes such as sex, colour, physical handicaps or the number of winters that have passed since birth. Age is particularly important. It is an attribute nearly perfectly synchronised to a modern complex industrialised society. It is a continuous variable where we can introduce as many intervals as we might need. We can split the population in two: children and adults. But we also can split it in ten: babies, pre-school children, school-children, teenagers, older youth, adults, prepensioned, pensioned, old people, the senile. And most important: the cutting points can be moved up and down according to social needs. The concept 'teenager' was particularly suitable 10 years ago. It would not have caught on if social realities had not been in accordance with the word. Today the concept is not often used in my country. The condition of youth is not over at 59. Young people have to wait even longer before they are allowed to enter the work force. The caste of those outside the work force has been extended far into the twenties. At the same time departure from the work force – if you ever were admitted, if you were not kept completely out because of race or sex-attributes – is brought forward into the early sixties in a person's life. In my tiny country of four million inhabitants, we have 800,000 persons segregated within the educational system. Increased scarcity of work has immediately led authorities to increase the capacity of educational incarceration. Another 600,000 are pensioners.

Segmentation according to space and according to caste attributes has several consequences. First and foremost it leads into a *depersonalisation* of social life. Individuals are to a smaller extent linked to each other in close social networks where they are confronted with *all* the significant roles of the significant others. This creates a situation with limited amounts of information with regard to each other. We do know less about other people, and get limited possibilities both for understanding and for prediction of their behaviour. If a conflict is created, we are less able to cope with this situation. Not only are professionals there, able and willing to take the conflict away, but we are also more willing to give it away.

Secondly, segmentation leads to destruction of certain conflicts even before they get going. The depersonalisation and mobility within industrial society melt away some essential conditions for living conflicts; those between parties that mean a lot to each other. What I have particularly in mind is crime against other people's honour, libel or defamation of character. All the Scandinavian countries have had a dramatic decrease in this form of crime. In my interpretation, this is not because honour has become more respected, but because there is less honour to respect. The various forms of segmentation mean that human beings are inter-related in ways where they simply mean less to each other. When they are hurt, they are only hurt partially. And if they are troubled, they can easily move away. And after all, who cares? Nobody knows me. In my evaluation, the decrease in the crimes of infamy and libel is one of the most interesting and sad symptoms of dangerous developments within modern industrialised societies. The decrease here is clearly related to social conditions that lead to increase in other forms of crime brought to the attention of the authorities. It is an important goal for crime prevention to re-create social conditions which lead to an increase in the number of crimes against other people's honour.

A third consequence of segmentation according to space and age is that certain conflicts are made completely invisible, and thereby don't get any decent solution whatsoever. I have here in mind conflicts at the two extremes of a continuum. On the one extreme we have the over-privatised ones, those taking place against individuals captured within one of the segments. Wife beating or child battering represent examples. The more isolated a segment is, the more the weakest among parties is alone, open for abuse. Inghe and Riemer (1943) made the classical study many years ago of a related phenomenon in their book on incest. Their major point was that the social isolation of certain categories of proletarised Swedish farm-workers was the necessary condition for this type of crime. Poverty meant that the parties within the nuclear family became completely dependent on each other. Isolation meant that the weakest parties within the family had no external network where they could appeal for help. The physical strength of the husband got an undue importance. At the other extreme we have crimes done by large economic organisations against individuals too weak and ignorant to be able even to realise they have been victimised. In both cases the goal for crime prevention might be to re-create social conditions which make the conflicts visible and thereafter manageable.

Conflicts as property

Conflicts are taken away, given away, melt away, or are made invisible. Does it matter, does it really matter? [...] Material compensation is not what I have in mind with the formulation 'conflicts as property'. It is the conflict itself that represents the most interesting property taken away, not the goods originally taken away from the victim, or given back to him. In our types of society, conflicts are more scarce than property. And they are immensely more valuable.

They are valuable in several ways. Let me start at the societal level [...]. Highly industrialised societies face major problems in organising their members in ways such that a decent quota take part in any activity at all. Segmentation according to age and sex can be seen as shrewd methods for segregation. Participation is such a scarcity that insiders create monopolies against outsiders, particularly with regard to work. In this perspective, it will easily be seen that conflicts represent *a potential for activity for participation*. Modern criminal control systems represent one of the many cases of lost opportunities for involving citizens in tasks that are of immediate importance to them. Ours is a society of task-monopolists.

The victim is a particularly heavy loser in this situation. Not only has he suffered, lost materially or become hurt, physically or otherwise. And not only does the state take the compensation. But above all he has lost participation in his own case. It is the Crown that comes into the spotlight, not the victim. It is the Crown that describes the losses, not the victim. It is the Crown that appears in the newspaper, very seldom the victim. It is the Crown that gets a chance to talk to the offender, and neither the Crown nor the offender are particularly interested in carrying on that conversation. The prosecutor is fed-up long since. The victim would not have been. He might have been scared to death, panic-stricken, or furious. But he would not have been uninvolved. It would have been one of the important days in his life. Something that belonged to him has been taken away from that victim.[1]

But the big loser is us – to the extent that society is us. This loss is first and foremost a loss in *opportunities for norm-clarification*. It is a loss of pedagogical possibilities. It is a loss of opportunities for a continuous discussion of what represents the law of the land. How wrong was the thief; how right was the victim? Lawyers are, as we saw, trained into agreement on what is relevant in a case. But that means a trained incapacity in letting the parties decide what they think is relevant. It means that it is difficult to stage what we might call a political debate in the court. When the victim is small and the offender big – in size or power – how blameworthy then is the crime? And what about the opposite case, the small thief and the big house-owner? If the offender is well educated, ought he then to suffer more, or maybe less, for his sins? Or if he is black, or if he is young, or if the other party is an insurance company, or if his wife has just left him, or if his factory will break down if he has to go to jail, or if his daughter will lose her fiancé, or if he was drunk, or if he was sad, or if he was mad? There is no end to it. And maybe there ought to be none. [...]

A further general loss – both for the victim and for society in general – has to do with anxiety-level and misconceptions. It is again the possibilities for personalised encounters I have in mind. The victim is so totally out of the case that he has no chance, ever, to come to know the offender. We leave him outside, angry, maybe humiliated through a cross-examination in court, without any human contact with the offender. He has no alternative. He will need all the classical stereotypes around 'the criminal' to get a grasp on the whole thing. He has a need for understanding, but is instead a non-person in a Kafka play. Of course, he will go away more frightened than ever, more in need than ever of an explanation of criminals as non-human.

The offender represents a more complicated case. Not much introspection is needed to see that direct victim-participation might be experienced as painful indeed. Most of us would shy away from a confrontation of this character. That is the first reaction. But the second one is slightly more positive. Human beings have reasons for their actions. If the situation is staged so that reasons can be given (reasons as the parties see them, not only the selection lawyers have decided to classify as relevant), in such a case maybe the situation would not be all that humiliating. And, particularly, if the situation was staged in such a manner that the central question was not meting out guilt, but a thorough discussion of what could be done to undo the deed, then the situation might change. And this is exactly what ought to happen when the victim is re-introduced in the case. Serious attention will centre on the victim's losses. That leads to a natural attention as to how they can be softened. It leads into a discussion of restitution. The offender gets a possibility to change his position from being a listener to a discussion – often a highly unintelligible one – of how much pain he ought to receive, into a participant in a discussion of how he could make it good again. The offender has lost the opportunity to explain himself to a person whose evaluation of him might have mattered. He has thereby also lost one of the most important possibilities for being forgiven. Compared to the humiliations in an ordinary court [...] this is not obviously any bad deal for the criminal.

But let me add that I think we should do it quite independently of his wishes. It is not health-control we are discussing. It is crime control. If criminals are shocked by the initial thought of close confrontation with the victim, preferably a confrontation in the very local neighbourhood of one of the parties, what then? I know from recent conversations on these matters that most people sentenced are shocked. After all, they prefer distance from the victim, from neighbours, from listeners and maybe also from their own court case through the vocabulary and the behavioural science experts who might happen to be present. They are perfectly willing to give away their property right to the conflict. So the question is more: are we willing to let them give it away? Are we willing to give them this easy way out?[2]

Let me be quite explicit on one point: I am not suggesting these ideas out of any particular interest in the treatment or improvement of criminals. I am not basing my reasoning on a belief that a more personalised meeting between offender and victim would lead to reduced recidivism. Maybe it would. I think it would. As it is now, the offender has lost the opportunity for participation in a personal confrontation of a very serious nature. He has lost the opportunity to receive a type of blame that it would be very difficult to neutralise. However, I would have suggested these arrangements even if it was absolutely certain they had no effects on recidivism, maybe even if they had a negative effect. I would have done that because of the other, more general gains. And let me also add – it is not much to lose. As we all know today, at least nearly all, we have not been able to invent any cure for crime. Except for execution, castration or incarceration for life, no measure has a proven minimum of efficiency compared to any other measure. We might as well react to crime according to what closely involved parties find is just and in accordance with general values in society.

A victim-oriented court

There is clearly a model of neighbourhood courts behind my reasoning. But it is one with some peculiar features, and it is only these I will discuss in what follows.

First and foremost; it is a *victim-oriented* organisation. Not in its initial stage, though. The first stage will be a traditional one where it is established whether it is true that the law has been broken, and whether it was this particular person who broke it.

Then comes the second stage, which in these courts would be of the utmost importance. That would be the stage where the victim's situation was considered, where every detail regarding what had happened – legally relevant or not – was brought to the court's attention. Particularly important here would be detailed consideration regarding what could be done for him, first and foremost by the offender, secondly by the local neighbourhood, thirdly by the state. Could the harm be compensated, the window repaired, the lock replaced, the

wall painted, the loss of time because the car was stolen given back through garden work or washing of the car ten Sundays in a row? Or maybe, when this discussion started, the damage was not so important as it looked in documents written to impress insurance companies? Could physical suffering become slightly less painful by any action from the offender, during days, months or years? But, in addition, had the community exhausted all resources that might have offered help? Was it absolutely certain that the local hospital could not do anything? What about a helping hand from the janitor twice a day if the offender took over the cleaning of the basement every Saturday? None of these ideas is unknown or untried, particularly not in England. But we need an organisation for the systematic application of them.

Only after this stage was passed, and it ought to take hours, maybe days, to pass it, only then would come the time for an eventual decision on punishment. Punishment, then, becomes that suffering which the judge found necessary to apply *in addition* to those unintended constructive sufferings the offender would go through in his restitutive actions *vis-à-vis* the victim. Maybe nothing could be done or nothing would be done. But neighbourhoods might find it intolerable that nothing happened. Local courts out of tune with local values are not local courts. That is just the trouble with them, seen from the liberal reformer's point of view.

A fourth stage has to be added. That is the stage for service to the offender. His general social and personal situation is by now well-known to the court. The discussion of his possibilities for restoring the victim's situation cannot be carried out without at the same time giving information about the offender's situation. This might have exposed needs for social, educational, medical or religious action – not to prevent further crime, but because needs ought to be met. Courts are public arenas, needs are made visible. But it is important that this stage comes *after* sentencing. Otherwise we get a re-emergence of the whole array of so-called 'special measures' – compulsory treatments – very often only euphemisms for indeterminate imprisonment.

Through these four stages, these courts would represent a blend of elements from civil and criminal courts, but with a strong emphasis on the civil side.

A lay-oriented court

The second major peculiarity with the court model I have in mind is that it will be one with an extreme degree of lay-orientation. This is essential when conflicts are seen as property that ought to be shared. It is with conflicts as with so many good things: they are in no unlimited supply. Conflicts can be cared for, protected, nurtured. But there are limits. If some are given more access in the disposal of conflicts, others are getting less. It is as simple as that.

Specialisation in conflict solution is the major enemy; specialisation that in due – or undue – time leads to professionalisation. That is when the specialists get sufficient power to claim that they have acquired special gifts, mostly through education, gifts so powerful that it is obvious that they can only be handled by the certified craftsman.

With a clarification of the enemy, we are also able to specify the goal; let us reduce specialisation and particularly our dependence on the professionals within the crime control system to the utmost.

The ideal is clear; it ought to be a court of equals representing themselves. When they are able to find a solution between themselves, no judges are needed. When they are not, the judges ought also to be their equals.

Maybe the judge would be the easiest to replace, if we made a serious attempt to bring our present courts nearer to this model of lay orientation. We have lay judges already, in principle. But that is a far cry from realities. What we have, both in England and in my own country, is a sort of specialised non-specialist. First, they are used *again and again*. Secondly, some are even *trained*, given special courses or sent on excursions to foreign countries to learn about how to behave as a lay judge. Thirdly, most of them do also represent an extremely *biased sample* of the population with regard to sex, age, education, income, class[3] and personal experience as criminals. With real lay judges, I conceive of a system where nobody was given the right to take part in conflict solution more than a few times, and then had to wait until all other community members had had the same experience.

Should lawyers be admitted to court? We had an old law in Norway that forbids them to enter the rural districts. Maybe they should be admitted in stage one where it is decided if the man is guilty. I am not sure. Experts are as cancer to any lay body. [...]

Behaviour experts represent the same dilemma. Is there a place for them in this model? Ought there to be any place? In stage 1, decisions on facts, certainly not. In stage 3, decisions on eventual punishment, certainly not. It is too obvious to waste words on. We have the painful row of mistakes from Lombroso, through the movement for social defence and up to recent attempts to dispose of supposedly dangerous people through predictions of who they are and when they are not dangerous any more. Let these ideas die, without further comments.

The real problem has to do with the service function of behaviour experts. Social scientists can be perceived as functional answers to a segmented society. Most of us have lost the physical possibility to experience the totality, both on the social system level and on the personality level. Psychologists can be seen as historians for the individual; sociologists have much of the same function for the social system. Social workers are oil in the machinery, a sort of security counsel. Can we function without them, would the victim and the offender be worse off?

Maybe. But it would be immensely difficult to get such a court to function if they were all there. Our theme is social conflict. Who is not at least made slightly uneasy in the handling of her or his own social conflicts if we get to know that there is an expert on this very matter at the same table? I have no clear answer, only strong feelings behind a vague conclusion: let us have as few behaviour experts as we dare to. And if we have any, let us for God's sake not have any that specialise in crime and conflict resolution. Let us have generalised experts with a solid base outside the crime control system. And a last point with relevance for both behaviour experts and lawyers: if we find them unavoidable in certain cases or at certain stages, let us try to get across to them the problems they create for broad social participation. Let us try to get them to perceive themselves as resource-persons, answering when asked, but not domineering, not in the centre. They might help to stage conflicts, not take them over.

From N. Christie, 'Conflicts as property', British Journal of Criminology, *1977, 17 (1): 1–15.*

Notes

1 For a preliminary report on victim dissatisfaction, see Vennard (1976).
2 I tend to take the same position with regard to a criminal's property right to his own conflict as John Locke on property rights to one's own life – one has no right to give it away (*cf.* C.B. MacPherson, 1962).
3 For the most recent documentation, see Baldwin (1976).

References

Baldwin, J. (1976) The Social Composition of the Magistracy. *British Journal of Criminology.*, 16, 171–174.

Baum, M. and Wheeler, S. (1968) Becoming an inmate. In Wheeler, S. (Ed.), ch. 7, pp. 153–187,*Controlling Delinquents*. New York: Wiley.

Bottoms, A.E. and McClean, J.D. (1976) *Defendants in the Criminal Process*. London: Routledge and Kegan Paul.

Kinberg, O., Inghe, G., and Riemer, S. (1943) *Incest-Problemet i Sverige*. Sth.

MacPherson, C.B. (1962). *The Political Theory of Possessive Individualism: Hobbes to Locke*. London: Oxford University Press.

Newman, O. (1972) *Defensible Space: People and Design in the Violent City*. London: Architectural Press.

Scott, P.D. (1959) Juvenile Courts: the Juvenile's Point of View. *British Journal of Delinqency*, 9, 200–210.

Vennard, J. (1976) Justice and Recompense for Victims of Crime. *New Society*, 6, 378–380.

30.2 Restorative Justice: an overview
Tony Marshall

What is Restorative Justice?

Restorative Justice is a problem-solving approach to crime which involves the parties themselves, and the community generally, in an active relationship with statutory agencies.

It is not any particular practice, but a set of principles which may orientate the general practice of any agency or group in relation to crime.

These principles are:

- making room for the personal involvement of those mainly concerned (particularly the offender and the victim, but also their families and communities)

- seeing crime problems in their social context

- a forward-looking (or preventative) problem-solving orientation

- flexibility of practice (creativity)

Restorative Justice may be seen as criminal justice embedded in its social context, with the stress on its relationship to the other components, rather than a closed system in isolation (see diagram below).

A commonly accepted definition used internationally is: *Restorative Justice is a process whereby parties with a stake in a specific offence collectively resolve how to deal with the aftermath of the offence and its implications for the future.*

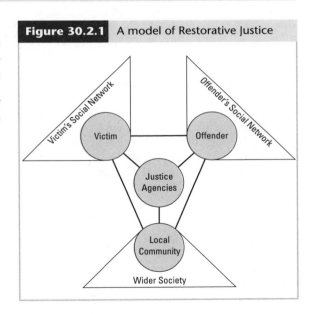

Figure 30.2.1 A model of Restorative Justice

What is Restorative Justice for?

The primary objectives of Restorative Justice are:

- to attend fully to *victims' needs* – material, financial, emotional and social (including those personally close to the victim who may be similarly affected)

- to prevent re-offending by *reintegrating offenders* into the community
- to enable offenders to assume active *responsibility* for their actions
- to recreate a *working community* that supports the rehabilitation of offenders and victims and is active in preventing crime
- to provide a means of *avoiding escalation* of legal justice and the associated costs and delays.

These might all be objectives of the current criminal justice system, and although primacy has been given in the new Crime and Disorder Act to the prevention of offending as the statutory aim of youth justice, the system only partially and haphazardly achieves this, or any other aim. It is not centrally concerned with victims and does not address most of their needs. Only limited action is taken to encourage the reintegration of offenders, and the evidence shows that this is largely unsuccessful. It requires only the passive acquiescence of offenders, who are not expected to take the initiative in making good what they have done but only to suffer their punishment. It is distant from the community and does little to encourage any role for it in the prevention of crime. Despite various programmes intended to divert offences from the full process and reduce costs and delays, their use without parallel attention to victims' needs and future prevention has sometimes led to the criticism that much crime is not taken sufficiently seriously. (The new Crime and Disorder Act seeks to deal with this last point by eliminating the use of multiple cautions and instituting opportunities for victim consultation and preventive measures, an approach which is in accord with Restorative Justice.)

Restorative Justice is based on the following *assumptions*:

- that crime has its origins in social conditions and relationships in the community
- that crime-prevention is dependent on communities taking some responsibility (along with local and central governments' responsibility for general social policy) for remedying those conditions that cause crime
- that the aftermath of crime cannot be fully resolved for the parties themselves without facilitating their personal involvement
- that justice measures must be flexible enough to respond to the particular exigencies, personal needs and potential for action in each case

- that partnership and common objectives among justice agencies, and between them and the community, are essential to optimal effectiveness and efficiency
- that justice consists of a balanced approach in which a single objective is not allowed to dominate the others.

Why is it called Restorative Justice?

Restorative Justice is centrally concerned with restoration, restoration of the victims, restoration of the offender to a law-abiding life, restoration of the damage caused by crime to the community. Restoration is not solely backward-looking; it is equally, if not more, concerned with the construction of a better society in the present and the future.

Other terms have been used to refer to basically identical ideas (see Marshall, 1997 for a discussion of these). The Relationships Foundation (previously the Jubilee Policy Group) has used the term Relational justice to emphasise the fact that this kind of justice is more concerned with the creation of positive relationships than traditional justice processes. Positive Justice was used by an eponymous group that advocated the same ideas as a means of moving away from the negative emphasis on punishment for its own sake to a more constructive approach to justice. Reintegrative Justice has also been used, both as a synonym for restorative and to refer more specifically to Braithwaite's (1989) theory of reintegrative shaming (see below, Theories of Restorative Justice).

The term Restorative Justice is not inherently better than any of the alternatives, but it has the longest history, is the internationally accepted term, and is the most commonly known in this country.

How did the idea of Restorative Justice arise?

The first use of the term is generally ascribed to Burnett (1977) referring to certain principles arising out of early experiments in America using mediation between victims and offenders (see Wright, 1991, for more on the early history of the idea). These principles have been developed further over time, as commentators have thought them through and as other innovative practices have been taken into account, but their basic justification is still grounded in practical experience. Innovation in criminal justice has mainly been in response to frustrations that many practitioners have felt with the limitations, as they perceived them, of traditional approaches. In the course of their normal work these practitioners started to experiment with new ways of dealing with crime problems. Practice developed through experience of what worked in terms of impact on offenders, satisfaction of victims, and public acceptability: In particular, it was realised that the needs of victims, offenders and the community generally were not independent and that justice agencies had to engage actively with all three in order to make any impact. For instance, public demands for severe punishment, which those working to reform offenders found to be counter-productive, could only be relieved if attention was paid to victims' needs and healing the community, so that offender rehabilitation could only occur in parallel with the satisfaction of other objectives. Similarly, the overloading of courts and other justice agencies was due to the increasing lack of capacity of local communities to manage their indigenous crime problems, so that escalating costs could only be prevented by agencies working in partnership with communities to reconstruct their resources for crime prevention and social control.

Restorative Justice is not, therefore, a single academic theory of crime or justice, but represents, in a more or less eclectic way, the accretion of actual experience in working successfully with particular crime problems. Although contributing practice has been extremely varied (including victim support, mediation, conferencing, problem-oriented policing and both community- and institution-based rehabilitation programmes), all these innovations were based on recognition of the need for engagement between two or more of time various parties represented in the diagram above. Coming from very different directions, innovating practitioners found themselves homing in on the same underlying principles (personal participation, community involvement, problem solving and flexibility). As practice is refined, so is the concept of Restorative Justice.

In the course of this development there has been much inspiration from examples of community justice still in use (or recently so) among other non-Western cultures, particularly the indigenous populations of such new world countries as North America (Native American sentencing circles) and New Zealand (Maori justice). These practices have particularly contributed to the development of family (or community) group conferencing (see below), and were effective in moving Restorative Justice ideas away from the relative individualism of victim/offender mediation practice, providing a new community-oriented focus. (A communitarian theme, however, was evident in the early development of mediation in the form of Victim–Offender Reconciliation Projects, VORPs, which represented an attempt by close-knit religious communities in North America to decrease reliance on formal justice.)

Relationship of Restorative Justice to Legal Justice

One of the prominent concerns both within and outside Restorative Justice has been the boundary between negotiatory practices and the workings of the criminal justice system. There are concerns that the due process safeguards for rights, equality and proportionality could all be lost. There are also concerns that the power of judicial agencies might undermine and convert the aims of restorative practices (Messmer and Otto, 1992). Some have argued for completely separate and parallel systems, neither interfering with the other. Others have countered that this would not lead to Restorative Justice at all, because all it gained would be destroyed by the alienating and negative effects of adversarial justice.

It is, in fact, difficult to see how, in practice, two independent systems could co-exist. There is bound to be some influence each way, and therefore the problem cannot be avoided. Even though Restorative Justice involves a greater or lesser degree of devolution of control to individual citizens and communities, it is now generally accepted that Restorative Justice can and should be integrated as far as possible with legal justice as a complementary process that improves the quality, effectiveness and efficiency of justice as a whole. It is this concept of integrated or 'whole' justice (Marshall, 1997) which underlies the concept of Restorative Justice outlined above. It is not just a matter of new and different practices, but of traditional practice too, informed by the same underlying principles. In this way the two processes reinforce one another to mutual benefit, and evolve towards a single system in which the community and formal agencies cooperate. It is in this context that issues of legality and control must be resolved.

Limitations of Restorative Justice

Restorative Justice practices rely in large part upon voluntary cooperation. If one party is not willing to participate, the range of options is reduced. If neither party is willing, there is no option but to let formal justice take its usual course. There is therefore no prospect of justice being wholly restorative and of formal justice being wholly replaced. Traditional justice forms will remain to deal with cases where Restorative Justice is inapplicable because of the circumstances, or fails through lack of cooperation or through failure to come to a mutually acceptable resolution.

This might seem a major drawback to Restorative Justice. Experience has indicated, however, that the majority of individuals offered a chance to participate would like to do so, and the rate of agreements is also high. Later failures to carry out agreements are, moreover, much lower than failures to pay fines or compensation ordered by the courts. Restorative practices are, by their nature, more accessible and attractive to individuals because they provide them with flexibility, for manoeuvre and are more easily understood than legal procedures. They also offer benefits that the formal system offers less certainly or not at all.

Another limitation to any practice which attempts to involve communities is the available level of resources and skills. Communities are not as integrated as they once were. There is a greater emphasis on individual privacy and autonomy, and major social divides occur between cultures and age groups. Greater community involvement would inevitably mean increased education, training and practical resources, more in some areas than in others. A third, related, limitation for Restorative Justice is the existence of social injustice and inequality in and between communities. While problems such as these continue the degree to which communities can be supportive, caring and controlling is restricted. Social divisions also make voluntary participation less likely or less effective. If Restorative Justice involves the community as a major player, there needs to be a community. The degree to which effective communities exist depends largely on other social policies apart from criminal justice. There are implications for education, housing, community development, employment opportunities, welfare, health and environmental services.

The last two limitations are, of course, equally barriers to the success of crime control by any system, retributive or restorative, and are therefore not reasons for not proceeding in a restorative direction, if this offers benefits in terms of victims' needs and the quality of justice.

Some people may conceive of Restorative Justice as applicable only to minor offences, which, if it were so, would be a major limitation. Again, practice has shown that there may be even more to gain by working in this way with serious crimes, especially in terms of victim benefits, but also in terms of prevention. Such practice would normally take place alongside criminal justice rather than as a replacement for it just as there are lower-order legal procedures for minor offences, so one may have to conceive of lower-order Restorative Justice practices for the same offences or for minor offenders in order to prioritise the cases where more effort may have a greater pay-off.

Theories related to Restorative Justice

The first writer to create a really integrated and comprehensive model of Restorative Justice was Howard Zehr, firstly in a small pamphlet called 'Retributive Justice, Restorative Justice' (1985), and subsequently in his book *Changing Lenses* (1990). He represented Restorative Justice as an 'alternative justice paradigm', opposed in all principal respects to the principles underlying legal or retributive justice. His work placed particular stress on benefits to victims and enabling offenders to assume active responsibility, for putting right the harm they had caused (both as a matter of natural justice and as having a more profound impact on the offender than simply receiving punishment from the court). The interaction between victim and offender, involving personal reconciliation, atonement and, potentially, forgiveness, was presented as entirely compatible with religious notions (especially, but not only, Christian), and given justification in those terms. The limitations of Zehr's early work were the attachment of Restorative Justice ideas to a single practical innovation, mediation (and a particular manifestation of such practice as represented by the VORPs), and its individualistic emphasis, largely neglecting public interests in crime in favour of the more or less private concerns of the victim and the offender. (In his most recent writings, however, Zehr has adopted a more inclusive focus – a wide angle lens! – and now stresses the potential variety of processes and the more general community interest – e.g. Zehr and Mika, 1998.)

Zehr's work was widely influential among the growing cohort of converts to such ideas, being particularly evident in the works of Mark Umbreit (1985) in America and Martin Wright (1991) and John Harding (1992) in Britain. These authors treated Restorative Justice as virtually synonymous with victim–offender mediation and continued the emphasis on private negotiation as a sufficient response to crime. Wright, for instance, presented Restorative Justice as a shift from criminal to civil law. This argument is traditionally backed by reference to an earlier paper by Nils Christie (1977) which treated crimes as conflicts between the parties that had been 'stolen out of their hands by the State and should be returned to the parties'. Christie's ideas were particularly influential in his home country, Norway, where they formed the ideological foundation for the unique Municipal Mediation Boards (Fjaerem, 1996). European theory itself developed predominantly in the direction of 'abolitionism' (Bianchi and van Swaaningen, 1986), a radical rejection of state intervention, under the influence of academics like Christie, Bianchi, and de Haan (1990), and has only recently embraced the more Anglo-American ideas of Restorative Justice, with the influence of Restorative Justice practitioners in Europe (particularly pioneers like Christa Pelikan in Austria, Ivo Aertsen in Belgium, Bonafe-Schmidt in France, and a number of people in Germany, some of whom directly imported personal experiences in the USA and elsewhere – e.g. Thomas Trenczek, Elmar Weitekamp and Heike Jung).

Wright was also much exercised by the problem of reconciling Restorative Justice procedures (i.e. in his case, victim–offender mediation) with the traditional justice system. This issue was made particularly clear by emerging research, such as that in Britain published by the Home Office (Marshall and Merry, 1990), and in America and Europe (e.g. Messmer and Otto, 1992, papers from an international NATO conference in Italy). The relationship between the two approaches was made particularly difficult by the apparent opposition between their underlying principles as represented in Zehr's two paradigms, and by the denial in Restorative Justice of the public-interest dimension. It was at about this time that criticism of the over-individualised nature of Restorative Justice thinking also began to emerge, in particular from Harry Mika (1992) in the USA and Tony Marshall (1994) in the UK. As early as 1987, however, Shonholtz in the USA was advocating community-based justice (with some influence from the European abolitionism movement. which was always chary of the ease with which victim–offender mediation could become incorporated by traditional legal values).

The social dimension of Restorative Justice was given a boost by ideas associated with the group forum approaches of indigenous cultures in North America and Pacific nations (e.g. Consedine, 1995) and formal cultural practices of apology and forgiveness in Japan (Haley, 1988). While there is a large literature on community justice (summarised in Marshall, 1985) which was important in the early days, largely in support of neighbourhood justice centres in the USA and elsewhere, more recently these ideas became associated, almost by accident, with a quite separate thread of criminological thought initiated by John Braithwaite (1989) in Australia. His work had developed the idea of reintegrative shaming, a theory of social control that argued that potential offenders were positively influenced by being shamed by their circle of acquaintances or their own community, but were negatively influenced by the alienative shaming of the state in the form of criminal punishment. He favoured locating social control in the community as far as possible. Several writers saw parallels with Restorative Justice thinking in Braithwaite's work (see especially Dignan, 1994). At about the same time Braithwaite himself began to make the same connections. In more practical terms, Braithwaite reinterpreted the New Zealand family group conferences in terms of reintegrative shaming, and this innovation was introduced experimentally in Australia with an explicit justification in terms of his shaming theory. The shaming idea gained further currency and was introduced even into probation and social work practice with offenders on an *ad hoc* basis, and was confused with notions of meeting the victim and mediation.

Reintegrative shaming is by no means universally accepted as part of Restorative Justice theory. Many people are unhappy with its overtones, as shaming can easily be misapplied in a negative way. For instance, it goes entirely against the grain of Braithwaite's original ideas for agents of the state to apply reintegrative shaming, as is happening when it is applied in social work contexts or even in family group conferences run by youth justice workers or the police. There is a basic contradiction in state agencies attempting to engineer a community-based process. While they might go as far as to set up the circumstances, through community involvement, in which reintegrative shaming might occur, whether or not it happens will depend on the individuals involved and so it cannot he used as a rationale for state intervention. In any case, Braithwaite's theory is only one of crime control and prevention, and does not encompass the victim interests and justice issues that are primary components of Restorative Justice as a whole (Bazemore, 1997).

As it currently stands, Restorative Justice still lacks a definitive theoretical statement, although works continue to be written that take thinking forward, such as Cragg (1992) and Bianchi (1994). The latter casts prisons in a restorative role (as much for the support and protection of the offender as for public protection). Dignan and Cavadino (1996) have made an attempt to integrate different models of Restorative Justice action. The most comprehensive statement and the one that most recognises the community role in Restorative Justice is contained in a number of brief papers by Kay Pranis (e.g. 1997), which attempt to encapsulate the essence of the more socialised conception of Restorative Justice. Marshall (1991b) represented an early attempt to present Restorative Justice in the context of holistic changes in the structure of community, society and political organisation, a line also followed by Weitekamp (1992).

Whether or not it is capable of becoming more than just a model of practice and becoming a complete theory of justice remains to be seen. The academic development of such a theory is still in the early days of development, particularly as terms of the formulation of a philosophy or 'ethics' of Restorative Justice, in which a number of commentators are currently engaged, such as Rob Mackay at Dundee (e.g Mackay, 1992), and the Penology and Victimology Research Group at Leuven in Belgium (e.g. Deklerck and Depuydt, 1997).

To practical developments this matters very little, and it may be advantageous that it remains an open model able to accept innovations as they occur, rather than a closed system of thought that might restrict options. It is its ability to absorb many different concerns that gives it appeal, and it is its grounding in successful practice that gives it persuasive justification. In this lies its strength and weakness. There is a grave danger that Restorative Justice may end up being all things to all men and women, concealing important divergences of practice and aim. Marshall (1996) identifies one such major rift between social work-orientated practice and the professional mediation stance.

Although no other criminological or justice theory can be held to underpin Restorative Justice, many academic theories and approaches have been incorporated in, or associated with, it at different stages. Perhaps the most fully compatible, although it is not then referred to in this context (with the exception of Marshall and Merry, 1990, and Haines, 1997), is Hirschi's (1969) control theory, which argues that state intervention cannot replace the power of community ties and community acceptance to control misbehavior. In many ways Braithwaite's ideas are a re-working of Hirschi, and the latter is similarly restricted in its applicability to Restorative Justice because of its lack of concern with justice per se and victims.

Matza's theory of neutralisation has also been applied to victim–offender mediation (e.g. Mackay, 1988, Marshall and Merry 1990, and Messmer, 1992). Matza argued that a major element in enabling offenders to commit crime while maintaining a positive self image was what they employed in number of techniques of neutralisation to dismiss or minimise the effects of their actions ('they can afford it', 'they'd never miss it') or to justify their actions ('they asked for it'). A confrontation with the victim makes it difficult to maintain such fictions and makes the offenders face up to the reality of the harm they cause.

Other strands of thought that have impacted on Restorative Justice include abolitionism (Bianchi and van Swaaningen, 1986), which advocates community control in place of state control; feminist criminology (e.g. Heidensohn, 1996; Pepinsky and Quinney, 1991), which emphasises personal relationships and community; peace-making (Pepinsky and Quinney, 1991) and conflict-resolution theory (Kennedy, 1990; Scimecca, 1991), which both treat crime as a conflict better resolved through participation and voluntary agreement than by dictate.

From T.F. Marshall, Restorative Justice: An Overview *(Restorative Justice Consortium), 1998, pp. 5–36.*

References

Barnett, R. (1977) Restitution: a new paradigm of criminal justice, *Ethics* 87:4, 279–301.

Bazemore, G. (1997) After shaming, whither reintegration: Restorative Justice and relational rehabilitation, In Bazemore, G. and Walgrave, L. (Eds) *Restoring Juvenile Justice*. Amsterdam: Kugler.

Bianchi, H. (1994) *Justice as Sanctuary: toward a new system of crime control*. Bloomington: Indiana University Press.

Bianchi, H. and van Swaaningen, R. (Eds) (1986) *Abolitionism*. Amsterdam: Free University Press.

Braithwaite, J. (1989) *Crime, Shame and Reintegration*. Cambridge: Cambridge University Press.

Christie, N. (1977) Conflicts as property. *British Journal of Criminology* 17, 1–15.

Consedine, J. (1995) *Restorative Justice: healing the effects of crime*. Lyttelton, NZ: Ploughshares Publications.

Cragg, W. (1992) *The Practice of Punishment: towards a Theory of Restorative Justice*. London: Routledge.

de Haan, W. (1990) *The Politics of Redress*. London: Unwin Hyman.

Deklerck, J. and Depuydt, A. (1997) An ethical approach to crime prevention. *European Journal on Criminal Policy and Research* 5:3, 71–80.

Dignan, J. (1994) Reintegration through reparation, a way forward for Restorative Justice? In Duff, Marshall, Dobash and Dobash (Eds) *Penal Theory and Practice*. Manchester University Press.

Dignan, J. and Cavadino, M. (1996) Towards a framework for conceptualising and evaluating models of criminal justice from a victim's perspective. *International Review of Victimology* 4, 153–182.

Fjaerem, A. (1996) The Norwegian system of mediation boards. Paper to Council of Europe Committee of Experts on Mediation in Penal Matters. Strasbourg Council of Europe.

Haines, K. (1997) Some principled objections to a Restorative Justice approach to working with juvenile offenders. Paper to the First International Conference on Restorative Justice for Juveniles, Leuven, 14 May.

Haley, J. (1988) Confession, repentance and absolution, in Wright and Galaway (Eds) *Mediation and Criminal Justice*. London: Sage.

Harding, J. (1982) *Victims and Offenders: needs and responsibilities*. London: Bedford Square Press.

Heidensohn, F. (1986) Models of Justice: Portia or Persephone. *International Journal of the Sociology of Law* 14, 287–298.

Hirschi, T. (1969) *Causes of Delinquency*. Berkeley: University of California Press.

Kennedy, L.W. (1990) *On the Borders of Crime: conflict management and criminology*. London: Longman.

Mackay, R. (1988) *Reparation in Criminal Justice*. Edinburgh: SACRO.

Mackay, R. (1992) A humanist foundation for restitution. Paper to Fulbright Colloquium, University of Stirling.

Marshall, T.F. (1985) *Alternatives To Criminal Courts*. Aldershot: Gower.

Marshall, T.F. (1991b) Criminal Justice in the New Community. Paper for British Criminology Conference, York.

Marshall, T.F. (1994) Grassroots initiatives towards Restorative Justice. In Duff, Marshall, Dobash and Dobash, *op.cit.*

Marshall, T.F. (1996) The evolution of Restorative Justice in Britain. *European Journal on Criminal Policy and Research* 4:4, 21–43.

Marshall, T.F. (1997a) Seeking the whole justice. In Hayman, S. (Ed) *Repairing the Damage: Restorative Justice in Action*. London: ISTD.

Marshall, T. and Merry, S. (1990) *Crime and Accountability*. London: HMSO.

Messmer, K. (1992) Communication in decision-making about diversion and victim/offender mediation. In Messmer and Otto, *op.cit.*

Messmer, K. and Otto, H. (Eds) (1992) *Restorative Justice on Trial*. Rotterdam: Kluwer.

Mika, H. (1992) Mediation interventions and Restorative Justice: responding to the astructural bias. In Messmer and Otto, *op.cit.*

Pepinsky, H. and Quinney, B. (Eds) (1991) *Criminology as Peacemaking*. Bloomington: Indiana University Press.

Pranis, K. (1997) Rethinking community corrections: restorative values and an expanded rule for the community. *ICCA Journal on Community Corrections*, 8:1, 36–39.

Scimecca, J.A. (1991) Conflict resolution and a critique of 'Alternative Dispute Resolution'. In Pepinsky and Quinney, *op.cit.*

Umbreit, M. (1985) *Crime and Reconciliation*. Nashville: Abingdon Press.

Weitekamp, E. (1992) Reparative Justice: towards a victim oriented system. *European Journal on Criminology, Policy and Research* 1:1, 70–93

Wright, M. (1991) *Justice for Victims and Offenders*. Milton Keynes: Open University Press.

Zehr, H. (1985) *Retributive Justice, Restorative Justice*. Elkhart: Mennonite Central Committee, US Office of Criminal Justice.

Zehr, H. (1990) *Changing Lenses*. Herald Press.

Zehr, H. and Mika, H. (1998) Fundamental concepts of Restorative Justice. *Contemporary Justice Review* 1, 47–55.

30.3 Responsibilities, rights and restorative justice
Andrew Ashworth

One of the aims of the restorative justice movement is to replace forms of state justice for a wide range of offences and offenders. This means changing the focus of the term 'criminal justice' itself, away from the assumption that it is a matter concerning only the state and the defendant/offender, and towards a conception that includes as stakeholders the victim and the community too. However, it will be argued here that such a process of change should not have the effect of depriving defendants/offenders of safeguards and rights that should be assured to them in any processes which impose obligations as the consequence of committing an offence. Important steps have been and are being taken to ensure that appropriate standards are respected in restorative processes and outcomes.

The responsibilities of the state

It is central to the philosophy of restorative justice that the stakeholders should be able to participate in dialogue about the offence. Undoubtedly the offender is one stakeholder, but who are the others? It may be claimed that the community and the victim also have a stake in the response to the offence but what about the state? [...]

In crude terms, the political theory would be that citizens agree to obey laws in return for protection of their vital interests, though keeping their right of self-defence for occasions of emergency when state protection is unavailable. As David Garland puts it, 'over time, the effective control of crime and the routine protection of citizens from criminal depredations had come to form elements of the promise that the state holds out to its citizens' (Garland 2001: 109–10). This serves as the basis of the justification for maintaining a police force, a system of public prosecutions, the courts, and other aspects of the criminal justice system. [W]e must acknowledge two major failures of the statist approach.

First, in many political systems the prevailing statist approach has neglected (some would say, reinforced) social inequalities.[...]

Second, and more deeply, there are countries in which the legitimacy of the state and its apparatus, including the criminal justice system, has suffered a serious collapse – obvious examples were South Africa (van Zyl Smit 1999; Shearing 2001) and Northern Ireland (McEvoy and Mika 2001). [...]

These deficiencies in relation to social disadvantage and governmental legitimacy have led many restorative justice advocates to the view that the state should not have a prominent position in the administration of criminal justice, and should instead have a residual role in providing facilities and in enforcing post-offence agreements reached by conferences, etc. [...] Are there duties that the state should retain, no matter that there are elements of 'rolling back' or 'hollowing out' the state's functions which lead to a measure of privatization and responsibilization? [...]

What reasons can be given for state control over punishment and official responses to offences? Two arguments are that criminal justice must be administered 'in the public interest', and that it should ensure respect for human rights. Since, as argued above, a defining feature of criminal offences is that they are offences against the state or collectivity, it is right that the state should ensure that the response is based on general principles duly established and applicable throughout the jurisdiction. This connects closely with the second argument about respect for human rights. The state surely owes it to offenders to exercise its power according to settled principles that uphold citizens' rights to equal respect and equality of treatment. Decisions on sentence should be taken by independent and impartial tribunals, operating on principle and transparently, within a legal framework. [...]

The state ought, out of fairness to the people in respect of whom its coercive powers are being exercised, to insist on 'rule of law' principles and so ensure consistency of response to offences. Insofar as restorative justice approaches are adopted, the state's responsibility should be to impose a framework that guarantees these safeguards to offenders – an aim no less worthy in those societies where state legitimacy is contested. [...] We should also recall that the state has responsibilities towards victims: in the context of restorative justice, this means that it is wrong in principle to place burdens on victims as part of any criminal justice initiative (Reeves and Mulley 2000).

The empowerment of communities

It is the hallmark of many restorative justice approaches that they draw into criminal justice both victims and the wider community. [...]

Much depends, of course, on the conception of community on which reliance is being placed. Every citizen may be seen as a member of several cross-cutting communities: each of us has 'a number of community attachments, articulated in terms of factors such as race, ethnicity, class, gender, age, sexuality, occupation' (Lacey 1998: 144). Some restorative justice advocates would probably claim to have an open and inclusive approach to 'community', but in practice most schemes seem to involve the families of victim and offender, and yet to regard the community (where there are 'community representatives') as a geographical entity. If this means that local communities can adopt separate standards, the result is likely to be a form of 'justice by geography' or 'postcode lottery'. Indeed, the empowerment of communities, howsoever defined, might involve a sacrifice of 'rule of law' values such as consistency, which, it was argued, ought to be standards for criminal justice. Is it right for the state, or for bodies exercising authority delegated by the state, to use its coercive powers differently against each of two people, one who commits an offence in one locality and another with exactly similar background who commits a similar offence in a different locality? Surely not; it happens in both 'conventional' and restorative justice systems, but the difference is that in the former it is regarded as a malfunction to be removed whereas in the latter it may be thought beneficial. [...] The issue cannot be argued to a conclusion here, but the very least that is required by the principle of the consistent use of state power over offenders is that local decision making should be constrained by general standards of procedural and substantive justice.

Turning from restorative processes to restorative outcomes, what is meant by the goal of 'community restoration'? This is regarded by most advocates as one desirable outcome of restorative justice processes, but its practical meaning turns on two issues which remain unsettled. One is the conception of community that is being used. If the broad aim is to restore the 'communities affected by the crime' (Braithwaite 1999: 6), as well as the victim and victim's family, this will usually mean a geographical community; but where an offence targets a victim because of race, religion, sexual

orientation etc., that will point to a different community that needs to be restored. This leads to the second issue: what exactly is community 'restoration', and on what criteria are the form and amount of community restoration to be calculated? Reintegration is a term often used in this context, but its practical implications remain unclear. [...]

A further issue of principle concerns impartiality. It is one thing for critics of 'conventional' criminal justice systems to argue that those systems fail to sentence 'objectively', despite their aspirations, because they fail to avoid discrimination on grounds of class, race or gender. It is quite another thing to devise a system that would avoid problems of bias, or of informal hierarchies growing up, or of local power structures tending to dominate (Lacey 1998: ch. 5). Advocates of community justice stress the importance of inclusion rather than exclusion, and the concept of community is often associated with self-regulation, consent and agreement (Pavlich 2001). There may be examples of sentencing circles and restorative justice conferences that appear to avoid these difficulties, but there is always the danger that, as Adam Crawford has warned, 'the normative appeal of community [may be] confused with empirical reality' [...]. Among the problems here might be that majorities in some communities might disagree with certain criminal laws, perhaps laws intended to protect the weak against the strong or to eradicate drunk driving (Johnstone 2001: 55–7). Allowing community-based tribunals to determine the response to such laws is fraught with difficulty. Impartiality is a key value in justice processes, and yet in restorative justice theory it stands in tension with other values such as participation, involvement and empowerment (see Johnstone 2001: 153–8). But the tension is not insoluble, since it would be possible to concede the case for greater participation by members of affected communities while insisting that the power of decision making remains in impartial hands.

Rights and responsibilities of the victim

It is common for those writing on restorative justice to insist that all parties 'with a stake in the offence' ought to be able to participate in the disposition of the case, through a circle, conference, etc. (e.g. Llewellyn and Howse 1998: 19). The victim certainly has 'a stake', and Christie's (1977) assertion that the 'conflict' in some sense 'belongs' to the victim has become a modern orthodoxy among restorative justice supporters (e.g. Morris and Maxwell 2000: 207, who write of 'returning the offence to those most affected by it and encouraging them to determine appropriate responses to it'). [...]

The politico-historical argument is that most modern legal systems exclude the victim so as to bolster their own power. Originally the state wanted to take over criminal proceedings from victims as an assertion of power, and what now passes for 'normal' is simply a usurpation that has no claim to be the natural order. My concern is not to dispute this rather romantic interpretation of criminal justice in early history (Daly 2000 does this splendidly; also Johnstone 2001: ch. 3) but rather to raise three points of principle which have a bearing on the nature and extent of victims' rights: the principle of compensation for wrongs, the principle of proportionality, and the principle of independence and impartiality.

The first point of principle is the most direct of all in its target. What I want to argue is that the victim's legitimate interest is in compensation and/or reparation from the offender, and not in the form or quantum of the offender's punishment. [. . .] English criminal courts are required to consider ordering the offender to pay compensation to the victim or victim's family, so far as the offender's means allow. However, in many cases the offender will not have the funds to pay realistic compensation. It is now recognized as part of the state's responsibility for criminal justice that it should provide a compensation fund for victims of crimes of violence, at least (see Ashworth 1986 and, on the current scheme, Miers 1997). This is not to deny that victims primarily have a right to compensation from the offender: that is clear on legal and moral grounds, if not always practical.

The key question is whether the victim's legitimate interest goes beyond reparation or compensation (and the right to victim services and support, and to proper protection from further harm), and extends to the question of punishment. It would be wrong to suggest that the victim has no legitimate interest in the disposition of the offender in his or her case, but the victim's interest is surely no greater than yours or mine. The victim's interest is as a citizen, as one of many citizens who make up the community or state. [...] If I am an ardent advocate of restorative justice or of indeterminate imprisonment for repeat offenders, I can petition my MP about it, or join a pressure group.

Just because a person commits an offence against me, however, that does not privilege my voice above that of the court (acting 'in the general public interest') in the matter of the offender's punishment. A justification for this lies in social contract reasoning, along the lines that the state may be said to undertake the duty of administering justice and protecting citizens in return for citizens giving up their right to self-help (except in cases of urgency) in the cause of better social order. [...]

The second point of principle concerns proportionality. Sentencing is *for* an offence, and respect for the offender as a citizen capable of choice suggests that the sentence should bear a relationship to the seriousness of the offence committed. To desert theorists this is axiomatic: punishment should always be proportionate to the offence, taking account of harm and culpability (von Hirsch 1993: ch. 2), unless a highly persuasive argument for creating a class of exceptional cases can be sustained. [...]

The principle of proportionality goes against victim involvement in sentencing decisions because the views of victims may vary. Some victims will be forgiving, others will be vindictive; some will be interested in new forms of sentence, others will not; some shops will have one policy in relation to thieves, others may have a different policy. If victim satisfaction is one of the aims of circles and conferences, then proportionate sentencing cannot be assured and may be overtaken in some cases by deterrent or risk-based sentencing. Two replies may be anticipated. First, it may be argued that in fact the involvement of victims assures *greater* proportionality (Erez and Rogers 1999; Erez 1999; cf. Sanders *et al.* 2001: 451): the actual harm to the victim becomes clear, and in general victims do not desire disproportionate sentences. But these are aggregative findings, whereas the point of the principle is to ensure that in no individual case is an offender liable to a disproportionate penalty. A second reply would be to concede that victim involvement should be subject to proportionality limits, so that no agreement reached in a circle or conference should be out of proportion to the seriousness of the offence. The significance of this concession depends on the nature of the proportionality constraint. [...]

The third point is that everyone should have the right to a fair hearing 'by an independent and impartial tribunal', as Article 6.1 of the European Convention on Human Rights declares. This right expresses a fundamental principle of justice. Under the European Convention it applies to the sentencing stage as much as to trials. Do conferences and other restorative justice processes respect the right? Insofar as a victim plays a part in determining the disposition of a criminal case, is a conference 'independent and impartial'? The victim cannot be expected to be impartial, nor can the victim be expected to know about the available range of orders and other principles for the disposition of criminal cases. All of this suggests that conferences may fail to meet the basic standards of a fair hearing, insofar as the victim or victim's family plays a part in determining the outcome.

Most restorative justice supporters will be unimpressed with this, because the argument simply assumes that what has become conventional in modern criminal justice systems is absolutely right. But the issue of principle must be confronted, since it is supported by the European Convention, the International Covenant on Civil and Political Rights and many other human rights documents. One reply from restorative justice supporters might be that the required 'impartiality' and 'objectivity' produce such an impersonal and detached tribunal as to demonstrate exactly what is wrong with conventional systems, and why they fail. But that reply neglects, or certainly undervalues, the link between independence, impartiality and procedural justice. Might it be possible to sidestep the objection by characterizing conferences and other restorative justice processes as alternatives to sentencing rather than as sentencing processes, and therefore not bound by the same principles? This might be thought apposite where any agreement reached in the conference or circle has to be submitted for approval by a court, and where the offender may withdraw from the conference and go to the court at any time.

This is an appropriate point at which to question the reality of the consent that is said to underlie restorative justice processes and outcomes. The general principle is that 'restorative processes should be used only with the free and voluntary consent of the parties. The parties should be able to withdraw that consent at any time during the process' (UN 2000: para. 7). This suggests that the offender may simply walk out and take his or her chances in the 'conventional' system. However, the result of doing so would usually be to propel the case into a formal criminal justice system that is perceived to be harsher in general, or that the offender may expect to be harsher on someone who has walked away from a restorative justice process. On

some occasions, then, as in plea bargaining (Sanders and Young 2000: ch. 7; Ashworth 1998: ch. 9), the 'consent' may proceed from a small amount of free will and a large slice of (perceived) coercion. Where the 'consent' is that of young people, and it is the police who explain matters to them, the danger of perceived coercion may be acute (Daly 2001). The United Nations draft principles attempt to deal with some of these issues, by providing that failure to reach agreement or failure to implement an agreement 'may not be used as a justification for a more severe sentence in subsequent criminal justice proceedings' (UN 2000: paras. 15, 16). But it is right to remain sceptical of the reality of consent, from the offender's point of view. [...]

The above discussion of the three principles of compensation for wrongs, of independent and impartial tribunals, and of proportionality of sentence, suggests that the substantive and procedural rights of victims at the stage of disposal (sentence) ought to be limited. This should apply whether the rights of victims are being considered in the context of restorative justice or of a 'conventional' sentencing system. The rights of victims should chiefly be to receive support, proper services, and (where the offender is unable to pay) state compensation for violent crimes. There are arguments for going further, so as to achieve some measure of victim participation: this would require the provision of better and fuller information to victims, and the objective would be to enable some genuine participation in the process of disposal 'without giving [victims] the power to influence decisions that are not appropriately theirs' (Sanders et al., 2001: 458). This would be a fine line to tread.

Exploring the 'default setting' – when restorative justice runs out

Although some restorative justice practitioners and writers express themselves as if there are no aspects of criminal justice with which restorative justice could not deal, most are realistic enough to recognize that provision must be made for some cases to be handled outside restorative justice processes. [...] Certain writers make much stronger claims for the ability of restorative justice to handle a wide range of disputes in criminal justice, schools, industry, and business regulation (e.g. Wachtel and McCold 2001). But even some of those recognize that there must be some form of 'background system' in place (Braithwaite 1999). If one adds together the groups of offenders for whom such a system may be needed

– those who refuse to participate in restorative justice, or whose victims refuse to participate,[1] or who have failed to comply with previous restorative justice outcomes – the numbers might be considerable. It has been argued above that some restorative justice processes themselves are incompatible with principles of justice on independence, impartiality, proportionality, and so on. How does the 'default' or 'background' system measure up to these principles?

Braithwaite explains his background system by reference to this enforcement pyramid, developed in relation to regulatory enforcement (1999: 61):

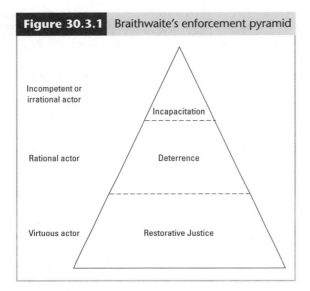

Figure 30.3.1 Braithwaite's enforcement pyramid

The idea is that one starts with restorative justice at the base of the pyramid. It may be tried more than once. If it clearly fails, then one would move to an 'active deterrence' strategy, which Braithwaite distinguishes carefully from the 'passive deterrence' described in most of the punishment literature (see Ayres and Braithwaite 1992: ch. 2).

To have this kind of deterrence in the background helps restorative justice to work, in Braithwaite's view. Nonetheless, he warns that:

> The problem is that if deterrent threats cause defiance and reactance, restorative justice may be compromised by what sits above it in a dynamic pyramidal strategy of deterrence and

incapacitation...The challenge is to have the Sword of Damocles always threatening in the background but never threatened in the foreground. (Braithwaite 1999: 63–4)

From the point of view of principle, this approach is troubling. It seems that, once we leave the softly, softly world of restorative justice, offenders may be delivered into raging deterrent and incapacitative strategies, with rogue elements like Uncle Harry calling the shots (see the remarkable paragraphs in Braithwaite 1999: 66–7, on Uncle Harry), and with only the vaguest of gestures towards 'guaranteeing offenders against punishment beyond a maximum' (*ibid.*: 105). [...]

We should not find these aspects of Braithwaite's restorative justice theory threatening, it is contended, if we looked at the practical meaning of the pyramid of enforcement and took account of the emphasis on penal parsimony in a republican system. But it is not enough to proclaim penal parsimony and yet to give such prominence, even in a 'background system', to deterrent and incapacitative strategies. What types of deterrent strategy are permissible, within what kinds of limits? What forms of incapacitation? To what extent does the background system permit, nay encourage, sentencing on the basis of previous record rather than present offence? The answers to these questions about restorative justice and recalcitrant offenders remain unclear (see von Hirsch and Ashworth 1998: 317–35), but the need for firm safeguards against undue severity does not disappear if a system is labelled 'restorative'. Penal history yields plenty of examples of apparently benign policies resulting in repressive controls.

From A. Ashworth, 'Responsibilities, rights and restorative justice', British Journal of Criminology, 42 (3): 578–595.

Note

1 Some RJ schemes are prepared to proceed with a conference in the absence of the victim, which expands the role of the facilitator or coordinator: see Daly (2001) on South Australia.

References

Ashworth, A. (1986) Punishment and compensation: State, victim and offender. *Oxford Journal of Legal Studies*, 6: 86–122.

Ashworth, A. (1998) *The Criminal Process*, 2nd edn. Oxford: Oxford University Press.

Ayres, I. and Braithwaite, J. (1992) *Responsive Regulation: Transcending the Deregulation Debate*. New York: Oxford University Press.

Braithwaite, J. (1999) Restorative Justice: Assessing optimistic and pessimistic accounts. *Crime and Justice: A Review of Research*, 25: 1–110.

Christie, N. (1977) Conflicts as property. *British Journal of Criminology*, 17/1: 1–15.

Daly, K. (2000) Restorative Justice: The real story. Unpublished paper presented to Scottish Criminology Conference; www.gu.edu.au/school/ccj/kdaly.html.

Erez, E. (1999) Who's afraid of the big bad victim? Victim impact statements as empowerment and enhancement of justice. *Criminal Law Review*, 545–56.

Erez, E. and Rogers, L. (1999) Victim impact statements and sentencing outcomes and processes: The perspectives of legal professionals. *British Journal of Criminology*, 39/2: 216–39.

Garland, D. (2001) *The Culture of Control: Crime and Social Order in Contemporary Society*. Oxford: Oxford University Press.

Johnstone, G. (2001) *Restorative Justice*. Cullompton: Willan Publishing.

Lacy, N. (1998) *Unspeakable Subject*. Oxford: Hart Publishing.

Llewellyn, J. J. and Howse, P. (1998) *Restorative Justice: A Conceptual Framework*. Ottawa: Law Commission of Canada.

McEvoy, K. and Mika, H. (2001) Punishment, policing and praxis: Restorative justice and non-violent alternatives to paramilitary punishments in Northern Ireland. *Policing and Society*, 11.

Meier, B.-D. (1998) 'Restorative Justice? New paradigm in criminal law?. *European Journal of Crime, Criminal Law and Criminal Justice*, 6: 125–36.

Morris, A. and Maxwell, G. (2000) The practice of family group conferences in New Zealand: Assessing the place, potential and pitfalls of Restorative Justice. In Crawford, A. and Goodey, J. (Eds) *Integrating a Victim Perspective within Criminal Justice*. Aldershot: Ashgate.

Pavlich, G. (2001) The force of community. In Strang, H. and Braithwaite, J. (Eds) *Restorative Justice and Civil Society*, 56–68. Cambridge: Cambridge University Press.

Reeves, H. and Mulley, K. (2000) The new status of victims in the UK: Opportunities and threats. In Crawford, A. and Goodey, J. (Eds) *Integrating a Victim Perspective within Criminal Justice*. Aldershot: Ashgate.

Sanders, A., Hoyle, C., Morgan, P. and Cape, E. (2001) Victim impact statements: Can't work, won't work. *Criminal Law Review*, 447–58.

Shearing, C. (2000) Punishment and the changing face of governance. *Punishment and Society*, 203–20.

Shearing, C. (2001) Transforming security: A South African experiment. In Strang, H. and Braithwaite, J. (Eds) *Restorative Justice and Civil Society*, 14–34. Cambridge: Cambridge University Press.

United Nations (2000) *Basic Principles on the Use of Restorative Justice Programmes in Criminal Matters*, www.restorativejustice.org/.ents/UNDecBasicPrinciplesofRJ.htm.

van Zyl Smit, D. (1999) Criminological ideas and the South African transition. *British Journal of Criminology*, 39/2: 198–215.

von Hirsch, A. (1993),*Censure and Sanctions*. Oxford: Oxford University Press.

von Hirsch, A. and Ashworth, A. (Eds) (1998) *Principled Sentencing: Readings on Theory and Policy*. Oxford: Hart Publishing.

30.4 Critiquing the critics: a brief response to critics of restorative justice Allison Morris

It is not unusual in the criminological literature to come across claims that 'reforms' have had unanticipated and negative consequences (see, for example, Platt 1969; Martinson 1974; Pease 1985; Bottoms 1987) and this claim has been made with respect to restorative justice. [...] This paper takes issue with these various claims.[1]

Critiquing restorative justice

For ease of presentation, I have grouped what I see as the main criticisms made about restorative justice[2] under the following headings: restorative justice erodes legal rights; restorative justice results in net-widening; restorative justice trivializes crime (particularly men's violence against women); restorative justice fails to 'restore' victims and offenders; restorative justice fails to effect real change and to prevent recidivism; restorative justice results in discriminatory outcomes; restorative justice extends police powers; restorative justice leaves power imbalances untouched; restorative justice leads to vigilantism; restorative justice lacks legitimacy; and restorative justice fails to provide 'justice'. I respond to these criticisms where I can at an empirical level but, on occasions, can really only refer back to restorative justice values to question the validity of the criticisms.

Claim: restorative justice erodes legal rights

A common criticism made of restorative justice is that it fails to provide procedural safeguards or to protect offenders' rights. [...]

Overall, there is nothing in the values of restorative justice which would lead to a denial or erosion of offenders' legal rights (through their broad emphasis on human rights). However, different examples of restorative justice have translated the protection of offenders' rights into practice in different ways. For example, in South Australia, young people participating in conferences can consult with lawyers prior to admitting the offence and prior to agreeing with the proposed outcome though lawyers tend not to be present at the conference itself. In Real Justice conferences in the United States, lawyers at conferences have a watching brief and they can interrupt proceedings if they feel that

the young person's legal rights are being breached (Paul McCold, personal communication). And, in New Zealand, if facilitators at a family group conference have any concerns about young offenders' legal rights, they may request the appointment of a lawyer (paid for by the state). In addition, young people referred to a conference by the Youth Court can have their court appointed lawyers (youth advocates)[3] with them during the family group conference, as can adult offenders involved in the court referred restorative justice pilots.[4]

And so it is difficult to accept, either with respect to the values of restorative justice or empirically with respect to these examples at least, the claim that restorative justice erodes offenders' rights.[5] What restorative justice does is place a different priority on the protection of offenders' rights by not adopting a procedure whereby offenders' lawyers are the main protagonists or spokespersons and their primary purpose is to minimize the offender's responsibility or to get the most lenient sanction possible.

And, of course, it is quite farcical for critics of restorative justice to imply that, in contrast, conventional criminal justice systems adequately protect offenders' legal rights.

Claim: restorative justice results in net-widening

It is commonly claimed that restorative justice processes widen the net of social control because they tend to focus on minor offenders at low risk of reoffending (presumably offenders who would otherwise be warned by the police or otherwise diverted) and because they tend to result in these minor offenders being given more incursive penalties than they would otherwise receive . [...]

In New Zealand, restorative justice processes are used not for relatively minor offenders but rather for the most serious and persistent offenders in the youth justice system and for relatively serious offenders in the adult criminal justice system. Family group conferences are held for about 15–20 per cent of youth offenders; the rest are simply warned or diverted by the police. Some examples of the kinds of offenders dealt with in family group conferences there (taken from Maxwell and Morris 1993) include a boy who broke into a house and raped a young woman; a group of school children who set fire to and destroyed an entire school block; a boy whose victim was beaten over the head during the process of a robbery; and a boy whose victim barely survived the assault and was left with permanent brain damage. As for the restorative justice pilots for adults, Maxwell *et al.* (1999) document that the two schemes in that evaluation dealt with aggravated robbery, threats to kill, driving causing death, driving with excess alcohol as well as the more 'routine' offences of wilful damage, theft and burglary.

However, some examples of conferencing – particularly those which operate as part of police diversion – do focus on more minor offences and it is possible that net-widening occurs here. Young and Goold (1999) certainly raised this concern with respect to restorative conferencing in the Thames Valley Police area at that time (see also Young 2001). On the other hand, Maxwell and Morris (1993) specifically examined net-widening in their research on family group conferences in New Zealand and found no evidence of it. Also, in the evaluation of the community panels in New Zealand, most offenders in the pilot groups experienced less incursive penalties than their matched controls who were dealt with solely in conventional criminal courts (Maxwell *et al.* 1999).

To repeat the point made earlier: the validity of this claim depends on the focus of particular examples of restorative justice and it certainly does not apply to all.

Claim: restorative justice trivializes crime

This claim is most frequently mentioned with respect to violence against women. Critics tend to see restorative justice processes as decriminalizing men's violence against their partners and as returning it to the status of a 'private' matter. Morris and Gelsthorpe (2000b) have already fully discussed this and I repeat here only the gist of their response to this criticism. Their main point is that the use of restorative justice processes does not signify the trivialization of any crime: the criminal law remains as a signifier and denouncer. In addition, however, restorative justice advocates believe that the offender's family and friends are by far the most potent agents to achieve this objective of denunciation. In the context of men's violence against their partners, denouncing the violence in the presence of the abuser's family and friends

means that the message is loud and clear for those who matter most to him.

More broadly, restorative justice arguably takes crime more seriously than conventional criminal justice systems because it focuses on the consequences of the offence for victims and attempts to address these and to find meaningful ways of holding offenders accountable. Crime, on the other hand, is trivialized by processes in which victims have no role (apart, in some situations, as witnesses) and in which offenders are not much more than passive observers.

Claim: restorative justice fails to 'restore' victims and offenders

By definition, we would expect restorative justice to 'restore' and it has to be accepted that there is some haziness in the restorative justice literature about what precisely this means. But, as noted earlier, for victims, I take it to mean restoring the victim's security, self-respect, dignity and sense of control. There is no doubt that research shows that victims who have taken part in restorative justice processes have high levels of satisfaction with reparative agreements, have reduced levels of fear and seem to have an improved understanding of why the offence occurred and its likelihood of recurrence (for empirical detail, see Daly 2001; Strang 2001; Umbreit *et al.* 2001). It is true, as some critics allege, that full monetary restoration is not always achieved as many offenders have limited resources. However, if we as a community take restorative justice seriously, this type of restoration could, and perhaps should, be a community (state) responsibility. But, more importantly, research consistently suggests that monetary restoration is not what victims want: they are much more interested in emotional reparation than material (Marshall and Merry 1990; Umbreit *et al.* 1994; Strang 2001). Now, of course, emotional reparation also does not always happen. But it seems to happen more often in restorative justice processes than it does not. And it certainly happens more often there than in conventional criminal justice processes.

For offenders, again as noted earlier, I take restoration to mean restoring responsibility to them for their offending and its consequences, restoring a sense of control to them to make amends for what they have done and restoring a belief in them that the process and outcomes were fair and just. The evidence seems clear that this can occur.

Claim: restorative justice fails to effect real change

Most critics of restorative justice are sceptical about what it has achieved. [...]

The major claim made by critics is that restorative justice has failed to reduce reoffending. It could reasonably be argued that reducing reoffending is not really an objective of restorative justice; its focus is holding offenders accountable and making amends to victims. However, it can also be reasonably argued, at least in principle, that if a particular process reflects restorative values and achieves restorative outcomes then we might expect reoffending to be reduced. Thus, if the offender accepts responsibility for the offending, feels involved in the decision about how to deal with that offending, feels treated fairly and with respect, apologizes and makes amends to the victim and takes part in a programme designed to deal with the reasons underlying his or her offending, then we could at least predict that s/he will be less likely to offend again in the future.

Critics of restorative justice feel otherwise, principally, it seems, because the assumed features of restorative justice do not coincide with the principles of effective treatment (as outlined in, for example, Andrews and Bonta 1994; Gendreau 1996). I need to make three points in response.

First, it is quite possible for the parties to reach an agreement, after a restorative process, which would involve a rehabilitative outcome based on the principles of effective treatment (as well as or instead of a reparative or, for that matter, a punitive outcome). I referred to this earlier in the discussion about 'restoring' offenders.

Second, critics seem to have confused here restorative justice processes and restorative outcomes and to have ignored the possibility that both may impact on reoffending. There is now some evidence of the importance of process in shaping attitudes and behaviour. [...]

Third, and more importantly, there is now a considerable amount of research which suggests that restorative justice processes and outcomes can reduce reconviction.[6]

Indeed, Latimer *et al.*'s (2001) meta-analysis concluded that, on average, restorative justice programmes had lower reconviction rates than conventional criminal justice approaches. Compared to comparison or control groups, offenders who participated in restorative justice programmes were significantly more successful at remaining crime free during the follow up periods.[7]

Claim: restorative justice results in discriminatory outcomes

Critics here claim that affluent communities are more likely to have the resources to develop restorative justice alternatives and that restorative justice reinforces existing race and class biases in the criminal justice system by excluding certain types of offenders from restorative justice processes.[8] The validity of this claim again depends on how (and where) the restorative justice process is implemented. It is certainly *possible* for restorative justice programmes to be set up on an ad hoc and selective basis. But this is not the result of endorsing restorative justice principles or values and so this criticism cannot be made with respect to restorative justice generally.

To again take New Zealand as an example: conferencing for young offenders there operates on a statutory basis, nationwide and, in certain circumstances, referral to a family group conference is mandatory. In many Australian states, restorative justice processes are also based in statute and operate state-wide. Referral to a conference, however, tends to be discretionary and there are suggestions that certain categories of offenders (Aboriginals) are under-represented in conferencing in some Australian states and are more likely to be referred directly to courts (Blagg 2001; Daly 2001).

Claim: restorative justice extends police powers

This criticism seems aimed primarily at the experiments in Australia, England and Wales and the Unites States with restorative conferencing located as part of police diversion. There, to the extent that the police dominate outcomes, it could be argued that police powers have been extended because they virtually become 'sentencers' as well as prosecutors (Young and Goold 1999; Young 2001). However, because of this, not all commentators see these examples of conferencing as meeting restorative values (Morris and Gelsthorpe 2000a). The earlier comments on net-widening are relevant to these conferences too.

On the other hand, family group conferencing in New Zealand can be seen as *curtailing* police powers. The police there cannot refer young people who have not been arrested directly to the Youth Court. They must first refer the young person to a family group conference. If the conference feels it can resolve the matter without it going to court, then that is the end of it. Thus, again, this criticism is valid only to the extent that particular programmes are not based on restorative justice principles or values – the empowerment of the key participants – and is not, therefore, valid with respect to all examples of restorative justice.

Claim: restorative justice leaves power imbalances untouched

A common argument against the use of restorative justice is the imbalance between supposedly powerless offenders and supposedly powerful victims. [...]

Within a restorative justice framework, power imbalances can be addressed by ensuring procedural fairness, by supporting the less powerful, and by challenging the more powerful. Thus restorative justice processes can provide a forum in which victims can make clear to offenders and, importantly, to their friends and families the effects of the offence on them but it can also provide a forum in which offenders can give victims some insight into the reasons for their offending.[9] Facilitators of restorative justice processes have a responsibility to create an environment that ensures that both victims and offenders can freely participate, by whichever way is necessary. In contrast, power imbalances between defendants and professionals are entrenched in conventional criminal justice systems and the image of an adversarial struggle between two lawyers of equal might is a fiction (McConville *et al.* 1993).

Claim: restorative justice encourages vigilantism

Restorative justice is sometimes equated with community or popular justice, which is, in turn, equated with vigilantism.[10] It is true that some forms of community justice can be repressive, retributive, hierarchical and patriarchal. But these values are fundamentally at odds with the defining values of restorative justice and cannot, therefore, be part of it. That is also why 'community' involvement in restorative justice processes needs to be defined quite narrowly and in such a way as to exclude the attendance of 'representative' members of geographical or social communities (except where it would be culturally appropriate to do so, as in North American sentencing circles). Also, if there are concerns about communities taking over this process for non-restorative purposes, checks could be introduced – for example, courts could provide some oversight of restorative justice outcomes for the purposes of ensuring that the outcomes are in accordance with restorative justice values. Finally, of course, vigilantism does not require the introduction of restorative processes to emerge.

Claim: restorative justice lacks legitimacy

Tyler (1990) found that citizens treated with respect and listened to by the police were likely to see the law as fair; conversely, when they were treated without respect and were not listened to they were likely to see the law as unfair. He distinguished between 'process control' and 'outcome control' and concluded that 'having a say' (that is, process control) was more important than determining the outcome of a decision. Tyler's research, however, was based in a context in which decisions were made by third parties (judges). To this extent, his conclusions about priorities may not be as relevant for restorative justice processes, which are premised on consensual decision making. [...]

Much of the evidence I have cited so far would support restorative justice's claims for legitimacy. And, again, one has to be sceptical about the assumed legitimacy of conventional criminal justice systems, at least for those groups that are marginalized, alienated and socially excluded.

Claim: restorative justice fails to provide justice

As noted earlier, just deserts theorists argue that the sanctions agreed to within a restorative justice framework may not be proportionate to the severity of the offence and are unlikely to be consistent. Such criticisms can be responded to in a number of ways. First, judges in conventional criminal justice processes do not always deal with like cases alike. However, that is hardly an adequate response.

Second, and related to the above point, the different reasons for these inconsistencies are crucially important. Inconsistencies on the basis of gender, ethnicity or socioeconomic status *per se* – which is what research on conventional criminal justice systems (Hood 1992; Hedderman and Gelsthorpe 1997) points to – can never be right.[11] Inconsistencies between outcomes which are the result of genuine and uncoerced agreement between the key parties, including victims, may be.

Third, restorative justice is premised on consensual decision making. It requires all the key parties – the victims, offenders and their communities of care – to agree on the appropriate outcome. The state continues to remain a party to decision making through its representatives – for example, the police or the judiciary – depending on the location of the particular restorative justice process in the criminal justice system. But what is different is that these representatives are not the 'primary' decision makers.

Finally, consistency and proportionality are constructs that serve abstract notions of justice. Ashworth and von Hirsch (1998: 334) refer to desert theory providing 'principled and fair guidance'. But there are a number of criticisms that can be made of this: in particular, the oversimplification of the gradation of offences (see Tonry 1994 for more details). There are some writers on restorative justice who refer in similar terms to 'uniformity', 'fairness' and 'equity' as means of ensuring that outcomes for offenders are not disproportionate to their culpability (see, for example, Van Ness 1993; Bazemore and Umbreit 1995). But, in my view, uniformity or consistency of approach (as opposed to uniformity or consistency in outcomes) is what is required and this is achieved by always taking into account the needs and wishes of those most directly affected by the offence: victims, offenders and their communities of care. Specifically from a restorative perspective, desert theory does not provide outcomes that are meaningful to them. Indeed, desert theory is silent on why equal justice for offenders should be a higher value than equal justice (or, indeed, any kind of justice at all) for victims.

From A. Morris, 'Critiquing the critics: a brief response to critics of restorative justice', British Journal of Criminology, 2002, 42(3): 596–615.

Notes

1 It is perhaps invidious in this introduction to identify certain writers on restorative justice and I may open myself up to challenge by choosing to quote these rather than others. However, these critical works can be taken as 'representative'. The criticisms in them are 'typical' and not individual or idiosyncratic.

2 This is not an exhaustive list of criticisms. I have not dealt with, for example, the claim that restorative justice fails to deter and is a 'soft option', that it uses victims to benefit offenders, that it cannot deal with persistent offenders and that it should not deal with men who are violent towards women. For my responses to these criticisms see Morris and Gelsthorpe (2000b) and Morris and Young (2000). See also Braithwaite (1999) for his responses to various criticisms of restorative justice.

3 These lawyers are specially selected for their personality, cultural background, training and experience as being suitably qualified to represent young people. They provide the young person with legal advice

generally, represent him or her in court, and can attend the young person's family group conference.

4 A quite different issue not explored in this paper is how lawyers should act in restorative justice processes. In a survey by Morris et al., (1997), a few of the youth advocates who attended conferences seemed to act in a way which was at odds with the principles of the restorative justice (for example, they spoke for the young persons rather than allowing or encouraging them to speak for themselves).

5 In some jurisdictions too, judges play a role in protecting offenders' rights. In court-referred family group conferences and in the court-referred restorative justice pilots in New Zealand, judges receive recommendations from the conferences and it is up to them to decide whether or not they accept them.

6 See, for example, Umbreit et al.'s (1994) comparison of four victim–offender mediation programmes in the United States compared with non-mediated and non-referred offenders; the meta-analysis by Bonta et al. (1998) of programmes using community service, restitution and mediation compared with programmes without these elements; McCold and Wachtel's (1998) evaluation of young offenders randomly assigned to conferences or to courts; Maxwell et al.'s (1999) comparison of 200 participants in two restorative justice pilot schemes in New Zealand with a matched sample of offenders who were dealt with solely through the criminal courts; and Sherman et al.'s (2000) comparisons of young people randomly assigned to conferences or to courts.

7 This contrasts with Miers et al.'s (2001) findings with respect to a number of restorative justice schemes in England. It is not clear, however, that all of these schemes really met the core values of restorative justice.

8 The way in which this criticism is framed, of course, reinforces that it is already acknowledged by critics of restorative justice that conventional criminal justice systems operate in a discriminatory way.

9 In the above examples, we might not think it appropriate to give all offenders an equal voice and this would have to be taken into account in trying to achieve a balance. With respect to men's violence against women, for example, Braithwaite and Daly (1994) refer to the fact that in some Maori tribes an accused male abuser would have no right to speak and that statements would have to be made by others on his behalf.

10 Ashworth and von Hirsch (1998: 303) certainly justify conventional criminal justice practices on the grounds that they displace vigilantism and prevent people from taking the law into their own hands.

11 I acknowledge that desert theorists would not support such inconsistencies either, but I prefer to respond to their criticisms of restorative justice by referring to how sentencing 'is' empirically rather than how it 'ought' to be ideally.

References

Andrews, D. and Bonta, J. (1994) *The Psychology of Criminal Conduct*. Cincinnati, OH: Anderson.

Ashworth, A. and von Hirsch, A. (1998), Desert and the three Rs. In von Hirsch, A. and Ashworth, A. (Eds) *Principled Sentencing: Readings on Theory and Policy*. Oxford: Hart Publishing.

Bazemore, C. and Umbreit, M. (1995) Rethinking the sanctioning function in juvenile court. *Crime and Delinquency*, 41: 296–316.

Blagg, H. (2001) Aboriginal youth and restorative justice: Critical notes from the Australian frontier. In Morris, A. and Maxwell, G. (Eds) *Restoring Justice for Juveniles: Conferences, Mediation and Circles*. Oxford: Hart Publishing.

Bonta, J., Wallace-Capretta, S. and Rooney, J. (1998) *Restorative Justice: An Evaluation of the Restorative Resolutions Project*. Ottawa, Ontario: Solicitor General Canada.

Bottoms, A. (1987) Limiting prison use in England and Wales. *The Howard Journal of Criminal Justice*, 26: 177–202.

Braithwaite, J. (1999) Restorative justice: Assessing optimistic and pessimistic accounts. In Tonry, M. and Morris, N. (Eds) *Crime and Justice: A Review of the Research*. Chicago, IL: Chicago University Press.

Daly, K. (2001) Conferencing in Australia and New Zealand: Variations, research findings and prospects. In Morris, A. and Maxwell, C. (Eds) *Restoring Justice for Juveniles: Conferences, Mediation and Circles*. Oxford: Hart Publishing.

Gendreau, P. (1996) The principles of effective intervention with offenders. In Harland, A. (Ed.) *Choosing Correctional Outcomes That Work*. Thousand Oaks, CA: Sage.

Hedderman, C. and Gelsthorpe, L. (1997) *Understanding the Sentencing of Women*. Home Office Research Study no. 170. London: HMSO.

Hood, R. (1992) *Race and Sentencing*. Oxford: Clarendon Press.

Latimer, J., Dowden, C. and Muise, D. (2001) *The Effectiveness of Restorative Justice Practice: A Meta-analysis*. Ottawa, Ontario: Department of Justice Canada.

Marshall, T. and Merry, S. (1990) *Crime and Accountability: Victim/Offender Mediation in Practice*. London: HMSO.

Martinson, R. (1974) What works? Questions and answers about prison reform. *Public Interest*, 35 (Spring): 22–54.

Maxwell, G. and Morris, A. (1993) *Families, Victims and Culture: Youth Justice in New Zealand*. Wellington, New Zealand: Social Policy Agency and Institute of Criminology.

Maxwell, G. Morris, A. and Anderson, T. (1999) *Community Panel Adult Pre-Trial Diversion: Supplementary Evaluation*. Wellington, New Zealand: Crime Prevention Unit Dept. of Prime Minister and Cabinet and Institute of Criminology.

McCold, P. and Wachtel, B. (1998) *Restorative Policing Experiment*. Pipersville, PA: Community Service Foundation.

McConville, M., Hodgson, J. Bridges, L. and Pavlovic, A. (1993) *Standing Accused: The Organisation and Practices of Criminal Defence Lawyers*. Oxford: Clarendon Press.

Morris, A. and Gelsthorpe, L. (2000a) Something old, something borrowed, something blue, but something new? A comment on the prospects for restorative justice under the Crime and Disorder Act 1998. *Criminal Law Review*, January: 18–30.

Morris, A. and Gelsthorpe, L. (2000b) Re-visioning men's violence against female partners. *The Howard Journal of Criminal Justice*, 39/4: 412–28.

Morris, A. and Young, W. (2000) Reforming criminal justice: The potential of restorative justice. In Strang, H. and Braithwaite, J. (Eds) *Restorative Justice: From Philosophy to Practice*. Aldershot: Ashgate.

Pease, K. (1985) Community service orders. In Tonry, M. and Morris, N. (Eds) *Crime and Justice: An Annual Review of the Research*, vol.6. Chicago, IL: University of Chicago Press.

Platt, A. (1969) *The Child Savers*. Chicago, IL: University of Chicago Press.

Sherman, L. Strang, H. and Woods, D. (2000) *Recidivism Patterns in the Canberra Reintegrative Shaming Experiment (RISE)*. Canberra: Australian National University.

Strang, H. (2001) Justice for victims of young offenders: The centrality of emotional harm and restoration. In Morris, A. and Maxwell, G. (Eds) *Restoring Justice for Juveniles: Conferences, Mediation and Circles*. Oxford: Hart Publishing.

Tonry, M. (1994) Proportionality, parsimony and interchangeability. In Duff, A., Marshall, S., Dobash, R.E. and Dobash, R.P. (Eds) *Penal Theory and Practice*. Manchester: Manchester University Press.

Tyler, T. (1990) *Why People Obey the Law*. New Haven, CT: Yale University Press.

Umbreit, M., Coates, R. and Kalanj, B. (1994) *When Victim Meets Offender*. Monsey, NY: Criminal Justice Press.

Umbreit, M., Coates, R and Vos, B. (2001) Victim impact of meeting with young offenders: Two decades of victim offender mediation practice and research. In Morris, A. and Maxwell, G. (Eds) *Restoring Justice for Juveniles: Conferences, Mediation and Circles*. Oxford: Hart Publishing.

van Ness, D. (1993) New wine and old wineskins: Four challenges of restorative justice. *Criminal Law Forum*, 4: 251–76.

Young, R. (2001) Just cops doing 'shameful' business?: Police-led restorative justice and the lessons of research. In Morris, A. and Maxwell, G. (Eds) *Restorative Justice for Juveniles: Conferences, Mediation and Circles*. Oxford: Hart Publishing.

Young, R. and Goold, B. (1999) Restorative police cautioning in Aylesbury – from degrading to reintegrative shaming ceremonies? *Criminal Law Review*, February: 126–38.

31

Race, crime and justice

31.1 The racism of criminalization: police and the reproduction of the criminal other
Tony Jefferson   742

31.2 From Scarman to Stephen Lawrence
Stuart Hall   747

31.3 In proportion: race, and police stop and search
P.A.J. Waddington, Kevin Stenson and David Don   754

31.4 Deadly symbiosis: when ghetto and prison meet and mesh
Loïc Wacquant   759

Introduction

To what extent is it possible to assume that the criminal justice system treats people fairly? Are we all equal in the eyes of the law? A source of continuing controversy in criminal justice concerns the suggestion that individuals and institutions are discriminatory in the way they deal with people of different ethnic origins. Specifically, it is argued that racist attitudes or institutional practices mean that minority ethnic groups are poorly treated and, consequently, end up over-represented in the criminal justice system.

In an early article in this field, Tony Jefferson **(Reading 31.1)** explores the parameters of the 'race/crime' debate. Much previous literature had explored, crudely put, two contrasting explanations for the over-representation of minorities in the criminal justice system: either that they committed more crime or, conversely, that the institutions of the criminal justice system operated in a racist manner. Jefferson's aim in his review is different, seeking rather to explore 'the contiguity between structural disadvantage, policing the powerless, and the notion of "the criminal". His central claim is that police racism is *not* about discriminating against young black males but rather about the production of a criminal 'Other' in which young black males figure prominently. Put differently, he suggests that this argument requires some refinement of our assumptions of criminal justice processes. Thus, referring to the nexus of criminalization, ethnicity and age he says that his research suggests that youthfulness is a better predictor of criminal justice involvement than ethnicity. He goes on to make similar points in relation to sex and class.

One of the terms in this field that is perhaps better known (though not necessarily better understood) than many is that of 'institutional racism'. As a result, in particular of the Stephen Lawrence case, the term has come to be attached to the practices of the police. Stuart Hall **(Reading 31.2)** argues that whilst police/black relations are an insufficient basis for assessing race relations in general in Britain they nonetheless provide a very important insight. Police racism or discriminatory activity has been a source of controversy for decades. Hall's account of developments takes in the Brixton riot in 1981 and Lord Scarman's subsequent inquiry and report, further riots later in the decade, including Broadwater Farm in 1985, and the murder of Stephen Lawrence and the Inquiry chaired by Sir William Macpherson.

One of the areas of police activity considered in some detail by both the Scarman and Stephen Lawrence Inquiries was that of stop-and-search. Police stop powers have long been a source of controversy and are generally understood to be used in a manner which disproportionately targets young black males. P.A.J. Waddington and colleagues **(Reading 31.3)** report the findings of a research study which sought to question existing assumptions about the disproportionate use of stop and search. The thesis they explore is one which considers the possibility that 'racial or ethnic groups place themselves at greater or lesser risk of being stopped by the police through their differential use of public space'. That is to say, they may be more or less 'available' to be stopped and searched depending on their visibility on the streets. Their conclusion is that Sir William Macpherson and his team were in error when they concluded that disproportionality in stop-and-search figures was evidence of racial stereotyping.

Nowhere perhaps is the disproportionate impact of criminalization of ethnic minorities more visible than in the United States (see Reading 21.4). Loïc Wacquant **(Reading 31.4)** argues that the prison is the latest in a long line of 'peculiar institutions' which have operated to restrict and confine African Americans. From slavery, through the Jim Crow laws and the emergence of the modern ghetto, the United States has had varied ways of managing its black population. The prison, and the emergent system of mass incarceration, continues this sequence.

Questions for discussion

1. What does Jefferson mean when he says that police racism is not about discriminating against young black males but rather about the production of a criminal 'Other' in which young black males figure prominently?

2. What is meant by the term 'institutional racism'? What difficulties, if any, do you see with this term?

3. What are the main differences between the treatment of institutional racism by Lord Scarman and Lord Justice Macpherson?

4. Why, according to Hall, had 'those expecting Macpherson to usher in a new epoch in black/police relations ... better think again'?

5. What are the main research methods used by Waddington *et al.* to assess the 'available population' on the streets? How satisfactory do you think those methods were?

6. On what basis do Waddington *et al.* conclude that Sir William Macpherson and his team were in error when they concluded that disproportionality in stop-and-search figures was evidence of racial stereotyping?

7. What are the main 'peculiar institutions' identified by Wacquant and what are their main features?

8. According to Wacquant, how did the ghetto become more like a prison and the prison more like a ghetto?

31.1 The racism of criminalization: police and the reproduction of the criminal other Tony Jefferson

In the original, longer version of this reading Tony Jefferson begins by defining key terms (race/racism & crime/criminalization) before then offering a brief overview of the changing ways in which the problem of delinquency has been framed at different points of history. In what follows – in the excerpt below – he examines the nature of the relationship between processes of criminalization and the structural issues of ethnicity, age, sex and social class. In the original version, which you should consult if you can, Jefferson then considers the Asian experience – one of under-policing, under-protection and less criminalization – before concluding that it is important that we shift our view from narrow arguments about ethnicity and crime to the broader territory of structural disadvantage, policing and criminalization – the context within which racial discrimination is located and criminal 'Others' are defined and reproduced.

The 'race/crime' debate: a brief overview of the empirical evidence

Various summaries of the relevant literature exist (cf. Reiner, 1985a and 1989; Benyon, 1986; Jefferson, 1988 and 1991; Walker, 1987; Fitzgerald, 1991). These are attempts to sift and sort the available evidence in some detail and come to considered, and considerably qualified, judgements of the state of the art. My present purpose is different. In the first place, my present argument is operating at a more general level than these summaries aspire to. Rather than confine myself to the narrow 'either/or' contours of the existing debate – do blacks commit more 'crime' or are the police racist (or both) – I wish to address a superordinate issue, namely, the contiguity between structural disadvantage, policing the powerless, and the notion of 'the criminal'. At this level, the issue of ethnicity is only a part of the picture, a point which has, I think, important political ramifications. Secondly, I am less interested in the detailed qualifications and points of dissension, more in making sense of the (by now considerable) broad areas of agreement. Thirdly, and again in line with the breadth of my argument, I shall draw freely from across the range of empirical evidence, research-based and otherwise. This predilection for the broad picture over its constituent parts stems from a strong feeling that the narrow scope and methodological punctiliousness evident in some research studies have had (paradoxically in the

light of their 'scientific' aspirations) a somewhat blinkering effect. So, a secondary thread in what follows is a critique of perhaps the dominant methodological approach in this area.

Let me start by listing the general points which can, I think, be safely drawn from the evidence:

(i) black (i.e. Afro-Caribbean) people are more likely, generally, to be criminalized (stopped and/or arrested) than Whites or Asians;

(ii) young people are more likely to be criminalized than older people;

(iii) females – white, black or Asian – are relatively absent from the criminalizing process;

(iv) black/white differences in rates of criminalization appear to be subject to an area effect;

(v) Asian males appear less likely to be criminalized than either their white or their black counterparts, irrespective of area (but see below);

(vi) broadly-speaking, differences in attitudes towards the police of these three groups follow the same trend as their collectively differential experiences of criminalization.

This parsimonious (but reasonably comprehensive) gutting of the literature is the empirical backcloth of my claim that police racism is *not* primarily about discriminating against young black males but rather about the production of a criminal Other in which, currently, young black males figure prominently. Taking each of the above points in turn, I hope first to demonstrate this, and then to show what hangs on it.

Criminalization and ethnicity

Over at least the last twenty years or so, relations between police and black people in many urban centres in Britain have been in a more-or-less continuous state of crisis. For some, the (black) robber, rioter and rastaman have come to form an unholy trinity symbolising the contemporary problems of crime, disorder and culture in modern Britain; for others, the swamping, stopping, surveillance tactics of metropolitan policing, especially the unacceptable (visored) faces of the

Special Patrol Groups, have become the aggressive cutting edge of state racism. But whether seen as a problem of 'crime and disorder' or racial harassment (or both) few would deny that regular, hostile interactions are depressingly characteristic of contemporary, urban police/black relations. Statistically this has manifested itself in the consistent over-representation of black people in studies of stops and of arrests (in so far as these have been done) (cf. Smith, 1983). Whilst the early to mid-seventies figures related purely to London – these being the only statistics then available – our more recent work in Leeds confirms this general finding (see Walker *et al.*, 1990; Jefferson and Walker, 1992; Jefferson *et al.*, 1992; though, as I argue below, this point is subject to numerous qualifications). Now for some this black over-representation constitutes a *prima facie* case of police racism: black people are stopped or arrested *because they are black*. But to stop there is to ignore other very relevant factors.

Criminalization and age

Take age. The above picture of the police and inner-city black communities locked in a cycle of near-permanent conflict is, in fact, quite generationally-specific. The older, first generation of black immigrants has a very different image: one of struggling to make ends meet, create a decent life, against the impossible odds of economic insecurity, political impotence, social ostracism and a relentless racism. Yet, in spite of everything they remain, in popular stereotype, hard-working, God-fearing and law-abiding. It is their offspring, often British born, which have become criminalized. This has produced an altogether different image – of a younger, second generation seen to be 'rising up angry', refusing 'shitwork' (where there is any to refuse) and generally struggling or 'hustling' to survive in a variety of ways – legal, semi-legal and illegal. The statistical evidence can be used to make a similar point, namely, that black over-representation, though it does not disappear entirely with the older age group, is significantly lower. The result generally is that youthfulness is regarded as a more reliable predictor of criminal justice involvement than ethnicity. Once again, our Leeds research endorsed this: though the arrest rate for older black males (in our study 'older' meant 22–35 and 'younger' 11–21, a fairly arbitrary division admittedly) like that for their younger counter-

parts, showed they were over-represented, it was lower than that for younger white males. So, without wishing to deny or belittle the horrendous experiences that some older black males and females have suffered in the arms of the law, it seems to me that, generally speaking, 'because they are black' should read 'because they are young and black'. But there is more to it than that of course, for there is also the question of sex.

Criminalization and sex

There are some things that are so taken-for-granted, so blindingly obvious, we become blinded by them. Failing to see the need to articulate them because 'everybody knows', we lose sight of the implications of not noticing. The relationship between sex and crime is a case in point. Whether we are talking of common or garden thieving, political terrorism, state violence, sexual abuse, or big city frauds, crime connotes the male sex. Of course women do these things too, but in the popular imagination crime is male – as it is, by a factor of about 6 to 1 in the official crime statistics (Riley, 1986).[2]

Yet this fact is so routinely ignored in the research in this area that you have to look closely to see whether women are included or not. Of course, in one sense it makes precious little difference: precisely because so few women, black or white, are stopped or arrested, their presence or absence in any study concerned to examine the ethnic dimension usually has no noticeable effect. Thus, though we chose to exclude women because we were interested specifically in questions around males, 'crime' and policing, it would have made virtually no difference to our Leeds arrest findings had we chosen otherwise; during the 6 month period when there were 318 stop searches and 5,488 arrests of males, for example, only 2 stop searches and 1,127 arrests of females (of whom 84 were black and 10 Asian) were recorded, insufficient to cause much of a blip in our statistical trends. But the effect of taking women for granted, whether formally included or excluded, is to give ethnicity a higher salience than it warrants; for if age moderates the impact of ethnicity, sex all but obliterates it. Nothing, neither age, nor ethnicity, nor class, compares with sex when it comes to predicting involvement in the criminal justice system. So, we ought to make a further amendment to the notion 'because they are black'; this should now read *'because they are young and male and black'*.

In some ways, I have simply been stating the obvious, namely, that the criminal justice system spends most of its time processing young men. But, my point here has been to tease out the implications of this for the ethnicity/'crime' debate. In so far as the debate has largely overlooked them, it has ended up, effectively, focusing on the salience (or otherwise) of ethnicity. However, when we keep age, sex and ethnicity equally in view, the order of salience becomes, very definitely, sex, age and then ethnicity. Given that, the relationship between racism and criminalization – my object in all this – has at least to be recast somewhat. The case for doing so becomes even more compelling when we include the question of class. Once again, everybody knows about the link between class and criminalization and how the depredations of the poor are more criminalized than those of the rich (cf. Cook, 1989). Yet the research that has focused on ethnicity has tended to obscure this – and, in consequence, its implications. The next section attempts to rectify this omission.

Criminalization and class

Perhaps the primary starting point for our Leeds research was the feeling that the existing research had been too cavalier on the question of ethnicity and class. Specifically, we felt that the use of the London statistics without controlling for the area of residence of Blacks and Whites was not really comparing like with like. In other words, the significantly higher arrest rates found for black people might, we thought, have a lot to do with where they lived, i.e. predominantly in the poorer, deprived and heavily policed parts of London. The white rate by contrast, being based on Whites living in the whole of London including its salubrious suburbs, might, we reasoned, be expected to be lower. Thus, we decided that until 'within area' comparisons were made the significance of the higher black rate must remain unclear. This then became the linchpin of our research design.

Our research findings, based on within area comparisons, bore out our reasoning with a vengeance. Though our comparative stop/search and arrest rates, when uncontrolled for area, echoed the P.S.I.'s London findings (Smith, 1983), namely, Blacks having the highest arrest rates (as we saw earlier) the picture changed dramatically once area controls were introduced. Then we found – somewhat to our surprise, the black rate was highest *only* in the areas with *low concentra-*

tions of Blacks and Asians; in the poorer areas where the majority of Blacks and Asians lived, it was younger *Whites* who had the highest arrest rate, one much higher than young Blacks. It is worth adding that arrest rates generally, in line with expectations, were higher in the younger age group and in the poorer areas.

When we examined the White rate in more detail, we found it increased along with increases in the numbers of Blacks and Asians living in an area, the numbers in privately rented accommodation, the unemployment rate, and the percentage of residents in social class 4 and 5. It thus appeared to confirm the long established correspondence between structural (i.e. class, roughly speaking) disadvantages and the processes of criminalization. The black rate puzzlingly, did not show the same neat correlations, being highest in the area with the least black and Asian residents, the smallest proportion in privately rented accommodation[3] and the lowest unemployment rate. The reasons for the surprising black arrest rate pattern invite interesting speculations – that Blacks are less willing to report and/or police to record black offenders in black neighbourhoods, which might explain the lower black rate in the areas where they tended to live; that such neighbourhood 'protections' do not apply in the white suburbs and/or black offenders in such areas will be concentrated in isolated pockets of poorer housing (this latter point we were able to confirm by personal observation) which might explain their higher rate in the 'whiter' areas.[4] But whatever the reasons, they should not obscure the importance of our finding about the white arrest rates. Clearly these confirm, for those in doubt, the continuing importance of socio-economic factors in criminalization, even as they also show that this 'fact' is complicated in ways that purely statistically-based analyses *have great difficulty in unravelling*.

This brings me to my methodological concerns. I write, I hasten to add, not as an outsider, berating statistics for not being ethnography, but as someone recently involved in a research study incorporating a statistically-based methodology as its analytical heart. Ruminating on that experience, not sniping from outside the statistical battlements, forces me to the following observations. Take the notion, so central to our critique and subsequent analysis, 'controlling for area'. Our contention was that the London statistics, which showed a higher black arrest rate across all offence categories, might be explained by reference to area, by the fact that black people live in the poorer, deprived parts of the city where involvement in processes of criminalization is more common generally. So our research design was deliberately constructed to ensure, as far as possible, that 'like' was being compared with 'like': that Black, White and Asian arrestees were similar in that they lived in the same small areas (enumeration districts). Thus, we made sure we were comparing males with males, the young with the young, those living in poorer areas with those living in poorer areas, on the grounds that sex, age and (to some extent) class were the key 'relevant characteristics' for the question of criminalization. The methodological logic – as beguiling as it is difficult to render operationally feasible – was that once these characteristics known to be implicated in the criminalization process were controlled for, any residual difference in rates could only be explained by reference to the one remaining characteristic, not controlled for but presumptively relevant, namely, ethnicity.[5]

The problem amounts to this: the more extensive and sophisticated the controls, the more the 'uncontrolled' difference (given the wide range of factors known to be implicated in the criminalization process) will be 'controlled' out: the less extensive and sophisticated the controls, i.e. the less the 'controlled' and 'uncontrolled' factors are disentangled, the less reliance can be placed on resulting differences. In other words, big differences are the result of poor controls and hence less meaningful; only as differences become smaller can more faith be placed in their meaning. Thus, the approach can only ever aspire to explain adequately *residual* differences. Given this, one could be forgiven for saying, 'why bother?'.

But this does not mean that the observational studies, British or North American, have escaped the methodological dilemma. In so far as they have also been committed to the identification of differences – in the police treatment of suspects, for example – that can be unreservedly attributed to ethnicity, the methodological problem is identical. Perhaps not surprisingly then, these studies have not confirmed 'the clear discriminatory pattern suggested by the quantitative evidence' (Reiner, 1985: 171); rather, once situational or interactional features known to be relevant to being arrested (such as demeanour, showing disrespect, co-operativeness, etc.) are controlled for, it becomes virtually impossible, as Reiner's comprehensive overview concludes, to detect a level of 'pure' racially-based discrimination:

Both the statistical and the observational evidence concur in suggesting that in so far as there is apparent discrimination in the statistical pattern of use of police powers, this is not the outcome for the most part of a separate element of 'pure' police discrimination. The basic source is the character of the situations in which police–black encounters often occur, and the way the mutual backcloth of suspicion and hostility leads to a spiral of conflicting interaction. (Reiner, 1985: 172–3)[6]

But let's use the observationally-based evidence also to get back to the question of class. What exactly does it mean to conclude, that 'the basic source' of the 'apparent discrimination' is 'the character of the situation' and 'the mutual backcloth of suspicion and hostility'? Think of the inner-city disturbances, now an intermittent feature of contemporary, urban police–community relations. Here the character of the situation and the mutual backcloth of suspicion and hostility produced, and continue to produce, bloody and sustained police–community conflicts; that was, and is, their principal meaning. But these confrontations were, and are, merely more focused outbursts in a situation characterised by hostility, regular skirmishes and generally a low-level guerilla war in which questions of legality, justice and accountability have long since lost what little concrete relevance they might once have had. But this contemporary, inner-city guerilla war is not confined to police and black youths, highly visible and politically important though this aspect has been. Rather, as everyone who wasn't fortunate enough to sleep through the 1980s knows, it is an exercise in containing the new lumpen or 'underclass' – those left behind or no longer needed in the new high-tech, post-industrial, 'sunshine valley' Britain – especially the 'social dynamite' constituted by its unwanted young, a growing army of the unemployed, the homeless and the disaffected. Black youth, the offspring of an immigrant labour force which appears now to be permanently 'on reserve' and, additionally, is discriminated against in housing and other markets, are (unsurprisingly) disproportionately represented within this raggle taggle army of the dispossessed.

In other words, the situational and interactional factors that account for conflictual police–public interactions now are much as they have always been, though perhaps Cohen's seminal account, 'Policing the Working Class City'

(1979) might now be better entitled, 'Policing the *Rough* Working Class City'. For those not yet convinced, perhaps the words of Sir Alfred Sherman, ex-head of the Thatcherite think tank, the Centre for Policy Studies, might carry more weight. Speaking to the Russians in 1983, he is alleged to have said, in reply to a question about whether cuts in pensions and unemployment benefits would provoke a social explosion:

> The unemployed and the lumpen never have been a revolutionary force. If the unemployed get lower benefits, they will be quicker to start looking for work, and they won't turn to political trouble-making. As for the lumpen, coloured people and Irish... the only way to hold them in check is to have enough well-armed police.
> (Quoted in *The Guardian*, 6 February, 1992: 9)

Following Sherman's blunt lead, and connecting this section with the previous ones, what all this amounts to is that being the wrong age, sex and class, in the wrong place at the wrong time, displaying the wrong demeanour and attitude, spells 'trouble' to police, whatever the colour of your skin: being black may add a further dimension, but it's being a toe-rag[7] that constitutes the crucial generic category; which brings us back to the quintessential modern delinquent, the rough working class adolescent male with whom we also ended the historical section. 'Because they are black' ought now to read, *'because they are young and male and "rough" working class and black'*. The problem black youths have is that their whole way of life, itself a complex outcome of a host of structural and cultural discriminations, renders escape from the toe-rag categorisation virtually impossible. Put another way, all black youths are 'always already' toe-rags in the suspicious eyes of the social guardians of law and order.

From T. Jefferson, 'The racism of criminalization: policing and the reproduction of the criminal other', in L. Gelsthorpe (ed.) Minority Ethnic Groups in the Criminal Justice System. *Papers presented to the 21st Cropwood Conference, 1992 (Cambridge: Institute of Criminology), 1993, pp. 26–46.*

Notes

1 Though, when considering women only, black women, like their male counterparts, appear to be over-represented in the processes of criminalization.

For example, nearly a quarter of all sentenced female prisoners are now black (Home Office Prison Statistics).

2 The fact that self-report studies reveal that girls and young women are more involved in offending than these figures suggest does not invalidate the point. On the contrary, because the finding demonstrates the difficulty of placing the female sex and crime in the same conceptual framework, it strengthens my point. On the question of sex and gender, when I say 'sex' I intend just that, not gender. To imagine 'the criminal' is to imagine a man, a member of the male sex, even though the behaviour in question also connotes masculinity, which is, of course, a function of gender. By the same token, official criminal statistics are kept by sex not gender, even though offending behaviour clearly has gendered characteristics. Unfortunately, many writers erroneously confuse these two terms, most ludicrously in quoting statistics broken down by gender. This particular piece of nonsense – a good example incidentally of how the anxiety to be politically correct can produce a patent absurdity – exhibits a delightful irony; in striving to show awareness of the sex/gender distinction it effectively collapses it.

3 Living in privately rented accommodation was a characteristic of white families, rather than black or Asian. It tends to correlate positively with low social class and relatively high offender rates (cf. Baldwin and Bottoms, 1976).

4 Since it appears that white victims are more likely to report the incident when their attacker is black (Stevens and Willis, 1979) this might, also, partly explain the higher black rate in these 'whiter' areas.

5 The more one thinks about it, the more potentially relevant 'factors-to-be-controlled' emerge. For example, if 'presence on the streets' is a factor in vulnerability to criminalization, this would need to be controlled for in pursuit of the ever-receding dimension of 'pure' racial discrimination. We did attempt in our Leeds study to look at the effect of 'way of life', measured by asking about evenings spent out, mode of travel, time of return, etc.

6 This means, of course, that once all other factors were controlled for there was some residual 'race' effect (the meaning of 'for the most part'). It may also suggest a need to recast our notion of discrimination so that it includes these indirect forms of discrimination.

7 The term was widely used by police officers in the force Grimshaw and I studied (Grimshaw and Jefferson, 1987) to refer, broadly, to members of low-status, powerless groups whom they regarded with distaste or as potentially troublesome e.g. drunks, punks, the homeless, etc. Lee's definition of who becomes 'police property' – 'a category becomes police property when the dominant powers of society (i.e. the economy, polity, etc.) leave the problems of social control to the police' (Lee, 1981; 53-4) – encompasses a similar notion and neatly summarises the generic category I have in mind.

References

Baldwin, J. and Bottoms, A.E. (1976) *The Urban Criminal*. London: Tavistock.

Benyon, J. (1986) A tale of failure: Race and policing. Policy papers in ethnic relations, no. 3. University of Warwick: Warwick.

Cohen, P. (1979) Policing the working-class city. In Fine, B. *et al.*, (Eds) *Capitalism and the Rule of Law*. London: Hutchinson, 118–36.

Cook, D. (1989) *Rich Law, Poor Law*. Milton Keynes: Open University Press,

Fitzgerald, M. (1991) Ethnic minorities and the criminal justice system in the UK: research issues. Paper presented to British Criminology Conference, York University, July.

Grimshaw, R. and Jefferson, T. (1987) *Interpreting Policework*. London: Unwin Hyman.

Home Office (1981) *Racial Attacks*. London: Home Office.

Jefferson, T. (1988) Race, crime and policing: empirical, theoretical and methodological issues. *International Journal of the Sociology of Law*, 16, 521–39.

Jefferson, T. (1991) Discrimination, disadvantage and police-work. In Cashmore, E. and McLaughlin, E. (Eds) *Out of Order? Policing Black People*. London: Routledge, 166–88.

Jefferson, T. and Walker, M.A. (1992) Ethnic minorities in the criminal justice system. *Criminal Law Review*. February, 83–95.

Jefferson, T., Walker, M.A. and Seneviratne, M. (1992) Ethnic minorities, crime and criminal justice: A study in a provincial city. In Downes, D. (Ed.) *Unravelling Criminal Justice*. London: Macmillan.

Lee, J.A. (1981) Some structural aspects of police deviance in relations with minority groups. In Shearing, L. (Ed.) *Organizational Police Deviance*. Toronto: Butterworth, 49–82.

Reiner, R. (1985a) Police and race relations. In Baxter, J. and Koffman, L. (Eds) *Police: The Constitution and the Community*. Abingdon: Professional Books, 149–87.

Reiner. R. (1989) Race and criminal justice. *New Community*, 16, 1, 5–21.

Riley, D. (1986) Sex differences in teenage crime: The role of lifestyle. *Research Bulletin*, no. 20. London: Home Office Research and Planning Unit, 34-8.

Smith, D.J. (1983) *Police and People in London. 1: A Survey of Londoners*. London: Policy Studies Institute.

Stevens, P. and Willis, C. (1979) *Race, Crime and Arrests*. Home Office Research Study, no. 58. London: HMSO.

Walker. M.A. (1987) Interpreting race and crime statistics. *Journal of Royal Statistical Society* A, 150, 39–56.

Walker, M.A., Jefferson, T., and Seneviratne, M. (1990) *Ethnic Minorities, Young People and the Criminal Justice System*. Main Report to ESRC., Ref. E06250023.

31.2 From Scarman to Stephen Lawrence
Stuart Hall

Nearly two decades separate the Report by Lord Scarman which brought the race riots of 1981 to some sort of official conclusion,[1] from the Report by Sir William Macpherson which in 1999 concluded the Official Inquiry into the death of the black teenager, Stephen Lawrence.[2] These have been momentous decades in the history of race and the future of Britain as a multicultural society. The routine way to assess this period is to ask whether, taking one thing with another, things haven't gotten better on the race-relations front? This way of framing the question assumes not only that some simple answer can be given, but that the verdict will be positive. The question, however, is not amenable to such simplistic optimisms.

It is better to see this period as defined by two more recent events, which stubbornly refuse to be conjugated one with the other. The first was the 1998 'Windrush' celebrations which marked the fiftieth anniversary of the arrival at Tilbury Docks of the *S.S. Empire Windrush* – the troopship which brought West-Indian service volunteers, on home leave in the Caribbean, back to Britain to be demobbed, and which also carried the first post World-War-Two West-Indian civilian migrants. The anniversary was widely construed as marking 'the irresistible rise of multi-ethnic Britain' and became the source of much self-congratulation.[3] The second was the Macpherson Inquiry into the attack, at 10.30 in the evening of 22 April 1993, on

Stephen Lawrence and Duwayne Brooks, as they waited at a bus-stop in Well Hall Road, Eltham, South London, by five white youths chanting: 'What, what, nigger?' Within sight of several witnesses, Stephen Lawrence was stabbed twice in the chest and died shortly after. The police refused to view the incident as a racial attack, treating Duwayne Brooks, who narrowly escaped with his life, as a suspect; and they failed to arrest anyone for weeks, despite considerable hearsay evidence. Instead, they pursued for several days the wholly unsubstantiated belief that there must have been a fight, somehow involving the two black boys. When five white youths were finally arrested, the identification collapsed and charges were abandoned. Following two internal reviews (the first, which exonerated the Metropolitan Police's handling of the original affair, later described by Macpherson as 'effectively indefensible'),[4] the Inquiry found that the Met's handling of the affair 'was marred by a combination of professional incompetence, institutional racism and a failure of leadership by senior officers'.[5] The incompetence – exposed day after day, as the whole police construction of the events collapsed before the eyes of press and public – was indeed staggering. But, Macpherson insisted in 1999, the incompetence could only be explained by 'pernicious and persistent institutional racism'.

These two events are paradigmatic of the state of play as to race in Britain today, and signify its unresolved contradictoriness. The first speaks to multicultural 'drift' – the increasing visible presence of black and Asian people in all aspects of British social life as a natural and inevitable part of the 'scene' – rather than an 'alien wedge', to borrow Mrs Thatcher's felicitous phrase – especially in the cities and urban areas. This is not the result of deliberate and planned policy but the unintended outcome of undirected sociological processes. Though visibly registering the new play of difference across British society, this creeping multiculturalism is, of course, highly uneven. Large tracts of the country, most significant centres of power and many so-called 'ethnic minority' people are largely untouched by it. Many white British people may accept it as a fact of life, but do not necessarily welcome it. Outside of its radius, the practices of racialized exclusion, racially-compounded disadvantage, household poverty, unemployment and educational under-achievement persist – indeed, multiply.

The second, however, is an ancient story, banal in its repetitive persistence. From the early race riots of Nottingham and Notting Hill in 1958, through the 1970s campaigns against 'sus' laws (permitting arbitrary stop-and-search), the death of Blair Peach from a police baton at a 1979 demonstration in Southall, the uproar following the death of Colin Roach in Stoke Newington police station in 1983 and the lack of explanation for many other black deaths in police custody, the Deptford Fire and the arson of Asian shops and homes, the 1980s 'disorders' in Brixton and at Broadwater Farm, Tottenham, to Stephen Lawrence's murder in 1993 or the flaming body of Michael Menson falling unheeded into the Thames in 1997, black people have been the subject of racialized attack, had their grievances largely ignored by the police, and been subjected to racially-inflected practices of policing. Each of those events was followed by a campaign, unofficial inquiries (I sat on two), recriminations from the authorities, promises of reform. Very little seems to have changed. Relations between black communities and police have continued to be a catalogue of disasters, marked by mistrust, prejudice and disrespect, often leading to tragedy.

Of course, the whole 'race-relations' situation in Britain cannot be accurately assessed from the perspective of black/police relations alone. But these do have a symptomatic value. [...] The excuse, which successive Chief Police Officers have peddled for twenty years, that since British society is 'racist' we must expect a proportionate number of police officers to be racists too, is not only cynical but constitutionally unacceptable. As Scarman himself observed, 'the standards we apply to the police must be higher than the norms of behaviour prevalent in society as a whole'.[6] A similar argument (popularly known as the 'rotten apples' theory) – that, since society contains a lot of villains, the police too will necessarily have its 'normal ration' of corrupt officers – could not be legitimately advanced; and when some such charge has been laid in the past, senior police have mobilized extraordinary manpower and resources to stamp it out. Racism, however, continues to be subject to a different logic.

This double standard is a testimony to the stubborn persistence of racial thinking as part of the deep, unconscious structure of British common sense, often crystallized in institutional cultures. It testifies to the pervasive disavowal and double-talk which across the years has covered over the yawning gaps between policy and practice in these institutions. The state of black/police relations thus gives us an unwelcome glimpse into how racialized difference is actually being negotiated at a deeper level, where unreconstructed attitudes find a sort of displaced but systematic expression in places which the utopian language of 'multicultural Britain' cannot reach.

The Scarman Report was the official response to an unprecedented level of racialized violence, rioting and public disorder in the streets, which erupted first in April 1980 in the St Paul's district of Bristol and spread, during 1981, to Brixton and Southall, Toxteth in Liverpool, Manchester Moss Side, Handsworth in Birmingham, Sheffield, Nottingham and other cities. It culminated with further rioting on 15 July 1981, following an aggressive police swoop on houses around the Railton Road area of Brixton, which the Police Complaints Board subsequently said showed 'an institutional disregard for the niceties of the law', and which resulted in extensive damage to property for which the Met paid compensation.[7] As is customary in such circumstances, contingent events sparked off the rioting, against the background of racial disadvantage, fears about rising crime and drug use, growing black youth unemployment and deepening despair amongst the black communities, compounded by the looming spectre of the Thatcherite assault on the structures of welfare support.

Lord Scarman's Report was no panacea, but it was distinctive for at least three reasons. First, it broke the prevailing law-and-order consensus by firmly locating the sources of unrest in 'insecure social and economic conditions and in an impoverished physical environment' – a 'set of social conditions which create a disposition towards violent protest'.[8] [...]

Secondly, Scarman put his trust in a much-expanded programme of police training on community and race issues as a way of trying to get to grips with the racialization of routine police work. [...]

His third strand was the statutory establishment of community consultative committees, designed to give the community an augmented voice and 'help to provide an agenda for a continuing dialogue between the police and the public about the nature of policing in today's society'.[9] These committees had some educational value, but they had no way of resolving the deep conflicts and intense hostilities which frequently surfaced, could not represent the diversity of community opinion with one voice and had no power to influence policing policy when it really mattered.[10]

Some parts of Scarman's reforms of policing were implemented, though inadequately. The wider social and economic reforms, however, were seriously out of key with the political temper of the times and triggered no significant political or policy response. In retrospect, Scarman was to bewail the 'lack of implementation of the social and economic recommendations' and to acknowledge that he should have been 'more outspoken about the necessity of affirmative action to overcome racial disadvantage'. [11]

Racial disorder flared again in 1985, first in Handsworth, where two Asian men died; it spread to Brixton, where a police officer's shot paralysed Mrs Cherry Groce during a house search for her son; thence to Toxteth, Peckham and Tottenham, where Mrs Cynthia Jarrett collapsed and died during a house search for evidence against her son (subsequently acquitted). In the rioting around the Broadwater Farm Estate, in Tottenham, PC Keith Blakelock was stabbed to death. Two features distinguished this period of unrest (in which incidentally both white and black youth were heavily involved). First, the violence was preceded by a much-increased, pro-active programme of police raids, aimed at drugs, drug pushers and concealed weapons. No effort was made to forewarn the very active Broadwater Farm community group until too late.[12] Secondly, the police response to urban unrest was notably vigorous. For the first time para-military policing tactics (including full riot-gear, plastic bullets and CS gas) were deployed on British streets in the effort, apparently, not to contain the violence but to 'win' the public-order 'war'.

This appeared to signal some sort of climacteric – or nadir – in black/police relations, which, as we've said, always have wider significance; and was followed by dire warnings of further unrest and violence. Yet, in fact, there were no parallel explosions in the subsequent decade. What, then, has been happening in the interim? Have black/police relations substantially improved? Have the policing reforms finally begun to bite? Have the precipitating socio-economic conditions improved so rapidly in the declining years of Tory rule and New Labour's New Dawn as to totally transform the situation?

Many complex factors have been at work here, only some of which can be briefly identified. The first is the rapid differentiation which has been taking place amongst the so-called ethnic minorities, undermining the tired notion of an undifferentiated block of 'ethnic minority' people, homogenously characterized by their 'otherness' (Them), versus an equally homogeneous white 'majority' (Us) to whose unified culture and 'way of life' the former must assimilate or perish. These fundamentally binary terms in which British race relations have been mapped have essentially collapsed. [...]

This greater social diversity includes the class trajectories of different groups. [...] The internal class gaps, between a minority rising middle class and the majority poor, already familiar from the post civil-rights African-American experience, are now beginning to show up here. [...]

Racial attacks on the homes and shops of Asian families have continued unabated. The stop-and-search and school-exclusion figures for blacks have been soaring again. The criminalization of areas of high immigrant settlement coupled with pervasive involvement in drugs have sharpened confrontations between a so-called 'villainous' minority and the police, which spill over into and infect general police/community relations.

Seen in this context, the Stephen Lawrence affair does not appear so aberrant as it did at first glance. There has been no slow, steady, evolutionary 'rise and rise' of a new multicultural spirit in Britain. There has been change – but racism just as deeply persists. Indeed, there is some evidence to suggest that, as multicultural drift has become increasingly a sort of tolerated norm, those opposed to it feel more, not less, threatened, as the tide imperceptibly shifts against them. This is compounded by the astonishing social diversity which has overtaken the so-called 'majority' population. We know that what is called 'the British way of life' is really a euphemism for the stabilized pattern of differences and inequalities which has come to be accepted as the natural order of things in Britain. But in almost every feature of that settled pattern, over the past two decades, change and diversity have intervened. Social, economic, cultural, technological and moral shifts, unsettling established patterns and norms, have combined with Britain's relative economic decline, the unrequited loss of imperial destiny and the onset of globalization, which relativizes the power of the nation-state and national culture, to produce nothing short of a crisis of British, and especially English, identity. What does it mean to be 'British' in a world in which Britain no longer rules the waves?

There is thus a growing sense of defensive embattlement, particularly amongst some of the English, in response to what that minority sees as the erosion of a distinctive and 'historic' (that is, a traditional) British way of life. [...]

On all three fronts, then – the multicultural, the European and the devolved kingdom – what passes for an 'English' nationalism feels deeply threatened and beleaguered. A spirit of what has properly, in the post-globalization sense, to be called an English cultural nationalism – an English 'fundamentalism' – has been slowly emerging into the light of day. This is the precondition for a revived – and transformed – type of 'cultural racism', to add to and to compound the other garden varieties. The small overtly-fascist political groupings have so far been able to politicize only a very small proportion of this subterranean sentiment (they have been much less successful at invading the political mainstream than Le Pen's blue-suited shock troops in France). However, they have touched the hearts of a small, dedicated band of converts amongst a section of white working-class young men, living in some of Britain's most depressed and forgotten corners. They have few employment or educational prospects, feel a deep sense of national shame and dispossession, practise their manoeuvres in the context of international sport (last bastion of territoriality in an increasingly de-territorialized world). They are the small seedbed of that form of violent collective projection which follows the classic logic – 'We are poor because the blacks are here'.

Against that background, the Inquiry into Stephen Lawrence's death was a remarkable affair. The murder occurred in precisely such an area as described above: one with a long history of racialized violence around schools, playgrounds and sports-fields (including incidents involving the five white suspects)[13] – and near Plumstead, where a police Racial Incident Unit had been established as early as December 1990, because of the high level of racial incidents. The Inquiry referred to several cases of black boys beaten up by white gangs between 1991 and 1993 'to highlight both the regularity of such offences and the lack ... of coordinated information about them'.[14] The area is also a well-known stamping-ground of the British National Party and of Combat 18.

The Inquiry would not have happened without the stubborn persistence of Stephen's parents, Neville and Doreen Lawrence, and the small campaign group which supported them. Liaison with the parents throughout the five-year investigation was, however, pathetic. They were sidelined, rarely informed about or kept in touch with developments, the construction being put about by the police that they had been 'nobbled' by anti-police political agitators. Duwayne Brooks, who had to run for his life from the attackers, and was wandering around at the scene of the crime distraught and agitated because of the lack of police follow-up to his leads and the ambulance delay, was treated by them as a hysterical and unreliable witness, rather than as a victim. Macpherson judged that he was 'stereotyped as a young black man' and that this played a part in 'the collective failure of those involved to treat him properly'.[15] The Metropolitan Police were obliged to apologize to all three unreservedly for their conduct. Whatever else happened when the police arrived on the scene – and the Report's view is that 'Anybody who listened to the evidence of the officers involved in the initial police action after the murder would...be astonished at the lack of command and lack of organization that took place'[16] – the suspects were not pursued; the search was fitful, disorganized, misdirected and fruitless. The police assumed – 'without any basis for such a conclusion',[17] and despite Brooks's testimony – that there had been a fight in which Lawrence and Brooks were somehow implicated. Despite the long history of racial incidents in the area, and the clear guidance from the Association of Chief Police Officers that the word of a participant involved in an incident who alleges that there was a racial motive must be believed until evidence to the contrary emerges,[18] no-one took Duwayne Brooks seriously; and experienced officers, up to and during the Inquiry, persisted in denying that racism had been involved.[19] There was an implicit, collective, 'institutional' refusal to define the incident as a racialized attack. This is the point at which gross and systematic professional incompetence by the police began to slide imperceptibly into the question of institutional racism. Thereafter, even when the five white suspects had been widely named and police attention was finally turned on them, both incompetence and racism remained in evidence. Two of the suspects, leaving home with something unusual in black binliners, were not followed nor the contents examined. Records of statements by local people naming the five suspects, including a lengthy and detailed account (Message 40) by a 'James Grant' (supposed to be a police informer), were not passed on. Some vital notes and notebooks, briefing documents, records of meetings, minutes of strategic decisions whether to arrest or not, have all gone missing – disappeared (despite almost continuous uproar about the case between 1993 and the Inquiry and two formal internal inquiries) down a very black hole.

The Report itself is a curious document. It fails altogether to place the event in the broader historical context of black/police relations and disconnects it from the local contexts of racial violence. On the other hand, its minute recording of evidence given at the Inquiry in painstaking sequence has its own impact, since the slow-motion unravelling in public of the justificatory narratives offered by the police constituted a drama of its own (the dramatized version which played to packed houses at the Tricycle Theatre needed only a carefully-edited transcript). The facet which has captured public attention is, of course, the issue of 'institutional racism', which thrust its way, 'unwittingly', into the centre of the Report. The issue remains controversial. Critics of the Report do not like it because, they say, its emphasis on 'unwitting' and 'unconscious' racism lets racists in general, and the police in particular, off the hook. They want a more moralized definition which forces racists to take responsibility for their actions. It is also said to be so general (applying equally to all institutions) that it leaves things where they are: if every institution is racist, then there is nothing to do but destroy them and start again – a recipe for inaction. Though these dangers do exist, I would argue that the official use of the term 'institutional racism' to characterize the conduct of the Metropolitan Police, from the lowest to the most senior ranks, is a real advance, in a long campaign which is unlikely to have many short-term or any total victories. Moreover, the idea of 'institutional racism' strikes at the heart of one very English kind of racism, which thrives, not against, but cosily inserted within, liberalism. Lord Scarman muddied the waters by suggesting the phrase could mean 'knowingly, as a matter of policy' – a wobble on which Sir Paul Condon, the Metropolitan Police Commissioner, then constructed a veritable mountain of prevaricating apologetics. Macpherson's definition accepts 'unwitting' and 'unconscious' and adds 'unintentional'.[20] Of course, there is a great deal of 'witting, conscious and intentional' racism about. But there is also a great deal which arises

> because of lack of understanding, ignorance or mistaken beliefs. . . from well-intentioned but patronising words or actions .... from unfamiliarity with the behaviour or cultural traditions of people ... from ethnic minorities .. . from racist stereotyping ... out of uncritical self-understanding born out of an inflexible police ethos of the 'traditional' way of doing things [which] thrive in a tightly knit community.[21]

The first part of that definition is weak – powerful racist stereotypes of 'the other' can hardly be effectively described as 'lack of understanding, ignorance or mistaken beliefs'. But it gets better as the sentence goes on. The idea could be much more sharply and succinctly expressed than it is in Macpherson, but the broader discussion in the Report does begin to capture its salient features[. . .]

The key points to bear in mind here are as follows. First, institutional racism does not require overtly racist individuals: it conceives racism as arising through social processes[. . .] Second, institutional racism has clearly taken the argument that *culture* regulates *conduct*. These behavioural norms are carried within the occupational culture of an organization, and transmitted by informal and implicit ways through its routine, everyday practices as an indestructible part of the institutional *habitus*. Racism of *this* kind becomes routine, habitual, taken for granted. It is far more effective in socializing the practice of officers than formal training or regulations. (The arduous reporting of racial incidents or domestic violence, by contrast, is defined, in the occupational culture, as 'rubbish' policing.) And it blocks a professional reflexivity from ever coming into operation. Far from being seen as exceptional, this 'unwitting' type of racism becomes part of the very working definition of 'normal police work'. It is perfectly possible for young officers whose promotion up the ranks and acceptance as 'regular cops' depends on imbibing as an unreflected practice this folk-wisdom of 'how to be a good copper' – to love reggae, eat Vindaloo curry every Saturday night, have a few black friends, and still think that 'good policing' requires them to act on the assumption that a young black man carrying a holdall at a bus-stop after dark almost certainly just committed a robbery and should be 'sussed' – stopped and searched. This is certainly not the *only* kind of racism which operates in our institutions, but it is one, distinct variety and, precisely because of its institutional embeddedness, one of the most difficult to identify and dismantle. It is not clear that the Macpherson recommendations can deal effectively with it. Sir William did try to put Sir Paul Condon on the spot by noting the latter's stubborn resistance, conducted as a war of attrition throughout the Inquiry ('I acknowledge the danger of the institutionalization of racism. However, labels can cause more problems than they solve').[22] Macpherson remarked that 'Any Chief Officer who feels unable so to respond [to the problem of institutional racism] will find it difficult to work in harmony and co-operation with the community in the way that policing by consent requires'.[23] What then are we to deduce from the fact that the Home Secretary chickened out and Sir Paul remained in office, successfully riding out the post Lawrence-Inquiry storm on the way to a happy retirement?

The police and press counter-campaign effectively diverted public attention to the two most questionable of Macpherson's seventy recommendations: number 38, proposing a review of the court's power to prosecute after acquittal if 'fresh and viable' evidence emerged, and number 39, constituting racist language or behaviour in private a prosecutable offence. This tactic, together with pervasive denials and disavowals, has served to obscure other more significant proposals, such as subjecting the police to extensive performance indicators on racial matters, bringing the Met under a proper police authority, opening the police to a Freedom of Information Act and to the Race Relations Act, from which they are currently exempt, granting disclosure of evidence by right to parties represented at an inquest, improving the monitoring and recording of racist incidents, underlining the witness's priority in defining a 'racist incident', and 'ensuring that serious complaints against officers are independently investigated'.[24] What has not been tackled is how to hold officers directly accountable in terms of preferment, and how to make the 'cost' of proven racist behaviour by police officers, witting or unwitting, directly impact on their careers, pay, promotion prospects and indeed job retention and retirement rewards. [...]

Those expecting Macpherson to usher in a new epoch in black/police relations had therefore better think again. The sound of police doors – and minds – slamming shut against the drubbing and exposure they have had to endure resounds across the land. This is not however to say that nothing has happened. By a strange quirk of fate, the Lawrences were so exceptional in their dignified forbearance throughout, so manifestly a serious, responsible and respectable couple, and Stephen Lawrence so manifestly a very bright student, good athlete, exemplarily behaved, with a promising career in architecture ahead of him, that they did obviously touch the hearts of some middle-class white folk who had hitherto reposed an unquestioning faith in the police and felt that all the talk about 'police racism' was really just 'a black thing'. There, but for the grace of God – they could see in the Lawrence family, people very much like themselves, with their own hopes and fears and aspirations, and many identified with their ordeal – as few would have done had Stephen been a ragamuffin with 'locks' or a rude-boy from Peckham. On such piquant, fragile and bizarre paradoxes does the universally acclaimed 'rise and rise' of multi-cultural Britain depend.

> *From S. Hall, 'From Scarman to Stephen Lawrence',* History Workshop Journal, *1999, 48, 187–197.*

Notes and references

1 Lord Scarman, *The Brixton Disorders 10–72 April 1981: Report of an inquiry by the Rt. Hon. The Lord Scarman, OBE*, Cmnd 8247, HMSO, London, 1982.
2 Sir William Macpherson of Cluny, *The Stephen Lawrence Inquiry Report*, Cm 4264–1, TSO, London, 1999.
3 Mike Phillips and Trevor Phillips, *Windrush: The Irresistible Rise of Multi-Racial Britain*, Harper Collins, London, 1998.
4 Macpherson, para 28.14, p. 197.
5 Macpherson, para 46.1, p. 317.
6 Scarman, 1981, para 4.64, p. 64, quoted in Macpherson 6.9 p. 21.
7 *Report of the Police Complaints Board 1982*, HC 278, HMSO, London, 12 April 1983, p. 1, quoted in John Benyon and John Solomos (eds), *The Roots Of Urban Unrest*, Pergamon Press, Oxford, 1987, p. 5.
8 Scarman, para 23.
9 Scarman, p. 99, quoted in Simon Holdaway, *The Racialization of British Policing*, Macmillan, Houndmills, 1996, p. 128. See the analysis of consultative committees in Michael Keith, 'Squaring circles', *New Community* 15: 1, pp. 63-77.
10 Lord Scarman, 'The Quest For Social Justice', in Benyon and Solomos (eds), *Roots of Urban Unrest*, p. 128.
11 See *The Broadwater Farm Inquiry: Report Of An independent inquiry Into Disturbances of October 1985 at the Broadwater Farm Estate, Tottenham*, chaired by Lord Gifford Q.C., Broadwater Farm Inquiry, 1986.
12 Macpherson, para 7.15, p.38.
13 Macpherson, para 7.23, p. 39.
14 Macpherson, para 5.12, p. 16.
15 Macpherson, para 11.1, p. 62.
16 Macpherson, para 11.13, p. 63.
17 Macpherson, para 19.37, p. 146.
18 Macpherson, paras 19.34–19.44, pp. 145-8.
19 Macpherson, para 6.34, p. 28.
20 Macpherson, para 6.17, p. 22.
21 Sir Paul Condon's letter to Inquiry of 2 Oct. 1998, cit.
22 Macpherson, para 6.25 p. 24.
23 Macpherson, para 6.48 p. 31.
24 Macpherson, p. 333.

31.3 In proportion: race, and police stop and search
P.A.J. Waddington, Kevin Stenson and David Don

Introduction

The exercise of the police power to stop and search members of the public is one that has long excited public controversy. Central to this controversy is the allegation that police officers use the discretion afforded by this power selectively to target sections of the population, especially ethnic minorities. This debate rages not only in Britain: in the United States and Canada, the issue of 'racial profiling' excites as much controversy as racial disproportionality does in the United Kingdom (Harris 1999; Petrocelli *et al.* 2003; Smith and Petrocelli 2001; Weitzer and Tuch 2002; Zingraff *et al.* 2000). Recently, this debate reached new heights of intensity in Britain, following the publication of the Macpherson Inquiry into the murder of Stephen Lawrence, which concluded that the over-representation of racial minorities in the national stop and search figures led to the 'clear core conclusion of racist stereotyping' (Macpherson of Cluny *et al.* 1999, para. 6.45(b)).

Stop and search as a policing power

The power to stop and search those whom the police suspect of wrongdoing is long established in British policing. Brogden (1985) suggests that it continues a tradition established prior to the creation of a professional police service and was intended to be used to harass marginal sections of the population – described in the 1824 Vagrancy Act as 'rogues, vagabond and incorrigible thieves'. Be that as it may, the power was extended haphazardly as policing in Britain developed. The Metropolitan Police and a handful of other forces had powers granted to them, but many others did not. Section 1 of the 1984 Police and Criminal Evidence Act (PACE) codified this power, extending it to all police officers and stipulating (mainly through Codes of Practice) how it was to be exercised. This was a development surrounded by controversy (Benyon and Bourn 1986). Annually published Home Office statistics demonstrate how the use of this power has grown enormously since PACE came into force, albeit that it has declined in recent years (Ayres *et al.* 2002).

The exercise of this power has been at the forefront of research into policing, in Britain and elsewhere. It is thought to epitomize the discretionary powers available to the most subordinate ranks in the police and the opportunities that these afford for discriminatory treatment. It is quintessentially a 'low visibility' decision (Goldstein 1960). [...]

There have long been suspicions that police officers exercise this power in a discriminatory fashion against marginal sections of the population. In the recent past, it has been the disproportionality of young black and Asian men who are stopped and searched that has commanded most attention from researchers and policy-makers alike. Norris *et al.* (1992) found not only that young blacks were stopped very much more frequently than other racial groups, but that these stops were made on a more speculative basis. FitzGerald and Hough found that being black was a good predictor for being stopped on foot and in a car, along with being under 30 years old and male (FitzGerald *et al.* 2002).

Explanations for this disproportionality have consistently emphasized the subjectivity of police officers (Bowling and Phillips 2001). This is hardly surprising, given the extent to which stop and search is the exercise of a discretionary legal power. Despite championing the notion that racism in policing was 'institutionalised', the Macpherson report (1999) attributed disproportionate levels of stop and search to 'stereotyping' – police racism may be 'unwitting', but nonetheless is an expression of the subjectivity of officers, albeit culturally shared. For instance, it is suggested that police are generally more suspicious of racial minorities than of white people (FitzGerald and Sibbitt 1997).

Yet, police attention may not be as misplaced as might be supposed. [...] [O]ver-representation of particular sections of the population indicates, but does not prove, that the power to stop and search is being selectively applied, for over-representation may be due to other factors, not least differential involvement in crime. Hence, the debate surrounding the over-representation of ethnic and racial minorities has tended to become polarized between those claiming that it reflects discriminatory police behaviour and others who assert that it is due to differential involvement in crime and disorder. We will argue that this dichotomy is unhelpful and that alternative explanations have greater validity.

What is undeniable is that the experiences of those stopped and searched has created and reinforced a sense of grievance and antagonism towards the police (Gilroy 1982; Hall *et al.* 1978; Porter 1996).

'Availability'

If disproportionality cannot easily be attributed to the prejudicial exercise of the power to stop and search by individual police officers, what else might explain it? An obvious candidate is that different racial or ethnic groups place themselves at greater or lesser risk of being stopped by the police through their differential use of public space. [...]

[I]f different racial or ethnic groups are disproportionately present or absent in public spaces, then they offer differential opportunities for the police to stop and search them. Home Office researchers (Miller and MVA 2000) systematically recorded the racial composition of people 'available' in areas of high crime/high stop and search. They concluded:

> Overall, across the five sites, the findings of this research did not suggest any general pattern of bias against people from minority ethnic groups either as a whole or for particular groups;

> white people tended to be stopped or searched at a higher rate to the available population;

> Asian people tended to be under-represented in those stopped or searched (with some exceptions); and

> black people have a more mixed experience, sometimes under-represented in stops and searches and sometimes over-represented.

In other words, the Home Office research challenges reliance upon the residential population as a proxy measure of the population available to be stopped and searched (cf. Zingraff *et al.* 2000). It also provides a simple remedy for avoiding reliance on such a proxy measure–sampling the 'available population'.

Research methods

This research was commissioned by the Thames Valley Police and was conducted in Reading and Slough. [...]

Four complementary research methods were employed: first, direct observation of the 'available population'; secondly, the viewing of Reading town centre CCTV footage; thirdly, analysis of the stop and search database, maintained by the police at Reading; and finally, interviews with officers about recent stop and searches that they had conducted.

Direct observation

The 'available populations' in both towns were sampled using methods derived from those employed by the Home Office research (Miller and MVA 2000). This entailed researchers driving along a route that took them through areas of high stop and search, systematically recording the ostensible race, age and sex of all pedestrians on the nearside footpath and public areas visible from the road. To facilitate consistency with the Home Office research and because the research was restricted to appearances, observers categorized race as 'white', 'black', 'Asian' and 'other'. Age was categorized as 'child', if the person appeared to be under 15 years old; 'young', if they appeared to be between 15 and 30; 'adult', if between 30 and 60; and 'old', if older than 60. Sex was categorized as 'male' and 'female'.

The route in each location remained constant, and was 23 miles in length in Reading and 24 in Slough. Each was designed to pass through areas where stop and search was prevalent. Police statistics identified the location of stop and searches quite narrowly (usually by street name) and, therefore, the route was not reliant upon aggregate statistics, such as those for beat areas. In each case, it took between 90 and 150 minutes to complete the route, depending on traffic conditions. Each daily period between 2 p.m. and 2 a.m. the following morning was divided into two hourly blocks and each block on every day of the week was observed in random order. Observations were limited to this 12-hour period each day because this is when stop and search activity is at its highest.

Estimating the composition of the 'available' population

When compared to the resident populations of each division (whether based on the 1991 Census, which was the only estimate available at the outset of the fieldwork, or the recently released 2001 Census), police stop and search figures certainly suggest significant disproportionality in both locations (Table 31.3.1). On the face of it, there is reason to believe that stop and search in these two towns reflects one aspect of 'institutional racism' because officers 'stereotype' members of the public. The strictures of the Macpherson report seem to have had, at best, only limited impact and disproportionality seems to continue.

However, when we consider the 'available population', we find a rather different picture. White people are much less evident amongst those available to be stopped and searched in both towns, especially in Slough. Black and Asian people are marginally, but crucially, more abundant in Reading and far more numerous in Slough. The result is that, in Reading, the pattern of stop and search reflects pretty closely the available population, whilst in Slough, there is significant disproportionality, with white people being over-represented amongst those stopped and searched and Asians under-represented.

Youth

It is, perhaps, questionable to rely on global estimates of the 'available population' (even if the public debate has relied upon global figures in relation to the resident population). It is widely known that stop and search falls heaviest upon young men and, therefore, that section of the population needs separate consideration. Table 31.3.2 displays the figures for the 'available population' of young men in Reading and Slough, disaggregated by race, alongside the stop and search figures. From these figures it will be seen that, in Reading, the picture remains remarkably consistent with the global data, probably because young people comprise 36 per cent of all those in the 'available population' in Reading. Whilst broadly consistent with the general position in Slough, the figures show that young white men are disproportionately stopped and searched even more than the white population, generally.

There is more to this issue of young men than meets the eye. Jefferson (1993) persuasively argues that race is only one, relatively minor component explaining why 'criminalization' (stop and search, and arrest) falls more heavily upon particular sections of the population. He points to how, historically, young men from the 'rough' working class, especially the immigrant Irish, were equated with the 'dangerous classes':

Table 31.3.1 Percentage racial breakdown of population, stop and search, and 'available population' in Reading and Slough

	Reading				Slough			
	Population (1991 Census) N = 147,300	Population (2001 Census) N = 143,096	Available population N = 14,898	Stop/search (2000–02) N = 7,934	Population (1991 Census) N = 148,580	Population (2001 Census) N = 119,067	Available population N = 8,819	Stop/search (2001) N = 711
Race								
White	91	87	74	75	79	64	42	54
Black	6	6	13	15	3	6	17	15
Asian	5	5	9	10	17	28	40	31
Other	1	2	4	0	1	2	1	0

Table 31.3.2 Percentage of 'available' young men in Reading and Slough compared to total stop and serach

	Reading			Slough		
	General	Young men	'Available'	General	Young men	'Available'
Race						
White	75	76	68	54	53	37
Black	15	12	16	15	14	19
Asian	10	12	10	31	33	43
Other	0	0	6	0	0	1

...from the late nineteenth century on the criminal Other has been, to all intents and purposes, a rough working class, adolescent male: the quintessential modern delinquent. (Jefferson 1993: 29)

Race became assimilated into this pre-existing pattern with the influx of 'New Commonwealth' immigration from the 1950s onwards, but race did not eclipse the influence of age, gender and class. Based on his analysis of a sample of residents of Leeds, he concludes that:

> what all this amounts to is that being the wrong age, sex and class, in the wrong place at the wrong time, displaying the wrong demeanour and attitude, spells 'trouble' to police, whatever the colour of your skin: being black may add a further dimension, but it's being a toe-rag that constitutes the crucial generic category; which brings us back to the quintessential modern delinquent, the rough working class adolescent male . . . . 'Because they are black' ought now to read, *'because they are young and male and "rough" working class and black'*. (Jefferson 1993: 35)

We are in no position to analyse the influence of social class, but our data lend support to Jefferson. Table 31.3.3 summarizes data comparing the available population with those stopped and searched. We see, as noted previously, that the proportion of white people stopped and searched either reflects their proportion in the available population or exceeds it. Whereas, young people and men, and especially the combined category of young men, are

Table 31.3.3 The availability and stop and searches according to race, age and gender

		Reading	Slough
White	Available	74	42
	Stopped and searched	75	54
Young	Available	60	57
	Stopped and searched	71	76
Men	Available	58	64
	Stopped and searched	91	91
Young men	Available	35	38
	Stopped and searched	64	63

far more likely to be stopped and searched than their proportions in the available population would lead us to expect. In terms of sheer proportionality, Jefferson is correct: it is young men who are vastly over-represented, irrespective of race or ethnicity.

Thus, it seems that a very different conclusion is reached from comparing stop and search figures with the composition of the 'available population' than with residential figures. First, it is difficult to see how these figures could be interpreted as an outcome of officers' stereotyping: if anything, it is white people who are disproportionately stopped and searched, especially in Slough. Secondly, and by the same token, racial minorities certainly appear no more inclined in general to conduct themselves in ways that arouse suspicion than are white people; indeed, they seem somewhat less prone to do so. Of course, it is perfectly possible that ethnic groups arouse police suspicions in different ways, but, overall, these cancel out marginally to the benefit of minorities.

Stop and search, and 'institutional racism'

This analysis and the Home Office (Miller and MVA 2000) research both suggest that Sir William Macpherson was in error in concluding that the disproportionality in stop and search figures was evidence of racial stereotyping. The attraction of the concept of 'institutional racism' is that it promises to raise criminological debate above the level of wilful police prejudice and stereotyping – what Keith calls 'pathology sociology' (quoted in Bowling and Phillips 2001: 137). Unfortunately, Sir William's 'clear core conclusion' that racial disproportionality in stop and search was attributable to 'stereotyping' perpetuated the emphasis given to the subjectivity of police officers as the prime causal influence.

Do our data mean that police officers are not 'institutionally racist'? Given the racial and ethnic divisions in many societies, not least in Britain, this seems highly improbable. What it does mean is that whatever mechanisms drive 'institutional racism', they are unlikely to be as simple as police officers' targeting people for stop and search on the basis of racial stereotypes. It is essential to recognize the complexity of the concept of institutionalized racism. The focus of this concept is the, perhaps unwitting, impact of routine, underlying institutional practices and also the structural conditions in which policing and criminal justice operate. For example, Bowling (1990;

1998) advanced our understanding of the inadequate police response to racist attacks, by shifting the focus of attention away from the supposed covert racism of officers to an analysis of how the universal tendency of police officers to consider incidents in isolation translated into a systematic failure to appreciate the significance of racial violence. It is our suspicion that understanding the 'institutionalized racism' of other policing practices (perhaps including stop and search) will require similarly sophisticated analysis.

Central to the latter conditions and a key concern of this article is the make-up of the street – rather than residential – populations who are available to be stopped and searched. Bowling and Phillips (2001) correctly point to the racialized nature of 'availability'. Racial patterning of unemployment, homelessness and school exclusion may be reflected in the composition of the 'available population' and, even if police proportionately select from amongst this 'available population', it remains the case that racial minorities may be more exposed to stop and search. By default, and particularly as night progresses, the urban streetscape increasingly becomes the domain of young men. Hence, the everyday practices of police patrol reflect, and perhaps reinforce, the deeper patterns of social change, division and inequalities that influence citizens' uses of public space (Bottoms and Wiles 1997). Moreover, the choices to deploy policing resources in public spaces, rather than, say, focusing on more or less visible offending by affluent populations in less public locations, embodies a politics of crime control that warrants further exploration (Stenson 1991). However, citizens' expectations mean that the maintenance of order and the control of crime in public places remains an inescapable core policing role in the liberal democracies (Stenson 2000; Waddington 1999), which brings officers disproportionately into contact with available street populations.

> From P.A.J. Waddington, K. Stenson and D. Don, 'In proportion: race, and police stop and search', British Journal of Criminology, 2004, *44(6): 889–914*.

References

Ayres, M., Perry, D. and Hayward, P. (2002) *Arrests for Notifiable Offences and the Operation of Certain Police Powers under Pace 12/02 England and Wales, 2007/02.* London: Home Office, Research, Development and Statistics Directorate.

Benyon, J, and Bourn, C. (Eds) (1986) *The Police: Powers, Procedures and Proprieties.* Oxford: Pergamon.

Bottoms, A. and Wiles, P. (1997) Environmental criminology', in Maguire, M. *et al.*, (Eds) *The Oxford Handbook of Criminology*, 305–359. Oxford: Clarendon Press.

Bowling, B. (1990) Conceptual and methodological problems in measuring race differences in delinquency: A reply to Marianne Junger. *British Journal of Criminology*, 30:483–492.

Bowling, B. (1998) *Violent Racism.* Oxford: Clarendon.

Bowling, B. and Phillips, C. (2001) *Racism, Crime and Criminal Justice.* Harlow, Essex: Longman.

Brogden, M. (1985), Stopping the people – crime control versus social control. In Baxter, J. and Koffman, L. (Eds) *Police: The Constitution and the Community*, 91–110. Abingdon, Oxon: Professional Books.

Fitzgerald, M., Hough, M., Joseph, I. and Qureshi, T. (2002) *Policing for London.* Cullompton, Devon: Willan.

Fitzgerald, M. and Sibbit, R. (1997) *Ethnic Monitoring in Police Forces: A Beginning.* London: Home Office Research and Statistics Directorate.

Gilroy, P. (1982) Police and thieves. In Centre for Contemporary Cultural Studies (Ed.) *The Empire Fights Back: Race and Racism in 70s Britain*, 143–182. London: Hutchinson.

Hall, S., Chritcher, C., Jefferson, T., Clarke, J. and Roberts, B. (1978) *Policing the Crisis.* London: Macmillan.

Harris, D.R. (1999) The stories, the statistics, and the law: Why 'driving while black' matters. *Minnesota Law Review*, 84: 265–326.

Jefferson, T. (1993) The racism of criminalization: Policing and the reproduction of the criminal Other. In Gelsthorpe, L. (Ed.) *Minority Ethnic Groups in the Criminal Justice System*, 26–46. Cambridge: Institute of Criminology.

Macpherson of Cluny, Sir William, advised by Cook, T., Sentamu, The Right Reverend Dr John and Stone, R. (1999) *The Stephen Lawrence Inquiry.* London: HMSO.

Miller, J. and MVA (2000) *Profiling Populations Available for Stops and Searches.* London: Policing and Reducing Crime Unit, Research, Development and Statistics Directorate, Home Office.

Norris, C., Fielding, N., Kemp, C. and Fielding, J. (1992) Black and blue: An analysis of the influence of race on being stopped by the police. *British Journal of Sociology*, 43(2), 207–224.

Petrocelli, M., Piquero, A.R. and Smith, M.R. (2003) Conflict theory and racial profiling: An empirical analysis of police traffic stop data. *Journal of Criminal Justice*, 31(1): 1–11.

Porter, S. (1996) Contra-Foucault: Soldiers, nurses and power. *Sociology*, 30(1): 59–78.

Smith, M. and Petrocelli, M. (2001) Racial profiling? A multivariate analysis of police traffic stop data. *Police Quarterly*, 4(1): 4–27.

Stenson, K. (1991) Making sense of crime control. In Stenson, K. and Cowell, D. (Eds) *The Politics of Crime Control*, 1–32. London: Sage.

Stenson, K. (2000) Some day our prince will come: Zero-tolerance policing and liberal government. In Hope, T. and Sparks, R. (Eds) *Crime, Risk and Insecurity*, 215–237. London: Routledge.

Waddington, P.A.J. (1999) *Policing Citizens*. London: UCL.

Weitzer, R. and Tuch, S.A. (2002) Perceptions of racial profiling: Race, class, and personal experience. *Criminology*, 40: 435–456.

Zingraff, M.T., Mason, H.M., Smith, W.R., Tomaskovic-Devey, D., Warren, P., Mcmurray, H.L. and Fenlon, C. R. (2000), *Evaluating North Carolina State Highway Patrol Data: Citations, Warnings, and Searches in 1998*. North Carolina State University.

31.4 Deadly symbiosis: when ghetto and prison meet and mesh Loïc Wacquant

Reframing black hyper-incarceration

Three brute facts stare the sociologist of racial inequality and imprisonment in America in the face as the new millennium dawns. First, since 1989 and for the first time in national history, African Americans make up a majority of those walking through prison gates every year. Indeed, in four short decades, the ethnic composition of the US inmate population has reversed, turning over from 70 percent white at the mid-century point to nearly 70 percent black and Latino today, although ethnic patterns of criminal activity have not been fundamentally altered during that period (LaFree *et al.*, 1992; Sampson and Lauritzen, 1997).

Second, the rate of incarceration for African Americans has soared to astronomical levels unknown in any other society, not even the Soviet Union at the zenith of the Gulag or South Africa during the acme of the violent struggles over apartheid. [...]

A third trend interpolates the social analyst of race, state, and punishment in the United States: the past two decades have witnessed a swift and steady *deepening of the gap* between the imprisonment rates of blacks and whites (from about one for 5 to one for 85), and this rising 'racial disproportionality' can be traced directly to a single federal policy, namely, the War on Drugs launched by Ronald Reagan and expanded by the administrations of George Bush and William Jefferson Clinton. [...]

These grim statistics are well-known and agreed among students of crime and justice – though they have been steadfastly ignored or minimized by analysts of urban poverty and policy, who have yet to register the enormously disruptive impact that imprisonment has on low-income black communities, as shown by Miller (1997). What remains in dispute are the causes and mechanisms driving this sudden 'blackening' which has turned the carceral system into one of a few national institutions dominated by African Americans, alongside professional sports and selected sectors of the entertainment industry. [...]

In this article, I put forth two interconnected theses, the first *historical*, replacing the carceral institution in the full arc of ethnoracial division and domination in the United States, the second *institutional*, explaining the astounding upsurge in black incarceration in the past three decades as a result of the obsolescence of the ghetto as a device for caste control and the correlative need for a substitute apparatus for keeping (unskilled) African Americans 'in their place', i.e. in a subordinate and confined position in physical, social, and symbolic space.

Four peculiar institutions

To ascertain the pivotal position that the penal apparatus has come to assume within the system of instruments of (re)production of ethnoracial hierarchy in the post-Civil Rights era, it is indispensable to adopt an historical perspective of the *longue durée* so as to situate the prison in the full lineage of institutions which, at each epoch, have carried out the work of race making by drawing and enforcing the peculiar 'color line' that cleaves American society asunder. Put succinctly, the task of *defining, confining, and controlling* African Americans in the United States has been successively shouldered by four 'peculiar institutions': slavery, the Jim Crow system, the urban ghetto, and the novel organizational compound formed by the vestiges of the ghetto and the expanding carceral system, as set out in Table 31.4.1.

however, the apparatus of ethnoracial domination would become less total and less capable of encompassing all segments and all dimensions of the social life of the pariah group. As African Americans differentiated along class lines and acceded to full formal citizenship, the institutional complex charged with keeping them 'separate and unequal' grew more differentiated and diffuse, allowing a burgeoning middle and upper class of professionals and salary earners to *partially* compensate for the negative symbolic capital of blackness by their high-status cultural capital and proximity to centers of political power, while

Table 31.4.1 The four 'peculiar institutions' and their basis

Peculiar institution	Form of labor	Core of economy	Dominant social type
Slavery (1619–1865)	unfree fixed labor	plantation	slave
Jim Crow (South, 1865–1965)	free fixed labor	agrarian and extractive	sharecropper
Ghetto (North, 1915–1968)	free mobile labor	segmented industrial manufacturing	menial worker
Hyperghetto + Prison (1968–)	fixed surplus labor	polarized postindistrial services	welfare recipient & criminal

The first three of these institutions, chattel slavery until the Civil War, the Jim Crow regime of racial exclusion operative in the agrarian South from Emancipation to the Civil Rights revolution, and the ghetto in the 20th century Northern industrial city, have, each in its own manner, served two joined yet discordant purposes: to recruit, organize, and extract labor out of African Americans, on the one hand; and to demarcate and ultimately seclude them so that they would not 'contaminate' the surrounding white society that viewed them as an irrevocably inferior and vile because devoid of ethnic honor. These two goals of *labor extraction and social ostracization* of a stigmatized category are in tension with one another. [...]

But the built-in instabilities of unfree labor and the inherent anomaly of caste partition in a formally democratic and highly individualistic society guaranteed that each 'peculiar institution' would in time be undermined by the weight of its internal contradictions as well as by mounting black resistance and external opposition, to be replaced by its successor regime. At each new stage,

lower-class blacks remained burdened by the triple stigma of 'race', poverty, and putative immorality.

1. Slavery (1619–1865)

From the first years of the colony to the Civil War, slavery was the institution that determined the collective identity and individual life chances of Americans of African parentage. [...] The forcible importation of Africans and West Indians, and the rearing of their descendants under bondage (the US enslaved population tripled to reach 4 million in the half-century after the slave trade was cut off in 1808), supplied the unfree and fixed workforce needed to produce the great staples that were the backbone of North America's preindustrial economy, tobacco, rice, sugar, and cotton.

In the early colonial period indentured servitude was economically more advantageous than slavery but, by the second half of the 17th century, the increase in life expectancy, the growth of the tobacco trade, the need to encourage further voluntary immigration and the relative powerlessness of African captives compared to European migrants and native Americans combined to make slaves the preferred source of labor (Morgan, 1975). After the Revolution, human bondage was abolished along the Eastern seaboard and prohibited north and west of the Ohio River, but it spread and solidified throughout the South, as the economic value of slaves rose in concert with the increase in the demand for cotton and the scarcity of labor in the new territories of the Southwest. Once it generalized, slavery transformed all of society, culture, and politics in its image, fostering the concentration of economic and state power in the hands of a small slaveholder class tied to lower-class whites by patronage relations and to their slaves by a paternalistic code and elaborate rituals of submission that reinforced the latter's lack of cultural autonomy and sense of inferiority (Williamson, 1986: 15–27). [...]

Slavery as a system of unfree labor thus spawned a suffusive racial culture which, in turn, remade bondage into something it was not at its outset: a color-coded institution of ethnoracial division.

2. Jim Crow (South, 1865–1965)

Emancipation posed a double and deadly threat to Southern society: the overthrow of bondage made slaves formally free laborers, which potentially eliminated the cheap and abundant workforce required to run the plantation economy; black access to civil and political rights promised to erode the color line initially drawn to bulwark slavery but since entrenched in both the South and the North of the country. In a first phase, during Reconstruction, the Dixie ruling class promulgated the Black Codes to resolve the first problem by establishing 'forced labor and police laws to get the freedman back to the fields under control' (Woodward, 1971: 250–1). In a second phase, through the 1880s, the white lower classes, pressed by the dislocations wrought by declining farm prices, demographic pressure and capitalist industrialization, joined with the plantation elite to demand the political disenfranchisement and systematic exclusion of former slaves from all major institutions (Wilson, 1980: 57–61): the Jim Crow regime of racial segregation was born which would hold African Americans in its brutal grip for nearly a century in the Southern states and beyond.

Under this regime, backed by custom and elaborate legal statutes, super exploitative sharecropping arrangements and debt peonage fixed black labor on the land, perpetuating the hegemony of the region's agrarian upper class. [...]

Most crucially, the second 'peculiar institution' sharply curtailed social contacts between whites and blacks by relegating the latter to separate residential districts and to the reserved 'colored' section of commercial establishments and public facilities, saloons and movie houses, parks and beaches, trolleys and buses, waiting rooms and bathrooms. Any and all forms of intercourse that might imply social equality between the 'races' and, worse yet, provide an occasion for sexual contact across the color line were rigorously forbidden and zealously surveiled, and any infringement, real or imagined, savagely repressed. [...] In the last two decades of the 19th century, some 2,060 African Americans were lynched, one third of them after being accused of sexual assault or mere improprieties towards white women (Williamson, 1982: 292).

3. The ghetto (North, 1914–1963)

The very ferocity of Jim Crow on both the labor and the ostracization fronts sowed the seeds of its eventual ruin, for blacks fled the South by the millions as soon as the opportunity came. Three forces combined to rouse them to desert Dixie and rally to the surging metropolitan centers of the Midwest and Northeast in the half-century following the outbreak of World War I. The first was the economic crisis of cotton agriculture caused by the boll weevil and later by mechanization, as well as arrested urbanization in the South due to the industrial underdevelopment of the region (Fligstein, 1981). The second was the booming demand for unskilled and semiskilled labor in the steel mills, packinghouses, factories and railroads of the North. [...] But economic push and pull factors merely set conditions of possibility: the trigger of the Great Migration that transformed the black community from a landless peasantry to an industrial proletariat, and with it the visage of American society *in toto*, was the irrepressible will to escape the indignities of caste and its attendant material degradation, truncated life horizon, and rampant violence – the out migration of blacks was heaviest in those counties of the Deep South where lynchings were most frequent (Tolnay and Beck, 1992). [...]

Yankee life did offer salutary relief from the harsh grip of Southern caste domination and significantly expand the life chances of the former sharecroppers, but it did not turn out to be the 'promised land' of racial equality, economic security, and full citizenship for which migrants yearned. For, in the Northern metropolis, African

Americans came upon yet another device designed to allow white society to exploit their labor power while keeping them confined to a separate *Lebensraum*: the ghetto. [...]

This 'black city within the white', as black scholars from DuBois and Frazier to Oliver Cox and Kenneth Clark have consistently characterized the ghetto (Wacquant, 1998a), discharged the same two basic functions that slavery and the Jim Crow system had performed earlier, namely, to harness the labor of African Americans while cloistering their tainted bodies, so as to avert both the specter of 'social equality' and the odium of 'miscegenation' that would inevitably result in loss of ethnic honor for whites. But it differed from the preceding 'peculiar institutions' in that, by granting them a measure of organizational autonomy, the urban Black Belt enabled African Americans to fully develop their own social and symbolic forms and thereby accumulate the group capacities needed to escalate the fight against continued caste subordination. For the ghetto in full-fledged form is, by its very makeup, a *double-edged sociospatial formation*: it operates as an instrument of exclusion from the standpoint of the dominant group; yet it also offers the subordinate group partial protection and a platform for succor and solidarity in the very movement whereby it sequesters it.

From communal ghetto to hyperghetto: how the ghetto became more like a prison

The *fin-de-siècle* hyperghetto presents four main characteristics that differentiate it sharply from the communal ghetto of the Fordist-Keynesian era and converge to render its social structure and cultural climate more akin to those of the prison.

1. Class segregation overlays racial segregation

The dark ghetto of mid-century held within itself a full complement of classes, for the simple reason that even the black bourgeoisie was barred from escaping its cramped and compact perimeter while a majority of adults were gainfully employed in a gamut of occupations. [...] The postwar ghetto was *integrated both socially and structurally* – even the 'shadies' who earned their living from such illicit trades as the 'numbers game', liquor sale, prostitution and other *risqué* recreation, were entwined with the different classes.

Today's black bourgeoisie still lives under strict segregation and its life chances continue to be curtailed by its geographic and symbolic conti-

guity with the African-American (sub)proletariat (Patillo-McCoy, 1999). Nonetheless, it has gained considerable physical distance from the heart of the ghetto by establishing satellite black neighborhoods at its periphery inside the city and in the suburbs. [...] The genealogical ties of the black bourgeoisie to the black poor have also grown more remote and less dense. What is more, the historic center of the Black Belt has experienced massive depopulation and deproletarianization, such that a large majority of its residents are no longer employed. [...]

This marked lowering and homogenization of the social composition of the ghetto makes it akin to the monotonous class recruitment of the carceral institution, dominated as the latter is by the most precarious fractions of the urban proletariat of the unemployed, the casually employed, and the uneducated. [...] Residents of the hyperghetto and clients of the carceral institution thus present germane profiles in economic marginality and social disintegration.

2. Loss of a positive economic function

The transformed class structure of the hyperghetto is a direct product of its evolving position in the new urban political economy ushered by post-Fordism. [...] Just as mechanization had enabled Southern agriculture to dispense with black labor a generation earlier, 'automation and suburban relocation created a crisis of tragic dimension for unskilled black workers' in the North, as 'for the first time in American history, the African American was no longer needed in the economic system' of the metropolis (Rifkin, 1995: 79). [...] At best, the hyperghetto now serves the *negative economic function of storage of a surplus population* devoid of market utility in which respect it also increasingly resembles the prison system.

3. State institutions of social control replace communal institutions

The organizations that formed the framework of everyday life and anchored the strategies of reproduction of urban blacks in the 1950s were group-based and group-specific establishments created and run by African Americans. The black press, churches, lodges and fraternal orders, social clubs and political (sub)machine knit together a dense array of resources and sociability that supported their quest for ethnic pride and group uplift. [...]

By the 1980s, the organizational ecology of the ghetto had been radically altered by the generalized devolution of public institutions and commercial establishments in the urban core as well as by the cumulative demise of black associations caused by the confluence of market withdrawal and state retrenchment (Wacquant, 1998a). [...]

The vacuum created by the crumbling of the ghetto's indigenous organizations has been filled by *state bureaucracies of social control*, themselves largely staffed by the new black middle class whose expansion hinges, not on its capacity to service its community, but on its willingness to assume the vexing role of *custodian* of the black urban sub-proletariat on behalf of white society.

4. Loss of 'buffering function' and the depacification of everyday life

Along with its economic function of labor pool and the extensive organizational nexus it supported, the ghetto lost its capacity to buffer its residents from external forces. It is no longer Janus-faced, offering a sheltered space for collective sustenance and self-affirmation in the face of hostility and exclusion, as in the heyday of the Fordist-Keynesian era. Rather, it has devolved into a one-dimensional machinery for naked relegation, a human warehouse wherein are discarded those segments of urban society deemed disreputable, derelict, and dangerous. And, with the conjoint contraction of the wage labor market and the welfare state in the context of unflinching segregation, it has become saturated with economic, social, and physical insecurity (Massey and Denton, 1993; Krivo and Peterson, 1996). Pandemic levels of crime [...] have further depressed the local economy and ruptured the social fabric. The depacification of everyday life, shrinking of networks, and informalization of survival strategies have combined to give social relations in the hyperghetto a distinct carceral cast (Kotlowitz, 1991; Jones and Newman 1997; Wacquant 1998b).

From 'big house' to warehouse: how the prison became more like a ghetto

The two decades following the climax of the Civil Rights movement not only witnessed a sea change in the function, structure and texture of the dark ghetto in the postindustrial metropolis. The racial and class backlash that reconfigured the city also ushered a sweeping transformation in the purpose and social organization of the carceral institution. Summarily put, the 'Big House' that embodied the correctional ideal of melioristic treatment and community reintegration of inmates[9] gave way to a race-divided and violence-ridden 'warehouse' geared solely to neutralizing social rejects by sequestering them physically from society – in the way that a classical ghetto wards off the threat of defilement posed by the presence of a dishonored group by encaging it within its walls, but in an ambience resonant with the fragmentation, dread, and despair of the post-Fordist hyperghetto.

1. The racial division of everything

The relatively stable set of positions and expectations defined primarily in terms of criminal statuses and prison conduct that used to organize the inmate world has been replaced by a chaotic and conflictual setting wherein 'racial division has primacy over all particular identities and influences all aspects of life' (Irwin, 1990: v; also Carroll, 1982; Johnson, 1996; Hassine, 1999: 71–8). The ward, tier, cell and bed-bunk to which one is assigned; access to food, telephone, television, visitation and in-house programs; one's associations and protections, which in turn determine the probability of being the victim or perpetrator of violence: all are set by one's ethnic community of provenance. Elective loyalty to inmates as a generic class, with the possibility of remaining non-aligned, has been superseded by forced and exclusive loyalty to one's 'race'.

2. The 'code of the street' overwhelms the 'convict code'

Along with racial division, the predatory culture of the street, centered on hypermasculinist notions of honor, toughness, and coolness has entered into and transfigured the social structure and culture of jails and prisons. The 'convict code', rooted in solidarity among inmates and antagonism towards guards (Sykes and Messinger, 1960), has in effect been swamped by the 'code of the street' (Anderson, 1998), with its ardent imperative of individual 'respect' secured through the militant display and actualization of readiness to mete out physical violence. Accordingly, 'the old 'hero' of the prison world – the 'right guy' – has been replaced by outlaws and gang members.

3. Purging the undesirables

The 'Big House' of the postwar decades was animated by a consequentialist theory of punishment that sought to resocialize inmates so as to lower the probability of re-offense once they returned to society, of which they were expected to become law-abiding if not productive members. Following the official repudiation of the philosophy of rehabilitation in the 1970s (Allen, 1981), today's prison has for sole purpose to *neutralize* offenders – both materially, by removing them physically into an institutional enclave, and *symbolically*, by drawing a hard and fast line between criminals and law-abiding citizens. [...]

When the prison is used as an implement for social and cultural purging, like the ghetto, it no longer points beyond itself; it turns into a self-contained contraption which fulfils its function, and thus justifies itself, by its mere existence. And its inhabitants learn to live in the here-and-now, bathed in the concentrate of violence and hopelessness brewing within the walls.

4. The proto-racialization of judicial stigma

The contemporary prison can be further likened to the ghetto in that, in the revanchist penal climate of the past two decades, the stigma of penal conviction has been prolonged, diffused, and reframed in ways that assimilate it to an ethnoracial stigma attached *ad aeternitum* to the body of its bearer. In other liberal-democratic societies, the status dishonor and civic disabilities of being a prisoner are temporary and limited: they affect offenders while they are being processed by the criminal justice system and typically wear off upon coming out of prison or shortly thereafter; to ensure this, laws and administrative rules set strict conditions and limits to the use and diffusion of criminal justice information. Not so in the United States, where, on the contrary, (1) convicts are subjected to ever-longer and broader post-detention forms of social control and symbolic branding that durably set them apart from the rest of the population; (2) the criminal files of individual inmates are readily accessible and actively disseminated by the authorities; (3) a naturalizing discourse suffused with genetic phraseology and animalistic imagery has swamped public representations of crime in the media, politics, and significant segments of scholarship.

5. Bifurcated socioracial patterning of carceral recruitment and authority

Today's prison further resembles the ghetto for the simple reason that an overwhelming majority of its occupants originate from the racialized core of the country's major cities, and returns there upon release, only to be soon caught again in the police dragnet to be sent away for another, longer sojourn behind bars in a self-perpetuating cycle of escalating socioeconomic marginality and legal incapacitation. [...]

The contemporary prison system and the ghetto not only display a similarly skewed recruitment and composition in terms of class and caste. The former also duplicates the authority structure characteristic of the latter in that it places a population of poor blacks under the direct supervision of whites – albeit, in this case, lower-class whites. [...]

The convergent changes that have 'prisonized' the ghetto and 'ghettoized' the prison in the aftermath of the Civil Rights revolution suggest that the inordinate and mounting over-representation of blacks behind bars does not stem simply from the discriminatory targeting of specific penal policies such as the War on Drugs, as proposed by Tonry (1995), or from the sheer destabilizing effects of the increased penetration of ghetto neighborhoods by the penal state, as Miller argues (1997). Not that these two factors are not at work, for clearly they are deeply involved in the hyper-incarceration of African Americans. But they fail to capture the precise nature and the full magnitude of the transformations that have interlocked the prison and the (hyper)ghetto via a relation of *functional equivalency* (they serve one and the same purpose, the coercive confinement of a stigmatized population) and *structural homology* (they comprise and comfort the same type of social relations and authority pattern) to form a *single institutional mesh* suited to fulfil anew the mission historically imparted to America's 'peculiar institutions'.

From L. Wacquant, 'Deadly symbiosis: when ghetto and prison meet and mesh', Punishment and Society, *2001, 3(1): 95–133.*

References

Allen, F.A. (1981) *The Decline of the Rehabilitative Ideal*. New Haven: Yale University Press.

Anderson, E. (1998) *Code of the Street. Decency, Violence, and the Moral Life of the Inner City*. New York: Knopf.

Berlin, I. (1998) *Many Thousands Gone: The First Two Centuries of Slavery in North America*. Cambridge MA: Harvard University Press.

Carroll, L. (1982) Race, ethnicity, and the social order of the prison. In Johnson, R. and Toch, H. (Eds) *The Pains of Imprisonment*. pp. 181–201. Beverly Hills: Sage.

Davis, F.J. (1992) *Who is Black? One's Nation Definition*. University Park: Penn State Press.

Drake, St. C. and Clayton, H. (1945) *Black Metropolis: A Study of Negro Life in a Northern City*. New York: Harper and Row.

Fligstein, N. (1981) *Going North: Migration of Blacks and Whites from the South, 1900–1950*. New York: Academic Press.

Hassine, V. (1999) *Life without Parole: Living in Prison Today*. (2nd ed.) Boston: Roxbury Publications.

Irwin, J. (1970 [1990]). *The Felon*. Berkeley: University of California Press, new edition.

Johnson, R. (1996). *Hard Time. Understanding and Reforming the Prison*. (2nd ed.) Belmont: Wadsworth Publishing.

Jones, LeA. and Newman, L (1997) *Our America: Life and Death on the South Side of Chicago*. New York: Washington Square Press.

King, D. (1995) *Separate and Unequal: Black Americans and the US Federal Government*. Oxford: Oxford University Press.

Kolchin, P. (1987) *Unfree Labor: American Slavery and Russian Serfdom*. Cambridge: The Belknap Press of Harvard University Press.

Kotlowitz, A. (1991) *There are No Children Here*. New York: Anchor Books.

Krivo, L.J. and Peterson, R.D. (1996) Extremely disadvantaged neighborhoods and urban crime. *Social Forces* 75(2): 619–650.

Lafree, G., Drass, K. and O'Day, P. (1992) Race and crime in post-war America: determinants of African American and white rates, 1957–1988. *Criminology*, 30: 157–88.

Massey, D. and Denton, N. (1993) *American Apartheid: Segregation and the Making of the Underclass*. Cambridge: Harvard University Press.

Mauer, M. (1997) Racial disparities in prison getting worse in the 1990s. *Over-crowded Times* 8(1): 8–13.

Miller, J.G. (1997) *Search and Destroy: African-American Males in the Criminal Justice System*. Cambridge: Cambridge University Press.

Morgan, E.S. (1975) *American Slavery, American Freedom: The Ordeal of Colonial Virginia*. New York: WW. Norton.

Myrdal, G. (1944 [1962]) *An American Dilemma: The Negro Problem and Modern Democracy*. New York: Harper Torchbook.

Patillo-McCoy, M. (1999) *Black Picket Fences: Privilege and Peril among the Black Middle Class*. Chicago: University of Chicago Press.

Patterson, O. (1982) *Slavery as Social Death*. Cambridge: Harvard University Press.

Rifkin, J. (1995) *The End of Work: The Decline of the Global Labor Force and the Dawn of the Post-Market Era*. New York: Tarcher and Putnam.

Sampson, R.J. and Lauritsen, J.L. (1997) Racial and ethnic disparities in crime and criminal justice in the United States. In Tonry, M. (Ed.), *Ethnicity, Crime, and Immigration: Comparative and Cross-national Perspectives*. Chicago: The University of Chicago Press, pp. 311–74.

Sykes, G. and Messinger, S. (1960) The inmate social system. In Cloward, R. *et al.*, *Theoretical Studies in the Social Organization of the Prison*. New York: Social Science Research Council, pp. 6–10.

Tolnay, S.E. and Beck, F.M. (1992) Racial violence and black migration in the American south, 1910 to 1930. *American Sociological Review*, 57(1): 103–116.

Tonry, M. (1995) *Malign Neglect: Race, Class, and Punishment in America*. New York: Oxford University Press.

Wacquant, L. (1998a) Negative social capital: State breakdown and social destitution in America's urban core. *The Netherlands Journal of the Built Environment*, 13–1: 25–40.

Wacquant, L. (1998b) 'Inside the zone: The social art of the hustler in the black American ghetto'. *Theory, Culture, and Society*, 15(2): 1–36.

Williamson, J. (1986) *A Rage for Order: Black-White Relations in the American South since Emancipation*. New York: Oxford University Press.

Wilson, W.J. (1980) *The Declining Significance of Race*. (2nd ed.) Chicago: The University of Chicago Press.

Wilson, W.J. (1987)*The Truly Disadvantaged: The Inner City, The Underclass and Public Policy*. Chicago: University of Chicago Press.

Woodward, C.V. (1971) *American Counterpoint: Slavery and Racism in the North-South Dialogue*. Boston: Little, Brown.

32

Gender, crime and justice

32.1 Women and criminal justice: saying it again, again and again
Loraine Gelsthorpe   770

32.2 The woman of legal discourse
Carol Smart   772

32.3 Women and social control
Frances Heidensohn   779

32.4 Common sense, routine precaution and normal violence
Elizabeth A. Stanko   786

32.5 Hegemonic and subordinated masculinities
James W. Messerschmidt   791

Introduction

Earlier in the book (Chapter 15) we considered feminist theory and what criminologists working in that tradition have to say about the gendered nature and consequences of criminal justice. In this chapter we revisit some of these concerns, but from a more empirically-oriented perspective. The central concerns, therefore, cover such matters as the differential treatment of men and women by criminal justice agencies, the ways in which experiences of crime and victimization are themselves gendered, and the differing ways in which men and women relate to issues of social control.

To begin with there is a short piece by Loraine Gelsthorpe **(Reading 32.1)**, the subtitle of which is 'saying it again, again and again'. The piece was prompted by the continuing upward trend in women's imprisonment and a series of new policy proposals in relation to the sentencing of female offenders. The underpinning concern is that all too seldom are the specific needs of women considered when designing and implementing criminal justice initiatives, and that this is not for the lack of commentators continually saying how important it is to 'gender proof' sentencing and other aspects of the system.

It is not just the activities and outcomes of criminal justice agencies that are gendered but, according to Carol Smart **(Reading 32.2)**, the law itself. She identifies three phases in the development of the idea that the law is gendered. These are, in turn, the 'law is sexist', 'the law is male' and 'the law is gendered'. According to Smart there is a complex set of differentiations going in the 'production of women' by law: not only is the female criminal a type that is to be differentiated from other women, but there has already been a prior process of differentiation in which the ideal of 'woman' is distinguished from 'man'. This leads her to conclude that while it is valid to say that the law can be seen as a system which discriminates against women it is also a system which produces gender differences and identities more generally.

Whereas, for good and fairly obvious reasons, much criminological work focuses on the 'control' of women by the criminal justice system there is also much to be learned, Frances Heidensohn argues **(Reading 32.3)**, by looking at women *in* control. In this regard she identifies four primary spheres in which women play important social control functions. Each of these has much to tell us about both the nature of social control and its highly gendered nature. Returning to the issue of the control of women, Heidensohn argues that criminology has paid too little attention to the issue of conformity. Paralleling her earlier discussion she identifies four levels on which to consider the control of women. What this helps clarify is the extent and depth of the social controls to which women are subject and, possibly therefore, why there are such substantial apparent differences in male and female rates of criminal offending.

The strategies adopted by men and women in relation to personal safety also differ markedly. In her analysis of 'everyday violence', Betsy Stanko **(Reading 32.4)** examines the 'routine precautions taken by women and men in a variety of different situations, including when on the street, in the workplace and at home. As she shows, 'keeping violence at bay is an active process', often requiring changes to habits and practices. One of the ironies of criminology is that although for the bulk of its history it has been preoccupied by male experiences and male offending – rendering women largely invisible – relatively little thought has been given to the issue of masculinity. Indeed, it is largely as a result of feminism that the subject of masculinity reached the criminological agenda. James Messerschmidt **(Reading 32.5)** introduces the terms 'hegemonic' and 'subordinated masculinities'. This distinction draws on Antonio Gramsci's notion of hegemony and essentially distinguishes between a dominant conception of what we understand by 'masculinity' and the variety of other masculinities that are in evidence in society. As he goes on to argue 'boys will be boys differently', and the fact that this is so potentially helps us understand criminality in its various forms.

Questions for discussion

1. What does Gelsthorpe mean by 'gender-proofing' sentencing provisions, and how might this be done?

2. According to Smart, what do the three phases in the development of the idea that the law is gendered consist of?

3. Give some examples of 'how the law works to produce gender'.

4. Identify the four areas identified by Heidensohn in which women play important social control functions.

5. Why is the subject of conformity of interest and value to criminologists?

6. What are the primary differences between the strategies for safety adopted by the women and the men in Stanko's discussion of routine precautions?

7. What is meant by the terms 'hegemonic' and 'subordinated masculinities'?

8. How useful do you think the terms 'hegemonic' and 'subordinated masculinities' might be to criminologists?

32.1 Women and criminal justice: saying it again, again and again Loraine Gelsthorpe

Since 2000 there has been heightened awareness of the upward trend in the imprisonment of women. Although women in prison presently constitute only 6% of the total prison population, between 1994 and 2004 the numbers of women in prison in England and Wales increased by over 150%. This is a startling increase, and a wide range of different explanations have been offered for it: changes in the nature and seriousness of women's crime, moves towards dealing with male and female offenders more 'equally', changes in sentencing patterns, changes in the 'type' of women being sentenced to imprisonment, increases in the length of women's sentences, more foreign national women being imprisoned for drugs offences, and even the idea that prison reforms have attracted prison sentences (with prison provision sometimes being perceived to be better than social services) have all been proffered. In the main, none of these explanations is adequate entirely on its own (Gelsthorpe and Morris 2002; Deakin and Spencer 2003; Hedderman 2004; Carlen 2002) yet all contribute to the depressing fact that imprisonment appears to be increasingly used as a ready resort rather than a last resort – in principle, if not in practice. One explanation that still carries favour within popular and public policy circles is that female emancipation has led to increases in women and girls' crime. But even recognition of sophisticated ideas about women's changing participation in social life comes nowhere near explaining the dramatic shift in the prison figures. The notion of a feminist backlash doesn't provide enormous help either, although there is awareness that new regimes of governance do bring women into the criminal justice net rather more than previously.

To add to this dismal scenario, between 20% and 25% of women in prison are likely to be on remand at any one point; most women serve sentences of under a year. A high proportion of women prisoners receive help for mental health/emotional problems in the year prior to custody, and a significant proportion of women in prison self-harm. In 2004, there were 13 deaths from self-inflicted injuries in women's prisons and four in 2005; two-thirds of women in prison have drug problems and a further two-thirds have dependent children (the

living arrangements of at least 8,000 children a year are affected owing to their mothers' imprisonment). Moreover, the House of Commons Home Affairs Select Committee's First Report on the rehabilitation of offenders published in 2005 merely added to well-rehearsed concerns about the continuing failure to adapt rehabilitative programmes to the needs of women.

In sum, although there have been some increases in women's crime, they do not amount to a radical change in patterns of offending which might account for the radical change in sentencing; women continue to commit property-related crimes in the main, they commit crimes less often than men and they commit less serious crimes than men on the whole. But more of them are being sentenced to imprisonment.

There have long been problems in the sentencing of women, not least because of the tendency to configure sentences on the basis of perceptions of women's 'needs' rather than their 'deeds'. Successive generations of scholars and practitioners alike have highlighted the ways in which common constructions of gender appropriate behaviour have shaped sentencing. The Criminal Justice Act of 1991 – with all its focus on desert and proportionality and formal procedural justice – seemingly did nothing to limit the ways in which traditional gender discourses clouded perceptions of seriousness and desert. The sentencing of women continued to suggest separations of 'troubled' and 'troublesome' behaviour (Hedderman and Gelsthorpe 1997).

The major review of sentencing which heralded the Criminal Justice Act 2003 (the Halliday Report, Home Office 2001) offered much potential to sort out sentencing. Beyond expressing disappointment that the review was not more far-reaching, Elaine Player (2005) has rightly pointed to the ways in which the new legislation both reflects the government's commitment to the formal equality of consistent sentencing (desert) whilst at the same time establishing new penal aims: punishment, the reduction of crime by deterrence, reform and rehabilitation, the protection of the public, and the making of reparation by offenders. Thus the way is made clear for needs and risks and individualised sentencing to come to the fore. Will this help women? Will it help keep more of them out of custody? Given what we know about the sentencing of women in the past, when concerns for proportionality have been both wittingly and unwittingly overshadowed by 'women's needs', this seems highly unlikely. On the contrary, the introduction of new penal aims may well introduce new risks for women offenders. The new aims, perhaps, give licence to what sentencers were doing anyway in their sentencing of women. Making desert but one of a number of aims perhaps gives a green light to uptariffing women on the sentencing ladder so that their needs can be addressed via different sentencing options.

In terms of the actual sentencing provisions in the Act, there are worries regarding the possibility that intermittent custody (part week in prison, part week out of prison) will have the unintended consequence of more women being sentenced to custody than hitherto (if mothers are at home for at least part of the week then it might be thought that their imprisonment will not be wholly disruptive of children's lives). Thus there is another green light here for uptariffing.

I have particular concerns about the new sentence called Custody Plus. This is a term used by the CJA 2003 to describe the licence component of a term of imprisonment of less than twelve months. So all sentences of less than twelve months will consist of (i) a short 'custodial period', and then (ii) a longer 'licence period' during which, by way of an innovation – the offender must comply with one or more requirements set by the court as part of the sentence (chosen from a statutory menu – but a shorter menu than that in relation to the generic community sentence – mental health treatment, drug rehabilitation, and alcohol treatment, for example, are all missing from the Custody Plus menu (presumably it is thought that such problems will be resolved during the custodial part of the sentence ...)). As noted, many women in prison do have mental health and substance abuse problems, but these are commonly enduring problems and not ones which are going to be resolved during a short custodial sentence. So their absence from the 'Plus' menu is both perplexing and worrying.

This new sentence also raises the spectre of sentencers of the past remanding women in custody to give them a 'dose of what they don't want' and 'to scare them off' and then giving them a community penalty to deal with 'what they need'.

There is surely a danger that Custody Plus will lower the custody threshold as courts are attracted to the 'short, sharp shock' element of the custody period – assured that it will be followed up by supervision and support in the community.

In early May 2006, Lord Bassam, Junior Government Minister, announced a delay in the implementation of Custody Plus on grounds that the probation service would not be able to cope at present (probation staff have claimed that they need at least a 15% increase in staffing). Given that probation practice is increasingly risk-driven (resources necessarily following those who present the highest risk of reoffending, and this is certainly confirmed in the NOMS National Offender Management Model), there are huge concerns that women, who tend to present lower risks as offenders, will not receive adequate attention and support from the probation service. This is not from a lack of good intention or willingness, but it reflects past practice and the lack of resources. We also know that there is a lack of women-specific community provision and work placements, and as a result, women have sometimes had to travel far to complete punishments in the community. Put this together with women's childcare responsibilities and we can see that it may be particularly difficult for women to complete the 'Plus' requirements of their sentences unless there is adequate probation service provision. The ultimate consequence of patchy or thin provision for women may mean breaches and more imprisonment for them.

In March 2005, Charles Clarke, then Home Secretary, announced the award of £9.15 million for pilot community initiatives specifically for women offenders over a four-year period. However, compared with the cost of imprisoning women (estimated at around £35,000 for every prisoner), this is a small sum of money, and there are only two such initiatives anyway. Would that there could be more such initiatives to support women in the community. This might circumvent the potential negative consequences of the 2003 Act. We've said it before, but we seem to have to say it again, and again, and again, that new sentencing provisions need to be 'gender proofed' in a way that ensures that women's needs are recognised.

From L. Gelsthorpe, 'Counterblast: women and criminal justice: saying it again, again and again', Howard Journal of Criminal Justice, *2006, 45(4): 421–424.*

References

Carlen, P. (Ed.) (2002) *Women and Punishment: The Struggle for Justice*. Cullompton: Willan.

Deakin, J. and Spencer, J. (2003) Women behind bars: explanations and implications. *Howard Journal*, 42, 123–36.

Gelsthorpe, L. and Morris, A. (2002) Women's imprisonment in England and Wales: A penal paradox. *Criminal Justice*, 2(3), 277–301.

Hedderman, C. (2004) Why are more women being sentenced to custody? In: G. McIvor (Ed.), *Women Who Offend*. London: Jessica Kingsley.

Hedderman, C. and Gelsthorpe, L. (1997) *Understanding the Sentencing of Women* (Home Office Research Study 170). London: Home Office.

Home Office (2001) *Making Punishments Work: Report of a Review of the Sentencing Framework for England and Wales* (The Halliday Report). London: Home Office.

House of Commons Home Affairs Select Committee (2005) Rehabilitation of Prisoners, HC 193–1.

Player, E. (2005) The reduction of women's imprisonment in England and Wales. *Punishment and Society*, 7(4), 419–39.

32.2 The woman of legal discourse
Carol Smart

How law is gendered

There are three phases we can identify in the development of the idea that law is gendered. These are basically stages of reflection in feminist theory which have provided a foundation of understanding and have been largely, but not entirely, superseded (see also Naffine, 1990). The first stage is epitomized by the phrase 'law is sexist', the second by the phrase 'law is male', and finally we reach the point of arguing that 'law is gendered'. These three levels of argument may be found to be deployed simultaneously in some feminist work on law, however, it is useful to differentiate between them in order to see what analytical promise each approach has.

Law is sexist

The starting point of the 'law is sexist' approach was the argument that in differentiating between men and women, law actively disadvantaged women by allocating to them fewer material resources (for example, in marriage and on divorce), or by judging them by different and inappropriate standards (for example, as sexually promiscuous), or by denying them equal opportunities (for example, the 'person' cases, Sachs and Wilson, 1978), or by failing to recognize the harms done to women because these very harms advantaged men (for example, prostitution and rape laws). These were (and remain) important insights, but the attribution 'sexist' really operated more as a strategy of redefinition than as a mode of analysis. Thus the attribution of the label 'sexist' was a means of challenging the normative order in law and reinterpreting such practices as undesirable and unacceptable.

Law is undoubtedly sexist at one level. However, this attribution did not really begin to tap the problem that law poses and does, I would suggest, slightly misrepresent the problem. The argument that law is sexist suggests that a corrective could be made to a biased vision of a given subject who stands before law in reality as competent and rational as a man, but who is mistaken for being incompetent and irrational. This corrective suggests that law suffers from a problem of perception which can be put right such that all legal subjects are treated equally. This form of argument is by no means a simplistic one. It is framed with different degrees of sophistication from those who suggest that the introduction of gender neutral language into law rids us of the problem of differentiation and hence discrimination (e.g., spouse instead of wife, parent instead of mother) to those who appreciate that discrimination is part of a system of power relations which needs to be addressed before the sexism can be 'extracted'. For the former, sexism is a surface problem to be tackled by re-education programmes and a rigorous policy of hiding visible signs of difference. For the latter, law is embedded in politics and culture and the route to fairer treatment for women lies in changes which will allow women to occupy different positions in society so that differentiation will become redundant.

The problem with these approaches is that the meaning of differentiation tends to become collapsed into the meaning of discrimination and the fulcrum of the argument rests with the idea that women are treated badly in law because they are differentiated from men. It is often remarked that this means that men are retained as the standard by which women must be judged. Irksome and nonsensical as this may seem, pointing it out only leads us to imagine that judging women by the standard of women is the solution. This may not be a great leap forward if those women who set the standard are white and middle class. If they are, we are left with an equally problematic legal system in which sexism is apparently eradicated but other forms of oppression remain. But this fallacy of substitution is not the core problem of a perspective which invokes the concept of sexism rather than gendering. The concept of sexism implies that we can override sexual difference as if it were epiphenomenal rather than embedded in how we comprehend and negotiate the social order. Stating it more boldly, sexual difference – whether we see it as constructed or not (Fuss, 1989) – is part of the binary structure of language and meaning. If eradicating discrimination is dependent on the eradication of differentiation, we have to be able to think of a culture without gender. Thus what seems like a relatively easy solution such as the incorporation of gender-neutral terminology into law, masks a much deeper problem. Moreover, as many feminists have argued, it is not at all certain that the desired outcome of feminism is some form of androgyny.

Law is male

The idea that 'law is male' arises from the empirical observation that most lawmakers and lawyers are indeed male. It transcends this starting point, however, because of the realization that maleness or masculinity, once embedded in values and practices, need not be exhaustively anchored to the male biological referent, i.e., men. Thus MacKinnon (1987) has made the point most eloquently when she argues that ideals of objectivity and neutrality which are celebrated in law are actually masculine values which have come to be taken as universal values. Thus, in comparison to the 'law is sexist' approach, this analysis suggests that when a man and woman stand before the law, it is not that law fails to apply objective criteria when faced with the feminine subject, but precisely that it does apply objective criteria and these criteria are masculine. To insist on equality, neutrality and objectivity is thus, ironically, to insist on being judged by the values of masculinity.

As with the 'law is sexist' approach, the 'law is male' perspective covers a range of more or less sophisticated positions. From the early work of Gilligan (1982) which *seemed* to attach male or masculine values to the biological referent and thus appeared biologically reductionist, to more recent work (Young, 1990; Tronto, 1989; Mossman, 1986) which details the exclusion of values of caring in preference for 'uncaring' (i.e., impartiality), or the actual rules and methods for arriving at the legal (and hence impartial) decision by systematic exclusion of other perspectives.

Yet, important as these insights are, they perpetuate a number of specific problems. Firstly, this approach perpetuates the idea of law as a unity rather than problematizing law and dealing with its internal contradictions. Secondly, and without necessarily being explicit, this approach presumes that any system founded on supposedly universal values and impartial decision making (but which is now revealed to be particular and partial) serves in a systematic way the interests of men as a unitary category. We can see, therefore, that while great care is taken in these arguments to effect a distance from a biological determinism, there lingers an unstated presumption that men as a biological referent either benefit or are somehow celebrated in the rehearsal of values and practices which claim universality while (in reality) reflecting a partial position or world view. Yet we know that law does not serve the interests of men as a homogeneous category any more than it serves the interests of women as a category. It might, of course, be argued that these authors do not make this connection between male value systems and the interests of men and that I am forcing their argument to the sort of limits where any argument would start to look absurd. But there is a reason for stretching this argument, perhaps unfairly, which does not lie in the rather futile desire to show that no feminist argument transcends biological reductionism.

Any argument that starts with ceding priority to the binary division of male/female or masculine/feminine walks into the trap of demoting other forms of differentiation, particularly differences within these binary opposites. Thus the third problem with this sort of approach is that divisions such as class, age, race, religion tend to become mere additives or afterthoughts. This process of adding 'variables' which appears on the face of it to overcome the criticism of racism and classism levelled against feminist theory, in fact merely compounds the problem by obscuring it.

Law as gendered

The shift between taking 'law as male' and taking 'law as gendered' is fairly subtle, and the transition does not entail a total rejection of all the insights of the former. But while the assertion that 'law is male' effects a closure in how we think about law, the idea of it as gendered allows us to think of it in terms of processes which will work in a variety of ways and in which there is no relentless assumption that whatever it does exploits women and serves men. Thus we can argue that '[t]he same practices signify differently for men and women because they are read through different discourses' (Hollway, 1984: 237). So we do not have to consider that a practice is harmful to women because it is applied differently in relation to men. Rather, we can assess practices like, for example, imprisonment without being forced to say that the problem of women's prisons is that they are not like men's. But further, the idea of 'law as gendered' does not require us to have a fixed category or empirical referent of Man and Woman. We can now allow for the more fluid notion of a gendered subject position which is not fixed by either biological psychological or social determinants to sex. Within this analysis we can turn our focus to those strategies which attempt to do the 'fixing' of gender to rigid systems of meaning rather than falling into this practice ourselves.

This means we can begin to see the way in which law insists on a specific version of gender differentiation, without having to posit our own form of differentiation as some kind of starting or finishing point. We can therefore avoid the pitfall of asserting a pre-cultural Woman against which to measure patriarchal distortions (i.e., a starting point), as well as avoiding a Utopianism which envisions what women will be once we overcome patriarchy (i.e., the finishing point). Thus we can take on board the sort of argument made by Allen (1987) in relation to the way in which law can only see and think a gendered subject without invoking the same form of differentiation ourselves. Her argument is worth rehearsing here. She

examines the use of the concept the 'reasonable man' in criminal law. It has always been taken to be an 'objective test' of *mens rea* (guilty intent) but Allen demonstrates the sheer impossibility of this proposition. She states:

> Legal discourse thus incorporates a sexual division not only into what the law can legitimately 'do,' in terms of particular provisions and procedures, but also, more profoundly, into what it can reasonably argue. Yet beneath even this we can trace a third and yet deeper level of sexual division in legal discourse – at the level of what the law can intelligibly think. What is revealed in these arguments is that ultimately legal discourse simply cannot conceive of a subject in whom gender is not a determining attribute: it cannot think such a subject.
>
> (Allen, 1987: 30)

With this approach we can deconstruct law as gendered in its vision and practices, but we can also see how law operates as a technology of gender (de Lauretis, 1987). That is to say we can begin to analyse law as a process of producing fixed gender identities rather than simply as the application of law to previously gendered subjects.

The revised understanding of 'law as gendered' rather than as sexist or male has led to a modified form of enquiry. Instead of asking 'How law can transcend gender?' the more fruitful question has become, 'How does gender work in law and how does law work to produce gender?' What is important about these enquiries is that they have abandoned the goal of gender neutrality. Moreover, law is now redefined away from being that system which can impose gender neutrality towards being one of the systems (discourses) that is productive not only of gender difference, but quite specific forms of polarized difference. Law is seen as bringing into being both gendered subject positions as well as (more controversially?) subjectivities or identities to which the individual becomes tied or associated. It is therefore appropriate, at this stage in the argument, to turn to the concept of law as a gendering strategy which needs to be read in conjunction with the idea of 'law as gendered'.

Law as a gendering strategy

In this section my argument will develop the point that Woman is a gendered subject position which legal discourse brings into being. This is of course a sweeping statement; one that will invoke the cry that women have always existed, they did not have to wait for law to give them entry into the Social, that law is hardly so powerful, that women are the product of natural, biological processes and so on. [...]

Woman is no longer self-evident (Riley, 1988; Hekman, 1990; Spelman, 1988; Butler, 1990; Fuss, 1939). Such a statement is, of course, an affront to common sense which knows perfectly well what women are and reacts keenly should anyone try to blur the naturally given boundaries between the two (also naturally given) sexes. Yet first we must concede a distinction between Woman and women. This is familiar to feminists who have for some centuries argued that the *idea* of Woman (sometimes the *ideal* of Woman) is far removed from real women. Moreover, feminism has typically claimed an access to real women denied those who perceive the world through patriarchal visions. So the distinction between Woman and women is not new but it has become more complex. For example, we have begun to appreciate that Woman is not simply a patriarchal ideal and that the women that feminism(s) invoke(s) are perhaps the Woman of/constructed by feminist discourse(s) rather than an unmediated reality simply brought to light. In other words, the claim to an absolute reality located in the body of women against which the excesses of patriarchy can be measured has become less tenable. Feminism does not 'represent' women. [...]

Some have argued that this form of thinking removes feminism's constituency and thus threatens feminism as a political and social movement. However, this assumes that both intellectual innovation and political work must have an absolute, unmediated object of knowledge on which to ground itself. This requirement seems to be set stringently for any forms of poststructuralist feminism, while many other feminisms are allowed to operate on the basis of 'as if'. Indeed, feminism has long taken issue with common sense and its counterpart the 'unmediated real'; recognizing the cultural and historical elements of knowledge and rejecting the claim to a transcendental authority. So if we accept that Woman and women are not reducible to biological categories or – at the very least – that biological signs are not essences which give rise to a homogeneous category of women, we can begin to acknowledge that there are strategies by which Woman/women are brought into being. These strategies (in which I include law as well as

discipline) vary according to history and culture, they are also contradictory and even ambivalent. They may also be strategies without authors in as much as we should not imagine that strategy here implies a plan, masterminded in advance by extra-cultural (Cartesian) actors.

There is, of course, a distinction to be made between the discursive production of a type of Woman and the discursive construction of Woman. I want to invoke both of these meanings because it is my argument that they work symbiotically. Put briefly the (legal) discursive construction of a type of Woman might refer to the female criminal, the prostitute, the unmarried mother, the infanticidal mother and so on. The discursive construction of Woman, on the other hand, invokes the idea of Woman in contradistinction to Man. This move always collapses or ignores differences within categories of Woman and Man in order to give weight to a supposedly prior differentiation – that between the sexes. Thus this prior differentiation acts as a foundationalist move on which other differentiations can be grounded. Thus the female criminal is a type who can be differentiated from other women but, at the same time, what she is is abstracted from the prior category of Woman always already opposed to Man.

Thus she may be an abnormal woman because of her distance from other women, yet simultaneously she celebrates the natural difference between Woman and Man. Only by understanding this double move can we comprehend what we might otherwise mistake for inconsistency or oversight. Rather than taking it as a contradiction which can be resolved by the application of a little logic, we should recognize that the very foundation of the discursive construct of modern Woman is mired in this double strategy.

Thus Woman has always been *both* kind and killing, active and aggressive, virtuous and evil, cherishable and abominable, not *either* virtuous or evil. Woman therefore represents a dualism, as well as being one side of a prior binary distinction. Thus in legal discourse the prostitute is constructed as the bad woman, but at the same time she epitomizes Woman in contradistinction to Man because she is what any woman could be and because she represents a deviousness and a licentiousness arising from her (supposedly naturally given) bodily form, while the man remains innocuous.

While these strategies which produce gender are many and varied, I want to tell a straightforward story so that I can reach my topic of law without too much further delay. It has been argued that the end of the eighteenth century and the nineteenth century in Britain marked an important moment in the history of gender. What was witnessed was a polarization of genders in which difference became increasingly fixed and rigid, and at the same time was naturalized (Davidoff and Hall, 1987; Jordonova, 1989; Laqueur, 1990). Scientific discourses were central to this process, giving new rigour to traditional religious and philosophical beliefs about the inferiority of women. Women became more and more closely associated with their bodies, and their bodies became both overdetermining and pathological. It becomes possible to argue that scientific, medical and later psychoanalytic discourses operated to create the very gender differences we have come to take for granted as natural but, more importantly, these discourses have rendered natural the ideal of natural differences. At the same moment, of course, feminism was constructing a very different Woman, one who was not a semi-invalid (if middle class) nor sexually licentious and vicious (if working class). Yet even this feminist discourse fixed difference in the realm of the natural.

For my analysis of law, the nineteenth century is also particularly significant. This century marks both the pinnacle of law's exclusion of women from civil society (e.g., the denial of the legal personality of married women) and the moment when written law began to inscribe in finer and finer detail the legal disabilities of Woman. (Put another way, we can say that gender became increasingly fixed in terms of its attributes and in terms of being increasingly polarized.) At the most basic of levels we can see that legislation dating from the eighteenth century and before was sketchy in its terms and succinct to a fault (at least to twentieth-century eyes). But the nineteenth century marks a moment in which there grows a greater refinement and a 'pinning down' of relevant categories and legal subjects.

We could therefore claim that nineteenth-century law brought a more tightly defined range of gendered subject positions into place. We can also see how law and discipline 'encouraged' women to assume these identities or subjectivities. This idea is perhaps best pursued with an example and the one I wish to trace concerns motherhood, but not the good mother, or even the 'good enough' mother – I am interested in the bad mother.

An example of law as a gendering strategy: specifying the category of the bad mother

Although I have specified the nineteenth century as a particularly significant moment in the fixing of gendered identities, I shall start my story earlier than this in order to identify how the nineteenth-century engagement of law and discipline, as two different forms of regulation, marks a break with earlier periods.

Thus my story begins in 1623 in England. In that year a new statute was introduced, creating a new crime and criminal. The statute made it a penal offence for a mother to kill her bastard infant on pain of death. The point about this new law was that the mother was to be presumed guilty if her infant died, and it was for her to provide evidence of her innocence. A presumption of guilt was extremely rare in English law and so the unmarried mother was brought into being in law as a culpable murderer. It should be stressed that at this time the state did not regulate marriage or even insist on formal marriage and so the condition of being married or not married was in some ways more fluid, especially as some people did not marry until they had several children together.

Thus we have the problematization of a specific form of motherhood. Its regulation was to take the form identified by Foucault (1977) as the power of the sovereign to inflict death. This woman is perhaps one of the first to enter into statute specifically as Woman. Her entry marks a number of associations which are implicit yet must be understood for the legislation to make any sense. Not only is she unmarried and hence without protection, she occupies a specific class position (i.e., poor), she is deprived of the material conditions to raise a child, yet she is to be put to death for seeking to escape her plight – even if the child died of natural causes (or the effects of poverty on pregnancy and childbirth).

This piece of legislation was so draconian that it was rarely enforced because juries failed to convict. We can, however, map how the strategy of inflicting harsh punishment on the few became translated into modes of discipline and surveillance of the many. The penalties became less harsh, but fewer women could escape the reach of the revised forms of legal categorization.

In 1753, Lord Hardwick's Marriage Act began the process of regulating marriage such that there no longer existed indeterminate states of semi-matrimony – women were either married or unmarried. In 1803, the draconian Infanticide Act of 1623 was transformed into legislation against the concealment of birth. A presumption of innocence was restored and the penalty much reduced. However, its aim was to bring more women into the reach of the law because there was no requirement to establish murder. In the same year (1803) the first criminal statute on abortion was introduced. Abortion at any stage of pregnancy was criminalized and, although there was a distinction made between the pre- and post-quickening stages, this was later removed. English law never criminalized the introduction and sale of information on birth control (as, for example, Canadian law did), but the spread of such information was effectively controlled by the use of private prosecutions against blasphemous or obscene libel. In 1882 the age of consent was raised to 13 and in 1885 to 16. Thus marriage could not take place before these ages and this exposed young women who became pregnant, but could not marry, to legal and philanthropic scrutiny. In 1913 the Mental Defective Act facilitated the incarceration of unmarried mothers on the grounds of moral imbecility or feeble-mindedness.

My point is not just that these different forms of law constructed a category of dangerous motherhood, but that the net of law widened at precisely the same time as it made it increasingly difficult to avoid unmarried pregnancy and childbirth. The end of the nineteenth and early part of the twentieth century also coincides with the problem of the surplus woman, who had no chance of marrying anyway because of the export of men to the colonies or their slaughter in various wars.

The penalties (especially for infanticide) became less harsh, but more women were caught in the net of inescapable motherhood. If they attempted to escape through the use of contraception or abortion they were condemned as prostitutes or (virtual) murderers, if they failed they were subject to newer forms of discipline in the shape of philanthropy and mental health legislation/provision. We can see, therefore, how motherhood was actually materially constructed as a 'natural', hence unavoidable, consequence of heterosex. Means of avoiding motherhood were denied to women, and the inevitability of the link between sex and reproduction was established through the harsh repression of those deploying traditional means of rupturing this link. [...]

The unmarried mother obviously served (and still serves) to reinforce our cultural understanding of what 'proper' motherhood means. In this sense she is a type of woman rather than Woman. Yet she simultaneously operates in the discourse as Woman because she always invokes the proper place of Man. She is the problem (supposedly) because she does not have a man. Therefore Man is the solution, he signifies the stability, legitimacy and mastery which is not only absent in her but inverted. The unmarried mother is therefore also quintessential Woman because she represents all those values which invert the desirable characteristics of Man.

At this point it may appear that my concerns are with the symbolic. However, my interests extend beyond this because my purpose in mapping the development of the legal subject 'unmarried mother' is to throw light on the dominant regime of meaning which always already treats this woman as problematic and destabilizing. Just as Foucault has shown that categories such as the criminal or the homosexual are not pre-existing entities to be investigated and understood by science, so we can also see that the unmarried mother comes into being as a consequence of specific strategies and knowledges. While she is not a fixed or unchanging category she enters into an established web of meanings which make instability and dangerousness virtually self-evident and matters of common sense.

The significance of this for the contemporary situation is that more and more women can be fitted into this category. The Act of 1623 that I started with affected relatively few women. Now the category includes the never married and the divorced lone mother. (The widow is rarely included because she is thought to keep the symbolic father alive, and so is hardly a lone mother.) More recently this category has extended further to include the 'surrogate' mother and the woman seeking infertility treatment. I should therefore like to close with a contemporary example. In 1990 the British Parliament passed a piece of legislation entitled the Human Fertilisation and Embryology Act. Section 13(5) reads,

A woman shall not be provided with treatment services unless account has been taken of the welfare of any child who may be born as a result of the treatment (including the need of that child for a father)...

This legislation also continues the fiction that a woman's husband is the father of her children even if he is not biologically related to them and creates a new form of illegitimacy by insisting that the husband and biological father of a child will not be treated as the legal father if his sperm was used or if an embryo of his was implanted after his death.

These measures are nonsensical unless you already know that the mother without a husband is a danger.

Concluding remarks

From where I stand, feminist socio-legal scholarship faces two main tasks at the beginning of the 1990s. The first is to grasp the nettle that law is not simply law, by which I mean it is not a set of tools or rules which we can bend into a more favourable shape. [...] Thus we should see the power of law as more than that negative sanction that holds women down. Law is also productive of gender difference and identity, yet this law is not monolithic and unitary.

Moreover, much more work needs to be done in tracing how women have resisted and negotiated constructions of gender, since we should not slip into a new form of determinism which suggests that, because power constructs, it produces women in some predetermined, calculated, powerless form. I am suggesting therefore that law remains a valid focus of feminist theoretical and political scrutiny, but that we need to recast our understanding of the relationship between 'law' and 'gender'.

From C. Smart, 'The woman of legal discourse', Social and Legal Studies, *1992, 1: 29–44.*

References

Allen, H. (1987) *Justice Unbalanced.* Milton Keynes: Open University Press.

Butler, J. (1990) *Gender Trouble.* London: Routledge.

Davidoff, L. and Hall, C. (1987) *Family Fortunes.* London: Hutchinson.

de Lauretis, T. (1987) *Technologies of Gender.* Bloomington, IN: Indiana University Press.

Foucault, M. (1977) *Discipline and Punish.* London: Allen Lane.

Fuss, D. (1989) *Essentially Speaking.* London: Routledge.

Gilligan, C. (1982) *In a Different Voice.* London: Harvard University Press.

Hekman, S. (1990) *Gender and Knowledge.* Boston, MA: Northeastern University Press.

Hollway, W. (1984) Gender difference and the production of subjectivity. In Henriques, J. *et al.* (Eds), *Changing the Subject.* London: Methuen.

Jordonova, L. (1989) *Sexual Visions.* London: Harvester.

Laqueur, T. (1990) *Making Sex.* Boston, MA: Harvard University Press.

MacKinnon, C. (1987) *Feminism Unmodified.* London: Harvard University Press.

Mossman, M.J. (1986) Feminism and legal method: The difference it makes. *Australian Journal of Law and Society* 3: 30–52.

Naffine, N. (1990) *Law and the Sexes.* Sydney: Allen & Unwin.

Riley, D. (1988) *Am I That Name?* London: Macmillan.

Sachs, A. and Wilson, J.H. (1978) *Sexism and the Law.* Oxford: Martin Robertson.

Spelman, E. (1988) *Inessential Woman.* Boston, MA: Beacon Press.

Tronto, J. (1989) Women and caring: What can feminists learn about morality from caring? In Jaggar, A. and Bordo, S. (Eds), *Gender/Body/Knowledge.* London: Rutgers University Press.

Young, I.M. (1990) *Justice and the Politics of Difference.* Princeton, NJ: Princeton University Press.

32.3 Women and social control
Frances Heidensohn

'Social control' is a term which has become associated with two rather different approaches to the study of crime and deviance. In the first place, it is a key concept in the interactionist and other approaches to deviance. [...] [Numerous] studies have demystified social control, showing, for example how attempts to combat crime by bringing in more policemen, can actually increase its recorded incidence, or that repeated imprisonment is very unlikely to 'reform' offenders. Second, a specific set of theories called 'control theories' has been developed over the past two decades which have emphasised bonding – in relation to family, peer group and school – as a control mechanism which reduces criminality. In further refinements, situational characteristics are linked to bonds to explain patterns of delinquency. Both approaches to social control have considerable salience for the understanding of female criminality.

Women in control

Women participate in a number of areas of society where their roles in the control of others are very important. These are:

1 the traditional domestic sphere of the home – 'the angel in the house';

2 the traditional community – the village street or tribe – 'the wisewoman and her kin';

3 the world of early modern welfare – what Hearn (1982) has called the 'patriarchal feminine';

4 the world of modern welfare, of the feminine semi-professional.

'The angel in the house'

Coventry Patmore's verses extolling the submissive, self-effacing wife are the poetic expression of an ideological view propounded by Rousseau and all-too-many other political philosophers (Elshtain, 1981). Women are the gentler, weaker sex. They bear and love children, they are also more childlike. It is therefore their duty to rear and nurture the next generation and to provide supportive services for their menfolk. Rousseau put it thus:

> Woman's reign is a reign of gentleness, tact, and kindness; her commands are caresses, her threats are tears. She should reign in the home as a minister reigns in the state...

and he of course advocated consequently differing educational paths for boys and girls. [...]

Elshtain summarised the importance of this concern for the female role for social control – for, indeed, the stability of society itself:

> Women are a softening influence; they purvey moral values and sentiments to the young; they are the civilizers of children, and, sometimes of men. It follows ... that when women are unchaste, unfaithful, unseemly, vain, or frivolous, *their ostensibly private behaviour is suffused with public implications*. Why? Because the basis of male public citizenship would disintegrate if his private world collapsed, as the citizen is also, necessarily a husband-father, the head of a household.
>
> (Elshtain, 1981, pp. 161–2, emphasis added)

[...] Even if voices such as these are now rather quieter about what women *cannot* do especially in the 'public' world of men, the tasks women are required to carry out to ensure stability in civil society are awesome.

Amongst the most conspicuous are that women are charged with producing fit, healthy children who will grow up to be well-adjusted citizens, accepting their gender roles, capable of benefiting from education and of contributing to society (Dally, 1982; Badinter, 1981; Oakley, 1980; Ehrenreich and English, 1979). While rearing the next generation, women must maintain high (indeed increasingly high) standards of domestic order so that their husbands and children have clean, comfortable refuges to return to from the toil of the day (Oakley, 1974; Wilson, 1977; Land, 1981).

It is also assumed that marriage to a 'good woman' will limit the delinquent proclivities of young men and that, once settled into a situation where he is cared for and occupied, a young criminal will mature out of his misdeeds (Mannheim, 1940; Fyvel, 1963). In recent times, with the development of more humane policies for the treatment of vulnerable groups such as mentally ill, mentally handicapped, disabled and elderly people, a new set of expectations are being – implicitly at least – focussed on women in the home. [...]

Failure by women to comply with these expectations is finally blamed by numerous observers for increases in public disorder. [...]

Although women with family responsibilities have been working outside the home as well as within in increasing numbers for the past thirty years, neither domestic expectations of them nor their achievements have diminished. Women still carry a double burden of two roles with very little help from husbands or partners. [...] Women, in short, in their roles as wives and mothers undertake the crucial basic tasks of care, containment and socialisation, crucial that is to the maintenance of order in society. Their investment, therefore, in that society's stability is clearly enormous despite, or perhaps because of the fact that their participation is within a context defined and dominated by men.

Wisewomen and their kin

We can distinguish at least four aspects of local community life in which women have played prominent and distinctive parts. The scripts they have followed have not had such prescriptive and exclusive moral requirements as those for the 'angel in the house'. Nevertheless, women have played vital and significant parts for social order:

1 in the maintenance of informal social networks;

2 in tending the sick, the old, etc., in their own communities;

3 in various types of ritual and other informal social control;

4 in using specialised skills and crafts as midwives, wisewomen, etc., for the community's benefit.

A considerable array of moralists and social scientists have agreed that women are the primary producers of the bonds and fabric of society. It is women who maintain links with the extended family (Young and Wilmott, 1957 and 1960; Frankenberg, 1976) and who compensate for deficiencies in local provision, whether in housing, pre-school care of children or informal supervision of the old (Cohen, 1978; Hadley and Hatch, 1981; Caplan and Bujra (eds), 1978) with their own work in a voluntary and unstructured capacity. Social relationships are the basis of normative order in society and it seems to be agreed that women do much of the work of succouring and sustaining those relationships.

Caring in their own localities for those who cannot care for themselves is a task left largely to women and expected of them. [...]

Pressures on women to participate in the maintenance of order through social relationships and community care have probably not diminished in industrial society, although their character has altered. There have, however, been considerable changes in women's informal participation in the control and chastising of deviant behaviour in local communities. Social historians have contributed very interesting analyses of the various ceremonies used in preindustrial and early modern societies to mock unruly or deviant behaviour or to prevent its continuance. [...] Men clearly played a part in these activities, though as Pearson notes, there were interesting acts of transvestism and 'misrule' in their participation (Pearson, 1983, pp. 197–202), but women's role was central to these rites in a way which largely ceased with the modern institutionalising of justice:

> Women had participated in the traditional forms of community regulation, but they were excluded almost completely from the formulation and administration of the new abstract forms of institutional control.
>
> (Dobash and Dobash, 1981)

These activities, as all observers emphasise, took place within the structure of patriarchal society and were designed to reinforce traditional norms and re-establish traditional patterns of behaviour. [...]

Far better documented are those contended areas of community life where traditional women's skills and craft roles have come into conflict with 'new men' who have sought to supersede them. Midwives were the original community health specialists, attending women in confinement and also overseeing aspects of child care. Several authors agree that medical men systematically conspired to down-grade and exclude the traditional midwife from obstetric care by establishing a paradigm of 'medical need' in childbirth. [...]

Two opposing trends can be noted in women's role in the maintenance of local communities. On the one hand industrialisation and the incorporation into formal, hierarchical structures of traditional customs led to women being excluded, except for a few middle class women, from activities to which they had once been central. On the other hand, the basic care and control tasks have increasingly been left to women who have been under growing pressure to shoulder them.

The patriarchal feminine and the semi-professions

So far we have looked at examples of women's role in social control without emphasising class distinctions. [...] Working-class women were increasingly excluded from the official public domain as working men fought for family wages and women became increasingly marginal and dependent in the labour market (Rowbotham, 1973, p.59). As we have seen, they were also being excluded at this time from informal community activities by the institutionalising of abstract justice. Middle- and upper-class women on the other hand, although they lived under the same economic and political disabilities as their poorer sisters, were participating more and more in voluntary welfare work. [...]

[T]heir work was primarily to gentle the masses, to make life for the poor a little more acceptable. Hearn in a very interesting analysis has shown how the development of what he called the 'patriarchal feminine' began in nineteenth-century voluntary organisations in which middle-class women served male professionals. Later, he argued, the semi-professions of nursing, midwifery, social work, etc., grew out of this basis, all retaining their subordination to male-dominated independent professions who still retain ultimate and true authority. Middle- and upper-class women have, then, some role and status in the public domain, but they are really, in Hearn's analysis, only able to keep these under the licence of patriarchal authority [...] It is women who overwhelmingly staff the socially-controlling semi-professions in health, education and social work, and it is usually women who hold the 'front-line' at the bedside, in benefit offices, the classroom, the courtroom or as 'gate-keepers' to welfare services. In that sense, these women and the public may believe that women are responsible for the system of social control. However, although the contribution made by women is immense – and it is, indeed impossible to imagine running welfare services without them – it is again true to say that women have been assimilated into the existing patriarchal system as professional handmaidens.

The control of women

Criminologists have, in general, looked too little at conformity, but this neglect is particularly striking with regard to women. [...] I shall look at the control of women on somewhat similar levels to those I used in the previous section, that is:

1 at home;

2 in public;

3 at work;

4 in social policies.

1. Domestic constraint

In a briskly polemical article entitled 'The coercion of privacy' DahI and Snare argued that women are privately and domestically imprisoned within the home:

> The nuclear family represents a prison comparable to the public institution carrying this label.
>
> (Dahl and Snare, 1978, p.22)

on a quantitative basis many more women are controlled through informal methods. A woman's seclusion fosters close control by children, husband and neighbours. Sociologically speaking the dominant tool is primary rather than secondary social control.

> (Dahl and Snare, 1978, p.21)

They went on to argue that women are too heavily supervised in the home to commit much crime and that this 'supervision' by husbands and family members is sanctioned, but not itself supervised. They seemed to mean preventive detention, rather than imprisonment as punishment [...].

Now to see the domestic life of women as a form of detention which constrains them from committing crimes may seem extreme, but consider this three-page advertisement which appeared in the glossy magazine *Options* in March 1984. It is headed 'Have you sentenced yourself to a life of hard labour?' In the centre is an authentic 'mugshot' and 'prison record' of a young woman whose 'crime' is given as 'housewife' and whose sentence is listed at '77 hours housework per week for life'. The copy then reads as follows:

> Next time your old man staggers home from the pub complaining about how hard he works, let him into a little secret. Which is that you probably work nearly twice as hard as he does. Because the average British housewife puts in a 77 hour week! No one should have to work that hard and no one needs to: some women manage to have plenty of free time. So what keeps your nose pressed firmly to the grindstone? In a word: You ... you're kept hard at it by a collection of attitudes and prejudices you're probably not even aware of!

That a bastion of commerce concurs in a feminist analysis of women's domestic oppression does not make that analysis correct, but it is a very significant congruence. [...]

In one sense, women can be seen as in private, solitary, domestic confinement, unlikely to stray because of both the role-constraints of motherhood and housewifery and the time-consuming nature of their tasks. Yet as many writers have pointed out, and feminists have increasingly stressed, women do not have the autonomy within the home that the term 'privacy' normally implies. If there are 'separate spheres' for men and women, this means in practice that women are banned from men's clubs, not that men are banned from clubbing women at home.

'Prison' is perhaps more a meaningful metaphor for women's domestic position than an actual description of it, but many women are clearly disciplined and dominated in the home by domestic violence in ways which enormously constrain and confine what they can do. [...]

Carlen made very clear and telling links between women's isolation in the family, domestic violence and women's crimes in Scotland. After marriage, she argued, the women in her study were increasingly isolated and dependent, yet they were expected to maintain children and household order, often without resources:

> Women who had entertained the romantic notion that marriage would give them protection, full adult status and companionship had found instead that it gave them the triple burdens of increased responsibility, increased dependency and a deadening sense of increasing isolation from the world outside the home!
>
> (Carlen, 1983, p. 45)

Many of these women had been battered but Carlen suggested marital violence was just one part of the 'non-penal and informal disciplining of women' (Carlen, 1983, p. 44). The family relationships of women, she observed, were full of contradictions; yet the ultimate contradictions were reached when the women stepped outside the 'discipline' and protection of family life into alcoholism and crime. They were then much more likely to be punished formally if they were defined as 'outwith', in Carlen's term, family structures and control, *despite the fact* that all the sheriffs, prison staff and social workers agreed that the women's home conditions were often intolerable (Carlen, 1983, pp. 66–7). The final irony Carlen observed is that, once they are imprisoned, the penal system attempts to reimpose a domestic form of control on the female inmates. [...]

It is not my intention to suggest that the majority of women spend their lives locked into the domestic equivalent of Parkhurst with gaolers who are likely to beat or terrorise them into submission. I am proposing an ideal-typical analysis of family life and social control which involves very different meanings for men and for women within the same institution. While most women may not experience direct violence, nor collapse under intolerable burdens, domestic life is constituted as an elaborate series of constraints and expectations for women, supported by a very pervasive value system. [...]

Marriage and domesticity provide powerful controlling mechanisms to ensure the good behaviour of adult women. They are all the more powerful since they can largely be imposed with the willing, even eager, acquiescence of women themselves.

2. Public propriety

It is useful to distinguish three aspects of the control of women's public behaviour. All (since we are now in the public realm of observed behaviour and formal control) are related to forms of officially-determined deviance. They are:

1 the male quasi-monopoly of force and violence

2 the notion of reputation and 'name'

3 the ideology of separate spheres.

1 *Male violence* Men have almost total power over both legitimate and illegitimate means of force in our society. Legitimate force is of course, meant to be used in the defence of vulnerable women, children and the old, not against them. (Modern and past history show that this is an optimistic view.) However, women are unlike some powerless groups in that they have traditionally neither used legitimate 'force' or illegal 'violence' to attain their ends. The typical victim of public violent attack appears to be young, fit and male (Hough and Mayhew, 1983, p. 17). However, the same Home Office study which reported this finding also noted the discrepancy between actual risk of street violence and perceived fears:

> Around a third of women (but only 5 per cent of men) said they sometimes avoided going out on foot after dark in their neighbourhood for fear of crime.
>
> (Hough and Mayhew, 1983, p. 23)

[...] These authors also suggested that victimisation rates among women and the old may be lower *because of* their fears, which prevent them from going out – especially at night, – or in inner city areas (see Harrison, 1983, pp. 339-46 for some sadly graphic case histories of victims).

To general fears of crime and lawlessness in public places, women have to add the fear of sexual assault. [...]

Statistically, the true risk of being sexually assaulted or raped may be quite low, lower, for example, than the risk of injury in a traffic accident. But it is the fear and the consequent helplessness that are traditionally engendered in women which are relevant here. Undoubtedly these act as controlling agents on women's behaviour.

2 *The fear of ill-repute* [...] The attentive reader will not be surprised to learn that it is largely men, with some support from the feminine community, who control female reputations. One of the best-documented examples of this is the way in which teenage working-class males define females publicly in terms of their sexuality, and how this inhibits the latter's behaviour, or as Lees economically put: 'How boys slag off girls' (Lees, 1983, p. 51). [...]

Women researchers have got rather closer to teenage girls and actually recorded their views. The end result however, is, depressingly similar. Wilson found that her sample of working-class inner-city girls [...] differentiated between permissible and improper levels of sexual activity. She claimed that these girls themselves defined and monitored the sex codes and conduct. It is apparent, however, that they only did so within a framework policed and controlled by boys and by parents. Boys punished deviant girls by getting 'the girl's name... passed around the streets as being easy' (Wilson, 1978, p.71). [...]

Lees observed that girls cannot fight back when boys call them 'bitch, slag, slut'. Girls have no such vocabulary of male-abusing labels, and in any case, while boys may label girls wrongly and unfairly and be believed, the reverse is not true. Keeping a good reputation is extremely difficult 'The girls tread a very narrow line'. They must have the right kind of dress, demeanour, make-up and even speech. The effects on behaviour in public places is absolutely crucial. [...]

Other forms of labelling of females by males have not been as fully anatomised. There is, however, considerable evidence of similar processes at work in the lives of adult women. Whitehead (1976), for example, in her account of 'sexual antagonism in Herefordshire' described incidents of abuse, horseplay and scandal-mongering in a border village. She noted how rumours and hostile encounters 'can be seen as situations in which joking abuse is used by men to control the behaviour of women' (Whitehead, 1976, p. 179). [...]

For some women, of course, loss of reputation is not merely an anxiety which limits their social and sexual lives. For prostitutes, for some women alcoholics and for some 'bad' mothers the consequences of being labelled deviant are far more serious than once they were for 'witches'. [...]

Carlen (1983, ch. 7) and Otto (1981) both pointed out that drinking is less acceptable for women than men. Heavy drinking and alcoholism are therefore much more damaging to a woman's good name and she is likely to be regarded as far more delinquent and much less acceptable. Otto suggested that this has to do with women's role as mothers, 'No one likes to believe that the hand that rocks the cradle might be a shaky one'.

3 *Separate spheres and a woman's place* It is, I hope, clear from the foregoing that even in our own society today, women's behaviour in public places is bound by different rules from that of men. The chief difference is that men monitor and control women's behaviour [...].

Women, strictly speaking, are only supposed to be 'at home' at home. The public domain is men's and they control access to it and behaviour in it. [...]

What is ultimately most 'controlling' about the separation of spheres is that the insulation and isolation of private domestic life prevents (or has done so until recently) personal issues becoming political ones and real changes which could improve the status of women being achieved. Thus wife-battering was a secret crime until recently, and even now victims get little support from the police. Loneliness and depression, child-care problems and health have also, until recent years, been either ignored and invisible or treated individualistically as aspects of medical- or psycho-pathology.

3. At work

Three notable factors about women's work today add to the already strong normative constraints under which they have to manage their lives:

1 most women carry the burden of two roles – they have to cope with home and work;

2 although job segregation means that most women work with other women at women's work, most of their supervisors are men;

3 sexual harassment at work.

1 *Dual roles* It is generally agreed that while women have very considerably increased their commitments to paid work outside the home over the past thirty years, men have not put in any extra compensating activity in the home (Land, 1981). Women in consequence, do as much housework whether they go out to work or not and achieve great feats of ingenuity in fitting work and home responsibilities together. It is clear, too, that most married women have gone to work because of family needs. Many more families would have suffered poverty, had it not been for women's wages. [...]

2 *Hierarchies at work* Much as in the domestic sphere, men hold the controlling powers and authority as foremen, supervisors and managers. Trade union officials too are usually male and have been sharply criticised for the way in which they have manipulated, controlled or prevented women's collective action (Cunnison, 1983). Lown summed up succinctly the process of dominance in the workplace as 'Not so much a factory, more a form of patriarchy' (Lown, 1983, p. 28) [...]

3 *Sexual harassment* [...] Sexual harassment is also another constraint which operates to confine and inhibit women's activities at work. Many women report having left jobs they liked because of constant harassment (Hadjifotiou, 1983) while others have been made acutely ill or depressed and have their promotion chances affected and their working lives made miserable. [...]

The incidence of such harassment appears to be high – 60 per cent of women interviewed in one survey reported at least one incident. Surveys have failed to find serious examples of men sexually harassed by their female colleagues (Hadjifotiou, 1983, pp. 10–11).

4. Social policies

Social policies are not usually regarded as instruments whose prime purpose is the definition and enforcement of prescriptions about gender roles, especially for women, but a growing body of analyses shows that such prescriptions underpin, or are an effective part of certain policies. Several areas of policies assume that gender-roles, especially in the family, take particular forms for both men and women. On men, for example, falls the obligation to maintain their wives and children and indeed their common-law partners. What notably characterises the way women's roles and actions are prescribed in welfare provisions is that since these tend to regard married women and some single women as 'dependant', constraints applied to women are reinforced. Thus some women have not been able to claim benefits in their own right nor for their dependants. [...]

The ways in which social security systems define women's role, discourage work outside the home for some groups of women and assume that others will look after dependants within the home, are very complicated and can change with time. [...]

In both the widely-expressed values of our society and in the structure of that society are embodied particular notions of normal women and controls to ensure their production and conformity. This all works very 'successfully' despite many inherent contradictions and the very considerable costs to individual women. That is why understanding the control of women is so important to our appreciation of their criminality. Obviously since women are, in Hagan's term, 'over-controlled' they commit less crime and fewer serious and repeated offences. Even when they do deviate they do so within a particular man-made framework of controls. [...] Barbara Wootton pointed out many years ago that if men behaved like women the courts and prisons would be empty. Strictly speaking, that is not true, but it is very interesting to speculate on the reversal of the present system of social order. Could boys and men be contained as comprehensively as women have been?

From F. Heidensohn, 'Women and social control', in F. Heidensohn Women and Crime, *2nd ed.* (Basingstoke: Macmillan), 1996, pp. 163–195.

References

Badinter, E. (1981) *The Myth of Motherhood*. London: Souvenir Press.

Caplan, P. and Bujra, J. (1978) *Women United, Women Divided*. London: Tavistock.

Carlen, P. (1983) *Women's Imprisonment*. London: Routledge & Kegan Paul.

Cohen, G. (1978) Women's solidarity and the preservation of privilege. In Caplan, P. and Bujra, J. (Eds).

Cunnison, J. (1983) Trade union activity. in Garmanikow, E. *et al.* (Eds) *Gender Class and Work*. London: Heinemann.

Dahl,T. S. and Snare, A. (1978) The coercion of privacy. In Smart, C. and Smart, B. (Eds) *Women, Sexuality and Social Control.*, London: Routledge & Kegan Paul.

Dally, A. (1982) *Inventing Motherhood*. London: Burnett Books.

Dobash, R and Dobash, R.E. (1981) Community response to violence against wives: Charivari, abstract justice and patriarchy. *Social Problems*, 28(5).

Ehrenreich, B. and English, D. (1979) *For Her Own Good*. London: Pluto Press.

Elshtain, J. (1981) *Public Man, Private Woman*. Oxford: Martin Robertson.

Frankenberg, R. (1976) Sex and gender in British community studies. In Barker. D.L. and Allen, S. (Eds) *Sexual Divisions and Society*. London: Tavistock.

Fyvel, T.R.(1963) *The Insecure Offenders*. Harmondsworth: Penguin.

Hadjifotiou, N. (1983) *Women and Harassment at Work*. London: Pluto Press.

Hadley, R. and Hatch, S. (1981) *Social Welfare and the Failure of the State*. London: Allen & Unwin.

Harrison, P. (1983) *Inside the Inner City*. Harmondsworth: Penguin.

Hearn, J. (1982) Notes on patriarchy, professionalization and the semiprofessions. *Sociology*, 16(2).

Hough, M. and Mayhew, P. (1983) *The British Crime Survey*, Home Office Research Study no. 76, London: HMSO.

Land, H. (1981) *Parity Begins at Home*, Equal Opportunities Commission and Social Science Research Council Joint Panel on Equal Opportunities, London.

Lees, S. (1983) How boys slag off girls. *New Society*, 13 October.

Lown, J. (1983) Not so much a factory, more a form of patriarchy: Gender and class during industrialisation. In Garmamikow, E. *et al.* (Eds). *Gender, Class and Work*. London: Heinemann.

Mannheim, H. (1940) *Social Aspects of Crime in England Between the Wars*. London: Allen & Unwin.

Oakley, A. (1974) *The Sociology of Housework*. Oxford: Martin Robertson.

Oakley, A. (1980) *Women Confined: Towards a Sociology of Childbirth*. Oxford: Martin Robertson.

Otto, S. (1981) Women, alcohol and social control. In Hutter, B. and Williams, G. (Eds). *Controlling Women*. London: Croom Helm.

Pearson, G. (1983) *Hooligan: A History of Respectable Fears*. London: Macmillan.

Rowbotham S. (1973) Hidden from History, London: Pluto Press.

Whitehead, A. (1976) Sexual antagonism in Herefordshire. In Barker, D.L. and Allen, S. (Eds) *Dependence and Exploitation in Work and Marriage*. London: Longman.

Wilson, E. (1977) *Women and the Welfare State*. London: Tavistock.

Wilson, E. (1983) *What is to be Done About Violence Against Women?* Harmondsworth: Penguin,

Young, M. and Wilmott, P. (1957) *Family and Kinship in East London*. London: Routledge & Kegan Paul.

32.4 Common sense, routine precaution and normal violence Elizabeth A. Stanko

This chapter is about everyday routines of safety. These are not the habits of paranoid people who find difficulty in coping with the ordinary demands of daily life, but behaviours typical of adults. People develop these routines in order to avoid being constantly preoccupied with security: little rituals which seem to reduce their anxiety about danger. They take these measures in their homes, on the street or at work as safeguards against being attacked.

Some habits do not seem to have any conscious origin, but they are things people say they have always done or were once told to do by someone in authority. Such tips for safety are incorporated into our lives without much question, and we come to consider them as just good common sense. We pass them on to our children in the hope that they, too, will be safer and avoid danger.

If there's an occasional familiar ring to what people say in what follows, it's because many of us do similar things, including having rituals for locking and unlocking doors, choosing routes to and from shopping or work, protecting valuables inside and outside our homes, carrying money, travelling to strange places and assessing the who, what and where of safety. Some of us have habits few know about and we keep it this way for fear others might consider us odd. [...]

Although greater precautions are taken by women, both sexes pick up clues about what safeguards to use from their own individual circumstances. [...]

So when people speak about rituals of safety, they are describing both their perceptions of their needs and the extent to which they are able to go about protecting themselves. The economic, social and political contexts in which they live their lives are rarely acknowledged, as these seem to be entirely taken for granted. But they all recognise the old adage: 'I'd rather be safe than sorry.'

Strategies for safety

On the street

I always have my keys in my hands wherever I go and I have a whistle and I always have my arms free. I always know right where I'm going and I never stop and look at things.

I've always been aware of someone walking behind me, and groups of youths, black or white. I'd cross over to the other side of the road. I always took my key out of my bag and put it in my pocket, just in case.

I have a couple of night classes. I'm usually by myself. I don't know. I usually don't think about being attacked or anything like that. I just kinda go. I don't focus on anybody. I just focus on where I'm heading to. I look straight ahead. I don't make eye contact. I usually don't carry too much money. And my clothes I wear to school are usually just jeans and a sweatshirt. I usually don't carry more than 5 dollars with me.[1]

Especially within an urban area, being 'street smart' means moving purposefully, alert and on-guard, unencumbered, and with the confidence that one could respond to danger quickly if need be. Risk comes from making eye contact, from unwittingly missing the signs of danger. These streetwise rituals, commonly used coming and going from home at night, include varying the routes home; walking on the streetside of the sidewalk or pavement; avoiding dimly lit areas, bus stops, or train platforms; walking assertively; selecting parking spaces carefully; avoiding certain districts at various times of the evening; never carrying valuables in a handbag; having friends or companions wait outside until one is safely inside one's home. Some people actually carry a limited amount of cash to surrender to muggers if the need should arise.

Certain routines are also treated as necessary in order to be able to leave home, sometimes during the day, but mostly at night. Micki participates in martial arts purposely as a hedge against personal danger, and she consciously monitors her surroundings at night.

I become more aware [when I am out at night]. I get ready in case something happens. Like if I have to run, yell, or fight. If I have my hands in my pockets, which I don't do anymore, I take them out. I walk 'bigger' and I try not to have anything on my person that would get in the way, like a loose jacket or something, or books. When I have a backpack, I don't sling it over one shoulder anymore. I put it over both so I can use my arms if I have to. But that sort of happens every day. I don't ever feel completely safe. I feel less safe at night. I don't know why night has these connotations but I guess studies have shown – I don't know if this is true or not, but this is one of my assumptions – that stranger attacks happen between six and midnight or something like that. I can't see as well then. And it's night, and the mystery of scary bushes and stuff like that. It's harder to be familiar with the environment. It's like two different environments almost. So I don't feel quite as safe then. I'm more cautious when I go out at night. It's also a stereotype – night-time is when these things happen, even though they happen all the time. So I'm used to walking real big.[...]

What I find so often in speaking with women is their own recognition of their special vulnerability as women on the street. This awareness is demonstrated in the way they are able to describe, sometimes in minute detail, the routes they take home, using their vehicles, if they have one, as devices to secure their own safety. Cars, for many women and some men, become mobile safety units. Soon after being physically assaulted by strangers while he was walking down the street, Alan remarks: 'I go out at night but only if I can use the car.' Men may be prompted by a specific threatening experience to find additional ways of increasing their personal safety. But for most women, it is a matter of everyday routine. [...]

To understand the logic of keeping safe, it is important to appreciate the ability to anticipate the possible 'aggravation' or trouble one may find on the street. Someone who has been menaced recently or has experienced memorable threats in the past, may become acutely aware of possible danger. Or someone may be living through a particularly trying time. The death of a loved one, a divorce or separation, or other life crises may bring on additional feelings of vulnerability. Sylvia assumes she will encounter harassment, at the very least, on her coffee break, if not greater problems from the probability of violence that surrounds drug deals. During the course of her working day, she sees countless others passing by the corner and how they are treated. She rightly places herself amongst the likely targets – why should she be any different?

What feels safe to some may feel unsafe to others. Just as the car can be a security device, it may also be the location of danger. Kathy describes leaving the shelter of her car, not just to get to her home, but anywhere:

My car is parked in a lot a little bit down, a block away. So I feel a little nervous at night when I go home. I only walk a block but I'm really aware of the block that I walk. [When I go out] I definitely try to park in well lit areas and I try to park close to the place [I'm going]. I'm really conscious about making sure that if I do go out that I park in somewhere safe. I lock my door [when I'm driving].[...]

Walking alone at night often gives rise to uneasy feelings in women and some men. But many have no choice but to either walk alone at night or stay indoors. 'I really don't like walking alone at night, anywhere,' states Kathy. Large-scale victimisation surveys, as I have already noted, support the findings that women express more concern than do men. These surveys also show that under 5% of those interviewed state that they never go out at night, because they fear for their personal safety; Among elderly women in inner-city areas, this figure rises to almost one in five, nearly 20%. Yet, most of us say that we do venture out at night.

So when we do walk down the street at night, and in some neighbourhoods even during the day, there are a variety of rules of thumb we adopt for protection. One woman, for instance, regularly visits the fish and chip shop on her way home so that if the need should arise, she can always run in there and feel secure. (She complains that this strategy caused her to gain weight, however!) Lester, an elderly gentleman from Central Massachusetts, copes by restricting his own behaviour:

I don't walk home after 8 o'clock at night from downtown. The idea of walking home from here at 10 or 11 o'clock at night doesn't appeal to me. That has cut into my life a little bit. Obviously though, in either daytime or night, in the crummy area around my house, I do my best to have eyes in the back of my head and be very alert to who is walking where. I am more firmly resolved not to let myself walk home drunk. [...]

If we live somewhere we know has frequent, random incidents of crime, we take additional precautions. One man reported that how he walked at night depended upon 'the neighbourhood in which I'm living'. Mike reports:

> Like I lived over on [a notorious street for crime] and I'd go out at night to the drug store to get some cigarettes or a newspaper or stuff like that. Basically my concern was not having too much money in my pockets when I go out. There were some of the men [where I worked] who had gotten jumped. I knew that some people's houses had gotten broken into. But largely it was the money situation which was a real concern, not wanting to lose too much money if I ever got jumped. I wasn't walking faster or being much more cautious or something. I think there was probably a certain amount of fear but not a whole lot.

Mike also said he worried about the possibility of a chance meeting with 'a couple of big guys... if I don't know them and I think they tend to be threatening.' The threat here is the threat of physical violence. It is the rare man who mentions the possibility of facing sexual violence, with an exception being the man who finds himself in prison. Both heterosexual and homosexual men aim their precautionary behaviour towards the avoidance and negotiation of physical safety. Margaret, who has lived in her neighbourhood for 27 years, perceives the time of day as a clue to her safety:

> It depends on the time [of the evening]. I think early in the evening I would do it [walk] without too much problem, but probably after 9.00 or so I would be careful. I used to go for walks a lot. It would get dark, and I would take a walk. And now I wouldn't do that.

In a further effort to protect themselves, some people carry objects which can be used for defence, such as lit cigarettes, keys between fingers, knitting needles (one of my own favourites), umbrellas, pens, or personal alarms. Others carry actual weapons. Cynthia reports:

> I have a key chain that has a [small] knife. I keep that in my hands but nobody bothers me but I keep it as a precaution. I look back [while I'm walking] once in a while. [...]

While some people carry objects in order to feel better, others pack weapons because they work, or participate in activities where violence is part of the scene.

What is especially interesting in the US, where many women express concerns about their own safety, is that it is men who are more likely to pack guns and knives.[2] In Britain, too, men more than women carry knives as weapons. Men bear arms to even the odds in any confrontation with other men, while women who have an object in their hands do so to help them feel more confident on the street or as a way to meet male intimidation. It is important to remember that men report that, by and large, they feel relatively safe.

Safety at work

The risk of attack at work, as well as during the journey there and back, is also of concern to many people. Nurses and other hospital staff, police officers, probation officers, prison officers, school teachers, bus drivers, shop clerks, bank tellers, security personnel, salespeople – they all have contact with those who may be a danger to them. Threat may be a regular part of the job, from bullying school children or troublesome colleagues to potentially violent clients and customers. Or it might come from the occasional stranger either at work or when commuting.

Again, it is women who report taking precautions aimed at both sexual and physical safety, while men speak only of physical safety. Sexual harassment at work – the composite of experiences of sexual degradation from verbal assault to sexual assault – should also be understood as an obstacle to the security of women and some men. One woman whose job was to canvass for a non-profit organisation in rural Massachusetts carried a can of mace (a personal safety device containing a liquid stunning agent) with her. Laura states:

> I carried my mace because I had a job canvassing [membership subscriptions] last summer. You went from door to door all throughout the night, asking people for money. They [the supervisors] dropped you off. You had a really long turf, and they'd meet you at the end. A lot of times there were certain places that were really creepy at night. It was basically country areas and really nice places, you know, because you wanted to get a lot of money. And there were some places. I know one night there was this fog and I couldn't see anything. It was half raining. And some guy told me, 'You shouldn't be walking around late at night,' and I was really feeling weird. I was walking away from his house and was getting the eeriest feelings in the world. I was holding on to it [the mace] for dear life. That happened to me a few times in that job. I

was doing it because I was getting a lot of money and I totally believed in the cause.

Robert, an electrician's apprentice in Central Massachusetts, tells of his concern for his safety at work, where the danger comes from colleagues:

> I had a situation at work within the last year. I almost got thrown down a flight of stairs by a guy about twice my size but it was strange because it was over something where he was angry over the fact that he was making only 25 cents more an hour than me. I guess he didn't have anyone to take it out on but me. I knew I couldn't take him on. And if no one was going to be on my side I was going to have to do something. A lot of people I work with I don't trust, and doing electrical work, it would be nice if I did. So I just watch my back. If I'm working on something, I'm going to check and double check because, not having trust is like the same as having incompetency. It's like somebody that's not going to turn off a switch when you're going to work on something.

The strategies we devise for safety on the job may include some of the things we already do on the street or at home. One woman, for instance, took her dog with her if she had to work late at night or on weekends. When estate agent Suzy Lamplugh disappeared from her office in West London in 1986, concern about the vulnerability of women at work rose to alarm levels. She went to show a house to a potential male buyer and never returned. Her diary indicated the time, place and name of the client, but there were no other clues about who he might have been. For a long time after her disappearance many women changed the way they interacted with male clients. Some estate agents in London now require all clients to meet the agents in the office first. Some agents will show houses only in pairs. In 1988, when a 14-year-old schoolboy disappeared while delivering newspapers and was later found murdered, two-thirds of the paper delivery children in that rural area left their jobs.

While this kind of acute anxiety rises and falls, perhaps partly due to particular highly-publicised incidents, some people feel acutely vulnerable and alter their work habits permanently. When danger occurs in the ordinary work routine, worry about safety may completely interfere with the ability to do one's job at all. Some leave because they are no longer able to cope with

the daily reminder that they could be attacked. Many others have been utterly silenced about their fears for safety because they fear being accused of incompetence.

Safety at home

> I just don't have much in the way of fear. One of the things I do, by the way, when I go home in the evening or anytime I go home, I always open the apartment door and look around to make sure there's nobody in there.

While 72-year-old Lester may not be afraid to enter his home, he none the less takes some precautions when he does. The simple procedure of looking around the home is one tactic people use as part of routine behaviour. Others keep televisions and radios on and lights burning when going out at night, or use electronic timers that automatically switch on such appliances when it gets dark. Dogs are trained to bark at intruders, perhaps frightening them away. Thanks to modern technology, people may even purchase a tape recording of a dog barking for their burglar alarm.

Nowadays locks that are highly elaborate, expensive and considered to be the most impregnable are growing in popularity. The majority of people say they regularly lock their doors when going out. Some household insurance companies even specify what kind of security a house must have in order to qualify for coverage. Indeed, firms specialising in domestic security are making bigger profits.

Protecting one's home against thieves is also procuring one's personal safety. Those who are burgled sometimes report feeling intimately violated as well. Others treat it as a hazard of contemporary urban living. No matter what the individual reaction, no one wants to confront an uninvited guest in their own home. Margaret, a 62-year-old woman, widowed and a resident of a small city in Massachusetts, has experienced four burglaries over the past six years.

> I guess I don't feel that it is as safe [as it was when I moved in 27 years ago]. I think it was the kind of thing that if I forgot to lock my door I didn't get frantic about it. Now I go around and check the locks. My windows have the nails through them and I have a whole lighting system set up so lights go on and off all over the place all the time. I have a very expensive light bill.

Gordon, a 23-year-old man, living in a small town in rural Massachusetts, states:

> There's two doors that lead out of the apartment and they both have chains on them and a deadbolt. When I'm in the apartment, I always have the deadbolt on the doors. One door is always locked. That's the door I never use. If you're in the bathroom or you're washing up or you're doing dishes, or something you can't hear if someone's coming in, and then it's too late. If someone comes in....Not that I anticipate it, but why risk it? And when I'm home for the evening, the door's always chained. I have a sliding glass door in my living room and even on a day like today when it's a beautiful day out I wouldn't leave it open even though my living room faces a quad in the [apartment] complex. [...]

People are able to describe the tactics they use to safeguard themselves against intrusion from outsiders. The 1984 US Victimisation Risk Survey, for example, shows that people have taken measures to protect their property in their home. One quarter of the respondents of this survey indicated they had engraved their property so that, in the event of a burglary, their valuables could be identified if recovered. The 1992 British Crime Survey finds that 20% of households in England and Wales keep an eye out for intruders on a more formal basis through neighbourhood watch schemes; US figures show that approximately 7% of US households participate in neighbourhood watch.[3] While the majority do not participate in organised neighbourhood activities to protect against burglary, they do take some measures to deter household crime by installing locks or by making the house look occupied at all times.

Yet, no matter how secure your home may be to intruders, if you live with someone who is violent, either physically or sexually, the potential for danger is locked in with you. The targets of this kind of violence, typically women and children, try all kinds of avoidance tactics. Rachel recalls:

> My dad would beat up my Mom, and me or one of my sisters would call the police if it got really bad. Or if my mom told me to call, and then they would come. I was really scared, for her and for me, because it was really obvious that if he was going to hurt her, he would hurt us too. I was really concerned about her, trying to figure out how to make it safe for her, to do something. It was frustrating because there was nothing really I could do, because he was so

much bigger and things like that. I was frustrated and angry.

[...] Just as the home can be the location for unsafety for those living with violence, it may also be seen as a fortress for locking out danger. Linda, who now lives in Central Massachusetts, moved from one city to another after the experience of rape by an intruder. She describes the hardware built into her present home:

> We built this house because I had been raped. We really built it. I think everybody thinks we're crazy. I've got locks, you know. Our doors are really good. We have grates on the basement windows, that sort of thing. Very small windows at the top. [The house is set up] high enough so that somebody can't look in. I keep the windows locked, lock the door at all times. I'm certain that someone could get in if they really wanted to, but when I look at the other houses around, it would be much harder to break into this one. So I feel apprehensive in general, but somewhat more safe within this house. I'm apprehensive going from here to the car and back...which I think is probably more my own psychological reality than actual. Well, I shouldn't say that. It [violence] happens all the time.

Anticipating trouble prompts some to keep their homes as uninviting as possible, reducing the possible attraction of the target. Jill, living in London, describes the logic behind the caution:

> I've got lovely ideas for the front of the house, but quite honestly I don't know if it's worth it. And it's not that doing it would actually cost very much money. It would simply be a coat of paint and maybe a couple of pots so we can plant things growing up the wall. It's a dreadful thing to say that you don't actually want to do the front of your house simply because you know you'll get burgled if you do. But I do keep a pretty low profile. I'm particularly cautious about the front door because it's right on the street so it would only take someone just a sort of a lean against it if it wasn't shut properly for the door to swing open. I don't have a peep hole but I've got a very big front window and I can normally see who's at the front door. And if the situation is such that I can't see who's at the front door and I don't really like the sound of it or if I'm not expecting someone, I will go upstairs and look out the window, open the window and see who's there.

Anticipating danger and avoiding violence

In general, to act sensibly we take measures to minimise risk. Doing so recognises the random and sometimes not-so-random features of everyday violence. Unfortunately, we are not always able to avoid danger despite all our efforts. [...] Keeping violence at bay is an active process. We change our everyday habits, develop elaborate precautionary strategies, and hope for the best.

From E. A. Stanko, 'Common sense, routine precaution and normal violence', E.A. Stanko in Everyday Violence: How Women and Men Experience Sexual and Physical Danger (London: Pandora), 1990, pp. 13–34.

Notes

1 The extracts are exact transcriptions. The text that appears in square brackets has been added by me in order to clarify the sense or the context of response to my question.
2 Research & Forecasts, Inc. with Ardy Friedberg, *America Afraid: How Fear of Crime Changes the Way we Live*, New York: New American Library, 1983, pp. 229–33; G. Hill, F. Howell and E. Driver, 'Gender, fear and protective handgun ownership', *Criminology*, vol.23, no. 3, pp. 541–52, 1985.
3 P. Mayhew, L. Dowds and D. Elliot, *The British Crime Survey 1988*, London: HMSO; US Department of Justice, *Report to the Nation on Crime and Justice*, 1988.

32.5 Hegemonic and subordinated masculinities
James W. Messerschmidt

Hegemonic and subordinated masculinities

Several pro-feminist men have begun to employ Antonio Gramsci's notion of 'hegemony' to distinguish between 'hegemonic masculinity' and 'subordinated masculinities' (Carrigan *et al.*, 1987; Connell, 1987; Frank, 1987). Gramsci (1978) used the term hegemony to refer to the ascendancy – obtained primarily by manufactured consent rather than by force – of one class over other classes. Ideological hegemony, as the dominant conception of reality, is manifest throughout social institutions and, therefore, comprises 'the "spontaneous" consent given by the great masses of the population to the general direction imposed on social life by the dominant fundamental group' (p. 12). According to Gramsci (p. 12), hegemony is achieved fundamentally through consent, yet force may at times be necessary for 'those groups who do not "consent" either actively or passively.'

Similarly, Connell (1987: 184) defines 'hegemonic masculinity' as the ascendancy of a certain form of masculinity that is 'embedded in religious doctrine and practice, mass media content, wage structures, the design of housing, welfare/taxation policies, and so forth'. Connell's notion of hegemonic masculinity is constructed in relation both to subordinated masculinities and to women; it is the dominant form of masculinity to which other types of masculinity are subordinated, not eliminated, and it provides the primary basis for relationships among men. Moreover, force and threat of force may be used to help maintain hegemonic masculinity (for example, violence against women and homosexuals).

Simply defined, in any culture, hegemonic masculinity is the idealized form of masculinity in a given historical setting. It is culturally honored, glorified, and extolled, and this 'exaltation stabilizes a structure of dominance and oppression in the gender order as a whole' (Connell, 1990: 94). In contemporary Western industrialized societies, hegemonic masculinity is defined through work in the paid-labor market, the subordination of women, heterosexism, and the driven and uncontrollable sexuality of men. Refined still further, hegemonic masculinity emphasizes practices toward authority, control, competitive individualism, independence, aggressiveness, and the capacity for violence (Connell, 1990, 1992; Segal, 1990). Hegemonic masculinity is substantially different from the notion of a 'male sex role,' because it allows us to move beyond universal and, therefore, categorical formulations of what constitutes 'male' behavior. With it, we are able to explain power relations among men based on a hierarchy of masculinities and see how such masculinities are socially constructed.

'Boys will be boys' differently

The two most significant and tenacious features associated with crime are age and gender. For example, young men account for a disproportionate amount of crime in all Western industrialized societies (Beirne and Messerschmidt, 1991; Chesney-Lind and Shelden, 1992). Moreover, although Albert Cohen's (1955) thesis on 'delinquent boys' can be legitimately criticized for the reasons outlined in Chapter 1, his awareness of a relationship between the school and youth crime should not be discounted. Research has shown that youth crime declines drastically when public schools are not in session and that youth who leave school during the academic year engage in less crime than those currently enrolled (Elliott and Voss, 1974; Messerschmidt, 1979). Yet schooling is one of the chief social milieux for the development of youth crime and also a social setting that has institutionalized gender and, therefore, patterned ways in which femininity and masculinity are constructed and represented. School, then, does not merely adapt to a natural masculinity among boys. Rather, it constructs various forms of masculinity (and femininity) and negotiates relations among them (Connell, 1987: 291–292). [...]

'Boys will be boys' differently, depending upon their position in social structures and, therefore, upon their access to power and resources. Social structures situate young men in a common relation to other young men and in such a way that they share structural space. Collectively, young men experience their daily world from a particular position in society and differentially construct the cultural ideals of hegemonic masculinity. Thus, within the school and youth group there are patterned ways in which masculinity is represented and which depend upon structures of labor and power in class and race relations. Young men situationally accomplish public forms of masculinity in response to their socially structured circumstances; indeed, varieties of youth crime serve as a suitable resource for doing masculinity

when other resources are unavailable. These forms of youth crime, as with other resources, are determined by social structures.

Social structures, masculinities, and crime in youth groups

Research on youth groups indicates that what young men and women do tends to mirror and recreate particular gender divisions of labor and power and normative heterosexuality. This appears to be so regardless of class and race position. From Thrasher's (1927) early research to the works of Cohen (1955), Cloward and Ohlin (1960), Short and Strodtbeck (1965), Klein (1971), Miller (1980), Quickei (1983), Schwendinger and Schwendinger (1985), Harris (1988) and Fishman (1988), women have been found to take on secondary or 'auxiliary roles' in the group if, in fact, they are involved in the group at all. Anne Campbell's (1984: 242–243) important ethnographic study of lower-working-class racial minority youth groups in New York City found that both men and women assume positions within the group that might be available to them in society at large:

> In straight society the central, pivotal figure is the male. His status in the world of societal and material success is the critical factor, while the woman supports, nurtures, and sustains him. The gang parodies this state of affairs, without even the economic infrastructure to sustain it, for the male rarely works and often it is the female who receives a more stable income through welfare. Nevertheless, the males constitute the true gang! Gang feuds are begun and continued by males; females take part as a token of their allegiance to the men.

Campbell (p. 266) argues further that specific girl groups:

> exist as an annex to the male gang, and the range of possibilities open to them is dictated and controlled by the boys. Within the gang, there are still 'good girls' and 'bad girls', tomboys and fallen women. Girls are told how to dress, are allowed to fight, and are encouraged to be good mothers and faithful wives. Their principal source of suffering and joy is their men. And though the girls may occasionally defy them, often argue with them, and sometimes patronize them, the men remain indisputably in control.

What Campbell's research indicates is that the gender social structures of labor and power shape interaction in youth groups, affording young men the opportunity to arrange social life to their advantage. Although these opportunities vary by race and by class, young men exercise authority and control in terms of gender, at least relative to young women of the same race and class. The youth group, then, is unmistakably a domain of masculine dominance, a domain that reflects the gender structures of labor and power in society and the related practices by which they are reproduced.

Besides overall dominance in youth groups, normative heterosexuality is a decisive 'measuring rod' for group participation. Indeed, young men often control and exploit the sexuality of young women. Campbell (1984: 245) reported that in one particular group, heterosexuality was so crucial to group membership by young women that when 'dykes' were discovered, they were 'multiply raped and thrown out of the club'. Similarly, the Schwendingers (1985: 167) found that 'sexist exploitation of girls is common to all stratum formations', from middle- to working-class youth groups.

Suspicion and jealousy being one of the most disruptive practices inside youth groups, serial monogamy is demanded and enforced. Jealousy by a young man is often interpreted by a young woman as evidence not of his control, but of his passionate attachment to her. Similarly, 'the beatings that she may receive at his hands when he believes that she has been unfaithful are interpreted as a direct index of his love for her' but 'his infidelity is blamed upon his desirability to other women, rather than seen as evidence of his less-than-total commitment to her' (Campbell, 1990: 174–175). Campbell (pp. 180–181) adds that both the men and women see the men as being:

> by nature, unable to refuse an offer of sex. Consequently, it is not the boy's fault when he strays but rather the other woman's. The confrontation is recast as between the girlfriend and her rival, rather than between the girl and the boy. Consequently, sexual betrayal is terminated by an attack on the rival, not on the boyfriend, who simply was following his nature.

Other research suggests similar heterosexual relations in lower-working-class (Fishman, 1988), working-class (Willis, 1977), and middle-class (Schwendinger and Schwendinger, 1985) youth groups. Accordingly, normative heterosexuality is constructed as a practice that helps to reproduce the subordination of young women and to form age-specific heterosexual styles of masculinity, a masculinity centering on an uncontrollable and unlimited sexual appetite. Normative heterosexuality, then, serves as a resource for the situated accomplishment of gender in youth groups.

Regardless of the degree of participation in youth groups by young women and the nature of youth sexuality in such groups, research clearly shows that various masculinities (as well as femininities) are constructed within these groups and, thus, the various forms of youth crime associated with those masculinities. William Chambliss's (1973) classic study 'The Saints and the Roughnecks' is notable in this regard. The Saints were 'eight promising young men – children of good, stable, white upper-middle-class families, active in school affairs, good pre-college students' (p. 24). They were successful in school, earned high grades (two boys had close to straight 'A' averages), and several held student offices. At the end of their senior year, the student body selected ten seniors as 'school wheels'; four were Saints.

As for youth crime, the Saints were involved primarily in practices that 'raised hell', such as traveling to nearby cities on weekend evenings (often under the influence of alcohol) to vandalize property, engage in a variety of 'pranks' and forms of 'mischief', and commit minor forms of theft. The Saints, however, never fought; in fact, they avoided physical conflict both inside and outside their group. Chambliss (p. 26) points out: 'The boys had a spirit of frivolity and fun about their escapades. They did not view what they were engaged in as "delinquency".'

Although the Roughnecks attended the same school as the Saints, they were six lower-working-class white boys. The Roughnecks avoided school as much as possible because they considered it a burden. They neither participated in school affairs, except for two who played football, nor earned good grades, averaging a 'C' or lower. Moreover, these boys were involved in more serious forms of delinquency. In addition to drinking, truancy, and vandalism, they engaged in major forms of theft and violence. The Roughnecks sometimes stole as a group (coordinating their efforts) or simply stole in pairs, rarely stealing alone. Regarding violence, the Roughnecks not only welcomed an opportunity to fight, but they went seeking it, frequently fighting among themselves; at least once a month the Roughnecks would participate in some type of physical fight (pp. 27–29).

Chambliss's study is important for showing that within this particular social setting, the same school, the Saints and the Roughnecks both used available class and race resources to shape particular types of public masculinity. It is not that the Roughnecks were masculine because of their violence and that the Saints were not masculine because of their pranks. Rather, the Saints and Roughnecks were constructing different personifications of masculinity and drawing on different forms of youth crime (e.g., pranks vs. violence) as resources for that construction.

Other research indicates similar processes occurring among masculine-dominated youth groups, enabling us to build on Chambliss's data. For example, Herman Schwendinger's and Julia Schwendinger's (1985) study, *Adolescent Subcultures and Delinquency*, attempts to explain the forms of youth crime that emerge at the group level and, in so doing, identify two types of group formations that young men dominate: the 'socialite' and 'street-corner youth'. The Schwendingers' data show that both groups construct different forms of masculinity and, therefore, exhibit varying types of youth crime. Yet the middle class 'Socs' (socialites) and the lower-working-class 'Eses' (street corner youth) both marshal gender and class resources in their struggle for power and status in the adolescent world.

Like the Saints, the Socs are 'less likely to be involved in the most serious violent and economic forms of delinquency' (p. 56), drawing on school resources and various forms of vandalism, drinking, gambling, petty theft, and truancy to construct a specific type of public masculinity. Although the Eses engage in the same types of delinquent activities, the most extreme forms of violence are found among these street-corner youth. In other words, both groups of young men pursue gendered strategies of action that reflect their relative class and race ethnicity position. Again, like the Saints, Socs have specific potential and opportunities that help construct less violent forms of masculinity. As the Schwendingers (p. 208) point out:

the Socs control the student organizations in their high schools, and the payoffs from this control are considerable. These advantages do not merely mean unique experiences, such as trips and contacts with prestigious youth in other schools, but also large and pleasant facilities in which to hold dances. Furthermore, their frequent control over the student council, cheerleading squad, and student monitor system reflects their integration with prevailing systems of institutionalized power and enables them to establish an authoritative position in the eyes of other youth.

Eses have no access to such resources and power, and thus accomplish gender in a different way. For the street-corner youth, masculinity does not derive from competition for school office but from violent conflicts with other street-corner men. Carlos, a member of a street-corner gang, told the Schwendingers (p. 171), 'In my territory that's the way they are now. That's the way we are. It seems to be the neighborhood that is the thing. You want to prove yourself to nobody but these people.'

For both the Saints/Roughnecks and Socs/Eses, the youth group is a critical organizing setting for the embodiment of public masculinity. It is within this group that young men's power over young women is normalized and that youth crime, as a social practice within the group, constructs gendered differences, weaving 'a structure of symbol and interpretation around these differences that naturalizes them' (Messner, 1989: 79). Yet, simultaneously, these findings exhibit clear differences in 'doing gender' for middle- and lower-working-class boys. In fact, the above findings require a more rigorous examination of class and race distinctions.

From J. Messerschmidt, Masculinities and Crime *(Lanham, MD: Rowman and Littlefield), 1993, pp. 81–92.*

References

Beirne, P., and Messerschmidt, J.W. (1991) *Criminology*. San Diego, CA: Harcourt Brace Jovanovich.

Campbell, A. (1984) *The Girls in the Gang*. Cambridge, MA: Basil Blackwell.

Campbell, A. (1990) Female participation in gangs. In *Gangs in America* (Ed.) Huff, C.R., pp.163–82. Newbury Park, CA: Sage.

Carrigan, T., Connell, B. and Lee, J. (1987) Hard and heavy: toward a new sociology of masculinity. In *Beyond Patriarchy: Essays by Men on Pleasure, Power and Change* (Ed.) Kaufman, M., pp.139–92. New York: Oxford University Press.

Chambliss, W.J. (1973). The saints and the roughnecks. *Society*, 11(1): 24–31.

Chesney-Lind, M. and Shelden, R.G (1992) *Girls, Delinquency and Juvenile Justice*. Pacific Grove, CA: Brooks/Cole.

Cloward, R.A., and Ohlin. L.E. (1960) *Delinquency and Opportunity*. New York: Free Press.

Cohen, A. (1955) *Delinquent Boys: The Culture of the Gang*. New York: Free Press.

Connell, R.W. (1987). *Gender and Power*. Stanford, CA: Stanford University Press.

Connell, R.W. (1990). The state, gender, and sexual politics: Theory and appraisal. *Theory and Society*,19 (4): 507–44.

Connell, R.W. (1992). Drumming up the Wrong Tree. *Tikkun, 7* (1): 31–36.

Elliott, D.S., and Voss, H.L (1974) *Delinquency and Dropout*. Lexington, MA: Lexington Books.

Fishman, L.T. (1988) The vice queens: An ethnographic study of black female gang behavior. Paper presented at the annual meeting of the American Society of Criminology.

Frank, B. (1987). Hegemonic heterosexual masculinity. *Studies in Political Economy* 24 (Autumn): 159–70.

Gramsci, A. (1978) *Selections from the Prison Notebooks*, (Ed.) Hoare, Q. and Smith., G.N. London: Lawrence and Wishart.

Harris, M.G. (1988) *Cholas: Latino Girls and Gangs*. New York: AMS.

Klein, M.W. (1971) *Street Gangs and Street Workers*. Englewood Cliffs, NJ: Prentice-Hall.

Messerschmidt, J.W. (1979) *School Stratification and Delinquent Behavior*. Stockholm: Gotab.

Miller, W.B. (1980) Gangs, groups and serious youth crime. In *Critical Issues in Juvenile Delinquency* (Ed.) Shichor, D. and Kelly, D.H., pp.115–38. Lexington, MA: Lexington Books.

Quicker, J.C. (1983) *Homegirls: Characterizing Chicano Gangs*. San Pedro, CA: International University Press.

Schwendinger, H. and Schwendinger, J. (1985) *Adolescent Subcultures and Delinquency*. New York: Praeger.

Segal, L. (1990) *Slow Motion: Changing Masculinities, Changing Men*. New Brunswick, NJ: Rutgers University Press.

Short, J.F. and Strodtbeck, F.L. (1965) *Gang Process and Gang Delinquency*. Chicago: University of Chicago Press.

Thrasher, F. (1927) *The Gang*. Chicago: University of Chicago Press.

Willis, P.E. (1977) *Learning to Labour*. Farnborough, England: Saxon House.

33

Criminal and forensic psychology

33.1 Individual factors in offending
David P. Farrington and Brandon C. Welsh   800

33.2 Adolescence-limited and life-course-persistent antisocial behavior: a developmental taxonomy
Terrie E. Moffitt   807

33.3 A sociogenic developmental theory of offending
Robert J. Sampson and John H. Laub   818

Introduction

KEY CONCEPTS	adolescence-limited antisocial behaviour; informal social control; life-course-persistent antisocial behaviour; risk and protective factors; social bonds

In recent times there has been a quickly developing interest in psychological approaches to criminology and, for a variety of reasons, they are set to become increasingly influential. In an earlier chapter (Chapter 7) we looked at a range of psychological theories and ideas. In this chapter we look at three separate – though linked – bodies of empirical research, each of which takes aspects of human biology and psychology and, via links with social and cultural factors, offers insights into the patterning of criminal behaviour.

For the past decade or more one of the most influential approaches to explaining patterns of offending behaviour has emanated from a variety of longitudinal studies – studies which follow cohorts of people over extended periods of time – and which have identified what are generally referred to as 'risk' and 'protective factors' linked with offending. Essentially, these factors are variables that predict an increased or decreased probability of later offending. They work cumulatively rather than individually, and cover a wide variety of influences including family factors, socio-economic, peer, school and community factors and, as outlined by David Farrington and Brandon Welsh **(Reading 33.1)**, individual factors. The most important of these, they suggest, are low intelligence and attainment, personality and temperament, empathy and impulsiveness.

One of the key assumptions underpinning much psychological criminology is, as Farrington and Welsh put it, 'that individual differences in criminal potential (or, more precisely, the rank orderings of individuals on criminal potential) are relatively stable over time and in different environments'. This leads scholars to search for persistent underlying tendencies which might explain the consistency of such (mis)conduct. An influential, and controversial, addition to this literature in recent years has been provided by Terrie Moffitt's theory of adolescence-limited and life-course-persistent antisocial behaviour **(Reading 33.2)**. In effect, she sets out to explain why it is that the majority of adolescents that get involved in criminal or antisocial conduct cease such involvement in their late teenage years, but a minority continue long into their adult lives. Her answer, crudely, is that these are analytically separable groups of people. Moreover, for that group whose offending is consistent across the life course the explanation must consequently be found early in their lives. This leads her to a theory that is partly neuropsychological, partly genetic and partly social. She concludes that the 'life-course-persistent antisocial syndrome... has many characteristics that, taken together, suggest psychopathology'. By contrast, the prevalence of the other model – adolescence-limited offending – is such that it is better considered as normative she argues.

The final excerpt comes from a book called *Crime in the Making* by Robert Sampson and John Laub **(Reading 33.3)** and offers a different approach and explanation of patterns of offending over the life course. It is worth offering a sentence or two by way of background to this study. It is based on the re-analysis of data that were originally collected in a lengthy period between the 1940s and

1960s by two American scholars, Sheldon and Eleanor Glueck (you will see references to 'the Gluecks' in the excerpt). In *Crime in the Making* Sampson and Laub look again at the original data and re-analyse it in order to examine the patterns of offending among the 500 males included in the original study. The key to their eventual explanation of the trends they identify is the idea of social bonds (see also the Readings in Chapter 11). Weak social bonds early in life are associated with juvenile delinquency but, similarly, weak or, alternatively, strengthening social bonds in adulthood may also be predictive of offending, or desistance from offending, later in life. More particularly, they point to key transitions in the life course.

Questions for discussion

1. What are the main individual risk factors as identified by Farrington and Welsh?

2. In what way might personality be said to be linked with patterns of offending?

3. Describe the characteristics of, and differences between adolescence-limited and life-course-persistent antisocial behaviour.

4. In what ways might adolescence-limited antisocial behaviour be considered 'normal' and life-course-persistent antisocial behaviour 'abnormal'? Are such descriptions helpful?

5. What are the three main components of Sampson and Laub's thesis?

6. How do social bonds relate to the presence or absence of offending over the life course according to Sampson and Laub? Give examples.

7. What are the main similarities and differences of the ideas outlined in each of the three readings in this chapter?

33.1 Individual factors in offending
David P. Farrington and Brandon C. Welsh

Individual factors

It is clear that individuals differ in their potential to commit criminal and related types of antisocial acts, given a particular opportunity, situation, or victim. [...] We use the word 'potential' (equivalent to 'tendency') in preference to 'propensity' or 'predisposition' to describe the key theoretical construct underlying regularities in behavior, in order to avoid possible connotations of biological determinism.

An important assumption is that individual differences in criminal potential (or, more precisely, the rank orderings of individuals on criminal potential) are relatively stable over time and in different environments. A great deal of criminal career research (Farrington, 1997b) shows continuity and relative stability in offending over time; even though the absolute level of offending, and different types of offending, vary with age, the 'worst' people at one age still tend to be the 'worst' at a later age. Similarly, criminal career research shows a great deal of versatility and not much specialization in offending (Farrington, 1991); it is almost as though the most antisocial people commit different types of offenses at random, depending, presumably, on situational factors. [...]

Among the most important individual factors that predict offending are low intelligence and attainment, personality and temperament, empathy, and impulsiveness.

Low intelligence and attainment

Intelligence is usually measured according to scores on IQ tests. The IQ (Intelligence Quotient) indicates the relationship between a child's 'mental age' (based on the test) and chronological age. [...] Low intelligence is an important predictor of offending, and it can be measured very early in life. For example, in a prospective longitudinal survey of about 120 Stockholm males, Hakan Stattin and Ingrid Klackenberg-Larsson (1993) reported that low intelligence measured at age 3 significantly predicted officially recorded offending up to age 30. Frequent offenders (with four or more offenses) had an average IQ of 88 at age 3, whereas nonoffenders had an average IQ of 101. All of these results held up after controlling for social

class. In the Perry Preschool project in Michigan, Lawrence Schweinhart, Helen Barnes, and David Weikart (1993) found that low intelligence at age 4 significantly predicted the number of arrests up to age 27. [...]

In the Cambridge Study, one-third of the boys scoring 90 or less on a nonverbal intelligence test (Raven's Progressive Matrices) at age 8–10 were convicted as juveniles, twice as many as among the remainder (Farrington, 1992c). Low nonverbal intelligence was highly correlated with low verbal intelligence (vocabulary, word comprehension, verbal reasoning) and with low school attainment at age 11, and all of these measures predicted juvenile convictions to much the same extent. In addition to their poor school performance, delinquents tended to be frequent truants, to leave school at the earliest possible age (15), and to take no secondary school examinations.

Low intelligence and attainment predicted both juvenile and adult convictions (Farrington, 1992b). Low intelligence at age 8–10 was also an important independent predictor of spouse assault at age 32 (Farrington, 1994a). In addition, low intelligence and attainment predicted aggression and bullying at age 14 (Farrington, 1989, 1993b), and low school attainment predicted chronic offenders (Farrington and West, 1993). Low nonverbal intelligence was especially characteristic of the juvenile recidivists (who had an average IQ of 89) and those first convicted at the earliest ages (10–13). Furthermore, low intelligence and attainment predicted self-reported delinquency almost as well as convictions (Farrington, 1992a), suggesting that the link between low intelligence and delinquency was not caused by the less intelligent boys having a greater probability of being caught.

Low nonverbal intelligence was about as strong a predictor of juvenile convictions as other important early risk factors (low family income, large family size, poor parental child-rearing behavior, poor parental supervision, and poor concentration or restlessness), but it was a weaker predictor than having a convicted parent or a daring (risk-taking) personality. Measures of intelligence and attainment predicted measures of offending independently of other risk factors such as family income and family size (Farrington, 1990).

Similar results have been obtained in other projects (Lynam, Moffitt, and Stouthamer-Loeber 1993; Moffitt and Silva, 1988a; Wilson and Herrnstein, 1985).

The key explanatory factor underlying the link between intelligence and delinquency may be the ability to manipulate abstract concepts. People who are poor at this tend to do badly in intelligence tests such as Raven's Progressive Matrices and in school achievement, and they also tend to commit offenses, probably because of their poor ability to foresee the consequences of their offending and to appreciate the feelings of victims (i.e., their low empathy). Certain family backgrounds are less conducive than others to the development of abstract reasoning. For example, lower class, economically deprived parents tend to talk in terms of the concrete rather than the abstract and tend to live for the present, with little thought for the future, as the sociologist Albert Cohen (1955, p. 96) pointed out many years ago. In some ways, it is difficult to distinguish a lack of concern for future consequences from the concept of impulsiveness (discussed later).

There has been a great deal of recent interest in the concept of 'emotional intelligence', which measures empathy, self-awareness, emotional control, and the ability to delay gratification. This is typically measured by items such as 'I easily recognize my emotions as I experience them' and 'I have control of my emotions' (Schutte et al., 1998). Emotional intelligence seems to reflect empathy and impulsiveness, which will be discussed later.

Low intelligence may be one element of a pattern of cognitive and neuropsychological deficits. For example, in the Dunedin (New Zealand) longitudinal study, Terrie Moffitt and Phil Silva (1988b) found that self-reported delinquency was related to verbal, memory, and visual-motor integration deficits, independently of low social class and family adversity. Neuropsychological research might lead to important advances in knowledge about the link between brain functioning and offending. For example, the 'executive functions' of the brain, located in the frontal lobes, include sustaining attention and concentration, abstract reasoning and concept formation, anticipation and planning, self-monitoring of behavior, and inhibition of inappropriate or impulsive behaviors (Moffitt and Henry, 1991; Morgan and Lilienfeld, 2000). [...]

Alternatively, it might be argued that IQ tests are designed to measure ability to succeed in school (which may be a different construct from 'intelligence'). Hence, low IQ predicts school failure, and there are many criminological theories suggesting that school failure leads to delinquency (e.g., through the intervening construct of status deprivation; see Cohen, 1955). Donald Lynam, Terrie Moffitt, and Magda Stouthamer-Loeber (1993) completed one of the most important attempts to test these and other possible explanations, using data collected in the Pittsburgh Youth Study. Their conclusions vary according to the ethnicity of the boys. For African American boys, they found that low verbal intelligence led to school failure and subsequently to self-reported delinquency, but for Caucasian boys the relationship between low verbal intelligence and self-reported delinquency held after controlling for school failure and all other variables. It may be that poor executive functioning and school failure are both plausible explanations of the link between low intelligence and offending.

Personality

Antisocial behavior is remarkably consistent over time; or, to be more precise, the relative ordering of individuals is remarkably consistent over time (Roberts and del Vecchio, 2000). Psychologists assume that behavioral consistency depends primarily on the persistence of underlying tendencies to behave in particular ways in particular situations. These tendencies, such as impulsiveness, excitement-seeking, assertiveness, modesty, and dutifulness, are termed personality traits. Larger personality dimensions, such as extraversion, refer to clusters of personality traits.   Before   1990, the best known research on personality and crime was probably that inspired by the British psychologist Hans Eysenck in his theory and personality questionnaires (1996). He viewed offending as natural and even rational, on the assumption that human beings are hedonistic, seek pleasure, and avoid pain. He assumed that delinquent acts such as theft, violence, and vandalism were essentially pleasurable or beneficial to the offender. In order to explain why everyone was not a criminal, Eysenck suggested that the hedonistic tendency to commit crimes is opposed by the conscience, which he viewed as a fear response built up from childhood in a conditioning process.

On the Eysenck theory, the people who commit offenses are those who have not built up strong consciences, mainly because they have inherently poor conditionability. Poor conditionability is linked to Eysenck's three dimensions of personality: extraversion (E), neuroticism (N), and psychoticism (P). Examples of E items on the questionnaires are 'Do you often make decisions on the spur of the moment?' (Yes) and 'Do you prefer reading to meeting people?' (No). The E items seem to measure either sociability or impulsiveness. Examples of N and P items are 'Do you worry about awful things that might happen?' (Yes; an N item) and 'Would it upset you a lot to see a child or animal suffer?' (No; a P item).

According to Eysenck, people who have a high level of the E dimension build up conditioned responses less well, because they have low levels of cortical arousal. People who are high on the N dimension also condition less well, because their high resting level of anxiety interferes with their conditioning. In addition, since the N dimension acts as a drive, reinforcing existing behavioral tendencies, neurotic extraverts should be particularly criminal. Eysenck also predicted that people who are high on the P dimension would tend to be offenders, because the traits included in his definition of psychoticism (emotional coldness, low empathy, high hostility, and inhumanity) were typical of criminals. However, the meaning of the P scale is unclear, and it might perhaps be more accurately labeled psychopathy. Marvin Zuckerman (1989) suggested that it should be termed 'impulsive unsocialized sensation-seeking'.

A review of studies relating Eysenck's personality dimensions to official and self-reported offending concluded that high N (but not E) was related to official offending, while high E (but not N) was related to self-reported offending (Farrington, Biron, and LeBlanc, 1982). High P was related to both, but this could have been a tautological result, since many of the items on the P scale reflected antisocial behavior or were selected in light of their ability to discriminate between prisoners and non-prisoners. In the Cambridge Study, those high on both E and N tended to be juvenile self-reported offenders, adult official offenders, and adult self-reported offenders but not juvenile offenders, according to official records. These relationships held independently of other criminogenic risk factors such as low family income, low intelligence, and poor parental child-rearing behavior. However, when individual items of the questionnaire were studied, it was clear that the items measuring impulsiveness caused the significant relationships (e.g., doing things quickly without stopping to think). Hence it seems likely that research inspired by the Eysenck theory mainly identifies the link between impulsiveness and offending (discussed later).

Since 1990, the most widely accepted personality system has been the 'Big Five' or five-factor model, developed by Robert McCrae and Paul Costa (1997, 2003). This model suggests that there are five key dimensions of personality: neuroticism (N), extraversion (E), openness (O), agreeableness (A), and conscientiousness (C). Openness means originality and openness to new ideas, agreeableness includes nurturance and altruism, and conscientiousness includes planning and the will to achieve. Openness and conscientiousness seem to be related to intelligence, or at least to social or emotional intelligence. These dimensions are measured using a personality inventory called the Neuroticism-Extraversion-Openness Personality Inventory (NEO-PI). Controversially, Robert McCrae and his colleagues (2000) argued that these personality dimensions are biologically based tendencies that follow intrinsic developmental pathways independently of environmental influences.

Because of its newness, the 'Big Five' personality model has rarely been related to offending. In Canada, Stephen Hart and Robert Hare (1994) found that psychopathy was most strongly (negatively) correlated with agreeableness and conscientiousness. Similarly, in an Australian study Patrick Heaven (1996) showed that agreeableness and conscientiousness were most strongly (negatively) correlated with self-reported delinquency. Much the same results were obtained in the Pittsburgh Youth Study when the five dimensions were measured using mothers' ratings (John, Caspi, Robins, Moffitt, and Stouthamer-Loeber, 1994), and the relevance of agreeableness and conscientiousness was confirmed in a detailed review (Miller and Lynam, 2001). It is informative to measure elements ('facets') of the larger dimensions. Joshua Miller, Donald Lynam, and Carl Leukefeld (2003) did this and concluded that low straightforwardness, low compliance, and low deliberation were particularly related to aggression and conduct problems in a Lexington (Kentucky) longitudinal study.

Empathy

There is a widespread belief that low empathy is an important personality trait that is related to offending, on the assumption that people who can appreciate or experience a victim's feelings (or both) are less likely to victimize someone. This belief also underlies cognitive-behavioral skills training programs that aim to increase empathy. However, its empirical basis is not very impressive. Therefore, because of inconsistent results, measures of empathy are not well validated or widely accepted, and there are no prospective longitudinal surveys relating early empathy to later offending.

A distinction has often been made between cognitive empathy (understanding or appreciating other people's feelings) and emotional empathy (actually experiencing other people's feelings). Darrick Jolliffe and David Farrington (2004) carried out a systematic review of 35 studies comparing questionnaire measures of empathy with official record measures of delinquent or criminal behavior. They found that low cognitive empathy was strongly related to offending, but low affective empathy was only weakly related. Most important, the relationship between low empathy and offending was greatly reduced after controlling for intelligence or socioeconomic status, suggesting that they might be more important risk factors or that low empathy might mediate the relationship between these risk factors and offending.

Impulsiveness

Impulsiveness is the most crucial personality dimension that predicts offending. Unfortunately, there are a bewildering number of constructs referring to a poor ability to control behavior. These include impulsiveness, hyperactivity, restlessness, clumsiness, not considering consequences before acting, a poor ability to plan ahead, short time horizons, low self-control, sensation-seeking, risk-taking, and a poor ability to delay gratification. Virtually all these constructs, measured in different ways, are consistently related to measures of offending (see, e.g., Blackburn, 1993, pp. 191–196; Pratt, Cullen, Blevins, Daigle, and Unnever, 2002).

Many studies show that hyperactivity predicts later offending. In the Copenhagen Perinatal project, psychologists Patricia Brennan, Birgitte Mednick, and Sarnoff Mednick (1993) discovered that hyperactivity (restlessness and poor concentration) at age 11–13 significantly predicted arrests for violence up to age 22, especially among boys who had experienced delivery complications. More than half of those with both hyperactivity and high delivery complications were arrested for violence, compared to less than 10% of the remainder. [...]

The most extensive research on different measures of impulsiveness was carried out in the Pittsburgh Youth Study by Jennifer White and her colleagues (1994). The measures that were most strongly related to self-reported delinquency at ages 10 and 13 were teacher-rated impulsiveness (e.g., 'acts without thinking'), self-reported impulsiveness, self-reported undercontrol (e.g., 'unable to delay gratification'), motor restlessness (from videotaped observations), and psychomotor impulsiveness (on the Trail Making Test). Generally, the verbal behavior rating tests produced stronger relationships with offending than the psychomotor performance tests, suggesting that cognitive impulsiveness (based on thinking processes) was more relevant to delinquency than behavioral impulsiveness (based on test performance). Future time perception and delay of gratification tests were only weakly related to self-reported delinquency.

Theories of impulsiveness

Many theories have been put forward to explain the link between impulsiveness and offending. One of the most popular suggests that impulsiveness reflects deficits in the executive functions of the brain, located in the frontal lobes (Moffitt, 1990). Persons with these neuropsychological deficits will tend to commit offenses because they have poor control over their behavior, a poor ability to consider the possible consequences of their actions, and a tendency to focus on immediate gratification. There may also be an indirect link between neuropsychological deficits and offending, which is mediated by hyperactivity and inattention in school and the resulting school failure. [...]

A related theory suggests that low cortical arousal produces impulsive and sensation-seeking behavior. Offenders have a low level of arousal as shown by their low alpha (brain) waves on the electroencephalogram (EEG) or by autonomic nervous system indicators such as heart rate, blood pressure, or skin conductance, or they show low autonomic reactivity (Raine, 1993). [...]

The Harvard scholars James Q. Wilson and Richard Herrnstein (1985) propounded an important criminological theory focusing on impulsiveness and offending. This theory suggested that people differ in their underlying criminal tendencies, and that whether a person chooses to commit a crime in any situation depends on whether the perceived benefits of offending are considered to outweigh the perceived costs. Hence Wilson and Herrnstein focus on cognitive (thinking and decision-making) processes.

The benefits of offending, including material gain, peer approval, and sexual gratification, tend to be contemporaneous with it. In contrast, many of the costs of offending, such as the risk of being caught and punished, and the possible loss of reputation or employment, are uncertain and long delayed. Other costs, such as pangs of conscience (or guilt), disapproval by onlookers, and retaliation by the victim, are more immediate. As many others have done, Wilson and Herrnstein emphasized the importance of the conscience as an internal inhibitor of offending, and suggested that it was built up in a social learning process according to whether parents reinforced or punished childhood transgressions.

The key individual difference factor in the Wilson-Herrnstein theory is the extent to which people's behavior is influenced by immediate as opposed to delayed consequences. They suggested that individuals vary in their ability to think about or plan for the future, and that this ability is linked to intelligence. The major determinant of offending is a person's impulsiveness. More impulsive people are less influenced by the likelihood of future consequences and hence are more likely to commit crimes.

In many respects, Michael Gottfredson and Travis Hirschi's (1990) theory is similar to the Wilson-Herrnstein theory. Gottfredson and Hirschi castigated criminological theorists for ignoring the fact that people differed in underlying criminal propensities and that these differences appeared early in life and remained stable over much of the life-course. They called the key individual difference factor in their theory 'low self-control', which referred to the extent to which individuals were vulnerable to the temptations of the moment. People with low self-control were impulsive, took risks, had low cognitive and academic skills, were self-centered, had low empathy, and had short time horizons. Hence they found it hard to defer gratification, and their decisions to offend were insufficiently influenced by the possible future painful consequences of offending. Gottfredson and Hirschi also argued that between-individual differences in self-control were present early in life (by age 6–8), were remarkably stable over time, and were essentially caused by differences in parental child-rearing practices.

Social cognitive skills

Many researchers have argued that offenders use poor techniques of thinking and problem-solving in interpersonal situations (Blackburn, 1993,

pp. 204–209). Offenders are often said to be self-centered and callous, with low empathy. They are relatively poor at role-taking and perspective-taking, and may misinterpret other people's intentions. Their lack of awareness or sensitivity to other people's thoughts and feelings impairs their ability to form relationships and to appreciate the effects of their behavior on other people. They show poor social skills in interpersonal interactions, fidgeting and avoiding eye contact rather than listening and paying attention.

It is further argued that offenders tend to believe that what happens to them depends on fate, chance, or luck rather than on their own actions. Such thinking makes them feel that they are controlled by other people and by circumstances beyond their control. Hence they think that there is no point in trying to succeed, so they lack persistence in aiming to achieve goals. Arguably, offenders often externalize the blame for their acts to other people rather than taking responsibility themselves, and expect people to believe far-fetched stories. Furthermore, they fail to stop and think before acting and fail to learn from experience. These social cognitive deficits are linked to offenders' concrete, as opposed to abstract, thinking and their poor ability to manipulate abstract concepts (Ross and Ross, 1995). While this constellation of features fits in with many previously cited characteristics of offenders, it has to be said that the evidence in favor of some of them (e.g., the poor social skills of delinquents) is not convincing. Perhaps the most elaborated theory to explain the development of social cognitive skills in relation to aggressive behavior is the social information processing model of the psychologist Kenneth Dodge (1991). According to this, children respond to an environmental stimulus by (1) encoding relevant cues, (2) interpreting those cues, (3) retrieving possible behavioral responses from long-term memory, (4) considering the possible consequences of alternative responses, and (5) selecting and performing a behavior. According to Dodge, aggressive children are more likely to interpret cues as hostile, to retrieve aggressive alternative responses, and to evaluate the consequences of aggression as beneficial.

There are other theories focusing on the thinking processes of offenders. The most popular 'rational choice' theory of crime events suggests that they occur in response to specific opportunities, when their subjectively perceived benefits (e.g., stolen property, peer approval) outweigh their subjectively perceived costs (e.g., legal punishment, parental disapproval). For example, the British psychologists Ronald Clarke and Derek Cornish (1985) outlined a theory of residential burglary that included such influencing factors as whether a house was occupied, whether it looked affluent, whether there were bushes to hide behind, whether there were nosy neighbors, whether the house had a burglar alarm, and whether it contained a dog.

Conclusions

Low intelligence and attainment, and low empathy and impulsiveness, are important risk factors for offending. All of these factors may reflect executive

functioning deficits in the brain. The fact that low attainment predicts offending has inspired programs (especially in preschool) designed to improve school attainment. Similarly, the idea that offenders have high impulsiveness and poor social skills has inspired cognitive-behavioral programs, such as 'reasoning and rehabilitation', designed to reduce impulsiveness and improve social skills.

> *From D.P. Farrington and B. Welsh,* Saving Children from a Life of Crime *(New York: Oxford University Press), 2007, pp. 37–54.*

References

Blackburn, R. (1993) *The Psychology of Criminal Conduct.* Chichester: Wiley.

Brennan, P.A., Mednick, B.R. and Mednick, S.A. (1993) Parental psychopathology, congenital factors, and violence. In *Mental Disorder and Crime,* Hodgins, S. (Ed.) Newbury Park, CA.: Sage.

Clarke, R.V. and Cornish, D.B. (1985) Modelling offenders' decisions: A framework for research and policy. In *Crime and Justice,* vol. 6, Tonry, M. and Morris, N. (Eds) Chicago: University of Chicago Press.

Cohen, A.K. (1955) *Delinquent Boys: The Culture of the Gang.* Glenoe, Ill.: Free Press.

Dodge, K.A. (1991) The structure and function of reactive and proactive aggression. In *The Development and Treatment of Childhood Aggression.* Pepler, D.J. and Rubin, K.H. (Eds.) Hillsdale, NJ: Erlbaum.

Eysenck, H.J. (1996) Personality and crime: Where do we stand? *Psychology, Crime and Law,* 2:143–152.

Farrington, D.P. (1989) Early predictors of adolescent aggression and adult violence. *Violence and Victims.* 4 : 79–100.

Farrington, D.P. (1990) Implications of criminal career research for the prevention of offending. *Journal of Adolescence,* 13: 93–113.

Farrington, D.P. (1991) Childhood aggression and adult violence: Early precursors and later life outcomes. In *The Development and Treatment of Childhood Aggression,* Pepler, D. and Rubin, K.H. (Eds) Hillsdale, N.J.: Erlbaum.

Farrington, D.P. (1992a) Explaining the beginning, progress and ending of antisocial behavior from birth to adulthood. In *Facts, Frameworks and Forecasts:Advances in Criminological Theory,* vol. 3, McCord, J. (Ed.) New Brunswick, N.J.: Transaction.

Farrington, D.P. (1992b) Juvenile delinquency. In *The School Years,* 2nd ed., Coleman, J.C. (Ed.) London: Routledge.

Farrington, D.P. (1993b) Understanding and preventing bullying. In *Crime and Justice,* vol. 17, Tonry, M. and Morris, N. (Eds) Chicago: University of Chicago Press.

Farrington, D.P. (1994a) Childhood, adolescent and adult features of violent males. In *Aggressive Behavior: Current Perspectives,* Huesmann, L.R. (Ed.) New York: Plenum.

Farrington, D.P. (1997b) Human development and criminal careers. In *The Oxford Handbook of Criminology* (2nd. edn), Maguire, M., Morgan, R. and Reiner, R. (Eds) Oxford: Clarendon Press.

Farrington, D.P. and West, D. J. (1993) Criminal, penal and life histories of chronic offenders: Risk and protective factors and early identification. *Criminal Behavior and Mental Health,* 3: 492–523.

Farrington, D.P., Biron, L. and LeBlanc, M. (1982) Personality and delinquency in London and Montreal. In *Abnormal Offenders, Delinquency, and the Criminal Justice System,* Gunn, J. and Farrington,D.P. (Eds) Chichester, England: Wiley

Gottfredson, M. and Hirschi, T. (1990) *A General Theory of Crime.* Stanford, Calif.: Stanford University Press.

Hart, S.D. and Hare, R.D. (1994) Psychopathy and the big five: Correlations between observers' ratings of normal and pathological personality. *Journal of Personality Disorders,* 8: 32–40.

Heaven, P.C.L. (1996) Personality and self-reported delinquency: Analysis of the 'big five' personality dimensions. *Personality and Individual Differences*, 20: 47–54.

John, O.P., Caspi, A., Robins, R.W., Moffitt, T.E. and Magda Stouthamer-Loeber, M. (1994) The 'little five': Exploring the nomological network of the five-factor model of personality in adolescent boys. *Child Development*, 6: 160–178.

Jolliffe, D. and Farrington, D.P. (2004) Empathy and offending: A systematic review and meta-analysis. *Aggression and Violent Behavior*. 9: 441–476.

Lynam, D., Moffitt, T. E. and Stouthamer-Loeber, M. (1993) Explaining the relation between IQ and delinquency: Class, race, test motivation, school failure or self-control? *Journal of Abnormal Psychology*,102: 187–96.

McCrae, R.R. and Costa, P.T. (1997) Personality trait structure as a human universal. *American Psychologist*, 52: 509–516.

McCrae, R.R. and Costa, P.T. (2003) *Personality in Adulthood: A Five-Factor Theory Perspective*. New York: Guilford Press.

McCrae, R.R., Costa, P.T., Ostendorf, F., Angleitner, A., Hrebickova, M., Avia, M.D., Sanz, J., Sanchez-Bernardos, M.L., Kusdil, M. E., Woodfield, R., Saunders, P.R. and B. Smith, P. B. (2000) Nature over nurture: Temperament, personality, and life span development. *Journal of Personality and Social Psychology* 78: 173–186.

Miller, J.D. and Lynam, D.R. (2001) Structural models of personality and their relation to antisocial behavior: A meta-analytic review. *Criminology*, 39: 765–798.

Miller, J.D., Lynam, D.R. and Leukefeld, C. (2003b) Examining antisocial behaviour through the lens of the five factor model of personality. *Aggressive Behavior*, 29: 497–514.

Moffitt, T.E. (1990) The neuropsychology of juvenile delinquency: A critical review. In *Crime and Justice*, vol.12, Tonry, M. and Morris, N. (Eds) Chicago: University of Chicago Press.

Moffitt, T.E. and Henry, B. (1991) Neuropsychological studies of juvenile delinquency and juvenile violence. In *Neuropsychology of Aggression*, Milner, J.S. (Ed.) Boston: Kluwer.

Moffitt, T.E. and Silva, P.A. (1988a) IQ and delinquency: A direct test of the differential detection hypothesis. *Journal of Abnormal Psychology*, 87:330–333.

Moffitt, T.E. and Silva, P.A. (1988b) Neuropsychological deficit and self-reported delinquency in an unselected birth cohort. *Journal of the American Academy of Child and Adolescent Psychiatry*. 27: 233–240.

Morgan, A.B. and Lilienfeld, S.O. (2000) A meta-analytic review of the relation between antisocial behavior and neuropsychological measures of executive function. *Clinical Psychology Review*, 20: 113–136.

Pratt, T.C., Cullen, F.T., Blevins, K.R., Daigle, L. and Unnever, J. D. (2002) The relationship of attention deficit hyperactivity disorder to crime and delinquency: A meta-analysis. *International Journal of Police Science and Management*, 4:344–360.

Raine, A. (1993) *The Psychopathology of Crime: Criminal Behavior as a Clinical Disorder*. San Diego, CA.: Academic Press.

Roberts, B.W. and del Vecchio, W.F. (2000) The rank-order consistency of personality traits from childhood to old age: A quantitative review of longitudinal studies. *Psychological Bulletin*, 126:3–25.

Ross, R.R. and Ross, R.D. (Eds.) (1995) *Thinking Straight: The Reasoning and Rehabilitation Program for Delinquency Prevention and Offender Rehabilitation*. Ottawa: Air Training and Publications.

Schutte, N.S., Malouff, Lena, J.M., Hall, B., Haggerty, D.J., Cooper, J.T., Golden, C.J. and Dornheim, L. (1998) Development and validation of a measure of emotional intelligence. *Personality and Individual Differences*, 25:167–177.

Schweinhart, L.J., Barnes, H.V. and Weilkart, D.P. (1993) *Signficant Benefits: The High/Scope Perry Preschool Study through Age 27*. Ypsilanti, MI: High/Scope Press.

Stattin, H. and Klackenberg-Larsson, I. (1993) Early language and intelligence development and their relationship to future criminal behavior. *Journal of Abnormal Psychology*, 102: 369–378.

White, J.L., Moffitt, T.E., Caspi, A., Bartusch, D.J., Needles,D. J. and Stouthamer-Loeber, M. (1994) Measuring impulsivity and examining its relationship to delinquency. *Journal of Abnormal Psychology*. 103: 192–205.

Wilson, J.Q., and Herrnstein, R.J. (1985) *Crime and Human Nature*. New York: Simon and Schuster.

Zuckerman, M. (1989) Personality in the third dimension: A psychobiological approach. *Personality and Individual Differences*. 10: 391–418.

33.2 Adolescence-limited and life-course-persistent antisocial behavior: a developmental taxonomy
Terrie E. Moffitt

There are marked individual differences in the stability of antisocial behavior. Many people behave antisocially, but their antisocial behavior is temporary and situational. In contrast, the antisocial behavior of some people is very stable and persistent. Temporary, situational antisocial behavior is quite common in the population, especially among adolescents. Persistent, stable antisocial behavior is found among a relatively small number of males whose behavior problems are also quite extreme. The central tenet of this article is that temporary versus persistent antisocial persons constitute two qualitatively distinct types of persons. In particular, I suggest that juvenile delinquency conceals two qualitatively distinct categories of individuals, each in need of its own distinct theoretical explanation. [...]

If correct, this simple typology can serve a powerful organizing function, with important implications for theory and research on the causes of crime. For delinquents whose criminal activity is confined to the adolescent years, the causal factors may be proximal, specific to the period of adolescent development, and theory must account for the *dis*continuity in their lives. In contrast, for persons whose adolescent delinquency is merely one inflection in a continuous lifelong antisocial course, a theory of antisocial behavior must locate its causal factors early in their childhoods and must explain the continuity in their troubled lives.

The dual taxonomy (and its two theories) that I propose in this article is best introduced with reference to the mysterious relationship between age and antisocial behavior. This relationship is at once the most robust and least understood empirical observation in the field of criminology.

Age and antisocial behavior

When official rates of crime are plotted against age, the rates for both prevalence and incidence of offending appear highest during adolescence: they peak sharply at about age 17 and drop precipitously in young adulthood. The majority of criminal offenders are teenagers: by the early 20s the number of active offenders decreases by over 50%, and by age 28, almost 85% of former delinquents desist from offending (Blumstein and Cohen, 1987; Farrington, 1986). With slight variations, this general relationship between age and crime obtains among males and females, for most types of crimes, during recent historical periods and in numerous Western nations (Hirschi and Gottfredson, 1983). A prototype of the empirical curve of criminal offenses average is shown in Figure 33.2.1.

Until recently, research on age and crime has relied on official data, primarily arrest and conviction records. As a result, the left-hand side of the age–crime curve has been censored. Indeed, in many empirical comparisons between early-onset and late-onset antisocial behavior, *early* has been artifactually defined as mid-adolescence on the basis of first police arrest or court conviction (cf. Farrington, Loeber, Elliott, *et al.*, 1990; Tolan, 1987). However, research on childhood conduct disorder has now documented that antisocial behavior begins long before the age when it is first encoded in police data banks, Indeed, it is now known that the steep decline in antisocial behavior between ages 17 and 30 is mirrored by a steep incline in antisocial behavior between ages 7 and 17 (Loeber, Stouthamer-Loeber, Van Kammen and Farrington, 1989; Wolfgang, Figlio, and Sellin, 1972). This extension to the age–crime curve is plotted in Figure 33.2.2. Furthermore, we may venture across disciplinary boundaries to add developmental psychologists' reports of childhood aggression (Pepler and Rubin, 1991) and mental health researchers' reports of conduct disorder (Kazdin, 1987) to criminologists' studies of self-reported delinquency and official crime. So doing, it becomes obvious that manifestations of antisocial behavior emerge very early in the life course and remain present thereafter.

Figure 33.2.1 Age-specific arrest rates for United States Federal Bureau of Investigation's (FBI) index offenses in 1980

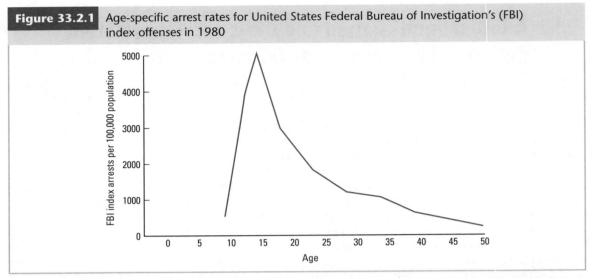

Note: Index offenses include homicide, forcible rape, robbery, aggravated assault, burglary, larceny, and auto theft. From 'Criminal Career Reaserch: Its Value for Criminology' by A. Blumstein, J. Cohen, and D.P. Farrington 1998, *Criminology*, 26 p.11. Copyright 1998 by the American Society of Criminology, adapted by permission.

Figure 33.2.2 The rate of new male offenders at each age per 1,000 male population

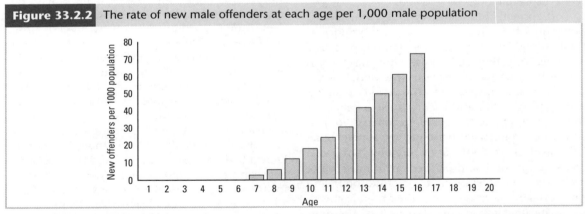

Note: Onset of offending was defined as the age at which a child was first taken into custody and designated delinquent by the police. Rates are based on a cohort of 9,945 boys born in 1945 in Philadelphia, Pennsylvania. From *Delinquency in a Birth Cohort* (p.132) by M.E. Wolfgang, R.M. Figlio, and T. Sellin, 1972, Chicago: The University of Chicago Press. Copyright 1972 by the University of Chicago. Adapted by permission.

With the advent of alternate measurement strategies, most notably self-reports of deviant behavior, researchers have learned that arrest statistics merely reflect the tip of the deviance iceberg (Hood and Sparks, 1970; Klein, 1989). Actual rates of illegal behavior soar so high during adolescence that participation in delinquency appears to be a normal part of teen life (Elliott, Ageton, Huizinga, Knowles, and Canter, 1983). With the liberty of some artistic license, the curved line plotted in Figure 33.2.3 may be taken to represent what is currently known about the prevalence of antisocial behaviors over the life course.

Although there is widespread agreement about the curve of crime over age, there are few convincing explanations for the shape of the curve. Until

Figure 33.2.3 Hypothetical illustration of the changing prevalence of participation in antisocial behaviour across the life course.

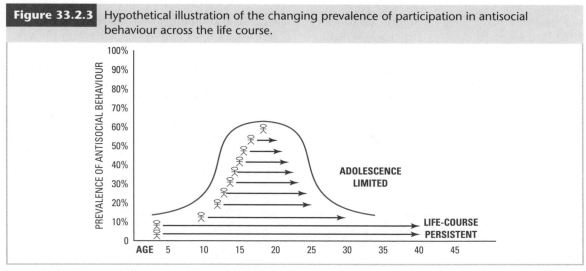

Note: The solid line represents the known curve of crime over age. The arrows represent the duration of participation in antisocial behaviour by individuals.

recently, scholars still disagreed about whether the adolescent peak represented a change in prevalence or a change in incidence: Does adolescence bring an increment in the number of people who are willing to offend or does the small and constant number of offenders simply generate more criminal acts while they are adolescent? Empirical evaluations now suggest that the former explanation is correct. In his English study of offense rates over age, Farrington (1983) showed that the adolescent peak reflects a temporary increase in the number of people involved in antisocial behavior, not a temporary acceleration in the offense rates of individuals. This finding has been replicated in American samples (Wolfgang, Thornberry, and Figlio, 1987). The small human figures under the curve of Figure 33.2.3 portray these changes in prevalence.

But whence the increase in the prevalence of offenders? One possibility is that some phenomenon unique to adolescent development causes throngs of new adolescent offenders to temporarily join the few stable antisocial individuals in their delinquent ways. Figure 33.2.3 depicts the typological thesis to be argued here. A small group of persons is shown engaging in antisocial behavior of one sort or another at every stage of life. I have labeled these persons life-course-persistent to reflect the continuous course of their antisocial behavior. A larger group of persons fills out the age–crime curve with crime careers of shorter

duration. I have labeled these persons adolescence-limited to reflect their more temporary involvement in antisocial behavior. Thus, timing and duration of the course of antisocial involvement are the defining features in the natural histories of the two proposed types of offenders.

Two oft-cited rules of thumb asserted by Robins (1978) seem to simultaneously assert and deny the life-course stability of antisocial behavior: 'Adult antisocial behaviour virtually requires childhood antisocial behaviour [yet] most antisocial youths do not become antisocial adults' (p. 611). In fact, research has shown that antisocial behavior is remarkably stable across time and circumstance for some persons but decidedly unstable for most other people.

The stability of antisocial behavior is closely linked to its extremity. The extreme frequency of crime committed by a very few males is impressive; it has been repeatedly shown that the most persistent 5% or 6% of offenders are responsible for about 50% of known crimes (see Farrington, Ohlin, and Wilson, 1986, for a review). [...]

I have already alluded to the small number of persons in the general population whose antisocial behavior is life-course-persistent. In fact, epidemiological research has shown that there is remarkable uniformity in the prevalence rates of different manifestations of severe antisocial behavior: Regardless of their age, under 10% of males warrant an 'official' antisocial designation. For example, about 5% of preschool boys are considered by their parents or caretakers to be 'very difficult to manage' (McGee, Partridge, Williams, and Silva, 1991). The prevalence of conduct disorder among elementary-school-aged boys has been found to be between 4% and 9% in several countries (Costello, 1989; Rutter, Tizard, and Whitmore, 1970). About 6% of boys are first arrested by police as preteens (Moffitt and Silva, 1988c; Wolfgang et al., 1972); such early arrest is important because it is the best predictor of long-term recidivistic offending. [...]

It is possible, of course, that the persons who constitute these epidemiological statistics at different ages are all different individuals. However, the longitudinal data suggest otherwise: It is more likely that the remarkable constancy of prevalence rates reflects the reoccurrence of the same life-course-persistent individuals in different antisocial categories at different ages. Robins (1966, 1978) has shown that there are virtually no subjects with adult antisocial personality disorder who did not also have conduct disorder as children. [...] The consistency is impressive: A substantial body of longitudinal research consistently points to a very small group of males who display high rates of antisocial behavior across time and in diverse situations. The professional nomenclature may change, but the faces remain the same as they drift through successive systems aimed at curbing their deviance: schools, juvenile-justice programs, psychiatric treatment centers, and prisons. The topography of their behavior may change with changing opportunities, but the underlying disposition persists throughout the life course.

Whereas a few males evidence antisocial behavior that emerges in toddlerhood and is persistent thereafter, the majority of boys who become antisocial first do so during adolescence (Elliott, Knowles, and Canter, 1981). This tidal wave of adolescent onset has been studied in the aforementioned representative sample of New Zealand boys (Moffitt, 1991). Between ages 11 and 15, about one third of the sample joined the delinquent life-styles of the 5% of boys who had shown stable and pervasive antisocial behavior since preschool. As a group these adolescent newcomers to antisocial ways had not formerly exceeded the normative levels of antisocial behavior for boys at ages 3, 5, 7, 9, or 11. Despite their lack of prior experience, by age 15, the newcomers equaled their preschool-onset antisocial peers in the variety of laws they had broken, the frequency with which they broke them, and the number of times they

appeared in juvenile court (Moffitt, 1991). On the basis of such commonly used indexes of adolescent delinquency, the two delinquent groups were indistinguishable. Thus, if the sample was viewed only as an adolescent cross section, researchers would lose sight of the two delinquent groups' very different developmental histories seeing only delinquents and nondelinquents. [...]

I have argued that juvenile delinquency conceals two categories of people. A very large group participates in antisocial behavior during adolescence. A much smaller group who continues serious antisocial behavior throughout adulthood, is the same group whose antisocial behavior was stable across the years from early childhood. The categories remain hypothetical types, because no longitudinal study has yet repeatedly measured antisocial behavior in a representative sample of the same individuals from preschool to midlife. I describe in the next sections the two hypothetical types of antisocial youth: life-course-persistent and adolescence-limited. I argue that the two groups differ in etiology, developmental course, prognosis, and, importantly, classification of their behavior as either pathological or normative.

Life-course-persistent antisocial behavior

As implied by the label, continuity is the hallmark of the small group of life-course-persistent antisocial persons. Across the life course, these individuals exhibit changing manifestations of antisocial behavior: biting and hitting at age 4, shoplifting and truancy at age 10, selling drugs and stealing cars at age 16, robbery and rape at age 22, and fraud and child abuse at age 30; the underlying disposition remains the same, but its expression changes form as new social opportunities arise at different points in development. This pattern of continuity across age is matched also by cross-situational consistency: Life-course-persistent antisocial persons lie at home, steal from shops, cheat at school, fight in bars, and embezzle at work (Farrington, 1991; Loeber, 1982; Loeber and Baicker-McKee, 1989: Robins, 1966, 1978; White et al., 1990). [...]

If some individuals' antisocial behavior is stable from preschool to adulthood as the data imply, then investigators are compelled to look for its roots early in life, in factors that are present before or soon after birth. It is possible that the etiological chain begins with some factor capable of producing individual differences in the neuropsychological functions of the infant nervous system. Factors that influence infant neural development are myriad, and many of them have been empirically linked to antisocial outcomes. [...]

There is good evidence that children who ultimately become persistently antisocial do suffer from deficits in neuropsychological abilities. I have elsewhere reviewed the available empirical and theoretical literatures; the link between neuropsychological impairment and antisocial outcomes is one of the most robust effects in the study of antisocial behavior (Moffitt, 1990b; Moffitt and Henry, 1991; see also Hirschi and Hindelang 1977). Two sorts of neuropsychological deficits are empirically associated with antisocial behavior: verbal and 'executive' functions. The verbal deficits of antisocial children are pervasive, affecting receptive listening and reading, problem solving, expressive speech and writing, and memory. In addition, executive deficits produce what is sometimes referred to as a comportmental learning disability (Price, Daffner, Stowe, and Mesulam, 1990), including symptoms such as inattention and impulsivity. These cognitive deficits and antisocial behavior share variance that is independent of social class, race, test motivation, and academic attainment (Moffitt, 1990b; Lynam, Moffitt, and Stouthamer-Loeber, 1993). In addition, the relation is not an artifact of slow-witted delinquents' greater susceptibility to detection by police: undetected delinquents have weak cognitive skills too (Moffitt and Silva, 1988a).

The evidence is strong that neuropsychological deficits are linked to the kind of antisocial behavior that begins in childhood and is sustained for lengthy periods. [...] Unfortunately, children with cognitive and temperamental disadvantages are not generally born into supportive environments, nor do they even get a fair chance of being randomly assigned to good or bad environments. [...] Vulnerable infants are disproportionately found in environments that will not be ameliorative because many sources of neural maldevelopment co-occur with family disadvantage or deviance.

Indeed, because some characteristics of parents and children tend to be correlated, parents of children who are at risk for antisocial behavior often inadvertently provide their children with criminogenic environments (Sameroff and Chandler, 1975). [...]

Parents and children resemble each other on temperament and personality. Thus, parents of children who are difficult to manage often lack the necessary psychological and physical resources to cope constructively with a difficult child (Scarr and McCartney, 1983; Snyder and Patterson, 1987). For example, temperamental traits such as activity level and irritability are known to be partly heritable (Plomin, Chipuer, and Loehlin, 1990). This suggests that children whose hyperactivity and angry outbursts might be curbed by firm discipline will tend to have parents who are inconsistent disciplinarians; the parents tend to be impatient and irritable too. The converse is also true: Empirical evidence has been found for a relationship between variations in parents' warmth and infants' easiness (Plomin, Chipuer, and Loehlin, 1990).

Parents and children also resemble each other on cognitive ability. The known heritability of measured intelligence (Plomin, 1990; Loehlin, 1989) implies that children who are most in need of remedial cognitive stimulation will have parents who may be least able to provide it. [...] Vulnerable children are often subject to adverse homes and neighborhoods because their parents are vulnerable to problems too (cf. Lahey *et al.*, 1990).

Importantly, although examples from behavior genetics research have been cited in the previous three paragraphs, the perverse compounding of children's vulnerabilities with their families' imperfections does not require that the child's neuropsychological risk arise from any genetic disposition. In fact, for my purposes, it is immaterial whether parent–child similarities arise from shared genes or shared homes. A home environment wherein prenatal care is haphazard, drugs are used during pregnancy, and infants' nutritional needs are neglected is a setting where sources of children's neuropsychological dysfunction that are clearly environmental coexist with a criminogenic social environment.

I believe that the juxtaposition of a vulnerable and difficult infant with an adverse rearing context initiates risk for the life-course-persistent pattern of antisocial behavior. The ensuing process is a transactional one in which the challenge of coping with a difficult child evokes a chain of failed parent–child encounters (Sameroff and Chandler, 1975). [...] Thus children's dispositions may evoke exacerbating responses from the environment and may also render them more vulnerable to criminogenic environments.

If the child who 'steps off on the wrong foot' remains on an ill-starred path, subsequent stepping-stone experiences may culminate in life-course-persistent antisocial behavior. For life-course-persistent antisocial individuals, deviant behavior patterns later in life may thus reflect early individual differences that are perpetuated or exacerbated by interactions with the social environment: first at home, and later at school. [...]

The theory begins with a trait: variation between individuals in neuropsychological health. The trait is truly underlying in that it seldom comes to anyone's attention unless an infant is challenged by formal examinations; it is manifested behaviorally as variability in infant temperament, developmental milestones, and cognitive abilities.

Next, the theory brings environments into play. Parents and other people respond to children's difficult temperaments and developmental deficits. In nurturing environments, toddlers' problems are often corrected. However, in disadvantaged homes, schools, and neighborhoods, the responses are more likely to exacerbate than amend. Under such detrimental circumstances, difficult behavior is gradually elaborated into conduct problems and a dearth of prosocial skills. Thus, over the years, an antisocial personality is slowly and insidiously constructed. Likewise, deficits in language and reasoning are incrementally elaborated into academic failure and a dearth of job skills. Over time, accumulating consequences of the youngster's personality problems and academic problems prune away the options for change.

This theory of life-course-persistent antisocial behavior emphasizes the constant process of reciprocal interaction between personal traits and environmental reactions to them. The original attribute is thus elaborated on during development, to become a syndrome that remains conceptually consistent, but that gains new behavioral components (Caspi and Bem, 1990). Through that process, relatively subtle childhood variations in neuropsychological health can be transformed into an antisocial style that pervades all domains of adolescent and adult behavior. It is this infiltration of the antisocial disposition into the multiple domains of a life that diminishes the likelihood of change. [...]

The life-course-persistent antisocial syndrome, as described here, has many characteristics that, taken together, suggest psychopathology. For example, the syndrome is statistically unusual; much research converges to suggest that it is characteristic of about 5% of males (Robins, 1985). Its rarity is thus consistent with a simple statistical definition of abnormality.

The theoretical syndrome is also characterized by tenacious stability across time and in diverse circumstances. [...] Life-course-persistent antisocial behavior is thus maladaptive in the sense that it fails to change in response to changing circumstances.

The syndrome of life-course-persistent antisocial behavior described here has a biological basis in subtle dysfunctions of nervous system (Moffitt, 1990b). (I reiterate my assertion that biological origins are in no way deterministic. Rather, individual variations in nervous system health provide raw material for subsequent person–environment interactions.) The syndrome is associated with other mental disorders. There is good evidence that such 'comorbidity' is associated with long-term continuity. An impressive body of research documents an overlap between persistent forms of antisocial behavior and other conditions of childhood such as learning disabilities and hyperactivity (cf. Moffitt, 1990a). [...]

Of course, no one or two of these parameters is enough to warrant the classification of life-course-persistent antisocial behavior as psychopathology. Nonetheless, when taken together they form a more persuasive argument that persons whose antisocial behavior is stable and pervasive over the life course may constitute a category that is distinct from persons whose antisocial behavior is short term and situational.

Adolescence-limited antisocial behavior

As implied by the proffered label, discontinuity is the hallmark of teenaged delinquents who have no notable history of antisocial behavior in childhood and little future for such behavior in adulthood. However, the brief tenure of their delinquency should not obscure their prevalence in the population or the gravity of their crimes. In contrast with the rare life-course-persistent type, adolescence-limited delinquency is ubiquitous. Several studies have shown that about one third of males are arrested during their lifetime for a serious criminal offense, whereas fully four fifths of males have police contact for some minor infringement (Farrington, Ohlin, and Wilson, 1986). Most of these police contacts are made during the adolescent years. Indeed, numerous rigorous self-report studies have now documented that it is statistically aberrant to refrain from crime during adolescence (Elliott *et al.*, 1983: Hirschi, 1969; Moffitt and Silva, 1988c).

Compared with the life-course-persistent type, adolescence-limited delinquents show relatively little continuity in their antisocial behavior.

Across age, change in delinquent involvement is often abrupt, especially during the periods of onset and desistence. [...]

Adolescence-limited delinquents may also have sporadic, crime-free periods in the midst of their brief crime 'careers'. Also, in contrast with the life-course-persistent type, they lack consistency in their antisocial behavior across situations. For example, they may shoplift in stores and use drugs with friends but continue to obey the rules at school. Because of the chimeric nature of their delinquency, different reporters (such as self, parent, and teacher) are less likely to agree about their behavior problems when asked to complete rating scales or clinical interviews (Loeber, Green, Lahey, and Stouthamer-Loeber. 1990; Loeber and Schmaling, 1985).

These observations about temporal instability and cross-situational inconsistency are more than merely descriptive. They have implications for a theory of the etiology of adolescence-limited delinquency. Indeed, the flexibility of most delinquents' behavior suggests that their engagement in deviant life-styles may be under the control of reinforcement and punishment contingencies.

Unlike their life-course-persistent peers, whose behavior was described as inflexible and refractory to changing circumstances, adolescence-limited delinquents are likely to engage in antisocial behavior in situations where such responses seem profitable to them, but they are also able to abandon antisocial behavior when prosocial styles are more rewarding. They maintain control over their antisocial responses and use antisocial behavior only in situations where it may serve an instrumental function. Thus, principles of learning theory will be important for this theory of the cause of adolescence-limited delinquency.

A theory of adolescence-limited delinquency must account for several empirical observations: modal onset in early adolescence, recovery by young adulthood, widespread prevalence, and lack of continuity. Why do youngsters with no history of behavior problems in childhood suddenly become antisocial in adolescence? Why do they develop antisocial problems rather than other difficulties? Why is delinquency so common among teens? How are they able to spontaneously recover from an antisocial life-style within a few short years? [...]

Why do adolescence-limited delinquents begin delinquency. The answer advanced here is that their delinquency is 'social mimicry' of the antisocial style of life-course-persistent youths. [...]

If social mimicry is to explain why adolescence-limited delinquents begin to mimic the antisocial behavior of their life-course-persistent peers, then, logically, delinquency must be a social behavior that allows access to some desirable resource. I suggest that the resource is mature status, with its consequent power and privilege.

Before modernization, biological maturity came at a later age, social adult status arrived at an earlier age, and rites of passage more clearly delineated the point at which youths assumed new roles and responsibilities. In the past century, improved nutrition and health care have decreased the age of biological maturity at the rate of three tenths of a year per decade (Tanner, 1978; Wyshak and Frisch, 1982). Simultaneously, modernization of work has delayed the age of labor-force participation to ever later points in development (Empey, 1978; Horan and Hargis, 1991; Panel on Youth of the President's Science Advisory Committee, 1974). Thus, secular changes in health and work have lengthened the duration of adolescence. The ensuing gap leaves modern teenagers in a 5- to 10-year role vacuum (Erikson, 1960). They are biologically capable and compelled to be sexual beings, yet they are asked to delay most of the positive aspects of adult life. In most American states, teens are not allowed to work or get a driver's license before age 16, marry or vote before age 18, or buy alcohol before age 21, and they are admonished to delay having children and establishing their own private dwellings until their education is completed at age 22, sometimes more than 10 years after they attain sexual maturity. They remain financially and socially dependent on their families of origin and are allowed few decisions of any real import. Yet they want desperately to establish intimate bonds with the opposite sex, to accrue material belongings, to make their own decisions, and to be regarded as consequential by adults (Csikszentmihalyi and Larson, 1984). Contemporary adolescents are thus trapped in a *maturity gap*, chronological hostages of a time warp between biological age and social age.

This emergent phenomenology begins to color the world for most teens in the first years of adolescence. [...] Thus, just as teens begin to feel the discomfort of the maturity gap, they enter a social reference group that has endured the gap for 3 to 4 years and has already perfected some delinquent ways of coping with it. Indeed, several researchers have noted that this life-course transition into high school society may place teens at risk for antisocial behavior. In particular, exposure to peer models, when coupled with puberty, is an important determinant of adolescence-onset cases of delinquency (Caspi, Lynam, Moffitt, and Silva, 1993; Magnusson, 1988; Simmons and Blyth, 1987).

Life-course-persistent youngsters are the vanguard of this transition. Healthy adolescents are capable of noticing that the few life-course-persistent youths in their midst do not seem to suffer much from the maturity gap. (At a prevalence rate of about 5%, one or two such experienced delinquents in every classroom might be expected.) Already adept at deviance, life-course-persistent youths are able to obtain possessions by theft or vice that are otherwise inaccessible to teens who have no independent incomes (e.g., cars, clothes, drugs, or entry into adults-only leisure settings). Life-course-persistent boys are more sexually experienced and have already initiated relationships with the opposite sex.[1] Life-course-persistent boys appear relatively free of their families of origin; they seem to go their own way, making their own rules. [...] Antisocial behavior becomes a valuable technique that is demonstrated by life-course-persistents and imitated carefully by adolescence-limiteds. The effect of peer delinquency on the onset of delinquency is among the most robust facts in criminology research (Elliott and Menard, in press; Jessor and Jessor, 1977; Reiss, 1986; Sarnecki, 1986).

One hypothesized by-product of the maturity gap is a shift during early adolescence by persistent antisocial youth from peripheral to more influential positions in the peer social structure. This shift should occur as aspects of the antisocial style become more interesting to other teens. [...]

Much evidence suggests that before adolescence, life-course-persistent antisocial children are ignored and rejected by other children because of their unpredictable, aggressive behavior (Coie *et al.*, 1988; Dodge *et al.*, 1982). After adolescence has passed, life-course-persistent adults are often described as lacking the capacity for loyalty or friendship (Cleckley, 1976; Robins, 1985). At first, these observations may seem contrary to my assertion that life-course-persistents assume social influence over youths who admire and emulate their style during adolescence. [...] In this theory, adolescents who wish to prove their maturity need only notice that the style of life-course-persistents resembles adulthood more than it resembles childhood. Then they need only observe antisocial behavior closely enough and long enough to imitate it successfully. What is contended is that adolescence-limited youths should regard life-course-persistent youths as models, and life-course-persistent teens should regard themselves as magnets for other teens. [...]

Life-course-persistents serve as core members of revolving networks, by virtue of being role models or trainers for new recruits (Reiss, 1986). They exploit peers as drug customers, as fences, as lookouts, or as sexual partners. Such interactions among life-course-persistent and adolescence-limited delinquents may represent a symbiosis of mutual exploitation. Alternatively, life-course-persistent offenders need not even be aware of all of the adolescence-limited youngsters who imitate their style. Unlike adolescence-limited offenders, who appear to need peer support for crime, life-course-persistent offenders are willing to offend alone (Knight and West, 1975). The point is that the phenomena of 'delinquent peer networks' and 'co-offending' during the adolescent period do not necessarily connote supportive friendships that are based on intimacy, trust, and loyalty, as is sometimes assumed. Social mimicry of delinquency can take place if experienced offenders actively educate new recruits. However, it can also take place if motivated learners merely observe antisocial models from afar.

For teens who become adolescence-limited delinquents, antisocial behavior is an effective means of knifing-off childhood apron strings and of proving that they can act independently to conquer new challenges (Erikson, 1960). Hypothetical reinforcers for delinquency include damaging the quality of intimacy and communication with parents, provoking responses from adults in positions of authority, finding ways to look older (such as by smoking cigarettes, being tattooed, playing the big spender with ill-gotten gains), and tempting fate (risking pregnancy, driving while intoxicated, or shoplifting under the noses of clerks). None of these putative reinforcers may seem very pleasurable to the middle-aged academic, but each of the aforementioned consequences is a precious resource to the teenager and can serve to reinforce delinquency. [...]

I suggest that every curfew violated, car stolen, drug taken; and baby conceived is a statement of personal independence and thus a reinforcer for delinquent involvement. Ethnographic interviews with delinquents reveal that proving maturity and autonomy are strong personal motives for offending (e.g., Goldstein, 1990). [...]

In summary, in this narrative account of the etiology of adolescent-onset delinquency I have emphasized three conditions: motivation, mimicry, and reinforcement. I have suggested that a secular change in the duration of adolescence has generated an age-dependent motivational state. In addition, life-course-persistent antisocial models must be available so that their delinquent behaviors can be imitated. Finally, adolescents' fledgling attempts to mimic antisocial styles will continue if they are socially reinforced by the 'negative consequences' of crime. [...]

By definition, adolescence-limited delinquents generally do not maintain their delinquent behavior into adulthood. The account of life-course-persistent persons I made earlier in this article required an analysis of maintenance factors. In contrast, this account of adolescence-limited delinquents demands analysis of desistence: Why do adolescence-limited delinquents desist from delinquency? This theory's answer: Healthy youths respond adaptively to changing contingencies. If motivational and learning mechanisms initiate and maintain their delinquency, then, likewise, changing contingencies can extinguish it. [...] Adolescence-limited delinquents gradually experience a loss of motivation for delinquency as they exit the maturity gap. Moreover, when aging delinquents attain some of the privileges they coveted as teens, the consequences of illegal behavior shift from rewarding to punishing, in their perception. An adult arrest record will limit their job opportunities, drug abuse keeps them from getting to work on time, drunk driving is costly, and bar fights lead to accusations of unfit parenthood. Adolescence-limited delinquents have something to lose by persisting in their antisocial behavior beyond the teen years.

There is some evidence that many young adult offenders weigh the relative rewards from illegal and conventional activities when they contemplate future offending. In a study of three samples, the effect of age on criminal participation was mediated by young men's expectations about whether illegal earnings would exceed earnings from a straight job (Piliavin, Thornton, Gartner, and Matsueda, 1986). Important for this theory, research shows that 'commitment costs' are among the factors weighed by young adults when they decide to discontinue offending. [...]

At the crossroads of young adulthood, adolescence-limited and life-course-persistent delinquents go different ways. This happens because the developmental histories and personal traits adolescence-limiteds allow them the option of exploring new life pathways. The histories and traits of life-course-persistents have foreclosed their options, entrenching them in the antisocial path. To test this hypothesis, research must examine conditional effects of individual histories on opportunities for desistence from crime. [...]

In an earlier section, it was contended that life-course-persistent antisocial behavior represented an especially pernicious and tenacious form of psychopathology. My view of adolescence-limited delinquency is strikingly different: its prevalence is so great that it is normative rather than abnormal. It is flexible and adaptable rather than rigid and stable; most delinquent careers are of relatively short duration because the consequences of crime, although reinforcing for youths caught inside the maturity gap, become punishing to youths as soon as they age out of it. Instead of a biological basis in the nervous system, the origins of adolescence-limited delinquency lie in youngsters' best efforts to cope with the widening gap between biological and social maturity. Moreover, neither this theory nor the empirical evidence suggests that there are links between mental disorders and short-term adolescent delinquency. [...]

It is my stance that individual characteristics will not predict adolescence-limited offending; it is a product of an interaction between age and historical period. True, past studies have reported low to moderate correlations between adolescent delinquency and individual difference variables (such as IQ). However, none of these studies excluded life-course-persistent subjects before analysis. Thus, it remains unclear whether the obtained correlations represent linear monotonic relationships between variables or 'outlier' effects of the extreme scores of life-course-persistent subjects. For example, in the New Zealand sample, the often-reported 8-point IQ difference (Hirschi and Hindelang, 1977) between delinquents and nondelinquents obtains, but it is the pooled result of a 1-point mean deficit for adolescence-onset delinquents and a 17-point mean deficit for childhood-onset delinquents. The same pattern obtains for measures of reading achievement and impulsivity (Moffitt, 1990a; White *et al.*, in press).

The evidence and the alternatives

In this theory of adolescence-limited delinquency, I have made several novel propositions. I have suggested that adolescence-onset delinquency constitutes social mimicry of a pathological type of antisocial child. I have suggested that the motivation for such mimicry follows from a maturity gap between biological adulthood and ascribed adulthood. I have suggested that delinquent mimicry is reinforced by its own consequences while a youth is inside the maturity gap. I have suggested that those consequences lose their rewarding properties after youths age out of the gap, extinguishing delinquency. All three of components of this theory are needed to support my assertion.

> *From T.E. Moffitt, 'Adolescence-limited and life-course-persistent antisocial behavior: a developmental taxonomy',* Psychological Review, *1993, 100: 674–701.*

Note

1   Several longitudinal studies have shown that a history of antisocial behavior predicts early sexual experience for males relative to their age peers (Elliott and Morse, 1987; Jessor, Costa, Jessor and Donovan, 1983; Weiher, Huizinga, Lizotte and Van Kammen, 1991). Specifically, almost all of the sexual experience of an early adolescent cohort is concentrated among the most seriously delinquent 5% of its boys (Elliott and Morse, 1987).

References

Blumstein, A. and Cohen, J. (1987) Characterizing criminal careers. *Science*, 237, 985–991.

Blumstein, A., Cohen, J., and Farrington, D.P. (1988) Criminal career research: Its value for criminology. *Criminology*, 26, 1–35.

Caspi, A. and Bem, D.J. (1990) Personality continuity and change across the life course. In Pervin, L. (Ed.) *Handbook of Personality Theory and Research*. pp. 549–575. New York: Guilford Press.

Caspi, A., Lynam, D., Moffitt, T.E., and Silva, P.A. (1993) Unraveling girls' delinquency: Biological, dispositional and contextual contributions to adolescent misbehavior. *Developmental Psychology*, 29, 19–30.

Cleckley, H. (1976) *The Mask of Sanity*. (5th ed.) St. Louis, MO: Mosby.

Coie, J. D., Belding, M. and Underwood, M. (1988) Aggression and peer rejection in childhood. In Lahey, B. and Kazdin, A. (Eds) *Advances in Clinical Child Psychology*, vol 2, pp. 125–158. New York: Plenum Press.

Costello, E.J. (1989) Developments in child psychiatric epidemiology. *Journal of the American Academy of Child and Adolescent Psychiatry*, 28, 836–841.

Csikszentmihalyi, M., and Larson, R. (1984) Being Adolescent: *Conflict and Growth in the Teenage Years*. New York: Basic Books.

Dodge, K. A., Coie, J. D. and Brakke, N. P. (1982) Behaviour patterns of socially rejected and neglected preadolescents: The roles of social approach and aggression. *Journal of Abnormal Child Psychology*, 10, 389–410.

Elliott. D.S., Ageton, S. S., Huizinga. U., Knowles, B. A., and Canter, R.J. (1983) *The Prevalence and Incidence of Delinquent Behavior*, 1976–1980. The National Youth Survey Report, no. 26. Boulder, CO: Behavioral Research Institute.

Elliott, D.S., Knowles, B., and Canter, R. (1981) The epidemiology of delinquent behavior and drug use among American adolescents: 1976–1980. The National Youth Survey Project Report, no. 14. Boulder, CO: Behavioral Research Institute.

Elliott, D. and Menard, S. (in press) Delinquent friends and delinquent behaviour: Temporal and developmental patterns. In Hawkins, D. (Ed.) *Some Current Theories of Deviance and Crime*. New York: Springer-Verlag.

Elliott, D.S. and Morse, B.J. (1987) Drug use, delinquency, and sexual activity. In Jones, C. and McAnarney, E. (Eds) *Drug Use and Adolescent Sexual Activity, Pregnancy and Parenthood*. pp. 32–60. Washington DC: US Government Printing Office.

Empey, L.T. (1978) *American Delinquency*. Homewood, IL: Dorsey Press.

Erikson, E.H. (1960) Youth and the life cycle. *Children Today*, 7, 187–194.

Farrington, D.P. (1983) Offending from 10 to 25 years of age. In Van Dusen, K. and Mednick, S.A. (Eds), *Prospective Studies of Crime and Delinquency*, pp. 17–38. Boston: Kluwer-Nijhoff.

Farrington, D.P. (1986) Age and crime. In Tonry, M. and Morris, N. (Eds) *Crime and Justice: An Annual Review of Research*, 7, 189–250. Chigago: Chicago University Press.

Farrington, D.P. (1991) Antisocial personality from childhood to adulthood. *The Psychologist*, 4, 389–394.

Farrington, D.P., Loeber, R., Elliott, D.S., Hawkins, D.J., Kandel, D.B., Klein, M. W., McCord, J., Rowe, D., and Tremblay, R. (1990) Advancing knowledge about the onset of delinquency and crime. In Lahey. B. and

Kasdin, A. (Eds.), *Advances in Clinical Child Psychology*, 13, 283–342. New York: Plenum Press.

Farrington, D., Ohlin, L., and Wilson, J.Q. (1986) *Understanding and Controlling Crime*. New York: Springer-Verlag.

Goldstein, A. P. (1990) *Delinquents on Delinquency*. Champaign, Il: Research Press.

Hirschi. T. (1969) *Causes of Delinquency*. Berkeley, CA: University of California Press.

Hirschi, T. and Gottfredson, M. (1983) Age and the explanation of crime. *American Journal of Sociology*, 89, 552–584.

Hirschi, T. and Hindelang, M.J. (1977) Intelligence and delinquency: A revisionist review. *American Sociological Review*, 42, 571–587.

Hood. R. and Sparks, R. (1970) *Key Issues in Criminology*. New York: McGraw-Hill.

Horan, P.M. and Hargis, P.G. (1991) Children's work and schooling in the late nineteenth-century family economy. *American Sociological Review* 56, 583–596.

Jessor, R. and Jessor, S.L (1977) *Problem Behavior and Psychological Development: A Longitundinal Study of Youth*. San Diego, CA: Academic Press.

Jessor, R., Costa, F., Jessor, L. and Donovan, J.E. (1983) The first time of intercourse: A prospective study. *Journal of Personality and Social Psychology*, 44, 608–626.

Kazdin, A.E. (1987) *Conduct Disorders in Childhood and Adolescence*. Newbury Park, CA: Sage.

Klein, M. (1989) Watch out for that last variable. In Mednick, S., Moffitt, T. and Stack, S.A. (Eds), *The Causes of Crime: New Biological Approaches*, pp. 25–41. Cambridge: Cambridge University Press.

Knight, B.J. and West, D.J. (1975) Temporary and continuing delinquency. *British Journal of Criminology*, 15, 43–50.

Lahey, B.B., Frick. P.J., Loeber, R., Tannenbaum, B.A., Van Horn, Y. and Christ, M.A.G. (1990) Oppositional and conduct disorder. A meta-analytic review. Unpublished manuscript.

Loeber, R. (1982) The stability of antisocial and delinquent child behavior: A review. *Child Development*, 53, 1431–1446.

Loeber, R., and Baicker-McKee, C. (1989) The changing manifestations of disruptive/antisocial behavior from childhood to early adulthood: Evolution or tautology? Unpublished manuscript. Western Psychiatric Institute. University of Pittsburgh, Pittsburgh. PA.

Loeber, R., Green. S., Lahey B., and Stouthamer-Loeber, M. (1990) Optimal informants on childhood disruptive behaviors. *Development and Psychopathology*, 1, 317–337.

Loeber, R., and Schmaling, K.B. (1985) Empirical evidence for overt and covert patterns of antisocial conduct problems: A meta-analysis. *Journal of Abnormal Child Psychology* ,13, 337–351

Loeber, R., Stouthamer-Loeber, M., Van Kammen, W., and Farrington, D.P. (1989) Development of a new measure of self-reported antisocial behavior for young children: Prevalence and reliability. In Klein, M. (Ed.) *Cross-National Research in Self Reported Crime and Delinquency*, pp. 203–226. Boston: Kluwer-Nijhoff.

Loehlin, J.C. (1989) Partitioning environmental and genetic contributions to behavioral development. *American Psychologist*, 44, 1285–1292.

Lynam, D., Moffitt, T. and Stouthamer-Loeber, M. (1993) Explaining the relationship between IQ and delinquency: Class, race, test motivation, school failure, or self-control? *Journal of Abnormal Psychology*, 102, 187–196.

Magnusson, D. (1988). *Individual Development from an Interactional Perspective: A Longitudinal Study*. Hillsdale, NJ: Erlbaum.

McGee, R., Partridge, F., Williams, S.M., and Silva, P.A. (1991) A twelve-year follow up of preschool hyperactive children. *Journal of the American Academy of Child and Adolescent Psychiatry*, 30, 224–232.

Moffitt, T.E. (1990a) Juvenile delinquency and attention-deficit disorder: Developmental trajectories from age 3 to 15. *Child Development*, 61, 893–910.

Moffitt, T.E. (1990b) The neuropsychology of delinquency: A critical review of theory and research. In Morris, N. and Tonry, M. (Eds) *Crime and Justice*, 12, 99–169. Chicago: University of Chicago Press.

Moffitt, T.E. (1991, September) Juvenile delinquency: Seed of a career in violent crime, just sowing wild oats, or both? Paper presented at the Science and Public Policy Seminars of the Federation of Behavioral, Psychological, and Cognitive Sciences, Washington, DC.

Moffitt, T.E. and Henry, B. (1991) Neuropsychological studies of juvenile delinquency and violence: A review. In Milner, J. (Ed.) *The Neuropsychology of Aggression* , p. 67–91. Norwell, MA: Flower Academic.

Moffitt, T.E. and Silva, P.A. (1988a) IQ and delinquency: A direct test of the differential detection hypothesis. *Journal of Abnormal Psychology*, 97, 330–333.

Moffitt, T.E. and Silva, P.A. (1988c) Self-reported delinquency: Results from an instrument for New Zealand. *Australian and New Zealand Journal of Criminology*, 21, 227–240,

Panel on Youth of the President's Science Advisory Committee. (1974) *Transition to Adulthood*. Chicago: University of Chicago Press.

Pepler, D. and Rubin, K. (Eds) (1991) *The Development and Treatment of Childhood Aggression*. Hillsdale, NJ: Erlbaum.

Piliavin, I., Thornton. C., Gartner. R., and Matsueda, R. (1986) Crime, deterrence, and rational choice. *American Sociological Review*, 51, 101–119.

Plomin, R. (1990) The role of inheritance in behavior. *Science*, 248, 183–188.

Plomin, R., Chipuer, H.M., and Loehlin, J.C. (1990) Behavioral genetics and personality. In Pervin, L.A. (Ed.) *Handbook of Personality Theory and Research*, pp. 225–243. New York: Guilford Press.

Price, B.H., Daffner, K.R., Stowe, R.M., and Mesulam, M. M. (1990) The compartmental learning disabilities of early frontal lobe damage. *Brain*, 113, 1383–1393.

Reiss, A.J., Jr. (1986) Co-offender influences an criminal careers. In Blumstein, A., Cohen, J., Roth, J.A. and Visher, C. (Eds).*Criminal Careers and Career Criminals*, pp. 121–160. Washington, DC: National Academy Press.

Robins, L.N. (1966) *Deviant Children Grown Up*. Baltimore, MD: Williams and Wilkins.

Robins, L.N. (1978) Sturdy childhood predictors of adult antisocial behaviour: Replications from longitudinal studies. *Psychological Medicine*, 8, 611–622.

Robins, L.N. (1985) Epidemiology of antisocial personality. In Cavenar, J. O. (Ed.) *Psychiatry*, 3, 1–14. Philadelphia: Lippincots.

Rutter, M., Tizard, J., and Whitmore, K. (1970) *Education, Health and Behaviour*. London: Longman.

Sameroff, A. and Chandler, M. (1975) Reproductive risk and the continuum of caretaking casualty. In Horowitz, F., Hetherington, M., Scarr-Salapatek, S. and Siegel, G. (Eds) *Review of Child Development Research*, 4, 187–244. Chicago: Chicago University Press.

Sarnecki (1986) *Deliquent Networks*. Stockholm: National Council for Crime Prevention.

Scarr, S., and McCartney, K. (1983) How people make their own environments: A theory of genotype – environment effects, *Child Development*, 54, 424–435.

Simmons, R.J., and Blyth, D.A. (1987) *Moving into Adolescence: The Impact of Pubertal Change and School Context*. New York: Aldine de Gruyter.

Snyder, J., and Patterson, G. (1987) Family interaction and delinquent behavior. In Quay, H. (Ed.) *Handbook of Juvenile Delinquency*, 216–243. New York: Wiley.

Tanner. J.M. (1978) *Fetus into Man*. Cambridge, MA: Harvard University Press.

Tolan, P. H. (1987) Implications of age of onset for delinquency risk. *Joural of Abnormal Child Psychology*, 15, 47–65.

Weiher, A. Huizinga, D. Lizotte, A.J. and Van Kammen, W. B. (1991) The relationship between sexual activity, pregnancy, delinquency, and drug abuse. In Huizinga, D., Loeber, R. and Thornberry, T. (Eds) *Urban Delinquency and Substance Abuse: A Technical Report*. (ch.6). Washington DC: Office of Juvenile Justice and Delinquency Prevention.

White, J., Moffitt, T.E., Caspi, A., Jeglum, D., Needles, D., and Stouthamer-Loeber, M. (in press). Measuring impulsivity and examining its relationship to delinquency. *Journal of Abnormal Psychology*.

White, J., Moffitt, T.E., Earls, F., Robins, L.N., and Silva, P.A. (1990) How early can we tell? Preschool predictors of boys' conduct disorder and delinquency. *Criminology*, 28, 507–533.

Wolfgang, M.E., Figlio, R.M., and Sellin, T. (1972) *Delinquency in a Birth Cohort*. Chicago: University of Chicago Press.

Wolfgang, M.E., Thornberry T.P., and Figlio, R.M. (1987) *From Boy to Man, from Delinquency to Crime*. Chicago: University of Chicago Press.

Wyshak, G., and Frisch, R.E. (1982) Evidence for a secular trend in age of menarche, *New England Journal of Medicine*, 306, 1033–1035.

33.3 A sociogenic developmental theory of offending
Robert J. Sampson and John H. Laub

Summary of theoretical model

Our theoretical framework has three major themes. The first is that structural context is mediated by informal family and school social controls, which in turn explain delinquency in childhood and adolescence. The second theme is that there is strong continuity in antisocial behavior running from childhood through adulthood across a variety of life domains. The third theme is that informal social capital in adulthood explains changes in criminal behavior over the life span, regardless of prior individual differences in criminal propensity. In our view, childhood pathways to crime and conformity over the life course are significantly influenced by adult social bonds.

Although we reject the 'ontogenetic' approach dominant in developmental psychology (see Dannefer, 1984), our theoretical framework nonetheless follows a developmental strategy (see Loeber and LeBlanc, 1990; Farrington, 1986b; Patterson et al., 1989). Loeber and LeBlanc (1990: 376) define 'developmental criminology' as strategies that examine within-individual changes in offending over time. Moreover, the developmental approach that we take views causality as 'best represented by a developmental network of causal factors' in which dependent variables become independent variables over time (Loeber and LeBlanc, 1990: 433). Developmental criminology recognizes continuity and change over time and focuses on life transitions as a way of understanding patterns of offending. This strategy has also been referred to as a 'stepping stone approach', where factors are time ordered by age and assessed with respect to outcome variables (see Farrington, 1986b).

A similar perspective can be found in interactional theory (see Thornberry, 1987 and Thornberry *et al.*, 1991). In our theoretical framework, we draw on the key idea of interactional theory that causal influences are bidirectional or reciprocal over the life course. Interactional theory embraces a developmental approach and argues convincingly that delinquency may contribute to the weakening of social bonds and informal social control over time. In particular, Thornberry maintains that interactional theory offers an explanation for continuity in criminal trajectories over time: 'The initially weak bonds lead to high delinquency involvement, the high delinquency involvement further weakens the conventional bonds, and in combination both of these effects make it extremely difficult to reestablish bonds to conventional society at later ages. As a result, all of the factors tend to reinforce one another over time to produce an extremely high probability of continued deviance' (Thornberry *et al.*, 1991: 30).

Thornberry's perspective is also consistent with a person-centered approach to development as described by Magnusson and Bergman (1988: 47). In our analysis of the Gluecks' qualitative data we focused explicitly on 'persons' rather than 'variables' by examining individual life histories over time (see Magnusson and Bergman, 1988 and 1990). This focus complemented our quantitative analyses and offered insight into the social processes of intraindividual developmental change in criminal behavior over the life course.

A summary representation of our sociogenic developmental theory as applied to the Gluecks' data is presented in Figure 33.3.1. In essence, this model explains probabilistic links in the chain of events from childhood to adult criminal behavior. It is our view that family and school processes of informal social control provide the key causal explanation of delinquency in childhood and adolescence. Structural background characteristics are important in terms of their effects on informal family and school processes, but these same characteristics have little direct influence on delin-

quency. Individual characteristics like temperament and early conduct disorder are also linked to both family and school social control processes as well as delinquency itself, but these same factors do not significantly diminish the effects of social bonding in family and school on delinquency.

The theory embodied in Figure 33.3.1 explicitly links delinquency and adult crime to childhood and adolescent characteristics as well as socializing influences in adulthood. Early delinquency predicts weak adult social bonds, and weak adult social bonds predict concurrent and later adult crime and deviance. The process is one in which childhood antisocial behavior and adolescent delinquency are linked to adult crime and deviance in part through weak social bonds. We also believe that salient life events and socialization experiences in adulthood can counteract, at least to some extent, the influence of early life experiences. For instance, late onset of criminal behavior can be accounted for by weak social bonds in adulthood, despite a background of non-delinquent behavior. Conversely, desistance from criminal behavior in adulthood can be explained by strong social bonds in adulthood, despite a background of delinquent behavior. In contrast to many life-course models, our theory emphasizes the quality or strength of social ties more than the occurrence or timing of life events (cf. Loeber and LeBlanc, 1990: 430–432). Thus, our theory provides a sociological explanation of stability and change in crime and deviance over the life course with an explicit focus on within-individual changes in offending and deviance.

Summary of empirical findings

Causes of delinquency

We found that the strongest and most consistent effects on both official and unofficial delinquency flow from the social processes of family, school, and peers. Low levels of parental supervision, erratic, threatening, and harsh discipline, and weak parental attachment were strongly and directly related to delinquency. In addition, school attachment had large negative effects on delinquency independent of family processes. Moreover, attachment to delinquent peers had a significant positive effect on delinquency regardless of family and school process. Despite this finding on peer influence, further analyses of delinquent siblings and attachment to peers revealed that family and school processes appear most important in the causal chain.

Figure 33.3.1 Dynamic theoretical model of crime, deviance, and informal social control over the life course of 1,000 Glueck men, circa 1925–1975

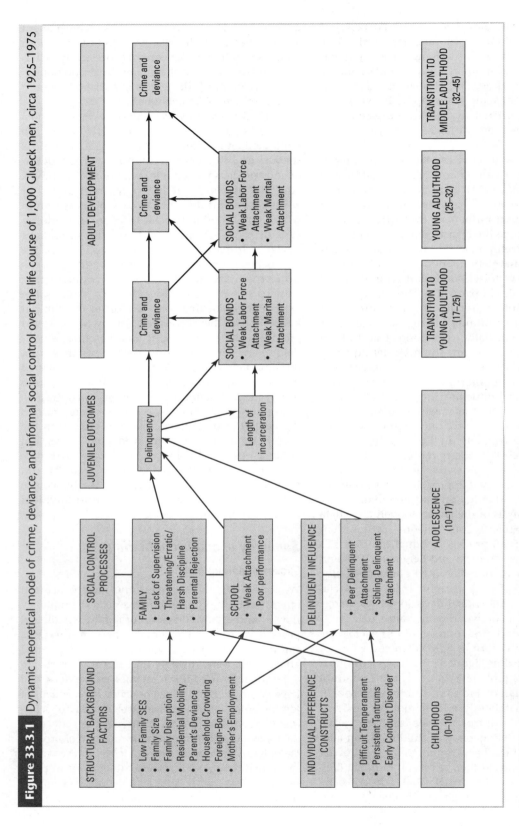

Note: In the *U/D* design, delinquent and nondelinquent males were matched on age, race/ethnicity, neighbourhood SES, and IQ.

At the same time, we found that structural background factors have little direct effect on delinquency, but instead are mediated by intervening sources of informal social control. Moreover, whereas difficult children who display early antisocial tendencies (for instance, violent temperament) do sort themselves into later stages of delinquency, the processes of informal social control explain the largest share of variance in adolescent delinquency.

Overall, the results support our integrated version of social control theory that recognizes the importance of both structure and process. When the bonds linking youth to society – whether through family or school – are weakened, the probability of delinquency is increased. Negative structural conditions (such as poverty or family disruption) also affect delinquency, but largely through family and school process variables.

Stability and change in criminal behavior over the life course

Independent of age, IQ, neighborhood SES, and ethnicity, the original delinquents and nondelinquents in the Gluecks' study displayed behavioral consistency – both homotypic and heterotypic – well into adulthood. Indeed, delinquency and other forms of antisocial conduct in childhood were strongly related to troublesome adult behavior across a variety of life's domains (for example, crime, military offenses, economic dependence, marital discord).

Consistent with a sociological theory of adult development and informal social control, however, we found that job stability and marital attachment in adulthood were significantly related to changes in adult crime – the stronger the adult ties to work and family, the less crime and deviance occurred among both delinquents and controls. We even found that strong marital attachment inhibits crime and deviance regardless of the spouse's own deviant behavior, and that job instability fosters crime regardless of heavy drinking. Moreover, social bonds to employment were directly influenced by State sanctions – incarceration as a juvenile and as an adult had negative effects on later job stability, which in turn was negatively related to continued involvement in crime over the life course. Although we found little direct effect of incarceration on subsequent criminality, the indirect 'criminogenic' effects appear substantively important.

Despite differences in early childhood experiences, adult social bonds to work and family thus had similar consequences for the life trajectories of the 500 delinquents and 500 controls. In fact, the parameter estimates of informal social control were at times nearly identical across the two groups, and the predictive power of early individual-difference constructs was virtually nonexistent once differences in juvenile delinquency were accounted for. These results were consistent for a wide variety of outcome measures, control variables (for example, childhood antisocial behavior and individual-difference constructs), and analytical techniques, including methods that account for persistent unobserved heterogeneity in criminal propensity.

Our strategy also included a new way of portraying life histories of individuals in context. Namely, our quantitative findings were systematically challenged through an intensive examination of qualitative data drawn from the Gluecks' original case files. Integrating divergent sources of information on life histories, the qualitative analysis supported the central idea of our theoretical model that there are both stability and change in behavior over the life course, and that these changes are systematically linked to the institutions of work and family relations in adulthood. Specifically, through an analysis of the narrative data found in the Gluecks' case files, we found that poor job stability and weak marital attachment to one's spouse increase the likelihood of criminal activity and deviant behavior. Conversely, the case records supported the idea that strong job stability and attachment to one's spouse reduce the likelihood of involvement in criminal and deviant behavior.

Taken as a whole, then, our qualitative and quantitative findings suggest that social ties embedded in adult transitions (for example, marital attachment, job stability) explain variations in crime unaccounted for by childhood propensities. This empirical regularity supports our dual concern with continuity and change in the life course (see also Rutter *et al.*, 1990).

Limitations

To be sure, one issue emerged in our qualitative data analyses that complicates our theoretical model – namely, that frequent drinking tends to undermine marital attachment and job stability for some sample members. We also observed for some individuals a reciprocal causal order – crime itself leading to poor job stability and weak marital attachment, which in turn leads to more crime. Consistent with these findings, Vaillant's extensive research on alcoholism has revealed that alcoholics create bad marriages far more often than bad marriages create alcoholics (1983: 97). Vaillant (1983: 6) has further noted that previous studies of delinquent populations have found that '*premorbid* antisocial behavior is associated with *subsequent* alcohol abuse' (see also Robins, 1966; McCord and McCord, 1960; Glueck and Glueck, 1968).

Unfortunately, the nature of the Gluecks' data precludes a definitive analysis of the reciprocal linkages among drinking, social bonds, and crime. As Vaillant (1983) notes, the overrepresentation of antisocial children in the Glueck studies makes it difficult to separate out the antecedents of alcoholism and antisocial behavior. Yet suggesting support for our informal social control framework, Vaillant (1983: 191) maintains that those alcoholics with the most to lose (for example, a job, spouse, or friend) have the best chance at recovery. Alcoholics with social ties to work and marital or other intimate relationships have a base of social support and are under continual supervision and monitoring. Moreover, on the basis of detailed quantitative analyses, we found that although drinking does seem to foster disrupted marriages

and job instability, this relationship does not explain the role of these two factors in fostering crime. Though limited in scope, analysis of simultaneous equation models also revealed that the concurrent effect of adult social bonds on adult crime remained when the reciprocal effect of crime itself was controlled. Therefore, while there is certainly much to be learned about the complex interactional nature of social bonding and drinking (see also Thornberry, 1987), the essential elements of our theoretical model appear robust.

> *From R. Sampson and J. Laub, 'Summing up and looking ahead', in R. Sampson and J. Laub* Crime in the Making: Pathways and Turning Points Through Life *(Cambridge, MA: Harvard University Press), 1993, pp. 243–250.*

References

Dannefer, D. (1984) Adult development and social theory: A paradigmatic reappraisal. *American Sociological Review*, 49: 100–116.

Farrington, D. P. (1986b) Stepping stones to adult criminal careers. In *Development of Antisocial and Prosocial Behavior*, (Ed.) Olweus, D. Block, J. and Radke-Yarrow, M. pp. 359–384 New York: Academic Press.

Glueck, S. and Glueck, E. (1968) *Delinquents and Nondelinquents in Perspective*. Cambridge, Mass.: Harvard University Press.

Loeber, R. and LeBlanc, M. (1990) Toward a developmental criminology. In *Crime and Justice*, vol 12 , (Eds) Tonry, M. and Morris, N. pp. 375–437. Chicago: University of Chicago Press.

Magnusson, D. and Bergman, L.R. (1988) Individual and variable-based approaches to longitudinal research on early risk factors. In *Studies of Psychosocial Risk: The Power of Longitudinal Data*, (Ed.) Rutter, M. pp. 45–61. Cambridge: Cambridge University Press.

Magnusson, D. and Bergman, L.R. (1990) A pattern approach to the study of pathways from childhood to adulthood. In *Straight and Devious Pathways from Childhood to Adulthood*, (Eds) Robins, L. and Rutter, M. pp. 101–115. Cambridge University Press.

McCord, W. and McCord, J. (1960) *Origins of Alcoholism*. Stanford: Stanford University Press.

Modell, J. (1989) *Into One's Own: From Youth to Adulthood in the United States, 1920–1975*. Berkeley: University of California Press.

Patterson, G.R., DeBaryshe, B.D. and Ramsey, E. (1989) A developmental perspective on antisocial behavior. *American Psychologist*, 44: 329–335.

Robins, L.N. (1966) *Deviant Children Grown Up*. Baltimore: Williams and Wilkins.

Rutter, M., Quinton, D. and Hill, J. (1990) Adult outcomes of institution-reared children: Males and females compared. In *Straight and Devious Pathways from Childhood to Adulthood*, (Eds) Robins, L.N. and Hinter, M. pp. 135–157. Cambridge: Cambridge University Press.

Thornberry, T.P. (1987) Toward an interactional theory of delinquency. *Criminology*, 25: 863–891.

Thornberry, T.P., Lizotte, A.J., Krohn, M.D., Farnworth, M. and Sung Joon Jang. (1991) Testing interactional theory: An examination of reciprocal causal relationships among family, school, and delinquency. *Journal of Criminal Law and Criminology*, 82: 3–35.

Valliant, G.E. (1983) *The Natural History of Alcoholism*. Cambridge, Mass.: Harvard University Press.

34

Globalisation, terrorism and human rights

34.1 Crime control as industry
Nils Christie   826

**34.2 Human rights and crimes of the state:
the culture of denial**
Stanley Cohen   827

**34.3 The new regulatory state and the
transformation of criminology**
John Braithwaite   837

34.4 Criminal justice and political cultures
Tim Newburn and Richard Sparks   844

Introduction

KEY CONCEPTS comparative criminology; crime control industry; denial; Gulag; human rights; Keynesian state; new regulatory state; policy learning; policy transfer; political cultures; risk management; state crime

Politicians seeking to explain elements of the financial crisis affecting the majority of developed economies in recent times – or perhaps avoid taking responsibility for it – have reached regularly for the term 'globalisation'. It is a word that has entered everyday language and is now used as a short-hand for a set of changes that give the feel of an interconnected and shrinking world; a world in which the means by which peoples, communications, goods and money travel are growing apparently ever quicker and where the importance of national boundaries is growing ever less. Such trends – though the empirical basis for them may be contested in some respects – have some fairly obvious implications for criminologists.

One possible implication of such a globalised world is that the power of international capital may make itself felt in the arenas of crime and its control. This is Nils Christie's **(Reading 34.1)** basic thesis. What he calls the 'crime control industry' is, he suggests, in an almost uniquely powerful position for the demand for the goods it supplies are almost bottomless. Where are the points of resistance, he asks, to the ever-growing numbers of people incarcerated in our prisons? Indeed, so serious is the potential for expansion he thinks that he draws a comparison with the Soviet Gulags and Nazi system of concentration camps (though without the threat of genocide he suggests). His conclusion – and one you might like to think over – is that the major crime-related danger in modern societies is not crime itself, but the way in which we respond to it (a similar point is often made about terrorism).

In a number of earlier sections of this book (especially Chapters 18 and 19) we noted how criminology for most of its history had been preoccupied with the crimes of the powerless and had paid relatively scant attention to those of the powerful. Stanley Cohen **(Reading 34.2)** focuses on 'crimes of the state' – the atrocities and sufferings that governments and elites impose on others. His central focus concerns the idea of 'denial' (in various forms) and the question of why when confronted, say, with egregious human rights violations our response is so often avoidance or indifference?

Underpinning much of the work in the general field of globalisation is the idea that what we are witnessing is a reworking of the nature, idea and significance of the nation state. According to John Braithwaite **(Reading 34.3)** the shift can be conceptualised as a move from a welfare state, centrally-organised and concerned to attempt to manage demand, to a new regulatory state which is increasingly market-oriented and reliant on privatized institutions and means of delivery. In the crime control arena we can see the impact of these changes in some of the developments highlighted by the Christie reading earlier (though in very different language) and in the spectacular rise of the private policing sector (see also Reading 25.4). One of the consequences of these long-term shifts, he argues, will be the eventual demise of criminology with its preoccupation with state agencies (police, courts, prisons) and old forms of regulation and control. Though he doesn't use the term, one senses that Braithwaite's view of criminologists that continue to be thus preoccupied is that this is another case of what Cohen would call 'denial'!

The ease of communication and travel in our globalised world opens up opportunities for connections, influences and interactions that did not exist before, or at least not in the form they now do so. In the final excerpt, Tim Newburn and Richard Sparks **(Reading 34.4)** examine a variety of issues that now confront the comparative criminologist – many of which coalesce around the question of how one understands and analyses the *similarities* and *differences* between nation states in their systems of regulation and crime control.

Questions for discussion

1. What does Nils Christie mean by the term 'crime control industry'?

2. To what extent is Christie right to argue that the crime control industry is in a most privileged position compared to most other industries?

3. Do you agree with Christie that the major danger of crime in modern societies is not crime itself but the ways in which we respond to it? Explain your reasons.

4. Describe the various forms of 'denial' outlined by Stan Cohen.

5. How does Cohen apply 'neutralization theory' to the issue of denial? How useful do you think this is?

6. What does Braithwaite mean by the term 'new regulatory state'? What are its main characteristics and how does it differ from the Keynesian welfare state?

7. Why, according to Braithwaite, do the changes associated with the emergence of the new regulatory state illustrate the limited relevance of criminology?

8. Why are 'political cultures' of importance and relevance to the comparative criminologist?

34.1 Crime control as industry
Nils Christie

Efficiency and decency

This book is a warning against recent developments in the field of crime control. The theme is simple. Societies of the Western type face two major problems: Wealth is everywhere unequally distributed. So is access to paid work. Both problems contain a potentiality for unrest. The crime control industry is suited for coping with both. This industry provides profit and work while at the same time producing control of those who otherwise might have disturbed the social process.

Compared to most other industries, the crime control industry is in a most privileged position. There is no lack of raw-material, crime seems to be in endless supply. Endless also are the demands for the service, as well as the willingness to pay for what is seen as security. And the usual industrial questions of contamination do not appear. On the contrary, this is an industry seen as cleaning up, removing unwanted elements from the social system.

Only rarely will those working in or for any industry say that now, just now, the size is about right. Now we are big enough, we are well established, we do not want any further growth. An urge for expansion is built into industrial thinking, if for no other reason than to forestall being swallowed up by competitors. The crime control industry is no exception. But this is an industry with particular advantages, providing weapons for what is often seen as a permanent war against crime. The crime control industry is like rabbits in Australia or wild mink in Norway – there are so few natural enemies around.

Belief in being at war is one strong driving force behind the development. A general adaptation to industrialized ways of thought, organization and behaviour is another. The institution of law is in a process of change. The old-fashioned symbol was Lady Justice, blindfolded, and with scales in her hand. Her task was to balance a great number of opposing values. That task is gone. A silent revolution has taken place within the institution of law, a revolution which provides increased opportunities for growth within the control industry.

Through these developments, a situation is created where a heavy increase in the number of prisoners must be expected. This may already be observed in the USA, which at present has reached the hitherto unheard of number of more than 1.2 million prisoners or 504 per 100,000 inhabitants. This is so high a level of prisoners that it cannot be compared to what is found in any industrialized country in the West. But why only 1.2 million? Why not two, three, or five million? And in view of the attempts to create a market-economy in the former USSR, why not a resumed use of Gulags there as well? And then, as the European welfare states decline, will these be able to resist the tempting models of the two forces now turned brothers?

But there are counter-forces in action. As will soon be documented, enormous discrepancies in prison figures exist between countries otherwise relatively similar. We are also confronted with 'unexplicable' variations within the same countries over time. Prison figures may go down in periods where they – according to crime statistics, economy and material conditions – ought to have gone up, and they may go up where they by the same reasons ought to have gone down. Behind these 'irregular' moves, we find ideas on what it is seen as right and fair to do to other beings, ideas which counteract 'rational' economic-industrial solutions. The first chapters of this book document the effects of these counter-forces.

My lesson from all this is as follows: In our present situation, so extraordinarily well suited for growth, it is particularly important to realise that the size of the prison population is a normative question. We are both free and obliged to choose. Limits to the growth of the prison industry have to be man-made. We are in a situation with an urgent need for a serious discussion of how large the system of formal control can be allowed to grow. Thoughts, values, ethics – and not industrial drive – must determine the limits of control, the question of when enough is enough. The size of the prison population is a result of decisions. We are free to choose. It is only when we are not aware of this freedom that the economic/material conditions are given free reign. Crime control is an industry. But industries have to be balanced. This book is about the drive in the prison industry, but also about the counter-forces in morality. [...]

Behind my warning against these developments lurks a shadow from our close history. Recent studies on concentration camps and Gulags have brought us important new insights. The old questions were wrongly formulated. The problem is not. How could it happen? The problem is rather: Why does it not happen more often? And when, where and how will it happen next time?[1] Zygmunt Bauman's book (1989) *Modernity and the Holocaust* is a landmark in this thinking.

Modem systems of crime control contain certain potentialities for developing into Gulags – Western type. With the cold war brought to an end, in a situation with deep economic recession, and where the most important industrial nations have no external enemies to mobilize against, it seems not improbable that the war against the inner enemies will receive top priority according to the well-established historical precendents. Gulags – Western type – will not exterminate, but they have the possibility of removing from ordinary social life a major segment of potential troublemakers for most of those persons' lives. They have the potentiality of transforming what otherwise

would have been those persons' most active lifespan into an existence very close to the German expression of a life not worth living... 'there is no type of nation-state in the contemporary world which is completely immune from the potentiality of being subject to totalitarian rule' says Anthony Giddens (1985, p. 309). I would like to add: The major dangers of crime in modern societies are not the crimes, but that the fight against them may lead societies towards totalitarian developments.

> *From N. Christie*, Crime and Control as Industry, *3rd edn (London: Routledge), 2000, pp. 11–14.*

Note

1. It can rightly be said: The question is not when or where the Holocaust will happen next. It is already happening. Western industrial and financial policy results each day in death and destruction in the Third World. Nonetheless, I will limit my attention to the situation within the industrial world. Crime control in the west is a microcosmos. If we understand what is happening within some of these countries, we may come closer to an understanding of Third World phenomena.

References

Bauman, Z. (1989) *Modernity and the Holocaust*. Ithaca, NY: Cornell University Press.

Giddens, A. (1985) *The Nation-State and Violence*. Cambridge: Polity Press.

34.2 Human rights and crimes of the state: the culture of denial Stanley Cohen

For personal and political reasons that I won't impose on you, I have gradually moved during the last decade from 'doing' criminology to 'doing' human rights.

Criminology and crimes of the state

It would be completely ludicrous to claim that Western criminology over the past decades has completely ignored the subject of state crime or the broader discourse of human rights.

The first significant confrontation with the subject came in the early phase of radical criminology in the late sixties. That favourite debate of the times – 'who are the *real* criminals?' – naturally turned attention from street crime to white collar/corporate crime and then to the wider notion of 'crimes of the powerful'. The particular context of the Vietnam War, pushed our slogans ('Hey, hey LBJ! How many kids have you killed today?') explicitly in the direction of 'crimes of the state'.

In criminology, this sentiment was expressed in the much cited paper by the Schwendingers (1970) entitled 'Defenders of Order or Guardians of Human Rights?' Looking back at this text, it appears a missed opportunity to deal with the core issues of state crime.

Quite rightly, the Schwendingers saw themselves going in the same direction, but a step further than Sutherland by invoking the criterion of *social injury* to define crime. In the case of white collar crime, this mandated us to go beyond criminal law into the areas of civil and administrative law. The Schwendingers then noted that if Sutherland had consistently followed what they rightly call his 'ethical' rather than legal categorisation, he should also have arrived at those other socially injurious actions which are not defined as either criminal or civil law violations. So far, so good. But their argument then goes awry.

Firstly, they cite as examples of other socially injurious action (their only examples) 'genocide and economic exploitation'. Now, besides the fact that these are hardly morally equivalent categories, genocide is crucially different from economic exploitation. It is recognised in current political discourse as crime by the state; it is clearly illegal by internal state laws; and since the Nuremberg Judgements and the 1948 UN Convention Against Genocide, it is a 'crime' according to international law. Genocide belongs to the same conceptual universe as 'war crimes' and 'crimes against humanity'. By any known criteria, genocide is more self evidently criminal than economic exploitation. [...]

I don't want to get into definitional quibbles. Enough to say that the extension of criminology into the terrain of state crimes, can be justified without our object of study becoming simply everything we might not like at the time. Let us see what happened after that mid-sixties to mid-seventies phase when questions about state crimes and human rights were placed on the criminological agenda by the radicals. What mostly happened was that the human rights connection became lost. In the discourse of critical criminology, the putative connection between crime and politics took two different directions, both quite removed from the idea of state crime.

The first was the short-lived notion of the criminal as proto-revolutionary actor and the extension of this to all forms of deviance. This whole enterprise – referred to as the 'politicisation of deviance' – was soon abandoned and eventually denounced as naïve, romantic and sentimental.[1] The second connection – which turned out the more productive – was the focus on the criminalising power of the state. This led to the whole revisionist discourse on the sociology of law, social control and punishment that has remained so salient and powerful.

But neither direction leads anywhere near towards talking about state crimes. The subject simply faded away from criminological view in the mid-seventies to mid-eighties. By the time left realist criminology appeared, we move entirely from 'crimes of state' back to the 'state of crime'. Today the subject has reappeared from two contexts, one *external* to the discipline, the other *internal*.

The *external* context is the incremental growth of the international human rights movement itself. [...] So this is one way – from the outside – that criminologists as citizens who read the news, must have become aware of the subject of human rights violations and crimes of the state. Not that you know about the awareness if you read criminological texts. There is, however, one *internal* way in which the subject has been registered in criminology. This is through the growth of victimology. There are many obvious echoes of human rights issues in victimological literature – whether in the feminist debate about female victims of male sexualised violence; in talking about children and children's rights; in the concern about victims of corporate crime, ecological abuse, etc. [T]hese external and internal inputs are slowly making their way into criminology. [...]

Despite this recent interest, major gaps in the criminological discourse remain:

a First, there is little understanding that a major source of criminalisation at national and international levels draws on the rhetoric human rights.

b Another importance defect in recent literature is its American focus. It is pre-occupied with 'exposures' – of the CIA (e.g., drug running in Vietnam), FBI surveillance methods, the global drug wars, international arms dealing, etc. This results in a certain ethnocentrism, but also allows the derivative subjects (political economy, globalisation, state propaganda, illegal clandestine operations, counter intelligence) to be denied as being 'normal politics' (like the white collar crime issue allowed the denial of 'normal business'). For my purposes here, I want to stress not the politicality of the subject but its criminality. For this, we don't need theories of state, we need merely to pick up the latest Amnesty Annual report.

c If we have missed something about law making, we have ignored even more the facts of victimisation. Again, there is a ritualistic acknowledgement of the damage, harm and violence that are obvious consequences of state crime – and then we return to easier topics. It is as if we don't want to face the facts; as if – to anticipate the substance of the second part of my lecture – we have denied their implications. I am aware that phrases such as 'crimes of the twentieth century' sound bombastic – but for vast populations of the world, this is a fair characterisation of those 'gross violations of human rights': genocide, mass political killings, disappearances, torture, rape by agent of state.[2]

This terrible record is known but (as I will show) simultaneously not known. [...] The reasons why we don't make these connections are less logical than epistemological. The political discourse of the atrocity is, as I will soon show, designed to hide its presence from awareness. This is not a matter of secrecy, in the sense of lack of access to information, but an unwillingness to confront anomalous or disturbing information. [...]

The standard vocabulary of official (government) denial weaves its way at times simultaneously, at times sequentially – through a complete spiral of denial. First you try 'it didn't happen'. There was no massacre, no one was tortured. But then the media, human rights organisations and victims show that it does happen: here are the graves; we have the photos; look at the autopsy reports. So you have to say that what happened was not what it looks to be but really something else: a 'transfer of population', 'collateral damage', 'self defence'. And then – the crucial subtext what happened anyway was completely justified – protecting national security, part of the war against terrorism. So:

It doesn't happen here. If it does, 'it' is something else. Even if it is what you say it is, it is not justified. [...]

Obviously, this is very complex territory – more complex than I can even hint at here – and it is understandable why mainstream criminology is reluctant to become too immersed in these debates. Their absence in 'left realist' criminology is stranger to explain. After all, the ontological base here is a realist philosophy which starts with harm, victimisation, seriousness, suffering and supposed indifference to all this by the adolescent left idealism of the sixties.

I will return to some possible explanations for this blindsight. On one level, this is nothing more sinister than a Western ethnocentrism preoccupied with its own national concerns and secure in the great achievement of liberal capitalism; the separation of crime from the state. On another more interesting level, this stems from the universal tendency to see only what is convenient to see.

The culture of denial

Let me now turn to my substantive topic – denial. How did I get to this subject?

During the last decade in which I lived in Israel, but especially the past five years of the *intifada* (the uprising of Palestinians in the Occupied Territories), I have been puzzled by the apparent lack of overt reaction (dissent, criticism, protest) in just those sectors of Israeli society where one would expect to be reacting more. In the face of clear information about what's going on – escalating levels of violence and repression, beatings, torture, daily humiliations, collective punishment (curfews, house demolition, deportations), death-squad-type killings by army undercover units – the level of shame, outrage and protest, is not psychologically or morally appropriate. [. .]

This is not Milgram's famous question of how ordinary people will behave in terrible ways, but rather how ordinary, even good people, will not react appropriately to knowledge of the terrible. Why, when faced by knowledge of others' suffering and pain – particularly the suffering and pain resulting from what are called 'human rights violations' – does 'reaction' so often take the form of denial, avoidance, passivity, indifference, rationalisation or collusion? I have mentioned the official state discourse: the pure denials (it didn't happen, they are lying, the media are biased, the world community is just picking on us) and the pure justifications (deterrence, self defence, national security, ideology, information gathering). But my concern is not the actor but rather (back, in a curious way, to labelling theory!) the audience. In the triangle of human suffering so familiar to criminologists – the victim, to whom things are done; the perpetrator, who is actively causing the suffering; the observer who sees and knows – my interest lies in this third corner: the audience, the observers, the bystanders. [...] What bodies of literature might be of relevance?

1. The psychology of denial

Orthodox psychoanalysis sees denial as an unconscious defence mechanism for coping with guilt and other disturbing psychic realities. Freud originally distinguished between 'repression' which applies to defences against internal instinctual demands and 'denial' (or what he called 'disavowal') which applies to defences against claims of external reality.

With a few exceptions, pure psychoanalytic theory has paid much less attention to denial in this sense than repression (but see Edelstein, 1989). We have to look in the more applied fields of psychoanalysis (or its derivatives) for studies about denial of external information. This yields a mass of useful material. There is the rich literature on denial of knowledge about fatal disease (especially cancer and more recently, AIDS) affecting self or loved ones. More familiar to criminologists, there is the literature on family violence and pathology: spouse abuse, child abuse, incest, etc. The concept of denial is standard to describe a mother's reaction on 'discovering' that her husband had been sexually abusing their daughter for many years: 'I didn't notice anything'. In this case, the concept implies that in fact the mother did 'know' – how could she not have? – but that this knowledge was too unbearable to confront.

The subject of denial has also been dealt with by cognitive psychology and information theory. Of particular interest is the 'denial paradox': in order to use the term 'denial' to describe a person's statement 'I didn't know', you have to assume that he or she knew or knows about what it is he or she claims not to know (otherwise the term 'denial' is inappropriate).

Cognitive psychologists have used the language of information processing, selective perception, filtering, attention span, etc, to understand the phenomenon of how we notice and

simultaneously do not notice (Goleman, 1985). Some have even argued that the neurological phenomenon of 'blindsight' suggests a startling possibility: that one part of the mind may know just what it is doing, while the part that supposedly knows, remains oblivious of this.

We are all familiar, from basic social psychology, with the notion of cognitive bias: the selection of information to fit existing perceptual frames. At the extreme, information which is too threatening to absorb is shut out altogether. The mind somehow grasps what is going on, but rushes a protective filter into place, steering information away from what threatens. Information slips into a kind of 'black hole of the mind' – a blind zone of blocked attention and self deception. Attention is thus diverted from facts or their meaning. Thus, the 'vital lies' sustained by family members about violence, incest, sexual abuse, infidelity, unhappiness. Lies continue unrevealed, covered up by the family's silence, collusion, alibis and conspiracies (Goleman, 1985).

Similar processes have been well documented outside both the social psychology laboratory and intimate settings like the family. The litany by observers of atrocities is all too familiar: 'we didn't see anything', 'no one told us', 'it looked different at the time'.[3]

In addition to psychoanalytical and cognitive theory, there is also the tradition in philosophical psychology concerned with questions of self knowledge and self deception. The Sartrean notion of 'bad faith' is of particular interest in implying – contrary to psychoanalytical theory – that the denial is indeed conscious.

2. Bystanders and rescuers

Another body of literature more obviously relevant (and more familiar to criminologists) derives from the victimological focus on the bystander. The classic 'bystander effect' has become a cliche: how witnesses to a crime will somehow disassociate themselves from what is happening and not help the victim. The prototype is the famous Kitty Genovese case. (One night in New York in 1964, a young woman, Kitty Genovese, was savagely assaulted in the street just before reaching her apartment. Her assailant attacked her over a period of forty minutes while she struggled, battered and screaming, to reach her apartment. Her screams and calls for help were heard by at least 38 neighbours who, from their own windows saw or heard her struggle. No one intervened directly or by calling the police. Eventually a patrol car arrived – too late to save her life.)

Studies of the bystander effect (Sheleff, 1978) suggest that intervention is less likely to occur under three conditions:

1 *Diffusion of responsibility* – so many others are watching, why should I be the one to intervene? Besides, it's none of my business.

2 *Inability to identify with the victim* – even if I see someone as a victim, I won't act if I cannot sympathise or emphathise with their suffering. We help our family, friends, nation, in-group – not those excluded from our moral universe. (*Journal of Social Issues*, 1990). In fact, those who are outside our moral universe may be blamed for their predicament (the common experience of women victims of sexual violence). If full responsibility is laid on the political out-group (they provoked us, they had it coming), this releases you from your obligation to respond.

3 *Inability to conceive of effective intervention* – even if you do not erect barriers of denial, even if you feel genuine moral or psychological unease ('I feel so awful about what's going on in Bosnia', 'I just can't get those pictures from Somalia out of my mind'), this will not necessarily result in intervention. Observers will not act if they do not know what to do, if they feel powerless and helpless themselves, if they don't see any reward in helping, or if they fear punishment if they help.

These processes are of obvious relevance to my work on human rights violations. There are immediate and literal 'bystanders': all massacres, disappearances and atrocities have their witnesses. And there are also metaphorical bystanders; remember the reader looking at the Amnesty adverts about street kids being killed in Brazil or dissidents being tortured in Turkey: Is this really my problem? Can I identify with these victims? What can I do about it anyway?

The obverse of the bystander effect has generated its own special discourse. Just as interesting as the social bases of indifference, are the conditions under which people are aroused to intervene – often at great personal cost and risk. There is a vast ranging literature here: experimental studies on the social psychology of altruism and pro-social behaviour; the sociology of charity and philanthropy;

philosophical and economic discussions of altruism (notably attempts to reconcile the phenomenon to rational choice theory); historical studies of helping, rescuing, altruism, the Good Samaritan. The best known of this work deals with rescuers of Jews in Nazi Europe (Oliner and Oliner, 1988).

3. Neutralisation theory

More familiar ground to criminologists, is the body of literature known as 'motivational accounts' or 'vocabulary of motives' theory [as] in Sykes and Matza's (1957) 'techniques of neutralisation' paper.

The theory assumes that motivational accounts which actors (offenders) give of their (deviant) behaviour must be acceptable to their audience (or audiences). Moreover, accounts are not just *post facto* improvisations, but are drawn upon in advance from the cultural pool of motivational vocabularies available to actors and observers (and honoured by systems of legality and morality). Remember Sykes and Matza's original list; each technique of neutralisation is a way of denying the moral bind of the law and the blame attached to the offence: denial of injury ('no one got hurt'); denial of victim ('they started it'; 'it's all their fault',); denial of responsibility ('I didn't mean to do it', 'they made me do it'); condemnation of the condemners ('they are just as bad') and appeal to higher loyalties (friends, gang, family, neighbourhood).

Something very strange happens if we apply this list not to the techniques for denying or neutralising conventional delinquency but to human rights violations and state crimes. For Sykes and Matza's point was precisely that delinquents are not 'political' in the sense implied by subcultural theory; that is, they are not committed to an alternative value system nor do they withdraw legitimacy from conventional values. The necessity for verbal neutralisation shows precisely the continuing bind of conventional values.

But exactly the same techniques appear in the manifestly political discourse of human rights violations – whether in collective political trials (note, for example, the Nuremberg trials or the Argentinian junta trial) or official government responses to human rights reports (a genre which I am studying) or media debates about war crimes and human rights abuses. I will return soon to 'literal denial', that first twist of the denial spiral which I identified earlier (it didn't happen, it can't happen here, they are all liars). Neutralisation comes into play when you acknowledge (admit) that something happened – but either refuse to accept the category of acts to which it is assigned ('crime' or 'massacre') or present it as morally justified. Here are the original neutralisation techniques, with corresponding examples from the realm of human rights violations:

i *denial of injury* – they exaggerate, they don't feel it, they are used to violence, see what they do to each other.

ii *denial of victim* – they started it, look what they've done to us; they are the terrorists, we are just defending ourselves, we are the real victims.

iii *denial of responsibility* – here, instead of the criminal versions of psychological incapacity or diminished responsibility (I didn't know what I was doing, I blacked out, etc.) we find a denial of individual moral responsiblity on the grounds of obedience: I was following orders, only doing my duty, just a cog in the machine. (For individual offenders like the ordinary soldier, this is the most pervasive and powerful of all denial systems.)

iv *condemnation of the condemners* – here, the politics are obviously more explicit than in the original delinquency context. Instead of condemning the police for being corrupt and biased or teachers for being hypocrites, we have the vast discourse of official denial used by the modern state to protect its public image: the whole world is picking on us; they are using double standards to judge us; it's worse elsewhere (Syria, Iraq, Guatamala or wherever is convenient to name); they are condemning us only because of their anti-semitism (the Israeli version), their hostility to Islam (the Arab version), their racism and cultural imperialism in imposing Western values (all Third World tyrannies).

v *appeal to a higher loyalty* – the original subdued 'ideology' is now total and self-righteous justification. The appeal to the army, the nation, the *volk*, the sacred mission, the higher cause – whether the revolution, 'history', the purity of Islam, Zionism, the defence of the free world or state security. As the tragic events of the last few years show, despite the end of the cold war, the end of history and the decline of meta narratives, there is no shortage of 'higher loyalties', old and new.

Let us remember the implications of accounts theory for our subject. Built into the offender's action,

is the knowledge that certain accounts will be accepted. Soldiers on trial for, say, killing a peaceful demonstrator, can offer the account of 'obeying orders' because this will be honoured by the legal system and the wider public. This honouring is, of course, not a simple matter: Were the orders clear? Did the soldier suspect that the order was illegal? Where in the chain of command did the order originate from? These, and other ambiguities, make up the stuff of legal, moral and political discourses of denial. [...] For illustration only, let me list some elementary forms of denial which these theories might illuminate.

I will distinguish three forms of denial, each of which operates at (i) the individual or psychic level and (ii) at the organised, political, collective or official level.

(I) Denial of the past

At the individual level, there are the complex psychic mechanisms which allow us to 'forget' unpleasant, threatening or terrible information. Memories of what we have done or seen or known are selected out and filtered. At the collective level, there are the organised attempts to cover up the record of past atrocities. The most dramatic and successful example in the modern era is the eighty years of organised denial by successive Turkish governments of the 1915–47 genocide against the Armenians – in which some one and half million people lost their lives (Hovanissian, 1986). This denial has been sustained by deliberate propaganda, lying and cover-ups, forging of documents, suppression of archives and bribing of scholars. The West, especially the USA, has colluded by not referring to the massacres in the UN, ignoring memorial ceremonies and by surrendering to Turkish pressure in NATO and other arenas of strategic cooperation.

The less successful example, of course, is the so called 'revisionist' history of holocaust of European Jews, dismissed as a 'hoax' or a 'myth'.

At both levels, we can approach the process of denial through its opposite: the attempt to recover or uncover the past. At the individual level, the entire psychoanalytic procedure itself is a massive onslaught on individual denial and self-deception. At the political level, there is the opening of collective memory, the painful coming to terms with the past, the literal and metaphorical digging up of graves when regimes change and try to exorcise their history.

(2) Literal denial

Here we enter the grey area sketched out by psychoanalysis and cognitive theory. In what senses can we be said to 'know' about something we profess not to know about? If we do shut something out of knowledge, is this unconscious or conscious? Under what conditions (for example, information overload or desensitisation) is such denial likely to take place?

There are many different versions of literal denial, some of which appear to be wholly individual, others which are clearly structured by the massive resources of the state. We didn't know, we didn't see anything, it couldn't have happened without us knowing (or it could have happened without us knowing). Or: things like this can't happen here, people like us don't do things like this. Or, you can't believe the source of your knowledge: – victims, sympathisers, human rights monitors, journalists are biased, partial or ignorant.

The psychological ambiguities of 'literal denial' and their political implications are nicely illustrated by the psychoanalyst John Steiner's re-interpretation of the Oedipus drama (Steiner, 1985 and 1990).

The standard version of the legend is a tragedy in which Oedipus is a victim of fate who bravely pursues the truth. At the beginning he does not know the truth (that he has killed his father, that he had sexual relations with his mother); at the end he does. This is taken as a paradigm for the therapeutic process itself: the patient in analysis to whom, gradually and painfully, the secrets of the unconscious are revealed. But alongside this version, Steiner shows, Sophocles also conveys a quite different message in the original drama: the message is that the main characters in the play must have been aware of the identity of Oedipus and realised that he had committed patricide and incest. There is a deliberate ambiguity throughout the text about the nature of this awareness – just how much did each character know? Each of the participants (including Oedipus himself) and especially the various court officials, had (good) different reasons for denying their knowledge, for staging a cover up. The Oedipus story is not at all about the discovery of truth, but the denial of truth – a cover up like Watergate, Iran Contra. Thus the question: how much did Nixon or Bush 'know'?

The ambiguity about how conscious or unconscious our knowledge is, how much we are aware of what we say we are unaware, is nicely captured in Steiner's title 'Turning a Blind Eye'. This suggests the possibility of *simultaneously* knowing and not knowing. We are not talking about the simple lie or fraud where facts are accessible but lead to a conclusion which is knowingly evaded. This, of course is standard in the organised government cover up: bodies are burnt, evidence is concealed, officials are given detailed instructions on how to lie. Rather, we are talking about the more common situation where 'we are vaguely aware that we choose not to look at the facts without being conscious of what it is we are evading' (Steiner, 1985, p 61).

(3) Implicatory denial

The forms of denial that we conceptualise as excuses, justifications, rationalisations or neutralisations, do not assert that the event did not happen. They seek to negotiate or impose a different construction of the event from what might appear the case. At the individual level, you know and admit to what you have done, seen or heard about. At the organised level, the event is also registered but is subjected to cultural reconstruction (for example, through euphemistic, technical or legalistic terminology). The point is to deny the implications – psychological and moral – of what is known. The common linguistic structure is 'yes, but'. Yes, detainees are being tortured but there is no other way to obtain information. Yes, Bosnian women are being raped, but what can a mere individual thousands of miles away do about it?'Denial of responsiblity', as I noted earlier, is one of the most common forms of implicatory denial. The sociology of 'crimes of obedience' has received sustained attention, notably by Kelman and Hamilton (1989). The anatomy of obedience and conformity – the frightening degree to which ordinary people are willing to inflict great psychological and physical harm to others – was originally revealed by Milgram's famous experiment. Kelman and Hamilton begin from history rather than a university laboratory: the famous case of Lieuenant Calley and the My Lai massacre during the Vietnam War in May 1968 when a platoon of American soldiers massacred some 400 civilians. From this case and other 'guilt free' or 'sanctioned' massacres, they extract a rather stable set of conditions under which crimes of obedience will occur:

i   *Authorisation*: when acts are ordered, encouraged, or tacitly approved by those in authority, then normal moral principles are replaced by the duty to obey;

ii *Routinisation*: the first step is often difficult, but when you pass the initial moral and psychological barrier, then the pressure to continue is powerful. You become involved without considering the implications; it's all in a day's work. This tendency is re-inforced by special vocabularies and euphemisms ('surgical strike') or a simple sense of routine. (Asked about what he thought he was doing, Calley replied in one of the most chilling sentences of all times: 'It was no big deal');

iii *Dehumanisation*: when the qualities of being human are deprived from the other, then the usual principles of morality do not apply. The enemy is described as animals, monsters, gooks, sub-humans. A whole language excludes them from your shared moral universe.

The conditions under which perpetrators behave can be translated into the very bystander rationalisations which allow the action in the first place and then deny its implications afterwards. As Kelman and Hamilton show in their analysis of successive public opinion surveys (in which people were asked both to imagine how they would react to a My Lai situation themselves and to judge the actual perpetrators), obedience and authorisation are powerful justifications. And observers as well as offenders are subject to desensitisation (the bombardment by horror stories from the media to a point that you cannot absorb them any more and they are no longer 'news') and dehumanisation.

My research on human rights organisations (national and international) deals with their attempts to overcome these barriers of denial. What is the difference between working in your own country and trying to arouse an international audience in distant and different places? What messages work best in mobilising public action (whether going to a demonstration, donating money or joining an organisation like Amnesty International)? Does focusing on a country work better than raising an issue (such as torture or the death penalty)? And which countries or which issues? Are some techniques of confronting denial – for example, inducing guilt or representing the horrors more vividly – counter-productive? Is there competition for the human rights message within the same audiences (for example, from the environmental movement)?...

Conclusion

Instead of a conclusion, let me instead end with two footnotes. One raises – dare I say – some meta-theoretical issues; the other introduces a little optimism into an otherwise bleak story.

(1) Meta theory

There are a number of trends in post modernist theory which – usually unwittingly – impinge on the human rights discourse. Let me mention a few such meta issues:

First, there is the question of moral relativism. This is the familiar claim – now supposedly finally vindicated – that if there is no universal, foundational base for morality (the death of meta-narratives), then it is impossible to stake out universal values (such as those enshrined in human rights standards). Then comes the derivative claim that such values and standards are Western, ethno-centric, individualistic, alien and imposed.

Now, whatever the historical record, this claim has some strange political, implications. The standard and age-old government denials of the applicability of international human rights norms – we are different, we face special problems, the world doesn't understand us – now acquire a new philosophical dignity. And further, the condemners are condemned for being ethnocentric and imperialist.

A similar problem comes from the assertion that local struggles for human rights lose their meaning because they are informed by the very universal foundations and master narratives now so thoroughly discredited or tarnished. This is again a complex debate; I side with those who argue that no amount of deconstructive scepticism should deny the force with which we defend these values. It is surely a bizarre sight for Western progressives to be telling human rights activists from the Third World or Eastern Europe that their struggle is, after all, not worth the candle.

A second problem is posed by the proclaimed end of history. This is the current round of the old 'end of ideology' game: the collapse of international socialism finally proving the triumph of Western democratic capitalism. Besides the poverty of the case itself, it can make little sense for those still living between death squads, famine, disease and violence. For them, history is not over. But even if one meta narrative has won and there is nothing left for 'history' in the industrialised world, then how does this world react to what is happening elsewhere? Why – if not because of racism, selfishness, greed, and the type of denial I've talked about – do the victors not devote more resources to achieve these values elsewhere?

A third post modernist theme is even more directly relevant to my subject here – and potentially even more destructive. This is the attack on all modes of rational enquiry which work with positivist categories of reality. The human rights movement can live without absolute, foundational values. But it cannot live with a theory which denies any way of knowing what has really happened.[4] All of us who carried the anti-positivist banners of the sixties are responsible for the emergent epistemological circus. Its apotheosis was reached a year ago. On 29 March 1991, shortly after the cessation of hostilities in the Gulf War – just as thousands were lying dead and maimed in Iraq, the country's infra-structure deliberately destroyed by savage bombing, the Kurds abandoned to their fate – the high priest of post-modernism, Jean Baudrillard, published an article entitled 'The Gulf War Has Not Taken Place' (Baudrillard, 1991b). The 'true belligerents' he argued, are those who thrive on the ideology of the truth of this war. He was only being consistent with an article he wrote a few days before the war (Baudrillard, 1991a) in which he predicted that it would never happen. The war existed only as a figment of media simulation, of imaginary scenarios that exceeded all limits of real world facticity. The war, Baudillard had solemnly declared, was strictly unthinkable except as an exchange of threats so exorbitant that it would guarantee that the event would not take place. The 'thing' would happen only in the minds of its audience, as an extension of the video games imagery which had filled our screens during the long build up. Dependent as we all were – prime time viewers as well as generals – on these computer generated images, we might as well drop all self-deluding distinctions between screen events and 'reality'. Given this 'prediction', it was unlikely that Baudrillard would be proved wrong if the war realty did break out. So indeed the 'war' – a free floating signifier, devoid of referential bearing – did not happen. To complain that he was caught out by events only shows our theoretical naivete, our nostalgia for the old truth-telling discourses. [...]

My point in raising this example is simple. If the Turkish government can deny that the Armenian genocide happened; if revisionist historians and neo-Nazis deny that the Holocaust took place; if powerful states all around the world today can systematically deny the systematic violations of human rights they are carrying out then we know that we're in bad shape. But we're in even worse shape when the intellectual *avant garde* invent a form of denial so profound, that serious people including progressives – will have to debate whether the Gulf War actually took place or not.

(2) Acknowledgement

Denial has it opposites. What has to be understood are the conditions under which denial does not occur, in which the truth (even if this concept is disappearing down the post modern black hole) is acknowledged, not just its existence but its moral implications.

After all, in the Milgram experiment, somewhere around 30% of the subjects (depending on the conditions) did not push the button. In Kelman and Hamilton's public opinion surveys, again another 30% would not obey orders to shoot innocent women and children. In the middle of even the most grotesque of state crimes, such as genocide, there are extraordinary tales of courage, rescuing and resistance. Acts of altruism, compassion and pro-social behaviour are woven into the social fabric. Above all, there is the whole human rights movement itself, which over the last three decades has mobilised an extraordinary number of people into wholly selfless behaviour to alleviate the suffering of others – whether by giving money, writing to a prisoner of conscience or joining a campaign.

In my initial interviews with human rights organisations, I was surprised to hear a sense of optimism. Yes, there are some people (referred to in the trade as the 'ostriches') who do not want to know. But most organisations were certain that their potential pool has not been reached. I mentioned to one of my interviewees the cynical notion of 'compassion fatigue' – that people are just too tired to respond, they can't bear seeing any more pictures of the homeless in the streets, victims of AIDS, children starving in Somalia, refugees in Bosnia. Her response was that the concept was a journalistic invention; what there is, is media fatigue.

This is where we return to the state of hyperreality which post modernist theories have so well exposed. The question is right open: Will the type of manipulation and simulation seen in the Gulf War dominate, creating indeed a culture of denial?

Or can we conceive of a flow of information which will allow people to acknowledgereality and act accordingly?

This might seem a pretentious question for us humble criminologists to consider, but I hope that you will allow me to get away with it.

From S. Cohen, 'Human rights and crimes of the state: the culture of denial', Australian and New Zealand Journal of Criminology, 1993, 26(2): 97–115.

Notes

1 I have examined elsewhere the move in alternative criminology from 'idealism' to 'realism', see Cohen (1988; 1990).
2 On rape and sexual abuse in custody, see Amnesty International reports in 1992, especially on India, Turkey, Philippines, Guatamala and Uganda.
3 For a nuanced historical reconstruction of the perceptions of villagers living next to the Mauthausen concentration camp complex, see Horowitz, 1992.
4 My minor personal involvement in this debate – as the object of a radical post-modern critique for foolishly using objective standards of knowledge (in a report on torture in Israel) is recorded in Cohen (1991).

References

Baudrillard, J. (1991a) The reality Gulf. *The Guardian*, 11 January.

Baudrillard, J. (1991b) La guerre du Golfe n'a pas eu lieu. *Liberation*, 29 March.

Cohen, S. (1988) *Against Criminology*. New Brunswick: Transaction.

Cohen, S. (1990) Intellectual scepticism and political commitment; The case of radical criminology. Bonger Memorial lecture. University of Amsterdam.

Cohen, S. (1991) Talking about torture in Israel. *Tikkun*, 6: 23–30, 89–90.

Edelstein, E.L. *et al* (Eds) (1989) *Denial: A Clarification of Concepts and Research*. New York: Plenum Press.

Goleman, D. (1985) *Vital Lies, Simple Truths: On the Psychology of Self Deception*. New York: Simon and Schuster.

Horowitz, G. (Ed.) (1986) *The Shadow of Death: Living Outside the Gates of Mauthausen*. New York: Free Press.

Hovanissian, R.C. (Ed.) (1986) *The Armenian Genocide in Perspective*. New Brunswick: Transaction.

Journal of Social Issues (1990) Special issue on 'moral exclusion', 46.

Kelman, H.C. and Hamilton, V.L. (1989) *Crimes of Obedience*. New Haven:Yale University Press.

Oliner, S. and Oliner, P. (1988) *The Altruistic Personality: Rescuers of Jews in Nazi Europe*. New York: Free Press.

Schwendinger, H. and Schwendinger, J. (1970) Defenders of order or guardians of human rights. *Issues in Criminology*, 7, 72–81.

Sheleff, L. (1978) *The Bystander*. Lexington.

Steiner, J. (1985) Turning a blind eye: The cover up for Oedipus. *International Review of Psycho-Analysis*, 12, 161–72.

Steiner, J. (1990) The retreat from truth to omnipotence in Sophocles: Oedipus at Colonus. *International Review of Psycho-Analysis*, 17, 227–37.

Sykes, G. and Matza, D. (1957) Techniques of neutralization: A theory of delinquency. *American Sociological Review*, 22, 664–70.

34.3 The new regulatory state and the transformation of criminology John Braithwaite

The forms of government and social relations that increasingly characterize contemporary society are giving rise to new ways of thinking about crime and crime control. In particular it is argued that although the discipline of criminology is currently well established in institutional terms, the intellectual tools of the discipline are of diminishing relevance to the social world that is now emerging.

The article describes the major developmental trends in government policy as involving a shift from a welfare state, governed by Keynesian techniques of demand management to a new form of regulatory state, premised upon a neo-liberal combination of market competition, privatized institutions, and decentred, at-a-distance forms of state regulation. These new styles of governance are premised upon a recognition of new social forces and mentalities, particularly of the globalizing logic of risk 'management, and they will increasingly reconfigure the social and political fields in ways that have consequences for the policing and control of crime.

Criminology's traditional focus upon street crimes and the institutions of police, courts and prisons may be decreasingly relevant to the new harms, risks and mechanisms of control that are emerging today. The innovative work of 'regulatory state scholars' such as Clifford Shearing is identified as pushing criminology in new directions that confound the discipline's traditional boundaries but which give it more leverage in the attempt to understand and respond to the control problems of the end of the century. The possibilities for restorative justice in the new context are also discussed, as are other methods for combating insecurity, and both are linked to the importance of developing forms of local knowledge that are informed by a sense of the global development context.

It is argued that the Keynesian state has been replaced by a new regulatory state that is a more Hayekian response to a risk society. Clifford Shearing is identified as a criminological theorist who has come to terms with these developments, especially in his collaborations with Phillip Stenning, David Bayley, Tony Doob and his colleagues at the Community Peace Foundation in Cape Town. Shearing *et al.* are forging a new paradigm (that incorporates the restorative justice paradigm) which might just transcend criminology and become something of general import to the social sciences.

Carved in stone

When I entered the University of Queensland in 1969, there was a large sandstone building with Zoology carved over the entrance. Next to it Botany was carved into the stone. Behind was a newer building called Microbiology. Today, these disciplinary divides don't mean much. The big organizing themes of the biological sciences are molecular biology (transformed by the DNA revolution), evolutionary biology and ecology – all themes that run right across the old biologies based on types of organisms.

Comparable change is descending upon the social sciences. This essay will attempt to explain why. It will contend that some of the scholars who are currently thought of as criminologists might become central influences in the social sciences, even though criminology itself, according to this analysis, is destined for decline. Most of the contributors to this collection, including this one, come from the discipline of sociology, which is already in decline. The risk is that in 20 years our collection will be read as a dialogue between a dead and a dying discipline.

But for the moment sociology is far from dead and criminology is booming. Criminologists have only recently begun to think of themselves as belonging to a discipline, though most continue to have a healthy scepticism of criminology going the way of disciplines they have escaped. In North America, where criminology is most disciplined, there now may well be more university scholars who identify themselves as criminologists than as philosophers or geographers. There are certainly more of the former in government research posts.

The criminology boom is not fed by the intellectual accomplishments of the field, but by the continuous growth in public sector employment in the criminal justice system combined with new expectations that police should be university graduates, and by even stronger growth in private policing. This criminology expansion is so sustained that the criminal justice building will probably still stand on the university campus a century from now. My prediction is that just as there is exciting biology going on in the zoology and botany buildings today, in future we might see criminology abandoned inside the criminal justice building in favour of studies of regulation, child development, restorative and procedural justice and other yet unforseeable organizing ideas. Why? Because of a shift from a Keynesian state to a new regulatory state. Perhaps 'new' should be in inverted commas because all its individual elements are old, and similarly with 'state' since the most important feature of the new regulatory state is that most of the regulation is neither undertaken nor controlled by the state.

The nightwatchman state which preceded the Keynesian state will be conceived as one where most of the steering and rowing (Osborne and Gaebler 1992) was done in civil society. The Keynesian state that succeeds it has the state do a lot of rowing, but was weak on steering civil society. The new regulatory state that is most recent in this chronology holds up state steering and civil society rowing as the ideal.

From the nightwatchman state to the Keynesian state

The nightwatchman state of classical liberal theory had functions more or less limited to protecting its citizens from violence, theft, fraud and promulgating a law of contract (Nozick 1974). Until the nineteenth century most of the steering and most of the rowing in the regulation of social life was done in civil society rather than by the state. Oliver McDonagh (1977) has documented the pattern of government growth in Victorian England that began the journey from the nightwatchman to the Keynesian state. Part of the same pattern was professionalizing the nightwatchman functions themselves with the Peelian revolution in policing from 1829.

The most decisive shift to the Keynesian state was the New Deal in the United States, when a great variety of national regulatory agencies assumed a degree of expert central state control of formerly unregulated activity. It took something as terrible as the great crash to end the nightwatchman state, with the libertarians fighting a rearguard action to the very end. When Richard Whitney, President of the New York Stock Exchange, appeared before Senate staff investigators who were setting up the Securities and Exchange Commission in 1933, he said: 'You gentlemen are making a great mistake. The Exchange is a perfect institution.' (McCraw 1984: 194).

Compared with what went before and with the more Hayekian policy that followed it, the Keynesian state justified quite a lot of rowing by the state, without paying much attention to steering regulatory activities in civil society. In practice, of course, it was still a liberal capitalist society where a great deal of steering and rowing continued to be undertaken by institutions of civil society such as the stock exchange. But the mentality of the Keynesian state was general belief that the state could do the job, including the job of policing; the debate was no longer with liberal minimalism (Hayek was a marginalized, 'out-of-touch' intellectual) but with socialism. Under the ideology of the Keynesian state, the response to every outbreak of disorder was to increase central state policing resources. Social workers, probation officers and other welfare workers employed by the state also acquired ever more resources and powers under the same Keynesian disposition.

From the Keynesian state to the new regulatory state

Following the lead of the Thatcher government in Britain, during the 1980s and 90s thousands of privatizations of public organizations occurred around the world. Contrary to the Hayekian philosophy of Thatcherism, deregulation did not always go hand in hand with privatization (Ayres and Braithwaite 1992: 7-12). Rather we saw what a number of scholars have discussed as the rise of a new regulatory state (Majone 1994; Loughlin and Scott 1997; Parker 1999a). Hence, when British telecommunications was deregulated in 1984, Oftel was created to regulate it; Ofgas with the regulation of a privatized gas industry in 1986, OFFER with electricity in 1989, OfWat with water in 1990, and the Office of the Rail Regulator for rail in 1993 (Baldwin et al. 1998). When the Thatcher government radically shifted the provision of nursing home beds from the public to the private sector (Day and Klein 1987), 200 little nursing home inspectorates were set up in district health authorities to upgrade the previously cursory regulatory oversight of the industry. This led Patricia Day and Rudolf Klein as early as the mid-80s to be speaking of the rise of a new regulatory state in the health and welfare sector, replacing the Keynesian welfare state. Privatization combined with new regulatory institutions is the classic instantiation of Osborne and Gaebler's (1992) prescription for governments to steer but not to row.

The rise of the new regulatory state was partly European catch-up with the New Deal, partly a fresh phenomenon shaped by European Commission imposition of regulatory standards on states (Majone 1994). IMF and World Bank conditionality requiring former communist and developing economies to implement 'good governance' initiatives have also been important in globalizing the new regulatory state (Braithwaite and Drahos 2000). But the new regulatory state is qualitatively different from the New Deal in its reliance on self-regulatory organizations (Clarke 1986), enforced self-regulation (Braithwaite 1982) and other responsive regulatory techniques that substitute for direct command and control. Responsive regulation also flows into strategies for regulating already private institutions through compliance systems, codes of practice and other self-regulatory strategies.

The decentring of the state and 'rule at a distance' are evident in other contemporary intellectual currents, including the 'regulated self-regulation' of neo-corporatist theory (Streeck and Schmitter 1985) and the work of Marsh and Rhodes (1992) on 'policy communities' and 'issue networks' as more important in some ways than states as policy makers (see Crawford 1997). The latter echoes Meidinger's (1987) analysis of 'regulatory communities' of state, business and NGO policy networks with a shared epistemic frame.

While the development of the concept of the new regulatory state by regulatory scholars predates the popularity of late-Foucauldian ideas of liberal governmentality, in the 1990s regulatory scholarship began to be influenced by Foucault's (1991) governmentality lectures. There is no doubt that at the end of his life Foucault was grasping at similar phenomena, albeit in a way that lacked the concrete referents of the scholars of the new regulatory state, or of his own earlier work on disciplinary power with its detailed analyses of practices such as imprisonment (Garland 1997).

For the late Foucault, successful government operates through a capacity of both those who govern and those who are governed to regulate their own behaviour. What Foucault meant by a progressive governmentalization of the state was a move away from direct domination or law enforcement toward indirect rule through invent-

ing technologies for the regulation of conduct, technologies which reshape the institutions within which individuals regulate their own conduct (Hindess 1996). Foucault believed that we 'live in an era of "governmentality" first discovered in the eighteenth century' (Foucault 1991: 91). This account is more or less compatible with the new regulatory state chronology of (1) eighteenth century 'police' in the pluralized, privatized regulatory sense that one sees for example in the writings of Adam Smith (1978), followed by (2) the rise of the Peelian project of a unified state monopoly of 'the police', culminating with (3) the ascendency of Keynesianism that re-pluralizes into (4) the new regulatory state from the 1980s. On both accounts, the Keynesian mentality obscures both the eighteenth and late twentieth century reality of a state that is not a unified set of instrumentalities. What we must study today is strategies of regulation by state and non-state actors, where the state is both a subject and an object of regulation (by the IMF, Moody's, the Security Council, the International Organization for Standardization and the World Trade Organization, among other institutions).

The substantive topics studied by eighteenth century scholars of police were almost identical in range to those researched by contemporary regulatory scholars, so many of whom moved beyond a base in criminology (like Clifford Shearing and his colleagues). In France and Germany in the eighteenth century, included among the topics covered by 'police regulations' were security, customs, trade, highways, foodstuffs, health, labour standards, fire, forests and hunting, streetlife, migration and immigrant communities (Pasquino 1991: 110). Both eighteenth century scholars of police, of which there were thousands (Pasquino 1991: 112), and the equally numerous researchers of the new regulatory state, share an interest in integrating explanatory and normative theories (e.g. Loader 1998; Crawford 1997). For most of the police scholars, the normative theory tended to utilitarianism: 'The object of police is everything that has to do with maintaining and augmenting the happiness of its citizens' (Von Hohental 1776). For the new regulatory scholars, the normative frame tends to involve a blend of neo-liberal and Keynesian welfarist objectives, well illustrated by Shearing's attraction to a neorepublican concern with freedom as non-domination (see Brogden and Shearing 1993). More broadly, new regulatory scholars blend police, liberal and Keynesian mentalities of governance. The marriage of police and the market effected in the writing of Adam Smith (1978)[1] is in turn married to a nostalgia for certain Keynesian virtues, as we will see below.

The new regulatory state has touched even the heartland of the Keynesian state in Australia, with job placement services for the unemployed being privatized and subjected to the regulatory standards of what was initially called the Employment Services Regulatory Authority. The criminal justice system has not been immune to the vectors of the new regulatory state. As in so many nations, in Australia we have seen ten private prisons built during the 1990s, though the new institutions for regulating them have been rather limited (Harding 1997; for Britain see Hood *et al.* 1998). Again, Hayekian marketization combined with Keynesian regulation of markets.

Much more dramatic has been the privatization of policing, with most developed economies having today more private than public police (Shearing and Stenning 1981, 1983, 1987). As early as the 1950s in the US private security personnel outnumbered public police. But the huge taxpayer investment in public police during the 1960s restored a roughly equal balance of the private and public by 1970, only to see the 1.1 million private police by 1982 standing at almost double the public police (Johnston 1992), increasing to 2 million in 1994, thrice the public police (Bayley 1994). In South Africa the preponderance of private over public police is much more profound than in the United States or Europe. There, not only have private replaced public police at sporting events, in high-rise buildings and in gated housing communities for the wealthy, but on the streets in the nightlife areas of the cities nightclubs and restaurants employ, the armed private security personnel who patrol to help us to feel safe as we park along the street. Increasingly, the governmental role is to regulate the standards of these private security providers. In Papua New Guinea, which may have even a worse crime problem than South Africa, the new regulatory state has on some occasions taken the fascinating form of Justice Ministers and Police Commissioners negotiating gang surrenders whereby Rascol gangs hand over their weapons and give various other self-regulatory undertakings in return, among other things, for help by the government to set them up in employment in the private security industry! (Dinnen 1996).

The biggest difference between the new regulatory state of criminal justice versus telecommunications, for example, is that whereas private sector growth has been coupled with public sector decline in telecommunications, this is far from universally true with criminal justice. Public prison building has been as expansive as private prison construction during the 1990s. Between 1970 and 1990 the number of public police increased from a low of 22 percent in Japan (which was the lowest per capita to start with) to a high of a 97 per cent increase in Australia (Bayley 1994: 37), with Britain and the United States falling in the middle at 35 per cent and 64 per cent growth respectively. Where we do find some public sector retrenchment with criminal justice is in the employment of social workers and with other types of welfare provision for offenders, ironically at a time when the evidence clearly no longer sustains a 'nothing works' conclusion. While the welfare state is wound back, the punitive state is not Andrew Scull's (1977) prediction that the fiscal crisis of the Keynesian welfare state would lead to decarceration has happened with mental patients but not with criminals. Indeed, we might say that with recent cuts to the defence establishments in most states, the Keynesian punitive state stands alone as the major exception to 'the hollowing out of the state' (Jessop 1993).

Associated with the neo-liberal economic policies of the 1980s and 90s have been much higher levels of unemployment than the levels possible in the Keynesian world of the 1950s, 60s and early 70s. Part of the ideological strategy of Bush-Reagan and Thatcher-Major, copied by many other states, was to blame the victims for a slothful welfare mentality, but most of all through the war on drugs. In the United States by 1994 there were 678,300 black men behind bars, more than were enrolled in higher education (Mortenson 1996: 4). The impression that the United States has a lower unemployment rate than some European nations today disappears if you correct the unemployment rate by adding those in prison. In 1980, there were 31,000 Americans in prison or jail for selling or using drugs; by 1994, there were 400,000 (mostly unemployed when arrested and black) (Reuter 1997: 264).

But the simultaneous expansion of the new regulatory state to monitor privatized security and the punitive state is beginning to take a financial toll. The state that has gone further than any other in winding back Keynesianism, New Zealand, has been the state that has gone furthest with the new social movement for 'restorative justice' (the most important manifestation of the new regulatory state in criminal justice). Part of the appeal was the fiscal windfall from reducing the number of juvenile justice institutional beds. A close competitor to New Zealand as the most liberal economy in the world is Singapore, the only state that has nominated 'restorative justice' as the officially sanctioned model of its juvenile (but not its adult) justice system (Singapore Subordinate Courts 1997). The Howard conservative government in Australia was elected in 1995 with a justice policy which committed it to expansion of restorative justice initiatives. In the event, while it has cut federal police numbers substantially and while all Australian jurisdictions do have some kind of restorative justice programmes, the expenditure on the latter has been minimal and the cuts to the former are being reversed. The US Attorney General and the British Home Secretary are giving speeches about picking up restorative justice initiatives without really taking any significant policy turns.

Risk society and the new regulatory state

Clifford Shearing (1995), who I will construe as the quintessential scholar of the new regulatory state, believes with Beck (1992), that we have become a risk society in which preventive governance (O'Malley (1992) calls it 'prudentialisin', Feeley and Simon (1994) an 'actuarial logic') has become more important. In this, Shearing follows in the footsteps of a variety of regulatory scholars, including Albert Reiss (1989), Carol Heimer (1985), Nancy Reichman (1986), Peter Manning (1989), Charles Perrow (1984), Ellen Baar (1989), Joseph Sanders (1989), Susan Shapiro (1989), Diane Vaughan (1989) and Keith Hawkins (1989) who made the study of risk a central theme of the sociology of regulation during the 1980s. Shearing sees a difference between feudal governmentality as decentralized rule from the centre (sovereignty devolved) and a marketized mentality that devolves authority itself. Here he picks up on Beck's (1992: 104) idea that the 'universalism of the market' engenders a mentality of loss-reduction, a risk-focused strategy. This combines with the imperative to respond to certain risks that are extreme (and extremely difficult to manage) which have come with the late twentieth century. Let me give two illustrations of what I want to construe as the key connections between risk society and the new regulatory state.

One of the ironies of financial markets is that the engineering of new products to spread risks (derivatives such as futures contracts) has increased systemic risks. The collapse of Barings, England's oldest merchant bank, once referred to as the 'sixth great power in Europe' (Ziegler 1988), by the derivatives trading of a single employee in Singapore, led the development of various risk-reduction strategies coordinated by the International Organization of Securities Commissions and the Basle Commission on Banking Supervision. But the most revealing response to the Barings collapse from the perspective of the new regulatory state was by J.P. Morgan, which had succeeded Barings and the Rothchilds in the late nineteenth century as the most powerful banking house in the world. J.P. Morgan released for general use in October 1994 its own proprietary risk management model, RiskMetrics, accompanied by the data set on the volatilities of different types of financial products used with the model (Dale 1996: 165). As a big player, J.P. Morgan realized that it was in a community of shared fate with smaller players like Barings which used less sophisticated risk management technologies than RiskMetrics. Trading in derivatives actually does not generate new kinds of risks, but risks that can get out of hand with a rapidity obscured by the complexity of secondary markets. The risks of derivatives trading had to be made more transparent to fend off the systemic risk of a major financial collapse.

The second illustration is another of a community of fate (Heimer 1985). Joe Rees (1994) showed how following Three Mile Island, the American nuclear industry shared self-regulatory technologies that they had previously kept secret from one another. They believed another Three Mile Island would see the mentality of the risk society wipe them all out. They set up an industry self-regulatory organization which seems to have been more effective than state regulation alone, though state regulation in the background was an important element of their success. For example, scrams (automatic emergency shutdowns) declined in the US from over seven per unit in 1980 to one in 1993. After the Chernobyl disaster, this self-regulatory programme globalized under the auspices of the World Association of Nuclear Operators (WANO). WANO pairs all nuclear power plants in Russia with sister plants mostly in Germany who help them upgrade to international standards of risk management.

What do these two cases illustrate?

1 The centrality of the mentality of risk management in regulation.

2 The globalizing logic of risk management and how it decentres the regulatory role of the state compared with transnational corporations, and

hybrid private/public international regulators such as WANO, IOSCO and the Basle Commission on Banking Supervision.

3 The possibilities for what Rees (1994) calls 'communitarian regulation' within communities of fate.

Fourthly, these cases illustrate the limited relevance of criminology, with its focus on the old state institutions of police-courts-prisons, to the crimes which pose the greatest risks to all of us. Even at the level of state institutions, one would never grasp from reading criminology journals that the combined numerical strength of public police had not only fallen behind that of private police, but by 1984 in Australia the combined strength of the 100 largest governmental business regulatory agencies had risen to approximately equal the number of public police (Grabosky and Braithwaite 1986). As in Adam Smith's (1978) account, the most consequential domain of 'police' is not the regulation of safety on the streets, but business regulation and self-regulation. 'Future generations will look back on our era as a time when one system of policing ended and another took its place' (Bayley and Shearing 1996: 585). Perhaps the alleged success story of state policing of hot-spots in New York under Mayor Giuliani is a different story of state policing resurgent. Yet the more neglected and more interesting Giuliani story from a new regulatory state perspective is the 1990s liberation of New York from the grip of organized crime told by

James Jacobs (1999). This was accomplished by a shift of reliance away from criminal enforcement (usually followed by the replacement of one jailed mafioso with another) and toward a regulatory strategy (e.g. using licensing powers to deny licences to mob-controlled firms).

From J. Braithwaite, 'The new regulatory state and the transformation of criminology', British Journal of Criminology, 2000, 40 (2): 222–238.

Note

1 Adam Smith's agenda of fostering competitive markets by eliminating both public and private monopolies and liberalizing trade is shared by most scholars of the new regulatory state. Where they differ is that new regulatory state researchers are highly attracted to many Keynesian forms of regulation, of banking, stock markets and labour standards, that would not have been in the least congenial to Smith. Moreover, new regulatory state students utterly reject Smith's ironically statist and authoritarian approach to 'security': 'In every civilized nation death has been the punishment of the murder(er), but in barbarious nations a pecuniary compensation was accepted, because then government was weak and durst not meddle in the quarrels of individuals unless in the way of mediation. . . In the laws of all nations we have the remains of this ancient state of weakness' (Smith 1978; 476) For new regulatory state theorists who find much that is attractive in decentralized restorative justice, this 'weakness' of pre-mercantilist states was an attractive one.

References

Ayers, I. and Braithwaite, J. (1992) *Responsive Regulation: Transcending the Deregulation Debate*. Oxford: Oxford University Press.

Baar, E. (1989) A balance of control: Defining the risk bearer's role in the regulatory equation. Paper presented to the Annual Meeting of the Law and Society Association, Madison, Wisconsin.

Baldwin, R., Hood, C. and Scott, C. (1998) Regulation grows up: Into its prime or mid-life crisis? In Baldwin, R., Hood, C. and Scott, C. (Eds) *Socio-legal Reader on Regulation*. Oxford: Oxford University Press.

Bayley, D.H. (1994) *Police the Future*. Oxford: Oxford University Press.

Bayley, D. and Shearing, C. (1996) The future of policing. *Law and Society Review* 30(3): 585–606.

Beck, U. (1992) *Risk Society: Towards a New Modernity*. Newbury Park: Sage.

Braithwaite, J. (1982) Enforced self-regulation: A new strategy for corporate crime control. *Michigan Law Review*, 80: 1466–507.

Braithwaite, J. and Drahos, P. (2000) *Global Business Regulation*. Melbourne: Cambridge University Press.

Brogden, M. and Shearing, C. (1993) *Policing for a New South Africa*. London: Routledge.

Clarke, M. (1986) *Regulating the City: Competition, Scandal and Reform*. Milton Keynes: Open University Press.

Crawford, A. (1997) *The Local Governance of Crime: Appeals to Community and Partnerships*. Oxford: Clarendon Press.

Dale, R. (1996) *Risk and Revolution in Global Securities Markets*. New York: Wiley.

Day, P. and Klein, R. (1987) Residential care for the elderly: A billion pound experiment in policy-making. *Public Money*, March, 19–24.

Dinnen, S. (1996) Challenges of order in a weak state. PhD dissertation. Canberra: Australian National University.

Feeley, M. and Simon, F. (1994) Actuarial justice: The emerging new criminal law. In Nelken, D. (Ed.) *The Futures of Criminology*. London: Sage.

Foucault, M. (1991) Governmentality. In Burchall, G., Gordon, C. and Miller, P. (Eds.) *The Foucault Effect: Studies in Governmentality*. London: Harvester Wheatsheaf.

Garland, D. (1997), 'Governmentality' and the problem of crime: Foucault, criminology, sociology. *Theoretical Criminology*, 1(2) 173–214.

Grabosky, P., and Braithwaite, J. (1993) (Eds) *Business Regulation and Australia's Future*. Canberra: Australian Institute of Criminology.

Harding, R.W. (1997) *Private Prisons and Public Accountability*. Buckingham: Open University Press.

Hawkins, K. (1989) 'Fatcats' and prosecution in a regulatory agency: a footnote on the social construction of risk. *Law and Policy*, 11(3).

Heimer, C. A. (1985) *Reactive Risk and Rational Action: Managing Moral Hazard in Insurance Contracts*. Berkeley: University of California Press.

Hindess, B. (1996) *Discourses of Power: from Hobbes to Foucault*. Oxford: Blackwell.

Hood, C., James, O., Jones, G., Scott, C. and Travers, T. (1998) *Regulation Inside Government: Waste Watchers, Quality Police and Sleazebusters*. Oxford: Oxford University Press.

Jacobs, J. B. Friel, C and Radick, R (1999) *Gotham Unbound: How New York City was Liberated from the Grip of Organized Crime*. New York: New York University Press.

Jessop, B. (1993) Towards a Schumpeterian welfare state? Preliminary remarks on post-Fordist political economy. *Studies in Political Economy*, 40: 7–39.

Johnston, L. (1992) *The Rebirth of Private Policing*. London: Routledge.

Loader, I. (1998) Criminology and the public sphere: Arguments for utopian realism. In Walton, P. and Young, J. (Eds) *The New Criminology Revisited*. London: Macmillan.

Loughlin, M. and Scott, C. (1997) The regulatory state. In Dunlevy, P., Holliday, I. and Peele, C. (Eds) *Developments in British Politics, 5*. London: Macmillan.

Majone, C. (1994) The rise of the regulatory state in Europe. *West European Politics*, 17:77–101.

Manning, P. (1989) Managing risk: Managing uncertainty in the British Nuclear Installations Inspectorate. *Law and Policy*, 11(3).

Marsh, D. and Rhodes, R. (1992) Policy communities and issue networks: Beyond typologies. In Marsh, D. and Rhodes, R. (Eds) *Policy Networks in British Government*, 249–68. Oxford: Clarendon Press.

Meidinger, E. (1987) Regulatory culture: A theoretical outline. *Law and Policy*, 9: 355.

McCraw, T.K. (1984) *Prophets of Regulation*. Cambridge, MA: Harvard.

McDonagh, O. (1977) *Early Victorian Government*. London: Weidenfeld and Nicolson.

Mortenson, T. (1996) Black men in college or behind bars. *Overcrowded Times*, 7(2):4.

Nozick, R. (1974) *Anarchy, State and Utopia*. Oxford: Blackwell.

Osborne, D. and Gaebler, T. (1992) *Reinventing Government*. New York: Addison-Wesley.

O'Malley, P. (1992) Risk, power and crime prevention. *Economy and Society*, 21(3): 252–75.

Parker, C. (1999a) *Just Lawyers*. Oxford: Oxford University Press.

Pasquino, P. (1991), Theatrum Politicum: The genealogy of capital – police and the state of prosperity. In Burchall, C., Gordon, C. and Miller, P. (Eds) *The Foucault Effect: Studies in Governmentality*. London: Harvester Wheatsheaf.

Perrow, C. (1984) *Normal Accidents: Living with High-Risk Technologies*. New York: Basic: Books.

Rees, J.V. (1994) *Hostages of Each Other: The Transformation of Nuclear Safely Since Three Mile Island*. Chicago: University of Chicago Press.

Reichman, N. (1986) Managing crime risks: Toward an insurance based model of social control. *Research in Law, Deviance and Social Control*, 8: 151–72.

Reiss, A.J. Jr (1989) The institutionalization of risk. *Law and Policy*, 11(3),392–402.

Reuter, P. (1997) Why can't we make prohibition work better? Some consequences of ignoring the unattractive. *Proceedings of the American Philosophical Society*, 141: 262–75.

Sanders, J. (1989) Firm risk management in the face of products liability rules. *Law and Policy*, 11(3).

Scull, A, T. (1977) *Decarceration: Community Treatment and the Deviant. A Radical View*. Englewood Cliffs, NJ: Prentice-Hall.

Shapiro, S. (1989) Libel lawyers as risk counselors: Pre-publication and pre-broadcast review and social construction of news. *Law and Policy*, 11(3).

Shearing, C.D. and Stenning, P.C. (1981) Modern private security: its growth and implications. In Tonry, M. and Morris, N. (Eds) *Crime and Justice: An Annual Review of Research*, 3: 193–245. Chicago: University Chicago Press.

Shearing, C. D. and Stenning, P. C. (1983) Private security: Implications for social control. *Social Problems*, 30(5): 493–506.

Shearing, C. D. and Stenning, P. C. (1987) (Eds) *Private Policing*, California: Sage.

Singapore Subordinate Courts (1997) *Excellence and Beyond*. Singapore: Singapore Subordinate Courts.

Smith, A. (1978) *Lectures on Jurisprudence*. Meek, R.L., Raphael, D.D. and Stein, P.C. (Eds) Oxford: Clarendon Press.

Streeck, W. and Schmitter, P. (1985) *Private Interest Government*. London. Sage.

Vaughan, D. (1989) Regulating risk: Implications of the Challenger accident. *Law and Policy*, 11, 330–49.

Von Hohental, P.C.C. (1776) *Liber de Politia*. Liptal.

Ziegler, P. (1988) *The Sixth Great Power: Barings 1762–1929*. London: Collins.

34.4 Criminal justice and political cultures
Tim Newburn and Richard Sparks

Introduction

The imperative to think about contemporary social analysis in terms of 'flows' and 'edges' has latterly become part of the common currency of much social theory and substantive research (Lash and Urry 1993; Urry 1999; Castells 2000; Bauman 2001b). The way in which the notion of globalization has burst the bounds of technical discussion (in which it was itself a fairly novel coinage only ten or fifteen years ago) and has become a standard term of public debate attests to the receptiveness of our wider political culture to these concerns, even if the concept of globalization has lost something in precision or specificity in the process. The case of criminal justice is an especially vexed and interesting one here, however. While it seems clear that policy-makers and senior practitioners increasingly occupy the 'space of flows' (Castells 2001) it is also the case that many of the key concerns of criminology and criminal justice – with police powers or with the punishment of offenders, for example – have classically been regarded as integral to, and even definitve of, the capacities and legitimation claims of the nation-state (Weber 1978). There are questions of sovereignty, of democratic accountability and, indeed, of national self-definition at stake in this field. We should therefore be ready to confront a quite complicated and contentious arena in which examples of 'policy transfer' and convergence, and the creation of specifically supranational institutions, jostle against restatements of state sovereignty and assertions of identity. David Garland (1996) has famously identified and analysed one half of this dialectic, namely the sense of a withering of state capacity in crime control and the menace this poses to the power to rule by sovereign command, as central to explaining the amplified importance of contemporary penal politics. We share this concern but think that the time is also ripe for a wider attempt at reorientation. In other words in seeking to pose contemporary and demanding questions about 'what is going on?' (let alone about 'what is to be done?') criminology and criminal justice as fields of study will have to address the tense and contradictory intersection between 'the space of flows' and 'the space of places', for it is here that new institutional forms emerge and political energies are generated.

We begin with two basic premises. First, that there is increasing evidence of certain forms of convergence in the languages and practices of crime control (Garland 2001). We plainly need to confront the emergence and promulgation of supranational legal orders, international standards and common intellectual currencies. Secondly, the mechanisms, directions and outcomes of such flows and transfers are both more complex and less well elucidated empirically and theoretically than is commonly assumed.

'Policy transfer' and 'lesson drawing'

The idea that policies and practices in one jurisdiction are affected, more or less directly, by those in another is by no means new. In the context of the broad sweep of changes associated with the idea of globalization it is, however, of increasing importance across the social sciences. There has, in this regard, been a developing interest within the fields of comparative politics and international relations in the idea of 'policy transfer' (Stone 1999; Dolowitz and Marsh 1996) and related but distinct ideas, including 'lesson-drawing' (Rose 1993), 'policy convergence' (Bennett 1991) and 'policy diffusion' (Eyestone 1977).

As we have separately noted elsewhere (Sparks 2001; Newburn 2002) the impulse to look across, to import novel ideas and replicate models encountered elsewhere can be traced back more or less to the inception of criminal justice institutions in their 'modern' forms. This is perhaps best attested in relation to penitentiary imprisonment. It stands behind John Howard's epic pilgrimage through the prisons of Britain and Europe or Beaumont and de Tocqueville's epistles home from the USA. [...] According to Tarde (1903) the purpose of scholarship in this area was 'to learn why, given one hundred innovations conceived at the same time – innovations in the form of words, in mythological ideas, in industrial processes, etc. – ten will spread abroad while ninety will be forgotten' (cited in Rogers 1995:40). One question before us now concerns the ways in which such processes of exchange may have intensified, accelerated and altered their media of transmission in recent times.

In its narrow form, the question can be reduced to the idea of 'policy transfer'. This may be seen as 'a process in which knowledge about policies, administrative arrangements, institutions etc. in one time and/or place is used in the development of policies, administrative arrangements and institutions in another time and/or place' (Dolowitz and Marsh 1996: 344). This definition of the process of policy transfer is broad enough to encompass essentially voluntary processes such as 'lesson drawing' and more structurally influenced notions such as 'convergence'. Previous work in this area has highlighted at least seven major questions.

The first of the questions concerns the reasons why particular policies, practices or ideas are transferred. Crudely, transfer may be analysed along a continuum from the broadly voluntary to the more coercive. At the largely voluntary end one example would be the many visits by politicians and professionals to the New York Police Department, particularly during the 'crime drop' of the 1990s, to examine the possibility of replicating the NYPD's use of information technology for the management of police performance (known locally as Compstat) to domestic forces. At the more coercive end are the changes wrought as a result of the existence of international treaties and other obligations. One of the most visible sites of such changes in the crime control sphere is the transnationalising effect of the processes and practices central to increasing European co-operation in field of policing and the impact of donor assistance on police reform in South Africa.

Secondly, any analysis of these processes requires us to ask: who is involved in the transfer of ideas, policies and practices? As Rogers (1995: 7) puts it, 'innovations do not sell themselves'. A number of actors, agencies and institutions may be involved in different ways in the process of transfer. They may include, *inter alia*, politicians, parties and governments, pressure groups and think-tanks, policy entrepreneurs and experts and transnational corporations and non-governmental institutions/networks. Though it may seem obvious to note that there are people, agencies and institutions involved in such processes, all too often work in this area talks of emergent systems of crime control as if they were entirely the product of structural forces that underpin them. While we don't for a moment deny the importance of struc-

tural forms of explanation, we need also to move beyond what Karstedt suggests are approaches that involve unilateral or deterministic concepts towards those that also recognise the 'path dependency' inherent in the notion of travel: 'decisions taken at crossroads, different destinations and different points of departure'.

Thirdly, there is the issue of *what* is transferred. Though the focus of much extant work in this area has tended to be on the most formal aspects of policy – programmes, instruments and institutions – as several of the chapters remind us, symbols and rhetoric maybe at least if not more important. This is particularly the case, it would appear, in the crime control arena. Moreover, the fact that transfer might be more common at the level of symbol than substance should not be taken as an indication of its relative unimportance, for as Muncie notes, 'it is vital not to lose sight of the fact that the discursive also has material effects'. Finally in this regard there is also what might be thought of as 'negative policy transfer' where the result of a particular influence is the non-adoption of a particular policy.

Fourthly is the question of from where are lessons drawn. Influences may be domestic and international. In terms of the topography of contemporary crime control it is undoubtedly the case that the USA is perceived to be the source of the greatest number of exported ideas and practices. [...] [However, it is all too easy for such American influence to be] misunderstood, misrepresented, exaggerated or simplified. Much of the political science literature focuses on the nature of the policies being transferred and how their complexity and feasibility affect the extent of transfer. By contrast, we argue that while these factors are undoubtedly important, it is the sociopolitical and cultural context in which 'transfer' occurs, or is attempted, that has the most profound effect on the eventual shape and style of the policy concerned. This raises two further questions about policy transfer. What are the constraints on such transfer and, linked to this, what are the different degrees of transfer or, put another way, how complete is the process? Is what is occurring something akin to 'copying' or, rather, is it a vaguer process of emulation in which inspiration is taken from a set of ideas or practices, but where the eventual result is the production of something quite distinctive? In part, as we have intimated, the likely answer to the latter question is, in particular cases, a product, at least in part, of the socio-political circumstances under which 'policy transfer' takes place.

Finally there is the question of how the process is related to policy 'success' or 'failure'. In part, this could be interpreted as simply a different way of assessing the degree of fidelity in the process of transfer. Seen more broadly, the question concerns the more general results of the spread of particular policies. Were they fully implemented? When implemented, did they achieve their intended goals? And so on. These, however, are not really questions addressed in this volume. It is not that they are not, or could not be, important. Rather, that they are rather narrowly technical in scope and lead us away from many of the broader political and normative questions that a focus on the spread of ideas, policies and practices can raise. Moreover, questions of policy 'success' or 'failure' also lead us quite quickly to some of the difficulties of the very idea of policy transfer.

As we said earlier, we could limit our focus to the narrow question of policy transfer. The notion is a suggestive and interesting one and, as we hope we have illustrated, raises some important questions. Yet it is insufficiently broad to allow some of the distinctive structural and cultural issues to come fully into play. It also suffers from a number of other difficulties. First, as Jones and Newburn outline, the term 'policy' is often rather taken for granted; it tends to be insufficiently specified in studies of 'transfer'. Related to this, 'transfer' is itself a somewhat problematic concept, inviting the assumption that there are conscious, intended processes at work. As a consequence it draws attention away from unintended consequences and, crucially, is generally based on a model of policy-making and policy development that is overly rational and which tends, either explicitly or implicitly, to see policy-making as a set of stages involving the creation of agendas, the selection between alternatives, the implementation (possibly following transfer) of the selected policy, followed by some assessment of its success or failure. Now there may be occasions where policymaking does indeed look like this. However, and this may be something specifically to do with criminal justice and penal policy – though we very much doubt it – the emergence and adoption of crime control practices, policies and technologies are subject to a much more complex mix of structural, subjective and simply serendipitous influences. And it is these as much as the more obvious accoutrements of policy-making (and transfer) that concern us here. Thus, [it is important] to move beyond the limiting vocabulary of policy transfer towards a more broadly conceptualised idea of comparative policy analysis. Such a project is itself, of course, far from unproblematic.

Some problems of comparative criminology

For all the reasons already stated, students of crime, punishment and control increasingly address the transnational scope of their subject, and are bound to do so with increasing urgency in coming years. This in no sense means that the traditions of comparative criminology (the contrastive exploration of problems, priorities, legal cultures, elite networks, public sensibilities and so on) are anywhere near being exhausted. Indeed, Nelken, in some of the most elegant and authoritative commentaries on the problems and prospects of comparative study in criminology and criminal justice (see, *inter alia*, Nelken 1994, 1997, 2000), more often suggests that this style of work is embryonic and unfulfilled than that it is, in any sense of the term, *finished*.

We expressly do not, therefore, suggest that a concern with flux, mobility and transfer simply supercedes one with difference, diversity or inter-cultural understanding. The cognitive, explanatory and ethical challenges posed by comparative research remain both daunting and exciting. Indeed, given that it has very often been suggested (for example, here in terms suggested by Giddens 1991) that one of the primary purposes of sociological work is to 'think oneself away' from the immediacy of local experience, there remains an abiding place for comparative reflection at every level of theory and research. Moreover, comparative study retains its essential role simply as a corrective against sweeping assertions of either difference or sameness. [...]

Among the more salutary discoveries of recent comparative research is that terms and institutions that at first blush look strikingly similar (indeed often consciously adopted or adapted from an imported model) turn out on closer examination to be distinct in interesting and meaningful ways. Thus for example the important work of Lacey and Zedner on concepts of 'security' and 'community' in Britain and Germany (1995, 1998; see also Bauman 2001a), and the growing international literature on 'prevention' and 'safety' (King 1989; Crawford 2000; Melossi and Selmini 2000), disclose both subtle and basic differences of meaning and application. On some occasions while there is a surface similarity –

in terms of symbolism or of diction – deeper analysis reveals often quite profound differences at the level of substance. [...] As Muncie argues, it is by no means always clear whether 'globalization' and its synonyms have broad applicability or merely serve to direct our attention to those transformations that fit neatly within our narrowly ethnocentric view of the world.

At the same time, and as we have implied, the future of comparative criminology is increasingly complicated by both those illegal flows and markets (movements of people, drugs, weapons, money and information) that expressly puncture national and jurisdictional boundaries and the varieties of police co-operation, international treaties, protocols and conventions designed to impede their mobility and promote common standards and practices. In many of their aspects these dialectics of crime and control systems are now familiar (if none the less bewildering) features of policy networks and of academic discourse. What remain arguably less well understood are the means whereby cultural and conceptual resources also escape their points of origin and become naturalised (and hence variously translated, inflected or hybridised) in other locations. [...] Who are their sponsors and entrepreneurs? How is a certain field made fertile for their reception?

And what of less flagrant or less overt sharings of knowledge or experimentation or innovation – a certain 'take' on risk, for instance, or a certain set of demands for auditing or accountability? Such questions also demand attention to the travels undertaken by criminological theories, explanatory models and terms as much as to policy enterprises as such. The international reach of certain of these (Braithwaite's (1989) account of shaming and reintegration springs to mind here) has been striking recently – but how are such effects accomplished and with what consequences? Indeed, this may be one of the more powerful illustrations of the power of criminology. For, despite the oft-lamented refrain that criminology and criminologists have remarkably little influence on their domestic policy-makers and practitioners, a shift of focus away from the minutiae of policy towards the narratives, rhetorics and metaphors developed by criminologists may provide more obvious examples of influence, particularly perhaps when their spread cross-nationally is taken into account. [...]

However, there is an inherent danger in all such activity. It is that in thinking about the global reach of ideas, policies and practices, our attention will tend to be drawn to convergence rather than divergence, to similarity rather than difference and to homogeneity rather than heterogeneity. Influential models and dictions meet resistances, counter-discourses and extant traditions and sensibilities. A crucial question for us, therefore, is how different are the ways in which ostensibly similar vocabularies are taken up and applied in the distinct settings they encounter? Just how diverse in terms of their social organisation, intellectual formation, political temper and points of intersection with policy networks and the wider public sphere are the 'criminologies' of contemporary European societies? How in turn do the latter intersect with and differ from the language and practice of crime control in North America or other regions of the world?

The importance of politics and political culture

While much that is common to the cultures of control in contemporary advanced economies is the result of broad social, cultural, political and economic pressures, so it is also the case that particular socioeconomic, cultural and political contexts frame and shape in very different ways apparently mobile policy ideas. Moreover, it is clear that the nature of the politico-cultural environment to which ideas, practices and policies travel has a very significant impact on the eventual shape and destiny of the 'import'; or even if there is any import at all. As Lacey (2003: 86) observes, it is crucial for us to recognise 'that the salience and politicisation of criminal justice vary from country to country' and that our understanding of this variation remains far from developed (Tonry 2001). Understanding similarities and differences in the pattern of contemporary systems of crime control – and understanding the movement and translation of commodities between and within these systems – is therefore arguably one of the key tasks facing criminology. Strictly speaking, translation, Melossi argues, is impossible. Rather, 'generally speaking any term, even the simplest, is embedded within a cultural context, or milieu, that gives it its meaning' (2000: 144). Of course, cultures are not hermetically sealed and it is the case that practices, policies and rhetorics travel and that, within limits, there can be, and are, common understandings. Nevertheless, his central argument is that we cannot and should not take for granted that surface similarities necessarily imply deeper convergences [...].

How to investigate such variation is a particularly challenging task. A recent interesting addition to the literature exploring this tension between broad structural changes and local socioeconomic circumstances is what Hall and Soskice (2001: 57) have called their 'Varieties of Capitalism' approach. This, they suggest, 'calls into question the monolithic political dynamic conventionally associated with globalisation'. In this thesis they identify two ideal types that they refer to as 'liberal market economies' and 'co-ordinated market economies'. These are distinguished by the way in which firms within such economies resolve the co-ordination problems they face in the spheres of industrial relations, vocational training and education, corporate governance, interfirm relations and in relation to their own employees. In Hall and Soskice's distinction, liberal market economies are ones in which firms primarily co-ordinate their activities through hierarchies and competitive market arrangements. By contrast, co-ordinated market economies are ones in which firms rely to a greater extent on non-market relationships for coordination – they are more collaborative than the competitive liberal market economy. For Hall and Soskice, the advantage of this approach is that it helps to explain some of the key questions in comparative political economy, in particular why some states respond differently to the pressures of globalisation and convergence and, more particularly, how some appear to have a 'comparative institutional advantage' over others. For the criminologist, this approach – or some variant of it – directs our attention to possible means of exploring international differences in levels of crime, insecurity and the nature of the political and social responses to them.

One of the potential benefits of paying close attention to the role and impact of political cultures in the diffusion and exchange of crime control ideas is that it will temper the tendency to impose too much order and rationality on the process of policy formation. As most students of policy-making will attest, the emergence of particular ideas is rarely the product of a process which bears any relation to a rational choice model. Rather, at best they tend to be the product of messy compromises and uneasy and temporary alliances and exigencies. One of the most astute observations made by one of the more interesting commentators in this field, John Kingdon (see Kingdon 1995), is that solutions and answers, and problems and questions circulate in what he calls the 'political stream', often remarkably independently of each other. In this regard, solutions seek problems just as much as problems seek solutions. This is not to say that our task as analysts is not to seek, or to impose, a degree of analytical order on these processes. What we are attempting to encourage here, however, is the acceptance of the existence of a greater degree of disorder, disharmony and incompatibility of explanation than is often allowed for in this particular social scientific terrain.

Concluding comments

There are a number of analytically separable, but inextricably linked, tensions running through current work around, and conceptualisations of, convergence and divergence in crime control in the west. First, and crudely, there is the tension between work which on the one hand tends to focus on the broad sweep of structural change and that which, on the other hand, considers the more particular concerns of policy development and change within particular jurisdictions. Secondly, there is the related tension between literatures which focus upon the macro-level concerns of globalization – and its related concepts and processes – and those which are more concerned with the meso- and micro-level issues of governance and governmentality. Thirdly, work of a more broadly structural character, concerned with globalization is, for the most part, primarily theoretical in character and, ironically given its overarching focus, somewhat 'placeless' in its concerns. As such, it is often quite distinct from, and in a certain amount of tension with, work that is more obviously concerned with politics and political culture which is heavy with meaning, tradition and symbol, very particularly located and, at least some of the time, more richly empirical in character. Now, clearly, we caricature somewhat in outlining these tensions and divergences for in practice the differences are not so visible or entrenched. Nevertheless, in taking forward the criminological enterprise in this area it is, we would suggest, necessary to recognise and seek to begin to overcome the difficulties inherent in marrying concerns which of necessity are simultaneously broadly generalised and empirically particular.

From T. Newburn and R. Sparks (eds), Criminal Justice and Political Cultures *(Cullompton: Willan), 2004, pp. 1–15.*

References

Bauman, Z. (2001a) *Community: Seeking Safety in an Insecure World.* Cambridge: Polity Press.

Bauman, Z. (2001b) *The Individualized Society.* Cambridge: Polity Press.

Bennett, C. (1991) What is policy convergence and what causes it? *British Journal of Political Science*, 21: 215–233

Braithwaite, J. (1989) *Crime, Shame and Reintegration.* Cambridge: Cambridge University Press.

Castells, M. (2000) *The Rise of the Network Society.* Oxford: Blackwell.

Castells, M. (2001) *The Internet Galaxy: Reflections on the Internet, Business and Society.* Oxford: Oxford University Press.

Crawford, A. (2000) Contrasts in victim/offender mediation and appeals to community in comparative cultural contexts: France and England and Wales. In Nelken, D. (Ed.) *Contrasting Criminal Justice.* Aldershot: Dartmouth.

Dolowitz, D. and Marsh, D. (1996) Who learns what from whom? A review of the policy transfer literature. *Political Studies*, 44: 343–57.

Eyestone, R. (1977) Confusion, diffusion and innovation. *American Political Science Review*, 71: 441–53.

Garland, D. (1996) The limits of the sovereign state: strategies of crime control in contemporary society. *British Journal of Criminology*, 36(4): 445–71.

Garland, D. (2001) *The Culture of Control.* Oxford: Oxford University Press.

Giddens, A. (1991) *Modernity and Self-identity: Self and Society in the Late Modern Age.* Cambridge: Polity Press.

Hall, P.A. and Soskice, D. (2001) Introduction. In Hall, P.A. and Soskice, D. (Eds) *Varieties of Capitalism: The Institutional Foundations of Comparative Advantage.* Oxford: Oxford University Press.

King, M. (1989) Social crime prevention *a la* Thatcher. *Howard Journal of Criminal Justice*, 28: 291–312.

Kingdon, J. (1995) *Agendas, Alternatives and Public Policies* (2nd edn.) New York, NY: HarperCollins.

Lacey, N. (2003) Principles, politics and criminal justice. In Zedner, L. and Ashworth, A. (Eds) *The Criminological Foundations of Penal Policy: Essays in Honour of Roger Hood.* Oxford: Clarendon Press.

Lacey, N. and Zedner, L. (1995) Discourses of community in criminal justice. *Journal of Law and Society*, 22(1): 301–20.

Lacey, N. and Zedner, L. (1998) Community in German criminal justice: a significant absence? *Social and Legal Studies*, 7: 7–25.

Lash, S. and Urry, J. (1993) *Economies of Signs and Space.* London: Sage.

Melossi, D. (2000) Translating social control: reflections on the comparison of Italian and North American cultures concerning social control, with a few consequences for 'critical' criminology. In Karstedt, S. and Bussmann, K.-D. (Eds) *Social Dynamics of Crime and Control.* Oxford: Hart Publishing.

Melossi, D. and Selmini, R. (2000) Social conflict and the microphysics of crime. The experience of the Emulia-Romagna Citta sicure project. In Hope, T. and Sparks, R. (Eds) *Crime, Risk and Insecurity.* London: Routledge.

Nelken, D. (Ed.) (1994) *The Futures of Criminology.* London: Sage.

Nelken, D. (1997) *Comparing Legal Cultures.* Aldershot: Dartmouth.

Nelken, D. (2000) *Contrasting Criminal Justice.* Aldershot: Dartmouth.

Newburn, T. (2002) Atlantic crossings: 'policy transfer' and crime control in the USA and Britain. *Punishment and Society*, 4(2): 169–94.

Rogers, E.M. (1995) *The Diffusion of Innovations* (4th edn). New York, NY: The Free Press.

Rose, R. (1993) What is lesson drawing? *Journal of Public Policy*, 11: 3–30.

Sparks, R. (2001) Degrees of estrangement: the cultural theory of risk and comparative penology. *Theoretical Criminology*, 5(2):159–76.

Stone, D. (1999) Learning lessons and transferring policy across time, space and disciplines. *Politics*, 19(1): 51–9.

Tarde, G. (1903) *The Laws of Imitation.* New York, NY: Holt.

Tonry, M. (2001) Symbol, substance and severity in western penal policies. *Punishment and Society*, 3(4): 417–36.

Urry, J. (1999) *Sociology beyond Societies.* London: Routledge.

Weber, M. (1978) *Economy and Society.* Vol. 1. Berkeley, CA: University of California Press.

35

Doing criminological research

35.1 The relationship between theory and empirical observations in criminology
Anthony Bottoms   854

35.2 The fieldwork approach
Howard Parker   860

35.3 A snowball's chance in hell: doing fieldwork with active residential burglars
Richard Wright, Scott H. Decker, Allison K. Redfern and Dietrich L. Smith   865

35.4 Doing research in prison: breaking the silence?
Alison Liebling   870

35.5 Feminist methodologies in criminology: a new approach or old wine in new bottles?
Loraine Gelsthorpe   875

35.6 Writing: the problem of getting started
Howard S. Becker   882

Introduction

KEY	chain referral; data; empirical observation; ethnography;
CONCEPTS	feminist methodology; participant observation; snowball sampling; theory

If you are currently studying criminology then the chances are that at some stage you will have to write a dissertation or an extended essay. You may even need to do some primary research of your own. Central to these tasks is attempting to understand how criminological research is undertaken. What are the main pitfalls and problems and what are the basic principles that researchers try to follow? The readings in this chapter offer a few examples (necessarily limited to particular types of research) which, though by no means comprehensive, should give a sense of both the excitement and some of the challenges of doing research, as well as some clues as to how to write up such research.

We begin with a piece by Anthony Bottoms **(Reading 35.1)** which analyses the relationship between theory and data. He suggests that there should be a continual dialogue between theory and data: theory allows messy data to be organised and corralled into some sort of order; data allow theories to be tested and refined. These are wise words and his example of the work of the Gluecks and Sampson and Laub (see also Reading 33.3) provides a neat illustration of many of the complexities, but also the great strides that can be made when careful use is made of systematically collected data in the context of a flexible and changing theoretical model.

In an important book entitled *View From the Boys*, Howard Parker **(Reading 35.2)** reports his ethnographic research with 'The Boys' in inner-city Liverpool in the 1970s. In the excerpt reprinted here he talks about some of the methodological issues, beginning with questions of 'access' (how to get accepted by The Boys) and moving on to some of the ethical issues (Where do loyalties lie? What should one do when confronted with criminal activity?). He refers to his methodological approach as 'participant observation' though he admits to doubts as to whether this is an appropriate description. Another tricky area of research is that involving those involved in relatively serious forms of offending 'in the field': how does one make contact, gain cooperation, retain trust, stay safe and so on? Richard Wright and colleagues **(Reading 35.3)** report on an innovative study with active residential burglars which involved both interviews and also taking offenders to the site of a recent burglary and asking them to reconstruct it in detail.

By contrast, Alison Liebling **(Reading 35.4)** reports on some of the difficulties of doing research in prison. Some of these difficulties are personal (issues that tend to be talked about much less in the methodology literature) and some professional/methodological. She raises a number of important issues. One concerns the role of emotions in research – the emotions of those being researched and those doing the research. Another is found in her observation that although the study she is reporting started out with all the social scientific methodological rigour the team could muster, once underway 'it was our judgement, intuition and creative instinct... which steered us through the exercise'. Finally, and importantly, she also raises the issue of gender and the ways in which this had an impact on the relationships both within the research team and between researchers and respondents. Aspects of the latter issue are picked up by Loraine Gelsthorpe **(Reading 35.5)** who asks what we mean when we talk of 'feminist research'. In short, is it merely a new label for rigorous research around a particular set of concerns, or does it involve something identifiably different from other methodologies. Having outlined the nature of feminist research she uses the example of a research project on prisons to illustrate some of the ways in which feminist methodology offers a challenge to traditional criminology.

My very favourite social scientific book about the nature of 'doing research' is actually a book about writing. Any of us doing research – whether it be an extended essay, a PhD, or some large-scale funded project – has to write it up. In my view, you only have to read a small selection of criminological research to see how little attention is paid to the craft of writing. Given that it is the crucial tool that enables ideas, findings and so on to be communicated this seems a little surprising. Anyway, the reality is that writing is not easy. There are many difficulties and many distractions. I strongly recommend that you browse through a few books about the craft of writing. They often contain very helpful advice. My favourite is Howard Becker's *Writing for Social Scientists* **(Reading 35.6)** and in the excerpt here he discusses the problem of 'getting started' with his usual combination of insight and wit. A treat to finish with.

Questions for discussion

1. Is Layder (as quoted by Bottoms) right when he argues that in many ways the really interesting questions for researchers 'concern the nature of the relations between theory and empirical research'? Why?

2. What difficulties can you think of in undertaking 'participant observation' research?

3. What is snowball sampling? What are its advantages and disadvantages?

4. Why was it important for Wright *et al*. to interview active burglars rather than get their sample from, say, local prisons?

5. In what ways is it important to recognise the emotions that may be involved in doing research (in prison or elsewhere)?

6. Is feminist methodology a new approach or old wine in new bottles?

35.1 The relationship between theory and empirical observations in criminology Anthony Bottoms

Among the leading US criminological researchers of the 1950s and 1960s were the Harvard-based husband-and-wife team, Sheldon and Eleanor Glueck. In 1950, they published *Unraveling Juvenile Delinquency* (Glueck and Glueck 1950), which was a comparative empirical study of 500 white male institutionalized juvenile delinquents (aged 10 < 17) and 500 male 'nondelinquents', the two samples being matched on an individualized case-by-case basis on four variables: age, type of home neighbourhood, measured IQ, and 'national origin' (based on parental and grandparental birthplace). In studying these samples, the researchers used interviews with research subjects, parents and teachers, as well as official records. Later, they also followed up the two samples to age 32, with a good re-contact rate (Glueck and Glueck 1968). In consequence, for these samples 'extensive data are available for analysis relating to criminal career histories, criminal justice interventions, family life, and recreational activities ... in childhood, adolescence and young adulthood' (Sampson and Laub 1993: 29).

The Gluecks' analyses of these data can reasonably be described as 'multidisciplinary' and 'multifactoral' (i.e. aiming to give weight to a somewhat eclectic mixture of different causative factors); as based on 'empiricism' (i.e. based on the view that data can be apprehended directly); and as atheoretical or even anti-theoretical (Sampson and Laub 1993: 41–5). For these reasons, and despite the admirable dataset, the Gluecks' research initially had a mixed reception. Reservations were expressed especially by sociologists, who considered that the Gluecks had 'downplayed or ignored traditional sociological variables like stratification, peer group, culture and community characteristics' (Sampson and Laub 1993: 43). However, these justified sociological criticisms were also fairly often mixed with an opposition that was clearly ideological, being based on a political rather than scientific aversion to the Gluecks' view that some of the causes of crime are biological (Sampson and Laub 1993: 41–2).

In the mid-1980s, after the deaths of both Eleanor and Sheldon Glueck, Robert Sampson and John Laub discovered – in the sub-basement store of the Harvard Law School Library – more than fifty unsorted cartons containing the Gluecks' data for the *Unraveling* study, and its subsequent follow-up. They recoded and computerized this information, and set out to understand more fully what these rich data could tell a fresh generation of criminologists about criminal career patterns from childhood through adolescence and up to age 32. Part of this task was straightforwardly empirical – for example, the Gluecks had carried out few multivariate (as opposed to bivariate) analyses, and they had not paid sufficient attention to the temporal order of events in their subjects' lives, a matter that is, of course, potentially crucial to the causal interpretation of the data. But as well as tackling these technical issues, Sampson and Laub (1993) also deliberately located their reanalysis of the Gluecks' data within the theoretical context of the criminology of the 1980s. In that decade, there took place a fierce debate between two opposing camps in developmental criminology. One of these (led by Gottfredson and Hirschi 1990) argued that the central key to understanding criminal propensity and criminal careers is 'low self-control', a trait that was postulated as fixed in individuals by about age 10, and thereafter stable throughout the life course. Given these views, Gottfredson and Hirschi naturally considered the detailed longitudinal study of offenders' lives to be unnecessary (Sampson and Laub 1993: 2). In the other camp, however, researchers such as David Farrington (see, e.g., Farrington 1994) argued that longitudinal research studies on criminal careers revealed more complex empirical patterns than Gottfredson and Hirschi were willing to concede. It can, however, reasonably be argued that the strength of the position of this second group lay very largely in empirical rather than theoretical arguments.

Sampson and Laub (1993: 2) were to an extent attracted by Gottfredson and Hirschi's approach, particularly 'because of its emphasis on the importance of families in explaining the origins of juvenile delinquency and because it highlighted continuities in behaviour at different stages in the life-course. On the other hand, they were 'troubled' by some features of the 'stability' thesis, and they doubted whether it took sufficient account of matters such as 'individual change and salient life events in adulthood'. Thus, Sampson and Laub set out the initial theoretical starting-point of their reanalysis of the Gluecks' data in the following manner:

> By using longitudinal data properly (that is, longitudinally) and in a theoretically informed fashion, we believed new insights could be gained into the causes of crime. In our view, the theoretical puzzle provided by the two sides in the [1980s] debate in essence can be reduced to the following challenge: can we develop and test a theoretical model that accounts for the unfolding of childhood antisocial behavior, adolescent delinquency, and adult crime in longitudinal perspective? In other words, can we unravel crime and deviance over the full life course?

(Sampson and Laub 1993: 2)

The term 'life course', at the end of the above quotation, is not used casually by the authors. Rather, it refers explicitly to Glen Elder's (1985) theorization of the 'life-course perspective' in social science, underlying which are two core concepts, namely 'trajectories' and 'transitions' which in certain circumstances can interlock to create a 'turning point':

> *Trajectories* may be described as pathways or lines of development throughout life. These long-term patterns of behavior may include work life, marriage, parenthood, or criminal behavior. *Transitions*, on the other hand, are short-term events embedded in trajectories which may include starting a new job, getting married, having a child, or being sentenced to prison...Transitional events may lead to *turning points*, or changes in an individual's life-course trajectory. For example, getting married may have a significant influence on a person's life and behavior, from changing where a person lives or works to changing the number and type of friends with whom one associates. Turning points may modify trajectories in ways that cannot be predicted from earlier events.

(Laub, Sampson, and Sweeten 2006: 314)

To use the language of Layder's 'adaptive theory', what Sampson and Laub are engaged in here is creating an initial 'theoretical scaffold' (the life course perspective', with its accompanying theoretical core concepts), which is intended to have a 'rela-

tively durable form since it adapts reflexively rather than automatically in relation to empirical data, although it should be 'capable of accommodating new information and interpretations by reconfiguring itself' (Layder 1998: 150). In practice, what has happened since 1993 is that Sampson and Laub's use of the framework of Elder's 'life-course perspective' has remained fully durable, but within this framework the content of their initial substantive theorisation has – as we shall now see – undergone some significant modifications.

As noted above, Sampson and Laub intended their theory (developed in interaction with the Gluecks' data) to be able to embrace both continuity and change in criminal careers; or, more specifically, to be able to explain (i) the development of childhood and adolescent delinquency; (ii) continuity between adolescent delinquency and adult offending; and (iii) changes in behaviour in the post-adolescent years. To meet this challenge, the initial formulation of the theory linked the life-course perspective to one other theoretical tradition, namely a developed and modified version of Hirschi's (1969) *control theory*. As Laub, Sampson, and Sweeten (2006: 315) subsequently put it, the organizing principle of the initial theory was that:

> delinquency or crime is more likely to occur when an individual's bond to society is attenuated ... Social ties also provide social and psychological resources that individuals may draw on as they move through life transitions. The concept of social bond echoes Toby's (1957) 'stake in conformity', suggesting that the stronger an individual's social bonds, the more that person risks by engaging in criminal behavior. From this general theoretical framework Sampson and Laub (1993) propose three major themes. First, structural context is mediated in fundamental respects by informal family and school social controls, which, in turn, explain delinquency in childhood and adolescence. Second, there is strong continuity in antisocial behavior running from childhood through adulthood across a variety of life domains. Finally, informal social control in adulthood explains changes in criminal behavior over the life span, independent of prior individual differences in criminal propensity.

In the present context, in order to keep the discussion within bounds, I shall restrict attention to the third of the above points, namely changes in adult criminal behaviour. Sampson and Laub's (1993) original reanalysis of the Gluecks' data on criminal careers up to age 32 led them to conclude that two fresh control factors in particular had the capacity to alter the criminal trajectories that might seem to have been established during adolescence, and thus to become 'turning points'.[1] These factors were described by Sampson and Laub as weak or strong 'labour force attachment' and weak or strong 'marital attachment',[2] and – it is worth restating – they were found in the empirical analysis to be important '*independent* of prior [adolescent] individual differences in criminal propensity' (Laub, Sampson, and Sweeten 2006: 315, emphasis added).

If we now review the story to this point, we can initially note that Sampson and Laub's reanalysis of the Gluecks' data was set firmly in the context of their theoretical reflections on the developmental criminology debates of the 1980s, and the use of Elder's 'life-course perspective'. Thus, they showed a clear awareness from the outset of the need to bring a coherent initial theoretical focus to data analysis, there being no theory neutral facts. Thereafter, however, their work was essentially inductive in approach, but this led in due course to the creation of a rather ambitious *hypothesis* embracing 'crime, deviance and informal social control over the life-course' (Sampson and Laub 1993: 244). This hypothesis then became available for others to test, and some scholars have indeed done just that. A recent overview of much relevant research, mostly supportive of the theory, will be found in Laub, Sampson, and Sweeten (2006).[3] A further and perhaps particularly interesting study (not discussed in Laub *et al.*'s 2006 article) is by Michael Ezell and Lawrence Cohen (2005), which was based on longitudinal analysis (using official data) of three independent samples of wards of the California Youth Authority (at different dates). The authors indicated that their data did not allow them 'to test the specific causal structures of a particular theory or set of theories'; but they were nevertheless able to 'evaluate the empirical validity of the longitudinal implications of three leading criminological theoretical perspectives' (Ezell and Cohen 2005: 258). Of these three, the one that was the most consistent with the California data was that of Sampson and Laub (Ezell and Cohen 2005:259).[4]

However, Sampson and Laub's theory has not remained unmodified since 1993. Naturally, their book was extensively reviewed, and some of these reviews posed constructively critical challenges to the authors. Laub and Sampson (2003: 7-8) later reported that they considered the 'most important' of these challenges to have been raised by John Modell (1994) in a book review in the *American Journal of Sociology*. Modell noted the authors' claims to have integrated a person-based and a variable-based analysis in *Crime in the Making* (Sampson and Laub 1993: 204), the former focused upon a qualitative analysis of the life history records of a subset of cases from the Gluecks' study, randomly selected from the cells of a typology. According to Modell, however, this qualitative analysis was 'not entirely satisfying' because the authors:

> cannot divorce themselves from a variables focus, and they virtually treat this small intensive sample as a microscopic quantitative test of their hypotheses. Nor are they adept at discerning (or portraying) the inner logic of lives as revealed in data such as these.[5]

Very bravely, Laub and Sampson (2003: 8) later said that, having reflected on Modell's critique, they felt 'compelled by the evidence to agree'. For this and other reasons, they therefore embarked upon the difficult task of tracing and interviewing a sub-sample of the Gluecks' original 500 delinquents, in a quest to understand retrospectively 'the inner logic of [their] lives' – or, in other words, to add an 'interpretative understanding' dimension to their earlier work.[6] At the same time, the opportunity was taken to update the quantitative (official records) follow-up of the originally delinquent sample up to the age of c.65. To the relief of the authors, the results from these further quantitative data analyses and the fresh interview data were congruent.

In the light of this further research, Laub and Sampson (2003) modified the original formulation of their theory. As regards desistance from or persistence in crime during adulthood, there were two main modifications, namely the addition of 'structured routine activities' and 'purposeful human agency' to the original key variable of social bonds/social control. The 'routine activities' addition is essentially an empirical modification of the original hypothesis:

> Structured routine activities modify the array of behavioral choices available to an individual ... The modified theory contends that structured routine activities condition the effect of social

controls on offending. Persistent offenders are notable in their lack of structured routine activities across the life course. On the other hand, increased structure surrounding routine activities facilitates desistance from crime regardless of prior offending trajectories.

(Laub, Sampson, and Sweeten 2006: 323)

The addition of 'human agency' to the theory is, however, rather more radical. Although the authors do not state the matter in this way, this amendment seems to amount to no less than a modification of some of the ontological assumptions of the original theory. As Laub, Sampson, and Sweeten (2006: 323) put the matter:

the concept of human agency might seem inconsistent with the social control perspective, since a key distinction of control theories is their assumption of universal motivation to offend. That is, in the absence of constraints (social controls), individuals will offend... However, in the revised age-graded theory a less stringent version of control theory is offered, assuming that human nature is malleable across the life course. In addition, the concept of human agency cannot be understood simply as a proxy for motivation. Rather, the concept of agency has the element of projective or transformative action within structural constraints. This goes beyond selection effects; that is, structures are in part determined by individual choices, and in turn structures constrain individual choices. Thus, the bi-directional interaction of choice and structure produces behavior that cannot be predicted from a focus on one to the other. The modified theory refers to agentic moves within structural context as 'situated choice'.

(Laub, Sampson, and Sweeten 2006: 323)

Perhaps curiously, however, although the authors introduced human agency into their theory in this way, they stopped short of any detailed exploration of what, in detail, the exercise of 'agency' might mean in a human subject, and how exactly this concept could bring further illumination to the task of explaining adult desistance or persistence. Impressed by Laub and Sampson's theoretical approach, but noting also this relative silence about agency, in a recent essay I attempted to advance the discussion by offering further theoretical suggestions about the potential role of human agency in desistance, drawing upon four different

theoretical treatments of the concept of 'agency' from mainstream sociology and philosophy (Bottoms 2006).

How can we best describe the addition of 'human agency' to the Laub/Sampson theorization? Essentially, I think, this has to be seen, in the language of Layder's adaptive theory as a significant modification of the original 'theoretical scaffold'. For Layder (1998: 150) a researcher's initially/constructed theoretical scaffold 'should never be regarded as immutable since it is capable of accommodating new information and interpretations by reconfiguring itself'. The incorporation of agency in the Sampson/Laub theorization is clearly more than just an attempt to add 'new information'; it is, instead, very much a 'new interpretation' which requires some definite ontological reconfiguration of the original scaffold. It is because this change is so potentially significant that Laub and Sampson are arguably open to criticism for not discussing more fully the implications of the modification.[7]

From the point of view of this chapter, one matter of special interest that arises from the introduction of agency into the Laub/Sampson theorization concerns the compatibility of the *explanation/causation* and *interpretative understanding* traditions. John Modell's (1994) review judged *Crime in the Making* to be deficient in understanding 'the inner logic of lives'; or, otherwise stated, to be lacking in interpretative understanding. Laub and Sampson's second book seeks to overcome this difficulty, and in doing so it explicitly rejects determinism (Laub and Sampson 2003: 34), so embracing aversion of free will,[8] while also being wary of rational choice theory.[9] Yet clearly, Laub and Sampson also remain committed to the explanatory/causal enterprise of explaining criminal careers. Can there truly be a co-existence of (i) explanation/cause and (ii) free agentic choice, viewed in terms of the meaning of the act to the actor, within his/her social context(s)?

We are in very deep waters here, but briefly, my contention would be that coherent co-existence is possible, but only if we develop a concept of *explanation* which does not make *prediction* its central characteristic.[10] As I explained the matter in a recent essay, referring explicitly to the context of desistance:

Let us assume that P, an ex-prisoner, has decided to try to desist for the sake of the future of his newborn child, but one day some of his former criminal associates offer him the opportunity to join in the planning for what looks to be a promising factory break-in, potentially yielding large rewards. Let us further (and, undoubtedly, with more philosophical difficulty) assume that P is truly free to accept or reject this offer; that is, that whichever option he chooses he will afterwards be able to genuinely to say, 'I could have acted otherwise'. In *explanatory* terms, it is actually not at all difficult for us to explain whichever choice he makes. We know why P has decided to try to desist, so if he says 'no' to his criminal associates, we can explain that decision as a natural consequence of the prior desistance decision. But we also know that the lure of the money, a desire for his friends' esteem, and so on, might indeed constitute a real temptation to join their enterprise; so if P does say 'yes' to his friends, we can explain that decision as well ... What is difficult for the social scientist, in circumstances such as these, is in fact not explanation, but the *prediction* of which choice P will make. It is, however, perfectly possible to envisage a version of social science that says it *cannot* effectively predict such decisions, though *ex post facto* it can explain.

(Bottoms 2006: 281–2)

Let me make one final observation. At the end of their 2003 book, Laub and Sampson reflected upon the key methodological difference between their initial and subsequent research on the Gluecks' sample, namely the addition of qualitative retrospective interviews in the second phase. They noted that the change in research method was linked to the modification to the substantive theory:

as much as our earlier theory was linked to our methodological and analytical approach (for example, regression models focusing on holding individual differences constant to see the effects of turning points), our revised theory here is also linked to our method and analytical strategy (for example, life-history narratives derived from the men themselves integrated with quantitative longitudinal data reconstructed from the Glueck archive supplemented by our own follow-up study at age 70). This merging of quantitative and qualitative data allowed us to gain insight into the life course of crime that would not [otherwise] have been possible.

(Laub and Sampson 2003: 293)

[I have advocated] the use, in appropriate contexts, of both qualitative and quantitative research methods. So, too, another prominent feature of the Laub-Sampson *oeuvre*, namely the obvious presence, throughout their research, of a continuing dialogue between theoretical reflection and empirical data-gathering and data analysis. As Derek Layder [has] put it in many ways 'the really interesting questions' for researchers 'concern the nature of the relations between theory and empirical research'; moreover, as we have also seen, there is a continual need to return to those questions throughout the research process. All this can be very challenging, it can also be exciting.

> From A.E. Bottoms, 'The relationship between theory and empirical observations in criminology', R. King and E. Wincup (eds) Doing Research on Crime and Justice, *2nd edn (Oxford: Oxford University Press), 2008, pp. 106–116.*

Notes

1 Other but more minor 'turning points' were also identified for men in the sample, for example military service in the Second World War.
2 'Attachment to spouse' was a composite variable derived from interview data. 'Weak attachment' was indicated by 'signs of incompatibility'; subjects with 'strong attachment' generally displayed 'close, warm feelings towards their wives, or were compatible in a generally constructive relationship' (Sampson and Laub 1993: 144). Thus, the variable does not simply measure marriage/non-marriage, but also the quality of conjugal relationships.
3 Of course, not all research testing the hypothesis is supportive. For example, although the empirical research base on the point remains slight, it seems that 'romantic partner attachment' might have different meanings and effects among female offenders than among males (Leverentz 2006).
4 The other theoretical perspectives considered were Gottfredson and Hirschi's (1990) self-control theory and Terrie Moffitt's 'dual taxonomy' theory (on which see, now, Moffitt 2006).
5 Modell (1994:1391) noted, however, that Sampson and Laub were working with secondary data only, and that the original 'interviews and notes may well lack insight'.
6 The interviewed subsample consisted of 52 of the original 500 delinquents, including 'persisters' and 'desisters' and those with 'zigzag criminal careers'.
7 It should perhaps also be noted that Laub and Sampson were not the first to include a specific discussion of agency in considering the topic of desistance: see Giordano *et al.* (2002), published

shortly before Laub and Sampson's revised theory. There remains, however, a theoretical disagreement between Laub and Sampson and Giordano *et al.*: see Laub, Sampson, and Sweeten (2006: 326).

8 Note that it is normally considered analytical to the concept of human agency that, if it exists, one can truly say, in any normal situation, that 'he/she could have acted otherwise': see, e.g., Giddens (1993: 61); Bhaskar (1979:146).

9 On rational choice theory see Laub and Sampson (2003:30-2). Note also the complex contextual (i.e., not simply rational choice) underpinnings of the authors' summary statement that: 'Offenders desist as a result of a combination of individual actions (choice) in conjunction with situational contexts and structural influences linked to important institutions that help sustain desistance. This fundamental theme underscores the need to examine both individual motivation and the social context in which individuals are embedded' (Laub and Sampson 2003:145).

10 This raises important questions about explanation in the social sciences, on which see more fully Hedstrom (2005).

References

Bhaskar, R. (1979) *The Possibility of Naturalism.* Brighton: Harvester.

Bottoms, A.E. (2006) Desistance, social bonds and human agency: A theoretical exploration. In Wikstrom, P.-O. and Sampson, R.J. (Eds) *The Explanation of Crime: Context, Mechanism and Development.* Cambridge: Cambridge University Press.

Elder, G.H. Jr (1985) Perspectives on the Life Course. In Elder, G.H.(Ed.) *Life Course Dynamics.* Ithaca, NY: Cornell University Press

Ezell, M.E. and Cohen, L.E. (2005) *Desisting from Crime: Continuity and Change in Long-Term Crime Patterns of Serious Chronic Offenders.* Oxford: Oxford University Press.

Farrington, D.P. (1994) Human development and criminal careers. In Maguire,M., Morgan, R. and Reiner, R. (Eds) *The Oxford Handbook of Criminology.* Oxford: Clarendon Press.

Giddens, A.(1993) *New Rules of Sociological Method* (2nd edn). Cambridge: Polity Press.

Giordano, P.C., Cernovich, S.A., and Rudolph, J.L. (2002) Gender, crime and desistance: Towards a theory of cognitive transformation. *American Journal of Sociology,* 107: 990–1064.

Glueck, S. and Glueck, E. (1950) *Unraveling Juvenile Delinquency.* Cambridge, Mass: Harvard University Press.

Glueck, S. and Glueck, E. (1968) *Delinquents and Nondelinquents in Perspective.* Cambridge, Mass: Harvard University Press.

Gottfredson, M.R. and Hirschi, T. (1990) *A General Theory of Crime.* Stanford, CA: Stanford University Press.

Hedstrom, P. (2005) *Dissecting the Social: On the Principles of Analytical Sociology.* Cambridge: Cambridge University Press.

Hirschi, T. (1969) *Causes of Delinquency.* Berkeley: University of California Press.

Laub, J.H. and Sampson, R.J. (2003) *Shared Beginnings, Divergent Lives: Delinquent Boys to Age 70.* Cambridge, MA: Harvard University Press.

Laub, J.H., Sampson, R.J. and Sweeten, G.A. (2006) Assessing Sampson and Laub's life-course theory of crime. In Cullen, F.T., Wright, J.P. and Blevins, K.R. (Eds) *Taking Stock: The Status of Criminological Theory.* New Brunswick: Transaction Publishers.

Layder, D. (1994) *Understanding Social Theory.* London: Sage.

Layder, D. (1998) *Sociological Practice: Linking Theory and Social Research.* London: Sage.

Leverentz, A.M. (2006) The love of a good man?: Romantic relationships as a source of support or hindrance for female ex-offenders. *Journal of Research in Crime and Delinquency,* 43: 459–88.

Modell, J. (1994) *Book review of Crime in the Making. American Journal of Sociology,* 99: 1389–91.

Moffit, T.E. (2006) A review of research on the taxonomy of life-course persistent versus adolescence-limited antisocial behaviour. In Cullen, F.T., Wright, J.P. and Blevins, K.R. (Eds) *Taking Stock: The Status of Criminological Theory.* New Brunswick: Transaction Publishers.

Sampson, R.J. and Laub, J.H. (1993) *Crime in the Making: Pathways and Turning Points through Life.* Cambridge, MA: Harvard University Press.

Toby, J. (1957) Social disorganization and stake in conformity: complementory factors in the predatory behaviour of hoodlums. *Journal of Criminal Law, Criminology and Police Science,* 48: 12–17.

35.2 The fieldwork approach
Howard Parker

I grew into, rather than systematically planned, this case study. It was the happy transactions at Sandhills which saw me moving towards The Boys. One of the requirements of the staff at Sandhills was that they should wherever possible be the same as, rather than different from, the visitors. The liaison was successful and it was in this highly favourable atmosphere that my credentials were checked out during the course of normal events. For my part and in retrospect Sandhills provided an almost perfect introduction into the specific style, dialect, dress, personal standards humour, aggressions, etc, of The Boys and other Roundhouse youngsters.

I left Sandhills to take up a research post in the university, close to the city centre. Almost immediately I was encouraged to carry out my own project, and various commitments aside I found that the post provided the time and flexibility to try a participant-observation study. Since out of simple enjoyment I had continued my contact with Roundhouse anyway and since I was now living in the city, the opportunity to look in greater depth at a community which fascinated me was seized upon. So by mid Year Two the study started in earnest, bolstered by many advantages including easy entry into the field.

At first I 'knocked around' the area and the local youth club during lunch breaks and in the evenings; initially it was the younger kids and The Girls who made me feel less uneasy. Of The Boys, Joey, Titch and Des were the friendliest with most others simply being civil and 'letting on' when they saw me. In fact getting started was the most anxiety-provoking period of the study. I no longer had a recognised role – Howard from Sandhills – and was without a *raison d'etre*. Initially I simply said I was hanging around: I'd got a new job at the university but it wasn't really under way yet so I was just bumming around. Any more sophisticated explanations were left till later, not least because I myself was not altogether sure what I was doing either.

Although at the time it seemed laborious, entry into Roundhouse adolescents' 'normal society' was easy and rapid. That old faithful 'the pub' was of course the answer. At first I would only go for an evening drink when specifically asked to, and fortunately Joey and Des made a point in asking me whenever I was around.[1] Once in 'The Turk', Sandhills acquaintances were warm and friendly and always ready to recall the good laughs of the summer just past. Again the 'He's OK'[2] epithet was important. I was a drinker, a hanger-arounder, and had been tested in illegal 'business' matters and could be relied on to say nothing since I 'knew the score'.

So by appearing for a couple of hours in the day and most nights during the week, I gradually moved inwards and started to comprehend more fully the nature and extent of The Boys' network. I got friendly with Emo, Arno, Golly, Tommy and Streak fairly quickly, although Fosser, later to be a good friend, was totally indifferent towards me for several months. I still felt insecure if Joey or Des were not around. A lot of local people who knew me from Sandhills assumed I was on the dole: I always denied this and said I worked at the university. It was only with a few of The Boys that I mentioned research, and then in terms of studying the way the police and the Courts operated. The message was always 'I'm on your side boys'. As I settled in as a regular face, I was several times congratulated on having such a cushy number for a job. To be paid for hanging around and a few hours' teaching seemed to appeal to The Boys, who appeared to condone rather than resent my good fortune.

My first request made at opportune moments was that if anybody was going to Court would they let me know and I would come along with them, as I wanted to study the prosecution process and perhaps hear what they thought about it. This ritual became well established, not least because I had a car, could help out with technicalities and later was willing to stand bail if nobody else could. Sitting for a couple of hours as 'two mates' in an alien world was a great consolidator of my loyalty to The Boys, and I later followed the process even further by visiting any of them who eventually got 'stuck down'.

My hanging around 'all the time' period came in the autumn (mid Year Two), when most of The Boys were unemployed and were spending their days knocking around the neighbourhood, standing on the Corner and following the routinised structure of the bumming days already discussed. Fitting into this set-up was not too difficult. Dress regulations were not unduly strict, and a dark pair of cord jeans and a leather jacket were as acceptable as all-blue denim or combinations of leather, cord and denim. I never attempted to copy dress style completely, adapting only to the extent of blunting differences. My own black shirt, black jeans, burgundy leather, style was always acceptable and indeed my leather (acquired locally at a very reasonable price!) became a bit of a joke and it was agreed that I most probably not only slept in it but copulated in it also. 'There's a leather going in the Block, Parker lad, 'bout time you went mad isn't it? They'll give you a needle at the Royal [hospital] to get that old one off.' (Joey)

No doubt everyone was aware that I spoke differently and 'posher' than they did. This was not a problem. It was more important to be able to understand 'scouse' than speak it: the scouser is bilingual, the outsider can be understood. Since as a Merseysider I could understand the dialect, my own pronunciation, although occasionally 'skitted' at, caused little comment once I was known. As time went on, or when drunk, I found myself swearing a lot more and using local esoteric words and phrases – divvy, tart, gear, busies, come'ed, bevvy, etc.[3] This helped too.

More importantly, blending in was facilitated by certain basic skills. One of the most important involved being 'quick': although I was regarded as normally 'quiet' and socially marginal, this placidity is not always a good idea. Unless you are to be seen as something of a 'divvy' you must be able to look after yourself in the verbal quickfire of the Corner and the pub. Thus although I rarely suffered the barrage of friendly abuse that some of the network received I felt it necessary from time to time to counter any 'quickies'.

Joey: Sideboards on you, it's Elvis the pelvis isn't it?

Self : That's all right la', yours'll grow one day.

Joey: Phh they better hadn't or there won't be room in our 'ouse.

Being able to kick and head a football reasonably accurately was also an important aspect of fitting into the scene. Again, whilst I was certainly 'no Kevin Keegan' and indeed occasionally induced abuse like 'back to Rugby Special', I was able to blend into a scene where kicking a ball around took up several hours of the week. I also followed

The Boys' football team closely each week and went to 'the match' with them when I could. This helped greatly. Indeed when everyone realised I supported Preston (as well as Liverpool, of course) it was always a good joke since they were so often getting beaten. 'Why don't you play for them they couldn't do any worse?' 'Is there a blind school in Preston?' (Danny)

During Year Two I made the usual block of minor mistakes mentioned elsewhere, including commenting on the sexuality of a passing girl (as is the custom) who turned out to be someone's sister.[4] Occasionally I would be confronted by a phrase which meant nothing to me and would reply incorrectly. Likewise I sometimes used words that no one else understood and received the deserved animadversion (see what I mean).

Looking back on the fieldwork I find it difficult to judge whether larger strategies were mistaken or not. The Flems affair discussed at the end of Chapter 5, for instance, was certainly a cop-out from the participant-observation role, yet on the other hand it allowed me to function on The Boys' behalf and show where my loyalties were. It is arguable, therefore, that on other occasions such as routine police stops I should have 'spoken up', which I didn't.

During Year Two I carried out about thirty taped interviews (T), with most of The Boys and a few of The Ritz. I bided my time in setting these up, usually tentatively suggesting to somebody he might come up to my room for a chat about things, the area, work, school, the police, etc. I would arrange a day not far ahead and then be around ready to cancel: 'It'll do again, anytime, let me know.' Usually I 'interviewed' two people at once and found this discussion-type conversation much more fruitful than the more structured affair. I sometimes found myself embarrassed by these occasions, however, and whilst the interviewees seemed to enjoy the novelty which broke up the day I was glad when they were all over. Again in retrospect it is hard to say whether interviews or taped conversations were a good idea. I tend to feel that most of the information would have come to me eventually anyway, but on the other hand the interviews did acquaint me better with the situation at the time and so help my comprehension progress more quickly. (I also had interviews with teachers, EWOs, health visitors, social workers, planners, the police and other officials during the fieldwork period.)

The end of Year Two had seen the catseye business evolve. My position in relation to theft was well established. I would receive 'knock off' and 'say nothing'. If necessary I would 'keep dixy' but I would not actually get my hands dirty. This stance was regarded as normal and surprised nobody; it coincided with the view of most adults in the neighbourhood. Further, given my job, relative affluence and 'middle-classness', it was also regarded as an expedient stance. I had things to lose by being caught. There were occasions when I in fact interfered with a car-radio theft and suggested to those about to get involved that given the situation and their strategy someone was likely to get caught. My advice was always taken. This reaction to anxiety[5] on my part can be seen as 'bad' participant observation since it was interfering with normal group behaviour. Yet on other occasions vetos came from other members of the network, for the same reasons, and were likewise considered. Thus in a sense my actions can also be seen as in harmony with the participant-observer role, depending on how one defines it, a point I will return to shortly.

Year Three saw me more relaxed, and for the most part I enjoyed my fieldwork, looking forward with everyone else to the regular nights out, camping holidays, trips off to Sandhills, etc, which broke up the more extensive periods of, for me at least, relative boredom. It was during the first half of Year Three that I found myself as accepted as I ever would be, in the thick of things and at my most functional. Due to my regular Court attendance I was being regarded as something of an expert in such matters and was able to give advice from time to time. I also found that people were asking me 'how so and so got on', what were his chances next time, etc.

One occupational hazard was drunkenness (and bankruptcy). The nights out achieved such a pitch at one time that I too became 'skint' by the end of the week. I survived most big drinking bouts as well as anybody, although on a couple of occasions I over-indulged. One evening in particular saw me 'rotten drunk' and slinging chairs across a club floor, demanding more of everything and generally making a fool of myself. The next day the feedback came in thick and fast: 'Who can't hold his ale then', 'Plonkie Parker', 'state of yous last night, lad'. These were the days when I was very nearly one of The Boys. My style, poise and humour were nearly there and I felt a genuine sense of belonging. It was a good feeling which dis-sipated only with the lessening of the network's solidarity towards the end of Year Three.

I made one big and indisputable mistake near the end of Year Three. It involved my mentioning a particular illegality and the name of its perpetrator to a man from Everomer I was friendly with, in the presence of Emo. Emo didn't know the outsider and for some reason found him untrustworthy. He thus interrupted our conversation to point out I had got my facts wrong. I hadn't, and since I didn't at the time understand Emo's motives I argued with him and added more 'incriminating' evidence to back my argument. Emo later told the 'offender' in question that I had been talking about his activities to an outsider who couldn't be trusted. This was fair enough, but having read the situation differently I knew the Everomer man could be trusted; I also knew he was in the same line of business. Nevertheless, I had made a mistake and had to suffer the consequences; for a couple of bad days I found myself much more upset than I wanted to be. Having always vowed that rather than dodge rumours and any confrontations I would face them, I made sure of finding 'him' before he found me, and asked him who he was calling a grass. I sorted things out with Emo and faced rumours head-on. It was a nerve-racking few days but things worked themselves out and I'm now probably the only person who still remembers the incident. I relate this affair because I think it makes an important point. The participant observer will almost certainly make mistakes and in the down-town situation this can well lead to him getting his head kicked in. If you intend to carry on the study your philosophy must be: better to have it kicked in today than next week. Unless you really have betrayed your subjects, you must ride your mistakes rather than retreat. Having made one big mistake, to have disappeared for a month would have been another. By then Mr X would have gone in every pub and asked everyone he saw where I was and told them an extreme version of why he was going to give me a hiding. If you confront Mr X on the same day the cloud bursts, he hasn't had time to tell anybody what a creep you are, nor can he be convinced by your disappearance that you really are guilty.

Dozens of other situations encountered and recorded by other (American) fieldworkers had to be faced: do you lend money, do you get involved in sexual escapades, do you act as a witness in Court? (For my part I felt acting as a witness in court would have jeopardised the project and I had to sit out police perjury without intervening.) There are no definite answers. It *all depends*, of course, and since the whole situation would be different for someone else, somewhere else, a long catalogue appears pointless.

Considering the study more generally, several points are pertinent. I have referred to 'participant observation', 'the third man' and 'the fieldwork' rather loosely throughout. Since in Britain at least we still await the 'obvious' example of a participant-observation study, there is a vagueness about what the method entails. Indeed it may well be misleading to regard participant observation as a single method at all. McCall and Simmons for instance talk of 'a characteristic blend or combination of methods and techniques that is employed in studying certain types of subject matter'.[6]

Although attempts are made at exact terminological definition of participant observation, for instance with regards the 'type' of participation, in this study at least, the mix has been too variable to allow such tidiness.[7] What I have aimed at throughout is to become an insignificant variable. That is whilst one can watch and/or take part in normal group activities and so contribute to the dialogue, one must not alter the group's processural direction. One may occasionally alter content, but never form. In these terms such events as, for example, my suggesting theft from a car be postponed because of strategic circumstances only, since it is part of *normal* behaviour by group members, altered the content of one particular evening but not the form taken by evenings during that period. This definition of participant observation is open to discussion, and since the whole research approach in question tends to be a personalised one, again I am merely elaborating on my own methodological approach. Thus whilst exactly what 'distortion' is may be somewhat ambiguous, I would not dispute Kluckhohn's very old maxim that as regards participant observation, 'The purpose is to obtain data about behaviour through direct contact and in terms of specific situations in which the distortion that results from the investigator's being an outside agent is reduced to a minimum.'[8]

Such a statement can of course be read on many levels. Research methodology is of course highly problematic, whatever technique is used. The sorts of doubts cast by the precision demanded from Schutz and the American ethnomethodologists for instance would demolish the validity of this little book with ease, with perhaps a consoling comment that it at least moved towards addressing itself to the commonsense meanings actors give to reality. But this is not the best of possible worlds and my view of sociology cannot allow the crippling limitations the ethnomethodologists demand. Sociology is also political and the sociologist needs to communicate to others outside his academic world. If he waits until he is absolutely sure about the truth of what he is saying, and works out in detail all the necessary qualifications and phenomenological brackets, he will never say anything but become like the Greek philosopher Cratylus who in the cause of such perfection was reduced to wagging his finger. What is more the ordinary man does not use such techniques and would find such an approach to writing about adolescence incomprehensible. For me the sociologist must become, in Alan Blum's terms, 'objective enough' to have something to say.

On the more practical level of gaining access to another's world, the problems of obtaining data are less complex. Each researcher's individual personality, like each fieldwork situation, is different and the only real test of feasibility in the end becomes 'suck it and see'. Although it is difficult to say exactly I would guess The Boys are more amenable to the outsider than some urban adolescent groups might be.[9] They seem willing to tolerate a wide variety of outsiders as onlookers though obviously long-term entry into their network requires a more sophisticated match. If I hadn't been young, hairy, boozy, etc, etc, willing to keep long hours, accept 'permissive' standards, the liaison would have failed. This project 'succeeded', at least in personal terms, because the personality and style of the researcher and of The Boys were compatible. Other liaisons that I might have attempted could well have failed. A nervous, very 'straight', guy has certain possibilities open to him which I haven't, and vice-versa. Given the general match in terms of age, style, etc, such a study is not as difficult as might at first appear; basic factors such as time and energy are as important as anything. Participant observation is not and should not be rejected as impractical, as often as it is. McCall and Simmons lead us in the right direction when they suggest: 'Virtually any mature social scientist can, with good sense and close attention to his methodology, carry out participant observation of at least, the less demanding varieties.'[10]

The problems do not of course finish once the fieldwork is under way or completed. One has great difficulty knowing what to record, how to record it and what to make of it anyway. Again in retrospect I was too selective in recording data. I did not take enough time in keeping my fieldwork diary, especially in recording what I considered mundane events. Quite often I would be obsessed with a small conversation piece to the exclusion of other events. Had I been more concerned with detailed writing earlier on I would have probably hit upon on-going social processes more rapidly than I did. My general conclusion here therefore is that keeping a detailed and accurate diary *may* be of great significance. Although it is probably a personal idiosyncrasy I also suffered a great deal from insomnia during Year Three. Thus even though I was coming in in the early hours and well plied with alcohol I still found the evening's events insisted on consideration before I could sleep. This sort of research is demanding right to the last.

The major problem in 'writing up' is an ethical one, however. The fieldwork data basically fell into three categories: that which I felt could definitely be published, that which could definitely not be published and that which I was unsure about. The third category was eventually broken up and distributed into the yes/no compartments through consultation with those involved and colleagues. Becker has pointed out in reviewing studies of this nature that publication will almost inevitably 'make somebody angry'.[11] This is probably true; my main concern is that no harm comes to The Boys. Thus what I have published is related to my knowledge of what Authority already knows about. The nature of The Boys' delinquency discussed is well known to Authority. The analysis blows no whistles but rather tries to explain what happens when whistles are blown. It is designed in this way and indeed suffers from it.

Finally, although I am unhappy with the finished product and a little depressed about having discovered such crippling limitations in my ability to 'getting things across', I am still satisfied the project was worth undertaking. It has impressed upon me and I hope it will on others how easy it is for sociological research to do grievous bodily harm to reality. How little we hear of reciprocity, dialectic,

process, change, innovation, back-tracking, in relation to delinquency, although in this longitudinal study that is what it was all about. Yet did not William Whyte assure us over thirty years ago: 'Only as I began to see changes in these groups did I realise how extremely important it is to observe a group over an extended period of time.'[12]

> *From H. Parker,* A View from the Boys *(London: David and Charles), 1974, pp. 214–233.*

Notes and References

1 William Whyte noted the importance of having the support of key individuals in any group studied ethnographically. *Street Corner Society*, University of Chicago Press, 1941 p 300.
2 'I found that my acceptance in the district depended on the personal relationships I developed far more than upon any explanations I might give,' Whyte, ibid, p 300.
3 Elliot Liebow also found that blunting and 'dulling' differences in dress and language was more practical than attempting a complete copy. *Tally's Corner*, Routledge & Kegan Paul, 1967, p 255.
4 Whyte, op cit, p 302. He mentions such mistakes also.
5 See 'Anxiety as a source of distortion' by M.S. and C.C. Schwartz in C.J. McCall and J.L. Simmons, *Issues in Participant Observation*, Addison-Wesley, 1969, p 200.
6 Ibid, p 1.
7 Although the Schwartzes, for instance, distinguish between two ideal types, the 'passive' and 'active' participant observer as distinctive roles, such a dichotomy is untenable for this study. See their article in McCall and Simmons, op cit, pp 89–505.
8 Florence Kluckhohn, quoted in R.A. Berk and J.M. Adams, 'Establishing rapport with deviant groups', *Social Problems*, 8, 1970–1, p 502.
9 James Patrick suggests a Glasgow gang of the 1960s was not very friendly, for instance. See *A Glasgow Gang Observed*, Eyre Methuen, 1973.
10 McCall and Simmons, op cit, p 28.
11 Howard Becker, 'Problems in the publication of field studies', in A.J. Vidich, J. Bensman and M.R. Stein (eds), *Reflections on Community Studies*, Wiley, New York, 1964, pp 267–84.
12 William Whyte, op cit, p 309.

35.3 A snowball's chance in hell: doing fieldwork with active residential burglars Richard Wright, Scott H. Decker, Allison K. Redfern and Dietrich L. Smith

Criminologists long have recognized the importance of field studies of active offenders. More than 2 decades ago, for example, Polsky (1969, p. 116) observed that 'we can no longer afford the convenient fiction that in studying criminals in their natural habitat, we would discover nothing really important that could not be discovered from criminals behind bars.' [...]

Although generally granting the validity of [this critique] most criminologists have shied away from studying criminals, so to speak, in the wild. Although their reluctance to do so undoubtedly is attributable to a variety of factors (e.g., Wright and Bennett 1990), probably the most important of these is a belief that this type of research is impractical. In particular, how is one to locate active criminals and obtain their cooperation? [...]

We recently completed the fieldwork for a study of residential burglars, exploring, specifically, the factors they take into account when contemplating the commission of an offense. The study is being done on the streets of St. Louis, Missouri, a declining 'rust belt' city. As part of this study, we located and interviewed 105 active offenders. We also took 70 of these offenders to the site of a recent burglary and asked them to reconstruct the crime in considerable detail.

Locating the subjects

In order to locate the active offenders for our study, we employed a 'snowball' or 'chain referral' sampling strategy. As described in the literature (e.g., Sudman 1976; Watters and Biernacki 1989), such a strategy begins with the recruitment of an initial subject who then is asked to recommend further participants. This process continues until a suitable sample has been 'built.'

The most difficult aspect of using a snowball sampling technique is locating an initial contact or two. [...] In attempting to find active offenders for our study, we avoided seeking referrals from criminal justice officials for both practical and methodological reasons. From a practical standpoint, we elected not to use contacts provided by police or probation officers, fearing that this would arouse the suspicions of offenders that the research was the cover for a 'sting' operation. One of the offenders we interviewed, for example, explained that he had not agreed to participate earlier because he was worried about being set up for an arrest: 'I thought about it at first because I've seen on T.V. telling how [the police] have sent letters out to people telling 'em they've won new sneakers and then arrested 'em.' We also did not use referrals from law enforcement or corrections personnel to locate our subjects owing to a methodological concern that a sample obtained in this way may be highly unrepresentative of the total population of active offenders. It is likely, for instance, that such a sample would include a disproportionate number of unsuccessful criminals, that is, those who have been caught in the past (e.g., Hagedorn 1990). Further, this sample might exclude a number of successful offenders who avoid associating with colleagues known to the police. Rengert and Wasilchick (1989, p. 6) used a probationer to contact active burglars, observing that the offenders so located 'were often very much like the individual who led us to them.'

A commonly suggested means of making initial contact with active offenders other than through criminal justice sources involves frequenting locales favored by criminals (see Chambliss 1975; Polsky 1969; West 1980). This strategy, however, requires an extraordinary investment of time as the researcher establishes a street reputation as an 'all right square' (Irwin 1972, p.123) who can be trusted. Fortunately, we were able to short-cut that process by hiring an ex-offender (who, despite committing hundreds of serious crimes, had few arrests and no felony convictions) with high status among several groups of Black street criminals in St. Louis. This person retired from crime after being shot and paralyzed in a gangland-style execution attempt. He then attended a university and earned a bachelor's degree, but continued to live in his old neighborhood, remaining friendly, albeit superficially, with local criminals. We initially met him when he attended a colloquium in our department and disputed the speaker's characterization of street criminals.

Working through an ex-offender with continuing ties to the underworld as a means of locating active criminals has been used successfully by other criminologists (see e.g., Taylor 1985). This approach offers the advantage that such a person already has contacts and trust in the criminal subculture and can vouch for the legitimacy of the research. In order to exploit this advantage fully, however, the ex-offender selected must be someone with a solid street reputation for integrity and must have a strong commitment to accomplishing the goals of the study.

The ex-offender hired to locate subjects for our project began by approaching former criminal associates. Some of these contacts were still 'hustling', that is, actively involved in various types of crimes, whereas others either had retired or remained involved only peripherally through, for example, occasional buying and selling of stolen goods. Shortly thereafter, the ex-offender contacted several street-wise law-abiding friends, including a youth worker. He explained the research to the contacts, stressing that it was confidential and that the police were not involved. He also informed them that those who took part would be paid a small sum (typically $25.00). He then asked the contacts to put him in touch with active residential burglars.

Figure 35.3.1 outlines the chain of referrals through which the offenders were located. Perhaps the best way to clarify this process involves selecting a subject, say 064, and identifying the referrals that led us to this person. In this case, the ex-offender working on our project contacted a street-wise, noncriminal acquaintance who put him in touch with the first active burglar in the chain, offender 015. Offender 015 referred 7 colleagues, one of whom – 033 – put us in touch with 3 more subjects, including 035, who in turn introduced us to 038, who referred 8 more participants. Among these participants was offender 043, a well-connected burglar who provided 12 further contacts, 2 of whom – 060 and 061 – convinced 064 to participate in the research. This procedure is similar to that described by Watters and Biernacki (1989, p. 426) in that 'the majority of respondents were not referred directly by research staff'. As a consequence, our sample was strengthened considerably. After all, we almost certainly would not have been able to find many of these individuals on our own, let alone convince them to cooperate.

Throughout the process of locating subjects, we encountered numerous difficulties and challenges. Contacts that initially appeared to be promising, for example, sometimes proved to be unproductive and had to be dropped. And, of course, even productive contact chains had a tendency to 'dry up' eventually. One of the most challenging tasks we confronted involved what Biernacki and Waldorf (1981, p. 150) have termed the 'verification of eligibility', that is, determining whether potential subjects actually met the criteria for inclusion in our research. In order to take part, offenders had to be both 'residential burglars' and 'currently active'. In practice, this meant that they had to have committed a residential burglary within the past 2 weeks. This seems straightforward, but it often was difficult to apply the criteria in the field because offenders were evasive about their activities. In such cases, we frequently had to rely on other members of the sample to verify the eligibility of potential subjects.

We did not pay the contacts for helping us to find subjects and, initially, motivating them to do so proved difficult. Small favors, things like giving them a ride or buying them a pack of cigarettes, produced some cooperation, but yielded only a few introductions. Moreover, the active burglars that we did manage to find often were lackadaisical about referring associates because no financial incentive was offered. Eventually, one of the informants hit on the idea of 'pimping' colleagues, that is, arranging an introduction on their behalf in exchange for a cut of the participation fee (also see Cromwell *et al.* 1991). This idea was adopted rapidly by other informants and the number of referrals rose accordingly. In effect, these informants became 'locators' (Biernacki and Waldorf 1981), helping us to expand referral chains as well as vouching for the legitimacy of the research, and validating potential participants as active residential burglars.

The practice of pimping is consistent with the low level, underworld economy of street culture, where people are always looking for a way to get in on someone else's deal. One of our contacts put it this way: 'If there's money to make out of something, I gotta figure out a way to get me some of it.' Over the course of the research, numerous disputes arose between offenders and informants over the payment of referral fees. We resisted becoming involved in these disputes, reckoning that such involvement could only result in the alienation of one or both parties (e.g., Miller 1952). Instead, we made it clear that our funds were intended as interview payments and thus would be given only to interviewees.

Figure 35.3.1 'Snowball' referral chart

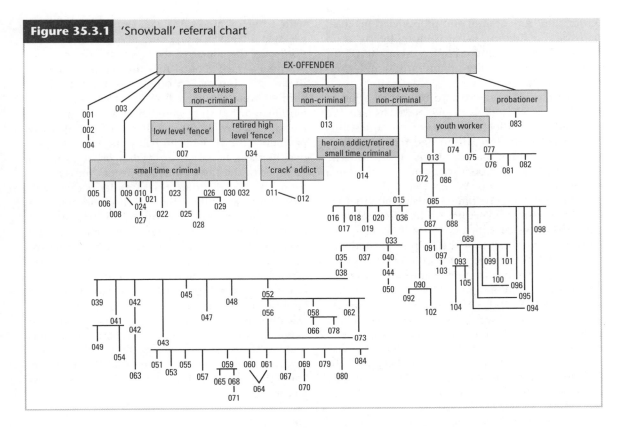

Field relations

The success of our research, of course, hinged on an ability to convince potential subjects to participate. Given that many of the active burglars, especially those located early in the project, were deeply suspicious of our motives, it is reasonable to ask why the offenders were willing to take part in the research. Certainly the fact that we paid them a small sum for their time was an enticement for many, but this is not an adequate explanation. After all, criminal opportunities abound and even the inept 'nickel and dime' offenders in the sample could have earned more had they spent the time engaged in illegal activity. Moreover, some of the subjects clearly were not short of cash when they agreed to participate; at the close of one interview, an offender pulled out his wallet to show us that it was stuffed with thousand dollar bills, saying:

> I just wanted to prove that I didn't do this for the money. I don't need the money. I did it to help out [the ex-offender employed on our project]. We know some of the same people and he said you were cool.

Without doubt, many in our sample agreed to participate only because the ex-offender assured them that we were trustworthy. But other factors were at work as well. Letkemann (1973, p. 44), among others, has observed that the secrecy inherent in criminal work means that offenders have few opportunities to discuss their activities with anyone besides associates – which many of them find frustrating. As one of his informants put it: 'What's the point of scoring if nobody knows about it.' Under the right conditions, therefore, some offenders may enjoy talking about their work with researchers.

We adopted several additional strategies to maximize the cooperation of the offenders. First, following the recommendations of experienced field researchers (e.g., Irwin 1972; McCall 1978; Walker and Lidz 1977; Wright and Bennett 1990), we made an effort to 'fit in' by learning the distinctive terminology and phrasing used by the offenders. Here again, the assistance of the ex-offender proved invaluable. Prior to entering the field, he suggested ways in which questions might be asked so that the subjects would better understand them, and provided us with a working knowledge of popular street terms (e.g., 'boy' for heroin, 'girl' for cocaine) and pronunciations (e.g., 'hair ron' for heroin). What is more, he sat in on the early interviews and critiqued them afterwards, noting areas of difficulty or contention and offering possible solutions.

A second strategy to gain the cooperation of the offenders required us to give as well as take. We expected the subjects to answer our questions frankly and, therefore, often had to reciprocate. Almost all of them had questions about how the information would be used, who would have access to it, and so on. We answered these questions honestly, lest the offenders conclude that we were being evasive. Further, we honored requests from a number of subjects for various forms of assistance. Provided that the help requested was legal and fell within the general set 'of norms governing the exchange of money and other kinds of favors' (Berk and Adams 1970, p. 112) on the street, we offered it. For example, we took subjects to job interviews or work, helped some to enroll in school, and gave others advice on legal matters. We even assisted a juvenile offender who was injured while running away from the police, to arrange for emergency surgery when his parents, fearing that they would be charged for the operation, refused to give their consent.

One other way we sought to obtain and keep the offenders' confidence involved demonstrating our trustworthiness by 'remaining close-mouthed in regard to potentially harmful information' (Irwin 1972, p. 125). A number of the offenders tested us by asking what a criminal associate said about a particular matter. We declined to discuss such issues, explaining that the promise of confidentiality extended to all those participating in our research.

Much has been written about the necessity for researchers to be able to withstand official coercion (see Irwin 1972; McCall 1978; Polsky 1969) and we recognized from the start the threat that intrusions from criminal justice officials could pose to our research. The threat of being confronted by police patrols seemed especially great given that we planned to visit the sites of recent successful burglaries with offenders. Therefore, prior to beginning our fieldwork, we negotiated an agreement with police authorities not to interfere in the conduct of the research, and we were not subjected to official coercion.

Although the strategies described above helped to mitigate the dangers inherent in working with active criminals (see e.g., Dunlap *et al.* 1990), we encountered many potentially dangerous situations over the course of the research. For example, offenders turned up for interviews carrying firearms including, on one occasion, a machine gun; we were challenged on the street by subjects who feared that they were being set up for arrest; we were caught in the middle of a fight over the payment of a $1 debt. Probably the most dangerous situation, however, arose while driving with an offender to the site of his most recent burglary. As we passed a pedestrian, the offender became agitated and demanded that we stop the car: 'You want to see me kill someone? Stop the car! I'm gonna kill that motherfucker. Stop the fuckin car!' We refused to stop and actually sped up to prevent him jumping out of the vehicle; this clearly displeased him, although he eventually calmed down. The development of such situations was largely unpredictable and thus avoiding them was difficult. Often we deferred to the ex-offender judgment about the safety of a given set of circumstances. The most notable precaution that we took involved money; we made sure that the offenders knew that we carried little more than was necessary to pay them.

Conclusion

By its nature, research involving active criminals is always demanding, often difficult, and occasionally dangerous. However, it is possible and some of the offenders included in such research may differ substantially from those found through criminal justice channels. It is interesting, for example, that those in our sample who had never been arrested for anything, on average, offended *more* frequently and had committed *more* lifetime burglaries than their arrested counterparts. These 'successful' offenders, obviously, would not have shown up in a study of arrestees, prisoners, or probationers – a fact that calls into question the extent to which a sample obtained through official sources is representative of the total population of criminals.

Beyond this, researching active offenders is important because it provides an opportunity to observe and talk with them outside the institutional context. As Cromwell *et al.* (1991) have noted, it is difficult to assess the validity of accounts offered by institutionalized criminals. Simply put, a full understanding of criminal behavior requires that criminologists incorporate field studies of active offenders into their research agendas. Without such studies, both the representativeness and the validity of research based on offenders located through criminal justice channels will remain problematic.

> *From R. Wright, S. Decker, A. Redfern and D. Smith, 'A snowball's chance in hell: doing fieldwork with active residential burglars'*, Journal of Research in Crime and Delinquency, *1992, 29: 149–161.*

References

Berk, R. and Adams, J. (1970) Establishing rapport with deviant groups. *Social Problems*, 18:102–17.

Biernacki, P. and Waldorf, D. (1981) Snowball sampling: Problems and techniques of chain referral sampling. *Sociological Methods & Research*, 10:141–63.

Chambliss, W. (1975) On the paucity of research on organized crime: A reply to Galliher and Cain. *American Sociologist*, 10:36–39.

Cromwell, P., Olson, J. and D'Aunn Avary. (1991) *Breaking and Entering: An Ethnographic Analysis of Burglary*. Newbury Park, CA: Sage.

Dunlap, E., Johnson, B., Sanabria, H., Holliday, E., Lipsey, V., Barnett, M., Hopkins, W., Sobel, I., Randolph, D., and Ko-Lin Chin. (1990) Studying crack users and their criminal careers: The scientific and artistic aspects of locating hard-to-reach subjects and interviewing them about sensitive topics. *Contemporary Drug Problems*, 17:121–44.

Hagedorn, J. (1990) Back in the field again: Gang research in the nineties. *In Gangs in America* (Ed.) Huff, C.R. pp. 240–59. Newbury Park, CA: Sage.

Irwin, J. (1972) Participant observation of criminals. In *Research on Deviance* (Ed.) Douglas, J. pp. 117–37. New York: Random House.

Letkemann, P. (1973) *Crime as Work*. Englewood Cliffs, NJ: Prentice-Hall.

McCall, G. (1978) *Observing the Law*. New York: Free Press.

Miller, S.M. (1952) The participant observer and over-rapport. *American Sociological Review*, 17:97–99.

Polsky, N. (1969) *Hustlers, Beats, and Others*. Garden City, NJ: Anchor.

Rengert, G. and Wasilchick, J.(1989) Space, dine and crime: Ethnographic insights into residential burglary. Final report submitted to the National Institute of Justice, Office of Justice Programs, US Department of Justice.

Sudman, S. (1976) *Applied Sampling*. New York: Academic Press.

Taylor, L. (1985) *In the Underworld*. London: Unwin.

Walker, A. and Lidz, C. (1977) Methodological notes on the employment of indigenous observers. pp. 103–23 In *Street Ethnography* (Ed.) Weppner, R. Beverly Hills, CA: Sage.

Watters, J. and Biernacki, P. (1989) Targeted sampling: Options for the study of hidden populations. *Social Problems*, 36:416–30.

West, W.G. (1980) Access to adolescent deviants and deviance. In *Fieldwork Experience. Qualitative Approaches to Social Research*, (Eds) Shafer, W., Stebbins, R. and Turowitz, A. pp. 31–44. New York: St. Martin's.

Wright, R. and Bennett,T. (1990) Exploring the offender's perspective: Observing and interviewing criminals. In *Measurement Issues in Criminology*, (Ed.) Kempf, K. pp. 138–51. New York: Springer-Verlag.

35.4 Doing research in prison: breaking the silence?
Alison Liebling

Prisons and the research enterprise

Why do people do research in prison? Any research is usually driven by personal curiosity, but often the particular world selected (or landed upon) and the particular topic chosen resonates with some conscious or unconscious value or interest whose origins pre-date the research project. So what particular features of the prison world draw the curious in? What are its key 'themes'? Prisons are potentially dangerous settings. What makes some people (like me) seek them out and others shun them? For those few who venture in, the answers will differ among researchers, whose antennae may be sensitized to different features of the prison community. What associations can we summon? They indicate much about us as well as about prison: confinement, authority, power, control, injustice, violence, relationship, hope, pain and sadness. Both extremes of human nature – its capacity for good and evil – are present in prison in perhaps their starkest form. All variations on human behaviour – from compassion and wisdom to abuse and life-threatening violence – are observable, or implicit, in the daily round of events. A curiosity about the human spirit and the institutions we create, and a concern that its better side be nurtured, however challenging the odds, may drive our research lives. Prisons are raw, and sometimes desperate, special places. They can also precipitate remarkable honesty.

It is possible to be driven at the professional level by the specific research questions in hand (what motivates prisoner behaviour? what brings the best out in staff? what kind of regime is constructive? how does one minimize harm – and create order? what leads to suicide?) as well as by the more fundamental 'golden threads' of the research enterprise, which persist between projects: how do we understand prisons, their function and their flaws? Are legitimate prisons possible? What do prisons – and those who live and work in them – tell us about the human condition? These are the issues that prisons as a research site continually raise. Although our research was carried out in five types of prisons of differing levels of security, it was in our maximum security (dispersal) prison – the

'deepest' and 'heaviest' prison (see Downes, 1988; King and McDermott, 1995) that our most acute experiences occurred.

The research experience

In many ways, this research *experience* emerged in its overall character as a largely qualitative exercise, with very strong structured and quantitative foundations. We elicited carefully planned, stringently gathered, quantifiable interview results and other quantitative data which was spilling from our desks and filing cabinets, onto our office floors, ready for analysis. We are still reflecting on what we have discovered, even though a detailed report has been written and submitted to the Home Office (Liebling *et al.*, 1997). Our quantitative results tell us part of what we have 'found'. To this extent, the core of our project was quantitative. The numbers of interviewees included in the research were relatively large. All of the material gathered in the before and after interviews was analysed statistically, and the content and conclusions of our final report were largely guided by the outcome of this process. In other respects, we are still coming to terms with our research experience. The fieldwork was complex, messy, 'deep'. The qualitative component (and tone) of the project steered our search through the data, guided our discussions about possibility, and structured the focus of our analysis. It informed our theoretical work, and directed our attention. But this has not been enough. As an enterprise, it is through our prolonged interaction with the world we entered, and alongside this our attempts to structure our exploration of it, but then through a prolonged period of reflection, that we might emerge with what we would be happy to call ('verstehen') understanding. We are not there yet – and very few funding sources are interested in employing us to do this bit.

Our core tool has been the interview. […] Our interviews were strenuously prepared, arranged and introduced in a way which would encourage openness and elaboration from prisoners and staff. Inevitably, there were sensitive areas where the information we sought was perceived as risky (e.g.

the use of drugs and the 'black economy') or as damaging to self-esteem (e.g. questions about fear). We did notice contradictions within the interview – so that direct questions about ever feeling fearful were often answered in the negative ('I've nothing to fear in here' – or I am not a prisoner who is picked on by others), whereas elsewhere in the interview, a spontaneous anecdote would be given which included references to feeling unsafe, afraid of other prisoners or being on the receiving end of an assault. These contradictions were relatively infrequent however, and were in fairly expected areas. We recorded answers as given, and used the information received elsewhere to make judgements about the accuracy or otherwise of our data. We were surprised by the willingness of (many) prisoners to talk to us at length about the going rate for and availability of drugs, the circulation of money and goods, the price of sexual favours, the behaviour of staff (their generous behaviour was as much a topic of note among prisoners as any indifferent or careless behaviour). We did give frequent reassurances about the confidentiality of the information, and hope that we were able to appear as well informed about prison life. Our questionnaire gave away the extent to which we already knew something (or had perceptions) of the prison world so that prisoners responded to us, on the whole, as informed, independent outsiders, who wanted to understand their world. We represented a form of contact with the outside world and as a way of relating to it. We were given several written texts by individual prisoners after the interviews – letters written directly to us, elaborating on points raised during the interviews, or poems and other accounts of life in prison.

It is important to acknowledge that our interviews were frequently very emotional, for interviewer and interviewee alike. Often, we emerged from these encounters exhausted, upset, occasionally uplifted, by the satisfaction of a good interview, with both parties gaining from the experience. Prisoners (and staff) occasionally shed tears, or became choked, or struggled with the questions. Our research participants did not want to be 'subjects' but acted as agents. They participated, made choices, drew us into relationships with them, and involved us in their world. They would return to a topic, change their first response – go deeper, and become fluent, trusting, more open, as the interview unwound. Or they would hesitate, answer abruptly when we asked about home, families, about fear. 'Do you have a partner or long-term

relationship outside?' The tone of the 'no' given would determine whether further probing was manageable – had prison affected this relationship? was the relationship surviving? The answers we received were often painfully honest – we heard tales of decreasing contact, uncertainty, the gradual dawning that life was carrying on outside without them, the final admission to themselves (perhaps for the first time, out loud) that separation and divorce was round the corner. 'I've lost everything', said many, 'I've nothing left out there'. Children disappeared into the world, no longer visiting their stranger-fathers. Wives and partners faded into history. These brave and terrible stories littered the interviews.

In other ways, we were continually thanked by prisoners, who welcomed the interest, the time and the reassurance of 'people who are interested in us'. One or two commented that: 'This is the most I have talked since I've been here!' They shook our hands, asked our names (and used them, often), greeted us warmly in corridors, and invited us into their cells for cups of tea (this latter offer was not often, but was very occasionally, accepted).

At one point, in our dispersal prison, we almost had to abandon method when the atmosphere on the last wing to be covered deteriorated. Prisoners had become increasingly angry – essentially about what they saw happening to them on the wing, but in direct proportion to this, about *not* being included in our research ('It's a conspiracy!') or about being asked to be interviewed ('How can *you* help us?!'). We managed to interview 12 of the original target sample of 18 (out of 22 names randomly selected) on this particular wing, but ceased approaching disgruntled prisoners eventually. We made up the final number with prisoners who were willing to be interviewed (and who were not on the 'suspected hostage-potential' list, being transferred out or too hostile) – or those very few who were apparently so determined to have their voices heard that we were anxious about the consequences of avoiding them! Here, we began to understand the staff and some of the pressures they work under a little better. [...]

On reflection, our research enterprise was launched with all the rigour and discipline of the 'social scientific' methodology we had at our disposal: careful observation and reporting, painstakingly prepared questionnaires, patiently gathered information, hours spent 'hanging-out' between formally arranged interviews. Once launched, it was our judgement, intuition and creative instinct, our various abilities to connect with others and our (ethnographically inclined) 'selves' which steered us through the exercise. Time invested in the field was crucial. [...] The experiences of living away from home, in countless different lodgings and circumstances, of spending time together as fieldwork colleagues (and gradually, as friends), of socializing with staff and others from the world we have become part of, is neglected, even in honest accounts of the research experience. We lived, albeit temporarily, in circumstances reminiscent of the prison experience without easy access to telephones, away from our friends, cut off from our lives, and propelled into others' worlds, with all the consequences staff reported to us of prolonged detached duty.

Likewise, the term 'observation' does not adequately capture the process of being present in others' worlds. We see, observe, but inwardly (subjectively) digest scenes and encounters; our inner lives interplaying with the lives of others. We watch, hear, take notes, drink tea, chat, experience periods of engagement, distraction, warmth, sadness or fear; we are entertained, frustrated, fascinated and puzzled – we are no more 'passive' agents in our research than our research 'partners' are. The term 'reserved participation' may be more appropriate than observation to capture this activity.

A key dimension to our project was the team. Several players, 10 in all, each with different roles, participated in the project. The team dimension was one of the most significant aspects of the project's success. Two project directors (one of whom managed to remain a fieldwork addict throughout), a statistician, a research assistant, one prison governor on secondment, four additional interviewers and a project secretary made up the staff of the project. Each of the team spent different amounts of time in the field and had different degrees of previous experience. Regular debriefing or discussion meetings – occasionally with the whole team, or more frequently with specific members with particular roles to play – became a key arena in which theoretical interpretations were generated and discussed, building upon the interplay between experience in the field, analysis of the data and reflection. This practice, which evolved, functioned both as a creative exercise, and a check on method and interpretation, and as a mode of support for those in the field. We also engaged in a dialogue with representatives of the field, discussing and presenting our interim results and impressions with different players from the world we studied at key points in the research.

The gender, age and background differences among us were also of significance as prisoners (and staff) took different members of the team into their confidence, or adopted different styles with each of us, and related different stories in markedly different ways during the informal (and probably to some extent the formal) stages of our research. There was a distinct difference between the 'man-to-man' conversations engaged in with our male fieldworker (whose previous 'real' work experience, age, Scottish accent, smoking habit and interest in football were particular assets) and the 'man-woman' conversations engaged in with the female members of the team, whose capacity for unconditional emotional support was assumed to be greater. In our female establishment, this pattern was occasionally reversed. It felt important for us to be able to discuss these differences and to 'see' the world we researched from others' perspectives.

Communicating about prison: inside out

Staff and governors often comment to us that they try 'not to take their work home'. They suggest that talking about work at home is difficult. Describing prison life to someone who has not experienced the prison world is extremely hard. People have prejudices, images, impressions, far removed from the lived reality of the prison environment. Its life is intense, varied, infused by collective meanings. The senses are immediately bombarded – smells, sounds, visions of expressions, incidents and activities, atmosphere, so much occurs in a moment. It was pointed out to us that we spent more time talking to staff and prisoners over a period of 14 months than most other people in the prison. This was our full-time and sole task. The experience of returning into our own worlds was disturbing; we experienced a sense of detachment and disorientation, and a frustration at wanting to share the experiences with others, and yet finding a way of describing what we had experienced almost impossible.

Many staff and governors working in prisons have touched on this problem of finding prison life difficult to share with others. Many comment after interviews that they have talked with us for the first time about some of their experiences of fear, isolation and the experience of being on the receiving end of others' aggression. It is not 'safe' to have these open conversations with their colleagues. By the end of our project, we understood how staff might feel tempted to avoid walking on to certain wings or landings, or tempted to minimize their contact with certain prisoners. We interviewed one prisoner who was not on our list, because the consequences of 'saying no' to him seemed so risky, in the circumstances. We were entering the world of intimidated, beleaguered and 'conditioned' staff. The question of how staff cope with the fluctuating possibility of abuse and violence, while maintaining a relationship with prisoners, has never been adequately addressed.

The political and penal climate

Without going into all the complexities of how prisons should be managed in order to achieve some balance between order, security and justice (see Sparks et al., 1996; Morgan, 1997; Tilt, 1997), or the results of our evaluation (Liebling et al., 1997), we were inevitably disturbed by some of the reactions of long-term prisoners to the changes brought about by the transformation in the political and penal climate between 1993/4 and 1995/6. A prisoner serving life with a minimum recommendation of 20 years for murder talked to us at length about his prison experience during an interview in his workshop – the lawnmower repair shop. He was a conscientious worker, and an articulate and reflective 40 year old. His previous sentences had included a five-year sentence for manslaughter. He had spent the first five years of this 20-year sentence aggressively resisting the system, being moved, segregated, punished and controlled. He arrived at our maximum security prison as a disciplinary transfer in 1990. To his surprise (and deep and prolonged suspicion), he found himself on X wing a new 'experiment' in long-term regimes. Staff called him by his first name ('I had forgotten what my first name was!'); they allowed him space, responded to his problems and the wing evolved in consultation with prisoners. He attended 'reasoning and rehabilitation' and 'alcohol awareness' courses, and after an initial period of disorientation, found himself seeing a psychologist on a one-to-one basis. This whole experience, he explained (on the wing and in work and 'treatment'), changed him utterly. He matured, grew to understand his previously violent, addictive and destructive behaviour, and gradually saw a way forward. He experienced guilt, regret and suffering. He learned new ways to relate to staff and to others. He put this transformation down to the open, responsive, tolerant and supportive regime, and the specialist help he received over a long period ('This prison actually made me a better person. They really cared. It made you feel part of something'). We had spoken to him on several occasions during the year

of our fieldwork. He had attended some of our group discussions and had talked to us informally. On our last visit, he was formally interviewed as part of our random sample. He knew us and our research well, and referred back to previous comments he had made to us throughout the interview, which was – despite its structure – like a continuation of our previous conversations. The current climate, he argued, was destructive. Relationships on his wing were fraught. Staff morale was low. His own attitude was changing – along with that of many others on the wing. The atmosphere was tense; tempers were high. He could see younger prisoners coming on to the wing, like he had been: young, challenging, energetic, aggressive, boisterous, impulsive, angry. 'They won't get the chance I had – to change', he said. 'No-one else coming to this prison gets the advantage of that experience. They've killed it. Gone overboard, All that trust is gone ... They're not gaining, but losing what they had. Sad, isn't it?' He still thought his work environment was constructive and that the works instructor treated him 'like someone on the out'. He felt trusted, and 'relied upon ... That makes you feel good'. He was brutally honest about the futility of prison, particularly without relationships and activities. It was a sad conversation, which left its mark for days afterwards. What do we do with such experiences? What was going on at the prison was complex; some of the changes (for example, to levels of safety) were necessary. We were in danger of 'going native' by this stage, identifying so powerfully with the feelings of prisoners and of some staff groups, that we were becoming less able to bear the interviews. It was time to leave the field. The task was now to reconcile our powerful emotions with our 'data'. Or was it?

Concluding observations

What does all of this tell us about the nature of prisons research? It is an enterprise made complex by the human nature of the researchers and the researched. It is an intense, risk-laden, emotionally fraught environment. It makes demands on fieldworkers which are at times barely tolerable. The risks of 'going native' are high – particularly when long periods of time are spent with staff and prisoners in 'the deep end' of prison life. Without this exposure, in the intimate 'places' and 'times' of the prison world, the research is superficial.

It is possible, in the light of the above account, and with the benefit of hindsight, to make a few observations about research, and about prisons, which I hope others will engage with and respond to. First, two observations about research, about the significance of the particular, and about the moral dimension of social research. First, *the significance of the particular*. How representative is any prison, or any individual prisoner, or member of staff, of the world we seek to understand? Does it matter, when we know that depth can only be reached through a detailed involvement in the particular life? Without the particular, there is little understanding. [...]

Human feeling, George Eliot argued, is the chief agent of morality. Subjectivity and objectivity need to be reconciled, not opposed to one another. Positivist science, she argued, strips human beings of their dignity and purpose. It is based on, and creates a false vision of, what it is to be human. Human sympathy can return the dignity of the individual responsibly to its place, centre stage. These two observations are linked. My personal position, arrived at over time, is that the significance of the particular and the careful consideration of the general are equally relevant to 'faithful representation'. Human feeling is a chief agent of realist research. In other words, our emotions do not need to be reconciled with our so-called data. They constitute data. They require critical reflection and triangulation, and 'faithful representation', but not selective inattention. [...]

Other key lessons from this research enterprise were that qualitative and quantitative methodologies used in tandem, together with an ongoing dialogue with those in administrative positions, and regular injections of 'involvement' and 'distance', create a tension out of which satisfying and credible research can be built. The checks of experience and emotion on the one hand, and structure and measurement on the other, interplay to form a deep kind of knowledge that feels like 'understanding'. An important lesson for us was that support (and time) needs to be built in to research which makes demands on the emotional lives of the researchers. Emotional experiences can be crucial clues in the process of research. Debriefing meetings, with a committed team – and preferably a theoretically informed 'outsider' – can generate order from chaos, and can capitalize on this process of working with different perspectives, around a solid core of painstakingly gathered data, whose meaning still has to be explored, on 'micro' and 'macro' levels, if such

simplistic divisions can be meaningful. Time is needed for critical, independent intellectual reflection on the deeper theoretical and methodological questions raised by empirical research. There is no doubt that, at its best, the careful 'art of research' is a deeply satisfying undertaking. Its joys and its pains are part of what makes it meaningful. [...]

Two further observations about prisons: one general and one specific. First, the general point. The pains of imprisonment are tragically underestimated by conventional methodological approaches to prison life. Prison is all about pain – the pain of separation and loss, the wrench of restricted contact in the context of often fragile relationships, of human failings and struggles. [...]

Finally, my last point and a particular reflection about prison. The research experience on which this article is based had a specific context, which perhaps brought to my attention these broad issues in a particularly stark form. The prison world changed rather drastically between 1995 and 1996. On reflection, I think what we encountered was, in Richard Sparks' words (Sparks, 1997), 'a moment of resistance'. Prisoners expressed (rather powerfully) feelings which now seem to make sense in terms of their reaction to their treatment, not by staff (for many staff actually resisted some of these changes too) but by politics. What our research project witnessed was a dehumanizing moment, whereby new managerialism met popular punitiveness (Bottoms, 1994). Prisoners (and staff) were on the receiving end of a rational choice model of human behaviour, a seemingly authoritarian era of prison management, and the concept of austerity. [...] All of these distinct and overlapping features of our social and political world resulted (and who knows for how long or whether the worst is over) in prisoners finding themselves not 'structurally redundant', as some argue, but structurally vital – as a means to political ends, as objects. [...]

So, am I a criminologist? Yes, I am also a human being, and any methodological approach which asks for separation between these two features of our lives or work is deeply flawed.

> From, A. Liebling, 'Doing research in prison: Breaking the silence?' Theoretical Criminology, *1999, 3: 147–161.*

References

Bottoms, A. (1994) The philosophy and politics of punishment and sentencing. In Clarkson, C. and Morgan, R. (Eds) *The Politics of Sentencing Reform.* Oxford: Oxford University Press (forthcoming).

Brown, A. and Gilligan, C. (1992) *Meeting at the Crossroads: Women's Psychology and Girls' Development.* Cambridge, MA: Harvard University Press.

Downes, D. (1988) *Contrasts in Tolerance: Post-War Penal Policy in the Netherlands and England and Wales.* Oxford: Clarendon Press.

Gelsthorpe, L. (1992) Response to Martyn Hammersley's paper 'On feminist methodology'. *Sociology*, 26 (2): 213–18.

King, R. and McDermott, K. (1995) *The State of Our Prisons.* Oxford: Oxford University Press.

Liebling, A., Muir, G., Rose, G. and Bottoms, A. (1997) An evaluation of incentives and earned privileges. Unpublished report submitted to Home Office: London.

Morgan, R. (1997) The aims of imprisonment revisited. In Liebling, A. (Ed.) *Security, Order and Justice*, pp. 62–70, proceedings of a Cropwood Conference at Fitzwilliam College, Cambridge, 5 January 1996.

Sparks, R. (1997) Recent social theory and the study of crime and punishment. In Maguire, M., Morgan, R. and Reiner, R. (Eds) *The Oxford Handbook of Criminology*, pp. 409–36. Oxford: Oxford University Press.

Sparks, R., Hay, W. and Bottoms, A. (1996) *Prisons and the Problem of Order.* Oxford: Oxford University Press.

Stanley, L. and Wise, S. (1983) *Breaking Out: Feminist Consciousness and Feminist Research.* London: Routledge.

Tilt, R. (1997) Thinking about the security/order/custody/control interface. In Liebling, A. (Ed.) *Security, Order and Justice*, pp. 3–3, proceedings of a Cropwood Conference at Fitzwilliam College, Cambridge, 5 January 1996.

Wolcott, H. (1995) *The Art of Fieldwork.* Walnut Creek: Altamira (Sage).

35.5 Feminist methodologies in criminology: a new approach or old wine in new bottles?
Loraine Gelsthorpe

What does it mean to label research as feminist research? There is no single, definitive answer and writers and researchers have seen various elements as the essentials of a feminist approach. These include the choice of topic, the aims of the research, the research process and the role of 'the researched'; but my main concern is with the potential impact of feminist approaches for criminological research.

What is feminist research?

This question has been the subject of much discussion in recent years [...] Four major themes emerge from these discussions, which also illuminate some of the dilemmas and pitfalls of adopting a specifically feminist method or of choosing to label particular methodological preferences as feminist.

The first concerns the choice of topic. As Renate Duelli Klein claims, 'the "what" to investigate must come prior to the decision of "how" to

go about doing research' (1983: 88). For most this has meant choosing topics which are relevant or sympathetic to women and to the women's movement. In essence, it has meant choosing topics which it is hoped will contribute to ending the oppression of women, that is, topics which have both political and practical import (Mies, 1983).

The concern to 'make women visible' has also led to the suggestion that feminist research must be 'on, by and for women' (Stanley and Wise, 1983:17–21). Some writers, however, have found this dictum problematical and Maureen Cain (1986a), for instance, argues that none of these three criteria is adequate as a test. She writes that 'a more valid test would interpret the social and political character of these "by, on and for" relationships, rather than treating the criteria themselves as empirical givens' (1986a: 255). Clearly, a socio-political analysis of this sort would make it possible to determine 'how, why and when' the 'by, on, and for' criteria for feminist scholarship could be usefully applied. This is essential in the field of criminology, for so much of the system revolves around men: it is mainly men who are labelled offenders, mainly men who police offenders, mainly men who sentence offenders (although it should be noted that in fact there are about as many female as male magistrates), and mainly men who are imprisoned. Maureen Cain (1986a) and Loraine Gelsthorpe and Allison Morris (1988) are thus among those who argue that men cannot be excluded from the enterprise. However, involving men does not necessarily mean conceding the whole terrain. Cain rationalizes men's involvement on the basis that feminist criteria are satisfied if those researched remain active and gendered subjects. Thus her revised version of the 'on, by, and for' dictum demands only that the subjectivity of those investigated should be taken into account.

The second theme concerns process. There is the by now familiar debate about the merits and demerits of qualitative and quantitative research, styles of interviewing and so on (Glaser and Strauss, 1967). Some writers further suggest that quantitative methods are inconsistent with feminist values, have an objective appearance and, therefore, have no place in feminist methodologies. Both Shulamit Reinharz (1979) and Evelyn Fox Keller (1980), for example, are keen to emphasize a preference for qualitative work and suggest that it better reflects the nature of human and, therefore, women's experiences. Indeed, they argue that quantitative methods cannot convey an in depth understanding of, or feeling for, those being researched and that they often ignore sex and gender differences or look at them without considering other mediating variables. However, the problem is perhaps not quantification itself but insensitive quantification. Some of the difficulties can be corrected (Eichler, 1988). Thus qualitative methods can be used in devising questionnaires for quantitative surveys (Hunt, 1986). Within criminology, large-scale quantitative surveys can be an important means of gaining an overall picture of events. The British Crime Surveys (Hough and Mayhew, 1983 and 1985; Mayhew *et al.*, 1989), for example, were primarily based on quantitative methods of data collection. Though initially criticized because of insensitive questioning, the surveys were refined to deal more sensitively with questions of sexual harassment and abuse. While there is always scope for further refinements, the surveys nevertheless provide important back-

ground data for feminist, as well as for other, researchers (Worrall and Pease, 1986).

Paradigms for traditional interviewing practice create problems for feminist researchers (and for research subjects). Ann Oakley (1981), for instance, argues that conventional methods of interviewing (whereby the process is seen as a one-way process, where researchers allocate 'the researched' an objectified function as data and where interviews are seen as having no personal meaning in terms of social interaction) invalidate women's subjective experiences as women and as people. She dismisses 'masculinist paradigms' of interviewing (and thus the masculinist view of social reality) in favour of an approach which acknowledges the subjectivity of the researcher and the researched and which exposes the notion of 'unbiased, objective interviews as myth'. Others in the field have endorsed this view (Bowles and Duelli Klein, 1983).

The third theme which can be discerned is that of the related issue of power and control. Liz Stanley and Sue Wise, among others, reject the traditional relationship between the researcher and the researched:

> It is obscene because it treats people as mere objects, there for the researcher to do research 'on'. Treating people as objects – sex objects or research objects – is morally unjustifiable.

> (1983:170)

Many have found a solution to this by adopting an interactive methodology which means that the principle of a hierarchical relationship between interviewer and interviewee is not adhered to and, as Robert Rapoport and Rhona Rapoport put it, 'an attempt is made to generate a collaborative approach to the research which engages both the interviewer and respondent in a joint enterprise'. Thus rather than minimizing the personal involvement of the interviewer the approach relies on forming a relationship between interviewer and interviewee 'as an important element in achieving the quality of the information... required' (1976: 31). [...]

Would we, indeed, should we, allow 'the researched' to have the last word? In practice, of course, research methodologies are often negotiated with those who are the subjects; but how far we are prepared to reject the traditional relationship between researcher and researched is another matter and not one which is easily resolved in a simple commitment to 'egalitarian research'. Few of us have absolute control over what we do. There are funding agencies to consider, research committees to appease, financial and time constraints to note.

There is another difficulty, too. The dismantling of power differentials between women is one thing; that between female researchers and men who are 'researched' is potentially quite another. While an 'interactive methodology' may have obvious value in research on, by, and for women, it is possible to envisage situations where men are the research subjects where such an interactive approach might be difficult to implement because of the attitudes of the men involved. This is simply to reiterate Cain's proposal that the 'on, by and for' criteria must be interpreted in a social and political context.

There is also a problem in that one cannot, and should not, assume that women who participate in other women's research necessarily share their politics (Acker *et al.*, 1983). There is a need for sensitivity; 'egalitarian research' cannot be adopted as a new orthodoxy. It is possible to imagine a situation where the researcher's interpretation is not only different from but potentially threatening and disruptive to the subject's world view. It may be, too, that the researched do not want to play the game this way. Joan Acker *et al.* describe a situation in which the women who were the subject of the research questioned the inclusion of life histories and extended quotes and urged the researchers to include more analysis. Thus the democratization of the research process is not necessarily easy or clear cut.

The work of Fiona Poland (1985) and Hilary Barker (1986) provides further illustration of the difficulties. Indeed, Barker suggests that we are in danger of creating a 'false-equality trap' whereby feminists negate their own possession of knowledge and skills in order to minimize differences between women. Thus hierarchies of skill superimpose upon the suppositions of sisterhood. But this does not mean that moves towards democratization have to be thrown out. The important point in this third theme is that hierarchical relationships are not denied but questioned. Feminist researchers do not regard it as reasonable to adopt a purely exploitative attitude to interviewees as sources of data. It may mean 'negotiating' the research focus and methods (depending on who is being researched, what the subject matter is and what the research objectives are). It may also mean being honest about the research – answering all questions about it as fully as required – and answering personal questions, too. [...] The researched have a perfect right to ask questions and they have a right to reasonable answers which

signify respect for them as people. In this way feminist researchers do at least approach *some* of the issues of power and control.

Finally, feminist research is characterized by a concern to record the subjective experiences of doing research. As Stanley and Wise point out:

> Whether we like it or not, researchers remain human beings complete with all the usual assembly of feelings, failings, and moods. And all of these things influence how we feel and understand what is going on. Our consciousness is always the medium through which the research occurs; there is no method or technique of doing research other than through the medium of the researcher.
>
> (1983:157)

Helen Roberts (1981) uses the concept of 'reflexivity' to describe the process through which feminist researchers locate themselves within their work. Indeed, this is seen as integral to a feminist approach to research. Of course, the concern to be open and honest about the research process and our part in it sometimes leads to accusations of a lack of objectivity but it is precisely this notion of 'objectivity' which feminist researchers aim to question and hold up to scrutiny. A rejection of the notion of 'objectivity' does not mean a rejection of a concern for being accurate (Du Bois, 1983). Other writers have expressed the importance of reflexivity rather differently. Stanley and Wise (1983), for example, write that 'the personal is political' and that experience must be prioritized – not only for the researched, but for the researcher too. As Angela McRobbie has pointed out, feminists doing research both draw on, and are constantly reminded of, their own experiences: 'Feminism forces us to locate our own autobiographies and our experience inside the questions we might ask' (1982: 52). This does not mean, of course, that our experience cannot inform our work on men. What is crucial is that feminist researchers explore the nature of their own experience (of women or men) and do not dismiss it as irrelevant.

There are other themes which are implicit in those which I have outlined. Feminist research is seen to be anti-positivist; it involves a link between beliefs, life and research; it is opposed to what is sometimes termed 'decorticated' theory – theory which is essentially speculative, concerned with abstractions and does not reflect knowledge grounded in lived experience. In contrast, feminist research is concerned with theory which arises out of experience. Further, in feminist research perspectives conventional 'value free' research is replaced by conscious partiality. (See Reinharz, 1979, for a fuller discussion.)

The challenge to traditional criminology

It is easy to see the difference that feminist approaches make to a subject like violence against women (see the introduction to this Part). It is perhaps less easy to see some of their wider applications.

'Transforming' research: a project on prisons

This research came about as part of the Economic and Social Research Council initiative on crime and the criminal justice system. The (male) director of the project employed two researchers (on a contract basis for a period of three years) to carry out qualitative and quantitative research on 'the concept of humane containment in a context of security and control' in a representative sample of prisons.

The research proposal made no mention of gender issues. However, the project director did consciously set out to employ at least one woman for the fieldwork and, in fact, both fieldworkers were women. The research study itself involved five prisons: Gartree, Nottingham, Ashwell, Featherstone and Winson Green, and we also carried out some pilot work in Stafford prison. We spent a period of three to four months in each prison, four days a week, though the days varied to try to cover every aspect of the regime and we maintained contact with the prisons, and individual prisoners, for much longer.

The research methodology was wide ranging and included questionnaires for prisoners and staff to complete, individual interviews, group discussions, observation, time-sampling and monitoring of shifts, menus, ethnic representation in 'good' prison jobs (in the kitchens and gardens), educational provision and opportunities and so on. It also involved discussions with senior management at a regional and national level as well as an examination of policy documents, assessment of staffing levels, analysis of medical records (to identify staff absenteeism and health problems) and a description of disciplinary procedures.

While the director had overall control of the project, the actual research process was open to negotiation. The first few months of the research saw many revisions and refinements to the 'data

collection instruments' – questionnaires, interview schedules and so on. Also, despite the fact that the original proposal made no mention of gender issues, these did have some consequences for the nature and structure of the research. This was not necessarily the result of any 'feminist input' but was a reflection of the fact that the two female researchers encountered a whole range of difficulties which were peculiar to them as women. Our male colleague did not experience the research in the same way.

The extent to which experience, age, sex and ethnicity influences the field researcher's role is often underplayed, if not ignored, in more traditional approaches to research which do not ask how far personal biography and experience influence the research role, what the significance of age is on field relations, what it is like to be a woman/man doing research in a male/female setting, or how a white/black researcher works in a research situation involving blacks/whites. Yet these are all important questions. In my research diary (which was hard to distinguish from a personal diary since I was concerned to record my experiences and interactions within the prison, rather than record so called 'objective observations'), I noted a number of points which were relevant to the influence of (my) gender, age and race.

One of my first experiences working in the prison was to realize, with some force, that I, and my female colleague, were quite out of place. We were incongruous in the nearly all-male environment. The only other women in the prisons were secretaries or probation officers. There was a female assistant governor in Birmingham but her position was rather unusual because she was also a union representative and in some sense considered a pseudo man because of this. It is not that she was labelled as such, but rather that she was accepted as 'one of the boys', albeit one of the management boys, because of her union interests. Indeed, she explained to us that this position gained her both respect and acceptance within the prison. Having no such kudos we were regarded with great suspicion. Prison officers frequently commented, 'What's a nice girl like you doing in a place like this?' or stressed that 'This is not a place for ladies'.

Suspicion of us as women, of course, was hard to distinguish from suspicion of us as researchers. Some officers thought it particularly devious of the government to employ 'women as spies'. Despite our protestations that we were not working for the government some individual officers remained hard to convince.

During our initial visits to the prisons we were normally cast in the role of casual visitors – often mistaken for trainee governors, representatives of the board of visitors or magistrates spending a day in prison as part of their training. Our induction period in each prison, however, marked the beginning of more intensive work within the prison and it was during this time that our research roles became blurred. Management insisted on announcing us as Dr Gelsthorpe and Dr McDermott, even though we asked them not to. My feeling at this time was that the intention behind this was to try and secure co-operation through our perceived status. Inevitably, it was assumed that we were medical doctors or psychiatrists (some of the visiting doctors were female). One incident which illustrates the confusion is where an officer in Stafford prison assumed that we would want to interview all those on his wing who were 'strange' or 'disturbed', and he duly selected prisoners for us on this basis.

Where we managed to disclaim the awkward prefixes to our names we were often cast in the role of students in a way that our male colleague, a professor, was not. We were respectively in our 30s, 40s and 50s. Being the youngest in the research team meant that it was assumed that I was the others' assistant and my decisions were sometimes questioned because of this. It was assumed that I had no authority to make decisions.

The term 'researcher' itself created some confusion in that it was often taken to mean 'psychological tester' (again, the staff and prisoners *were* familiar with female psychologists). However, the 'observation' part of our role was widely and, apparently, clearly understood. We presented ourselves as observers of the prison who wished to learn what went on, where it went on and how staff and prisoners felt about it.

This being so, it still did not mean that we were welcomed. Indeed, we experienced considerable 'testing out'. Having said that we wanted to consider every aspect of the regime in each prison – daytime, night-time and so on, prison staff asked us to be there from 6.30 am. until 10 p.m. and then back again at 6.30 a.m. to see if we were 'man' enough to take it. This was not simply because we were female, of course, but it was an indication of their suspicion and resentment of our intrusion. Although we said we were there to learn we were often regarded as 'experts' who were there to spy and then 'tell them how to do the jobs they had been doing for umpteen years'.

Acceptance in the prison environment was slow and painful. It partly came through the role foisted upon us. The more we talked with both staff and prisoners the more we gained a reputation as 'good listeners'. Prisoners were often desperate for someone to talk to and, in essence, we became 'counsellors'. It is hard to negate the influence of our gender in this since our male colleague had very different experiences when he visited the prisons. Whereas our 'interviews' more often than not became 'conversations' – partly through our approach and partly through the fact that the long, structured interview schedule proved to be impracticable – his did not. Interestingly, our male colleague felt excluded from the research to some degree. This was in part a reflection of the fact that his role meant that he spent less time in the prisons. But it also reflected a difference in approach. As a research team we experienced some tension because of our perceived 'over-involvement' and the implication that the men only talked to us because we were female.

Finally, my recorded reflections on the research experience included responses to both racism and sexism. Racist and sexist comments in the prison were prevalent. But while racist comments divided the male staff and prisoners, sexist comments united them in a way which transcended the unequal power relationship between them and emphasized the fundamental power differential between men and women. If nothing else, they could share jokes about us, pass comments on the way we dressed and award us marks on our perceived attractiveness (or otherwise).

How, then, was the research transformed? At what point did 'feminism' or feminist concerns enter the research process? We did not have control over the choice of topic or over the methodology, though we had some influence over the latter. Our discussions about methodology were influenced by feminist preferences, by our experiences as female researchers and by our sense of what was 'good research'; but it is hard to distinguish between these factors or to weigh up their relative importance. Combined, however, they did influence our approach to the research and there were specific consequences for both the nature and structure of the research, particularly for the style of interviewing and the content of discussions. Our respective 'feminist perspectives' increased our awareness of gender issues within the prison; but not everything about the way we worked can be put down to some abstract or theoretical feminist stance. I cannot separate a feminist and a non-feminist me. Therefore, the way in which I conducted the research had as much to do with my collective experiences – as a researcher, as a woman, as someone with a particular history – as well as to any specific elements of feminism. Thus, although I may attempt to record my experience of the research – to make clear my values, choices and so on – the choices are not always conscious or politicized. Awareness of gender issues is much more diffuse.

Where my feminist commitment was apparent – quite consciously – was in a concern not to view those we spoke with as research 'objects' or 'mere informants'. Although our conversations with the prisoners involved an unequal balance of power – our clothes, tape recorders and freedom to walk around and out of the prison gave us authority, much as we tried to resist it – our vulnerability as women enabled us to share the men's vulnerability as prisoners at least to some extent. And we gained acceptance by wholeheartedly adopting the role ascribed to us – as counsellors – making ourselves more vulnerable as a condition of that acceptance. While feminist researchers might applaud this, honesty compels me to acknowledge that we did it to gain acceptance for ourselves as much as for the prisoners. It would be dishonest to describe it as a wholly 'feminist' move. We were uncomfortable in the prisons, out of place and finding it hard to achieve acceptance to the point where prisoners would talk to us freely and not say the kind of things they thought we wanted to hear. The role of counsellor provided a chance to make the experience more meaningful for us as well as for them.

A more overt feminist commitment arose in our refusal to restrict conversations to the research questions and we frequently abandoned formal interviews altogether in the face of someone's distress or concern to express a particular point. Distress and concern to express a particular viewpoint were valuable indicators of a prisoner's experience of imprisonment. Structured and semi-structured interview schedules were obstacles to attempting to understand that experience. Indeed, at times, between us, we identified the questions which were important to the prisoner. More importantly, we tried to include in our discussions with the men, whether prisoners or prison officers, some reference to the impact of their life in prison on their partners, wives and children.

We also attempted, though not always successfully, to meet both women visiting men in prison and the partners of prison officers, in order to learn from them directly something of their prison experiences. Thus we tried to gain some insights into the meaning of imprisonment for the women who served out the men's sentences or worked out their men's shifts at home, for these experiences affected men's experience of prison life.

I am not suggesting that this was the 'right' approach. The point is that as feminist women we felt it inappropriate to deny women's experiences in a project designed to focus on men and their experiences. Gender awareness meant that we had to analyse men in relation to women as well as in relation to other men and, in the research process at least, if not in the reporting of the research,[1] to include something of women's experiences. The general consensus of the research team was that feminism had in these ways added an important dimension to the project. [...]

My purpose in writing in this way is twofold. I wanted to convey something of the difficulty of distinguishing between feminist research and simply 'good' research. Is feminist research merely 'old wine in new bottles'? If we accept that feminist research can be carried out with men as the focus (and carried out by men) then it may be that we are left with 'good' research. I do not believe that it is as important for feminists to try to lay sole claim to 'good research' as it is to challenge the supremacy of more conventional methods and approaches.

From L. Gelsthorpe, 'Feminist methodologies in criminology: a new approach or old wine in new bottles?', in L. Gelsthorpe and A. Morris (eds) Feminist Perspectives in Criminology (Milton Keynes: Open University Press), 1990, pp. 89–105.

Note

1 The researchers have produced a number of papers to date (see, for example, Roy King and Kathy McDermott 1989) but none of these has made specific reference to gender issues.

References

Acker, J., Barry, K. and Esseveld, J. (1983), Objectivity and truth: Problems in doing feminist research, *Women's Studies International Forum*, 6 (4), 423–35.

Barker, H. (1986) Recapturing sisterhood: a critical look at 'process' in feminist organising and community work, *Critical Social Policy*, 6, 80–90

Bowles, C and Duelli Klein, R. (Eds)(1983) *Theories of Women's Studies*. London: Routledge and Kegan Paul.

Cain, M. (1986a) Realism, feminism, methodology and law, *International Journal of the Sociology of Law*, 14, 255–67

Du Bois, B. (1983). Passionate scholarship: Notes on values, knowing and method in feminist social science. In Bowles, C. and Duelli Klein, R. (Eds) *Theories of Women's Studies*. London: Routledge and Kegan Paul.

Eichler, M. (1988) *Nonsexist Research Methods: A Practical Guide*. Boston: Allen and Unwin.

Gelsthorpe, L. and Morris, A. (1988) Feminism and criminology in Britain. In Rock, P. (Ed.) *A History of British Criminology*. Oxford: Clarendon Press.

Glaser, B. and Strauss, A. (1967) *The Discovery of Grounded Theory: Strategies for Quantitative Research*. Chicago: Aldine.

Hough, M. and Mayhew, P. (1983) *The British Crime Survey: First Report*. London: HMSO, Home Office Research Study No. 76.

Hough, M. and Mayhew, P. (1985) Taking Account of Crime: Key Findings from the British Crime Survey. London: HMSO, Home Office Research Study No. 85.

Hunt, A. (1986) Use of quantitative methods in researching issues which affect women. *Methodological Issues in Gender Research*, 10, 12–19.

Keller, E. Fox (1980) Feminist critique of science: a forward or backward move? *Fundamenta Scientiae*, 1, 341–9.

King, R. and McDermott, K. (1989) British prisons, 1970–1987: The ever deepening crisis. *British Journal of Criminology*, 29 (2), 107–28.

Klein, R. Duelli (1983) How to do what we want to do: thoughts about feminist methodology. In Bowles, C. and Duelli Klein, R. (Eds) *Theories of Women's Studies*. London: Routledge and Kegan Paul.

McRobbie, A. (1982) The politics of feminist research: between the talk, text and action. *Feminist Review*, 12, 46–57.

Mayhew, P., Elliott, O. and Dowds, L. (1989) *The 1988 British Crime Survey*. London: HMSO, Home Office Research Study No. 111.

Mies, M. (1983) Towards a methodology for feminist research. In Bowles, G. and Duelli Klein, R. (Eds) *Theories of Women's Studies*. London: Routledge and Kegan Paul.

Oakley, A. (1981) Interviewing women: a contradiction in terms. In Roberts, H. (Ed.) *Doing Feminist Research*. London: Routledge and Kegan Paul.

Poland, F. (1985) *Breaking the Rules*. Manchester: University of Manchester, Department of Sociology, Studies in Sexual Politics No. 4.

Rapoport, R. and Rapoport, R. (1976) *Dual Career Families Re-examined*. London: Martin Robertson.

Reinharz, S. (1979) *On Becoming a Social Scientist: From Survey Research and Participant Observation to Experiential Analysis*. San Francisco: Jossey-Bass.

Roberts, H. (Ed.) (1981) *Doing Feminist Research*. London: Routledge and Kegan Paul.

Stanley, L. and Wise, S. (1983) *Breaking Out: Feminist Consciousness and Feminist* Research. London: Routledge and Kegan Paul.

Worrall, A. and Pease, K. (1986) Personal crime against women: evidence from the 1982 British Crime Survey. *The Howard Journal of Criminal Justice*, 25 (2) 118–24.

35.6 Writing: the problem of getting started
Howard S. Becker

Some very common, quite specific writing difficulties have their origins in this attitude: the problem of getting started and the problem of 'which way to organize it'. Neither one has a unique solution to be discovered. Whatever you do will be a compromise between conflicting possibilities. That doesn't mean that you can't arrive at workable solutions, only that you can't count on finding the one perfect one that was there all along waiting to be found.

Most writers, even professionals, have trouble getting started. They start over and over again, destroying reams of paper, working over the first sentence or paragraph again and again as they find each successive try unsatisfactory in some new way. They start that way because they believe that there is One Right Way. If they can only find the Right Way to begin, they think, everything else will take care of itself, all the other problems that they fear are lurking ahead of them will disappear. They set themselves up to fail.

Suppose I am reporting on my study of Chicago schoolteachers. (I have immodestly used this ancient document, my own PhD thesis, as an example because I know it well, and because the problems it exemplifies still bother students, who find the solutions I discuss helpful.) The study dealt with, loosely speaking, race, class, professional culture, and institutional organization. How shall I begin? I could say: 'Schoolteacher culture defines lower-class, and especially black, students as difficult to work with. As a result, teachers avoid those schools, transferring to higher-class schools as soon as their seniority makes it possible, and that in turn means that lower-class schools are always staffed by new, inexperienced teachers.' Even though I am talking about a thesis completed and accepted in 1951, I still have trouble writing a concise introductory sentence. (Imagine me trying to do it in 1951, when I still wasn't sure what the thesis was about.) When I look at the sentence I just typed, I might think, 'Wait a minute, do I really want to say "schoolteacher culture"? After all, it's not exactly culture in the strict anthropological sense, is it? I mean, they don't pass it on from generation to generation, and it doesn't cover all aspects of life, isn't really a "design for living".

If I call it culture, I'm sure to get in trouble, and I'll deserve it, because I will be saying something I might not mean.' So I put that sheet in the wastebasket, and try again.

I might substitute 'shared beliefs' for 'culture' and feel happier with that. But then I would see that I was talking about class and remember what a tangle of implications surrounds every one of the many ways sociologists talk about class. Whose version would I mean? W. Lloyd Warner's? Karl Marx's? I might decide to go back over the literature on class again before using such an expression. So I would put another sheet in the typewriter. But now I might notice that I had said 'As a result of something teachers something-or-other.' That is a pretty direct causal statement. Do I really think that social causality works like that? Shouldn't I use some less committing expression? In short, every way to say it would start me down some path I hadn't fully explored and might not want to take if I really understood what it would commit me to. The simplest remarks would have implications I might not like, and I wouldn't even know I was implying them. (Curious readers can see what I actually did by consulting Becker 1980.)

That is why people make outlines. Maybe working the whole puzzle out in outline will show you where you are going, help you catch all the implications, evade all the traps, and get it all to come out right. You will find the One Right Way. An outline can help you get started, even if it won't find the Way, but only if it is so detailed as to be the actual paper whose skeleton it pretends to be. That just gives you the same problem in a slightly different form.

Introductions raise the problem of unwanted implications in a specially difficult way. Everett Hughes told me, when I was still in graduate school, to write introductions last. 'Introductions are supposed to introduce. How can you introduce something you haven't written yet? You don't know what it is. Get it written and then you can introduce it.' If I do that, I discover that I have a variety of possible introductions available, each one right in some way, each giving a slightly different twist to my thought. I don't have to find the One Right Way to say what I want to say; I have to find out what I want to say. But I can do that more easily after I have said it all and know pretty much what I mean than when I am writing the first sentence. If I write my introductory sentences after I finish the body of my text, the problem of the One Right Way is less compelling.

Fearing commitment to the implications of an initial formulation also accounts for people beginning with the vacuous sentences and paragraphs so common in scholarly writing. 'This study deals with the problem of careers' or 'Race, class, professional culture, and institutional organization all affect the problem of public education.' Those sentences employ a typical evasive maneuver, pointing to something without saying anything, or anything much, about it. What about careers? How do all those things affect public education? People who make outlines do the same thing by making topic rather than sentence outlines. The minute you turn the topic headings into nonvacuous sentences, the problems the outline solved return.

Many social scientists, however, think they are actually doing a good thing by beginning evasively. They reveal items of evidence one at a time, like clues in a detective story, expecting readers to keep everything straight until they triumphantly produce the dramatic concluding paragraph that summarizes argument and evidence at once. They may do this out of a scientific prudery which forbids stating a conclusion before laying out all the evidence (which ignores the excellent example of mathematical proofs that begin by stating the proposition to be proved). Investigators frequently report survey research results this way. A table shows, for example, that class and racial prejudice are directly related. The next table shows that that is true only when you hold education constant. Further tables showing the effect of age or ethnicity complicate matters further, and so on down a long road of items before whatever conclusion the assemblage warrants finally appears.

I often suggest to these would-be Conan Doyles that they simply put their last triumphant paragraph first, telling readers where the argument is going and what all this material will finally demonstrate. That flushes out the other reason for this caginess: 'If I give the ending away at the beginning, no one will read the rest of what I've written.' But scientific papers seldom deal with material suspenseful enough to warrant the format. If you put the paragraph that gives the secret away at the beginning, you can then go back and say explicitly what each section of your work con-tributes to reaching that result, instead of having to hide its function in noncommittal prose.

Suppose you are reporting, as Prudence Rains (1971) did, the results of a study of unwed mothers. You could, in classical evasive style, begin your book like this: 'This study investigates the experiences of unwed mothers, with special attention to their careers, moral aspects of their situations, and the influence of social agencies.' Giving nothing at all away, that beginning would leave the reader with a collection of unrelated tokens to be exchanged later in the book (if the author delivers on the IOU) for sentences asserting real relationships between real entities.

Fortunately, Rains did not do that. She wrote, instead, a model introduction, which explains exactly what the rest of the book then analyzes in detail. I quote it at length:

> Becoming an unwed mother is the outcome of a particular sequence of events that begins with forays into intimacy and sexuality, results in pregnancy, and terminates in the birth of an illegitimate child. Many girls do not have sexual relations before marriage. Many who do, do not get pregnant. And most girls who get pregnant while unmarried do not end up as unwed mothers. Girls who become unwed mothers, in this sense, share a common career that consists of the steps by which they came to be unwed mothers rather than brides, the clients of abortionists, contraceptively prepared lovers, or virtuous young ladies.
>
> The most significant aspects of this career are moral ones, for sexuality, pregnancy, and motherhood are matters closely linked to conceptions of feminine respectability and intimately connected to women's conceptions of themselves. Becoming an unwed mother is not simply a private and practical trouble; it is the kind of trouble that forces public accounting, raises retrospective questions, and, above all, calls into question the kind of person the unwed mother was and is.
>
> The moral career of an unwed mother is, in this sense, like the moral careers of other persons whose acts are treated as deviant, and whose selves become publicly implicated. Important, if not central, to the moral career of such a person are the social agencies with which he may come into contact as a result of his situation. Social agencies and institutions, whether geared to rehabilitation, incarceration, help, or

punishment, provide and enforce interpretations of the person's current situation, of the past that led to it, and of the possibilities that lie ahead.

(Rains 1971, 1–2)

That introduction, laying out the map of the trip the author is going to take them on, lets readers connect any part of the argument with its overall structure. Readers with such a map seldom get confused or lost. Evasive vacuous sentences, however, are actually good ways to begin early drafts. They give you some leeway at a time when you don't want or need to be committed, and most important, they let you start. Write one down and you can go ahead without worrying that you have put your foot on a wrong path, because you haven't really taken a step yet. You just have to remember, when you have written the rest of what you have to say, to go back and replace these placeholders with real sentences that say what you mean.

Suppose I take this advice and start somewhere else. If I don't begin at the beginning, where do I begin? What do I write first? Won't anything I write commit me as much as a first sentence? Doesn't every sentence somehow contain in itself, at least by implication, the whole argument? Sure. So what? Remember that any sentence can be changed, rewritten, thrown out or contradicted. That lets you write anything at all. No sentence commits, not because it doesn't prefigure your argument in just the way people fear, but because nothing bad will happen if it is wrong. You can write utter nonsense, things that turn out not to be what you think at all, and nothing will happen. Try it.

Once you know that writing a sentence down won't hurt you, know it because you have tried it, you can do what I usually ask people to try; write whatever comes into your head, as fast as you can type, without reference to outlines, notes, data, books or any other aids. The object is to find out what you would like to say, what all your earlier work on the topic or project has already led you to believe. (I here 'invented' the device known to teachers of composition as 'freewriting,' which is described fully in Elbow 1981, 13–19.)

If you can bring yourself to do this you will make some interesting discoveries. If you follow the directions and write whatever comes into your head, you will find that you do not have the bewildering variety of choices you feared. You can see, once you have your work on paper, that most of it

consists of slight variations on a very few themes. You do know what you want to say and, once you have the different versions before you, you can easily see how trivial the differences are. Or if there are real differences (though there seldom are), you now know what your choices are.

(The same trick helps students who get hung up trying to frame a dissertation topic. I ask them to write down, in no more than one or two sentences, one hundred different thesis ideas. Few people get past twenty or twenty-five before they see that they only have two or three ideas, which are almost always variations on a common theme.)

If you write this way, you usually find out, by the time you get to the end of your draft, what you have in mind. Your last paragraph reveals to you what the introduction ought to contain, and you can go back and put it in and then make the minor changes in other paragraphs your new-found focus requires.

In short, by the time we come to write something, we have done a lot of thinking. We have an investment in everything we have already worked out that commits us to a point of view and a way of handling the problem. We probably couldn't, even if we wanted to, handle the problem any differently from the way we will end up handling it. We are committed, not by the choice of a word, but by the analysis we have already done. That's why it makes no difference how we begin. We chose our path and destination long before.

Writing an unthought-out, unplanned draft (what Joy Charlton once inelegantly but accurately called a 'spew' draft) demonstrates something else. You can't deal with the welter of thoughts that flash through your head when you sit at your keyboard trying to think where to begin. No one can. The fear of that chaos is one reason for the rituals the students in my seminar described. First one thing, then another, comes into your head. By the time you have thought the fourth thought, the first one is gone. For all you know, the fifth thought is the same as the first. In a short time, certainly, you have gone through your whole repertoire. How many thoughts can we have on one topic?

Trying to evaluate, elaborate, and relate all that we know on a given topic can easily overload the capacity of our working memory. Trying to compose even a single sentence can have the same effect, as we try to juggle grammatical and syntactical alternatives plus all the possibilities of tone, nuance, and rhythm even a simple sentence offers. Composing, then, is a cognitive activity that constantly threatens to overload short-term memory.

(Flower 1979, 36)

That's why it is so important to write a draft rather than to keep on preparing and thinking about what you will write when you do start. (Joseph Williams suggests reserving the word draft for the first version that aims at coherence, to emphasize that freewriting produces a collection of working notes that shouldn't be mistaken for something more organized.) You need to give the thoughts a physical embodiment, to put them down on paper. A thought written down (and not immediately thrown into the wastebasket) is stubborn, doesn't change its shape, can be compared with the other thoughts that come after it. You can only learn how few thoughts you really have if you write them all down, set them side by side and compare them. That's one reason why dictating an early draft onto tape, even if you do the transcription yourself, is useful. You can't throw away a page of a tape very easily; you can still erase a foolish thought, but it is a lot of trouble, and most people find it easier just to keep talking and make changes on a typed version. Making the words physically real, then, does not commit you to dangerous positions. Just the opposite. It makes sorting out your thoughts easier. It makes writing the first sentences easier by letting you see what you want to say.

From H. Becker, Writing for Social Scientists *(Chicago: University of Chicago Press), 1986, pp. 48–56.*

References

Becker, H. S. (1980) *Outsiders: Studies in the Sociology of Deviance.* Glencoe: Free Press.

Elbow, P. (1981) *Writing with Power: Techniques for Mastering the Writing Process.* New York: Oxford University Press.

Flower. L. (1979) *Writer-Based Prose: A Cognitive Basis for Problems in Writing.* College English 41 (September): 19–37.

Rains, P.M. (1971) *Becoming an Unwed Mother.* Chicago: Aldine Publishing Company.

Publisher's Acknowledgements

We have made every attempt to obtain permission to reproduce material in this book. Copyright holders who we may have inadvertently failed to acknowledge should contact Willan Publishing.

We are very grateful to the following for permission to reproduce material in this volume:

Chapter 1
1.2 The author and Wadsworth, a part of Cengage Learning, Inc. www.cengage.com/permissions for Box, S., *Deviance, Reality and Society* (London: Holt, Reinhart and Winston), 1981, pp. 1–5. Copyright © 1982 by Wadsworth. **1.3** The author and SAGE publications, London, Los Angeles, New Delhi and Singapore for Muncie, J., 'The construction and deconstruction of crime', from Muncie, J. and McLaughlin, E. (eds) *The Problem of Crime* (London: Sage), 2001, pp. 9–23. **1.4** The author and Taylor & Francis Books UK for Christie, N., *A Suitable Amount of Crime* (London: Routledge), 2004, pp. 10–12.

Chapter 2
2.1 The author and Oxford University Press for Gatrell, V.A.C., *The Hanging Tree* (Oxford: Oxford University Press), 1996, pp. 6–10. **2.2** The author and Palgrave Macmillan for Ignatieff, M. (1978) *A Just Measure of Pain: The penitentiary in the industrial revolution 1750–1850* (New York: Pantheon), 1978, pp. 15–21. **2.3** The author and Pearson Education for Emsley, C. (2005) *Crime and Society in England 1750–1900*, 3rd ed (Harlow: Longman), 2005, pp. 178–185. **2.4** The author for Ignatieff, M., 'Police and people: the birth of Mr Peel's blue locusts', New Society, Aug 1979 (Vol. 49, pp. 443–445).

Chapter 3
3.1 The author and Wadsworth, a part of Cengage Learning, Inc. www.cengage.com/permissions for Box, S., *Deviance, Reality and Society* (London: Holt, Reinhart and Winston), 1981, pp. 157–163. Copyright © 1982 by Wadsworth. **3.3** The authors and Criminal Justice Press for Hough, M., Maxfield, M., Morris, B. And Simmons, J., 'British Crime Survey after 25 Years', in Hough, M. and Maxfield, M. (eds) *Surveying Crime in the 21st Century*, Crime Prevention Studies, Vol. 22 (Monsey, NY: Criminal Justice Press), 2007, pp. 9–22. **3.4** The author and Polity Press Ltd for Reiner, R., *Law and Order* (Cambridge: Polity Press), 2007, pp. 61–70.

Chapter 4
4.1 The author and SAGE publications, London, Los Angeles, New Delhi and Singapore for Katz, J., 'What makes crime 'news'?' from *Media, Culture and Society*, 1987 (Vol. 9, pp. 47–75). **4.2** The authors and Wiley-Blackwell for Schlesinger, P., Tumber, H. and Murdock, G. (1991) 'The media politics of crime and justice', *British Journal of Sociology*, 1991 (Vol. 42, pp. 397–420). **4.3** The author and Bloomsbury Academic, an imprint of A&C Black Publishers for Livingstone, S., 'On the continuing problem of media effects', in Curran, J. and Gurevitch (eds) *Mass Media and Society*, 2nd edition (London: Arnold), 1996, pp. 305–324. **4.4** The author and Taylor & Francis Books UK for Cohen, S., *Folk Devils and Moral Panics*, 3rd edn (London: Taylor & Francis), 2002, pp. 161–171.

Chapter 5
5.1 The editor, translator and Cambridge University Press for Beccaria, C., *On Crimes and Punishments and Other Writings*, edited by Richard Bellamy and translated by Richard Davies (Cambridge: Cambridge University Press), 1767/1995,

pp. 9–113. **5.2** The editors and translators and Duke University Press for Lombroso, C. and Ferrero, G. 'The Female Born Criminal', from Nicole Rafter and Mary Gibson, translators and eds *Criminal Woman, the Prostitute and the Normal Woman* (Duke University Press), 1893/2004, pp. 182–192. **5.3** Charles H. Kerr Publishing Co., Chicago for Ferri, E., *The Positive School of Criminology* (Chicago: Charles H. Kerr Publishing Co.), 1913, pp. 49–94.

Chapter 6

6.1 The author and the American Society of Criminology for Rafter, N.H., 'Criminal anthropology in the United States', from *Criminology*, 1992 (Vol. 30, pp. 535–545). **6.2** The author and Taylor & Francis Group LLC for Duster, T., *Backdoor to Eugenics* (New York: Routledge), 2003, pp. 92–101. **6.3** The author and Springer Science and Business Media for Raine, A., 'Biosocial studies of antisocial and violent behaviour in children and adults', from *Journal of Abnormal Child Psychology*, 2002 (30, 4, pp. 311–326). **6.4** The author and Taylor and Francis Group LLC for Kanazawa, S., 'Evolutionary psychology and crime', from Walsh, A. and Beaver, K. (eds) *Biosocial Criminology* (New York: Routledge), 2009, pp. 90–110.

Chapter 7

7.2 The author and Transaction Publishers for Akers, R.L., *Social Learning and Social Structure: A general theory of crime and deviance* (Boston: Northeastern University Press), 1998, pp. 322–413. **7.3** The authors and Simon & Schuster, Inc. for Wilson, J.Q. and Herrnstein, R., *Crime and Human Nature* (New York: Simon and Schuster), 1985, pp. 43–63. Copyright © 1985 by James Q Wilson and Richard J. Herrnstein. All rights reserved. **7.4** The authors and The Free Press, a Division of Simon & Schuster, Inc. for Herrnstein, R. and Murray, C., *The Bell-Curve: Intelligence and class structure in American life* (New York: The Free Press), 1994, pp. 241–251. Copyright © 1995 by Richard J. Herrnstein and Charles Murray. All rights reserved.

Chapter 8

8.1 The translators , the editor and The Free Press, a Division of Simon & Schuster, Inc. for Durkheim, E., *The Rules of Sociological Method*, translated by Sarah A. Solovay and John H. Mueller and edited by George, E.G. Caitlin (New York: Free Press) 1895/1964, pp. 65–73. Copyright © 1938 by George E.G. Caitlin. Copyright © renewed 1966 by Sarah A. Solovay, John H. Mueller, George E.G. Caitlin. All rights reserved. **8.3** The author and Oxford University Press for Agnew, R., *Pressured into Crime: An overview of general strain theory* (Los Angeles: Roxbury), 2006, pp. 1–17. **8.4** The author and Transaction Publishers for Rosenfeld, R. and Messner, S.F., 'Crime and the American Dream', from Adler, F. and Laufer, W. (eds) *The Legacy of Anomie Theory* (New Brunswick: Transaction), 1995, pp. 159–181. **8.5** The author and SAGE publications, London, Los Angeles, New Delhi and Singapore for Young, J., *The Vertigo of Late Modernity* (London: Sage), 2007, pp. 2–14.

Chapter 9

9.1 The authors and the University of Chicago Press for Shaw, C.R. and McKay, H.K., *Juvenile Delinquency and Urban Areas* (Chicago: University of Chicago Press), 1972, pp. 170–189. **9.2** The author and The Free Press, a Division of Simon & Schuster, Inc. for Cohen, A., *Delinquent Boys: The culture of the gang* (New York: Free Press), 1955, pp. 12–133. Copyright © 1955 by the Free Press. Copyright © renewed 1983 by Albert K. Cohen. All rights reserved. **9.3** The author and Palgrave Macmillan for Cohen, P., 'Subcultural conflict and working-class community', *Working Papers in Cultural Studies No. 2* (University of Birmingham: CCCS); reprinted as Ch. 2 in Cohen, P. (ed.), *Rethinking the Youth Question* (Basingstoke: Macmillan), 1972, pp. 48–62. **9.4** The authors and Taylor & Francis Books UK for Clarke, J., Hall, S., Jefferson, T. and Roberts, B., 'Subcultures, cultures and class', in Hall, S. and Jefferson, T. (eds) *Resistance Through Rituals* (London: Hutchinson), 1976, pp. 71–74. **9.5** The author and Annual Reviews for Ferrell, J., 'Cultural criminology', from *Annual Review of Sociology*, 1999 (Vol. 25, pp. 395–418). Copyright © 1999 by Annual Reviews www.annualreviews.org.

Chapter 10

10.1 The author and McGraw Hill USA for Lemert, E., 'Primary and secondary deviance', from *Social Pathology* (New York: McGraw Hill), 1951, pp. 75–78. **10.3** The author and The Free Press, a Division of Simon & Schuster, Inc. for Becker, H.S., *Outsiders* (New York: The Free Press), 1963, pp. 1–18. Copyright © 1963 by the Free Press. Copyright © renewed 1991 by Howard S. Becker. All rights reserved. **10.4** The author and Wiley-Blackwell for Plummer, K., 'Misunderstanding labelling perspectives', in Downes, D. and Rock, P. (eds) *Deviant Interpretations* (Oxford: Martin Robertson), 1979, pp. 85–121. **10.5** The author for Young, J., *The Drugtakers* (London: Paladin), 1971, pp. 107–119.

Chapter 11

11.2 The author and Transaction Publishers for Hirschi, T., *Causes of Delinquency* (Berkeley: University of California Press), 1969, pp. 16–34. **11.3** The authors and Stanford University Press for Gottfredson, M.R. and Hirschi, T., *A General Theory of Crime* (CA: Stanford University Press), 1990, pp. 87–91. Copyright © 1990 by the Board of Trustees of the Leland Stanford Jr. University. **11.4** The author and SAGE publications, London, Los Angeles, New Delhi and Singapore for Braithwaite, J., 'Charles Tittle's *Control Balance* and criminological theory', *Theoretical Criminology*, 1997 (Vol. 1, 1, pp. 77–97).

Chapter 12

12.1 The author and Springer Science and Business Media for Chambliss, W., 'Toward a political economy of crime', from *Theory and Society*, 1975 (Vol. 2, 1, pp. 149–170). **12.2** The author and SAGE Publications, London, Los Angeles, New Delhi and Singapore for Scraton, P. and Chadwick, C., 'The theoretical and political priorities of critical criminology', from Stenson, K. and Cowell, D. (eds) *The Politics of Crime Control* (London: Sage), 1991, pp. 161–185. **12.3** The author and Oxford University Press for Young, J., 'Radical criminology in Britain', from *British Journal of Criminology*, 1988 (Vol. 28, 2, pp. 159–183). **12.4** The author and SAGE Publications, London, Los Angeles, New Delhi and Singapore for de Haan, W., 'Abolitionism and crime control: A contradiction in terms', in Stenson, K. and Cowell, D. (eds) *The Politics of Crime Control* (London: Sage), 1991, pp. 203–205; 212–215.

Chapter 13

13.1 The authors and SAGE Publications, London, Los Angeles, New Delhi and Singapore for Matthews, R. and Young, J., 'Reflections on realism', from Young, J. and Matthews, R. (eds) *Rethinking Criminology: The realist debate* (London: Sage), 1992, pp. 1–23. **13.2** The author and SAGE Publications, London, Los Angeles, New Delhi and Singapore for Young, J., 'The failure of criminology: the need for a radical realism', from Matthews, R. and Young, J. (eds) *Confronting Criminology* (London: Sage), 1986, pp. 4–30. **13.3** The author and the IEA for Murray, C., *The Emerging Underclass* (London: IEA), 1990, pp. 1–35. **13.4** The authors for Wilson, J.Q. and Kelling, G., 'Broken windows', *Atlantic Monthly*, March 1982 (Vol. 127 pp. 29–38).

Chapter 14

14.1 The author and Oxford University Press for Garland, D., *The Culture of Control* (Oxford: Oxford University Press), 2001, pp. 127–131. **14.2** The author and Oxford University Press for Clarke, R.V.G., 'Situational crime prevention: theory and practice', from *British Journal of Criminology*, 1980 (Vol. 20, 2, pp. 136–147). **14.3** The authors and the Home Office for Felson, M. and Clarke, R.V.G., *Opportunity Makes the Thief: Practical theory for crime prevention* (London: Home Office), 1998, pp. 9–35. **14.4** The authors and the American Sociological Association for Cohen, L. and Felson, M., 'Social change and crime rate trends: A routine activity approach', from *American Sociological Review*, 1979 (Vol. 44, pp. 588–608).

Chapter 15

15.1 The author and Social Justice for Klein, D., 'The etiology of female crime', from *Issues in Criminology*, 1973 (Vol. 8, pp. 3–30). **15.2** The author and SAGE

Publications, London, Los Angeles, New Delhi and Singapore for Chesney-Lind, M., 'Girls, crime and woman's place: Toward a feminist model of female delinquency', from *Crime and Delinquency*, 1989 (Vol. 35, pp. 5–29). **15.3** The authors and Taylor & Francis Ltd for Daly, K. and Chesney-Lind, M., 'Feminism and criminology', from *Justice Quarterly*, 1988 (Vol. 5, pp. 497–538). **15.4** The author for Smart, C. 'Feminist approaches to criminology or postmodern woman meets atavistic man', in Gelsthorpe, L. and Morris, A. (eds) *Feminist Perspectives in Criminology* (Milton Keynes: Open University Press), 1990, pp 70–84.

Chapter 16

16.1 The authors and the American Society of Criminology for Feeley, M. and Simon, J., 'The new penology: notes on the emerging strategy of correction and its implications', from *Criminology*, 1992 (Vol. 30, 4, pp. 449–474). **16.2** The author and SAGE Publications, London, Los Angeles, New Delhi and Singapore for Young, J., *The Exclusive Society* (London: Sage), 1999, pp.68–77. **16.3** The author and Taylor & Francis Ltd for O'Malley, P., 'Risk, power and crime prevention', from *Economy and Society*, 1992 (Vol. 21, 3, pp. 252–275). **16.4** The authors and SAGE Publications, London, Los Angeles, New Delhi and Singapore for Shearing, C. and Stenning, P., '"Say Cheese!" The Disney order that is not so Mickey Mouse', from Shearing, C. and Stenning, P. (eds) *Private Policing* (Newbury Park, CA: Sage), 1987, pp. 317–323.

Chapter 17

17.1 The author and Hart Publishing for Rock, P., 'On Becoming a Victim', from Hoyle, C. and Wilson, R. (eds) *New Visions of Crime Victims*, 3rd edition (Oxford: Hart Publishing), 2002, pp 1–22. **17.2** The author for Shapland, J., 'Fiefs and peasants: accomplishing change for victims in the criminal justice system', from Maguire, M. and Pointing, J. (eds) *Victims of Crime: A New Deal?* (Milton Keynes: Open University Press), 1988, pp. 187–194. **17.3** The authors for Radford, J. and Stanko, E.A., 'Violence against women and children: the contradictions of crime control under patriarchy', from Hester, M., Kelly, L. and Radford, J. (eds) *Women, Violence and Male Power* (Buckingham: Open University Press), 1996, pp. 65–80. **17.4** The author and A B Academic Publishers for Farrell, G., 'Multiple victimization: Its extent and significance', from *International Review of Victimology*, 1992 (Vol. 2, pp. 85–102).

Chapter 18

18.1 The author and Yale University Press for Sutherland, E., *White-collar Crime: The uncut version* (New Haven, CT: Yale University Press), 1983, pp. 3–10. **18.3** The author and Wadsworth, a part of Cengage Learning Inc. www.cengage.com/permissions for Friedrichs, D., *Trusted Criminals: White-collar criminals in contemporary society* (Belmont: Wadsworth), 1996, pp. 5–17. Copyright © 1996 by Wadsworth. **18.4** The author and Rutgers University Press for Rothe, D., 'Iraq and Halliburton', from Michalowski, R. and Kramer, R., *State-Corporate Crime: Wrongdoing at the intersection of business and government* (New Brunswick, NJ: Rutgers University Press), 2006, pp. 215–228.

Chapter 19

19.1 The author and Harper Collins for Cressey, D., *Theft of the Nation* (New York: Harper and Row), 1969, pp. 109–126. **19.2** The author and New York University Press for Jacobs, J., *Gotham Unbound* (New York: New York University Press), 1999, pp. 33–47. **19.3** The author and Indiana University Press for Chambliss, W., *On the Take* (Bloomington: Indiana University Press), 1988, pp. 61–80. **19.5** The author and Wiley-Blackwell for Levi, M., 'Perspectives on "Organised Crime": An Overview', from *Howard Journal*, 1998 (Vol. 37, 4, pp. 335–345).

Chapter 20

20.1 The author and the University of California Press for Shover, N., 'The social organization of burglary', from *Social Problems*, 1973 (Vol. 20, 4, pp. 499–514). **20.2** The authors and Oxford University Press for Zimring, F. and Hawkins, G., *Crime is not the problem: lethal violence in America* (New York: Oxford University Press), 1997, pp. 51–123. **20.3** The author and Oxford University Press for Eisner, M., 'Modernization, self-control and lethal violence', from *British Journal of Criminology*, 2001 (Vol. 41, 4, pp. 618– 638). **20.4** The author and Oxford University Press for Bowling, B., 'Racial harassment and the process of victimization', from *British Journal of Criminology*, 1993 (Vol. 33, 2, pp. 231–250).

Chapter 21
21.1 The authors and Oxford University Press for Hobbs, R., Hadfield, P., Lister, S. and Winlow, S., *Bouncers: Violence and Governance in the Night-time Economy* (Oxford: Oxford University Press), 2003, pp. 36–43. **21.2** The author and SAGE publications for Inciardi, J., 'Heroin use and street crime', from *Crime and Delinquency*, 1971 (Vol. 25, pp. 335–346). **21.3** The author and the AAAS for Nadelmann, E., 'Drug prohibition in the United States: Costs, consequences and alternatives', from *Science*, 1989 (Vol. 245, pp. 939–47). **21.4** The author and the New Press www.thenewpress.com for Mauer, M., *Race to Incarcerate* (New York: W.W. Norton), 1999, pp. 142–161. Copyright © 1999 by Marc Mauer.

Chapter 22
22.1 The translator and Penguin Group UK for Foucault, M., 'The Birth of Prison' from Foucault, M., translated by Alan Sheridan, *Discipline and Punish* (Harmondsworth: Penguin), 1982, pp. 3–31. **22.3** The author and Oxford University Press for von Hirsch, A., *Censure and Sanctions* (Oxford: Oxford University Press), 1993, pp. 115–132. **22.4** The authors and Oxford University Press for Zimring, F., Hawkins, G. and Kamin, S., *Punishment and Democracy: Three Strikes and You're Out in California* (New York: Oxford University Press), 2001, pp. 17–19; 109–119.

Chapter 23
23.1 The author and Stanford University Press for Packer, H.L., *The Limits of the Criminal Sanction* (CA: Stanford University Press), 1968, pp. 149–173. **23.2** The author and Elsevier Ltd. for Heidensohn, F., 'Models of justice: Portia or Persephone? Some thoughts on equality, fairness and gender in the field of criminal justice', from *International Journal of the Sociology of Law*, 1986 (Vol. 14, 3, pp. 287–298). **23.3** The author for Tyler, T., *Why People Obey the Law* (Yale: Yale University Press), 1990, pp. 161–166. **23.4** The author and SAGE publications for Sherman, L., 'Defiance, deterrence and irrelevance: A theory of the criminal sanction', from *Journal of Research in Crime and Delinquency*, 1993 (Vol. 30, pp. 445–473).

Chapter 24
24.1 The authors and SAGE publications for Brantingham, P.J. and Faust, F.L., 'A conceptual model of crime prevention', from *Crime and Delinquency*, 1976 (Vol. 22, pp. 284–296). **24.2** The authors and the University of Chicago Press for Clarke, R.V.G. and Mayhew, P. 'The British Gas Suicide Story and its Criminological Implications', from Morris, N. and Tonry, M. (eds) *Crime and Justice*, 1988 (Vol. 10, pp. 79–116). **24.3** the authors and the AAAS for Sampson, R., Raudenbusch, S. and Earls, F., 'Neighbourhoods and violent crime: A multilevel study of collective efficacy', from *Science*, 1997 (Vol. 277, pp. 1–7). **24.4** The author and The Random House Group Ltd for Jacobs, J., *Death and Life of Great American Cities* (London: Jonathan Cape) 1962 pp 29–46.

Chapter 25
25.1 The author and Oxford University Press for Bayley, D. 'What do the police do?', from Bayley, D., *Police for the Future* (New York: Oxford University Press), 1996, pp. 29–41. **25.2** The author and Pearson Education, Inc. Upper Saddle River, NJ for Skolnick, J., 'A sketch of the policeman's working personality', from Skolnick, J., *Justice Without Trial*, 3rd edition (New York: Wiley), 1994, pp. 264–279. **25.3** The author and ABC-CLIO LLC for Klockars, C.B., 'The rhetoric of community policing', in Greene, J.R. and Mastrofski, S. (eds) *Community Policing: Rhetoric or Reality* (New York: Praeger), 1988, pp. 442–459. **25.4** The authors and Wiley-Blackwell for Bayley, D. and Shearing, C., 'The Future of Policing', from *Law and Society Review*, 1996 (Vol. 30, 3, pp. 585–606).

Chapter 26

26.1 The author and The University of Chicago Press for Garfinkel, H. (1956) 'Conditions of successful degradation ceremonies', from *American Journal of Sociology*, March 1956 (Vol 61, 5, pp. 420–424). **26.2** The author and Wiley-Blackwell for Carlen, P., *Magistrates Justice* (Oxford: Martin Robertson), 1976, pp. 18–38. **26.3** The author and Oxford University Press for Rock, P., 'The adversarial system', from Rock, P., *The Social World of an English Crown Court: Witness and Professionals in the Crown Court Centre at Wood Green* (Oxford: Oxford University Press), 1993, pp. 30–40. **26.4** The author and Palgrave Macmillan for McBarnett, D., *Conviction: Law, the state and the construction of justice* (Basingstoke: Macmillan), 1981, pp. 154–162.

Chapter 27

27.1 The author for Carlen, P., 'Crime, inequality and sentencing', from Carlen, P. and Cook, D. (eds) *Paying for Crime* (Milton Keynes: Open University Press), 1989, pp. 8–28. **27.2** The author and Springer Science and Business Media for Cohen, S., 'The punitive city: Notes on the dispersal of social control', from *Contemporary Crises*, 1979 (Vol. 3, 4, pp. 339–363). **27.3** The author for Bottoms, A.E., 'Neglected features of contemporary penal systems', from Garland, D. and Young, P. (eds) *The Power to Punish* (Aldershot: Gower), 1983, pp. 173–180. **27.4** The authors and SAGE Publications, London, Los Angeles, New Delhi and Singapore for Millie, A., Jacobson, J. and Hough, M., 'Understanding the growth of the prison population in England and Wales', from *Criminology and Criminal Justice*, 2003 (Vol. 3, 4, pp. 369–387).

Chapter 28

28.1 The author and Oxford University Press for Garland, D, *Punishment and Modern Society* (Oxford: Oxford University Press), 1990, pp. 143–151. **28.2** The author and SAGE Publications, London, Los Angeles, New Delhi and Singapore for Sparks, R., 'Prisons, punishment and penality' in McLaughlin, E. and Muncie, J. (eds) *Controlling Crime* (London: Sage), 1996, pp. 199–207. **28.3** The author and Penguin Group UK and Random House Inc., New York for Goffman, E., *Asylums* (Harmondsworth: Penguin), 1968, pp. 23–47. **28.4** The authors and Willan Publishing for Carlen, P. and Worrall, A., *Analysing Women's Imprisonment* (Cullompton: Willan Publishing), 2004, pp. 28–42.

Chapter 29

29.1 The author and Palgrave Macmillan for Pearson, G., *Hooligan: A history of respectable fears* (Basingstoke: Macmillan), 1983, pp. 3–14. **29.2** The author and *The Weekly Standard* for Dilulio, John, 'The Coming of the Super-Predators', from *The Weekly Standard*, 27 November 1995. **29.3** The author and SAGE Publications, London, Los Angeles, New Delhi and Singapore for Goldson, B., 'Penal custody: intolerance, irrationality and indifference', from Goldson, B. and Muncie, J. (eds) *Youth, Crime and Justice* (London: Sage), 2006, pp. 139–156. **29.4** The authors and SAGE Publications, London, Los Angeles, New Delhi and Singapore for Cavadino, M. and Dignan, J., *Penal Systems* (London: Sage), 2006, pp. 199–212.

Chapter 30

30.1 The author and Oxford University Press for Christie, N., 'Conflicts as property', from *British Journal of Criminology*, 1977 (Vol. 17, 1, pp. 1–15). **30.2** The author and the Home Office for Marshall, T., *Restorative justice: an overview* (Home Office: Restorative Justice Consortium),1998, pp. 5–36. **30.3** The author and Oxford University Press for Ashworth, A., 'Responsibilities, rights and restorative justice', from *British Journal of Criminology*, 2002 (Vol. 42, 3, pp. 578–595). **30.4** The author and Oxford University Press for Morris, A., 'Critiquing the critics: a brief response to critics of restorative justice', *British Journal of Criminology*, 2002 (Vol. 42, 3, pp. 596–615).

Chapter 31

31.1 The author for Jefferson, T., 'The Racism of Criminalization: Police and the reproduction of the criminal other', in Gelsthorpe, L. (ed) *Minority Ethnic Groups in* *the Criminal Justice System*, papers presented to the 21ˢᵗ Cropwood Conference, 1992 (Cambridge: Institute of Criminology), 1993, pp. 26–46. **31.2** The author and Oxford University Press for Hall, S., 'From Scarman to Stephen Lawrence', *History Workshop Journal*, 1999 (Vol. 48, pp. 187–197). **31.3** The authors and Oxford University Press for Waddington, P. A. J., Stenson, K. and Don, D., 'In Proportion: Race, and Police Stop and Search', *British Journal of Criminology*, 2004, (Vol. 44, 6, pp. 889–914). **31.4** The author for Wacquant, L., 'Deadly Symbiosis: When Ghetto and Prison Meet and Mesh', from *Punishment and Society*, 2001 (Vol. 3, 1, pp. 95–133).

Chapter 32
32.1 The author and Wiley-Blackwell for Gelsthorpe, L., 'Counterblast: Women and Criminal Justice: Saying it Again, Again and Again', from *Howard Journal of Criminal Justice*, 2006 (Vol. 45, 4, pp. 421–424). **32.2** The author and SAGE Publications, London, Los Angeles, New Delhi and Singapore for Smart, C., 'The woman of legal discourse', from *Social and Legal Studies*, 1992 (Vol. 1, pp. 29–44). **32.3** The author and Palgrave Macmillan for Heidensohn, F., 'Women and social control', in Heidensohn, F., *Women and Crime*, 2nd edn (Basingstoke: Macmillan), 1996, pp. 163–195. **32.4** The author for Stanko, E., 'Common sense, routine precaution and normal violence', from Stanko, E., *Everyday Violence: How Women and Men Experience Sexual and Physical Danger* (London: Pandora), 1990, pp. 13–31. **32.5** The author and Rowman & Littlefield Publishers Inc. for Messerschmidt, J., *Masculinities and Crime* (Lanham, Maryland: Rowman & Littlefield), 1993, pp. 81–92.

Chapter 33
33.1 The authors and Oxford University Press for Farrington, D.P. and Welsh, B., *Saving Children from a Life of Crime* (New York: Oxford University Press), 2007, pp. 37–54. **33.2** The author and the American Psychological Association for Moffitt, T., 'Adolescence-limited and life-course persistent antisocial behavior: A developmental taxonomy', from *Psychological Review*, 1993 (Vol. 100, pp. 674–701). Copyright © 1993 by the American Psychological Association. **33.3** The authors and Harvard University Press for Sampson, R. and Laub, J., *Crime in the Making: Pathways and turning points through life* (Cambridge, MA: Harvard University Press), 1993, pp. 243–250. Copyright © 1998 by the President and Fellows of Harvard College.

Chapter 34
34.1 The author and Taylor & Francis Books UK for Christie, N., *Crime Control as Industry*, 3rd edn (London: Routledge), 2000, pp. 11–14. **34.2** The author and the Australia and New Zealand Society of Criminology for Cohen, S., 'Human rights and crimes of the state: The culture of denial', *Australian and New Zealand Journal of Criminology*, 1993 (Vol. 26, 2, pp. 97–115). **34.3** The author and Oxford University Press for Braithwaite, J., 'The new regulatory state and the transformation of criminology', from *British Journal of Criminology*, 2000 (Vol. 40, 2, pp. 222–238). **34.4** The authors and Willan Publishing for Newburn, T. and Sparks, R., 'Criminal justice and political cultures', from Newburn, T. and Sparks, R. (eds) *Criminal Justice and Political Cultures* (Cullompton: Willan Publishing), 2004, pp. 1–15.

Chapter 35
35.1 The author and Oxford University Press for Bottoms, A.E., 'The relationship between theory and empirical observations in criminology', in King, R. and Wincup, E. (eds) *Doing Research on Crime and Justice*, 2ⁿᵈ ed. (Oxford: Oxford University Press), 2008, pp. 106–116. **35.2** The author and David and Charles for Parker, H., *A View From the Boys* (London: David and Charles), 1974, pp.214–224. **35.3** The authors and SAGE publications for Wright, R., Decker, S., Redfern, S. and Smith, D., 'A snowball's chance in hell: Doing fieldwork with active residential burglars', from *Journal of Research in Crime and Delinquency*, 1992 (Vol. 29, pp. 149–161). **35.4** The author and SAGE Publications, London, Los Angeles, New Delhi and Singapore for Liebling, A., 'Doing research in prison: breaking the silence?', from *Theoretical Criminology*, 1999 (Vol. 3, pp. 147–73). **35.5** The author for Gelsthorpe, L., 'Feminist methodologies in criminology: a new approach or old wine in new bottles?', from Gelsthorpe, L. and Morris, A. (eds) *Feminist Perspectives in Criminology* (Milton Keynes: Open University Press), 1990, pp. 89–105. **35.6** The author and the University of Chicago Press for Becker, H., *Writing for Social Scientists* (Chicago: University of Chicago Press) 1986, pp. 48–56.

Index

Names in bold are those of authors whose contributions appear in this book.
Index entries in bold also refer to a key concept which appears at the beginning of one or more chapters.

abolitionism 257, 271–3, 723, 724
  on crime control 273
  as a political strategy 272
  as a social movement 271
  as a theoretical perspective 271–2
Abraham, Lynne 684
absorption 637–8
actuarialism 358, 367–72
  and the risk society 367–8
  recalcitrant modernity and the critics of risk 370–2
  six components of risk 368–9
  Umwelt and the management of risk 369–70
actus reus 11
Adderley's Bill 37
Adler, M. 11
administrative criminology 267, 269–70
adolescence 129
adolescence-limited anti social behaviour 809, 812–15
  maturity gap 813
  social mimicry 813
Adolescent Subcultures and Delinquency 794
adoption studies 115, 117, 120–1
adult social bonds 821
adversarial justice 602, 613–18
Advisory Council on the Penal System (ACPS) 54
aetiological crisis 256, 267–8, 269, 285, 286
African Americans
  ghetto 761–2
  Jim Crow 761
  prison population 759
  slavery 760–1
  war on drugs 506–10
Afro-Caribbeans, criminalization and 742–3
age, criminalization and 743–4
age-crime curve 129–31, 808–9
Age of Extremes 181
aggression 490–1
Agnew, R. 169
AIDS 501, 503
Akers, R.L. 142
alcohol abuse, cost of 502
alcohol-related violence 490–3
  disinhibitor effect 490
  marketing strategies 493
alcoholism 212, 821
Althusserian functionalism 285
American Bar Foundation study 52
American Dream 174–80
  anomic tendencies of the 174–6

anomie, weak social controls and crime 179–80
  and the institutional balance of power 176–9
Americal lethal violence 470–5
  circumstances and demography of 472–4
  demography of homicide 474–5
  profile of 470–1
  trends over time 471–2
American Revolution and capital punishment 23
amplification 66, 67, 82–4
anger 549
Angry Brigade Trial 202
anomie 144, 145, 146, 147, 160–1, 165–9, 174–85, 224, 228, 229
  strain towards 168–9
Anthony, Susan B. 337
anthropological factor of crime 100–3
anti-prison movements 271
anti-social behaviour orders (ASBOs) 184
anti-social conduct/behaviour 12, 16, 184, 268, 690, 801
  age and 807–10
  see also adolescence-limited anti social behaviour; life-course persistent antisocial behaviour
apartheid 759
Aristotle 608
arrests 575, 595
Ashworth, A. 726
assault, in eighteenth century 28, 29
assizes 29
atavism 109, 329
attorneys 468–9
attrition model 271
authoritative intervention 572–99
available population 755–8
avocational crime 427

'backlash' against feminist perspectives 671
bail 29
bankruptcy fraudsters 458
barbarism on sidewalks 568
Barings Bank, collapse of 841
Bauman, Zygmunt 827
Bayley, David 574, 585–92
Beccaria, C. 88
Becker, H.S. 216, 882
Becoming Deviant 228
Beetham, David 661
behaviour, interpreting meaning of 47
behaviour systems 464
benefit of clergy 25–6
benefit system 293
Bentham, Jeremy 653–4
bias
  class 45, 214, 218, 421
  judicial 45–6
  media 68, 71
bifurcation 268, 659 *see also* punitive bifurcation

'Big Five' model   802
'Big House'   763–4
bill of indictment   29–30
binge drinking   184
'biology of crime'   115
biosocial explanations   106
biosocial interaction   106, 119–25
  birth complications   123–4
  genetics   120–1
  pregnancy complications   122–3
Birmingham Six   659
blackguarding   615
Black Act   20, 25
Black Codes   761
Black Death   14
black letter law   2, 11, 12
Blackstone, William   25, 26
Blair, Tony   690
Bloody Code   20, 23, 25, 26
blue locusts   20, 31–4
Boies, H.M.   110, 111
Bonanno crime family   445
bond to society   236–40
bondsmen   468–9
boot camps   364
born criminal   108–10, 111
  see also female born criminal
Bottoms. A.   640, 854
'boundary crisis'   80
Box, S.   7, 44
Boyson, Rhodes   681
Bowling, B.   481
Braithwaite, John   246 , 723, 730, 837
Brantingham, P. J.   554
Brave new World   382
breach of trust   4
Brighton Rock   682
British/Birmingham School of Cultural Studies   203
British Crime Survey   42, 54–9, 61, 283
  context   54
  design elements   56
  influence on criminological research and justice
    policy   57–8
  key contributions since 1982   55
  making a case for National Crime Survey   54–5
  origins of   54
British National Party   750
British Union of Fascists   481
'British way of life'   750
broken homes   157
broken windows   276, 277, 295–300, 369
  experimental tests on theory   296
Brooks, Duwayne   748, 750
Brothers in Crime   335
Brown and Root   431
bullying   694
burglary   464–9
  bondsmen and attorneys   468
  external social organization   466
  fence   467–8
  internal social organization   464–6
  tipsters   466–7
Bush, George W.   431, 759

'Butskellite' compromises   262
bystander effect   830–1

California, sentencing in   524–8
  determinate sentencing   526
  indeterminate sentencing   525–6
  jurisprudence of imprisonment   526–7
  proportionality and disparity   527–8
  Three Strikes   524, 527
Cambodia genocide   248
Cambridge Study   800, 802
capable guardians   318, 321–2
capital punishment   659
capitalism   258, 264, 283–4
  in the United States   177
  welfare   262
carbon monoxide, removal from gas supply   559
carceral continuum   656–7
carceral punishment   640–3, 759
cardinal proportionality   523–4
Carlen, P.   608, 628, 670
Caroline, Queen   32
Cavadino, M.   698
censure   2, 13–14, 212, 512, 520–4
censure-based justifications for punishment   520–2
  hard treatment   521–2
  reason for   521
Chadwick, K.   261
chain referral   865–6
chain rule   609
Chambliss, W.J.   258, 449
Changing Lenses   722
Cheney, Dick   431–5
Chesney-Lind, M.   335, 340
Chicago study   542–4
child imprisonment, conditions and treatment   692–4
child-rearing
  and low self-control   244–5
  in single-parent communities   290
children, violence against   402–8
Children Act 1908   691
Children and Young Persons' Act 1969   629
'childsaving movement'   336, 337
chivalry   332, 334
choice, crime as   149–53, 307–8
  conditioning   151–2
  reinforcers   149, 150–1
  theory as a whole   152–3
Christie, N.   17, 712, 826
CIA   455
Cicourel, A.V.   48
citizen patrols   299
'civil death'   665
civilizing process   462, 476, 480
Clarke, J.   201
Clarke, R.V.   307, 312, 559
class, structural location   262–3
class bias   45, 214, 218
class conflict   258
class, criminalization and   744–6
class system   258–63
classicism   86, 88–103
Clinton, Bill   690, 759

cocaine 502–3
coercive sexuality 402–8
cognitive ability and criminal behaviour 154–8
    intelligence as a preventative 154–5
    interpreting self-report data 155
    IQ and types of criminal behaviour 155–6
    role of a broken home 157
    role of education 157
    role of socioeconomic background 156–7
cognitive bias 830
Cohen, A.K. 194
Cohen, L.E. 318
Cohen, P. 198
Cohen, S. 79, 633, 827
coining offences 22, 26, 27
collective efficacy 552, 563–7
Combat 18 750
Combination Acts 29
commercial crime 425
Common Culture 182
community action, offenders dealt with by 27
community-based crime prevention 596
community-based justice 723
community block grants 598
community conferencing 703–4
community consultative committees 749
community control 634
community corrections 629–30, 640, 642
community policing 585–92, 596, 598
    areal decentralization of command 588–9
    civilianization 590–1
    mixed metaphors of reduced crime 587
    mystification of the concept of community 585–7
    police-community reciprocity 585
    reorientation of patrol 589–90
community restoration 727
community service 642–3, 659, 660
comparative criminology, problems of 846–7
comparative youth justice 698–706
    justice model 700–1
    minimum intervention model 701–3
    neo-correctionalist model 704–6
    restorative justice model 703–4
    welfare model 698–700
compensation for wrongs 728
computer-assisted self-interviewing (CASI) 56
concentration camps *see* total institution
conditional discharge, women and 670
conditioning 138, 151–2
conflict-resolution theory 724
conflicts 712–18
    lay-oriented court 717–18
    as property 715–17
    professional thieves 713–14
    structural thieves 714–15
    victim-oriented court 717
conscience 151–2, 15
consent, underlying restorative justice processes 729
consequences of crime for society 259
conservative demonisation 182–3
contemporary classicism 304–23
contrepreneurial crime 427
control-balance theory 246–53

control ratios and types of deviance 249–52
control ratios, provocation and opportunity 252–3
effects of redistributing control 247–9
importance of Tittle's contribution 246–7
Control Balance:Toward a General Theory of Deviance 246
control ratios 246–53
control theories 234–54
    control balance and criminological theory 246–53
    control theory of delinquency 236–40
    general theory of crime 241–5
    neutralization 234–6
control theory of delinquency 236–40, 855
    attachment 236–7
    belief 238–40
    commitment 237–8
    involvement 238
    motivation 240
control of women 781–4
    domestic constraint 781–2
    public propriety 782
    at work 783–4
conviction 602, 619–23
corporal punishment 556, 626, 640, 641, 682
corporate crime 426
correctional continuum 626, 634, 638
Cortez and the Conquistadors 248
Cosa Nostra 440–3
    control of Fulton Fish Market 445–8
    domination of Local 359 445
Council of Europe 455
counting prisoners 671–2
    average population 671–2
    rates of imprisonment 672
    reception 672
counting rules 42, 62–3
courteous society 476
Cressey, D.R. 140, 143–4, 239, 440
crime
    becoming safer 292
    black letter law approach 11, 12
    juristic view 5
    statistics 17
    useful role of 164
crime, definitions of 11–16
    as criminal law violation 11–12
    as historical invention 14–15
    as ideological censure 13–14
    as social construct 13
    as social harm 15–16
    as violation of moral codes 12–13
Crime and Disorder Act 1998 691
Crime and Human Nature 278
'crime as opportunity' 304
crime control 532–5
crime control industry 826–7
    criminal process 533
    values 532–4
Crime in the Making 856, 857
crime patterns and trends 59–63
crime prevention, conceptual model of 554–8
    primary prevention 556
    secondary prevention 556
    tertiary prevention 555–6

crimes of obedience 833–4
  authorisation 833
  dehumanisation 834
  routinisation 834
crimes of the state 827–36
  bystanders and rescuers 830
  culture of denial 829–30
  neutralization theory 831–4
  psychology of denial 830
crimes of the suites 425
crimes without victims 488, 497
Criminal, The 110
criminal, juristic view of 5
criminal anthropology in the United States 108–12
  born criminal 108–10
  and eugenics 111–12
  as a science 108
  other criminal types 110–11
criminal-by-passion 110, 111
criminal class, creation of 34–8
criminal coping 169, 171
criminal investigation 576–7
  triage strategy 577
Criminal Justice Act 1982 400
Criminal Justice Act 1991 659, 671, 770
Criminal Justice Act 2003 770
  section 95 671
Criminal Justice and Police Act 2001 691
Criminal Justice and Public Order Act 1994 690
Criminal Justice Bill 1986 400
criminal justice, political cultures and 844–8
criminal justice fiefdom 386, 397–401
criminal justice system, victim services and 398–9
Criminal Man and Crime: Its Causes and Remedies 111
criminal 'other' 740, 742–6
  age 743
  class 744–6
  ethnicity 742–3
  sex 743
criminal sanctions 530, 542–50
criminal types 110–11
Criminality of Women, The 333
criminalization 4–6
  of drugs 500
  of popular culture 205
  and racism 742–6
criminaloids 110, 111
criminology
  classic school of 99–100
  positive school of 99–103
critical criminology, theoretical and political priorities of
    261–5
  class analysis and the determining context of
      production 262–3
  establishing a framework for critical analysis 261–2
  feminist critiques and the determining context of
      patriarchy 264–5
  racism, crime and the politics of neocolonialism 263–4
crombies 198, 199
crop eradication/substitution programs (illicit drugs) 499
cross-examination 615
cross-national comparisons, crime data 462, 476–80
Crown Court 613–17

blackguarding 615
cross-examination 615
defence counsel 614–15
emotion 617
good manners 617
juries 615
opening statement 614
prosecution 614, 616
verbal abuse 616
verdict 616
Crown Prosecution Service 398, 399
Cullen, F.T. 630
cultural criminology 182, 203–6
  crime as culture 204–5
  culture as crime 205
  historical and theoretical frameworks 203–4
  media constructions of crime and crime control 205
  methodological frameworks 204
  politics of culture, crime and cultural criminology 206
cultural goals 165–6
Culture of Control, The 17
cultural transmission 188–206
Cusody Plus 771

Daly, K. 340
Damiens the regicide 514–15
'dark figure' of crime 54, 55
Davis, J. 34
day fine system 631–2
De Haan, W. 14, 15, 271
decadence 250
decarceration 634, 703
Decker, S.H. 865
defective delinquency theory 109
defence counsel 614–15
defendants 610–11
defiance 250–2, 530, 531, 545–50
  anger and displaced just deserts 549
  defining sanctions as unfair 548
  mainstream 547–8
degeneration 94, 102, 109–10
degradation ceremonies 604–6
delinquency 655, 656
delinquent girls *see* female delinquency
delinquent subculture 194–8, 234 *see also* juvenile
      delinquency
  appeal of 197–8
  content of 194–5
  pressure towards conformity 195
  problem solving 195
  subcultural solutions 195–6
  subcultural solutions to status problems 196–7
demographics 117
denial 829–36
  implicatory 833–4
  literal 833
  of the past 832
deregulation 838
detectives 576–7
  developing legal expertise 577
Detention and Training Order
detention centres, re-introduction of 689
determinate and indeterminate sentences 512, 513,
      524–8, 690

deterrence 545–50, 657–62
developmental criminology 818–19
deviance
  definitions of 215–17
  'holy trinity' of 9
  of those in power 116
  perpetuation of 215
  responses of others 217–18
  sociology of 214–15
  submissive 250
  withdrawn or escapist 250
deviancy amplification 225–9
  five types of 225–7
deviation, primary and secondary *see* primary and
      secondary deviance
differentiation 750
Dignan, J. 698
Dilulio, J.J. 648
discipline 640–8
  three mechanisms of 640
Discipline and Punish 640–1, 642, 652, 655
differential association 138, 140–2, 143–4,
      147–8, 234
differential reinforcement 138, 142, 144
differential social organization 137, 143–4,
      147–8, 188, 191–3
discretion 45, 46, 47, 52
discrimination 742–6, 772–3
disculturation 664
dishonest poor 289
Disney World 379–82
  control strategies 380–1
  physical barriers 380
  picture spots 381–2
  queueing 381
  recorded messages 381
disorderly behaviour 296–8
dispersal of discipline 640–3
dispersal of social control 633–9
  absorption 637–8
  blurring the boundaries 634–6, 640
  decarceration 634
  from prison to community 633–4
  masking and disguising 636–7
  penetration 637, 640
  re-integration 637–8
  thinning the mesh 635–6, 640
  widening the net 635–6, 640
displacement 302, 307–18, 374, 549, 561–2
disproportionality 754, 755, 757, 759
distributive justice 536, 542–4
doli incapax 705
domestic violence 386, 391, 392, 402–8, 410, 411, 414,
      549
dominant ideology 66, 71
Don, D. 754
double deviance 536–41
double jeopardy 536–41, 670–1
Drahms, A. 109, 110
drug prohibition in the US 499–505
  alternatives to 501–5
  costs and consequences of policies 500–1

dangerous consequences of 500–1
  limits of policies 499–500
  see also war on drugs
drug takers
  attitudes of ideological 228–9
  attitudes of illicit 228
  attitudes of sick 229
drug taking, social reaction against 224–9
drug testing 364
dual role, of women 784
Due Process 532–5
Dunedin longitudinal study 801
Durkheim, Emile 48, 162, 214
Duster, T. 113

Earls, F. 563
East India Company 29
Eaton, Daniel Isaac 26
economic crime 425
economic inactivity 291–2
economic power and origins of criminal law 14
education 157, 177, 178, 190, 193
Eisner, M. 476
electronic monitoring 364
Elias, Norbert 476, 480
elite crime 425
embedded control strategies 380
Emergence of the Risk Society, The 367
emotional intelligence 801
empathy, as a factor of offending 802–3
empirical observation 854–9
employment
  ex-convicts chances of finding 36, 37
  necessity of to support family 178
Emsley, C. 27
enforcement 2, 13, 25
enforcement pyramid 730
enterprise crime 427
Erikson, K.T. 214
ethnic minorities 747–53
ethnography 203–6
etiology of criminal behaviour 259
etiology of female crime 328–35
  Lombroso, Cesare 328–30
  Pollak, Otto 333–4
  Thomas, W.I. 330–3
eugenics 106, 111–12
European Convention on Human Rights 728–9
European Convention on Mutual Assistance 458
European Court of Human Rights 398
European modernity 476
European Union (EU) 455, 457
evidence 614
evolutionary psychology 127–33
  age 129–30
  gender 129
  intelligence 131–3
executions 22–4
experienced vicarious and anticipated strains 160,
      171
exploitation 249, 252
export controls, flaunting of by arms manufacturers 15

extenuating circumstances 101
external social organisations 466
Eysenck, Hans, three dimensions of personality 801–2

'facts at issue' 613
failure of criminology 282–8
fairness 548
family
    breakdown in relationships 12
    child-rearing and self-control 244–5
    decline of 680
    disputes 575
    ineffectiveness of in high-rate delinquent
        communities 191–2
family group conferencing 703–4, 732–3
Farrell, G. 409
Farrington, D.P. 800
fashion style and deviancy 80
Faucher, Leon 515–16
faulty products, marketing of 15
Faust, F.L. 554
fear displacement 284
fear of crime 54, 57, 283, 295, 370–2, 598
fear of disorderliness 295, 297
Federal Communications Commission 77
Feeley, M.M. 360
Felson, M. 312, 318
female born criminal 93–38
    affections and passions 94
    contradictions 95–6
    cruelty 93–4
    dress 95
    eroticism and virility 94
    greed and avarice 95
    hatred 95
    instigation 96
    intelligence 96
    lasciviousness 97
    love 95
    method of committing crime 96
    obstinacy in denial 97
    religiosity 95
    revelation of crime 97
    sentimentalism 96
    variety of crimes 93
    vengeance 94–5
    writing and painting 96
    see also born criminal
female delinquency 332–3, 335–9
Female Offender, The 329
female poverty 670
feminism 340–7, 404–7
    defining 342–3
    feminist analysis 341–2
    first wave 342
    five elements of thought 343
    lack of objectivity 340–1
    myths about 340–2
    narrow focus on women 341
    second wave 340, 342
    standpoint 352–3
feminist criminology 328–55, 724
feminist approaches to criminology 347–55

appliance of science 347–8
debate over postodernism 349–50
empiricism 351–2
feminist intervention 351–4
search for theory, cause and solution 348–9
feminist empiricism 327, 351–2
feminist methodology 853, 875–80
feminist perspectives 344
feminist postmodernism 353–4
feminist research 875–80
    challenge to traditional criminology 878
    project on prisons 878–80
    themes of 875–8
feminist thought, relevance of to criminology 343–5
fence 467–8
Ferrell, J. 203
Ferrero, G. 93
Ferri, E. 99
Festival of Light 202
fetal nicotine exposure 122–3
Fielding, Sir John 28
fieldwork and research 860–80
    active residential burglars 865–9
    feminist 878–80
    research in prison 870–4
    'The Boys' 860–4
fiefs and peasants 397–401
fighting 491
finance crime 427
first-wave feminism 342
First World Dream 181, 182
folk devils 34, 35, 38, 66, 82, 203, 205
Fordist-Keynesian era 762, 763
forgery
    and counterfeiting statutes 25
    death penalty for 22, 25
Foucault, Michel 37–8, 261, 514, 640–3, 652–3, 654–7
France, executions in 23
fraud 457–8
free markets 276
Friedrichs, D.O. 425
Fry, Elizabeth 22
Fulton Fish Market 444–8
    Cosa Nostra's control of 445
    defrauding suppliers 447
    extorting Christmas payments 446–7
    loading companies' parking racket 447
    rental of union signs 446
    stealing seafood 447
    unloading cartel 447
    watchman's association protection racket 445–6
    workings of the market 444
Fulton Patrol Association 446

gang culture 194–8
Garden House Trial 202
Garfinkel, H. 604
Garland, D. 304, 625
garotting 20, 34–8
gas suicides 559–62
    detoxification and decline in suicide 560–1
    detoxification of domestic gas 560
    lessons for displacement 561

Gatrell, V. 22
Gelsthorpe, L. 770, 875
gender-proofing 770–1
gendering strategies 772–8
General Household Survey (GHS) 54, 60
general intelligence 132, 133
general rehabilitation model of sentencing 628
general strain theory (GST) 169, 170, 172–3
general theory of crime 241–5
   causes of 243–4
   child-rearing and self-control 244–5
   elements of self-control 242–3
   manifestations of low self-control 243
   self-control and alternative concepts 241–2
Genes, Mind and Culture 114
genetics 106, 113–17, 199–21, 811
   explanation of criminal behaviour 140–2
Genovese crime family 445–7
'ghetto' 761–2 *see also* hyperghetto
ghetto dwellers 500, 501
Gilbert, K.E. 630
globalization 358, 844–8
Gluecks' study 821, 822, 854–8
Goffman, E. 664
Golden Gate Bridge, and suicide 559
Goldson, B. 689
'good burglar' 464–9
Gottfredson, M.R. 241
governmental crime 426
greasers 82, 199
Great Migration 761
Great Transformation 634, 640
greed 248, 423
Greene, Graham 682
group autonomy 195
Guildford Four 659
guillotine 23
Gulag 824, 826–7
Gurr, Ted Robert 476

habitual criminals 110
Hadfield, P. 490
halfway house 635
Hain, Peter 202
Hall, S. 747
Halliburton 430–5
   Cheney connections 431
   contracts 431–2
   overcharges, kickbacks and cost overruns 432–5
hallucinogens 503
hanging 22–3, 25
Harding, Arthur 27
Harding, John 723
Hawkins, G. 470, 524
health and safety standards, failure to enforce 15
hegemonic and subordinated masculinities 791–4
Heidensohn, F. 536, 779
heredity 108, 109, 110, 111, 114, 115
heritability 116, 121
heroin use 501, 502
heroin use and street crime survey 496–9
   criminal histories 497
   current criminal activity 497
   drug use patterns 496–7

Herrnstein, Richard 114, 149, 154, 278
heterosexuality, in youth groups 793
hidden female crime 333–4
hierarchies at work 784
high school rebellion 237
higher court, trial in 29
highway robbery 24, 35
hippies 81, 82, 83, 199, 202
Hirschi, T. 236, 241
Hirschi's control theory 724
history of crime and punishment 22–39
Hitler, Adolf 248, 249
HIV 501
Hobbs, D. 490
Hobsbawm, Eric 181
Home Office 54, 55
Homeless Persons Act 1977 293
homicide 128, 172, 566 *see also* American lethal violence
hooligans 678, 680–3
Hoover, J. Edgar 248
hot products 305, 315
hot spots 252, 305, 314, 390, 411, 491
'hot times' 491
Hough, M. 54, 644
house arrest programs 364–5
Hughes, Howard 250
'human agency' 857
human anatomy and deviant behaviour 8
human nature 127
human rights 596–7, 726–30, 824
   and crimes of the state 827–36
   violation of as definition of crime 15
humiliation 249
Huxley, Aldous 382
hyperactivity, as a factor of offending 803
hyperghetto 762–4
   institutions 762–3
   loss of 'buffering functions' 763
   loss of positive economic function 762
   segregation 762
   see also ghetto

ideal types, criminal process models 530, 532–5
Ignatieff, M. 24, 31, 37
ill repute, fear of 783
Illegitimacy 12, 289–90
imitation 138, 141, 142
immediate gratification, of criminal acts 242
'immigrants'/'foreigners', in court 611–12
impartiality 727, 728–9
imprisonment 659–61
   in eighteenth century 24, 29
   stigmatizing consequences of 45
impulsiveness, as a factor of offending 803–4
incapacitation 362, 657–62, 730
incarceration rates 116
Inciardi, J.A. 496
indefinite discipline 638, 642
indeterminate sentencing 525
Infanticide Act 1623 777
informal social control 552, 553, 563–7
injurious practices 15

inmates 664–8
innovation 160, 167
instinctive criminal 110
institution of privacy 46, 47
institutional racism 748, 751–2, 754
institutionalized intolerance 691
institutionalized norms 165–6
insurance cover 61
intelligence 154–8, 800–1
  of born criminals 109
  of female born criminals 96
  genetics and 114
  as a preventative 154–5
  of women 330
intelligence-led policing 458
intensive supervision programs 364–5
interactional theory 819
interactionist school of sociology 13
interdiction 488, 499–505
internal social organisation 464–6
internalization of norms 237
International Covenant on Civil and Political Rights 729
IQ 154–8, 800, 801
  black and white differences 114, 116
  delinquents and non-delinquents 131, 154
  and frequency of offending 154
  size of gap 154
  and types of criminal behaviour 155–6
Iraq and Halliburton 430–5
Jackroller, The 335

Jacobs, J. 568
Jacobs, J.B. 443
Jacobson, J. 644
Jackson, Michael 250
Jagger, Mick 202
Jefferson, T. 742
Jenkin, Patrick 682
Jim Crow 761
Joint Committee Against Racialism (JCAR) 481–2
Joseph, Sir Keith 680, 682
judges, dual function of 621
judicial bias 45–6
junior criminal courts 700
juridical criminals 110
juridical punishment 626, 640–3
juries 615
justice by geography 727
justice model
  of sentencing 628–9
  youth justice 700–1
justice for women 536–8
juvenile delinquency 49, 132, 234
  in urban areas 190–3
  see also delinquent subculture
Juvenile Delinquency in Urban Areas 335
Juvenile Justice and Delinquency Prevention Act 1974
    338

Kamin, S. 524
Kanazawa, S. 127
Katz, J. 68
Kelling, G.L. 295

Keynesian state 837, 838, 840
kickbacks 434
Kirkholt Burglary Prevention Project 412–13, 414
Kitsuse, J.I. 48
Klein, D. 328
Klockars, C.B. 585
Kornhauser, Ruth 175–6
Kray twins 453–4

labelling 210, 220–3, 307, 701
  biases and limitations of 220
  irrelevance of to certain problem areas 221
  'man on his back' bias 221
  neglect of becoming deviant 220–1
  neglect of power 222–3
  neglect of structure 223
larceny 24, 26, 28, 77, 172
late modernity 160, 181–5
Laub, John 818, 854–8
Law and Order society 202, 203
law enforcement 45–6, 619–23
  gap between rhetoric and law 620–1
  managing the ideological gap 621–3
  rhetoric of justice 619–20
Lawrence, Stephen 747–8, 750
laws
  interpretation of 89
  obsurity of 90
learned helplessness 250–1
left idealism 285, 286
left realism 276, 282–8
legal discourse, women of 772–8
  example of law as a gendering strategy 776–8
  law as a gendering strategy 774–6
  law is gendered 774
  law is male 773–4
  law is sexist 772–3
legalization of controlled drugs 501–5
legitimacy 542–4, 661–2
Lemert, E.M. 212
lesson-drawing 844
Levi, M. 454
lethal violence *see* American lethal violence;
        modernization, self-control and lethal violence
licensed premises and increase in assaults 491
Liebling, A. 870
life-course persistent antisocial behaviour 809,
        810–12
  link with neuropsychological deficits 811
  resemblance of parents and children 811
'life-course' theory 854–8
'lifestyle analysis' 304
Legitimation of Power, The 661
liminal zones 488, 493
Lister, S. 490
Little Red School Book affair 202
Livingstone, S. 75
loan sharks 468
Local 359 443, 445, 446
  domination of by Cosa Nostra 445
Logistics Civil Augmentation Program (LOGCAP) 431
Lombroso, Cesare 93, 328–30

London Garrotting panic 1862 34–8
  magistrates and judges role in 36
  police's role in 36
Longford Report 202
'low self-control' 854

McBarnet, D. 619
'machismo' 199
Macpherson, Sir William 747, 757
Macpherson Inquiry 747–8, 750–3
mafia 438, 439, 442, 443–8, 451–2, 456, 457
'magical' solutions, subcultures and 188, 198
magistrates' courts 608–12
  acoustics 609
  beyond absurdity 612
  humiliation 609
  interrogation 609
  placing and spacing 608–9
  time saving 609–10
Major, John 689, 690
male violence 782
mandatory penalties/sentences 509, 513, 524–8
Maori justice 721
marginalization 262–3
  of women 264
marijuana 499, 502
  for medical purposes 501
  smokers 500
marketing of faulty products 15
markets, organized crime 438
Marriage Act 1753 777
Marshall, T. 719
Martinson, R. 517
Marx, Karl 258–9
Marxian paradigm 259–60
Marxist theory of crime and criminal law 13
mass media 66
  distortion of crime 282–3
Matthews, R. 278
Matza, David 228, 234
Mauer, M. 506
Maxfield, M. 54
Mayhew, P. 559
McKay, H.D. 190
means of production 256, 258
mechanistic explanation, criminal behaviour 140
media 68–84
  patterns of coverage in press and television 71–4
  reader interest 68–70
media effects 66, 75–8
  comparison with control groups 77–8
  contested findings of experimental research 75–7
  scope and context of 75
Mednick, Sarnoff 115
Mein Kampf 249
Melly, George 83
men
  age 129–31
  compared to women 129
mens rea 11
Mental Defective Act 1913 777
mental hospital see total institution
Merseyside Crime Survey 284

Merton, R.K. 48, 49–52, 145, 165–9, 174–6, 180, 336
mesh-thinning 635–6, 642
Messerschmidt, J.W. 791
Messner, S.F. 124
meta theory 834–5
Metropolitan Police 31, 748 see also new police
Michael, J. 11
midwives 780
Milgram experiment 835
Millie, A. 644
minimum intervention model 701–3
  systems management 702
minor physical anomalies (MPAs) 122
minority groups
  convicted with lesser evidence 45
  privacy rights ignored 46
Modernity and the Holocaust 827
modernization, self-control and lethal violence 476–80
  England 477–8
  main patterns and secular trends 478–80
  measurement issues 478
  secular declining trend 480
modes of adaptation 160, 167
  conformity 167
  innovation 167
  rebellion 168
  retreatism 168
  ritualism 167–8
Mods and Rockers 79–84, 198, 199, 202, 620
Moffitt, T.E. 807
monetary success 166, 170, 175, 177, 178–9
money-laundering legislation 458
monopoly, state's on police 593, 595
moonlighting 594
moral career 664
'moral decline' in Britain 680–3
moral indignation 604
moral panics 20, 34–3, 66, 188, 201–3
  end of 82
  sociology of 79–84
moral poverty 686–8
moral propaganda 37
morality 2, 331–2, 542
Morris, A. 732
Morris, B. 54
mortification 664–8
Moss, Kate 184
motivated offenders 318, 321
motivation, towards crime 246
motor-bike boys 201 see also scooter boys
multiple/repeat victimization 386, 409–15
  and the British Crime Survey 411–12
  evidence from a local crime survey 412
  preventing 412–14
Muncie, J. 11
Municipal Mediations Board 723
Murray, Charles 12, 154, 288
Murdock, G. 71

Nadalmann, E.A. 499
National Commission on the Causes and Prevention of Violence 318
National Council on Alcoholism 502

National Crime Recording Standard 62
National Crime Squad 455
National Crime Victimization Survey (NCVS) 55
National Criminal Intelligence Service 455
National Front 481
National Institute on Drug Abuse (NIDA) 502
nationwide criminal cartel and confederation 440
natural and sexual selection 127, 131, 133n
Negroes 218, 219
neighborhoods and violent crime 563–6
    homicide 566
    measures 565
    perceived violence 565–6
    research design 565
    violent victimization 566
Neighbourhood Watch Schemes 790
neocolonialism 256, 263–4
neo-correctionalist model 704–6
    fast-tracking procedures 705
    systems management techniques 705
    transfer procedures 705
Nero 250
net-widening 635–6, 671, 732–3
neutralization 232, 234–6, 239, 724, 831–2
    appeal to higher loyalies 235–6, 832
    condemnation of the condemners 235, 832
    denial of injury 235, 832
    denial of responsibility 234–5, 832
    denial of the victim 235, 832
New Blue Line, The 585
'new criminologies of everyday life' 302, 304–6
New Labour 690
New Left 267, 268, 285
new penology 358, 360–6
    drugs and punishment 363–4
    expansion of penal sanctions 363
    in perspective 362
    innovation 364–5
    new discourse 360
    new objectives 360–1
    new techniques 361–2
new police 20, 31–4
    and the poor 32–3
    cooperation of public 33
    resistance to 31–2
new regulatory state 824, 837–42
New Right 375, 376, 680
Newburn, T. 844
Newgate prison, hangings at 23
news 66, 68–70
newsworthiness 66, 68–70
night-time economy 490–3
*No More Excuses: A New Approach to Tackling Youth Crime In
    England and Wales* 690
non-conformity 12
'non-crimes' 15
Normanton, Matthew 25
normal, Durkheim and 160, 162–4
'normal ordinary person', in court 162
normalization 650, 653
normative perspective 542, 544
norms 4–6, 138, 140–2, 165–6
Notting Hill Riots 83, 201

nouveaux riches estate holders 25
'nuts'/'nutcases', in court 611

objective and subjective strains 160, 171
objectivity/subjectivity, feminism and 341, 351
obstetrics 121–2
    minor physical anomalies (MPAs) 122
    nicotine exposure 122–3
occasional criminal 110
occupational crime 427
offending, individual factors in 800–5
    empathy 802–3
    impulsiveness 803–4
    low intelligence and attainment 800–1
    personality 801–2
    social cognitive skills 804–5
Office of Population, Census and Surveys (OPCS) 54
official deviants, studies of 8–9
official statistics 42, 44–53
    appropriateness and reliability of 49–50
    discretion of law enforcement personnel 52
    divergence with crime news 68
    social construction of 44–7
Old Bailey 24
O'Malley, P. 373
ontogenetic approach 818
ontological insecurity 160, 181, 183
opening statement 614
opium 499
opportunity 302, 312–18, 562
    concentrated in time and space 314
    crime can be prevented by reducing 316
    crime not usually displaced by reducing 316–17
    depend on everyday movements of activity 314
    focused reduction can produce wider declines in crime
        317
    highly specific 313–14
    one crime produces opportunities for another
        314–15
    plays a role in causing all crime 312–13
    social and technological changes 316
    some products are more tempting 315–16
ordinal proportionality 523–4
organized crime 438, 440–60
    in Britain 457–8
    control of in UK 458–9
    definition of 454
    nature of 456–7
othering, two modes of 182–3
outsiders 210, 216–20
    conflicting attitudes towards rules 218–19
overcharging 432–4

Packer, H.L. 532
Paisley, journeymen weavers 24, 25
'Paki-bashing' 481
panopticon 653–4
para-military policing tactics 749
parkas 198, 199
Parker, H. 860
Parsons, P.A. 110, 111, 112
participant observation 852, 860–9
pathological, Durkheim and 160, 162–4, 212, 420

patriarchal feminine 780–1
patriarchy 256, 264–5, 326, 345n, 386, 402–9
patrol 572, 574–6
  arrests 575
  'cats-in-a-tree' situation 575
  family disputes 575
  pacifying situations of potential conflict 575
  reported crime 574
  traffic law violations 574
patterns of crime 59
Pavlov's dog 151
Pearson, G. 680
Pearson, J. 453
peculiar institutions 741, 759–64
penal custody of children 689–95
  bullying 694
  conditions and treatment 692–4
  educational needs 693
  expansion of 691–2
  racism 692
  reductionist agenda 689
  rush to custody 690
penal justice, new age of 514–17
penal range 659–61
penal severity 512, 516–28
penalties, fall in number 292–3
penetration, social control and 636–8
penitentiary 20, 37
perceived coercion 729
permissive revolution 202
permissive society 79, 80, 680
Perry Preschool project 800
Persephone model 540–1
persistent young offenders 689–90
personality, as a factor in offending 801–2
'petty' criminals 4, 423
Philadelphia Quakers and capital punishment 23
physiological defect and deviant behaviour 8
Pilkington, Hugh 34
pillory 26, 516
pious perjury 20, 26
Pitt's Police Bill of 1785 32
Pittsburgh Youth Study 803
Plummer, K. 220
plunder 250
Poisson model of victimisation 410
police
  foot patrol 295–6, 298
  organizing principles in the administration of justice
    45–8
  performance measurement regime 62
  powers 37, 458
  role of 297–8
  see also policeman's 'working personality'
police, activities of 574–9
  criminal investigation 576–7
  other work 578
  patrol 574–6
  traffic 577–8
  variations in police work 578–9
Police and Criminal Evidence Act 1984 (PACE) 754
Police Bill 1829 32
policing 592–9

accountability 597
civilian employees 594
equity 596
human rights 596–7
moonlighting 594
pluralizing 594, 595, 596, 597
private security 593
safety 595–6
searching for identity 593–5
see also community policing
Policing the Crisis 268
policeman's 'working personality' 580–5
  correlates of social isolation 583
  police solidarity 581
  police solidarity and danger 581–2
  social isolation 581
  social isolation and authority 582–3
  symbolic assailant and police culture 580
policy transfer 844–8
political cultures 844–8
political economy of crime 258–60
Pollak, Otto 333–4
polygamy 127–8, 131
'Portia' model of rights 536, 539
positive school of criminology 99–103
  three causes of crime 100
positivism 86, 93–103, 106, 267, 268, 269, 347–8
  biological 106, 108–33
  psychological 140–58
postmodern feminism 326, 347–55
postmodernism, debate over 349–50
postmodernity 358
poverty 100, 420–1, 563
power, dynamics and visibility of 261–2
Power Elite, The 431
Powers of the Criminal Courts (Sentencing) Act 2000 691
predation 250–2
press reaction to crime 34–8
presumption of guilt 533–4
presumption of innocence 533–4
prevention 302, 552, 553, 554–70, 587–8
primary and secondary deviance 212–13
  sequence leading to secondary 213
primary and secondary reinforcers 138, 150–1
Principles of Criminology 143
prison population in England and Wales 644–8, 691
  changes in custody rates 645
  child prisoners 691–2
  greater use of custody 647
  length of sentence passed 645–7
  tougher sentencing 647–8
prison reform 517–20
prisons 652–62, 763–4
  became like ghettos 763–4
  Bentham's Panopticon 653
  carceral continuum 656–7
  contested nature of punishmment 657–62
  discipline and democracy 654–5
  'failure' of 655–6
  normalizing deviance 653
  problem of legitimacy 661–2
  training the body 652–3
Prisoners and Paupers 110

private security   358, 572, 593, 594
   accountability   597
privatization   838–40
   of policing   840
   of prison buildings   840
probation orders   660
procedural justice   542, 543–4
procedural safeguards   710, 732
professional crime   438–60
Progressive movement   337
prohibition   488, 499–504
Project on Human Development in Chicago
      Neighborhoods (PHDCN)   565
property crime   59, 464–9
proportionality   512–13, 520–4, 527–8, 728, 770, 771,
      736
   criteria for   523–4
   rationale for   522
prosecution   27–30
   witnesses   615
prosecutors and courts   27–30
'prostitution business'   37
provocation   246, 252–3
psychological defect and deviant behaviour   8
psychological mechanism   127–33
psychological positivism   140–58
psychological reactance theory   250–1
public denunciation   604–6
public hangings, abolition of   23
Public Order Act 1936   682
punishment   20, 88–92, 657–62
   choice of   659–61
   consequences   88–9
   in eighteenth century   24–6
   essentially contested concept   658–9
   interpretation of the law   89
   lenience   91–2
   origin of   88
   prompt   91
   proportion between crimes and   90–1
   right to punish   88
'Punishment, Custody and the Community'   629
punitive bifurcation   660 *see also* bifurcation
punitive city   633–9 642
punitive mechanisms   512
Puritan beliefs, of deviant behaviour   8

Quango cull   54
quarter sessions   28, 29

race
   influence of   101
   IQ differences   116
racial disorder in Britain   748–9, 750
racial harassment   463, 481–5
racial profiling   754
racial stereotyping   741, 754, 757
racial violence   481–5
   crime surveys and prioritization   482
   criminal incidents and criminology   482–3
   defining as a crime   481–2
   emergence of a social problem   481
   implications for policy development   484–5

   implications for survey research   484
   process of victimization   483–4
racism   263–4, 692, 740–1
   of criminalization   742–6
racketeering   438, 443–8
radical and administrative criminology/ies   256–73
   advantages of   269
   definition of   267
   developing paradigm   268–9
   emergence of administrative   269–70
   exterior history   267
   interior history   267–8
   and radical realism   278–9
radical and critical criminology   258–73
radical realism   278–9, 282–8
   see also realism
Radford, J.   402
Rafter, N.H.   108
Raine, A.   119
rape   128
   crisis centres   406
   within marriage   405
rates of crime   42–63
rational choice   138, 140, 149–58, 302, 304,
      305–6, 804
rationalizations   234
Raudenbusch, S.W.   563
Raven's Progressive Matrices   801
reaction formation   190
Reader's Guide to Periodical Literature   113
Reaffirming Rehabilitation   630
Reagan, Ronald   759
'real crime'   12
realism   278–300
   and feminist criminology   279–80
   left and right   278
   and modernism   279
   nature of left   282–8
   not empiricism   284
   square of crime   280–1
   see also radical realism
rebellion   160, 168, 229
recidivism   361, 512, 517–20
reconciliation, victim-offender projects   704
recorded crime   59–63, 368
Redfern, A.K.   865
reductionist agenda   689
Rees, Merlyn   683
reproduction and crime   127–33
reflexivity   368
reform, unwillingness to deal with   268–9
Reform Act 1832   23
refraction   369
'regular villains', in court   611
'regulatory offences'   12
regulatory state and transformation of criminology
      837–42
   Keynesian state to new regulatory state   838–41
   nightwatchman state to Keynesian state   838
   risk society and the new regulatory state   841–2
rehabilitation   512, 517–20, 628–33
rehabilitationist penology   628
Reiner, R. 59

reinforcers   138, 149, 150–1
reintegration   637–8, 710, 719–36
reintegrative shaming   723–4
religion, as a means to stop super-predators   687–8
research *see* fieldwork and research
reserve   368
respect   548, 609
respectable crime   425
respectable fears   678, 680–3
respectability, and white-collar crime   428
Responsibility for Crime   110
restorative justice   726–30, 841
  'default setting'   729–30
  definition and principles   719
  development of   720–1
  empowerment of communities   727
  model   703–4
  limitations to   722
  primary objectives   719–20
  relationship to legal justice   721
  responsibilities of the state   726
  rights and responsibilities of the victim   727–9
  theories related to   722–4
restorative justice, response to critics   732–6
  encourages vigilantism   735
  erodes legal rights   732
  extends police powers   734–5
  fails to provide justice   735–6
  lacks legitimacy   735
  leaves power imbalances untouched   735
  fails to effect real change   734
  fails to 'restore' victims and offenders   733–4
  results in discriminatory outcomes   734
  results in net-widening   732–3
  trivializes crime   733
retaliatory aggression   491
retreatism   160, 168
retribution   629, 658
'revolving door' effect   431
rewards
  for return of property   28
  of crime   149–53
right realism   276, 278
Riot Act   25
rising expectations   368
risk   358, 360–78
  recalcitrant modernity and critics of   370–2
  power and crime prevention   373–8
  six components of   368–9
  and white-collar crime   428–9
risk and protective factors   800–5
risk management   358, 363, 373–8, 841
risk society and the new regulatory state   841–2
ritual, capital punishent as   24–6
ritualism   160, 167–8
robber barons   422, 423
Rock, P.   388, 613
Rosenfeld, R.   174
Rothe, D.   430
'rotten apples' theory   748
rough music   20, 27–8
routine activities   488, 491
routine activity theory   302, 304, 318–22

composition of crime trends   321
  related property trends and relation to human
    activity patterns   320
  related trends in business establishments   320–1
  trends in human activity patterns   319–20
routine precautions   316, 768–9, 786–91
  anticipating danger and avoiding violence   791
  at home   789–90
  on the street   786–8
  at work   788–9
rule breaking   216–19
rule enforcement   216–19
'rule of law'   726, 727
'runner'   611
Rwanda genocide   248

'Safe and Clean Neighborhoods Program'   295
safety strategies   786–94
Sampson, Robert   563, 818, 854–8
sanctions   547
Saunders, Cornelius   27
Savanna-IQ Interaction Hypothesis   131–3
Scarman, Lord   747, 748
Scarman Report   749
Schlesinger, P.   71
Schwendinger, H. and J.   792, 793, 794, 828
scooter boys   199   *see also*   motor-bike boys
Scotland, executions in   22–3, 24n4
Scottish youth justice system   702
scouting trips   465–6
Scraton, P.   261
search warrants, application by victims   29
Seattle's crime network   449–52
second-wave feminism   340, 342
secondary prevention   554, 556
Secret Intelligence Services (MI6)   455
Secure Training Order   690, 691
Security Service Bill 1996   455
Security Services (MI5)   455
segmentation   714–15
selective process of justice system   44–5
  organizing principles of   45–8
self-control   241–5, 232
  and alternative concepts   241–2
  causes of   243–4
  child-rearing and   244–5
  elements of   242–3
  manifestations of low   243
self-fulfilling prophecy   215, 227, 228
self-harm, in prison   674, 694, 770
self-reported offending   56, 802
Sellin, T.   12
sentencing   628–33, 645–7
  democratic approach to   632
  equality of impact   631–2
  feasibility and social circumstances   631
  four models of   628–30
  state-obligated rehabilitation   630
  to promote good   631
sentencing circles   721, 727
severity of punishment   88–92
sex, criminalization and   743–4
Sex and Society   330

sexism   772–3
sexual harassment at work   784, 788
sexual violence   *see* violence against women and children
shame   547
Shapland, J.   397
Shaw, C.R.   190
Shearing, C.D.   379, 592
Sherman, L. W.   545
short-run hedonism   195
'short, sharp shock'   683, 689
Shover, N.   464
sidewalks, safety on   568–70
Simmons, J.L.   12, 54
Simon, J.   360
single-parent households   290
situational controls   305
situational crime prevention   304, 307–11, 373–8, 561–2
   crime as the outcome of choice   307–8
   dispositional theories and their preventative implications   307
   increasing risks of getting caught   309–10
   objections to   310–11
   and the offender   374–5
   preventative implications of a 'choice' model   308
   problem of displacement   308–9
   reducing physical opportunities for crime   308–9
   as risk management   373–4
   and social justice   376–7
   and the victim   376
'situational man'   305
skinheads   83, 198–200, 202, 204, 481
Skolnick, Jerome   580, 585–92
slavery   760–1
Smart, C.   347, 772
Smith, Adam   839–40
Smith, D.L.   865
snowball sampling   865–6
social bond theory   236–40
social bonds   798–9, 818–22
social change and crime rate trends   318–22
social cognitive skills, as a factor of offending   804–5
social construction
   of crime   13
   official statistics   44–8
social control, women and   779–84
social disorganization   142–8
social harm   2–3, 12, 15–16
social information processing model   804
social injury   12, 424, 828
social justice   626
   crime prevention and   376–7
   sentencing   628–32
social learning   142–8
social order   11–16
social problems interconnected   293–4
social reaction
   against drugtaking   224–9
   outsiders   216–19
   primary and secondary deviation   212–13
   to youth   201–3
social structure   142–8

and anomie   165–9
   main components of SSSL model   145–8
Social Structure and Anomie (SS&A)   174–6
Social Structure and Social Learning (SSSL) theory of crime   142, 145–8
'socialite'   794
socialized welfare tribunals   698
sociogenic developmental theory of offending   818–22
   causes of delinquency   819–21
   limitations   821–2
   stability and change over life course   821
   summary of   818–19
Socrates   164
Sparks, R.   657, 844
Springbok Tour protesters   202
'square john'   467
square of crime   280–1
standpoint feminism   280, 352–3
Stanko, E.A.   402, 786
state-corporate crime   419, 427, 430–5
state crime   425, 430–5, 827–36
state legitimacy   726
state-obligated rehabilitation   630–3
   sentencing principles   630
   suggested sentencing reforms   631–2
'State-organised Crime'   455
statistics   360
   unwillingness to deal with   268
status offences   326–55
Stenning, P.C.   379
Stenson, K.   754
stepping stone approach, pattern of offending   819
sterilization of criminals   112, 115–16
stigmatization   213, 252
stop and search   754–8
   availability   755
   estimating composition of 'available' population   756
   and institutional racism   757–8
   as a policing power   754–5
   youth   756–7
strain theory   170, 239
strains   160, 169–73
   definition of   170
   experienced, vicarious and anticipated strains   171
   general strain theory   170
   increased likelihood of crime   171–3
   objective and subjective   171
   other versions of strain theory   170
Strawson, P.F.   521
'street-corner youths'   794
stressors   160, 169–73
structural disadvantage   742–6
structural functionalism   285
subcultures   188
   and class   201–4
   conflict and the working-class community   198–201
   delinquent   194–7
substantive unfairness   548
suicide/attempted suicide, in prison   674, 694
suitable targets   318, 321–2
summary offences   29
Sumner, C.   14
super-predators   684–8

supergrasses 457
supervision, women and 670
supply side criminology 305
surplus labour 263
surplus population 263
surveillance 629, 631
Surveying Victims 54, 410
'sus' laws 46, 748, 752
suspended prison sentence 671
Sutherland, Edwin 2, 4, 11, 12, 15, 140, 143–4, 146–7,
    234, 238, 246, 259, 336, 420, 423–4,
    425–8, 828
Skyes, G.M. 234

Taft-Hartley Act 446
Tappan, P.W. 4, 11, 423, 426
Targeted Policing Initiative 492
technocrime 427
Teddy Boys 79–80, 82, 481
television, effect on behaviour 75–80, 131–2
telluric factors of crime 100, 102
territoriality 200
tertiary prevention 544–6, 552
Thatcher Government 276, 292, 838
Thatcher, Margaret 376, 680–1, 683, 689, 748
'The Saints and the Roughnecks' 793–4
theft, in eighteenth century 27
theory, and empirical observations 854–9
Thomas, W.I. 330–3
Thompson, E.P. 15
Three Strikes legislation 524, 527
ticket of leave men 34, 38
tipsters 466–7
Tittle, Charles 246–53
tobacco companies, 'culpable negligence' of 15
tobacco use, health costs of 502
torture, as a public spectacle 516
total institution 664–8
    admission procedures 665
    exposure 667
    humiliation 666–7
    loss of identity 666
    obedience tests 665
    personal possessions 665
    role dispossession 664–5
    sexual molestation 667–8
    uncleanliness 667
toxic waste, international dumping of 15
traffic law violations 574
traffic police 577–8
transportation 20
    to the colonies 22, 25–6
trends in crime 60–3
    period 1 late 1950s-1980 60–1
    period 2 1980s-1992 61
    period 3 1992 onwards 61–3
trust, white collar crime and 427–8
Tumber, H. 71
tunnel vision 284
twin studies 115, 120
Tyler, T.R. 542

Umbreit, Mark 723

Umwelt 369–70
UN Convention Against Genocide 828
UN Convention on the Rights of the Child 702–3
Unadjusted Girl, The 330, 332
underclass 288–94
    causation 292
    concept of 288–9
    crime and the 290–1
    illegitimacy and the 289–90
    self-government 294
    size of British 292–4
    unemployent and the 291
'underworld anti-trust suit' 450
unemployment 840
unethical practices, corporate managers 12
'unfair-advantage' theory 520
Uniform Crime Report 318
Unraveling Juvenile Delinquency 854
unsolved crime, amount of 577
urban decay 297
urban growth, and new police 32
urban riots 297

vagrancy laws 14
values, conflict of 192
'Varieties of Capitalism' 848
VAT evasion 458
verdicts 616
victim-oriented court 717
victim rights/responsibilities 726–30
victims 388–94
    limitations of knowledge about 390–1
    problem of identity 391–4
    rediscovery of 389–90
victims' needs 719–22
victim-offender mediation 704, 723
Victim-Offender Reconciliation Projects 704
Victims of Personal Crime 410
victimization 283, 393, 482
    racial 483–5
    violent 566
    see also multiple/repeat victimization
victimization survey 286
victimology 828
victims movement 390
Victim-Offender Reconciliation Projects (VORPs) 704, 721,
    722
Victim Support (voluntary organisation) 406, 412
victim support 397–401
    legislation or persuasion 399–401
    'rights'-based strategy 397, 398
    services involving criminal justice system 398–9
vigilante groups 299
'villains', in court 611
violence 263
violence against women and children 402–8
    criminal violence is private violence 407–8
    feminist concerns 404–7
    legislative change 405–6
    naming of types of abuse 403
    police practice 406–7
    problems of definition 402–3
    sexual violence 403

virtue 246–7
IVA model 315
von Hirsch, A. 520

Wacquant, L. 759
Waddington, P.A.J. 754
war on drugs 506–10, 759
   drug sales and arrests 508
   drug use and arrests 506–8
   sentencing for drug offenses 509
war on terrorism 431, 432
weight of consumer goods 320
welfare capitalism 262
welfare dependency 290
welfare model, youth justice 698–700
Welfare State 267, 268
Welsh, B.C. 800
whipping 26, 37
white collar crime 420–36
   definition of 425–9
   financial cost of 422–3
   in industry 422
   in medical profession 422
   multistage approach to 426–7
   in politics 422
white collar criminal 423–5
Whitehouse, Mary 202
Whitelaw, William 689
Wilkes and Liberty rioters 24
Wilkins, L. 13, 225
Willis, Paul 182
Wilson, Edward 114
Wilson, J.Q. 149, 295
Windrush celebrations 747
Winlow, S. 490
witnesses 615, 617
Wollstonecraft, Mary 247, 248
women
   Lombroso on 328–30
   Pollak on 333–4
   sentencing of 770–1
   Thomas on 330
   violence against 402–8
women in control 779–81
   angel in the house 779–80
   patriarchal feminine and semi-professions 780–1
   wisewomen and their kin 780
   see also control of women

women in prison 670–5
   age and motherhood 673
   average population 671–2
   disciplinary offences 674
   discrimination and section 95 publications 671
   drugs, sexual abuse and mental health 675
   ethnic group and nationality 673
   number of 672
   offences and previous convictions 673–4
   rates of prisoners 672
   receptions 671
   reconvictions 674–5
   sentence lengths 674
   sentencing 670–1
   suicide 674
women-centred justice 536–41
Women's Aid 406
World Association of Nuclear Operators 841
Werrall, A. 670
Wright, Martin 723
Wright Mills, C. 431
Wright, R. 865
writing, the problem of getting started 882–5

Young, J. 181, 224, 267, 278, 282, 367
Young Offenders 689
Young Offender Institutions 693–4
youth 201–3
youth crime 684–8, 792–4
   becoming more dangerous 686
   intra-racial 685
youth groups 792–4
   girl groups 792–3
   masculine dominance 793
   suspicion and jealousy 793
   'The Saints and the Roughnecks' 793–4
youth justice 689–95, 698–706
   justice model 700–1
   minimum intervention model 701–3
   neo-correctionalist model 704–6
   restorative justice model 703–4
   welfare model 698–700
Youth Justice Board 694

Zehr, Howard 722–3
Zimbardo, Philip 296
Zimring, F.E. 470, 524
zonal hypothesis 188